The BIRDER'S HANDBOOK

A Field Guide to the Natural History of North American Birds

Including All Species that Regularly Breed North of Mexico

Paul R. Ehrlich

David S. Dobkin

Darryl Wheye

ILLUSTRATED BY SHAHID NAEEM

A Fireside Book Published by Simon & Schuster Inc.
New York   London   Toronto   Sydney   Tokyo

Designed by Oporornis Agilis
Manufactured in the United States of America

10 9 8 7 6 5 4 3 2 1

10 9 8 7 6 5 4 3 2 1 Pbk.

Library of Congress Cataloging in Publication Data
Ehrlich, Paul R.
    The birder's handbook : a field guide to the natural his-
tory of North American birds / Paul R. Ehrlich, David S.
Dobkin, and Darryl Wheye.
        p. cm.
    1. Birds—North America—Identification. 2. Birds—
North America.
I. Dobkin, David S.   II. Wheye, Darryl.   III. Title.
QL681.E37 1988
598.297—dc19   87-32404
ISBN 0-671-62133-5   CIP

ISBN 0-671-65989-8   Pbk.

Dedicated to:
Ruth Ehrlich;
Gabriel, Adria,
and Elliot Dobkin;
Ida Wheye;
and all those
who share with us
the pleasure of
watching birds

Contents

Introduction

How often have you come across a bird on a spring morning and stood motionless in an effort to determine what it was doing; to see whether it was near its nest, and if so, what kind of nest it built, or to see why it was holding its tail in an unusual position? Have you wondered what it ate, how many mates it had, how many eggs would occupy its nest, how long it would take them to hatch, or how helpless its hatchlings would be? While there are excellent field guides to help identify that bird, none provide comprehensive information on what it is doing, and why.

This field guide takes up where the others leave off—that is once you have identified a bird. First, you can refer to an up-to-date condensed description of the biology of the species you have in view, and then you can read two or three brief essays which expand on that information and fit your bird into "the big picture" of avian ecology, behavior, and evolution. As you become familiar with this book's format, you will find that it also serves as a guide to what is *not* known about the biology of North American birds. We have indicated where, by making careful observations, you can contribute to the science of ornithology (see "Observing and Recording Bird Biology," p. XXVII).

The Birder's Handbook: A Field Guide to the Natural History of North American Birds includes all bird species (some 650 of them) *known to nest regularly* on the continent, north of the Mexican border (with the exception of some exotic species that have escaped from captivity) and all the now-extinct birds known to have nested here since the arrival of Europeans.

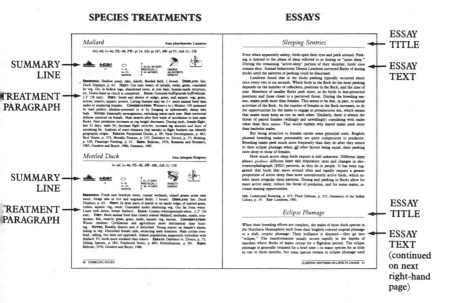

SPECIES TREATMENTS   ESSAYS

ESSAY TITLE

SUMMARY LINE

TREATMENT PARAGRAPH

ESSAY TEXT

SUMMARY LINE

TREATMENT PARAGRAPH

ESSAY TITLE

ESSAY TEXT (continued on next right-hand page)

Just as identification guides often present text on left-hand pages and illustrations on right-hand pages, this guide puts facing pages to different uses. Short synopses, called "species treatments," describing the biology of individual species are on left-hand pages of the main section of the book. The species are arranged in approximately the same order found in the second edition of the National Geographic Society's *Field Guide to the Birds of North America* (1987), the most recent standard identification guide at this writing and the one that follows most closely the sequence of species in the latest (1983, 1985, 1987) revision of and supplements to the *Checklist of North American Birds* produced by the American Ornithologists' Union (AOU). At the end of each species treatment you will find a list of essays (and the page number on which each starts) giving especially pertinent background material, followed by several references in the bibliography (p. 672) which provide entry to the detailed literature on the species.

The essays are presented on the right-hand pages facing these species treatments. They vary in length and cover important and interesting biological topics—how flamingos feed, how different species of warblers divide hunting areas in conifer trees, how species are formed, how raptors can be conserved, why shorebirds sometimes stand on one foot, why birds rub themselves with ants, how migrating birds find their way, why the Passenger Pigeon became extinct, what determines how often hummingbirds feed, and what duck displays mean, just to name a few of the numerous topics addressed. Also included is a series of biographical sketches of bird biologists who have made important contributions to understanding our birds, and some notes on the origins and meanings of North American bird names. To the degree possible, these essays are placed opposite species to which they are most relevant.

We have attempted in this small volume to condense the information that otherwise can be found only in a library of ornithological books and journals. The only other book that has attempted to present roughly equivalent coverage is now hopelessly out of date and *weighs eight pounds*. To achieve compactness we have had to use a highly condensed format for the presentation of data on the species treated. It therefore is important to read the next section, "How to Use This Book," so that the information will be readily accessible to you when birding.

How to Use this Book

Read this section and check the treatments of some familiar birds before you take the *Handbook* into the field with you. Because the information in the treatments is concentrated, it will take a little practice before you gain access to all of it rapidly.

RIGHT-HAND PAGES—ESSAYS

Essays are generally placed close to species they relate to. If you are searching for information on a particular topic, refer to the subject index (p. 743) or to p. 736, where we have provided a "Guide to Essay Topics" that groups the essays by general content and will help you delve more systematically into the topics covered in the *Handbook*. At the ends of essays we have cross-referenced other related essays. We have tried to list the most closely related essay first, especially where it gives more general background information. For instance, the essay "Parasitic Swallows" deals with swallows laying eggs in the nests of other members of the same colony—an example of "brood parasitism." The first essay cross-referenced at the end of "Parasitic Swallows" is "Brood Parasitism," which gives a more general discussion of the phenomenon. References at the ends of the essays direct you to further readings on the same general topic.

LEFT-HAND PAGES—SPECIES TREATMENTS

Treatments of the nearly 650 species that regularly breed north of Mexico are given on the left-hand pages in the main section of the book. Decisions on which species to exclude were sometimes "judgment calls"—to avoid confusion we have listed on p. 666 species described in the National Geographic guide but not included here. That list will permit you to determine whether a species you can't find is missing because its name has changed or because we consider it a nonbreeder. Note also that we have included treatments of those species known to have gone extinct in North America in historic times.

Each treatment is divided into three parts:

1. Treatment Heading

The first part of the heading consists of the common name of the species, followed by its latinized "specific" name. The latter consists of two parts, a generic name (always capitalized) and a specific name (never capitalized). The generic name identifies the immediate group to which the bird belongs, and the specific name denotes the exact member of the genus. The latinized name of the American Robin is *Turdus migratorius*. *Turdus* is a genus of large thrushes; other members of that genus include *Turdus merula*, the Blackbird of Europe, and *Turdus grayi*, the Clay-colored Robin, which occurs casually in the southern tip of Texas but is excluded from this guide as a nonbreeder. Following the specific name is the name of its author—the person who first applied the latinized name to the species. Linnaeus

(p. 629), the father of scientific taxonomy, was the first to apply a two-part latinized name to the American Robin, so it is called *Turdus migratorius* Linnaeus. We include the authors not just for preciseness, but for your convenience in familiarizing yourself with the fascinating history of North American ornithology. Above the latinized species name we note those species that are members of a "superspecies" (a group of closely related, similar species with geographic distributions that usually do not overlap) with other North American birds, and a numerical designation for the superspecies to which it belongs. A list of all the North American superspecies that explains the composition of each numbered superspecies can be found on p. 379, following the end of the Superspecies essay.

Finally, so that you can quickly find a picture of the bird being discussed, the line below the rule of the heading lists the location where the species is illustrated in the most recent editions of the standard field guides (NG = National Geographic; G = Golden; PE = Peterson East; PW = Peterson West; AE = Audubon East; AW = Audubon West; AM = Audubon Master). If the bird is illustrated in an identification guide on a page opposite its description, the page number of the description is given; if it appears on a separate plate, then "pl" precedes the number of the plate. Note that in some cases birds' names have changed since the identification guides were published and will not match those found in this guide.

2. Summary Line

Immediately beneath the heading is an abbreviated, partly pictorial "summary line" presenting a combination of symbols, words, abbreviations, and numbers, that supplies at a glance the following basic information:

(1) Typical nest location and height.
(2) Type of nest.
(3) How sexes divide the task of nest building.
(4) Whether eggs are marked or unmarked.
(5) Usual number of eggs in a clutch.
(6) Predominant type of breeding system (whether the species is monogamous, a cooperative breeder, etc.).
(7) How sexes divide the task of incubation.
(8) Usual number of days from start of incubation to hatching.
(9) Stage of development at hatching (precocial/altricial).
(10) Usual number of days between hatching and fledging.
(11) How the sexes divide the task of caring for the young.
(12) Major types of food eaten during the breeding season.
(13) Basic methods of obtaining food (foraging).

The summary line for an imaginary bird is shown and explained opposite this page.

More details on interpreting the summary line are given below, and in the end papers. Note that in the summary lines we use M to indicate the

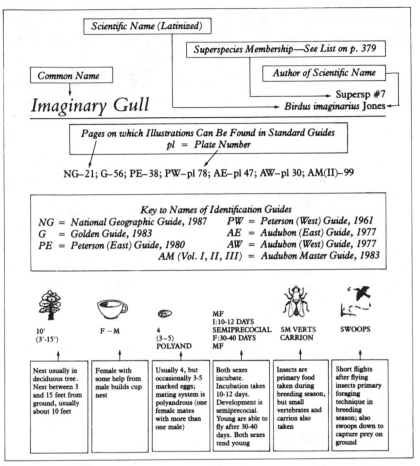

Scientific Name (Latinized)

Superspecies Membership—See List on p. 379

Common Name

Author of Scientific Name

Imaginary Gull

Supersp #7

Birdus imaginarius Jones

Pages on which Illustrations Can Be Found in Standard Guides
pl = Plate Number

NG–21; G–56; PE–38; PW–pl 78; AE–pl 47; AW–pl 30; AM(II)–99

Key to Names of Identification Guides

NG = National Geographic Guide, 1987   PW = Peterson (West) Guide, 1961
G = Golden Guide, 1983   AE = Audubon (East) Guide, 1977
PE = Peterson (East) Guide, 1980   AW = Audubon (West) Guide, 1977
AM (Vol. I, II, III) = Audubon Master Guide, 1983

10'
(3'-15')

F – M

4
(3–5)
POLYAND

MF
I:10-12 DAYS
SEMIPRECOCIAL
F:30-40 DAYS
MF

SM VERTS
CARRION

SWOOPS

Nest usually in deciduous tree. Nest between 3 and 15 feet from ground, usually about 10 feet	Female with some help from male builds cup nest	Usually 4, but occasionally 3-5 marked eggs; mating system is polyandrous (one female mates with more than one male)	Both sexes incubate. Incubation takes 10-12 days. Development is semiprecocial. Young are able to fly after 30-40 days. Both sexes tend young	Insects are primary food taken during breeding season, but small vertebrates and carrion also taken	Short flights after flying insects primary foraging technique in breeding season; also swoops down to capture prey on ground

male, and F to indicate the female. Plurals are simply shown by doubling the codes: MM = males; FF = females.

3. Treatment Paragraph

The largest part of the treatment, a paragraph giving expanded information on the biology of the species, follows the summary line. The sequence of topics is: **BREEDING** habitat and number of broods per year; a brief description of **DISPLAYS** that might be observed (in species with numerous recorded displays this will be a sample only); characteristics of the **NEST** and its construction; color, markings, and average size of **EGGS**; **DIET**; **CONSERVATION** status, wintering range if it extends south of the U.S.-Mexico border, comments on human interference, and, if parasitized by cowbirds, its relative frequency as a cowbird host; **NOTES** of interest in addition to the previous categories; **ESSAYS** in this book that are especially relevant to the species; **REFERENCES** listed in the bibliography (p. 672) that provide access to the literature pertaining to the species.

Dealing with Uncertainty

There is a great deal of information in the ornithological literature that is only anecdotal and in need of confirmation, and much in books designed for birders that is inaccurate. Where we have presented unconfirmed information in either the summary line or the treatment paragraph it is accompanied by a question mark. We also have used question marks when we ourselves have made an extrapolation. For instance, those hummingbird species that have been studied have been found to be promiscuous, and we have designated most unstudied hummingbird species as "PROMISC?". Our policy has been to use such guesswork (always accompanied by the "?") where information from a closely related species can help make a strong inference about a species that has been less studied. It is critical to keep in mind, however, that *even closely related birds can be remarkably different in their biological attributes,* and that projections of the behavior of one species based on that of a close relative can be dead wrong. *Throughout the treatments you should consider the "?" to be a signal to alert you to an opportunity to contribute to the knowledge of avian biology.* A question mark in parentheses in the summary line applies to the full range of numbers or to both sexes that precede it. For example, "MF?" means the participation of the female is uncertain; "MF(?)" means the uncertainty extends to both sexes.

Be alert to the possibility that exceptions to the information given in the summaries may occur. If we report that the typical range of nest heights is between 20' and 30', with a total range of 5' to 50', do not assume that a nest at 3' or 55' is necessarily that of another species; recorded ranges are seldom all-inclusive.

Finding something that differs markedly from the information given is a sign that caution and careful observation are called for. If you just saw a Carolina Wren lay an egg in an open cup nest, double check the identity of the bird; it would be an unusual event indeed, but not impossible.

What follows is a key to the treatment summary line and then a detailed description of the treatment paragraph.

Key to the Summary Lines

(1) **NEST LOCATION:** Since many species are quite flexible in situating their nest, the symbol often represents only the *most likely* location. The symbol for the primary site is given at the left-hand margin of the summary line. Secondary locations are indicated by words or abbreviations shown below that symbol. These words are shown in the list beginning on the next page just under their symbols. For a very few unusual sites the location is given by a word only (no symbol). In the summary line, the numbers just under the location information indicate the most likely height in feet above ground, and the numbers in parentheses (if present) indicate the general range of heights at which nests of the species have been found. The heights indicated apply only to those nest locations given *above* the numbers, not

below. A species whose nests are found in trees as high as 50 feet, in shrubs, and on the ground will be shown as 0'–50'.

Note that in this key the most abbreviated form of a word is always given, although where space permitted we spelled words out in the summary line.

Locations Defined by Topographic Features:

BANK

Bank. Includes river banks, areas of soft soil on steep island slopes, etc., where nest burrows are excavated.

GROUND

Ground. Includes nests placed among the roots, or in niches among the roots of fallen trees, among tules and reeds (in marshes), among grasses, on bare rock, or simply scraped in the dirt or sand.

CLIFF

Cliff. Includes nests situated in natural crevices or on ledges of cliffs typically offering a commanding view of a defensible position, and sometimes chosen when no suitable trees are available.

Locations Defined by Supporting Plant Structures:

SHRUB

Shrub. Includes nests placed within any multi-stemmed woody plant (i.e., one that does not have a distinct single trunk extending several feet between the ground and the lowest branching point).

DECID

Deciduous tree. Includes nests placed in any broad-leaved tree, whether it sheds all of its leaves in the fall ("deciduous") or not ("live"): oaks, maples, poplars, hickories, magnolias, etc. *Also used for species that use broad-leaved and coniferous trees more or less indiscriminately.*

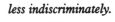

CONIF

Coniferous tree. Includes nests placed in any tree that bears cones: pines, spruces, junipers, firs, etc.

SNAG

Snag. Nests in a standing dead tree. *Also used for species that use cavities in dead and live trees more or less indiscriminately.*

TANGLE

Vine tangle. Includes nests in vines, brambles, brush piles, etc.

FLOATING

Floating on water. Almost always anchored to live emergent or submerged vegetation.

(2) **NEST TYPE:** The symbol shows the type of nest most frequently used by that species. Birds of the same species tend to construct similar nests, but the *materials* available often differ from area to area. (See essays: Masterbuilders, p. 445; Nest Materials, p. 369; Nest Lining, p. 391.) Secondary nest types are listed beneath the symbol and usually discussed in the treatment paragraph.

SCRAPE

Scrape. A simple depression usually with a rim sufficient to prevent eggs from rolling away. Those of many duck species are almost bowl-shaped. Occasionally with lining added.

CUP

Cup. Typical of songbirds, this is the archetypal "bird nest." Hemispherical inside with a rim height several times the diameter of the eggs. In some cases bulky, but always with a deep depression.

SAUCER

Saucer. A shallow cup with the height of the rim not more than two times the diameter of the eggs. Also a flattened nest of pliable vegetation as in some wetland birds.

PLATFORM

Platform. A structure in a tree, on a cliff, or providing a dry place above marshy ground or water, usually big enough for the bird to land on, with or without a distinct depression to hold the eggs. Typical of many raptors and birds of wetlands.

CAVITY

Cavity. Either excavated, as is typical of woodpeckers, or natural cavity found in dead or dying limb or tree. Sometimes a cup or other structure is built within.

CREVICE

Crevice. Eggs placed in a crack in the face of a cliff, between boulders, in a human-made structure, etc.

BURROW

Burrow. Eggs placed in a chamber at the end of a tunnel. Tunnels either excavated by the birds (most kingfishers, puffins, storm-petrels) or usurped from small mammals, especially ground squirrels and prairie dogs.

PENDANT

Pendant. An elongate saclike nest suspended from a branch.

SPHERICAL

Spherical. Globe-shaped or ball-shaped. A roughly round structure, fully enclosed except for a small opening usually on the side or at one end.

(3) **WHO BUILDS THE NEST**: The male (M) and/or female (F) code(s) below the nest symbol indicate which sexes participate in nest building. If both sexes participate, but one does much more than the other, there is a minus sign (−) preceding the symbol of the less-involved sex, and that sex is presented second. In cooperative breeders, if birds other than the breeding adults help with construction, there is a plus sign (+) following the codes for the breeding adults.

(4) **EGGS**: The symbol 🥚 is used if the eggs have markings, ◯ if it is unmarked. The number(s) just below the symbol indicate the most common clutch size, or the range (there is often individual and/or geographic variation in clutch size). The number(s) in parentheses below that line or to its right indicate more extreme values recorded in the literature. In many species the data on clutch size are limited. Furthermore it is often difficult to determine when clutch sizes at the higher end of the range indicate the production of two or more females laying in the same nest (we have tried to exclude such values here), and when clutch sizes at the lower end of the range indicate incomplete production. Clutch size can also be affected by a female's age, by whether the clutch is produced early or late in the season, by whether it is the female's first clutch or a replacement clutch, as well as by other factors (see essays: Average Clutch Size, p. 51; Variation in Clutch Sizes, p. 339; Brood Parasitism, p. 287; and Cooperative Breeding, p. 283).

(5) **MATING SYSTEM**: The following abbreviations found below the clutch size listed beneath the drawing of the egg indicate which breeding system is typical for the species.

MONOG	Monogamy. One male mates with one female (see essay: Monogamy, p. 597).
POLYGYN	Polygyny. One male mates with two or more females (see essay: Polygyny, p. 443).
POLYAND	Polyandry. One female mates with two or more males (see essay: Polyandry, p. 133).
PROMISC	Promiscuity. Males and females mate more or less indiscriminately (see essays: Promiscuity, p. 145; Leks, p. 259).
POLYGAM	Polygamy. Both polygyny and polyandry occur.
COOP	Cooperative. Two females rear broods in the same nest simultaneously and/or non-breeding birds serve as helpers at the nest of one or more breeding pairs (see essay: Cooperative Breeding, p. 283).

Monogamy is, by far, the most common mating system in birds, and unless there is evidence to the contrary, we have assumed a species to be monogamous. Note that very often a small percentage of birds in a population deviate from the mating system of the majority. It is not, for example, unusual in an otherwise monogamous population to find 5 percent of the males polygynous. Conversely, in virtually every population of a polygynous species there will be at least a few monogamous pairs. In our classifications, *unless at least 15 percent* of the birds use the minority system (given in parentheses), it usually will not be identified in the summary line. Here again, careful observations are needed to see if nonmonogamous systems, especially polygyny, are more widespread than currently thought.

(6) **INCUBATING SEX:** The male (M) and/or female (F) codes at the top of the fourth column of the summary line indicate whether both parents, or only one parent, incubates. As in nest construction, if both sexes are involved but one spends much more time on the nest, there is a minus sign (−) before the symbol of the less-involved sex, and it is listed second; in cooperative breeders, if birds other than the breeding adults are involved, there is a plus sign (+) following the symbols of the pair.

(7) **LENGTH OF INCUBATION:** The number(s) following the "I:" are the usual number of days (or recorded range of days) from the start of incubation to hatching. Note that hatching of a clutch is often synchronized by delaying the start of incubation until the last egg is laid. Incubation time is somewhat geographically variable within species, and your accurate observations could add to our knowledge of that variation. Numbers appearing in parentheses represent recorded extreme values.

(8) **DEVELOPMENT AT HATCHING:** Birds show great variation in their degree of development at hatching, and we show the maturity of hatchlings

for each species on the line under the incubation time. In North America there are no fully developed (PRECOCIAL 1) young at hatching. Our most fully developed young at hatching are classified "PRECOCIAL 2," exemplified by ducklings and shorebird chicks. They are downy, open-eyed, mobile at birth, and find their own food while following their parent(s). At the opposite extreme, our songbirds are "ALTRICIAL"—born naked, immobile, and wholly unable to feed themselves.

Developmental patterns are explained fully in the essay Precocial and Altricial Young (p. 581). In North America seven conditions of young at hatching are found:

PRECOCIAL 2	Mobile, downy, follow parents, find own food.
PRECOCIAL 3	Mobile, downy, follow parents, are shown food.
PRECOCIAL 4	Mobile, downy, follow parents, fed.
SEMIPRECOCIAL	Mobile, remain at nest, fed.
SEMIALTRICIAL 1	Immobile, downy, eyes open, fed.
SEMIALTRICIAL 2	Immobile, downy, eyes closed, fed.
ALTRICIAL	Immobile, downless, eyes closed, fed.

Other than in the summary line, the word "precocial" used alone in this guide refers to the first four categories collectively; similarly the word "altricial" refers collectively to the last three categories.

(9) TIME FROM HATCHING TO FLEDGING: The number(s) under the development pattern, following an "F:", are the usual number of days (or recorded range of days) until precocial young are able to fly competently and the time required before altricial young leave the nest (altricial species may not be able to fly competently when they depart the nest). Numbers in parentheses represent recorded extreme values. Again, fledging times are variable and your accurate observations may be useful. Note that fledging rarely means the end of parental care. Precocial young of some species, such as oystercatchers, stay with and are helped by the parents long after they can fly; after they have left the nest, altricial young may be fed more than twice as long as they were fed in the nest.

(10) WHO TENDS THE YOUNG: How the parents divide the feeding (and guarding) of the young is shown just under the hatch-to-fledge time. For precocial species whose young are not fed by the parents, this indicates who tends the young while they feed. The letters coding the sex of the tending parent are the same as those used in (3) above.

(11) DIET DURING BREEDING: The symbol shows the primary type of food eaten *during the breeding season*. Secondary types of food commonly taken may be shown by words or abbreviations below the symbol. Many of these words are shown in the list below just under their symbols. Additional specific food items taken less frequently are listed in the treatment paragraph and details of primary food types are often given there (since the symbols cover broad categories). Remember, many species have an entirely

different winter diet, and if so, this is usually described in the treatment paragraph.

Animal Foods Include:

SM MAMMAL

Small Mammals. Anything from shrews to ground squirrels and rabbits, but most often rodents.

BIRDS

Birds. May include their eggs—if so, that will be mentioned in the treatment paragraph.

SM VERTS

Small Terrestrial Lower Vertebrates. Includes reptiles (lizards, snakes, etc.) and amphibians (salamanders, frogs, etc.).

FISH

Fishes. Sometimes includes fry and eggs, in which case that usually will be mentioned in the treatment paragraph.

INSECTS

Terrestrial Invertebrates. May include insects, spiders, mites, snails, slugs, worms, millipedes, sowbugs, etc. Usually predominance of insects.

AQ INVERTS

Aquatic Invertebrates. May include aquatic insects, crayfish, shrimp, snails, bivalves, etc.

CARRION

Carrion. Prey found dead.

Plant Foods Include:

NECTAR

Nectar. The sugary solution found in many flowers.

FRUIT

Fruits. Includes berries, which are simple fleshy fruits.

GREENS

Greens. May include leafy parts of both aquatic and terrestrial plants.

NUTS

Nuts. Hard, dry, single-seeded fruits, often acorns and beechnuts.

SEEDS

Seeds. Includes grains, sunflower seeds, conifer seeds, etc.

OMNIVORE

Omnivorous. A variety of plants and animals too diverse to specify here; neither plant nor animal food usually comprises less than one-third of diet.

Many birds, especially passerines, that eat both seeds and insects take proportionately more insects when seasonally available. Although seed-feeding birds frequently consume gravel to aid in grinding seeds, we have not included grit in our description of diets.

(12) FORAGING TECHNIQUES: The major method each species uses to obtain food during their breeding season is the last symbol on the right in the summary line. The symbol is often supplemented by a word or abbreviation that indicates less frequently used foraging techniques. These words are shown below just under their symbols. In the case of foraging techniques we again find gaps in the record, offering ample opportunities to provide the missing information. Note both *primary* and *secondary* techniques may be used to obtain *primary* food items.

Techniques for Picking Food from Ground Surface or Plants While Walking or Clinging Include:

GRND GLEAN

Ground Gleaning. Picking up items from the surface of soil, turf, sand, etc. Includes scavenging dead aquatic organisms from shorelines.

FOLIAGE GLEAN

Gleaning from Foliage and Occasionally from Branches. Takes invertebrates and/or fruit from vegetation, not from the surface of the ground.

BARK GLEAN

Gleaning from Tree Trunks and Branches. Describes foraging that only rarely includes removal of invertebrates from foliage as well. Includes excavating and drilling into bark.

Hovering Techniques Include:

HOV & GLEAN

Gleaning while Hovering. Takes nectar, insects or berries from plants above the ground while hovering.

HOVER & POUNCE

Hovering and Pouncing. Hovering before swooping or dropping down on prey.

Other Flying Techniques Include:

HAWKS

Hawking. Sallies from perch on short flights to capture flying insects.

AERIAL FORAGE

Aerial Foraging. While in prolonged continuous flight, captures flying insects.

AERIAL PURSUIT

Aerial Pursuit. Chases and catches birds in midair, stoops (drops on flying birds from above, killing them in midair with a blow from the talons), or snatches them from their perches.

SWOOPS

Swoops. Snatches up prey from ground in talons after gliding descent from perch with wings spread.

HIGH PATROL

High Patrol. Soars at high altitude in search of carrion or prey.

LOW PATROL

Low Patrol. Seeks prey in low searching flight.

Aquatic Techniques Include:

HIGH DIVES

High Dives. Drops from height into water, usually to catch fish, but sometimes to take waterfowl or other prey.

SKIMS

Skims. Flys low over water (Black Skimmers' lower mandibles penetrate surface); and snatches up fishes or aquatic invertebrates.

SURFACE DIVES

Surface Dives. Floats and then dives; swims underwater using feet and/or wings.

SURFACE DIPS

Surface Dips. Takes food from the water's surface or from just below while floating or swimming on the surface.

DABBLES

Dabbling. Floating on surface in shallow water, pivots headfirst downward while raising hindquarters above water to reach submerged plants or animals on or near substrate (mud, sand).

STALK & STRIKE

Stalks and Strikes. Hunting by standing motionless on bank or in water and spearing fishes, frogs, etc.

Probes below Surface. Foraging for food beneath surface of substrate (mud, sand) either in or near shallow water. Also often includes taking food from within the water column.

PROBES

INTERPRETING THE TREATMENT PARAGRAPHS

As in the summary line, the information in the treatment paragraph is also necessarily condensed, so you should be aware of the following assumptions. First, birds are complex, adaptable animals, and although certain aspects of behavior within some species are relatively stereotyped, many vary as local environmental conditions vary. Thus a species that normally lines its nest with fine grasses may substitute a bit of fleece snagged on a barbed-wire fence surrounding a sheep pen or shredded plastic insulation from an old power cable, if either is conveniently near the nest site. In addition to behavior, the physiological, reproductive, and other biological characteristics of most widespread birds vary geographically. For instance, a species may raise only one brood per season in the northern part of its range, but rear two or even three farther south. Within a species, clutch and egg sizes may differ between birds nesting in desert regions and those in well-watered localities. Western coastal populations may have access to insects during the rather mild winters, while east coast representatives may be restricted mostly to berries after the first hard frost.

Thus, because space limitations in the book prevent detailing these patterns of variation, we present *the most common* biological features and behaviors, and try to indicate the range of variation. But not every individual will fall within a given range.

The statements in the paragraph are telegraphic and most of the material is self-explanatory, but keep the following in mind:

BREEDING. Only the breeding habitat—where nesting occurs—is given. Birds may very often be found in quite different kinds of environments when foraging, after breeding, during migration, or in the winter. The habitat description is followed by the number of broods per season.

DISPLAYS. Courtship has not been systematically described in many birds, particularly those active at night. If described in the literature, we attempt here to give at least some major features of courtship displays. In addition, as you will see in various essays, displays used in courtship and in aggression are frequently similar. For this reason, we will often describe displays that you might observe without ascribing a function to them. Because of space constraints, in many cases you will have to infer the form of the display from its name (e.g., "head pumping" meaning moving the head up and down). Careful observations of display behavior and the contexts in which it occurs are badly needed for many species.

NEST. Positions of nests (e.g., relative to the trunk for cup nests in trees) are often listed, as are alternate sites, but materials used tend to be so extremely variable (see essays: Nest Materials, p. 369; Nest Lining, p. 391) that they usually have been condensed to a minimum. In most cases we indicate whether nests are reused for subsequent broods within a season or whether nests are reused in successive years (nest is "perennial"). Often the amount of time required to build the nest is given.

EGGS. These vary in color and markings, even within clutches. Colors may change as incubation advances, and eggs often become stained in the nest, particularly if situated on the ground. Egg identification thus is often very difficult even when a photograph is available. It is, however, usually easy to exclude many possibilities on the basis of our brief description of color, markings, and average size. Egg size (length) is given in both inches (") and millimeters (mm). Remember that one inch is 25.4 mm, so that eggs described in the literature as 37, 38 or 39 mm long will be recorded as 1.5" due to our rounding. Conversion to inches was done before averages in mm were rounded to the nearest mm. Note that egg size is also variable: if one species is listed as having a size of 19 mm and another of 18 mm, it is quite likely that some eggs of the first species will be smaller than some of the second species, and vice versa. If, on the other hand, one species is listed as 19 mm and the other 25 mm, egg size will provide a pretty good clue to which species' nest you are observing. Also bear in mind that eggs may vary in size with the order in which they are produced and that eggs from early clutches often tend to be larger than later ones. *Above all, remember it is illegal to disturb the eggs of most species without appropriate permits.*

DIET. This usually expands the information on breeding-season diet presented in the summary line, may list foods eaten during the nonbreeding season if different, and occasionally adds brief comments on foraging. Animal prey usually are listed first, followed by plant matter. Very often items given in the summary line are not repeated here.

CONSERVATION. Information about the wintering range provides important clues about the future conservation status of migrants traveling to Latin America where accelerating deforestation and other forms of habitat destruction are increasingly evident and may greatly affect the size of breeding populations within "our" area. Therefore we describe here the wintering range in some detail if significant numbers of North American individuals spend the nonbreeding season outside of the United States and Canada. If the species is resident or migrates within our area, this is stated briefly. Migrating birds occasionally stray far off course, but we have excluded "casual" or "rare" sightings since they are not important to the species' conservation status. Critical as wintering grounds can be to the survival of a species, *remember that many threats to the persistence of our avifauna involve human activities within the United States and Canada.*

Significant documented interference by humanity (hunting, habitat destruction associated with the encroachment of civilization and concomitant land, water, and food contamination, competition from introduced species) is also included here, as are efforts that are, or could be, implemented to circumvent such interference. Inclusion in The Blue List (p. 11) or Endangered Species status (see Birds and the Law, p. 293), is noted here as well.

Standard enemies are not discussed here. Given the chance, predators such as domestic cats or Sharp-shinned Hawks will snatch up any small bird; and foxes, raccoons, jays, ravens, and many others will rob any nest they can. We do, however, note the degree of parasitism by cowbirds, since expansion of cowbirds' ranges has made them especially important enemies of some species, such as Kirtland's Warbler (see essay: Conservation of Kirtland's Warbler, p. 527). We also indicate nesthole usurping by European Starlings, House Sparrows, etc., when it is thought to influence conservation status.

NOTES. In this section we include interesting additional information that does not conveniently fit elsewhere. In many cases some of the most important and unusual aspects of the biology of the species will be described here.

ESSAYS. Near the end of the treatment paragraph we list a few of the essays that seem especially pertinent to the species, and give the page numbers on which those essays begin. For instance, after watching a hummingbird for a while you might wonder why it spends so much time perching—and you'll find an answer in the essay Hummingbird Foraging Bouts (p. 331). Naturally, we can't list every pertinent essay in every species treatment, so each essay itself is cross-referenced to other essays on related topics. By referring to cross-linked essays we hope you will gradually (and relatively painlessly) acquire an overview of modern bird biology. To the same end, we have sometimes referred you to more general essays when the bird in question has relatively little known about its biology, and none (or only one or two) of the more specific essays are pertinent. We hope that each time you see an especially interesting bird in the field you will try to read some of the associated essays—in many cases they can greatly enhance your appreciation of the species you have under observation. For an overview of the topics covered in the essays, see the Guide to Essay Topics, p. 736.

REFERENCES. Citations in this section direct you to sources listed in the bibliography (p. 672) that can give you further information on a species. For example, *Blackbirds of the Americas* by Gordon Orians (with marvelous illustrations of behavior by artist Tony Angell) is a recent (1985) account of this group of birds and is listed as "Orians, 1985" at the end of the treatment paragraphs of all species of blackbirds. Simply turn to the alphabetized bibliography to find the complete reference for the book. Wherever possible we have tried to list two or three recent references for a species in order to provide entry to the literature relevant to that species. We have tried to select recent papers with wide-ranging references, even if the topic of that paper is narrow. By using the bibliographies in the cited papers and books you can easily work back into the pertinent older literature. *For this reason many "classic" references are omitted, since these will be found in the bibliographies of more recent work.*

Observing and Recording Bird Biology

We wrote this field guide largely to provide North American bird watchers with a portable, easily accessed source of information on our birds. Throughout the book, areas where knowledge of the North American avifauna is incomplete or unconfirmed, or where information is entirely lacking, are indicated by a question mark. For many species, even common ones, the literature provides only anecdotal reports on, for example, the length of incubation and fledging periods. Similarly, for many widespread species, data on breeding biology are often based on a limited number of studies from only a restricted portion of their range. Because many features (such as clutch size, prey items fed to young, incubation and fledging periods, and even the preferred nest site) can vary geographically, the understanding of even comparatively abundant species may be woefully incomplete. Thus one use of the *Handbook* is as a guide to the kinds of observations needed to advance knowledge of North American birds.

Active birders are constantly refining their ability to watch, interpret, and record various aspects of bird behavior and ecology. The most important habit to develop is that of carrying a small field notebook and *writing down* observations in the field while details are still fresh in your mind.

How to Record

There are several ways to organize your notebook; the two most popular are *by species* and *by date*. Other possibilities include organizing by habitat, by geographic region, etc.

Most people find that in a notebook organized by species, it is most convenient to include observations for only one species per page, although entries for more than one date (in chronological order) can go on the same page. Organization by date is usually more convenient for entering data, but often is not so convenient when the time comes to look up what you recorded. In either case, each day's entry should start with the date, the geographic location, any pertinent information concerning the habitat, a brief description of weather conditions, and the time of your observations. Time is most conveniently noted with a 24-hour clock, so that 6 A.M. is 0600 and 6 P.M. is 1800. If you do not prefer to do this, be sure to include A.M. and P.M. in order to avoid confusion. Scientists ordinarily keep a second copy of their notes for safety's sake. If observations are worth making, they're worth preserving; be sure to store your duplicate notes in a different building from the originals.

What to Record

Many useful data can be obtained simply by recording counts: how many eggs in a clutch, how many fledglings being fed, how many birds in a shorebird flock, how many standing on one leg, and so on. Similarly, behaviors can be easily quantified. For example, one can note the number of feeding trips made to the nest by parent birds per 10 minutes of watching the nest, or the duration of dives made by a duck.

It is very important, and far more useful for making comparisons, to quantify your observations wherever possible rather than simply describing a situation in general terms. Say, for example, that you are watching the foraging behavior of a Wilson's Warbler on a sunny day. Rather than simply recording, "Wilson's Warbler foraging for insects in a tree, 10:00–10:23 A.M.," you could quantify your observations by recording:

> "Wilson's Warbler foraging for insects in variety of deciduous trees (list species of trees if known), 10:00–10:23 A.M.: Hawking—3 times, Foliage Gleaning—6 times, Hover Gleaning—13 times."

You now have a 23-minute sample of foraging behavior for one individual at one point in the breeding cycle, at a given time of day, in a given type of habitat under certain weather conditions. Additional information that might be recorded includes height for each foraging attempt, diameter of the branch on which each occurred, surface of the leaf (top or bottom) gleaned for each instance of foliage gleaning, and other birds foraging in the same vicinity. You might wish to sample for shorter periods of time—say, 10 minutes of continuous observation of one bird—and then move on to locate a different individual and similarly observe and record its foraging behavior. Repeating this procedure over a number of days and at different times of day would soon give you a pretty good picture of the relative use of different foraging techniques by Wilson's Warblers under different circumstances.

Another observational strategy involves locating one or more active nests and following the families throughout the breeding cycle. Again, it is important to quantify your observations and record clutch size, which bird incubates, duration of incubation period, which bird feeds the nestlings, duration of nestling period, etc. Here, too, more detailed aspects of behavior can be quantified, such as duration of incubation by one bird before it leaves to forage or is relieved by the other parent, or the proportion of time spent singing by the territorial male during the course of the breeding cycle. The latter will tell you whether singing decreases or increases at different points in the cycle.

In all of your bird watching it is extremely important to remember that you are an *observer* not a *participant*. In other words, you want to be as unobtrusive (to the bird) as possible. Do not interfere with nests, and always remain at sufficient distance from the birds you are watching to avoid modifying the very behaviors that you are seeking to observe. Remember that capture or marking of virtually all species of wild birds and even possession of dead ones, except by individuals possessing valid permits or authorization from the appropriate government agencies (see essay: Bird Banding and Marking, p. 95), are prohibited by provincial, federal, and state laws.

Remember also that what a bird does and why it does it are two different things. You can readily devise ways of quantifying and recording the behavior of a bird, but you should resist the temptation of attributing motivations to that behavior—e.g., "the male sang an average of 9 songs during each 3-minute period, *trying to attract a mate.*" In fact, the male may have been already mated and singing quite hostilely toward the male on an adjacent territory. What you do know unambiguously, however, is that he sang an average of 9 songs every 3 minutes.

What to Do with Your Data

A fine way to make your observations widely available to the birding community, and thus add to the growing body of information on North American birds, is to contribute them to any of several cooperative research programs of the National Audubon Society, United States Fish and Wildlife Service, or Laboratory of Ornithology at Cornell University. Such "cooperative research" programs, described below, coordinate the observations of a large number of people collecting similar kinds of information in many different locations.

The Christmas Bird Count sponsored by the National Audubon Society is one of the oldest cooperative research projects in North America. Organized in 1900, this data-gathering effort now involves more than 40,000 people and collects millions of records annually. These records consist of the number of birds of each species seen within 15-mile-diameter circles on a single day within two weeks of Christmas. The data collected are used to analyze early-winter population trends of individual species, monitor changes in relative abundance of species over large geographic areas, and assess the changing status of wintering populations.

The Breeding Bird Census, begun in 1937 and also sponsored by the National Audubon Society, records the number of breeding pairs on particular study sites that vary from about 10 to more than 400 acres in size. Each census includes at least eight visits to the same site during a single breeding season. Some 2000 volunteers, who know local birds both by sight and sound, participate annually. The goal is to make repeated censuses on the sites over successive years in order to gain understanding of local and regional population trends and collect information on the habitat requirements for breeding species. Since 1949 The Winter Bird Populations Study has conducted similar censuses during the winter, often using the same sites, with the goal of understanding wintering populations. These programs are administered through *American Birds*. For information and forms write to:

American Birds
National Audubon Society
950 Third Avenue
New York, NY 10022

Two major projects sponsored by the Cornell Laboratory of Ornithology collect detailed information on the nesting biology of North American birds. The Nest Record Card Program was started in 1965 and now includes more than 300,000 records of individual bird nests. Each record may include a description of the nesting habitat, clutch size, length of incubation and nestling periods, fledging success, and a variety of other pertinent pieces of information. Besides adding to our knowledge of breeding biology, these records also can be extremely useful for understanding reproductive success. The lab also sponsors the Colonial Bird Register, which contains more than 37,000 records collected over the past 20 years. Each record contains the number of breeding pairs in a colony (or mixed colony) of colonially breeding waterbirds, including pelicans, cormorants, herons, egrets, ibises, gulls, terns, and alcids. More than 60 species are included.

Data from all of these research programs are now stored at the Laboratory of Ornithology. You can obtain further information on them as well as standard forms for submitting your data by writing to:

Bird Population Studies
Cornell Laboratory of Ornithology
Sapsucker Woods Road, Cornell University
Ithaca, NY 14850

Other important cooperative research projects in North America include the United States Fish and Wildlife Service's Breeding Bird Survey, the Philadelphia Academy of Natural Sciences' Pan American Shorebird Program, Manomet Bird Observatory's International Shorebird Survey, the Hawk Migration Association of North America's Hawk Migration Surveys, and the compilation of Breeding Bird Atlases sponsored by various state and provincial agencies. You can seek information on these projects through the Audubon Society.

A more ambitious means of sharing your observations is to publish them. The variety of potential topics suitable for a short paper is nearly endless. We suggest that you become familiar with the style and topics covered in your local, regional, or even national birding magazines or appropriate scientific journals (see Sources of Information Used in This Guide, p. 670) to get some idea of what sorts of information might be most useful to collect and how it might be most effectively presented.

Finally, if you are just beginning to study birds, we urge you to contact your local branch of the Audubon Society (or other birding groups) and see if there are some bird study tours that you can participate in. You will learn a great deal by going into the field with experienced birders. People you meet through the Society should also be able to advise you on the best ways of making your observations available to others.

The BIRDER'S HANDBOOK

Common Loon

Gavia immer Brünnich

NG–18; G–18; PE–32; PW–pl 1; AE–pl 188; AW–pl 169; AM (I)–36

     MF
I: 26–31 DAYS
SEMIPRECOCIAL
F: 75–80 DAYS
MF

MF | 2 | AQUATIC
 | (1–2) | INVERTS
 | MONOG

BREEDING: n lakes, ponds. 1 brood. **DISPLAYS:** Bill dipping, splash-diving, "penguin dancing" (vertical position with wings outspread). Yodel call signals territorial ownership. **NEST:** On aquatic veg at edge of shallow water. Wet mass of aquatic veg. Occ concealed. Perennial. Continues building during incubation. Occ simple scrape. **EGGS:** Olive-brown/olive-green, sparsely marked with black/brown. 3.5″ (89 mm). **DIET:** Fish usu pursued and swallowed underwater, some aquatic inverts, esp crustaceans. Young fed small fish, aquatic inverts. **CONSERVATION:** Winters s to n Mexico on coasts, bays, estuaries. Blue List 1981–82; Local Concern 1986: loss of nesting habitat, acid rain threatens lake fish used as food. Will use artificial nesting platforms. **NOTES:** Adults perform distraction display. Young hatch asynchronously; downy chicks ride on back of swimming adult. Eyes adapted for both aerial and underwater vision. Wintering birds use individual feeding territories in day, gather in "rafts" at night, suggesting loosely cohesive social system. Known in Europe as Great Northern Diver. **ESSAYS:** Swimming, p. 73; Loon Nurseries, p. 3; Blue List, p. 11; Transporting Young, p. 103; Distraction Displays, p. 115. **REFS:** Barklow, 1979; Klein, 1985; McIntyre, 1978, 1986b; Rummel and Goetzinger, 1978.

Yellow-billed Loon

Supersp #1

Gavia adamsii Gray

NG–18; G–18; PE–32; PW–4; AW–pl 168; AM (I)–38

     MF
I: 27–29 DAYS
SEMIPRECOCIAL
F: ? DAYS
MF

MF | 2
 | MONOG

BREEDING: Tundra lakes. 1 brood. **DISPLAYS:** Courtship of bill dipping and splash-dive, followed by search-swimming and inviting. Territorial behavior incl calls, alert posture, circle dance, bill dipping, and silent splash-diving. Also rushing, jumping, and fencing-posturing, in which the bird rises nearly straight up, treads water with bill held to breast and wings folded or extended. **NEST:** Simple depression in grass usu on island in lake. Occ of twigs, grass. Male selects site. **EGGS:** Brown, marked with brown. 3.5″ (89 mm). **DIET:** Mostly fish, few aquatic inverts. **CONSERVATION:** Primarily Eurasian; winters on seacoasts, bays, estuaries, occ lakes. Small numbers and limited breeding habitat in N.A. threatened by Arctic development; occ caught in commercial fish nets. **NOTES:** Young brooded in nest or elsewhere onshore for first few days; downy chicks ride on back of swimming adult. Eyes adapted for both aerial and underwater vision. Males and females may winter separately in different areas. Known in Europe as White-billed Diver. **ESSAYS:** Swimming, p. 73; Loon Nurseries, p. 3; Transporting Young, p. 103; Superspecies, p. 375. **REFS:** Cramp and Simmons, 1977; Klein, 1985; Remsen and Binford, 1975; Sjolander and Agren, 1976.

Loon Nurseries and Populations

During breeding, Common Loons require not only a suitable site for a nest but also a "nursery" pool. Preferably, the nest floats or is at the water's edge where the drop-off is steep enough to permit underwater arrival and departure by the adults. Ideally, the nursery pool contains water clear enough for the birds to spot their prey, shallow enough to limit the size of predatory fishes and turtles, reasonably free of scouting eagles and gulls, and rich enough to furnish an eleven-week supply of food for the two chicks. That diet initially includes plant material, crayfish, aquatic invertebrates and small fishes; but as the chicks develop, the proportion of fishes increases until they become the major food item. Often, the nursery pool is situated a relatively long swim away from the nest site. Although the young spend up to 65 percent of their first week being carried on the back of an adult, they are not transported from nest to nursery; they swim there when they are less than two days old. The best territories provide a view of neighboring territories and a pool that suffers neither wind nor wave action sufficient to separate the young from their parents and make them vulnerable to predation.

How well these requirements are met varies, as does the breeding success of the birds. Unfortunately, declines in Common Loon populations have been precipitous. The rising popularity of boating is thought to be responsible for a dramatic increase in predation on eggs as loons are inadvertently frightened off their nests by the frequent passing of boats. In the northeastern United States loon populations were reduced to between 35 and 75 percent of their previous levels between 1965 and 1985. According to the calculations of biologist Judith McIntyre, in New York only 70 percent of those lakes used for breeding in 1960 were still occupied in 1978.

In some areas, lakes are occupied but breeding success is greatly reduced. In Robert Alvo's study of 84 lakes in Ontario, 62 percent of the loon broods on acidified lakes died compared with 14 percent on healthy lakes. Although adult loons can fly to neighboring lakes to feed themselves, their young cannot. Young loons reared on acidified lakes simply starve to death. The weakened, starving young are unable to sit up when transported over water, and instead lie toward the rear of the parent's back, dragging their feet. Adult loons, nonetheless, persist in attempting to rear broods in northern food-poor acid lakes. Disasters for loons, however, have not been restricted to the north. Off Florida, in the Gulf of Mexico, as many as 7,000 Common Loons died in 1983, presumably from complications following mercury poisoning.

Efforts to reverse this downward trend have focused especially on upgrading conditions in loon breeding habitats. Wildlife protection agencies and researchers are attempting to offset the effects of human disturbance, fluctuations in water levels, and chronic water pollution (especially acidification). In one successful management program being tested from Minnesota to New Hampshire, small sedge mats or cedar rafts filled with

Arctic Loon

Supersp #2
Gavia arctica Linnaeus

NG–18; G–18; PE–32; PW–pl 1; AE–pl 187; AW–pl 167; AM (I)–36

MF 2 F –M
(1–3) I: 28–30 DAYS
MONOG SEMIPRECOCIAL
F: 60–65 DAYS
MF

BREEDING: Tundra and taiga lakes. 1 brood. **DISPLAYS:** Bill dipping and splash-diving in pairs, followed by underwater rushing. **NEST:** On aquatic veg at edge of shallow water. Wet mass of roots, stems and accompanying mud torn from ground. **EGGS:** Brownish, sparsely marked with browns. 3.3″ (84 mm). **DIET:** Mostly fish, also few insects, crustaceans, mollusks, frogs; occ much aquatic veg. In winter almost entirely fish. **CONSERVATION:** Winters mostly in Eurasia, occ in N.A. from w Alaska s to BC. **NOTES:** Recently split into two species (Arctic and Pacific Loons) based on studies of breeding biology in U.S.S.R. In N.A. breeds only in Cape Prince of Wales region of w Alaska. Adults occ fly miles from nest to foraging grounds. Solitary individuals on empty lakes emit prolonged, eerie call, audible for miles. Eyes adapted for both aerial and underwater vision. Known in Europe as Black-throated Diver. **ESSAYS:** Swimming, p. 73; Loon Nurseries, p. 3; Species and Speciation, p. 355. **REFS:** Cramp and Simmons, 1977; Klein, 1985.

Pacific Loon

Supersp #2
Gavia pacifica Lawrence

NG–18; G–18; PE–32; PW–pl 1; AE–pl 187; AW–pl 167; AM (I)–36

MF (?) 2 F –M
(1–2) I: 23–25 DAYS
MONOG SEMIPRECOCIAL
F: 60–65 DAYS
MF

BREEDING: Tundra and taiga lakes. 1 brood. **DISPLAYS:** Bill dipping and splash-diving in pairs, followed by underwater rushing. **NEST:** On aquatic veg at edge of shallow water. Wet mass of roots, stems and accompanying mud torn from ground. Completed after first egg is laid. **EGGS:** Brownish, sparsely marked with browns. 3.0″ (76 mm). **DIET:** Mostly fish, also few insects, crustaceans, mollusks, frogs; occ much aquatic veg. In winter almost entirely fish. **CONSERVATION:** Winters s to n w Mexico. **NOTES:** Recently split into two species (Arctic and Pacific Loons) based on studies of breeding biology in U.S.S.R. This is the widespread form in N.A. Adults occ fly miles from nest to foraging grounds. Solitary individuals on empty lakes emit prolonged, eerie call, audible for miles. Young hatch asynchronously. Eyes adapted for both aerial and underwater vision. Incl in European form known as Black-throated Diver. **ESSAYS:** Swimming, p. 73; Loon Nurseries, p. 3; Species and Speciation, p. 355. **REFS:** American Ornithologists' Union, 1985; Godfrey, 1986; Klein, 1985; Petersen, 1979.

vegetation have been anchored in lakes to serve as artificial nesting islands. Breeding success has increased through their use, as nests can be positioned away from the heaviest recreational pressures and freed from the threats of flooding or water drawdowns. Ensuring that associated nursery pools remain productive enough to sustain chicks for up to two months will be central to the success of management programs.

In 1986, more than $15,000 was distributed through the North American Loon Fund to further research on loon management. There is already a little cheering news from the front. Some loons on lakes with heavy canoe traffic are becoming accustomed to the disturbance and are no longer deserting their nests. Also, surveys in 1986 indicate that the rapid decline in the number of lakes used by loons for breeding in New York has been halted, at least temporarily. Even after chronic degradation of loon habitat has been stopped—and it won't be until acid precipitation has been controlled—relentless pressure by bird enthusiasts to restore and then maintain lake quality will be absolutely necessary.

SEE: Transporting Young, p. 103; Dabblers vs. Divers, p. 75; Swimming, p. 73; Helping to Conserve Birds—National Level, p. 363; Parental Care, p. 555; Habitat Selection, p. 463. REFS: Alvo, 1986; McIntyre, 1983, 1986; Ream, 1976.

Visual Displays

When a bird moves or holds itself in a way that signals information to another bird of the same or different species, it is said to be performing a "display." Thus a pigeon leaping into flight at the sight of a hawk, only coincidentally alerting other members of its flock in the process, is moving but not displaying. In contrast, a male grouse strutting on a lek (a traditional courting ground) is displaying—passing information about its desirability as a mate to females of its own species. Displays may include vocalizations, as they do in the case of the grouse—and in the broad sense, vocalizations alone are displays. But because ornithologists often consider vocalizations separately, for our discussion we will define as displays only ritualized movements or postures.

Displays are usually classified according to their apparent function: courtship, aggression, begging, greeting, and so on. The strutting male grouse is performing one of the myriad kinds of courtship display seen in birds. Often courtship displays accent a striking feature of the bird's plumage. The conspicuous, labored flight displays of the male Red-winged Blackbird exaggerate its red shoulder patches. The display flight of the male Yellow-headed Blackbird is performed with the body cocked upward so that its prominent yellow head is held high.

On the other hand, some male birds do not advertise with physical attributes; they demonstrate skills. Male terns court females by displaying a

Red-throated Loon

Gavia stellata Pontoppidan

NG–20; G–18; PE–32; PW–pl 1; AE–pl 186; AW–pl 166; AM (I)–34

			F –M		
PLATFORM	2		I: 24–29 DAYS		
MF (?)	(1–3)		SEMIPRECOCIAL	AQUATIC	
	MONOG		F: 49–51 DAYS	INVERTS	
			MF		

BREEDING: Ponds and small lakes in coastal and alpine tundra; coastal flats s of tundra. 1 brood. **DISPLAYS:** Bill dipping and splash-diving; fast underwater rushing. **NEST:** Saucer or scrape of grass, twigs, usu on muddy ground with slight rise within 1' of water, occ platform of mud and veg. Lined with finer materials, few feathers. **EGGS:** Brownish-olive, usu marked with blackish-brown. 2.9" (73 mm). **DIET:** Mostly small fish, obtained by diving; also some frogs, aquatic inverts, and insects. Young fed mostly small fish. **CONSERVATION:** Winters along coasts s to n w Mexico. **NOTES:** Only loon capable of taking flight from land rather than by running across water. Adults use distraction display. Young hatch asynchronously; chicks ride on backs of swimming adults. Unlike other loons, usu nest on small ponds with no food and must oft fly to lakes or ocean to forage. Never fly to nest, always land on water. Eyes adapted for both aerial and underwater vision. Known in Europe as Red-throated Diver. **ESSAYS:** Swimming, p. 73; Loon Nurseries, p. 3; Transporting Young, p. 103; Distraction Displays, p. 115. **REFS:** Bundy, 1976; Cramp and Simmons, 1977; Klein, 1985; Reimchen and Douglas, 1984.

Western Grebe

Supersp #3
Aechmophorus occidentalis Lawrence

NG–20; G–20; PE–34; AW–pl 174; AM (I)–46

			MF		
MF	3–4		I: 23 DAYS		
	(2–7)		PRECOCIAL 4	AQUATIC	
	MONOG?		F: 63–77 DAYS	INVERTS	
			MF		

BREEDING: Marshes, lakes. 1 brood. **DISPLAYS:** Elaborate mutual displays performed by 2 or more birds in predictable sequences: "rushing" by 2 males, male and female, or several males and a female; "weed dance" with male and female holding plants in bills; "greeting" by pairs rejoining after separation. **NEST:** Floating platform in shallow water; compact mass of fresh and decayed veg, oft coated with aquatic veg, usu anchored to or built up over live veg. Open or concealed. **EGGS:** Bluish-white, chalky, nest-stained buff/brown. 2.3" (58 mm). **DIET:** Mostly fish, aquatic inverts, few amphibians, feathers. Young fed adults' feathers. **CONSERVATION:** Winters s to c Mexico. Blue List 1973–82, Special Concern 1986. Plume hunters devastated populations. **NOTES:** Colonies of tens to hundreds of nests; gregarious year-round. Recently split into two species (Western and Clark's; Western is the dark-faced form); double-noted advertising call prevents hybridization. Tend to fed nearer to shore than Clark's Grebe, suggesting possibility of reduced foraging overlap. Bare skin patch on head of young flushes dark red when begging or in distress. Chicks carried on adults' backs; young fed while carried. **ESSAYS:** Eating Feathers, p. 13; Visual Displays, p. 5; Transporting Young, p. 103; Plume Trade, p. 37; Species and Speciation, p. 355; Blue List, p. 11; **REFS:** Nuechterlein, 1981a, 1985; Nuechterlein and Storer, 1982.

fresh-caught fish. Courting male European Gray Herons perform ritualized hunting movements, erecting head feathers, pointing their bills downward and clashing their mandibles together. Many male passerines, when courting, also lower their bills as if pecking at something below them. Perhaps, next to singing, the most common component of courtship displays in male songbirds is vibration of the wings; other components include fluffing of the body feathers, bill raising, thrusting the head forward, and running using short steps.

Birds also use a great diversity of agonistic displays (those used in threats and actual combat). Male Mourning Doves may bow repeatedly and then lift their heads and coo when defending their territories. Canada Geese often pump their heads up and down just before attacking. Male Gray Catbirds, disputing the boundary between their territories, will fluff their feathers, spread and often lower their tails, and as a last resort, raise their wings. In the same situation Eastern Kingbirds spread their tails to display their white terminal band. Similarly, Tufted Titmice assume a horizontal posture, may open their bills while slightly spreading their wings, and lunge at the intruder. Aggressive geese may rear up and spread their wings when on land; aggressive loons rear up in the water. In established dominance hierarchies, dominant birds often use threat displays against subordinates. Subordinates signal their submission with other displays—in passerines often by crouching with feathers fluffed and head withdrawn.

Quite different from these sexual and agonistic displays are begging displays, which are employed both by chicks to solicit parental feeding and by some females to solicit courtship feeding. Greeting displays are used when one parent relieves the other at the nest, and may serve to prevent aggressive interactions. Pairs of adult Adelie Penguins do bowing displays and exchange vocal greetings at "changings of the guard," thus making large colonies extremely noisy. And, finally, there are social displays that

Named elements of the courtship display of the Western Grebe. Clockwise from upper left: rushing, weed-dancing, dip-shaking and bob-preening.

Clark's Grebe

Aechmophorus clarkii Lawrence

NG–20; PE–34; PW–pl 1; AM (I)–46

| MF | 3–4
(2–7)
MONOG? | MF
I: 23 DAYS
PRECOCIAL 4
F: 63–77 DAYS
MF | AQUATIC
INVERTS | |

BREEDING: Marshes, lakes. 1 brood. **DISPLAYS:** Elaborate mutual displays performed by 2 or more birds in predictable sequences: "rushing," "weed dance," and "greeting" as in Western Grebe. **NEST:** Floating platform in shallow water as in Western Grebe. **EGGS:** Bluish-white, chalky, nest-stained buff/brown. 2.3" (58 mm). **DIET:** Mostly fish, aquatic inverts, few amphibians, feathers. Young fed adults' feathers. **CONSERVATION:** Winters s to c Mexico. Blue List 1973–82, Special Concern 1986. Plume hunters devastated populations. **NOTES:** Colonies of tens to hundreds of nests; gregarious year-round. Recently split into two species (Clark's and Western; Clark's is the light-faced form); single-note advertising call prevents hybridization. Tend to feed farther from shore than Western Grebe, suggesting possibility of reduced foraging overlap. Range overlaps widely with Western Grebe but rare among n populations. Bare skin patch on head of young flushes dark red when begging or in distress. Chicks carried and fed on adults' backs. **ESSAYS:** Eating Feathers, p. 13; Visual Displays, p. 5; Transporting Young, p. 103; Plume Trade, p. 37; Species and Speciation, p. 355; Blue List, p. 11. **REFS:** American Ornithologists' Union, 1985; Nuechterlein, 1981b; Storer and Nuechterlein, 1985.

Red-necked Grebe

Podiceps grisegena Boddaert

NG–20; G–20; PE–34; PW–pl 1; AE–pl 185; AW–pl 175; AM (I)–44

| MF | 4–5
(2–6)
MONOG | MF
I: 22–23 DAYS
PRECOCIAL 4
F: 49–70 DAYS
MF | FISH | |

BREEDING: Shallow lakes, large ponds edged with reeds or sedges. Occ along quiet rivers. Usu 1, rarely 2 broods. **DISPLAYS:** On water male and female call together; call ends like horse whinny. Male and female approach, head and bill at 45°, birds nearly facing until close, then swim parallel, calling. **NEST:** Floating platform in shallow water; anchored, mass of fresh and decayed reeds. **EGGS:** Bluish-white, nest-stained. 2.1" (54 mm). **DIET:** Aquatic insects and inverts, fish, amphibians. Feather ball in stomach. **CONSERVATION:** Winters along coasts of N.A. Blue List 1974–81, Local Concern 1986. Recent declines due to egg inviability and shell thinning from pesticides and PCBs, and to increased egg predation by raccoons. **NOTES:** Usu solitary; occ nests in small colonies. Young hatch asynchronously; initially fed by carrying or attending adult and brooded on platforms. Take-off awkward; tends to escape by swimming. Flight swift. **ESSAYS:** Eating Feathers, p. 13; Visual Displays, p. 5; Transporting Young, p. 103; Plume Trade, p. 37; Blue List, p. 11; Swimming, p. 73; Eye Color, p. 233; DDT and Birds, p. 21; Precocial and Altricial Young, p. 581. **REFS:** Cramp and Simmons, 1977; De Smet, 1987; Godfrey, 1986.

apparently help to keep flocks unified. Displays are, in fact, a major part of the "glue" that binds avian societies together.

How this glue evolved remains a matter of conjecture and dispute. It was the courtship display of the Great Crested Grebe (which is much like that of the Western Grebe illustrated above) that led the pioneering British behaviorist and evolutionist Julian Huxley to develop the concept of "ritualization"—the gradual evolutionary transformation of an everyday movement into an increasingly effective signal. For instance, preflight movements—crouching, slight spreading of the wings, and raising of the tail—have been modified in many birds into signals. When wooing a female, the male Great Cormorant begins an exaggerated takeoff leap, but does not leave the ground.

One of the most interesting ideas on the origins of display behavior was developed in the middle of this century by the celebrated ethologist (student of behavior in natural environments) Niko Tinbergen and his colleagues. Tinbergen suggested that internal conflicts between different behavioral "systems" or tendencies—such as the desire to threaten and the urge to court—are responsible for the generation of displays.

For instance, after vigorously defending its territory, a male bird may approach a female with ambivalence over whether to attack or woo her. As a result, he may do neither, but instead channel his energies into behavior that is irrelevant to either aggression or mating—say pulling at a tuft of grass or preening. Such "displacement activities" can then become incorporated into courtship displays, and "emancipated" from their previous functions. Thus when displacement preening becomes part of courtship, it also becomes more conspicuous and stereotyped than normal preening, and becomes useful as a signal, not as an aid in maintaining the bird's feathers. Similarly, males of many species have incorporated components of courtship fighting (battles between rivals during the courtship season) into their courtship displays. For example, among passerines, bill raising is used widely, in some species in fighting, in others in courtship, and in a few species in both. In many finches the preliminary male courtship display is a modified head-forward threat posture.

Although some behaviorists think that virtually all displays arise from conflicts between internal tendencies, experiments have so far failed to confirm this. As a result, scientists are now turning away from Tinbergen's approach, and looking at the possible evolution of displays without reference to conflicting "underlying tendencies" in the nervous system. Evolution has modified an enormous variety of activities into displays, from food exchange, as in courtship feeding (originating as food exchange between parent and chick), to stylized fishing movements used in heron courtship. We expect the perspectives of those researchers investigating the overt behavior of the animal and those studying the functioning of its nervous sys-

Horned Grebe

Podiceps auritus Linnaeus

NG–22; G–20; PE–34; PW–pl 1; AE–pl 184; AW–pl 181; AM (I)–42

MF · 4–7 (3–7) MONOG · MF I: 22–25 DAYS PRECOCIAL 4 F: 45–60 DAYS MF · FISH

BREEDING: Marshes, ponds, and lakes, occ along sluggish streams. Pothole marshes in aspen habitat of s w Manitoba supports highest densities. Usu 1 brood. **DISPLAYS:** Elaborate courtship of varied postures incl "rushing" (both birds rise out of water while side-by-side), weed ceremony, and much head shaking. **NEST:** Floating platform in shallow water, oft anchored in emergent veg; of underwater plants, rotting veg, rubbish, mud. Building continues during laying and incubation. **EGGS:** Bluish-white, chalky, usu nest-stained. 1.7" (44 mm). **DIET:** Aquatic insects, also crustaceans, mollusks. Stomach usu contains feather ball. In winter mostly fish, crustaceans. **CONSERVATION:** Winters within N.A. Blue List 1986; apparently declining. **NOTES:** Usu solitary, but occ may fish in flocks. Feathers occ half of stomach contents, may dive up to 3 minutes and travel 500' underwater. Young hatch asynchronously; eat adults' feathers. **ESSAYS:** Eating Feathers, p. 13; Commensal Feeding, p. 35; Visual Displays, p. 5; Transporting Young, p. 103; Plume Trade, p. 37; Blue List, p. 11; Swimming, p. 73; Eye Color, p. 233; Precocial and Altricial Young, p. 581. **REFS:** Ferguson and Sealy, 1983; Storer, 1969; Sugden, 1977.

Eared Grebe

Podiceps nigricollis Brehm

NG–22; G–20; PE–34; PW–pl 1; AE–pl 183; AW–pl 180; AM (I)–44

MF · 3–5 (1–6) MONOG · MF I: 20–22 DAYS PRECOCIAL 4 F: 21 DAYS MF · FISH

BREEDING: Marshes, ponds, lakes. Usu 1 brood, occ 2. **DISPLAYS:** Courtship and pair-bond maintenance: "penguin dance" with partners facing; stereotyped preening; "cat" attitude (elbows and crest raised) by one bird when partner approaches submerged. **NEST:** Floating platform in shallow water; of fresh and decayed veg, anchored in emergent veg. Build more than 1 nest. **EGGS:** Bluish-white, chalky, nest-stained buff or brown. 1.7" (43 mm). **DIET:** Mostly aquatic insects and larvae, also fish, crustaceans, mollusks, amphibians, feathers. **CONSERVATION:** Winters s to Guatemala. Milliners used feathers for hats, capes, and muffs. Eggs once taken for food. **NOTES:** Dense colonies in shallow water. Young hatch asynchronously; dive and hide, remaining submerged with bill exposed. Chicks ride and are fed on adults' backs. Young of several broods join to form creches. Mono Lake, CA and Great Salt Lake, UT serve as staging areas for fall migration; brine shrimp then comprise >90% of diet. Known in Europe as Black-necked Grebe. **ESSAYS:** Eating Feathers, p. 13; Visual Displays, p. 5; Transporting Young, p. 103; Plume Trade, p. 37; Creches, p. 191; Swimming, p. 73; Eye Color, p. 233; Precocial and Altricial Young, p. 581. **REFS:** Cramp and Simmons, 1977; Godfrey, 1986; Winkler and Cooper, 1986.

tem to gradually converge. That convergence, we hope, will supply a deeper understanding of displays and other behavioral phenomena.

SEE: Leks, p. 259; Territoriality, p. 387; Distraction Displays, p. 115; Dominance Hierarchies, p. 533; Shorebird Communication, p. 139; Duck Displays, p. 63; American Coots, p. 105; Redwing Coverable Badges, p. 611. REFS: Andrew, 1961; Baerends, 1975; Hinde, 1955; Wilson, 1975.

The Blue List

In 1971, the National Audubon Society's ornithological field journal, *American Birds*, began publishing a list, the Blue List, to provide early warning of those North American species undergoing population or range reductions. The Blue List was designed to identify patterns of impending or ongoing serious losses in regional bird populations, not to duplicate the function of the U.S. Fish and Wildlife Service's Threatened and Endangered Species List. Many species on the Blue List remain locally common, but appear to be undergoing noncyclic declines. In contrast, by the time a species is officially listed as Endangered, it often is on its last legs.

Throughout the decade following its inception, *American Birds* solicited reports and recommendations from its readership to incorporate into an annual update of the list. Regional editors forwarded these reports and recommendations to the publication, where nominations to and deletions from the list were compiled. In 1981, *American Birds* published a summarizing "decade list." It included the 69 birds nominated for listing that year as well as all of the species that had previously appeared on the Blue List. Updates of the Blue List continue, and at this writing (1987), 22 species were officially Blue-Listed and another 52 merited "Special" or "Local" Concern. Blue List status is noted under the "CONSERVATION" section of the respective species treatments.

The effectiveness of the Blue List depends on the accuracy of the data supplied by regional compilers and the responsiveness of government agencies accountable for species conservation. Submission of data to the editors of the Blue List is a way for field observers to influence policies of state and federal agencies concerned with avian research and species protection. More information is available from: American Birds Blue List, c/o *American Birds*, National Audubon Society, 950 Third Avenue, New York, NY 10022.

SEE: Birds and the Law, p. 293; Helping to Conserve Birds—National Level, p. 363; Metallic Poisons, p. 137; Wintering and Conservation, p. 513. REFS: Arbib, 1971; Tate, 1981, 1986.

Pied-billed Grebe

Podilymbus podiceps Linnaeus

NG–22; G–20; PE–34; PW–pl 1; AE–pl 180; AW–pl 176; AM (I)–40

MF	5–7 (3–10) MONOG?		F –M I: 23 DAYS PRECOCIAL 4 F: ? DAYS MF	FISH

BREEDING: Usu well-vegetated lakes, ponds, sluggish streams and marshes. 1 brood, 2 in s. **DISPLAYS:** Courtship more vocal than visual; male-female duet call. In territorial display at border, males turn away from each other and call, heads held high, bills up, then swing back face to face. **NEST:** Inconspicuous, shallow sodden platform of decaying veg anchored in open water among reeds or rushes. Of reeds, grass, oft plastered with soft green scum. **EGGS:** Bluish-white, chalky, nest-stained buff/brown. 1.7″ (43 mm). **DIET:** Aquatic insects, also snails, fish, frogs; incidental aquatic veg. Feather balls found in stomach. In winter occ forage in salt water. **CONSERVATION:** Winters s to Panama; s populations sedentary. Adaptable, found in developed areas. **NOTES:** Most solitary of all N.A. grebes. For proper development, eggs must lose water but this is a problem in hot, wet nest; facilitated by having 3× more pores for water diffusion, compared with similar eggs of other species. Young carried on back of adult, occ even during dives. Sinks to hide, leaving only head exposed. **ESSAYS:** Eating Feathers, p. 13; Transporting Young, p. 103; Plume Trade, p. 37; Swimming, p. 73; Precocial and Altricial Young, p. 581. **REFS:** Davis et al., 1984; Godfrey, 1986.

Least Grebe

Tachybaptus dominicus Linnaeus

NG–22; G–20; PE–298; PW–pl 1; AE–pl 179; AM (I)–40

MF	4–5 (3–6) MONOG?		MF I: 21 DAYS PRECOCIAL 4 F: ? DAYS MF	FISH

BREEDING: Freshwater lakes, streams, ponds, lagoons and temporary water bodies, usu in sluggish, quiet habitats. 2–3 broods? **DISPLAYS:** Practice reverse mounting (female mounts male, no cloacal contact), which may strengthen pair bond. "Inviting" head posture differs from other grebes. No rearing or wing-quivering. Duet trills. **NEST:** Exposed in middle of secluded pond: floating platform of decaying plants in shallow water, or anchored among emergent veg. Building continues throughout incubation. Used for successive broods. **EGGS:** Bluish-white, chalky, nest-stained buff/brown. 1.3″ (34 mm). **DIET:** Insects (mostly aquatic), few crustaceans, tadpoles, fish; also some algae. Swallows fewer feathers than fish-eating grebes. Oft picks insects from veg and from water's surface. **CONSERVATION:** Winter resident. **NOTES:** Occ loosely colonial. Nest throughout year, if weather permits. As in most grebes, commonly cover nest when leaving. Regularly sunbathe. Vigorous bathing sends up spray 2–3′ high. Oft in small flocks when not breeding. **ESSAYS:** Eating Feathers, p. 13; Transporting Young, p. 103; Plume Trade, p. 37; Swimming, p. 73; Precocial and Altricial Young, p. 581; Temperature Regulation, p. 149; Visual Displays, p. 5. **REFS:** Palmer, 1962; Storer, 1976.

Eating Feathers

Perhaps because the idea of swallowing hair is so unpleasant to us, it is difficult to believe the stories of birds deliberately eating their feathers. Nonetheless, some do and they do so regularly. Grebes, for example, consume their feathers by the hundreds. Feathers taken from parents are found in the stomachs of chicks only a few days old. Fifty percent of the stomach contents of a Horned or Pied-billed Grebe may be feathers. This odd behavior seems to have a purpose.

The action of the gizzard in these primarily fish-eating birds is insufficient to crush the bones that are swallowed. The feather balls are thought to protect the stomach by padding the sharp fish bones and slowing down the process of digestion so that the bones dissolve rather than pass into the intestine. This notion is supported by the observation that the Least Grebe, which of all the grebes consumes the fewest fish, also accumulates the smallest feather ball. Comparative studies of the gizzards and digestive physiology of fish-eating birds are needed to test this hypothesis. If it is supported, the question will then be why grebes have not evolved digestive tracts that can function efficiently without being stuffed with feathers.

SEE: Swallowing Stones, p. 269; Winter Feeding by Redpolls and Crossbills, p. 641; Feathered Nests, p. 605. REF: Storer, 1976.

Bird Names—I

No one is sure of the origin of the name grebe. It may come from the Breton word *krib*, for "crest." While loons may be thought to have been named for their crazy calls, the term actually is a corruption of the word *loom* which means "lame" in the language of the Shetland Islands (and refers to the awkwardness of these birds on land). Pelican, curiously, traces back to the Greek for "woodpecker," a term used by ancients for any bird with an impressive bill. Gannet is from the Anglo-Saxon for "little goose"; gannets were long thought to be close relatives of geese.

Anhinga means "water turkey" in the South American native language Tupi. The Anhinga (*Anhinga anhinga*) is unique among North American birds in having all its names the same. Bittern comes from Old English for "bellowing of a bull," referring to its call. Heron comes from the Middle English name for "herons"; Egret comes from the French and Old High German meaning "small heron." Flamingo is from the Spanish for "flame" (red). Stork and "starch" have the same roots in Old English, indicating the bird's stiff posture. Crane comes from the Anglo-Saxon *cran*—"to cry out."

REFS: Choate, 1985; Owen, 1985.

Northern Fulmar

Fulmarus glacialis Linnaeus

NG–26; G–24; PE–76; PW–pl 2; AE–pl 40; AW–pl 25; AM (I)–54

| GROUND | SAUCER MF (?) | 1 MONOG | MF I: 50–60 DAYS SEMIALTRICIAL 2 F: 46–51 DAYS MF | AQUATIC INVERTS OFFAL | HIGH DIVES LOW PATROL |

BREEDING: Sea cliffs, occ low, rocky isles. 1 brood. **DISPLAYS:** Female resting on ledge, male alights, bill open, head back, waving head side-to-side and up-down calling. **NEST:** Scrape on small grassy shelf of steep cliff, or saucer of veg on ground. Usu lined with fine material. **EGGS:** Off-white, oft nest-stained, occ marked with reddish-brown. 2.9″ (74 mm). **DIET:** Incl crustaceans, squid, jellyfish, other marine inverts, esp with high oil or fat content. Takes offal from whaling and fishing ships. Drinks seawater. Young fed oily regurgitant. **CONSERVATION:** Pelagic in winter, ranges to s Baja. **NOTES:** Long-term pair bond; strong nest site tenacity. Nocturnal at breeding colonies, less active on moonlit nights. "Foul gull" name for defensive vomiting of oil from stomach by young and adults; if sprayed on another bird, results in permanent wetting causing waterlogging and oft leads to drowning. Age at first breeding 6–12 years. Oft soars after ships. Female has sperm-storage glands, allowing separation of pair for several weeks prior to egg laying. Eggshells thicker than burrow-nesting petrels', which are less exposed. **ESSAYS:** Seabird Nesting, p. 197; Drinking, p. 123; Avian Smell, p. 15; Site Tenacity, p. 189; Salt Glands, p. 29; Bills, p. 209. **REFS:** Cramp and Simmons, 1977; Hatch, 1983, 1987; Ollason and Dunnet, 1986; Swennen 1974, Warham, 1983.

Manx Shearwater

Puffinus puffinus Brünnich

NG–28; G–28; PE–74; PW–pl 2; AE–320; AW–pl 67; AM (I)–66

| MF | 1 MONOG | MF I: 50–54 DAYS SEMIALTRICIAL 2 F: 70–75 DAYS MF | AQUATIC INVERTS OFFAL | HIGH DIVES SURFACE DIPS |

BREEDING: Isles with rocky cliffs. 1 brood. **DISPLAYS:** Male prospects for burrow, then calls from on or inside to attract females. Pair duets. **NEST:** Prefers to burrow among rocks, but also can excavate in soil; tunnel at least 4′, in lower slopes usu at junction of veg and rocks. Chamber lined with dry grass, leaves. Perennial. **EGGS:** White. 2.4″ (61 mm). **DIET:** Fish, crustaceans, squid, surface-floating offal; few aquatic plants. Can pursue prey underwater. **CONSERVATION:** Pelagic in winter, ranges s to Bermuda, rarely more than 10 miles from shore. **NOTES:** Colonial; only one N.A. colony exists (in Newfoundland), composed mostly of young breeders or birds too young to breed. Strictly nocturnal in colony, less active on moonlit nights. Does not breed until fifth or sixth year. Long-term pair bond. Male incubates first; each shift lasts ca. 6 days (range 1–26). Strong fidelity to nest burrow and to mate. Sexes can be distinguished by calls. Uses primarily visual cues to locate nest burrow in the dark. **ESSAYS:** Navigation and Orientation, p. 559; Feeding Young Petrels, p. 15; Parent-Chick Recognition, p. 193; Pelagic Birds, p. 657; Monogamy, p. 597. **REFS:** Cramp and Simmons, 1977; James, 1986; Nuttall et al., 1982; Storey and Lien, 1985.

Feeding Young Petrels

Petrels, albatrosses, shearwaters, and fulmars are commonly known as "tubenoses." All are marine birds with extremely large nostrils (thus the name) and a well-developed olfactory center in the brain. It is thought that these birds are able to find other individuals, good foraging areas, food, breeding areas, and/or nest sites by smell alone. They often feed very far from land, converting the oil-rich prey in their stomachs into a store of oil and partially digested flesh. The birds regurgitate the mix for their young when they return to their nests, often after an absence of days to weeks.

Tubenoses always produce a clutch of one, and the single chick matures very slowly. At one extreme, large albatrosses may take a year to fledge, while small storm-petrels are flight-ready in about two months. Tubenose young store large deposits of fat that may function to tide them over the long intervals between feedings. But the young of species, such as Manx Shearwaters, that are fed frequently (only about 5 percent of feeding intervals extend beyond three days) also have abundant fat deposits. These stores may allow for earlier fledging or may safeguard against uncertainties in hunting success after fledging.

Field studies have been conducted to examine whether foraging rates of the adults are determined by unpredictable food supplies or instead are dictated by the needs of the chicks. In one such study, a detailed analysis of feeding rates (frequency of feeding and meal size) was undertaken for Leach's Storm-Petrels on an island in the Bay of Fundy, New Brunswick. The results showed that time between consecutive feedings was only rarely as long as the period that the chicks could survive on their fat stores. Indeed the rate at which the storm-petrel chicks were fed seemed determined by their needs rather than the ability of the adults to find food. More research will be required to determine whether this is true for all tubenoses and, if so, to further examine the true function of fat storage in the chicks of these birds.

SEE: Coloniality, p. 173; Average Clutch Size, p. 51; Sea Bird Nesting Sites, p. 197; The Avian Sense of Smell, p. 15. REF: Ricklefs et al., 1985.

The Avian Sense of Smell

Most birds are primarily "sight animals" as their superb eyes, colorful plumage, and nonacoustic signals attest. But their sense of hearing is obviously also very acute—as in the case of night-hunting owls, which use sound to locate their prey. Most birds seemingly would have little use for smell; in the airy treetops odors disperse quickly and would be of minimal help in locating obstacles, prey, enemies, or mates. Yet the apparatus for detecting odors is present in the nasal passages of all birds. Based on the

Leach's Storm-Petrel

Oceanodroma leucorhoa Vieillot

NG–34; G–30; PE–76; PW–pl 2; AE–pl 83; AW–pl 62; AM (I)–72

| BANK | M | 1 MONOG | MF
I: 38–46 DAYS
SEMIALTRICIAL 2
F: 63–70 DAYS
MF | AQUATIC
INVERTS
OFFAL | |

BREEDING: Coastal islands. 1 brood. **DISPLAYS:** Male calls female to burrow; cop in burrow. **NEST:** On bank, grassy slope, or in field among stumps, rocks; burrows 1′–3′, occ 6′, branched, end in enlarged chamber. Nest, if present, is loose, flat, thin pad of dry veg. Perennial. Male digs with bill, feet. **EGGS:** Cream/white, oft nest-stained, occ marked with reddish/purplish, wreathed. 1.3″ (33 mm). **DIET:** Skims ocean surface for fish, squid, crustaceans, floating oil (from large, dead animals). Will follow wounded marine mammals. Occ forage for exposed prey at edge of potentially dangerous gull feeding-flocks. Young fed oily regurgitant independently by each parent every 2–3 nights. **CONSERVATION:** Pelagic in winter, ranges s to Galapagos (w) and Brazil (e). **NOTES:** Colonial. Strictly nocturnal on breeding ground; less active on moonlit nights. Incubation exchange ca. every 3 days; sitter loses 11% of body weight during each stint. Mate retention between years dependent on site tenacity to specific burrow; most mate switches occur with neighbors. Orientation to nest site based partly on olfactory cues. Female has sperm-storage gland in oviduct, permitting separation of pair for several weeks preceding egg laying. **ESSAYS:** Navigation and Orientation, p. 539; Feeding Young Petrels, p. 15; Seabird Nesting, p. 197; Avian Smell, p. 15; Pelagic Birds, p. 657; Site Tenacity, p. 189. **REFS:** Boersma, 1986; Cramp and Simmons, 1977; Morse and Kress, 1984; Ricklefs, 1987; Watanuki, 1986.

Black Storm-Petrel

Oceanodroma melania Bonaparte

NG–36; G–30; PW–pl 2; AW–385; AM (I)–74

| CLIFF | MF (?) | 1 MONOG? | ?
I: >18 DAYS
SEMIALTRICIAL 2
F: ? DAYS
? | OFFAL | SURFACE DIPS |

BREEDING: Coastal islands with cliffs. 1 brood. **DISPLAYS:** ? **NEST:** In old burrow of Cassin's Auklet or amid boulders, in crevice. Lays egg on bare ground or few twigs. **EGGS:** Dull white, somewhat nest-stained, occ marked with lavender/reddish, wreathed. 1.4″ (37 mm). **DIET:** Little known. Scavenges fat or oil of large, dead animals from ocean surface; crustaceans, possibly fish, plankton. **CONSERVATION:** Pelagic in winter, ranges s to Peru. **NOTES:** Do not occupy nest in advance of egg deposition as do shearwaters; usu colonial. Active at breeding grounds only at night; when confronted eject oily stomach contents up to 3′. Slowly fly 1′–2′ above waves. First breeding n of Mexico recorded 1976 on Santa Barbara Island, CA. **ESSAYS:** Pelagic Birds, p. 657; Avian Smell, p. 15; Skimming, p. 195; Feeding Young Petrels, p. 15; Navigation and Orientation, p. 559. **REF:** Palmer, 1962.

relative size of the brain center used to process information on odors, physiologists expect the sense of smell to be well developed in rails, cranes, grebes, and nightjars and less developed in passerines, woodpeckers, pelicans, and parrots. By recording the electrical impulses transmitted through the bird's olfactory nerves, physiologists have documented some of the substances that birds as diverse as sparrows, chickens, pigeons, ducks, shearwaters, albatrosses, and vultures are able to smell.

The sense of smell seems better developed in some avian groups than others. Kiwis, the flightless birds that are the national symbol of New Zealand, appear to sniff out their earthworm prey. Sooty Shearwaters and Northern Fulmars are attracted from downwind to the smell of fish oils, squid, and krill, and when tested, investigate the area around a wick releasing such odorants. Other tubenoses such as the Ashy Storm-Petrel and Pink-footed Shearwater are also attracted to the same stimuli.

When they return at night from foraging in the Bay of Fundy, Leach's Storm-Petrels appear to use odor to locate their burrows on forested Kent Island, New Brunswick. They first hover above the thick spruce-fir canopy before plummeting to the forest floor in the vicinity of their burrows. Then they walk upwind to them, often colliding with obstacles on the way. In one experiment the storm-petrels moved toward a stream of air passing over materials from their own burrow, rather than one passing over similar materials from the forest floor. In another experiment, individuals whose nostrils were plugged or whose olfactory nerves had been severed were unable to find their way back to their burrows. These results suggest that the storm-petrels locate their burrows by smell where there is heavy forest cover; they do not seem to use smell to find their burrows on unforested Pacific Islands. Interestingly, there is also some evidence that the smells in air currents near their lofts help pigeons navigate.

There has been a long controversy over the degree to which vultures use odor to help them find food. Mostly the argument has been over whether sight or smell is more important, but it has also been suggested, by those with a flair for the absurd, that vultures listen for the noise of the chewing of carrion-feeding rodents or insects or even use an as yet undiscovered sense. Nonetheless, the sight-odor argument remains unsettled. While Turkey Vultures, for example, seem to have a good sense of smell, quite likely it is not good enough to detect the stench of decomposing food from their foraging altitudes. Experiments have shown that their threshold for detecting the odors of at least three different products of decay is too high to permit sniff location from high altitude. Whether or not the birds are more sensitive to the smells of other components of decomposition remains to be determined. More work will need to be done before we know whether vultures use sight or smell or both to locate the dead animals they feed on.

SEE: Hawk-Eyed, p. 229; What Do Birds Hear?, p. 299; How Owls Hunt in the Dark, p. 291. REFS: Bang and Wenzel, 1985; Grubb, 1974; Smith and Paselk, 1986; Wenzel, 1973.

Ashy Storm-Petrel
Oceanodroma homochroa Coues

NG–36; G–30; PW–pl 2; AW–pl 64; AM (I)–72

			MF		
CREVICE	1		I: 44? DAYS	AQUATIC	SURFACE
	MONOG		SEMIALTRICIAL 2	INVERTS?	DIPS
			F: ? DAYS	ALGAE?	
			?		

BREEDING: Islands with natural cavities or providing burrows. 1 brood. **DISPLAYS:** Lengthy. Nights spent on breeding grounds, chiefly in burrow followed by 1 week of constant residence. **NEST:** Preference for natural cavities, also under loosely piled rocks, stone walls, driftwood and turf. No nest constructed; occ uses pebble pile, rarely lined. Nest burrow has distinctive musky odor. **EGGS:** Dull, creamy white, unmarked or wreathed with faint reddish-brown dots. 1.2" (30 mm). **DIET:** Little known; probably fish, crustaceans, marine algae. Young fed regurgitant of marine inverts. **CONSERVATION:** Pelagic in winter, ranges to Baja and San Benito Islands. **NOTES:** Colonial. Incubation shifts exchange at night. Young do not leave nest until fully feathered. Ejects bright orange oil under duress. **ESSAYS:** Avian Smell, p. 15; Feeding Young Petrels, p. 15; Pelagic Birds, p. 657; Skimming, p. 195; Navigation and Orientation, p. 559; Monogamy, p. 597. **REF:** Palmer, 1962.

Fork-tailed Storm-Petrel
Oceanodroma furcata Gmelin

NG–36; G–30; PW–pl 2; AW–383; AM (I)–72

			MF		
MF	1		I: 46–51 (37–68) DAYS	CRUSTACEANS	SURFACE
	MONOG		SEMIALTRICIAL 2		DIPS
			F: 51–61 DAYS		
			MF		

BREEDING: On rocky islands. 1 brood. **DISPLAYS:** Mutual preening between pair accompanied by vocalizations. **NEST:** Burrow in soft soil on slopes or at base of cliff. Enlarged chamber, scantily lined with grass. Also in crevices, 8"–3' deep. Probably perennial. **EGGS:** Dull white, wreathed by dark purple/black specks. 1.3" (34 mm). **DIET:** Incl oil and animal detritus picked from ocean surface, seek oils seeping from wounded marine mammals; follow large floating carcasses. Young fed oil regurgitant. **CONSERVATION:** Pelagic in winter off w N.A. Regurgitant can be used to monitor petroleum, plastic particles and other sublethal doses of oceanic pollutants. **NOTES:** Colonial; nocturnal activity. Long-term pair bond. Pairs spend much time together in burrow prior to egg laying. Eggs may remain unattended for days at a time; low metabolism of embryo at cool burrow temperatures, slow development, and low water loss from egg permit extended neglect. Incubation shifts of 1–5 (usu 2–3) days. Adults assist emergence of young from shell; chicks brooded 1–8 (usu 3–5) days; begin to explore outside of burrow several days before fledging. Follows ships; oft attracted like moths to light. **ESSAYS:** Geometry of Selfish Colony, p. 19; Incubation Time, p. 481; Pelagic Birds, p. 657; Avian Smell, p. 15. **REFS:** Boersma et al., 1980; Quinlan, 1983; Simons, 1981; Vleck and Kenagy, 1980.

Geometry of the Selfish Colony

In a classic article entitled "The geometry of the selfish herd," ecologist W. D. Hamilton presented a model to explain why animals often are found in aggregations—flocks, herds, schools, etc. The basic assumption of the model was rather simple: animals do not crowd together to benefit the group, but for purely "selfish" reasons.

Hamilton's scheme assumed that a predator would always attack the nearest prey. In that circumstance, it would always be to the advantage of potential victims to approach each other. Side by side, two of them would each have only half the "domain of danger" that one alone would have, since each would be closer to a predator approaching from only half the possible directions. If four crowd together, each is exposed to predation from only one quarter of the possible directions (that is, the domain of danger is halved again). And so it goes—the larger the herd or colony, the less the exposure of a given individual. Those able to reach the center of the crowd would be safest of all.

Some evidence of this can be seen in observations of fishes attempting to move into the middle of a school when a predator approaches, sheep trying to butt their way into the center of a flock when harried by sheepdogs, and Gray-breasted Martins in Mexico trying to remain near the center of nocturnal roosting aggregations on power lines. Could Hamilton's model fit other aggregations of birds? Research by Susan E. Quinlan, of the Alaska Department of Fish and Game, who studied predation by river otters on storm-petrel colonies at Fish Island in the Gulf of Alaska, indicates that it could. Quinlan suggested that river otters prey heavily on seabirds under special circumstances only, such as a decline in the availability of an important aquatic food. She found that in 1976 and 1977 the otters were the primary cause of mortality among breeding Fork-tailed Storm-Petrels on Fish Island, killing about a quarter of those breeding in burrows on the soil-covered plateau in the island's center. (The petrels breeding in the other habitat, rocky slopes dropping to the shoreline, suffered little predation, but exact data could not be obtained because of the difficulty of locating the nests.)

The density of Fork-tailed Storm-Petrel nests varied over the plateau, and depredations by the otters were greatest where the density was lowest. Birds in denser parts of the colony were safer, even though there is no mobbing reaction to intruders to explain the greater security of "inside" birds. Quinlan suggested that although the probability of a group of nests being detected increased as they crowded close together, above a certain density this disadvantage was overcome by the reduction in the chance of being eaten. This could be due to the selfish herd effect, the domains of danger of each nest in high-density areas being very small. She predicted that large colonies in general will suffer less than small ones from irregular otter predation.

More research needs to be done to test whether these birds really do

Magnificent Frigatebird

Fregata magnificens Mathews

NG–38; G–34; PE–78; PW– 14; AE–pl 85; AW–pl 57; AM (I)–104

2'–15'	MF	1	MF	AQUATIC	PIRACY
GROUND		MONOG	I: >50? DAYS	INVERTS	
			ALTRICIAL		
			F: 170 DAYS		
			MF		

BREEDING: Islands with mangroves, low trees and shrubs on undisturbed coasts. 1 brood. **DISPLAYS**: Males display in small groups inflating red gular sacs, opening wings and drumming against gular sacs. Male shakes head side-to-side, calls, spreads wings and fluffs green iridescent scapulars. Male rubs pouch against female. **NEST**: Oft in thickets; frail, of sticks, twigs, sparsely lined with grass. Small for size of bird. Male chooses site for nest and gathers material, female builds. **EGGS**: White. 2.7" (68 mm). **DIET**: Inverts include jellyfish, crustaceans; occ turtles, offal. Never alights, picks from surface in flight. **CONSERVATION**: Pelagic in winter, s to n Peru, n Argentina. **NOTES**: Colonial. Nest never left unattended; colony members steal materials, eat eggs, young. Male and female brood. Female tends and feeds young for ca. one year; male leaves at ca. 3 months. Initial breeding deferred several years. Unlike males, females probably do not breed annually. Adults more adept than immatures at piracy. Helpless if enter water; soaring wings and weak legs prevent takeoff. **ESSAYS**: Piracy, p. 159; Coloniality, p. 173; Sexual Selection, p. 251. **REFS**: Gochfeld and Burger, 1981; Harrington et al., 1972; Nelson, 1975; Trivelpiece and Ferraris, 1987.

Brown Pelican

Pelecanus occidentalis Linnaeus

NG–40; G–32; PE–78; PW–14; AE–pl 176; AW–pl 155; AM (I)–90

8'–200'	MF	3	MF	
CLIFF		(2–4)	I: 28–30 DAYS	
GROUND		MONOG	ALTRICIAL	
			F: 71–88 DAYS	
			MF	

BREEDING: Open coastal habitat on islands without mammalian predators. 1 brood. **DISPLAYS**: Female squats on bare ground; male slowly and silently circles female, slightly lifting wings and tilting neck back. Female rises from squat and flies to water, male follows. **NEST**: Usu on mangrove treetops or scrape on ground; variable in size and structure. Tree nests well built of sticks, reeds, grass. Perennial. Male gathers material, female builds. **EGGS**: White, stained. 3.0" (76 mm). **DIET**: Esp anchovies in breeding season, some prawns. Young fed regurgitant. Pouch serves as fishnet on dive; on surfacing, points bill down to drain pouch, then up to swallow fish. **CONSERVATION**: Winters s along coasts of Americas. Suffered eggshell thinning by pesticides, also habitat loss; by 1970, only viable N.A. populations were in FL. Now recovering on e and w coast; only in TX and LA still Endangered Species. **NOTES**: Colonial in nesting and feeding. Females do not breed before third year, males even later. Arboreal young stay in nest almost 2× longer (63 days) than ground young (35 days). Eyes not adapted for underwater vision. Live 25–30 years. **ESSAYS**: DDT and Birds, p. 21; Birds and the Law, p. 293; Bills, p. 209. **REFS**: Briggs et al., 1983; Schreiber, 1977, 1980.

constitute a "selfish colony," but Quinlan's results show that here, as elsewhere, ecological theory can suggest reasons for observed bird behavior—in this case why some Fork-tailed Storm-Petrel nest burrows have as many as five other burrows within a radius of two yards. A good model may eventually prove to be incorrect or inapplicable in a given case, but models provide a framework for designing field research.

SEE: Mobbing, p. 425; Sleeping Sentries, p. 61; Facts, Hypotheses, and Theories, p. 567. REFS: Hamilton, 1971; Quinlan, 1983; Watt and Mock, 1987.

DDT and Birds

Birds played a major role in creating awareness of pollution problems. Indeed, many people consider the modern environmental movement to have started with the publication in 1962 of Rachel Carson's classic *Silent Spring*, which described the results of the misuse of DDT and other pesticides. In the fable that began that volume, she wrote: "It was a spring without voices. On the mornings that had once throbbed with the dawn chorus of robins, catbirds, doves, jays, wrens, and scores of other bird voices there was now no sound; only silence lay over the fields and woods and marsh." *Silent Spring* was heavily attacked by the pesticide industry and by narrowly trained entomologists, but its scientific foundation has stood the test of time. Misuse of pesticides is now widely recognized to threaten not only bird communities but human communities as well.

The potentially lethal impact of DDT on birds was first noted in the late 1950s when spraying to control the beetles that carry Dutch elm disease led to a slaughter of robins in Michigan and elsewhere. Researchers discovered that earthworms were accumulating the persistent pesticide and that the robins eating them were being poisoned. Other birds fell victim, too. Gradually, thanks in no small part to Carson's book, gigantic "broadcast spray" programs were brought under control.

But DDT, its breakdown products, and the other chlorinated hydrocarbon pesticides (and nonpesticide chlorinated hydrocarbons such as PCBs) posed a more insidious threat to birds. Because these poisons are persistent they tend to concentrate as they move through the feeding sequences in communities that ecologists call "food chains." For example, in most marine communities, the living weight (biomass) of fish-eating birds is less than that of the fishes they eat. However, because chlorinated hydrocarbons accumulate in fatty tissues, when a ton of contaminated fishes is turned into 200 pounds of seabirds, most of the DDT from the numerous fishes ends up in a relatively few birds. As a result, the birds have a higher level of contamination per pound than the fishes. If Peregrine Falcons feed on the seabirds, the concentration becomes higher still. With several concentrating steps in the food chain below the level of fishes (for instance, tiny

American White Pelican
Pelecanus erythrorhynchos Gmelin

| MF | 2
(1–3)
MONOG | MF
I: 29–36 DAYS
ALTRICIAL
F: 60 + DAYS
MF |

BREEDING: Islands in inland rivers and bays free of mammalian predation. 1 brood. **DISPLAYS**: In courtship, female bows to male by raising breast, elevating folded wings, arching neck and pointing bill down against breast. Male responds by close approach, expands pouch, extends neck over female and sways head. Pair also perform strutting walk, oft joined by others. **NEST**: Scrape rimmed with dirt and rubbish, or with stems, wood bits, and fine material. **EGGS**: White, oft nest-stained. 3.5″ (90 mm). **DIET**: Mostly fish, occ salamanders, crayfish. Young fed regurgitant, later fed fish. Swims at surface and submerges head to catch fish; consumes about 3 lb/day. Occ fish cooperatively. **CONSERVATION**: Winters s through lowlands to Nicaragua. Blue List 1972–81, Special Concern 1982, Local Concern 1986; reduced in w U.S. from 23 colonies to 5, but stable. **NOTES**: Colonial, oft assoc with Double-crested Cormorant. Unlike Brown Pelican, buoyant, not built for diving. Young brooded 15–18 days. Second chick in brood usu dies from starvation due to harassment by its older sibling. Conspicuous spring flights over breeding grounds attract arriving migrants and promote breeding synchrony. **ESSAYS**: Plume Trade, p. 37; Variation in Clutch Sizes, p. 339; Brood Reduction, p. 307; Blue List, p. 11; Coloniality, p. 173. **REFS**: Evans and Cash, 1985; Evans and McMahon, 1987; Knopf, 1979; Sidle et al., 1985.

Northern Gannet
Sula bassanus Linnaeus

| GROUND | M –F | 1
MONOG | MF
I: 42–44 DAYS
ALTRICIAL
F: 91 (84–97) DAYS
MF | SQUID |

BREEDING: Flat-topped open islands, coastal rocky slopes and cliffs. 1 brood. **DISPLAYS**: Nest exchange sequence: pair face, wings slightly raised, tails spread, bow, sky-point, and repeatedly dip bill to breast of mate; then preen and exchange duties on nest. Sequence occ carried out alone. **NEST**: Of seaweed, grass, flotsam; repaired yearly with soil accumulating beneath. **EGGS**: Light bluish-white, nest-stained. 3.1″ (78 mm). **DIET**: Esp herring and mackerel from surface schools; dives from up to 90′ above surface. Young fed regurgitant, later fed fish. **CONSERVATION**: Pelagic in winter off e N.A. Oft drowned in commercial fishnets. **NOTES**: Nest in dense colonies. Long-term pair bond. Special reinforced skull cushions dive impact. Young grow rapidly; fledge by launching from cliff and landing ¼–½ mile out to sea. Breeds to northern limit of warm/cold water mixing. Prebreeders range among colonies before making permanent choice of future breeding colony. **ESSAYS**: Bills, p. 209; Incubation Time, p. 481; Brood Patches, p. 427; Swimming, p. 73; Vocal Functions, p. 471; Color of Birds, p. 111. **REFS**: Kirkham et al., 1985; Montevecchi et al., 1984; Nelson, 1978.

aquatic plants → crustacea → small fishes), very slight environmental contamination can be turned into a heavy pesticide load in birds at the top of the food chain. In one Long Island estuary, concentrations of less than a tenth of a part per million (PPM) of DDT in aquatic plants and plankton resulted in concentrations of 3–25 PPM in gulls, terns, cormorants, mergansers, herons, and ospreys.

"Bioconcentration" of pesticides in birds high on food chains occurs not only because there is usually reduced biomass at each step in those chains, but also because predatory birds tend to live a long time. They may take in only a little DDT per day, but they keep most of what they get, and they live many days.

The insidious aspect of this phenomenon is that large concentrations of chlorinated hydrocarbons do not usually kill the bird outright. Rather, DDT and its relatives alter the bird's calcium metabolism in a way that results in thin eggshells. Instead of eggs, heavily DDT-infested Brown Pelicans and Bald Eagles tend to find omelettes in their nests, since the eggshells are unable to support the weight of the incubating bird.

Shell-thinning resulted in the decimation of the Brown Pelican populations in much of North America and the extermination the Peregrine Falcon in the eastern United States and southeastern Canada. Shell-thinning caused lesser declines in populations of Golden and Bald Eagles and White Pelicans, among others. Similar declines took place in the British Isles. Fortunately, the cause of the breeding failures was identified in time, and the use of DDT was banned almost totally in the United States in 1972.

The reduced bird populations started to recover quickly thereafter, with species as different as ospreys and robins returning to the pre-DDT levels of breeding success in a decade or less. Furthermore, attempts to reestablish the peregrine in the eastern United States using captive-reared birds show considerable signs of success. Brown Pelican populations have now recovered to the extent that the species no longer warrants endangered status except in California. The banning of DDT has helped to create other pesticide problems, however. The newer organophosphate pesticides that to a degree have replaced organochlorines, such as parathion and TEPP (tetraethyl pyrophosphate), are less persistent so they do not accumulate in food chains. They are, nonetheless, highly toxic. Parathion applied to winter wheat, for instance, killed some 1,600 waterfowl, mostly Canada Geese, in the Texas panhandle in 1981.

Unfortunately, however, DDT has recently started to become more common in the environment again; its concentration in the tissues of starlings in Arizona and New Mexico, for example, has been increasing. While the source of that DDT is disputed, what is certain is that DDT has been shown to be present as a contaminant in the widely used toxin dicofol (a key ingredient in, among others, the pesticide Kelthane). Dicofol is a chemical formed by adding single oxygen atoms to DDT molecules. Unhappily, not all the DDT gets oxygenated, so that sometimes dicofol is contaminated with as much as 15 percent DDT.

Anhinga

Anhinga anhinga Linnaeus

NG–44; G–36; PE–40; AE–pl 100; AM (I)–102

TREE	MF	4	MF	AQUATIC	
4'–20'		(2–5)	I: 26–29 DAYS	INVERTS	
		MONOG	ALTRICIAL	SM VERTS	
			F: ? DAYS		
			MF		

BREEDING: Freshwater swamps, lakes and sluggish streams. 1? brood. **DISPLAYS:** Courting male performs spiral aerial display; perched, performs wing-waving displays and "reverse bow" by raising tail and bringing neck back with head touching back. **NEST:** Prefers willow clumps; conspicuous, loosely built, bulky platform of sticks, twigs, dead leaves, etc., unlined or lined with green leaves and finer materials. Perennial sites. Male chooses site, brings materials. Oft appropriate heron or egret nest. **EGGS:** Light bluish-white, nest-stained. 2.1" (53 mm). **DIET:** Usu swallows food at surface. Avoids hunting in salt water. Spearlike bill used to impale prey, which are oft tossed in air, swallowed head first. Young fed by regurgitation. **CONSERVATION:** Mainly resident in winter, some s to c Mexico. **NOTES:** Usu colonial, oft with egrets and herons. Young hatch asynchronously; brooded continuously by male and female until day 12. Young use bill and feet to climb, but return to nest until fledged. Plumage is very wettable but characteristic spread-wing posture functions to absorb solar energy in cool weather to offset low metabolic rate and high rate of heat loss. Can control buoyancy like grebes. **ESSAYS:** Spread-Wing Postures, p. 25; Feathers, p. 309; Preening, p. 53. **REFS:** Burger et al., 1978; Hennemann, 1985; Owre, 1967.

Great Cormorant

Phalacrocorax carbo Linnaeus

NG–44; G–36; PE–40; AE–pl 102; AM (I)–92

TREE	MF	4–5	MF	
		(1–6)	I: 29–31 DAYS	
		MONOG	ALTRICIAL	
			F: 50 DAYS	
			MF	

BREEDING: Coastal cliffs, lakes and rivers. 1 brood. **DISPLAYS:** Perched male flaps wings to invite female, followed by billing, then roles reverse: female perches, male flies. At nest, pair intertwine necks. **NEST:** Usu on higher portions of rocky cliffs. Bulky, of twigs, branches, grass, seaweed, lined with fine material. Added to yearly. Guano coats vicinity. **EGGS:** Faint green/blue, nest-stained. 2.6" (65 mm). **DIET:** Occ also crustaceans. Young fed regurgitant, first dripped from bill, later offered tureenlike from adult's bill. **CONSERVATION:** Winters near breeding grounds, along e coast of N.A. Regarded as competitor by commercial fishermen. **NOTES:** Colonial, oft assoc with Double-crested Cormorants. Used by fishermen in s e Asia to capture fish, usu with neck rings to prevent swallowing, but well-trained birds need no rings. Eyes adapted for aerial as well as underwater vision. **ESSAYS:** Visual Displays, p. 5; Coloniality, p. 173; Seabird Nesting, p. 197; Bathing and Dusting, p. 429. **REFS:** Cramp and Simmons, 1977; Drury and Hatch, 1985; Erskine, 1972; Milton and Austin-Smith, 1983.

Overall, the 2.5 million pounds of dicofol used annually in pesticides contain about 250 thousand pounds of DDT. In addition, little is known about the breakdown products of dicofol itself, which may include DDE, a breakdown product of DDT identified as the major cause of reproductive failure in several bird species. Finally, DDT itself may still be in use illegally in some areas of the United States, and migratory birds such as the Black-crowned Night-Heron may be picking up DDT in their tropical wintering grounds (where DDT application is still permitted). Unhappily tropical countries are becoming dumping grounds for unsafe pesticides that are now banned in the United States. As the end of the century approaches, the once hopeful trend may be reversing, so that DDT and other pesticides continue to hang as a heavy shadow over many bird populations.

SEE: Metallic Poisons, p. 137; Hatching, p. 233; Wintering and Conservation, p. 513; Conservation of Raptors, p. 247. REFS: Beaver, 1980; Bonney, 1986; Carson, 1962; Ehrlich et al., 1975; Henny et al., 1984; Spitzer et al., 1978; White et al., 1982.

Spread-Wing Postures

Some birds adopt characteristic poses in which they extend and often slightly droop their wings. This behavior is commonly described as "sunbathing" or "wing-drying." Cormorants and Anhingas frequently assume these postures, which are also seen in both Brown and White Pelicans, as well as in some storks, herons, vultures, and hawks.

The structure of cormorant and Anhinga feathers decreases buoyancy and thus facilitates underwater pursuit of fishes. Hence their plumage is not water-repellent, but "wettable." It has been suggested that the function of the spread-wing postures in these birds is to dry the wings after wetting. Biologists once thought that deficient production of oils from the preen gland necessitate wing-drying behaviors. We now know, however, that the degree of waterproofing of feathers is primarily due to their microscopic structure, not to their being oiled. In addition to helping wing feathers to dry, other suggested functions for these postures include regulating body temperature ("thermoregulation"), realigning of feathers, forcing parasites into motion to ease their removal, and helping the perched bird to balance.

Spread-wing postures may serve different purposes in different species. Anhingas, for example, have unusually low metabolic rates and unusually high rates of heat loss from their bodies. Whether wet or dry, they exhibit spread-wing postures mostly under conditions of bright sunlight and cool ambient temperatures, and characteristically orient themselves with their backs to the sun. Thus, it appears that Anhingas adopt a spread-wing posture primarily for thermoregulation—to absorb solar energy to supplement their low metabolic heat production and to offset partly their inordinately

Olivaceous Cormorant

Supersp #4
Phalacrocorax olivaceus Humboldt

NG–44; G–36; PE–40; AE–pl 101; AM (I)–94

| 3'–20'
GROUND | MF (?) | 4
(2–6)
MONOG? | ?
I: ? DAYS
ALTRICIAL
F: ? DAYS
MF | FROGS | |

BREEDING: Rivers, lakes, marshes and seacoasts. 1? brood. **DISPLAYS:** ? **NEST:** Sturdy platform with shallow depression; of small sticks, compactly arranged on forking branches of live or dead support. Also on bare ground. **EGGS:** Light bluish-white, oft nest-stained. 2.1″ (54 mm). **DIET:** Occ hunt cooperatively, beating water with wings, confusing fish; also take some frogs, insects. **CONSERVATION:** Winter resident. **NOTES:** Nests in small colonies. Grunts like pig when frightened. Eyes adapted for aerial as well as underwater vision. Unlike other N.A. cormorants, oft perches on branches or wires; occ feeds with wings and tail spread. Adults much more efficient foragers than are young birds which must spend relatively more time foraging. **ESSAYS:** Spread-Wing Postures, p. 25; Commensal Feeding, p. 35; Swimming, p. 73; Coloniality, p. 173; Superspecies, p. 375. **REFS:** Morrison et al., 1978; Palmer, 1962.

Double-crested Cormorant

Supersp #4
Phalacrocorax auritus Lesson

NG–46; G–36; PE–40; PW–pl 17; AE–pl 99; AW–pl 76; AM (I)–94

| TREE
6'–150' | MF | 3–4
(2–7)
MONOG | MF
I: 25–29 DAYS
ALTRICIAL
F: 35–42 DAYS
MF | AQUATIC
INVERTS | SURFACE
DIPS |

BREEDING: Lakes, rivers, swamps, seacoasts, along coastal cliffs. 1 brood. **DISPLAYS:** Complex courtship—males pursue females, splash forcefully with both wings, swim rapidly in zigzag until heads submerged, dive and surface holding veg which male drops near female or tosses in air. **NEST:** On tree or ground, but not both in same colony; platform of sticks, seaweed, and other drift material. Usu lined with finer materials. Stick and twig tree nests may have green leaves. **EGGS:** Light blue/bluish-white, usu nest-stained. 2.4″ (61 mm). **DIET:** Primarily schooling fish; rarely other small verts. Young fed regurgitant, first dripped from bill, then offered in tureenlike bill. **CONSERVATION:** Winters s to w c Mexico, Bahamas and Greater Antilles. Blue List 1972–81, Special Concern 1982, Local Concern 1986; populations appear to be increasing. **NOTES:** Usu colonial; within colonies, earliest breeders usu older, experienced nesters. Young hatch asynchronously. Young brooded almost continuously for 12 days; can maintain body temperature at 14–15 days. Eyes adapted for aerial as well as underwater vision. Energetic, aggressive defense of eggs and young from avian predators (esp Northwestern Crow, Glaucous-winged Gull). Regurgitates pellets. Vandalized colonies are abandoned. **ESSAYS:** Incubation Time, p. 481; Blue List, p. 11; Pellets, p. 297; Coloniality, p. 173; Seabird Nesting, p. 197. **REFS:** Dunn, 1976; McNeil and Léger, 1987; Siegel-Causey and Hunt, 1981; Vermeer and Rankin, 1984.

high rate of heat loss due to convection and (when wet) evaporation from their plumage.

Cormorants, in contrast, apparently use spread-wing postures only for drying their wings and not for thermoregulation. Although cormorant plumage also retains water, only the outer portion of the feathers is wettable, so an insulating layer of air next to the skin is maintained when cormorants swim underwater. This difference in feather structure may explain why cormorants can spend more time foraging in the water than Anhingas, and why cormorants can inhabit cooler climes, while the Anhinga is restricted to tropical and subtropical waters.

Spread-wing postures appear to serve for both thermoregulation and drying in Turkey Vultures. These birds maintain their body temperature at a lower level at night than in the daytime. Morning wing-spreading should provide a means of absorbing solar energy and passively raising their temperature to the daytime level. Field observations indicate that this behavior is associated with the intensity of sunlight and also occurs more frequently when the birds are wet than when they are dry.

SEE: Metabolism, p. 325; Temperature Regulation and Behavior, p. 149; Black and White Plumage, p. 177.   REFS: Clark, 1969; Clark and Ohmart, 1985; Elowson, 1984; Hennemann, 1982, 1983, 1985; Mahoney, 1984; Simmons, 1986.

Who Incubates?

Which parent incubates varies greatly among species, as we indicate in the species treatments. In most birds, parents share incubation. Double-crested Cormorants, like many other birds that share the task, relieve each other regularly, every hour or so. In other birds, including some sandpipers, pigeons, and doves, the female incubates at night while the male takes his turn during "working hours"—about 9 A.M to 5 P.M. Both sexes of most woodpeckers alternate during the day, but the male sits on the eggs at night. Starlings, on the other hand, share the task during the day, but the female alone incubates at night. In monogamous species in which both adults incubate the same clutch, the eggs usually are covered most of the time. That is the case in the African Common Waxbill, an estrildid finch, one of the most extreme examples of shared incubation: in this species the pair spends virtually full time sitting together on the clutch.

The female is the only incubator in hummingbirds, many raptors, many passerines, and all North American polygynous species (those in which one male has more than one mate). Often the male is not without duties; he may feed the incubating female and stand watch from a nearby perch. Female hornbills, brightly colored Old World birds with large, downcurved bills, lay their eggs in cavities. The female then seals herself into the cavity with the eggs, using first mud and then feces mixed with

Brandt's Cormorant

Phalacrocorax penicillatus Brandt

NG–46; G–36; PW– 17; AW–pl 77; AM (I)–96

		MF		
MF	4	I: ? DAYS		
	(3–6)	ALTRICIAL		
	MONOG	F: ? DAYS		
		MF		

BREEDING: Usu on open ground in rocky areas along seacoasts, less oft inshore on brackish bays. 1 brood. **DISPLAYS:** Male 2-part courtship: "flutter"—bill up, tail cocked and spread, neck feathers fluffed, blue gular pouch distended, wings fluttering; "stroke"—head thrust forward and downward in hammerlike rocking. **NEST:** Avoids perpendicular cliffs used by Pelagic Cormorant. No sticks in nests; instead, uses seaweed, other marine veg. Nests perennial; fresh material added to guano-coated, rotted debris. Male gathers material, female builds. **EGGS:** Light blue/ bluish-white, nest-stained. 2.4" (62 mm). **DIET:** Fish obtained by diving, oft caught near substrate. **CONSERVATION:** In winter ranges s to s Baja, and widely in Gulf of CA. **NOTES:** Nests closely packed in colonies on clifftops or on grassy slopes. Adults do not leave nest unattended since Western Gulls steal eggs and young. Eyes adapted for aerial as well as underwater vision. Regurgitates pellets. Very tame. **ESSAYS:** Spread-Wing Postures, p. 25; Coloniality, p. 173; Seabird Nesting, p. 197; Pellets, p. 297. **REFS:** Ainley et al., 1981; Palmer, 1962.

Pelagic Cormorant

Phalacrocorax pelagicus Pallas

NG–46; G–36; PW–17; AW–pl 74; AM (I)–98

			MF	
GROUND	MF	3–5	I: 26–31 DAYS	
		(3–7)	ALTRICIAL	AQUATIC
		MONOG	F: ? DAYS	INVERTS
			MF (?)	

BREEDING: Rocky seacoasts and island cliffs. 1 brood. **DISPLAYS:** ? **NEST:** On highest, steepest, least accessible rocky cliffs facing water. Nest made of sticks, seaweed and grass, debris, or only moss; added to yearly. One sex gathers material, other sex builds, may reach 6' high. **EGGS:** Light blue/bluish-white, usu nest-stained. 2.4" (60 mm). **DIET:** Primarily solitary fish; also some marine inverts. **CONSERVATION:** Winters s to c Baja. **NOTES:** Colonial. Breeders remain in colony in daytime; nonbreeding individuals return in evening. Young hatch asynchronously. Ineffective defense of eggs and young against aerial predators; relies primarily on inaccessibility of cliff-nesting habitat to deter predators. Taken in commercial fishing nets at depths to 120'. Slow in takeoff, does not use feet to run on water surface, but flight faster and more graceful than larger cormorants. Eyes adapted for aerial as well as underwater vision. Shy. **ESSAYS:** Spread-Wing Postures, p. 25; Coloniality, p. 173; Seabird Nesting, p. 197; Pellets, p. 297; Diving and Flightlessness, p. 203. **REFS:** Ainley et al., 1981; Siegel-Causey and Hunt, 1981; Vermeer and Rankin, 1984.

food remains (in some species the male helps make the seal), leaving only a narrow vertical slot through which the male passes her food. Males of some hornbill species feed the female throughout incubation and raising of the young; in others the female breaks out when the young are partially grown and helps with the feeding chores.

In polyandrous birds (those in which one female mates with more than one male), like jacanas and phalaropes, it is common for the male to be the sole incubator. Polyandry is relatively rare, though, and in only about 5 percent of bird species do males do all the incubating. In certain polyandrous shorebirds, such as Spotted Sandpipers and Temminck's Stints, the female lays more than one clutch. She then incubates the clutch in one nest, and her mates incubate those in others.

In the remaining 20 percent or so of bird species the pattern is variable, with one or both sexes incubating according to circumstances. What controls the distribution of the incubation task is not thoroughly understood, but ecological factors such as distance to food supplies, climate, and predation pressures must all play roles. For example, seabirds that must travel long distances to feed, clearly cannot leave all of the incubation chores to a single parent.

SEE: Incubation: Heating Eggs, p. 393; Incubation Time, p. 481; Polyandry, p. 133; Hatching Asynchrony and Brood Reduction, p. 507. REF: White and Kinney, 1974.

Salt Glands

Biologists long wondered how birds such as albatrosses, which spend months at sea, are able to survive without fresh water to drink. Seawater has about three times the salt content of the body fluids of the birds; in order for them to filter out the salts taken in with each quart of seawater, the birds would have to produce two quarts of urine—clearly impossible.

How oceanic birds manage to maintain their salt balance has been figured out in the past few decades. Evolution has provided marine species with enlarged nasal glands, known as salt glands, to regulate the salt content of the blood. Nasal glands are found above the eyes at the base of the bill of all birds. Those in land birds are normally inactive. Oceanic birds drink seawater, and the glands remove salt from the blood, producing a concentrated waste fluid that has a salt content of about 5 percent. The salty solution either dribbles out of the bill or, in petrels, is blown forcibly from the nostrils. With the aid of the salt glands, the normal salt content of the body fluids can be rapidly restored after a seawater drink. Although avian physiologists have investigated the operation of the salt glands in detail in cormorants, among others, and have uncovered some clues to their remarkable efficiency at removing salt from the blood, the functioning of the glands is still not entirely understood.

Red-faced Cormorant

Phalacrocorax urile Gmelin

NG–46; G–36; PW–17; AW–pl 75; AM (I)–100

  ?

MF (?)   3–4   MF (?)   AQUATIC

MONOG?   I: 21? DAYS   INVERTS

ALTRICIAL

F: 60? DAYS

MF (?)

BREEDING: Cliffs along seacoasts, rocky islands. 1 brood. **DISPLAYS:** Male advertises holding nest material in bill. **NEST:** Neatest of cormorant nests; large, securely plastered on wide rock shelves projecting from low cliffs. Constructed from green grass and sod, or from seaweed and other marine veg gathered by diving. Some lined with gull feathers. **EGGS:** Light bluish-white, nest-stained. 2.4" (60 mm). **DIET:** Young fed liquefied regurgitant, then increasingly solid diet of fish, crab, and shrimp. **CONSERVATION:** Winter resident. **NOTES:** Colonial; close sitters on nest, do not harass neighbors in colony. Will oft fly to incoming boats. Eyes adapted for aerial as well as underwater vision. **ESSAYS:** Coloniality, p. 173; Seabird Nesting, p. 197; Feathered Nests, p. 605; Spread-Wing Postures, p. 25. **REF:** Palmer, 1962.

Least Bittern

Ixobrychus exilis Gmelin

NG–48; G–98; PE–104; PW–pl 4; AE–pl 17; AW–pl 11; AM (I)–108

0'–3'   MF   4–5   MF   AQUATIC   GROUND

(To 8')   (2–7)   I: 19–20 DAYS   INVERTS   GLEAN

MONOG   SEMIALTRICIAL 1   INSECTS

F: 25 DAYS

MF

BREEDING: Emergent veg in freshwater, occ coastal brackish marshes, mangroves. 2 broods. **DISPLAYS:** Voice plays important role. Greeting ceremony: noncontact and contact bill clappering; territorial displays incl much posturing. **NEST:** Usu near or over water. On ground in emergent veg or in low shrub; of emergent veg, sticks. Little, if any, rim. **EGGS:** Bluish-white/greenish-white. 1.2" (31 mm). **DIET:** Also insects, amphibians, small mammals. Young fed regurgitant. **CONSERVATION:** Winters s to Costa Rica (w) and throughout Greater Antilles to n Colombia (e). Blue List 1979–86; widely reported as declining and has disappeared from some areas, esp in w. **NOTES:** Solitary to loosely colonial. Adults approach nest on foot. Clutches larger in n. Shy, cryptic, holds reedlike pose. Young are adept climbers. Marsh Wrens stab eggs. Flies rapidly with fast, but weak wingbeats. Possibly preys on eggs and young of nearby Yellow-headed Blackbirds. **ESSAYS:** Blue List, p. 11; Feathers, p. 309; Precocial and Altricial Young, p. 581. **REF:** Hancock and Kushlan, 1984.

Interestingly, Mallard ducklings experimentally exposed to high concentrations of salt in their drinking water developed larger salt glands than ducklings given less salty water. Apparently in species that may be exposed to water of different salinities, the glands are able to respond to the differing needs of individuals.

Birds are not the only organisms that have evolved glands for the excretion of salt. The famous marine iguanas of the Galapagos periodically snort sprays of salt from their nostrils, and some turtles, bony fishes, and sharks also have the glands, which are located in body areas as different as the rectum and the gills.

SEE: Bird Droppings, p. 263; Metabolism, p. 325; Hummingbirds, p. 333.

Feathered Dinosaurs?

For years biologists have half-jokingly referred to birds as "feathered reptiles." In part, it is a ploy to annoy bird lovers with the thought that the objects of their fancy are just singing lizards wrapped in stretched-out scales called "feathers." Yet the phrase reflects an important biological reality: birds *are* undeniably the modified descendants of reptiles, as their body structure and habit of laying eggs out of water clearly show.

The fossil record of ancient birds is not extensive. One probable reason is that birds have hollow bones to lighten them for flight, and those bones crush easily and tend to disintegrate before fossilization is complete. Also, probably few early birds lived in areas (such as swamps and estuaries) where fossils are readily preserved. The existence of several superb specimens of *Archaeopteryx* preserved in slate compensates for this paucity of fossils. Some 140 million years ago, at the end of the Jurassic period, *Archaeopteryx* was a denizen of warm swamps in what is now Bavaria in Germany.

Archaeopteryx makes an ideal "missing link," showing characteristics intermediate between reptiles and birds. It had teeth like those of reptiles, but feathers almost identical with those of modern birds. Its long bony tail was reptilian, but had feathers attached to it. Its elongated forelimbs resembled those of modern birds, but each had three movable clawed fingers, which presumably were useful for climbing trees. (Chicks of the South American hoatzin, the only living bird with clawed forelimbs, do use them in clambering through branches.) Although *Archaeopteryx* had another feature that today is unique to birds, a "wishbone" (furcula) formed by the fusion of the collarbones (clavicles), it lacked a robust, bony keel (part of the sternum) to which strong flight muscles could be attached. *Archaeopteryx* certainly could not fly as well as a modern bird.

Archaeopteryx tells us a great deal about what the distant ancestors of modern birds were like, but we run into controversy again when trying to trace *Archaeopteryx* back to its reptilian ancestors. One view, still held by many paleontologists, suggests that about 200 million years ago its ancestral

American Bittern
Botaurus lentiginosus Rackett

| F | 4–5
(2–7)
POLYGYN? | F
I: 28–29 DAYS
SEMIALTRICIAL 1
F: ? DAYS
F | AQUATIC
INVERTS
SM VERTS | GROUND
GLEAN |

BREEDING: Emergent veg of freshwater and brackish marshes. ? brood. **DISPLAYS:** Male arches back, shortens neck, lowers abdomen, displays and booms like grouse; also expands white patches on back. Male and female perform repeated aerial display. Male booms throughout day. **NEST:** On dry ground above water or mud in tall emergent veg. Occ over deep water or in grass with arch. Scanty, of sticks, grass, sedge. Separate paths for nest exit and entrance. Male believed to choose site. **EGGS:** Buff-brown/olive-buff. 1.9″ (49 mm). **DIET:** Varied, any animal it can catch incl small mammals, insects. Young fed regurgitant. **CONSERVATION:** Winters s to s Mexico, Greater Antilles. Blue List 1976–86; declining throughout range, esp in central portions, likely caused by loss of marsh habitat. **NOTES:** Solitary, territorial males advertise with booming call. Adult very slow and cautious when approaching nest. Cryptic, holds reedlike pose. Nest becomes very foul. Young leave nest at two weeks. Redhead may dump eggs in nest. Heavy, hurried flight. **ESSAYS:** Blue List, p. 11; Feathers, p. 309; Precocial and Altricial Young, p. 581; Parasitized Ducks, p. 89. **REF:** Hancock and Kushlan, 1984.

Black-crowned Night-Heron
Nycticorax nycticorax
Linnaeus

| SHRUB
15′–30′
(0′–60′) | MF | 3–5
(1–7)
MONOG | MF
I: 24–26 DAYS
SEMIALTRICIAL 1
F: 42–49 DAYS
MF | AQUATIC
INVERTS |

BREEDING: Marshes, swamps, ponds, lakes, lagoons, mangroves; occ grassland, rice fields. 1 brood. **DISPLAYS:** On tree male bows, stretches neck, erects breast feathers and back plumes, calls. Female responds similarly. Pair bills, plumage smooth. **NEST:** In tree, shrub, cattails, occ concealed in dense undergrowth. Oft fragile, loose, of sticks, twigs, reeds; occ substantial. Scantily lined with finer materials. Perennial. **EGGS:** Light bluish/greenish. 2.0″ (52 mm). **DIET:** Mainly fish, usu from within territory; also insects, eggs and young birds (esp terns, heron, ibis), small mammals, amphibians (esp in spring), other lower verts. Young fed regurgitant, later mostly fish, unpredigested. **CONSERVATION:** Winters s to S.A., but esp Cuba and C.A. Blue List 1972–81, Special Concern 1982, Local Concern 1986; stable or increasing in most areas. **NOTES:** Usu in small to large colony. Pair defend nest. First breed at 1–3 yr, usu 2–3. Clutch larger in n. Young hatch asynchronously; very noisy. Forage at dawn, dusk, and at night. Roost in trees. In day, attacked by "day" herons. **ESSAYS:** Feathers, p. 309; Precocial and Altricial Young, p. 581; Blue List, p. 11; Coloniality, p. 173; Communal Roosting, p. 615. **REFS:** Custer et al., 1983; Hancock and Kushlan, 1984; Tremblay and Ellison, 1980.

line split off from a group of reptiles, the thecodonts. Thecodonts are considered ancestral to crocodiles, dinosaurs, and pterosaurs (contemporaries of dinosaurs that could fly but were unrelated to birds). Some thecodonts resembled crocodiles or Komodo dragons, but two recently discovered 200-million-year-old chickadee-sized thecodont fossils show interesting birdlike features. One has similarities in the skull and signs of featherlike structures; the other has clavicles fused into a furcula and elongated scales.

More recently, paleontologist John Ostrom has concluded that, instead of being derived from thecodonts, the birds are descended directly from a group of relatively small, agile, predatory dinosaurs called coelosaurs. Some coelosaurs were quite ostrichlike, and the forelimbs of others were constructed very much like those of *Archaeopteryx*.

The debate between these views impinges on another still raging in paleontology—were the dinosaurs "warm-blooded"? Some claim that the metabolism (the chemical and physical processes that maintain life) of dinosaurs was more like that of birds and mammals than reptiles. They credit the dinosaurs with evolving highly efficient circulatory systems, regulating their body temperature by generating their own heat, and being relatively smart. Others remain convinced that dinosaurs, like modern reptiles, were "cold-blooded" creatures that regulated their temperature behaviorally, moving in and out of the sun, orienting at different angles to it, and becoming torpid when it was cold and sunless.

Definitive resolution of this debate, and of ones over the ancestors of the birds and the flying abilities of *Archaeopteryx*, seems unlikely in the near future. Fuel is certain to be added to the fire by the recent discovery, by paleontologist Sankar Chatterjee of Texas Tech University, of two fragmentary, crow-sized skeletons some 75 million years older than *Archaeopteryx*. They have keellike development of their breastbones and lack teeth, both more birdlike characteristics than those of *Archaeopteryx*. The fossils appear to be the remains of birds that could fly at least short distances. Perhaps *Archaeopteryx* will eventually prove to have been on a stubby evolutionary side branch, rather than a direct connector of dinosaurs and modern birds.

Some enthusiasts for the "warm-blooded dinosaurs" theory have gone so far as to suggest that dinosaurs be moved out of the reptiles and classified with the birds. There is a certain charm to the notion that the dinosaurs did not disappear 65 million years ago, and that some can be found today sitting on the edge of our feeders or singing territorial songs in the local woodlot. This nomenclatural change would seem premature, however, especially since the name of the older group might catch on and, as paleontologist Alan Charig has pointed out, lead us to change some old proverbs. Do we really want to say "a dinosaur in the hand is worth two in the bush," or dinosaurs of a feather flock together"?

SEE: *Hesperornis* and Other Missing Links, p. 93; How Do Birds Fly?, p. 161; Adaptations for Flight, p. 507; Origin of Flight, p. 397; Natural Selection, p. 237. REFS: Charig, 1979; Desmond, 1975; Martin, 1983; Ostrom, 1979.

Yellow-crowned Night-Heron

Nycticorax violaceus
Linnaeus

NG–48; G–98; PE–104; AE–pl 19; AM (I)–120

			MF I: 21–25 DAYS SEMIALTRICIAL 1 F: 25 DAYS MF		
SHRUB 30'–40' (1'–50')	MF	4–5 (4–8) MONOG		INSECTS FISH	GROUND GLEAN

BREEDING: Marshes, swamps, lakes, lagoons, tidal mud flats, rocky shores, and mangroves, breeding in trees in wooded habitats near water, also suburbs, parkland. 1? brood. **DISPLAYS:** Greeting ceremony: crest raising and calling; noncontact and contact bill clappering. Territorial display incl circle flight. **NEST:** In clumped trees, shrubs, on dry land. Nest usu substantial, of sticks, twigs, occ lined with rootlets, leaves. Occ perennial. **EGGS:** Light bluish-green. 2.0" (51 mm). **DIET:** Crustacean specialist, esp crayfish, crabs, also lower verts, fish, insects, leeches, young birds. **CONSERVATION:** Winters s to s Panama and Grenadines. **NOTES:** Solitary or small loose colonies. Secretive, less gregarious than Black-crowned. Young seldom fed directly from bill. Forages at night and in dim light. Tall trees usu used for roosting; larger bill permits larger prey than similarly sized herons. Island forms have larger bills. **ESSAYS:** Coloniality, p. 173; Communal Roosting, p. 615; Visual Displays, p. 15. **REF:** Hancock and Kushlan, 1984.

Green-backed Heron

Butorides striatus Linnaeus

NG–50; G–96; PE–104; PW–pl 4; AE–pl 18; AW–pl 7; AM (I)–118

			MF I: 21–25 DAYS SEMIALTRICIAL 1 F: 34–35 DAYS MF	
SHRUB 10'–20' (0'–30')	MF	2–4 (2–7) MONOG		INSECTS AQUATIC INVERTS

BREEDING: Forested margins of ponds, rivers, lakes, marshes, swamps, mangroves. Occ 2 broods. **DISPLAYS:** Raises crest when excited. Male erects neck plumes, swells throat, and calls while strutting (hopping from foot to foot) before female. Territorial display incl forward stretch exposing red mouth lining while calling. **NEST:** In absence of trees and shrubs, on tussock in emergent veg. Usu concealed, flat, of interwoven sticks (occ green) and twigs near or over water. Usu unlined or occ lined with finer materials after laying. **EGGS:** Light greenish/bluish-green. 1.5" (38 mm). **DIET:** Fish, insects, aquatic and terrestrial inverts, lower verts. Mostly fish in late summer. Young fed solid regurgitant. **CONSERVATION:** Winters s through Antilles to n S.A. Common in most of U.S., but locally rare in w. **NOTES:** Usu solitary, occ small colony. Young hatch asynchronously, climb expertly; tended by adults for >1 month after leaving nest. Forages on territory by slowly stalking prey or crouching and waiting for food to come by; occ rakes shallow water bottom with foot to stir up prey. Formerly known as Little Green Heron. **ESSAYS:** Tool Using, p. 435; Nest Lining, p. 391; Visual Displays, p. 5. **REF:** Hancock and Kushlan, 1984.

Commensal Feeding

Some birds eat alone. For those that do not, the choice of a dining partner can be surprising. Why should a phalarope associate with an avocet, or a coot with a swan? Often, it is because a feeding association benefits the participants by enhancing foraging success while increasing protection from predators. For example, by simply standing close to a foraging White Ibis, a Great Egret can snatch stray prey scared to the surface by the ibis but beyond the ibis' reach. In return, the egret warns the shorter, less wary ibis of predators. But not all foraging associations are mutually beneficial.

In commensal associations, members of one species assist the foraging of another, but incur no significant costs and receive no benefits. One of the more common commensal associations involves "beaters," which stir up prey, and "attendants," which simply follow in their footsteps taking whatever comes their way. Many waterbirds, marsh birds, and shorebirds attend particular beater species. Great and Snowy Egrets, for example, attend cormorants; Snowy Egrets, Tricolored Herons and Great Egrets attend mergansers. Some attendants will follow more than one beater species. Enterprising American Coots attend Canvasbacks, Tundra Swans, Mallards, pintails, and Redheads. In water of swimming depth, Wilson's Phalaropes will follow Northern Shovelers; where they can wade, they will often forage behind American Avocets.

Beater-follower associations are not restricted to waterbirds, of course. On land, Cattle, Snowy, and Great Egrets attend cattle, European Robins follow wild pigs, antbirds follow army ants, and African drongos (jay-sized insectivores) follow many species of mammals and birds in anticipation of insects flushed by the "beaters." Interestingly, an African drongo can be sustained following a single elephant, but when following small antelopes, it requires a small herd.

The distance separating attendants from their beaters is not uniform. It depends on the habitat, the type of prey and the ease of its capture, and the speed of the feeders. Consequently, it is not always easy to determine whether two birds seen near each other are feeding commensally. In his study of slow-walking Little Blue Herons following White Ibises, ornithologist James Kushlan compared the foraging success of "attending" (venturing to within one meter of the ibis beater) and "independent" (staying farther away) heron individuals. Kushlan found that attending herons caught twice as many prey as those feeding alone and that the increase reflected more frequent feeding attempts (presumably because the beater stirred up more prey), rather than more successful feeding attempts.

Commensal feeding arrangements can also involve food recycling. In New Guinea, the diet of Shining Starlings includes fruits with large, hard pits. The starlings digest the fleshy coating but regurgitate the pit. Opportunistic Emerald Doves, whose strong stomachs are able to grind tough materials, take in these stripped pits and digest them. Sparrows and finches that feed on seeds in horse manure provide a similar example.

Tricolored Heron

Egretta tricolor Müller

NG–50; G–96; PE–100; PW–pl 4; AE–pl 13; AM (I)–114

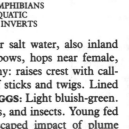

SHRUB	MF	3–4	MF I: 21–25 DAYS		
2'–12'		(3–7)	SEMIALTRICIAL 1	AMPHIBIANS	
(To 30')		MONOG	F: 35 DAYS MF	AQUATIC INVERTS	

BREEDING: Marshes, ponds and rivers, breeding usu near salt water, also inland freshwater habitats. 1 brood. **DISPLAYS:** Perched male bows, hops near female, raises and lowers back and head plumes. Greeting ceremony: raises crest with calling, bill clappering. **NEST:** Flat, loosely built platform of sticks and twigs. Lined with fine twigs, grass, leaves. Rarely on or near ground. **EGGS:** Light bluish-green. 1.7" (44 mm). **DIET:** Fish, also small verts, aquatic inverts, and insects. Young fed regurgitant. **CONSERVATION:** Winters s to Panama. Escaped impact of plume trade partly bcause of plume color. **NOTES:** Colonial, oft large colonies, either alone or mixed with other species. One adult always on duty at nest. Young are expert climbers at 3 weeks; able to swim. Forages in shallow water, oft estuarine and brackish habitats. Crouches and waits, stalks, or runs after prey; occ uses foot stirring and foot raking to flush prey from substrate in shallow water. **ESSAYS:** Commensal Feeding, p. 35; Plume Trade, p. 37; Precocial and Altricial Young, p. 581; Coloniality, p. 173. **REFS:** Hancock and Kushlan, 1984; Recher and Recher, 1980.

Little Blue Heron

Egretta caerulea Linnaeus

NG–50; G–96; PE–100; PW–pl 4; AE–pl 16; AM (I)–112

SHRUB	MF	2–5	MF I: 20–23 DAYS		
1.5'–40'		(1–6)	SEMIALTRICIAL 1	AMPHIBIANS	
		MONOG	F: 42–49 DAYS MF	AQ INVERTS INSECTS	

BREEDING: Marshes, ponds, lakes, meadows, streams and mangroves. 1 brood. **DISPLAYS:** Males: stretching; bill clappering; wing preening; circle flight. Pair: snap; mutual rubbing; preening; bill clappering. **NEST:** Oft above water in low tree, shrub. Small, flimsy, frail platform of sticks and twigs, slightly hollowed. Unlined or lined with finer materials. **EGGS:** Light bluish-green. 1.7" (44 mm). **DIET:** Wide variety of prey, but mostly fish, usu larger than taken by other similar-sized herons. Young fed regurgitant. **CONSERVATION:** Winters s to c S.A. Not decimated by plume trade. **NOTES:** Nests colonially, usu without other species. "Extramarital cop" rare but nearby male will intrude on unguarded female at her nest. Until end of egg laying, male seldom leaves nest >5 min; does not feed. Brooding ends during third week. Large nocturnal roosts; nonbreeders oft roost and mingle with breeders. Possible nest site competition with Cattle Egret. As in many other herons, young forage less efficiently than older birds. Stalks prey or stands and waits to strike. **ESSAYS:** Commensal Feeding, p. 35; Plume Trade, p. 37; Communal Roosting, p. 615; Coloniality, p. 173; Nest Lining, p. 391. **REFS:** Hancock and Kushlan, 1984; Rodgers, 1980; Werschkul, 1982.

Three of the more common forms of commensal feeding in North American woodlands involve woodpeckers. Some hummingbirds, warblers, and kinglets drink sap oozing from sapsucker "wells" (holes drilled into trees by the sapsuckers), and other species, including bluebirds and nuthatches, follow insect-seeking woodpeckers to snap up prey they miss. After Pileated Woodpeckers clear the outer bark from a section of tree trunk, Hairy Woodpeckers, which are not bark removers, may seek insects then exposed close enough to the surface to exploit. In the case of these woodpeckers, however, it has yet to be demonstrated that the associations exact no cost (in missed food) to the producer.

There may be no out-and-out exceptions to the ecological slogan, "There is no free lunch," but while not obviously damaging to their benefactors, some species definitely gain from the actions of others with whom they forage.

SEE: Mixed-Species Flocking, p. 433; Coevolution, p. 405; Bird Communities and Competition, p. 605; Interspecific Territoriality, p. 385. REFS: Anderson, 1974; Diamond, 1981; Diamond et al., 1977; Kilham, 1980a; Kushlan, 1978b; Siegfried and Batt, 1972; Williams, 1953; Willis and Oniki, 1978.

Plume Trade

During two walks along the streets of Manhattan in 1886, the American Museum of Natural History's ornithologist, Frank Chapman, spotted 40 native species of birds including sparrows, warblers, and woodpeckers. But the birds were not flitting through the trees—they had been killed, and for the most part, plucked, disassembled, or stuffed, and painstakingly positioned on three-quarters of the 700 women's hats Chapman saw. The North American feather trade was in its heyday.

Throughout the preceding 30 years, general economic prosperity of a growing middle class had provided opportunities to purchase nonessentials. Emulating the fashionable elite, men selected fedoras with feather trim and women adorned their hair, hats, and dresses with "aigrettes" (sprays) of breeding plumage taken from a variety of birds. Accordingly, women's hats became larger, hat ornamentation (reminiscent of that found on dress military headgear) became more lavish, and the feather trade expanded its enterprise to include marketing the remains of some 64 species from 15 genera of native birds.

Herons were favored. The Great Egret and especially the more plentiful, more widely distributed, more approachable, and more delicately plumed Snowy Egret, suffered great losses. These birds had evolved extravagant breeding plumage as sexual advertisements to attract their mates. The feathers, apparently, had such a similar effect on 19th-century men that sources of supply began to disappear. So extensive was the decoupling of egrets and their skins that egrets were adopted as the symbol of the bird

Reddish Egret

Egretta rufescens Gmelin

NG–50; G–96; PE–100; AE–pl 15; AM (I)–114

SHRUB	MF	3–4	MF I: 25–26 (?) DAYS SEMIALTRICIAL 1	AQ INVERTS	
0'–10'		(2–7)	F: 45 DAYS	SM VERTS	
(To 20')		MONOG	MF		

BREEDING: Brackish marshes and shallow coastal habitats, esp mangrove. 1? brood. **DISPLAYS:** Circle flight; pursuit flight; greeting ceremony: head-toss, snap, noncontact/contact bill clappering. **NEST:** Usu in small trees or shrubs; occ on ground. Flat platform of sticks, occ twigs, rootlets, grass. Little or no lining. **EGGS:** Light bluish-green. 2.0" (51 mm). **DIET:** Most, if not all, food obtained in salt water. Young fed by regurgitation. **CONSERVATION:** Some resident in winter or wander within U.S.; remainder s to El Salvador. Blue List 1972–80, Special Concern 1981–86. Plume hunters decimated populations but may have overlooked one TX colony. Colonies disappeared from FL 1927–37, but reestablished. Approximately 2,000 pairs nest in U.S. **NOTES:** Nests in colonies, oft near water. Territory defended by pair. Young leave ground nests at 28–35 days; leave colony at 9–10 weeks. Red phase may hatch white morphs. Forages very actively for a heron —pursues schools of fish in shallow water; occ stirs bottom by raking with foot to expose prey. **ESSAYS:** Blue List, p. 11; Plume Trade, p. 37; Coloniality, p. 173. **REF:** Hancock and Kushlan, 1984.

Cattle Egret

Bubulcus ibis Linnaeus

NG–52; G–94; PE–102; PW–pl 4; AE–pl 4; AW–pl 5; AM (I)–116

SHRUB	MF	3–4	MF I: 22–26 DAYS SEMIALTRICIAL 1	SM VERTS	
3'–30'		(2–5)	F: 30 DAYS		
(0.5'–65')		MONOG	MF		

BREEDING: Wet pastures, plowed fields, marshes, lawns. 1 brood. **DISPLAYS:** Pair bond incl neck stretch with side-to-side sway, mutual back preening, contact bill clappering. Greeting ceremony incl erected plumes and flattened crest. **NEST:** Of reeds, sticks, twigs, vines. Building continues throughout incubation. Male collects sticks, female builds. **EGGS:** Light blue-green/bluish-white. 1.9" (48 mm). **DIET:** Also mollusks, crustaceans, earthworms, nestlings. Prey (esp insects) flushed by large grazing animals; occ aggressively defend area around grazer. **CONSERVATION:** Winters s to S.A. Invading species: spread from Africa to S.A. about 1880, reached FL and TX in 1940s and 1950s; range expanded rapidly n and w. Deforestation, irrigation, and cattle industry provide foraging habitat. **NOTES:** Highly colonial, up to 1,000s per colony. Steals materials from other nests and competes for nests with other herons in n. One bird always attends nest. Young hatch asynchronously; brooded 2 weeks, leave nest at 20 days, independent at 45 days. Can withstand water stress better than other herons. Roost communally in trees, departure synchronized. Attracted to field fires, flying directly into smoke, taking small verts and inverts. **ESSAYS:** Avian Invaders, p. 633; Mixed-Species Flocking, p. 433; Commensal Feeding, p. 35. **REFS:** Burger, 1978; Hancock and Kushlan, 1984; Weber, 1975.

BIRD SPECIES	NUMBER OF HATS SEEN	BIRD SPECIES	NUMBER OF HATS SEEN
Grebes	7	Blue Jay	5
Green-backed Heron	1	Eastern Bluebird	3
Virginia Rail	1	American Robin	4
Greater Yellowlegs	1	Northern Shrike	1
Sanderling	5	Brown Thrasher	1
Laughing Gull	1	Bohemian Waxwing	1
Common Tern	21	Cedar Waxwing	23
Black Tern	1	Blackburnian Warbler	1
Ruffed Grouse	2	Blackpoll Warbler	3
Greater Prairie Chicken	1	Wilson's Warbler	3
Northern Bobwhite	16	Tree Sparrow	2
California Quail	2	White-throated Sparrow	1
Mourning Dove	1	Snow Bunting	15
Northern Saw-whet Owl	1	Bobolink	1
Northern Flicker	21	Meadowlarks	2
Red-headed Woodpecker	2	Common Grackle	5
Pileated Woodpecker	1	Northern Oriole	9
Eastern Kingbird	1	Scarlet Tanager	3
Scissor-tailed Flycatcher	1	Pine Grosbeak	1
Tree Swallow	1		

Modified from Strom, 1986.

preservation movement. Writers such as Herbert Job began to focus their protests on the robbing of heron rookeries:

> Here are some official figures of the trade from one source alone, of auctions at the London Commercial Sales Rooms during 1902. There were sold 1,608 packages of . . . herons' plumes. A package is said to average in weight 30 ounces. This makes a total of 48,240 ounces. As it requires about four birds to make an ounce of plumes, these sales meant 192,960 herons killed at their nests, and from two to three times that number of young or eggs destroyed. Is it, then, any wonder that these species are on the verge of extinction?

There was no question that plume trading had become a very lucrative business. "In 1903," Job continued, "the price for plumes offered to hunters was $32 per ounce, which makes the plumes worth about twice their weight in gold." (Later they were to bring $80!) It should not be surprising that the millinery trade, an industry employing 83,000 people (1 of every 1,000 Americans) in 1900, stood fast against claims of cruelty and exploitation and offered the public false assurances. It was carefully explained, for instance, that the bulk of feather collection was limited to shed plumes—those found scattered on the ground within rookeries. In truth, those "dead plumes" brought only one-fifth the price of the live, unblem-

Snowy Egret
Egretta thula Molina

NG–52; G–94; PE–102; PW–pl 4; AE–pl 1; AW–pl 1; AM (I)–112

SHRUB | MF | 3–5 | MF
I: 20–24 DAYS
SEMIALTRICIAL 1 | FISH
5'–10' | | (3–6) | F: 30 DAYS | INSECTS
(0'–30') | | MONOG | MF

BREEDING: Marshes, lakes, ponds, shallow coastal habitats. 1 brood. **DISPLAYS**: With erect plumes: territorial display incl crest raising, accompanied by calls; in courtship: male stretches neck, points bill skyward and calls; circle flight, tumbling flights. **NEST**: Rarely in cactus or on ground; flat, flimsy, of sticks. Lined with fine twigs, rushes. Occ in marsh veg. Male collects material, female builds. **EGGS**: Light bluish-green. 1.7" (43 mm). **DIET**: Also small verts. **CONSERVATION**: Winters s to n S.A. Decimated by plume hunters; subsequent range expansion beyond prehunting limits. DDE (probably from Mexico) leads to nest failure in ID populations. **NOTES**: Highly colonial, usu in mixed colonies. Asynchronous hatching oft leads to starvation of smallest chicks. Young leave nest at 20–25 days. Most diverse foraging techniques of any heron; active pursuit of prey compared with most herons, egrets. Uses yellow feet to stir mud to flush prey. Occ feeds following Glossy Ibis (or other species) and capturing food stirred up by ibis. Communal roost at night when not breeding, oft moving to and from roost in flocks. **ESSAYS**: Plume Trade, p. 37; DDT and Birds, p. 21; Communal Roosting, p. 615; Commensal Feeding, p. 35; Brood Reduction, p. 307; Range Expansion, p. 459. **REFS**: Erwin, 1983; Hancock and Kushlan, 1984; Raye and Burger, 1979.

Great Egret
Casmerodius albus Linnaeus

NG–52; G–94; PE–102; PW–pl 4; AE–pl 2; AW–pl 3; AM (I)–110

SHRUB | MF | 3 | MF
I: 23–26 DAYS
SEMIALTRICIAL 1 | SM VERTS
8'–40' | | (1–6) | F: 42–49 DAYS | AQUATIC
(3'–90') | | MONOG | MF | INVERTS

BREEDING: Marshes, swamps, irrigation ditches, tidal estuaries, fresh- and brackish-water margins. 1 brood. **DISPLAYS**: Territorial defense incl: erect posturing, supplanting flights. Courtship: advertising calls, circle flight, neck stretch skyward, snap. Greeting ceremony: erects plumes, raises wings. **NEST**: Frail, of sticks, twigs. Unlined or lined with fine materials. Occ perennial. **EGGS**: Light blue or light bluish-green. 2.2" (57 mm). **DIET**: Also insects, lower verts, small birds. Young usu fed frogs, crayfish, fish; regurgitant delivered directly into nestlings' mouths, later into nest. **CONSERVATION**: Winters s to C.A. Decimated by plume hunters. Clutch and brood sizes have increased since 1972 ban on DDT. **NOTES**: Usu in colonies of 10 to 1,000s. Most cosmopolitan of all herons. Young leave nest at 3 weeks. Forages alone or in groups, oft by slowly walking in shallow water, occ commensally with White Ibis or other species. Forages in mixed flocks, occ stealing from smaller species—piracy 5 × more efficient than foraging. Formerly known as American or Common Egret. **ESSAYS**: Plume Trade, p. 37; DDT and Birds, p. 21; Communal Roosting, p. 615; Commensal Feeding, p. 35. **REFS**: Hancock and Kushlan, 1978a, 1984; Mock, 1978; Pratt and Winkler, 1985.

ished, little-worn ones. To counteract the charges of cruelty, claims were circulated that most feather trim was either artificial or produced on foreign farms that exported molted feathers. The demand for egret feathers, nonetheless, began to slip.

No sooner was the public weaned off egrets than it fixed its attention on seabirds of the Atlantic coast. And harvesting did not stop there. Hunting of West Coast terns, grebes, White Pelicans, and albatrosses for ornamental feathers also expanded.

By the turn of the century many millions of birds were being killed by plume hunters each year. Preservationists struggled to enact laws to prevent the killing, possession, sale, and importation of plume birds and ornamental feathers. They disseminated their information through numerous periodicals (including *Bird Lore* and *Audubon Magazine*), many books, and the campaigns of the American Ornithologists' Union (founded in 1883), the Audubon Society, and other conservation organizations. The Audubon Society offered public lectures on such topics as "Woman as a bird enemy" and erected Audubon-approved millinery displays. It also selected regulatory committees to audit the millinery sold in key areas. These actions helped more women to recognize their role in the issue and more men in the millinery trade (whose livelihoods had come from encouraging those women into that role) to change their orientation as interest in feathered fashions subsided.

Thus ended the "Age of Extermination," and by World War I, embellishing attire with breeding plumes had become a thing of the past. How much this change was due to the effects of hunting and trade regulations and how much was the result of rising prices for dwindling supplies is still not clear. Nor is it evident whether changes in the everyday lives of women simply eliminated opportunities to wear oversized, constraining hats, or whether a growing inclination toward promoting humanitarian ideals reduced the allure of feathered garb. Regardless, displaying feathers became, once again, an avian trait.

SEE: Birds and the Law, p. 293; Metallic Poisons, p. 137; Helping to Conserve Birds—National Level, p. 363; Bird Biologist—Frank M. Chapman, p. 43. REFS: Bent, 1926; Buchheister and Graham, 1973; Doughty, 1975.

Great Blue Heron

Ardea herodias Linnaeus

NG–54; G–94; PE–100; PW–pl 4; AE–pl 14; AW–pl 15; AM (I)–108

30'–70' MF 3–5 MF AQ INVERTS
(10'–130') (1–7) I: 28 DAYS SM VERTS
MONOG SEMIALTRICIAL 1
F: 56–60 DAYS
MF

BREEDINIG: Freshwater and brackish marshes, swamps, lakes, rivers, mangroves. 1 brood. **DISPLAYS:** Male at nest: neck stretch and fluff, circle flight, twig shake. Pair: crest raising, bill clappering. Displays more varied than those of egrets, but used less oft and continue after pair-bond formation. **NEST:** Also occ in shrub, rarely on ground, rock ledge, coastal cliff. Large, flat, well made of interwoven sticks. Lined with twigs and leaves; repaired nests oft lined with green needles. **EGGS:** Light bluish-green. 2.5" (64 mm). **DIET:** Mostly fish, but opportunistic, incl human food scraps, nestlings, small mammals. Young fed fish. **CONSERVATION:** Winters s to n S.A. Blue List 1980–81, Special Concern 1982, Local Concern 1986; numbers increasing but much Atlantic coast habitat gone. **NOTES:** Nests in colonies, variable in size, occ solitary; in mixed colonies, Great Blue nests higher. Avg clutch size increases with latitude to 5 in s Canada. As in most herons, foraging success improves with age: adults 2× as successful as young, which expend far more energy in foraging. White morphs ("Great White Heron") found only in marine habitats. **ESSAYS:** Piracy, p. 159; Variation in Clutch Sizes, p. 339; Blue List, p. 11; Coloniality, p. 173. **REFS:** Gibbs et al., 1987; Hancock and Kushlan, 1984; Pratt and Winkler, 1985.

Wood Stork

Mycteria americana Linnaeus

NG–54; G–100; PE–106; PW–pl 4; AE–pl 9; AW–pl 13; AM (I)–128

50'–80' MF 3 MF AMPHIBIANS
(12'–90') (2–4) I: 28–32 DAYS AQUATIC
MONOG SEMIALTRICIAL 1 INVERTS
F: 55–60 DAYS
MF

BREEDING: Marshes, swamps, mangroves, and adjacent streams. 1? brood. **DISPLAYS:** ? **NEST:** Prefers top of large cypress standing in water. Flimsy platform of large sticks, added to continually, slightly depressed. Lined sparsely with fine materials and green leaves, placed far out on horizontal limb. **EGGS:** White to off-white. 2.7" (68 mm). **DIET:** Chicks fed regurgitated fish. **CONSERVATION:** Winters within U.S. Endangered Species due to habitat destruction and alteration. U.S. population estimated at 10,000 in 1984; C.A. and S.A. populations apparently stable. **NOTES:** Highly colonial with 5–25 nests per tree, occ touching. Colonies will skip breeding due to lack of food, and will desert eggs and young if prolonged rains occur in dry season; such rains preclude effective foraging because water table does not drop and fish consequently do not become concentrated in relatively small pools. Does not breed before fourth year. Forages by moving open bill in water until contact with prey item triggers rapid bill-snap reflex; sighting of prey not required. Oft shuffles feet while feeding, presumably to flush fish. **ESSAYS:** Birds and Law, p. 293; Bills, p. 209; Coloniality, p. 173. **REFS:** Kale, 1978; Kushlan and Frohring, 1986; Ogden, 1985; Ogden et al., 1976.

Bird Biologist—Frank M. Chapman

The rise of the American Museum of Natural History in New York as a center of ornithology can be traced largely to the work of Frank M. Chapman (1864–1945), who became curator of the collections there in 1908. Chapman wrote the best North American bird guide of the turn-of-the-century period, started the journal *Bird-Lore* (which eventually evolved into *Audubon*), and developed innovative museum exhibits in which birds were displayed in their natural habitats. Through all of these endeavors he succeeded in encouraging many young people to become familiar with bird biology, and he also did fine scientific work on the ecology, distribution, and life histories of birds, especially those of the tropics.

SEE: Plume Trade, p. 37. REFS: Kastner, 1986; Stresemann, 1975.

Flamingo Feeding

Flamingos are filter feeders, and in that respect resemble whales and oysters more than they do most birds. Many complex rows of horny plates line their beaks, plates that, like those of baleen whales, are used to strain food items from the water. The filter of the Greater Flamingo traps crustaceans, mollusks, and insects an inch or so long. The Lesser Flamingo has such a dense filter that it can sift out single-celled plants less than two hundredths of an inch in diameter.

Flamingos feed with their heads down, and their bills are adapted accordingly. In most birds a smaller lower beak works against a larger upper one. In flamingos this is reversed; the lower bill is much larger and stronger, and the fat tongue runs within the bill's deep central groove. To complete the jaw reversal, unlike other birds (and mammals) the upper jaw is not rigidly fixed to the skull. Consequently, with the bird's head upside down during feeding the upper bill moves up and down, permitting the flamingo's jaws to work "normally."

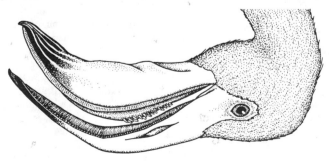

Greater Flamingo

Phoenicopterus ruber Linnaeus

NG–54; G–100; PE–110; AE–pl 12; AM (I)–130

MF

1
(1–2)
MONOG

○

MF
I: 28–32 DAYS
SEMIPRECOCIAL
F: 75–77 DAYS
MF

ALGAE

FILTER
FEEDS

BREEDING: Mud flats, lagoons, and lakes, usu highly saline. 1 brood. **DISPLAYS:** In large groups, mostly ritualized preening and stretching with head waving, rapid opening and closing of wings. **NEST:** Packed on mud mounds in shallow water. Clay scooped with lower mandible, spread, flattened with feet, and piled up while still wet. Clay gathered from 3 pits which eventually join to form moat around pile. Cup-shaped top. When available, leaves, roots, and twigs used. Perennial. **EGGS:** White, rarely pinkish-white. 3.6″ (91 mm). **DIET:** Filters insects, crustaceans, mollusks, tiny fish, algae. Young initially fed parental "crop-milk" secretions. **CONSERVATION:** Winter resident. **NOTES:** Colonial. Long-term pair bond. Formerly probably bred in FL Keys; FL population semidomesticated. Young remain in nest 5–8 days, straight-billed for 2 weeks; form creches after leaving nest. **ESSAYS:** Flamingo Feeding, p. 43; Swallowing Stones, p. 269; Walking vs. Hopping, p. 69; Bird Milk, p. 271; Bird Biology and the Arts, p. 47; Creches, p. 191. **REF:** Cramp and Simmons, 1977.

Glossy Ibis

Supersp #5
Plegadis falcinellus Linnaeus

NG–56; G–100; PE–108; AE–pl 27; AM (I)–124

SHRUB
TREE

MF

○
2–4
(1–5)
MONOG

F–M
I: 21 DAYS
SEMIALTRICIAL 1
F: 28+ DAYS
MF

INSECTS
SMALL
VERTS

GROUND
GLEAN

BREEDING: Marshes, swamps. 1 brood. **DISPLAYS:** Nest relief ceremony: billing and preening while cooing; billing and cooing continue until young fledge. Flock circle flights not limited to breeding season. **NEST:** In trees or shrubs over water, or on ground. Large cupped platform of sticks, twigs or aquatic veg; lined, occ with leaves. Doubles in size by time of hatching, material added until fledging; male adds branches at each turn during incubation. **EGGS:** Dull blue/greenish-blue. 2.0″ (52 mm). **DIET:** Aquatic inverts (esp crayfish), insects, water snakes. **CONSERVATION:** Winters s to n w Costa Rica, through Caribbean to n Venezuela. Breeding range expanding n since 1940. **NOTES:** Nests in colonies, oft mixed with herons, egrets. Nest constantly guarded. Female incubates at night; male part of day. Hatching increasingly asynchronous with increasingly unpredictable food supply. Chick takes regurgitant from adult's bill; after 14 days regurgitant dumped into nest. Within 7 weeks young join parents on feeding trips. Oft forage commensally with Snowy Egrets; probing ibises make prey more available to visually hunting egrets. Grackles pirate food. **ESSAYS:** Commensal Feeding, p. 35; Who Incubates?, p. 27; Range Expansion, p. 459; Piracy, p. 159; Communal Roosting, p. 615. **REFS:** Burger and Miller, 1977; Cramp and Simmons, 1977; Erwin, 1983; Miller and Burger, 1978.

Part of the flamingo's filter feeding is accomplished simply by swinging the head back and forth and letting the water flow through the bill. The tongue also can be used as a pump to pass water through the bill's strainer more efficiently. It moves quickly fore and aft in its groove, sucking water in through the filter as it pulls backward, and expelling it from the beak as it pushes forward. The tongue may repeat its cycle up to four times a second.

Flamingos are not the only avian filter feeders, however. Some penguins and auks have simple structures to help them strain small organisms from water, and one Southern Hemisphere genus of petrels (*Pachyptila*, prions or whalebirds) and some ducks have filtering devices. The Northern Shoveler, the most highly developed filter feeder among the ducks, has specialized plates lining its long, broad bill. The Mallard also has a broad bill, horny plates, and an enlarged tongue. But the pumping action of the ducks is different, and their tongues are housed in the upper mandible, rather than in the lower as in the flamingos.

The flamingo's marvelously adapted tongue almost became its downfall. Roman emperors considered it a delicacy and were served flamingo tongues in a dish that also included pheasant brains, parrotfish livers, and lamprey guts. Roman poets decried the slaughter of the magnificent birds for their tongues (much as early American conservationists lamented the slaughter of bison for theirs). One poet, Martial, wrote (as Stephen Jay Gould recently translated):

My red wing gives me my name, but epicures regard my tongue as tasty.
But what if my tongue could sing?

SEE: Determining Diets, p. 535; Shorebird Feeding, p. 125; Bills, p. 209; Swallowing Stones, p. 269.   REFS: Gould, 1985; Jenkin, 1957; Olson and Feduccia, 1980.

White-faced Ibis

NG–56; G–100; PE–108; PW–pl 4; AE–pl 28; AW–pl 14; AM (I)–124

SHRUB	MF	3–4	MF I: 21–22 DAYS SEMIALTRICIAL 1	INSECTS	GROUND
TREE		(2–7)	F: 28+ DAYS	SMALL	GLEAN
0'–6'		MONOG	MF	VERTS	

BREEDING: Marshes, swamps, ponds and rivers, mostly freshwater habitats. 1 brood. **DISPLAYS**: Nest relief ceremony: billing and preening while cooing. Flock circle flights not limited to breeding season. **NEST**: In aquatic veg, shrub, low tree, occ over water, usu on ground. Deeply cupped platform of coarse emergent veg, sticks. Lined with finer materials. **EGGS**: Greenish-blue/bluish-green. 2.0" (52 mm). **DIET**: Aquatic inverts (esp crayfish), insects, earthworms, fish, small verts; occ aquatic veg. **CONSERVATION**: Winters s to n S.A. Declining throughout N.A. range. Draining of wetlands poses threat. Rice farmers' use of pesticides and herbicides may threaten TX and LA populations. **NOTES**: Nests in small colonies. Nest constantly guarded. Female incubates at night; male part of day. Chick takes regurgitant from adult's bill. Grackles pirate food. **ESSAYS**: Commensal Feeding, p. 35; Piracy, p. 159; Who Incubates?, p. 27; Coloniality, p. 173; Visual Displays, p. 5; Bills, p. 209. **REFS**: Burger and Miller, 1977; Ryder, 1967.

White Ibis

NG–56; G–100; PE–108; AE–pl 25; AM (I)–122

8'–15'	MF	2–3	MF I: 21–23 DAYS SEMIALTRICIAL 1	FISH	GROUND
		(4–5)	F: 28–35 DAYS	SM VERTS	GLEAN
		MONOG	MF (?)		

BREEDING: Marshes, mangroves, lakes, estuaries. 1? brood. **DISPLAYS**: Bill, face, gular pouch, and legs of male become red; calling distends pouch. Territorial defense varied, incl bill snap, gular inflation, pursuit flight, supplanting. Pair formation incl twig grasp, preening, bill snap, stretching, billing. **NEST**: Near water, occ in shrub or on low, matted veg. Loose, of dry sticks, live twigs, leaves, roots; added to continually. Lined with green leaves. **EGGS**: Buff/bluish- or greenish-white, marked with brown, occ unmarked. 2.3" (58 mm). **DIET**: Esp crabs, crayfish, snails, also snakes, insects. Young fed regurgitant. **CONSERVATION**: Winters within U.S. **NOTES**: Large dense colonies with thousands of nests. Nest occ usurped by neighboring pair. Clutches larger in inland than in coastal colonies. Young leave nest at ca. 3 weeks. Commonly robbed of prey by other species in mixed feeding groups of wading birds. Males spend more time feeding than females do. Fish Crow is major egg predator, usu destroying entire clutch. Huge summer roosts harbor up to 80,000 birds. Fly in Vee occ extending >1 mile. **ESSAYS**: Commensal Feeding, p. 35; Piracy, p. 159; Flying in Vee Formation, p. 59; Communal Roosting, p. 615; Visual Displays, p. 5. **REFS**: Bildstein, 1987; Courser and Dinsmore, 1975; Frederick, 1986, 1987; Kushlan, 1977, 1979.

Bird Biology and the Arts

Artists throughout history have drawn inspiration from the birds. Part-bird, part-human forms have frequently been used to depict either supernatural phenomena or enhanced human abilities, especially those of vision (bird heads) and speed (bird wings). Perhaps the oldest artistic representation of birds or parts of birds is a prehistoric bird-headed man dating from 15,000 to 10,000 B.C. It is painted on one of the walls of the Lascaux Cave in France—the often-described treasure-house of Stone Age art.

Ancient Egyptians considered birds "winged souls"; they occasionally used them to symbolize particular gods. The symbol for Horus, the god of the sun (and the local god of the Upper Nile), was the head or body of a falcon. In a statue of King Chefren from Giza on his throne (c. 2500 B.C.), the king is not seated alone—the falcon of Horus is perched behind his head, and its wings enfold the king's shoulders. The bird appears to be watching over the king and his realm. Raptors subsequently have often been used to represent national power—right down to the national symbol of the United States. (The founding fathers, we would like to think, did not recognize the Bald Eagle's habit of scavenging dead fish and feeding at dumps.) Whereas predatory birds are often used in art to symbolize power, doves (frequent prey to raptors) often depict peace.

Symbolic winged chimeras like Pegasus, the flying horse, are recurrent. The power of the sphinx, indicated by the merging of a human head onto a lion's body, is sometimes augmented by the wings of a bird. If the Great Sphinx had wings, they are long gone, but those of the winged Sphinx of Naxos (500 B.C.) remain resplendent. Both victory and liberty continue to be associated with bird wings. They are, for example, the outstanding feature of the renowned Hellenistic marble sculpture the "Winged Victory" of Samothrace (200 B.C.). That partly airborne goddess, in turn, became the prototype for countless modern political paintings and cartoons.

Goldfinches, which appear commonly in illuminated manuscripts in the Middle Ages, were associated with the Christ child. In southern Italy and Sicily goldfinches were commonly released at the time a figure representing the risen Christ appeared at Easter celebrations. Could the predilection of goldfinches for prickly thistles have recalled the crown of thorns and thus led to their association with Christ? During the Renaissance most paintings were religious and bird-winged angels were common. It would seem that the countless depictions of the Annunciation differ most in the use of wings from different bird species.

Native Americans living on the northwest coast of our continent were consummate bird artists. They used stylized depictions of ravens (which were considered gods and played a central role in their religion), eagles, and oystercatchers, etc., in carved masks and rattles as well as on painted screens, drums, and boxes. While the symbolic use of birds (and parts of their anatomy) is ancient, depictions of bird biology are by no means a

Roseate Spoonbill

Ajaia ajaja Linnaeus

NG–56; G–100; PE–110; AE–pl 11; AM (I)–126

SHRUB
10'–15'
GROUND

 MF

 3
(1–5)
MONOG

MF
I: 22–23 DAYS
SEMIALTRICIAL 1
F: 35–42 DAYS
MF

 AQ INVERTS
INSECTS

SWEEPS

BREEDING: Marsh, swamp, pond, river, lagoon. 1 brood. **DISPLAYS**: Pair bonding incl stick presentation, bill clappering, close perching. Cop at nest. Nest relief call. **NEST**: In branches of dense veg above water, occ on ground; well built, deeply cupped, stick, twig platform. Lined with green and dry finer materials. Male presents nest materials to female, she builds. **EGGS**: Dirty white, marked with brown, occ wreathed. 2.6″ (65 mm). **DIET**: Sweeps bill through water snapping it shut on fish, crustaceans, insects, detected by feel. Few aquatic plants. Grunts while hunting. **CONSERVATION**: Winter resident. Populations decimated for wing feathers used in ladies' fans. Expanded range since 1940 but drainage for mosquito control and real estate development continue to threaten foraging habitat. **NOTES**: Nests in small colonies, oft mixed with herons, egrets. Nest relief 2–3 times daily. Juveniles tagged in FL disperse up to 250 miles, return in fall. Usu in small flocks. Although eggs in some areas show relatively high pesticide levels, nest success not impaired; apparently less sensitive than some other species of waterbirds. **ESSAYS**: Plume Trade, p. 37; Incubation Time, p. 481; Visual Displays, p. 5; DDT and Birds, p. 21. **REFS**: Robertson et al., 1983; White et al., 1982.

Sandhill Crane

Grus canadensis Linnaeus

NG–58; G–102; PE–106; PW–pl 4; AE–pl 30; AW–pl 16; AM (I)–312

 MF

 2
(1–3)
MONOG

MF
I: 28–32 DAYS
PRECOCIAL 4
F: 65 DAYS
MF

 GROUND
GLEAN

BREEDING: Shallow wetlands, freshwater margins. 1? brood. **DISPLAYS**: Courtship incl loud rattling calls accompanied by elaborate dances and threat postures. Dance incl head bobbing, bowing and leaping, grass tossing, and running with wings extended. Pair at nest usu duet at dawn and dusk. **NEST**: Occ concealed, bulky, large pile of dead sticks, moss, reeds, grass. Requires surrounding water or undisturbed habitat. **EGGS**: Buff/olive, marked with olive/brown. 3.8″ (96 mm). **DIET**: Opportunistic. Mostly aquatic inverts, insects, worms, also small mammals, young birds and eggs, lower verts; seeds, grass shoots, grain, bulbs, berries, lichen, aquatic plants. **CONSERVATION**: Winters s to c Mexico, except resident Gulf Coast subspecies, which is Endangered; drainage of habitat since 1950s has resulted in decline. **NOTES**: Long-term pair bond; rare mate swapping reported. Young may remain with adults for 10 months. In FL, winter rain increases breeding success; heavy spring rain decreases it. **ESSAYS**: Bird Biology and the Arts, p. 47; Birds and the Law, p. 293; Visual Displays, p. 5. **REFS**: Johnsgard, 1983; Layne, 1983; Mallory, 1987; Reinecke and Krapu, 1986.

modern invention. For instance, a stylized tick bird picking parasites from the back of a bull is painted on a piece of pottery dating to the late Mycenaean, more than a thousand years before Christ, and an early English book contains a picture of an owl being mobbed.

The realistic depiction of birds in nature become increasingly evident in 18th-century Western and Eastern paintings, but illustrating bird biology was not elevated to its current position as an art form until the work of John James Audubon in the early 1800s. Audubon was among the first artists to accurately portray bird biology and certainly the first to consistently paint his subjects with such drama as to establish himself as a significant figure in art history as well. Reproductions of his life-size watercolors were printed in the famous "Double Elephant Folio" of the *Birds of America*. The outlines were printed from huge engraved copper plates, and the coloring done expertly by hand. The pictures often illustrated aspects of bird biology: varying plumages, nesting, feeding, defending against predators, displaying, and so on. Less than 130 of the 200 original hand-colored sets of 435 plates have survived intact. The value placed on them as works of art can be judged from the prices commanded by the individual plates from sets that have been broken up. At an auction in late 1985 many plates, including the Flamingo, the Trumpeter Swan, the Gyrfalcons, and the Snowy Owls, sold for over $25,000 each. Top dollar, $35,200, was paid for an example of Audubon's portrayal of a group of seven long-gone Carolina Parakeets.

Bird vocalizations, of course, often figure in works of literature, especially poetry, as the words of Milton, Keats, Shelley, and others about the songs of nightingales remind us. The call of the European Cuckoo has been featured in the chorus of at least one lullaby. Perhaps the most widespread transference of themes from the avian world to the world of human art has occurred in the dance. The peoples of the northwestern coast have exceptional raven and oystercatcher dances. The courtship rituals of cranes are mimicked in the dances of African tribes, the Ainu of Japan, Australian Aborigines, and Native Americans. One might even imagine that cranes have, directly or indirectly, influenced ballet in much the same way Peter Tchaikovsky was influenced by swans more than a century ago when he composed Swan Lake.

The symbolic use of birds continues today unabated. For example, many television advertisements feature the Bald Eagle or assorted hawks to suggest patriotism, dependability, speed, or machismo. The "proud" peacock is the symbol of a major network. Film clips of birds flying, feeding, singing, and courting are also frequently used in nature and public affairs programs to indicate the peaceful, primeval conditions that are rapidly disappearing from our planet. Bird art seems to be getting more popular as the birds themselves start to disappear. Modern bird paintings, prints, and sculptures are in much demand, especially as the works of Audubon and other avian "old masters" are unavailable to most. Children raised with the image of an all-knowing "Big Bird" may well see birds differently than their parents, raised with Woody Woodpecker and Daffy Duck, did, but it seems

Whooping Crane
Grus americana Linnaeus

NG–58; G–102; PE–106; PW– 71; AE–pl 29; AM (I)–314

MF   2   MF
      (1–3)   I: 29–31 DAYS   GROUND
      MONOG   PRECOCIAL 4   GLEAN
                 F: 80–90 DAYS
                 MF

BREEDING: Wilderness wetlands: freshwater marsh, wet prairie. 1 brood. **DISPLAYS:** Typically cranelike dancing and posturing in courtship, incl head bobbing, bowing, leaping, flapping, grass tossing, and elaborate threat postures accompanied by trumpeting. **NEST:** Soft grass gathered in firm heap with slight depression placed on mound of coarse grass, reeds, or sod near or surrounded by water. **EGGS:** Cream/olive buff, marked with brown. 3.9″ (98 mm). **DIET:** Crustaceans, fish, small verts, insects, small mammals; roots, berries, grain. **CONSERVATION:** Winters within U.S. Endangered, on verge of extinction; increased from 15 birds in 1941 to 170 (incl captives) in 1986. Eggs have been introduced successfully into nests of Sandhill Cranes to increase total production in wild. **NOTES:** Long-term pair bond. Female usu incubates at night. Young leave nest within few hours of hatching; take 3–5.5 years to reach sexual maturity. Very wary. 46 years of census data at Aransas National Wildlife Refuge in TX show a striking 10-year cycle in numbers of overwintering birds, but cause unknown. Roost standing in shallow water. Pairs and families defend large winter territories. **ESSAYS:** Variation in Clutch Sizes, p. 339; Average Clutch Size, p. 51; Territoriality, p. 387; Bird Biology and the Arts, p. 47; Birds and the Law, p. 293; Visual Displays, p. 5. **REFS:** Binkley and Miller, 1983; Boyce and Miller, 1985; Godfrey, 1986; Lewis, 1986.

Tundra Swan
Supersp #6
Cygnus columbianus Ord

NG–60; G–40; PE–43; PW–pl 5; AE–pl 174; AW–pl 156; AM (I)–136

M –F   4–5   F –M
      (2–7)   I: 35–40 DAYS   AQUATIC   DABBLES
      MONOG   PRECOCIAL 2   INVERTS   GROUND
                 F: 60–70+ DAYS   GLEAN
                 MF

BREEDING: Islets, peninsulas, and elevated spots amid open tundra ponds, lakes, etc. 1 brood. **DISPLAYS:** Males high-stepping walk with arched neck lifted, wings outstretched. Pair occ bow and constantly call throughout routine. After several minutes fly ca. 100 yards, repeat sequence. **NESTS:** On elevated hummock; of grass, moss. Male selects site; occ perennial. **EGGS:** Creamy white, nest-stained. 4.2″ (107 mm). **DIET:** Largely aquatic veg, also grass, freshwater inverts, insects. Young feed for first month mostly on aquatic inverts. **CONSERVATION:** Winters within U.S. Older birds very tough, never much hunted but flightless young were eaten. Early nesting (while land still impassable) responsible for continued preservation. **NOTES:** Nests solitary. Pair formation in fall; long-term pair bond. To become airborne must run 15′–20′ on water into wind. Young led to water as parents begin molt; remain with parents for first year. In severe weather on n migration wings collect ice. Formerly known as Whistling Swan. **ESSAYS:** Monogamy, p. 597; Preening, p. 53; Breeding Season, p. 55. **REFS:** Bellrose, 1976; Scott, 1977; Stewart and Manning, 1958; Van Wormer, 1972.

Human Dancing and Crane Displays

certain that birds and their biology will, in one way or another, remain embedded in the arts and in the human psyche for a long time to come.

SEE: Visual Displays, p. 5.   REFS: Angell, 1978; Hutchinson, 1978.

Average Clutch Size

Clutch size is the number of eggs laid in a single nesting. When clutch sizes within populations are censused and then the number of young successfully reared is determined, it often turns out that the average clutch size is slightly below that which produces the greatest number of successfully reared young. One would expect clutch sizes to be evolutionarily determined to maximize reproduction. Why, then, would females lay "too few" eggs in a clutch? The reason is that evolution should, if possible, maximize reproduction *over the lifetime of a female*, not reproduction per brood. By being slightly conservative in the size of the clutches they produce, females may reduce the stresses of brood rearing and increase their chances of living through the following winter and producing more clutches.

Some birds, rather than laying fewer eggs than they can successfully rear, always lay more. Whooping Cranes lay clutches of two eggs, but almost always rear but one young. Presumably, it takes relatively little energy to lay the second egg, even though only one chick can be reared. The second egg is "insurance" against loss of an egg to accident or predation.

Trumpeter Swan

Cygnus buccinator Richardson

NG–60; G–40; PW–pl 5; AW–pl 157; AM (I)–140

| MF | 4–6
(2–9)
MONOG | F
I: 33–37 DAYS
PRECOCIAL 2
F: 91–119 DAYS
MF | AQUATIC
INVERTS | DABBLES |

BREEDING: Usu freshwater, occ brackish habitats, veg margin around ponds, lakes. 1 brood. **DISPLAYS:** Mutual spreading and raising of wings, wing quivering, head bobbing, and trumpeting, all assoc with nesting and nest defense by pair. **NESTS:** Oft on muskrat house, surrounded by water. Of aquatic and emergent veg, down, and feathers. Perennial. Built in 2–5 weeks. **EGGS:** Cream/white, nest-stained. 4.4" (111 mm). **DIET:** Leaves, seeds, and roots of aquatic veg; insects, crustaceans, occ small verts. Young feed on aquatic inverts first month. **CONSERVATION:** Winters within N.A. Local Concern 1986; large proportion of N.A. birds winter in small area of MT, ID, WY juncture. Pushed out of U.S. breeding grounds by development and agriculture; near extinction by 1930s. Full protection enabled recovery; reintroduced to parts of former U.S. range. **NOTES:** Largest N.A. wildfowl. Nests solitary. Territory requires sufficient open water for takeoff and landing. Pair formation in fall; long-term pair bond. Female incubates for long uninterrupted periods. Young remain in nest 24 hours; do not ride on adults' back. **ESSAYS:** Birds and the Arts, p. 47; Monogamy, p. 597; Blue List, p. 11. **REFS:** Banko, 1960; Bellrose, 1976; Cooper, 1979; Van Wormer, 1972.

Mute Swan

Cygnus olor Gmelin

NG–60; G–40; PE-42; AE–pl 173; AM (I)–140

| MF | 4–8
(4–10)
MONOG | F –M
I: 36 (35–41) DAYS
PRECOCIAL 2
F: 115–155 DAYS
MF | AQUATIC
INVERTS | DABBLES |

BREEDING: Lake, pond, marsh and sluggish river with emergent veg. 1 brood. **DISPLAYS:** In courtship: mutual head turning with breasts nearly touching and neck feathers fluffed. Territorial defense: "alighting display" (male and female land on water splashing conspicuously) and "rotation display" (neighboring males repeatedly and synchronously rotate 360° on shared border). **NESTS:** On ground near water; of cattail, reeds, roots, coarse aquatic veg, lined with fine materials, feathers and down. **EGGS:** Light gray/bluish-green. 4.5" (113 mm). **DIET:** Over 95% aquatic veg; few insects, aquatic inverts. Young feed mostly on aquatic inverts for first month. **CONSERVATION:** Winter resident. Introduced from Europe and established, esp on e coast. **NOTES:** Reproductive success improves with age through first 4 nesting attempts. Females begin breeding at earlier age than males; most females pair by second year, nest by third year. Pair formation in fall. Fiercely defend territory. Young oft ride on parents' back. **ESSAYS:** Bird Biology and the Arts, p. 47; Dabblers vs. Divers, p. 75; Feathered Nests, p. 605; Nest Lining, p. 391; Monogamy, p. 597. **REFS:** Bellrose, 1976; Lind, 1984; Reese, 1980.

Conservationists sometimes take advantage of the insurance egg, removing it from the nest to hatch the chick for captive or foster breeding programs.

SEE: Variation in Clutch Sizes, p. 339; Indeterminate Egg Layers, p. 165; Natural Selection, p. 237; Hatching Asynchrony and Brood Reduction, p. 307. REFS: Koenig, 1984; Lack, 1947, 1968; Winkler and Walters, 1983.

Preening

Preening is a commonly observed behavior involving the careful cleaning, rearrangement, and oiling of the feathers with the bill. Preening is essential in preserving those delicate structures so critical both for flight and, because of their insulating properties, for regulating body temperature. Most birds have a "preen gland" on the rump at the base of the upper tail feathers. The bill is used to work oil squeezed from this gland into the feathers, and head scratching may be an attempt to distribute preen oil over the head, where the bill obviously cannot do the job. The oil apparently has several functions: to help keep the feathers flexible and waterproof and to inhibit the growth of fungi and bacteria.

In Ross' Gulls and some other gulls and terns, the preen oil contains a pink colorant. The intensity of color seems to depend on the diet and whether or not the bird is in breeding condition. But in these species the head gets little color, apparently because of the difficulty of spreading the oil on the head.

SEE: Feathers, p. 309; Temperature Regulation and Behavior, p. 149; Head Scratching, p. 543. REF: Grant, 1986.

Trumpeter Swan taking oil from its preen gland to spread on its feathers.

Greater White-fronted Goose

Anser albifrons Scopoli

NG–62; G–44; PE–44; PW–pl 5; AE–pl 169; AW–pl 165; AM (I)–144

| F | 5–6
(4–7)
MONOG | F
I: 23–25 DAYS
PRECOCIAL 2
F: 45 DAYS
MF | AQUATIC
INVERTS | DABBLES
GROUND
GLEAN |

BREEDING: Small lakes, ponds, deltas, estuaries, sloughs; dwarf-shrub tundra. 1 brood. **DISPLAYS:** See: Duck Displays, p. 63. **NESTS:** Mass of feathers, coarse grass, lichen, moss, dry leaves. Sparse lining of finer materials; down added during laying. **EGGS:** Buffy-cream/pinkish-white, nest-stained. 3.1" (79 mm). **DIET:** Grass shoots, berries, grain shoots and seeds (occ causing commercial damage), nuts, occ aquatic insects and larvae. **CONSERVATION:** Winters s to. n and c Mexico. **NOTES:** Ground snow-covered upon arrival on breeding grounds. Most nest failures from flooding and predation. Clutch size decreases when nesting begins late. Young do not scatter when alarmed, but run forward in mass. Pair bond rarely formed in first year, usu begin breeding at 3 years. High, wedge-shaped flocks similar to Canada Goose, usu led by old male. **ESSAYS:** Flying in Vee Formation, p. 59; Monogamy, p. 597; Variation in Clutch Sizes, p. 339; Breeding Season, p. 55; Feathered Nests, p. 605. **REFS:** Bellrose, 1976; Ely and Raveling, 1984.

Snow Goose

Chen caerulescens Linnaeus

NG–64; G–44; PE–42; PW–pl 5; AE–pl 171; AW–pl 159; AM (I)–144

| F | 3–5
(1–6)
MONOG | F
I: 23–25 DAYS
PRECOCIAL 2
F: 45–49 DAYS
MF | AQUATIC
INVERTS | DABBLES
GROUND
GLEAN |

BREEDING: Usu near water on open tundra or on ridge. 1 brood. **DISPLAYS:** See: Duck Displays, p. 63. **NESTS:** Oft on tussock built up with mud and grass. Depression lined with down and grass. **EGGS:** White, usu nest-stained. 3.2" (80 mm). **DIET:** Shoots and roots of sedges, grass, bulbs, aquatic veg; insects, aquatic inverts. In autumn, berries, cultivated grain, aquatic plants. **CONSERVATION:** Winters s to n e coastal Mexico. E Canada population esimated 2.4 million, increasing at rate of 130,000/yr. **NOTES:** Colonial, to tens of thousands; females usu return to natal colony to breed, oft choosing old site (if previously successful). Early clutches larger, but subject to higher predation; late ones smaller, usu produced by younger females. Females first breed at 2–4 years. Long-term pair bond. Clutch size increases with age and/or experience up to third breeding attempt. Incubating female will retrieve eggs found within ca. 4' of nest. Crowding, stress, may lead to egg dumping: up to 80% of nests receive dumped eggs in harsh springs. Late springs inhibit nesting; some years simply skipped. Two color phases; dark phase previously considered separate species (Blue Goose). **ESSAYS:** Breeding Season, p. 55; Taxonomy and Nomenclature, p. 515; Hybridization, p. 501; Variation in Clutch Sizes, p. 339; Site Tenacity, p. 189. **REFS:** Boyd et al., 1982; Findlay and Cooke, 1982; McLandress, 1983.

Breeding Season

Evolution generally has adjusted the timing of avian breeding seasons to maximize the number of young produced. In the temperate, subarctic, and arctic zones, the overriding factor is the availability of food. Abundant nourishment is needed, not only by growing nestlings and juveniles, but also to meet increased energy demands of breeding adults. For females those increased demands include the energetic burden of producing eggs; males need additional energy to support vigorous displays and to defend territories. One or both adults generally participate in the work of building a nest, foraging for more than one individual (mate or chicks), and in some cases territorial defense or guarding young from predators.

For most birds the young hatch and grow when insects are abundant. In the arctic and subarctic, egg laying is concentrated primarily in May and June to take advantage of the late June–early July flush of mosquitoes, blackflies, butterflies, and other six-legged prey. The supply is rich near the pole, but the season is short, and birds must court, mate, and nest well before the risk of frigid storms is over. In fact, geese that nest in the arctic arrive on the breeding grounds before the snow is gone, in order to start incubating as soon as nest sites are clear. The geese depend on reserves of body fat to sustain them in an initially food-poor environment.

In general, the number of passerine broods raised annually decreases as the poles are approached. Widely distributed species in North America that manage to rear only one brood at the northern edge of their ranges, may rear two or more at their southern limits. In temperate areas, many passerine species commonly renest if a clutch or brood is lost; in contrast, many nonpasserines can produce only one brood. In some nonpasserines, such as arctic-breeding geese, the reproductive organs begin to shrink as soon as the eggs are laid. These birds have neither the energy reserves to lay replacement eggs if a clutch is lost, nor sufficient time to rear the young of a second clutch even if one could be produced. In fact, the young of arctic-breeding geese often do not have time to mature fully before winter conditions return, and seasons without successful breeding are common for species such as Snow and Ross' Geese.

Although not the only factors, assured food supplies and accompanying benign weather are by far the most common influences that affect the timing of the avian breeding seasons. To find examples of other factors, however, we must look outside of North America. For instance, to reduce predation on eggs and young, the Clay-colored Robin (which only rarely nests in South Texas) breeds in the dry season in Panama, when food is relatively scarce. Fewer losses to predators more than compensate for the risk of starvation for the chicks.

In addition to such ultimate causes favoring the evolution of breeding at a particular time, we must consider environmental changes that are proximate causes of the triggering of breeding behavior. The overwhelming majority of bird species living outside of the tropics sense that it is time to start

Ross' Goose

Chen rossii Cassin

NG–64; G–44; PE–42; PW–pl 5; AE–389; AW–pl 158; AM(I)–146

| F | 3–5
(1–6)
MONOG | ⬭ | F
I: 21–24 DAYS
PRECOCIAL 2
F: 40–45 DAYS
MF | AQUATIC
INVERTS | DABBLES
GROUND
GLEAN |

BREEDING: Islands in tundra lakes. 1 brood. **DISPLAYS:** See: Duck Displays, p. 63. **NESTS:** Usu under low veg, esp shrubs. Small depression lined with dry grass and roots. Down added as incubation advances. **EGGS:** White. 2.9" (74 mm). **DIET:** Aquatic veg, grass shoots, etc.; terrestrial and aquatic inverts. **CONSERVATION:** Winters within U.S. Population increasing: >100,000 counted in 1983 among 30 colonies in c Canadian Arctic. **NOTES:** Oft nests in assoc with Lesser Snow Goose in large colonies. Usu does not breed until third year, occ in second year. Family groups arrive together on breeding grounds. Smallest N.A. goose, occ hybridizes with Snow Goose. Two color phases but darker form extremely rare. **ESSAYS:** Breeding Season, p. 55; Taxonomy and Nomenclature, p. 515; Hybridization, p. 501; Feathered Nests, p. 605; Coloniality, p. 173. **REFS:** Bellrose, 1976; Godfrey, 1986; Kerbes et al., 1983; McLandress, 1983.

Emperor Goose

Chen canagica Sevastianov

NG–64; G–42; PW–pl 5; AW–pl 160; AM (I)–148

| F | 4–7
(3–12)
MONOG | 🥚 | F
I: 23–27 DAYS
PRECOCIAL 2
F: 50–60 DAYS
MF | AQUATIC
INVERTS | DABBLES
SURFACE
DIPS |

BREEDING: Low tundra marshes, usu near coast on margins of ponds, lakes and potholes. 1 brood. **DISPLAYS:** Male walks around female swinging head, calling. See: Duck Displays, p. 63. **NESTS:** On elevated sites near tidal pools usu with unhindered sea view; occ among scattered alders. Unconcealed, small depression. Lined with fine grass, leaves, down added as clutch is completed. **EGGS:** Creamy/white, nest-stained, variegated or fine buff mottling. 3.2" (80 mm). **DIET:** Sedges, grass, algae, berries; mostly aquatic inverts, esp mussels. Forage on seashore. **CONSERVATION:** Pelagic in winter off s and s e AK. Continued steady decline over past 20 years due to excessive taking of eggs and adults on breeding grounds. **NOTES:** Rather gregarious, nesting in loose colonies. Probably do not breed until third year; likely mate for life. After incubation begins, female on nest nearly 100% of time to hatching, leaving for only ca. 10 min once every 2 days; loses 20% of body mass during incubation. Male rarely near nest, approaches only when nest threatened. Rarest N.A. goose. **ESSAYS:** Monogamy, p. 597; Coloniality, p. 173; Feathered Nests, p. 605; Pelagic Birds, p. 657. **REFS:** Bellrose, 1976; Petersen, 1985; Thompson and Raveling, 1987.

breeding by the lengthening of the days as spring approaches. Day length, per se, has relatively little to do with breeding success, although, of course, long hours of daylight to forage—especially for time-constrained bird populations in the Far North—can be very important. But evolution seems to have latched on to day length as a "timer" of activities, since it is a signal that can be used to forecast future events. If, for instance, birds that breed in the arctic did not start to develop their reproductive organs until insects were abundant, the insects would be gone before the eggs hatched. The day length cue for development occurs long before the insects emerge. Other factors, such as weather (and associated abundance of food), also play important roles in starting the reproductive process, and especially in fine-tuning responses to the cues already provided by day length. For example, if Red-winged Blackbirds are experimentally provided with abundant food, they will begin laying their eggs three weeks earlier than birds without supplemented diets.

At least some birds also have "biological calendars"—internal timing devices that are independent of external environmental cues and tell them when it is time to breed. Consider experiments involving the Short-tailed Shearwater, a Southern Hemisphere species that "winters" in the summer off the Pacific coast of North America but breeds on islands near Australia. Birds were kept in a laboratory for over a year and subjected to a constant light regime, 12 hours of light and 12 hours of darkness, for the entire period. In spite of this constancy, their reproductive organs developed and their feathers molted at the same time as those of Short-tailed Shearwaters in the wild. The physiological basis for biological clocks and calendars—the mechanisms by which they function—remains one of the great mysteries of biology.

SEE: Hormones and Nest Building, p. 547; Metabolism, p. 325; Polyandry in the Spotted Sandpiper, p. 131; Variation in Clutch Sizes, p. 339; Pelagic Birds, p. 657. REFS: Marshall and Serventy, 1959; Morton, 1971.

Bird Biologist—Konrad Lorenz

Although he was born in Vienna (1903), and spent his entire career in Europe, Konrad Lorenz has had a substantial impact on the study of bird behavior in North America. He cofounded, with Nikolaas Tinbergen (p. 71), the discipline of ethology—the study of animal behavior in natural settings. For example, he did the seminal work on the phenomenon of "imprinting" through which young precocial birds (Lorenz worked with geese) learn to recognize and follow whatever object moves in their visual field during a brief critical period shortly after they are hatched. Lorenz found that he could substitute for the parent geese and easily get the young to imprint on him. Lorenz did other work on avian biology, on such things

Canada Goose

Branta canadensis Linnaeus

NG–66; G–42; PE–44; PW–pl 5; AE–pl 170; AW–pl 162; AM (I)–150

  ⬭

F	4–7	F	INVERTS	DABBLES
	(4–10)	I: 25–30 DAYS		GROUND
	MONOG	PRECOCIAL 2		GLEAN
		F: 40–73 DAYS		
		MF		

BREEDING: Freshwater and brackish marshes, meadows, small islands. 1 brood. **DISPLAYS:** Courting male holds head 1″ off ground, bill open, tongue raised, hissing loudly, quills shaking, approaches female, and passes neck around hers. **NESTS:** Usu near water, of dry grass, forbs, moss, sticks, aquatic veg, etc., feathers; down added as incubation begins. Occ of conifer needles, bark chips, lined with down. Occ use abandoned nest, esp if ground snow-covered; occ human-made structure. **EGGS:** White, nest-stained. 2.9″–3.6″ (74–90 mm). **DIET:** Shoots, roots, and seeds of grass and sedges, bulbs, grain, berries; also insects, crustaceans, mollusks. Mostly grain and foliage in winter. **CONSERVATION:** Winters s to n Mexico. Aleutian Canada Goose is Endangered. Most grain consumption is postharvest. Flocks oft found in urban parks with lakes or rivers; semi-domesticated. **NOTES:** Long-term pair bond. Strong fidelity to nesting territory. Breeding usu in third year, occ in second year. Male usu leads young on water; if disturbed, young dive. Male performs distraction display. Sentinels constantly guard foraging flocks. **ESSAYS:** How Long Can Birds Live?, p. 643; Visual Displays, p. 5; Flying in Vee Formation, p. 59; Metallic Poisons, p. 137; Birds and the Law, p. 293; Site Tenacity, p. 189. **REFS:** Bellrose, 1976; Craven, 1984; Godfrey, 1986; Prevett et al., 1985.

Brant

Branta bernicla Linnaeus

NG–66; G–42; PE–44; PW–pl 6; AE–pl 172; AW–pl 164; AM (I)–148

  ⬭

F	3–5	F	AQUATIC	DABBLES
	(3–8)	I: 24 (22–26) DAYS	INVERTS	GROUND
	MONOG	PRECOCIAL 2		GLEAN
		F: 40–50 DAYS		
		MF		

BREEDING: Low arctic tundra, river deltas, water-pocketed sandy areas and shallows. 1 brood. **DISPLAYS:** See: Duck Displays, p. 63. **NESTS:** Depression amid tussocks, lined with bits of seaweed and copious down; where available, lined wth moss or lichen. Occ in sand, moss or grass on marshy lake islands. Covered with down when unattended. **EGGS:** Creamy white/buff, stained. 2.9″ (73 mm). **DIET:** Sedges, grass, algae, moss, lichen; also crustaceans, mollusks, worms, insects. Some grain in winter. **CONSERVATION:** Winters s to s Baja. Decline linked to disappearance of most important food, eelgrass, along much of Atlantic coast since 1930s (same in England). **NOTES:** Long-term pair bond. Unusually late Arctic spring occ results in no reproduction that year. Strong nest site tenacity. Usu do not breed before 3 years old. Clutch size commonly 5 in w. Young of several broods join to form group at sea. Days to fledging = 40–45 for Black Brant, 45–50 for Atlantic Brant. Mainland nesting possible since decline of Arctic fox. **ESSAYS:** Diet and Nutrition, p. 587; Site Tenacity, p. 189; Feathered Nests, p. 605; Breeding Season, p. 55. **REFS:** Bellrose, 1976; Cramp and Simmons, 1977; Smith et al., 1985.

as the functions of displays, the life history of jackdaws, the courtship of ducks, and the sociology of colonial species.

Many of Lorenz's ideas on imprinting, aggression, and other topics are no longer accepted. He remains, however, a giant figure in the history of ethology—a pioneer of the view that the behavior of animals evolved in the same manner as their morphological features. In 1973 he shared a Nobel Prize with Tinbergen and Karl von Frisch, who had discovered the dance language of honeybees.

Flying in Vee Formation

We commonly see ducks and geese flying in a regular V-shaped formation, but why they do so remains something of a mystery. One theory has been that all but the lead bird are able to gain lift from the wing-tip vortices produced by the bird in front of them. Those vortices are formed by air rushing up over the tip from the high-pressure area under the wing into the low-pressure area above the wing. The following bird, if it is in just the right position, will remain within the upward flow of the vortices. Calculations indicate that such an advantage could greatly boost the range of a flock of birds over that of a bird flying alone.

Theoretically, to be most efficient, the wing-tip of a following bird should remain within about one-fourth of a wingspan from that of a bird in front of it. Motion pictures of flying flocks reveal, however, that in practice Canada Geese do not travel in formations that allow flight efficiency to be much increased by this mechanism. Instead, scientists have suggested that flying in vee formation is a way of maintaining visual contact and avoiding collisions. Further study is clearly required before the reason for flying in vees becomes clear.

SEE: How Do Birds Fly?, p. 161; Skimming: Why Birds Fly Low Over Water, p. 195. REFS: Gould and Heppner, 1974; Lissaman and Schollenberger, 1970; May, 1979.

Mallard

Anas platyrhynchos Linnaeus

NG–68; G–46; PE–48; PW–pl 14; AE–pl 107; AW–pl 97; AM (I)–158

			F	
			I: 28 (26–30) DAYS	
F	7–10	◯	PRECOCIAL 2	GREENS
	(6–15)		F: 42–60 DAYS	AQ INVERTS
	MONOG		F	INSECTS

BREEDING: Shallow pond, lake, marsh, flooded field. 1 brood. **DISPLAYS:** See: Duck Displays, p. 63. **NEST:** Usu near water; of cattails, reeds, grass, concealed by veg. Occ in hollow logs, abandoned nests, at tree base, human-made structure, etc. Down-lined as clutch is completed. **EGGS:** Greenish-buff/grayish-buff/whitish. 2.3" (58 mm). **DIET:** Seeds and shoots of sedge, grass, and aquatic veg, grain, acorns; insects, aquatic inverts. Laying females may eat 2× more animal food than males or nonlaying females. **CONSERVATION:** Winters s to c Mexico. Oft poisoned by lead pellets; alkaline-poisoned in w by foraging in ephemerally damp lake beds. **NOTES:** Seasonally monogamous, switching mates each year. Male territorial defense centered on female. Male deserts after first week of incubation to join male flocks. Nest predation increases as veg height decreases. During molt, female flightless 32 days, male 34; decrease flight muscles, increase leg muscles and layer of insulating fat. Analysis of trace elements (esp metals) in flight feathers can identify geographic origin. **ESSAYS:** Parasitized Ducks, p. 89; Vocal Development, p. 601; Bird Voices, p. 373; Metallic Poisons, p. 137; Dabblers vs. Divers, p. 75; Molting, p. 529; Flamingo Feeding, p. 43. **REFS:** Bellrose, 1976; Bossema and Roemers, 1985; Gooders and Boyer, 1986; Swanson, 1985.

Mottled Duck

Anas fulvigula Ridgway

N–68; G–46; PE–48; AW–388; AM (I)–158

			F	
			I: 25–27 DAYS	
F	8–10	◯	PRECOCIAL 2	INSECTS
	(5–13)		F: 60–70 DAYS	GREENS
	MONOG		F	

BREEDING: Fresh and brackish water, coastal wetlands, inland grassy areas near water; forage also in rice and ungrazed fields. 1 brood. **DISPLAYS:** See: Duck Displays, p. 63. **NEST:** In drier parts of marsh or on sandy ridge; of matted grass, rushes, aquatic veg, reeds. Concealed under sheltering veg. Occ far from water. Lined with down, breast feathers. **EGGS:** Creamy-white/greenish-white. 2.2" (56 mm). **DIET:** More animal food than closely related Mallard; mollusks, snails, crustaceans, fish, insects; grass, grain, seeds, aquatic veg, berries. **CONSERVATION:** Winter resident. Civilization and agriculture more detrimental than hunting. **NOTES:** Readily deserts nest if disturbed. Young scatter on female's alarm, hiding in veg. Disturbed female calls, attracting male attention. Male circles overhead, calling, but does not approach. Inland populations apparently hybridize with Mallard. FL birds more streaked than others. **ESSAYS:** Dabblers vs. Divers, p. 75; Sibling Species, p. 383; Feathered Nests, p. 605; Hybridization. p. 501. **REFS:** Bellrose, 1976; Gooders and Boyer, 1986.

Sleeping Sentries

Even when apparently asleep, birds open their eyes and peek around. Peeking is limited to the phase of sleep referred to as dozing or "quiet sleep." During the remaining "active-sleep" portion of their slumber, birds' eyes remain shut. Animal behaviorist Dennis Lendrem surveyed flocks of dozing ducks until the patterns of peeking could be discerned.

Lendrem found that in the ducks peeking typically occurred about once every two to six seconds. Which birds in the flock do the most peeking depends on the number of coflockers, positions in the flock, and the time of year. Members of smaller flocks peek more, as do birds in less-protected positions and those closer to a perceived threat. During the breeding season, males peek more than females. This seems to be due, in part, to sexual activities of the flock. As the number of females in the flock increases, so do the opportunities for the males to engage in promiscuous sex, which means that males must keep an eye on each other. Similarly, there is always the threat of paired females (willingly and unwillingly) copulating with males other than their mates. That would explain why mated males peek more than bachelor males.

But being attractive to females carries some potential costs. Brightly plumed breeding males presumably are quite conspicuous to predators. Breeding males peek much more frequently than they do after they return to their eclipse plumage when, all other factors being equal, their peeking rates drop to those of females.

How much active sleep birds require is still unknown. Different sleep phases produce different heart and respiratory rates and changes in electroencephalograph (EEG) patterns, as they do in people. It has been suggested that birds that move around often and rapidly require a greater proportion of active sleep than more intermittently active birds, which exhibit more irregular sleep patterns. Dozing and peeking in flocks allow for more active sleep, reduce the threat of predation, and for some males, increase mating opportunities.

SEE: Communal Roosting, p. 615; Flock Defense, p. 235; Geometry of the Selfish Colony, p. 19. REF: Lendrem, 1983.

Eclipse Plumage

When their breeding efforts are complete, the males of most duck species in the Northern Hemisphere molt from their brightly colored nuptial plumage to a dull, cryptic plumage. Their brilliance is dimmed—they go into "eclipse." The transformation usually occurs rapidly in the depths of marshes where flocks of males retreat for a flightless period. The eclipse plumage is generally retained for a brief time—in many species for as little as one to three months, but some species remain in eclipse plumage until

American Black Duck

Anas rubripes Brewster

NG–68; G–46; PE–48; PW–pl 14; AE–pl 133; AM (I)–156

			F		
			I: 26–29 (23–33) DAYS		
TREE	F	8–10	PRECOCIAL 2	SEEDS	
STUMP		(6–12)	F: 58–63 DAYS	TUBERS	
To 45'		MONOG	F		

BREEDING: Freshwater and brackish wetlands esp with emergent veg. Usu 1 brood. **DISPLAYS:** See: Duck Displays, p. 63. **NEST:** In concealing grass tussock in wooded swamp, thicket, wood border, or meadow. Depression neatly filled with dry grass, leaves, etc. Rarely in tree using abandoned nest. Down lining added during incubation. **EGGS:** Creamy-white/greenish-buff. 2.4″ (59 mm). **DIET:** Incl insects, worms, snails; aquatic veg, seeds, grass, forbs, berries, also grain. **CONSERVATION:** Winters within N.A. Blue List 1980–81, Special Concern 1982, 1986. Populations decreasing from aerial spraying for spruce budworm, habitat destruction, acid rain, overhunting, competition and hybridization with Mallard. **NOTES:** Hybridizes extensively with Mallard throughout large overlapping range where Mallard has been introduced by game-farm releases; genetically, the two species are essentially identical. Previously most abundant duck breeding in U.S. Pair bond lasts until ca. 20 days after incubation starts. Young mobile 1–3 hours after hatching; if disturbed, female feigns injury. Female leaves brood to forage elsewhere, reducing competition for food. Hen-brood bond terminates at 6–7 weeks. **ESSAYS:** Dabblers vs. Divers, p. 75; Blue List, p. 11; Hybridization, p. 501; Distraction Displays, p. 115; Monogamy, p. 597. **REFS:** Ankney et al., 1986; Bellrose, 1976; Luoma, 1987; Ringelman et al., 1982; Seymour and Titman, 1978; Spencer, 1986.

Gadwall

Anas strepera Linnaeus

NG–70; G–48; PE–48; PW–pl 14; AE–pl 135; AW–pl 125; AM (I)–168

			F		
			I: 24–27 DAYS		
	F	8–11	PRECOCIAL 2	INSECTS	SURFACE
		(5–13)	F: 48–56+ DAYS	AQUATIC	DIVES
		MONOG	F	INVERTS	

BREEDING: Freshwater (and rarely brackish) marshes, brushy, grassy areas away from water; on lake islands. 1 brood. **DISPLAYS:** In courtship, male raises black posterior out of water and shows speculum while bobbing head. See: Duck Displays, p. 63. **NEST:** Usu concealed in dense grass, tall reeds, or under brush; made of nearby veg. Building continues during laying. Lined with finer materials; down added during incubation. **EGGS:** White. 2.2″ (55 mm). **DIET:** Grass, aquatic plants, nuts, grain; aquatic inverts, small verts. Dives for food more than most dabblers. In winter, mostly aquatic veg, algae. **CONSERVATION:** Winters s to s Mexico. Range expanding e. **NOTES:** Nesting success oft higher than other dabblers. Strong female nest site tenacity. Nest parasitism by other Gadwalls and by scaup, not uncommon. Breeding season later than most other ducks. Gadwalls feed farther from shore than do other dabblers. **ESSAYS:** Dabblers vs. Divers, p. 75; Piracy, p. 159; Parasitized Ducks, p. 89; Site Tenacity, p. 189. **REFS:** Bellrose, 1976; Gooders and Boyer, 1986; Hepp, 1985; Hines and Mitchell, 1983, 1984.

the following spring. With the next molt, the male returns to his fancy breeding garb. In those species that lose their eclipse plumage early, the rapid loss of their camouflage pattern is apparently more than compensated for by the advantage of impressing females in advance of the impending breeding season.

SEE: Molting, p. 529; The Color of Birds, p. 111; Feathers, p. 309.

Duck Displays

Most ducks confine their displays to the water (or land) surface, since their heavy weight relative to their wing area ("high wing loading") dictates continuous flapping and makes complex maneuvers, such as hovering and soaring, difficult or impossible. Aerial communication is thus largely restricted to short, ritualized flights (ordinarily close to the water surface) and vocalizations, including contact calls that help maintain flock coherence in these rapid fliers that often go long distances between landings.

Most people's first observations of duck behavior probably are of Mallard courtship. Mallards perform in the fall and winter as well as the spring, so there is plenty of opportunity to watch their displays. They are also often rather tame, and perform in the open—this is a good thing since, while frequent, their displays are subtle and brief. Males swimming in the presence of females may be seen shaking their heads (head-shake display) and tails (tail-shake), often doing the former with their breasts held clear of the water and their necks outstretched. They also raise their wingtips, heads and tails briefly and then swim with their necks outstretched and held close to the water (head-up-tail-up). Groups of four to five males may swim around females, arching their necks, whistling, then lowering their bills below the water surface and jerking their bills up to their breasts while spurting water toward the preferred female (water-flick or grunt-whistle). The water-flick may take only a fraction of a second to complete. The drakes in male groups give short, nasal "raeb-raeb" (two-syllable) calls, and short high-pitched whistles.

Female Mallards and other female ducks often demonstrate (inciting displays) and call to provoke males to attack other males or females. In some circumstances these displays may allow the female to observe the performance of males and to evaluate them as potential mates. To elicit displays from a group of males, a female Mallard may swim with her neck outstretched and her head just above the water (nod-swimming). When a strange male approaches a female Mallard, she often will do an inciting display, swimming after her preferred mate while producing a rapid staccato series of quacks and flicking her beak back and downward to the side. As pairs are formed, both sexes may be observed lifting a wing, spreading the feathers to expose the speculum (the patch of bright color at the trailing

Green-winged Teal

Anas crecca Linnaeus

NG–70; G–50; PE–52; PW–pl 14; AE–pl 105; AW–pl 121; AM (I)–154

  ◯ F
I: 21–23 DAYS
PRECOCIAL 2
F: 34 DAYS
F

F 8–9 AQUATIC DABBLES
(5–15) INVERTS
MONOG

BREEDING: Densely vegetated inland freshwater lake, marsh, pond, pool, shallow stream. 1 brood. **DISPLAYS:** See: Duck Displays, p. 63. **NEST:** Well concealed in clump of tall grass, forbs, brush, or at base of log or shrub. Occ in vicinity of burn, occ far from water. Nest of soft grass, forbs, twigs and leaves. Lined with finer materials and increasing amounts of down. **EGGS:** Cream/light olive buff. 1.8″ (46 mm). **DIET:** In summer: aquatic inverts, tadpoles; seeds of emergent and aquatic veg. In fall: grain, grass, seeds, plant shoots. Young feed on insects, other inverts, veg gleaned from water's edge, aquatic veg. **CONSERVATION:** Winters s to Baja, c Mexico and Bahamas. According to Audubon (1840) individual gunners in w shot 6 dozen/day upon first arrival of migrants. **NOTES:** Young have fastest growth rate of all N.A. ducks. Male usu abandons nest before incubation begins. Female covers eggs when off nest. **ESSAYS:** Bird Communities and Competition, p. 605 ; Metallic Poisons, p. 137; Feathered Nests, p. 605; Dabblers vs. Divers, p. 75. **REFS:** Bellrose, 1976; Gooders and Boyer, 1986; Hepp, 1985.

American Wigeon

Anas americana Gmelin

NG–72; G–48; PE–50; PW–pl 14; AE–pl 106; AW–pl 119; AM (I)–170

  ◯ F
I: 23–25 DAYS
PRECOCIAL 2
F: 37–48 DAYS
F

F 7–10 AQUATIC
(6–12) INVERTS
MONOG

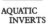

BREEDING: Marshes, freshwater areas with exposed shoreline, lakes, islands. 1 brood. **DISPLAYS:** See: Duck Displays, p. 63. **NEST:** Oft far from water. Concealed; filled with dry grass and plant stems, lined with finer materials. Down added as incubation advances. **EGGS:** White. 2.1″ (54 mm). **DIET:** Grass, grain, aquatic veg, fewer seeds than most dabblers; aquatic inverts, mollusks, insects. **CONSERVATION:** Winters s to n S.A. **NOTES:** Pair bond lasts through first or second week of incubation. Male reproductive success related to persistent aggression, dominance, mate attentiveness, and displaying, esp aerial chases. Males in full plumage acquire mates earliest; males unable to acquire mates usu smaller and have lower energy (protein and lipid) reserves. If young disturbed, female feigns injury while young scatter; when young hidden, female flies away. **ESSAYS:** Bird Communities and Competition, p. 605; Dabblers vs. Divers, p. 75; Diet and Nutrition, p. 587; Metallic Poisons, p. 137; Monogamy, p. 597; Feathered Nests, p. 605; Distraction Displays, p. 115. **REFS:** Bellrose, 1976; Gooders and Boyer, 1986; Wishart, 1983.

edge of the wing), and placing the beak behind the raised wing as if preening. Then just before copulation, the male and female typically float face-to-face and pump their heads up and down.

Similar courtship can be seen in other dabbling or "puddle" ducks (in North America members of the genus *Anas*—who are able to spring into the air without running across the water surface). The displays of the Black Duck are, in particular, almost identical with those of the Mallard. Nevertheless, significant differences in patterns of communication exist among members of the genus, differences that have evolved in response to varying ecological situations. Shovelers, for example, are specialized for the time-consuming process of sieving plankton from the waters of small, permanent ponds. A male defends a small, discrete territory around his mate, with whom he has a strong, long-lasting relationship; consequently he rarely spends time in "extramarital" pursuits.

Northern Shovelers and their close relatives within the genus *Anas* (Blue-winged and Cinnamon Teal, Garganey) are known collectively as the "blue-winged ducks" because of their powder-blue or grayish upper-wing coverts. Blue-winged ducks have evolved a conspicuous "hostile pumping" display. The head, with crown feathers depressed and bill slightly elevated, is repeatedly raised high while giving "took" calls out of phase with the pumping. This sequence is used both as a short-distance territorial display ("stay away from my mate/nest") and long-distance territorial threat display ("stay out of my feeding territory").

Unlike relatively sedentary shovelers, pintails (again, a member of the genus *Anas*) range far and wide to forage in temporary bodies of water, and tend to nest in sparse cover at a great distance from water. In addition, male pintails spend only part of their time with their mates, and devote some of their time trying to copulate with other females; as a result female pintails tend to be frequently harassed. It seems likely that close defense of a territory is profitable for the male shoveler because concentrated food resources allow him to provide an area where his mate can obtain sufficient food free from harassment. No such strategy is feasible for the male pintail because of the dispersed nature of that species' food resources. Therefore Northern Pintails and their relatives (e.g., Green-winged Teal) have not evolved a conspicuous long-range territorial threat display; they need only guard nests and mates, not feeding territories.

This discussion of Mallards, shovelers and pintails only scratches the surface of the complexity and variety of duck displays. For example, Robert Alison studied the displays of Oldsquaw, whose "ahr-ahr-ahroulit" vocalizations are familiar background music to those who have spent time in the northern tundra. He distinguished a *dozen* distinct displays performed by courting males alone: the lateral head-shaking, bill-tossing, rear end, porpoising, wing-flapping, body-shaking, parachute, breast, turning-the-back-of-the-head, bill-dipping, steaming, and neck-stretching displays. Some of these are accompanied by unique vocalizations. Females, in turn, perform chin-lifting, soliciting, and hunch displays; though the precise functions of

Northern Pintail

Anas acuta Linnaeus

NG–72; G–48; PE–50; PW–pl 14; AE–pl 115; AW–pl 124; AM (I)–160

| F | 6–9
(6–12)
MONOG | F
I: 22–25 DAYS
PRECOCIAL 2
F: 36–57 DAYS
F | GREENS | GROUND
GLEAN |

BREEDING: Grassland, cultivated field, tundra, sandy flat, island in boreal forest lake, marsh, pond. 1 brood. **DISPLAYS:** See: Duck Displays, p. 63. **NEST:** Occ far from water, concealed in grass, stubble, etc. Filled with dry grass, leaves. Lined with finer materials. Down added as incubation advances. **EGGS:** Olive-green/ olive-buff. 2.2″ (55 mm). **DIET:** About 90% veg, incl seeds, aquatic veg, sedge, grain; minnows, aquatic inverts, insects, tadpoles. **CONSERVATION:** Winters s to n S.A. Nests placed in stubble fields oft plowed up. Oft poisoned by ingested lead shot. **NOTES:** Clutch size small for dabbling duck. Female nest site tenacity not well developed. Male deserts female early in incubation. Female feigns injury in defense of young. Ranks third as game bird after Mallard and American Black, in both abundance and distribution. **ESSAYS:** Metallic Poisons, p. 137; Dabblers vs. Divers, p. 75; Commensal Feeding, p. 35; Nest Lining, p. 391; Feathered Nests, p. 605; Distraction Displays, p. 115; Site Tenacity, p. 189. **REFS:** Bellrose, 1976; Gooders and Boyer, 1986; Hepp, 1985.

Northern Shoveler

Anas clypeata Linnaeus

NG–74; G–50; PE–52; PW–pl 14; AE–pl 108; AW–pl 96; AM (I)–166

| F | 9–12
(6–14)
MONOG | F
I: 22–25 DAYS
PRECOCIAL 2
F: 38–66 DAYS
F | AQUATIC
INVERTS | |

BREEDING: Freshwater shallows, esp muddy, sluggish habitats and surrounding marsh veg; also wet, prairie meadows. 1 brood. **DISPLAYS:** See: Duck Displays, p. 63. **NEST:** Usu in short grass on boggy edge of water, occ in field, meadow, or emergent veg. Concealed depression filled with dry grass, other veg. Lined with down as incubation advances. **EGGS:** Olive-buff/greenish-gray. 2.0″ (52 mm). **DIET:** Aquatic veg, esp plankton; snails, clams, aquatic insects. Feeds primarily by straining small plants and animals from water's surface through comblike edge of bill; also feeds along mudflat margins. **CONSERVATION:** Winters s to n S.A. **NOTES:** Females incubate more sporadically than other ducks, spend more time foraging. Some males remain paired and stay on territories throughout incubation. Oft nests late, esp in n. **ESSAYS:** Metallic Poisons, p. 137; Dabblers vs. Divers, p. 75; Commensal Feeding, p. 35; Incubation Time, p. 481; Breeding Season, p. 55; Feathered Nests, p. 605. **REFS:** Afton, 1979a, b; Bellrose, 1976; Gooders and Boyer, 1986.

these displays are still unclear, they occur with different frequencies in different situations: male-male encounters; male-female encounters; pre- and post-copulation, etc.

The problem of thoroughly analyzing such displays is not trivial. Benjamin Dane (now of Tufts University) and his colleagues studied 22,000 feet of film of displaying Common Goldeneyes. They used a stop-action projector to view each frame individually, counting frames (the film was exposed at a constant 24 frames per second) to determine the duration of a given display. It was thus possible to time each display accurately and to determine the probability of one display following another at each stage of the courtship. The projector was also used to analyze display-response interactions between individuals. One of the most interesting findings was the rather uniform timing of some of the displays—the head-throw of the Goldeneye took an average of 1.29 seconds to perform, and some 95 percent of head-throws were timed at between 1.13 and 1.44 seconds.

The great complexity of duck courtship displays probably has evolved because ducks tend to concentrate in small areas to breed, and closely related species often give their displays in plain view of each other (and of human observers, which makes them a joy to study). This has created considerable evolutionary pressure for each species to develop distinctive displays, so that hybridization among different species displaying together will be minimized. Thus, for example, the displays of Barrow's Goldeneyes are very different from those of Common Goldeneyes until the precopulatory stage is reached. In spite of this, some hybrids between Barrow's and Common Goldeneyes occur, but with nowhere near the frequency of hybrids between Mallards and Black Ducks, which have very similar displays.

A major problem that needs more investigation is exactly how context affects communication. Does a certain display given by a mated male convey different information from the same display given by a courting male? Does the distance between signaler and receiver influence meaning? How about orientation (face-to-face, side-to-side, etc.)? When and why does consistent alternation of two displays occur?

Recent advances (and price reductions) in portable video cassette recorder systems may open wide the door to advanced analysis of behavior—all that is needed is the development of appropriate telephoto lenses. With the participation of increasing numbers of birders and ornithologists, the meaning of many of the complex (and often rapidly performed) displays of ducks may be clarified, increasing our understanding of why these displays have evolved.

SEE: Visual Displays, p. 5; Shorebird Communication, p. 139; Sexual Selection, p. 251; Dabblers vs. Divers, p. 75. REFS: Alison, 1975; Cramp and Simmons, 1977; Dane et al., 1959; Dane and Van der Kloot, 1964; Johnsgard, 1965; McKinney, 1975.

Blue-winged Teal

NG–74; G–50; PE–52; PW–pl 14; AE–pl 136; AW–pl 120; AM (I)–164

			F		
F	8–11		I: 24 (23–27) DAYS	GREENS	DABBLES
	(6–15)		PRECOCIAL 2	AQUATIC	
	MONOG		F: 35–44 DAYS	INVERTS	
			F		

BREEDING: Prairie potholes of Northern Plains, marsh, also pond, slough, lake, sluggish stream. 1 brood. **DISPLAYS:** See: Duck Displays, p. 63. **NEST:** Overarching veg oft conceals nest of grass, cattail. Lined with finer materials. Down added after clutch well under way. Occ foundation wet, but eggs stay dry. Female, oft accompanied by male, selects site. **EGGS:** Creamy-white/olive-white. 1.8″ (47 mm). **DIET:** Seeds of aquatic veg, greens; in autumn, grain important; aquatic inverts (esp snails), insects. **CONSERVATION:** Winters s to c Peru, c Argentina and s Brazil, but most N.A. birds winter in C.A. **NOTES:** Nests occ parasitized by other duck species. Male deserts female near end of incubation. Female feigns injury in defense of young, which hide in veg. Breeding range overlaps with closely related Cinnamon Teal, with whom it hybridizes. **ESSAYS:** Metallic Poisons, p. 137; Dabblers vs. Divers, p. 75; Parasitized Ducks, p. 89; Hybridization, p. 501. **REFS:** Bellrose, 1976; Gooders and Boyer, 1986; Stewart and Titman, 1980; White et al., 1981.

Cinnamon Teal

NG–74; G–50; PE–52; PW–pl 14; AE–pl 112; AW–pl 117; AM (I)–164

			F		
F	7–12		I: 21–25 DAYS	INSECTS	DABBLES
	(4–16)		PRECOCIAL 2	MOLLUSKS	
	MONOG		F: 49 DAYS		
			F		

BREEDING: Alkaline wetland in arid area, shallow lake margin with emergent veg, pond, lagoon, slough, sluggish stream, marsh. 1 brood. **DISPLAYS:** See: Duck Displays, p. 63. **NEST:** Usu in marsh or adjacent meadow; depression concealed by woven veg. Lined sparsely with bits of grass; copious down added as clutch is completed. Nest occ wet and bulky. **EGGS:** Pinkish-buff. 1.9″ (48 mm). **DIET:** Mostly aquatic veg seeds; also insects, snails. Forage in shallow water along shorelines. **CONSERVATION:** Winters s to n S.A. Populations decline in response to encroachment of civilization and agriculture (draining wetlands for cultivation and diverting water for irrigation). **NOTES:** Redheads oft parasitize; Mallards and Ruddy Ducks also parasitize, occ remove teal eggs. Clutches >11 may be result of parasitization. Pair bond maintained throughout most of incubation. Young hide by diving or seeking veg cover; adult feigns injury before flying away. Hybridizes with Blue-winged Teal. **ESSAYS:** Metallic Poisons, p. 137; Dabblers vs. Divers, p. 75; Species and Speciation, p. 355; Parasitized Ducks, p. 89; Hybridization, p. 501; Feathered Nests, p. 605; Distraction Displays, p. 115; Monogamy, p. 597. **REFS:** Bellrose, 1976; Gooders and Boyer, 1986.

Botulism

Annually, millions of waterfowl die around the world because of a toxin produced by a bacterium, *Clostridium botulinum*. The bacterium multiplies in the oxygen-poor environments created by decaying plant and animal matter (the bacterium is "anaerobic"—it is poisoned by oxygen). In the process the *clostridia* produce the toxin, which may then be acquired by birds feeding on rotting plants or flesh. The toxin affects the birds' nervous systems, causing as the most obvious symptom a paralysis which prevents flight. The neck may be held to the side, and walking may be difficult or impossible. Birds die from drowning or respiratory failure.

Although botulism most commonly attacks aquatic birds (an estimated quarter of a million ducks succumbed on the Great Salt Lake in 1932), it has been identified in over 20 avian families. Epidemics usually occur in the summer when high temperatures, low water levels, low oxygen levels, and high alkalinity of lakes and marshes create ideal conditions for the multiplication of *Clostridium* and, therefore, production of the toxin.

SEE: Metallic Poisons, p. 137; Disease and Parasitism, p. 399; Helping to Conserve Birds—Local Level, p. 361.

Walking vs. Hopping

A bird moving along a telephone wire does not walk like a tightrope artist; instead, the bird will "sidestep," "switch-sidle," or "hop." Sidestepping (the way that people typically move along a ledge) involves alternately lifting each foot and moving it to the side while continuing to keep the same foot ahead. Switch-sidling means moving to the right or to the left by crossing one foot over the other in an exaggerated "pigeon-toed" step. Hopping, of course, requires moving both feet simultaneously.

When unconstrained by such a narrow perch, many birds walk or run using the alternating strides typical of most bipeds. Others, particularly small, arboreally inclined species, commonly hop. It is uncertain why hopping is more common in smaller birds. The evidence seems to point to economy of effort: short-legged birds move farther in a single hop than they do taking several steps, whereas it is more economical for larger birds, with longer strides, to move one leg at a time.

Although birds of the same taxonomic groups frequently share a common pattern of locomotion on the ground, the patterns often have exceptions. Most passerines hop, but others, such as larks, pipits, starlings, and meadowlarks, typically stride. Within the family Corvidae, jays hop whereas crows stride. Diverse species, including robins, ravens, and blackbirds, both hop and stride. Whether a physically unconstrained bird hops or strides is not just a question of anatomy; speed also affects choice of locomotion—a hopper in a hurry tends to break into a run.

Ruddy Duck
Oxyura jamaicensis Gmelin

NG–76; G–62; PE–60; PW–pl 13; AE–pl 111; AW–pl 116; AM (I)–206

F
6–8
(6–10)
MONOG

F
I: 23–26 DAYS
PRECOCIAL 2
F: 42–48 DAYS
F

GREENS

BREEDING: Usu densely vegetated freshwater marsh, occ lake, pond. 1 brood, 2 in s. **DISPLAYS:** "Bubbling" by male used both in courtship and aggression toward other males. See: Duck Displays, p. 63. **NEST:** In tall emergent veg, built of same. Lined sparsely with finer materials. Occ uses abandoned coot or Redhead nest. **EGGS:** Creamy white, nest-stained. 2.5" (62 mm). **DIET:** Mostly aquatic insect larvae, also aquatic snails, other inverts; aquatic veg, esp in winter. Most food obtained by straining animals from soft substrate ooze. **CONSERVATION:** Winters s to n C.A. and Bahamas. **NOTES:** Brood parasite, oft laying eggs in nests of other ducks, esp Redhead, Canvasback, also grebes, rails. Parasitism rate not necessarily related to environmental conditions; parasitism higher among Ruddies than between Ruddies and other species. Male deserts prior to or early in incubation; males oft seen accompanying females with broods, but these males are not the broods' parents, apparently simply males attracted to females. Young soon capable of diving effectively but helpless on land. **ESSAYS:** Parasitized Ducks, p. 89; Dabblers vs. Divers, p. 75; American Coots, p. 105; Brood Parasitism, p. 287; Parental Care, p. 555; Monogamy, p. 597. **REFS:** Bellrose, 1976; Gooders and Boyer, 1986; Joyner, 1977, 1983; Siegfried, 1976.

Masked Duck
Oxyura dominica Linnaeus

NG–76; G–62; PE–298; PW–pl 13; AM (I)–208

F
4–10
MONOG

F
I: 28 DAYS
PRECOCIAL 2
F: ? DAYS
F

INSECTS

BREEDING: Densely vegetated fresh and brackish pools, ponds, lagoons, swamps, ricefields, and sluggish streams. 1 brood. **DISPLAYS:** See: Duck Displays, p. 63. **NEST:** Neat, almost cuplike; of grass. Sparsely lined. **EGGS:** White/buff. 2.5" (63 mm). **DIET:** Plant materials, some insects, crustaceans. **CONSERVATION:** Winter resident. **NOTES:** Poorly known. A tropical duck whose range is expanding n. Clutches larger than 10 presumably result from 2 females laying in same nest. Secretive and difficult to observe but relatively tame. Oft skulks raillike through emergent veg, which wears away feather tips, esp of tail. **ESSAYS:** Dabblers vs. Divers, p. 75; Feathers, p. 309; Sleeping Sentries, p. 61. **REFS:** Bellrose, 1976; Gooders and Boyer, 1986.

Leg length is not only related to locomotory mode but also associated, among other things, with foraging style. For example, among ground gleaners and waders, species with shorter legs forage in shallower debris or water. Some ground foragers (especially buntings, towees, juncos, and sparrows) are more likely to use a method of foraging called "double-scratching," a maneuver involving little more than hopping in place. But here, too, there is no simple division between birds that hop, stride, and double-scratch. Some striders double-scratch and some hoppers do not.

Recording the locomotory patterns in local bird species in different circumstances could be helpful in determining, for example, the conditions under which birds that typically hop when on perches (such as jays, flickers, and House Sparrows) continue to hop when on the ground and under which conditions they do not.

SEE: Swimming, p. 73; Songbird Foraging, p. 381; Feet, p. 239; Visual Displays, p. 5; Avian Snowshoes, p. 255; How Do We Find Out About Bird Biology?, p. 319. REFS: Dagy, 1977; Hailman, 1973.

Bird Biologist—Nikolaas (Niko) Tinbergen

Dutch biologist Niko Tinbergen was a central figure in establishing the science of ethology—the study of animal behavior in natural settings. Born in 1907, he has worked on many different kinds of animals from stickleback fishes to butterflies. His influence on North American bird biology has been substantial, especially because of his work on Herring Gulls (and his book *The Herring Gull's World*), and other investigations of avian ethology. Virtually all work on bird behavior today owes something to Tinbergen's ideas and approaches. His work earned him a Nobel Prize, which he shared with the great ethologist, Konrad Lorenz (p. 57) and Karl von Frisch, who had demonstrated that honeybees communicated the distance and direction of food sources to each other by dancing on the face of their honeycomb.

Fulvous Whistling Duck
Dendrocygna bicolor Vieillot

NG–76; G–52; PE–48; PW–pl 13; AE–pl 166; AW–pl 122; AM (I)–134

| TREE | F | 12–13
(6–16)
MONOG | MF
I: 24–26 DAYS
PRECOCIAL 2
F: 55–63 DAYS
MF | SEEDS | GROUND
GLEAN |

BREEDING: Shallow fresh and brackish water marshes, lagoon, field. 1 brood. **DISPLAYS:** See: Duck Displays, p. 63. **NEST:** Oft on levee above flooded ricefield; well-woven nest bowl. Female trims surrounding reed, sedge within 4'–5'. Occ built up 6" above ground on hummock in marsh, between ponds, or in swamp. Lined with grass, weeds, but no down. **EGGS:** White/buff white, oft stained. 2.1" (53 mm). **DIET:** Seeds incl esp rice, also alfalfa, corn. **CONSERVATION:** Winters s to s Mexico. Blue List 1972–79, Special Concern 1982, 1986; declining in s w. **NOTES:** More gooselike than ducklike. Long-term pair bond. Brood parasites: females oft lay in each other's nests, as well as in those of other species; >60 eggs recorded in parasitized ("dump") nests. Nests oft unattended for long periods. Largely nocturnal feeders. Formerly known as Fulvous Tree Duck. **ESSAYS:** Blue List, p. 11; Parasitized Ducks, p. 89; Who Incubates?, p. 27; Variation in Clutch Sizes, p. 339. **REFS:** Bellrose, 1976; Flickinger, 1975; Gooders and Boyer, 1986.

Black-bellied Whistling Duck
Dendrocygna autumnalis
Linnaeus

NG–76; G–52; PE–298; PW–pl 13; AE–pl 168; AM (I)–134

| 8'–30'
GROUND | F | 12–14
(9–18)
MONOG | MF
I: 25–30 DAYS
PRECOCIAL 2
F: 53–63 DAYS
MF | | |

BREEDING: Fresh and brackish marshes, pond and stream borders with floating veg and exposed mud, open woodland. 2? broods. **DISPLAYS:** See: Duck Displays, p. 63. **NEST:** Usu in tree cavity in woodland regardless of proximity to water. Lined only with rotted chips. Also nests on ground among rushes, weeds, or grass on lake margin. Occ uses human-built structures. **EGGS:** White/creamy white, oft nest-stained. 2.0" (52 mm). **DIET:** Oft forage in cultivated fields for seeds, grain; <10% snails, insects. **CONSERVATION:** Winter resident. Hunted mostly in Mexico. Will use nest boxes. **NOTES:** Long-term pair bond. Strong fidelity to nest area. Male incubates, atypical of waterfowl but typical of whistling ducks. Brood parasitism with "dump" nests produced by >1 female common; results in clutches of up to 101 eggs! Young remain in nest 18–24 hours, then one by one, jump to ground when called by female; once accumulated, brood moves to water. Parents remain with brood for at least 6 months. Formerly known as Black-bellied Tree Duck. **ESSAYS:** Site Tenacity, p. 189; Who Incubates?, p. 27; Parasitized Ducks, p. 89; Brood Parasitism, p. 287; Incubation Time, p. 481. **REFS:** Bellrose, 1976; Bolen and McCamant, 1977; Delnicki and Bolen, 1976; Gooders and Boyer, 1986.

Swimming

One of the most graceful sights in the animal world is a penguin swimming underwater. With seemingly no effort, they rocket around using their wings to "fly" through the ocean. Swimming penguins change the angle of the leading edge of their wings, lowering them on the downstroke and raising them on the upstroke, so that both strokes propel the bird forward, resulting in smooth progression through the water. The penguins' body feathers are short, and thus trap little air, and their bones are quite solid for birds. Both features reduce buoyancy, thereby helping penguins to remain submerged.

Underwater "fliers" are mostly seabirds with short wings, including cormorants, guillemots, auks, shearwaters, and diving petrels. To work well in water, wings must be short and muscular. Long, slender wings are fine for soaring, but are poor instruments for flying in a medium as thick as water—they cannot be moved rapidly against the friction. But with their stubby wings, underwater fliers tend to make poor aviators, and some, such as penguins, have given up flying altogether. Diving petrels, however, fly reasonably well with rapid wing beats, and upon plunging into water simply continue to fly through it.

Most birds that swim in fresh water propel themselves with their feet. This is also true for underwater fliers when they are on the surface. The most advanced practitioners of this technique are the loons. Veritable submarines, loons are long, slender, and streamlined, with two powerful propellerlike legs attached to the rear of their body and tipped with webbed feet. Like penguins (and other diving birds such as auks, grebes, and cormorants) they have relatively solid bones and float low. And, like submarines, they can dive deep; Common Loons have been recorded at depths of 600 feet in the Great Lakes.

Other birds that dive but are also accomplished fliers, such as terns, gannets, and pelicans, are quite buoyant because of their hollow bones, numerous air sacs, and the air that remains trapped in their feathers. They turn the trick of submerging much as buoyant human beings often do—by diving from a considerable height and allowing their momentum to help carry them well below the surface. Kingfishers seem to use a similar technique, but often take their prey very close to the surface. In contrast, grebes can squeeze much of the air out of their feathers, and partially deflate their air sacs, "trimming" themselves to float at any level or to submerge. Cormorants and Anhingas have wettable feathers which help them sink but which also apparently commit them to long sessions of sun-drying with spread wings.

Birds that are foot-propelled in water generally hold their wings tightly while diving and swimming, so as to streamline the body. Eider and scoter ducks, however, keep their wings partially open and use them for both paddling and steering. Oddly, the American Dipper often just walks along

Wood Duck

Aix sponsa Linnaeus

NG–78; G–52; PE–50; PW–pl 13; AE–pl 119; AW–pl 114; AM (I)–152

>30'
NESTBOX
2'–65'

F

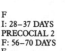

○
10–15
(6–15)
MONOG

F
I: 28–37 DAYS
PRECOCIAL 2
F: 56–70 DAYS
F

SEEDS

BREEDING: Wooded swamp, bottomland slough, flooded forest, pond, marsh. 1 brood, occ 2, esp in s. **DISPLAYS:** Courtship and pair formation begin in autumn, continue into spring. Courtship bouts in groups avg 11 birds, males outnumbering females; always incl vocalizations. See: Duck Displays, p. 63. **NEST:** Prefer tree cavity. Lined with wood chips, down. Occ use abandoned nest hole of other species, rock fissure. Perennial. **EGGS:** Creamy white. 2.0" (51 mm). **DIET:** Seeds, acorns, berries, grain; aquatic and terrestrial insects, other inverts. **CONSERVATION:** Winters s to Cuba and Bahamas. Market-hunted for plumage, food, and eggs; nest habitat lost through development and forestry practices; by early 1900s verged on extinction, but made comeback. Readily use nest boxes. **NOTES:** Older males pair earlier in season than yearlings. Females show extremely strong nest site tenacity. Clutches of 15–50 result from 2–10+ females contributing to individual nests ("dumped"); dumping increases with increased density of nest boxes. Female will repel parasitizing females from her nest. Young remain in nest 24 hours; sharp-clawed, can climb up to 8' out of cavity. If disturbed, young submerge like grebe or dive to reach cover. **ESSAYS:** Site Tenacity, p. 189; Plume Trade, p. 37; Parasitized Ducks, p. 89. **REFS:** Armbruster, 1982; Bellrose, 1976; Drobney and Fredrickson, 1979; Gooders and Boyer, 1986; Semel and Sherman, 1986.

Canvasback

Aythya valisineria Wilson

NG–78; G–54; PE–58; PW–pl 11; AE–pl 110; AW–pl 95; AM (I)–172

F

○
7–9
(7–12)
MONOG

F
I: 24–29 DAYS
PRECOCIAL 2
F: 56–68 DAYS
F

AQUATIC
INVERTS

BREEDING: Open, freshwater marsh, pond, lake, river, bay, bordered by emergent veg. 1 brood. **DISPLAYS:** See: Duck Displays, p. 63. **NEST:** Well-concealed, rimmed, basket-shaped on bulky emergent veg over water up to knee-deep. Lined with finer materials and down. Occ uses muskrat house; rarely on dry ground. **EGGS:** Grayish- or greenish-olive. 2.4" (62 mm). **DIET:** Aquatic veg; aquatic inverts, esp small clams. **CONSERVATION:** Winters s to s Mexico. Blue List 1975–81, Special Concern 1982, 1986. Draining and cultivation of prairie potholes and freshwater marshes have reduced breeding grounds. **NOTES:** Females highly "philopatric" (oft return to natal area to breed); males virtually never do so. Mated pair never rejoin as pair in subsequent years. Male deserts when clutch complete. Nests oft parasitized by Redhead. Females retain fat store during laying but lose nearly 70% during incubation. **ESSAYS:** Blue List, p. 11; Metallic Poisons, p. 137; Parasitized Ducks, p. 89; Dabblers vs. Divers, p. 75; American Coots, p. 105; Commensal Feeding, p. 35; Brood Parasitism, p. 287. **REFS:** Anderson, 1985; Bellrose, 1976; Gooders and Boyer, 1986; Noyes and Jarvis, 1985.

Diving ducks. On the left, a Surf Scoter keeps its wings partially extended to help in propulsion and maneuvering; on the right, a Canvasback propels itself with legs alone.

the bottom. When suspended in midwater, however, these passerines use their wings to swim.

SEE: How Do Birds Fly?, p. 161; Soaring, p. 215; Feet, p. 239; Diving and Flightlessness, p. 203; Dipping, p. 483; Spread-Wing Postures, p. 25.

Dabblers vs. Divers

Nothing is more fundamental to animals than eating. Consequently, it is possible to organize a view of animal communities on the basis of who eats what, where, and when, and who prevents whom from eating. Many ecologists think that closely related species tend to evolve strategies that minimize how much they compete for food. Such "resource partitioning" has been the subject of numerous investigations into the foraging behavior of birds.

Not all species of waterfowl are highly competitive for food during breeding. Some, including geese and eiders that nest in the Far North, have minimal foraging requirements when on their breeding grounds because they build up sufficient stores of fat during the winter or when visiting their staging areas during migration. Other migratory species, however, such as diving and dabbling ducks that breed in the pothole region of the northern prairies, wait until they arrive at their breeding grounds to meet the bulk of their dietary demands and may often compete for food. The shallow potholes (small ponds) they use during breeding formed during alternating periods of glaciation and semiarid conditions. The water in the pools continually fluctuates in depth and salinity, and consequently in the size of the resident communities of plants and animals that can be supported. These pools have provided ideal conditions for studying the behavior of these ducks in detail.

Once assembled on the prairies in the spring, divers and dabblers ap-

Redhead

Aythya americana Eyton

| F | 11 (9–13) MONOG | F I: 24–28 DAYS PRECOCIAL 2 F: 56–73 DAYS F | AQUATIC INVERTS | DABBLES |

BREEDING: Large marsh, prairie slough and pothole, lake, lagoon, and bay with emergent veg. 1 brood. **DISPLAYS:** See: Duck Displays, p. 63. **NESTS:** Usu concealed in emergent veg over shallow water. Heavy basket of rushes or cattails atop matted dead aquatic veg anchored to emergent veg. Lined with finer materials and down. Occ on dry ground. **EGGS:** Pale olive buff. 2.4″ (61 mm). **DIET:** Aquatic veg; aquatic inverts, esp insects, crustaceans, snails. **CONSERVATION:** Winters s to Guatemala, Cuba, Jamaica, and Bahamas. **NOTES:** Females follow one of three nesting strategies: (1) incubate their own clutch, (2) incubate their own clutch and "dump" some eggs in other nests, or (3) entirely parasitic, laying their eggs in other nests and having no nest of their own. Laying in nests of other Redheads is more successful than laying in nests of other species (chief victim is Canvasback, but other ducks readily parasitized, as well). Females use ca. 50% of fat stores (energy reserves) during early period of laying and 30% through incubation. **ESSAYS:** Parasitized Ducks, p. 89; Metallic Poisons, p. 137; Commensal Feeding, p. 35; Dabblers vs. Divers, p. 75; Brood Parasitism, p. 287; American Coots, p. 105. **REFS:** Bellrose, 1976; Gooders and Boyer, 1986; Joyner, 1983; Noyes and Jarvis, 1985.

Ring-necked Duck

Aythya collaris Donovan

| FLOATING | F | 8–10 (6–14) MONOG | F I: 26–27 (25–29) DAYS PRECOCIAL 2 F: 49–56 DAYS F | AQUATIC INVERTS |

BREEDING: Freshwater marsh, slough, bog, wooded lake, swamp, rarely saline habitats. 1 brood. **DISPLAYS:** See: Duck Displays, p. 63. **NEST:** Dry and semidry sites near water, on hummock, or in clumped bushes at water's edge, occ over shallow water. Building does not precede laying, but begins by 3rd–4th egg. Compact, of bent fine grass, moss, other nearby material. Lined abundantly with down. **EGGS:** Olive-gray/olive-brown/buff. 2.3″ (58 mm). Varied, but consistent within clutch. **DIET:** Proportion of animal food is habitat-dependent. As with most waterfowl, proportion of inverts (esp aquatic insects, snails) increases after arrival on breeding grounds. Young eat mostly inverts, esp for first 2–3 weeks. **CONSERVATION:** Winters s to West Indies and Panama. Breeding range expanded e in mid-1900s. Lead shot poisoning not uncommon. **NOTES:** Male remains with mate through most of incubation, occ to hatching. Pair together when female off nest. In n e usu nest in low-productivity wetlands oft avoided by other ducks. Young and adult food habits usu more generalized than those of other members of this genus. **ESSAYS:** Bird Communities, p. 605; Dabblers vs. Divers, p. 75; Metallic Poisons, p. 137; Feathered Nests, p. 605; Color of Eggs, p. 305. **REFS:** Bellrose, 1976; Gooders and Boyer, 1986; Hohman, 1985, 1986.

pear to divide their habitat in a manner analogous to the way in which some warbler species divide trees in which they forage. This partitioning presumably has evolved to protect access to their preferred food items, which for breeding females consist of protein-rich aquatic insects, other invertebrates, and aquatic vegetation. During the period between their arrival and the laying of their eggs, females are essentially feathered eating machines, foraging from 50 to 70 percent of the day.

Diving ducks, or "divers," are ducks that propel themselves underwater with large feet attached to short legs situated far back on the body. "Dabblers," in contrast, have smaller feet and their legs are situated farther forward. While a few dabblers may occasionally dive to feed or to escape predators, typically they skim food from the surface or feed in the shallows by tipping forward to submerge their heads and necks. The table below lists the North American ducks generally included in the groups dabblers and divers. We have also listed a substantial group of species that dive after their food, but often are not meant when one refers to divers. Note that many of the ducks that dive also dabble. Although the Wood Duck (not listed) dabbles and shares with the dabblers the ability to take-off vertically, it is not ordinarily included in the dabblers.

In one study, wildlife biologists analyzed the patterns of foraging in three diving ducks whose ranges converge in the prairie pothole region. Presumably, in the past few thousand years, Redheads moved there from the southwest, Canvasbacks moved in from the east, and the range of Lesser Scaups expanded southward. These species may coexist within a given pool, but each occupies a particular area of water. Canvasbacks have the most specialized diet and usually take food from the bottom in open water near the center of the pool; females prefer immature aquatic insects and snails, often selected from relatively scarce species. Redheads have less specialized bills and presumably a more generalized diet of aquatic invertebrates and

DABBLERS, DIVERS, AND DUCKS THAT DIVE

DABBLERS (Anas)	DIVERS AND STIFF-TAILED DIVERS (Aythya; Oxyura)	DUCKS THAT DIVE (But are not usually referred to as "Divers"; often called "Sea Ducks")
Green-winged Teal		
American Black Duck	Canvasback	
Mottled Duck	Redhead	Eiders (Somateria, Polysticta)
Mallard	Ring-necked Duck	Scoters (Melanitta)
Northern Pintail	Greater Scaup	Harlequin Duck (Histrionicus)
Blue-winged Teal	Lesser Scaup	Oldsquaw (Clangula)
Cinnamon Teal	Ruddy Duck	Goldeneyes (Bucephala)
Northern Shoveler	Masked Duck	Bufflehead (Bucephala)
Gadwall		Mergansers (Mergus,
American Wigeon		Lophodytes)

Greater Scaup

Aythya marila Linnaeus

NG–80; G–54; PE–58; PW–pl 11; AE–pl 124; AW–pl 93; AM (I)–178

FLOATING	F	7–10	F	AQUATIC
		(5–11)	I: 24–28 DAYS	PLANTS
		MONOG	PRECOCIAL 2	
			F: 35–42 DAYS	
			F	

BREEDING: Ponds and small lakes in forested or open tundra and n border of taiga, and islands in large taiga lakes. 1 brood. **DISPLAYS:** See: Duck Displays, p. 63. **NEST:** Usu concealed depression supported by tall, dead marsh grass, usu from 4″ above water in swales to 50′ from water on high, dry hummock. Sparsely lined with fine grass and down, added to during incubation. **EGGS:** Dark olive buff. 2.5″ (62 mm). **DIET:** Primarily mollusks, also other aquatic inverts; aquatic plants may predominate in inland freshwater habitats. **CONSERVATION:** Winters s to Baja. **NOTES:** Occ lays eggs in nests of other Greater Scaups; clutches >11 likely result from such brood parasitism. Nests occ clustered, appearing semicolonial. Male deserts when incubation begins. Females oft combine broods and cooperatively tend and defend. Can dive to 20′ and stay underwater 1 minute. Small to large winter flocks, occ with Lesser Scaup. **ESSAYS:** Dabblers vs. Divers, p. 75; Parasitized Ducks, p. 89; Brood Parasitism, p. 287; Feathered Nests, p. 605; Swimming, p. 73. **REFS:** Bellrose, 1976; Gooders and Boyer, 1986.

Lesser Scaup

Aythya affinis Eyton

NG–80; G–54; PE–58; PW–pl 11; AE–pl 123; AW–pl 92; AM (I)–180

	F	9–12	F	AQUATIC
		(8–14)	I: 21–28 DAYS	PLANTS
		MONOG	PRECOCIAL 2	
			F: 45–50 DAYS	
			F	

BREEDING: Oft upland areas near pond or small lake, marsh, prairie potholes. 1 brood. **DISPLAYS:** See: Duck Displays, p. 63. **NEST:** In fairly open, dry habitat within 150′ of water, nest concealed by veg, rarely over water. Lined with grass, down; uses less down in nest than do other ducks. Built as eggs are laid. **EGGS:** Olive/olive-buff. 2.3″ (57 mm). **DIET:** Aquatic inverts, esp amphipods; aquatic veg. **CONSERVATION:** Winters s throughout C.A. and West Indies to n S.A. **NOTES:** Male deserts when incubation begins, occ remains until middle of incubation. Young led to water; if disturbed, dive and disperse. Young form creches, several broods oft combined and tended by 1–3 females. Nests holding >14 eggs are due to >1 female laying in nest. Clutch size increases with age of female; nest success of females >2 years old is greater than that of 1- and 2-year-old females. Occ feeds at night. Large winter flocks, occ with Greater Scaup. **ESSAYS:** Eye Color, p. 233; Bird Communities and Competition, p. 605; Metallic Poisons, p. 137; Dabblers vs. Divers, p. 75; Creches, p. 191; Parasitized Ducks, p. 89; Variation in Clutch Sizes, p. 339. **REFS:** Afton, 1984; Bellrose, 1976; Gooders and Boyer, 1986.

aquatic vegetation. They usually forage in open areas of shallower water near the edge of the pools and eat the most abundant food items; their diet changes in accordance with the relative abundance of food available. The foraging activity of the Lesser Scaups is dictated by their bills, which are specialized for straining small crustaceans (amphipods) from the water. The scaups usually seek food in the same central area as Canvasbacks, but remain in the open water column above the bottom.

When dabblers first arrive on their breeding grounds they eat seeds and waste grain exposed by snowmelt. As the season progresses and the emergent aquatic vegetation grows, their mainstay of surface-associated invertebrates increases in availability. But surface-feeding dabblers are not restricted to shallow water. Gadwalls, for example, feed as far from shore as Lesser Scaup and Redheads. Gadwalls, however, avoid direct competition with these two divers (and other dabblers) during the breeding season by delaying the onset of nesting.

The segregation of divers and dabblers within a pothole is not determined simply by the distribution of preferred foods, important as that is. It is also influenced by the access to takeoff and landing areas in the pool. Dabblers have large wings relative to body weight and fly slowly, which enables them to drop down onto small areas with precision. Divers, on the other hand, have small wings relative to body weight and fly faster, but must remain in open water with sufficient runway space because they lack the ability to land on a dime and must run along the water surface to become airborne.

Of course, such patterns of habitat division among divers and dabblers is not limited to species breeding in the prairie pothole region. The division of foraging habitats by these waterfowl is relatively consistent in different geographic regions although there is some variation according to the mix of species.

Many questions concerning competition and resource partitioning remain unresolved, but evidence from studies on divers and dabblers seems to support one tenet of ecological theory, that space is easier to divide than food.

SEE: Bird Communities and Competition, p. 605; MacArthur's Warblers, p. 523; Swimming, p. 73; Loon Nurseries and Populations, p. 3; Breeding Season, p. 55. REFS: Hines and Mitchell, 1983; Hohman, 1985; Noyes and Jarvis, 1985; Siegfried, 1976; Swanson et al., 1985; Toft et al., 1982.

Common Eider
Somateria mollissima Linnaeus

NG–82; G–58; PE–56; PW–pl 12; AE–pl 117; AW–pl 109; AM (I)–182

		F		
F	4–5	I: 25–30 DAYS		
	(3–6)	PRECOCIAL 2		DABBLES
	MONOG	F: 65–75 DAYS		SURFACE
		FF		DIPS

BREEDING: Shores of ponds and lagoons with outlet to rocky seacoast. Oft on islands free from mammalian predators, esp Arctic fox. 1 brood. **DISPLAYS:** See: Duck Displays, p. 63. **NEST:** Oft concealed in sheltered spot on open grassy site, under rock shelf or veg, usu within 100' of water; of matted seaweed, moss, grass, sticks, unlined or with down lining. Occ perennial. **EGGS:** Light olive-green/brownish-olive. 3.0" (76 mm). **DIET:** Almost entirely mollusks, echinoderms, crustaceans, a few fish. **CONSERVATION:** Pelagic in winter off n e and n w N.A.; populations increasing and stabilizing since 1930 low. Common and King down commercially valued; collected during incubation: 35–40 nests make 1 lb. Down removal usu does not cause nest desertion. **NOTES:** Nests in colonies, oft near gulls and terns; females may fight over choice nest sites. Pair bond apparently long-term, but male deserts female when well into (or occ prior to) incubation, and migrates to sea. Female takes little or no food throughout incubation! Creches begin to form soon after nest exodus and may last until fledging; composed of 2 or more broods and usu 2 or 3 females. **ESSAYS:** Creches, p. 191; Feathered Nests, p. 605; Plume Trade, p. 37; Monogamy, p. 597. **REFS:** Bellrose, 1976; Cooch, 1965; Gooders and Boyer, 1986; Munro and Bédard, 1977; Schamel, 1977.

King Eider
Somateria spectabilis Linnaeus

NG–82; G–58; PE–56; PW–pl 12; AE–pl 118; AW–pl 106; AM (I)–184

		F		
F	4–5	I: 22–24 DAYS		
	(2–6)	PRECOCIAL 2		DABBLES ?
	MONOG	F: >30<50 DAYS		
		F		

BREEDING: Freshwater arctic ponds and pools, rocky tundra. 1 brood. **DISPLAYS:** See: Duck Displays, p. 63. **NEST:** Usu 10'–50' from water, but occ much farther. Lined with fine materials, breast feathers, and down. **EGGS:** Olive buff. 2.7" (68 mm). **DIET:** Mostly mollusks, few crustaceans, aquatic insects; very small percentage of aquatic veg. **CONSERVATION:** Pelagic in winter off n e and n w N.A. **NOTES:** Second deepest diver among waterfowl (Oldsquaw is number one); may go down 200' (33 fathoms). Does not breed until second (possibly third) year. At start of incubation, male deserts and joins large male flocks on traditional molting areas. Sitting female well camouflaged. Occ brood parasitism: clutches of 8 or more likely due to >1 female laying in nest. Young of several broods form creches attended by 1–9 females. Development of young appears to be very rapid but further study is needed. **ESSAYS:** Color of Birds, p. 111; Creches, p. 191; Feathered Nests, p. 605; Plume Trade, p. 37; Molting, p. 529; Brood Parasitism, p. 287. **REFS:** Bellrose, 1976; Cramp and Simmons, 1977; Gooders and Boyer, 1986.

How Fast and High Do Birds Fly?

Generally birds follow the facetious advice often given to pilots—"fly low and slow." Most cruise speeds are in the 20-to-30-mph range, with an eider duck having the fastest accurately clocked air speed of about 47 mph. During a chase, however, speeds increase; ducks, for example, can fly 60 mph or even faster, and it has been reported that a Peregrine Falcon can stoop at speeds of 200 mph (100 mph may be nearer the norm). Interestingly, there is little relationship between the size of a bird and how fast it flies. Both hummingbirds and geese can reach roughly the same maximum speeds.

There is, of course, a considerable difference between the speed at which a bird *can* fly and the speed at which it normally *does* fly. When the bird is "around home" one might expect it to do one of two things, minimize its energy use per unit time, that is, minimize its metabolic rate, or maximize the distance it travels per unit of energy expended. A vulture loitering in the sky in search of prey might, like the pilot of an observation aircraft, maximize endurance; a seabird traveling to distant foraging grounds might, like a Concorde encountering headwinds on a transoceanic flight, maximize range. Staying up longest does not necessarily mean going farthest. A bird might be able to stay aloft 6 hours at 15 mph (maximum endurance, covering 90 miles) or 5 hours at 20 mph (maximum range, covering 100 miles). Birds can also choose to maximize speed, as when being chased by a predator or racing to defend a territory. Or they can choose some compromise between speed and range.

In order to determine what birds normally do, Gary Schnell and Jenna Hellack of the University of Oklahoma used Doppler radar, a device similar to that used by police to catch speeders, to measure the ground speeds of a dozen species of seabirds (gulls, terns, and a skimmer) near their colony. They also measured wind speeds with an anemometer, and used those measurements to estimate the airspeeds of the birds. (The wind speeds were generally measured closer to the ground than the birds were, which led to some errors of estimation, since friction with the surface slows air movements near the ground.)

Airspeeds were found to be mostly in the 10-to-40-mph range. The power requirements of each bird at each speed could be calculated, and that information was used to establish that the birds were generally compromising between maximizing their range and minimizing their metabolic rates—with more emphasis on the former. Airspeeds varied a great deal, but near the minimum metabolic rate rather large changes in airspeed did not require dramatic rises in energy consumption. For example, a gull whose most efficient loiter airspeed was 22 mph could fly at anything between 15 and 28 mph without increasing its metabolic rate more than 15 percent.

Most birds fly below 500 feet except during migration. There is no reason to expend the energy to go higher—and there may be dangers, such as exposure to higher winds or to the sharp vision of hawks. When migrating, however, birds often do climb to relatively great heights, possibly to

Spectacled Eider

Somateria fischeri Brandt

NG–82; G–58; PW–pl 12; AW–pl 107; AM (I)–186

F	4–6 (1–8) MONOG	F I: 24 DAYS PRECOCIAL 2 F: 50–53 DAYS F	AQUATIC PLANTS	SURFACE DIPS SURFACE DIVES

BREEDING: Sedge and grass margin of tundra ponds, lakes, deltas, and tidal inlets. 1 brood. **DISPLAYS:** See: Duck Displays, p. 63. **NEST:** Usu well concealed in grass tussock close to pond margin, on knoll, or small island. Of sedge, grass, lined with down added as incubation advances, occ lined with moss. **EGGS:** Olive green. 2.7″ (68 mm). **DIET:** Mollusks, aquatic insects; seeds and vegetative parts of aquatic plants, berries. **CONSERVATION:** Pelagic in winter off n w N.A. **NOTES:** Male deserts at start of incubation or shortly thereafter. Female is a very close sitter on nest. Unlike other eiders, broods seldom combine into creches. Range very restricted for an arctic bird. **ESSAYS:** Feathered Nests, p. 605; Plume Trade, p. 37; Monogamy, p. 597; Pelagic Birds, p. 657; Who Incubates?, p. 27; Creches, p. 191. **REFS:** Bellrose, 1976; Cramp and Simmons, 1977; Gooders and Boyer, 1986.

Steller's Eider

Polysticta stelleri Pallas

NG–82; G–58; PW–pl 12; AW–pl 108; AM (I)–188

F	6–8 (5–10) MONOG	F I: ? DAYS PRECOCIAL 2 F: ? DAYS F	AQUATIC PLANTS	SURFACE DIVES

BREEDING: Grassy margin of tundra ponds and lakes, occ barren rocky habitats, but always near coast. 1 brood. **DISPLAYS:** See: Duck Displays, p. 63. **NEST:** Bulky, lined with fine material, breast feathers, and down. Down content increases as incubation advances. **EGGS:** Olive buff, mottled with darker shades, usu nest-stained. 2.4″ (61 mm). **DIET:** Mostly marine inverts, esp crustaceans, mollusks, also aquatic insects; aquatic veg, berries. **CONSERVATION:** Pelagic in winter off s AK, Aleutians. **NOTES:** Probably does not breed until second or third year. Forms large flocks along rocky coasts. Male deserts soon after incubation begins. Broods occ join but large creches are not formed. During molt, selects marine inverts with high caloric content to meet increased energy demands of growing new flight feathers. **ESSAYS:** Feathered Nests, p. 605; Plume Trade, p. 37; Monogamy, p. 597; Pelagic Birds, p. 657; Molting, p. 529; Metabolism, p. 325; Creches, p. 191. **REFS:** Bellrose, 1976; Gooders and Boyer, 1986; Petersen, 1981.

avoid dehydration in the warmer air near the ground. Migrating birds in the Caribbean are mostly observed around 10,000 feet, although some are found half and some twice that high. Generally long-distance migrants seem to start out at about 5,000 feet and then progressively climb to around 20,000 feet. Just like jet aircraft, the optimum cruise altitude of migrants increases as their "fuel" is used up and their weight declines. Vultures sometimes rise over 10,000 feet in order to scan larger areas for food (and to watch the behavior of distant vultures for clues to the location of a feast). Perhaps the most impressive altitude record is that of a flock of Whooper Swans which was seen on radar arriving over Northern Ireland on migration and was visually identified by an airline pilot at 29,000 feet. Birds can fly at altitudes that would be impossible for bats, since bird lungs can extract a larger fraction of oxygen from the air than can mammal lungs.

SEE: Wing Shapes and Flight, p. 227; Soaring, p. 215; Flying in Vee Formation, p. 59; Adaptations for Flight, p. 507; Birds vs. Airplanes, p. 83. REFS: Murphy, 1986; Schnell and Hellack, 1978, 1979.

Birds vs. Airplanes

Birds have always been hazardous to airplanes, and vice versa. The first plane brought down was a Wright biplane that crashed in 1912 on the shoreline near Long Beach, California, after sea gulls became entangled in the wires that braced its wings. Modern aircraft remain susceptible to damage by collision with birds. A duck traveling at 60 mph meeting the windshield of a jet going 500 mph will impact at 560 mph, and would go through an unreinforced windshield like a bomb (fortunately, jet windshields are reinforced). Most serious aviation "bird strikes," however, take place at low altitudes and slower speeds. Michael Grzimek, the son of a well-known zoologist, Bernhard Grzimek, was tragically killed doing research in East Africa when the wing of his light aircraft was struck by a Griffon Vulture. Airliners taking off or landing sometimes have power failures when birds are ingested by their jet engines, and this has caused the most serious accidents so far. In 1960 an Electra propjet taking off from Boston sucked half a dozen starlings from a large flock into its turbines, lost power, and crashed, killing all 62 passengers and crew. Seven people died when the engines of a business jet ingested starlings on takeoff from Atlanta.

All in all, there are thousands of bird-aircraft collisions annually, fortunately no others yet with a death toll approaching that of the Electra disaster (although 139 passengers barely escaped with their lives from a bird-induced DC-10 crash at New York's Kennedy Airport in 1975). At Kennedy, between 1973 and 1981 gulls accounted for about 70 percent of bird strikes, ducks about 9 percent, shorebirds 4 percent, and owls 3 percent. Herring and Great Black-backed Gulls were less, and young gulls more, likely to be

Labrador Duck

Camptorhynchus labradorius Gmelin

(Extinct: not in field guides except PE–55; see fig. p. 85)

  ? ? F?

F? ? I: ? DAYS SEAWEED SURFACE
MONOG? PRECOCIAL 2 DIPS
F: ? DAYS
F

BREEDING: Unknown. Thought to have bred in Labrador. Essentially maritime. 1? brood. **DISPLAYS:** See: Duck Displays, p. 63. **NEST:** Audubon reported nests resembled those of eiders; of large fir twigs, lined with dry grass and much down. **EGGS:** Eggs possibly attributable to this species measure 2.4″ (61 mm). **DIET:** Marine inverts; seaweed. Reported to have foraged like Spoonbill. **CONSERVATION:** Probably pelagic in winter off n e N.A. Never abundant, had very limited breeding range. Extinction probably result of habitat loss and hunting. **NOTES:** Last known specimen shot 1875, on Long Island. Total of American and European collections includes 42 specimens, with 31 in N.A. **ESSAYS:** Labrador Duck, p. 85; Bills, p. 209; Northern Penguin, p. 199; Feathered Nests, p. 605. **REF:** Greenway, 1967.

Black Scoter

Melanitta nigra Linnaeus

NG–84; G–60; PE–54; PW–pl 12; AE–pl 131; AW–pl 110; AM (I)–192

  ⬭ F

F 6–8 I: 30–31 DAYS
(5–11) PRECOCIAL 2
MONOG F: 45–50 DAYS
F

BREEDING: Grassy or shrubby tundra with freshwater lakes and pools. 1 brood. **DISPLAYS:** See: Duck Displays, p. 63. **NEST:** Usu near water margin in grass or within willow stand on small island. Concealed. Well lined with fine materials and feathers. **EGGS:** Light pinkish-buff. 2.4″ (62 mm). **DIET:** Mollusks, crustaceans; few aquatic plants. Also insects and seeds in interior. **CONSERVATION:** Winters along N.A. coasts. **NOTES:** Male deserts shortly after start of incubation. While still small, young brooded at night. Broods occ merge to form creches. Does not breed until third (occ second) year. Can dive to 40′, but usu dives to 20′ or less. Formerly known as Common Scoter. **ESSAYS:** Feathered Nests, p. 605; Swimming, p. 73; Nest Lining, p. 391; Creches, p. 191; Pelagic Birds, p. 657. **REFS:** Bellrose, 1976; Cramp and Simmons, 1977; Gooders and Boyer, 1986.

hit than their proportional abundances would suggest. On the other side of the equation, the new wide-bodied jets had collisions with birds disproportionately more than did narrow bodies.

Many techniques have been tried to keep feathered aircraft away from aluminum ones, from scaring birds with firecrackers, distress calls, and giant eyeballs painted on the fan spinners of jet engines, to closing food-rich dumps near airports or letting grass between runways grow tall enough to obscure predators and thus discourage birds from landing there. Nothing has worked well enough to preclude a possible repetition of the 1960 tragedy, so that finding ways to discourage birds from frequenting airports continues to challenge ornithologists.

SEE: How Fast and High Do Birds Fly?, p. 81; Flying in Vee Formation, p. 59; Adaptations for Flight, p. 507. REFS: Burger, 1985; Smith, 1986.

The Labrador Duck

Ducks are hunted yet species survive, in part because of the support they get from duck hunters interested in maintaining their sport. But one North American duck that was hunted went extinct before duck hunters became organized as conservationists. The fathers of North American ornithology, Alexander Wilson and John James Audubon, knew the now extinct Labrador Duck (*Camptorhynchus labradorius*) as the Pied Duck; it was also known by some early hunters as the Sand-shoal Duck because it frequented sandbars. Wilson's account, written at the start of the last century, described it as "a rather scarce species on our coasts." Audubon commented: "A bird-stuffer whom I knew at Camden had many fine specimens, all of which he had procured by baiting fish-hooks with the common mussel, on a 'trot-line' sunk a few feet below the surface, but on which he never found one alive, on account of the manner in which these Ducks dive and flounder when securely hooked."

Little is known of the biology of this sea duck, whose closest living

White-winged Scoter

Melanitta fusca Linnaeus

NG-84; G-60; PE-54; PW-pl 12; AE-pl 130; AW-pl 112; AM (I)-196

F

9
(5-12)
MONOG

F
I: 28 (25-30) DAYS
PRECOCIAL 2
F: 63-75 DAYS
F

BREEDING: Open tundra or prairie with ponds, lakes, sluggish streams, islands in large lakes, occ mixed tundra-taiga. 1 brood. **DISPLAYS:** See: Duck Displays, p. 63. **NEST:** Concealed, oft under dense shrubbery, nettles, usu 75'-350' from water. Lined with down, added when clutch complete. Nest site oft reused. **EGGS:** Light ocher/pinkish. 2.6" (65 mm). **DIET:** Mollusks, crustaceans, aquatic insects; about 10% aquatic veg. **CONSERVATION:** Winters mostly along N.A. coasts. Declined in parklands and boreal forests of n Alberta, coastal and interior AK, s w Manitoba; possibly due to commencement of hunting season 2-3 weeks before young fly in some areas. **NOTES:** Begin nesting later than all our other ducks. Females show strong nest site tenacity. Brood parasitism: occ lay eggs in nests of other White-winged females and other duck species; clutches >12 result of >1 female laying in nest. Hens usu brood chicks for 12-24 hours after hatching. Form creches of mixed-age broods, some of 150+, attended by 1-3 hens. Dive to 40', strong swimmers. Like other divers, have high wing-loading, must run across water surface to take off. **ESSAYS:** Dabblers vs. Divers, p. 75; Creches, p. 191; Parasitized Ducks, p. 89; Site Tenacity, p. 189. **REFS:** Bellrose, 1976; Brown and Brown, 1981; Brown and Fredrickson, 1987.

Surf Scoter

Melanitta perspicillata Linnaeus

NG-84; G-60; PE-54; PW-pl 12; AE-pl 129; AW-pl 113; AM (I)-194

F

5-8
MONOG

F
I: ? DAYS
PRECOCIAL 2
F: ? DAYS
F

BREEDING: Bogs, ponds or sluggish streams in brushy or forested habitats. 1 brood. **DISPLAYS:** Much courtship occurs in groups. See: Duck Displays, p. 63. **NEST:** Oft in clump of small spruce or dwarf willow, or placed in grass tussock. Reportedly occ far from open water. Lined with feathers and down. **EGGS:** Pinkish- or buffy-white. 2.4" (62 mm). **DIET:** Mostly mollusks, crustaceans, also aquatic insects; very little aquatic veg. Fish eggs occ constitute 90% of diet. **CONSERVATION:** Winters s along coasts to n e Mexico. Apparently declined extensively in early 1900s; numbers now stable. **NOTES:** Breeding biology least known of all N.A. ducks. Frequently "scotes" (scoots) through breaking waves while feeding offshore. **ESSAYS:** Dabblers vs. Divers, p. 75; Skimming, p. 195; How Do We Find Out About Bird Biology?, p. 319; Swimming, p. 73. **REFS:** Bellrose, 1976; Gooders and Boyer, 1986.

relatives seem to be the eiders. It is perplexing that the species became extinct so rapidly because, although it could be found in markets for sale, it was not considered a desirable game bird, and market hunters presumably did not persecute it. As Wilson put it: "Its flesh is dry, and partakes considerably of the nature of its food." Hunting may have helped it on its way out, and so may the decline of mussels and other shellfish as people polluted the East Coast (the Labrador Duck had a unique bill; apparently it was our only mussel-feeding duck). Its breeding grounds were never discovered, but it has been suggested that it nested on a few islands off Labrador, where harvesting of seabird eggs may have caused or contributed to its demise. For whatever reason, this rarity left our fauna precipitously; it was no longer marketed after 1860, and 1875 was the year of the last certain sighting.

SEE: The Northern Penguin, p. 199; The Passenger Pigeon, p. 273; Our Only Native Parrot, p. 279; Conservation of Kirtland's Warbler, p. 527.   REFS: Audubon, 1843; Halliday, 1978; Wilson, 1824; Zusi and Bentz, 1978.

Bird Biologist—George Miksch Sutton

Many distinguished ornithologists since Audubon (p. 413) have combined an artistic talent with a love of birds. George Miksch Sutton (1898–1982) developed a passion for drawing birds when he was a boy in Nebraska. He obtained his doctorate at Cornell, his thesis being a report on the ornithological aspects of his year-long biological survey of Southampton Island in northern Hudson Bay (beautifully described in Sutton's book *Eskimo Year*). He had a lifelong interest in the North and its birds, but he studied bird biology in many areas of our continent, including Mexico. He wrote a dozen books, and some 250 ornithological papers, and produced hundreds of beautiful paintings and drawings of birds to illustrate his works and those of others. An extremely generous man, George Sutton was one of the most beloved ornithologists of this century.

Harlequin Duck

Histrionicus histrionicus Linnaeus

NG–84; G–56; PE–56; PW–pl 12; AE–pl 120; AW–pl 115; AM (I)–190

  ○

F
F   6–8   I: 28–30 DAYS   DABBLES
                 (5–10)   PRECOCIAL 2
                 MONOG   F: 60–70 (?) DAYS
                                  F

BREEDING: Rocky coastal islets, forested mountain streams with fast-flowing water, occ on open tundra. 1 brood. **DISPLAYS:** See: Duck Displays, p. 63. **NEST:** Usu under shrub 60′–90′ from water. Occ in rock crevice among boulders, tree cavity, or puffin burrow. Of dried grass, lined with fine materials and down. **EGGS:** Light buff/cream. 2.3″ (58 mm). **DIET:** Crustaceans, mollusks, aquatic insects, few fish. Walk on bottom of swift streams like Dipper when foraging, searching among rocks. **CONSERVATION:** Winters along N.A. coasts. **NOTES:** Male deserts at start of incubation. Fledging rates are relatively high, oft 50–70%. Do not breed before second year. This is our only "torrent duck", a species dependent on rough, turbulent streams—usu those draining lakes, which tend to be more food-rich than simple run-off drainage. Use wings and feet in dives. **ESSAYS:** Dabblers vs. Divers, p. 75; Dipping, p. 483; Swimming, p. 73; Feathered Nests, p. 605; Nest Lining, p. 391. **REFS:** Bellrose, 1976; Cramp and Simmons, 1977; Gooders and Boyer, 1986.

Oldsquaw

Clangula hyemalis Linnaeus

NG–86; G–60; PE–56; PW–pl 12; AE–pl 116; AW–pl 98; AM (I)–192

F
F   6–7   I: 26 (24–29) DAYS
                 (5–11)   PRECOCIAL 2
                 MONOG   F: 35–40 DAYS
                                  FF

BREEDING: Tundra near shallow freshwater lakes and along coast, also use taiga. 1 brood. **DISPLAYS:** See: Duck Displays, p. 63. **NEST:** Oft within 30′ of water, concealed in veg. Neat, of moss, sedge, grass, lined with leaves, down. Female selects site. **EGGS:** Olive-buff/greenish-yellowish. 2.1″ (53 mm). **DIET:** Aquatic inverts, esp crustaceans, mollusks, insects, also fish; little aquatic veg. **CONSERVATION:** Winters along N.A. coasts and on Great Lakes. **NOTES:** Deepest diving duck, plummets to more than 200′ (33 fathoms), submerging for up to 1.5 min. Oft nest in loose colonies. Usu do not breed in first year. Females show stronger nest site tenacity than males, although some pairs remate in successive years. Brood parasitism: clutches >11 eggs result from females laying in nests of other Oldsquaws. Mainland nests better concealed than island nests. Young form creches usu of 3–4 broods but may reach up to 135 ducklings, usu attended by older females. Young develop extremely rapidly. Female performs distraction display. **ESSAYS:** Dabblers vs. Divers, p. 75; Site Tenacity, p. 189; Distraction Displays, p. 115; Parasitized Ducks, p. 89; Creches, p. 191; Monogamy, p. 597; Swimming, p. 75. **REFS:** Alison, 1975, 1976; Bellrose, 1976; Cramp and Simmons, 1977; Gooders and Boyer, 1986.

Parasitized Ducks

If a bird of one species parasitizes a bird of another by laying an egg in its nest, the act is relatively easily detected by a human observer. The host and parasite eggs and the host and parasite young usually differ—but people's sensory systems are better equipped to discern these differences than are those of birds. A cowbird laying its egg in the nest of a small warbler is pretty obvious, so interspecific brood parasitism has received a great deal of attention from ornithologists.

*Intra*specific brood parasitism, an individual laying eggs in the nest of another of the same species, is not nearly as easily detected by birds or people—parasitic eggs and young are very similar to those of the host. If both the host and parasite female are unbanded, even an observed incident of one female laying in another's nest may go unrecognized as such.

Intraspecific parasitism is common among ostriches and their relatives, game birds, and a few passerines (such as Cliff Swallows). Many cases, however, involve ducks. A female duck that is parasitized by another of the same species may have her own reproductive output reduced in several ways. Both hatching success of her own eggs and survival of her hatchlings may be reduced, and the larger brood may attract more predators. The female may face the numerous risks and stresses of reproduction for relatively little benefit, if a substantial portion of the clutch is not her own.

What can the host female do in the face of parasitic attack? She can desert the clutch and start over, thus not spending her efforts on a mix of her own and "adopted" offspring, but then she wastes the resources tied up in her own eggs. She can identify the parasitic eggs and discard them. Or if she senses from the presence of more eggs in the nest than she laid that she has been parasitized, but cannot discriminate the other female's eggs, she can adjust the number of eggs she lays subsequently so as to maximize survival of her own offspring.

Female Common Goldeneyes are apparently incapable of recognizing the eggs of other females, perhaps because goldeneyes nest in deep, dark cavities. A test was carried out in a Swedish population of goldeneyes in which there was evidence of a regular decline in fledging success with clutch size. Experimenters simulated parasitism by adding one, four, or seven eggs to clutches of goldeneye females in nest boxes. The goldeneyes' reactions were recorded—did they continue to lay, start to incubate, or desert the nest? When one or four eggs were added to the females' clutches, the rate of nest desertion was no higher than it was in "control" nests, which had no added eggs. If seven eggs were added, however, the female never incubated.

When females were "parasitized" with only one additional egg, they laid significantly more eggs than if four "parasitic" eggs were added to their clutches. In addition, if four eggs were added before a female had laid five eggs of her own, she adjusted her final output downward, whereas if the four interloper eggs were added to the nest after the female had laid five to

Barrow's Goldeneye

Bucephala islandica Gmelin

NG–86; G–56; PE–60; PW–pl 11; AE–pl 125; AW–pl 104; AM (I)–198

0'–50'　　　F　　　9–10　　　F
　　　　　　　　　　(6–15)　　I: 32–34 DAYS
　　　　　　　　　　MONOG　　PRECOCIAL 2
　　　　　　　　　　　　　　　F: ca. 56 DAYS
　　　　　　　　　　　　　　　F

BREEDING: Near densely vegetated lakes and ponds with abundant aquatic veg. 1 brood. **DISPLAYS**: See: Duck Displays, p. 63. **NEST**: In live or dead tree; occ in rock crevice. Lined with down as incubation advances, added mostly as clutch nears completion. **EGGS**: Dark green/light olive. 2.4" (61 mm). **DIET**: In fresh water, aquatic insects, crayfish, some aquatic veg. In salt water, mostly mollusks, crustaceans. **CONSERVATION**: Winters within N.A. Will use nest boxes. **NOTES**: Female site tenacity strong—oft returns to same nest. Pair bond lasts over successive years, although male deserts incubating, females. Unpaired males oft return to same breeding area; fidelity to wintering site may be equally strong. Do not breed until second year. Young remain in nest for 24–36 hours. Deserted broods occ join female-tended brood. Yearlings and failed nesters (females) "prospect" for future nest sites while other females are incubating, or shortly after hatching. Rarely (<2% of population) polygynous. Oft swim to lake center rather than fly when alarmed. Dive for up to 50 seconds. **ESSAYS**: Site Tenacity, p. 189; Creches, p. 191; Dabblers vs. Divers, p. 75; Monogamy, p. 597; Polygyny, p. 443; Feathered Nests, p. 605. **REFS**: Bellrose, 1976; Gooders and Boyer, 1986; Savard, 1982, 1985, 1986.

Common Goldeneye

Bucephala clangula Linnaeus

NG–86; G–56; PE–60; PW–pl 11; AE–pl 126; AW–pl 105; AM (I)–196

6'–60'　　　F　　　7–10　　　F
GROUND　　　　　　(5–15)　　I: 28–32 DAYS
　　　　　　　　　　MONOG　　PRECOCIAL 2
　　　　　　　　　　　　　　　F: 56–60 DAYS
　　　　　　　　　　　　　　　F

BREEDING: Ponds, lakes, rivers and coastal bays, wooded marshy habitat. 1 brood. **DISPLAYS**: See: Duck Displays, p. 63. **NEST**: Cavity in tree near water. Lined with chips and down, increasing to thick blanket as incubation advances. **EGGS**: Light-green/olive-green. 2.4" (60 mm). **DIET**: In fresh water, aquatic insects, crayfish, fish; some aquatic veg. In salt water, crustaceans, mollusks. **CONSERVATION**: Winters within N.A. Readily use nest boxes. **NOTES**: Where nests scarce, females parasitize each other, resulting in clutches oft >30 eggs; if parasite's egg(s) added early in laying, nesting female proportionately reduces the number of eggs she lays. Young remain in nest 24–42 hours. Deserted broods occ aggregate in creches. Do not breed until second year. Yearlings and failed nesters (females) "prospect" for future nest sites while other females are incubating, or shortly after hatching. Males winter farther n than females, who winter farther n than juveniles. **ESSAYS**: Parasitized Ducks, p. 89; Dabblers vs. Divers, p. 75; Creches, p. 191; Feathered Nests, p. 605; Migration, p. 183. **REFS**: Andersson and Eriksson, 1982; Bellrose, 1976; Dane and Van der Kloot, 1964; Eadie and Gauthier, 1985; Gooders and Boyer, 1986.

eight eggs of her own, she did not (natural clutch sizes are mostly in the range of eight to twelve).

These experiments clearly showed that goldeneye females can adjust their egg laying to compensate for parasitic eggs added to their clutches. This is not surprising, since goldeneyes are indeterminate layers—they do not, like many songbirds always lay exactly the same number of eggs per clutch.

Why should intraspecific brood parasitism have evolved so commonly in ducks? One suggestion is that many ducks, especially cavity nesters, suffer from a shortage of suitable nest sites. This could drive several females to lay in the same nest, but in the goldeneye population under study, less than a third of the nest boxes were used, so this is certainly not a universal reason. In addition, ducks seem to be better able than smaller birds are to find nests of other females of their own species. Also duck young are precocial, which can lessen the host's burden when caring for the young of parasites. Altricial birds, in contrast, should be under heavy selection to avoid being parasitized by their own kind. Loss of young to starvation is commonly observed in such birds, indicating that a high price would be paid for rearing an "adopted" offspring.

Another factor may be that a female duck often returns to nest near the place of her birth. Thus sisters or mothers and daughters would tend to nest in the same area, and therefore in many cases parasitize each other. This would reduce somewhat the evolutionary costs of being parasitized, since the host often would be rearing young carrying copies of the same genes. That would also reduce selection pressures on the hosts to evolve defenses against being parasitized.

Finally, ducks, unlike many passerines, do not defend the immediate vicinity of their nests during the laying period, easing the access of parasitic females to the nest. This exposes ducks to interspecific parasitization as well, generally by other ducks. The Redhead appears to be our most persistent parasitic duck. In one study on artificial islands in reservoirs in Alberta, Redheads parasitized 19 percent of 685 duck nests, laying an average of 2.68 eggs per parasitized nest. Mallard nests were most frequently parasitized, but the percentage of parasitic eggs per nest was highest when Lesser Scaups were the hosts.

Why don't more passerines exhibit intraspecific parasitism? Have they evolved powerful defenses to prevent parasitism by members of their own species? Studies were done in which the eggs of three colonial passerines—Pinyon Jays, Barn Swallows, and Great-tailed Grackles—were exchanged between nests of the same species. The experiments produced no evidence that members of these species can discriminate their own eggs from those of other individuals. Perhaps the birds have other mechanisms for repelling brood parasites of the same species, such as defense of the nest. Another possibility is that the costs of being a parasite are too high for most birds with altricial young. Nest failures are frequent, and time taken sneaking around trying to parasitize another nest must be subtracted from time that

Bufflehead

Bucephala albeola Linnaeus

NG–86; G–56; PE–60; PW–pl 13; AE–pl 127; AW–pl 103; AM (I)–200

2'–10'	F	8–10	F I: 29–31 (28–33) DAYS	
(To 50')		(6–12)	PRECOCIAL 2	
BANK		MONOG	F: 50–55 DAYS	
			F	

BREEDING: Mixed conifer-deciduous woodland near lake, pond. 1 brood. **DISPLAYS:** See: Duck Displays, p. 63. **NEST:** Usu within 650' of water; in natural or woodpecker-excavated (esp flicker) cavity. Where cavities scarce, will use burrow in earthen bank. Unlined or use remnants of previous nesters; down added. Perennial. **EGGS:** Ivory-yellow/light olive-buff. 1.8" (46 mm). **DIET:** Mostly aquatic insects and seeds of aquatic veg in fresh- and brackish-water habitats; crustaceans, snails, other mollusks and some aquatic veg in saltwater habitats. Fish important in winter. **CONSERVATION:** Winters s to c Mexico. Will use nest boxes where tree cavities scarce. **NOTES:** Long-term pair bond; strong fidelity to breeding and wintering areas. Young remain in nest for 24–36 hours; merging of broods is uncommon. Paired goldeneyes usu dominate territory-defending Bufflehead, but Bufflehead can expel goldeneye yearlings, females, and unpaired males. Yearlings and failed nesters (females) "prospect" for future nest sites while other females are incubating, or shortly after hatching. When feeding in small groups, one sentry usu stays on surface while others dive. **ESSAYS:** Dabblers vs. Divers, p. 75; Sleeping Sentries, p. 61; Interspecific Territoriality, p. 385. **REFS:** Eadie and Gauthier, 1985; Erskine, 1972; Gauthier, 1987; Gooders and Boyer, 1986; Savard, 1982.

Common Merganser

Mergus merganser Linnaeus

NG–88; G–62; PE–62; PW–pl 13; AE–pl 114; AW–pl 101; AM (I)–204

15'–50'	CREVICE	8–11	F I: 28–35 DAYS	AQUATIC
GROUND	F	(6–13)	PRECOCIAL 2	INVERTS
		MONOG	F: 65–85 DAYS	
			F	

BREEDING: Lakes and rivers in mountainous and forested areas, oft inland. 1 brood. **DISPLAYS:** See: Duck Displays, p. 63. **NEST:** Usu cavity in decid tree; also in earthen bank or rock crevice, beneath boulders, under shrubs, in root hollows, occ in abandoned nests. Usu large, bulky bed of dead weeds, fibrous root, leaves, moss, feathers. Lined with feathers and down. Occ perennial. Female selects site. **EGGS:** Light buff/ivory-yellow. 2.6" (64 mm). **DIET:** Usu fish. In spring, when prey scarce, take frozen, rotted fish, other lower verts, inverts. **CONSERVATION:** Winters s to n Mexico. **NOTES:** Females exhibit strong nest site tenacity. Where suitable nest sites are limited, egg dumping occurs resulting in clutches occ >13 eggs. Does not breed before second year. Male departs at onset of incubation. Young remain in nest 24–48 hours. Deserted broods join female-tended brood. Long takeoff run because of high wing-loading, but strong flier. Known in Europe as Goosander. **ESSAYS:** Dabblers vs. Divers, p. 75; Creches, p. 191; Wing Shapes and Flight, p. 227; Site Tenacity, p. 189; Feathered Nests, p. 605; Who Incubates?, p. 27. **REFS:** Bellrose, 1976; Cramp and Simmons, 1977; Gooders and Boyer, 1986.

could be used in building nests, laying eggs in the home nest, feeding, and other activities that affect the success of the bird's own nesting attempt. In short, the costs of being a parasite may often outweigh the benefits in altricial birds, which may explain why intraspecific parasitism does not seem to be widespread in passerines.

SEE: Brood Parasitism, p. 287; Parasitic Swallows, p. 401; Altruism, p. 453; Precocial and Altricial Young, p. 581; Site Tenacity, p. 189.   REFS: Andersson and Eriksson, 1982; Giroux, 1981; Lanier, 1982; Yom-Tov, 1980.

Hesperornis and Other Missing Links

In the interim between *Archaeopteryx* and living birds there are relatively few fossil "missing links" that cast more light on the origins of birds. The most informative (and oldest) are from the late Cretaceous period, some 70 million years ago. They are mostly fossils of two marine birds, the gull- or tern-like *Ichthyornis*, which had a deep sternum indicating powerful flight muscles, and the cormorantlike *Hesperornis*. The latter retained *Archaeopteryx*-style teeth, presumably used (like the serrations in a merganser's bill) for gripping fishes; it is not clear whether *Ichthyornis* had teeth or not.

Over the past 50 million years birds have left many fossils. They are most interesting for showing us kinds of bird that have gone extinct—such as *Diatryma*, a six-foot-tall North American flightless predator with an impressive hooked bill. Evident in the fossil record from North America are some groups of birds now entirely lost from the continent. At one time, for example, we had pratincoles (relatives of plovers) and accipitrid vultures, both groups now restricted to the Eastern Hemisphere.

SEE: Feathered Dinosaurs, p. 31; Natural Selection, p. 237; Bills, p. 209.   REF: Martin, 1983.

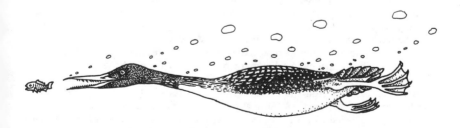

Like a primitive cormorant, an extinct Hesperornis *pursues a fish through the ocean some 70 million years ago. It had teeth like* Archaeopteryx, *which were presumably used as the serrations in the bill of a merganser are today, for gripping slippery prey.*

Red-breasted Merganser
Mergus serrator Linnaeus

NG–88; G–62; PE–62; PW–pl 13; AE–pl 113; AW–pl 100; AM (I)–204

			F		
 F	8–10 (5–11) MONOG?		I: 30 (29–35) DAYS PRECOCIAL 2 F: 59 (<65) DAYS F	CRUSTACEANS	

BREEDING: Rivers, ponds, lakes, coasts, usu on small islands of inland waters with low shrubby veg. 1 brood. **DISPLAYS:** See: Duck Displays, p. 63. **NEST:** Usu sheltered under low veg, among tree roots, piles of driftwood, or logs, usu within 25' of water. Well lined with veg, feathers and down. **EGGS:** Olive-buff. 2.5" (65 mm). **DIET:** Mostly fish, also crustaceans, aquatic insects. **CONSERVATION:** Winters s to s Baja. **NOTES:** Individuals known to fish in cooperative manner to drive fish into shallow water. Nests oft close together, appearing colonial; gregarious throughout summer. Do not breed before second year. Male departs after incubation begins. Broods frequently combine and are attended by one to several females. Male rarely seen near nest. High wing-loading requires long takeoff run. **ESSAYS:** Wing Shapes and Flight, p. 227; Creches, p. 191; Commensal Feeding, p. 35; Dabblers vs. Divers, p. 75; Feathered Nests, p. 605; Who Incubates?, p. 27. **REFS:** Bellrose, 1976; Cramp and Simmons, 1977; Gooders and Boyer, 1986.

Hooded Merganser
Lophodytes cucullatus Linnaeus

NG–88; G–62; PE–62; PW–pl 13; AE–pl 128; AW–pl 102; AM (I)–202

			F		
15'–20'	F	10–12 (7–13) MONOG	I: 32–33 (28–41) DAYS PRECOCIAL 2 F: 71 DAYS F	AQUATIC INVERTS	

BREEDING: Forested habitats near water, lakes, swamps, marshes, estuaries. 1 brood. **DISPLAYS:** See: Duck Displays, p. 63. **NEST:** Tree cavity near water, rarely in hollow log. Lined with grass, leaves, down. Perennial. **EGGS:** White, oft nest-stained. 2.1" (54 mm). **DIET:** Mostly fish, but also many crustaceans, insects, some lower verts and mollusks. **CONSERVATION:** Winters s to coastal n Mexico. Will use nest boxes and cavities used by Wood Ducks. **NOTES:** Females lay in each other's nests resulting in dump nests with up to 36 eggs. Male deserts female early in incubation. Known to share incubation with Wood Duck or goldeneye females. In early summer, immature birds reportedly inspect nest sites for future nesting. Broods do not combine as they do in other mergansers. Female performs distraction display. Very fast flier. In winter, arrive singly or in flocks up to 16, but usu in pairs to form single species roost (on water) in groups of 100–200; actively display until dark. **ESSAYS:** Distraction Displays, p. 115; Communal Roosting, p. 615; Dabblers vs. Divers, p. 75; Parasitized Ducks, p. 89; How Fast and High Do Birds Fly?, p. 81; Who Incubates?, p. 27. **REFS:** Barbour, 1982; Bellrose, 1976; Gooders and Boyer, 1986; McGilvrey, 1966.

Bird Biologist—Alexander Wetmore

Spencer Fullerton Baird (p. 569) was the first secretary of the Smithsonian Institution, and the first ornithologist to hold that position. Alexander Wetmore (1886–1978) was the sixth secretary of the Institution, and the second ornithologist so honored. Wetmore published very widely on bird migration, taxonomy, biogeography and paleontology (155 papers on fossil birds alone), and promoted the study of bird biology through involvement in the affairs of many scientific organizations. He was especially helpful to Arthur Bent (p. 637), supporting Bent's work on the life histories of North American birds. Wetmore replaced Robert Ridgeway (p. 119) as the leading ornithologist on our continent.

SEE: Taxonomy and Nomenclature, p. 515.

Bird Banding and Marking

On occasion you may see birds with metal or plastic bands on their legs. Each year more than half a million birds in North America are marked with small metal bands that are placed around the lower portion of one leg. These birds are banded by licensed "cooperators" of the U.S. Fish and Wildlife Service (FWS), and every band carries a unique serial number and the abbreviated name and address of the FWS Bird Banding Laboratory (BBL) in Laurel, Maryland. When birds are shot by hunters, found dead, or recaptured by banders, the serial number is transmitted to the BBL. Through such banding and recovery efforts, ornithologists have greatly increased their understanding of migration routes, the timing of migration, wintering areas used by our birds, the age structure of populations, individual longevity, and site fidelity to breeding and wintering areas.

Although the first banding organization was established in 1909, the U.S. and Canadian governments did not create formal centers for the collection and maintenance of banding records until the early 1920s. Since that time, more than 40 million birds have been banded in North America. Much of the initial impetus for government involvement in bird banding derived from a need to understand and monitor the migration patterns and population dynamics of migratory game birds in order to adjust seasonal hunting limits for each species. In spite of the massive numbers of birds banded annually, less than 5 percent are recaptured or recovered. Waterfowl, gallinaceous birds, and doves yield a higher return percentage through the cooperation of licensed hunters.

Limpkin

Aramus guarauna Linnaeus

NG–96; G–102; PE–108; AE–pl 23; AM (I)–310

			MF I: ? DAYS	SNAILS	
SHRUB	MF	4–8	PRECOCIAL 4	AQ INVERTS	STALK
TREE		(3–8)	F: ? DAYS	LIZARDS	& STRIKE
0'–45'		?	?	INSECTS	

BREEDING: Swampy forests, mangroves, marshes. 2, possibly 3 broods. **DIS-PLAYS:** ?   **NEST:** On banks, beneath shrubs, or in shallows in clumped veg. Large hollowed reed and grass mat interwoven with live veg, or attached to stump or shrub. Lined with fine materials. Occ in tree.   **EGGS:** Olive buff/cream buff, marked with brown. 2.3" (59 mm).   **DIET:** Aquatic inverts incl esp snails and mussels; lower verts, esp frogs and lizards; also worms and aquatic insects.   **CONSERVATION:** Winter resident.   **NOTES:** Occ nests in loose colonies. Breeding biology relatively unknown. Bill asymmetric, tip curved to right (esp lower mandible), making it well adapted for extracting snails from shells. A slight space oft occurs behind tips of mandibles and may serve to grasp snail shells when foraging tactilely and then carrying them to shore for opening.   **ESSAYS:** Bills, p. 209; Thin as a Rail, p. 99; How Do We Find Out About Bird Biology?, p. 319; Coloniality, p. 173.   **REF:** Snyder and Snyder, 1969.

King Rail

Supersp #10
Rallus elegans Audubon

NG–96; G–106; PE–112; AE–pl 254; AM (I)–302

		MF I: 21–24 DAYS		
M–F	10–12	PRECOCIAL 4	INSECTS	GROUND
	(6–15)	F: 63+ DAYS	FISH	GLEAN
	MONOG	MF		

BREEDING: Freshwater swamps and marshes, ricefields, also coastal brackish marshes. 2? broods.   **DISPLAYS:** Courtship by male mostly involves walking with tail raised to expose white undertail feathers. After pairing, when female approaches, male assumes head downward, tail-raised position and swings bill from side to side.   **NEST:** On hummock, usu 6"–8" above water, amid aquatic veg. Concealed under canopy. Well-made basket of dry aquatic veg, deeply hollowed. Occ in grass with dry grass arching over it.   **EGGS:** Buff, spotted with browns. 1.6" (41 mm).   **DIET:** Aquatic inverts incl esp crustaceans; also frogs; some seeds, grain (esp in winter). Eject pellets.   **CONSERVATION:** Winters s to c Mexico, Cuba. Blue List 1976–82, Special Concern 1986; declined from habitat loss and pesticides; numbers now appear low but stable.   **NOTES:** Oft return to nest in same area in successive years. Defend territory against other rail species. Adults perform distraction display. Young remain with adults >1 month. Overlaps breeding range with Clapper Rail where fresh and brackish water meet (tidal rivers and creeks along Gulf and Atlantic); mixed pairs and hybrids occur.   **ESSAYS:** Thin as a Rail, p. 99; Blue List, p. 11; Hybridization, p. 501; Site Tenacity, p. 189; Pellets, p. 297; Interspecific Territoriality, p. 385; Distraction Displays, p. 115.   **REFS:** Meanley, 1969; Ripley, 1977.

Capture of birds for banding is accomplished through a variety of techniques, depending on the species. Nylon mesh nets, resembling very fine badminton nets and known as "mist nets," are used to capture a wide variety of species ranging in size from hummingbirds to jays, depending on the mesh diameter of the net. (Mist nets were originally developed by the Japanese, who used them to capture birds for food; their original name in Japanese translated to "suicide nets," because any bird entangled in the net wound up in the cooking pot.) Small single- and multi-celled wire traps can be used to capture small ground-feeding species. Waterfowl are often captured by baiting them to an area and then shooting large nets (cannon nets) over the entire flock or by herding them into "corrals" during the annual molt period when they are flightless. State or provincial as well as federal permits are necessary for banding all species, and special authorization from the banding agencies is required to capture and band waterfowl, eagles, and endangered species.

In addition to standard metal FWS leg bands, a variety of other types of markers are employed when studies require the identification of individual birds in the field. Colored plastic leg bands generally used in combination (e.g., red over black on right leg, FWS band on left leg), numbered (or lettered) colored wing streamers, plastic or aluminum neck collars (on geese, swans, and Sandhill Cranes), plastic saddles across the upper bill of ducks, and tiny radio transmitters attached to the backs of larger birds (e.g., birds of prey) or surgically implanted in the abdominal cavity of smaller birds have all been employed by researchers engaged in projects ranging from the study of individual behavior to attempts to discover the wintering areas and migration routes of individual breeding populations. Colored dyes applied directly to the feathers are sometimes used for short-term individual recognition, lasting until the bird molts. Care must be exercised in altering plumage characteristics so as not to disrupt the effectiveness of displays that employ such features. For example, experimenters studying the displays of Red-winged Blackbirds found that applying black dye to the red epaulettes affected the ability of males to attract mates and to maintain territories against unaltered males. Less dramatic effects on behavior, nesting success, and survival have been noted occasionally for selected species, but most studies indicate little if any adverse effects of markers. All such "auxiliary" markers must be approved and coordinated through the BBL. This prevents duplication of markers in different studies of the same species, since such duplication could result in ambiguous sightings.

Success of banding and marking efforts depend a great deal on birders. If you find a dead or injured bird wearing an FWS band, record the serial number as well as the other information that a bander would record: species, sex, age (if it can be determined from plumage or skull characteristics), condition of the bird, and precise geographic location. If the bird is dead,

Clapper Rail

NG–96; G–106; PE–112; PW–pl 24; AE–pl 253; AW–pl 243; AM (I)–300

| M–F | 7–11 (5–12) MONOG | | MF
I: 20–23 DAYS
PRECOCIAL 4
F: 63–70 DAYS
MF (?) | INSECTS
FISH | GROUND
GLEAN |

BREEDING: Salt and brackish marshes, mangrove swamps, freshwater marshes in s w. 2? broods (esp in s). **DISPLAYS:** Male walks with uplifted tail, approaches female, points bill to ground and swings it from side to side; male also postures with neck stretched upward, bill open, and approaches female. Courtship feeding. **NEST:** Elevated on firm bank occ under small bush. Concealed, occ domed, basket of aquatic veg and tide-deposited materials. Ramps oft evident in adjacent veg. Occ extra nests. **EGGS:** Buff/olive-buff, marked with brown. 1.7" (42 mm). **DIET:** Crustaceans (esp crabs), also snails, worms, frogs; seeds. Eject pellets. **CONSERVATION:** Winters within N.A. Special Concern 1986; mangrove-dwelling FL subspecies declining. CA and AZ subspecies Endangered. Habitat loss and pesticides threaten these, s, and s e populations. **NOTES:** Hybridizes with King Rail where ranges overlap. Incubation begins midway through laying, thus hatching asynchronous. Constructs brood nests; parental care lasts 5–6 weeks. Nest dome both protects from aerial predators and keeps eggs contained during tidal flooding. **ESSAYS:** Thin as a Rail, p. 99; Blue List, p. 11; Birds and the Law, p. 293; Transporting Young, p. 103; Courtship Feeding, p. 181; Hybridization, p. 501; Pellets, p. 297. **REFS:** Massey et al., 1984; Meanley, 1985.

Virginia Rail

Rallus limicola Vieillot

NG–98; G–104; PE–112; PW–pl 24; AE–pl 252; AW–pl 242; AM (I)–302

| MF | 7–12 (5–13) MONOG | | MF
I: 18–20 DAYS
PRECOCIAL 4
F: 25 DAYS
MF | AQUATIC
INVERTS
SEEDS | GRND GLEAN
STALK
& STRIKE |

BREEDING: Freshwater, occ brackish, marshes, usu in cattails, reeds, dense grass. 2? broods. **DISPLAYS:** With wings open and raised above body, male runs before female, twitching his tail quickly. At each pass, pauses and rises to full height, bows, and female bows in response. Courtship feeding and mutual preening. **NEST:** In tussock or clumped veg, pile of matted reeds; layers of coarse aquatic veg and grass, occ only reeds. Usu in drier area, occ over water or mud. Concealed oft with sedge or reed canopy. Occ lined with fine materials. **EGGS:** Off-white/buff, spotted with brown, occ gray, oft wreathed. 1.3" (32 mm). **DIET:** Incl snails, earthworms, occ fish. **CONSERVATION:** Winters s to c Guatemala. **NOTES:** Young hatch asynchronously, can swim on first day. Chicks fed largely by parents until 2–3 weeks old. Uses brood nests. Adults perform distraction display. Broods raised to independence as a family group in breeding territory; adults then shift home range out of brood-rearing territory. **ESSAYS:** Thin as a Rail, p. 99; Transporting Young, p. 103; Precocial and Altricial Young, p. 581; Courtship Feeding, p. 181; Nest Lining, p. 391. **REFS:** Horak, 1970; Johnson and Dinsmore, 1985; Kaufmann, 1987; Reynard, 1974.

remove the band and send it along with the pertinent information to:

U.S. Fish & Wildlife Service
Bird Banding Laboratory,
Laurel, Maryland 20708

If you spot a bird with any auxiliary markers, note the same kinds of information, including habitat and the specific numbers, colors, and position of the additional markers. This information too should be sent to the BBL, which in turn will forward it to the researcher who originally marked the bird. In both cases, you will receive information concerning the original locality and date where the bird was banded, and if auxiliary markers were present, sometimes a short summary of the research project employing the markers will be provided.

SEE: Migration, p. 183; Birds and the Law, p. 293; How Long Can Birds Live?, p. 643. REF: Marion and Shamis, 1977.

Thin as a Rail

Why, since rails are widely distributed, are many of them absent from life lists of most birders? It is not because rails have especially sparse populations; six of the nine species breeding in North America are so abundant that hunting them is legal; only King, Yellow, and Black Rails are protected in the United States. Rather, many members of this family are so secretive that they move about unnoticed; when necessary, rails can melt into the marsh vegetation without causing much of a ripple. In situations where other marsh birds take flight and depart emitting harsh calls, rails often move silently. As Audubon wrote of the Clapper Rail in his *Birds of America* (1842):

> On the least appearance of danger, they lower the head, stretch out the neck, and move off with incomparable speed, always in perfect silence . . . they have a power of compressing their body to such a degree as frequently to force a passage between two stems so close that one could hardly believe it possible for them to squeeze themselves through.

Unlike highly visible, skittering shorebirds that run and pause in pursuit of the tide line, deliberate stepping, cryptically colored rails are usually

Sora

Porzana carolina Linnaeus

NG–98; G–104; PE–114; PW–pl 24; AE–pl 249; AW–pl 245; AM (I)–304

			MF I: 18–20 DAYS		
GROUND	MF	10–12 (6–13) MONOG	PRECOCIAL 4 F: 21–25 DAYS MF	INSECTS AQUATIC INVERTS	PROBES

BREEDING: Usu freshwater marshes, occ flooded fields. 2? broods. **DISPLAYS**: Pair perform ritualized mutual preening, occ bowing and facing away. **NEST**: Built up to 6″ above water. Occ in meadows. Concealed under arching veg. Well-made basket of dead aquatic veg supported by surrounding stems. Lined with finer materials. Path oft evident. Tends to nest over deeper water than does Virginia Rail. Built in 3–4 days. **EGGS**: Brown and buff, marked with brown. 1.2″ (32 mm). Occ placed in layers. **DIET**: Mostly seeds; also snails, other inverts. **CONSERVATION**: Winters s through C.A. and West Indies to c S.A. **NOTES**: Hatching asynchronous. Young readily drop into water and dive; fed largely by adults for up to 3 weeks. Flooding of nest sites common hazard. Broods raised to independence as a family group in breeding territory; adults then shift home range out of brood-rearing territory. Adult iris color changes from reddish-brown to black in breeding season. **ESSAYS**: Thin as a Rail, p. 99; Bathing and Dusting, p. 429; Precocial and Altricial Young, p. 581; Eye Color, p. 233; Nest Lining, p. 391. **REFS**: Horak, 1970; Johnson and Dinsmore, 1985; Kaufmann, 1987; Rundle and Sayre, 1983.

Yellow Rail

Coturnicops noveboracensis Gmelin

NG–98; G–104; PE–114; PW–pl 24; AE–pl 251; AW–pl 244; AM (I)–298

		F I: 16–18 DAYS		
MF	8–9 (3–10) MONOG	PRECOCIAL 4 F: 35 DAYS F?	INSECTS FISH	GROUND GLEAN

BREEDING: Marshes, wet meadows, and other freshwater habitats. ? brood. **DISPLAYS**: Nuptial song of clicking or "kicker" notes; usu heard at night. In captivity, male preens, male and female make up to 6 scrapes before selecting one. **NEST**: Above damp soil on bare ground or flattened veg. Canopy of veg pulled to cover mat of fine dead grass a few inches deep, coiled or shaped by body. Occ suspended over water. Materials occ carried from great distance. Lined with fine materials. Entrance via small hole in canopy. Female continues to add material during incubation. **EGGS**: Creamy buff, occ spotted with reddish-brown, capped. 1.1″ (28 mm). **DIET**: Incl freshwater snails, other small inverts. **CONSERVATION**: Winters within U.S. **NOTES**: Male territories apparently overlap greatly. Freeze rather than run when confronted, relying on camouflage. Secretive but rather indifferent to humans. **ESSAYS**: Thin as a Rail, p. 99; Bathing and Dusting, p. 429; Precocial and Altricial Young, p. 581; Nest Lining, p. 391. **REFS**: Bookhout and Stenzel, 1987; Elliot and Morrison, 1979; McKee, 1987; Reynard, 1974.

hard to spot against their noncontrasting backgrounds. Indeed, rails may consider themselves invisible, for even on the rare occasion when they are in the open, they often act as though they cannot be seen. Such apparent indifference to discovery is sometimes mistaken for boldness, but more likely indicates that they do not recognize a human being 20 yards away as a potential threat. Even their fibrous, domed nests fade into the grass. Their generally elusive behavior causes difficulty for conservationists trying to census rail populations to learn enough about their ecology to implement effective management practices.

For seventy years mystery surrounded the calls of the rails and, for a while, their voices were misdescribed and misattributed. Since rails are rarely heard and more rarely seen, it remained difficult to positively identify the producer of a call until the use of tape recordings to attract the bird became practical. Many rails limit calling to the breeding season, often awaiting the break of day or onset of darkness. Besides the infrequent acoustic advertisements, telltale evidence of rails consists of little more than their tracks, pelleted remains of meals, and inch-sized white splatters of droppings.

Rail disappearing acts also work in water. They can readily submerge their normally buoyant bodies, dive when pressed, and speed their paddling by using wings underwater. So effectively do they maintain a low profile that their main nonhuman predators are pike, black bass, and other predatory fish which feed on their young.

Not only do rails usually elude their predators, they seem to delude their prey. During a tail-jerk display a rail's tail is cocked upward and its head (which usually bobs as it steps) is frozen still. This posture is thought by some to permit a steady view of the foraging area while misleading small prey to mistake its tail for its head.

Many birders hope to spot rails at dawn or dusk low tides when the birds reputedly come forth to bathe and preen at the water's edge or to forage on temporarily exposed mud-dwelling prey. Other enthusiasts venture to marshlands when very high tides compress the amount of space and covering vegetation available to both rails and stalk-climbing snails that rails eat. Along the Atlantic coast, hunters of Clapper Rails (Marsh Hens) usually await the first full-moon tide of September. When this tide is pumped by a north wind, which forces the water level exceptionally high and pushes the birds to even higher ground, it is known as Marsh Hen Tide.

Rails are subject to periodic calamities; floods destroy nests and young, and during their nighttime migrations, heavy fog can take them off-course, even into cities. In 1977 a storm brought an early freeze and reduced by two-thirds the breeding success of Clapper Rails in New Jersey. In 1940 one hurricane left an estimated 15,000 of these rails dead in South Carolina, and in 1976 another storm killed some 20,000 in New Jersey.

Ironically, the remarkable ability of rails to reestablish after natural disasters could lead to their demise, for their ability to respond to nature's

Black Rail

Laterallus jamaicensis Gmelin

NG–98; G–104; PE–114; PW–pl 24; AE– 400; AW–pl 247; AM (I)–300

| MF | 6–10
(6–13)
MONOG | MF
I: 16–20 (?) DAYS
PRECOCIAL 4
F: ? DAYS
? | SEEDS
AQUATIC
INVERTS | GROUND
GLEAN |

BREEDING: Fresh, brackish and salt marshes, occ in wet savanna, rarely in dry grassland. 2? broods. **DISPLAYS:** Male and female have distinctively different songs; sing only at night (oft for many hours) just prior to and at start of breeding season. **NEST:** In 18″–24″ grass in open habitat. Deep cup concealed by veg. Fine woven coil of soft grass blades, sedge, or other available veg. Canopy also serves to exclude sun. Path evident through adjacent area. **EGGS:** White/pinkish-white/creamy-white, dotted with brown. 1.0″ (26 mm). **DIET:** Mostly insects, also crustaceans; seeds of aquatic veg. **CONSERVATION:** Winters within U.S. Populations in w declining due to habitat destruction. **NOTES:** Secretive. Like other rails, most easily seen when high tides force birds into highest portions of marshes. Highly scattered disjunct populations; poorly known. **ESSAYS:** Thin as a Rail, p. 99; Transporting Young, p. 103; Bathing and Dusting, p. 429; Precocial and Altricial Young, p. 581; Hormones and Nest Building, p. 547; How Do We Find Out About Bird Biology?, p. 319. **REFS:** Burtt, 1987; Repking and Ohmart, 1977; Reynard, 1974; Ripley, 1977.

Purple Gallinule

Porphyrula martinica Linnaeus

NG–100; G–106; PE–64; AE–pl 248; AM(I)–304

| MF | 6–8
(5–10)
COOP | MF
I: 22–25 DAYS
PRECOCIAL 4
F: ca. 63 DAYS
MF + |

BREEDING: Marshes, esp with dense emergent veg. 2? broods. **DISPLAYS:** ? **NEST:** Usu over deep water (4′–10′), often on floating island of high, dense aquatic veg. Partly concealed by arched canopy. Hollowed platform of green and dry stems and leaves interwoven with anchoring plants. Soggy and wet below, dry above, with inclined ramp leading down to water. Usu build extra nests. **EGGS:** Cinnamon-pink/buff, marked with brown. 1.5″ (39 mm). **DIET:** Mostly seeds, fruit, grain, and plants; also snails, aquatic insects, inverts, frogs, occ eggs and young of marsh birds. In autumn, mostly rice. **CONSERVATION:** Winters s to West Indies, n Argentina. **NOTES:** Live in family groups of up to 14 (avg 4–5); nonbreeders help feed young and defend young and territory. Young hatch asynchronously. Adults and young move to second nest to brood, usu within 30′ of original site. Breeding biology not well known in N.A. Walk on floating veg. **ESSAYS:** Cooperative Breeding, p. 283; Thin as a Rail, p. 99; Precocial and Altricial Young, p. 581; Transporting Young, p. 103; Feet, p. 239. **REFS:** Hunter, 1985, 1987; Krekorian, 1978; Ripley, 1977.

inconstancy may promote false confidence in marshland managers who assume rails will recover from human interference with equal success. Pollution in salt-marsh habitats cannot necessarily be counterbalanced by the apparent physical hardiness of rails. In Georgia, for example, 95 percent of rails tested in one area near an industrial plant had unacceptably high concentrations of mercury in their muscles—levels high enough to make eating them ill-advised. It would not be surprising if searching for these furtive creatures proves ever more frustrating. The disappearance of a rail seen ambling amid the marsh grasses may be illusory, but the disappearance of high-quality rail habitat is not.

SEE: American Coots, p. 105; Saving a Subspecies, p. 571; Metallic Poisons, p. 137. REFS: Audubon, 1842; Bollinger and Bowes, 1973; Menley, 1985; Reynard and Harty, 1968; Ripley, 1977.

Transporting Young

Much like the stories of babies being delivered from the sky to the bassinet by a stork, the accounts of young birds being carried from elevated tree nests to the ground in the bill of their mother appear to be fairy tales—or, at best, descriptions of very atypical behavior. Reports of chicks jumping to the ground rather than being carried from the nest by a parent are far more common.

Aerial carrying has been reported in 16 species of seven waterfowl groups as well as Virginia and Clapper Rails, gallinules, willets, woodcocks, chachalacas, and a cuckoo. Nevertheless, ornithologists remain uncertain of both the conditions leading to it and how it is accomplished. Making observations is difficult, given that aerial transport occurs either discreetly under the cover of dim light or in panic situations when a parent is confronted by a predator. Thus, most information remains anecdotal. It is not clear, for example, whether a parent holds its chick in its bill, carries it on its back, or clutches it between its legs. In addition to aerial carrying there are also a few reports of birds using their wings to clap chicks to their sides and proceeding on foot.

Much more is known about birds that carry their young while swimming. Worldwide, three species of swan, at least seven species of duck, and various other birds of the wetlands have been frequently observed chauffeuring their young as the accompanying American Coot illustration shows. In all cases, the young initiate the ride and are readily able to hang on by clamping their bills over the feathers of the adult should it decide to dive. Ferrying by adults over water is apparently most advantageous in species that fly infrequently, that have large bodies and small broods, and whose young grow slowly.

Careful observations are needed to document how frequently and

Common Moorhen

Gallinula chloropus Linnaeus

NG–100; G–106; PE–64; PW–pl 24; AE–pl 247; AW–pl 246; AM(I)–306

| GROUND | CUP | 5–8 | MF
I: 19–22 DAYS
PRECOCIAL 4 | SNAILS | GRND GLEAN |
| SHRUB | MF | (2–13)
COOP | F: 40–50+ DAYS
MF+ | INSECTS
SEEDS | FOLIAGE
GLEAN |

BREEDING: Freshwater marshes, lakes, and ponds, usu with emergent veg and grassy edges. Occ 2, rarely 3, broods. **DISPLAYS:** With head low, wings partly raised and open, elevates tail exposing white undertail feathers. Male bends head down and in toward feet; male and female bow. **NEST:** Usu over water (with ramps leading down to water), occ on ground or in low shrub. Occ with canopy. Well-rimmed cup of conspicuous bleached aquatic plants, lined with grass. Unused nests, brooding and roosting platforms nearby. Occ use old nest of jays, magpies. **EGGS:** Cinnamon/buff, marked with reddish-brown or olive. 1.7″ (44 mm). **DIET:** Mostly aquatic veg; also mollusks (esp snails), worms; berries; fruit. **CONSERVATION:** Winters s to c S.A. **NOTES:** Cooperative breeder with young of first brood oft aiding in care of subsequent broods and in defense of territory. Brood parasitism: clutches >13 likely result from >1 female laying in nest. Younger birds lay smaller clutches than older birds and lay later. Young usu hatch asynchronously. Wing spur aids young in climbing. **ESSAYS:** Cooperative Breeding, p. 283; Thin as a Rail, p. 99; Variation in Clutch Sizes, p. 339; Brood Parasitism, p. 287; American Coots, p. 105. **REFS:** Cramp and Simmons, 1980; Petrie, 1986.

American Coot

Fulica americana Gmelin

NG–100; G–106; PE–64; PW–pl 24; AE–pl 134; AW–pl 111; AM(I)–308

| 0′–2′ | MF | 8–12 | MF
I: 21–25 DAYS
PRECOCIAL 4 | | GRND GLEAN |
| | | (2–12)
MONOG | F: 49–56(?) DAYS
MF | | FOLIAGE
GLEAN |

BREEDING: Freshwater lakes, ponds, marshes, rivers. Usu 1 brood, occ 2. **DISPLAYS:** Male paddles after female, flapping wings; female dives if too closely pressed. Male paddles with head and neck on water, wingtips raised above, spreads and elevates tail to display white patches. Female assumes similar pose. **NEST:** Usu over water (1′–4′ deep), in veg tall enough to conceal; large floating cup of dead stems on platform anchored to veg, lined with finer materials. Other platforms for resting/roosting, esp brood platform built mostly by male. **EGGS:** Pinkish-buff, marked with blackish-brown. 1.9″ (49 mm). **DIET:** Mostly aquatic veg, algae; also fish, tadpoles, crustaceans, snails, worms, aquatic and terrestrial insects, eggs of other marsh-nesting birds. Pirates plants from ducks. **CONSERVATION:** Winters s to s C.A. Golf course and gun club pest. **NOTES:** Clutch overlap occurs during seasons when breeding starts early enough for 2 broods. Younger birds tend to nest later than older birds; later clutches smaller. Brood parasitism: clutches >12 likely from >1 female. Young hatch asynchronously. **ESSAYS:** American Coots, p. 105; Piracy, p. 159; Feet, p. 239; Vocal Development, p. 601; Variation in Clutch Sizes, p. 339; Commensal Feeding, p. 35. **REFS:** Gorenzel et al., 1982; Hill, 1986; Ryan and Dinsmore, 1979, 1980.

under what circumstances parent birds carry their young. But birders fortunate enough to witness parental transport should be cautious: some species feign carrying their young. The Eurasian (and perhaps American) Woodcock uses this type of distraction display to lure predators away from its chicks. Such displays may effectively fool predators and foil their attempts to locate young. Birders with pencil in hand need to be careful that they, too, don't fall for this ruse.

SEE: Parental Care, p. 555; Carrying Eggs, p. 361; Distraction Displays, p. 115; Loon Nurseries and Populations, p. 3; Precocial and Altricial Young, p. 581.   REFS: Johnsgard and Kear, 1968; Lowe, 1972.

American Coots

American Coots are noted for many qualities, some considerably less redeeming than others. Conspicuous, noisy, and aggressively territorial, they select from a repertoire of some 14 displays to communicate among themselves. To signal their social intentions coots vary body postures, adjust the position of the white undertail coverts, alter the degree to which they arch the wings over the back, change the angle of erect neck feathers and, when aroused, swell the frontal "nose" shield.

Many coot displays are associated with strident, year-long territorial defense. Generally, it is the male that confronts perceived threats. When the male partner is absent however, the female becomes demonstrative, reacting first to intruding females before confronting intruding males. When an intruder appears, the resident approaches it by modifying its normal slow paddling into a hastened patrol swim and then makes a wake-forming charge that may end in a splattering, rapid run across the surface. Such confrontations may lead to combat. While fighting, a coot usually sits back on the water and grabs its opponent with one long-clawed foot while attempting to slap the contender with the free one and jab it with its bill. Apparently, the aim is to push the opponent onto its back and, in some

Northern Jacana

Jacana spinosa Linnaeus

NG–102; G–110; PE–298; PW–pl 24; AE–pl 250; AM(I)–340

M

4
(3–5)
POLYAND

M
I: 22–24 DAYS
PRECOCIAL 2
F: 28 DAYS
M

GROUND
GLEAN

BREEDING: Freshwater marshes with floating veg, wet pastures and meadows, pond, lake and stream edges. Multiple broods. **DISPLAYS:** ? **NEST:** Of green veg on floating veg sufficient to keep eggs contained. **EGGS:** Brown with fine black scrawls. 1.2″ (30 mm). **DIET:** Insects usu taken from floating mat of veg, occ forage in cultivated fields; occ take small fish. **CONSERVATION:** Winter resident. **NOTES:** Polyandry typical—each female has 1–4 mates. Sex role reversal—male does all of incubating (only male has brood patches) and virtually all care of young; male does most of brooding, female occ broods in bad weather. Female role is substantial in defense of eggs and young (female is 70% heavier than male). Male performs distraction display in defense of young: crouches and extends wings, alternately slaps wings and/or feet against ground (or floating veg). Young fly at ca. 35 days. **ESSAYS:** Polyandry, p. 133; Monogamy, p. 597; Feet, p. 239; Passerines and Songbirds, p. 395; Brood Patches, p. 427; Distraction Displays, p. 115. **REFS:** Jenni and Betts, 1978; Stephens, 1984.

Black Oystercatcher

Supersp #11
Haematopus bachmani Audubon

NG–102; G–110; PW–pl 26; AW–pl 218; AM(I)–334

MF

2
(1–3)
MONOG

MF
I: 24–29 DAYS
PRECOCIAL 3
F: 35 + DAYS
MF

BREEDING: Rocky coast and islands; occ on sand beaches. 1 brood. **DISPLAYS:** Noisy pre-cop ground display with bowing. See: Shorebird Communication, p. 139. **NEST:** Usu above high tide line in weedy turf, beach gravel, or rock depression, generally with unobstructed view; usu lined with rock shards or shell bits. **EGGS:** Cream buff/olive buff, marked with brown, black. 2.2″ (57 mm). **DIET:** Various marine inverts, esp mussels, worms, echinoderms; also fish, crustaceans, barnacles, limpets. **CONSERVATION:** Winter resident. **NOTES:** Long-term pair bond. Feeding territories defended year-round. Ravens are major egg predators. Hybrid zone with American Oystercatcher in c Baja. Good swimmer and diver. More than 4 eggs indicates more than one female using nest (dump nest). Young precocial, but dependent on adults for extended period; begin to fly at ca. 35 days. Formerly known as American Black Oystercatcher. **ESSAYS:** Oystercatchers and Oysters, p. 109; Bills, p. 209; Empty Shells, p. 165; Shorebird Feeding, p. 125; Hybridization, p. 501; Parental Care, p. 555. **REFS:** Groves, 1984; Hartwick and Blaylock, 1979; Morrell et al., 1979.

cases, hold it underwater. Quite impressive, this sequence can be seen in coots four days old.

Not all displays directed toward unfamiliar coots are antagonistic, however. Coots communicate distress to each other by exposing their undertail coverts or displaying a swollen shield when alarmed by potential dangers such as hawks, airplanes, or predatory mammals. Similarly, aggressive displays are not restricted to avian intruders. If approached or harassed by other vertebrates, including people, coots will assert themselves by erecting their feathers so that they appear larger than life. Interestingly, coots do not perform distraction displays, even though Clappers and other rails do.

Not only are coots demonstrative, they are also hardy. For example, they can adjust well to hot temperatures. They have lobed feet, unique among gallinules, which, in addition to their use in battle, can effectively conduct heat out of the body. By immersing their feet in water, European Coots were able to tremendously increase their rate of heat loss and very quickly cool down when experimentally subjected to a temperature increase from 50° to 104°F.

American Coots are opportunistic feeders. In addition to hunting for themselves, however, they also feed commensally by taking leftovers from other species such as dabbling ducks, or they pirate plants brought to the surface by diving ducks such as Canvasbacks. Young coots are opportunistic as well. Groups of up to five juveniles may pirate aquatic vegetation from the bills of ducks and swans.

Overall, coot breeding behavior is not unlike other rails. Coots select breeding areas rich in nesting materials and build up to nine bulky, floating structures. They lay eggs in only one or two of them; the others are used for displaying, copulating, or brooding. Since incubation is not initiated until the fourth or fifth egg is laid, ample time is available beforehand for other birds to parasitize the clutch. But, American Coots, unlike the even more aggressive South American Red-fronted Coots, rarely host the eggs of other species. Redheads and Ruddy Ducks, the two common brood parasitic waterfowl in North America, reputedly ignore the very abundant American Coot nests. Ornithologist Milton Weller tried an experiment to find out why. Weller inserted chicken eggs into 43 coot nests at varying stages of nesting. The reason for the 100 percent failure of these eggs could not be pinpointed, but it appears that coots have somehow evolved a way to circumvent brood parasitism that requires neither the vigilance nor concerted effort seen in many other species.

Coots are among the least graceful of marsh birds. Commonly called "splatterers," they scramble across the surface of the water with wings flapping not only to confront intruders but also to become airborne. Coots bob their heads while walking, quite likely because the head movements help them to judge the distance to their prey. While foraging on insects, they bob quickly; while eating greens, they bob slowly. Appearing somewhat like aquatic pigeons, coots also bob their heads while swimming.

Since coots appear neither comical, vulnerable, nor inspirational, the

American Oystercatcher

Supersp #11
Haematopus palliatus Temminck

NG–102; G–110; PE–116; AE–pl 242; AM(I)–332

MF	3	MF
	(2–4)	I: 24–29 DAYS
	MONOG	PRECOCIAL 3
		F: 35+ DAYS
		MF

BREEDING: Sandy and rocky coasts and islands. 1 brood. **DISPLAYS:** Pre-cop on ground—male lowers tail and retracts head, repeatedly calls softly and stealthily advances toward female. See: Shorebird Communication, p. 139. **NEST:** On open, flat, loose substrate (oft sand or gravel) with good view. Oft amid shells, pebbles, marsh grass; occ rimmed with shells, usu unlined. Tracks lead to nest. **EGGS:** Olive buff, sparsely marked with brown. 2.2" (56 mm). **DIET:** Also marine worms, crabs, echinoderms, occ fish. **CONSERVATION:** Winters s to Guatemala and Honduras (w); West Indies and coastal S.A. (e). Conversion of beaches has forced oystercatchers from much of former breeding habitat. Range expanding northward in e. **NOTES:** Solitary, occ loosely colonial. 200-mile-wide hybrid zone with Black Oystercatcher in c Baja. Oft high egg losses to avian predators; renest up to 4–5 times; chick survival to adulthood usu high. First clutches usu 3 eggs, replacement clutches usu 2 eggs. Young depend almost entirely on adults for food; require long period for learning to open mollusks. Small clutch size possibly related to extended period of requisite parental care. **ESSAYS:** Oystercatchers and Oysters, p. 109; Bills, p. 209; Empty Shells, p. 165; Shorebird Feeding, p. 125; Parental Care, p. 555; Variation in Clutch Sizes, p. 339. **REFS:** Johnsgard, 1981; Nol et al., 1984.

American Avocet

Recurvirostra americana Gmelin

NG–102; G–110; PE–116; PW–pl 26; AE–pl 244; AW–pl 220; AM(I)–338

MF	4	MF	SWEEPS
	(3–5)	I: 22–29 DAYS	
	MONOG	PRECOCIAL 2	PROBES
		F: 28–35 DAYS	
		MF	

BREEDING: Marshes, mud flats, ponds, alkaline lakes, estuaries. 1 brood. **DISPLAYS:** Courtship: wades, bows, crouches, dances with wings spread. Prostrate female extends head, neck, wings. See: Shorebird Communication, p. 139. **NEST:** Among tufts of veg on gravel, sand, mud flats below brush. Lining variable, oft dry grass, mud chips. **EGGS:** Olive-buff, marked with brown, black. 2.0" (50 mm). **DIET:** Mostly crustaceans, insects; aquatic veg, seeds. About ⅔ animal. Usu forages by sweeping bill back and forth beneath water's surface, finding food by feel. **CONSERVATION:** Winters s to s Mexico. **NOTES:** Loosely colonial. Loud calls and mobbing of predator typical defense on breeding grounds; group distraction display. Male and female develop brood patches; male incubates more frequently for first 8 days, then primarily female for next 16. Young hatch synchronously. Activity peaks in early morning and in afternoon. Food stirred up by American Avocets taken by commensal Wilson's Phalaropes following behind. **ESSAYS:** Bills, p. 209; Feet, p. 239; Shorebird Feeding, p. 125; Commensal Feeding, p. 35; Distraction Displays, p. 115; Brood Patches, p. 427. **REFS:** Gibson, 1971, 1978; Grant, 1982; Hamilton, 1975.

public is often unsympathetic to their problems. American Coot flocks may number up to 1,500 individuals, and the birds may readily attain "pest" status. In 1986, for example, employees at a California golf course shot 400 coots in an effort to keep them off the grass. Apparently their droppings accumulated on the putting greens and resulted in raised golf scores and tempers. But when coots disappear, they usually toll the bell for other species as well. In Hawaii, for example, where coot numbers were reduced to 1,500 by the mid-1970s and the island population was considered endangered, their decline was also an indicator of the rapid disappearance of island wetlands, an important habitat for many other Hawaiian species.

SEE: Brood Parasitism, p. 287; Piracy, p. 159; Temperature Regulation and Behavior, p. 149; Thin as a Rail, p. 99; Hawaiian Bird Biology, p. 651. REFS: Brent et al., 1985; Gullion, 1952, 1953, 1954; Ripley, 1977; Weller, 1971.

Oystercatchers and Oysters

Anyone who has tried to open oysters or other bivalves can empathize with the challenge facing oystercatchers, for they subsist in large part on those mollusks. Bivalves have powerful "adductor" muscles that hold the two shells together; prying them open is no easy task for us, even with the aid of a stout, sharp knife. Yet oystercatchers, birds a mere foot-and-a-half long, accomplish the feat quickly (often in under 30 seconds) and apparently with ridiculous ease.

How they do it has been elucidated by careful studies of the common Eurasian Oystercatcher, a bird in the same superspecies as the American Oystercatcher. The trick, in part, lies in having the right tool—a long, stout bill with mandibles that are triangular in cross section and reinforced so that they do not bend easily. But the success of the oystercatcher depends mainly upon use of one of two learned techniques. Oystercatchers are either stabbers or hammerers.

Stabbers sneak up on open mollusks and plunge their bills between the shells, severing the adductors before the bivalve can "clam up." The meat is then neatly chiseled away from each shell, shaken free, and eaten. Hammerers, in contrast, loosen the bivalve from its moorings and then shatter one shell with a rapid series of well-directed, short, powerful blows. The bill is then inserted through the hole, the adductors are cut, the shells pried apart, and the mollusk removed and devoured.

Young oystercatchers learn the techniques by observing their parents, who feed them for variable periods, often continuing beyond fledging. In fact, adults and young may associate for up to a year. During this period, the offspring gradually refine their skills as stabbers or hammerers, and learn to take other prey including crabs, marine worms, and, when feeding inland, earthworms and (to a lesser degree) a variety of insects. When oys-

Black-necked Stilt
Himantopus mexicanus Müller

NG–102; G–110; PE–116; PW–pl 26; AE–pl 243; AW–pl 219; AM(I)–336

MF
I: 22–26 DAYS

| MF | 4
(3–5)
MONOG | | MF
I: 22–26 DAYS
PRECOCIAL 2
F: 28–32+ DAYS
MF (?) | INSECTS | GROUND
GLEAN |

BREEDING: Marshes, wet savannas, mud flats, shallow ponds and flooded fields. 1? brood. **DISPLAYS:** Courtship: male alternately pecks ground/water and preens breast, female elongates, male circles female flicking water with bill. See: Shorebird Communication, p. 139. **NEST:** Variable, may be open or partly concealed; on dry, water-bounded mound above tide line, on flooded flats with 360° view. Eggs oft wet. Occ of mud, sticks, shells, and debris, lined with pebbles, shell bits, sticks. **EGGS:** Buff, marked with dark brown, black. Oft nest-stained. 1.7″ (44 mm). **DIET:** Esp brine flies, crayfish, brine shrimp, snails, few fish, tadpoles; some seeds. **CONSERVATION:** Winters s to s S.A. **NOTES:** Loosely colonial. In hot environments, "belly-soaking" (transport of water in the ventral feathers) by incubating adults cools the incubating bird, the eggs or chicks, and increases nest humidity; in a single day, >100 trips for water can occur. Adults distract predators using aerial, mock incubation, and feigned injury displays. Young hide when threatened; swim using wings. **ESSAYS:** Shorebird Feeding, p. 125; Temperature Regulation, p. 149; Distraction Displays, p. 115; Spacing of Wintering Shorebirds, p. 147; Shorebird Migration and Conservation, p. 119. **REFS:** Grant, 1982; Hamilton, 1975.

Snowy Plover
Charadrius alexandrinus Linnaeus

NG–104; G–114; PE–120; PW–pl 25; AE–pl 233; AW–pl 182; AM(I)–322

| M | 3 (2–3)
MONOG
(POLYGAM) | | MF
I: 27–28 (25–32) DAYS
PRECOCIAL 2
F: 31 DAYS
MF | AQUATIC
INVERTS | PROBES |

BREEDING: Beaches and dry mud or salt flats; sand margins of rivers, lakes, and ponds. 1 (e), oft 2 (w) broods. **DISPLAYS:** Courtship: nest scrape display—male points bill to scrape, raises far wing, ruffles throat feathers, cop at nest. See: Shorebird Communication, p. 139. **NEST:** Scrape marked with twigs, debris, oft amid grass tufts; lined with bits of concealing ornaments. Male makes 1–2 extra scrapes. **EGGS:** Buff, marked with black. 1.2″ (30 mm). **DIET:** Insects, worms, crustaceans, mollusks, fish. **CONSERVATION:** Winters from Bahamas s to Venezuela (e) and from n w Mexico s to Chile (w); CA population partially resident. Blue List 1972–82, Special Concern 1986. **NOTES:** Occ loosely colonial. Monogamous e of Rockies with male and female attending young and having only one clutch per season; in w, female deserts young within 6 days, male attends them for 29–47 days. After deserting, ca. 33% of females renest with new male, ca. 50% of males renest with new mate: serial polyandry and serial polygyny. Male incubates 10% of day and all night. "Run and peck" visual foraging and "pattering" (vibrates leg to scare up prey). Known in Europe as Kentish Plover. **ESSAYS:** Blue List, p. 11; Polyandry, p. 133; Polygyny, p. 443; Shorebird Migration and Conservation, p. 119. **REFS:** Cramp and Simmons, 1983; Lessels, 1984; Purdue, 1976; Warriner et al., 1986.

tercatchers eat large crabs, they turn the victim on its back, kill it with a stab through the center of the nervous system, and then demolish the shell by hammering. Presumably they detect worms with extremely sensitive nerve endings at the bill tip. These sensory receptors are thought to be specialized to respond to vibrations (similar receptors are found on the bills of other shorebirds that probe for prey).

Observations on feeding techniques of closely related North American oystercatchers would be most interesting; we anticipate that patterns will be similar to those described here.

SEE: Shorebird Feeding, p. 125; Parental Care, p. 555; Bills, p. 209. REFS: Cramp and Simmons, 1983; Heppleston, 1971; Norton-Griffiths, 1967; Tinbergen and Norton-Griffiths, 1964.

The Color of Birds

Birds are, hands down, the most colorful terrestrial vertebrates—only insects and coral reef fishes rival them among animals. Birds, like butterflies and moths, have two basic sources of color. The more common is pigments, which are chemical compounds located in the feathers or skin. Pigments absorb some wavelengths of light and reflect others; it is the reflected light that reaches our eyes. The color we perceive is a function of the wavelength of the light stimulating the receptors of our retinas. In the visual part of the electromagnetic spectrum, we see the shortest wavelengths as "violet" and the longest as "red." Thus a cardinal has pigment in its feathers that absorbs all the wavelengths *except* the ones that, when they enter our visual system, register as red. When no light is reflected we see black; when all wavelengths are reflected we see white.

Blue and iridescent colors in birds are never produced by pigments, however. They are "structural colors." The blues are produced by minute particles in the feather that are smaller in diameter than the wavelength of red light. These particles are able to influence only shorter wavelengths, which appear blue, and are "scattered"—reflected in all directions. Thus structural blue colors remain the same when they are viewed at different angles in reflected light. If, however, they are viewed by transmitted light (that is, with the feather between the light source and the observer), the blue disappears.

Iridescent colors are produced by differential reflection of wavelengths from highly modified barbules of the feathers that are rotated so that a flat surface faces the incoming light. The detailed structure of the barbule reflects some wavelengths and absorbs others, and the reflected wavelength changes with the angle of reflection. The structural color is registered by the eye in response to the reflected wavelengths and changes with the angle formed by the light, the reflecting surface, and the eye.

Piping Plover
Charadrius melodus Ord

NG–104; G–114; PE–120; PW–pl 25; AE–pl 234; AM(I)–326

   MF
I: 25–31 DAYS
MF   4   PRECOCIAL 2
(3–5)   F: 20–32 DAYS
MONOG   MF

 INSECTS   PROBES

BREEDING: Mostly sand, occ gravel, or pebble beaches, esp among scattered grass tufts. 1 brood. **DISPLAYS:** Courtship: circular or figure-eight flight; on ground male whistles, crouches, circles female, spreads wings and trailing tail, puffs feathers, holds up head, stretches neck, stamps feet. See: Shorebird Communication, p. 139. **NEST:** In sand or gravel, conspicuous scrape well above tide line, oft lined with bits of concealing objects. Extra scrapes are made but not used. **EGGS:** Buff, marked with brownish-black. 1.2″ (31 mm). **DIET:** Incl marine worms, crustaceans, mollusks, eggs of marine inverts. **CONSERVATION:** Winters in U.S., occ through Bahamas, Greater Antilles. Blue List 1972–82, Special Concern 1986. Endangered Species: <20 breeding pairs left in Great Lakes region (1986), seriously threatened elsewhere (<4500 birds remain). Hunting brought close to extinction. Extensive habitat loss from development and recreation; vehicles oft destroy nests. **NOTES:** Monogamy occ long-term (2–3 years). Breeding site tenacity strong, esp in males. Both sexes brood. Females oft desert broods before males, oft within one week posthatching. Performs distraction display. **ESSAYS:** Blue List, p. 11; Empty Shells, p. 165; Birds and the Law, p. 293; Shorebird Feeding, p. 125; Shorebird Migration, p. 119; Site Tenacity, p. 189; Monogamy, p. 597; Nest Lining, p. 391. **REFS:** Cairns and McLaren, 1980; Haig and Oring, 1987.

Wilson's Plover
Charadrius wilsonia Ord

NG–104; G–114; PE–120; AE–pl 237; AM(I)–322

   MF
I: 23–24 DAYS
M   3   PRECOCIAL 2
(2–4)   F: 21 DAYS
MONOG   MF

 INSECTS   GROUND
GLEAN

BREEDING: Sand beaches, tidal mud flats and savanna pools, usu near coast. 1 brood. **DISPLAYS:** Courtship: male makes several scrapes; circles crouching female with head lowered, tail low and spread, wings drooped, and stamps feet. Threat: male erects throat feathers, confronts upright or in crouching chase. See: Shorebird Communication, p. 139. **NEST:** On sand or gravel above tide line, near object amid bits of broken shell, small stones, driftwood, rubbish, scattered forbs and grass; unlined or lined with bits of same. Occ concealed by beach plants. **EGGS:** Cream/buff, marked with dark brown, black. 1.4″ (36 mm). **DIET:** Esp crabs, sand worms, also insects. Feed night and day. **CONSERVATION:** Winters s through Caribbean–Gulf Atlantic region to n S.A. **NOTES:** Loosely colonial, occ assoc with oystercatchers, terns. Female incubates most of day, male incubates all or most of night. Distraction display: threatened female decoys using calls while lying on side gasping. **ESSAYS:** Shorebird Feeding, p. 125; Spacing of Wintering Shorebirds, p. 147; Shorebird Migration and Conservation, p. 119; Distraction Displays, p. 115; Who Incubates?, p. 27. **REFS:** Bergstrom, 1986; Johnsgard, 1981.

Just as bird songs did not evolve to please the human ear, bird colors did not evolve to delight our eyes. The most spectacular colors typically function to impress members of the same species. The classic example is the tail of the peacock, but the brilliant colors of the breeding male Scarlet Tanager or male King Eider illustrate the same phenomenon. Nondemonstrative colors frequently help a bird avoid predation. The camouflage of a King Eider female on its nest is an example of such cryptic coloration.

Many inconspicuous birds exhibit what is known as "countershading"; they are darkest along the back, and gradually become lighter until the belly is pure white. Countershading tends to eliminate a sharply defined shadow, since the bird absorbs the most light above, where the light is brightest, and reflects the most light below, where the light is dimmest. The vast majority of shorebirds are countershaded, although as in the Snowy Plover the division between darker back and lighter belly may be rather sharp.

"Disruptive" coloration—the use of striking patterns to break up the outline of the bird—is another technique for avoiding detection. Killdeer and Semipalmated Plovers, for example, are very difficult to see in some circumstances. The extreme in cryptic coloration, of course, is found among those birds that simply take on the color of the background against which they live. Ptarmigans in their pure white winter plumage are the classic example.

Birds often use colors to identify themselves to other members of their flock and thus to hold it together. Examples are the color patterns revealed in flight by shorebirds such as Ruddy Turnstones and Willets. Colors, such as those inside the mouths of gaping chicks, may also function to stimulate parental feeding. Other colors may direct the feeding movements of the young, as does the red spot on the bill of the Herring Gull, which encourages the young to solicit food and to stick its head into the adult's mouth.

Some colors are apparently produced incidentally by pigments deposited for other reasons. For instance, feathers of the wingtips are subjected to

Disruptive coloration in the Killdeer. The alternating bands of white and black on the head and neck break up the outline of the bird and make it more difficult to see against a variegated background than a bird that is uniformly light or dark.

Semipalmated Plover

Charadrius semipalmatus Bonaparte

NG–104; G–114; PE–120; PW–pl 25; AE–pl 236; AW–pl 183; AM(I)–324

M	4
	(3–4)
	MONOG

MF
I: 23–25 DAYS
PRECOCIAL 2
F: 22–31 DAYS
MF

INSECTS
SEEDS

BREEDING: Sandy habitat, grassy or mossy tundra. 1 brood. **DISPLAYS**: Male crouches low, tail spread, wings partly open, feathers puffed, calls with increasing speed. See: Shorebird Communication, p. 139. **NEST**: Wind-sheltered but in full sun, amid sparse veg; unlined or lined with bits of concealing objects. **EGGS**: Brown/olive buff, marked with dark brown, black. 1.3″ (33 mm). **DIET**: Mollusks, crustaceans, worms, insects. Unlike Least and Semipalmated Sandpipers with which it associates in winter, runs with head held before stabbing prey. **CONSERVATION**: Winters s through West Indies and along coasts to c Chile and s Argentina. Declined drastically in 1890s from hunting. **NOTES**: Cryptic; adults skulk away when confronted at nest. Roost above high-tide line and sleep during high tide. Flock members frequently alternate positions and postures during roosting. **ESSAYS**: Color of Birds, p. 111; Shorebird Feeding, p. 125; Spacing of Wintering Shorebirds, p. 147; Shorebird Migration and Conservation, p. 119; Nest Lining, p. 391; Communal Roosting, p. 615; Mixed-Species Flocking, p. 433. **REFS**: Johnsgard, 1981; Sutton and Parmelee, 1955.

Killdeer

Charadrius vociferus Linnaeus

NG–106; G–114; PE–120; PW–pl 25; AE–pl 235; AW–pl 187; AM(I)–328

M	4
	(3–5)
	MONOG

MF
I: 24–28 DAYS
PRECOCIAL 2
F: 25 DAYS
MF

BREEDING: Fields, meadows, pastures, mud flats, freshwater margins, occ on coasts. Oft 2 broods. **DISPLAYS**: Male courtship on ground and in air with loud calling and sham nest-scraping movements. See: Shorebird Communication, p. 139. **NEST**: Variable. In open, with extended view, oft assoc with human habitation, or near little or no veg on soft substrate offering camouflaging stones, gravel, pebbles, etc., oft far from water. Unlined or lined with local materials, occ well lined with grass. **EGGS**: Buff, marked with blackish-brown, occ wreathed or capped. 1.4″ (37 mm). **DIET**: About 75% insects, remainder wide variety of inverts; ca. 2% weed seeds. **CONSERVATION**: Winters s to C.A., Caribbean, n S.A., s w to Chile. Once locally reduced by hunting. **NOTES**: Males show stronger nest-site tenacity than do females. Mates oft retained in successive seasons. Incubating adults belly-soak to cool eggs in hotter part of range. Adult performs conspicuous broken-wing distraction display. **ESSAYS**: Masterbuilders, p. 445; Eggs and Their Evolution, p. 301; Incubation: Heating Eggs, p. 393; Color of Birds, p. 111; Distraction Displays, p. 115; Site Tenacity, p. 189. **REFS**: Lenington and Mace, 1975; Phillips, 1972.

more wear than those nearer the base of the wing. And feathers containing pigments are more resistant to wear than those without. That is thought to be the reason that the wingtips of many mostly white birds, such as many gulls, terns, pelicans, and gannets, are dark.

SEE: Feathers, p. 309; Molting, p. 529; Eclipse Plumage, p. 61; Bird Badges, p. 591; Black and White Plumage, p. 177; Visual Displays, p. 5.

Distraction Displays

Some nesting birds make themselves as conspicuous as possible when approached by a predator. Rather than attempting to cover their nests, eggs, or young, these birds deliberately attract the attention of the intruder, usually behaving in an exaggerated manner. Although they may occasionally show mild aggression by, for example, rapidly opening and closing the bill, more often they feign an injury, exhaustion, or illness to divert the predator from the nest or the young.

Broken-wing displays are most easily provoked and most realistic in shorebirds, waterfowl, and other species with ground nests. The displays typically involve spreading and dragging of a wing or tail, while slowly fluttering away from the nest or young, and may include calling or flashing of brightly contrasting feathers.

Some displays give the impression of a running small mammal. For instance, in the "rodent-run" display of the tundra-nesting Purple Sandpiper, the bird drags its wings (creating the illusion of a second pair of legs), erects its feathers (providing some resemblance to fur), and "squeals" while it dodges between imaginary barriers.

There is little doubt that effectively leading a predator away from the nest would be strongly favored by natural selection, but how these stylized antics evolved remains controversial among behaviorists. Some conclude

A Killdeer feigning injury to lure a predator away from its nest.

Mountain Plover

Charadrius montanus Townsend

NG–106; G–112; PW–pl 25; AW–pl 233; AM(I)–328

M

3 (1–4)
MONOG
(POLYAND)

MF
I: 28–31 DAYS
PRECOCIAL 2
F: 33–34 DAYS
MF

BREEDING: At moderate elevations on open plains, esp shortgrass prairie. 2 broods. **DISPLAYS:** Falling leaf and butterfly aerial displays; bowing and calling. See: Shorebird Communication, p. 139. **NEST:** On flat between hummocks, occ amid cacti or scattered shrubs; oft near old cow pats. Lined with cow manure chips, rootlets, grass. Cryptic (as are adults from rear). First egg laid in bare scrape; lining added during incubation. Builds >1 nest. **EGGS:** Usu dark olive-buff, marked with black, wreathed. 1.5″ (38 mm). Oft become embedded in mud, so turning impossible. **DIET:** Esp grasshoppers, crickets, beetles, flies. **CONSERVATION:** Winters s to s Baja, n Mexico. Important game bird of market hunters prior to 1900. Range contracting due to agricultural conversion of shortgrass prairie. **NOTES:** Breeding system characterized by rapid, multiple clutches, oft with sequential polyandry as females desert first clutch. Male incubates first clutch, female incubates second. Second clutch started 11–13 days after completion of first. Not found on shore; not mountain-dwelling either. Incubating or brooding bird performs distraction display using vocalizations and feigning injury. Selectively inhabit prairie dog towns in some regions. **ESSAYS:** Polyandry, p. 133; Shorebird Feeding, p. 125; Shorebird Migration, p. 119; Wintering Shorebirds, p. 147; Distraction Displays, p. 115. **REFS:** Graul, 1975; Graul and Webster, 1976; Knowles et al., 1982.

Black-bellied Plover

Pluvialis squatarola Linnaeus

NG–108; G–112; PE–118; PW–pl 25; AE–pl 240; AW–pl 190; AM(I)–316

MF

4
(3–4)
MONOG

MF
I: 26–27 DAYS
PRECOCIAL 2
F: 35–45 DAYS
MF

PROBES

BREEDING: Tundra, low-lying coast. 1 brood. **DISPLAYS:** Male butterfly flight in courtship. See: Shorebird Communication, p. 139. **NEST:** In dry, exposed site where snow melts first, with extensive view, occ on peat ridge in marsh. Cryptic. Lined with lichen or grass by female; scrape made by male. **EGGS:** Pink/green/ brown, marked with blackish-brown, olive, wreathed. 2.0″ (52 mm). **DIET:** Also earthworms. In migration, mostly polychaete worms, clams, also other marine inverts. **CONSERVATION:** Winters s through West Indies to coasts of Chile and n Argentina. **NOTES:** Female deserts chicks at 12 days; male remains until chicks independent at ca. 23 days. Oft nest within 300′ of previous year's nest. Does not breed before second or third year. When foraging, birds having just captured prey take fewer steps than those who fail. Oft very aggressive on wintering grounds, hold feeding territories. Known in Europe as Grey Plover. **ESSAYS:** Spacing of Wintering Shorebirds, p. 147; Shorebird Feeding, p. 125; Shorebird Migration and Conservation, p. 119; Parental Care, p. 555; Wing Shapes and Flight, p. 227. **REFS:** Baker, 1974; Cramp and Simmons, 1983; Hussell and Page, 1976.

that distraction displays are a product of the conflicting desires of the parent to approach the predator aggressively, to return to the nest, and to retreat. Others suggest that they evolved directly as a predator defense, with more stylized sequences found in species that have had longer association with heavy predation. In either case, fear is a prerequisite; tame birds cannot be induced to perform distraction displays. Similarly, distraction displays may be reduced or eliminated from the behavioral repertoire through habituation to repeated nondamaging intrusions by predators (or experimenters).

The most conspicuous and risky distraction displays occur when parental investment is greatest. Since the timing of maximum parental investment differs between altricial and precocial species, so too does the point in the breeding cycle when the adults give their most daring displays. Experimenters have measured, for example, how close to the nest an intruder can approach before a distraction display is elicited and how far from the nest the parent moves before performing. In altricial birds distraction displays are generally most conspicuous and, therefore, most risky to the parent just before the young fledge. At that point, parental investment is at its peak and the opportunity for renesting may already have been lost. For precocial birds, displays are most conspicuous and risky just at hatching, when the adults have made their maximum investment in the young. After that point, as the importance of parental care gradually declines, so do the displays.

SEE: Visual Displays, p. 5; Precocial and Altricial Young, p. 581; Mobbing, p. 425; Duck Displays, p. 63; Shorebird Communication, p. 139; Altruism, p. 453; Gulls Are Attracted to Their Predators, p. 169; Bird-Brained, p. 415; Parental Care, p. 555. REFS: Armstrong, 1949; Barash, 1975; Hinde, 1954a, b.

Bird Names—II

Plover is from the Latin *pluvia*, rain. It has been claimed that the name refers to either the ease with which the birds can be caught in the rain, or that they sing in the rain. Neither is correct, and its true origins remain unrecorded. Semipalmated from *semi* plus *palma* in Latin means "half-palmed" and refers to the partially webbed foot of that plover. Wilson's Plover, of course memorializes the father of scientific ornithology in America, Alexander Wilson (p. 277).

Goose and swan trace to the Anglo-Saxon words for those birds; teal to the Dutch word for "teal"; ibis to the same name in Greek (which itself may have been Egyptian in origin). Phalarope is an example of a common name borrowed from the scientific *Phalaropus*, from *Phalaris* plus *pous*, which in turn means "coot-footed" in Greek. The name refers to the birds' lobed toes. Avocet is based on the Latin name *avis* for small, or graceful. Curlew and Willet are simply renditions of the birds' calls; the origin of godwit is unknown.

REFS: Choate, 1985; Owen, 1985.

Lesser Golden Plover

Pluvialis dominica Müller

NG–108; G–112; PE–118; PW–pl 25; AE–pl 194; AW–pl 189; AM(I)–318

			MF I: 26–27 DAYS		
M	4 (3–4) MONOG		PRECOCIAL 2 F: 22? DAYS MF		 PROBES

BREEDING: Grassy tundra. 1? brood. **DISPLAYS:** Territorial: aerial. Courtship: male approaches female on ground, wings closed, body low, tail up, neck extended. See: Shorebird Communication, p. 139. **NEST:** On high, dry, exposed portions of tundra; lined with dry grass, dead leaves, lichen or moss. **EGGS:** Cinnamon/light-pink/buff, or cream, marked with brown, black. 1.9" (48 mm). **DIET:** Also worms, spiders; occ grass seed, berries. **CONSERVATION:** Winters s to middle S.A. Once flights darkened sky, but market hunting (48,000 shot in one day near New Orleans in 1861) reduced numbers greatly. **NOTES:** Noisy, fastest-flying wader. Pair bond may be long-term. Male incubates first, female later. Two subspecies overlap in n w AK but hybridization does not occur and subspecies may be elevated to species status; separated possibly as result of genetically differentiated migration routes. Extended molt requires ca. 125 days. **ESSAYS:** Birds and the Law, p. 293; Wing Shapes and Flight, p. 227; Shorebird Feeding, p. 125; Shorebird Migration and Conservation, p. 119; Spacing of Wintering Shorebirds, p. 147; Molting, p. 529; Hybridization, p. 501; Species and Speciation, p. 355; Who Incubates?, p. 27; Monogamy, p. 597. **REFS:** Connors, 1983; Johnsgard, 1981.

Marbled Godwit

Limosa fedoa Linnaeus

NG–110; G–116; PE–126; PW–pl 26; AE–pl 231; AW–pl 210; AM(I)–366

			? I: 21–23 (?) DAYS		
?	4 (3–5) MONOG ?		PRECOCIAL 2 F: 21 DAYS MF	 INSECTS	 GROUND GLEAN

 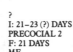

BREEDING: Shortgrass prairie, pastures, marshes, flooded plains. ? brood. **DISPLAYS:** Figure-8 and pursuit flights; nest scrape display. See: Shorebird Communication, p. 139. **NESTS:** Usu dry spot in shortgrass prairie wetland; occ far from water. Hollow in beaten-down grass, occ woven roof. Lined with dry grass. **EGGS:** Olive buff, marked with brown, wreathed. 2.2" (57 mm). **DIET:** In winter mostly mollusks, snails, crustaceans, worms, leeches. Usu feed by feel, oft forage at night, head oft submerged. Move inland to feed at high tide. **CONSERVATION:** Winters s along coasts, rarely s of Mexico. Range declining as breeding habitat converted to agriculture. **NOTES:** Loosely colonial. Late summer daily time divided as follows: 60% foraging, 20% sleeping, 17% preening and bathing; 2% walking, flying, not moving. Feeding less efficient in wind, usu avoided. Usu feed in midthigh water. During foraging individual distance of ca. 2' maintained. Mixed flocks (to 50) of adults and juveniles before fall migration. **ESSAYS:** Determining Diets, p. 535; Shorebird Feeding, p. 125; Shorebird Migration and Conservation, p. 119; Spacing of Wintering Shorebirds, p. 147. **REFS:** Ryan et al., 1984; Wishart and Sealy, 1980.

Bird Biologist—Robert Ridgway

Robert Ridgway (1850–1929) curated the bird collections of first the Smithsonian Institution and then (after it was established as a separate division to house the Smithsonian's collections) the U.S. National Museum from 1869 to 1929. In that epic sixty-year tenure he continued the work of his mentor, Spencer Fullerton Baird (p. 569), with whom he co-authored (along with Thomas Brewer, p. 647) the five-volume *A History of North American Birds*. He played an important role in the production of the first American Ornithologists' Union (AOU) *Check-list of North American Birds* and served on the committee that produced the second and third editions. He produced 8 volumes of his monumental *Birds of North and Middle America* (1901–1919), as well as hundreds of other publications. He was the leading American ornithologist of his generation, a kindly man who was always willing to give his time to encourage beginners.

REFS: Kastner, 1986; Stresemann, 1975.

Shorebird Migration and Conservation

As a group, shorebirds undertake some of the most spectacular of long-distance migrations of any North American birds. Nearly two-thirds of the species that breed in North America journey from their arctic nesting grounds to winter in Central and South America, and then return to the Arctic the following spring. Many species traverse more than 15,000 miles in this annual circuit. Some fly at altitudes exceeding 10,000 feet and achieve cruising speeds approaching 50 mph. From sightings of marked individuals, we know that at least some birds on nonstop flights cover nearly 2,000 miles in less than two days. Hudsonian Godwits may fly 8,000 miles nonstop between breeding and wintering areas, unless brief stopovers are made at as-yet-undiscovered spots somewhere in South America. The surprising migration feats of Sanderlings were discovered only recently by ornithologist Pete Myers. Their hitherto unsuspected circumnavigation of the Americas each year follows a route east across the top of North America and down the Atlantic coast in the autumn to their wintering grounds in Chile and Peru, and back north in the spring through the western United States to their arctic breeding grounds.

Although more than 20 million shorebirds migrate through the United States to the Arctic each year, Myers and his colleagues have captured the attention of the ornithological and conservation communities with their recent discovery that the long-term survival of even abundant species may be in jeopardy. Their studies show that Sanderlings, Ruddy Turnstones, Red Knots, Dunlins, and White-rumped, Baird's, Stilt, Western, and Semipalmated Sandpipers form enormous concentrations at several key staging areas along their migration route. Each of these spots is critical for success-

Bar-tailed Godwit

Limosa lapponica Linnaeus

NG–110; G–116; PE–294; PW–pl 26; AW–501; AM(I) –364

MF (?)	4	MF I: 20–21 DAYS		INSECTS	
	(2–4)	PRECOCIAL 2			
	MONOG	F: ? DAYS MF			

BREEDING: Coastal tundra, sedge-dwarf shrub tundra in foothills. 1 brood. **DISPLAYS:** Territorial male calls loudly and constantly. Male display flight of alternate glides and strong wingbeats. See: Shorebird Communication, p. 139. **NEST:** In moss, lichen or between grass clumps on dry portion of elevated ridges or slopes. Haphazardly lined with moss, lichen, or birch leaves; occ heavily with grass, some woven into circular nest. Reportedly occ steals nest from ptarmigan. **EGGS:** Greenish-brownish with few small scattered brown marks, occ unmarked, occ grayish/black marks forming wreath. 2.2″ (55 mm). **DIET:** Incl mollusks, crustaceans, marine worms, occ fish; about 1% veg. **CONSERVATION:** Winters in Old World. **NOTES:** Substantial sexual dimorphism in bill length: female's bill ca. 30% longer than male's. Female incubates in day, male at night. Breeds at two years. Foraging success of individuals greater in flocks than when solitary. Winter flocks of mixed sexes and ages. **ESSAYS:** Shorebird Feeding, p. 125; Shorebird Migration and Conservation, p. 119; Spacing of Wintering Shorebirds, p. 147; Who Incubates?, p. 27. **REFS:** Cramp and Simmons, 1983; Evans and Smith, 1975; Smith and Evans, 1973.

Hudsonian Godwit

Limosa haemastica Linnaeus

NG–110; G–116; PE–126; PW–pl 26; AE–pl 232; AM(I) –362

MF	4	MF I: 22–25 DAYS		WORMS	
	(3–4)	PRECOCIAL 2		MARINE	
	MONOG ?	F: 30 DAYS MF		INVERTS	

BREEDING: Sedge, moss, and lichen tundra close to water. 1 brood. **DISPLAYS:** Shorebird Communication, p. 139. **NESTS:** usu concealed by veg, oft on dry hummock, in grass, tussock, or beside fallen tree, oft spruce. Lined with few decayed leaves. **EGGS:** Olive-buff/brownish-olive, marked sparsely with olive-brown, few black spots forming wreath. 2.2″ (55mm). **DIET:** Mostly marine inverts in winter. **CONSERVATION:** Winter s to Tierra del Fuego. Nearly exterminated by market hunters; until ca. 1960 thought threatened, but now considered safe, simply rarely seen because of extreme, virtual nonstop long-distance migration and remote breeding grounds. **NOTES:** Female incubates in day, male at night. Female does not flush easily from the nest. Migrates in large flocks. **ESSAYS:** Shorebird Feeding, p. 125; Shorebird Migration and Conservation, p. 199; Spacing of Wintering Shorebirds, p. 147; Who Incubates?, p. 27; Migration, p.183. **REFS:** Hagar, 1966; Johsgard, 1981.

ful migration of these species, providing superabundant food resources that enable the birds to quickly replenish their energy reserves and continue on. In North America, five such sites support more than a million shorebirds annually: Alaska's Copper River Delta, Washington's Gray's Harbor, eastern Canada's Bay of Fundy, Kansas' Cheyenne Bottoms, and the beaches of Delaware Bay in New Jersey and Delaware. More than 80 percent of the entire North American population of some species may join ranks at any of these key locations; virtually all Western Sandpipers and Dunlins use the Copper River site. Other similarly vital locations have been identified throughout the Americas. These few critical staging areas underpin the entire migration system of New World shorebirds. As Myers points out, such enormous concentrations dependent upon so few widely spaced locales breaks the usual link between a species' abundance and its immunity to extinction.

The series of critical stopover sites is typified by Delaware Bay. The arrival and departure of 500,000 to 1,500,000 shorebirds within a span of three to four weeks is synchronized with the annual breeding cycle of the bay's enormous population of horseshoe crabs, for it is the eggs of the crabs that supply the energy required by the birds to complete their spring journey to the Arctic. Each evening, after day-long feasting on crab eggs, the birds move east to roost in tidal marshes and on the outer beaches of the Atlantic coast. Coastal and wetland development have forced the birds into ever smaller foraging and roosting sites as the number of suitable areas has dwindled. On high-tide nights, more than 100,000 shorebirds may be packed into a few hundred yards of beach.

Fortunately, efforts are now under way to link the staging sites connecting wintering and breeding areas into a system of sister reserves. Shorebird biologists, backed by the World Wildlife Fund–U.S., the International Association of Fish and Wildlife Agencies, and the National Audubon Society are working toward establishment of these critical reserves throughout the Americas. Success hinges on persuading local, regional, and national governments that such a system is not only desirable but absolutely necessary to ensure the survival of migratory shorebirds. As a first step, in May of 1986 the governors of New Jersey and Delaware mandated the lower estuary of Delaware Bay as a reserve for shorebird conservation.

SEE: Spacing of Wintering Shorebirds, p. 147; Shorebird Feeding, p. 125; Sandpipers, Social Systems, and Territoriality, p. 155; Birds and the Law, p. 293; Migration, p. 183. REFS: Myers, 1986; Myers et al., 1987.

Eskimo Curlew

Numenius borealis Forester

NG–112; G–118; PE–126; AM(I)–358

?	4		?	BERRIES	PROBES
	(3–4)		I: ? DAYS	AQUATIC	
	MONOG ?		PRECOCIAL 2	INVERTS	
			F: ? DAYS		
			?		

BREEDING: Open tundra. 1? brood. **DISPLAYS**: Undescribed. See: Shorebird Communication, p. 139. **NESTS**: Lined with few decaying leaves, occ a sprinkling of hay. **EGGS**: Olive, occ brown, marked with blackish-brown, wreathed. 2.0" (51mm). **DIET**: In spring: insects (esp grasshoppers, their eggs, ants); berries. In winter: insects; snails; berries. **CONSERVATION**: Winters s to s S.A. Endangered Species; formerly very abundant, now nearly extinct from excessive hunting in late 1800s. Once called "doughbirds" for the thick layer of fat developed for migration; canned for winter in Labrador—birds weighed 1 lb each. 1976 sighting in w Hudson Bay. **NOTES**: Little additional information available. **ESSAYS**: Birds and the Law, p. 293; Shorebird Feeding, p. 125; Shorebird Migration and Conservation, p. 119; Spacing of Wintering Shorebirds, p. 147; How Do We Find Out About Bird Biology?, p. 319. **REF**: Gollop et al., 1986.

Whimbrel

Numenius phaeopus Linnaeus

NG–112; G–118; PE–126; PW–pl 26; AE–pl 245; AW–pl 216; AM(I)–358

?	4		MF	BERRIES	PROBES
	(3–4)		I: 27–28 DAYS	AQUATIC	
	MONOG		PRECOCIAL 2	INVERTS	
			F: 35–42 DAYS		
			MF		

BREEDING: Sedge meadows, bogs, tundra, heath. 1 brood. **DISPLAYS**: Aerial courtship display: male starts low, then circles high and glides down; repeats. See: Shorebird Communication, p. 139. **NEST**: Unconcealed, usu near perch in dry portion of wet swale. Well defined or merely pressed into veg. Scantily lined with bits of dry grass, moss, or lichen. **EGGS**: Green/olive to light brownish-buff, marked with olive/reddish-brown. 2.3" (58 mm). **DIET**: Aquatic inverts incl esp crustaceans, also worms, mollusks; few seeds and leaves. In late summer, berries become esp important. **CONSERVATION**: Winters s to s Chile and s Brazil. **NOTES**: Occ nests in loose colony. Long-term pair bond. May not breed until third year. Hummock-bog habitat supports highest nest success; its greater structural complexity affords better nest concealment, and higher nest density improves group defense and results in lower predation. Birds nesting in hummock-bog habitat were more likely to return to the same site than birds in sedge meadow or heath tundra. Young migrate 1 week or more after adults depart. **ESSAYS**: Shorebird Feeding, p. 125; Shorebird Migration and Conservation, p. 119; Spacing of Wintering Shorebirds, p. 147; Site Tenacity, p. 189; Habitat Selection, p. 463. **REFS**: Cramp and Simmons, 1983; Skeel, 1983.

Drinking

As for all living things, water is essential to the survival of birds. All birds lose water to their environment by evaporation from the moist lining of the lungs as they breathe, and although they lack specialized sweat glands, birds also lose water through the skin. Water is also lost when waste products are excreted. The rate of water loss depends on several factors. A key one, of course, is weather. In hot, dry conditions water loss is high, as birds use evaporation to cool themselves. Another factor is the size of the bird. Water loss, like heat loss, is relatively higher in small birds compared with large, because of the greater surface area in relation to volume in small birds. A bird's pattern of activity—how much it flies as opposed to rests, for example—will also influence the rate of water loss.

Most birds drink to make up for the loss, and do so by dipping the bill and then tipping the head back to let the water run down into the throat to be swallowed, which may explain the apparent "sky-pointing" behavior in long-billed species such as curlews. Many small birds use dewdrops as a source of water. Pelicans sometimes drink by holding their beaks open in the rain. Northern Fulmars, doves, and pigeons drink more like horses, immersing the bill and sucking up the water.

Not all land birds need to drink water, however. Hummingbirds, with their largely liquid diet of nectar, normally face a problem of flooding rather than dehydration. Birds of arid areas may either go very long periods without drinking or never drink at all. They manage this in part by manufacturing water, as we all do, in the process of "burning" their food (cellular respiration). They also obtain water from their food (even dry seeds contain some), and they conserve water.

The main function of a bird's kidneys is to remove from the blood the nitrogen-containing wastes formed during the breakdown of proteins—and to do so while maintaining the proper balance of water, salts, and other materials in the body. In arid environments birds can remove these wastes while passing very little water in the urine.

Most mammals excrete these wastes largely in the form of urea, a rather poisonous compound that must be diluted with considerable water. Birds excrete uric acid, which does not dissolve easily in water, is relatively nontoxic, and can be voided nearly dry. Birds, however, must use much more energy to produce the uric acid than mammals do to produce urea. Thus they pay a price for their efficient water retention. Like birds, reptiles excrete uric acid and also pay a high energetic price. Presumably the excretion of uric acid originally evolved in both groups to permit the laying of terrestrial eggs. Fish and amphibian eggs can pass water-soluble nitrogen compounds, ammonia and urea, into the water in which they are bathed. Reptile and bird embryos must store their nitrogenous wastes inside the egg, and to keep from poisoning themselves, they manufacture uric acid. With vast new terrestrial environments thus opened to reptiles and their

Bristle-thighed Curlew

Numenius tahitiensis Gmelin

NG–112; G–118; PW–pl 26; AW– 761; AM(I) –360

MF(?)   4   ?   MF(?)
     MONOG?   I: ? DAYS
     PRECOCIAL 2
     F: ? DAYS
     MF(?)

BREEDING: Montane tundra. 1? brood. **DISPLAYS**: Undescribed. See: Shorebird Communication, p. 139. **NEST**: On flat, dry, exposed ridges; in lichen with little, if any, lining. **EGGS**: Olive, marked with brown blotches. ca. 2.6" (65mm). **DIET**: Blueberries, crowberries, presumably insects, too. Steals eggs. In winter: plant material, crustaceans, gastropods. **CONSERVATION**: Winters on Pacific islands. Very rare. Unusually small range for a shorebird; exact breeding location was discovered only in late 1940s. **NOTES**: Little studied; only known breeding area is in w Alaska. **ESSAYS**: Shorebird Feeding, p. 125; Shorebird Migration and Conservation, p. 119; Spacing of Wintering Shorebirds, p. 147; How Do We Find Out About Bird Biology?, p. 319; Feathers, p. 309. **REFS**: Johnsgard, 1981; Kyllingstad, 1987.

Long-billed Curlew

Numenius americanus Bechstein

NG–112; G–118; PE–126; PW–pl 26; AE–pl 246; AW–pl 217; AM(I)–360

?   4   MF   MARINE   GROUND
     (3–5)   I: 27–30 DAYS   INVERTS   GLEAN
     MONOG   PRECOCIAL 2
     F: 32–45 DAYS
     MF

BREEDING: Prairies, grassy meadows, usu near water. 1 brood. **DISPLAYS**: Pair does aerial flight display, nest-scraping display. See: Shorebird Communication, p. 139. **NEST**: In damp grassy hollow or on slope. Occ on substantial platform with 1½" rim. Occ near dry cow pats. Lined thinly with grass, weeds, cow pat chips. **EGGS**: Olive buff, olive, green, buffy white, marked with brown/olive. 2.6" (65 mm). **DIET**: Mostly insects, also worms, burrow-dwelling crustaceans, mollusks, toads, eggs and nestlings of other birds; few berries. **CONSERVATION**: Winters s along beaches, mud flats to Honduras, Costa Rica. Blue List 1981–82, Special Concern 1986. Breeding range much reduced and shrinking. Recent studies also indicate some losses from organochlorine poisoning, but primary problem is habitat loss and degradation. **NOTES**: Adult males cooperatively mob nest predators. Nests usu placed no closer than 750' apart. Males show stronger tendency than females to return to natal area to breed (philopatry); males first breed at 3+ years. Male incubates first, then only at night (female in day). Largest shorebird. **ESSAYS**: Birds and the Law, p. 293; Shorebird Feeding, p. 125; Blue List, p. 11; Site Tenacity, p. 189; DDT and Birds, p. 21; Mobbing, p. 425; Who Incubates?, p. 27. **REFS**: Allen, 1980; Redmond and Jenni, 1982, 1986.

avian descendants, the energetic cost of uric acid production by the embryo proved a bargain. Evolution then simply coopted its "invention" for adult birds and reptiles, as well.

SEE: Salt Glands, p. 29; Bird Droppings, p. 263; Temperature Regulation and Behavior, p. 149; Hummingbirds, Nectar, and Water, p. 333; Metabolism, p. 325; Eggs and Their Evolution, p. 301.

Shorebird Feeding

Trying to watch warblers feeding is a neck-and-patience-straining exercise —as Robert MacArthur found in the course of his classic study of how these small insect-eaters divide their food resources. Such "resource partitioning" by birds can be observed in much greater comfort, however, while seated behind a spotting scope (perhaps in a shelter) watching waders forage in an estuary.

In such a situation you might see an American Avocet, with its up-curved bill. Its bill seems less strange when you notice how the avocet uses

Left: American Oystercatcher opening mussels. Center: Ruddy Turnstone foraging under rocks. Right, bottom to top: Semipalmated Plover (searches surface); probing species that forage at different depths—Sanderling, Red Knot, Greater Yellowlegs, Marbled Godwit, Long-billed Curlew.

Willet

Catoptrophorus semipalmatus Gmelin

NG–114; G–122; PE–128; PW–pl 31; AE–pl 229; AW–pl 215; AM(I)–350

?	4 (4–5) MONOG	MF I: 22–29 DAYS PRECOCIAL 2 F: ? DAYS MF	GROUND GLEAN

BREEDING: Marshy lake margins and adjacent uplands (w); salt marshes, intertidal zone (e). 1 brood. **DISPLAYS:** Nest relief ceremony incl male bow. Prominent white-wing flash in courtship. See: Shorebird Communication, p. 139. **NEST:** Conspicuous, elaborate, or concealed by short, thick veg (esp where wet) on open beach or flat. Grasses bent to form hollow, lined with few dead rushes, dry grass/sedge, etc. Completed during laying. Female chooses site. **EGGS:** Olive, marked with olive-brown. 2.1″ (53 mm). **DIET:** Aquatic insects, worms, crustaceans, mollusks, fish. **CONSERVATION:** Winters s along coast to n Chile (w) and throughout West Indies to n Brazil (e). Moderately abundant, partly from tolerance of mowing and burning. Market hunters depleted population n of VA; now recovering and range expanding in e. **NOTES:** Semicolonial, oft nesting synchronously. Maintain separate feeding and nesting territories. Strong fidelity to mate and to feeding territory between years. Male incubates at night, occ during midday. Female abandons mate and brood 2–3 weeks posthatch; male attends brood for 2 more weeks. Oft wade to belly and swim. Adults leave breeding grounds before young fledge. Oft defend winter territories along sandy beaches. **ESSAYS:** Transporting Young, p. 103; Determining Diets, p. 535; Color of Birds, p. 111; Site Tenacity, p. 189; Spacing of Wintering Shorebirds, p. 147; Parental Care, p. 555. **REFS:** Howe, 1982; Ryan and Renken, 1987; Sordahl, 1979; Wilcox, 1980.

Greater Yellowlegs

Tringa melanoleuca Gmelin

NG–114; G–120; PE–128; PW–pl·31; AE–pl 228; AW–pl 207; AM(I)–344

?	4 MONOG?	MF(?) I: 23 DAYS PRECOCIAL 2 F: 18–20 DAYS MF	INVERTS

BREEDING: Muskeg, tundra. 1 brood. **DISPLAYS:** See: Shorebird Communication, p. 139. **NEST:** Slight depression in moss on small hummock, usu near water by branch or log, occ sheltered. Leaves blow in, or barely lined with grass. **EGGS:** Buff, marked with dark brown, wreathed. 1.9″ (49 mm). **DIET:** Small fish, also insects, snails, worms, tadpoles; berries. Oft forages by skimming surface in shallow water. **CONSERVATION:** Winters s to Tierra del Fuego. **NOTES:** Very noisy on nesting ground; female close sitter. If clutch lost, renests within 60′–90′ of first nest. Frequently stands on one foot. Defends foraging territory in winter. Small, very vocal winter flocks. **ESSAYS:** Shorebird Feeding, p. 125; Shorebird Migration and Conservation, p. 119; Spacing of Wintering Shorebirds, p. 147; Temperature Regulation and Behavior, p. 149. **REFS:** Cramp and Simmons, 1983; Johnsgard, 1981; Myers and Myers, 1979.

it as a scythe, swinging it back and forth in the water, stirring the bottom and snatching up insects and small crustaceans thus exposed. Nearby a Black-necked Stilt stalks its victims in water six inches or more deep, a habitat inaccessible to the stubby-legged Western Sandpipers snatching invertebrates from the surface of an adjacent mud flat. On the same flat a Long-billed Curlew uses its nine-inch, curved, forcepslike bill to probe the burrow of a large marine worm, while a Dunlin uses its short beak to feel for smaller worms or insect larvae just below the mud's surface. A Semipalmated Plover collects prey from the surface, hunting by sight and alone where the pattering feet of a flock will not warn sensitive prey to withdraw into their burrows.

Although crowded together at high tide, shorebirds begin to sort themselves out into preferred feeding habitats as the tide recedes. Least Sandpipers remain on drier, algae-covered mud; beyond them, Red Knots and Dunlins concentrate on bare, wet mud. Farther out, the long-legged Short-billed Dowitchers wade while rapidly probing the mud beneath the shallow water, accompanied by Greater Yellowlegs skimming prey from the water surface or swinging their bills back and forth to snare small fishes. On sandy, wave-washed soils Sanderlings dash nimbly back and forth at the very edge of the ebb and flow, probing the sand for tiny shrimplike crustaceans.

Ruddy Turnstones, as their name suggests, fill their bellies in quite a different way—they turn over rocks, shells, and even cowpies to expose concealed prey and sometimes dig deeply into sand. Oystercatchers, similarly well named, can extract a mussel's meat from between its shells, but that's a story for another essay.

In a single year, one oystercatcher can consume more than a hundred pounds of mussel meat. Indeed, each day many shorebirds take in about a third of their weight in food. When you see huge mixed-species flocks of shorebirds feeding on an estuary, you can view it as a tribute to the great biological productivity of those environments, and an example of the ways that evolution has managed to limit the degree to which each species must compete with others for its food.

SEE: Oystercatchers and Oysters, p. 109; MacArthur's Warblers, p. 523; Determining Diets, p. 535; How Do We Find Out About Bird Biology, p. 319. REFS: Burger and Olla, 1984; Evans et al., 1984; Wander, 1985.

Lesser Yellowlegs

Tringa flavipes Gmelin

NG–114; G–120; PE–128; PW–pl 31; AE–pl 227; AW–pl 206; AM(I)–346

			MF(?)		
?	4		I: 22–23 (?) DAYS		
	(3–4)		PRECOCIAL 2	CRUSTACEANS	GROUND
	MONOG?		F: 18–20 (?) DAYS	FISH	GLEAN
			MF		

BREEDING: Tundra, muskeg, woodland clearings, burned areas. 1? brood. **DISPLAYS**: See: Shorebird Communication, p. 139. **NEST**: Depression oft near log, snag, among burned debris, occ sheltered by veg, occ in moss, occ far from water. Lined with few decayed leaves or bits of grass under eggs. **EGGS**: Yellowish-grayish buff, marked with dark brown, wreathed. 1.7″ (42 mm). **DIET**: Mostly terrestrial and aquatic insects, also small fish, crustaceans. Nonbreeding incl worms, snails. Oft picks food from surface of water; wades to breast level. **CONSERVATION**: Winters s through West Indies, to Tierra del Fuego. **NOTES**: Very noisy on nesting grounds. Prefers drier areas for nesting than Greater Yellowlegs, but oft assoc. Young hatch synchronously. Defends winter foraging territories. One record of nest found with 6 eggs and 2 incubating birds. **ESSAYS**: Shorebird Feeding, p. 125; Shorebird Migration and Conservation, p. 119; Spacing of Wintering Shorebirds, p. 147; Temperature Regulation and Behavior, p. 149. **REFS**: Cramp and Simmons, 1983; Johnsgard, 1981; Myers and Myers, 1979.

Solitary Sandpiper

Tringa solitaria Wilson

NG–116; G–120; PE–128; PW–pl 31; AE–pl 216; AW–pl 191; AM(I)–350

			F?		
DECID	F?	4	I: 23–24 (?) DAYS		
TREE		(4–5)	PRECOCIAL 2	AQUATIC	GROUND
3.5′–40′		MONOG	F: ? DAYS	INVERTS	GLEAN
			?		

BREEDING: Taiga, muskeg. ? brood. **DISPLAYS**: See: Shorebird Communication, p. 139. **NEST**: Uses deserted, occ new, passerine nests (oft of Common Grackle, Rusty Blackbird, Cedar and Bohemian Waxwings, American Robin, Gray Jay, Eastern Kingbird), usu in conifer, occ decid tree. Pair select nest site together. If original lining gone, female may reline. Usu returns to previously used nests. **EGGS**: Greens/cream-buff, marked with dark brown, usu wreathed. 1.4″ (36 mm). **DIET**: Aquatic and terrestrial insects, spiders, worms, mollusks, crustaceans, frogs. Agitates water by trembling lead foot, presumably to stir up prey. **CONSERVATION**: Winters s to Peru, s c Argentina, and Uruguay. **NOTES**: Only female has brood patch. Breeding biology little known. Characteristically keeps wings raised briefly after landing; frequently bobs and teeters. **ESSAYS**: Shorebird Feeding, p. 125; Shorebird Migration and Conservation, p. 119; Spacing of Wintering Shorebirds, p. 147; Site Tenacity, p. 189; How Do We Find Out About Bird Biology?, p. 319; Brood Patches, p. 427. **REFS**: Cramp and Simmons, 1983; Johnsgard, 1981; Oring, 1973.

Mice and Ground-Nesting Birds

Classically rats, ground squirrels, foxes, coyotes, and other mammals have been recognized as important predators of the eggs of birds that nest on the ground. And mice long have been suspected to be major destroyers of tern eggs. Now, there is substantial evidence that these small rodents may have a significant impact on the reproductive success of shorebirds. During an intensive study of a Spotted Sandpiper population nesting on an island in a Minnesota lake, two ornithologists, Stephen Maxson and Lewis Oring, noticed that many nests contained fewer eggs than the usual clutch of four. They discovered that this was due, at least in part, to overnight damage to a single egg in the clutch, and (often) the subsequent disposal of that egg by the adult birds. Usually the damaged egg had two punctures, about as far apart as mouse incisors, and mouse droppings were often found near the nests; on several occasions, incubating sandpipers were seen chasing mice that approached their nest during the daytime. Oddly, the mice did not eat the damaged eggs, although sometimes albumin leaked from them and presumably was consumed. If the albumin was not eaten, the behavior of the mice is more difficult to understand. Also the failure of the birds to defend their eggs better at night remains to be explained. Over a three-year period, between 6 and 34 percent of the sandpiper eggs failed to hatch because of mouse damage.

Outside of the arctic and (in one report) temperate grasslands, this is the first documented evidence of small rodents like mice as enemies of birds. Since the two species of mice incriminated in the destruction of Spotted Sandpiper eggs are widespread and common in North America, mouse predation on eggs, and perhaps young, of ground-nesting birds may be more important than has been thought previously.

SEE: Empty Shells, p. 165; Polyandry in the Spotted Sandpiper, p. 131; Sandpipers, Social Systems, and Territoriality, p. 155; The Decline of Eastern Songbirds, p. 495; Gulls Are Attracted to Their Predators, p. 169. REF: Maxson and Oring, 1978.

Bird Biologist—William Bartram

Alexander Wilson (p. 277) and John James Audubon (p. 413) are known as the fathers of North American ornithology; William Bartram (1739–1823) is known as the grandfather. Bartram traveled through Florida, Georgia, and South Carolina observing and making notes on the avifauna. His *Travels through North and South Carolina, Georgia, East and West Florida* contained information on nesting, migration, and other aspects of bird biology. Above all, Bartram helped and encouraged Wilson in the production of the great classic *American Ornithology*.

REF: Kastner, 1986.

Spotted Sandpiper

Actitis macularia Linnaeus

NG–116; G–124; PE–132; PW–pl 32; AE–pl 215; AW–pl 192; AM(I)–354

MF

4
(1–4)
POLYAND

M
I: 20–24 DAYS
PRECOCIAL 2
F: 17–21 DAYS
M

AQUATIC
INVERTS

BREEDING: Wide variety of habitats: semiopen veg from sea level to alpine near water. Usu 2–3, exceptionally to 5 broods. **DISPLAYS:** See: Shorebird Communication, p. 139. **NEST:** Elevated site in grass, among rocks, within moss, forbs, shrubs, tangle on slope, in wooded areas near log, etc. Bulkier in n. Of dry moss, lined with grass, moss, occ feathers. **EGGS:** Brownish/greenish/pinkish-buff, marked with dark brown. 1.3″ (32 mm). **DIET:** Largely flying insects, also worms, fish, crustaceans, mollusks, carrion. Deftly captures flying insects; also picks from water's surface. **CONSERVATION:** Winters s to n Chile, n Argentina, Uruguay. **NOTES:** Usu nests solitary, occ loosely colonial. Polyandrous females arrive before males on breeding grounds; males also defend territories. Experienced females have more mates, and produce more eggs, chicks, and fledglings than inexperienced females. Female lays up to 5 complete clutches; male provides most or all care for only a single nest and brood. Most consistent source of egg loss in 10-yr MN study was mice. Constantly bobs and teeters on ground. Can swim, dive, perch on wires. Roosts in loose flocks. **ESSAYS:** Polyandry in Spotted Sandpiper, p. 131; Polyandry, p. 133; Mice and Ground-Nesting Birds, p. 129; Spacing of Wintering Shorebirds, p. 147. **REFS:** Cramp and Simmons, 1983; Oring et al., 1983.

Wandering Tattler

Heteroscelus incanus Gmelin

NG–118; G–124; PW–pl 31; AW–pl 226; AM(I)–352

?

4
MONOG?

MF
I: 23–25 DAYS
PRECOCIAL 2
F: ? DAYS
MF

CRUSTACEANS

BREEDING: Mountainous, hilly habitat usu among scrubby veg along rocky, mossy streams, lakes, in wet meadows, creek bottoms, occ in clearings away from water. ? brood. **DISPLAYS:** See: Shorebird Communication, p. 139. **NEST:** On gravel bar of mountain stream. Unlined or compactly lined with fine roots, bits of dry leaves, twigs. **EGGS:** Greenish, marked with dark brown, wreathed. 1.7″ (43 mm). **DIET:** Aquatic insects, amphipods, mollusks, crabs. In migration, crustaceans, marine worms, mollusks. Oft wades submerging bill or head. **CONSERVATION:** Winters along Pacific coast to Peru; on rocky coasts. **NOTES:** Presumably named by hunters for annoying alarm call. Female does not flush easily from nest. Habitually bobs and teeters while foraging. Feet unwebbed but can swim, even as chicks. Usu only associates with other Wandering Tattlers, occ forming groups, but usu solitary. Flies out calling to meet intruders at nesting ground, otherwise quiet. First eggs and nest not discovered until 1912. **ESSAYS:** Sandpipers, Social Systems, and Territoriality, p. 155; Shorebird Feeding, p. 125; Shorebird Migration and Conservation, p. 119; Spacing of Wintering Shorebirds, p. 147; Temperature Regulation and Behavior, p. 149. **REFS:** Johnsgard, 1981; Weeden, 1965.

Polyandry in the Spotted Sandpiper

The most widespread sandpiper in North America is the Spotted, and it has one of the most unusual breeding systems found in birds—polyandry (one female mating with more than one male). Unlike most sandpipers, the Spotted has invaded temperate areas to breed. Apparently it has found polyandry to be the most successful reproductive strategy for taking advantage of the relatively long breeding season (compared with the season in the arctic and subarctic breeding areas used by most members of this family). The Spotted Sandpiper can be characterized as a "pioneering species" that quickly and frequently colonizes new sites, emigrates in response to reproductive failure, breeds at an early age, lives a relatively short time (breeding females live an average of only 3.7 years), lays many eggs per female per year, and has relatively low nest success.

Initiation of breeding in the Spotted Sandpiper is influenced by the abundance of insects, and cessation of breeding normally occurs abruptly in early July, in anticipation of the decline of insect populations later in the month (hatchlings from later clutches would starve). Females arrive first on the breeding grounds and must compete for males as they appear. Their vigorous displays occasionally lead to physical combat. Characteristically, females defend territories encompassing the individual territories of their male consorts. Ornithologist Lewis Oring and his colleagues have uncovered fascinating details of Spotted Sandpiper breeding biology through their long-term study of an island population in Minnesota.

The maximum clutch size in these sandpipers is four eggs, each of which weighs about 20 percent of the adult female's body weight. Apparently, it is physiologically impossible for a female to increase the clutch size beyond four, but during the six-to-seven-week breeding season she can lay up to five complete clutches of four eggs each. Each clutch requires about three weeks of incubation, so a female would be hard-pressed to hatch and raise even two broods. Multiple mates enable a female to increase her reproductive output by freeing her from the responsibility for incubation and care of the young.

Nonetheless, because of a chronic shortage of available males, females produce an average of only eight eggs per breeding season, although physiologically capable of producing twenty. That explains why females compete so vigorously for mates; indeed, it is fighting among females that limits the number of breeding females on the island. Early in the season there are fewer males than females present. As more males arrive over the following few weeks, the ratio of available males to females becomes more even but only temporarily. When males begin to incubate clutches, they are effectively removed from the pool of prospective mates and, at the same time, the females completing clutches are available again for remating. During the second half of the breeding season, it is not unusual to find six or seven females for every potentially available male.

Wood Sandpiper

Tringa glareola Linnaeus

NG–118; G–120; AM(I)–348

TREE	?	4 (3–4) MONOG	MF I: 22–23 DAYS PRECOCIAL 2 F: 28–30 DAYS M –F	INVERTS	GROUND GLEAN

BREEDING: Taiga along pond edges. 1 brood. **DISPLAYS:** See: Shorebird Communication, p. 139. **NEST:** Usu moss depression where dwarf birch, willow, etc., offer cover or in hummock on dry ground. Lined with grass. Also uses abandoned cup nests of thrush, shrike. Occ reused. **EGGS:** Light-green/creamy-white/buff, marked with reddish-brown, wreathed. 1.5″ (38 mm). **DIET:** Aquatic and terrestrial insects, worms, spiders. In migration, mollusks, fish, frogs, small amount of plant material. Occ forages by sweeping bill from side to side in water and by jumping from ground to capture flying insects. **CONSERVATION:** Winters in Old World. **NOTES:** Appears loosely colonial when nesting in low-lying areas. Female deserts male and brood 7–10 days posthatch, occ sooner. **ESSAYS:** Sandpipers, Social Systems, and Territoriality, p. 155; Shorebird Feeding, p. 125; Shorebird Migration and Conservation, p. 119; Spacing of Wintering Shorebirds, p. 147; Parental Care, p. 555; Site Tenacity, p. 189. **REF:** Cramp and Simmons, 1983.

Wilson's Phalarope

Phalaropus tricolor Vieillot

NG–120; G–126; PE–136; PW–pl 25; AE–pl 207; AW–pl 203; AM(I)–408

M		4 (3–4) MONOG (POLYAND)	M I: 16–21 DAYS PRECOCIAL 2 F: ? DAYS M	SEEDS	PROBES

BREEDING: Freshwater marshes, sloughs, wet meadows, islands; occ saline habitat. 1, occ 2 broods. **DISPLAYS:** Aerial courtship: chase of male by female; swimming near male, female expands neck feathers, stretches neck, gives repeated "chugging" call. **NEST:** Open or well concealed in sparse veg on damp ground, oft surrounded by water. Lined with grass, occ densely. Male makes several scrapes (female chooses one), lines scrape after first egg laid. **EGGS:** Buff, marked with brown, black. 1.3″ (33 mm). **DIET:** Aquatic insects, few crustaceans, amphipods, spiders; seeds of aquatic plants. Spears prey at or near surface (spins up to 60 revolutions/minute stabbing water on each turn). **CONSERVATION:** Winters mostly in w S.A. on altiplano of Bolivia, Chile, Argentina, usu in shallow, highly saline and alkaline lakes. Threatened by wetland loss in breeding range and migration. **NOTES:** Occ loosely colonial. Sex role reversal, occ with sequential polyandry. Male, female perform distraction display. Paired males more aggressive than unpaired. Oft feeds in assoc with other species, esp American Avocet, Northern Shoveler; feeding with latter 3× as effective as feeding alone. **ESSAYS:** Sexual Selection, p. 251; Polyandry, p. 133; Migration, p. 183; Distraction Displays, p. 115; Commensal Feeding, p. 35. **REFS:** Howe, 1975; Kagarise, 1979; Mahoney and Jehl, 1985; Reynolds et al., 1986.

This shortage of males, rather than any scarcity of food resources, limits the reproductive effort of female Spotted Sandpipers. Not surprisingly, experienced females acquire more mates, lay more eggs, produce more chicks, and successfully fledge more young than do inexperienced females.

Spotted Sandpipers thus forgo the advantages of having two parents care for eggs and chicks. At least in the study population, however, that does not seem to affect the fledging rate greatly, and the Spotted Sandpipers' reproductive strategy seems to be highly successful.

SEE: Polyandry, p. 133; Monogamy, p. 597; Polygyny, p. 443; Promiscuity, p. 145; Sandpipers, Social Systems and Territoriality, p. 155; Spacing of Wintering Shorebirds, p. 147. REFS: Lank et al., 1985; Oring et al., 1983.

Red-necked Phalarope "spinning." Phalaropes have a characteristic mode of feeding— they spin like tops on the water surface, presumably to stir the bottom and cause food items to rise from the bottom and become accessible. The dense breast plumage of phalaropes traps a great deal of air, and makes them very buoyant, so they have difficulty dabbling, which they occasionally do.

Polyandry

The mating of one female with more than one male while each male mates with only one female is known as polyandry (literally, "many males"). It is a rare mating system, occurring in less than one percent of all bird species, and is found mostly in shorebirds. Polyandry is often accompanied by a reversal of sexual roles in which males perform all or most parental duties and females compete for mates. The common pattern of sexual dimorphism is often reversed in polyandrous birds: the female is often larger and more colorful than the male. This reversal confused early biologists and led Audubon to mislabel males and females in all of his phalarope plates.

Two types of polyandry have been documented: simultaneous polyandry and sequential polyandry. In simultaneous polyandry, each female holds a large territory containing the smaller nesting territories of two or

Red-necked Phalarope

Phalaropus lobatus Linnaeus

NG–120; G–126; PE–136; PW–pl 25; AE–pl 206; AW–pl 205; AM(I)–410

M

4
(2–4)
POLYAND

M
I: 19 (17–21) DAYS
PRECOCIAL 2
F: 20 DAYS
M

SEEDS

PROBES

BREEDING: Grass-sedge borders of pond, lake. 1, occ 2 broods.   **DISPLAYS:** Female solicits male with low call, crouches on water as male hovers before mounting. See: Shorebird Communication, p. 139.   **NEST:** In tussock or sunk in moss, oft sheltered by low veg. Lined with few bits of grass, leaves. Constructed by male accompanied by female, who chooses scrape in which to lay.   **EGGS:** Olive, marked with browns. 1.1″ (29 mm).   **DIET:** Aquatic insects, crustaceans, mollusks, zooplankton.   **CONSERVATION:** Wintering mostly pelagic off s S.A.   **NOTES:** Sex role reversal; sequential polyandry in ca. 10% of females. Non-territorial. Only males have brood patches. Female deserts as male begins incubation. Young can swim immediately upon hatching. Brooding males occ adopt orphans. Phalaropes are most pelagic of shorebirds: have salt glands; air trapped in feathers of belly keeps buoyant; submerging difficult, no diving. Most abundant, widely distributed phalarope. Late summer 10s to 100s of thousands assemble at mouth of Bay of Fundy. Formerly known as Northern Phalarope.   **ESSAYS:** Migration, p. 183; Sexual Selection, p. 251; Polyandry, p. 133; Salt Glands, p. 29; Pelagic Birds, p. 657; Hormones and Nest Building, p. 547; Brood Patches, p. 427.   **REFS:** Cramp and Simmons, 1983; Reynolds, 1987; Reynolds et al., 1986.

Red Phalarope

Phalaropus fulicaria Linnaeus

NG–120; G–126; PE–136; PW–pl 25; AE–pl 208; AW–pl 204; AM(I)–412

MF

4
(2–4)
POLYAND

M
I: 18–20 DAYS
PRECOCIAL 2
F: 16–21 DAYS
M

INSECTS
SEEDS

PROBES

BREEDING: Coastal sedge-moss tundra with freshwater ponds. Usu 2 broods.   **DISPLAYS:** Courtship: circle flight by female to attract male; swimming female follows male with head drawn in between her shoulders. See: Shorebird Communication, p. 139.   **NEST:** Usu near water, on sand, moss, lichen, grass, oft lined with grass, moss; occ built up, saucer-shaped. Both sexes make scrapes, female selects one in which to lay, male lines it.   **EGGS:** Olive buff, occ olive brown, marked with dark brown, wreathed. 1.3″ (32 mm).   **DIET:** Mostly aquatic insects; at sea, fish, marine inverts. Oft forages by spinning up to 40 revolutions/minute. Occ leaps from ground to catch flying insects.   **CONSERVATION:** Wintering mostly pelagic off coast of N.A. and S.A. s to Patagonia, Falklands.   **NOTES:** Loosely colonial. Sex role reversal with sequential polyandry. Only males have brood patches. Most pelagic of phalaropes: have salt glands; air trapped in belly feathers maintains buoyancy; submerging difficult, no diving. Known in Europe as Grey Phalarope.   **ESSAYS:** Sexual Selection, p. 251; Polyandry, p. 133; Migration, p. 183; Salt Glands, p. 29; Pelagic Birds, p. 657; Brood Patches, p. 427.   **REFS:** Cramp and Simmons, 1983; Kistchinski, 1975; Mayfield, 1978b; Schamel and Tracy, 1977.

more males who care for the eggs and tend the young. In our region, only Northern Jacanas characteristically practice this form of polyandry. Females may mate with all of their consorts in one day and provide each male with help in defending his territory. A female will not copulate with a mate while their eggs are being incubated or during the first six weeks of the life of the chicks. If a clutch is lost, she will quickly copulate with the broodless male and lay a new batch of eggs within a few days.

A very rare variation on the preceding theme is "cooperative simultaneous polyandry," in which more than one male mates with a single female and the single clutch of mixed parentage is reared cooperatively by the female and her several mates. This arrangement occurs in some populations of Harris' Hawks and occasionally in Acorn Woodpecker groups.

In sequential polyandry (the most typical form of this mating system), a female mates with a male, lays eggs, and then terminates the relationship with that male, leaving him to incubate the eggs while she goes off to repeat this sequence with another male. Spotted Sandpipers, Red-necked and Red Phalaropes are examples of sequentially polyandrous species that breed in North America. A possible evolutionary precursor of sequential polyandry is found in Temminck's Stint, Little Stint, Mountain Plover, and Sanderling. In these species, each female lays a clutch of eggs that is incubated by the male, followed by a second clutch that she incubates herself. These two-clutch systems can be envisioned as a step toward the sort of sequential polyandry seen in the Spotted Sandpiper, but females of that species never incubate a clutch alone unless their mate is killed—even when resources are abundant.

There is an interesting sidelight to the story of polyandry in birds. In polygynous mammals (one male mating with several females) such as lions and gorillas, infanticide can occur when a new male takes over a harem. By killing the young of the previous harem ruler, the new male presumably brings females back into heat. This gives him a chance to increase his own reproductive contributions and, perhaps, to reduce use of resources by unrelated offspring. In Northern Jacanas it has been reported that females taking over the territories of other females occasionally practice infanticide, destroying the offspring of previous females. The males attempt to defend their broods (which represent their genes, but not those of the new female), just as lionesses attempt to defend their cubs from infanticidal male lions taking over a pride. However, the actual killing of young has not been observed—only empty nests. If substantiated, this behavior in jacanas is the first known example of infanticide being used as a reproductive strategy by females.

SEE: Polyandry in the Spotted Sandpiper, p. 131; Monogamy, p. 597; Polygyny, p. 443; Cooperative Breeding, p. 283; Leks, p. 259; Natural Selection, p. 237. REFS: Erckmann, 1983; Oring, 1982, 1986.

Short-billed Dowitcher

NG–122; G–124; PE–124; PW–pl 31; AE–pl 212; AW–pl 212; AM(I)–402

	MF(?)	4	MF	INSECTS	
		(3–4)	I: 21 DAYS	SEEDS	
		MONOG?	PRECOCIAL 2		
			F: ? DAYS		
			M		

BREEDING: Grass or moss tundra, wet meadows, bogs in boreal forests. ? broods. **DISPLAYS:** See: Shorebird Communication, p. 139. **NEST:** In clump of moss. Scantily lined with fine twigs, leaves, fine grass. **EGGS:** Light olive buff or brown, marked with brown. 1.6″ (41 mm). **DIET:** Aquatic insects, mollusks, crustaceans, marine worms, spiders; seeds of aquatic plants. On coast, also takes crab eggs. Systematically stabs mud. **CONSERVATION:** Winters s to c Peru, e c Brazil. Formerly popular game bird; populations were severely depleted. **NOTES:** More commonly associated with salt water than is Long-billed Dowitcher. Male reportedly rolls eggs to new site if nest threatened. Males outnumber females. Relatively unsuspecting and approachable. Adept swimmer. Forms mixed flocks with sandpipers, plovers. **ESSAYS:** Shorebird Feeding, p. 125; Spacing of Wintering Shorebirds, p. 147; Shorebird Migration and Conservation, p. 119; Sandpipers, Social Systems, and Territoriality, p. 155; Mixed-Species Flocking, p. 433. **REFS:** Cramp and Simmons, 1983; Johnsgard, 1981; Miller et al., 1983.

Long-billed Dowitcher

NG–122; G–124; PE–124; PW–pl 31; AE–pl 213; AW–pl 213; AM(I)–404

	MF(?)	4	M –F	INSECTS	
		MONOG?	I: 20–21 DAYS	SEEDS	
			PRECOCIAL 2		
			F: ? DAYS		
			M –F		

BREEDING: Grass tundra, wet meadows. ? broods. **DISPLAYS:** See: Shorebird Communication, p. 139. **NEST:** On small rise in wet meadow, usu near shallow water. Scrape in decayed grass or moss. Bottom oft wet. Meagerly lined with withered leaves, grass. **EGGS:** Brownish or greenish, marked with brown, wreathed. 1.7″ (42 mm). **DIET:** Aquatic insects, mollusks, crustaceans, marine worms, spiders; seeds of aquatic plants. Forages in shallow fresh water at margin, probing mud, oft immersing head. **CONSERVATION:** Winters s through Mexico (mostly w portions) to Guatemala. **NOTES:** Pair initially incubate, later only male. Young can be herded by hovering adult. More commonly associated with fresh water than is Short-billed Dowitcher. **ESSAYS:** Shorebird Feeding, p. 125; Spacing of Wintering Shorebirds, p. 147; Shorebird Migration and Conservation, p. 119; Sandpipers, Social Systems, and Territoriality, p. 155; Who Incubates?, p. 27. **REFS:** Cramp and Simmons, 1983; Johnsgard, 1981; Miller et al., 1984.

Metallic Poisons

Hunters annually kill millions of ducks and geese intentionally with shotguns. Sadly, they also kill a large number of these birds accidentally. Lead pellets that do not end up in the hunters' targets plummet into ponds, lakes, and marshes where they are often ingested by aquatic birds. It has been estimated that 1400 pellets (about half a pound) are left behind for every bird carried out. A single pellet swallowed with food or taken as grit and ground in the gizzard can introduce enough lead into the bloodstream to kill a duck. Such poisoning of birds by lead ingestion has occurred on a large scale—over 100,000 Mallards died in Illinois in 1948; more than 500 Whistling Swans were killed in a North Carolina refuge in 1974. In all some 1.5 to 3 million waterfowl die from lead poisoning annually. Since 1980 more than sixty Bald Eagles, which prey on waterfowl, have acquired the poison from them and have also died.

Mallards, Northern Pintails, Redheads, Ring-necked Ducks, Canvasbacks, Lesser Scaups and Canada Geese seem to suffer the heaviest mortality because they eat hard seeds and grains similar in appearance to lead shot, because they dig with their bills for tubers and seeds of aquatic vegetation in areas where the pellets are lodged, or (as in the Mallard) have high carbohydrate diets. Northern Shovelers, Blue-winged Teal, Green-winged Teal, and Wood Ducks all take softer food, forage without digging, or have high protein diets, and have lower mortality rates. Poisoned waterfowl show characteristic behaviors, including holding wings in a "roof-shaped" or drooped position, a walking with staggering gait, showing reluctance to fly, seeking isolation, or remaining behind after others migrate.

In the United States, the lead poisoning problem has become sufficiently serious for the Fish and Wildlife Service to announce a gradual ban on lead shot beginning in the 1987–88 season, making its use illegal in the United States by 1991. Steel substitutes are not as desirable from the point of view of ballistics and shotgun barrel wear, however, and it is not clear whether the ban will be instituted. Clearly, it is in the interest of both birders and hunters that this problem be resolved. Weights used by anglers also cause lead poisoning of waterfowl, but probably have minor impact in comparison with lead shot.

Although lead is the major metallic toxin threatening North American bird populations, mercury is another source of poisoning. It may be ingested by eating contaminated fish or along with seeds that have been treated with pesticides containing the element. The use of organic mercury pesticides on rice fields was responsible for extirpating White Storks from Japan; substantial mercury pollution of lakes and streams already exists on our continent, adding to the serious stresses already placed on bird populations by other human activities.

SEE: DDT and Birds, p. 21; Birds and Oil, p. 207; Botulism, p. 69; Disease and Parasitism, p. 399. REF: Sanderson and Bellrose, 1986.

Stilt Sandpiper

Calidris himantopus Bonaparte

NG–124; G–122; PE–128; PW–pl 31; AE–pl 230; AM(I)–398

| M | 4 MONOG | MF
I: 19–21 DAYS
PRECOCIAL 2
F: 17–18 DAYS
MF | AQUATIC PLANTS | |

BREEDING: Sedge tundra near water, usu near wooded border of taiga. 1 brood. **DISPLAYS:** Male display flight: sequential hovering over spots in territory; flaps wings continually while singing, chattering, and calling. See: Shorebird Communication, p. 139. **NEST:** Near water, on higher dry area, partly concealed by tuft of veg. Lined with few decayed leaves, grass. Male initiates scrapes; female chooses. Site oft perennial. **EGGS:** Ivory-yellow/olive-buff, marked with brown, some wreathed. 1.4″ (36 mm). **DIET:** Incl worms, insect larvae, mollusks; seeds, roots, leaves of aquatic plants. In winter, feeds with dowitchers in tight flocks, oft wading belly-deep. Oft immerses head when probing substrate. **CONSERVATION:** Winters s through S.A. but mostly from Bolivia, s c Brazil s to n Chile, coastal Argentina. **NOTES:** Larger females select smaller males as mates. Both sexes have brood patches. Male incubates during day, female at night. Female leaves male and brood after hatching; male deserts chicks after 14 days. Like tattlers, lift wings slightly upon alighting. Prefer sheltered areas in migration and in winter. **ESSAYS:** Shorebird Feeding, p. 125; Wintering Shorebirds, p. 147; Shorebird Migration, p. 119; Sandpiper Social Systems, p. 155. **REFS:** Johnsgard, 1981; Miller, 1983.

Common Snipe

Gallinago gallinago Linnaeus

NG–124; G–126; PE–124; PW–pl 31; AE–pl 255; AW–pl 214; AM(I)–406

| F | 4 (3–4) MONOG? | F
I: 18–20 DAYS
PRECOCIAL 2
F: 19–20 DAYS
MF | EARTHWORMS | |

BREEDING: Wet grass habitat from tundra to lowland, hilly regions. 1 brood. **DISPLAYS:** Male spreads outer tail feathers during aerial dives making characteristic fluttering sound; also performed during migration and in winter. Bleating flight over home range. See: Shorebird Communication, p. 139. **NEST:** In small clump of grass under low veg, occ concealed by bent-over grass. Molded of short, dead grass, leaves, or moss. Lining of fine grass. Occ compact and cup-like, of fine grass. Female builds 4–5 scrapes, molding with breast. **EGGS:** Brownish/olive-buff, marked with dark brown, wreathed. 1.5″ (39 mm). **DIET:** Insects, crustaceans, mollusks; little veg. Forms pellets of indigestible parts. Heavy drinker. **CONSERVATION:** Winters s through S.A. Popular game bird. **NOTES:** Solitary and secretive. Females initially promiscuous, become monogamous when nest site selected. Not easily flushed from nest; explosive noisy takeoff when flushed. Distraction display performed. Adults divide brood and tend them separately. Pliable bill can bend, hunt by feel; to swallow prey, serrated bill and tongue spikes move food forward. Probable fidelity to wintering grounds. Formerly Wilson's Snipe. **ESSAYS:** Nonvocal Sounds, p. 313; Pellets, p. 297; Displays, p. 115; Shorebird Feeding, p. 125. **REFS:** Arnold and Jirovec, 1978; Cramp and Simmons, 1983; Tuck, 1972.

Shorebird Communication

Communication in shorebirds, as in other birds, can be very confusing to the observer. Their displays are extremely varied and often complex, and, above all, the meaning of both displays and calls appears to depend upon the ecological and social contexts in which they are given. During winter, shorebirds are often found in flocks in estuarine mud flats and other open habitats. When breeding they usually nest on the ground, most often in the open. Thus highly visible, they are especially suitable subjects for studies of avian visual communication. Indeed, plumage color and pattern are perhaps the simplest bases of shorebird communication, and in the breeding season usually suffice to signal a bird's gender.

While their acoustic communication is not as well studied as that of passerines, shorebirds also signal extensively with sound. Shorebird vocalizations tend to match the context of their open habitats. Loud, low-frequency, repeated sounds are used during aerial displays, as territorial signals and to attract mates. Oystercatchers and others, for example, have evolved loud, piercing calls that carry over the crashing surf of rocky coasts. Such sounds will remain recognizable over greater distances than more complex, high-frequency songs—they are less attenuated by distance and their repetitiousness helps to differentiate them from background noise. Exchanges between parents and offspring at the nest and other short-distance acoustic communication are not, of course, subject to the same constraints.

The sounds produced by shorebirds vary greatly, both from individual to individual and in the same individual in different situations. For instance, many species of calidridine sandpipers (members of the tribe Calidridini, which includes our smallest sandpipers) produce two distinct types of call: a trill lasting almost a second, and a much shortened, frequency-modulated call. Edward H. Miller, who has studied acoustic communication in shorebirds extensively, reports that one male Least Sandpiper rarely trilled, while another male almost never gave the short call. Furthermore, the mix of trills and short calls uttered by a single sandpiper would change as the individual changed its direction of flight toward or away from an intruder.

Shorebirds also communicate with a wide range of visual displays, some aerial, some on the ground. Aerial displays are especially suited to communication in the open habitats, since the display can be viewed without obstruction over relatively long distances (woodland birds make much less use of aerial displays). The aerial display of an old-world shorebird, the Northern Lapwing (found casually in our area), has been studied in great detail. The male Lapwing starts a typical display sequence with "butterfly flight" (slow, deep wingbeats), followed by a zigzag flight in which the body is rotated from side to side around its long axis. During that phase, the bird produces a humming sound with its specially modified outer primary feathers. Then the Lapwing flies low and soundlessly with slow, shallow wingbeats, finishing that phase with a steep climb. At the end of the climb

American Woodcock
Scolopax minor Gmelin

NG–124; G–126; PE–124; AE–pl 256; AM(I)–408

		F	EARTHWORMS	
		I: 20–21 DAYS		
F	4	PRECOCIAL 2	INSECTS	
	(3–5)	F: 14 DAYS		
	PROMISC	F		

BREEDING: Moist woodland, mixed forest, thickets along boggy streams, occ wet meadows, abandoned fields, conifer plantations. 1 brood. **DISPLAYS:** Male begins advertising flight when still on wintering ground; oft performed at night on breeding ground, ending in "falling-leaf" flight to alight on ground and walk stiff-legged to female. See: Shorebird Communication, p. 139. **NEST:** Variable. Within 300' of display area; under brush, tall weeds, tree, or in rocky hollow, oft near support. Usu amid abundant fallen leaves. Lined with dead leaves, conifer needles, occ rimmed with twigs. **EGGS:** Pinkish-buff/cinnamon, marked with brown, somewhat wreathed. 1.5" (38 mm) (large for size of bird). **DIET:** Eats more than its weight in earthworms daily; if unavailable, consumes other soil inverts. **CONSERVATION:** Winters within U.S. Popular game bird. Pesticides pose problem in parts of range. **NOTES:** Nocturnal, solitary. Performs distraction display. Three outer primaries modified to produce whistle in flight. Shares feeding ground with other woodcocks. Foot stamping helps locate prey. "Poke holes" identify feeding spots. **ESSAYS:** Hawk-Eyed, p. 229; Transporting Young, p. 103; Nonvocal Sounds, p. 313; Distraction Displays, p. 115; Promiscuity, p. 145. **REFS:** Gregg and Hale, 1977; Rabe et al, 1983; Sheldon, 1967.

Black Turnstone
Supersp #12
Arenaria melanocephala Vigors

NG–126; G–128; PW–pl 25; AW–pl 221; AM(I)–370

		MF		
		I: 21–22 DAYS		
MF(?)	4	PRECOCIAL 2	BERRIES	
	MONOG	F: ? DAYS		
		MF		

BREEDING: Coastal salt-grass tundra. 1 brood. **DISPLAYS:** Male's high whistling flight (probably result of feathers resisting wind) continues through incubation. Female zigzag flight usu brings her back to starting position. See: Shorebird Communication, p. 139. **NEST:** Depression in flattened dead grass or mud on grass-covered point or islet, oft near water. Lined with bits of grass. **EGGS:** Variable; yellowish-olive, marked with brown, wreathed. 1.6" (41 mm). **DIET:** Barnacles, snails, mollusks, crustaceans. **CONSERVATION:** Winters s along rocky coasts to s Baja, c Sonora. **NOTES:** Nests colonially. Both sexes have brood patches. Forages quickly, building small piles of detritus. Aggressive at foraging spot, defending from all. Cryptic when motionless, but usu in constant motion. Frequently wet; oft bathes. **ESSAYS:** Color of Birds, p. 111; Shorebird Feeding, p. 125; Spacing of Wintering Shorebirds, p. 147; Shorebird Migration and Conservation, p. 119; Sandpipers, Social Systems, and Territoriality, p. 155; Brood Patches, p. 427; Coloniality, p. 173; Bathing and Dusting, p. 429. **REF:** Johnsgard, 1981.

there is a period of straight flight during which two distinct "motifs" of its song are sung, and a third started. The third motif is finished during a steep bank and vertical dive. The bird may then repeat some of the earlier display components.

Other shorebirds have similar components in their aerial displays. As examples, oystercatchers may perform butterfly flights, Solitary Sandpipers do low display flights, and Common Snipe include dives in their high display flights. Aerial displays are very diverse, with variation in height, direction (straight, circling, undulating, etc.), wingbeat amplitude (shallow, deep), wingbeat frequency (rapid to glide), patterns of plumage display (especially tails or wings spread or flashed), calling during flight, and post-landing behavior (deliberately exaggerated wing-folding, strutting). Descent from flight displays, with the frequent production of nonvocal sounds, is thought to convey a great deal of information about the signaler's change of behavior.

As previously mentioned, the problem with interpreting shorebird aerial displays is that they are used in a wide variety of situations. For example, the Lapwing display may occur in response to predators, when a male returns to its territory, in response to other males, in response to females, and "spontaneously" (when there is no obvious triggering stimulus). Furthermore, the precise form of the display varies with the stage of the breeding cycle, the time of day, the weather, and the audience.

Context seems to play a similar role in giving meaning to the ground displays of shorebirds. For instance, five different displays used by Black-tailed Godwits in aggressive encounters have been studied in detail. They include two "upright" displays in which the legs are stretched, one with the back plumage smooth or slightly ruffled, the other with it ruffled. In each, the wings, tail, and bill are in different positions. The nonupright displays are "forward" (body almost horizontal, legs not stretched, neck extended, plumage very ruffled, bill usually down); "crouch" (body horizontal, legs deeply bent, neck withdrawn, plumage ruffled or smoothed, bill in various positions); and "tilt" (body slanted forward with breast near ground, legs deeply bent, neck withdrawn, plumage smooth, bill forward).

Analysis of these five displays and their variations revealed no simple association with attack or retreat behavior. Neither was any component of the displays (e.g., ruffling of plumage, lowering of bill) clearly a sign of attack or retreat. Again it appears that details of the context in which the displays occur (rather than the attack-retreat dichotomy) are required for their interpretation. Indeed, attacking Black-tailed Godwits within six feet of their opponents showed a different array of displays from those of godwits separated by a dozen feet or more.

Often the same general elements are used in both aggressive and sexual displays, so that their interpretation depends entirely on the audience or the stage of the breeding cycle. Male Least Sandpipers use a forward tilt, elevated tail, and wing-up display when approaching other individuals of either sex. Courtship displays are differentiated from antagonistic ones only

Ruddy Turnstone

Arenaria interpres Linnaeus

NG–126; G–128; PE–118; PW–pl 25; AE–pl 196; AW–pl 186; AM(I)–368

F   4   MF   AQUATIC   PROBES

MF
I: 22–24 DAYS
PRECOCIAL 2
F: 19–21 DAYS
MF

4
(3–4)
MONOG

AQUATIC
INVERTS
BERRIES

BREEDING: Dry, dwarf-shrub tundra, usu near water. Attracted to gull and tern breeding colonies. 1 brood. **DISPLAYS:** See: Shorebird Communication, p. 139. **NEST:** Usu on open tundra, rarely in rock crevice or in veg. Lined with withered leaves, moss, grass, or seaweed. **EGGS:** Olive-buff/olive-green, marked with browns, black, wreathed. 1.6″ (41 mm). **DIET:** Incl worms, mollusks, snails, crustaceans, bird eggs (esp terns). In addition to flipping and turning over stones, "roots" around in beach detritus. **CONSERVATION:** Winters s along rocky coasts to Tierra del Fuego. **NOTES:** Known to take eggs of other birds, incl House Sparrow; would eat booby and frigatebird eggs, too, but shell too tough. Pair bond occ lasts >1 year. Male pugnacious at nest. Both sexes have brood patches. Female leaves before young fledge. Age of first breeding 2 years. Forage singly or in small mixed flocks; defend temporary feeding territories when prey are patchily distributed but clumped. In spring migration, will dig down 2″ to uncover buried horseshoe crab eggs in Delaware Bay. **ESSAYS:** Shorebird Feeding, p. 125; Shorebird Migration and Conservation, p. 119; Sandpipers, Social Systems, and Territoriality, p. 155; Spacing of Wintering Shorebirds, p. 147; Brood Patches, p. 427. **REFS:** Brearey and Hilden, 1985; Cramp and Simmons, 1983; Sullivan, 1986.

Surfbird

Aphriza virgata Gmelin

NG–126; G–128; PW–pl 32; AW–pl 222; AM(I)–370

MF   4   MF   AQUATIC   PROBES

MF
I: ? DAYS
PRECOCIAL 2
F: ? DAYS
MF

4
MONOG

AQUATIC
INVERTS
SEEDS

BREEDING: Open rocky habitat above treeline in interior mountains. 1 brood. **DISPLAYS:** Males have three common types of breeding vocalizations: songs, rhythmically repeated calls, and "laughs." Male display flight performed with long gliding phases (no hovering) while calling. See: Shorebird Communication, p. 139. **NEST:** In open, natural erosional depressions on dry, rocky ground covered with 2″ high veg. Lined with grayish-green lichen and moss on sides, dead leaves on bottom. **EGGS:** Buff, marked with brown. 1.7″ (44 mm). **DIET:** Incl spiders, snails, mussels, barnacles, crustaceans; very few seeds. **CONSERVATION:** Winters s along rocky Pacific coast to Straits of Magellan. **NOTES:** Breeding biology and behavior virtually unknown. Nest and eggs discovered in mid-1920s. **ESSAYS:** Sandpipers, Social Systems, and Territoriality, p. 155; Shorebird Feeding, p. 125; Spacing of Wintering Shorebirds, p. 147; Shorebird Migration and Conservation, p. 119; How Do We Find Out About Bird Biology?, p. 319. **REFS:** Johnsgard, 1981; Miller et al., 1987.

by being more slowly paced and more stereotyped (showing less variation). Male Killdeer may do a "forward-tipped, neck-extended" display during which the legs are often kicked backward (scraping), when defending their territories against other males, then advertising for mates, during nest building, and as a precopulatory display.

Certain kinds of display show constancy of context not only within but also between species. For example, Semipalmated, Mountain, and Little Ringed Plovers (the latter a European species similar to the Semipalmated), among many others, all show a similar threat posture in which the body is kept horizontal, the flank feathers are spread over the closed wings, and the head withdrawn, giving the individual a flattened appearance.

To make sense of communication in shorebirds, careful notes should be made of the detailed form of the communication itself as well as of the context in which it occurs. Keep records of the physical environment (season, time of day, weather, illumination, background noise, etc.), the state of the communicating bird itself (sex, maturity, breeding condition, activity before, during, and after communicating—feeding, flying, nest building, resting, etc.), and the identity of birds of the same species, other bird species, or other animals to whom the communication might be directed (for instance, conspecifics of the same or opposite sex, individuals of closely related species that might compete for resources, potential predators). Pay particular attention to subtle movements, such as bobbing of the head, a slight change in the angle at which the body is held, or an extension of the wings before they are folded after landing. These may seem insignificant, but they may carry important messages for other birds.

SEE: Visual Displays, p. 5; Duck Displays, p. 63; Environmental Acoustics, p. 441; Spacing of Wintering Shorebirds, p. 147. REF: Miller, 1984.

Bird Names—III

Piping means "chirping." Sandpipers are thus birds that "chirp in the sand." Most sandpiper names are descriptive—the Stilt Sandpiper for its long legs, the Solitary Sandpiper because it rarely is found in flocks. The Western Sandpiper breeds in Alaska, but, confusingly, winters on the east coast as well as the west. Surfbirds are appropriately named for their preference for wintering on rocky ocean shorelines. Tattlers' calls were thought to warn other birds of the approach of a hunter. The generic name of tattlers, *Heteroscelus*, means "different leg" in Greek—it refers to the small scaling on the feet, which differentiates tattlers from other sandpipers. The Wandering Tattler, *Heteroscelus incanus*, ranges very widely, accounting for its common name, but *incanus* is Latin for "gray," and refers to the colors of the upper parts.

The weird name dowitcher is actually a corruption of "Duitsch" (Dutch) or "Deutscher" (German) Snipe. The name may be associated with

Rock Sandpiper

NG–126; G–128; PW–pl 25; AW–pl 211; AM(I)–392

M –F	4	MF			
	MONOG	I: 20 DAYS			
		PRECOCIAL 2	AQUATIC		
		F: ? DAYS	INVERTS		
		M –F	SEEDS		

BREEDING: Grassy or mossy tundra in coastal or montane habitat. 1 brood. **DISPLAYS:** Advertising display incl hovering flight with trills and whistles. See: Shorebird Communication, p. 139. **NEST:** Oft in moss or lichen, oft slightly elevated. Only used once. Unlined or lined with few bits of grass, leaves, lichen. Male does most of scraping, female continues to line nest after completion. **EGGS:** Variable. Olive, marked with brown, occ wreathed. 1.5″ (39 mm). **DIET:** Also worms, other inverts; occ algae, berries. **CONSERVATION:** Winters within N.A. **NOTES:** Adult very likely to return annually to same nesting area (i.e., strongly "philopatric"). Males dispersed widely over available tundra. Occ only male or female incubates. Performs distraction display. Chicks accompanied by male, rarely female or both. Young flatten on call from adult. Swims readily but not oft. In winter, oft assoc with Black Turnstones, Surfbirds, along rocky coasts. **ESSAYS:** Sandpipers, Social Systems, and Territoriality, p. 155; Shorebird Feeding, p. 125; Site Tenacity, p. 189; Shorebird Migration and Conservation, p. 119; Distraction Displays, p. 115; Who Incubates?, p. 27; Mixed-Species Flocking, p. 433. **REFS:** Myers et al., 1982; Pitelka et al., 1974.

Purple Sandpiper

NG–126; G–128; PE–132; AE–pl 217; AM(I)–390

     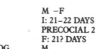

M	4	M –F		
	(3–4)	I: 21–22 DAYS		
	MONOG	PRECOCIAL 2	AQUATIC	PROBES
		F: 21? DAYS	INVERTS	
		M	PLANTS	

BREEDING: Mossy tundra, heath, barren coastal flats. 1 brood. **DISPLAYS:** Male advertising display: hovering, gliding to ca. 100′ high, trilling. Prominent wing-lift in antagonistic situations. See: Shorebird Communication, p. 139. **NEST:** On moist or dry tundra or on mountain ridges; within lichen or low veg, amply lined with grass. Male makes 2–5 scrapes, female selects one. **EGGS:** Light olive/light buffy brown, marked with browns, black, wreathed. 1.5″ (37 mm). **DIET:** Also spiders, crustaceans, mollusks, fish; aquatic veg, seeds. **CONSERVATION:** Winters within N.A.; winters farther n along Atlantic coast than any other shorebird. Numbers increasing and range expanding. **NOTES:** Males evenly spaced across tundra. Upon early arrival on breeding ground, pick animal foods from ice crevices. Very tame. Both sexes have brood patches. Female deserts at or just before hatching. Flights very short; rather sedentary. In winter, oft assoc with Ruddy Turnstones, Sanderlings, along rocky coasts. **ESSAYS:** Sandpipers, Social Systems, and Territoriality, p. 155; Range Expansion, p. 459; Shorebird Migration and Conservation, p. 119; Spacing of Wintering Shorebirds, p. 147; Shorebird Feeding, p. 125; Breeding Season, p. 55; Brood Patches, p. 427; Mixed-Species Flocking, p. 433. **REFS:** Cramp and Simmons, 1983; Pitelka et al., 1974.

the early Dutch population of New York and may have originated to distinguish it from the Common Snipe. Woodcocks are so named because of their woodland habitat; the generic name of woodcocks, *Scolopax*, means "woodcock" in Greek.

Shovelers are, of course, named for their large, shovel-shaped bills, which they use to strain small food from the water. Once they were known as "shovel bills," "broad bills" or "spoonbills." The meaning of the name scoter is obscure—it may have the same origin as the word "scoot," meaning to "hurry away." It may also be related to "coot," a name some hunters use for scoters. The generic name, *Melanitta*, simply means "black duck" in Greek. The Latin trivial name *nigra* also means "black" so that the name of the Black Scoter, *Melanitta nigra*, translates as "black black duck."

The term scaup may come from the English "scalp," meaning (besides what your hair grows on) "a ledge exposed at low tide." "Scaup banks" may have shellfishes growing on them on which the birds feed, and scaup may have originally meant "shell," so that these ducks may actually have a name with the same roots as "scallop." Then again, "scaup" may be a rendition of the bird's call. Merganser, on the other hand, has a clear origin—it is from the Latin for "diving goose." ("*Anser*," the genus of geese, has the same root.) The origins of Gadwall are obscure; the name may be connected to the Anglo-Saxon *gad*, meaning "a point," and referring to the fine teeth on the bill.

Sora is simply the Native American name for the same bird; Limpkin probably means "little limper," referring to the bird's unusual halting gait, although some think the name refers to its melancholy call. Rail seems to come from the Old French "raale" meaning "to make a scraping noise." *Gallinule* means "little hen" in Latin.

REFS: Choate, 1985; Owen, 1985.

Promiscuity

Some species of birds do not form pair bonds; but instead consort only briefly—for minutes or hours. The male's investment in offspring is limited to sperm, and the female raises the young alone. Male hummingbirds, for instance, court females for a short time, mate, and then resume their quest for other females. Males of many grouse species and some shorebirds display on leks (mating grounds used each year) to attract females that depart immediately after mating. The males may subsequently mate with additional females. Such mating systems, in which no pair bond is formed, are termed promiscuous. Presumably promiscuous mating systems can evolve only where the advantage of the male remaining with the female to help in raising the young is negligible.

SEE: Monogamy, p. 597; Polygyny, p. 443; Leks, p. 259; Polyandry, p. 133; Cooperative Breeding, p. 283; Parental Care, p. 555.

Red Knot
Calidris canutus Linnaeus

NG–128; G–130; PE–124; PW–pl 31; AE–pl 211; AW–pl 223; AM(I)–372

			MF I: 21–23 DAYS		
M –F(?)	4 (3–4) MONOG?		PRECOCIAL 2 F: 18–20 DAYS MF	SEEDS	PROBES

BREEDING: Wet, low tundra to dry slopes and ridges. 1 brood. **DISPLAYS:** Advertising display: male performs high flights, periodically hovering at 150'–300'. See: Shorebird Communication, p. 139. **NEST:** On grass hummock, usu near water. Lined with leaves, lichen. **EGGS:** Olive buff, marked with brown, black, wreathed. 1.6" (41 mm). **DIET:** Also spiders. In migration, takes esp mollusks, snails, horseshoe crab eggs, marine worms, fish. **CONSERVATION:** Winters s to Tierra del Fuego. Stops briefly along N.A. coast in fall to accumulate fat for nonstop migration to S.A. Once most abundant shorebird in N.A., but slaughtered during migrations from late 1800s to early 1900s. **NOTES:** First nest found in 1909 during Admiral Perry's expedition to North Pole. Large territories, males spaced far apart. Performs distraction display. Female leaves before young fledge. Mob jaegers, striking them from below. Remain more clustered on ground than other waders. Feeds in large winter flocks, oft with dowitchers. **ESSAYS:** Sandpiper Social Systems, p. 155; Shorebird Feeding, p. 125; Shorebird Migration, p. 119; Wintering Shorebirds, p. 147; Mobbing, p. 425. **REFS:** Cramp and Simmons, 1983; Harrington, 1986.

Dunlin
Calidris alpina Linnaeus

NG–128; G–130; PE–132; PW–pl 25; AE–pl 209; AW–pl 188; AM(I)–394

			MF I: 21–22 DAYS		
MF	4 (2–4) MONOG		PRECOCIAL 2 F: 19–21 DAYS MF		PROBES

BREEDING: Wet coastal tundra. 1, occ 2 broods. **DISPLAYS:** Display flight at 50'–100' incl brief glides alternating with shallow flutters, assoc with song and rhythmically repeated calls. See: Shorebird Communication, p. 139. **NEST:** On hummock, oft concealed in veg. Lined with withered willow leaves and lichen. **EGGS:** Light olive-buff/light blue-green, marked with red-brown, wreathed. 1.4" (34 mm). **DIET:** Also spiders, worms, mollusks; seeds in spring. In winter and migration takes mollusks, crustaceans, marine worms. **CONSERVATION:** Winters s along w coast to Baja, Sonora, and along e coast s to Yucatan. **NOTES:** In Finland, occ sequential polyandry. Most do not breed until second year. Strong fidelity to breeding territory oft leads to renewal of pair bond in successive years. Female incubates mostly at night, male in day. Female oft leaves chicks well before they fledge. Large territories incl nesting and occ feeding areas. Performs distraction display. Predation on juveniles may be higher than on adults in mixed winter flocks. Highest overwinter weight gains found in populations specializing on marine worms. Males tend to winter farther n than females. **ESSAYS:** Birds and the Law, p. 293; Sandpiper Social Systems, p. 155; Shorebird Feeding, p. 125; Shorebird Migration, p. 119; Wintering Shorebirds, p. 147; Site Tenacity, p. 189. **REFS:** Cramp and Simmons, 1983; Kus et al., 1984; Miller, 1983; Soikkeli, 1970.

Spacing of Wintering Shorebirds

Shorebirds feeding in groups along our coasts and along the margins of inland lakes and rivers are a familiar sight to most North American bird watchers. Such scenes are common during migration and, in many places, throughout the winter as well. The spacing systems found among wintering shorebirds cover a spectrum from individual feeding territories to large, tightly integrated foraging flocks.

At one extreme of the territoriality-flocking continuum are species such as Solitary and Spotted Sandpipers, Wilson's Plover, and Wandering Tattler which are usually seen as isolated individuals and only rarely seen in small groups. At the opposite extreme are Stilt Sandpipers, Surfbirds, Red Knots, and Long- and Short-billed Dowitchers, which are virtually always found in moderate-to-large cohesive flocks. Most shorebird species, however, fall somewhere in between, and many exhibit varying "spacing behaviors" depending upon location, time of day, and density of food resources.

Behaviors involved in defense of a feeding-site often differ from those seen in defense of a breeding territory. Conspicuous terrestrial visual displays are exhibited during feeding territoriality, for example, but aerial displays and extensive vocalizations are absent.

Like breeding territories, some feeding territories tend to have well-defined boundaries, and continued occupation for weeks or even months. But here again, a continuum exists from these to territories defended for only a few hours or a few days. Some birds defend "portable" territories with boundaries that shift as food resources move (e.g., sand-dwelling invertebrates in the wave-wash zone along a beach whose abundance varies as the tide rises or falls). An extreme example is a Sanderling defending an area around a foraging Black Turnstone. As the turnstone flips through beach litter, the Sanderling forages in the newly exposed substrate (an example of "commensal feeding," in which the Sanderling benefits without harming the turnstone). When the turnstone moves along the beach, the Sanderling follows, essentially defending a moving territory centered on the turnstone.

The preponderance of evidence from migration and wintering studies indicates that nonbreeding (wintering) territoriality is primarily resource-based, appearing and disappearing in response to changes in resource abundance and density. Whether or not wintering shorebirds are territorial also is sensitive to the risk territory-holders run of being eaten by falcons. Solitary small shorebirds have been shown to be more susceptible to falcon predation than those in flocks. Territoriality is most common at intermediate food densities and in places where, or at times when, the risk of predation on the territory-holder is low. When food is scarce, territoriality disappears because the amount of food within a defensible area is simply insufficient to meet the energy needs of the territory-holder. Similarly, when food is superabundant, territoriality disappears, in part because the energy cost of trying to keep out invading birds attracted to the rich food supply is

Sanderling
Calidris alba Pallas

NG–128; G–130; PE–130; PW–pl 32; AE–pl 220; AW–pl 193; AM(I)–374

M –F   4 (3–4)   MF   GROUND
   MONOG   I: 24–31 DAYS   GLEAN
   (POLYAND)   PRECOCIAL 2
      F: 17 DAYS
      MF

BREEDING: Dry sedge, barren or stony tundra. 1, occ 2 broods. **DISPLAYS:** Unpaired male advertises and defends territory with flight displays (incl hovering) and ground displays. See: Shorebird Communication, p. 139. **NEST:** Lined with grass, leaves, lichen. Female selects one of several scrapes. **EGGS:** Greenish-olive to buff, marked with dark brown, occ wreathed. 1.4″ (36 mm). **DIET:** Also spiders, veg in spring; on coast probe for marine inverts within 10 mm of surface. Probes with bill partly open. **CONSERVATION:** Winters s through West Indies and along coasts of S.A. to Tierra del Fuego. **NOTES:** Males widely scattered on arctic tundra, occ clumped. Sequential polyandry occurs but usu monogamous. Male and female occ incubate separate clutches, care separately for young. Performs distraction display. Some males return to previous breeding grounds; strong fidelity to wintering grounds. Size of winter feeding territory decreases as prey density increases, largely due to greater intruder presence in areas of high prey density; feeding flocks are open groups, membership shifts rapidly as flock moves along beach. **ESSAYS:** Who Incubates?, p. 27; Sandpiper Social Systems, p. 155; Polyandry, p. 133; Shorebird Migration, p. 119; Wintering Shorebirds, p. 147. **REFS:** Cramp and Simmons, 1983; Myers, 1983; Myers et al., 1980; Parmelee and Payne, 1973.

White-rumped Sandpiper
Calidris fuscicollis Vieillot

NG–130; G–132; PE–134; PW–pl 32; AE–pl 226; AM(I)–384

M?   4   F   SEEDS   PROBES
   POLYGYN   I: 21–22 DAYS
      PRECOCIAL 2
      F: 16–17 DAYS
      F

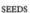

BREEDING: Mossy or grassy tundra near water. 1 brood. **DISPLAYS:** Advertising flight: male performs both high hovering and low flights with trills and whistles. See: Shorebird Communication, p. 139. **NEST:** On grassy hummock on ridge. Of grass or moss, partly concealed by dry grass, lined with few dry leaves, esp of willow. **EGGS:** Olive-buff/light-green, marked with brown, wreathed. 1.3″ (34 mm). **DIET:** Also worms, snails. Oft entirely immerses head while probing. **CONSERVATION:** Winters extensively in S.A. mostly e of Andes s to Tierra del Fuego. **NOTES:** Males on variably sized territories usu containing >1 nest and incl feeding areas. Length of incubation bouts and duration of feeding trips away from nest determined by metabolic needs of female resulting from weather on preceding and current day. Winters farther s than most "peeps" (small *Calidris* sandpipers); usu in flocks, occ with Baird's or Pectoral Sandpipers. Many defend winter feeding territories. **ESSAYS:** Shorebird Migration, p. 119; Sandpiper Social Systems, p. 155; Shorebird Feeding, p. 125; Wintering Shorebirds, p. 147; Polygyny, p. 443; Incubation: Heating Eggs, p. 393; Temperature Regulation, p. 149. **REFS:** Cartar and Montgomerie, 1987; Pitelka et al., 1974.

too great. Likewise, the size of individual territories also shows plasticity that depends both directly and indirectly on the density of prey. Flexibility is clearly a key feature of spacing systems exhibited by nonbreeding shorebirds.

Territorial defense in wintering shorebirds shows striking parallels with defense of feeding territories by hummingbirds. Central to both groups is the nature of their food resources; only spatially clumped, energy-rich, and temporally renewable types of food can be defended—features shared by such disparate types of food as nectar produced by flowers and invertebrates whose availability shifts with the tides.

SEE: Shorebird Feeding, p. 125; Shorebird Communication, p. 139; Shorebird Migration and Conservation, p. 119; Territoriality, p. 387; Sandpipers, Social Systems, and Territoriality, p. 155; Commensal Feeding, p. 35.   REFS: Myers, 1984; Myers et al., 1979.

Temperature Regulation and Behavior

The ability to maintain a high and constant body temperature enables birds to exploit a remarkable range of habitats—tropical, temperate, and polar. This achievement is not without cost, however. The "expense" of metabolic heat production must be repaid by taking in sufficient energy to balance what has been expended, and mechanisms must be available to shed excess heat when necessary. If the environmental temperature falls, birds raise their metabolic rate to prevent their internal temperature from falling as well. In contrast, if the environmental temperature becomes too hot, birds must mobilize water to lose heat through evaporative cooling (as we do when we perspire) and avoid death from overheating. Since birds have no sweat glands, heat must be lost through the respiratory tract by panting, or in non-passerines by the rapid vibration of the upper throat and thin floor of the mouth ("gular flutter").

To minimize the energy cost of temperature regulation ("thermoregulation"), birds use a variety of morphological and behavioral traits to adjust their rates of heat loss and heat gain. Unfeathered (uninsulated) body surfaces serve as important sites for heat exchange with the environment. When heat-stressed, therefore, some birds, such as Black Vultures, excrete onto their unfeathered legs to increase heat loss by evaporation.

When it is cold, the lack of insulation on the legs makes them a site of potential heat loss. To minimize such loss, the arteries and veins in the legs of many birds lie in contact with each other and function as a countercurrent heat exchange system to retain heat. Arterial blood leaves the bird's core (trunk) at body temperature, while venous blood in the bird's foot is quite cool. As the cool blood returns toward the core, heat moves by conductance from the warm arteries into the cool veins. Thus, arterial blood

Western Sandpiper

Calidris mauri Cabanis

NG–130; G–132; PE–134; PW–pl 32; AE–pl 222; AW–pl 194; AM(I)–378

M –F	4 MONOG	MF I: 20–22 DAYS PRECOCIAL 2 F: 19–21 DAYS MF	PROBES

BREEDING: Sedge-dwarf shrub tundra. 1 brood. **DISPLAYS**: Advertising flight: male flies to 20′ with little hovering; trills. See: Shorebird Communication, p. 139. **NEST**: On slightly elevated shrubby tundra near water; lined with grass, tiny leaves, moss. Occ domed with sedge, grass, low heath veg. **EGGS**: Buffy cream/dark buff, marked with brown, occ black. 1.2″ (31 mm). **DIET**: Almost entirely insects; mostly marine inverts in nonbreeding season. **CONSERVATION**: Winters s along both coasts to n Peru (w) and Surinam (e). Although very small, once regarded as game. **NOTES**: Large densely packed breeding colonies spread across tundra. Occupies drier areas than Semipalmated Sandpiper. Family groups remain together until young are able to fly. Adults depart breeding area in midsummer; young migrate 2–3 weeks later. Constantly moving and whistling at water's edge. **ESSAYS**: Shorebird Migration and Conservation, p. 119; Sandpiper Social Systems, p. 155; Shorebird Feeding, p. 125; Spacing of Wintering Shorebirds, p. 147; Coloniality, p. 173; Temperature Regulation and Behavior, p. 149. **REFS**: Butler et al., 1987; Holmes, 1973; Myers et al., 1982.

Least Sandpiper

Calidris minutilla Vieillot

NG–130; G–132; PE–134; PW–pl 32; AE–pl 223; AW–pl 195; AM(I)–382

M –F	4 MONOG	M –F I: 19–23 DAYS PRECOCIAL 2 F: ? DAYS M –F	AQUATIC INVERTS SEEDS	PROBES

BREEDING: Mossy or wet grassy tundra, occ in drier habitats with scattered shrubs. 1 brood. **DISPLAYS**: Advertising flight: male flies at 35′–100′, alternating brief glides and bouts of rapid fluttering. See: Shorebird Communication, p. 139. **NEST**: In grass, moss, or sedge hummock in sphagnum bog or dry upland habitat. Lined with dry leaves, bits of dry grass. Both sexes present during scrape-making. **EGGS**: Olive buff/pinkish, marked with dark brown, wreathed. 1.1″ (29 mm). **DIET**: On coast, also crustaceans, worms, mollusks. **CONSERVATION**: Winters s to c and e Peru. **NOTES**: Males evenly spaced in marsh-bog habitat. Territory usu for nest site only, occ also for foraging and brood-rearing; usu feed in undefended, communal area distant from nesting ground. Male assumes increasing role in incubation and is largely responsible for care of young. After nesting, adults and chicks move to undefended, communal feeding grounds. Flocks with Semipalmated Plovers, other "peeps" (small *Calidris* sandpipers). Extremely rapid wing beats and zigzag flight. **ESSAYS**: Shorebird Migration and Conservation, p. 119; Sandpipers, Social Systems, and Territoriality, p. 155; Shorebird Feeding, p. 125; Spacing of Wintering Shorebirds, p. 147; Who Incubates?, p. 127; Parental Care, p. 555. **REFS**: Cramp and Simmons, 1983; Johnsgard, 1981; Miller, 1983.

reaching the feet is already cool and venous blood reaching the core has already been warmed. In addition, by constricting the blood vessels in its feet a bird may further decrease heat loss by reducing the amount of blood flow to its feet at low temperatures. Thus while the core temperature of a duck or gull standing on ice may be 104° F, its feet may be only slightly above freezing.

Behavior also can play a significant role in reducing the amount of heat lost from unfeathered surfaces. By standing on one leg and tucking the other among its breast feathers, a duck or gull on ice reduces by half the amount of unfeathered limb surface area exposed; by sitting down and thus covering both legs, heat loss from the limbs is minimized. In cold weather, juncos, sparrows, and other finches foraging on the ground frequently drop down and cover their legs and feet with their breast feathers while pausing in their search for food. On cold or windy days, shorebirds often can be seen resting with their beaks tucked away among their feathers, sometimes combined with standing on one leg or sitting. And, of course, birds can further enhance their effective insulation by fluffing out their feathers to increase the thickness of their "coat."

Behavioral thermoregulation may be accomplished by other means, as well. Subtle changes in posture or orientation toward or away from the sun can alter heat gain and loss. Gulls, for example, usually nest in open habitats with little or no available shade and often face problems of overheating. Nesting Herring Gulls will rotate 180° to constantly face the sun on hot, windless days. This effectively minimizes the amount of radiative heat gain by minimizing the surface area exposed to direct solar radiation and by allowing the gulls to present only their most reflective plumage (white head, neck, and breast) to direct sunlight. Gulls use their unfeathered legs and feet to prevent overheating by standing—better yet, by standing in water. Gull chicks lack thermoregulatory ability until they are several days old and face acute problems of overheating. In many shadeless colonies, such as

Shorebirds retracting legs and placing heads beneath wings to retard heat loss. Left to right: American Oystercatchers, Semipalmated Sandpiper, Sanderling, Western Sandpiper.

Semipalmated Sandpiper
Calidris pusilla Linnaeus

NG–130; G–132; PE–134; PW–pl 32; AE–pl 221; AW–pl 196; AM(I)–376

     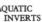

| MF | 4 (2–4) MONOG | MF I: 20 (18–22) DAYS PRECOCIAL 2 F: 19 DAYS MF | AQUATIC INVERTS | PROBES |

BREEDING: Open tundra, usu near water. 1 brood. **DISPLAYS:** Display flight: male rapidly hovers at 15′–30′; assoc with songs, "motorboat" calls. See: Shorebird Communication, p. 139. **NEST:** On hummock or knoll amid short veg. Lined with grass, moss, dry leaves. Male may build 10–12 scrapes, female lines 2 or 3 (only 1 is used) and continues to line during incubation. **EGGS:** Yellow to buff, marked with brown. 1.2″ (30 mm). **DIET:** In winter and migration takes aquatic insects, mollusks, worms, crustaceans. Forages with head down, running just above tide line or at water's edge. Can retrieve prey too large to swallow. Also forage on floating veg. **CONSERVATION:** Winters in Bahamas, Guatemala, s mostly to n S.A., esp in Surinam. 800,000 gather in Bay of Fundy in August for s migration. **NOTES:** Males evenly but densely spaced on breeding grounds. Mate retained between years in ca. 50% of pairs, but has little effect on nesting success; site tenacity secondarily produces mate fidelity. Male prepares night brooding scrape for 6–8 days posthatch. Female deserts 2–8 days posthatch. Older females have higher nest success. Young females have smaller eggs and later hatch. After fledging, male and young join wandering flocks. **ESSAYS:** Sandpiper Social Systems, p. 155; Shorebird Migration, p. 119; Wintering Shorebirds, p. 147; Site Tenacity, p. 189. **REFS:** Ashkenazie and Safriel, 1979; Gratto et al., 1983, 1985; Miller, 1983.

Baird's Sandpiper
Calidris bairdii Coues

NG–130; G–132; PE–134; PW–pl 32; AE–pl 225; AW–pl 197; AM(I)–386

| M –F | 4 (2–4) MONOG | MF I: 20–22 DAYS PRECOCIAL 2 F: 16–20 DAYS M –F | SPIDERS | |

BREEDING: Dry coastal and alpine tundra. 1 brood. **DISPLAYS:** Advertising display: male performs high hovering flight with trills. At onset of breeding season, displaying males concentrated, as if on leks. See: Shorebird Communication, p. 139. **NEST:** Cryptic; in drier regions beside grass tuft, rock, etc. Occ concealed. Depression lined with dead leaves (oft willow), lichen, or grass. **EGGS:** Pinkish-buff/olive-buff, marked with dark brown. 1.3″ (33 mm). **DIET:** Feed with other Baird's running in 30′ spurts on soft mud or in shallow water; rarely probe. In fall, oft forage in beach wrack. **CONSERVATION:** Winters s to Tierra del Fuego and Patagonia; mostly in s S.A. **NOTES:** Males evenly spaced in drier coastal and mountain habitat. Perform distraction display. Migrate through center of N.A.; adults, rarely seen on coasts, perform 4000 mile nonstop flight from n prairies to n S.A. **ESSAYS:** Shorebird Migration and Conservation, p. 119; Sandpipers, Social Systems, and Territoriality, p. 155; Shorebird Feeding, p. 125; Spacing of Wintering Shorebirds, p. 147; Leks, p. 259; Distraction Displays, p. 115. **REFS:** Jehl, 1979; Johnsgard, 1981; Myers et al., 1982; Pitelka et al., 1974.

those of California Gulls, chicks avoid heat stress by standing in the shade provided by their parents.

In cooler weather, rather than increasing their metabolic rate, birds can save energy by using environmental heat to raise their body temperature passively. Anhingas, for example, do this by sunning with wings spread, while many small- and medium-sized species, especially passerines, assume sunning postures in which they squat or sit with their feathers slightly erected and wings drooped. Usually the bird is oriented so the back is fully exposed to the sun's direct rays. Interestingly, Greater Roadrunners and some grebes that sunbathe in this way have either back feathers with black bases or black-pigmented back skin, both of which presumably facilitate heat absorption.

Birds have evolved the ability to maintain their body temperature at a somewhat lower level during periods of inactivity or in response to food deprivation. This "regulated hypothermia" achieves significant energy savings for many species ranging from passerines to raptors. For example, when deprived of food in winter, Red-tailed Hawks drop their nocturnal body temperature by 5° to 7°F below their daytime temperature. Hummingbirds, swifts, and poorwills enter a state of torpor in which body temperature may drop as much as 50°F for several hours during the night or for days during extremely inclement weather. Although the energy savings are great in birds that enter torpor, they face increased danger of predation because they are unable to respond quickly. There is also a substantial metabolic cost incurred by arousal from torpor that demands immediate payback in food intake. Nevertheless, recent studies indicate that the ability to enter shallow torpor for short periods may be much more widespread among birds than previously believed.

Keep thermoregulatory needs in mind when you are watching birds. Indeed, temperature-regulating actions of shorebirds and gulls are among the most readily observed and interpreted of bird behaviors.

SEE: Metabolism, p. 325; Black and White Plumage, p. 177; Spread-Wing Postures, p. 25; Winter Feeding by Redpolls and Crossbills, p. 641; Feet, p. 239; Bird Droppings, p. 263. REFS: Chaplin et al., 1984; Chappell et al., 1984; Larochelle et al., 1982; Lustick et al., 1978; Walsberg, 1983.

Bird Biologist—S. C. Kendeigh

S. Charles Kendeigh (1904–86) was born in Ohio, and had a distinguished career as an ornithologist and ecologist, working primarily at the University of Illinois. He did pioneering work on the ecology and physiology of birds, ranging over a wide variety of topics from thermoregulation and energy requirements in relation to size to the evolution of parental care and community ecology. He was active in both conservation and nature education.

Pectoral Sandpiper

Calidris melanotos Vieillot

NG–134; G–130; PE–130; PW–pl 32; AE–pl 219; AW–pl 198; AM(I)–386

| F | 4 PROMISC | F
I: 21–23 DAYS
PRECOCIAL 2
F: 21 DAYS
F | | GROUND
GLEAN |

BREEDING: Wet coastal or drier upland tundra. 1 brood. **DISPLAYS:** Advertising display: male performs low ritualized flight with hollow hoot. See: Shorebird Communication, p. 139. **NEST:** Of grass and leaves usu concealed in grass or depression; occ near water's edge. Lined with bits of dry grass and small dry leaves. Female selects site. **EGGS:** Cream/olive-buff, marked with brown. 1.4″ (37 mm). **DIET:** Also amphipods, spiders, worms; seeds. **CONSERVATION:** Winters s to c Chile, s Argentina. **NOTES:** Two sacs beneath skin of male become twice normal size during courtship to produce booming sound. Variably sized male territories, oft small, used for mating, feeding, roosting, and nesting, but nesting female not necessarily fertilized by the territory-holder; suggests antecedent to lek-type of mating system. Females not territorial. Performs distraction display. Most males depart for migration before eggs hatch; females depart well before young. **ESSAYS:** Sandpipers, Social Systems, and Territoriality, p. 155; Shorebird Feeding, p. 125; Leks, p. 259; Shorebird Migration and Conservation, p. 119; Spacing of Wintering Shorebirds, p. 147; Distraction Displays, p. 115; Promiscuity, p. 145. **REFS:** Myers, 1982; Pitelka, 1959; Pitelka et al., 1974.

Upland Sandpiper

Bartramia longicauda Bechstein

NG–134; G–122; PE–130; PW–pl 31; AE–pl 218; AW–pl 208; AM(I)–356

| MF? | 4 MONOG | MF
I: 21–27 DAYS
PRECOCIAL 2
F: 30–31 DAYS
MF | SEEDS | |

BREEDING: Grassland, esp prairie, dry meadow, fields, forest openings and (in AK) scattered woodland at timberline. ? broods. **DISPLAYS:** Courtship flight incl singing and wing spreading while flying in wide circles. See: Shorebird Communication, p. 139. **NEST:** Depression concealed on drier portions of habitat amid grass arching over grass scrape. Lined with bits of dry grass. **EGGS:** Cream/pinkish-buff, marked with red-brown. 1.8″ (45 mm). **DIET:** Also terrestrial inverts; grain. **CONSERVATION:** Winters s to c Argentina, Uruguay. Blue List 1975–86; declining in e portion of range as habitats (old fields) mature to woodland or are replaced by suburbanization. Rare cowbird host. Numbers greatly diminished as market hunters shifted from Passenger Pigeon to Upland Sandpiper as prime target in 1880s, but numbers increased and range expanded w as it adapted to open cropland, etc. **NOTES:** Nests in loose colony. Seldom found near water. Does not fly directly to nest. Young have disproportionately large legs. Performs distraction display. Formerly known as Upland Plover. **ESSAYS:** Blue List, p. 11; Sandpipers, Social Systems, and Territoriality, p. 155; Shorebird Feeding, p. 125; Shorebird Migration and Conservation, p. 119; Range Expansion, p. 459; Distraction Displays, p. 115. **REFS:** Higgins and Kirsch, 1975; Johnsgard, 1981.

Sandpipers, Social Systems, and Territoriality

Studies of breeding sandpipers in different arctic and subarctic habitats have shown how differences in mating systems and territoriality may be related to ecological factors such as the distribution and abundance of food resources and the need to avoid predators. For instance, in northern Alaska where food is relatively scarce and unpredictable, monogamous Dunlins establish territories sufficiently large to provide the pair with enough food to carry it through the leanest of years. This keeps densities of breeding populations low; when male Dunlins holding territories were removed experimentally, other males promptly replaced them. The replacements apparently had either been nonterritorial or occupied inferior locations.

In contrast, in the southern part of Alaska where the longer growing season provides a more predictable and abundant food supply, the territories are smaller and the population density higher. In both situations, however, the nests are well spaced because of male aggressiveness. Experimental evidence shows that wide spacing of nests in gull colonies reduces predation, and that may apply to sandpipers also. Since foxes, weasels, gulls, and jaegers prey heavily on sandpiper nests, one result of such spacing may be higher nesting success. Dunlins are monogamous, and the pair bond allows one adult to incubate while the other forages. In addition to limiting egg predations, the presence of both parents on the territory reduces egg chilling, which otherwise would delay the chicks' hatching and could reduce their chances of survival.

Some monogamous species, such as the Western Sandpiper, do not defend feeding territories. The Western's nesting habitat is patchily distributed but located close to abundant food. Western Sandpipers nest in "islands" of shrubby vegetation in the tundra that provide some protection from predators, but feed outside of their territories. Monogamous, territorial social systems like those of the Dunlin and Western Sandpiper are also found in the Red Knot, Surfbird, and the Purple, Semipalmated, Least, Baird's, Rock, and Stilt Sandpipers.

Other species of sandpipers exhibit a variety of nonmonogamous mating systems. Sanderlings, Temminck's Stints, and Little Stints (neither of the latter two breed in our area) are serially polyandrous—a female lays two or three clutches, which are normally fathered by more than one male, and the males care for them, or she lays two clutches and the male broods one clutch and the female a second one. White-rumped, Curlew, and Sharp-tailed Sandpipers are polygynous. Those males displaying on the best territories may have more than one mate, but do not assist in incubation. Pectoral Sandpipers, Buff-breasted Sandpipers, and Ruffs (which rarely breed in our area) are promiscuous. Males display vigorously, the Buff-breasted and Ruffs on leks, but play no part in incubation, and females may associate with several males in close succession.

This second group of sandpipers shows much more variation in territorial strategies and reproductive effort than do the monogamous species.

Buff-breasted Sandpiper

Tryngites subruficollis Vieillot

NG–134; G–122; PE–130; PW–pl 32; AE–pl 224; AM(I)–400

F	4	F	
	(2–4)	I: ? DAYS	
	PROMISC	PRECOCIAL 2	
	F	F: ? DAYS	
		F	

BREEDING: Dry grassy tundra. 1 brood. **DISPLAYS:** Males display in groups up to 15 on leks; wing flashing, jumping, low flutter flights; males call but song is absent. **NEST:** Shallow depression in moss or grass on dry upland; lined with few dead leaves or moss. **EGGS:** Buff/white/olive, marked with brown, occ wreathed. 1.5″ (37 mm). **DIET:** Also spiders; few seeds from aquatic veg. **CONSERVATION:** Winters in Paraguay, Uruguay and n Argentina. Numbers severely diminished by intense hunting in late 1800s. Problem now of agricultural conversion of upland winter habitat. **NOTES:** Feeding and nesting do not occur on male display territory. Males depart breeding area before eggs hatch. Many defend winter territories which they abandon temporarily when raptors fly near. **ESSAYS:** Leks, p. 259; Sandpipers, Social Systems, and Territoriality, p. 155; Shorebird Migration and Conservation, p. 119; Spacing of Wintering Shorebirds, p. 147; Shorebird Feeding, p. 125; Temperature Regulation and Behavior, p. 149. **REFS:** Myers, 1979; Oring, 1964; Prevett and Barr, 1976.

Parasitic Jaeger

Stercorarius parasiticus Linnaeus

N–142; G–138; PE–82; PW–pl 3; AE–pl 89; AW–pl 53; AM(II)–38

MF	2	MF	SMALL	PIRACY
	(1–2)	I: 25–28 DAYS	MAMMALS	
	MONOG	SEMIPRECOCIAL	FISH	
		F: 25–30 DAYS		
		MF		

BREEDING: Barren or dwarf-shrub coastal tundra. 1 brood. **DISPLAYS:** Courtship feeding. **NEST:** On low, mossy hummock, or other slight rise. Usu unlined but occ scantily lined with leaves, lichen, and grass. Male selects site, female does most of building. **EGGS:** Olive-green/gray/brown, marked with browns, occ wreathed. 2.2″ (57 mm). **DIET:** Primarily birds, but varies with locality; takes passerines, seabirds, young and eggs of many species; also small mammals, offal, carrion, insects, fish; occ seeds, berries. In winter takes mostly fish, largely by piracy. **CONSERVATION:** Mostly pelagic in winter, s to s S.A., e Argentina. **NOTES:** Gull-like birds with hawk-like characteristics. Hunts alone, in pairs, trios, occ to 5. Follows mammalian predators (incl biologists and birders!) through waterfowl and seabird colonies, snatching eggs from untended nests. Oft colonial. Long-term pair bond. Pale and dark forms behave differently: pale matures younger; dark males preferred by females and nest earlier in season. Dark form favored in n, light in s; usu the rarer form has better hunting success. Young hatch asynchronously; smaller chick usu disappears within few days of hatching. Distraction display: vigorous wing-flapping, jumping, and loud whimpering. Also known as Arctic Skua. **ESSAYS:** Brood Reduction, p. 307; Pelagic Birds, p. 657; Piracy, p. 159; Courtship Feeding, p. 181; Geometry of the Selfish Colony, p. 19. **REFS:** Birt and Cairns, 1987; Cramp and Simmons, 1983; Maher, 1974; Martin and Barry, 1978; O'Donald, 1983.

They are more "opportunistic," adapting their strategies to local conditions, especially the temporary availability of abundant food. For instance, instead of being conservative like Dunlins and setting up a territory that will contain enough food in any circumstances, Pectoral Sandpipers acquire fat reserves during their northern migration that permit them to ride out periods of food shortage. Like the White-rumped Sandpiper, they may breed at very high densities, with males holding small territories, since a continuous food supply is assured. Rather than guarding their nest to avoid predation, Pectorals keep the nest hidden, and incubation by only one adult reduces telltale traffic to and from the nest. Single adult incubation may also help to conserve food supplies for that adult and the young, since a second adult will not be depleting resources near the nest.

Opportunistic arctic breeders accept the increased hazards of nesting in highly productive locations such as lowland marshes. They get a rich harvest of insects in exchange, but risk increased predation associated with more closely spaced nests and flooding by summer rains (water runs off the tundra very rapidly because it cannot soak into the ground, which is frozen just below the surface).

The various mating systems offer different advantages, and those advantages accrue differentially to the two sexes. The females of polyandrous species gain more than males. They are freed from the necessity of incubating the first clutch, so their reproductive output is increased. Polygynous males with good territories may greatly increase their reproductive output, gaining more benefit than the two or more females sharing the territory. This may generate an evolutionary pressure toward a lek system that frees the female, once mated, from any constraints inherent in the male's territorial needs. The best territory for a displaying male may not be the best one for a female to use for nesting and rearing her young. Females in promiscuous species are free to optimize their choice of nest sites.

Several of the sandpiper species usually considered monogamous are occasionally polygamous (polygynous or polyandrous) and show other tendencies toward more opportunistic strategies, such as communal feeding away from the territory while maintaining a monogamous pair bond. Also, they will renest if the first clutch is lost—suggesting a possible evolutionary stepping-stone to the strategy of the male rearing the first clutch and the female the second, which in turn could open the door to polyandry.

We have simplified the account here, and more research is needed to confirm various aspects of sandpiper social systems, but as you can see, different members of this structurally rather uniform group of birds have developed very different ways of solving the problems of successful reproduction in northern environments.

SEE: Monogamy, p. 597; Polygyny, p. 443; Polyandry, p. 133; Polyandry in the Spotted Sandpiper, p. 131; Leks, p. 259; Territoriality, p. 387; Shorebird Communication, p. 139.   REFS: Myers, 1987; Pitelka et al., 1974; Tinbergen et al., 1967.

Pomarine Jaeger

Stercorarius pomarinus Temminck

| MF | 2 (1–3) MONOG | | MF I: 25–27 DAYS SEMIPRECOCIAL F: 31–37 DAYS MF | BIRDS | PIRACY |

BREEDING: Coastal flats, wet mossy tundra. 1 brood. **DISPLAYS:** Pair bond formation: birds face each other, vibrate wings; courtship feeding. **NEST:** Slight depression on drier spots of low tundra; unlined or with bits of moss, other veg. **EGGS:** Brownish-olive, sparsely marked with brown. 2.4″ (62 mm). **DIET:** Primarily lemmings, other rodents; occ adults, young, and eggs of seabirds. Captures prey with beak, not feet. When not breeding, takes fish, offal, carrion; occ by piracy. Young fed by regurgitation. **CONSERVATION:** Mostly pelagic in winter, s to Peru and Galapagos (w), and West Indies to coastal S.A. (e). **NOTES:** Chief lemming predator across the coastal plains of N.A. and Asia; breeding density fluctuates drastically between years as it tracks the regular cycling of lemming populations. Unable to breed when mammal populations crash; ability to take birds and other alternate foods on breeding grounds is limited. Youngest chick oft attacked by older sib. Chicks leave nest at 2–4 days; tended by adult up to 2 weeks post-fledging. Remarkably agile in flight. Known as Pomarine Skua in Europe. **ESSAYS:** Brood Reduction, p. 307; Pelagic Birds, p. 657; Monogamy, p. 597; Courtship Feeding, p. 181; Piracy, p. 159. **REFS:** Cramp and Simmons, 1983; Maher, 1974.

Long-tailed Jaeger

Stercorarius longicaudus Vieillot

| MF | 2 (1–2) MONOG | | MF I: 23–25 DAYS SEMIPRECOCIAL F: 22–28 DAYS MF | BIRDS INSECTS BERRIES | PIRACY |

BREEDING: Sparsely vegetated flats in open and alpine tundra, oft on or near slope. 1 brood. **DISPLAYS:** Noisy male-male interactions. Spectacular acrobatic aerial courtship. **NEST:** Depression in mossy top of knoll on slightly elevated ground. **EGGS:** Brownish/olive, marked with brown, wreathed. 2.2″ (55 mm). **DIET:** Primarily small mammals, also birds, insects, bird eggs, pirated fish, offal; berries. Young fed rodents, birds, insects, berries. **CONSERVATION:** Pelagic in winter, usu off S.A. from Ecuador to Chile and in Atlantic s to Argentina. **NOTES:** Long-term pair bond. Breeding dependent on rodent abundance. Female does most of brooding and feeding of young; male hunts and defends territory. Distraction display seldom performed. Young tended ca. 3 weeks post-fledging. Swims lightly and gracefully, holding tail up; does not dive. Known in Europe as Long-tailed Skua. **ESSAYS:** Brood Reduction, p. 307; Piracy, p. 159; Pelagic Birds, p. 657; Parental Care, p. 555. **REFS:** Cramp and Simmons, 1983; Maher, 1974.

Piracy

Evolution pays no attention to the commandment "Thou shalt not steal." Birds steal from each other just about anything that is not nailed down. They steal mates, nesting material, eggs, and prey. The term "piracy," however, is generally restricted to the harassment of one bird by another in order to force the first to give up food. In scientific jargon, such piracy is referred to as "kleptoparasitism."

Jaegers and skuas (both close relatives of gulls) are classic avian pirates that attack other birds in midair and make them relinquish their food. Gulls themselves also pirate food from other birds, including auks, shorebirds, and other gulls. The victims of these pirates may have food snatched from their bills, may be forced to regurgitate, or if pursued by jaegers, may occasionally become prey themselves. Jaegers and skuas obtain much of their food in this way, as do frigatebirds. The latter are lightly built to permit aerobatic flight, and possess feathers that are not very resistant to wetting. They are thus dependent on other birds, including gulls, to do their fishing for them.

Piracy is also commonly practiced by some raptors. In one unusual case, a European Sparrowhawk had its food snatched by a Merlin, which, in turn was robbed by a Honey Buzzard (a Eurasian accipiter), which lost it to a Peregrine Falcon. Turkey Vultures are known to force nestling Great Blue Herons to regurgitate their last meal, which is scooped up and later fed to the vultures' own chicks. Raptors get the tables turned on them occasionally, sometimes being forced to give up their catch to birds such as crows and magpies. Apparently this behavior on the part of the passerine pirates is derived from mobbing.

Interestingly, dabbling ducks, including American Wigeons and Gadwalls, often pirate aquatic vegetation from coots. The latter can dive deeper, and thus the ducks can dine on pond weeds that ordinarily would be out of their reach. They also may save energy in some circumstances by pirating rather than dabbling, since American Coots have been observed to simply

A Pomarine Jaeger harries a Herring Gull.

Heermann's Gull

Larus heermanni Cassin

NG–144; G–146; PW–pl 33; AW–pl 28; AM(II)–50

	MF		
SAUCER	3	I: 28? DAYS	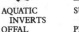
MF?	(2–3)	SEMIPRECOCIAL	AQUATIC
	MONOG	F: ? DAYS	INVERTS
		MF	OFFAL

SAUCER MF? — 3 (2–3) MONOG — MF I: 28? DAYS SEMIPRECOCIAL F: ? DAYS MF — AQUATIC INVERTS OFFAL — SURFACE DIPS PIRACY

BREEDING: Isolated coasts or flat, rocky islets, usu with grass clumps. 1 brood. **DISPLAYS**: Congregated females call and squat; males approach. Pairs bill and call. Courtship feeding oft part of nest relief. **NEST**: Usu well-formed scrape, unlined. In grass makes compact saucer of twigs, dry grass, weeds, and feathers. **EGGS**: Grayish-cream, marked with lavender/brown/blue, occ wreathed. 2.3" (59 mm). **DIET**: Incl shrimp, mollusks, insects, occ scavenge shores, oft in vicinity of kelp beds. **CONSERVATION**: Winters s to Pacific coast of Guatemala. **NOTES**: Colonial. Oddly, range expands to n and s in winter. Embryo is more susceptible to over-heating than to chilling; incubation appears most important as means of shading eggs to protect from lethal temperatures in hot desert breeding environment. Breeding biology little known. Oft pirate prey from pelicans, gannets, and boobies, usu forcing latter two species to disgorge. Flocks with other gulls. Adult plumage attained in third year. **ESSAYS**: Piracy, p. 159; Gull Development, p. 171; Coloniality, p. 173; Gulls and Predators, p. 169; Incubation: Heating Eggs, p. 393; Mixed-Species Flocking, p. 433. **REFS**: Bartholomew and Dawson, 1979; Bennett and Dawson, 1979; Burger, 1987; Cramp and Simmons, 1983.

Franklin's Gull

Larus pipixcan Wagler

NG–144; G–148; PE–88; PW–pl 33; AE–pl 45; AW–pl 31; AM(II)–44

MF	3	MF		
	(2–4)	I: 24–25 DAYS	EARTHWORMS	HAWKS
	MONOG	SEMIPRECOCIAL	FISH	HOVER &
		F: 32 DAYS		POUNCE
		MF		

BREEDING: Prairie freshwater marshes, sloughs and marshy lakes. 1 brood. **DISPLAYS**: Courtship: female begs for food, male regurgitates, both head toss. **NEST**: Usu in water 2'–3' deep, anchored to large floating platform of dead reeds. Well-maintained nest of coarse veg, lined with finer materials. Materials added throughout incubation and brooding; oft stolen from unguarded nests. **EGGS**: Buff/greenish-buff, marked sparsely with brown. 2.1" (52 mm). **DIET**: Oft follow agricultural machinery to forage on flushed insects, worms; chicks fed mostly earthworms. **CONSERVATION**: Winters on Pacific coast of S.A. s to s Chile. **NOTES**: Gregarious, nest in large colonies. Breeding cycle well synchronized within colony subareas. Very wary on breeding grounds; desert nest if too disturbed. Like other gulls, prior to egg laying leave colony at night. Rarely give distraction display. Young remain on nest platform 25–30 days. Early-season fledglings have higher survival rate than late-season birds. Parent-chick recognition occurs later than in ground-nesting gulls. Oft compete with coots for nest sites. Adult plumage attained in second year. **ESSAYS**: Parent-Chick Recognition, p. 193; Gull Development, p. 171; Vocal Development, p. 601; Coloniality, p. 173; Gulls and Predators, p. 169. **REFS**: Burger, 1972, 1974.

drop their food plants immediately upon surfacing when approached by a pirate. Although coots can be quite aggressive, they seldom attack the pirates, perhaps because the extensive preening required after agonistic interactions would consume too much time that could be more profitably spent feeding. Coots can be pirates as well as victims; groups of two to five juvenile coots have been known to snatch aquatic vegetation from the bills of diving ducks and swans.

But most groups of birds do not practice piracy. It is unknown in most songbirds and not recorded in pigeons, doves, or game birds. Apparently piracy is a behavior that evolves under rather special ecological circumstances. Most birds seem to have the greatest reproductive success collecting their own food, rather than running the risks of stealing it from others.

SEE: Natural Selection, p. 237; Dabblers vs. Divers, p. 75. REFS: Amat and Soriguer, 1984; Ryan, 1981.

How Do Birds Fly?

Hold a strip of paper lengthwise and blow along the top of it and you will see in action the physical principle that governs the flight of both birds and airplanes: the higher the velocity of air passing over a surface, the lower the pressure on that surface. Wings are held at an angle relative to the airflow and shaped in a manner that causes the air to move more rapidly over their upper surfaces than beneath their lower ones. As you can see in the diagram, the airflow splits at the leading edge of the wing and rejoins at the trailing edge. The air moving over the top travels a greater distance to get past the wing than does air going under the bottom of the wing, and therefore the "over" air must move faster to "catch up" with the "under." This difference in speed, according to the principle first enunciated in 1738 by the Swiss physicist Daniel Bernoulli, reduces the pressure on the upper wing surface. You can think of the upper air thinning out as it races to cover a greater distance in the same time as the air going under the wing. The lower pressure can be thought of as sucking the wing upward, creating "lift" which counters the downward pull of gravity—just as blowing over the top of the strip of paper causes it to rise against the force of gravity that is pulling it downward. That is a simplified description of how much of the lift of a wing is generated; the details we'll leave in the realm of mathematical aerodynamics. It will suffice here to note that a bird or an airplane will remain airborne at a given altitude when its lift is equal to its weight.

The angle at which the wing meets the airflow is known as the "angle of attack." As that angle is increased, the bird is able to fly at a slower speed. If the angle of attack is increased too much, however, the smooth flow of the air over the wing's upper surface is disrupted, lift is lost, and the

Laughing Gull

Larus atricilla Linnaeus

NG–144; G–148; PE–88; PW–pl 33; AE–pl 43; AM(II)–42

			MF I: 20 DAYS		
SAUCER	3		SEMIPRECOCIAL	GARBAGE	HIGH
MF	(2–4)		F: 35 DAYS	SNAILS	DIVES
	MONOG		MF	INSECTS	PIRACY

BREEDING: Marshes, scattered patches of long grass in sand. 1 brood. **DISPLAYS:** Long calls, head tosses, and crooning directed at potential mate by courting male. **NEST:** Esp in tall grass, also in grass under bushes, between dunes, oft concealed in surrounding veg. Scrape minimally lined; saucer elaborately interwoven of coarse grass lined with fine grass, sticks, debris. Building continues throughout reproductive cycle in areas subject to flooding. **EGGS:** Olive-buff/olive-brown, marked with brown, wreathed. 2.1″ (54 mm). **DIET:** Also fish, rarely seabird eggs and chicks. Young initially fed half-digested regurgitant. **CONSERVATION:** Winters s on coast to n Peru (w) and to Colombia e to Amazon delta (e). **NOTES:** Nests in colonies, occ with 1000s of nests; occ assoc with terns, Black Skimmers. Herring Gulls oft prey on eggs and young, compete for nest sites within established Laughing Gull colonies. Nest in center of colony more successful, eggs larger, hatch earlier, females older, than nests on perimeter. Adults forage more successfully than young birds. Adult plumage attained in third year. **ESSAYS:** Parent-Chick Recognition, p. 193; Vocal Functions, p. 471; Gull Development, p. 171; Coloniality, p. 173; Geometry of the Selfish Colony, p. 19; Gulls and Predators, p. 169. **REFS:** Burger, 1976; Burger and Gochfeld, 1985; Montevecchi, 1978; Schreiber and Schreiber, 1980.

Bonaparte's Gull

Larus philadelphia Ord

NG–146; G–148; PE–88; PW–pl 33; AE–pl 48; AW–pl 29; AM(II)–48

			MF(?) I: 24 DAYS		
GROUND	MF(?)	3	SEMIPRECOCIAL	AQUATIC	HIGH DIVES
4′–20′		(2–4)	F: ? DAYS	INVERTS	GROUND
		MONOG	MF	FISH	GLEAN

BREEDING: In open conif woodland near ponds, lakes. 1? brood. **DISPLAYS:** ? **NEST:** Uses abandoned tree nests placed on branch several feet from trunk, or occ build on ground, of twigs bound with turf, lined with hay and moss. **EGGS:** Brown/buff, marked with brown. 2.0″ (50 mm). **DIET:** Mostly insects; in migration takes (esp) fish, also shrimp, other crustaceans, worms. Foraging flight higher when feeding on fish than when feeding on insects. Dips for insects trapped in water surface layer. **CONSERVATION:** Winters s to w c Mexico. **NOTES:** Quite ternlike in flight. Breeding biology not well known. Immatures forage less efficiently than adults. Bay of Fundy is major staging area prior to autumn migration. Adult plumage attained in second year. **ESSAYS:** Empty Shells, p. 165; Gull Development, p. 171; Coloniality, p. 173; Gulls Are Attracted to Their Predators, p. 169. **REFS:** Braune, 1987a, b; Braune and Gaskin, 1982; Burger, 1987; MacLean, 1986.

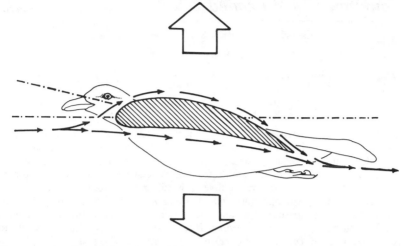

Diagram of gull in flight. Upper thick arrow: lift. Lower thick arrow: gravity. Thin arrows indicate airflow over wing—note the longer route over the top of wing, necessitating higher speed of airflow which generates lift. Long, lower dot-dash line: axis of airflow. Upper, shorter dot-dash line: axis of wing. The angle between the dot-dash lines is the angle of attack.

wing "stalls." Both birds and airplanes tend to increase the angle of attack and then stall their wings in the process of slowing down and landing.

The secondary feathers (inner portion of the wing) remain close together, making an airfoil similar to that of an airplane's wing. On the leading edge of a bird's wing is a structure called the "alula" (a few feathers on the bird's "thumb"), which forms a slot that helps to smooth the airflow at high angles of attack. The alula, like similar slots on the wings of many airplanes, helps to maintain lift at lower airspeeds.

Bird generate the necessary lift by moving forward through the air. They produce forward motion in a manner similar to the way propeller-driven aircraft do. Birds, lacking propellers, accomplish this feat in part with their primary feathers (the ones toward the end of the wing). The upper surfaces of those feathers are oriented partly forward, and on the downstroke the wings tend to move downward and forward. On the downstroke much of the "lift" the primaries create pulls the bird ahead because the low-pressure surfaces of the primaries are directed forward (that forward-directed lift is called "thrust"). The wings are often folded near the body on the upstroke (during which the wings also move backward), and the primaries are separated from each other to reduce air resistance. The primaries also twist in their orientation so that they can still provide some thrust on the upstroke, while the secondaries still provide lift (they also contribute to propulsion).

SEE: Wing Shapes and Flight, p. 227; Soaring, p. 215; Skimming: Why Birds Fly Low Over Water, p. 195; How Fast and High Do Birds Fly?, p. 81. REFS: Penny-cuick, 1975; Rueppell, 1977.

Common Black-headed Gull
Larus ridibundus Linnaeus

NG–146; G–148; PE–88; AE–pl 46; AM(II)–48

MF   3
MF
I: 23–26 DAYS

(2–3)   SEMIPRECOCIAL   SURFACE
MONOG   F: 35–42 DAYS   DIPS
MF   PIRACY

BREEDING: Coastal marsh, lakes, rivers. 1 brood. **DISPLAYS:** Pair formation: male performs forward-leaning and head-flagging. **NEST:** On ground, of dried grass. Male selects site and begins building; male and female maintain and add material through incubation. Material oft stolen from unguarded nests. **EGGS:** Dull green/gray/brownish, marked with brown/olive. 2.1" (52 mm). **DIET:** Insects, worms, aquatic inverts, etc.; scavenges garbage. **CONSERVATION:** Winters within N.A. or in Old World. European populations have undergone enormous expansion in numbers and range during this century; recently colonized from Europe, likely to become increasingly common breeder in N.A. **NOTES:** Colonial, nesting within established colonies of other similar species, esp Laughing Gull. As in other gulls, third eggs in 3-egg clutches tend to be somewhat smaller, which accounts for significantly lower survival in third-egg chicks compared with chicks from first and second eggs. Very rarely give distraction display. Breeding plumage attained in second year. Known in Europe as Black-headed Gull. **ESSAYS:** Empty Shells, p. 165; Average Clutch Size, p. 51; Parent-Chick Recognition, p. 193; Gull Development, p. 171; Coloniality, p. 173; Gulls and Predators, p. 169; Range Expansion, p. 459. **REFS:** Cramp and Simmons, 1983; Holt et al., 1986; Lundberg and Vaisanen, 1981; Ulfstrand, 1979.

Little Gull
Larus minutus Pallas

NG–146; G–148; PE–88; AE–pl 47; AM(II)–46

MF   2–3
MF
I: 23–25 DAYS

(2–5)   SEMIPRECOCIAL   CRUSTACEANS
MONOG   F: 21–24 DAYS   FISH
MF

BREEDING: Grassy lowland, freshwater marshes. 1 brood. **DISPLAYS:** Complex territorial displays that blend into courtship; engages in courtship feeding, female begs from hunched posture. **NEST:** Lined with grass, reeds, leaves. **EGGS:** Yellowish/olive-brown/greenish-gray, marked with reddish-brown/gray. 1.6" (41 mm). **DIET:** Mainly insects; in winter takes mostly fish, marine inverts. Oft picks food from surface of water while in flight. **CONSERVATION:** Winters within U.S. or in Old World. **NOTES:** Smallest gull. Colonial; within colony, nests oft close together. Eurasian species now breeding in Great Lakes region. Very tame. Oft gregarious. Swallowlike and butterflylike flight resembles tern more than gull. Adult plumage attained in second year. **ESSAYS:** Gull Development, p. 171; Coloniality, p. 173; Courtship Feeding, p. 181; Gulls Are Attracted to Their Predators, p. 169; Range Expansion, p. 459. **REFS:** Cramp and Simmons, 1983; Veen, 1980.

Indeterminate Egg Layers

Some birds, such as Barn Swallows, doves, shorebirds, Tricolored Blackbirds, large raptors, and many small songbirds, lay a precise number of eggs in each clutch. Removing one or more eggs, adding additional ones, or the hatching of some, will not lead the female to deviate from the predetermined number. Other birds, however, respond to the loss of eggs by laying more. The domestic hen is the best-known example; take away each egg she lays, and she can lay at a rate of very nearly an egg a day for a year (a talent which, of course, has been enhanced through selective breeding). A Northern Flicker normally lays 6 or 7 eggs. When, however, all eggs after the first were removed from the nest of one female, she laid 71 eggs in 73 days.

Such "indeterminate" layers, nonetheless, stop laying when they are sitting on the "proper" number and are left undisturbed. There is some sort of feedback from the number of eggs being incubated to the hormonal system that controls production of eggs by the ovary (only one ovary functions in the vast majority of birds). A clue to the mechanism has been provided by studies of Black-headed Gulls. Courtship in these birds stimulates the ovary to start producing eggs, and the female begins incubation with the first egg. The process of incubation starts to shut down the ovaries. One or two eggs may already be far enough along to complete their development and be laid, but not three. Therefore the female gull will lay a total of two or three eggs, but not four. If she is supplied with a wooden egg to incubate before the development of the first egg in her ovary has proceeded far enough, she will lay no eggs at all.

SEE: Average Clutch Size, p. 51; Variation in Clutch Sizes, p. 339; Hormones and Nest Building, p. 547.

Empty Shells

Birds appear to have an aversion to empty eggshells. Upon discovery, shells are typically picked up with the bill, flown from the nest, and dropped at some distance. Grebes thrust their eggshells under the water, releasing them far from the nest. Adult hawks usually eat the shells. Many birds with precocial young desert both nest and eggshells, herding their chicks elsewhere. These devices for distancing chicks from the remains of the eggs attracted the attention of the pioneer ethologist Niko Tinbergen, who studied the shell-disposal behavior of Common Black-headed Gulls—a European species that is starting to colonize eastern North America.

Common Black-headed Gulls normally fly away with the eggshell within a couple of hours after a chick hatches; sometimes they carry it off within minutes. Tinbergen hypothesized that the bright white lining of the shell would make the nest easier to detect by predators. But predators such

Ross' Gull

Rhodostethia rosea MacGillivray

NG–146; G–146; PE–84; PW–pl 33; AW– 339; AM(II)–80

			MF		
MF(?)	3		I: 21–22 DAYS	FISH	GROUND
	(2–3)		SEMIPRECOCIAL	AQUATIC	GLEAN
	MONOG		F: 20+ DAYS	INVERTS	
			MF		

BREEDING: Arctic coastal tundra, river deltas, usu near tundra-taiga boundary. 1 brood. **DISPLAYS**: Courtship: near nest, face each other, raise tail, and call softly; side-by-side, circle one another. **NEST**: Near water; shallow, in grass, on moss hummock, lined with fine materials. **EGGS**: Olive, faintly marked with reddish-brown, occ wreathed. 1.7″ (44 mm). **DIET**: Marine inverts incl crustaceans, mollusks, worms; occ offal. Hover glean from surface of water, oft dipping in from above. Young initially fed regurgitant. **CONSERVATION**: Wintering unknown, likely pelagic in open arctic waters. First known N.A. breeding in 1980, in Churchill, Manitoba. Global population <10,000. **NOTES**: Most strictly arctic of all gulls. More tern-like than gull-like. Female performs distraction display. After 5 days, young see adults only for feeding; by day 15, fed 4×/day, making colony look deserted. Dark patch under eye possibly reduces ice and water glare (similar to "war paint" used by baseball players). Pink coloration diet dependent. Adult plumage attained in second year. **ESSAYS**: Gull Development, p. 171; Coloniality, p. 173; Gulls and Predators, p. 169. **REFS**: Chartier and Cooke, 1980; Cramp and Simmons, 1983; Divoky, 1976.

Ring-billed Gull

Larus delawarensis Ord

NG–148; G–146; PE–86; PW–pl 33; AE–pl 38; AW–pl 24; AM(II)–54

		MF		
MF	2–4 (1–7)	I: 21 DAYS		HIGH DIVES
	MONOG	SEMIPRECOCIAL		SURFACE
	(POLYGYN)	F: ? DAYS		DIPS
		MF		

BREEDING: Rocky islets or isolated coasts, occ marshes. 1 brood. **DISPLAYS**: Courting pair face each other, one lowers head, flattens crown, elongates; pair then alternately circle several times, raise heads and call. Female oft assumes "submissive" hunched posture. **NEST**: Open or concealed among rocks on matted veg; of grass, forbs, rubbish, etc., lined with fine grass, feathers. Occ simple lined scrape. **EGGS**: Buffy white, marked with browns. 2.3″ (59 mm). **DIET**: Fish, insects, worms, rodents, bird eggs, offal; in winter, much garbage. Chicks' diet parallels adults' diet. **CONSERVATION**: Winters s to s Mexico, Bahamas, and Greater Antilles. Increased in response to food provided by garbage dumps. **NOTES**: Colonial, occ assoc with California Gulls, terns, ducks, cormorants. Polygyny and females associating without males are rare (less than 1% of nests in large colonies) and account for all nests with >4 eggs. Mate change oft with neighbor of previous year, result of esp strong nest site tenacity. Young remain in nest on day of hatching. Frequent pirate. Adult plumage attained in third year. **ESSAYS**: Parent-Chick Recognition, p. 193; Vocal Development, p. 601; Gull Development, p. 171; Site Tenacity, p. 189; Coloniality, p. 173; Gulls and Predators, p. 169. **REFS**: Boersma and Ryder, 1983; Conover, 1984; Southern et al., 1985.

as Herring Gulls and Carrion Crows seemed to have little trouble locating blotched, khaki-colored eggs that seem well camouflaged to the human eye. Furthermore, there are risks involved in shell disposal. When the gull leaves to dispose of the shell, the chicks and any remaining eggs are exposed for up to ten seconds, more than enough time for a winged predator to zoom in, grab one of them, and depart.

Tinbergen tested his hypothesis in several ways. In an area patrolled by predators, he distributed a mix of gull eggs, some unmodified and some painted white. The results were unambiguous: although both kinds of eggs were found and eaten, the white ones were discovered more frequently. Then he and his coworkers put out two sets of unmodified gull eggs, some alone and some accompanied by empty eggshells placed about four inches away. The eggs were covered with a few grass straws to help camouflage them, and those with the shells nearby were covered a little better than the lone eggs. Again, the results were clear: even though they were better camouflaged, eggs near shells were three times more likely than lone eggs to be found and eaten by gulls and crows.

Further experiments showed that the farther from an intact egg the eggshell was placed, the safer the intact egg. And the gulls, when presented with variously colored but otherwise identical eggshell "dummies" (bent strips of metal), were most likely to remove from their nests those resembling real eggshells. There was a lesser tendency to dispose of dummies with very conspicuous colors like red or blue, and *no* tendency to remove green dummies that blended well with the surrounding grass. Color, not shape, proved to be the crucial clue eliciting shell disposal. These two experiments reinforced the idea that eggshell removal improved protection from predators. The experiment with dummies indicated, in addition, that evolution had produced in the gulls a response that reduced the conspicuousness of the nest not only through removal of shells and other prominent objects, but through maintenance of vegetation that might help camouflage eggs and brood.

Tinbergen went on to discover a great deal about how the gulls differentiate between an egg, a half-hatched chick, and an empty eggshell. To determine whether the thin edge of a broken shell was the main characteristic telling the adult that it was not an egg, he did a series of tests using modified eggs—blown eggs with the shell intact but empty; blown eggs with additional flanges of broken eggshell glued to them; eggshells open and filled with either plaster or cotton wool; and eggshells open and filled with lead weighing as much as a chick. His results showed that it is the weight of the chick that apparently prevents the gulls from disposing of a hatching egg with a thin edge before the chick is free. If a gull started to pick up a shell containing a lead weight in it, it stopped immediately. Not a single "chick-weighted" shell was removed from the nest.

The gulls' shell-disposal behavior seems to be grounded in both instinct and learning. First-time breeders remove shells experimentally placed in their nests even before they have laid their first egg, presumably an act

Thayer's Gull

NG–152; G–144; PE–86; AE–pl 35; AW–pl 17; AM(II)–60

  ?

  ?

MF(?)

2
(2–3)
MONOG

MF(?)
I: ? DAYS
SEMIPRECOCIAL
F: ? DAYS
MF(?)

BREEDING: On cliffs facing maritime sounds. 1 brood. **DISPLAYS:** ? **NEST:** Near veg on rocks close to sea. **EGGS:** Mottled brown or olive. 2.9″ (74 mm). **DIET:** Omnivore. Eats everything from decaying fish to berries, eggs, and young of other gulls. **CONSERVATION:** Winters s to c Baja. **NOTES:** Interbreeds to an unknown extent with Iceland Gull, forming mixed colonies on Baffin Island. Adult plumage attained in fourth year. Formerly considered as a race of the Herring Gull; breeding biology is largely unstudied. **ESSAYS:** Hybridization, p. 501; Gull Development, p. 171; Parent-Chick Recognition, p. 193; Gulls Are Attracted to Their Predators, p. 169; Coloniality, p. 173; Superspecies, p. 375; How Do We Find Out About Bird Biology?, p. 319. **REF:** Smith, 1966.

Herring Gull

NG–150; G–144; PE–86; PW–pl 33; AE–pl 37; AW–pl 18; AM(II)–58

CLIFF
TREE
(<60′)

MF

3
(1–4)
MONOG

MF
I: 24–28 DAYS
SEMIPRECOCIAL
F: 35 DAYS
MF

SURFACE
DIPS
HIGH DIVES

BREEDING: Rocky terraces, grassy hummocks on sandy coasts, tundra, lakeside cliffs, grassy islands, salt marsh. 1 brood. **DISPLAYS:** Complex soliciting; courtship feeding; "choking" (swollen neck held in "S," breast pointed at ground). Male head tosses, neck stretches, calls. **NEST:** Of grass, moss, debris, lined with fine grass, feathers; oft concealed under veg. Perennial site, constantly rebuilt. **EGGS:** Olive/ light-blue/cinnamon, marked with brown. 2.9″ (72 mm). **DIET:** Scavenger, eats anything from garbage to berries; opportunistic predator on adult birds, eggs and young of other gulls. **CONSERVATION:** Winters s (mostly pelagic and along coasts) through West Indies and C.A. Increased numbers and expanding range due to reduced egg predation by humans and increased availability of garbage to supplement diets. **NOTES:** Colonial, usu near water. Occ polygyny and female-female "pairings" reported in Great Lakes. Young solicit feeding by bowing to adult, and touching or holding adult's bill. Both sexes brood. Young form creches; fed for up to 40 days postfledging (very long for gull). Esp strong site tenacity. Competes with Great Black-backed Gull for best nesting habitat. Frequent pirate. Adult plumage attained in fourth year. **ESSAYS:** Feeding Birds, p. 349; Eye Color, p. 233; Creches, p. 191; Empty Shells, p. 165; Gulls and Predators, p. 169; Parent-Chick Recognition, p. 193; Site Tenacity, p. 189. **REFS:** Burger, 1983, 1984; Cramp and Simmons, 1983; Morris and Haynes, 1977.

programmed into their genes. But birds that have been given dummy eggs of unnatural colors (including black) to incubate, preferentially remove dummy shells of the same color. Such preferential association seems to be a learned response "fine-tuning" their instinctive egg-removal reaction.

Tinbergen observed that oystercatchers and Ringed Plovers removed eggshells from their nests much more rapidly than did the gulls. He concluded that the slowness of the gulls was related to their colonial nesting habits. Some Common Black-headed Gulls will gulp down their neighbors' pipped eggs or freshly hatched chicks. Apparently it pays parent gulls to stay with the chicks until they are dry and fluffy, in order to prevent cannibal gulls from attacking them. Oystercatchers and plovers, being solitary nesters, do not run the same risk by leaving the nest early to dispose of shells.

SEE: Gull Development, p. 171; Hatching, p. 233; Parental Care, p. 555; Bird-Brained, p. 415. REF: Tinbergen, 1963.

Gulls Are Attracted to Their Predators

When a weasel, fox, or other predator enters a breeding colony of gulls, numerous birds gather in the air above the intruder, making it very conspicuous. Gulls come from a considerable distance and circle or hover over the predator for quite a while, sometimes even landing in its vicinity before returning to their territories. With the exception of those whose nests are immediately threatened, the gulls show little inclination to attack. Instead they appear nervous and ready to flee.

Experiments using models of predators show that breeding Herring and Lesser Black-backed Gulls are more attracted to models that have a dead gull placed close to them than they are to the models alone. Furthermore, once gulls have seen a predator model with a dead gull, they are more attracted to it if experimenters place it within the colony again on the same day, even without the dead gull. Indeed, there is some evidence that the heightened reaction to the predator lasts at least a day after it is seen with the dead bird. This heightened reaction is specific to the predator model seen with the corpse—there is no increased reaction to a model of a different predator subsequently presented in the same place. After seeing a predator model with a dead gull, the live gulls alight farther from the model on subsequent encounters. They remain attracted, but are more cautious.

These results indicate that the attraction of the gulls to their enemies is a method of learning about them. Apparently they can generalize—they draw conclusions about the predator after another gull has had a lethal encounter with it. This is a beneficial reaction, since mammalian predators such as weasels and foxes may engage in "surplus killing"—dispatching more victims than they can consume. Also these hunters can specialize for a

California Gull

NG–150; G–144; PE–86; PW–pl 33; AW–pl 19; AM(II)–56

			MF		LOW DIVES
	MF	2–3	I: 25 (23–27) DAYS		
		(1–5)	SEMIPRECOCIAL	INVERTS	
		MONOG	F: 45 DAYS	VERTS	
			MF		

BREEDING: Isles, open sand or gravel with scattered grass, or along lake and pond shores. 1 brood. **DISPLAYS:** Very similar to other members of superspecies #15. **NEST:** Of sticks, dried weeds, rubbish, feathers. **EGGS:** Brown/olive/gray/olive-buff, marked with dark brown/gray. 2.7″ (68 mm). **DIET:** Also worms, mice, other birds and their eggs, garbage; in winter, takes crabs and fish but mostly scavenges (esp fish). **CONSERVATION:** Winters s to n w Mexico. **NOTES:** Colonial, nests occ clustered within 2′–3′ of each other. Inland breeder. This is the bird that saved Mormons from great plague of grasshoppers in 1848, and inspired seagull monument in Salt Lake City. More time spent preening and sleeping and less in defense than denser-nesting but similar Ring-billed Gulls. Feeding rate, nest attendance, reproductive success, central nesting position, all increase with age. Clutches of >3 result from abnormal female-female "pairs," with no male involved. Usu do not breed until fourth year when adult plumage is attained. **ESSAYS:** Hybridization, p. 501; Gull Development, p. 171; Parent-Chick Recognition, p. 193; Gulls Are Attracted to Their Predators, p. 169; Coloniality, p. 173; Superspecies, p. 375. **REFS:** Conover, 1984; Pugesek, 1983; Winkler, 1985.

Glaucous Gull

NG–152; G–140; PE–84; PW–pl 33; AE–pl 36; AW–pl 20; AM(II)–72

			MF		PIRACY
GROUND	MF	3	I: 27–28 DAYS		
		(2–4)	SEMIPRECOCIAL		
		MONOG	F: 45–50(?) DAYS		
			MF		

BREEDING: Rocky coasts or margins and islands of tundra lakes. 1 brood. **DISPLAYS:** Complex soliciting, courtship feeding. Cop follows courtship feeding, "choking" (swollen neck held in "S," breast pointed at ground). Male head tosses, neck stretches, calls. **NEST:** Large mounds of soft grass and other materials, oft lined with fine veg, feathers. Added to yearly, probably by same pair. **EGGS:** Buffy olive, marked with brown. 3.0″ (76 mm). **DIET:** Fish, marine inverts, carrion, also seabird eggs and young (oft taken from nearby breeders), small mammals, insects; berries. Pirates from other birds (esp eiders) by chasing them until they disgorge their food. Also takes small seabirds, esp young on fledging flight from breeding colony. **CONSERVATION:** Winters within N.A. **NOTES:** Colonial (usu <50 nests per colony), oft with other species, or solitary (esp inland). Adults defend eggs and chicks vigorously. Young tended by parents >2 weeks postfledging. Adult plumage attained in fourth year. **ESSAYS:** Hybridization, p. 501; Gull Development, p. 171; Parent-Chick Recognition, p. 193; Gulls and Predators, p. 169; Coloniality, p. 173; Courtship Feeding, p. 181; Piracy, p. 159; Parental Care, p. 555. **REFS:** Cramp and Simmons, 1983; Stempniewicz, 1983.

period of time on one group of prey. An animal that has killed one gull may be more likely to kill others; individual foxes have been observed habitually killing gulls in breeding colonies. It requires little imagination, then, to see the potential adaptive advantage for gulls of investigating predators.

SEE: Natural Selection, p. 237; Flock Defense, p. 235; Bird-Brained, p. 415; Coloniality, p. 173; Distraction Displays, p. 115. REF: Kruuk, 1976.

Gull Development

Gull chicks are semiprecocial: they hatch with their eyes open, covered with down, and able to walk; but unlike fully precocial chicks, they remain in or near the nest for the first two or three weeks. For the next several weeks they hide in nearby vegetation (when available) until they fledge. Both adults feed the chicks regurgitated meals at least through fledging and, in some species (such as the Herring Gull), for a considerable postfledging period. To elicit the adult's feeding response, the chicks peck at the adult's bill, which is often adorned with a "target"—a contrasting spot.

When juvenile gulls are fledged they do not look like their parents, but instead have a distinctive streaked brown plumage. As the birds mature, the patterns of the plumage change, and these changes differ among gull species. Some gulls, such as Franklin's and Bonaparte's, develop adult plumage and breed when they are two years old. Others do not reproduce until they are three (i.e., Ring-billed, Heermann's Yellow-footed) or four years old (i.e., California, Western, Thayer's, Herring, and Lesser and Great Black-backed Gulls). The largest gulls, such as the Herring and the Black-backs, may even take five years to reach maturity. Adults usually have different breeding and winter plumages; thus, to identify gulls one must often differentiate among five or more color patterns within a species.

Occasionally immature gulls may form pairs, construct nests, and copulate, but not lay eggs. Such "practice" may increase the gulls' chances of success once their testes and ovaries mature and they are actually able to reproduce.

SEE: Precocial and Altricial Young, p. 581; The Color of Birds, p. 111; Black and White Plumage, p. 177; Eye Color and Development, p. 233. REFS: Grant, 1986; Tinbergen, 1953.

Iceland Gull

NG–152; G–140; PE–84; AE–pl 34; AM(II)–62

GROUND	MF(?)	2–3 MONOG	MF(?) I: ? DAYS SEMIPRECOCIAL F: ? DAYS MF(?)		SURFACE DIPS GROUND GLEAN

BREEDING: Steep cliffs and ledges facing sounds and fjords, usu well inland from ocean. 1 brood. **DISPLAYS:** ? **NEST:** Bulky, of moss, grass, usu on cliff ledge (oft above kittiwakes). **EGGS:** Clay-colored, marked with brown. 2.7″ (68 mm). **DIET:** Mainly fish, also bird eggs and young, crustaceans, mollusks, offal, carrion; berries. Oft feeds like tern, diving from about 15′, occ submerging completely. Occ scavenges beaches. **CONSERVATION:** Winters within N.A. Commensal relationship with humans: valued by fishermen to indicate presence of fish. **NOTES:** Nests in single- or multi-species colonies. Swims well. Adult plumage attained in fourth year. **ESSAYS:** Hybridization, p. 501; Gull Development, p. 171; Parent-Chick Recognition, p. 193; Gulls Are Attracted to Their Predators, p. 169; Coloniality, p. 173; Seabird Nesting Sites, p. 197; Commensal Feeding, p. 35. **REFS:** Cramp and Simmons, 1983; Smith, 1966.

Mew Gull

NG–148; G–146; PE–290; PW–pl 33; AW–pl 23; AM(II)–52

CONIF FLOATING 0′–20′	CUP MF	3 (2–3) MONOG	MF I: 24–26 DAYS SEMIPRECOCIAL F: 30–32 DAYS MF		SURFACE DIPS PIRACY

BREEDING: Rocky or sandy coasts and inland lakes and rivers. 1 brood. **DISPLAYS:** Courtship: female approaches male in hunched posture, head flags, begs food. **NEST:** Scrape in highest part of habitat: river bar, dry land, or marsh; scantily lined with dry grass. Alternatively, a shallow cup on platform of seaweed, twigs, lichens and moss in top of low-growing spruce, on stump, piling. In marsh habitat, oft build floating platform. Occ on flat gravel rooftop. Site oft perennial. **EGGS:** Brown/olive-buff, marked with brown, occ wreathed. 2.2″ (57 mm). **DIET:** Insects, earthworms, fish, mollusks, crustaceans, occ young birds, mice; grain, garbage. Pirates food from other gulls. Chicks fed much fish. **CONSERVATION:** Winters s to n Baja. **NOTES:** Nests in small colonies or as solitary pairs. Named for high-pitched mewing call given in breeding colony. Oft return to breed in natal colony. Adults demonstratively defensive at nest; oft perform distraction display. Protective cover is critical factor in selection of nest site. Drops sea urchins from heights onto beach to crack. Adult plumage attained in third year. Known in Europe as Common Gull. **ESSAYS:** Gull Development, p. 171; Coloniality, p. 173; Gulls and Predators, p. 169; Parent-Chick Recognition, p. 193. **REFS:** Burger and Gochfeld, 1987; Cramp and Simmons, 1983; Vermeer and Devito, 1986, 1987.

Coloniality

Why do some birds, but not others, nest in tightly packed colonies? About one avian species in eight is a colonial nester, either with its own kind or in mixed-species aggregations. The habit is widespread taxonomically; African weavers, relatives of House Sparrows, do it, and so do penguins, Brewer's Blackbirds, and sea gulls. As with other forms of gregariousness, whether colonial nesting evolves in a species depends on the balance between the advantages and disadvantages of the behavior from the viewpoint of the individuals involved. Social interactions related to foraging seem to be one major reason for the maintenance of coloniality in species with unpredictable food supplies that are patchy but locally abundant.

In eastern Washington, Brewer's Blackbirds forage in short vegetation around ponds and streams, mostly close to the colony site, but sometimes a mile or more away. The birds appear to dine primarily on emerging damselflies and other insects, and seem to concentrate their feeding in areas where prey are most abundant. Since the blackbirds exploit resources that are variable in space and time, natural selection does not favor individual territories for resource control. Instead coloniality apparently developed because it allows less-adept birds to follow more-successful foragers when they leave the colony to feed, and perhaps also because it provides some protection against predation.

The Brewer's Blackbird is not the only species that learns about food sources from other foragers. Cliff Swallows that have been unsuccessful in finding food, return to the colony and follow a successful forager to a food source. Most seabirds that nest together also forage together, suggesting that they too, can benefit from each others' good fortune on the hunt.

Some birds, however, nest colonially and forage alone; others forage in flocks and nest alone. Do these make the "information-center" hypothesis less likely? Not necessarily. Herons, which rely on stealth and must forage alone, still apparently learn a great deal about the productivity of remote feeding sites from other birds in their breeding colonies. Flock-feeding ducks do not breed colonially, presumably because their ground nests would be highly vulnerable to predators if grouped in colonies. But the ducks do come together daily in communal "loafing areas"—and information can be exchanged there, rather than at a nesting colony.

In the "information-center" hypothesis, reduced danger of predation is only a secondary benefit of coloniality. While increased numbers do increase chances of detecting the approach of a predator, beyond a colony size of a few hundred individuals the advantage of adding more sentries is vanishingly small. If predator detection were the major advantage of colonial breeding, why should some colonies have thousands of individuals? One possibility is that it leads to "predator saturation." Eggs and nestlings represent a large food resource, but they are present for only a short time. That time may be too brief for some predators to build or maintain populations

Great Black-backed Gull

NG–154; G–142; PE–86; AE–pl 42; AM(II)–74

			MF		
MF	2–3		I: 26–29 DAYS		HIGH
	(1–5)		SEMIPRECOCIAL		DIVES
	MONOG		F: 49–56 DAYS		
			MF		

BREEDING: On rocky coasts, isles, grassy slopes, occ on lakes, salt marshes. 1 brood. **DISPLAYS:** Courtship on territory: female assumes hunched posture, pair preen heads, courtship feed, head toss. **NEST:** Bare or grassy areas, rock outcrops; large mound of seaweed, sod, moss, rubbish, lined with fine grass. If turf dense, no nest built. **EGGS:** Olive-buff/brown, marked with brown. 3.1″ (78 mm). **DIET:** Birds, eggs, fish (oft pirated), squid, small mammals, carrion, offal; berries, grain. **CONSERVATION:** Winters s to Bermuda. **NOTES:** Colonial, oft assoc with Common Eider, Herring Gull, Double-crested Cormorant, terns; occ solitary. Pair bond may last >1 breeding season. Occ hybridizes with Herring Gull. Nest robbers, capable of altering distribution of terns and eiders. Adult plumage attained in fourth year. **ESSAYS:** Feeding Birds, p. 349; Hybridization, p. 501; Gull Development, p. 171; Parent-Chick Recognition, p. 193; Gulls Are Attracted to Their Predators, p. 169; Coloniality, p. 173; Courtship Feeding, p. 181. **REFS:** Butler and Janes-Butler, 1983; Butler and Trivelpiece, 1981; Cramp and Simmons, 1983; Verbeek, 1979.

Western Gull

NG–156; G–142; PW–pl 33; AW–pl 22; AM(II)–68

GROUND	MF(?)	3	F – M	AQUATIC	HIGH DIVES
		(1–5)	I: 26 (25–29) DAYS	INVERTS	GROUND
		MONOG	SEMIPRECOCIAL	OFFAL	GLEAN
			F: 42–49 DAYS		
			MF		

BREEDING: Offshore rocky isles, coastal cliffs. 1 brood. **DISPLAYS:** ? **NEST:** On cliff ledge, grassy hillside, human-built structures. Bulky, of dried grass, forbs, occ in open, occ partly sheltered. Perennial. **EGGS:** Buff/cinnamon-brown/gray, mottled, but variable within and between clutches. 2.9″ (72 mm). **DIET:** Incl clams, crabs, sea urchins, young birds, seabird eggs, small verts, carrion. **CONSERVATION:** Winters s to s Baja. Pesticides implicated in eggshell thinning and aberrant female-female pairing (oft with clutches of 4–5) on Santa Barbara Island. **NOTES:** Colonial, oft assoc with other seabirds. Nest oft adjacent to water for drinking/cooling; belly-soaks to wet eggs for cooling. Embryos can survive short exposure to 114°F (46° C)—unusually heat-tolerant for gulls. Within clutches, size, weight and survival related to laying sequence. During incubation, one parent guards while other sits on nest. Perform distraction display. Dropping shelled prey from air apparently learned behavior. Young disperse from colony at ca. 70 days; parental care occ extends beyond dispersal. Adult plumage attained in fourth year. **ESSAYS:** Hybridization, p. 501; Gull Development, p. 171; Parent-Chick Recognition, p. 193; Gulls and Predators, p. 169; DDT and Birds, p. 21; Temperature Regulation, p. 149. **REFS:** Hand et al., 1981; Hunt and Hunt, 1975; Spear et al., 1986, 1987.

large enough to take full advantage of the resource. On the other hand, large colonies sometimes *expose* their members to predation—since some predators will be attracted to vulnerable colonies and kill many, or even all, of the individuals in the colony.

The "information-center" hypothesis gains plausibility when we consider the occurrence of colonial nesting in species that appear to have little need for mutual predator defense, such as many Old World vultures and (before its decline) the California Condor. Closely related pairs of species, in which one is colonial and one is not, offer further support. The Eurasian Lesser Kestrel breeds in colonies, while the closely related Common Kestrel, whose range partly overlaps the Lesser's, is usually a solitary breeder. It seems unlikely that the Lesser Kestrel cannot find safe places to nest where it feeds, and instead travels considerable distances to gain further security by becoming a member of a colony. The reason for the difference is probably related to diets rather than predator pressures. The Lesser Kestrel feeds mostly on insects, and presumably can learn from other colony members where locusts or other suitable prey are abundant. The Common Kestrel, on the other hand, preys largely on vertebrates—and its success may well be predicated on intimate knowledge of a limited territory.

The avoidance of predation does seem to be the major reason for coloniality in at least some species whose prey is more uniformly or predictably distributed. For example, gaining information about food supplies seems unlikely to be an important reason for the formation of Bank Swallow aggregations. These birds do not forage in groups, 10-day-old young weigh less in large colonies than in small, and in times of hunger, survival of young is lower in large than in small colonies. There is, however, evidence for the antipredator hypothesis in this case. Predators are sometimes deterred by mobs of swallows, and mobs are bigger in the larger colonies. Also, central nests suffer less from predation than do peripheral nests, and larger colonies have proportionately more central nests.

The predator hypothesis is also given some support by the demise of the bird that was the all-time champion colonial nester. The Passenger Pigeon once nested in colonies of billions of birds covering many square miles. When its numbers were reduced to the point at which large colonies could no longer be formed, it declined to extinction in spite of the presence of abundant habitat and food and the absence of further human molestation. In large colonies, the birds presumably saturated local predators; nests of scattered survivors simply may have been too vulnerable to predation. Therefore the Passenger Pigeon may have evolved the need for the presence of large numbers before it would be stimulated to breed.

Perhaps the resolution of the information vs. predation dispute lies in the suggestion that young birds in a colony benefit most from acquiring information, while older birds gain more through protection from predation. Older, more experienced birds are almost always better able to find food than inexperienced individuals. They, however, would suffer more

Glaucous-winged Gull

Supersp #15
Larus glaucescens Naumann

NG–156; G–140; PW–pl 33; AW–pl 21; AM(II)–70

| GROUND | MF(?) | 2–3
(1–3)
MONOG | MF
I: 27–29 DAYS
SEMIPRECOCIAL
F: 35–54 DAYS
MF | OFFAL
FISH
GARBAGE | SURFACE
DIPS |

BREEDING: Coastal cliffs, grassy slopes, bare flats esp on small islands. 1 brood. **DISPLAYS:** Experiments indicate tendency to display to approaching threats and attack receding ones. Lowered head/neck position assoc with fewer attacks. **NEST:** Bulky, of seaweed, kelp, grass, etc. Older birds use more protected sites. **EGGS:** Buff/olive, marked with brown. 2.8″ (71 mm). **DIET:** Oft scavenge esp at canneries, fishing vessels. Usu seek fish for young; mussels less-preferred, indicate food shortage for colony. Frequent pirate. **CONSERVATION:** Winters s primarily in coastal waters to s Baja. Greatly expanded range and numbers in past 50 years to incl inland areas in Pacific n w. **NOTES:** Colonial. Usu return each year to same breeding colony, oft re-pairing with mate of previous year. Extensively hybridizes with Western Gull along WA coast. Gregarious with own and other gull species. Oft crack mollusks by dropping from height. Third egg in 3-egg clutches is smaller, weighs less. Adult plumage attained in fourth year. **ESSAYS:** Hybridization, p. 501; Gull Development, p. 171; Gulls Are Attracted to Their Predators, p. 169; Coloniality, p. 173; Range Expansion, p. 459. **REFS:** Hoffman et al., 1978; Irons et al., 1986; Murphy et al., 1984; Reid, 1987; Verbeek, 1986.

Black-legged Kittiwake

Rissa tridactyla Linnaeus

NG–158; G–146; PE–86; PW–pl 33; AE–pl 39; AW–pl 26; AM(II)–76

| MF | 2
(1–3)
MONOG | MF
I: 23–32 DAYS
SEMIPRECOCIAL
F: 43 DAYS
MF | AQUATIC
INVERTS
OFFAL | HIGH DIVES
GROUND
GLEAN |

BREEDING: Island, steep coastal cliff. 1 brood. **DISPLAYS:** Advertising male performs "choking," rhythmic jerking of head, neck, and bill. Pair formation and mating at nest. **NEST:** Rounded and deep, of seaweed, sod, moss; mud-cemented onto narrow ledge that oft supports only 50% of nest. Lined with fine grass. Perennial. **EGGS:** Buff/brown to off-white, marked with olive, brown. 2.3″ (57 mm). **DIET:** Incl crustaceans, mollusks. Occ pirates, mostly from subadults. Young fed regurgitant. **CONSERVATION:** Winters s along coasts to n w Baja (w), Bermuda (e). **NOTES:** Calls name. Nests in large colonies. Oft re-pairs with mate of previous year, leading to greater reproductive success than experienced breeders with new mates. Much fighting over nest sites and stealing of nest materials. First egg larger in normal 2-egg clutch; first-egg chick hatches first, begs more oft, grows faster, is more aggressive, oft ejects sib from nest (siblicide). Unlike ground-nesting gulls, young are conspicuous, remain at nest until fully fledged. Buoyant, swallowlike flight. Adult plumage attained in second year. **ESSAYS:** Seabird Nesting, p. 197; Parent-Chick Recognition, p. 193; Monogamy, p. 597; Vocal Functions, p. 471; Brood Reduction, p. 307; Piracy, p. 159. **REFS:** Braun and Hunt, 1983; Cramp and Simmons, 1983; Galbraith, 1983; Maunder and Threfall, 1972.

competition for the food they find if they are followed by colony mates to the feeding grounds. So why do they join colonies and accept that competition rather than nest alone? The answer may be that older birds are also more dominant birds, and can acquire the safest nesting sites in the center of the colony. Younger birds, in contrast, may accept a higher risk of losing their eggs and young at the periphery of the colony, but their feeding success is enhanced by the presence of more experienced birds for them to follow.

SEE: Geometry of the Selfish Colony, p. 19; Flock Defense, p. 235; Parasitic Swallows, p. 401; Communal Roosting, p. 615; Mixed-Species Flocking, p. 433; Mobbing, p. 425; The Passenger Pigeon, p. 273; Disease and Parasitism, p. 399. REFS: Blockstein and Tordoff, 1985; Brown 1986; Brown and Brown, 1986; Elgar and Harvey, 1987; Hoogland and Sherman, 1976; Horn, 1968; Hunt et al., 1986; Krebs, 1974; Ward and Zahavi, 1973; Weatherhead, 1985; Wittenberger and Hunt, 1985.

Black and White Plumage

All else being equal, black or dark-colored objects more readily absorb heat than do white or light-colored objects. Therefore, compared to birds with white plumage, birds with black plumage should be better able to absorb radiant solar energy and use it to warm themselves at low temperatures. On the other hand, dark-colored birds should have a problem with overheating in hot environments for the same reason. In nature, however, "all else" is rarely equal, and this simple dichotomy of black plumage as a good absorber of radiant energy and white plumage as a good reflector seldom holds true. If it did, birds with black or dark plumage would not occur in arid regions or other habitats with abundant sunshine and little shade, and birds with white or very light plumage would not be found in very cold environments. In fact, black or dark-colored birds such as blackbirds, Phainopepla, Lark Bunting, ravens, vultures, several hawks, and the darker gulls and herons do inhabit deserts, arid prairies, and southern portions of North America that have high daytime temperatures and abundant sunlight. Likewise, ptarmigan, light-colored gulls, and egrets are found at higher altitudes and latitudes with cooler temperatures.

This apparent paradox can be resolved by considering other avenues of heat exchange between a bird and its environment. Heat will be gained from or lost to the environment depending on whether a bird is hotter or cooler than its surroundings. If body temperature is lower than the air temperature, then heat will tend to flow from the external environment to the bird, which will warm up and possibly face a problem of overheating. The reverse is true when the bird's temperature exceeds the environmental temperature —it may become chilled. The bird's structural adaptations and behavior

Red-legged Kittiwake
Rissa brevirostris Bruch

NG–158; G–146; PW–pl 33; AW–pl 27; AM(II)–78

| | MF(?) | 2
(1–3)
MONOG | MF
I: 23–32 DAYS
SEMIPRECOCIAL
F: 38–48 DAYS
MF | AQUATIC
INVERTS
OFFAL | HOVERS &
PICKS |

BREEDING: On steep island cliffs. 1 brood. **DISPLAYS:** Male advertising incl "choking," rhythmic jerking of head, neck, and bill. Pair formation and mating at nest. **NEST:** Deep, of seaweed, dry grass, moss, cemented with mud onto ledges. Lined with dry grass. Occ uses building ledges and caves. **EGGS:** Bluish/buff/pinkish/brown/white, marked with olive/brown, wreathed. 2.2″ (56 mm). **DIET:** May scavenge offal from fishing vessels, takes drift marine inverts (crustaceans, mollusks). Drinks exclusively salt water. Young fed regurgitant. **CONSERVATION:** Winter resident near breeding areas. **NOTES:** Calls name. Nests in colonies, usu with Black-legged Kittiwake and oft assoc with murres and other seabirds. Breeding biology very similar to Black-legged Kittiwake. Stealing of nest materials common; pair alternately guard nest. Unlike ground-nesting gulls, cliff-bound young are conspicuous, remaining at nest until fully fledged. Sharp claws adapted to clinging and climbing on cliff. Large eyes may be adaptation to low light levels of high latitude wintering areas. Adult plumage attained in second year. **ESSAYS:** Seabird Nesting, p. 197; Parent-Chick Recognition, p. 193; Coloniality, p. 173; Salt Glands, p. 29; Drinking, p. 123. **REFS:** Byrd, 1978; Storer, 1987.

Ivory Gull
Pagophila eburnea Phipps

NG–158; G–140; PE–84; PW–pl 33; AE–pl 32; AM(II)–82

     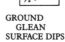

| CLIFF | SCRAPE
MF | 1–2
MONOG | F –M
I: 24–26 DAYS
SEMIPRECOCIAL
F: >35 DAYS
MF | AQUATIC
INVERTS
OFFAL | GROUND
GLEAN
SURFACE DIPS |

BREEDING: On steep cliffs or low rocky islets near ice or snow. 1 brood. **DISPLAYS:** Various displays (long call, head toss, choking) and courtship feeding precede cop. **NEST:** Usu bulky, of debris and seaweed, with shallow depression; occ little or no nest. Building may continue through incubation. **EGGS:** Bluish-olive, marked with brown. 2.4″ (61 mm). **DIET:** Occ scavenges on carrion (whale, walrus, and seal carcasses) and mammal feces; oft forages with kittiwakes, Sabine's Gulls, and picks food from surface while in flight. Chicks fed fish, crustaceans. Like many other gulls, produces pellets of indigestible parts of food. When not breeding forages at edge of pack and drift ice. **CONSERVATION:** Winters in Arctic seas. Colonies very sensitive to disturbance by aircraft, and readily desert nests. **NOTES:** Colonies small, usu <20 pairs, oft mixed with other seabirds. Incubation bouts vary from few minutes to 11 hours. Light, graceful flight. Solitary or in small flocks when not breeding. Adult plumage attained in second year. **ESSAYS:** Gull Development, p. 171; Parent-Chick Recognition, p. 193; Gulls and Predators, p. 169; Coloniality, p. 173; Pellets, p. 297; Courtship Feeding, p. 181; Mixed-Species Flocking, p. 433. **REFS:** Bateson and Plowright, 1959; Cramp and Simmons, 1983; Divoky, 1976.

mediate heat gain and loss by means of conduction (by placing some portion of the body in contact with a surface of different temperature), convection (by exposing the body surface to the wind), radiation (by either emission or absorption of radiant energy, a passive result of the bird/environment temperature difference), and evaporation (by losing body heat via wetting of the plumage or skin or through water vapor in exhaled breath).

The relationship between plumage color and radiative heat gain and loss is not so straightforward as previously believed. The simple rule of black/absorbing and white/reflecting is modified by whether feathers are sleeked or erected, by wind speed, and by how deeply the absorbed radiation actually penetrates through the plumage. At low wind speeds and with feathers sleeked, black plumages acquire higher heat loads than do white plumages, but the heat is absorbed mostly near the outer surface. As wind speed increases, the relative heat gains by white and black plumages converge; the portion of radiation that is not reflected by white plumage penetrates deeper than in black plumage and convection is thus less effective at removing heat from white than from black plumages. With erect feathers, black plumage actually gains less heat than white plumage when wind speeds are moderate or high. Thus, under conditions routinely encountered in arid habitats, birds with dark-colored plumage stay cooler than birds with light-colored plumage! Conversely, at low ambient temperatures and higher wind speeds, erect white plumage gains heat better and is more resistant to heat loss because of better penetration by solar radiation and better resistance to convective heat loss.

This is not to say that thermoregulatory considerations have been the only, or even the most important, selective forces in the evolution of white and black plumages. Surely white plumage in some polar birds has been of overriding importance as camouflage. Similarly, black plumage is very conspicuous in open or light-colored surroundings that are typical of deserts, grasslands, and marshes. Hence, its value as a long-distance signal must also be considered when viewing the evolution of dark plumages in birds of arid or other open habitats. And finally, some plumages, such as the wingtips of many gulls and terns, apparently are black because the dark pigment increases the durability of the feathers.

SEE: Metabolism, p. 325; Temperature Regulation and Behavior, p. 149; Feathers, p. 309; Color of Birds, p. 111; Spread-Wing Postures, p. 25. REFS: Ellis, 1980; Walsberg, 1982; Walsberg et al., 1978; Wunder, 1979.

Sabine's Gull

Xema sabini Sabine

NG–158; G–148; PE–88; PW–pl 33; AE–pl 44; AW–pl 30; AM(II)–82

MF(?)	2		MF	AQUATIC	HOVERS &
	(1–3)		I: 23–26 DAYS	INVERTS	PICKS
	MONOG		SEMIPRECOCIAL	INSECTS	SURFACE DIPS
			F: ? DAYS		
			MF		

BREEDING: Wet coastal meadows and salt-grass flats, oft near tidal beach. 1 brood. **DISPLAYS:** Male attracts female to territory with variety of hunched and arched displays and calling; courtship feeding prior to cop. **NEST:** Depression lined with bits and fragments of veg or unlined. **EGGS:** Brown/olive/buff, faintly marked with brown, occ wreathed. 1.8" (46 mm). **DIET:** Small fish, many insects, also mollusks, aquatic worms, crustaceans, occ eggs and young birds. Do not dive; pick food from water while in flight. Feed on mud flats scavenging dead and dying fish. **CONSERVATION:** Wintering area is Panama s to c Chile and less oft in Atlantic (mostly tropical). **NOTES:** Usu small colonies of 6–15 pairs, occ to 60, oft near Arctic Terns. Hover over breeding sites when disturbed, but relatively silent. Variable distraction display. Young less active than most gulls. More tern-like than gull-like. Continuous wingbeats in flight; seldom, if ever, soars. Adult plumage attained in second year. **ESSAYS:** Gull Development, p. 171; Parent-Chick Recognition, p. 193; Gulls and Predators, p. 169; Coloniality, p. 173; Courtship Feeding, p. 181; Distraction Displays, p. 115. **REF:** Cramp and Simmons, 1983.

Common Tern

Sterna hirundo Linnaeus

NG–162; G–152; PE–96; PW–pl 36; AE–pl 61; AW–pl 44; AM(II)–92

MF	3		MF	AQUATIC
	(1–3)		I: 21–27 DAYS	INVERTS
	MONOG		SEMIPRECOCIAL	INSECTS
			F: 26–27 DAYS	
			MF	

BREEDING: Usu island or coastal beach with sparse matted veg, grassy areas. 1 brood, rarely 2. **DISPLAYS:** Male struts, waddles around female, neck fully extended, bill upward, breast expanded, tail cocked; ritually feeds female, oft interrupted by competing male arriving with food to lure same female. **NEST:** Usu in sand, shells, pebbles, or beach wrack, shaped by body. Lined with grass, shells, seaweed. Occ no nest. **EGGS:** Buff/olive/brown, marked with dark brown, oft wreathed. 1.6" (42 mm). **DIET:** Fish (90% of diet), crustaceans, occ insects. **CONSERVATION:** Winters s to Peru, n Argentina. Blue List 1981–82, Special Concern 1982, Local Concern 1986. Millinery trade devastated populations. MA and Great Lakes populations declining, latter partly from rising water levels and nest site losses to expanding populations of Ring-billed Gulls. **NOTES:** Colonies of tens to thousands. Pair occupy and defend feeding territory away from breeding colony, esp prior to incubation; defense mostly by male. Third egg smallest and least likely to survive. Second clutches rarely successful. Habitually defecate at lowest point of aggressive dive, oft hitting attacker with feces. **ESSAYS:** Courtship Feeding, p. 181; Parent-Chick Recognition, p. 193; Blue List, p. 11; Plume Trade, p. 37. **REFS:** Burger and Lesser, 1979; Cramp, 1985; Morris and Wiggins, 1986; Nisbet, 1983; Wiggins et al., 1984.

Courtship Feeding

During the breeding season you may have watched one adult bird feed another. Whether it occurs when pairs are first getting established or sometime later after incubation has begun, this behavior is known as "courtship feeding." In most species males present solid or regurgitated food to the soliciting female. In species in which the females do the courting, the roles may be reversed.

Courtship feeding is frequently seen in terns. For instance, in an effort to lure females to their territories in the nesting area, a male Common Tern carries a fish around the breeding colony and displays it to prospective mates. After a pair bond is formed, during the "honeymoon period" the male tern actually feeds the female, and soon thereafter they begin to copulate. During the following five to ten days, both sexes feed themselves, but the male also frequently feeds the increasingly dependent female. For the few days prior to egg laying the female is fed almost exclusively by the male, but this activity declines rapidly as the second and third eggs are laid.

It is generally thought that courtship feeding serves more than a ceremonial or pair-bonding function—that it provides the female with considerable nutritional benefit. In turn, the number of eggs and total clutch weight are partly determined by the female's nutritional status. Careful measurements suggest that the total weight of a Common Tern's clutch is correlated with the amount of food the male delivers, especially during the honeymoon. Male Common Terns in one Massachusetts colony were unable to deliver as much food to their mates as males in a second colony. In the colony where the males were less successful, the females laid fewer and lighter eggs. Thus the amount of food the male provides may limit female reproductive output.

If the female's nutritional status is so critical to her reproduction, why does she gradually stop feeding herself prior to egg laying? The probable answer is that she is too heavy to hunt efficiently. Before laying her three-egg clutch a female Common Tern weighs half again as much as she does when not breeding. Terns forage by cruising at low speed and making precise dives at fishes. A female's additional weight would increase the energy requirements of flight, and perhaps make controlled dives too difficult.

This does not mean that improving the female's nutrition is the only function of courtship feeding. In gulls, it is also an important inducement to copulation (as it may be in the Common Tern). It may also serve to facilitate the formation of the pair bond and reduce aggression between the male and female. Still, when a male warbler, crossbill, chickadee, or tern is seen feeding a female, it seems apparent that he is increasing his own reproductive success by keeping her fat and healthy.

SEE: Average Clutch Size, p. 51; Visual Displays, p. 5.   REFS: Nisbet, 1977; Tasker and Mills, 1981.

Arctic Tern
Sterna paradisaea Pontoppidan

NG–162; G–152; PE–96; PW–pl 36; AE–pl 63; AW–pl 46; AM(II)–94

| | MF | 2
(1–3)
MONOG | MF
I: 20–24 DAYS
SEMIPRECOCIAL
F: 21–28 DAYS
MF | AQ INVERTS
OFFAL
INSECTS | |

BREEDING: Offshore islands, rocky or grass-covered coasts, tundra, occ along inland lakes and rivers. 1 brood. **DISPLAYS:** Courtship: conspicuous aerial; on ground, oft raise and extend wings, also courtship feeding. **NEST:** In sand, gravel, moss, or amid shells or rocks. Occ lined with bits of dry grass or shells. **EGGS:** Buff/olive/ brown, marked with dark brown, oft wreathed. 1.6″ (41 mm). **DIET:** Incl crustaceans. Also scavenge. After wet periods feed earthworms to chicks. Oft hover before diving; occ pick from surface, occ pirate. **CONSERVATION:** Mostly pelagic in winter in Antarctic waters s from c Chile, and c Argentina. Millinery threat once severe. **NOTES:** Usu colonial, occ assoc with Common and Aleutian Terns. Long-term pair bond; contact re-established upon return to breeding colony. Strong fidelity to territory. Vigorous nest defense; nest attended 98% of time. Family remains together into migration. Usu breeds at 3 years. Migration can cover 11,000 miles from Arctic to Antarctic. Spends more hours in daylight in both summer and winter than do most other animals. **ESSAYS:** Migration, p. 183; Plume Trade, p. 37; Site Tenacity, p. 189; Courtship Feeding, p. 181; Piracy, p. 159. **REFS:** Cramp, 1985; Godfrey, 1986; Skipnes, 1983.

Gull-billed Tern
Sterna nilotica Gmelin

NG–164; G–154; PE–94; PW–pl 36; AE–pl 68; AW–pl 41; AM (II)–84

| FLOATING | MF | 2–3
(1–4)
MONOG | MF
I: 22–23 DAYS
SEMIPRECOCIAL
F: 28–35 DAYS
MF | AQUATIC
INVERTS
FISH | HOVER &
POUNCE |

BREEDING: Gravel, sand, or shell beaches, occ on grassy portions of islands and salt marshes. 1 brood. **DISPLAYS:** Large, complex repertoire incl aerial displays and courtship feeding. **NEST:** Depression rimmed with sand, shells, sticks, grass, oft concealed in detritus among shells. Lined with shells, grass, sedge; occ unlined. **EGGS:** Buff, marked with browns. 1.9″ (47 mm). **DIET:** Mostly insects, usu hawked over agricultural fields; also spiders, frogs, crustaceans; rarely bird eggs and young, small mammals, and rarely dives for fish. **CONSERVATION:** Winters s to Peru (w), n Argentina (e). Onetime marsh nester, now mostly restricted to beaches. Reportedly declining; numbers reduced by egg collection and plume trade —exterminated from n portion of breeding range. **NOTES:** In colonies or solitary, oft assoc with Common Tern, Black Skimmer. Long-term pair bond. Site tenacity weak. Clutch size decreases and incubation investment increases through season. Hatching asynchronous. Fledglings fed at least 2–3 months. Usu breeds at 5 years. Defecates on intruder during aggressive swoop. **ESSAYS:** Plume Trade, p. 37; Visual Displays, p. 5; Courtship Feeding, p. 181; Coloniality, p. 173; Site Tenacity, p. 189; Average Clutch Size, p. 51; Parental Care, p. 555. **REFS:** Cramp, 1985; Møller, 1981, 1982; Sears, 1978, 1981.

Migration

The arrival of birds in the spring and their disappearance at the end of the breeding season is one of the most familiar aspects of North American bird biology. Seasonal migration enables birds to avoid the physiological stresses of unfavorable climates and to exploit food supplies that are available for only limited periods each year. Thus, many species can breed at high latitudes during the brief but insect-rich arctic summer, and then fly south to the more hospitable climate of the southern United States, Central America, of South America. While we may think of them as "our" birds that go south for the winter, it may be more logical to think of them as southern species that make a relatively brief foray north to breed.

Seasonal migration presumably evolved as a means of increasing lifetime reproductive output. It permits exploitation of areas that either are more productive or provide less competition than the wintering grounds. Moreover, daylight periods in spring and summer are longer at higher latitudes, resulting in more hours per day in which birds can gather food.

Preparation for migration involves both physiological and behavioral changes. Physiological preparation includes the accumulation of fat to provide fuel for prolonged flight. Not uncommonly, passerines lose one-fourth to one-half of their body weight during overwater migration. Behavioral changes are especially prominent in nocturnal migrants, which alter their activity rhythms during darkness and begin to preferentially orient in the direction that they will soon be flying.

Most long-distance migrants, especially smaller birds, fly at night; they may travel continuously or land daily around sunrise to rest and forage. When traveling over water or unsuitable habitats, birds that normally stop each day may fly without a break for longer periods. For example, Blackpoll Warblers migrate overland in spring, but autumn migrants travel nonstop over open ocean from southeastern Canada and the northeastern United States to their wintering grounds in northern South America. Migrants that move only relatively short distances within our region usually travel during the day, generally spending only a few hours of the morning in migration. Aerial foragers, such as swallows and swifts, do not stop but simply feed in flight as they are migrating.

Migration in North America is essentially north-south along four principal routes or "flyways"; Pacific, Central, Mississippi, and Atlantic (see maps below). In Europe and Asia, some migration routes are oriented more east-west, although latitudinal change is still significant. About 150 species of land and freshwater birds that breed in our region winter to the south in Central and South America and the West Indies.

Different species characteristically migrate different distances between wintering and breeding areas. The Arctic Tern, as its name implies, breeds in the high Arctic, winters near the southern tip of South America and as far south as Antarctica. In contrast, Clark's Nutcracker often migrates only a

Roseate Tern

Sterna dougallii Montagu

MF
I: 21–26 DAYS

| MF | 1–2
(1–3)
MONOG | MF
I: 21–26 DAYS
SEMIPRECOCIAL
F: 27–30 DAYS
MF | AQUATIC
INVERTS | |

BREEDING: Usu on offshore islands with sandy, rocky, pebble beaches, among boulders and in open bare or grassy habitat. 1 brood. **DISPLAYS:** Courtship: aerial chase in groups of 3–8; male and female stretch necks upward, strut with drooping wings and elevated tails, or stand side-by-side and call. Courtship feeding. **NEST:** Occ concealed in beach grass, vines, herbaceous plants; also lays among rocks or on sand. Occ lined with bits of dry grass, seaweed, rubbish, oft added during incubation. **EGGS:** Buff/olive-buff, marked with brown, occ wreathed. 1.7" (42 mm). **DIET:** Occ mollusks. Congregate where large fish drive small fish to surface. Oft hover before diving. Pirate food from own and other species. **CONSERVATION:** Winters West Indies s to e Brazil. Blue List 1972, 1979–86. Likely to be listed soon as Endangered. **NOTES:** Colonial, oft assoc with other terns, esp Common Terns. "Greyhound" of the terns. Clutches larger than 2 eggs may be result of 2 females. Hatching asynchronous. Female broods while male guards. Fledglings fed for at least 8 weeks. Usu breed at 3 years. **ESSAYS:** Blue List, p. 11; Piracy, p. 159; How Fast and High Do Birds Fly?, p. 81; Commensal Feeding, p. 35; Coloniality, p. 173. **REFS:** Cramp, 1985; Dunn, 1973; LeCroy and Collins, 1972.

Forster's Tern

Sterna forsteri Nuttall

| GROUND | SAUCER
MF | 3
(2–5)
MONOG | MF
I: 23–24 DAYS
SEMIPRECOCIAL
F: ? DAYS
MF | INSECTS
AQUATIC
INVERTS | AERIAL
FORAGE |

BREEDING: Freshwater and saltwater marshes, marshy borders of ponds and lakes. 1 brood. **DISPLAYS:** ? **NEST:** Deeply hollowed, well rounded, compactly woven platform; lined with bits of reeds, grass. Also makes depression in mud and sand or pats down grass and soil, lined with shells, grass. Oft on muskrat houses, occ nests of Western Grebe. **EGGS:** Buff, marked with dark brown, oft wreathed. 1.7" (43 mm). **DIET:** Insects taken flying over marshes. Also dead fish, live and dead frogs. **CONSERVATION:** Winters s to Guatemala (w), Bahamas and Greater Antilles (e). Oft assoc with wetlands affected by agriculture but impact on terns unknown. **NOTES:** Usu in loose colony; oft assoc with Yellow-headed Blackbird. Site tenacity weak. Larger clutches typically result of 2 females. Usu large, elaborate, well-built nests, similar to those of Franklin's Gull. Vigorous nest defense. Nests occ parasitized by American Coots and Red-necked Grebes. Hostile to other birds, incl Franklin's Gull. **ESSAYS:** Parent-Chick Recognition, p. 193; Swimming, p. 73; Site Tenacity, p. 189; Coloniality, p. 173; Brood Parasitism, p. 287. **REFS:** Bergman et al., 1970; McNicholl, 1982; Salt and Willard, 1971.

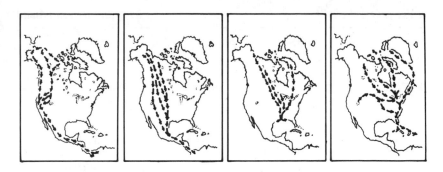

few miles to move from its high-elevation breeding sites in the Rockies or Sierras to lower elevations within the same mountain ranges.

In many bird species, males winter farther north than females or juveniles. Where females are larger than males (as in many birds of prey) or where dominance relationships between the sexes are reversed (as in polyandrous Spotted Sandpipers and phalaropes), females often winter farther north. Three hypotheses have been advanced to explain this phenomenon of differential migration—males, females, and sometimes different age groups within each sex wintering at different latitudes. The body-size hypothesis suggests that larger birds have greater cold tolerance and enhanced ability to fast through periods of inclement weather, and therefore can better endure the rigors of winter. Hence, smaller individuals should migrate farther south. A second explanation is based on dominance relationships within a species: in general, smaller individuals are subordinate to larger ones and therefore should migrate farther south. Third, the arrival-time hypothesis states that if members of one sex experience more intense competition for breeding resources than the other, then individuals of that sex should benefit by early return to the breeding grounds. This can best be achieved by wintering as close as possible to breeding areas.

Because males are larger than females in most migratory species, and because older birds tend to be larger than younger birds, it is often difficult to distinguish among these three hypotheses, which obviously are not mutually exclusive.

Just as many species show strong fidelity to breeding sites to which they return each year to nest, many migrants show some degree of site fidelity to wintering areas. Recent studies of Yellow-rumped Warblers, however, indicate much greater plasticity in choice of wintering site than previously thought. Ornithologists Scott Terrill and Robert Ohmart found that warblers wintering in desert riparian habitats shifted to similar but more southerly habitats in response to changing climatic conditions that led to a scarcity of their insect prey. These observations suggest that birds maintain a physiological readiness to continue their migration in a properly oriented direction well into the winter months. How widespread this ability is among migratory species remains to be determined.

Aleutian Tern

Sterna aleutica Baird

NG–162; G–156; PW–pl 36; AW–pl 50; AM(II)–94

MF(?)	2 (1–3) MONOG?	MF(?) I: 21 DAYS SEMIPRECOCIAL F: ? DAYS MF(?)	AQUATIC INVERTS?	

BREEDING: On small offshore islands and grassy or mossy coastal flats near lagoons or river mouths. 1 brood. **DISPLAYS:** ? **NEST:** Very cryptic, usu with view to water, eggs usu laid within matted grass or moss patches; occ little more than depression. **EGGS:** Clay-yellow/olive-buff, heavily marked with dark brown, occ wreathed. 1.7″ (42 mm). **DIET:** Little known, but probably similar to that of Arctic Tern. **CONSERVATION:** Pelagic in winter but precise range unknown. **NOTES:** Nests in loose colonies, oft assoc with Arctic Tern. Easily disturbed in breeding colony, readily flee nests; no active defense of nest, rely on concealment and crypticity. In mixed colonies with Arctic Terns, benefit from Arctic Tern's aggressiveness toward predators. Will not renest if first clutch destroyed. Young tended at colony 2 weeks postfledging. Forages up to 30 miles from colony. Whistling call very unternlike. **ESSAYS:** Precocial and Altricial Young, p. 581; How Fast and High Do Birds Fly?, p. 81; Coloniality, p. 173; Monogamy, p. 597. **REFS:** Baird, 1978; Buckley and Buckley, 1979; Cramp, 1985.

Least Tern

Sterna antillarum Lesson

NG–166; G–152; PE–96; PW–pl 36; AE–pl 69; AW–pl 42; AM(II)–96

F?	2 (1–3) MONOG	MF I: 20–22 DAYS SEMIPRECOCIAL F: 19–20+ DAYS MF	AQUATIC INVERTS	SKIMS

BREEDING: Open, flat beaches, river and lake margins, usu near shallow water. 1 brood, occ 2 in s. **DISPLAYS:** Courtship: male advertising flight with fish in bill, chased upwards by 1–6 birds, then glide down. Courtship feeding. **NEST:** Usu unlined. Rarely on flat rooftop. **EGGS:** Olive-buff/buff, marked with dark brown. 1.2″ (31 mm). **DIET:** Incl esp crustaceans, insects. More prolonged hovering than other terns. **CONSERVATION:** Winters s to n w S.A., e to Brazil. Endangered Species; declining in most areas. Depredations of cats, rats, and humans oft cause colony desertion. Snowfencing effectively provides shade for chicks and protection from chick predators. Nearly exterminated by plume hunters; typical seasonal kill of 100,000 at turn of century. **NOTES:** Small to large colony, occ solitary. Breeds at 2 yr. Incubating bird cools eggs by dipping into water and shaking water on eggs. Before onset of egg laying, uses nocturnal roosts away from breeding area, reducing amount of time colony subject to nocturnal predators. Adult can recognize mate by call. Hovers and defecates over intruders. Pebbles or shells on sand with short, sparse veg is favored e colony site. **ESSAYS:** Birds and the Law, p. 293; Vocal Functions, p. 471; Plume Trade, p. 37; Temperature Regulation, p. 149. **REFS:** Atwood, 1986; Cramp, 1985; Fisk, 1975; Kotliar and Burger, 1986; Moseley, 1979.

SEE: Navigation and Orientation, p. 559; Shorebird Migration and Conservation, p. 119; Breeding Season, p. 55; Bird Banding and Marking, p. 95; Site Tenacity, p. 189; Irruptions, p. 639; Wintering and Conservation, p. 513. REFS: Gauthreaux, 1982; Keast and Morton, 1980; Ketterson and Nolan, 1983; Mead, 1983; Myers, 1981; Terrill and Ohmart, 1984.

Bird Names—IV

Tern comes from the Old Norse (*taerne*) and the Swedish (*tarna*) names for these birds. Forster's Tern is named after Johann Reinhold Forster who, in the 18th century, accompanied Captain Cook on his voyage around the world and wrote on the birds of Hudson Bay. The first specimen of the Sandwich Tern was shot in the town of that name in Kent, England; similarly the first specimen of the Caspian Tern came from the Caspian Sea. Noddy means "stupid," and the name was given because nesting noddies are tame and easily approached.

The origins of the word gull are thought by some to be the same as those of "gullet," "gulp," and "gullible" (all based on the Latin *gula*, throat). It might, therefore, refer to the birds' scavenging habits. On the other hand, the name might be onomatopoetic. The name of the Mew Gull, however, does not come from the sound it makes, but from the Old English *mew*, meaning "a gull." Bonaparte's Gull was named after the father of avian taxonomy, Charles Bonaparte (p. 463), Ross' Gull after the famed arctic explorer Sir James Ross, and Franklin's Gull after the doomed explorer Sir John Franklin, whose disappearance stimulated much arctic exploration by the expeditions that searched for his party. Dr. Adolphus Heermann, who had a gull named after him, was a collector of eggs and birds on a railroad survey in 1853–54. Joseph Sabine shot the first Sabine's Gull, found as a vagrant in England, and named it for his brother Sir Edward Sabine, a well-known astronomer and physicist. REFS: Choate, 1985; Owen, 1985.

Bird Biologist—David Lack

Although David Lack (1910–73) was British, his impact on ornithology in North America (and elsewhere) was monumental. He helped develop radar during World War II, and then later pioneered its use in studying bird migration. After the war he became Director of the Edward Grey Institute of Field Ornithology at Oxford, and remained in that position for the rest of his life. Much of his work was on island bird faunas, starting with a seminal investigation of the Galapagos finches that had so fascinated Darwin (p. 475). He did pioneering work on the evolution of reproductive strategies in birds, and also encouraged long-term studies of bird population biology, publishing two books on that subject, *The Natural Regulation of Animal Numbers* (1954) and *Population Studies of Birds* (1966).

Black Tern
Chlidonias niger Linnaeus

NG–166; G–156; PE–98; PW–pl 36; AE–pl 75; AW–pl 43; AM(II)–102

GROUND   SCRAPE   3   MF
           MF   (2–4)   I: 21–22 DAYS
                    MONOG   SEMIPRECOCIAL   AQUATIC   SKIMS
                               F: 21–28 DAYS   INVERTS
                               MF   FISH

BREEDING: Freshwater marshes, sloughs, wet meadows. 1 brood, occ 2 in s. **DIS-PLAYS:** Courtship flight: spiralling ascent by 2–20 birds followed by steep downward glide; male advertising flight at 30′–50′ carrying fish in bill, female follows, oft ends in courtship feeding. **NEST:** In dense emergent veg; some nests elaborate, most only loose floating mat of damp veg raising eggs just above water. Eggs oft wet. Oft on muskrat house, occ in abandoned grebe nest; occ no nest. **EGGS:** Dark olive/buff, marked with dark brown, usu wreathed. 1.3″ (33 mm). **DIET:** Hawk insects over meadows and marshes; follow plows. In interior, largely insectivorous; also crayfish, mollusks, etc., fish plucked from surface. Young fed mostly insects. **CONSERVATION:** Winters along both coasts from Panama s to Peru and Surinam. Blue List 1978–86; declining in many areas due largely to loss of wetland habitat. Greatly reduced hatching success in upper midwest may be due to agricultural chemicals. **NOTES:** Small, loose colony, oft assoc with Forster's Terns; oft return to breed in natal colony. Breed at 2 years. Young develop more rapidly than do other terns, apparently result of small size. Nest success exceptionally low. Gregarious all year. Oft hovers. **ESSAYS:** Blue List, p. 11; Coloniality, p. 173; Precocial and Altricial Young, p. 581; Courtship Feeding, p. 181. **REFS:** Bergman et al., 1970; Cramp, 1985; Davis and Ackerman, 1985; Dunn, 1979.

Elegant Tern
Sterna elegans Gambel

NG–168; G–154; PW–pl 36; AW–pl 49; AM(II)–88

  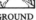

          MF(?)   1   ?
                        (1–2)   I: 20+ DAYS
                        MONOG   SEMIPRECOCIAL
                               F: ? DAYS
                               MF(?)

BREEDING: Salt marsh dikes, sand beaches, and flats. 1? brood. **DISPLAYS:** Courtship: pair run side by side with forward part of wings extended down away from body, necks stretched upward, and bills alternately raised and lowered in unison. **NEST:** Shallow scrape, oft within 20 yards of water. **EGGS:** Pinkish-buff/white, marked with dark brown. 2.1″ (54 mm). **DIET:** Oft hovers before diving for fish. Also scavenges. **CONSERVATION:** Winters along Pacific coast from Guatemala s to c Chile (most commonly from Ecuador s). Range expansion since 1959 colonization of San Diego Bay. **NOTES:** Colonial. Highly dependent on anchovies for feeding chicks; reproductive success strongly correlated with anchovy abundance. Chicks form creches. After breeding, moves n before migrating s. **ESSAYS:** Coloniality, p. 173; Parent-Chick Recognition, p. 193; Creches, p. 191; Range Expansion, p. 459; Swimming, p. 73. **REFS:** Gallup and Bailey, 1960; Schaffner, 1986.

Site Tenacity

The tendency to return each season to the same nest site or breeding colony is known as "site tenacity," "site fidelity," or "philopatry." The realization that site tenacity exists grew out of ornithologist Oliver Austin's long-term studies of Common Terns in Massachusetts. Austin found that individual terns tended to return to the same colony site and often to the same nest site within the colony. From banding studies, he discovered that this tendency increases with the age of the bird. Subsequent field studies have shown that this behavior occurs to varying degrees in a wide variety of North American birds including Common Goldeneye, Least Tern, Black Skimmer, Spotted Sandpiper, Long-billed Curlew, Broad-tailed Hummingbird, Bank Swallow, and Barn Swallow.

Avian biologists think the major advantage of returning to an established breeding site is that the bird's familiarity with the area results in reduced susceptibility to predation and other adverse conditions. Studies have shown that sex and age of the nesting bird, prior reproductive success at the particular site, and physical stability of the nest site are all important factors affecting site tenacity.

For all of the aforementioned species, birds that successfully rear young are more likely to return to the nest site the following year than birds that are unsuccessful. A finer discrimination is made by Black Skimmers, which are more likely to abandon a colony site following predation than following flooding. Presumably future failures as a result of predation are more predictable than those resulting from flooding.

One very important factor influencing the evolution of site tenacity is the degree of predictability or physical stability of the nest site. This is demonstrated by cliff-nesting Black-legged Kittiwakes, other gulls, and many alcids, which return repeatedly to the same sites (cliffs tend to be there year after year). At the opposite extreme of physical stability are nest sites on open sand or mud beaches, river sandbars, and the banks of watercourses subject to periodic inundation. Species nesting in these places, such as Least, Royal, and Sandwich Terns, exhibit little site tenacity (since the sites themselves are ephemeral). Barn Swallows and Bank Swallows provide another good example of well-developed versus poorly developed site tenacity in two related species that select very different sorts of nest sites. Barns stand for many years; banks are prone to erosion.

The repeated use of a nest or colony site is a behavioral property of the individual bird. Specific nest sites, however, may be used over time by a succession of individuals for a variety of reasons that are inherent properties of the site, leading to recognition of that site as a quality nest location. Such properties include physical stability, protection from predators and inclement weather, and association with a rich food supply. Ornithologist Raleigh Robertson and his colleagues in Ontario found that in any given year the breeding success of Eastern Kingbirds in a particular territory was related to breeding success there in the previous year. Pairs nesting in previously

Sandwich Tern

Sterna sandvicensis Latham

NG–168; G–154; PE–94; AE–pl 67; AM(II)–90

MF

1–2
(1–3)
MONOG

MF
I: 24–25 DAYS
SEMIPRECOCIAL
F: 30–35 DAYS
MF

AQUATIC
INVERTS

SKIMS
HAWKS

BREEDING: Coastal beaches, flats, and islands. 1 brood. **DISPLAYS:** During early laying period, upward-spiraling flights with much chattering. **NEST:** Unlined scrape, or no scrape at all, placed above tide line, occ among shells, on open sand. **EGGS:** Pinkish-buff/olive-buff, marked with blackish-brown. 2.0″ (51 mm). **DIET:** Oft hovers before diving for fish. Incl shrimp, marine worms, squid, occ insects. **CONSERVATION:** Winters s throughout West Indies to s Brazil and Uruguay (e), along coast from c Mexico s to Peru (w). **NOTES:** Colonial, virtually always assoc with Royal Tern. Long-term pair bond. Usu breed at 3–4 years; clutch size increases with age. Recognizes own chicks at 4–5 days. Chicks form mixed creches with Royal Tern chicks. Parents feed young until they are able to join on hunts. As in many other terns, fishing ability increases with experience; manifested by diving from increasing heights, indicating hunting over greater range of water depths. Swift, strong flight. Royal and Sandwich Terns assoc year-round; return to breeding ground together. **ESSAYS:** Coloniality, p. 173; Parent-Chick Recognition, p. 193; Creches, p. 191; Mixed-Species Flocking, p. 433. **REFS:** Buckley and Buckley, 1972; Cramp, 1985; Dunn, 1972; Langham, 1974.

Royal Tern

Sterna maxima Boddaert

NG–168; G–154; PE–94; PW–pl 36; AE–pl 64; AW–pl 48; AM(II)–86

MF

1
(1–2)
MONOG

MF
I: 30–31 DAYS
SEMIPRECOCIAL
F: 28–35 DAYS
MF

AQUATIC
INVERTS

SKIMS

BREEDING: Open sand beaches, esp isolated, sparsely vegetated, predator-free sandbars. 1 brood. **DISPLAYS:** Courtship feeding: fish or crab offered by male. Courtship incl spiraling aerial flight by 3+ birds; male struts before female. **NEST:** Oft amid shells, sparse veg; unlined or lined with shell fragments, fishbones. Nest rim built up by adult defecation. **EGGS:** Buff/white, marked with dark reddish-brown, occ wreathed. 2.5″ (63 mm). **DIET:** Hovers before diving. Incl esp crabs, also squid, shrimp. Skims to drink and after eating crab. Occ pirates fish, esp from Brown Pelican. **CONSERVATION:** Winters s along coastal lagoons, estuaries, rarely lakes, to Peru, Uruguay, and Argentina. **NOTES:** Large, dense colonies up to 10,000 nests, oft assoc with other terns, esp Sandwich; Laughing Gull assoc with Royals all year, eats eggs but ignored by terns and not viewed as predator! Colony oft destroyed by high tides and storms; commonly renest or reestablish colony, en masse, elsewhere. Young join creche at 2–3 days; adults recognize their own chicks in creches by chick's response to their calls. **ESSAYS:** Parent-Chick Recognition, p. 193; Creches, p. 191; Coloniality, p. 173; Site Tenacity, p. 189; Piracy, p. 159. **REFS:** Buckley and Buckley, 1972, 1977; Cramp, 1985; Loftin and Sutton, 1979.

successful territories were twice as likely to fledge young as pairs nesting in previously unsuccessful territories. Of course, scarcity of other suitable nest sites in an area may also promote site tenacity.

Occupation of "traditional" nesting locations and roosts over many generations will often occur in species exhibiting site tenacity. Such behavior is prominent among swifts. Black, White-throated, and Chimney Swifts in North America, as well as Chestnut-collared and Short-tailed Swifts in Trinidad, West Indies, are known to use sites over periods that far exceed the life expectancies of individual birds. Long-term use of a single site in North America is exemplified by White-throated Swifts that David Dobkin and colleagues found nesting in the same rock outcrop in Nevada's Toiyabe Range where they had been recorded nesting 54 years earlier by naturalist Jean Linsdale of the University of California's Museum of Vertebrate Zoology.

SEE: Habitat Selection, p. 463; Coloniality, p. 173; Seabird Nesting Sites, p. 197; Pelagic Birds, p. 657. REFS: Blancher and Robertson, 1985; Dobkin et al., 1986; McNicholl, 1975.

Creches

The fledglings of some bird species such as Greater Flamingos, Royal and Sandwich Terns, eiders, ostriches, and a number of penguins separate from their parents and form a group, or "creche." Whether parents continue to feed their own chicks, or the chicks feed themselves, supervision of the creche (when it occurs) is usually delegated to a small number of guardians. The guardians, of course, are related to only a small number of the young in the group. It is curious that "altruistic" guarding of unrelated young, presumably a dangerous, tiring responsibility, has evolved. Upon closer scrutiny, however, the behavior is not as altruistic as it appears.

Chick-creching generally occurs among birds that breed in large, loose colonies and whose eggs all hatch at about the same time. The day-care system permits a fledgling to lose itself in a crowd and reduce its risk of predation (dilution principle). In the case of young remaining dependent on their parents for food, creching frees the adults to spend more time foraging. Evolutionary theory suggests that creching is likely to develop when the young reared in a gang have a better chance of surviving than those reared alone, so that the birds practicing creche formation contribute more of their genes to the next generation than those that do not form creches.

It is not so easy, however, to predict which adults will adopt guarding behavior. In some species, this role is taken by nonbreeding adults (occasionally "aunts," or adults whose broods were lost, etc.), but in others, such as African ostriches, dominant pairs compete for the opportunity to gather the young of others to their group. Such herding of young is reminiscent of

Caspian Tern

Sterna caspia Pallas

NG–168; G–154; PE–94; PW–pl 36; AE–pl 65; AW–pl 47; AM(II)–86

MF

2–3
(1–4)
MONOG

MF
I: 20–22 DAYS
SEMIPRECOCIAL
F: 30–40 DAYS
MF

AQUATIC
INVERTS

BREEDING: Flat sand or gravel beaches, shell banks, occ marshes. 1 brood. **DISPLAYS:** Courtship complex and variable incl aerial chases. **NEST:** Varies with location; eggs placed on rocks, in sand, or concealed among driftwood, shells, and rubbish. Lined with moss, grass, seaweed. Occ builds up rim. **EGGS:** Pinkish-buff, marked with browns. 2.6″ (65 mm). **DIET:** Hovers before diving for fish; also takes crustaceans. Occ pirate. **CONSERVATION:** Winters primarily in coastal bays, estuaries, lakes, marshes and rivers s to Colombia, Venezuela. Colonies oft robbed of eggs in past. Human intrusion in breeding colony reduces reproductive success. **NOTES:** Usu small, occ large colonies, rarely solitary. Largest, strongest, fiercest, least gregarious tern. Usu breed at 4–5 years. Larger clutches in n. Pacific coast population (6,000 pairs in 1982) nests primarily on human-made habitats and shows 70% increase since 1960. Mate retention between years related to nest site stability, not to previous nesting success. Early nests more successful—nest predation increases with season. Young recognize call of parents. Longest parental care known for terns: feed juveniles 5–7 months postfledging. Flight gull-like. **ESSAYS:** Parent-Chick Recognition, p. 193; Coloniality, p. 173; Site Tenacity, p. 189. **REFS:** Cramp, 1985; Cuthbert, 1985a, b; Gill and Mewaldt, 1983.

Sooty Tern

Sterna fuscata Linnaeus

NG–170; G–156; PE–98; PW–265; AE–pl 71; AM(II)–100

MF

1
MONOG

MF
I: 27–30 DAYS
SEMIPRECOCIAL
F: 56 DAYS
MF

SQUID
OFFAL

HOVERS
& PICKS

BREEDING: Pelagic, island sand or coral beaches, usu among scattered grass, 1? brood. **DISPLAYS:** Courtship: male throws head back like some gulls, swells throat, circles female while calling, caressing, then taking flight. **NEST:** Occ lined with soft leaves, occ eggs laid directly on grass or sand. On ledge, may construct pebble or rock rim. **EGGS:** White, marked with red-brown, lavender, rarely black, wreathed. 2.0″ (50 mm). **DIET:** All food snatched from surface of water. **CONSERVATION:** In winter, ranges widely in tropical and subtropical waters. Valued by commercial fishermen who "commensally" track flocks over schooling fish. **NOTES:** Large colony. Noisy on breeding ground. Pair defends 14″ to 2′ diameter area around nest. Incubation shifts last 24 hours, changeover at night. Incubating bird cools egg by dipping feet, bill, and breast into water and transporting water to nest. Parents continue feeding young at least 3 weeks postfledging. Can breed at 4 yr, but usu wait until 6–8 yr. Tortuga colony continuous since 1516. Waterlog easily, neither dive nor sit on water. Soar with frigatebirds. **ESSAYS:** Preening, p. 53; Parent-Chick Recognition, p. 193; Coloniality, p. 173; Commensal Feeding, p. 35; Temperature Regulation, p. 149. **REFS:** Brown, 1977; Dinsmore, 1972; Johnston, 1979.

an African catfish that gathers the offspring of cichlid fishes into a school of its own young. The little cichlids are kept to the outside, where they (rather than the young of the catfish) are the first to be discovered by predators. Data are needed on relative position and mortality of adopted offspring in relation to the chicks most closely related to the adults guarding the creche to determine whether such supervision is truly altruistic.

SEE: Geometry of Selfish Colony, p. 19; Parental Care, p. 555; Parent-Chick Recognition in Colonial Nesters, p. 193; Altruism, p. 453.   REF: Hurxthal, 1986.

Parent-Chick Recognition in Colonial Nesters

In spite of the apparent chaos of seabird nesting colonies, returning adults invariably manage to locate and feed only their own offspring, indicating that some form of parental recognition of chicks (or vice versa) must exist. The timing and development of recognition, as well as whether it is accomplished by parent or chick or both, have been explored in species of shearwaters, penguins, gulls, terns, alcids, and swallows. These studies have all shown that recognition develops only in species in which circumstances, such as the young wandering away from the nest or being gathered in communal groups ("creches") for feeding, could lead to confusion. The onset of recognition coincides with the time when young of different broods begin to mingle. Where such intermixing does not occur (such as in Manx Shearwaters that nest individually in isolated burrows), researchers have found no evidence of recognition between parents and their chicks (the parents *do*, however, recognize their burrows or nest sites).

Many investigations have employed the technique of exchanging broods at different ages to determine whether recognition exists and how it occurs. Among gulls and terns, the age at which recognition develops is related to the timing of young leaving the vicinity of the nest. For example, in the ground-nesting Sooty Tern, adults reject strange chicks that are more than 4 days old. The tree-nesting Brown Noddy does not discriminate between its own and strange chicks until about 14 days, which is the age when young leave the nest. Black-legged Kittiwakes nest on cliff ledges, and young do not mix until they fledge; adults do not discriminate between their own and other chicks. In contrast, ground-nesting Herring Gulls reject foreign chicks beginning at about 5 days, but in cliff-nesting populations, where young leave the nest later, adults will still accept transfer chicks that are one to two weeks old. Franklin's Gulls, with widely spaced floating nests, do not discriminate among chicks less than one to two weeks old.

Development of recognition has been most thoroughly studied in the Laughing Gull by ethologist Colin Beer. Chicks remain close to the nest for 3 or 4 days, and although they recognize their parents' calls beginning at 1 to 3 days, their discriminatory ability becomes much sharper starting at 5 to

Brown Noddy

Anous stolidus Linnaeus

NG–170; G–156; PE–98; PW–265; AE–pl 73; AM(II)–104

| TREE
To 12'
GROUND | F | 1
MONOG? | MF
I: 35–38 DAYS
SEMIPRECOCIAL
F: 40–48 DAYS
MF | SQUID | |

BREEDING: Pelagic, island beaches, rock ledges. 1 brood.   **DISPLAYS:** Courtship: male stands near female, nods and bows; female attempts to extract fish from throat of male, alternates feeding attempts with nodding.   **NEST:** Shallow, bulky, loose, of dead bay-cedar branches, seaweed; in cedar or cactus. Lined with shells and coral. Added to yearly, becoming enormous. Ground nests rare in N.A. Steals materials from unguarded nests. Male feeds female while she builds.   **EGGS:** Pinkish-buff, marked with dark reddish-brown, wreathed. 2.1″ (52 mm).   **DIET:** Fly at 5′–10′, usu only touch water to drink (salt water), bathe, or snatch prey. Occ hover, seldom dive.   **CONSERVATION:** Pelagic in winter, mostly near breeding grounds.   **NOTES:** Nests in loose colonies. Named for famed indifference to people. Arrive at night on breeding ground 1–2 weeks before laying. Nest relief every 24 hours, at night. Young capable of climbing by day 20 but remain at nest until able to fly. Parental recognition of chicks apparent only after fledging; parents occ still feed fledglings at 100+ days. Roost in low shrubs fringing shore. Assoc with Sooty Tern at sea.   **ESSAYS:** Parent-Chick Recognition, p. 193; Coloniality, p. 173; Courtship Feeding, p. 181; Salt Glands, p. 29.   **REFS:** Brown, 1977; Riska, 1984, 1986.

Black Skimmer

Rynchops niger Linnaeus

NG–170; G–156; PE–98; AE–pl 70; AM(II)–106

| | MF(?) | 4
(3–5)
MONOG | MF
I: 21–23 DAYS
SEMIPRECOCIAL
F: 23–25 DAYS
MF | AQUATIC
INVERTS | |

BREEDING: Coastal beach, sandbar, shell bank, island, salt marsh, locally on gravel rooftops. 1 brood.   **DISPLAYS:** Aerial display: rival males attempt to overtake female while calling; zigzagging close pursuit, each male briefly passing female with wing extended.   **NEST:** Unlined scrape among shells.   **EGGS:** Bluish-white/buff/pinkish-white, marked with dark brown. 1.3″ (34 mm).   **DIET:** Incl crustaceans. Tactile hunter, rarely locate prey by sight; never dive.   **CONSERVATION:** Winters s to s Chile and c Argentina. Millinery trade oft turned them into hat decorations; eggs taken by humans. Even slight human disturbance in colony reduces reproductive success.   **NOTES:** Usu small colony, rarely 100–200 nests; oft assoc with terns, gulls, plovers. Males incubate and brood more than females do, but females defend from predators and feed more than males do. Colony site more likely to be abandoned following predation than following flooding. Young hatch asynchronously, fed regurgitant deposited onto ground (lower mandible does not elongate until almost adult size), later directly fed whole fish. Young hide by scratching themselves into a hollow and kicking up sand cover. Only bird to close pupil into vertical slit.   **ESSAYS:** Skimming, p. 195; Bills, p. 209; How Do Birds Fly?, p. 81; Plume Trade, p. 37; Who Incubates?, p. 27.   **REFS:** Blake, 1985; Burger, 1981, 1982.

6 days. Learning occurs in stages as the young gulls are exposed to different adult calls. Adults identify their chicks by the response that their calls elicit, rather than by the calls of the chicks. Similarly, Ring-billed Gulls recognize their chicks by sight instead of by their vocalizations.

In species with altricial young, the timing of recognition is also correlated with the potential for confusion with young from different broods. Adult Common Murres nesting on crowded cliff ledges can recognize their own chicks shortly after hatching; the chicks learn their parents' call while still in the egg! For most altricial species, the critical time requiring discrimination comes at fledging. Young of the colonial Bank Swallow fledge at 18–19 days. Until then, parents need simply return to the correct burrow to ensure that they are feeding their own young. Experiments confirm that exchanged chicks are readily accepted until they reach 15 days of age, when their begging calls are replaced by brood-specific "signature" calls that the adults use to discriminate between their own and other young.

Why is the development of parent-offspring recognition delayed until shortly before it is required? The likely answer is that there is an evolutionary cost involved in recognition prior to the onset of chick mobility. Not only would earlier recognition be superfluous for the purpose of rejecting alien chicks, it could even lead to evicting one's own chick by mistake!

SEE: Vocal Functions, p. 471; Vocal Development, p. 601; Coloniality, p. 173; Creches, p. 191. REFS: Beecher et al., 1981; Beer, 1979; Falls, 1982.

Skimming: Why Birds Fly Low Over Water

A flock of sea ducks, pelicans, or sandpipers skimming low over the water's surface is a common seashore sight. Far from shore, shearwaters often closely follow the contours of the waves, and gaggles of auklets fly rapidly just above the water. Skimming permits the birds to take advantage of an aerodynamic phenomenon known as "ground effect." The patterns of airflow around a wing that is operating close to a surface are modified by that surface in a manner that reduces drag, the resistance of the air to the progress of the wing. Sometimes overloaded airplanes are sometimes incapable of climbing out of the ground effect even though they can maintain flight close to the ground.

Thus, everything else being equal, it is more efficient to fly close to a surface than far from it. But things are rarely equal, which is why birds most often tend to take advantage of the ground effect when the "ground" is water. The ground effect only occurs when the flying object is much less than a wingspan from the surface—and at such an altitude over land a bird would be continually flying among obstacles, through grass, and so on. Only water is sufficiently uncluttered to permit such close safe passage.

SEE: How Fast and High Do Birds Fly?, p. 81; How Do Birds Fly?, p. 161; Soaring, p. 215. REF: Pennycuick, 1975.

Razorbill

Alca torda Linnaeus

NG–172; G–160; PE–36; AE–pl 91; AM(II)–112

MF

1
(1–2)
MONOG

MF
I: 35–37 DAYS
SEMIPRECOCIAL
F: 16–25+ DAYS
MF

CRUSTACEANS

BREEDING: Coastal cliff, rocky shore, island. 1 brood. **DISPLAYS:** Courtship: male throws head back with bill pointed vertically, mutual preening, billing. **NEST:** Usu on upper cliff ledge, in crevice or cavity under overhanging rock. Bed of pebbles may help to drain water; incubating bird occ places bits of veg, pebbles, beneath egg. **EGGS:** Light bluish- or greenish-white/white, marked with browns, black, oft wreathed. 3.0″ (76 mm). **DIET:** Chicks fed fish. Feed at 6′–35′, occ to max depth of 375′. Dive up to 50 sec; bring several fish per trip to young. **CONSERVATION:** Pelagic in winter, off n e N.A. Birds and eggs hunted through early 1900s; widespread decline in many areas this century. DDT and PCB levels in 1983 unchanged from 1970. **NOTES:** Large colonies (occ with murres), occupied several weeks prior to laying. Long-term pair bond. Strong fidelity to nest site, esp by male. Incubation shifts of 12–24 hours. Younger birds tend to lay later in season, have lower breeding success. First breed at 4 or 5 years. Young brooded only intermittently after 5 days; enter sea at 16–20 days, then cared for by male for several weeks. **ESSAYS:** Seabird Nesting, p. 197; Diving, p. 203; Pelagic Birds, p. 657; Site Tenacity, p. 189; DDT, p. 21. **REFS:** Cramp, 1985; Nettleship and Birkhead, 1985.

Common Murre

Uria aalge Pontoppidan

NG–172; G–160; PE–36; PW–108; AE–pl 94; AW–pl 79; AM(II)–110

NO NEST

1
MONOG

MF
I: 32–33 (30–35) DAYS
SEMIPRECOCIAL
F: 19–21+ DAYS
MF

BREEDING: Coastal cliff, offshore rocky flat island. 1 brood. **DISPLAYS:** Courtship: male throws head back with bill pointed vertically, mutual bowing, billing, preening. **NEST:** Mostly on lower or middle cliff face, rarely in rock crevice. Egg laid on bare rock. **EGGS:** Variable, blue/green/white/brown, marked with brown/black. 3.2″ (81 mm). Adults recognize own eggs by color and markings. **DIET:** Also few crustaceans, mollusks, worms. Dives >1 minute to depths of 100′, max to 550′. **CONSERVATION:** Pelagic in winter off N.A. Exterminated from much of range by mid-1800s. Highly aggregated in e N.A.: 90% breed at 3 sites in Canada; increasing but susceptible to oil spills, pollution. **NOTES:** Very large colonies; arrive several weeks before laying. High fidelity to nest site. Pair bond likely long-term. Incubating birds densely packed, touching neighbors. Pyriform-shaped egg maximizes surface area contacting brood patch. Incubates in semi-upright stance with feet holding egg in place; incubation shifts of 12–24 hours. Young leave nest at ¼ adult weight, tended by male for several weeks. First breed at 4–6 years. Known as Guillemot in Europe. **ESSAYS:** Seabird Nesting, p. 197; Eggs, p. 301; Natural Selection, p. 237; Chick Recognition, p. 193. **REFS:** Burger and Simpson, 1986; Cairns et al., 1987; Cramp, 1985; Murphy et al., 1986; Nettleship and Birkhead, 1985.

Seabird Nesting Sites

Pelagic birds—species spending most of their time over the open ocean—often differ in their foraging behavior and the types of prey they take. Different pelagic species frequently nest together, however, on barren islands and seaside cliffs, because such locations are in relatively short supply. All do not, however, choose the same part of the habitat for nesting. For

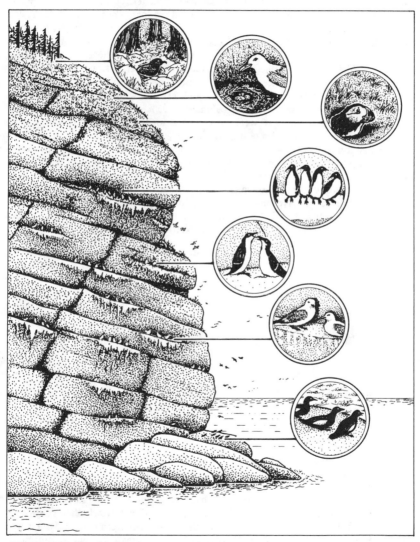

Stratification of seabird nesting sites on Gull Island, off Newfoundland coast. Bottom to top: Black Guillemots, Black-legged Kittiwakes, Razorbills, Common Murres, Atlantic Puffins, Herring Gulls, Leach's Storm-Petrels.

Thick-billed Murre
Uria lomvia Linnaeus

NG–172; G–160; PE–36; PW–108; AE–pl 93; AW–pl 78; AM(II)–112

 NO NEST MF
I: 30–35 DAYS
1 SEMIPRECOCIAL MARINE
MONOG F: 21 (16–30) DAYS INVERTS
MF

BREEDING: Coastal cliffs. 1 brood. **DISPLAYS:** "Butterfly" flight, mutual preening, head-vertical and mutual bowing all used in pair formation and maintenance. **NEST:** On narrow cliff ledge, oft too narrow for >1 bird. Egg laid on bare rock. **EGGS:** Bluish-greenish white/cream/olive-buff, marked with brown, usu wreathed. Occ unmarked. 3.2″ (81 mm). **DIET:** Incl esp crustaceans, also worms, mollusks. Chicks fed 90% fish. Regularly feeds at or near bottom to 330′. **CONSERVATION:** Pelagic in winter off N.A. Some colonies declined 20%–40% since mid-1950s due to hunting, oil pollution and esp drowning in commercial fish nets. **NOTES:** Breeds in very large colonies: >95% (e) occur in 11 colonies of >10,000 pairs each. Spend 4–6 weeks at colony prior to laying. Likely high fidelity to nest site. Incubation and brooding continuous; egg held against brood patch by feet. Incubation shifts of 12–72 hours, mainly by male at night. Young depart nest at ¼ adult weight, tended by male for several weeks. Adults oft forage 15–60 miles from colony. Early breeders more successful than late breeders. Glaucous Gull is major predator of eggs and chicks. Known as Brünnich's Guillemot in Europe. **ESSAYS:** Seabird Nesting, p. 197; Diving and Flightlessness, p. 203; Birds and Oil, p. 207; Eggs, p. 301; Site Tenacity, p. 189. **REFS:** Cramp, 1985; Gaston, 1985a, b, 1987; Gaston and Nettleship, 1981; Nettleship and Birkhead, 1985.

Dovekie
Alle alle Linnaeus

NG–172; G–160; PE–38; AE–pl 96; AM(II)–108

TALUS
SLOPE MF
I: 28–31 DAYS
CLIFF MF 1 SEMIPRECOCIAL FISH
MONOG F: 26–30 DAYS
MF

BREEDING: Talus slopes, coastal cliffs. 1 brood. **DISPLAYS:** Vociferous aerial flock displays precede egg laying. Greeting display with head bowing. **NEST:** Eggs laid on bed of pebbles, occ with fragments of veg. **EGGS:** Bluish-white or -green, usu unmarked. 1.9″ (48 mm). **DIET:** Primarily planktonic crustaceans; fed to chick and transported in adult's throat pouch. **CONSERVATION:** Pelagic in winter off n e N.A. Oft suffers from oil spills. Has declined in Iceland, possibly elsewhere; data lacking. **NOTES:** Colonial. Most numerous seabird in n Atlantic and most abundant alcid in world, but probably <1000 pairs breed in e N.A. Breeding synchronization higher among nearby pairs than in colony as a whole. Young fledging without accompanying adult oft captured by Glaucous Gulls. Unclear whether adult continues to tend fledged young at sea. Forage up to 60 miles from colony. Dive times usu 20–30 sec, probably reaching 60′–80′ (10–13 fathoms). Known in Europe as Little Auk. **ESSAYS:** Coloniality, p. 173; Diving and Flightlessness, p. 203; Seabird Nesting Sites, p. 197; Birds and Oil, p. 207. **REFS:** Cramp, 1985; Nettleship and Birkhead, 1985; Roby et al., 1981.

example, on Gull Island off the coast of Newfoundland, Black Guillemots nest along the cliff base in crevices and between boulders. Above them, on rocky projections too small for other species, Black-legged Kittiwakes rear their young. Higher still, Common Murres are found on wider ledges, while Razorbills hide their eggs in niches scattered throughout the cliff face. On steep, grassy clifftop slopes, Atlantic Puffins dig nest burrows in the soft peat, and in flatter areas Herring Gulls construct nests. Beneath the spruce and fir forest covering the peak of the island, the burrows of half a million Leach's Storm-Petrels lie concealed.

Almost five thousand miles to the west, on St. George Island in the Bering Sea off the coast of Alaska, Black-legged Kittiwakes and Common Murres prefer nest sites similar to those used on Gull Island. Roughly two million birds nest on St. George, however, and the mix of species there differs from that found on Gull Island. Some of the other species on St. George include Red-legged Kittiwakes, which, like their cousins, also prefer narrow ledges but choose those beneath overhanging rocks, and Red-faced Cormorants, which prefer deep ledges, sometimes using ones that slope toward the sea—as long as they are not beneath an overhang. Thick-billed Murres are found on moderately deep, flat ledges under a low overhang, and Northern Fulmars nest on soil-covered bedrock ledges or ledges with enclosed sides.

Ledge depth, ledge slope, and the size of overhang are key features that differentiate nesting habitats on St. George Island. Not surprisingly, the use of seaward-sloping ledges is limited to those birds, such as Northern Fulmars, kittiwakes, and Red-faced Cormorants, that build nests. Ornithologists R.C. Squibb and G.L. Hunt, Jr., who measured the physical characteristics of 288 nest sites on St. George Island, found that preferences of the species overlapped somewhat, and that there was some competition between species for nest sites. They also caution that the patterning of nest site partitioning on St. George Island might not be characteristic of other islands or other mixes of nesting species.

Cliffs where several species of seabirds nest together are some of the best places for you to observe habitat selection in action. Additional quantitative analyses of differences between sites, and at the same site from season to season, would be most informative.

SEE: Habitat Selection, p. 463; Pelagic Birds, p. 657; Coloniality, p. 173. REFS: Squibb and Hunt, 1983; Threlfall, 1985.

The Northern Penguin

Few people realize that the original "penguin" bred on our shores. The designation was first applied to the extinct flightless bird now known as the Great Auk or Garefowl, as its latinized generic name, *Pinguinus*, attests. This fish-hunting diver stood some two and a half feet tall, and was widely

Great Auk

Pinguinus impennis Linnaeus

(Extinct: not in field guides; see fig. p. 201)

 NO NEST

1
MONOG?

MF(?)
I: 39–45(?) DAYS
SEMIPRECOCIAL?
FLIGHTLESS
MF (?)

BREEDING: Formerly on offshore rocky islands. 1? brood. **DISPLAYS**: Courtship probably involved head shaking and bobbing with opened yellow mouth. **NEST**: Egg laid on bare or guano-covered rock. **EGGS**: Dirty white/yellowish buff, marked with brown/black, oft wreathed. 4.9″ (124 mm). **DIET**: Mostly fish. Probably foraged near bottom at depths down to 250′ (42 fathoms) or more. **CONSERVATION**: Pelagic in winter off n e N.A. Extinct. Last verified record June 3, 1844, in Iceland. Became extinct so fast that at one point it was considered a myth. Slaughtered for food, bait, fat, feathers, and finally by collectors. About 80 skins are preserved. **NOTES**: Bred in large colonies. The "original penguin," largest and only non-fossil flightless alcid. Walked upright. Estimates of breeding data and diet largely extrapolated from other alcids. Likely incubated in upright posture like murres. Chicks may have left nest and entered sea at about 9 days. **ESSAYS**: Northern Penguin, p. 199; Diving and Flightlessness, p. 203; Coloniality, p. 173. **REFS**: Bengston, 1984; Nettleship and Birkhead, 1985.

Black Guillemot

Supersp #17
Cepphus grylle Linnaeus

NG–174; G–160; PE–38; PW–108; AE–pl 92; AM(II)–114

GROUND   MF   2
                        (1–2)
                        MONOG

MF
I: 28–32 (23–39) DAYS
SEMIPRECOCIAL
F: 34–39 (30–40) DAYS
MF

MARINE
INVERTS

BREEDING: Rocky shores, on coastal cliffs and at base among boulders. 1 brood. **DISPLAYS**: Communal courtship displays in water early in season; strut on land, then mutual head-bobbing. **NEST**: Also on beaches amid flotsam and boulders, and in artificial "crevices" (e.g., holes in breakwaters). Eggs usu laid in cup of small stones. **EGGS**: Dull white/cream/buff, marked with dark brown, black, wreathed. 2.3″ (60 mm). **DIET**: Incl crustaceans, mollusks, worms. Dives to depths of 165′ for up to 75 sec per dive. Young fed mostly fish captured in shallow water near colony. **CONSERVATION**: Pelagic in winter. Stable or increasing; oil pollution and drowning in commercial fish nets may pose future threats. **NOTES**: Breeds mostly in loose aggregations (5–200 pairs) or in large (up to 10,000 pairs) colonies in high arctic, occ solitary. Long-term pair bond. Return to colony 4+ weeks prior to laying. Strong fidelity to nest site. Younger birds lay later than older birds; begin breeding as early as second year. Three- and occ 4-egg clutches involve >1 female. Chick growth rates higher, less variable, than most Atlantic alcids. Young fledge at night, unaccompanied by adult. Feed mainly inshore, rarely >10 miles from colony. **ESSAYS**: Seabird Nesting Sites, p. 197; Diving and Flightlessness, p. 203; Site Tenacity, p. 189; Coloniality, p. 173; Birds and Oil, p. 207; Black and White Plumage, p. 177. **REFS**: Cairns, 1987; Cramp, 1985; Nettleship and Birkhead, 1985.

Great Auks

distributed in the North Atlantic. The Great Auk was swift and agile in the water, but clumsy and vulnerable on land. Its breeding colonies on offshore islands served as butcher shops for seamen; the birds could be herded right across gangplanks and onto boats. Great Auks disappeared from Britain around 1760; soon thereafter their value increased as they were slaughtered for their feathers in addition to their meat. Their eggs were collected and their chicks were used for fish food. Audubon reported early in the nineteenth century: "When I was in Labrador, many of the fishermen assured me that the 'Penguin,' as they name this bird, breeds on a low rocky island to the south-east of Newfoundland, where they destroy great numbers of the young for bait."

As human numbers increased, those of the Great Auk decreased. Mother Nature may have pitched in with some bad luck. The "Little Ice Age," which began around the 13th century and lasted to about the turn of the present century, probably made life difficult for these large alcids, surrounding many of their best breeding islands with ice, giving polar bears access to their colonies, and perhaps reducing supplies of fish upon which the auks depended. As a final blow from nature, in 1830 one of the breeding sites, the rocky island of Geirfuglasker off Iceland, disappeared in a volcanic eruption. Presumably, however, some of the breeding birds from Geirfuglasker simply moved to the adjacent island of Eldey. So this large, and thus presumably always relatively scarce, alcid appears to have been in ecological trouble and suffering population declines just at the time people stepped up its exploitation.

The Great Auk never got a chance to respond, as some of its relatives have, to recent amelioration of climatic conditions in the North Atlantic. In June of 1844 the last two individuals known to be taken by human beings were captured by Icelanders on Eldey. They were turned over to a dealer, and the fate of their skins is not known, although some of their internal organs are preserved in the University of Copenhagen's Museum of Zoology.

The last reported sighting of the Northern Penguin was off Newfound-

Pigeon Guillemot

Supersp #17
Cepphus columba Pallas

NG–174; G–160; PW–pl 108; AW–80; AM(II)–116

| BURROW
MF | 2
(1–2)
MONOG | MF
I: 30–32 DAYS
SEMIPRECOCIAL
F: 35 (29–39) DAYS
MF | MARINE
INVERTS | |

BREEDING: Coastal cliff or cave, rocky island. 1 brood. **DISPLAYS:** Courting pairs engage in billing accompanied by twittering and a trilled song. Conspicuous "water-dance" performed in groups with much diving, flapping, and paddling, but function unknown. **NEST:** Also under loose rocks or boulders. Excavates burrow using beak and claws. Eggs placed on rock chips, pebbles, debris gathered at nest. Perennial. **EGGS:** Greenish-, bluish-white/white, marked with browns, black. 2.4″ (61 mm). **DIET:** Incl crustaceans, mollusks. Chicks fed mostly fish. **CONSERVATION:** Pelagic in winter along w coast of N.A. **NOTES:** Nests in small colonies. Pair bond apparently long-term and nest site fidelity is high. In years when food is abundant, males occupy breeding territories earlier, spend more time there, clutches are started earlier, and average clutch size is larger. Short incubation shifts of 30 min to 1 hour each (max 17 hours). Young fledge at night. Diving time up to 75 seconds. **ESSAYS:** Seabird Nesting Sites, p. 197; Diving and Flightlessness, p. 203; Coloniality, p. 173; Site Tenacity, p. 189; Monogamy, p. 597; Average Clutch Size, p. 51; Who Incubates?, p. 27. **REFS:** Drent, 1965; Nelson, 1987.

Marbled Murrelet

Brachyramphus marmoratus Gmelin

NG–174; G–164; PW–pl 35; AW–365; AM(II)–116

| TREE
0′–150′ | MF(?) | 1
MONOG | MF
I: 27–30 DAYS
SEMIPRECOCIAL
F: 27 DAYS
MF | AQUATIC
INVERTS |

BREEDING: Conifer forest near coast, inland lakes. 1? brood. **DISPLAYS:** ? **NEST:** Depression usu on n-facing open ground on islands or well inland, partly encircled by guano. Also nests in rock crevices and high in trees. **EGGS:** Light-greenish-yellow/light-olive-green, marked with lavender, blue, brown, black. 2.4″ (60 mm). **DIET:** Incl esp crustaceans. Usu inshore feeder, within 500′ of shore and 100′ (17 fathoms) deep. Adults usu return to nest with single fish. **CONSERVATION:** Usu pelagic in winter along w N.A. **NOTES:** Nests usu solitary. First N.A. nest discovered in 1974, in tree near Santa Cruz, CA. As of 1987, fewer than 10 nests known, all from CA, WA and AK. Incubation shifts of 24 hours. Young avoid direct sunlight; n-facing site possibly helps to avoid overheating. Chicks fed only at night; must successfully reach sea or lake on first flight, which may be from >20 miles inland. Feeding areas remain relatively constant during breeding. Egg laying may coincide with cyclic availability of prey. **ESSAYS:** Diving and Flightlessness, p. 203; Temperature Regulation, p. 149; Swimming, p. 73; Pelagic Birds, p. 657. **REFS:** Carter and Sealy, 1986; Day et al., 1983; Sanger, 1987; Sealy, 1975; Simons, 1980.

202 GUILLEMOTS/MURRELETS

land in 1852. Now only the name penguin lives on, transferred to the ecologically similar but unrelated birds of the Antarctic and southern oceans. Outside of that isolated continent, flightless birds have proven highly vulnerable to human-caused extinction. Perhaps, then, it is not surprising that North America's flightless bird, the Great Auk, was among the first to go.

SEE: The Passenger Pigeon, p. 273; Our Only Native Parrot, p. 279; The Labrador Duck, p. 85. REFS: Audubon, 1844; Bengtson, 1984; Halliday, 1978.

Diving and Flightlessness

Flightless Emperor and King Penguins can dive to a depth in excess of 130 fathoms (780 feet; 238 meters)—more than the length of two and a half football fields. The depth attained by their North Atlantic ecological equivalent, the Great Auk, is unknown since the species is extinct. That flightless alcid probably torpedoed down more than 100 fathoms, but foraged mainly on the continental shelf at depths of less than 40 fathoms. Why, unlike South American penguins and the Great Auk, are the extant North Atlantic alcids capable of flight? Colin Pennycuick, a leading student of bird flight, suggests that penguin ancestors opted to get bigger in order to swim better and gave up their racing flight—one with a hummingbirdlike wingbeat frequency. Penguin specialist Bernard Stonehouse suggests that the capabilities for flight and prolonged, deep diving are mutually limiting, and apparently coexist only in alcids weighing two pounds or less. Murres, the largest alcids, weigh nearly two pounds and the Little Blue, the smallest penguin, weighs just over two pounds. Stonehouse suspects that if murres increased in size, they would probably evolve ever smaller wings, and eventually become flightless.

It seems reasonable to assume that heavier, flightless penguins should forage in deeper water than alcids, and they probably do (records are scanty). Recent studies indicate, however, that alcids attain depths greater than previously estimated. Most earlier (and some current) data were derived from the accidental entanglement of diving birds in commercial fishing nets. Such reports are particularly unreliable because birds may be captured at any point while the net is descending or ascending, rather than at the maximum depth recorded. Now, data are often provided by assessing stomach contents for fish type and extrapolating probable foraging depths from information about the habits of those fish.

In addition, a new technique—one using a small, simple depth gauge attached by string to a metal leg band—is coming into use. (The string wears through in a short time so that, if the gauge is not recovered, the length of time the bird will be burdened with it is limited.) A gauge consists of a five-to-eight-inch length of plastic tubing coated on the inside with water-soluble powder (confectioner's sugar). Increasing pressure as the bird

Kittlitz's Murrelet

Brachyramphus brevirostris Vigors

NG–174; G–164; PW–pl 35; AW–364; AM(II)–118

 NO NEST
?
I: ? DAYS
1 SEMIPRECOCIAL
MONOG? F: 21? DAYS
?

BREEDING: In coastal mountains, oft near glaciers. 1? brood. **DISPLAYS**: ?
NEST: Well inland, usu on n-facing slope. Oft at base of slope, also cliffs and barren
ground on coasts, ledges and talus above timberline. Egg laid on bare ground amid
lichen-covered rocks. **EGGS**: Light-yellow/light-olive-green, variably marked. 2.4″
(60 mm) **DIET**: Esp crustaceans. **CONSERVATION**: Usu pelagic in winter or along
rocky seacoasts of n w N.A. **NOTES**: Young avoid direct sunlight; n-facing nest site
likely helps to avoid overheating. Young from inland nests probably swim down
streams to reach the sea. Flight swifter than other murrelets. Only 14 definite and 3
probable nests, all from AK, are sum total of our knowledge. Very poorly
known. **ESSAYS**: Diving and Flightlessness, p. 203; Temperature Regulation,
p. 149; How Do We Find Out About Bird Biology?, p. 319; Pelagic Birds,
p. 657. **REF**: Day et al., 1983.

Xantus' Murrelet

Synthliboramphus hypoleucus Xántus de Vesey

NG–176; G–164; PW–pl 35; AW–397; AM(II)–120

MF
I: 34 (27–44) DAYS
BURROW 2 PRECOCIAL 2
MF(?) (1–2) F: ? DAYS
MONOG MF(?)

BREEDING: Offshore islands. 1 brood. **DISPLAYS**: ? **NEST**: Usu on high, rugged
craggy site; oft under large rocks or dense veg. Also uses rabbit and Burrowing Owl
burrows, human-built structures. No nest construction or burrow excavation; eggs
laid on bare rock or in shallow depression where substrate soft. Perennial. **EGGS**:
Vary within clutch. Usu greenish with brown/lavender marks, occ light blue/dark
brown with spots. 2.1″ (54 mm). Usu 8 days (range 5–12) between eggs. **DIET**:
Poorly known. **CONSERVATION**: Winters s to s Baja. Usu pelagic. **NOTES**: Nests
in small colonies. Strong nest site fidelity and long-term pair bond. Active at night
during breeding season. Nest relief every 3–4 (range 1–6) days. Nests well concealed
in crevices, but irregular attendance can result in nearly half of all eggs being lost to
deer mice. Young extremely precocial for seabirds: usu escorted to sea by adults 2
nights after hatching. Following period of intense vocalization, family emerges from
nest and adults lead young a few feet downslope then fly to sea; now alone, chicks
move to cliff edge and jump or are blown off cliff into surf >200′ below. Chicks may
be guided by adults' calls in the distance below; reunited adults and chicks immediately move well offshore. **ESSAYS**: Diving and Flightlessness, p. 203; Pelagic
Birds, p. 657; Mice and Ground-Nesting Birds, p. 129; Site Tenacity, p. 189; Monogamy, p. 597. **REF**: Murray et al., 1983.

DIVING DEPTHS OF SELECTED BIRDS

SPECIES AND BODY LENGTH

	DOVEKIE 8-1/4"	BLACK GUILLEMOT 13"	COMMON PUFFIN 12-1/2"	RAZOR-BILL 17"	COMMON MURRE 17-1/2"	GREAT AUK 30"	EMPEROR PENGUIN 42"

DEPTHS IN FATHOMS

```
 5    ? ?                                                                  ? ?
10     ?
15     ?
20     ?
25
30
35
40                                                             ?
45                                                             ?
50                                                             ?
55                                                             ?
60                                                             ?
65                                                             ?
70                                                             ?
75                                                             ?
80                                                             ?
85                                                             ?
90                                                             ?
95                                                             ?
100                                                            ?
105                                                            ?
110                                                            ?
115
120
125
130
```

? ? Unknown normal depth   ? Estimated maximum depth
⊔ Normal recorded depth   ⊥ Maximum recorded depth

dives deeper forces water farther and farther into the tube. After a bird is retrieved, its greatest diving depth is determined by measuring the distance from the mouth of the tube to where the powder has dissolved. Calibration shows these gauges to be accurate to within a few percent.

The evidence obtained by these new techniques remains scanty but, so far, it substantiates the hypothesis that different species characteristically dive to different depths and that larger species generally dive deeper than smaller ones. Exactly how penguins and alcids compare will, however, have to await further studies.

SEE: Swimming, p. 73; Adaptations for Flight, p. 507; How Do Birds Fly?, p. 161; Pelagic Birds, p. 657. REFS: Burger and Simpson, 1986; Nettleship and Birkhead, 1985; Pennycuick, 1975; Piatt and Nettleship, 1985; Sealy, 1975; Stonehouse, 1975.

Ancient Murrelet

Synthliboramphus antiquus Gmelin

NG–176; G–164; PW–pl 35; AW–399; AM(II)–122

CREVICE 2
MF(?) (1–2)
MONOG

MF
I: 33–36+ DAYS
PRECOCIAL 2
F: ? DAYS
MF

BREEDING: Along rocky seacoasts on offshore islands. 1 brood. **DISPLAYS**: Courtship on nesting slopes at night. **NEST**: In burrows excavated near log, tree roots, or on grassy slope. Also under rocks. Lined with dry grass and leaves. **EGGS**: Buff, marked with light brown/lavender. 2.4″ (61 mm). **DIET**: Mostly planktonic crustaceans during early breeding; later take fish. Change in diet due to change in available prey. Forage offshore up to 12 miles and 165′ (28 fathoms) deep. **CONSERVATION**: Usu pelagic in winter s to Baja, occ on large inland bodies of water. **NOTES**: Nests in large colonies. Strong nest site tenacity and long-term pair bond. Each egg constitutes 22% of female's weight. Patchy food distribution requires long feeding periods and presumably leads to long (72 hr) incubation shifts exchanged at night; nocturnal on breeding grounds. Occ nest abandonment for 1–3 days by feeding adults leads to longer incubation periods. Young leave nest and go to sea as described for Xantus' Murrelet; mutual call recognition between chicks and parents aids relocation at sea. Feed usu in A.M. in flocks, diving against the current. **ESSAYS**: Diving and Flightlessness, p. 203; Pelagic Birds, p. 657; Incubation Time, p. 481; Site Tenacity, p. 189. **REFS**: Jones et al., 1987; Sealy, 1975b, 1976, 1984.

Cassin's Auklet

Ptychoramphus aleuticus Pallas

NG–176; G–164; PW–pl 35; AW–pl 87; AM(II)–124

CREVICE 1
MF MONOG

MF
I: 38 DAYS
SEMIPRECOCIAL
F: 41 DAYS
MF

BREEDING: Rocky, offshore islands, isolated cliffs. Occ 2 broods. **DISPLAYS**: Before leaving nest area for the day, pair display consists of backstep, bounce, and bow. **NEST**: On slope or in relatively flat area; entrance oft obscured. Occ in cave. Eggs laid on twigs, nest remnants. Usu perennial, burrow requires 2+ months to dig. **EGGS**: Creamy white, unmarked, oft nest-stained. 1.9″ (47 mm). **DIET**: Mostly zooplankton, also crustaceans, squid, marine insects. Food transported to young in throat pouch. Young fed pigeon milklike regurgitant, small marine inverts, and larval fish until fully fledged. **CONSERVATION**: Winters s to s Baja. Usu pelagic, occ along rocky seacoast. **NOTES**: Colonial. Feeds during day; active in nest colony at night. Most breed at 3 years. Incubation shifts of 24 hours. Strong nestsite tenacity; long-term pair bond. Nest excavation using claws and bill oft interrupted by bowing, calling and fighting with neighbors. Young avoid light; chick alone in burrow except for first 5–6 days, when parents alternately brood. As fledging approaches, chick oft at nest entrance, occ takes short walks and flaps wings. Adults and young oft taken by gulls, esp Western Gull. **ESSAYS**: Diving and Flightlessness, p. 203; Pelagic Birds, p. 657; Site Tenacity, p. 189; Bird Milk, p. 271. **REFS**: Manuwal, 1979; Vermeer, 1984; Vermeer et al., 1979.

Birds and Oil

A recurring sight on television news programs is dedicated naturalists attempting to save birds that have had their feathers contaminated with oil discharged into oceans, bays, or rivers. When oil tankers clean their tanks or suffer accidental spills, marine birds, such as loons, grebes, murres, puffins, razorbills, auklets, gulls, and ducks, are placed in jeopardy. Many birds may smell fresh oil and flee the area of a spill; unfortunately, many others cannot.

For a short time after oil is released, it may contain toxins that can be inhaled and ingested by birds in the process of preening and can cause pneumonia, kidney and liver damage, and other problems. Experiments with Black Guillemots indicate that swallowing even very small amounts of oil can lead to considerable physiological stress, interfere with adult foraging, and reduce the growth rates of young. A little oil on eggs during the first half of incubation can prove toxic to the developing embryo inside.

Even after the toxins have dissolved or evaporated, many hazards remain. The relatively inert oil mats the plumage, reducing its insulating and buoying properties. The soiled birds, swimming continually in an attempt to remain warm and afloat, eventually succumb to exhaustion.

Oiled birds rescued before they enter the last stages of distress can be saved by careful feeding, warming, and washing with detergent. Treatment is a time-consuming process, but records indicate that up to two out of every three oiled birds may be saved. Such statements can be misleading, however, in several ways. For example, volunteers are unlikely to rescue more than a small fraction of the affected birds after a major spill. At best their attempts may help to preserve a rare species in the path of a spill. In addition, volunteers usually are mobilized only in the face of major disasters, with the constant attrition that accompanies low-level, chronic oceanic oil pollution generally being neglected.

The degree to which chronic oil contamination of the sea contributed to long-term declines of Razorbill, Common Murre, and Atlantic Puffin populations in the North Atlantic, is controversial; oil pollution probably has been one factor among many. About 3.5 million tons of oil—about a tenth of a percent of the amount pumped from the ground annually—is spilled into the oceans each year. This spillage will, we hope, become smaller since seagoing nations have been instituting ever more stringent measures to eliminate the problem at its source: strict sanctions have been imposed against those who deliberately inject oil into the oceans. Furthermore, superior methods of containing accidental spills when they occur are being developed.

Ironically, the birds themselves may help to control the problem. The residues of petroleum ingested at sea have been detected in the stomach oil of storm-petrels. These and other tubenoses forage at the surface (where pollutants are concentrated), feed intermittently over large areas, digest oils

Rhinoceros Auklet

Cerorhinca monocerata Pallas

NG–180; G–162; PW–pl 35; AW–pl 85; AM(II)–130

MF   1   MF
      MONOG   I: 45 (39–52) DAYS   MARINE
             SEMIPRECOCIAL   INVERTS
             F: 48–55 DAYS
             MF

BREEDING: Rocky, shrub- or grass-covered slopes on islands. 1 brood. **DISPLAYS:** Billing maintains pair bond. Burrow defense and ownership proclaimed by standing upright, oft with wings partly spread, bill open and pointing up while hissing. **NEST:** On wide range of slope gradients, oft ocean-facing or wooded, turf-covered banks. Tunnel 5'–20' long, 5" across, with 1–2 side branches and chamber. Entrance usu near stump, tree, or under log. Of minimal twigs, moss, ferns formed into shallow saucer. **EGGS:** Dull white, unmarked or marked with lavender/gray/browns, occ wreathed. 2.7" (69 mm). **DIET:** Esp sardines; incl crustaceans. Pursuit diving elicits tight schooling of prey concentrating them toward surface. **CONSERVATION:** Winters s to Baja. Usu pelagic or found along rocky seacoasts. **NOTES:** Usu at colony only at night, at sea during the day (but also at some colonies in day). Usu incubates 24 hours before relief. Chick brooded ca. 4 days (range 0–9). In experimental exchange rearing with Tufted Puffin chicks, adopted feeding patterns of foster-parent puffins. Forages in mixed-species flocks. **ESSAYS:** Diving and Flightlessness, p. 203; Pelagic Birds, p. 657; Coloniality, p. 173; Incubation Time, p. 481; Mixed-Species Flocking, p. 433. **REFS:** Grover and Olla, 1983; Thoresen, 1983; Wilson and Manuwal, 1986.

Crested Auklet

Aethia cristatella Pallas

NG–178; G–162; PW–pl 35; AW–pl 86; AM(II)–128

1   MF
MONOG?   I: 34–41 DAYS
        SEMIPRECOCIAL?
        F: 35 DAYS
        MF

BREEDING: Rocky seacoasts and islands. ? broods. **DISPLAYS:** Much honking and grunting on breeding grounds. **NEST:** On talus slopes, among beach boulder rubble, occ in cliff. Egg laid in depression or on small bed of stones; no nest materials added. **EGGS:** White, unmarked. 2.1" (54 mm). **DIET:** Mostly crustaceans. Dives to 200' (33 fathoms). **CONSERVATION:** Usu pelagic in winter but also found off rocky islands and seacoasts of AK. **NOTES:** Colonial, oft with Least and occ Whiskered Auklets; adults arrive at colony 4–6 weeks before laying. Egg laying highly synchronous within colony over 10–12 day period. Young remain hidden in nest until fully fledged; parent brings food in throat pouch. Chicks begin to thermoregulate at 3–4 days; fledge during darkness. Fly low over water. Known to have 2 peak daylight activity periods. Adults important in diets of Glaucous-winged Gulls. **ESSAYS:** Diving and Flightlessness, p. 203; Pelagic Birds, p. 657; Coloniality, p. 173; Skimming, p. 195. **REFS:** Bédard, 1969; Knudtson and Byrd, 1982.

slowly, and regurgitate samples of the oil readily. Therefore, it has been suggested that the Procellariiformes could become part of an oceanic pollution monitoring system.

SEE: Metallic Poisons, p. 137; DDT and Birds, p. 21; Population Dynamics, p. 575; Helping to Conserve Birds—Global Level, p. 367; Pelagic Birds, p. 657. REFS: Boersma, 1986; Nettleship and Birkhead, 1985.

Bills

Birds pay a price for the advantages of flight. They must commit their forelimbs almost entirely to that enterprise. As a result the bill often must assume responsibility for diverse functions for which many mammals use their forelimbs—grasping, carrying, scratching, fighting, and digging.

The bill (or "beak") consists of the upper and lower jaws (mandibles), ensheathed in a layer of toughened skin. The horny outer layer tends to be especially thick near the tip, where the most wear occurs. The edges of the bill may be sharpened for cutting, or serrated for grasping, but the edges of some bills, including those of ducks, are blunt and relatively soft except at the tip, which is hardened. Ducks often must sort insects and seeds from murky water, and the edges of their bills are richly supplied with touch receptors that help them to detect their food.

In most birds the upper mandible is perforated by nostrils, although in some high-diving birds like gannets the external nostrils are missing; gannets avoid flooding by being "mouth breathers" and keeping their mouth shut when they hit the ocean. Similarly the nostrils of woodpeckers are protected from being flooded with "sawdust" by feathers or by being reduced to narrow slits. In the marine Procellariiformes (albatrosses and their relatives) the nostrils are a tube (storm-petrels) or pair of tubes (albatrosses, shearwaters, and fulmars) on top of the bill.

In most birds the horny sheath exfoliates (peels) and is continuously replenished from underneath. Sometimes the sheath develops special protuberances that are used in courtship and subsequently shed. The large, eye-catching grooved bill of the breeding Atlantic Puffin returns to its smaller and duller appearance after the fancy scales peel away at the end of the reproductive season.

As tools, bills are not used just for eating food, but also for catching it, prying up bark that conceals it, filtering it from water, killing it, carrying it, cutting it up, and so on. Bills also serve for preening, nest building, excavating, egg turning, defending, attacking, displaying, scratching, hatching, climbing, and so on. Small wonder that bill size and shape are characteristics that vary enormously from species to species and among major groups. And small wonder that the adaptations of bills to these various functions have long fascinated ornithologists.

Whiskered Auklet

Aethia pygmaea Gmelin

NG–178; G–162; PW–pl 35; AW–394; AM(II)–128

?
I: 35+ DAYS
SEMIPRECOCIAL?
F: ? DAYS
?

1
MONOG?

BREEDING: Rocky seacoasts and islands. ? broods. **DISPLAYS:** ? **NEST:** On talus slope, among beach boulders, and on high slopes of lava flows. Eggs laid directly on rock, occ soil substrate; no nest materials added. **EGGS:** White, unmarked. 1.9″ (48 mm). **DIET:** Crustaceans. **CONSERVATION:** Usu pelagic in winter or found off rocky Aleutian Islands. **NOTES:** Colonial, occ with Crested and Least Auklets. Rarest, least-known auklet. Egg laying highly synchronous within colony over 10–12 day period. Food for chick transported by adult in throat pouch. Chicks fledge in the darkness. **ESSAYS:** Diving and Flightlessness, p. 203; Pelagic Birds, p. 657; Coloniality, p. 173; How Do We Find Out About Bird Biology?, p. 319. **REF:** Knudtson and Byrd, 1982.

Least Auklet

Aethia pusilla Pallas

NG–178; G–164; PW–pl 35; AW–pl 89; AM(II)–126

MF
I: 31 (28–36) DAYS
SEMIPRECOCIAL
F: 29 (26–31) DAYS
MF

1
MONOG?

BREEDING: Rocky seacoasts and islands. ? broods. **DISPLAYS:** ? **NEST:** On talus slope, among beach rock rubble, occ in coastal cliff. No nest materials added; egg laid on bare rock, bed of small stones, or on ground. **EGGS:** White, unmarked. 1.6″ (40 mm). **DIET:** Small crustaceans taken in shallow water and from substrate in very deep water, usu near shore. **CONSERVATION:** Usu pelagic in winter or along rocky seacoasts and islands. Valued as food by Inuit; easily netted on nightly return to breeding colony. **NOTES:** Colonial, oft with Crested, occ Whiskered Auklets. Arrive in large flocks at breeding colony 4–6 weeks before laying. Strong nest site fidelity. Occ exhibit 2 peak daylight activity periods. Egg laying highly synchronous within colony over 10–12 day period. Incubation shifts avg 24 hours. Chicks brooded continuously by adults until they begin to thermoregulate at 5–6 days, then intermittently to day 18; fledge in darkness. Food for chick transported by adult in throat pouch. Adults are important in diets of Peregrine Falcons and Glaucous-winged Gulls. **ESSAYS:** Diving and Flightlessness, p. 203; Pelagic Birds, p. 657; Coloniality, p. 173; Temperature Regulation, p. 149; Site Tenacity, p. 189. **REFS:** Bédard, 1969; Knudtson and Byrd, 1982; Roby and Brink, 1986.

The most obvious adaptations of bills are those related to feeding. Birds that catch fishes with their bills must maintain a tenacious grip on slippery prey. Thus albatrosses and pelicans have hooked upper bill tips, and mergansers have serrated margins. Most waders hunt by probing in mud and sand, and have long, slender, forcepslike bills for finding and grasping their prey. Avocets, however, tend to feed more at the water's surface and swing their upward-curved bills from side to side. Oyster-catchers have especially stout bills designed for hammering and prying open recalcitrant mollusks. Hummingbirds also probe, and their fine bills are well designed for finding the nectar in deep tubes formed by the fusion of flower petals (corolla tubes). In tropical species the bills may have closely coevolved with specific flowers. The straight 4-inch bill of the Swordbill—the length of the bird's body and twice as long as the bill of any other hummer—permits it to drink nectar from (and pollinate) a passion flower with a corolla tube 4.5 inches deep. The half-arc bill of the Sicklebill hummers fits exactly in the sharply curved corollas of *Heliconia* flowers (South American relatives of *Strelitzia*, the "bird-of-paradise" flower).

Whip-poor-wills and their relatives have a wide-gaping bristle-fringed bill that acts as an aerial vacuum cleaner, sweeping in insects during flight. And tyrant flycatchers, such as kingbirds, pewees, phoebes, *Myiarchus* and *Empidonax* flycatchers, have ligaments connecting the upper and lower jaws that act as springs to snap the gaped jaw shut when an insect is snared.

Used for hunting and excavating nest cavities in wood, the powerful bill of a woodpecker is shaped like a pickaxe, and has an end like a chisel. The apparatus that supports the use of the bill is impressive: strong, grasping feet that work in concert with stiff tail feathers to form a triangular brace allowing the bird to position itself for its strenuous pecking against trunks or branches. Its very long, sensitive "tongue" (actually a complex extensible bone-muscle apparatus with a short tongue on the end of it) may wrap all the way around the bird's skull under the skin when it is retracted and is used to extract insects from holes and recesses.

Birds such as warblers and creepers that glean foliage or bark for insects tend to have slender bills that may or may not be downcurved. Those subsisting on seeds, such as sparrows, buntings, and other finches, have short, stout bills adapted for cracking and husking seeds. The stout, crossed mandibles of crossbills have evolved for the job of extracting seeds from conifer cones. The bills of omnivores like crows have an intermediate shape between those of insectivores and those of seed-eaters.

Interestingly, the bills of passerines that move about actively searching for bugs on leaves in our deciduous forests are shorter and wider than those of tropical forest species that feed in the same way. It has been proposed that the difference is related to differences in the insects that make up the major food sources in the two habitats. Highly mobile Orthoptera (katy-dids, crickets) and Blattodea (roaches) are abundant in the tropics. They are thought to be best grabbed with the long, slender, fast-closing bills of the

Parakeet Auklet

Cyclorrhynchus psittacula Pallas

NG–178; G–164; PW–pl 35; AW–pl 88; AM(II)–124

CLIFF

○
1
MONOG?

MF
I: 35–36 DAYS
SEMIPRECOCIAL?
F: 35 DAYS
MF

FISH

BREEDING: Rocky seacoasts. ? broods. **DISPLAYS:** ? **NEST:** Oft on densely vegetated slope or under loose pile of boulders on beach. No nesting materials added; egg placed on bare rock, soil, or bed of loose pebbles. **EGGS:** White/bluish-white, unmarked. 2.1″ (54 mm). **DIET:** Mostly planktonic crustaceans obtained while swimming at or near surface or by diving. **CONSERVATION:** Usu pelagic in winter off AK, or found along coasts. **NOTES:** Adults arrive on breeding grounds 4–6 weeks before laying. Food carried to chick in throat pouch of adult. By day 25 chicks reach maximum size, but weight decreases by 25% at fledging. Oft assoc with Crested and Least Auklets. Snow may delay breeding until late June. **ESSAYS:** Diving and Flightlessness, p. 203; Pelagic Birds, p. 657; Breeding Season, p. 55; Mixed-Species Flocking, p. 433. **REFS:** Bédard, 1969; Sealy and Bédard, 1973.

Atlantic Puffin

Supersp #18
Fratercula arctica Linnaeus

NG–180; G–162; PE–38; AE–pl 95; AM(II)–132

CLIFF

CREVICE
M

○
1
MONOG

MF
I: 39–45 DAYS
SEMIPRECOCIAL
F: 38–44 (34–74) DAYS
MF

MARINE
INVERTS

BREEDING: Earthen slopes and rocky areas on offshore islands. 1 brood. **DISPLAYS:** Courtship incl swimming in crowded groups, males rising, flapping wings, jerking heads past vertical in "head flick." Pair engage bills, then bill and neck. **NEST:** Burrow in open or under rock in loose soil; tunnel usu ca. 3′, ending in chamber. Crevice oft in cliff or among rocks. Usu lined with grass, leaves, feathers, occ unlined. **EGGS:** White/cream, occ faintly marked with lilac. 2.5″ (63 mm). **DIET:** Incl crustaceans, squid. Chicks fed almost exclusively fish. Usu forage near colony, but occ >10 miles, usu at depths <100′, rarely to 200′ (33 fathoms). **CONSERVATION:** Pelagic in winter off N.A. Serious decline in 1800s from commercial egging and hunting, continued in 1900s mostly in s; limited recent recovery in n. Reintroduced in ME. **NOTES:** Large colonies, those on cliffs smaller. Usu breed at 5–6, occ 3 years. Return to colony 3–4 weeks prior to laying. Strong nest site fidelity and long-term pair bond. Laying synchrony is high in groups of adjacent burrows. Incubating bird holds egg against brood patch with wing. Chick brooded 6–7 days; fledge at night. Bill develops bright plates prior to breeding. Formerly known as Common Puffin. **ESSAYS:** Bills, p. 209; Seabird Nesting, p. 197; Diving and Flightlessness, p. 203; Site Tenacity, p. 189. **REFS:** Boag and Alexander, 1986; Burger and Simpson, 1986; Cramp, 1985; Harris, 1984; Nettleship and Birkhead, 1985.

Left to right (and top to bottom): Northern Fulmar, Red Crossbill, Lesser Goldfinch, Atlantic Puffin, American Crow, Ruby-throated Hummingbird, Common Merganser, Prothonotary Warbler, Northern Gannet, Common Nighthawk, Black Skimmer, Hairy Woodpecker.

tropical birds—bills that are also handy for deftly removing the spiny legs of such prey. In the temperate forest sluggish caterpillars abound. They require no dexterity to catch, but a stout forceps to hold them while they are beaten into immobility. Thus a great deal can be surmised about birds' feeding habits simply from examination of their bills. One should always keep in mind, however, that bills do serve other functions.

Skimmers have one of the most interesting bills of all. Since, when foraging, they fly with their lower mandible slicing through the water, the mandible would be quickly eroded away by friction if it did not grow at roughly twice the rate of the upper mandible. Skimmers in zoos, deprived of the opportunity to skim, soon have lower mandibles much, much longer than the upper.

SEE: Flamingo Feeding, p. 43; Feet, p. 239; Bird Communities and Competition, p. 605; Coevolution, p. 405.   REF: Greenberg, 1981.

Horned Puffin

Fratercula corniculata Naumann

NG–180; G–162; PW–108; AW–pl 83; AM(II)–134

| CLIFF | CREVICE MF | 1 MONOG? | MF I: 40–42 DAYS SEMIPRECOCIAL F: 34–40 DAYS MF | MARINE INVERTS | |

BREEDING: Rocky islands. 1 brood. **DISPLAYS:** ? **NEST:** Burrow usu near cliff edge; tunnel 1′–3′ with enlarged chamber. Gathers minimal mass of grass. Holes and natural crevices among boulders used where available. Burrows perennial. Nest sites vary moving inland; presence of fox determines placement. **EGGS:** Off-white, lightly spotted. 2.8″ (72 mm). **DIET:** Incl esp squid, mollusks; some seaweed. **CONSERVATION:** Pelagic in winter off N.A. **NOTES:** Colonial; visits and remains at colony in daytime. Young call when unattended. Adults forage in inshore waters when feeding chicks; deliver food by dropping it on floor of nest burrow, oft near entrance. Habitually circle overhead if disturbed. **ESSAYS:** Bills, p. 209; Seabird Nesting Sites, p. 197; Diving and Flightlessness, p. 203. **REF:** Wehle, 1983.

Tufted Puffin

Fratercula cirrhata Pallas

NG–180; G–162; PW–108; AW–pl 82; AM(II)–130

| CLIFF | CREVICE MF | 1 MONOG? | MF I: 41 DAYS SEMIPRECOCIAL F: 45 DAYS MF | MARINE INVERTS | |

BREEDING: Coastal slopes, headland, rocky island with cliffs. 1 brood, 2 in s. **DISPLAYS:** ? **NEST:** On turf-covered slope or on clifftop; shallow, 2′–9.5′ tunnel ending in chamber. Occ lays egg on simple pile of grass and feathers. Also in rock piles, rarely under matted veg forming saucer-shaped nest with rim of aquatic veg. Straw lining oft stolen from gulls. **EGGS:** Bluish-white/off-white, marked with gray/light brown, occ wreathed. 2.8″ (72 mm). **DIET:** Incl squid, mollusks, sea urchins, also algae. Fish caught by underwater pursuit, carried crosswise in bill. Chicks fed fish, marine inverts; parents drop food on burrow floor, oft near entrance. **CONSERVATION:** Pelagic in winter off w N.A. **NOTES:** Colonial; active at colony in daytime. As fish feeder, nests later than plankton feeders. Prefers steep slope and high elevation for easy takeoff from nesting site. In experimental exchange rearing with Rhinoceros Auklet chicks, adopted feeding patterns of foster-parent auklets. Kittiwakes pirate fish from returning parents. **ESSAYS:** Bills, p. 209; Seabird Nesting Sites, p. 197; Diving and Flightlessness, p. 203; Piracy, p. 159; Breeding Season, p. 55. **REFS:** Vermeer, 1979; Vermeer and Cullen, 1979; Wehle, 1983.

Bird Biologist—Robert Cushman Murphy

A voyage taken to Antarctic waters as naturalist on the whaling brig *Daisy* in 1912 shaped the ornithological career of Robert Cushman Murphy (1887–1973). It started him on the road to becoming *the* expert on marine birds, and gave him the opportunity to write a classic volume on travel, *Logbook for Grace*, describing his voyage for the bride he had been obliged to leave behind. He spent his career at the American Museum of Natural History. There his first task (in 1906, before he entered college) was to help Frank Chapman (p. 43) read proof on *Warblers of North America*. He remained Chapman's junior colleague until that luminary retired in 1942. Murphy did much field work in the Southern Hemisphere, and published his beautifully written classic *Oceanic Birds of South America* in 1936. It is a must for anyone who wishes to enjoy fully birding trips off our coasts. Murphy was a lifelong conservationist, and in his latter years focused on the slaughter of the great whales, which he had observed from the *Daisy*.

SEE: Pelagic Birds, p. 657.

Soaring

Some land birds, such as vultures and certain hawks, sustain flight for long periods without flapping their wings. They take advantage of updrafts produced when the wind blows over hills and mountain ridges or make use of rising columns of warm air called "thermals." Vultures stay within thermals by flying slowly in tight circles. They have short, broad wings and a low wing loading (ratio of bird weight to wing area) that allows them to remain aloft and to be highly maneuverable at slow speeds. They also have a low aspect ratio (ratio of length to width of the wing), something that is dictated by their takeoff requirements. Low-aspect-ratio wings generally produce a lot of drag—that is, resistance from the air through which they are moving. Air from high-pressure areas beneath the wings tends to flow over the wingtips into the low-pressure areas above the wings. That flow produces wingtip turbulence, drag-creating disturbances of the smooth flow of air. A low-aspect-ratio wing, important for maneuvering, nevertheless creates a great deal of drag, something that is very undesirable in a soaring bird.

Vultures alleviate this problem slightly by flying with their primary feathers extended, creating slots between them. Each primary serves as an individual high-aspect-ratio wing, reducing wingtip turbulence and lowering the stalling speed of the wing so that the bird can remain aloft at a slower speed. This helps vultures to circle perpetually in thermals, maintaining thrust by gliding downward, but staying aloft by sinking at a rate slower than the hot air is rising.

It has been possible to measure a vulture's rate of sink by flying in

Turkey Vulture

Cathartes aura Linnaeus

NG–182; G–66; PE–160; PW–pl 18; AE–pl 317; AW–pl 307; AM(I)–212

NO NEST	◯	MF		
		I: 38–41 DAYS		
SNAG	2	SEMIALTRICIAL 2		
0'–20' +	(1–3)	F: 66–88 DAYS		
	MONOG	MF		

BREEDING: Open habitats in both lowlands and mountains. 1 brood. **DISPLAYS:** Courtship incl following-flights with male(?) occ diving at female. **NEST:** Also in cave (esp in w) or in hollow stump with narrow entrance. Rarely a minimal nest of raked stones, dry leaves, wood chips. **EGGS:** White, occ marked with brown. 2.8" (71 mm). **DIET:** Virtually any dead animal down to size of tadpole. Young fed regurgitant. **CONSERVATION:** Winters s to Bahamas, throughout C.A., Greater Antilles and S.A. Blue List 1972, 1980, Special Concern 1981–82, Local Concern 1986; reportedly decreasing in s Great Plains and parts of s. Eggshell thinning still a widespread problem. **NOTES:** Experimental evidence suggests carrion found by sight and scent. In contrast to Black Vulture, does not renest if clutch destroyed. Young brooded continuously for 5 days by both parents. Roost communally throughout year. **ESSAYS:** Soaring, p. 215; Avian Smell, p. 15; Spread-Wing Postures, p. 25; Blue List, p. 11; Temperature Regulation, p. 149; Communal Roosting, p. 615. **REFS:** Clark and Ohmart, 1985; Stager, 1964; Wilbur and Jackson, 1983.

Black Vulture

Coragyps atratus Bechstein

NG–182; G–66; PE–160; PW–pl 18; AE–pl 318; AW–pl 306; AM(I)–210

NO NEST	🥚	MF		
		I: 37–48 DAYS		
STUMP	2	SEMIALTRICIAL 2	VERTS	
0'–8' +	(1–3)	F: 80–94 DAYS		
GROUND	MONOG	MF		

BREEDING: Open lowland, garbage dumps, occ highland; avoids heavily forested regions. 1 brood. **DISPLAYS:** Courtship oft incl trio of males posturing at and flying after female. Complex aerial display starting with rapid, prolonged spiral, usu above cliffs. Pair bills. **NEST:** Occ in opening amid dense veg, on or in stump. **EGGS:** Light grayish-green, occ bluish-white, usu marked with browns, lavender, wreathed. Occ nearly plain. 3.0" (76 mm). **DIET:** Occ capture young birds, small mammals, other verts. Depend more on sight for finding food than do Turkey Vultures. Young fed regurgitant. **CONSERVATON:** Winter resident. Blue List 1972, 1981, Special Concern 1982, Local Concern 1986; decreased in s e and at n w edge of range but apparently expanding to n e. Loss of suitable tree cavities for nests due to fire control, and widespread eggshell thinning from pesticides are partly responsible for decrease. **NOTES:** Most colonial of vultures in both nesting and roosting. Family units maintained throughout year; preferentially assoc with other families, raising possibility of extended kin associations using communal roosts as information centers for locating good foraging areas. Roosts larger in winter (up to ca. 400 birds), avg ca. 33% turnover nightly. When confronted, regurgitate with power and speed. **ESSAYS:** Soaring, p. 215; Diet and Nutrition, p. 587; Avian Smell, p. 15; Spread-Wing Postures, p. 25; Communal Roosting, p. 615; Temperature Regulation, p. 149. **REFS:** McHargue, 1981; Rabenold, 1986, 1987; Wilbur and Jackson, 1983.

A soaring California Condor spreads its primary feathers so that each acts as a small, high-aspect-ratio wing. This reduces turbulence at the wingtips and lowers the stall speed, helping the condor to stay aloft circling slowly in thermals (columns of rising warm air).

aircraft in close formation with them. Turkey Vultures have a minimum sink rate of 2 feet per second, while Black Vultures have a minimum rate of 2.6 feet per second. Black Vultures, therefore, need stronger thermals than Turkey Vultures, which helps to explain why they are restricted to the southern United States while Turkey Vultures can penetrate the relatively cool climes of southern Canada.

Albatrosses and other seabirds such as shearwaters and petrels also soar. But their techniques are different from those of vultures. Albatrosses have long, slender wings with a high aspect ratio. They have the longest wings of any birds; the wingspan of the Wandering Albatross is in the vicinity of 10 feet. The high-aspect-ratio wings of soaring seabirds minimize drag, since the amount of wingtip is small in comparison with the length of the wing. The wing loading of albatrosses is very high also. Indeed, it is thought that albatrosses are close to the structural limits of wing length and wing loading.

Albatrosses and other soaring seabirds use their high wing loading and high-aspect-ratio wings to take advantage of the slope lift, updrafts created on the windward slopes of waves in the same manner they are created on mountain ridges. Albatrosses are able to proceed upwind by zigzagging along in the slope lift, and can even soar in windless conditions if there are waves. The waves push air upward as they move, and the albatrosses stay in that rising air. Seabirds can also extract some energy from the altitudinal gradient in the wind, which is slowed by friction near the water and increases in speed with height above its surface. That process has been called "dynamic soaring," but recent work by a leading authority on bird flight, Colin Pennycuick, indicates that slope soarers gain relatively little energy in that way. For instance, in typical wind conditions in the South Atlantic, dynamic soaring would permit albatrosses to rise about 10 feet above the surface, but they are regularly observed to soar to near 50 feet.

SEE: How Do Birds Fly?, p. 161; Wing Shapes and Flight, p. 227; How Fast and High Do Birds Fly?, p. 81.   REFS: Pennycuick, 1982; Raspet, 1950.

California Condor

Gymnogyps californianus Shaw

NG–182; G–66; PW–pl 18; AW–pl 337; AM(I)–214

 NO NEST

MF
I: 42–50 DAYS
SEMIALTRICIAL 1
F: 180 DAYS
MF

1
MONOG

BREEDING: Mountains, to moderate elevation, esp brushy or rocky outcrops with ample ledge and cliff nest sites. 0 or 1 brood. **DISPLAYS**: In courtship, male faces female, wings outstretched, tail dragging, and approaches her with his head bent exposing back of neck. **NEST**: On inaccessible cliff, cave floor or cavity in giant sequoia. Egg laid on bed of coarse gravel, with few twigs, leaves, etc. Most perennial. **EGGS**: Greenish-white/bluish-white. 4.3″ (110 mm). **DIET**: Dead red meat, salmon; does not eat most birds or squirrels. Group of 4 known to drag 100 + lb body of grizzly 200 yards. **CONSERVATION**: Winter resident. Endangered Species; no longer in the wild. **NOTES**: Although usu breed only every other year, capable of successfully nesting annually; rarely do so but can lay replacement clutch within breeding season. Long-term pair bond. Likely avg output is 2 young every 3 years. By fledging, wing span 8′, weight 20 pounds, length 46″, but able to fly no more than a few yards; dependent on adult for 6 months postfledging. Soar to 15,000′. **ESSAYS**: Conservation of the California Condor, p. 219; Birds and the Law, p. 293; Variation in Clutch Sizes, p. 339; Coloniality, p. 173. **REFS**: Ogden, 1985b; Snyder and Hamber, 1985; Snyder et al., 1986; Wilbur and Jackson, 1983.

Golden Eagle

Aquila chrysaetos Linnaeus

NG–184; G–78; PE–158; PW–pl 18; AE–pl 308; AW–pl 332; AM(I)–254

F – M
I: 43–45 DAYS
SEMIALTRICIAL 1
F: 66–75 DAYS
MF

TREE   MF   2   BIRDS   SWOOPS
10′–100′ +   (1–4)   REPTILES
                          MONOG   INSECTS

BREEDING: Open habitats, esp in mountains and hills. 1 brood. **DISPLAYS**: Upward spiral then nose-dive, wings half open, gliding up then diving and calling, usu alone, occ in pairs. **NEST**: Sticks interwoven with brush, leaves, etc. Lined with fine materials. Oft 2–3 (occ more) nests used alternately; perennial, becoming very large. **EGGS**: White/cream-buff, marked with brown; 1 egg usu unmarked. 2.9″ (75 mm). **DIET**: Esp jackrabbits; other prey (incl carrion) when mammals scarce. **CONSERVATION**: Winters s to n Mexico highlands. Protected since 1962 after >20,000 destroyed in 10 years mostly by sheep ranchers in spite of little evidence of livestock depredation; now stable or increasing. Also subject to powerline electrocution, poison intended for coyotes, etc. **NOTES**: Long-term pair bond. Male captures more food than female during incubation and chick rearing; male feeds female on nest, rarely feeds young directly or broods. Male incubates small amount, only in day. Oft use aromatic leaves in nest to deter insect pests. Larger sibling oft kills smaller. In most of w, territories occupied year-round. Subadult birds occ breed. Hunt solo or in pairs. Occ roost communally in winter when prey densities high. **ESSAYS**: DDT, p. 21; Brood Reduction, p. 307. **REFS**: Beecham and Kochert, 1975; Collopy, 1984; Cramp and Simmons, 1980; Steenhof et al., 1983.

Conservation of the California Condor

The California Condor is on the verge of extinction. There were three individuals, all males, known to be living free in late 1986. That was a drop from fifteen wild birds (including five breeding pairs) known to have been present in 1984. Twenty-one condors were also alive in captivity toward the end of 1986. The species is a relic of the ice ages; its preserved remains have been found in the La Brea tar pits. With its giant relative *Teratornis merriami* it picked the bones of mammoths and American camels that had expired in the ooze. *Teratornis,* even bigger than the condor—its 12-foot wingspread and 50-pound weight making it perhaps the biggest bird ever to take to the air—died out long before Europeans arrived in North America. By 1492 the condor was already retreating westward. Its bones were discovered in Florida early on, and recently its former presence in upper New York state was confirmed by Richard Laub of the Buffalo Museum of Science and David Stedman of the New York State Museum. When the '49ers were trekking to California, the condor had retired behind the Rockies, and it survived into the 20th century only in California and Baja California.

By World War II breeding condors were limited to California's southern Sierra Nevada, the Coast Range behind Santa Barbara, and the east-west ranges (Tehachapi Mountains) that connect the two across the southern end of the San Joaquin Valley. Considerably more than sixty birds were alive then. Since that time, the population has gradually declined. The causes of the condor's plight are several: shooting by hunters, poisoning with bait intended for coyotes, contamination of their food with DDT, other pesticides and lead, egg collecting by unscrupulous oologists, general harassment, food scarcity (mammoths and camels no longer exist in California and numbers of domestic stock are declining), and habitat destruction.

The question of how to save the condors has been strongly debated in the conservation community. A distinguished panel set up jointly by the National Audubon Society and the American Ornithologists' Union despaired of being able to save the species in the wild. The panel was convinced that irresponsible hunters would continue to shoot the condors, that the birds could not be protected from pesticide contamination, and that their habitat would continue to shrink and deteriorate. To learn more of their biology, the panel recommended initiation of a "hands-on" conservation program, including capturing of most remaining adults, keeping them captive long enough to determine their sex (by means of a simple surgical procedure), and placing radio transmitters on them, before releasing them.

The centerpiece of the program, which was adopted, was captive breeding. The single egg normally laid in each nest would be removed (the female will often lay a second) and the young condor would be reared under laboratory conditions. The goal was to establish a captive population that later could be used to restock empty habitat.

The program was challenged by other conservationists for scientific, political, esthetic, and ethical reasons. Would the interference with the birds

Bald Eagle

Haliaeetus leucocephalus Linnaeus

NG–184; G–78; PE–158; PW–pl 18; AE–pl 305; AW–pl 335; AM(I)–224

    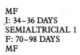

			MF I: 34–36 DAYS		
30'–60'	MF	2	SEMIALTRICIAL 1	BIRDS	LOW
(10'–180')		(1–3)	F: 70–98 DAYS	SMALL	PATROL
CLIFF		MONOG	MF	MAMMALS	SWOOPS

BREEDING: Coasts, rivers and large lakes in open areas. 1 brood. **DISPLAYS:** Spectacular aerial courtship, incl locking talons and descending in series of somersaults. **NEST:** Oft in fork of tall tree; of large sticks, veg, etc., deeply lined with fine materials. Cliff nests range from minimal sticks to massive structure. Occ >1 nest. Perennial, known to use >35 yr. **EGGS:** Bluish-white, oft nest-stained. 3.0" (76 mm). **DIET:** Esp salmon, up to 15 lb (oft dead or dying); also small mammals (esp rabbits), waterfowl and seabirds, carrion, rarely other verts. **CONSERVATION:** Winters s to coastal Baja. Endangered Species in most of U.S.; Threatened Species in WA, OR, MN, WI, MI. U.S. breeding population outside AK in 1982 <1500 pairs; declined due to habitat loss and reproductive impairment from pesticides and heavy metals. **NOTES:** Adopted as U.S. national emblem in 1782 because of fierce demeanor; in fact, somewhat timid carrion-feeder. Long-term pair bond. Young hatch asynchronously; smallest oft dies. Concentrations of 3000–4000 birds occur along Chiklat River, AK, during salmon run. Immature birds oft pirate fish from other species (esp crows); piracy from other Bald Eagles rarely successful. **ESSAYS:** DDT and Birds, p. 21; Metallic Poisons, p. 137; Birds and the Law, p. 293; Raptor Hunting, p. 223; Bird Biology and the Arts, p. 47; Conservation of Raptors, p. 247; Brood Reduction, p. 307; Piracy, p. 159; Monogamy, p. 597. **REFS:** Brown and Amadon, 1968; Fischer, 1985; Green, 1985; Lincer et al., 1979.

Mississippi Kite

Ictinia mississippiensis Wilson

NG–186; G–68; PE–150; PW–pl 17; AE–pl 304; AM(I)–222

			MF I: 31–32 DAYS		
30'–135'	MF	1–2	SEMIALTRICIAL 1		HIGH
(4'–135')		(1–3)	F: 34 DAYS		PATROL
		MONOG	MF		SWOOPS

BREEDING: Trees usu near waterway in forest, open woodland, semiarid rangeland. 1? brood. **DISPLAYS:** Already paired upon arrival in spring; little courtship. **NEST:** On upper branches, small forks, or occ horizontal limbs; bulky but flat, of coarse sticks, twigs. Lined with green leaves, Spanish moss. Perennial. **EGGS:** White/bluish-white, unmarked or faintly spotted, oft nest-stained. 1.6" (41 mm). **DIET:** Mostly large insects, few bats, amphibians, lizards. Flocks up to 20 follow livestock for flushed insects. **CONSERVATION:** Winters s to c S.A. Increasing since 1950s, breeding range expanding w, possibly due to tree planting for erosion control. **NOTES:** Nests in loose colonies. Congregate at communal perches and foraging areas; oft soar communally while hunting insects. Quiet. Reproductive success not related to nesting density. **ESSAYS:** Decline of Eastern Songbirds, p. 495; Range Expansion, p. 459; Masterbuilders, p. 445; Raptor Hunting, p. 223. **REFS:** Brown and Amadon, 1968; Glinski and Ohmart, 1983.

accelerate their decline? How much would the additional knowledge of condor biology really help in preserving them? Was enough known about captive breeding of condors to assure the success of attempts to rear them in the laboratory (the species has never been bred in captivity)? If there were no condors left in the wild to show the released birds where to forage and nest, would the releases survive? Political activists wondered if a successful captive breeding program would remove the constraints on development of the condor's habitat The presence of the giant birds protected an important habitat containing many other valuable but less spectacular species. And if the habitat disappeared, then there would be no place to release captive-bred birds in the future.

Other conservationists claimed that it was the free-flying condor that should be preserved, not a dreary zoo-bred captive. Naturalist Carl Koford, perhaps *the* leading expert on the condor, claimed that "Handling, marking and caging greatly diminish the recreational value of wild condors." Nature writer Kenneth Brower expressed a related viewpoint poetically: "Perhaps feeding on ground squirrels, for a bird that once fed on mastodons, is too steep a fall from glory. If it is time for the condor to follow *Teratornis*, it should go unburdened by radio transmitters." Opponents of the hands-on approach preferred a naturalistic recovery plan designed by Koford that involved improving the condors' environment—reducing pesticide use, supplementing food supplies, improving protection from hunters, and reducing competition from Turkey Vultures and other abundant scavengers.

We will never know whether that approach would have worked, but it clearly would have been a gigantic gamble. Even with an endangered species listing, a wilderness refuge, and the involvement of more biologists than there were condors, the birds were still dying out. The U.S. Fish and Wildlife Service and the California Fish and Game Commission chose the interventionist approach, with early results that were mixed. The population in captivity increased, while that in the wild dwindled away. The last wild condor, a seven-year-old male with the code name AC-9, was captured in April, 1987. There are still plans to release condors back into nature once their numbers have been increased, and by late 1986 $9 million had been appropriated for acquisition of a 13,000-acre tract of land containing critical condor habitat. Unfortunately, in that same year analysis of a smashed wild condor egg showed high levels of breakdown products of DDT. In addition, in the vicinity of condor habitat, hunters still leave behind bullet-riddled carcasses that are a source of lead-poisoning. Urban areas are still expanding, and oil and wind energy development is still planned. Even if the captive breeding program is an outstanding success, the prospects for reestablishing a thriving wild population in southern California seem bleak. It has been suggested that the Grand Canyon might be a more suitable release area. The environment in that national park can be closely controlled, and the condors could be readily viewed by millions of people. It is an idea worth considering if enough birds become available for release, even though

American Swallow-tailed Kite

Elanoides forficatus
Linnaeus

NG–186; G–68; PE–150; AE–pl 302; AM(I)–218

60'–130'	MF	2 (2–4) MONOG	MF I: 28 DAYS SEMIALTRICIAL 1 F: 36–42 DAYS MF	SMALL VERTS	SWOOPS

BREEDING: Lowland forest, esp swampy areas extending into open woodland. 1? brood. **DISPLAYS**: In flight: easy sailing, curving chase oft over water. On perch: mutual approach on horizontal limb, face-off, female quickly turns or backs under limb. Courtship feeding. **NEST**: Usu in treetop concealed by thick foliage; on foundation of preceding year's nest. Of sticks, twigs, moss, pine needles, leaves, lichen. Lined with fine materials, few feathers. **EGGS**: White, marked with browns, occ lavender, oft concentrated at end. 1.8″ (47 mm). **DIET**: Large insects, also incl nestlings, lizards, occ fruit. Usu eats in flight. **CONSERVATION**: Winters from Colombia and Venezuela s. Marsh drainage, deforestation, and shooting responsible for reduction in population and range. **NOTES**: Occ nest in loose colonies of a few pairs. Bathe and drink by skimming water surface like swallow. Occ soar at great heights. Up to 200 pieces used in nest, carried individually, may require up to 800 miles of flight. **ESSAYS**: Decline of Eastern Songbirds, p. 495; Raptor Hunting, p. 223; Hawk-Eyed, p. 229; Drinking, p. 123; Soaring, p. 215; Masterbuilders, p. 445. **REFS**: Brown and Amadon, 1968; Kilham, 1980b; Snyder, 1974.

Black-shouldered Kite

Elanus caeruleus Desfontaines

NG–186; G–68; PE–150; PW–pl 17; AE–pl 303; AW–pl 319; AM(I)–220

15'–60' (5'–60')	MF	4–5 (3–6) MONOG	F I: 30 DAYS SEMIALTRICIAL 1 F: 35–40 DAYS MF	INSECTS	

BREEDING: Savanna, riparian woodland, marsh, partially cleared or cultivated fields, grassy foothills. Occ 2 broods. **DISPLAYS**: Slow circling flight by pair, one passes below, rolls onto back as if to pass food, but interlocks feet with mate. **NEST**: In treetop, camouflaged from below but open above. Flimsy to well made, large and deep; of twigs, lined with grass, stubble, rootlets, moss, inner bark, etc. Oft perennial. **EGGS**: White, marked with brown. 1.7″ (42 mm). **DIET**: Esp California vole and other rodents, also birds, snakes, lizards, frogs, and large insects. **CONSERVATION**: Winters within U.S. N.A. range greatly expanded since 1960; probably the only raptor to have benefited from agricultural expansion. Aided by high adaptability to habitat disruption and increased abundance of rodents. **NOTES**: Under favorable conditions, nest semicolonially. Male does all of hunting for female and young from incubation until near fledging. Food transferred from hunter to mate in midair. Oft hover with legs dangling. Roost communally in winter (to >100 birds) but usu hunt solitarily. Formerly known as White-tailed Kite. **ESSAYS**: Raptor Hunting, p. 223; Communal Roosting, p. 615; Range Expansion, p. 459. **REFS**: Brown and Amadon, 1968; Cramp and Simmons, 1980; Eisenmann, 1971; Warner and Rudd, 1975.

a Grand Canyon population would probably need supplemental feeding of large animal carcasses on a regular basis.

Only time will tell, but the condor case illuminates the importance of prominent endangered organisms in helping with the most crucial of all conservation tasks—the protection of large tracts of relatively undisturbed habitat. It also shows how difficult decision-making becomes when it involves attempts to save organisms on the brink of extinction. In this case the controversy seriously split the conservation community, with people dedicated to the condors' welfare taking diametrically opposed views. But perhaps the most important point to be made about the California Condor is one of Ken Brower's: "When the *vultures* watching your civilization begin dropping dead . . . it is time to pause and wonder." We would add "and to act."

SEE: DDT and Birds, p. 21; Conservation of Raptors, p. 247. REFS: Ehrlich and Ehrlich, 1981; Emslie, 1987; Koford, 1953; Vitousek et al., 1986; Wilcove and May, 1986.

Raptor Hunting

One of the most spectacular sights in the world of birds is a kill of another bird by a stooping Peregrine Falcon. The falcon plunges steeply downward, wings partially closed, at speeds that can exceed 150 miles an hour. It was long thought that falcons and other raptors struck with their feet clenched like a fist. High-speed cinematographic studies, however, have shown that they strike their prey from above with all four toes fully extended. The Peregrine's victim is often ripped by the falcon's talons, producing a shower of feathers. Usually the prey is picked up off the ground afterward, although occasionally the falcon will stoop again and gather the tumbling bird before it falls to the ground.

Peregrines use other modes of hunting as well, sometimes diving past their prey and then zooming up from beneath to snatch it from behind and below, or simply catching a small bird from above with their talons. Sometimes they will patrol low over the ground like a harrier, attempting to flush game birds. The hunting success of Peregrines can vary widely with location, season, and even sex, as Cornell ornithologist Tom Cade showed with an interesting comparison. One breeding male in the eastern United States, hunting Blue Jays almost exclusively, caught 93 percent of his targets one season. A breeding female in Australia was successful only 31 percent of the time, but she captured mostly coots which were more than five times as heavy as the Blue Jays. Considering that the female probably weighed half again as much as the male, and analyzing the energy costs and benefits of both hunting patterns, Cade concluded that it took the male 49 kilocalories (kcal, what dieters normally just call a "calorie") to deliver 1,000 kcal of prey to the eyrie, while the female expended just 43 kcal to get the same job

Snail Kite

Rostrhamus sociabilis Vieillot

NG–188; G–68; PE–150; AE–pl 320; AM(I)–220

			MF	SNAILS	
			I: 26–30 DAYS		
SHRUB	M –F	3 (2–4)	SEMIALTRICIAL 1		SWOOPS
3'–9'		MONOG	F: 23–28 DAYS		
GROUND		(POLYGAM)	MF		

BREEDING: Subtropical freshwater marshes. 1 brood, oft 2 when food abundant. **DISPLAYS:** Pair soar high above marsh, suddenly fold wings and plunge short distance; occ dart at each other, stretching legs as if to grapple. **NEST:** In low tree, on hummock of marsh grass or in flooded bushes. Loose platform of green/dry sticks, leafy twigs. Lined with fine materials and leaves (usu green). **EGGS:** White, marked with brown, occ nearly plain. 1.7″ (44 mm). **DIET:** Nearly exclusively freshwater snails of the genus *Pomacea*. Grab in talons from substrate or water's surface, perch to eat. **CONSERVATION:** Winter resident. Endangered Species; FL population reduced to 20 by 1964 from marsh draining and shooting, esp at Lake Okeechobee. Recovering: 1983 estimate of 700 individuals. **NOTES:** Nests in loose colonies of a few pairs. Nest success increases with higher water levels, which result in greater snail abundance; in wet years, breeding extends over 10 months, male or female oft desert nestlings and remate. Breed as early as 10–12 months. Males do most of hunting for pair. Young independent at 10 weeks. FL population is n extreme of this tropical species. Formerly known as Everglade Kite. **ESSAYS:** Birds and the Law, p. 293; Diet and Nutrition, p. 587; Polygyny, p. 443; Polyandry, p. 133; Raptor Hunting, p. 223. **REFS:** Beissinger, 1986, 1987; Beissinger and Snyder, 1987; Snyder and Snyder, 1969; Sykes, 1983; Sykes and Kale, 1974.

Hook-billed Kite

Chondrohierax uncinatus Temminck

NG–188; G–68; AM(I)–218

			?	SNAILS	
			I: ? DAYS		
20'	MF	2–3	SEMIALTRICIAL 1		BARK
		MONOG	F: ? DAYS		GLEAN
			?		

BREEDING: Open swampy areas, lowland forest ranging from marsh to woodland. 1 brood. **DISPLAYS:** Courtship flight: pair circle together closely, dive at each other, and call frequently. **NEST:** Flimsy; of dead twigs and branches with shallow depression. **EGGS:** White, marked with brown. 1.8″ (45 mm). **DIET:** Mostly tree and land snails, rarely frogs, salamanders, insects. **CONSERVATION:** Winter resident. First N.A. nesting record in 1976 at Santa Ana National Wildlife Refuge; tropical species at n edge of range in s TX. Subspecies on Grenada and Cuba listed as Endangered (sub)Species. **NOTES:** More variable in bill size and plumage than any other raptor. Soars, occ in flocks to 25 birds. After capturing snail, flies to tree branch, braces snail against branch with left foot, inserts bill into opening of shell and breaks it open. Relative bill size accurately predicts relative size of snails captured. **ESSAYS:** Raptor Hunting, p. 223; Determining Diets, p. 535; Birds and the Law, p. 293; Soaring, p. 215. **REFS:** Brown and Amadon, 1968; Paulson, 1983; Smith and Temple, 1982a, b.

A Merlin stoops on an Inca Dove, killing it with a slashing blow of its open feet.

done. The female is more efficient, but is limited in the amount of time she can hunt because of her nest guarding duties. The somewhat less-efficient male probably delivered more nourishment to the young because he could spend more time hunting.

As a group, raptors exhibit an extraordinary variety of hunting techniques. Aside from owls (which are sometimes considered raptors) almost all are diurnal hunters, but a few like the European Hobby (a smaller relative of the Peregrine) will pounce on mice in the moonlight. Some are like the Peregrine in that they hunt at high speed. The Sharp-shinned Hawk, for example, often flashes through relatively thick woodland, maneuvering skillfully and often snatching passerines right from their perches. Others, like American Kestrels, Black-shouldered Kites, and the young of the very successful Red-tailed Hawk, often hover when hunting, and then drop steeply down on their targets. And still others, including adult Red-tails, soar as they watch for prey on the ground. But most hunting by raptors probably is done from perches with a commanding view from which the bird can scan the surrounding terrain with its telescopelike vision, where it can glide rapidly to gather in its prey. Interestingly, whether an American Kestrel hovers or perch-hunts depends in large part on whether there is a good breeze to hover in. Whichever technique is used, most prey of raptors are killed by the talons of the contracting foot being driven into their bodies; if required, the hooked bill is used to give a coup-de-grace. The exceptions are falcons, which ordinarily kill by biting into the necks of victims not dispatched in mid-air. (Owls also bite the necks of their prey.)

Of course, there are some birds of prey (in addition to falcons) that employ rather specialized hunting techniques. Perched or hovering Ospreys plunge into water to grab living fish; Snail and Hook-billed Kites course around like harriers in pursuit of their less-than-agile preferred food: snails.

SEE: Hawk-Eyed, p. 229; How Owls Hunt in the Dark, p. 291; Size and Sex in Raptors, p. 243. REFS: Brown and Amadon, 1968; Cade, 1982; Goslow, 1971; Ratcliffe, 1980; Rudolph, 1982.

Northern Harrier

Circus cyaneus Linnaeus

NG–188; G–70; PE–152; PW–pl 16; AE–pl 309; AW–pl 317; AM(I)–224

SHRUB <5'	F – M	5 (4–9) MONOG (POLYGYN)	F I: 31–32 DAYS SEMIALTRICIAL 1 F: 30–35 DAYS MF	SMALL VERTS	

BREEDING: Prairie, savanna, slough, wet meadow, marsh. 1 brood. **DISPLAYS:** Courting male performs series of dives from near stall, incl barrel-rolls in multiple U-shaped loops. **NEST:** Flimsy; on slightly elevated ground or in thick veg; of sticks, grass, etc., loosely lined with fine materials. **EGGS:** Bluish-white, usu unmarked, but 10% spotted with browns. 1.8" (47 mm). **DIET:** Esp voles, also birds, snakes, frogs, insects (esp grasshoppers), carrion. **CONSERVATION:** Winters s to n Colombia, n Venezuela, and Barbados. Blue List 1972–86; declining from loss of habitat and effects of pesticides: 20% of eggs showed shell thinning in 1970. **NOTES:** Like owls, has curved, sound-reflecting facial ruff which, with characteristic low (<7') flight, enables location of prey by sound. In 25 year WI study, 25% of nests were assoc with polygynous matings, oft involving subadult females; increased incidence of polygyny assoc with high vole populations. Female feeds and broods young. Females aggressively exclude males from preferred feeding areas in nonbreeding season. Outside of breeding season, roost communally on ground. Formerly known as Marsh Hawk; known as Hen Harrier in Europe. **ESSAYS:** Blue List, p. 11; Eye Color, p. 233; Raptor Hunting, p. 223; Polygyny, p. 443; DDT and Birds, p. 21; Size and Sex in Raptors, p. 243. **REFS:** Brown and Amadon, 1968; Hamerstrom et al., 1985; Rice, 1982; Temeles, 1986.

Sharp-shinned Hawk

Accipiter striatus Vieillot

NG–190; G–70; PE–152; PW–pl 16; AE–pl 294; AW–pl 325; AM(I)–226

DECID 10'–60' (10'–90')	?	4–5 (3–8) MONOG	F I: 32–35 DAYS SEMIALTRICIAL 1 F: 24–27 DAYS MF	

BREEDING: n woodland, mountainous conif/decid forest. 1? brood. **DISPLAYS:** Courting pair circle, land in tree, and call; courtship oft near nest. **NEST:** By trunk; broad and flat, of sticks, twigs. Lined with finer twigs, outer bark strips, grass, conif needles. Occ use old crow/squirrel nests, adding fresh materials. **EGGS:** White/bluish-white, marked with browns, wreathed. Occ unmarked; some clutches mixed. 1.5" (38 mm). **DIET:** Among accipiters, takes greatest proportion of birds as prey; only rarely takes small mammals, frogs, lizards, insects. **CONSERVATION:** Winters s through C.A. to c Panama, Greater Antilles. Blue List 1972–86; dramatic decline in e U.S. in early 1970s: 8%–13% of eggs showed shell thinning. **NOTES:** Juveniles may comprise up to 60% of breeding females in some populations. Male does virtually all of hunting from incubation to early nestling stage. Young dependent on adults for 21–28 days postfledging. Oft migrates in large numbers. **ESSAYS:** Wing Shapes and Flight, p. 227; Blue List, p. 11; Eye Color, p. 233; Adaptations for Flight, p. 507; Raptor Hunting, p. 223; DDT, p. 21. **REFS:** Henny et al., 1985; Kerlinger and Lehrer, 1982; Platt, 1976; Reynolds and Meslow, 1984.

Wing Shapes and Flight

One can tell a great deal about how a bird lives just from its wing shape. Most passerines, doves, woodpeckers, and game birds have wings that taper down more or less to a point at their outer tip. Those wings have a low aspect ratio (ratio of length to width), designed for rapid takeoff and swift twisting flight, but not for sustained high speed. Narrowing the tips reduces the area subject to the drag-inducing formation of vortices. At each wingtip a spiraling vortex is formed as air spills from the high-pressure area under the wing into the low-pressure area over it. Tapering, low-aspect-ratio wings are found on birds that must be fast and agile in order to outmaneuver both their prey and their predators.

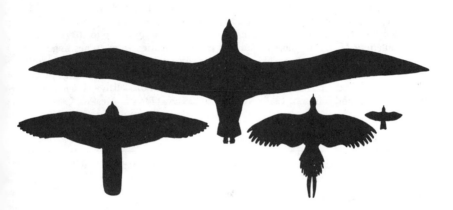

Top: albatross. Bottom, left to right: falcon, pheasant, passerine.

Slots between feathers at the tip of the wing lower the speed at which air flowing over the wingtip can cause enough turbulence to initiate a "stall" (reducing lift so that the bird starts descending). Slots thus aid low-speed maneuvering and are better developed in small, agile birds such as wood warblers than in less-active species such as House Sparrows. They are also prominent features on the wings of crows and their relatives and of game birds.

Flat, rather high-aspect-ratio wings lacking slots, and with feathers at the base that streamline the trailing edge in with the body, are found in falcons, swallows, plovers, and other specialists in high-speed flight. In contrast, hawks that soar in open country have lower-aspect-ratio wings; and Sharp-shinned Hawks that hunt in woodlands (and owls that also hunt there) and must be able to turn rapidly have an even lower aspect ratio. Wings that are more cambered (arched in cross section), with low aspect

Cooper's Hawk

Accipiter cooperii Vieillot

NG–190; G–70; PE–152; PW–pl 16; AE–pl 293; AW–pl 327; AM(I)–228

| | | | F –M
I: 32–36 DAYS | | |
| CONIF
35'–45'
(10'–60') | M –F | 4–5
(3–6)
MONOG | SEMIALTRICIAL 1
F: 27–34 DAYS
MF | SMALL
MAMMALS | |

BREEDING: Usu decid, occ conif, forest, woodland, esp riparian. 1? brood. **DISPLAYS**: Courtship flights with wings describing deep arc. **NEST**: Broad and flat or narrow and deep, of sticks, twigs, in crotch of conif, by trunk in decid tree; rarely on ground. Lined with chips, outer bark strips, occ green conif needles, down (oft added during and after laying). Occ use old crow nest. Male selects site. **EGGS**: Bluish-white/greenish-white, usu nest-stained, spotted with browns. 1.5" (39 mm). **DIET**: Also few reptiles, amphibians. Hunts with low dash through woods. **CONSERVATION**: Winters s through Mexico to Guatemala and Honduras. Blue List 1972–81, Special Concern 1982, Blue List 1986. Serious decline began reversal in e after 1972 ban of DDT. **NOTES**: Juvenile females occ comprise up to 20% of breeding population. Male does most of hunting from incubation to early nestling stage. Young hatch nearly synchronously but size difference apparent; dependent on adults for 30–40 days postfledging. **ESSAYS**: Blue List, p. 11; Raptor Hunting, p. 223; Hawk-Eyed, p. 229; DDT, p. 21; Brood Reduction, p. 307. **REFS**: Henny et al., 1985; Kennedy and Johnson, 1986; Nelson, 1968; Reynolds and Meslow, 1984.

Northern Goshawk

Accipiter gentilis Linnaeus

NG–190; G–70; PE–152; PW–pl 16; AE–pl 296; AW–pl 326; AM(I)–230

| | | | F –M
I: 36–38 DAYS | | |
| DECID
20'–60'
(18'–75') | M –F | 3–4
(2–5)
MONOG | SEMIALTRICIAL 1
F: 35–42 DAYS
MF | SMALL
MAMMALS | LOW
PATROL |

BREEDING: Mixed, oft mostly conif, forest, open woodland. 1 brood. **DISPLAYS**: Flying with slow wingbeats, male or female dives and swoops over territory. **NEST**: In crotch or by trunk, occ in aspen, oft in decid tree in s e part of range; slightly hollowed, occ compact, of sticks, twigs. Lined with bark strips, evergreen sprigs, grass, feathers. Perennial. **EGGS**: Bluish-white/off-white, occ nest-stained, occ spotted with brown. 2.3" (59 mm). **DIET**: Forages low in woodland taking slightly more birds (mostly ground-dwelling) than mammals. **CONSERVATION**: Winters s to n Mexico. Previously declining in n but range expanding to s e; eggshell thinning reported from some areas in early 1970s. **NOTES**: Female esp defensive at nest, boldly attacks humans. Pair bond may be long-term. Up to 25% breed first year, 25% second year, 50% not until third year. Male does most of hunting from incubation to early nestling stage; female broods and feeds young. Smaller male more agile than female, usu captures smaller, more agile prey. Young dependent on adults for 30–40 days postfledging. Invade s regions in winter ca. every 10 years, apparently assoc with crash of prey populations in n. **ESSAYS**: Heath Hens, p. 257; Irruptions, p. 639; Raptor Hunting, p. 223; DDT, p. 21; Size and Sex, p. 243. **REFS**: Cramp and Simmons, 1980; Henny et al., 1985; Mueller et al., 1977; Reynolds and Meslow, 1984; Speiser and Bosakowski, 1987.

ratio and well-developed slots, characterize vultures and other soaring land birds, while extremely high-aspect-ratio wings characterize albatrosses and other oceanic "slope soarers."

SEE: How Do Birds Fly?, p. 161; Soaring, p. 215; How Fast and High Do Birds Fly?, p. 81; Hovering Flight, p. 323; Flying in Vee Formation, p. 59.

Hawk-Eyed

Birds and people are "sight animals." For both, the eyes are the dominant sense organs, vastly more important than their inferior sense of smell. The reasons for our sensory similarity to birds can be found in human evolutionary history. At one point the ancestors of *Homo sapiens* were small, tree-dwelling primates. When leaping from limb to limb and snatching of insect prey with the hands, sharp, binocular vision was very handy; those of our forebears that tried instead to smell the location of a branch on which to land were unlikely to survive to reproduce. And since in the breezy treetops odors quickly dissipate, they do not provide good cues for detecting food, enemies, or mates. Birds, flying higher and faster than primates leap, naturally also evolved sight as their major device for orienting to the world.

Most birds have binocular vision. It is especially well developed in predators that must precisely estimate ever-changing distances to moving prey. Their eyes tend to be rotated toward the front of the head, so that the visual fields of each eye overlap to some degree. This trend is most pronounced in owls, whose eyes are almost as completely overlapping in field as ours. Small birds that are likely to be prey for raptors tend to have their eyes set on the sides of the head, permitting them to watch for danger in all directions. At the opposite extreme from the owls are the woodcocks, mud probers with eyes set high and back on the head, out of the way of vegetation and splattering mud and in a position to look out for predators. In fact, the woodcock has better binocular vision to the rear than to the front!

Shorebirds, waterfowl, pigeons, and other birds that have minimal binocular vision seem to depend on differences in apparent motion between close and distant objects for much of their depth perception. When a bird's eye is moving, closer objects appear to move at a faster rate than do distant objects—a phenomenon familiar from the way roadside telephone poles seen from the window of a moving car appear to pass more rapidly than the distant landscape. Presumably to enhance this distance-measuring method, shorebirds, and waterfowl often bob their heads up and down, and pigeons move theirs back and forth while walking. Even birds with relatively good binocular vision may use apparent motion to aid them in estimating distance; perched New Guinea kingfishers often "post" up and down on their legs before diving after prey. To see how this works, move your head with one eye closed and note the relative motion of close and distant objects.

Red-shouldered Hawk

Buteo lineatus Gmelin

NG–192; G–74; PE–156; PW–pl 15; AE–pl 298; AW–pl 312; AM(I)–236

			MF I: 28 DAYS		
20'–60'	MF	3	SEMIALTRICIAL 1	REPTILES	HIGH
(10'–200')		(2–4)	F: 39–45 DAYS	AMPHIBIANS	PATROL
		MONOG?	MF	BIRDS	

BREEDING: Riparian forest, wooded swamp. 1 brood. **DISPLAYS**: 1–4 birds soar, flap, swoop and dive while calling over territories. May rise in wide spirals 1,500'–2,000' over nest, flap, dive, descend to original spot in series of dives and sideslips. **NEST**: Usu by trunk, occ in conif in w; of sticks, twigs, inner bark strips, dry leaves, moss, lichen, conif needles. Lined with fine materials, green leaves (replenished from incubation on). Perennial. **EGGS**: White/bluish-white, oft nest-stained, marked with brown. 2.1″ (53 mm). **DIET**: Inc rodents, snakes, lizards, insects, also occ snails. Old nest oft becomes eating platform. **CONSERVATION**: Winters within U.S. Blue List 1972–86; declining or now stabilized at low numbers; known to accumulate organochlorine pesticides and PCBs, but habitat loss is the major threat. **NOTES**: Pair or kin may use same territory for many years. Usu first breed at 2 years. Can tolerate human disturbance if mature trees/high canopy maintained. Young hatch asynchronously, differ in size. Hunt in forest edge and open woodland near meadows and fields. **ESSAYS**: Blue List, p. 11; Hawk-Eyed, p. 229; Metallic Poisons, p. 137; Raptor Hunting, p. 223; DDT and Birds, p. 21; Nest Sanitation, p. 315; Brood Reduction, p. 307. **REFS**: Bednarz and Dinsmore, 1981; Brown and Amadon, 1968; Henny et al., 1973; Wiley, 1975.

Broad-winged Hawk

Buteo platypterus Vieillot

NG–192; G–74; PE–156; PW–pl 20; AE–pl 297; AM(I)–238

			F–M I: 28–32 DAYS	
30'– 50'	MF	2–3	SEMIALTRICIAL 1	BIRDS
(3'–90')		(1–4)	F: 35 DAYS	REPTILES
		MONOG	MF	INSECTS

BREEDING: Dense decid and mixed forest; occ in open woodland, oft near water. 1 brood. **DISPLAYS**: Aerial courtship: pair flap, soar in circles, darting at and passing close to each other. **NEST**: Usu in crotch of decid tree, occ in conif by trunk. Relatively small, loose, of sticks, twigs, dead leaves. Lined with inner bark strips, lichen, few outer bark chips, evergreen sprigs, green leaves. Usu annual. Built in 3–5 weeks; female does all or most of lining. Occ use old nest of crow, squirrel, hawk. **EGGS**: White/bluish-white, marked with brown, wreathed; occ unmarked. 1.9″ (49 mm). **DIET**: Opportunistic, also takes nestlings. Sedentary hunter; usu cannot catch adult birds. Occ hawks insects. **CONSERVATION**: Winters s from Guatemala through C.A. to e Peru, Bolivia, and s Brazil. **NOTES**: Pair bond occ lasts >1 year. Only female has brood patch; male provides food for incubating mate. Young hatch asynchronously, chick size differs. Female broods; begins hunting when nestlings 1–2 weeks old. Oft migrate in large flocks. **ESSAYS**: Decline of Eastern Songbirds, p. 495; Pellets, p. 297; Brood Reduction, p. 307; Brood Patches, p. 427. **REFS**: Fitch, 1974; Matray, 1974; Rosenfield, 1984; Rusch and Doerr, 1972.

The term "hawk-eyed" accurately describes many birds. For example, both raptors that must see prey at great distances and seed eaters that must pick tiny objects off the ground have eyes designed for high "visual acuity" —the capacity to make fine discriminations. There is, in fact, evidence that hawks can distinguish their prey at something like two or three times the distance that a human being can detect the same creature. Interestingly, even with such visual acuity, Cooper's Hawks are known to hunt quail by their calls.

One way that birds have attained such a high degree of acuity is by having relatively large eyes. A human eye weighs less than 1 percent of the weight of the head, whereas a starling's eye accounts for some 15 percent of its head weight. But more than size alone appears to account for the astonishing performance of the eyes of hawks. Evolution has arranged the structure of their eyes so that each eye functions very much like a telescope. The eye has a somewhat flattened lens placed rather far from the retina, giving it a long "focal length," which produces a large image. A large pupil and highly curved cornea admit plenty of light to keep the image on the retina bright.

Visual acuity in birds is also enhanced by the structure of the retina itself, which has tightly packed receptors and possesses other adaptations for producing a fine-grained image. Most of those receptors are the type called "cones." "Rods," the receptors of the vertebrate retina that are specialized to function in dim light, are relatively rare. Thus daytime acuity is, in part, achieved at the expense of night vision—a small price to pay for birds that are inactive at night anyway. In those relatively few species that are nocturnal, such as owls, rods predominate.

Considering the frequent evolution of gaudy colored plumage, it is not surprising that birds active in the daytime have color vision (nocturnal birds are thought to be color blind), and that color perception is often obvious in bird behavior. One can watch a hummingbird moving from red flower to red flower; bowerbirds show color preferences when decorating their bowers. Just how refined that color vision may be has proven difficult to determine. However, the diversity of visual pigments found in birds' eyes, and the presence of an array of brightly colored oil droplets inside the cones, suggest that avian color perception may surpass our own. There is also evidence that some birds' eyes are sensitive to ultraviolet light. In hummingbirds the adaptive significance of this is clear, since some flowers from which they drink nectar have patterns visible in the ultraviolet end of the light spectrum. Why pigeons have the ability to see ultraviolet remains a mystery. Equally surprising is the recently discovered ability of pigeons to detect the plane of polarized light. This probably serves them well in homing.

SEE: Raptor Hunting, p. 223; The Color of Birds, p. 111; How Owls Hunt in the Dark, p. 291; Bird-Brained, p. 415; What Do Birds Hear?, p. 299; The Avian Sense of Smell, p. 15. REFS: Goldsmith, 1980; Snyder and Miller, 1978.

Gray Hawk

Buteo nitidus Latham

NG–192; G–76; PW–pl 20; AW–pl 340; AM (I)–236

40'–60'	?	2	?	BIRDS	LOW PATROL
(30'–125')		(1–3)	I: 32 DAYS	SMALL	HIGH
		MONOG	SEMIALTRICIAL 1	MAMMALS	PATROL
			F: 30 DAYS		
			?		

BREEDING: Riparian woodland, open woodland, pastureland. 1 brood. **DISPLAYS**: Aerial display: male closely follows female in sailing chase, spiraling, both calling same nonshrill note, becoming less vocal when paired. **NEST**: Concealed in tree-tops, esp sycamore or cottonwood; small platform of mostly green twigs and sticks. Lined with green leaves, usu plucked from within reach of nest. **EGGS**: White/bluish-white, seldom marked, but oft nest-stained. 2.0″ (51 mm). **DIET**: Lizards, snakes, small mammals, game bird young, occ fish, large insects. **CONSERVATION**: Winters from n Mexico s to n w Costa Rica. **NOTES**: If female dies, male assumes full parental care. If nest approached, bird not sitting on nest gives whistling protest. Flight swift, graceful, more similar to *Accipiter* than *Buteo*. **ESSAYS**: Hawk-Eyed, p. 229; Raptor Hunting, p. 223; Size and Sex in Raptors, p. 243; Nest Sanitation, p. 315; Parental Care, p. 555. **REFS**: Brown and Amadon, 1968; Clark, 1987.

Red-tailed Hawk

Buteo jamaicensis Gmelin

NG–194; G–72; PE–154; PW–pl 15; AE–pl 300; AW–pl 314; AM(I)–246

15'–70'	MF	2–3	F – M	BIRDS	SWOOPS
(0'–120')		(1–5)	I: 30–35 DAYS	REPTILES	
CLIFF		MONOG	SEMIALTRICIAL 1	INSECTS	
			F: 45–46 DAYS		
			MF		

BREEDING: Woodland and open country with scattered trees, desert. 1? brood. **DISPLAYS**: Aerial display: pair spiral, recross, male usu circling behind and above female. Male may stoop at female, feet touching or interlocking as female rolls over. Courtship feeding. **NEST**: In crotch of large tree with commanding view; bulky, of sticks and twigs, lined with inner bark strips, evergreen sprigs, green leaves; greens renewed. May use old raptor nest as base. Alternately uses several perennial nests. **EGGS**: White/bluish-white, spotted with brown or unmarked. 2.4″ (60 mm). **DIET**: Mostly (85%+) rodents; also amphibians, crayfish, fish, and offal. **CONSERVATION**: Winters s to Panama. Much reduced in e by early bounty; continued steady decline from human persecution and habitat loss, also some egg-shell thinning. **NOTES**: Most common and widespread *Buteo*. Interspecifically territorial with Swainson's Hawk. Female oft returns to previous nesting territory. Young hatch asynchronously. Harlan's Hawk, formerly considered separate species, now considered form of Red-tail. **ESSAYS**: Eye Color, p. 233; Size and Sex in Raptors, p. 243; Raptor Hunting, p. 223; Metallic Poisons, p. 137; Site Tenacity, p. 189; Nest Sanitation, p. 315; Brood Reduction, p. 307; Courtship Feeding, p. 181. **REFS**: Brown and Amadon, 1968; Janes, 1984a, b; Mader, 1978.

Eye Color and Development

The color of a bird's eye (usually the color of the iris) results from both pigments and phenomena such as the diffraction of light. Avian eye colors range from dark brown and yellow through red, blue, and green to metallic silver and gold. In some species, eye color differs between the sexes, as in bright yellow-eyed male and brown-eyed female Brewer's Blackbirds. The nearly identical sexes of the European Starling can be differentiated by the presence of a yellow ring along the edge of the iris in females.

In many species, eye color changes as the bird matures and can serve as a means of determining an individual's age. Although the physiology of iris pigmentation is poorly understood, changes in color with age and with season are likely to be under hormonal control, especially where colors are closely associated with the sexual cycle. Changes of eye color with age are found in a wide variety of avian families including the loons, grebes, ducks, hawks, pheasants, gulls, alcids, woodpeckers, mimic thrushes, vireos, and blackbirds. Species requiring more than a year to pass from juvenile to adult plumage (such as the Bald Eagle and Herring Gull) generally show a concurrent change in eye color. Some specific examples of age-related changes are Lesser Scaup and Northern Harrier (from brown to yellow), Sharp-shinned Hawk (bright yellow to red), Red-tailed Hawk (yellow to red-brown), American Crow (blue or blue-gray to brown), Dark-eyed Junco (gray or gray-brown to red-brown), and Common Grackle (brown, turning paler with age). The evolutionary significance of these changes is not clear, but in some birds they may serve to help determine the maturity of potential mates.

SEE: The Color of Birds, p. 111; How Long Can Birds Live?, p. 643. REF: Trauger, 1974.

Hatching

The hard shell of a bird's egg is composed of a protein skeleton supporting a heavy deposit of calcium carbonate (largely) and other minerals. It is marvelously adapted to bear the weight of the incubating parent, conserve moisture, permit the exchange of gases, and resist the attacks of some predators. But it presents the developed chick with a problem—how to get out.

The chick solves the problem with two devices. It grows an "egg tooth" at the end of the upper mandible, and it develops powerful "hatching muscles" on the back of its head and neck. Then, as development comes to an end, the chick swallows much of the liquid in the egg, and pulls the remaining membrane-wrapped yolk into its abdomen. It then works its head into the airspace in the egg (formed by evaporation of liquids from the egg and their absorption by the chick), where it can breathe air and peep. Fi-

Swainson's Hawk

Buteo swainsoni Bonaparte

NG–194; G–74; PE–154; PW–pl 15; AE–pl 299; AW–pl 308; AM(I)–240

20'–30'	?	2–3	F –M		
(6'–70')		(2–4)	I: 28–35(?) DAYS	SMALL	
CLIFF		MONOG	SEMIALTRICIAL 1	VERTS	
			F: 30 DAYS	INSECTS	
			MF		

BREEDING: Savanna, prairie, desert, open pine-oak woodland, cultivated lands with scattered trees. 1 brood. **DISPLAYS:** Vigorous, aerial acrobatics, soaring over nest; occ 20'–30' dive preceded and followed by flat, circular flight, vigorous flapping, vertical climb, stall, dive, return to nest. **NEST:** Built of large sticks, twigs, brambles, grass, etc. Lined, occ layered, with inner bark, fresh leaves, flower clusters, down, feathers. Occ use abandoned nest of other birds (esp magpie). About 50% of nests reused. **EGGS:** Bluish-greenish-white/white, sparsely marked with brown; ca. 20% of eggs unmarked. 2.2″ (57 mm). **DIET:** Also rabbits, lizards, snakes, frogs, toads, birds (mostly fledglings), occ feed heavily on large insects. **CONSERVATION:** Winters primarily on pampas of s S.A. Blue List 1972–82, Special Concern 1986; current status unclear. Even minor disturbance occ causes nest desertion. Many shot while perched along roads. Expanding cultivation has increased breeding opportunities, esp in n Great Plains. **NOTES:** 30% of nest failures in agricultural shelter belts due to hail and wind destruction of nests. Young hatch asynchronously; remain with parents until migration. Before WW II, flocks of >2,000 common in n migration; annual trip is 11,000–17,000 miles. **ESSAYS:** Hawk-Eyed, p. 229; Size and Sex in Raptors, p. 243; Raptor Hunting, p. 223; Brood Reduction, p. 307; Migration, p. 183. **REFS:** Bechard, 1982; Brown and Amadon, 1968; Dunkle, 1977; Gilmer and Stewart, 1984; Olendorff, 1974.

Rough-legged Hawk

Buteo lagopus Pontoppidan

NG–196; G–72; PE–156; PW–pl 15; AE–pl 295; AW–pl 316; AM(I)–252

CONIF	MF (?)	2–7	F –M	INSECTS	SWOOPS
TREE		MONOG	I: 28–31 DAYS		
20'–30'			SEMIALTRICIAL 1		
			F: 39–43 DAYS		
			MF		

BREEDING: Open conif forest, tundra. 1 brood. **DISPLAYS:** Aerial display over territory: pair closely spiral, call (combination of whistle and hiss), and soar. Male performs U-shaped dives. **NEST:** In treetop if available, occ on steeply banked slope, rarely on ground; of sticks, grass, weed stalks and excrement. Lined with grass, down and feathers. Perennial. **EGGS:** Greenish-white/white, occ marked with brown. 2.2″ (57 mm). **DIET:** Occ birds, carrion. Oft hunts at dusk. **CONSERVATION:** Winters within N.A. Inadvertently poisoned by bait intended for mammals and oft shot when feeding on road kills in winter. **NOTES:** Larger clutches occur in years of high lemming abundance. Male does most or all of foraging from incubation until fledging. Young hatch asynchronously. Migrates in loose flocks. Roosts communally in winter, usu in conifers. Known as Rough-legged Buzzard in Europe. **ESSAYS:** Irruptions, p. 639; Hawk-Eyed, p. 229; Raptor Hunting, p. 223; Clutch Sizes, p. 339; Roosting, p. 615; Brood Reduction, p. 307. **REFS:** Andersson and Wiklund, 1987; Brown and Amadon, 1968; Cramp and Simmons, 1980.

nally, by contracting the hatching muscles the chick forces the egg tooth against the shell, making the first hole in the haven that has become its prison. It uses head and leg movements to complete the breakout. Within a short time after hatching, the egg tooth drops or wears off, and the hatching muscles atrophy. In some species, such as the Red-tailed Hawk, the egg tooth may last several weeks.

Hatching takes from hours to days, depending on the species. Albatrosses are the record holders. They may take as many as six days to hatch. In most species hatching tends to occur in the morning, possibly because it allows time for a feeding before nightfall. It appears that the alternation of day and night is perceived within the egg, thus permitting the chick to hatch at the best possible time.

SEE: Eggs and Their Evolution, p. 301; Incubation Time, p. 481; Incubation: Heating Eggs; p. 393; Life in the Egg, p. 457.

Flock Defense

One of the advantages that animals may obtain by grouping is a better chance of avoiding predators. Assuming a predator generally will attack the closest individual, a bird can reduce its "domain of danger," the area in which it can be the closest prey to a predator, by joining a flock. Where there is cover, of course, hiding rather than flocking may be a more effective predator defense strategy.

Simply reducing the domain of danger may not be enough to cause the evolution of flocking behavior, even in open country. Flocking may, in fact, backfire. The flock may be so conspicuous or represent so much potential food that it attracts predators that might otherwise miss or ignore a lone bird. However, there are other possible advantages of flocking. For instance, in some situations being in a flock may reduce the amount of time each bird must spend watching for predators, and thus increase the amount of time it has for feeding or other activities. Suppose a certain bird must spend half of its time feeding in order to survive, and can watch for predators the other half. A cat might sneak up on the bird by moving only when the bird was busy feeding. If two birds forage together, and they feed and look out at random, one bird or the other will be looking out three-fourths of the time. A little arithmetic shows that ten birds feeding together will have at least one individual watching for predators 99.9 percent of the time.

This bit of theory is supported by results from an interesting experiment with Laughing Doves (also called Senegal Turtledoves, a species from Africa and south-central Asia that is invading Europe and has been introduced into western Australia). Experimenters used bait to attract natural flocks of the doves and then "flew" a model hawk down a slanting wire toward them. The entire procedure was filmed, and the reactions of the

Ferruginous Hawk

Buteo regalis Gray

NG-196; G-72; PE-154; PW-pl 15; AW-pl 315; AM(I)-250

			MF I: 28–33 DAYS		
20'–40'	MF	2–4	SEMIALTRICIAL 1	BIRDS	SWOOPS
(6'–55')		(2–6)	F: 44–48 DAYS	REPTILES	
CLIFF		MONOG	MF	INSECTS	

BREEDING: Open country, usu prairies, plains, and badlands. 1 brood. **DISPLAYS:** Aerial courtship: soaring pair "parachuting" with wings held above back; male dives at female, pair grapple with talons. **NEST:** In tree with commanding view; of heavy sticks, cow dung, bones, rubbish. Lined with grass, inner bark strips, roots, etc., occ green leaves. Perennial, occ immense. Also on ground, bank, butte, slope. Old nest occ repaired and used. **EGGS:** White/bluish-white, marked with brown, occ nearly unmarked. 2.4" (61 mm). **DIET:** Almost exclusively small mammals, esp ground squirrels and jackrabbits, also snakes, lizards, large insects. **CONSERVATION:** Winters s to c Mexico. Blue List 1972–81, Special Concern 1982–86; now rare in many parts of range. Many shot while perched along roads. **NOTES:** In some areas, number of nesting pairs, number of eggs laid, and number of young fledged vary in synchrony with jackrabbit abundance. Will drive away Great Horned Owl. Wind may blow eggs from nest. Magpie oft shares old nest, taking lower site. **ESSAYS:** Blue List, p. 11; Hawk-Eyed, p. 229; Raptor Hunting, p. 223; Variation in Clutch Sizes, p. 339; Population Dynamics, p. 575. **REFS:** Fitzner et al., 1977; Gilmer and Stewart, 1983; Schmutz and Fyfe, 1987; Smith et al., 1981.

White-tailed Hawk

Buteo albicaudatus Vieillot

NG-196; G-76; PW-pl 19; AE-pl 301; AM(I)-242

			FM? I: ? DAYS		
SHRUB	?	2–3	SEMIALTRICIAL 1	SMALL	HOVER &
YUCCA		(1–4)	F: ? DAYS	VERTS	POUNCE
5'–15' (2'–40')		MONOG	MF (?)	INSECTS	

BREEDING: Coastal grassland, savanna, semiarid brushland. 1 brood. **DISPLAYS:** Talon-grappling occurs, probably as part of courtship. **NEST:** Unkempt, large platform with commanding view; of sticks and twigs. Lined with few green twigs, grass, green leaves, and breast feathers. Perennial. Occ built atop crow or caracara nest. Building of new nest takes up to 5 weeks. **EGGS:** White/bluish-white, sparsely marked with brown. About ⅓ of eggs unmarked. 2.3" (59 mm). **DIET:** Mostly small mammals (esp rabbits and woodrats), also snakes, lizards, frogs, large insects, occ ground-dwelling birds. Attracted to grass fires to take fleeing small mammals. **CONSERVATION:** Winter resident. Marked decline from 1930s to late 1960s largely due to habitat loss; significant eggshell thinning has occurred since 1947. **NOTES:** Not a close sitter, if disturbed at nest soars above intruder; if female leaves nest, male joins her. Strong nest-site tenacity. Breeding biology not well known. Tropical species with northernmost breeding in s TX. **ESSAYS:** Hawk-Eyed, p. 229; Raptor Hunting, p. 223; Size and Sex in Raptors, p. 243; Site Tenacity, p. 189; DDT, p. 21; How Do We Find Out About Bird Biology?, p. 319. **REFS:** Brown and Amadon, 1968; Morrison, 1978.

birds analyzed in slow motion. When flock sizes were between 4 and 15 birds, the size of the flock and the speed with which they became aware of the hawk and fled were directly related: the more birds, the quicker the reaction. Flocks of less than 4, however, reacted even faster than flocks of 4 to 15; but because they were always skittish and had many "false alarms," they did not feed well. In contrast, flocks of more than 15 birds had slower reaction times; often because they became engrossed in battles over the food. Similar results have been obtained from observations of falcons attacking wintering shorebirds on a California estuary. Hunting success was high when solitary shorebirds were the prey and when large flocks were attacked. Success was low when flocks of intermediate size were the targets.

So, at least over an intermediate range of flock sizes, the notion that more eyes are better than fewer seems to hold. In that range, larger flocks may detect predators more easily. Furthermore, flock members may reduce their chances of being eaten once the predator is detected. The sudden flight of large numbers of birds, or their simultaneous calls, may temporarily bewilder a predator and allow the flock to escape. It may also be more difficult for a predator to pick a victim from a wheeling flock than to catch a lone individual. This phenomenon is well known to the duck hunter who blasts away at an entire flock and does not hit a single bird.

Finally, flocks of birds may turn the tables on predators. Both European Starling and Red-winged Blackbird flocks have been observed to attack their attackers and force them into water or onto the ground.

SEE: Mobbing, p. 425; Geometry of the Selfish Colony, p. 19; Mixed-Species Flocking, p. 433; Altruism, p. 453. REFS: Hamilton, 1971; Myers, 1984; Siegfried and Underhill, 1975.

Natural Selection

The characteristics of birds result from evolutionary processes, the most important process being natural selection. It was Charles Darwin who first pointed out that just as stockmen shaped their herds by selecting which animals would be allowed to breed, so too nature shaped all organisms by "selecting" the progenitors of the next generation. Darwin's thinking had been influenced by the great economist Thomas Malthus, who emphasized the capacity of people and other organisms to multiply their numbers much more rapidly than their means of subsistence. Darwin realized, therefore, that most individuals born of any species could not have survived long enough to reproduce. He concluded that those that had been able to survive and reproduce had not been a random sample of those born, but rather variants especially suited to their environments.

Darwin knew nothing about genetics; the work of Gregor Mendel remained undiscovered until early in this century—almost 50 years after the

Common Black-Hawk
Buteogallus anthracinus Deppe

NG–198; G–76; PW–pl 19; AW–pl 339; AM(I)–232

20'–30'	?	1–2	MF		
(15'–100')		(1–3)	I: 34 DAYS		
		MONOG	SEMIALTRICIAL 1		
			F: ? DAYS		
			MF		

BREEDING: Usu near water; lowland forest, swamp, riparian forest. 1 brood. **DISPLAYS:** Courting male performs series of ascents and dives, oft while calling and dangling feet; pair oft flutter wings in display flight. **NEST:** Bulky platform in crotch of tree, usu cottonwood, sycamore, or large mesquite; occ built on mistletoe, of dry sticks and mistletoe. Lined with fine grass, green leaves, string. Occ simple. Perennial. **EGGS:** White, sparsely marked with brown, occ unmarked. 2.3″ (57 mm). **DIET:** Perches, oft over water, seeking mostly frogs, crayfish, fish, snakes, also stalks sandbars and mud flats, wading and grabbing crabs, etc. Occ takes small mammals, rarely insects. **CONSERVATION:** Winters s through Mexico. Rare and apparently declining in U.S. **NOTES:** On nest, female very shy. Less common than similar Zone-tailed Hawk. Breeding biology not well known. **ESSAYS:** Hawk-Eyed, p. 229; Raptor Hunting, p. 223; Size and Sex in Raptors, p. 243; How Do We Find Out About Bird Biology?, p. 319. **REFS:** Brown and Amadon, 1968; Clark, 1987.

Harris' Hawk
Parabuteo unicinctus Temminck

NG–198; G–74; PW–pl 15; AE–pl 311; AW–pl 311; AM(I)–234

CACTUS	F – M	3–4 (1–5)	MF	SNAKES	SWOOPS
10'–30'		POLYAND	I: 33–36 DAYS	BIRDS	
		(COOP)	SEMIALTRICIAL 1	INSECTS	
			F: 43–49 DAYS		
			MF		

BREEDING: Savanna, semiarid woodland and semidesert, esp near water. Oft 2 broods. **DISPLAYS:** ? **NEST:** Of sticks, twigs, forbs, roots. Lined with green mesquite, green shoots and leaves, grass, bark, roots. **EGGS:** White/bluish-white; 50% unmarked, 50% marked with browns, lavender. 2.1″ (54 mm). **DIET:** Hunts mostly in dim light by dashing into thicket for rabbits and other prey. Occ hunt in pairs. **CONSERVATION:** Winter resident. Blue List 1972–81, Special Concern 1982, Local Concern 1986; declining in parts of range, recently reintroduced in some areas. **NOTES:** Simultaneous polyandry common: in one study, nearly half of nests were tended by polyandrous trios; both males help incubate, feed, and brood young. Rather than polyandry, many nesting groups (up to 5 adults) are cooperative breeders, with helpers oft males that have remained in their natal territory. Young hatch asynchronously, differ in size; remain with parents and share their food for at least 3–6 months. When rabbits abundant (at least in NM), second brood oft reared in late summer or autumn. **ESSAYS:** Polyandry, p. 133; Blue List, p. 11; Conservation of Raptors, p. 247; Brood Reduction, p. 307; Cooperative Breeding, p. 283; Raptor Hunting, p. 223. **REFS:** Bednarz, 1987a, b; Brown and Amadon, 1968; Mader, 1978, 1979; Whaley, 1986.

publication of *Origin of Species*. We now know that variation among individuals is due to both environmental and hereditary factors. The latter result from the joint action of mutation (changes in the genes themselves) and, in birds and all other sexually reproducing organisms, recombination. Basically, recombination is the reshuffling of genes that occurs during the process of sperm and egg production. Because of mutation and recombination, each individual bird is genetically unique—that is, each has a unique "genotype." Geneticists typically examine only a small portion of the genetic endowment of an individual, such as the two pairs of genes (out of many thousands) that cause a cock's comb to be single and large or pea-shaped and small. Thus one might speak of the "single-comb" and "pea-comb" genotypes.

In modern evolutionary genetics, natural selection is defined as the differential reproduction of genotypes (individuals of some genotypes have more offspring than those of others). Natural selection would be occurring if, in a population of jungle fowl (the wild progenitors of chickens), single-comb genotypes were more reproductively successful than pea-comb genotypes. Note that the emphasis is not on *survival* (as it was in Herbert Spencer's famous phrase "survival of the fittest") but on *reproduction*. Thus while selection can occur because some individuals do not survive long enough to reproduce, sterile individuals also lack "fitness" in an evolutionary sense, as do individuals unable to find mates. We emphasize that fitness here refers only to the reproductive success of a kind of individual—if big, handsome, male grouse madly displaying on a lek turn out to have fewer offspring than smaller, drab males that skulk in the bushes and waylay females, it is the wimpy males that are more fit.

Natural selection provides a context in which to view the physical and behavioral characteristics of birds. Whether it is the large size of a female Harris' Hawk in comparison with the male, the territorial behavior of a sandpiper, the bill shape of a Clark's Nutcracker, or the coloniality of a Common Murre, a key question to ask is "how did natural selection manage that?"

SEE: Selection in Nature, p. 477; Altruism, p. 453; Sexual Selection, p. 251; Coevolution, p. 405; Size and Sex in Raptors, p. 243; Geometry of the Selfish Colony, p. 19. REFS: Ehrlich, 1986a; Ehrlich and Roughgarden 1987; Futuyma, 1979.

Feet

Avian feet, like bills, tell us a great deal about the taxonomic relationships, behavior, and ecology of birds. More than half of the 8,600 species of birds, for example, are passerines, birds characterized largely by the form of their feet. The Passeriformes, or perching birds, have feet with four separate toes, three of them directed forward, and one (first, or inner, the homologue

Zone-tailed Hawk

Buteo albonotatus Kaup

NG–198; G–76; PW–pl 19; AW–pl 341; AM(I)–244

25'–50'	?	2	MF		
(25'–100')		(1–3)	I: 35 DAYS		
		MONOG	SEMIALTRICIAL 1	BIRDS	
			F: ? DAYS		
			MF (?)		

BREEDING: Arid semi-open country, esp open pine-oak woodland in hills and mountains. ? broods. **DISPLAYS:** Talon-grappling occurs in courtship flight and/or in aggressive interactions. **NEST:** Oft in large tree, esp cottonwood, rarely mesquite, occ pine, along stream. Bulky platform of large sticks, considerably hollowed. Lined with twigs bearing green leaves. **EGGS:** White/bluish-white, dotted with lavender/yellowish-brown, occ concentrated on end. 2.2″ (57 mm). **DIET:** Snakes, lizards, frogs, fish, also small mammals. Hunts in slow soaring glide, diving on prey from above. **CONSERVATION:** Partly migratory in winter; s perhaps through C.A. **NOTES:** Gliding flight with wings set at an angle that strongly resembles that of Turkey Vulture, among which it often flies; such "aggressive mimicry" (a predator mimicking a non-predator) may deceive prey into believing hawk is harmless Turkey Vulture. Screams in flight and upon intrusion at nest, which it defends vigorously. **ESSAYS:** Hawk-Eyed, p. 229; Soaring, p. 215; Size and Sex in Raptors, p. 243; Raptor Hunting, p. 223. **REFS:** Brown and Amadon, 1968; Hubbard, 1974; Willis, 1963; Zimmerman, 1976.

Short-tailed Hawk

Buteo brachyurus Vieillot

NG–198; G–76; PE–156; AE–pl 319; AM(I)–240

15'–60'	FM?	2	?		
(8'–100')		(1–3)	I: ? DAYS		
		MONOG	SEMIALTRICIAL 1		
			F: ? DAYS		
			?		

BREEDING: Open country, from mangrove and cypress swamps to open pine-oak woodland; avoids dense forest. ? broods. **DISPLAYS:** ? **NEST:** In treetops; bulky, of fresh green sprigs (esp cypress or magnolia), twigs and leaves, bits of moss and lichen. Lined with fine materials. Will use abandoned nest of heron. **EGGS:** Off-white/bluish-white, occ marked with brown. 2.1″ (53 mm). **DIET:** Primarily birds, captured by swift dives into trees and shrubs from high, slow, soaring flight. **CONSERVATION:** Winters within FL. May be threatened by destruction of breeding habitat (mature cypress swamps and riparian hardwoods). **NOTES:** Not well studied. Usu seen soaring on midday thermal or perched on tall tree in dense woodland. During nest building, female places stick while male hovers >50' above tree, like White-tailed Hawk. Screams upon intrusion at nest. Occ seen flying with Swallow-tailed Kite, Turkey and Black Vultures. Very wary. Tropical species reaching its n extreme in FL. **ESSAYS:** Hawk-Eyed, p. 229; Size and Sex in Raptors, p. 243; Raptor Hunting, p. 223; How Do We Find Out About Bird Biology?, p. 319. **REFS:** Brown and Amadon, 1968; Kale, 1978.

of our big toe) directed backward. All four passerine toes join the leg at the same level. Foot structure varies among the other major taxonomic groups. Some swifts have all four toes pointing forward; kingfishers have the middle and outer toes fused for part of their length; woodpeckers have two toes pointed forward and two backward (except for the "three-toed" woodpecker, in which the first toe has been lost). The four toes of raptors are highly separated. Owls can turn their fourth (outer) toe either forward or backward. Many waterbirds and shorebirds have three toes pointed forward, but the hind toe is often greatly reduced and raised so that it joins the leg above the level of the other toes and loses contact with the ground. The toes of some are completely webbed, and those of others, including such shorebirds as American Avocets, are partially webbed.

These differences, of course, are related to the life-styles of the birds. The independent, extremely flexible tocs of the passerines, along with the completely opposed first toe, are ideal for grasping perches. All swifts have strong claws for clinging to vertical surfaces. In some, like the White-throated, the toes all point forward in a dead individual, but in life the inner two actually work against the outer two in grasping the soft materials the swifts use in making their nests. The fused toes of kingfishers help in excavating nest tunnels; the opposing toes of woodpeckers aid in clinging to tree trunks.

Birds of prey have powerful feet, strong, sharp, highly curved claws and roughened pads on the undersides of their toes to help them to readily

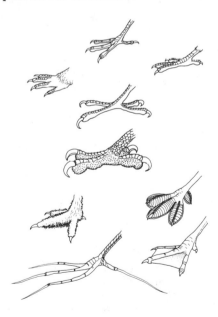

Top to bottom: passerine, kingfisher (right), swift (left), woodpecker, Osprey, grebe (right), ptarmigan (left), jacana (left), duck.

Osprey
Pandion haliaetus Linnaeus

NG–200; G–78; PE–158; PW–pl 20; AE–pl 306; AW–pl 304; AM(I)–216

10'–60'   MF   3   F –M
(0'–200')   (2–4)   I: 32–43 DAYS
CLIFF   MONOG SEMIALTRICIAL 1
               F: 48–59 DAYS
               MF

BREEDING: Along rivers, lakes, and coasts. 1 brood. **DISPLAYS:** Courting pair in swift pursuit flight, soar, circle, dodge with rapid turns and quick swoops. **NEST:** In decid or conif tree (dead or alive), near or over water, also atop pole. Of sticks, sod, cow dung, seaweed, rubbish, etc. Perennial, becoming very large. **EGGS:** White/pinkish-white/pinkish-cinnamon, marked with brown/olive, rarely unmarked. 2.4" (61 mm). **DIET:** Usu hovers at 30'–100' and dives, mostly for fish (live or dead); also takes rodents, birds, small verts, crustaceans. Young fed regurgitant first 10 days. Brood of 3 requires 6 lb of fish daily. **CONSERVATION:** Winters s to Chile, n Argentina. Blue List 1972–81, Special Concern 1982, Local Concern 1986; populations crashed (esp in e) 1950s–1970s from exposure to DDT, encroachment onto breeding grounds, and shooting. Coastal populations now recovered aided by DDT ban and conservation programs incl successful use of artificial nesting platforms. **NOTES:** Female fed entirely by mate from pair formation through egg laying; courtship feeding may ensure mate fidelity. Male occ does up to 30% of incubation. Male delivers food to female at nest; she then feeds young. Female does most of brooding. Young hatch asynchronously. Subject to piracy by Bald Eagle, frigatebird. Only raptor whose front talons turn backward. **ESSAYS:** DDT, p. 21; Feet, p. 239; Raptor Hunting, p. 223; Conservation, p. 247; Blue List, p. 11; Poisons, p. 137; Courtship Feeding, p. 181. **REFS:** Cramp and Simmons, 1980; Levenson, 1979; Poole, 1985; Reese, 1977; Van Daele and Van Daele, 1982.

Aplomado Falcon
Falco femoralis Temminck

NG–200; G–80; PW–pl 17; AW–pl 322; AM(I)–260

YUCCA   ?   3   F – M(?)   INSECTS   HAWKS
7'–25'   (3–4) I: ? DAYS   SWOOPS
            MONOG SEMIALTRICIAL 2
                  F: ? DAYS
                  MF(?)

BREEDING: Open country, mostly grassland and arid woodland, also desert. 1? brood. **DISPLAYS:** Uses "chip" call to attract attention of mate. **NEST:** Usu an abandoned nest of raven or hawk atop low tree or yucca; of twigs, lined with bits of grass. **EGGS:** White/pinkish-white, marked with brown. 1.8" (45 mm). **DIET:** Esp doves, blackbirds; also rodents, bats, reptiles, frogs, large insects. **CONSERVATION:** Winter resident. Endangered (sub)Species; now being reintroduced in TX. Likely declined from habitat loss to agricultural expansion and from eggshell thinning by pesticides. C.A. populations stable. **NOTES:** Pair oft hunt cooperatively (throughout year), esp when taking birds; pairs >twice as successful as solo falcons hunting birds. Fledglings also hunt together. Usu hunts at dawn and dusk. **ESSAYS:** Masterbuilders, p. 445; Raptor Hunting, p. 223; Wing Shapes and Flight, p. 227; DDT and Birds, p. 21; Conservation of Raptors, p. 247. **REFS:** Brown and Amadon, 1968; Cade, 1982; Hector, 1985, 1986.

grasp prey. The fish-eating Osprey also has spines on the pads on the soles of its toes for holding on to slippery fishes. Birds that spend a lot of time walking tend to have flat feet with a reduced backward-pointing toe; and if, like shorebirds, they often walk on soft surfaces, they usually have some webbing between the toes. And those, such as game birds, that scratch a great deal have blunt, thick claws attached to powerful legs. Ptarmigans, which walk on snow, have heavily feathered (highly insulated) feet that function as snowshoes. Ravens in the arctic have up to six times thicker, horny insulating soles on their feet than do tropical ravens. Birds with bare legs, especially those with webbed feet, avoid problems of heat loss from their extremities by circulatory adaptations.

Birds that swim generally have webbing between their toes so that the feet can be used to paddle. Lobes, rather than webbing, are often found on the toes of birds, such as American Coots, that divide their time between swimming and walking on mud. Jacanas have extremely long toes that spread their weight enough to permit them to walk on floating aquatic vegetation, including lily pads—giving them the common name "lily trotters."

SEE: Swimming, p. 73; Temperature Regulation and Behavior, p. 149; Passerines and Songbirds, p. 395; Avian Snowshoes, p. 255.

Size and Sex in Raptors

In most birds, males are larger than females, but in some birds, such as many shorebirds and birds of prey, the reverse is true. No one is certain why there is this "reversed sexual size dimorphism" in raptors, but a number of interesting hypotheses have been advanced. All are based on a well-established correlation: this size difference between the sexes is less pronounced in species that pursue sluggish prey than in those that pursue birds. Vultures, whose prey are least agile of all, show little sexual size difference. Mammal-hunting buteos, such as the Red-tailed Hawk, evolved males that are somewhat smaller than females, whereas in bird-hunting accipiters and falcons, females may be half again as heavy as males.

One explanation for the females' larger size suggests that it protects them from aggressive males that are well equipped with sharp talons and beaks, and the killer instincts to go with them. According to this theory, over evolutionary time, females have preferred to mate with smaller, safer males—in fact, the female may have to be able to dominate the male for proper pair bonding to occur and for the male to remain in his key role as food provider to both female and young. Such a system would involve sexual selection for smaller size in males. Bird-hunting raptors are assumed to show aggression most suddenly, and to represent the greatest threat to their mates, and they are the ones exhibiting the greatest size difference.

Crested Caracara

Polyborus plancus Miller

NG–200; G–78; PE–160; PW–pl 19; AE–pl 312; AW–pl 305; AM(I)–256

			MF I: 28 DAYS		
SHRUB 15'–30' (8'–80')	?	2–3 (2–4) MONOG?	SEMIALTRICIAL 2 F: 30–60 DAYS MF	SMALL VERTS	LOW PATROL HIGH PATROL

BREEDING: Open country, esp semiarid brushland, also pastureland, cultivated areas and semidesert; usu arid, but also moist habitats. 1, possibly 2 broods. **DISPLAYS:** Males fight in air in breeding season, which may function as sexual display. **NEST:** With commanding view oft in palmetto (occ pine), also in giant cacti. Bulky, loose, and deeply hollowed, of sticks, vines, twigs. Lined with fine materials. Occ shared by smaller birds (incl Great-tailed Grackle). Perennial. **EGGS:** White/pinkish-white, marked with browns, rarely unmarked. 2.3″ (59 mm). **DIET:** Opportunistic; also fish, turtle eggs, small mammals, reptiles, inverts. Long legs and flat claws permit running for quick prey and scratching ground for slow. **CONSERVATION:** Winter resident. Blue List 1972–79, 1981, Special Concern 1982–86; apparently declining throughout range, largely from habitat loss to agriculture. **NOTES:** National bird of Mexico. Oft seen feeding with and harassing vultures, forcing them to disgorge food. Usu seen in pairs. Roosts in tall tree groves. Behaves in flight like Northern Harrier. Breeding biology little known. **ESSAYS:** Blue List, p. 11; Raptor Hunting, p. 223; How Do We Find Out About Bird Biology?, p. 319; Piracy, p. 159. **REFS:** Brown and Amadon, 1968; Kale, 1978.

American Kestrel

Falco sparverius Linnaeus

NG–202; G–80; PE–162; PW–pl 16; AE–pl 314; AW–pl 331; AM(I)–256

		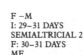	F –M I: 29–31 DAYS		
12'–80' CLIFF		4–5 (3–7) MONOG	SEMIALTRICIAL 2 F: 30–31 DAYS MF	SM VERTS SMALL MAMMALS	HAWKS SWOOPS

BREEDING: Open or partly open habitats with scattered trees, also cultivated and urban areas. 1 brood, 2 in s and when small mammal prey very abundant. **DISPLAYS:** Male flies rapidly in wide circles above perch, bends quivering wingtips down, calls, occ joined by female before realighting on perch. Pair bow, female constantly calling. Desert populations incorporate courtship feeding. **NEST:** Little, if any, nesting material. **EGGS:** White/pinkish-white, marked with browns, occ lavender, occ unmarked. 1.4″ (35 mm). **DIET:** Also occ birds. In desert, young eat only insects for first week, later also mice. Occ aerially forage for insects. **CONSERVATION:** Winters s to Panama. Readily uses nest box. **NOTES:** Oft uses same nest for second brood; male feeds fledglings of first brood and incubating female. Caches verts, usu in grass clumps. Competes with other hole-nesters for nest sites. Promiscuous matings occ occur before monogamous bonds form. In winter, individuals defend territories; females prefer habitat that is open and sparsely vegetated, males prefer denser veg. Formerly known as Sparrow Hawk. **ESSAYS:** Hovering Flight, p. 323; Raptor Hunting, p. 223; Hoarding Food, p. 345; Size and Sex in Raptors, p. 243; Courtship Feeding, p. 181; Habitat Selection, p. 463. **REFS:** Cade, 1982; Collopy, 1977; Mills, 1976; Mueller, 1977; Toland, 1985.

In experimental pairings set up so that male American Kestrels were the larger of the pair, Cornell ornithologist Tom Cade found that the females did not suffer from an avian version of wife abuse. The size difference in kestrels was not very great, however, so this may not be a definitive test of the hypothesis. It seems that while sexual selection may play a role, there probably is more to it.

Another hypothesis proposes that the size differences allow the two sexes to hunt different prey and thus reduce competition for food. Competition is thought to be more severe among bird hunters than among other hawks, since their small agile prey are able to flee in three dimensions and are thus effectively scarcer than, say, carrion or ground squirrels. Indeed, there are data indicating that the hunting success of bird-chasing raptors is only about half that of raptors preying on mammals, and only a sixth that of raptors eating insects. Tom Cade has suggested that, for bird eaters, available food supply in the nesting territory can become limiting, making it adaptive for the male to specialize on small prey and for the female to specialize on large prey. The male feeds the female and young at the beginning of the nesting season; the female becomes an active hunter when the nestlings are larger, and the adults then tend to partition the prey resource in their territory.

But if reducing intersexual competition for food is the reason for the size difference in raptors, why aren't males sometimes the larger sex? One possible reason is that females need to be larger because they must accumulate reserves in order to produce their eggs. Another is that females do not forage for a substantial period while incubating eggs and brooding young. They avoid the risks of the hunt during that time, but they must rely on the small male to feed the entire family. Small fleet prey, aerial or terrestrial, are more abundant than large sluggish prey, so that over time smaller male bird-eating raptors would be favored over larger, less agile ones, because they would be better providers. For species that take more sluggish prey, however, small males would not be so advantageous, which might explain the relationship between prey speed and the male-female size discrepancy.

SEE: Sexual Selection, p. 251; Polyandry, p. 133; Raptor Hunting, p. 223. REFS: Cade, 1982; Lewin, 1985; Mueller and Meyer, 1985; Temeles, 1985.

Bird Names—V

When falconry was in vogue, merlin was the name used for a female falcon. Falcon itself comes from the Latin *falx* ("sickle"), for the sicklelike talons and beak. Peregrine means "wanderer," from the same Latin source as "peregrinate" and "pilgrim." Aplomado has its origin, along with "plumb," in *plumbum*, the Latin word for "lead"; the name refers to the leaden color of this falcon's plumage or its vertical stoop. Kestrel appears to derive from the bird's call; there are many explanations for the "gyr" in Gyrfalcon.

Merlin

Falco columbarius Linnaeus

NG–202; G–80; PE–162; PW–pl 16; AE–pl 313; AW–pl 328; AM(I)–258

| | | | F –M
I: 28–32 DAYS | | |
| 15'–35'
(8'–60')
CLIFF | CAVITY
F? | 4–5
(2–7)
MONOG | SEMIALTRICIAL 2
F: 30–35 DAYS
MF | SMALL
MAMMALS
INSECTS | HAWKS |

BREEDING: Open habitats, nests primarily in open woodland, savanna; occ in cities. 1 brood. **DISPLAYS:** Pair perform aerial acrobatics high over nest site. **NEST:** Oft use abandoned nest of crows, magpies, hawks, occ relined with twigs and feathers; also use tree cavity with commanding view, cliff, or scrape on ground in treeless country. **EGGS:** White, marked with reddish-brown, some nearly unmarked. 1.6" (40 mm). **DIET:** Oft >90% birds. Rather than stooping, oft take prey in fast, low horizontal flight. **CONSERVATION:** Winters s through C.A., West Indies to n S.A. Blue List 1972–81, Special Concern 1982–86; uncommon, status unclear. Showing effects of pesticides in e Canada and of mercury buildup in w Canada. **NOTES:** Male arrives on breeding grounds before female, usu returning to same area each year. Male does all of hunting from courtship through incubation, occ through nestling period. Yearlings, esp males, occ serve as helpers in territory defense, feeding of female, etc. Females take heavier prey than do males; seasonal changes in diet correspond to prey availability. Formerly known as Pigeon Hawk. **ESSAYS:** Size and Sex, p. 243; Raptor Hunting, p. 223; Conservation, p. 247; Cooperative Breeding, p. 283; Metallic Poisons, p. 137; DDT, p. 21. **REFS:** Becker, 1985; Cade, 1982; Cramp and Simmons, 1980; James and Oliphant, 1986; Newton et al., 1984.

Prairie Falcon

Falco mexicanus Schlegel

NG–204; G–80; PE–162; PW–pl 17; AW–pl 320; AM(I)–264

| | | | F –M
I: 29–33 DAYS | | |
| 30'–40'
(20'–400') | CREVICE | 4–5
(2–7)
MONOG | SEMIALTRICIAL 2
F: 35–42 DAYS
MF | SM MAMMALS
INSECTS
LIZARDS | LOW
PATROL |

BREEDING: Open habitat in mountainous regions, shortgrass prairie, alpine tundra. 1 brood. **DISPLAYS:** Male performs aerial gymnastics, cutting parabolas and calling in front of perched female; she calls, occ joins flight. Male also struts on nesting ledge. **NEST:** On cliff ledge, occ in rock crevice, always facing open habitat. Usu unlined. Rarely use earthen bank. **EGGS:** White/pinkish-white, marked with browns. 2.1" (52 mm). **DIET:** Can overtake most birds directly, flushing ground dwellers by flying low, but also hovers and stoops for other prey. **CONSERVATION:** Winters s to Baja, n Mexico. Some eggshell thinning and mercury poisoning reported (accumulated esp from taking seed-eating Horned Lark). Declining in UT, w Canada, and agricultural CA. **NOTES:** Weak nest site tenacity. Clutches smaller in e portion of range. In nest defense, male circles above, female leaves nest only as last resort. Parental care of young continues after fledging. Female ca. 33% larger than male. With lighter wing loading, outflies Peregrine at high altitude. **ESSAYS:** Raptor Hunting, p. 223; Size and Sex in Raptors, p. 243; Conservation of Raptors, p. 247; Wing Shapes, p. 227; Metallic Poisons, p. 137; Site Tenacity, p. 189. **REFS:** Allen et al., 1986; Cade, 1982; Enderson, 1964; Marti and Braun, 1975.

Ernest Choate, who wrote the excellent *Dictionary of American Bird Names,* prefers the one that traces it to the German *geier,* greedy.

Hawk comes from the same Anglo-Saxon root as "have" (in the sense of "grasp"). Harris' Hawk was named after Edward Harris, a close friend of Audubon. "Ferruginous" refers to the reddish color of the Ferruginous Hawk.

Osprey derives from the Latin *ossifraga,* meaning "bone breaker"; the name got transferred from the Lämmergeier, an Old World vulture that drops bones from heights so that it can eat marrow from the shattered fragments. Caracara seems to be onomatopoetic. Eagle comes from the Latin *aquila,* eagle. Condor goes back through Spanish to the native Peruvian name for the bird, *kuntur.* REFS: Choate, 1985; Owen, 1985.

Conservation of Raptors

In some areas populations and species of raptors are threatened with extinction—more so than many other kinds of birds. There are five reasons. First, raptors are often directly persecuted by people who believe (usually erroneously) that these birds are a threat to livestock. The antiquated notion that birds of prey are "varmints" remains entrenched, and many otherwise law-abiding farmers and ranchers kill hawks and eagles, while some "hunters" take potshots at them. This is illegal, since raptors are federally protected against wanton shooting.

Second, a great many hawks, falcons, and owls are taken for an illegal taxidermy trade, mainly in Europe. Reportedly thousands of Northern Goshawks are slaughtered and stuffed each year in China alone.

Third, falcons are illegally trapped by smugglers lured by the enormous price that the birds will bring in the Middle East, where falconry is a high-prestige activity for the elite. The majority of falcons used by the Arabs are migrant Sakers *(Falco cherrug)* from Asia. Sakers are a species that is rather like a slightly smaller version of the Gyrfalcon. Gyrfalcons themselves, because of their long wings and large size, are especially prized. Members of the Middle Eastern royal families have reportedly paid up to $100,000 each for healthy specimens of these arctic raptors, of which perhaps only 4,000–5,000 live in North America. It is not clear, however, whether hunting, trapping, or nest-robbing of falcons has ever led to widespread permanent reductions in falcon populations. Cornell ornithologist Tom J. Cade suspects that birds killed by hunters or taken by falconers are largely part of the "expendable" surplus produced by falcon populations.

Fourth, raptors are generally rather long-lived birds and feed high on food chains, which makes them more susceptible than short-lived or plant-eating species to poisoning by pesticides and other pollutants. Poisons accu-

Peregrine Falcon

Falco peregrinus Tunstall

NG–204; G–80; PE–162; PW–pl 17; AE–pl 315; AW–pl 323; AM(I)–260

TREE	F	3–4	F –M	
50'–200' +		(2–6)	I: 29–32 DAYS	
		MONOG	SEMIALTRICIAL 2	
			F: 35–42 DAYS	
			MF	

BREEDING: Open habitats from tundra, savanna, and seacoasts to high mountains; also open forest, tall buildings. 1 brood. **DISPLAYS**: Aerial displays, courtship feeding, all with calls. **NEST**: Well-rounded scrape in accumulated debris on ledge, occ lined with grass. Rarely uses old tree nest or cavity. Cliff sites used traditionally for many years. **EGGS**: White/pinkish-cream, occ marked with brown/red. 2.1" (53 mm). **DIET**: Stoops or flies fast and low after wide variety of birds, esp doves and pigeons, also shorebirds, waterfowl, and passerines. **CONSERVATION**: Winters s through C.A. and West Indies to Tierra del Fuego. Endangered Species (arctic subspecies Threatened); serious decline since 1940s result of eggshell thinning from pesticides and PCB poisoning. Now being reintroduced to parts of former range. **NOTES**: Worldwide range more extensive than any other bird. Initially male does most of hunting, female broods and feeds chicks. Pairs roost together, hunt cooperatively. As in other falcons, female larger than male: eats first, dives first when hunting in pairs, takes larger prey. **ESSAYS**: Conservation, p. 247; Birds and the Law, p. 293; How Fast?, p. 81; Raptor Hunting, p. 223; Size and Sex, p. 243; Courtship Feeding, p. 181. **REFS**: Cade, 1982; Cade et al., 1971; Craig, 1986; Cramp and Simmons, 1980; Ratcliffe, 1980; Temple, 1977.

Gyrfalcon

Falco rusticolus Linnaeus

NG–204; G–80; PE–162; PW–pl 17; AE–pl 316; AW–pl 309; AM(I)–262

TREE	4	F –M	SMALL	LOW
30'–300' +	(3–5)	I: 34–36 DAYS	MAMMALS	PATROL
	MONOG	SEMIALTRICIAL 2		SWOOPS
		F: 49–56 DAYS		
		MF		

BREEDING: Arctic tundra with rock outcrops and cliffs, open conif forest, rocky seacoasts. 1 brood. **DISPLAYS**: Aerial courtship display incl diving. **NEST**: Marked by excrement, food debris, pellets. Old stick nest of raven or raptor oft used; lined with accumulated debris. Perennial. **EGGS**: White/yellowish-white, spotted with cinnamon-brown, occ nearly plain. 2.3" (59 mm). **DIET**: Esp ptarmigan, also grouse, seabirds, waterfowl, shorebirds. Apt to perch on rock outcrop while searching for movement or fly fast and low, "contour hugging" to surprise prey. **CONSERVATION**: Winter resident but some s movement within N.A. Rare over entire range. **NOTES**: Numbers vary with ptarmigan abundance; will skip breeding when prey scarce. Female 30–40% heavier than male. Male provides all food from incubation through early nestling period; female does all or most of brooding. Young dependent on parents for 30+ days postfledging. Capable of climbing sharply to rise above flying prey. **ESSAYS**: Bird Biology and the Arts, p. 47; Conservation of Raptors, p. 247; Raptor Hunting, p. 223; How Fast?, p. 81; Size and Sex in Raptors, p. 243; Pellets, p. 297; Variation in Clutch Sizes, p. 339. **REFS**: Brown and Amadon, 1968; Cade, 1982; Cramp and Simmons, 1980; Jenkins, 1978.

mulate in organisms over time, and poisons become concentrated as they move up food chains. There is no question that toxic substances have had catastrophic impacts on the populations of some raptors. Peregrine Falcons, for instance, were eliminated from much of North America through the large-scale use of DDT and its relatives, which began shortly after World War II. By 1964 Peregrines had been exterminated east of the Mississippi. They subsequently continued to decline sharply in the West and North.

Laws have been promulgated to limit the use of persistent pesticides that threaten raptors. The application of DDT has been largely banned in the United States since 1972, although it is a contaminant in dicofol (the main ingredient of Kelthane), a related chlorinated hydrocarbon pesticide, which is legally used. (There may also be illegal use of DDT itself.)

Finally, raptors, especially large ones, often suffer from habitat destruction, which makes areas with sufficient space for home ranges or suitable nesting sites scarce. This is the overriding problem for tropical forest eagles.

Laws now attempt to protect raptors from the depredations of hunters. Some individuals have been prosecuted under the Endangered Species Act for killing Bald Eagles. Fines as high as $5,000 and jail terms of up to six months have been dealt out to those convicted of this crime, which is being taken more seriously as time passes. And in 1984, the U.S. Fish and Wildlife Service arrested 39 people suspected of being involved in illegal commerce in falcons.

In addition to legal protection, steps can be taken to help preserve raptor populations in deteriorating habitats. For example, provision of artificial nesting sites has led to an increase in Osprey populations and shows potential for doing the same for Bald Eagles. In one ingenious program, Osprey nest poles were dropped like darts from helicopters into coastal salt marshes. Another helpful step toward protecting many large raptors, as we are often reminded through magazine and television advertisements, has been providing insulated perches on the tops of power poles carrying high-voltage power lines.

Populations of the Peregrine Falcon have been reestablished in areas from which it had been exterminated. Tom Cade pioneered a program of captive breeding and releasing primarily in the eastern United States, where DDT-induced breeding failures had led to the falcon's extirpation. After the use of DDT was banned in 1972, the birds could once again survive there; with skill and persistence Cade's team started the species on the road to recovery in the wild. Recovery to the pre-DDT level of some 400 breeding pairs in the eastern United States may be rapid. In 1978 no pairs nested in the East; in 1984, 27 pairs did. In 1985 there were 38 breeding pairs, and young were fledged by at least 16 pairs. In addition, during the summer of 1985, 125 young Peregrines reared in captivity were released in the eastern United States and 135 in the West. In 1986 there were 43 territorial pairs, and 25 of them fledged 53 young.

Legal protection against shooting, capturing and poisoning, habitat improvement, and reestablishment programs all help preserve birds of prey,

Ruffed Grouse

Bonasa umbellus Linnaeus

NG–210; G–86; PE–144; PW–pl 21; AE–pl 268; AW–pl 263; AM(I)–282

F	9–12 (6–15) PROMISC	F I: 23–24 (21–28) DAYS PRECOCIAL 3 F: 10–12 DAYS F	FOLIAGE BROWSE GROUND GLEAN

BREEDING: Decid and decid-conif forest with dense understory; strongly assoc with aspen. 1 brood. **DISPLAYS:** Males display on individual territories where they "drum" (usu on log) with rapid forward and upward strokes of the wings, the drumming accelerating then decelerating; males erect crest and neck ruff feathers, fan tail, and strut. **NEST:** Oft concealed at base of tree, under branches of fallen tree or next to log; deep hollow, facultatively lined with preened feathers. **EGGS:** Buff, lightly spotted with browns. 1.5" (39 mm). **DIET:** About 80% buds, leaves, flowers, seeds, and fruit; 20% insects, spiders, snails, small verts. Young feed largely on insects, inverts. **CONSERVATION:** Winter resident. **NOTES:** Although promiscuous, does not lek. Female aggressively defends young or performs distraction display. Young remain with female until early autumn. Solitary in winter, usu roost by diving into and then burrowing through snow; occ in small unisexual groups. Brood occ remains together through winter. **ESSAYS:** Leks, p. 259; Avian Snowshoes, p. 255; Environmental Acoustics, p. 441; Nonvocal Sounds, p. 313; Promiscuity, p. 145; Distraction Displays, p. 115. **REFS:** Archibald, 1976; Gullion, 1984; Johnsgard, 1973; Wittenberger, 1978.

Blue Grouse

Dendragapus obscurus Say

NG–210; G–86; PW–pl 21; AW–pl 261; AM (I)–274

F	7–10 (6–12) PROMISC	F I: 25–26 DAYS PRECOCIAL 3 F: 7–10 DAYS F	SEEDS BERRIES INSECTS	FOLIAGE BROWSE

BREEDING: Montane conif and conif-decid forest. 1 brood. **DISPLAYS:** Males solitary on dispersed territories; male expands circle of white, black-tipped feathers on neck, hoots and grunts, may include flutter-jump display. **NEXT:** Oft hidden under branches of fallen tree, under shrub, or beside log; shallow depression lined with available veg, usu a few feathers. **EGGS:** Buff, marked with brown, occ unmarked. 2.0" (50 mm). **DIET:** Mostly leaves (esp conif needles), also flowers, fruit; insects, esp grasshoppers. Young feed heavily on insects. Conif needles main winter food. **CONSERVATION:** Winter resident, with some local movement. **NOTES:** Males can individually recognize each other by their distinctive territorial hooting. First-year males rarely establish breeding territories, thus do not breed. Males inflate neck sacs to amplify their hooting. Juvenile females oft disperse farther than juvenile males. Protectively colored adults oft "freeze" in trees, leading to local name "fool grouse." **ESSAYS:** Leks, p. 259; Avian Snowshoes, p. 255; Vocal Functions, p. 471; Promiscuity, p. 145. **REFS:** Falls and McNicholl, 1979; Lewis, 1985; Lewis and Jamieson, 1987.

but in the long run these measures alone will not be enough. Without public education about raptors' esthetic and direct economic value, laws are likely to contain too many loopholes and will likely be enforced with insufficient vigor. And as with the entire extinction problem, long-term solutions almost certainly will depend on changing attitudes toward our fellow creatures, and reduction of the appropriation of Earth's resources by *Homo sapiens*. Until then, habitat destruction will continue to accelerate the loss of species—both spectacular ones that attract our interest and more obscure ones on which our favorites (and we) often depend.

SEE: Birds and the Law, p. 293; DDT and Birds, p. 21; Conservation of the California Condor, p. 219; Botulism, p. 69. REFS: Cade, 1982; Robbins, 1985; Sibley, 1985; Temple, 1978; Vitousek et al., 1986.

Sexual Selection

It was Charles Darwin who originally proposed that the so-called secondary sexual characteristics of male animals—such as the elaborate tails of peacocks, bright plumage or expandable throat sacs in many birds, large racks in mooses, deep voices in men—evolved because females preferred to mate with individuals that had those features. Sexual selection can be thought of as two special kinds of natural selection, as described below. Natural selection occurs when some individuals out-reproduce others, and those that have more offspring differ genetically from those that have fewer.

In one kind of sexual selection, members of one sex create a reproductive differential among themselves by competing for opportunities to mate. The winners out-reproduce the others, and natural selection occurs if the characteristics that determine winning are, at least in part, inherited. In the other kind of sexual selection, members of one sex create a reproductive differential in the other sex by preferring some individuals as mates. If the ones they prefer are genetically different from the ones they shun, then natural selection is occurring.

In birds, the first form of sexual selection occurs when males compete for territories, as is obvious when those territories are on leks (traditional mating grounds). Males that manage to acquire the best territories on a lek (the dominant males) are known to get more chances to mate with females. In some species of grouse and other such birds, this form of sexual selection combines with the second form, because once males establish their positions on the lek the females then choose among them.

That second type of sexual selection, in which one sex chooses among potential mates, appears to be the most common type among birds. As evidence that such selection is widespread, consider the reversal of normal sexual differences in the ornamentation of some polyandrous birds. There, the male must choose among females, which, in turn, must be as alluring as

Spruce Grouse
Dendragapus canadensis Linnaeus

NG–210; G–86; PE–146; PW–pl 21; AE–pl 270; AW–pl 262; AM(I)–272

F	4–7	F I: 17–24 DAYS		FOLIAGE BROWSE
	(2–10) PROMISC	PRECOCIAL 3 F: 10 DAYS F	BERRIES	GROUND GLEAN

BREEDING: Mature, old growth conif forest, oft with dense understory. 1 brood. **DISPLAYS**: On individual territories, males "drum" with wings (rapidly beating them) while rising in air alongside "traditional" tree; in w, male claps wings together above his back before returning to ground. Male also partially spreads tail and erects combs for female. **NEST**: Oft hidden under branches of fallen tree or beside log; shallow depression lined with conif needles, dry leaves, grass, usu a few feathers. **EGGS**: Buff, marked with browns, occ nearly plain. 1.7″ (44 mm). **DIET**: Mostly spruce, fir, and jackpine buds and needles; also berries, seeds, fruit; insects, esp grasshoppers. Shifts exclusively to browsing in conif trees in autumn and winter; dietary shift accompanied by increased size of gastrointestinal tract to digest conif foliage. **CONSERVATION**: Winter resident. **NOTES**: Spacing behavior of adults appears to regulate spring density by forcing young birds, for which no territories are available, to disperse. Female defends territory against other females using vocalizations and wing-flapping noises. Female defends young, performs distraction display. Protectively colored adults oft "freeze" in trees, leading to local name "fool hen." Solitary or in mixed-sex flocks in winter. **ESSAYS**: Leks, p. 259; Precocial Young, p. 581; Nonvocal Sounds, p. 313; Promiscuity, p. 145. **REFS**: Boag et al., 1979; Ellison, 1973; Nugent and Boag, 1982; Robinson, 1980.

White-tailed Ptarmigan
Lagopus leucurus Richardson

NG–212; G–88; PW–pl 21; AW–pl 273; AM (I)–280

F	4–8 MONOG	F I: 22–24 DAYS PRECOCIAL 3 F: 7–10 DAYS F	 INSECTS	

BREEDING: Alpine tundra. 1 brood. **DISPLAYS**: In courtship: male calls, alternates fast and slow strutting; red combs over eyes swollen. **NEST**: Usu exposed on alpine turf or under shrub; shallow depression lined with fine grass, lichens, small leaves, feathers. **EGGS**: Buff, marked with dark browns. 1.7″ (43 mm). **DIET**: Buds, leaves, and flowers of (esp) willows; few insects. Twig tips and buds browsed in winter. Young feed on both insects and veg. **CONSERVATION**: In winter moves to lower elevations. Introduced and established in Sierra Nevada. **NOTES**: Male may remain with female through hatching but usu deserts during incubation. Female delays nesting until fully in cryptic plumage. Nests covered with veg until clutch complete. Female is extremely close sitter, oft can be touched before she will flush from nest. Female performs distraction display incl hissing and clucking. Female eats white feathers and retrieves eggs to reduce conspicuousness of nest. Unisexual flocks or solitary in winter. **ESSAYS**: Avian Snowshoes, p. 255; Monogamy, p. 597; Feet, p. 239; Color of Birds, p. 111; Feathered Nests, p. 605. **REFS**: Giesen and Braun, 1979; Giesen et al., 1980; Johnsgard, 1973.

possible. Consequently in polyandrous species the *female* is ordinarily more colorful—it is her secondary sexual characteristics that are enhanced. This fooled even Audubon, who confused the sexes when labeling his paintings of phalaropes. Female phalaropes compete for the plain-colored males, and the latter incubate the eggs and tend the young.

There is evidence that female birds of some species (e.g., Marsh Wrens, Red-winged Blackbirds) tend to choose as mates those males holding the most desirable territories. In contrast, there is surprisingly little evidence that females preferentially select males with different degrees of ornamentation. One of the most interesting studies involved Long-tailed Widowbirds living in a grassland on a plateau in Kenya. Males of this polygynous six-inch weaver (a distant relative of the House Sparrow) are black with red and buff on their shoulders and have tails about sixteen inches long. The tails are prominently exhibited as the male flies slowly in aerial display over his territory. This can be seen from more than half a mile away. The females, in contrast, have short tails and are inconspicuous.

Nine matched foursomes of territorial widowbird males were captured and randomly given the following treatments. One of each set had his tail cut about six inches from the base, and the feathers removed were then glued to the corresponding feathers of another male, thus extending that bird's tail by some ten inches. A small piece of each feather was glued back on the tail of the donor, so that the male whose tail was shortened was subjected to the same series of operations, including gluing, as the male whose tail was lengthened. A third male had his tail cut, but the feathers were then glued back so that the tail was not noticeably shortened. The fourth bird was only banded. Thus the last two birds served as experimental "controls" whose appearance had not been changed, but which had been subjected to capture, handling, and (in one) cutting and gluing. To test whether the manipulations had affected the behavior of the males, numbers of display flights and territorial encounters were counted for periods both before and after capture and release. No significant differences in rates of flight or encounter were found.

The mating success of the males was measured by counting the number of nests containing eggs or young in each male's territory. Before the start of the experiment the males showed no significant differences in mating success. But after the large differences in tail length were artificially created, great differentials appeared in the number of new active nests in each territory. The males whose tails were lengthened acquired the most new mates (as indicated by new nests), outnumbering those of both of the controls and the males whose tails were shortened. The latter had the smallest number of new active nests. The females, therefore, preferred to mate with the males having the longest tails.

The widowbird study required considerable manipulation of birds in a natural environment that was especially favorable for making observations. Evidence for female choice of mates has also been accumulated without

Rock Ptarmigan

Lagopus mutus Montin

NG–212; G–88; PE–148; PW–pl 21; AE–pl 264; AW–pl 272; AM(I)–278

F	6–9 MONOG		F I: 21–24 DAYS PRECOCIAL 3 F: 10–12 DAYS F	BERRIES INSECTS	

BREEDING: High, rocky alpine tundra. 1 brood.   **DISPLAYS:** Courtship: males call and strut, red combs over eyes swollen, head stretched out, tail raised and spread, wings drooped; interspersed with aerial display.   **NEST:** Oft exposed; shallow depression lined with grass, moss, few feathers.   **EGGS:** Cinnamon, buff, marked with dark browns. 1.6″ (42 mm).   **DIET:** Leaves and flower buds of shrubs and trees (esp willow and birch); seeds, moss. In winter, browse on twigs and buds, dig seeds from snow. Young feed on both insects and plants.   **CONSERVATION:** In winter moves to lower elevations.   **NOTES:** Male may remain with female through hatching but usu deserts during incubation. Female covers nest with veg until clutch complete. Young independent at 10–12 weeks. Unisexual flocks, pairs, or solitary in winter. Known in Europe as the Ptarmigan.   **ESSAYS:** Avian Snowshoes, p. 255; Monogamy, p. 597; Feet, p. 239; Feathered Nests, p. 605; Parental Care, p. 555.   **REFS:** Cramp and Simmons, 1980; MacDonald, 1970; Theberge and Bendell, 1980; Weeden and Theberge, 1972.

Willow Ptarmigan

Lagopus lagopus Linnaeus

NG–212; G–88; PE–148; PW–pl 21; AE–pl 263; AW–pl 269; AM(I)–276

F	7 (5–14) MONOG (POLYGYN)		F I: 21–22 DAYS PRECOCIAL 3 F: 10–12 DAYS MF	SEEDS BERRIES INSECTS	FOLIAGE BROWSE GROUND GLEAN

BREEDING: Low tundra, esp shrubby areas, less commonly in clearings below treeline. 1 brood.   **DISPLAYS:** Courting males call and strut, red combs over eyes swollen, head thrown back, tail raised and spread, wings drooped; followed by flight display with descending spiral.   **NEST:** Oft exposed on tundra; shallow depression lined with leaves, grass, few feathers.   **EGGS:** Bright red when laid, but wet red pigment is usu rubbed off in places, dries blackish-brown, rubbed areas show creamy, rarely reddish, ground color. 1.7″ (43 mm).   **DIET:** Leaves, flower buds, and twigs of willows, birches, and alders. Twigs of willows, etc., in winter. Young feed on insects, many spiders, little veg.   **CONSERVATION:** In winter moves to lower elevations.   **NOTES:** Male remains with female and young; males contribute more to rearing and survival of offspring than males of any other grouse species. But widows and paired females are equally successful in rearing young. 5%–10% of males are polygynous. Eggs covered by grass or leaves during period of laying. Young usu independent at 8–10 weeks. Form unisexual winter flocks. Known as Willow or Red Grouse in Europe.   **ESSAYS:** Avian Snowshoes, p. 255; Monogamy, p. 597; Feet, p. 239; Parental Care, p. 555; Color of Eggs, p. 305.   **REFS:** Cramp and Simmons, 1980; Hannon and Smith, 1984; Martin, 1984, 1987; Martin and Cooke, 1987.

such intervention in the course of a 30-year study of Parasitic Jaegers (known in Great Britain as "Arctic Skuas") on Fair Isle off the northern tip of Scotland. The jaegers are "polymorphic"—individuals of dark, light, and intermediate color phases occur in the same populations. Detailed studies by population biologist Peter O'Donald of Cambridge University and his colleagues indicate that females prefer to mate with males of the dark and intermediate phases, and as a result those males breed earlier than light-phase males. Earlier breeders tend to be more successful breeders, so the females choices increase the fitness of the dark males. O'Donald concludes that the Fair Isle population remains polymorphic (rather than gradually becoming composed entirely of dark individuals) because light individuals are favored by selection farther north, and "light genes" are continuously brought into the population by southward migrants.

Further work, including some, we hope, on North American species, is required to determine the details of female choice in birds. The effort required will be considerable, and suitable systems may be difficult to find, but the results should cast important light on the evolutionary origin of many physical and behavioral avian characteristics.

We know remarkably little about the origins of sexual selection. Why, for example, do female widowbirds prefer long-tailed males? Possibly females choose such males because the ability to grow and display long tails reflects their overall genetic "quality" as mates—and the females are thus choosing a superior father for their offspring. Or the choice may have no present adaptive basis, but merely be the result of an evolutionary sequence that started for another reason. For instance, perhaps the ancestors of Long-tailed Widowbirds once lived together with a population of near relatives whose males had slightly shorter tails. The somewhat longer tails of males of the "pre-Long-tailed" Widowbirds were the easiest way for females to recognize mates of their own species. Such a cue could have led to a preference for long tails that became integrated into the behavioral responses of females. Although we are inclined to think the former scenario is correct, the data in hand do not eliminate the second possibility.

SEE: Natural Selection, p. 237; Leks, p. 259; Polyandry, p. 133; Polygyny, p. 443; Dominance Hierarchies, p. 533. REFS: Andersson, 1982; O'Donald, 1983. Payne, 1984.

Avian Snowshoes

Of all our birds that must frequently traverse snow on foot, only ptarmigan and other grouse have evolved structures to facilitate walking on snow. In winter, most grouse acquire a fringe of scales along each toe, which enlarges the surface area of the foot. The ptarmigan have gone further to increase the surface area of their feet: in winter plumage, they develop highly modified dense feathering covering both surfaces of their feet, and their claws become significantly longer. It is likely that winter foot feathering also pro-

NG–214; G–88; PE–146; AE–pl 261; AW–pl 254; AM(I)–286

F	10–12	F	
	(7–17)	I: 23–24 DAYS	GREENS
	PROMISC	PRECOCIAL 3	INSECTS
		F: 7–10 DAYS	FRUIT
		F	

BREEDING: Tallgrass prairie. 1 brood. **DISPLAYS:** Courtship: "booming" March–May; males spaced ca. 30' apart, occupy lek; male inflates air sacs on sides of neck, tail erect, wings drooped, then rapidly drops head and deflates sacs with "boom." Jumping displays follow and males run at each other with tail and neck tufts erect, sacs inflated. **NEST:** Usu concealed in grass or shrubs in open habitat; shallow depression lined with dead leaves, feathers, grass. **EGGS:** Olive, spotted with dark brown. 1.8″ (45 mm). **DIET:** Oct–April, largely seeds, also waste grain, acorns. May–Oct, ca. ⅓ of diet insects, esp grasshoppers. **CONSERVATION:** In winter locally migratory. Seriously declining due to habitat conversion for agriculture, oil and gas development. E subspecies (Heath Hen, formerly in fire-maintained grasslands and blueberry barrens) now extinct; dark race from s w LA and e TX (Attwater's Prairie-Chicken) Endangered (sub)Species. **NOTES:** Eggs left covered during laying and before incubation. Male Ring-necked Pheasants disrupt leks and attack adults; also reduce nesting success by laying their eggs in prairie-chicken nests. Winter flocks unisexual or mixed. **ESSAYS:** Birds and the Law, p. 293; Heath Hens, p. 257; Leks, p. 259; Vocal Development, p. 601; Promiscuity, p. 145; Sexual Selection, p. 251. **REFS:** Hamerstrom, 1980; Hamerstrom and Hamerstrom, 1973; Johnsgard, 1973; Vance and Westemeier, 1979.

Lesser Prairie-Chicken
Supersp #8
Tympanuchus pallidicinctus Ridgway

NG–214; G–88; PE–146; PW–pl 21; AE–pl 262; AW–pl 255; AM(I)–286

F	11–13	F	
	PROMISC	I: 22–24 DAYS	ACORNS
		PRECOCIAL 3	SEEDS
		F: 7–10 DAYS	GREENS
		F	

BREEDING: Shortgrass prairie. 1 brood. **DISPLAYS:** Courtship: "gobbling" March–May; males occupy lek, usu on slight rise covered with short grasses. Male inflates air sacs on sides of neck, tail erect and wings drooped, then rapidly drops head and deflates sacs with "gobble." Jumping displays follow and males run at each other with tail and neck tufts erect, sacs inflated. **NEST:** Usu concealed in grass or shrubs in open situations; shallow depression lined with grass. **EGGS:** Cream or yellowish-white, finely dotted with pale brown, olive. Oft unmarked. 1.6″ (42 mm). **DIET:** Esp grasshoppers; also takes leaves, plant galls, and waste grain (latter esp in autumn and winter). **CONSERVATION:** Winter resident, but some s movement. Declining; current populations occupy <10% of range occupied prior to 1900. **NOTES:** Unusually mobile for gallinaceous bird; may move several miles daily to feed on waste grain. Winter flocks of mixed sexes. **ESSAYS:** Birds and the Law, p. 293; Heath Hens, p. 257; Leks, p. 259; Vocal Development, p. 601; Promiscuity, p. 145; Sexual Selection, p. 251. **REFS:** Crawford and Bolen, 1975, 1976; Crawford and Stormer, 1980.

vides thermal insulation, but its effectiveness has not been measured. Experiments using feathered and plucked ptarmigan feet on soft snow clearly demonstrate that foot feathering eases walking in these birds much the way snowshoes aid people. The feathers increase the bearing surface of the foot by about 400 percent and reduce the distance the foot sinks in snow by roughly 50 percent.

SEE: Temperature Regulation, p. 149; Feet, p. 239. REF: Hohn, 1977.

Heath Hens and Population Sizes

The Greater Prairie-Chicken (*Tympanuchus cupido pinnatus*) can still entertain us with the booming displays of its males. But the first variety of this species to be described scientifically, the Heath Hen (*Tympanuchus cupido cupido*), is gone forever.

The Heath Hen was once common in brushy areas on the eastern seaboard, but it was good to eat and the human population on the coastal plain was exploding. It was so common an item in diets that, in New England, servants made not having to eat Heath Hen more than a few times a week a condition of employment. In addition it appears that the hens were easy prey for introduced predators, especially cats, and susceptible to diseases introduced with pheasants and domestic chickens. By the mid to late 1800s, habitat destruction and relentless hunting had exterminated the Heath Hen everywhere but on Martha's Vineyard Island. By the turn of the century, fewer than 100 birds remained. A portion of the island was set aside as a refuge in 1907, and a predator control program was begun. By 1916 the Heath Hen population had recovered to some 2,000 individuals, but then disaster overtook it. A natural fire in 1916 destroyed much of the remaining habitat and most of the nests. During the following winter an unusual concentration of goshawks placed heavy predation pressure on the birds that escaped the fire.

The 100–150 individuals that escaped both flames and hawks increased to some 200 by 1920, but then disease pushed the number of Heath Hens below 100 once again. From there on it was downhill, and the last living Heath Hen was recorded in early 1932. In its final years the population suffered from a surplus of males and a shortage of fertility.

Populations are subject to three kinds of chance events that can threaten their survival—deleterious environmental changes, random variation in breeding success of individuals, and random changes in genetic composition ("genetic drift") that will lead to loss of genetic variability and may result in lowered fertility. All three are more likely to influence small rather than large populations. If the entire island of Martha's Vineyard had been a Heath Hen preserve, or if (more reasonably) a second colony had been established on Nantucket or the nearby mainland, the birds would

Sharp-tailed Grouse
Tympanuchus phasianellus Linnaeus

NG–214; G–86; PE–146; PW–pl 21; AE–pl 260; AW–pl 252; AM(I)–288

| F | 10–14
(5–17)
PROMISC | F
I: 21–24 DAYS
PRECOCIAL 3
F: 7–10 DAYS
F | SEEDS
BERRIES
INSECTS | FOLIAGE
BROWSE |

BREEDING: Grassland, savanna, partially cleared boreal forest, shrubland, sage-brush. 1 brood. **DISPLAYS:** Courtship: "dancing" occurs April–May. Males occupy lek, usu on small knoll; male inflates sacs on sides of neck, with tail erect and wings drooped, then rapidly drops head and deflates sacs with a weak "coo." Jumping displays follow, males run at each other with tail and neck tufts erect, sacs inflated. **NEST:** Usu concealed in grass or under shrub; shallow depression lined with grass, leaves, ferns, etc. **EGGS:** Light brown, dotted with reddish brown, lavender, occ unmarked. 1.7″ (43 mm). **DIET:** Incl leaves, buds, flowers, nuts, fruit. Young highly insectivorous. Also takes waste grain in winter. **CONSERVATION:** Winter resident. Blue List 1972, 1978–82, Special Concern 1986; declining in some areas. **NOTES:** Occ interbreeds with Greater Prairie-Chicken. Hard seeds may substitute in gizzard for gravel where latter is scarce. Forms mixed-sex winter flocks of 10–35, occ to 100. **ESSAYS:** Leks, p. 259; Vocal Development, p. 601; Blue List, p. 11; Promiscuity, p. 145; Hybridization, p. 501; Swallowing Stones, p. 269; Sexual Selection, p. 251. **REFS:** Evans and Moen, 1975; Hamerstrom, 1963; Moyles, 1981.

Sage Grouse
Centrocercus urophasianus Bonaparte

NG–214; G–86; PW–pl 21; AW–pl 253; AM(I)–284

| F | 6–9
(6–13)
PROMISC | F
I: 25–27 DAYS
PRECOCIAL 3
F: 7–10 DAYS
F | INSECTS | FOLIAGE
BROWSE

GROUND
GLEAN |

BREEDING: Sagebrush communities. 1 brood. **DISPLAYS:** Groups of males occupy leks in April–May, strut and inflate neck sacs until nearly reaching ground; with tail erect and fanned, rapidly throw head back with wings held rigid and almost touching ground, and deflate sacs with loud popping. **NEST:** Concealed under sagebrush; shallow depression slightly lined with grass, sage leaves. **EGGS:** Olive, yellowish, greenish, finely dotted with browns. 2.2″ (55 mm). **DIET:** Incl flowers and buds from forbs. Almost exclusively sagebrush leaves in autumn and winter. **CONSERVATION:** Locally migratory in winter. Blue List 1972–81, Special Concern 1982–86; habitat conversion to agriculture, grazing, and herbicide use to eradicate sagebrush have extirpated from much of former range, declining esp in n w. **NOTES:** Within sage community, wet meadows or green areas are required by broods for insect foraging. Lack muscular gizzard of relatives, thus limited to relatively soft food. Form unisexual winter flocks. **ESSAYS:** Leks, p. 259; Blue List, p. 11; Sexual Selection, p. 251; Promiscuity, p. 145. **REFS:** Autenrieth, 1986; Braun et al., 1977; Gibson and Bradbury, 1986, 1987; Wiley, 1973.

have been much more secure. Then a larger portion of the Heath Hen population would have escaped the fire, and the goshawks would have left more Hens even if they managed to eat the same proportion of the more numerous survivors of the fire (fires and population increases of predators are examples of deleterious environmental events).

Once the population was below 100, the failure of a few nests or the presence of a single skilled predator could greatly influence the dynamics of the population. Similarly, the fertility of the hens may well have been reduced by genetic drift. In short, once a population drops below a critical size, its chances of extinction tend to increase greatly. A major challenge of the newly emerging ecological subdiscipline of conservation biology is to determine how large populations must be to have a reasonable assurance of survival—that is, to determine "viable population sizes." Such a determination is currently needed for the small, dark, southeast Texas form of this species, Attwater's Prairie-Chicken (*Tympanuchus cupido attwateri*), which is seriously endangered, and probably for the remainder of Greater Prairie-Chicken populations as well as those of the Lesser Prairie-Chicken, all of which appear to be threatened.

SEE: The Passenger Pigeon, p. 273; Our Only Native Parrot, p. 279; The Labrador Duck, p. 85; Population Dynamics, p. 575. REFS: Halliday, 1978; Shaffer, 1981; Soulé, 1986.

Leks

The mating system of some species of birds involves males displaying communally at a traditional site (one used year after year). The traditional site is known as a "lek" or, sometimes, an "arena." In North America, males of certain members of the grouse family (prairie-chickens, Sharp-tailed Grouse, and Sage Grouse) compete for mates at leks. During their displays, they call (often with a "popping," "gobbling," or "booming" sound) and inflate brightly colored air sacs on their necks, while repeatedly carrying out a ritualized dance. Females approach the lek, choose and mate with a male from the displaying group, and then leave to nest and rear the young alone.

The male grouse hold territories on the lek, with the dominant male usually claiming the most central position. The central male also normally mates with the most females; in general a male's success at attracting females is highly correlated with his position on the lek, which in turn is largely determined by his place in the male dominance hierarchy. This leads to relatively few males siring most of the young. In one study, about a third of the males performed three quarters of the copulations; in another, one male was involved in 17 of 24 observed matings.

Not all species of grouse establish leks. Spruce, Blue and Ruffed Grouse display at dispersed sites, although, as in lekking species, the females do not remain with the males after mating. In contrast, European Red

Northern Bobwhite
Colinus virginianus Linnaeus

NG–216; G–92; PE–148; PW–pl 22; AE–pl 257; AW–pl 282; AM(I)–292

| MF | 12–16
(6–28)
MONOG | MF
I: 23–24 DAYS
PRECOCIAL 3
F: 6–7 DAYS
MF | SEEDS
INSECTS | |

BREEDING: Tall grassland, brushy fields, open woodland, cultivated fields. 1 brood. **DISPLAYS:** Courtship: male with feathers erect, wingtips touching ground and elbows thrown forward to produce "feathered wall"; turns head to side displaying white markings, makes short rushes toward female. Combat (occ fatal) with rival male if present. **NEST:** Shallow depression lined with grass, etc., concealed by woven arch of veg; small side entrance. **EGGS:** White to creamy, occ buff, unmarked. 1.2″ (30 mm). **DIET:** Incl leaves, fruit, buds, tubers; spiders, snails, small verts. Roughly 85% veg, 15% animals over year but more insects in summer. **CONSERVATION:** Winter resident. Blue List 1980–81, Special Concern 1982, Local Concern 1986; largely recovered from severe 1979–80 winter. Endangered (sub)Species (Masked Bobwhite) reintroduced from Mexico (where it is close to extinction due to overgrazing of native grassland habitat) into former U.S. range in s AZ. **NOTES:** Feed and roost in covey (flock consisting of 2 or more family groups) of up to 30 except when nesting; coveys begin to form when young reach 3 weeks. Covey nestles together at night, tails inward, heads outward. Parents perform distraction display. **ESSAYS:** Quail Eggs and Clover, p. 265; Blue List, p. 11; Birds and the Law, p. 293. **REFS:** Roseberry and Klimstra, 1984; Rosene, 1969; Scott, 1985.

Montezuma Quail
Cyrtonyx montezumae Vigors

NG–216; G–90; PW–pl 22; AW–pl 283; AM(I)–290

| F –M | 10–12
(6–14)
MONOG | F
I: 25–26 DAYS
PRECOCIAL 3
F: 10 DAYS
MF | BULBS
INSECTS
NUTS
SEEDS | DIGGING
GROUND
GLEAN |

BREEDING: Open oak and open pine-oak woodland with bunchgrass understory. 1 brood. **DISPLAYS:** ? **NEST:** Shallow depression lined with grass, roofed and overhung with grass. Better constructed than other quail nests. **EGGS:** White to creamy, unmarked but oft very nest-stained. 1.2″ (32 mm). **DIET:** Also some fruit; insects more important than literature suggests. Also acorns, esp in autumn. **CONSERVATION:** Winter resident. Severely affected by cattle grazing and forest clearing. **NOTES:** Called "fool quail" because it remains still and depends on camouflage rather than running or flying. Breeding triggered by summer rains. Female and male brood chicks. Performs distraction display to divert attention from young. Strong feet and relatively large claws used to dig out plant bulbs. Closely tied to oak distribution, preferring the cooler microclimates provided by n-facing slopes. Fall coveys of 6–10, presumably single family units, inhabit small home ranges. Roost on ground. Formerly known as Harlequin or Mearn's Quail. **ESSAYS:** Precocial and Altricial Young, p. 581; Quail Eggs and Clover, p. 265; Distraction Displays, p. 115; Feet, p. 239; Temperature Regulation, p. 149; Breeding Season, p. 55. **REFS:** Johnsgard, 1973; Leopold et al., 1981; Leopold and McCabe, 1957.

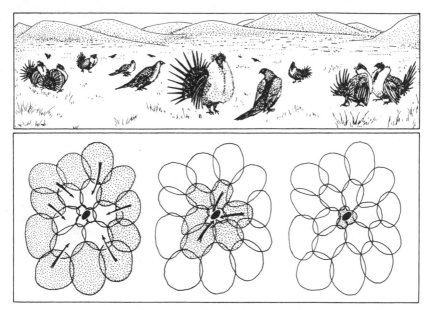

Above: male Sage Grouse displaying on lek. Below: map of territories on lek in three consecutive seasons. Males on the periphery of the lek in one breeding season, if they survive to the next breeding season, move into more central (and more desirable) territories. Thus older, more experienced males end up on the most desirable central territories, where they have the greatest chance of mating, since females prefer central males.

Grouse remain paired for much of the year, and males may help rear the young.

The grouse mating systems seem to be determined in part by habitat. Lekking species tend to live in open country; species with males that display in isolation tend to be forest dwellers. Natural selection may not have favored the evolution of leks in northern forest habitats that provide predators an opportunity to approach leks with little chance of detection. In the tropics, however, many groups of birds (e.g., cotingas, manakins, hermit hummingbirds) display at leks on forest floors.

Other birds with lek mating systems include some birds of paradise, some weavers, and some shorebirds (including the Buff-breasted Sandpiper, which breeds on the northern fringes of our continent). The grouse, however, are our most prominent performers. Many birds, such as cranes, have spectacular displays and elaborate courtship dances. These birds are not lekking, however, because the males do not attempt to attract females by displaying competitively and repeatedly at traditional sites season after season, and because males and females form pair bonds rather than mating promiscuously.

SEE: Polygyny, p. 443; Monogamy, p. 597; Promiscuity, p. 145; Territoriality, p. 387; Dominance Hierarchies, p. 533; Heath Hens p. 257; Visual Displays, p. 5.   REFS: Bradbury and Gibson, 1983; Payne, 1983; Wiley, 1978.

Scaled Quail

Callipepla squamata Vigors

NG–216; G–90; PE–148; PW–pl 22; AE–pl 258; AW–pl 284; AM(I)–294

F	12–14	F –M
	(9–16+)	I: 21–23 DAYS
	MONOG	PRECOCIAL 3
		F: ? DAYS
		MF

LEAVES
FRUIT
INSECTS

BREEDING: Semiarid plains, desert grassland, arid scrub. 1 brood. **DISPLAYS**: Male frontal display with head raised, crest up or down, wings drooped; lateral display with flanks spread and crest raised. **NEST**: Usu concealed in grass or shrubs; shallow depression lined with grass and a few feathers. **EGGS**: White to creamy, some unmarked, some speckled with browns. 1.3″ (32 mm). **DIET**: Esp weed seeds; eats more grass seed than other quail. **CONSERVATION**: Winter resident. **NOTES**: Male oft acts as sentinel on slightly elevated perch while female and chicks feed. Form coveys of up to 150 birds (avg 30) when not breeding. Occ hybridizes with Gambel's Quail, esp in areas where native habitats have been disrupted by agriculture and grazing. **ESSAYS**: Precocial and Altricial Young, p. 581; Quail Eggs and Clover, p. 265; Hybridization, p. 501; Flock Defense, p. 235. **REFS**: Anderson, 1978; Campbell et al., 1973; Johnsgard, 1973.

Gambel's Quail

Supersp #9
Callipepla gambelii Gambel

NG–218; G–90; PW–pl 22; AW–pl 276; AM(I)–294

F	10–12	F
	MONOG	I: 21–24 DAYS
		PRECOCIAL 3
		F: 10 DAYS
		MF

LEAVES

BREEDING: Hot, dry deserts with mesquite or other thorny cover but oft with water nearby, also riparian and juniper-pine woodland. 1 brood, 2 in exceptionally good years. **DISPLAYS**: Male struts around female, bowing head; males fight. **NEST**: Shallow depression lined with dead leaves, twigs, grass, oft under veg, positioned so shaded at midday. Occ to 10′ above ground in old bush or tree nest of Roadrunner, thrasher or Cactus Wren. **EGGS**: Dull white to buff, marked with browns. 1.2″ (31 mm). **DIET**: Also plant shoots, some fruit; few insects. **CONSERVATION**: Winter resident. **NOTES**: Most arid-adapted of quail. Activity in summer is constrained by hot weather: bimodal pattern with morning and late afternoon foraging separated by long quiet period. During winter, similar bimodal pattern occurs, apparently to avoid raptor predation. Two females oft lay in same nest. Male and female brood. Gregarious, living in coveys of 20–40 (occ to nearly 200) birds in fall and winter. Roost in bushes or in low, dense trees. **ESSAYS**: Bird Droppings, p. 263; Temperature Regulation, p. 149; Quail Eggs and Clover, p. 265. **REFS**: Goldstein, 1984; Goldstein and Nagy, 1985; Gullion, 1960.

Bird Droppings

"Droppings" is the term ornithologists use to describe the excrement of birds because, unlike mammalian feces, it includes kidney products in addition to alimentary wastes. This combining of the two waste products reduces water loss, especially in desert species such as Gambel's Quail. Bird droppings, of course, vary: those of granivores are very hard and finely ground, those of frugivores are minimally cemented; and those of insectivores differ with the proportion of soft- and hard-bodied insects taken.

Droppings also vary in their impact on the human community; small amounts go unnoticed but larger accumulations may be destructive, causing diseases and killing plants. When local accumulations are overwhelming, as in the case of guano desposits, the resulting fertilizer may be mined for use elsewhere.

Guano is the Spanish form of the Peruvian (Quechua Indian) word for the droppings of seabirds. Fish-eating seabirds deposit nitrogen- and phosphate-rich guano at their large, perennial colonies. The cycling of nitrogen and phosphorus through ecosystems differs: nitrogen can exist as a gaseous compound and return from sea to land via the atmosphere, but phosphorus cannot and has no easy return route after it is washed from the land into the sea. Along with the fishing industry's harvesting of ocean fish and shellfish, seabirds play a crucial role in returning phosphorus to the land and completing its cycle. Sales of the rich fertilizer mined from these sites have made important contributions to several South American economies. The Blue-footed Booby (*Sula nebouxii*), although not a North American breeder, is a casual visitor, and our only representative of the "guano" birds.

It was once thought that concentrations of waterfowl droppings were detrimental to farming, and flocks were discouraged from congregating in pastureland. Apparently, however, the droppings do no harm to forage or to grazing livestock. In some situations, in fact, mineral-rich droppings left by visiting birds are of value to both the plants and the grazing herbivores. In some areas, cattle and sheep have been conditioned to overcome any distaste for goose droppings, and augment their diet by consuming coated plants. The excrement of domestic birds, in fact, has several markets. Experiments using poultry litter and conventional fertilizer in land reclamation around old coal fields have shown comparable grass seed germination rates. In another application, the replacement of up to 25 percent (by volume) of sheep and cattle feed with chicken droppings has been shown to be a nutritionally sound practice.

Consumption of bird droppings is not limited to the fertilizing of plants and the feeding of livestock. Certain birds reputedly recycle their own excrement. Some species are known to swallow the fecal sacs of their young, thus gaining additional nutritional return for their foraging efforts. Many reports of the usefulness of their own excrement to birds are in need of further study. There are scattered observations of seabirds that "dive bomb" a pirating foe or a predator at a nesting colony and descriptions of droppings

California Quail

Callipepla californica Shaw

NG–218; G–90; PW–pl 22; AW–pl 278; AM(I)–296

F   12–16   F   FOLIAGE
MONOG   I: 18–23 DAYS   ACORNS
    PRECOCIAL 3
    F: 10 DAYS
    MF

BREEDING: Habitat generalist: chaparral, scrub, brushy and cultivated areas, suburbs, occ open woodland. 1 brood, 2 in exceptionally favorable years. **DISPLAYS:** Courtship: male bows, fluffs feathers, droops wings and, with tail spread, may rush toward female. Males oft fight. **NEST:** Usu concealed in grass or shrubs or next to log or rock, occ to 10′ above ground in bush or tree; shallow, covered depression lined with dead leaves, grass. **EGGS:** White to creamy, marked with dull browns. 1.2″ (31 mm). **DIET:** Also some fruit; insects, spiders, snails, etc., account for <5% of diet. **CONSERVATION:** Winter resident. **NOTES:** Gregarious, forming coveys of up to 200 (rarely to 300+) birds in fall and winter. Male acts as sentry throughout year. Female broods chicks. Remain on ground and run very rapidly, flying as last resort. Roost in dense trees or shrubs, not on ground. **ESSAYS:** Quail Eggs and Clover, p. 265; Precocial and Altricial Young, p. 581; Flock Defense, p. 235. **REFS:** Gutiérrez, 1979–80; Gutiérrez et al., 1983; Leopold, 1977; Zink et al., 1987.

Mountain Quail

Oreortyx pictus Douglas

NG–218; G–90; PW–pl 22; AW–pl 277; AM(I)–296

F?   9–10   MF   BULBS
    (6–15)   I: 21–24 DAYS   GREENS
    MONOG   PRECOCIAL 3   INSECTS
    F: ? DAYS
    MF

BREEDING: Overgrown cleared areas and "burns" in montane conif forest, coastal conif forest, chaparral, pinyon-juniper woodland. 1 brood, occ 2 at low elevations. **DISPLAYS:** Male frontal display with wings partly spread. **NEST:** Usu concealed by shrubs, at base of tree, or beside fallen log; shallow depression lined with leaves, pine needles, grass, and a few feathers. Oft near water. **EGGS:** Pale cream, buff, salmon, unmarked. 1.4″ (35 mm). **DIET:** Also fruit, berries; insects <5% of diet. **CONSERVATION:** In winter moves to lower elevations. **NOTES:** Parents defend young more vigorously than any other quail. Males apparently incubate regularly. Gregarious, coveys usu family groups of up to 14, but occ up to 30 birds may aggregate in fall and winter. Frequently dig for bulbs of plants. Unique among N.A. quail in undergoing altitudinal migration on foot between breeding and wintering ranges. **ESSAYS:** Precocial and Altricial Young, p. 581; Quail Eggs and Clover, p. 265; Parental Care, p. 555; Who Incubates?, p. 27; Feet, p. 239. **REFS:** Brennan et al., 1987; Gutiérrez, 1979–80; Leopold et al., 1981.

used to cement in place nests situated on windswept sites. As is so often the case, your careful observations could help expand our understanding of the conditions under which such purposive use of droppings occur.

Bird droppings can be detrimental to the timber industry, however. Entire plots in plantations may be damaged or killed by salts leaching from accumulated droppings of European Starlings, blackbirds, and other communally roosting birds. (The damage appears to resemble that once left beneath Passenger Pigeon roosts.) Foresters are presently trying to develop simple management practices that can move the birds frequently from plot to plot and convert the problem into an asset.

Bird droppings are implicated in one human disease, histoplasmosis, a noncontagious respiratory ailment that is especially common in the Ohio River Valley. Histoplasmosis is caused by the airborne spores of a fungus, *Histoplasma capsulatum*, that thrives in acid-rich soils fertilized by the droppings of chickens, grackles, Red-winged Blackbirds, European Starlings, etc. Massive bird kills have been part of histoplasmosis control programs. One technique involves spraying roosting colonies with a detergent solution that removes body and feather oils. The solution is applied during wet, cool weather, often by spraying from high-pressure hoses of fire trucks. The soaked birds, robbed of their weatherproofing oils, are unable to maintain their normal body temperatures at air temperatures below 45° F. Hopefully, resorting to this type of procedure will soon be superseded by less drastic measures that reduce the birds' breeding success or displace their colonies.

SEE: European Starlings, p. 489; The Passenger Pigeon, p. 273; Disease and Parasitism, p. 399; Parental Care, p. 555; Seabird Nesting Sites, p. 197; Communal Roosting, p. 615; Hummingbirds, Nectar, and Water, p. 333. REFS: Anderson and Braun, 1985; Crockett and Hansley, 1977; Hardy, 1978; Lawes and Kenwood, 1970; Marriott, 1973.

Quail Eggs and Clover

The rate of quail reproduction in the more arid portions of their ranges is closely related to the amount of rainfall. For example, in very dry years on the King Ranch of Texas, most Northern Bobwhites do not breed and populations drop to low levels. When rains are ample, however, the birds reproduce normally. In semiarid parts of California, those years with enough rain to produce spectacular displays of wild flowers also tend to be good years for the reproduction of California Quail.

But how do the rains regulate the breeding of the quail? They seem to do so, in part, by influencing the chemistry of the plants, especially legumes (members of the pea family) that the quail eat. A diet containing an extract from subterranean clover ("subclover"—a low-growing clover that buries its seed heads in the soil) has been shown to greatly reduce egg production

Chukar
Alectoris chukar Gray

NG–220; G–92; PE–302; PW–pl 22; AW–pl 281; AM(I)–270

F?	9–16 (7–20) MONOG (POLYGYN)	F I: 22–24 DAYS PRECOCIAL 3 F: 7–10 DAYS F –M?	LEAVES INSECTS FRUIT	

BREEDING: Rocky, grassy, arid mountain slopes, riparian brush, open desert. 1 brood. **DISPLAYS:** Courtship: male lateral display with head tilted, followed by circling of female while remaining in same posture or with head low, body horizontal, and one wing lowered. **NEST:** Concealed amid rocks or brush; shallow depression lined with dried grass, feathers. **EGGS:** Yellow-white, spotted with brown. 1.7" (43 mm). **DIET:** Esp grasshoppers. **CONSERVATION:** Winter resident. Native of Asia; widely introduced in N.A. but successfully established only in arid w, usu only where cheatgrass (*Bromus tectorum*) is available. **NOTES:** Role of male in incubation and rearing is unclear; either deserts early in incubation or remains through hatching and rearing. Young stay with parents until start of next breeding season. Usu found near water; studies on Chukars from Israel suggest they require drinking water except when succulent forage is available. Form fall coveys of 5–40 (usu ca. 20) birds. Roost on ground in circle, similar to bobwhite. **ESSAYS:** Avian Invaders, p. 633; Monogamy, p. 597; Polygyny, p. 443; Drinking, p. 123. **REFS:** Cramp and Simmons, 1980; Degen et al., 1984; Leopold et al., 1981.

Gray Partridge
Perdix perdix Linnaeus

NG–220; G–92; PE–148; PW–pl 22; AE–pl 267; AW–pl 285; AM(I)–268

F	15–17 (5–22 +) MONOG	F I: 23–25 DAYS PRECOCIAL 3 F: 13–15 DAYS MF	LEAVES INSECTS

BREEDING: Culviated areas in plains with native grassland or other cover. 1 brood. **DISPLAYS:** Courtship: male assumes upright posture, calls and jerks tail up and down; lateral display with body tilted toward female emphasizing male's barred flank. **NEST:** Usu concealed in grass or shrubs; shallow depression lined with leaves, straw, grass. Eggs covered by grass or leaves for up to 3 weeks during laying. **EGGS:** Olive, occ white, unmarked. 1.4" (37 mm). **DIET:** Esp seeds of cultivated grain, shoots of grass, clover. **CONSERVATION:** Winter resident. Introduced; native of Eurasia. **NOTES:** Female leads chicks, male oft acts as rearguard. Both adults perform distraction display. Form fall coveys of up to 30 (usu 12–15) birds; in cold weather, covey nestles together at night, tails inward, heads outward. Covey usu stays together in flight when flushed. **ESSAYS:** Distraction Displays, p. 115; Flock Defense, p. 235; Temperature Regulation, p. 149; Parental Care, p. 555. **REFS:** Cramp and Simmons, 1980; Leopold et al., 1981; Weigand, 1980.

by quail. That plant, among others, produces "phytoestrogens," chemical compounds that are similar to the hormones involved in regulating reproduction in birds and mammals. The phytoestrogens may play a role in protecting the plants against predation by herbivores. Their importance in regulating the reproduction of animals that eat them was first noted when subclover was found to inhibit the breeding of Australian sheep.

Stunted plants of drought years have higher phytoestrogen content than do plants with the luxuriant growth of high-rainfall years. Much higher levels of those compounds were found in samples of food removed from the crops of California Quail in 1972, a low-rain, low-reproduction year, than in samples from 1973, a high-rain, high-reproduction year.

Other factors may also help to regulate quail breeding. One is the quantity of nutritious legume seeds available (they were almost three times as abundant in the diet in 1973 as in 1972). Another is rainfall itself, which could contribute some direct stimulus for breeding. But diet appears to play the major role, and that long-evolved role may, ironically, end up depressing the size of some quail populations. Subclover, an exotic species probably originating in the Mediterranean region, is being used increasingly as a forage crop in California. It is possible that this human-induced change will reduce breeding in California Quail even in places and years with more than adequate rainfall.

SEE: Coevolution, p. 405.   REFS: Leopold et al., 1976; Leopold, 1977.

Bird Biologist—Alden H. Miller

The 1930s through the 1950s was a transitional period in which the focus of bird biology shifted from systematics and biogeography to ecology, behavior, and physiology. Alden H. Miller (1906–65) was a leader in ornithology during that period. He was a professor of zoology at the University of California at Berkeley and, from 1940 until his death, director of the Museum of Vertebrate Zoology at that institution. His predecessor in the latter position was his major professor, Joseph Grinnell (p. 411).

Miller published more than 250 scientific papers on the ecology, biogeography, systematics, morphology, and reproductive physiology of birds, all informed by his deep interest in evolution. They included a detailed study of the anatomy of the Hawaiian Goose (Nene), a classic monograph on the genus *Junco*, and a fine analysis of the distribution of California birds. Many of Miller's students are leaders of American ornithology today.

Ring-necked Pheasant

Phasianus colchicus Linnaeus

NG–222; G–92; PE–144; PW–pl 22; AE–pl 274; AW–pl 267; AM(I)–272

F

10–12
(6–15+)
POLYGYN
F

F
I: 23–25 DAYS
PRECOCIAL 3
F: 12 DAYS
F

BREEDING: Open country, cultivated areas, marsh, woodland, forest edge. 1 brood. **DISPLAYS:** Courtship: male on "crowing territory" rises high on feet and calls loudly while rapidly but briefly flapping wings; struts in semicircles around female, head tucked, tail spread, and wing toward female drooped. **NEST:** Usu concealed in grass, weeds; shallow depression, occ barely lined with leaves, grass. **EGGS:** Brownish-olive, occ pale blue, unmarked. 1.6″ (42 mm). **DIET:** Insects, terrestrial and aquatic inverts, small verts; seeds, grain, fruit. **CONSERVATION:** Winter resident. Asian species widely introduced. Occ damages grain crops. **NOTES:** Females form group that assoc with, and is defended by, one male. Strong breeding territory tenacity by male. Hens are occ brood parasites, laying eggs in nests of ducks or other gallinaceous birds. Female performs distraction display. Male rarely accompanies hen and chicks. Young independent at 10–12 weeks. Roost in trees or on ground, occ loosely communal. Fall and winter flocks oft up to 30–40 birds, usu sexes separate; strong dominance hierarchy in flock. **ESSAYS:** Population Dynamics, p. 575; Eye Color, p. 233; Dominance Hierarchies, p. 533; Brood Parasitism, p. 287; Distraction Displays, p. 115; Polygyny, p. 443; Site Tenacity, p. 189. **REFS:** Cramp and Simmons, 1980; Leopold et al., 1981; Snyder, 1984; Whiteside and Guthery, 1983.

Wild Turkey

Meleagris gallopavo Linnaeus

NG–222; G–84; PE–144; PW–69; AE–pl 269; AW–pl 266; AM(I)–290

F

10–12
(6–20)
POLYGYN
F

F
I: 27–28 DAYS
PRECOCIAL 3
F: 6–10 DAYS
F

BREEDING: Mature decid and decid-conif forests, open woodland, esp in mountains. 1 brood. **DISPLAYS:** Males gobble and strut with plumage erect, tail fanned, head ornaments swollen, and wings drooped with quills rattling. **NEST:** Usu concealed in grass or shrubs; shallow depression lined with a few dead leaves, grass. **EGGS:** Buff to white, marked with dull brown. 2.5″ (63 mm). **DIET:** Mostly seeds, nuts (esp acorns), fruit, leaves of many plants; also insects, esp grasshoppers, terrestrial inverts, small verts. **CONSERVATION:** Winter resident. Reintroduced to much of range where formerly extirpated by habitat loss and diseases spread by domestic poultry (latter still problem in e and s e). **NOTES:** Nearly became national bird of U.S., losing by one vote in congressional ballot. Female performs distraction display. Chicks roost under body, wings, and tail of female until ca. 4 weeks old. Family groups and broodless females coalesce into flocks when young are several weeks old. Roost in trees. Winter flocks, either unisexual or mixed, usu to 40–50, much larger in some areas. **ESSAYS:** Visual Displays, p. 5; Swallowing Stones, p. 269; Polygyny, p. 443; Distraction Displays, p. 115. **REFS:** Hewitt, 1967; Lewis, 1973.

Swallowing Stones

The gizzard, a muscular section of the stomach lined with horny plates or ridges, may be characterized as the teeth and jaws of some birds. It is there that grains, acorns, nuts, mussels, and similar hard-shelled materials that have been swallowed whole are rotated two to three times a minute and crushed. The gizzard can be extraordinarily effective; objects that require more than 400 pounds of pressure per square inch to crush have been flattened within 24 hours when experimentally fed to a turkey. The grinding action of the gizzard is often aided by swallowed sand, grit, or a few pebbles. In Ostriches, the grit may include stones up to an inch in diameter.

In the era when diets were still commonly chronicled by listing stomach contents recovered from dissected birds, a detailed list of gizzard contents was readily available. Today's surveys, however, are often limited to observations of foraging birds. Such observations verify that the accumulation of grinding materials in gizzards is not simply the result of inadvertently swallowing the materials along with food; granivorous birds are often seen swallowing selected stones, and Red Grouse in Europe have been observed to migrate when deep snow covers their grit supply.

The size of the gizzard and the characteristics of the grinding aids vary depending on diet and available materials. If the composition of the diet changes during the year, so may the quantity or coarseness of the grinding materials in the gizzard. Also, when preferred grinding aids are scarce, others may be substituted; when stones are unavailable, the indigestible heads of beetles, hard seeds, or fruit pits help to crush subsequent meals.

The grinding aids are rather coarse in herbivores (finches, gallinaceous birds, shorebirds, wildfowl, etc.) and in those insectivores, such as goatsuckers, that consume hard-bodied beetles. The gizzards of frugivores (fruit-eaters), nectarivores (nectar-eaters), and birds taking soft-bodied insects may be very reduced and hold only fine sand or no grinding aids at all. In carnivores, such as owls, the gizzard functions differently. In these birds, it accumulates and consolidates undigestible portions of prey items into pellets and retains them until they are ejected.

Some birds with special digestive problems have evolved special solutions to them. Grebes, for example, which ingest sharp, potentially harmful fish bones, also habitually swallow their own feathers. Feather balls are commonly found in their stomachs and are thought to embed dangerous bone tips.

The minerals of some grinding materials may provide necessary supplements. During egg laying, for instance, sources of calcium are actively sought by females of some species, and as in the case of the Ring-necked Pheasant, its availability may limit breeding ranges.

The gizzard is credited with permitting more diversified diets by making available the nutrients in well-sealed seeds or armored animals. Thus, by ingesting fairly coarse grit, Greater Flamingos are able to digest snails

Plain Chachalaca

Ortalis vetula Wagler

NG–222; G–84; PE–302; PW–62; AE–pl 272; AM(I)–266

10'–15'
(2'–35')

2–3
(2–4)
MONOG

F
I: 25 (22–27)DAYS
PRECOCIAL 4
F: 14-21(?)DAYS
MF

BUDS
INSECTS

GROUND
GLEAN

BREEDING: Dense riverine forest and thickets, forest edge. 1 brood. **DISPLAYS:** Males engage in dawn vocal contests from tops of tallest trees, producing a cacophony of calls of "chachalac." Male then descends from tree and struts among females. **NEST:** Near water and berry supply; on limb, in vines supported by tree, or in crotch; crude, of sticks, grass, leaves, Spanish moss, etc. Usu in refurbished nest of cuckoo, thrasher, ani, or eggs may be laid in chance accumulation of leaves in tree crotch. Does not build nest. **EGGS:** Creamy, dull white, unmarked. 2.3" (58 mm). **DIET:** Also fruit, foliage, flowers; few snails. Young initially fed by regurgitation. **CONSERVATION:** Winter resident. Winter survival likely has increased as result of supplemental foraging at backyard feeders. **NOTES:** Young fed by parents; leave nest within 2 hours of hatching, urged to ground by female. Both parents brood. Largely arboreal. Habitat oft flooded which may account for tree-nesting habit—unusual for gallinaceous birds. Gregarious in fall, forming loose feeding flocks. **ESSAYS:** Transporting Young, p. 103; Feeding Birds, p. 349; How Do We Find Out About Bird Biology?, p. 319; Vocal Functions, p. 471. **REFS:** Delacour and Amadon, 1973; Marion, 1976; Marion and Fleetwood, 1978.

Band-tailed Pigeon

Columba fasciata Say

NG–224; G–166; PW–pl 23; AW–pl 347; AM (II)–138

DECID
TREE
6'–30'

MF

1
(1–2)
MONOG

MF
I: 18–20 DAYS
ALTRICIAL
F: 25–27 DAYS
MF

BERRIES
GRAIN

GROUND
GLEAN

BREEDING: Oak forest and woodland, conif forest. 2, occ 3 broods. **DISPLAYS:** Courtship: male performs rapid flapping flight, alternating with short glides; in tree, male bows to female. **NEST:** Usu at fork of horizontal branch or at trunk in conif or oak tree; crude, shallow, of crossed twigs with little or no cross-weaving, occ lined with a few pine needles. **EGGS:** White, unmarked. 1.6" (40 mm). **DIET:** Esp acorns, also seeds. Young fed crop milk for ca. 3 weeks. **CONSERVATION:** Winters s to n c Nicaragua. Susceptible to overhunting; once nearly exterminated. **NOTES:** Usu nest as scattered pairs. Gregarious, oft seen in flocks of dozens. Nomadic, moving in search of mast crops (esp acorns and pinyon seeds), and likely breeding opportunistically in response to abundant food supplies. **ESSAYS:** Bird Milk, p. 271; Brood Patches, p. 427; Passenger Pigeon, p. 273. **REFS:** Goodwin, 1983; Gutiérrez et al., 1975; Leopold et al., 1981.

that they filter from the bottom mud and thus avoid competition with sand-ingesting Lesser Flamingos, whose diets are limited to algae and diatoms. For many aquatic birds today, however, this trait has a maladaptive side effect: the swallowing of lead pellets as grinding aids. Hunters and conservationists alike have been in search of replacement ammunition made of nontoxic materials (such as steel), but a substitute has yet to satisfy both groups fully. Aquatic birds will continue swallowing grinding materials; the question is whether they will continue to poison themselves by swallowing lead.

SEE: Flamingo Feeding, p. 43; Metallic Poisons, p. 137; Pellets, p. 297; Eating Feathers, p. 13; Determining Diets, p. 535; Diet and Nutrition, p. 587; Metabolism, p. 325. REFS: Barrentin, 1980; Jenkinson and Mengel, 1970; Rundle, 1982; Sanderson and Bellrose, 1986.

Bird Milk

Like mammals, the young of some birds are fed on special secretions from a parent. Unlike mammals, however, both sexes produce it. The best known of these secretions is the "crop milk" that pigeons feed to squabs. The milk is produced by a sloughing of fluid-filled cells from the lining of the crop, a thin-walled, saclike food-storage chamber that projects outward from the bottom of the esophagus. Crops are presumably a device for permitting birds to gather and store food rapidly, minimizing the time that they are exposed to predators. Crops tend to be especially well developed in pigeons and game birds.

Crop milk is extremely nutritious. In one study, domestic chicks given feed containing pigeon crop milk were 16 percent heavier at the end of the experiment than chicks that did not receive the supplement. The pigeon milk, which contains more protein and fat than does cow or human milk, is the exclusive food of the nestlings for several days after hatching, and both adults feed it to the squabs for more than two weeks. The young pigeons are not fed insects as are the chicks of many seed-eating birds; instead, the crop milk provides the critical ration of protein.

The milk of Greater Flamingos contains much more fat and much less protein than does pigeon milk, and its production is not localized in a crop, but involves glands lining the entire upper digestive tract. Interestingly, the milk contains an abundance of red and white blood cells, which can be seen under the microscope migrating like amoebas through the surface of the glands. Young flamingos feed exclusively on this milk for about two months, while the special filter-feeding apparatus that they will later employ for foraging develops.

Emperor Penguin chicks may also be fed milk in some circumstances. Each male incubates a single egg on his feet, covered with a fold of abdominal skin, for two months of the Antarctic winter, fasting while the female is

Red-billed Pigeon

Columba flavirostris Wagler

NG–224; G–166; PW–pl 23; AE–604; AM(II)–138

6′–30′

MF

○

1
(1–2)
MONOG

MF(?)
I: ? DAYS
ALTRICIAL
F: ? DAYS
MF(?)

NUTS
FRUIT

GROUND
GLEAN

BREEDING: Heavily wooded areas near water. >1? broods. **DISPLAYS:** ? **NEST:** Usu at fork of horizontal branch; sparse, shallow structure of crossed twigs, lined with weed stems, grass, rootlets. **EGGS:** White, unmarked. 1.5″ (38 mm). **DIET:** Not well known: nuts, esp acorns, berries appear to be mainstays. Young presumably fed crop milk for 2–3 weeks. **CONSERVATION:** Winter resident. **NOTES:** Solitary or gregarious, occ seen in flocks of 20–50. Adult distraction display: bird drops from nest, flutters and flaps wings. Said to be largely arboreal. Breeding biology virtually unknown. **ESSAYS:** Drinking, p. 123; Bird Milk, p. 271; Hawk-Eyed, p. 229; Distraction Displays, p. 115; How Do We Find Out About Bird Biology?, p. 319. **REF:** Goodwin, 1983.

White-crowned Pigeon

Columba leucocephala Linnaeus

NG–224; G–166; PE–180; AE–pl 328; AM(II)–138

0′–15′
(0′–30′)

MF(?)

○

2
(1–2)
MONOG

MF
I: ? DAYS
ALTRICIAL
F: 21 DAYS
MF(?)

BREEDING: Mangrove islets and swamps in s FL. 1–3 broods. **DISPLAYS:** Male advertising call in early A.M.: stands erect, bill closed, throat inflated, emits series of low-pitched notes. Male struts before female. **NEST:** Usu at fork of horizontal branch; shallow, of loosely crossed twigs, lined with grass, rootlets. Occ on ground. **EGGS:** White, unmarked. 1.4″ (37 mm). **DIET:** Variety of tropical fruit, berries. Young fed crop milk for 3 days, then milk-fruit mixture. **CONSERVATION:** Winters s on Caribbean islands esp Bahamas, Cuba, Hispaniola, and s to w Panama; a few remain in FL. Dredging and filling have reduced habitat, clearing of important food plant (poisonwood) has reduced breeding season foods. Poaching in Bahamas and elsewhere poses major threat. **NOTES:** Nests in colonies in coastal mangroves, usu one nest per tree. Birds move inland daily to feed on fruit. Female incubates at night, male during day. Red-winged Blackbirds oft destroy eggs and chicks in unattended nests. Highly arboreal. Distribution and timing of seasonal movements tied to availability of tropical fruits. **ESSAYS:** Passenger Pigeon, p. 273; Bird Milk, p. 271; Brood Patches, p. 427; Who Incubates?, p. 27; Coloniality, p. 173. **REFS:** Goodwin, 1983; Kale, 1978; Laycock, 1987.

out at sea feeding. If the female has not returned with food by the time the chick hatches, the male feeds it for a few days on milk secreted by the esophagus. After its brief diet of milk, the chick will be fed by regurgitation alternately by the male and female as they travel one at a time to the sea to hunt.

Thus three very different groups of birds have evolved the capacity to produce milk as solutions to very different problems: the need for protein and fat in the pigeons, which feed very little animal material to the squabs; the need for liquid food consumption during the development of the specialized feeding apparatus of the flamingos (which would make any other form of food difficult for the chicks to ingest); and the need for a convenient food supplement when breeding on the barren Antarctic ice shelf favored by penguins.

SEE: Flamingo Feeding, p. 43; Brood Patches, p. 427; Urban Birds; p. 629.   REFS: Hegde, 1973; Lang, 1963.

The Passenger Pigeon

In all probability, the Passenger Pigeon was once the most abundant bird on the planet. Accounts of its numbers sound like something out of Alfred Hitchcock's *The Birds* and strain our credulity today. Alexander Wilson, the father of scientific ornithology in America, estimated that one flock consisted of two billion birds. Wilson's rival, John James Audubon, watched a flock pass overhead for three days and estimated that at times more than 300 million pigeons flew by him each hour. Elongated nesting colonies several miles wide could reach a length of *forty miles*. In these colonies, droppings were thick enough to kill the forest understory.

Passenger Pigeons were denizens of the once great deciduous forests of the eastern United States. The birds provided an easily harvested resource for native Americans and early settlers. To obtain dinner in the nesting season one needed only to wander into a colony and pluck some of the fat squabs that had fallen or been knocked from their nests. Audubon wrote in his classic *Birds of America*, "The pigeons were picked up and piled in heaps, until each [hunter] had as many as he could possibly dispose of, when the hogs were let loose to feed on the remainder."

Market hunters prospered, devising a wide variety of techniques for slaughtering the pigeons and collecting their succulent squabs. Adults were baited with alcohol-soaked grain (which made them drunk and easy to catch), and suffocated by fires of grass or sulfur that were lit below their nests. To attract their brethren, captive pigeons, their eyes sewn shut, were set up as decoys on small perches called stools (which is the origin of the term stool pigeon for one who betrays colleagues). Squabs were knocked from nests with long poles, trees were chopped down or were set on fire to

Rock Dove

Columba livia Gmelin

NG–224; G–166; PE–180; PW–pl 23; AE–pl 327; AW–pl 346; AM(II)–136

BUILDING			MF I: 16–19 DAYS		
CLIFF	F – M	2 (1–2) MONOG	ALTRICIAL F: 25–26 DAYS MF		

BREEDING: Cities, towns, rural areas, but always near human habitations. 4–5 or more broods. **DISPLAYS:** Courting male inflates neck, spreads tail, and with much bowing accompanied by polysyllabic cooing, pursues female on ground, following and circling around her. **NEST:** On building ledge, under eaves, under bridges, etc.; rarely on cliff ledge, the presumed ancestral type of nest site. Loose saucer of roots, stems, leaves, etc., no lining. **EGGS:** White, unmarked. 1.6" (39 mm). **DIET:** Esp grain, occ green leaves, inverts. Young initially fed crop milk. **CONSERVATION:** Winter resident. Introduced. **NOTES:** Gregarious, oft seen in flocks when roosting, feeding or flying; prefer to breed in groups. Impressive flight capability, marked by much gliding and wheeling; oft glide to landing. May breed at 6 months. Young brooded for 7 days. Urban feeding groups are not closed flocks; individuals sample many feeding sites, temporarily adopting particularly good sites. Marked individual feeding preferences. **ESSAYS:** Bird Milk, p. 271; Navigation and Orientation, p. 559; Urban Birds, p. 629; Feral Birds, p. 654; Monogamy, p. 597. **REFS:** Cramp, 1985; Giraldeau and Lefebvre, 1985; Lefebvre, 1985.

Passenger Pigeon

Ectopistes migratorius Linnaeus

(Extinct: not in field guides)

			MF I: 13 DAYS		
			ALTRICIAL		
10'–50'	MF	1 MONOG	F: 13–15 DAYS MF	SEEDS INSECTS	FOLIAGE GLEAN

BREEDING: In crowded colonies in beech woods; probably 1 brood, perhaps occ 2. **DISPLAYS:** Male sidled up to female on branches, pressed close. Some flapping of half-spread wings, cooing. **NEST:** Up to hundreds of crude frail structures supported in branching forks, occ causing trees to collapse. **EGGS:** White. 1.5" (38 mm). **DIET:** Primarily mast—beechnuts, acorns, chestnuts, other forest nuts and fruits, berries, grain, and grass seeds, supplemented with insects, earthworms, other inverts. Natural salt licks oft visited. Young fed crop milk. **CONSERVATION:** Forced to extinction by market hunters. Native Americans never killed nesting adults, and never killed in excess of anticipated need. **NOTES:** Migrations not well documented, but winter range was apparently restricted, with AR the northern boundary. **ESSAYS:** Passenger Pigeon, p. 273; Bird Milk, p. 271; Birds and the Law, p. 293; Our Only Native Parrot, p. 279; Communal Roosting, p. 615; Coloniality, p. 173; Bird Droppings, p. 263. **REFS:** Goodwin, 1983; Schorger, 1955.

Old magazine illustration of hunters shooting passenger pigeons. Note the density of the flight. (From copy in Schorger, 1955.)

make the squabs jump from nests. Disruption of the colonies was so severe that wholesale nest abandonment was common and breeding success much reduced.

So successful were the market hunters that pigeons became cheap enough for use as live targets in shooting galleries. Laws intended to protect the pigeons did not help. In 1886 an editor's note in *Forest and Stream* said:

> When the birds appear all the male inhabitants of the neighborhood leave their customary occupations as farmers, bark-peelers, oil-scouts, wild-catters, and tavern loafers, and join in the work of capturing and marketing the game. The Pennsylvania law very plainly forbids the destruction of the pigeons on their nesting grounds, but no one pays any attention to the law, and the nesting birds have been killed by thousands and tens of thousands.

As railroads penetrated the upper Middle West after the Civil War, many millions of pigeons were shipped to cities along the Atlantic seaboard, since, by then, clearing of oak and beech forests and hunting had already exterminated the birds on the East Coast. Extinction of the Passenger Pigeon came with stunning rapidity. Michigan was its last stronghold; about three million birds were shipped east from there by a single hunter in 1878. Eleven years later, 1889, the species was extinct in that state. Although small groups of pigeons were held in various places in captivity, efforts to maintain those flocks failed. The last known individual of the species, a female named Martha, died in 1914 in the Cincinnati Zoo and is now on display in the U.S. National Museum of Natural History.

Of course, market hunting ended as soon as harvesting the birds was

Common Ground-Dove
Columbina passerina Linnaeus

NG–228; G–168; PE–180; PW–pl 23; AE–pl 325; AW–pl 344; AM(II)–146

SHRUB   FM?   2   MF   BERRIES
0'–12'   (2–3)   I: 12–14 DAYS
            MONOG   ALTRICIAL
                    F: 11 DAYS
                    MF

BREEDING: Woodland edge, open country with trees, sandy cultivated fields, suburbs. 2–4 broods. **DISPLAYS:** Courtship: male struts in front of female, puffing out feathers and bowing head, softly cooing. **NEST:** Very flimsy, simple, almost flat, of a few loose sticks, grass, rootlets; also slight depression in ground with little or no lining. Occ reuse nest for subsequent broods. **EGGS:** White, unmarked. 0.8″ (22 mm). **DIET:** Little known; seeds, berries, few insects. Young presumably fed crop milk. **CONSERVATION:** Winter resident. Rare cowbird host. **NOTES:** Very terrestrial, as name implies. Walks briskly, nodding head. Oft forage in small groups. Flocks in winter. **ESSAYS:** Bird Milk, p. 271; Wing Shapes and Flight, p. 227; How Do We Find Out About Bird Biology?, p. 319; Determining Diets, p. 535. **REFS:** Goodwin, 1983; Phillips et al., 1964.

Inca Dove
Columbina inca Lesson

NG–228; G–168; PE–180; PW–pl 23; AE–pl 326; AW–pl 345; AM(II)–144

10'–12'   FM?   2   MF
(4'–25')   MONOG   I: 14 DAYS
GROUND   ALTRICIAL
                       F: 14–16 DAYS
                       MF

BREEDING: Woodland edge, open country with trees, riparian thickets, scrub, around cultivated fields, esp cities and suburbs, mostly in arid or semiarid areas. 2–5 broods. **DISPLAYS:** Courtship: male struts in front of female, cooing, bows with tail held vertically and fanned. Males engage in furious combat. **NEST:** Compact, shallow, of sticks, twigs, grass, rootlets, unlined or lined with grass. Occ refurbishes nests of other birds. **EGGS:** White, unmarked. 0.9″ (22 mm). **DIET:** Little known; primarily seeds. Young presumably fed crop milk. Drinking water required. **CONSERVATION:** Winter resident. **NOTES:** Outer wing feathers produce characteristic buzzing sound in flight. Gathers in winter flocks of up to 50. In winter roosts communally in conif trees and shrubs, decid trees, building ledges, etc., oft lowering nocturnal body temperatures. On cold winter days, groups up to 12 occ closely huddle in "pyramids" with birds perched in 2 or 3 tiers on backs of those on limb or ledge. **ESSAYS:** Temperature Regulation, p. 149; Bird Milk, p. 271; Drinking, p. 123; Communal Roosting, p. 615; Nonvocal Sounds, p. 313. **REFS:** Goodwin, 1983; Johnston, 1960; Quay, 1982; Robertson and Schnapf, 1987.

no longer economically profitable. That point was reached when tens of thousands of the birds still flew within large stretches of suitable habitat. Much of that habitat still exists today, although many of the largest nut-producing trees that were common in the heyday of the pigeon were logged. Why, then, did the birds go extinct? No one knows for sure, but it appears that to survive they needed to nest in vast colonies. Perhaps this permitted them to "swamp" predators with their enormous numbers, so that the relatively few predators in the area of a roost were unable to make a significant dent in the huge breeding colonies. And since these colonies dispersed as soon as breeding was over, predators were prevented from building up their populations on the basis of such an ephemeral resource. In any case, the fate of the Passenger Pigeon illustrates a very important principle of conservation biology: it is not always necessary to kill the last pair of a species to force it to extinction.

Sad to say, the lesson of the Passenger Pigeon has not been learned. At the present time the White-crowned Pigeon is threatened by the horrendous slaughter of nesting birds on its Caribbean breeding grounds.

SEE: Saving a Subspecies, p. 571; Conservation of the California Condor, p. 219; The Northern Penguin, p. 199; Island Biogeography, p. 549; The Decline of Eastern Songbirds, p. 495. REFS: Blockstein and Tordoff, 1985; Brisbin, 1968; Schorger, 1955.

Bird Biologist—Alexander Wilson

Alexander Wilson (1766–1813) was one of the two fathers of North American ornithology. The other was John James Audubon (p. 413). Wilson got started before Audubon, arriving in the U.S. from his native Scotland in 1794 and shooting a Red-headed Woodpecker on his first day. He roamed the eastern states collecting bird specimens and making detailed observations on the biology of the species he encountered. His own field work and the observations of a growing army of bird watchers provided the basis for his classic work, nine large volumes entitled *American Ornithology; or, the Natural History of the Birds of the United States,* which was published between 1808 and 1814, the last two volumes posthumously. Both his taxonomic work and observations have stood the test of time much better than those of his more famous rival.

REF: Kastner, 1986.

White-tipped Dove

Leptotila verreauxi Bonaparte

NG–228; G–168; PW–pl 23; AE–pl 324; AM(II)–146

| 5'–12' | FM? | 2 MONOG | ? I: 14 DAYS ALTRICIAL F: ? DAYS MF | FRUIT | FOLIAGE GLEAN |

BREEDING: Riparian woodland and adjacent cultivated areas. ? broods. **DISPLAYS:** ? **NEST:** At fork of inclined branch; flimsy, usu of crossed sticks and twigs or grass, weed stems, etc. **EGGS:** Creamy buff when laid, fading to dull white, unmarked. 1.2" (31 mm). **DIET:** Little known; probably incl berries. Young presumably fed crop milk. **CONSERVATION:** Winter resident. **NOTES:** Highly terrestrial; forages under dense cover. Little studied. Formerly known as White-fronted Dove. **ESSAYS:** Drinking, p. 123; Bird Milk, p. 271; How Do We Find Out About Bird Biology?, p. 319. **REF:** Goodwin, 1983.

Mourning Dove

Zenaida macroura Linnaeus

NG–226; G–166; PE–180; PW–pl 23; AE–pl 322; AW–pl 349; AM(II)–142

| CONIF GROUND 0'–40' | MF | 2 (2–3) MONOG | MF I: 13–14 DAYS ALTRICIAL F: 12–14 DAYS MF | GRAIN | FOLIAGE GLEAN |

BREEDING: Desert (near water) to open woodland, agricultural areas with scattered trees, suburbs. Typically 2–3, but occ 3–6 broods. **DISPLAYS:** Courtship: male performs gliding, spiraling aerial display over female with wingtips held below body; on ground struts before female with feathers spread and head nodding. **NEST:** In fork of horizontal tree branch, on ground, on deserted nest of other species, or anywhere else providing solid support; flimsy, usu of crossed sticks and twigs (occ grass, weed stems) lined with fine materials. Female builds but male brings materials. Built in 1–3 days; oft reused. **EGGS:** White, unmarked. 1.1" (28 mm). **DIET:** Seeds, incl waste grain from cultivated fields, compose >99% of diet. Young fed crop milk for 3 days, then also seeds; entirely seeds by 6–8 days. **CONSERVATION:** Winters s to c Panama. Rare host of both cowbird species. Range expanding northward. **NOTES:** Champion of multiple-brooding among N.A. birds. Most abundant dove in N.A.; most widely hunted and harvested game bird. Pair bonds occ persist >1 nesting season. Flock for much of year, but not colonial breeder. Eggs always covered: male incubates most of day, female remainder of day, all night. Clutches of 3–4 likely due to brood parasitism by another Mourning Dove. Males produce crop milk 4–6 days longer than females. **ESSAYS:** Visual Displays, p. 5; Feeding Birds, p. 349; Bird Milk, p. 271; Who Incubates?, p. 27; Range Expansion, p. 459; Brood Parasitism, p. 287. **REFS:** Leopold et al., 1981; Leopold and Dedon, 1983; Westmoreland et al., 1986.

Our Only Native Parrot

The famous Passenger Pigeon is not the only North American bird that once flocked in large numbers that has gone extinct in historic times. The Carolina Parakeet (or, as it was sometimes called by Europeans, the "Illinois Parrot") declined and disappeared from the same eastern American forests on about the same schedule. The parakeet, the only member of the parrot family native to the United States, was a beautiful bird with a yellow head and orange mask, green body, and bluish wings and tail. Had they been just beautiful, they might have lasted, but they were also abundant agricultural pests. John James Audubon wrote in the mid-1800s:

> The stacks of grain put up in the field are resorted to by flocks of these birds, which frequently cover them so entirely, that they present to the eye the same effect as if a brilliantly coloured carpet had been thrown over them. . . . They assail the pear and apple trees, when the fruit is yet very small and far from being ripe.

Farmers naturally objected to these activities and hunted the parakeets in earnest. Both Audubon and that other pioneer student of North American bird biology, Alexander Wilson, commented on a trait of the parakeets that helped seal their doom—flocks would return to fallen comrades, perhaps to mob the "predator." Wilson described this behavior:

> Having shot down a number, some of which were only wounded, the whole flock swept repeatedly around their prostrate companions, and again settled on a low tree, within twenty yards of the spot where I stood. At each successive discharge, tho showers of them fell, yet the affection of the survivors seemed rather to increase; for after a few circuits around the place, they again alighted near me, looking down on their slaughtered companions with such manifest symptoms of sympathy and concern, as entirely disarmed me.

The parakeets were also hunted for "sport" and trapped for sale as cage birds. As is so often the case in the ongoing extinction story, habitat destruction and degradation probably played a role in their demise as well. It also has been suggested that the importation of honeybees may have helped them on their way. The bees occupied holes that the parakeets needed for nests, and honey collectors cut down old trees with nest cavities. Nevertheless, large stretches of riverine forest, the preferred parakeet habitat, persist to this day, as do other hole-nesting eastern birds. Thus it may be that, like the Passenger Pigeon, the Carolina Parakeet simply faded away when it became too scarce to form large social groups that were essential to its survival. The last known survivor died, like Martha the last Passenger Pigeon, in the Cincinnati Zoo. It passed away in 1914.

Ironically, there are now several members of the parrot family living in

White-winged Dove
Zenaida asiatica Linnaeus

NG–226; G–166; PE–180; PW–pl 23; AE–pl 321; AW–pl 348; AM(II)–142

4'–25'

MF

2
(1–4)
MONOG

MF
I: 13–14 DAYS
ALTRICIAL
F: 13–16 DAYS
MF

FRUIT

FOLIAGE
GLEAN

BREEDING: Riparian woodland or thickets (esp mesquite) in arid areas. 2 or 3 broods. **DISPLAYS:** Courtship: male raises tail high and tips body forward, then quickly spreads and closes tail, flashing prominent black and white pattern; also performs circling aerial display with stiff wings. **NEST:** At fork of inclined branch (oft mesquite in w), or atop deserted nest of other species; flimsy, usu of crossed sticks and twigs or grass, weed stems. Female selects site and builds in 2–4 days; male brings nest materials. Occ reused. **EGGS:** Creamy buff to white, unmarked. 1.2" (31 mm). **DIET:** Incl waste grain from cultivated fields, cactus fruit, berries, acorns. Young fed crop milk, plus seeds after 4 days. **CONSERVATION:** Winters s to Costa Rica. **NOTES:** Nesting varies from isolated pairs to extensive colonies. Flees nest readily, rarely performs distraction display. Incubation by male in day, female midafternoon through night. May fly long distances from breeding colony to forage and drink. Gregarious, feeding in large flocks, esp after breeding; roosts in nesting trees. Desert populations rely largely on cactus fruit for water. **ESSAYS:** Drinking, p. 123; Bird Milk, p. 271; Distraction Displays, p. 115; Who Incubates?, p. 27. **REFS:** Cottam and Trefethen, 1968; Leopold et al., 1981.

Carolina Parakeet
Conuropsis carolinensis Linnaeus

(Extinct: not in field guides, see fig., p. 281)

5'–30'

?

2–3
?

?
I: 19–20(?) DAYS
ALTRICIAL
F: 18–19(?) DAYS
?

FRUIT

BREEDING: Riverine forest, cypress swamps and decid woodland, foraging in open habitats incl cultivated lands and gardens. ? broods. **DISPLAYS:** ? **NEST:** Mostly in decid, occ conif, trees with up to 50 nests per tree. Ornithologists never examined nest in wild. Reportedly placed in abandoned chip-lined or unlined cavities, incl woodpecker holes. **EGGS:** White. 1.4" (34 mm). **DIET:** Seeds from wide variety of fruit, esp apple, peach, etc., also mulberry, pecan, grape, dogwood, grains. Before agriculture, seeds of grass, maple, elm, pine, etc. **CONSERVATION:** Extinct. Maintained 20 years, bred successfully in Cincinnati Zoo; last one died 1914. Considered agricultural pest before 1900. Coveted as game bird, as cage bird, and for plumage. **NOTES:** At night roosted communally in hollow trees, as many as 30 per tree; if hollow too crowded, some hung on outside. **ESSAYS:** Our Only Native Parrot, p. 279; Avian Invaders, p. 633; Communal Roosting, p. 615; Birds and the Arts, p.47. **REF:** Greenway, 1967.

the United States, such as the Australian Budgerigar, the South American Monk Parakeet, and the Mexican Yellow-headed Parrot. Escaped cage birds of these and other parrot species have established free-living colonies in Florida and southern California. They symbolize a thriving commercial traffic in these beautiful and intelligent birds which endangers many other members of the parrot family. In the twelve months ending September 1984, 913,653 birds were legally imported into the United States, many of them parrots. And for every three parrots that enter legally, one is smuggled in. Profits can be high—a smuggler buying a Palm Cockatoo for $650 in Indonesia in 1983 could sell it for $10,000 to $15,000 in the United States.

The brute figures on importing, legal and illegal, show only the tip of the iceberg. Many birds are injured and killed (or their nesting disturbed) in the process of capture, and many die in transit. For example, about one in four of the Crimson Rosellas imported into the United States from Australia dies in route. The best way to protect these birds in the wild is to pass national legislation forbidding the sale of wild-caught birds, while encouraging breeding of parrots for sale. Such legislation is already on the books in New York State. Birds reared by aviculturalists will be fitted with seamless leg bands placed on them when they are young, providing a snug fit and revealing mark to distinguish them from illegal, wild-caught birds. Such a program would greatly reduce the smuggling trade, promote aviculture, and help guard parrots and other birds from the fate of the Carolina Parakeet— although many tropical species would still be greatly at risk from deforestation.

SEE: The Passenger Pigeon, p. 273; Heath Hens and Population Sizes, p. 257; The Northern Penguin, p. 199; Disappearing Ivorybill, p. 357; Plume Trade, p. 37; The Labrador Duck, p. 85; Feral Birds, p. 654; Conservation of the California Condor, p. 219. REFS: Audubon, 1842; Halliday, 1978; Turner, 1985; Wilson, 1811.

Carolina Parakeets feeding in a pear orchard.

Elegant Trogon

Trogon elegans Gould

NG–232; G–192; PW–pl 38; AW–pl 457; AM(II)–214

| 12'–40' | ? | 3–4 | ?
I: ? DAYS | FRUIT | HOVER & |
| BANK | | (2–4)
? | ALTRICIAL
F: ? DAYS
? | | GLEAN |

BREEDING: Open woodland, pine-oak association, scrub, usu in arid or semiarid habitats, occ in humid woodland. ? broods. **DISPLAYS:** ? **NEST:** In tree hollow (esp sycamore) abandoned woodpecker hole, and earthen bank. Lined with straw, trash, moss, wool, vines, thistledown, down, and feathers. **EGGS:** White/light bluish-white. 1.1" (29 mm). **DIET:** Wide variety of flying insects; fruit. **CONSERVATION:** Winter resident. **NOTES:** Young are silent. Pairs roost together in dense veg. Breeding biology unknown. Formerly known as Coppery-tailed Trogon. **ESSAYS:** Color of Birds, p. 111; How Do We Find Out About Bird Biology?, p. 319. **REF:** Phillips et al., 1964.

Smooth-billed Ani

Crotophaga ani Linnaeus

NG–234; G–172; PE–182; AE–pl 577; AM(II)–154

| 6'–30' | MF+ | 2–4
COOP | MF+
I: 14 DAYS
ALTRICIAL
F: ? DAYS
MF+ | SMALL
VERTS
FRUIT | |

BREEDING: Open brushland or scrub, open woodland, fields, plantations, usu near water. ? broods. **DISPLAYS:** ? **NEST:** Usu low in tree. Large, loosely constructed twig mass, lined with leaves. **EGGS:** Blue. 1.4" (35 mm). **DIET:** Incl esp lizards, also cattle parasites, snails; berries, seeds. Capture lizards from veg above ground, as well as from ground. **CONSERVATION:** Winter resident. Apparently declining, perhaps due to habitat loss. **NOTES:** Live in groups containing 1 or more monogamous pairs on year-round territories; groups easily approached. All group members contribute to nest building, rearing young, and defense of territory. Breeding pairs within group lay eggs in communal nest. May breed opportunistically in response to food availability. Known to steal food from Gray Kingbird. **ESSAYS:** Cooperative Breeding, p. 283; Monogamy, p. 597; Breeding Season, p. 55; Piracy, p. 159. **REF:** Vehrencamp, 1978.

Cooperative Breeding

"Cooperative" or "communal" breeding occurs when more than two birds of the same species provide care in rearing the young from one nest. About 3 percent (approximately 300 species) of bird species worldwide are cooperative breeders. There are two types of cooperative arrangements: those in which mature nonbreeders ("helpers-at-the-nest" or "auxiliaries") help protect and rear the young, but are not parents of any of them, and those where there is some degree of shared parentage of offspring. Cooperative breeders may exhibit shared maternity, shared paternity, or both.

The best-studied North American cooperative breeders, the Scrub Jay, Gray-breasted (Mexican) Jay, Groove-billed Ani, and Acorn Woodpecker, differ from each other in the details of their breeding biology. Scrub Jays in Florida represent a group of populations that probably were once in contact with the widespread western populations but are now totally isolated. Only in Florida are Scrub Jays cooperative breeders, and there they reside in permanent, group-defended territories. Ornithologists Glen Woolfenden and John Fitzpatrick have found that groups consist of a permanently bonded monogamous pair and one to six helpers, generally the pair's offspring of previous seasons. About half the territories are occupied by pairs without helpers, and most other pairs have only one or two helpers. Although pairing and breeding can occur after one year spent as a helper, birds often spend several years as nonbreeding auxiliaries. Males may remain in this subsidiary role for up to six years; females generally disperse and pair after one or two years of helping. Helpers participate in all nonsexual activities except nest construction, egg laying, and incubation. Pairs with helpers are more successful—they fledge one and a half times more young than pairs without helpers.

Florida Scrub Jays are largely restricted to the scattered and now much reduced oak scrub habitat; reproductive success outside of oak scrub is very poor. All available habitat is occupied, and populations appear to be stable from year to year, which means young birds are unlikely to find vacant space to set up territories of their own. In contrast, western Scrub Jays generally are not space-limited, and the probability of a young bird leaving home and finding a territory in which to breed is high.

Like the Florida Scrub Jay, the closely related Gray-breasted Jay of the southwestern U.S. lives in permanent group-defended territories, and breeding adults are monogamous. Studies by ethologist Jerram Brown and his colleagues have shown that the cooperative system of this species is more complex than that of its southeastern relatives in several ways. Gray-breasted Jay groups are much larger, ranging from 8 to 18 individuals; thus, they usually include offspring from more than just the preceding year. Within each group, two and sometimes three breeding pairs nest separately but simultaneously each season, and some interference among them often occurs. Interference usually involves the theft of nest-lining materials, but can include the tossing of eggs from nests by females of rival nests. Al-

Groove-billed Ani

Crotophaga sulcirostris Swainson

NG–234; G–172; PE–182; PW–pl 38; AE–pl 578; AM(II)–154

6'–12'
(2'–25')

MF+

3–4
(3–8)
COOP

MF+
I: 13–14 DAYS
ALTRICIAL
F: 7 DAYS
MF+

SMALL
VERTS
FRUIT

BREEDING: Scrub, cultivated lands, savanna, marshes. Occ 2 broods. **DISPLAYS:** Male feeds female in courtship. Reverse mounting occurs. **NEST:** Bulky, loose, of twigs, lined with leaves picked green. Built in 3–21 days. **EGGS:** Blue. 1.2″ (31 mm). Placement within nest can determine viability. **DIET:** Incl cattle parasites; berries. **CONSERVATION:** Winters within U.S. **NOTES:** Live in groups of 1–4 monogamous pairs, oft with an additional male or female helper, on permanent year-round territories. All group members contribute to nest building, rearing young, and territorial defense. All females in group usu breed, laying their eggs in communal nest. Females attempt to toss each other's eggs from the nest. All group members incubate singly, but dominant male does all nighttime incubation and brooding. Young leave nest after 6 days and stop returning to it to sleep after 1 week; short flight possible after 10 days, can fully fly at ca. 17 days. Young disperse at 6–9 months. **ESSAYS:** Cooperative Breeding, p. 283; Monogamy, p. 597; Courtship Feeding, p. 181. **REFS:** Vehrencamp, 1977, 1978.

Greater Roadrunner

Geococcyx californianus Lesson

NG–236; G–172; PE–182; PW–pl 38; AE–pl 271; AW–pl 264; AM(II) –152

SHRUB
CACTUS
3'–15'

?

4–6
MONOG

M –F
I: 20 DAYS
ALTRICIAL
F: 18 DAYS
MF

MAMMALS
REPTILES

BREEDING: Desert scrub, chaparral, edge of cultivated land, arid open areas with scattered brush, pine-oak woodland. Occ 2 broods. **DISPLAYS:** Male parades with head held high and stiff, wings and tail drooped; precedes male mating song. Male also bows, alternately lifts and drops wings while spreading tail. **NEST:** Usu in low tree, thicket, or cactus clump. Of sticks, lined with leaves, grass, feathers, mesquite pod, snakeskin, roots, and manure flakes. Occ atop woodrat nest. **EGGS:** White with chalky yellowish coat. 1.5″ (39 mm). **DIET:** Animals (90%) incl insects, lizards, snakes, rodents, birds (esp passerines); fruit (esp cactus), seeds. **CONSERVATION:** Winter resident. **NOTES:** Performs distraction display to protect nest. Pair bond may be permanent; pairs territorial all year. Male does most of incubation, esp at night; nocturnally incubating males maintain normal body temperatures, but females and nonbreeding males drop their body temperature to as low as 33° C to save energy. Young hatch asynchronously; catch their own food within 3 weeks. Generated large folklore incl reputation for encircling rattlesnakes with cactus spine fence upon which they impale. Run 15 mph. **ESSAYS:** Feet, p. 239; Birds and the Arts, p. 47; Temperature Regulation, p. 149; Distraction Displays, p. 115; Monogamy, p. 597; Who Incubates?, p. 27. **REFS:** Ohmart, 1973; Vehrencamp, 1982; Whitson, 1975.

though the laying female does all the incubating, she is fed on the nest both by her mate and by auxiliaries. Nestlings receive more than half of their feedings from auxiliaries.

Although the Groove-billed Ani breeds in southern Texas, our knowledge of its breeding biology comes from the work of sociobiologist Sandra Vehrencamp and her colleagues who studied the species in Costa Rica. The groups defending permanent territories consist of one to four monogamous breeding pairs that occasionally include an unpaired helper. All members of the group participate in building a single nest into which all females lay their eggs. Incubation and care of the young are shared by all members of the group. Beyond a certain clutch size, some eggs tend to be buried and fail to receive proper incubation, leading to a decreased probability of any given egg hatching.

Unlike the "cooperative" breeders that they appear to be, female anis engage in behaviors that increase the probability of their own eggs being the successful ones in the communal clutch. The most effective of these behaviors is the tossing of other females' eggs from the nest. In spite of the increased competition and conflict, multipair groups manage to fledge more young per individual than do single pairs in similar habitats.

Long-term studies of Acorn Woodpeckers have been conducted by a succession of ornithologists, including M. H. and B. R. MacRoberts, Walter Koenig, Ron Mumme, and Frank Pitelka at the University of California's Hastings Natural History Reservation in central coastal California. There Acorn Woodpecker groups are composed of up to 15 members whose territories are based on the defense and maintenance of granaries in which they store acorns. Groups consist largely of siblings, their cousins, and their parents. Some of the sexually mature birds are non-breeding helpers. Within each group, up to four males may mate with one (or occasionally two) females, and all eggs are laid in a single nest. Thus paternity and sometimes maternity of the communal clutch is shared.

Per capita reproductive success generally increases with group size up to 7 or 8 members, and then declines. Clutches produced by two females are somewhat less successful than those of single females due to behavioral interference between the two females and some egg tossing. Although there is some geographic variation in the size of groups and other aspects of the Acorn Woodpecker system, it breeds cooperatively throughout its range.

Why has evolution produced cooperative breeding systems? Initial hypotheses were based on kin selection (seemingly "selfless" behavior like helping at the nest being favored because it increases the reproductive success of relatives genetically similar to the helper) or on maximizing of reproductive output. As more cooperatively breeding species have been examined worldwide, these explanations generally have not been supported. Instead, cooperative systems appear to arise when environmental constraints force birds into breeding groups because the opportunities for younger birds to breed independently are severely limited. Limitations may include a shortage of territory openings because higher quality habitats are saturated with

Yellow-billed Cuckoo

Coccyzus americanus Linnaeus

NG–236; G–172; PE–182; PW–pl 38; AE–pl 522; AW–pl 562; AM(II)–150

SHRUB	MF	4	MF		HOVER &
4′–8′		(1–8)	I: 9–11 DAYS		GLEAN
(3′–20′)		MONOG?	ALTRICIAL		HAWKS
			F: 7–8 DAYS		
			MF		

BREEDING: Open woodland, esp with dense undergrowth, parks, riparian woodland and thickets. 1 brood, 2? in s. **DISPLAYS:** Courtship feeding: calling male alights by perched female, mounts shoulder, and places food in her bill. **NEST:** Unkempt, of twigs, lined with rootlets, dried leaves, rimmed with pine needles, etc. Incomplete at onset of laying. **EGGS:** Light blue fading to light greenish-yellow. 1.2″ (31 mm). **DIET:** Esp hairy caterpillars, also few bird eggs, frogs, lizards; berries, fruit. Young fed insect regurgitant. **CONSERVATION:** Winters n S.A. s to e Peru, Bolivia and n Argentina. Blue List 1972–81, 1986; w populations much reduced, proposed for Endangered status. Declining in most other areas, as well. **NOTES:** Occ parasitizes Black-billed Cuckoo, rarely other birds. Breeding oft coincides with outbreaks of cicadas, tent caterpillars, etc.; prey abundance may lead to production of excess eggs and thus to brood parasitism. Young hatch asynchronously. Egg-to-fledge time esp short; can climb about branches at ca. 1 week, fly at ca. 3 weeks. First fledglings attended by male, second by female. **ESSAYS:** Decline of Eastern Songbirds, p. 495; Brood Parasitism, p. 287; Blue List, p. 11; Courtship Feeding, p. 181; Breeding Season, p. 55; Birds and the Law, p. 293. **REFS:** Hamilton and Hamilton, 1965; Nolan and Thompson, 1975; Potter, 1980.

Black-billed Cuckoo

Coccyzus erythropthalmus Wilson

NG–236; G–172; PE–182; PW–pl 38; AE–pl 521; AM(II)–150

?

SHRUB	MF?	2–3	MF		
2′–6′		(2–5)	I: 10–13 DAYS		
(0.2′–20′)		MONOG?	ALTRICIAL		
			F: 7–9 DAYS		
			MF		

BREEDING: Decid/conif forest and open woodland. ? broods. **DISPLAYS:** Courtship feeding. **NEST:** Placed horizontally against tree trunk, also on log, occ in vine tangle or on ground. Built of twigs, lined with ferns, grass, burrs, catkins, roots, etc. **EGGS:** Blue-green, occ marked with same. 1.1″ (27 mm). **DIET:** Esp hairy caterpillars, also takes mollusks, fish, small verts, bird eggs; fruit, berries. Young fed mostly caterpillars. **CONSERVATION:** Winters from n S.A. (also Trinidad) s to Ecuador, n Peru and c Bolivia. **NOTES:** Only rarely parasitic, laying in nest of Yellow-billed Cuckoo. Larger clutches apparently assoc with caterpillar outbreaks. Young hatch asynchronously. Egg-to-fledge time esp short; can leave nest and climb around branches at ca. 1 week, fly at ca. 3 weeks. When out of nest in tree or shrub, young assume erect motionless posture, with up-pointed bill when approached by predator (incl human!). **ESSAYS:** Decline of Eastern Songbirds, p. 495; Brood Parasitism, p. 287; Courtship Feeding, p. 181. **REFS:** Nolan and Thompson, 1975; Sealy, 1978, 1985.

established breeders; a shortage of sexual partners (generally females), indicated by the skewed sex ratios that are common in groups; and unpredictable availability of resources, which could make it too risky for individual pairs to commit themselves to reproduce in any given year. That cooperative breeding is a common strategy in arid and semiarid portions of Africa and Australia lends strong support to this line of reasoning. Cooperative breeding may be viewed primarily as a means by which young adults put off the start of their own breeding in order to maximize their lifetime reproductive output, and in the process occasionally promote genes identical with their own via kin selection.

SEE: Natural Selection, p. 237; Altruism, p. 453; Population Dynamics, p. 575. REFS: Brown, 1978, 1987; Emlen and Vehrencamp, 1983; Fitzpatrick and Woolfenden, 1984; Koenig et al., 1984; Skutch, 1987; Stacey and Koenig, 1984; Woolfenden and Fitzpatrick, 1978, 1984, 1986.

Brood Parasitism

Some species of birds thrive not by carefully rearing their own young, but by pawning that task off on adults of other species. The European Cuckoo, whose distinctive call is immortalized in the sound of the "cuckoo clock," is the bird in which this habit has been most thoroughly studied. Female European Cuckoos lay their eggs only in the nests of other species of birds. A cuckoo egg usually closely mimics the eggs of the host (one of whose eggs is often removed by the cuckoo). The host may recognize the intruding egg and abandon the nest, or it may incubate and hatch the cuckoo egg. Shortly after hatching, the young European Cuckoo, using a scooplike depression on its back, instinctively shoves over the edge of the nest any solid object that it contacts. With the disappearance of their eggs and rightful young, the foster parents are free to devte all of their care to the young cuckoo. Frequently this is an awesome task, since the cuckoo chick often grows much larger than the host adults long before it can care for itself. One of the tragicomic scenes in nature is a pair of small foster parents working like Sisyphus to keep up with thc voracious appetite of an outsized young cuckoo.

Interestingly, different females within a population of European Cuckoos often parasitize different host species. Some cuckoos may specialize in parasitizing the nests of Garden Warblers; others of the same population may lay in the nests of Reed Warblers, and yet others may lay in nests of White Wagtails. The eggs of each female very closely mimic those of the host selected (even though one host may have large, densely spotted eggs, and another may have smaller, unmarked pale blue eggs), and the mimetic patterns are genetically determined. The different genetic kinds of females (called "gentes") apparently mate at random with males. How these gentes are maintained within the cuckoo populations is not fully understood.

Mangrove Cuckoo

Coccyzus minor Gmelin

NG–236; G–172; PE–182; AE–pl 523; AM(II)–152

?   2

I: ? DAYS
ALTRICIAL
F: ? DAYS
?

?

BREEDING: Mangrove swamp, tropical hardwood forest, also scrub, open woodland. 2? broods. **DISPLAYS**: ? **NEST**: Flimsy, flat structure made of dry twigs. **EGGS**: Initially blue fading to light greenish-yellow. 1.2″ (31 mm). **DIET**: Also spiders, frogs; fruit, berries. **CONSERVATION**: Winters (mostly?) within U.S. Range may be expanding in FL. **NOTES**: Alights in tree at full speed. Reproductive biology essentially unknown. **ESSAY**: How Do We Find Out About Bird Biology?, p. 319. **REF**: Kale, 1978.

Common Barn-Owl

Tyto alba Scopoli

NG–238; G–176; PE–174; PW–120; AE–pl 291; AW–pl 302; AM(II)–156

BUILDING
CAVE

5–7
(3–11)
MONOG

F
I: 30–34 DAYS
SEMIALTRICIAL 2
F: 52–56 DAYS
MF

BIRDS

SWOOPS

BREEDING: Open and partly open habitats, esp grassland, farmland, oft in or near towns. 1, occ 2 broods. **DISPLAYS**: Male claps wings together in courtship flight; ritually presents food to female. **NEST**: Also in cliff crevice, occ excavate burrow in arroyo wall. Usu unlined, occ lined with wood chips, sticks, etc. **EGGS**: White, oft nest-stained. More elliptical than eggs of other owls. 1.7″ (43 mm). **DIET**: Mostly rodents (esp voles), rarely amphibians, reptiles, insects. Ejects pellets. **CONSERVATION**: Winters within U.S. Blue List 1972–81, Special Concern 1982–86; widely declining largely due to habitat loss as grassland and farmland reduced by suburbanization. Readily use nest boxes. **NOTES**: Clutch size reflects prey availability and severity of preceding winter; fledging success also low following severe winter. Male feeds female throughout incubation. Young hatch asynchronously, spanning up to 14 days. Male and female brood. Sway lowered head from side-to-side when confronted. Roosts diurnally, occ communally, leaving roost singly before sunset and circling upon departure. **ESSAYS**: How Owls Hunt in the Dark, p. 291; Pellets, p. 297; Blue List, p. 11; Brood Reduction, p. 307; Variation in Clutch Sizes, p. 339. **REFS**: Bunn et al., 1982; Colvin, 1985; Cramp, 1985; Earhart and Johnson, 1970; Marti and Wagner, 1985.

The North American Yellow-billed and Black-billed Cuckoos only rarely lay their eggs in the nests of other species, but occasionally lay some of their eggs in the nests of other members of their species. Our cuckoos usually build nests of their own and rear their own young. Only about 40 percent of cuckoo species worldwide are brood parasites, the rest care for their own eggs and young.

Brood parasitism is much less common in other groups of birds. It is found in about 1 percent of bird species, including members of such diverse groups as ducks, weavers, and cowbirds. In North America the only obligate brood parasites (those which must parasitize and cannot build nests of their own) are the Bronzed and Brown-headed Cowbirds, which may be important enemies of other birds. The Brown-headed Cowbird has been recorded as a parasite of more than 200 other species. Cowbird eggs do not closely mimic host eggs, nor do the young oust host eggs and young from the nest. But cowbirds do tend to hatch earlier than their hosts, to grow faster, and to crowd out or at least to reduce the food intake of the host's young.

Cowbirds thus can place powerful selection pressure on a host bird species to learn to recognize and reject cowbird eggs. Behaviorist Stephen Rothstein of the University of California at Santa Barbara has shown experimentally that some North American species have, indeed, learned to do this. He placed artificial and real Brown-headed Cowbird eggs in the nests of 43 other species, and found that those species divided rather neatly into "acceptor species" and "rejector species." Acceptors include many warblers, vireos, phoebes, and Song Sparrows, while robins, catbirds, Blue Jays, and Brown Thrashers are rejectors. The Song Sparrow just happens to have eggs very similar in size and spotting pattern to those of the cowbird, and almost invariably raises the cowbird young. In contrast, catbirds and robins, which lay unmarked blue eggs, almost invariably eject cowbird eggs from their nests. Phoebes, strangely, usually have unmarked eggs but are acceptors—perhaps their habit of nesting in dark recesses has reduced their awareness of egg pattern.

Rothstein found very little sign of transitional species—that is, ones with some individuals that accepted and others that rejected. The reason, he hypothesized, was that once the genetic ability to reject appeared in a species, it would spread very rapidly and very soon all individuals would be rejectors. That notion is certainly supported by rates of parasitism observed in acceptor species. In various studies, for example, 40 to 70 percent of the nests of Red-eyed Vireos were parasitized, about 20 percent of Eastern Phoebe nests were parasitized, and about 40 percent of Song Sparrow nests were parasitized. Reduction in the fledging rate of parasitized nests was well over 50 percent in the vireos and phoebes, and about 40 percent in the Song Sparrows.

A central mystery remains, however. Acceptors and rejectors do not represent different taxonomic groups, they do not have different lengths of association with cowbirds, most have eggs that can be easily distinguished

Short-eared Owl

Asio flammeus Pontoppidan

NG–238; G–174; PE–172; PW–120; AE–pl 284; AW–pl 291; AM(II)–174

  ○ F

			I: 26–28 DAYS		
F	4–7		SEMIALTRICIAL 2	BIRDS	SWOOPS
	(4–14)		F: 31–36 DAYS	INSECTS	
	MONOG		MF		

BREEDING: Prairie, meadow, tundra, marsh, savanna. 1 brood. **DISPLAYS:** Male calls in high courtship flight over nest, flapping, soaring, occ swooping with wings clapping below body. In pairs, male oft swoops down toward female from above while holding wings back and calling. Courtship feeding. **NEST:** Oft concealed by low veg; unlined or sparsely lined with grass, weeds, occ feathers. Occ perennial. Rarely in burrow. **EGGS:** White/cream-white. 1.5″ (39 mm). **DIET:** Esp rodents. Hunts at dawn and dusk. **CONSERVATION:** Winters s to c Mexico. Blue List 1976–86; declining in most of range, esp in prairie provinces, Pacific coast, parts of s e. **NOTES:** Irruptive, nomadic movements to locate areas with high rodent populations, then settle and breed. Clutch size larger when prey reach peak numbers. Male feeds incubating female. Young hatch asynchronously, sibs variously sized; fly at ca. 42 days. Adults perform distraction display. Roost on ground, oft communally, esp in winter. Where prey sufficient, maintain winter territories. Occ hunt communally where prey abundant. **ESSAYS:** Blue List, p. 11; Irruptions, p. 639; Nonvocal Sounds, p. 313; Pellets, p. 297; Brood Reduction, p. 307; Distraction Displays, p. 115. **REFS:** Burton, 1984; Clark, 1975; Cramp, 1985.

Long-eared Owl

Asio otus Linnaeus

NG–238; G–174; PE–172; PW–120; AE–pl 281; AW–pl 289; AM(II)–174

 ABANDONED NEST ○ F

			I: 26–28 DAYS	
25′–35′	F	4–5	SEMIALTRICIAL 2	BIRDS
(10′–40′)		(3–8)	F: 23–26 DAYS	
GROUND		MONOG	MF	

BREEDING: Conif and mixed conif-decid forest, esp near water; occ decid forest, also parks, orchards, farm woodland. 1 brood. **DISPLAYS:** Courtship: male flies in erratic zigzag with deep, slow wingbeats, occ gliding and clapping wings together beneath body. Courtship feeding. **NEST:** Usu in abandoned nests (esp crow, also squirrel, hawk, magpie, heron, raven). Perennial. Rarely scrape on ground, of small sticks, inner bark strips, pine needles. Female selects site. **EGGS:** White. 1.6″ (40 mm). **DIET:** Overwhelmingly rodents, rarely amphibians, reptiles, fish, insects. Hunts over open areas, strictly nocturnal. Ejects pellets. **CONSERVATION:** Winters s to c Mexico. **NOTES:** Occ nests in loose colonies; prey density may determine breeding density. Pair bond long-term where sedentary on year-round territories. Male feeds incubating female. Young hatch asynchronously; female broods. Young fly at ca. 34 days; parents feed them for 56–63 days. Perform distraction display in groups when colonial. Family unit retained perhaps until winter. Roosts, oft communally, in dense cover, less oft in caves, rock crevices. **ESSAYS:** Nonvocal Sounds, p. 313; How Owls Hunt in the Dark, p. 291; What Do Birds Hear?, p. 299; Pellets, p. 297; Brood Reduction, p. 307; Distraction Displays, p. 115. **REFS:** Cramp, 1985; Marks, 1984, 1986; Marti, 1976; Wijnandts, 1984.

from cowbird eggs, and they are capable of ejecting cowbird eggs from their nests. Why then have some species evolved the ability to reject, and others not. Rothstein suggests that nest concealment, large bill (to make ejection easier), and chance may play key roles. More careful observation and experiment will be needed before we will know if he is right.

Brood parasitism is not restricted to females of one species laying eggs in the nests of other species. In addition to some of our North American cuckoos, females of a wide variety of species sometimes lay eggs in the nests of other females of the same species. This behavior is examined in other essays.

SEE: Parasitized Ducks, p. 89; Parasitic Swallows, p. 401; Coevolution, p. 405; The Decline of Eastern Songbirds, p. 495; Monogamy, p. 597; Conservation of Kirtland's Warbler, p. 527; Cowbirds, p. 619. REFS: Heinrich, 1986; Payne, 1977; Rothstein, 1971, 1975a, b, 1976a; Wickler, 1968.

How Owls Hunt in the Dark

Nocturnal owls are formidable, silent hunters. Their silence on the wing derives from the structural modification of the first primary feather on each wing, a trait shared by all owls. The forward edge of the feather is serrated rather than smooth, which has the effect of disrupting the flow of air over the wing in flight and eliminating the vortex noise created by airflow over a smooth surface. Thus equipped, owls arrive upon their prey without a sound.

Owls, especially those that hunt at night, are able to locate even faint sounds with remarkable accuracy. The best studied of these nocturnal predators is the Barn Owl. Extensive experiments conducted by neurobiologists Marc Konishi and Eric Knudsen in totally darkened, soundproofed rooms have unequivocally demonstrated that Barn Owls can locate and capture prey by sound alone. The Barn Owl's sensitive hearing is enhanced by its facial ruff, a concave surface of stiff dark-tipped feathers. The ruff functions as a reflector, channeling sounds into the ears. Once a sound is detected, the owl orients toward it and accurately pinpoints its location to within 1.5 degrees in both horizontal and vertical planes.

The cue used to determine whether a sound comes from the right, left, or straight ahead is the difference in time that it takes for a sound to reach each ear. When the sound source is dead ahead, no time differential occurs. Another cue, the difference in intensity of sound received by each ear, is used to localize a sound vertically. Barn Owls (*Tyto* species), along with owls of at least eight other genera, have asymmetrical openings to their ears—as shown in the accompanying figure. A sound coming from above will seem slightly louder in the ear with the higher opening; if a sound is equally loud in both ears then the source must be at eye level.

The owls' ears are linked to specialized cells contained within a discrete

Great Horned Owl
Bubo virginianus Gmelin

NG–238; G–174; PE–172; PW–120; AE–pl 282; AW–pl 288; AM(II)–162

	ABANDONED NEST		F – M		
30'–50'	F?	2–3	I: 26–35 DAYS		
(15'–70')		(1–6+)	SEMIALTRICIAL 2	BIRDS	
CLIFF		MONOG?	F: 35 DAYS	SM VERTS	
			MF	INSECTS	

BREEDING: Conif or decid forest and woodland, swamp, orchard, park, riparian forest, semidesert. 1 brood. **DISPLAYS:** Male performs noisy aerial courtship display; ritually feeds female. Pair bill, bob, call, and click. **NEST:** In abandoned tree nest of raptor, corvid, occ squirrel; also tree cavity, cave, crevice, stump, and on ground in log, among rocks; of sticks, moss, hair, shredded bark, rootlets, etc., lined slightly with feathers and down. Perennial. **EGGS:** Dull white. 2.2" (55 mm). **DIET:** Esp rabbits and rodents, pheasants, quail, passerines, occ fish, amphibians, reptiles, scorpions. Mainly nocturnal, but also hunts crepuscularly. Ejects pellets. **CONSERVATION:** Winter resident. Occ uses nest box. **NOTES:** Incubating bird oft snow-covered in n; early eggs may freeze. Population density in n tracks snowshoe hare density; disperse when hare numbers crash. Young hatch asynchronously; rapidly develop ability to regulate body temperature, fly at 63–70 days, fed for several months. Adults perform distraction display. Daytime roost in dense conif near trunk. Most do not breed before second year. Arctic populations eat more birds. Cache prey; defrost frozen cache by "incubating" it ("prey thawing"). **ESSAYS:** Irruptions, p. 639; Pellets, p. 297; How Owls Hunt in the Dark, p. 291; Mobbing, p. 425; Brood Reduction, p. 307; Breeding Season, p. 55. **REFS:** Adamcik and Keith, 1978; Marti, 1974; Turner and McClanahan, 1981.

Barred Owl
Supersp #20
Strix varia Barton

NG–240; G–176; PE–174; PW–120; AE–pl 285; AM(II)–170

		F		
20'–50'	?	I: 28–33 DAYS		
(15'–80')		SEMIALTRICIAL 2	BIRDS	HOVER &
	2–3	F: 42 DAYS	SM VERTS	POUNCE
	(2–4)	F – M		
	MONOG?			

BREEDING: Dense conif and mixed conif/decid forest, wooded swamps and river valleys. 1 brood. **DISPLAYS:** Loud vocals by perched male and female. Pair nod, bow with half-spread wings, wobbling and twisting head side to side. **NEST:** Also use abandoned nests (esp hawk, also squirrel, crow), scraping hollow in remnant lining; may add green sprigs to open nest, but no material added to cavity. Perennial. Rarely on ground. **EGGS:** White. 2.0" (50 mm). **DIET:** Esp mice, squirrels, hares, shrews, also crayfish, amphibians, reptiles, rarely fish, insects. Ejects pellets. Oft hunts diurnally. Feeding perch near nest. **CONSERVATION:** Winter resident. Range expanding to the n w. **NOTES:** Male feeds incubating female. Young from small cavity nests may leave earlier than young in roomier cavities; parental care extends beyond 4 months. Light, quiet, slow-flapping flight, oft gliding. Audibly snaps beak. Drinks and bathes. Not easily disturbed from daytime roost. **ESSAYS:** Pellets, p. 297; How Owls Hunt in the Dark, p. 291; Mobbing, p. 425; What Do Birds Hear?, p. 299; Altricial Young, p. 581; Parental Care, p. 555. **REFS:** Burton, 1984; Devereux and Mosher, 1984; Earhart and Johnson, 1970.

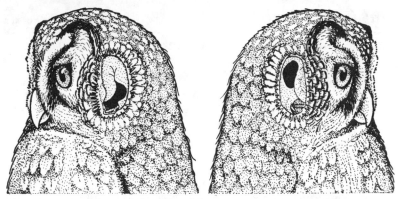

Both sides of owl's head with feathers pulled back to expose asymmetry of the ears.

region of the midbrain. Each cell is sensitive to a unique combination of time and intensity differentials and responds only to sound issuing from one small area in space. The Barn Owl's brain thus contains a "neural map" of auditory space. So armed, it is little wonder that the Barn Owl has been so successful that today it is arguably the most widespread bird species on Earth.

But their auditory systems are not the only reason that some owls can hunt successfully in the dark. Their sensory abilities are coupled with sedentary habits. As shown in studies of Tawny Owls in England, individuals hold a hunting territory in which they operate night after night. Familiarity with the environment, especially such things as the heights of favorite perches above the ground, seems to be essential to the owls' ability to pounce on prey. Hearing helps to replace the absence of sight, but intimate knowledge of the habitat completes the job.

SEE: What Do Birds Hear?, p. 299; Raptor Hunting, p. 223; Size and Sex in Raptors, p. 243; Site Tenacity, p. 189; Pellets, p. 297.   REFS: Knudsen, 1980; Konishi, 1983; Martin, 1986.

Birds and the Law

Most people interested in birds know that millions of Passenger Pigeons were killed for sale as food, but few realize that an enormous variety of other native birds once found their way to markets and dining tables. Reading his classic *Birds of America*, published in the early 1840s, one is quickly impressed with the number of species with which John James Audubon had firsthand experience. His numerous comments on hunting and eating eggs and adults applied not just to game birds such as ducks, geese, and prairie-chickens, but also to others such as Dunlin ("...my party shot a great number of them, on account of the fatness and juiciness of their flesh"), Eskimo Curlew, Belted Kingfisher ("...the eggs are fine eating"), Ameri-

Great Gray Owl

Strix nebulosa Forster

NG–240; G–176; PE–174; PW–120; AE–pl 286; AW–pl 290; AM(II)–172

	ABANDONED NEST		F		
			I: 30 DAYS		
10'–50'		2–4	SEMIALTRICIAL 2	BIRDS	SWOOPS
		(2–5)	F: 21–28 DAYS		
		MONOG	MF		

BREEDING: Boreal and dense conif forest, bogs. 1 brood. **DISPLAYS:** Pair forma-tion incl male aerial display assoc with courtship feeding; also mutual preen-ing. **NEST:** Usu in abandoned hawk or eagle nest of sticks and moss. Occ on stump-top, rarely on ground. **EGGS:** White. 2.1″ (54 mm). **DIET:** Mostly voles. **CONSERVATION:** Winters within N.A. Will use artificial nest sites created by topping trees and hollowing out trunks. **NOTES:** Male feeds female from incu-bation through small nestling stage. Female broods chicks nearly continuously for 14 days. Distraction display rarely given. Young return to roost in nest well after depar-ture and remain with parents for up to several months postfledging; fly at 60–65 days. Largest, but not heaviest N.A. owl, and one of the most diurnal. May be nomadic, settling where prey populations are dense. Plunge-dives into snow to catch rodents detected by sound. **ESSAYS:** Irruptions, p. 639; How Owls Hunt in the Dark, p. 291; What Do Birds Hear?, p. 299; Mobbing, p. 425; Courtship Feeding, p. 181. **REFS:** Burton, 1984; Cramp, 1985; Hilden and Helo, 1981; Nero, 1980.

Spotted Owl

Supersp #20
Strix occidentalis Xántus de Vesey

NG–240; G–176; PW–120; AW–pl 293; AM(II)–170

			F		
			I: 28–32 DAYS		
CLIFF	PLATFORM	1–2	SEMIALTRICIAL 2	BIRDS	
80'	SCRAPE	(1–3)	F: 34–36 DAYS	REPTILES	
(30'–160')	F	MONOG	MF	INSECTS	

BREEDING: Dense conif (esp old growth fir) and decid (esp in shaded, steep-walled canyons) forests. 1 brood. **DISPLAYS:** Male calls from perch near nest before and after cop. **NEST:** Cliff sites (mostly in s w) usu in wooded canyons, also use abandoned platform nest (esp raven, eagle, hawk) in tree, scrape on cave floor, rock crevice. Simple depression scraped in debris. Perennial. **EGGS:** White with faint tinge of buff. 2.0″ (50 mm). **DIET:** Mostly rodents and a few lagomorphs. Ejects pellets. **CONSERVATION:** Winter resident or altitudinal migrant. Blue List 1980–86; declining due to habitat destruction (logging) and fragmentation. Politics of logging have precluded Endangered Species status. Each pair requires 1400–4500 acres for home range; in 1979, 100 acres of Douglas fir in OR were worth $1,600,000. **NOTES:** Lifetime site tenacity by pair; pairs do not breed yearly. Sur-vival of young to breeding age very low. Female broods; male feeds female and young until young are 2 weeks old. Intolerant of even moderately high temperatures partly due to thick plumage and consequent inefficient ability to dissipate heat; select day-time summer roosts for cool microclimate: on n-facing slope with dense overhead canopy. Decidedly nocturnal. Regularly cache excess food. **ESSAYS:** Blue List, p. 11; How Owls Hunt in the Dark, p. 291; Site Tenacity, p. 189; Helping to Con-serve Birds—National Level, p. 363. **REFS:** Barrows, 1981; Dawson et al., 1987; Forsman and Meslow, 1986; Forsman et al., 1984; Salwasser, 1986.

can Robin ("... every gunner brings them home by bagsful, and the markets are supplied with them at a very cheap rate"), and Dark-eyed Junco ("... flesh is extremely delicate and juicy"). He reported some forty-eight thousand Golden Plovers slaughtered by French gunners near New Orleans in a single day.

In Audubon's time attitudes on wildlife were much like those that prevailed in the days of the Roman Empire. Until they were shot or trapped, birds were the property of no one; once killed, they became the property of the shooter or trapper. The exceptions were those birds found on private land, which could be taken only by the owner. Early on in Europe, wildlife became the property of royalty. Later, ownership was assigned to the state, but the latter doctrine was slow to emerge on the frontier continent of North America. Not until the middle of the last century were state and provincial laws enacted in attempts to protect birds—and the first laws were concerned with the preservation of game species.

It was not until the turn of this century, however, that the U.S. federal government got into the business of protecting birds. Largely in response to the fate of the Passenger Pigeon and the excesses of plume hunters, the Lacey Act was promulgated in 1900, making illegal the interstate transport of birds killed in violation of state laws. However, the turning point in bird conservation came in 1918 when legislation was enacted to implement the landmark Migratory Bird Treaty, which had been signed in 1916 between the United States and Great Britain (on behalf of Canada). The treaty designated three groups of migratory birds: game birds, insectivorous birds, and other nongame birds, and provided a season in which the birds of each group could not be taken "except for scientific or propagating purposes under permits." With minor exceptions for hunting by Native Americans, the closed season on the last two categories was year-round. For migratory game birds, hunting seasons were not to exceed three and a half months. The taking of nests and eggs of all migratory birds was prohibited, except for scientific purposes. Thus ended the hobby of oology, or egg collecting. Penalties for breaking the law were six months in prison and $500 in fines, or both.

Similar treaties were signed with Mexico in 1936, Japan in 1972, and the Soviet Union in 1976. In the Mexican treaty additional groups of birds were specified, more or less completing the basic legal protection of North American birds. The U.S. federal government had already taken steps to safeguard one prominent nonmigratory species; in 1940 the U.S. Congress became convinced that the American national symbol was threatened with extinction, and passed the Bald Eagle Protection Act. That law has twice been strengthened by amendments, most recently in 1972 after Wyoming ranchers were caught poisoning eagles and shooting them from helicopters.

Starting in 1966, Endangered Species Acts extended the principle embodied in the Bald Eagle Act to all species that could be demonstrated to be in jeopardy. As of 1986 thirteen species and eleven subspecies of North American birds are listed as endangered—according to the law "in danger

Snowy Owl
Nyctea scandiaca Linnaeus

NG–240; G–176; PE–174; PW–120; AE–pl 292; AW–pl 303; AM(II)–164

  ◯

		F		
		I: 32–34 DAYS		
F?	3–4	SEMIALTRICIAL 2	BIRDS	
	(3–9+)	F: 16 DAYS	FISH	
	MONOG	MF		

BREEDING: Tundra, esp among mounds, hillocks, or rocks. 1 brood. **DISPLAYS:** Male performs jerky, undulating courtship flight ending in near vertical landing. On ground, with wings spread, male dances stiffly while holding dead lemming. **NEST:** On hummock, esp on bare-topped gravel bank. Unlined or minimally lined with moss, lichen, and grass plucked from near rim. **EGGS:** White. 2.2″ (56 mm). More elongate than those of most owls. **DIET:** Lemmings, other rodents; if scarce, increases variety of prey, even taking marine inverts. **CONSERVATION:** Winters within N.A. **NOTES:** Breeding and clutch size closely track lemming abundance; forgo breeding when lemmings scarce. Male feeds incubating female. Adults perform distraction display. Young hatch asynchronously, the first nearly fledged by hatching of the last; brooded almost continuously by female for 3 weeks, fly at 51–57 days. Families remain together at least into autumn. Rarely perch in trees. In winter males nomadic; females territorial, maintaining area with combination of vocal and visual displays. Geese and eiders nest near owl nests for protection from Arctic fox. **ESSAYS:** Irruptions, p. 639; Bird Biology and the Arts, p. 47; Brood Reduction, p. 307; Courtship Feeding, p. 181; Distraction Displays, p. 115. **REFS:** Boxall and Lein, 1982; Burton 1984; Cramp, 1985; Taylor, 1973.

Western Screech-Owl
Supersp #19
Otus kennicottii Elliot

NG–242; G–174; PW– 123; AW–pl 286; AM(II)–160

   ◯

		F ?		
		I: 21–30 DAYS		
CACTUS	2–5	SEMIALTRICIAL 2	INSECTS	
5′–30′	(2–6)	F: 28 DAYS	SM VERTS	
	MONOG	MF	BIRDS	

BREEDING: Woodland (esp oak and riparian), scrub, orchards, woodlots. 1? brood. **DISPLAYS:** Similar to Eastern Screech-Owl. **NEST:** In tree or saguaro cavity, hollow stump, also use abandoned magpie nest, crevice in building. Add no lining material; eggs laid on remnant materials, fur and feathers of prey. **EGGS:** White. 1.4″ (36 mm). **DIET:** Varies regionally—incl arthropods, amphibians, reptiles, fish. Hunt soon after dusk, flying over open areas but never far from trees. **CONSERVATION:** Winter resident. Compete for nest cavities with other small species. Use nest boxes. **NOTES:** Male feeds female during incubation; female is close sitter. Pair oft in nest cavity in day. May attack intruder at nest. Highly nocturnal. Adults perform distraction display. **ESSAYS:** Mobbing, p. 425; Great Plains Hybrids, p. 625; How Owls Hunt in the Dark, p. 291; Distraction Displays, p. 115. **REFS:** Burton, 1984; Marks and Marks, 1981; Marti and Hogue, 1979.

of extinction throughout all or a significant portion of its range"—and thus have achieved an especially high level of protection as wards of the U.S. Fish and Wildlife Service. The endangered species are the Brown Pelican, Whooping Crane, Wood Stork, Piping Plover, Eskimo Curlew, Least Tern, California Condor, Bald Eagle, Peregrine Falcon, Red-cockaded Woodpecker, Ivory-billed Woodpecker, Bachman's Warbler, and Kirtland's Warbler, and the subspecies include the Everglade Snail Kite, Attwater's Prairie-Chicken, and the Northern Aplomado Falcon. In addition, the San Clemente Sage Sparrow, *Amphispiza belli clementeae*, is listed as threatened, which means it is considered likely to become endangered. Some 40 other species and subspecies, such as the Long-billed Curlew, Golden-cheeked Warbler, and two Florida subspecies of the Seaside Sparrow (a third, the Dusky, is now extinct) were candidates for listing. Citizens can petition to have species and subspecies of birds listed, but clear evidence that the petition is warranted is required to get the government to take action.

Under special permits, protected nongame species (but not endangered species) may be killed if they become serious local pests. This provision has been used primarily with regard to species of blackbirds and cowbirds when their gigantic fall and winter roosting flocks become nuisances, although control programs have not been without controversy. House Sparrows and starlings, both nonnative species, are not protected. No other birds, except those for which there are designated hunting seasons, can be legally killed, trapped, harassed, or possessed (including birds found dead). Even "adoption" of young birds that appear to have been deserted by their parents is illegal without a permit. If found, these apparently unattended young should be left alone, as, more often than not, the adults are not far away. In the United States or Canada, anyone molesting protected birds in any way should be reported to the state or provincial Department of Fish and Game or the U.S. Fish and Wildlife Service.

SEE: Conservation of the California Condor, p. 219; Conservation of Raptors, p. 247; Conservation of Kirtland's Warbler, p. 527; Saving a Subspecies, p. 571; The Blue List, p. 11; Helping to Conserve Birds—National Level, p. 363; Wintering and Conservation, p. 513.   REF: Council on Environmental Quality, 1977.

Pellets

Owls do exactly what children are warned against—they swallow their food whole, or nearly so. When they eat a small vertebrate, they digest all but the bones and fur or feathers. They regurgitate those remains in the form of a hard, felted or feathered pellet—one per victim. Where owls feed on insects, each regurgitated pellet contains the indigestible parts of the exoskeletons of numerous individuals.

Ejecting indigestible portions of food in the form of pellets is also common in raptors and gulls, and has ben recorded in many other groups of

Eastern Screech-Owl

NG–242; G–174; PE–172; AE–pl 279; AM(II)–160

15'–50' 4–5 F – M
         (2–8) I: 26 DAYS
         MONOG SEMIALTRICIAL 2   SM VERTS
                F: 27 DAYS   SM MAMMALS
                MF   BIRDS

BREEDING: Open woodland, decid forests, parks, towns, scrub, riparian habitats. 1 brood. **DISPLAYS:** Courtship on perch: male bows, raises wings, snaps bill, blinks at female and approaches; male brings food to female, lays it before her, with much hopping and bowing. Established pair mutually preen, also duet. **NEST:** Usu in tree cavity, hollow stump. Use remnant lining material, also feathers and fur debris from food. **EGGS:** White. 1.4" (34 mm). **DIET:** Also other arthropods, fish; marked regional differences. **CONSERVATION:** Winter resident. Blue List 1981, Special Concern 1982, 1986; apparently declining in e, s e, and midwest. Numbers reduced by creosote use on telecommunication poles used for nesting. Use nest boxes. **NOTES:** Pair oft in nest together, roost together. Male feeds incubating female. Female is close sitter. Young hatch synchronously. Nocturnal and crepuscular. Roost in hollow tree or in dense foliage near trunk. Abundant in suburban/urban habitats with mature trees for nesting and roosting. Live Blind Snakes brought to nest, live in debris where they eat insect larvae and may reduce insect parasitism of nestlings; owlets from nests with snakes grow faster and have lower mortality than broods without snakes. Home range size varies seasonally. **ESSAYS:** Mobbing, p. 425; Great Plains Hybrids, p. 625; How Owls Hunt in the Dark, p. 291; Blue List, p. 11; Courtship Feeding, p. 181. **REFS:** Gehlbach, 1986; Gehlbach and Baldridge, 1987; Smith and Gilbert, 1984; Van Camp and Henny, 1975.

Whiskered Screech-Owl

Otus trichopsis Wagler

NG–242; G–180; AW–622; AM(II)–162

18' 3 ?
     (3–4) I: ? DAYS
     MONOG? SEMIALTRICIAL 2
             F: ? DAYS
             ?

BREEDING: Montane oak and oak-conif forest. ? broods. **DISPLAYS:** Mutual preening, billing, and syncopated duet performed by pair. **NEST:** Eggs laid on remnant lining materials. **EGGS:** White. 1.3" (33 mm). **DIET:** Mostly large insects, other arthropods, rarely rodents. Hunts making short flights from perch or ground, catching prey in talons. **CONSERVATION:** Winter resident. **NOTES:** Nesting biology little known but presumably like that of other screech-owls. Nocturnal. Daytime roost in oaks, sycamores, and junipers; perching near trunk. Rarely seen over 30', usu below 15'. Perched with feathers fluffed and leaning forward, becomes cryptic limb bulge, perched further out on limb tilts body, mimicking leaf clusters. Oft bathe and preen; clean feathers essential to soundless flight. **ESSAYS:** Mobbing, p. 425; How Owls Hunt in the Dark, p. 291; What Do Birds Hear?, p. 299; Precocial and Altricial Young, p. 581. **REFS:** Angell, 1974; Earhart and Johnson, 1970; Martin, 1974; Smith et al., 1982.

birds, including flycatchers, corvids, herons, sandpipers, kingfishers, and even honeyeaters (primarily Australian birds that supplement their nectar/fruit diets with insects).

Pellets, especially those of birds that swallow their prey whole, provide ornithologists with records of what the birds are eating at various times and in various places. The hard pellets last a long time in dry climates and can be collected in numbers near roosts. If soaked in warm water, carefully dissected, and examined under magnification, the identity of vertebrate prey often can be determined from the bones. The pellets of raptors such as eagles and hawks are less useful, since they tear much of the flesh from their victims, and do not swallow the bones.

SEE: Diet and Nutrition, p. 587; Determining Diets, p. 535; Swallowing Stones, p. 269.

What Do Birds Hear?

The rich acoustic complexity of the vocalizations of many songbirds has long implied, at the very least, that the birds are able to perceive the diversity of such sounds. Widespread vocal learning and the faithful reproduction of complicated songs among the songbirds has now demonstrated that birds can hear what others are "saying." One wonders, however, just how much of the detailed acoustic and temporal complexity seen in a sonagram (a visual representation of a song) birds actually perceive.

The ability of birds to discriminate between sounds of different frequencies and degrees of loudness appears to be no better than that of humans. As a group, birds are most sensitive to sounds in the frequency range of 1–5 kilohertz (kHz; a thousand cycles per second), with an absolute upper limit (except for owls) of about 10 kHz. Even birds that use echolocation for maneuvering in the dark (Oilbirds and cave swiftlets) rely primarily on sounds in the 2–8 kHz range, in contrast to bats, which use ultrasonic frequencies.

The hearing abilities of fewer than 20 species have been tested rigorously under controlled laboratory conditions, but the results appear to indicate that all species can hear each other's vocalizations, as well as their own. The avian ear appears to be capable of separating sounds that are as close together as two to three thousandths of a second, which is comparable to or somewhat better than what can be seen in a sonagram.

SEE: Sonagrams: Seeing Bird Songs, p. 563; How Owls Hunt in the Dark, p. 291; Hawk-Eyed, p. 229; The Avian Sense of Smell, p. 15; Bird Voices, p. 373. REF: Dooling, 1982.

Flammulated Owl

Otus flammeolus Kaup

NG–244; G–180; PW–123; AW–pl 297; AM(II)–158

○
3–4
(2–4)
MONOG

F –M
I: 26 DAYS
SEMIALTRICIAL 2
F: ? DAYS
MF

BARK
GLEAN

BREEDING: Montane forest, esp ponderosa pine association. 1? brood. **DISPLAYS:** ? **NEST:** Uses abandoned woodpecker holes, esp those of flickers. Adds no lining, laying eggs on remnant materials found in hole. **EGGS:** White with faint creamy tint. 1.1″ (29 mm). **DIET:** Also other arthropods (spiders, centipedes and scorpions). Captures flying insects in and around trees while in flight; takes remainder from branches, trunks, occ from ground. **CONSERVATION:** Winters from c Mexico s to highlands of Guatemala and El Salvador. Will use nest boxes. **NOTES:** Occ nests in loose colonies. Strictly nocturnal. Sings mostly on moonlit nights. Male feeds incubating female. Broods fledge over 2 nights; sibs fledging on same night remain together, tended by one adult. Postfledging day roosts remain within ca. 300′ of nest for 2 weeks. Fledglings begin following adults on foraging trips within 7–10 days; independent at ca. 4 weeks postfledging. **ESSAYS:** Pellets, p. 297; How Owls Hunt in the Dark, p. 291; Mobbing, p. 425. **REFS:** Balda et al., 1975; Bergman, 1983; Earhart and Johnson, 1970; Linkhart and Reynolds, 1987.

Elf Owl

Micrathene whitneyi Cooper

NG–244; G–180; PW–123; AE–pl 287; AW–pl 294 AM(II)–168

CACTUS

15′–35′
(To 60′)

○
2–3
(1–5)
MONOG

F
I: 24 DAYS
SEMIALTRICIAL 2
F: 28–33 DAYS
M –F

HOVER &
POUNCE
HAWKS

?

BREEDING: Desert with giant cacti, oak and riparian woodland, esp with sycamores. 1 brood. **DISPLAYS:** Males sing from within cavity to attract females. **NEST:** In abandoned woodpecker hole in saguaro; also in decid tree or snag. No lining material added. **EGGS:** White. 1.1″ (27 mm). **DIET:** Also other arthropods, rarely lizards and snakes. Hunts at dusk and throughout night. **CONSERVATION:** Winters in n c and c Mexico. Range contracting in e and w portions; being reintroduced in CA where <10 breeding pairs remain. Competes with other small birds for nest holes. **NOTES:** Smallest owl in the world: sparrow size, but very loud. Males arrive on breeding grounds before females, locate 1 or more potential nest cavities. Male regularly feeds female from courtship until young are half-grown. Female roosts in nest from 1–2 weeks prior to egg laying through most of nestling period. When not breeding, roosts in dense cover in desert and oak habitat. Well camouflaged, sits motionless and erect. **ESSAYS:** How Owls Hunt in the Dark, p. 291; What Do Birds Hear?, p. 299; Precocial and Altricial Young, p. 581. **REFS:** Burton, 1984; Earhart and Johnson, 1970; Goad and Mannan, 1987; Ligon, 1968.

Eggs and Their Evolution

Females of all vertebrates produce eggs, but the reptiles "invented" the eggshell—a device that could keep the egg from drying out and allow reproduction away from water (or, at least, from extremely moist environments). With the exception of the platypus and echidna, mammals provide the developing embryo with a suitable environment within the mother's womb. The other major group of reptile descendents, the birds, not only have continued the reptilian tradition, but have evolved eggs of an improved design in a wide variety of sizes, shapes, colors, and textures.

Bird eggs are virtually self-contained life-support systems. All they require for the embryo to develop properly are warmth and oxygen. Oxygen diffuses into the egg through microscopic holes formed by the imperfect packing of the calcium carbonate crystals that compose the eggshell. There are not many of these pores—for example, they make up only about 0.02 percent of the surface of a duck egg. Carbon dioxide and water vapor diffuse outward through the same pores. Birds can lay their eggs in even drier environments than reptiles, because when the fatty yolk is broken down to provide energy for the developing embryo, water is produced as a by-product. Reptile eggs primarily use protein as a source of energy and do not produce as much "metabolic water."

The proportion of yolk differs between altricial and precocial birds. The former, which hatch so undeveloped that they require significant parental care and thus need less stored energy, generally have eggs that contain about 25 percent yolk. Precocial birds, which can walk and feed themselves shortly after hatching, have eggs with about 40 percent yolk (67 percent in megapodes, inhabitants of Australia and Pacific islands which upon hatching are virtually ready to fly). Interestingly, in spite of this difference, and although bird eggs range in weight from about one hundredth of an ounce (small hummingbird) to three and a half pounds (ostrich), all bird eggs lose water amounting to about 15 percent of their original weight during incubation. This careful control is probably a result of the necessity to keep the water content of the developing chick's tissues constant even though metabolic water is continually being produced.

Small birds tend to lay *proportionately* large eggs; the egg of a wren weighs about 13 percent of the wren's weight, while an ostrich egg weighs less than 2 percent of an adult's weight. As might be expected, the eggs of precocial birds tend to be heavier in proportion to body weight than those of altricial birds—the parents must "invest" more in the egg to give the chick the energy and materials required for more advanced development within the confines of the shell.

Although most are "egg-shaped," some eggs, such as those of owls, are nearly spherical. Fast-flying, highly streamlined birds such as swifts and hummingbirds tend to lay long, elliptical eggs, while those of auks, guillemots, and shorebirds are more pointed at the narrow end. Such "top-

Ferruginous Pygmy-Owl
Glaucidium brasilianum Gmelin

NG–244; G–180; PW–123; AW–pl 296; AM(II)–166

10'–20'		◯	F –M I: 28 DAYS	?
		3–4 (3–5) MONOG?	SEMIALTRICIAL 2 F: 27–30 DAYS MF	SMALL VERTS

BREEDING: Desert with large cacti, arid open and riparian woodland, thorn scrub. 1? brood. **DISPLAYS:** ? **NEST:** In natural cavity or abandoned woodpecker hole. No lining material added. **EGGS:** White. 1.1″ (29 mm). **DIET:** Not well known; possibly largely insects and other arthropods, also lizards, birds, and small mammals. **CONSERVATION:** Winter resident. **NOTES:** Active mostly at dawn and dusk. Hatch synchronously but young compete aggressively for food, resulting in size differences among siblings. Male feeds female and young. Oft jerks tail up and down when perched. **ESSAYS:** How Owls Hunt in the Dark, p. 291; What Do Birds Hear?, p. 299; Precocial and Altricial Young, p. 581; Brood Reduction, p. 307; How Do We Find Out About Bird Biology?, p. 319. **REFS:** Angell, 1974; Burton, 1984; Earhart and Johnson, 1970.

Northern Pygmy-Owl
Glaucidium gnoma Wagler

NG–244; G–180; PW–123; AW–pl 295; AM(II)–166

8'–20'		◯	F I: 28 DAYS	
		3–4 (2–7) MONOG?	SEMIALTRICIAL 2 F: 27–28 DAYS MF	INSECTS BIRDS SM VERTS

BREEDING: Dense montane mixed conif/decid and pine-oak forests. 1? brood. **DISPLAYS:** Courtship incl erratic, chasing twilight flight near nest. Low trilling call by perched female, joined by male. Ritual feeding of female by male. **NEST:** In abandoned woodpecker hole or natural cavity. No lining material added beyond occ feathers. Occ perennial. **EGGS:** White. 1.1″ (29 mm). **DIET:** Mostly rodents. Mostly diurnal, hunts primarily at dawn and dusk. **CONSERVATION:** Winter resident. **NOTES:** Young hatch asynchronously. Male brings food, female feeds young. Very aggressive for size. Hair, feathers, and bone are not swallowed, so no pellets are formed. Caches portion of larger prey. Roosts in tree cavity. On Pacific coast prefers canopy, but elsewhere lives in lower strata of forest. **ESSAYS:** How Owls Hunt in the Dark, p. 291; What Do Birds Hear?, p. 299; Precocial and Altricial Young, p. 581; Hoarding Food, p. 345; Courtship Feeding, p. 181; Brood Reduction, p. 307. **REFS:** Angell, 1974; Burton, 1984; Earhart and Johnson, 1970; Gashwiler, 1960.

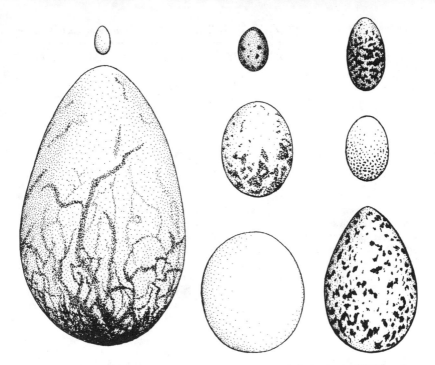

Left-hand column: Ruby-throated Hummingbird, Great Auk (extinct). Middle column: Acadian Flycatcher, Snail Kite, Great Horned Owl. Right-hand column: Common Nighthawk, Eastern Meadowlark, Long-billed Curlew.

shaped" eggs can be closely packed with the pointy ends inward, helping adults to efficiently cover them during incubation. Top-shape appears to be especially advantageous for birds that nest on bare ground or cliffs because, when disturbed, pointy eggs tend to roll in circles, rather than away from the nest (and possibly over the cliff).

Bird eggs vary enormously in color, and there is also variation in the surface texture of eggs—for instance, those of many ducks are greasy and water-repellent. Shells vary in thickness, too, and may be subject to thinning and weakening by environmental pollutants that interfere with the bird's calcium metabolism.

Why have birds not "advanced" beyond egg laying and started to bear their young alive like mammals? People have claimed that viviparity (live-bearing) is incompatible with flight, but bats disprove that hypothesis. Daniel Blackburn of Vanderbilt University and Howard Evans of Cornell point out that the evolutionary path to viviparity usually involved retaining eggs for longer and longer periods until they finally hatch within the female's body. Blackburn and Evans argue that egg retention would offer little advantage to birds, and several disadvantages. Among the latter are a loss of productivity—since females obviously could not retain many eggs until they hatched—and probably increased risk to the mother associated with

Northern Saw-whet Owl

Aegolius acadicus Gmelin

NG–246; G–178; PE–176; PW– 123; AE–pl 289; AW–pl 298; AM(II)–178

14'–60'

5–6
(4–7)
MONOG?

F –M
I: 26–28 DAYS
SEMIALTRICIAL 2
F: 27–34 DAYS
?

BIRDS

BREEDING: Dense conif and mixed conif-decid forest, wooded swamps, bogs. 1? brood. **DISPLAYS:** Vocal display: incessant, breathless repetition of single "whoop" syllable, occ changing key. **NEST:** In abandoned woodpecker (esp flicker and Pileated) holes, natural cavities. No lining materials added beyond occ feathers. **EGGS:** White. 1.2″ (30 mm). **DIET:** Mainly rodents; also takes insects. Ejects pellets. **CONSERVATION:** Winters within N.A. Will use nest boxes. **NOTES:** Smallest owl in e. Named for vocalization reminiscent of sharpening of saw blade. If disturbed at nest, refuses to leave cavity. Young hatch asynchronously. Very tame and retiring. Roosts diurnally, perched or in tree hole. Nocturnal hunter; most active at dusk and just before dawn. Assumes incubating posture to thaw frozen prey; probably caches prey. **ESSAYS:** How Owls Hunt in the Dark, p. 291; What Do Birds Hear?, p. 299; Precocial and Altricial Young, p. 581; Hoarding Food, p. 345; Pellets, p. 297; Brood Reduction, p. 307. **REFS:** Bondrup-Nielsen, 1977; Earhart and Johnson, 1970; Schaeffer, 1973.

Boreal Owl

Aegolius funereus Linnaeus

NG–246; G–178; PE–176; PW–123; AE–pl 290; AW–pl 300; AM(II)–176

10'–20'

4–6
(3–10)
POLYGAM

F
I: 27–28 DAYS
SEMIALTRICIAL 2
F: 28–33 DAYS
MF

BIRDS

BREEDING: Dense n conif and mixed conif-decid forest, muskeg, bogs. 1 brood. **DISPLAYS:** Female approaches courting male, he flies into prospective nest hole and vocalizes; male retrieves food from cache and presents to female. **NEST:** In abandoned woodpecker hole or natural cavity with well-matted bed of decayed chips and feathers. No lining materials added. **EGGS:** White. 1.3″ (32 mm). **DIET:** Also rarely frogs, insects. **CONSERVATION:** Winters within N.A. Will use nest box. **NOTES:** Both polygyny and sequential polyandry (documented in European populations) may be common but difficult to detect because nests are far apart (0.3 to >1 mile). Female in nest fed by male from ca. 1 week prior to laying until ca. 3 weeks posthatching. Secondary polygynous broods suffer greater losses because male provides less help feeding female and young owlets. Egg laying may take up to 12 days; young hatch asynchronously, vary greatly in size, brooded ca. 3 weeks, fed for 3–6 weeks postfledging. Irruptive, though may be mostly females that move. Assumes incubating posture to thaw frozen prey; caches food in crevices, tree forks, etc. Roosts diurnally in barns, dense veg. Known in Europe as Tengmalm's Owl. **ESSAYS:** Irruptions, p. 639; Polygyny, p. 443; Polyandry, p. 133; Brood Reduction, p. 307; Hoarding Food, p. 345; Parental Care, p. 555. **REFS:** Bondrup-Nielsen, 1977; Cramp, 1985; Earhart and Johnson, 1970; Hayward et al., 1987; Solheim 1983.

the added burden of weight. In addition, in many species, the contribution of the male to the care of offspring would be lost and it has recently been suggested that a female bird's body may be too hot for proper egg development. It seems likely, therefore, that evolving viviparity would be a step backward for birds—they are doing just fine laying eggs.

SEE: Incubation: Heating Eggs, p. 393: Average Clutch Size, p. 51; Variation in Clutch Sizes, p. 339; DDT and Birds, p. 21; Empty Shells, p. 165. REFS: Aderson, et al., 1986; Blackburn and Evans, 1987; Carey, 1983; Diamond, 1982a; Lewin, 1986.

Color of Eggs

Bird eggs show an enormous diversity of colors. Some bird groups that are considered relatively "primitive," such as cormorants and pelicans, are thought to have retained the pale, uniform white or bluish color typical of their reptilian ancestors. In more "advanced" groups, unmarked white eggs are found mostly among some cavity-nesting species where there is no need for the eggs to be camouflaged. Other cavity nesters, such as certain titmice, have spotted eggs—presumably an indication that they once nested in the open. Pale eggs are also common among some duck species that cover them with bits of nesting materials when they take a break from brooding, or among those species such as doves, owls, and herons that start incubating as soon as the first egg is laid and never leave them exposed.

Seabird species that nest in gigantic colonies tend to have eggs that are extremely variable in both color and markings. Their colors, like all egg colors, are from pigments produced by glands in the female's oviduct. As the egg moves down that tube the colors are squeezed out onto the shell. As ecologist Bernd Heinrich put it: ". . . the motion of the egg affects the color patterns. It is as if innumerable brushes hold still while the canvas moves. If the egg remains still there are spots, and if it moves while the glands continue secreting, then lines and scrawls result."

Chester Reed, an early egg collector, assumed that murres didn't know whose egg they were attending when they returned to their colony, but actually the variability of designs produced by the oviduct "brushes" permits individuals to recognize their own "painting." Experiments have shown that murres learn the pattern of their own egg and will reject others. If its egg becomes discolored gradually with guano, a murre will continually adjust the image of the "proper" egg and will reject an unstained egg of its own basic pattern. Thus the birds are not genetically programmed to recognize their own egg pattern, but rather learn the pattern of the egg they've laid and then continually update its image.

In most birds, however, the colors of the eggs in one way or another help with their concealment, as anyone who has sought Arctic Tern or Killdeer eggs against a pebbly background can testify. How, though, can one explain exceptions where one might expect camouflage, as in the case of the

Northern Hawk-Owl

Surnia ulula Linnaeus

NG–246; G–178; PE–176; PW–123; AE–pl 288; AW–pl 292; AM(II)–164

			F		
			I: 25–30 DAYS		
10'–40'	PLATFORM	5–7	SEMIALTRICIAL 2	BIRDS	HOVER &
		(3–9+)	F: 25–35 DAYS	INSECTS	POUNCE
		MONOG	MF		LOW PATROL

BREEDING: n conif and mixed conif-decid forest, wooded swamp. 1 brood. **DISPLAYS:** Courtship feeding occurs toward end of courtship, assoc with food caching. Paired birds duet. **NEST:** Also use stump tops, abandoned basket and platform nests (esp of crows and birds of prey). Mold chips into depression, but do not add additional materials. **EGGS:** White. 1.6″ (40 mm). **DIET:** Seasonally variable: mostly mice, lemmings, shrews and insects in summer, proportionately more birds, incl ptarmigan, in winter. **CONSERVATION:** Winters within N.A. Will use nest box. **NOTES:** Clutch size varies with rodent abundance. Young hatch asynchronously. Male feeds female from several days before egg laying through hatching. Fearless and aggressive toward nest intruders. Family group maintained until following spring. Hunts mostly crepuscularly as well as in daytime; straight, rapid, low hawklike flight and gliding; also hovers. Relies largely on sight. Surprisingly approachable. **ESSAYS:** How Owls Hunt, p. 291; What Birds Hear, p. 299; Irruptions, p. 639; Altricial Young, p. 581; Brood Reduction, p. 307; Courtship Feeding, p. 181; Vocal Functions, p. 471. **REFS:** Burton, 1984; Cramp, 1985.

Burrowing Owl

Athene cunicularia Molina

NG–246; G–178; PE–176; PW– 123; AE–pl 283; AW–pl 301; AM(II)–168

		F –M?		
		I: 21–28 DAYS		
M –F	7–9	SEMIALTRICIAL 2	RODENTS	HOVER &
	(6–11)	F: 28 DAYS	LIZARDS	POUNCE
	MONOG	MF	BIRDS	GRND GLEAN

BREEDING: Grassland, prairie, savanna, open areas near human habitation, esp golf courses, airports. 1 brood. **DISPLAYS:** Courtship: ritual feeding; pair choose nest site, stand atop burrow, quietly call, neck, and bill, also stretch legs and wings. **NEST:** In mammal burrow, occ enlarged by kicking dirt backward. Nest chamber lined with cow chips, horse dung, food debris, dry grass, weeds, pellets, feathers. Occ unlined. Perennial. **EGGS:** White, nest-stained. 1.2″ (31 mm). **DIET:** Hunts anytime, day or night; perches on burrow or fence post in day. Occ hawks insects. **CONSERVATION:** Winters s to Guatemala and El Salvador. Blue List 1972–81, Special Concern 1982, 1986; isolated FL population seriously declining; also declining on Pacific coast. Poisoning and nest site loss result from human efforts to control squirrels and prairie dogs. **NOTES:** Usu nest in small colonies within ground squirrel and prairie dog colonies. Pair bond usu >1 year. Female remains inside burrow during most of egg laying and incubation, fed by male through brooding; begins foraging for self and young when they are 3–4 weeks old. Burrow oft swarming with fleas; new burrow oft chosen 2–4 weeks after young emerge. Families remain together into Sept. When disturbed in burrow, mimics rattlesnake's rattle. **ESSAYS:** Blue List, p. 11; Vocal Copying, p. 469; Nest Sanitation, p. 315. **REFS:** Marti, 1974; Martin, 1973; Rich, 1986; Thomsen, 1971.

unmarked blue eggs of robins and catbirds? Their uniform colors may now permit easy identification of the eggs of nest-parasitic cowbirds, which may pose a greater threat to the survival of the brood than do nest robbers. It is doubtful, however, if robins and catbirds were in wide contact with cowbirds before deforestation and the importation of cattle opened the East to those parasites.

SEE: Incubation: Heating Eggs, p. 393; Variation in Clutch Sizes, p. 339; DDT and Birds, p. 21; Empty Shells, p. 165; Life in the Egg, p. 457. REFS: Heinrich, 1986; Lack, 1958.

Hatching Asynchrony and Brood Reduction

Whether eggs in a single clutch will hatch simultaneously or sequentially over an extended period of time is determined by the onset of incubation. In many birds, including most precocial species, incubation does not begin until the last egg has been laid, resulting in all of the eggs hatching within a few hours of each other. In contrast, many other birds begin incubation prior to laying the last egg of the clutch. This results in asynchronous hatchings separated by anywhere from a few hours to several days, depending on how soon incubation commences following the start of egg laying.

In altricial and semialtricial species, asynchronous hatching gives the first chicks to leave the egg a head start at vigorously begging for food and successfully attracting parental attention. The influential British ornithologist David Lack viewed the evolution of asynchronous hatching as a parental strategy for raising the largest number of offspring that food resources will allow when the abundance of food for the chicks cannot be predicted at the time that eggs are laid. The matching of offspring number with food availability is thus achieved by means of brood reduction: with asynchronous hatching, the smallest chick or chicks do not garner "their fair share" and will only survive in years of abundant food.

Elimination of the smallest chicks usually occurs by starvation as result of competition with their larger siblings for parental feeding, from overt parental neglect, or psychological and physical intimidation by their larger siblings. Brood reduction by means of starvation routinely occurs in almost all of our gulls and raptors, and is commonly seen in birds as diverse as cormorants, herons, egrets, terns, Red-cockaded Woodpeckers, Curve-billed Thrashers, some corvids, and Common Grackles. Size disparity among chicks is exacerbated in gulls by the laying of different-sized eggs in which egg weight typically decreases with laying order.

Eagles and boobies exhibit "obligate siblicide," in which the larger chick invariably kills its smaller sibling. For example, of more than 200 records of two-egg clutches followed in the Black Eagle of southern Africa, only one record exists of both chicks surviving to fledging. Obligate sibli-

Chuck-will's-widow

Caprimulgus carolinensis Gmelin

NG–248; G–182; PE–184; AE–pl 278; AM(II)–186

 NO NEST

F
I: 20+ DAYS
2 SEMIPRECOCIAL BIRDS
? F: 17 DAYS
F

BREEDING: Decid forest, pine-oak and live-oak woodland. 1 brood. **DISPLAYS:** Courtship: (one of few daylight activities) male struts to watching female, wings drooping, tail spread, puffs and calls, jerking body. Inactive close perching follows display. **NEST:** None. Lays eggs in approximately same dead-leaf-covered area each year. **EGGS:** Variable. Cream/pink/white, usu with brownish/purplish-gray mottling. 1.4″ (37 mm). If nest disturbed, eggs moved. **DIET:** Occ small birds (incl swallows, warblers, hummingbirds—all swallowed whole) taken during their migration. **CONSERVATION:** Winters s through Bahamas, Greater Antilles, C.A. to Colombia. **NOTES:** Nocturnal. Largest goatsucker (anatomically similar to owls), huge mouth covered with insect-trapping bristles opens 2″; silent flight. Usu roosts in same place each day, perching motionless on ground or lengthwise on branch. **ESSAYS:** Decline of Eastern Songbirds, p. 495; Precocial and Altricial Young, p. 581. **REFS:** Hoyt, 1953; Rohwer, 1971.

Whip-poor-will

Caprimulgus vociferus Wilson

NG–248; G–182; PE–184; PW–pl 38; AE–pl 277; AW–pl 248; AM(II)–188

 NO NEST

MF
I: 19–20 DAYS
2 SEMIPRECOCIAL
MONOG F: 20 DAYS
MF

BREEDING: Open arid and humid woodland, from lowland moist/decid forest to montane forest and pine-oak woodland. 1, occ 2 broods. **DISPLAYS:** Male calls, female alights, male quietly advances undulating and bobbing, circles female, purring. Also, female struts, wings and tail spread, neck low, "chuckling." Or, male waddles to female, she grunts with head low and trembles; male approaches, bills, keeps close. **NEST:** None. On well-drained ground near edge of woods. Depression around eggs results from incubation. **EGGS:** White, dotted with brown/olive/lavender. Occ unmarked? 1.2″ (30 mm). **DIET:** Esp moths. **CONSERVATION:** Winters s through C.A. to w Panama. Blue List 1980–81, 1986; continuing to decline in many areas. **NOTES:** Reproductive cycle synchronized with lunar cycle to result in moonlit nights when foraging to feed nestlings. Foraging based primarily on sight of prey, not sound. Adults perform distraction display. Male assumes care of brood if female begins second clutch. Species not identified until early 1800s; previously perceived as voice of nighthawk. **ESSAYS:** Bills, p. 209; Decline of Eastern Songbirds, p. 495; Blue List, p. 11; Metabolism, p. 325; Distraction Displays, p. 115. **REFS:** Babcock, 1975; Bruce, 1973; Mills, 1986.

cide also occurs among pelicans, owls, and cranes. In obligate siblicide, which occurs even when food supplies are abundant, the second egg serves as insurance against loss of the first egg from infertility, predation, or damage, rather than as a means of rearing two chicks.

In the 25–40 years since Lack's studies, information about many additional species has accumulated, and hatching asynchrony is now thought to be more common than synchronous hatching among altricial birds. Ornithologists now think that asynchronous hatching is not a strategy for achieving brood reduction in many species. They have advanced other hypotheses to explain its evolution. Sociobiologists Anne Clark and David Wilson argue that high nest predation rates can encourage the evolution of asynchronous hatching as a means of minimizing the total amount of time that eggs and nestlings spend in the nest. Asynchronous hatching also can be interpreted for some insectivorous species as an adaptation to "speed up" hatching so that at least some of the nestlings can capitalize on rapidly (but unpredictably) peaking food resources (such as outbreaks of forest caterpillars).

This "new view" of the adaptive significance of hatching asynchrony helps to explain the increasing egg weight often seen from first to last egg laid among many asynchronously hatching passerines. These weight differences represent differing proportions of nutrients and energy invested in different eggs within clutches, with the greatest investment going into the last egg of the clutch. This pattern is clearly inconsistent with the notion of facilitating brood reduction, and appears to be a means of compensating for the delay in hatching and development by providing the last chick with more resources initially.

SEE: Incubation Time, p. 481; Precocial and Altricial Young, p. 581; Eggs and Their Evolution, p. 301; Variation in Clutch Sizes, p. 339; Average Clutch Size, p. 51. REFS: Clark and Wilson, 1981; Lack, 1968; Mock, 1984; O'Connor, 1978; Stinson, 1979.

Feathers

Birds are *defined* by feathers—no bird lacks them, no other animal possesses them. Feathers are also a symbol of lightness. Therefore, a measure of their importance to birds is that, on average, they make up about 6–9 percent of a bird's weight. Birds produce them in very large numbers—roughly between 1,000 (hummingbirds) and 25,000 (swans) typical (or "contour") feathers adorn their bodies, supplemented by down and other specialized feather types.

Contour feathers have the familiar "crow quill" form. The bare part of the shaft that is held in a socket (follicle) in the skin is called the "quill." On each side of the rest of the shaft, the "rachis" supports an intricate web of

Buff-collared Nightjar

Caprimulgus ridgwayi Nelson

NG–248; G–182; AM(II)–188

 NO NEST ?

?
I: ? DAYS
SEMIPRECOCIAL
F: ? DAYS
?

? ?

BREEDING: Usu in arid habitat: open woodland, incl scrub, decid forest. ? broods. **DISPLAYS:** ? **NEST:** ? **EGGS:** ? **DIET:** Presumably flying insects like other members of the family. **CONSERVATION:** Winter resident. **NOTES:** Details of breeding biology and ecology virtually unknown. Voice very staccato, insectlike. Also known as Ridgway's Whip-poor-will. **ESSAYS:** Bills, p. 209; How Do We Find Out About Bird Biology?, p. 319; Metabolism, p. 325. **REF:** Bent, 1940.

Common Pauraque

Nyctidromus albicollis Gmelin

NG–250; G–182; PW–pl 38; AE–pl 276; AM(II)–184

 NO NEST

MF
I: ? DAYS
SEMIPRECOCIAL
F: ? DAYS
MF

2
?

  HAWKS

BREEDING: Open woodland, forest edge and clearings, arid scrub, riparian woodland and brush. ? broods. **DISPLAYS:** Separated by 1'–6', two birds face each other silently, rock up and down, occ flutter up a few feet flashing white in wings and tail; function unknown. **NEST:** Eggs laid on bare, level ground, oft near river or canyon, but not in rocky hills frequented by nighthawks. Female reportedly moves nesting location when disturbed. **EGGS:** Salmon/pinkish-buff, marked with cinnamon. 1.2" (30 mm). **DIET:** Young fed regurgitant. **CONSERVATION:** Winter resident. **NOTES:** Perches diurnally on ground near cover, occ within 1' of ground; typically flies within 10' of ground. In lower Rio Grande Valley, oft perches at night on road where readily located by light reflecting from their eyes. Longer-legged than most goatsuckers; more active on feet, oft runs and hops to flycatch. Occ hawks insects from low perch. Calls at dusk and throughout moonlit nights during breeding. Adults alternate incubation and brooding every 2–3 hours, male early A.M., female at night. **ESSAYS:** Temperature Regulation, p. 149; Metabolism, p. 325; Swallowing Stones, p. 269; Visual Displays, p. 5; Who Incubates?, p. 27. **REF:** Oberholser, 1974.

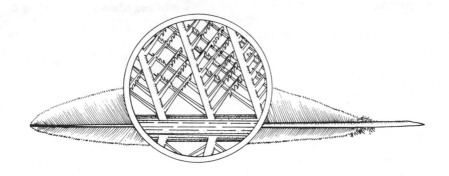

the "vane." The flat, flexible vane is one of nature's marvels. Under high magnification, the numerous parallel "barbs" of the vane, running diagonally outward from the rachis, look like feathers in miniature. The barbs have parallel "barbules" running diagonally outward from their shafts— more than a million barbules per feather.

But under the superhigh magnification of the electron microscope, the resemblance of barbs to feathers ends. The barbules on the side of each barb toward the feather tip are armed with minute hooks; those on the side toward the feather base (quill) have smooth ridges on their upper edges. The hooklets on the outer barbules of one barb attach it to the ridges on the inner barbules of the other. By this mechanism, the barbs, and thus the entire feather, zip together into a functional unit, capable of resisting a rapidly moving airstream. Should the structure of the feather be disrupted by, say, an encounter with a twig, the bird can simply rejoin the barbs by drawing its beak over the feather during preening.

Down feathers, in contrast, have barbules without hooklets. Usually they lie beneath contour feathers, and provide the bird with insulation. The base of many contour feathers also has barbules lacking hooklets, thus providing a fluffy, insulating layer that lies close to the skin. Next to the base of some contour feathers are simple, hairlike feathers called "filoplumes," which are attached to special sensory receptors in the skin. When the feathers become ruffled, they disturb the filoplumes which in turn stimulate the receptors. Each receptor has a "direct line" to the central nervous system, so that it provides very accurate information on feather disturbance to the bird, which then can do appropriate preening. It also seems likely that the filoplumes, sensing changes in feather position caused by airflow over a flying bird, may play an important role in the sensory control of flight.

There are other kinds of specialized feathers. For instance, some birds —such as pigeons, hawks, herons, bitterns, and parrots—have "powder down" feathers that produce, or disintegrate into, fine powder. These feathers may be concentrated in dense patches (herons) or scattered (hawks). The powder is distributed by preening and helps to waterproof and preserve the other feathers. It may also give the feathers a metallic

Common Poorwill

Phalaenoptilus nuttallii Audubon

NG–248; G–182; PE–184; PW–pl 38; AW–pl 249; AM(II)–184

NO NEST		MF		
SCRAPE	2	I: ? DAYS		
	?	SEMIPRECOCIAL		HOVER &
		F: ? DAYS		GLEAN
		MF		

BREEDING: Usu semiarid and arid habitat: scrub, brush, prairie, rocky canyon, open woodland. ? broods. **DISPLAYS:** ? **NEST:** Eggs laid on gravel or flat rock, occ in full sun, but usu partly shaded near shrub. Usu in vicinity of steep hill and dead grass. Occ slight depression scraped in dirt. Perennial site. **EGGS:** Usu pinkish-white/pinkish-cream, darkly mottled with lavender. 1.0″ (26 mm). **DIET:** Hunts insects by skimming silently, low to ground. Ejects pellets. **CONSERVA-TION:** Winters s to c Mexico. **NOTES:** If disturbed on nest, adult tumbles, hisses with widely opened mouth like snake; otherwise motionless. Strictly nocturnal, more oft heard than seen. Flits like moth on silent wings. Drinks on the wing by fluttering open-mouthed over surface of water. Wintering birds in s portions of U.S. range occ in torpid ("hibernating") condition. Formerly known as Poorwill. **ESSAYS:** Distraction Displays, p. 115; Metabolism, p. 325; Temperature Regulation, p. 149; Pellets, p. 297. **REF:** Fears, 1975.

Common Nighthawk

Supersp #21
Chordeiles minor Forster

NG–250; G–182; PE–184; PW–pl 38; AE–pl 275; AW–pl 250; AM(II)–182

NO NEST		F –M		
	2	I: 19 DAYS		GROUND
	(1–3)	SEMIPRECOCIAL		GLEAN
	?	F: 21 DAYS		
		MF		

BREEDING: Open and semiopen habitats esp savanna, grassland, fields, cities and towns. ? broods. **DISPLAYS:** Courtship oft at dusk: male calls, circling, hovering or soaring above intended nest site, swoops down with a pronounced hollow "boom," almost crashing near mate. Boom produced by vibrating primaries. Male lands, spreads tail, rocks body, remains upright near passive female; puffs throat, calls, exposing white throat. Aerial display and booming continue throughout nesting. **NEST:** If depression apparent, result of sitting adult. Prefer sandy soil in s; also lays eggs on stump, old robin nest, gravel rooftop. **EGGS:** White/olive, with olive mottling. 1.2″ (30 mm). **DIET:** Young fed regurgitant. **CONSERVATION:** Winters throughout S.A. to n Argentina. Blue List 1975–86; reported declining in many parts of range. Became common in cities after introduction of gravel roofs in mid-1800s. **NOTES:** Feeds at dusk, night, and in day. Performs distraction display. Young feed selves by day 25. Largely excluded from desert habitats by Lesser Nighthawk. Interspecifically territorial with Antillean Nighthawk in FL Keys. **ESSAYS:** Blue List, p. 11; Interspecific Territoriality, p. 385; Masterbuilders, p. 455; Nonvocal Sounds, p. 313; Distraction Displays, p. 115. **REFS:** Caccamise, 1974; Stevenson et al., 1983.

appearance. Powder down feathers tend to be abundant in birds, such as some pigeons and parrots, that lack preen glands.

Facial bristles are another kind of specialized feather. These feathers are concentrated around the mouths of flycatchers, swallows, Common Poorwills, crows, and ravens and may function like the whiskers of a cat to amplify sensations of touch. When bristles cover the nostrils, as they do in some woodpeckers, they may help to filter out wood or other particles.

Feathers are raised, lowered, or rotated by muscles that attach to the walls of their sockets. This helps them to perform their functions—first and foremost flight, but also several others. Fluffing or sleeking the feathers varies the thickness of the feather-plus-air insulating layer, controls heat exchange with the environment, and thus helps the bird to regulate its temperature. Feathers shield the bird from injury, sunburn, and rainfall. Tail feathers prop woodpeckers in position for their powerful pecking and act as a rudder for stiff-tailed Ruddy Ducks swimming underwater. Colorful feathers are used in displays, and drab ones often provide camouflage. Feathers not only define the bird, but are essential to its existence.

SEE: Molting, p. 529; Preening, p. 53; Bathing and Dusting, p. 429; Anting, p. 487; Head Scratching, p. 543; Black and White Plumage, p. 177; Eclipse Plumage, p. 61. REF: Necker, 1985.

Nonvocal Sounds

When we think of bird sounds, singing is the first thing that comes to mind. But many birds have found other ways of generating acoustical signals to serve functions usually accomplished by songs. Some bird sounds used in territorial and courtship displays are produced with their bills, feet, wings, or tails. Many songbirds clack their bills, but otherwise the use of such sounds in displays is limited primarily to species with poor singing abilities and occurs infrequently among the passerines.

Mated storks and albatrosses often communicate with bill clattering and bill tapping, but the best-known use of bills to produce auditory displays among North American birds is the drumming of several woodpecker species. Both sexes engage in loud rhythmical drumming by striking their bills against a hollow or dried branch or, to the annoyance of many homeowners, metal gutters, stovepipes, drainpipes, and even trashcans! In the Yellow-bellied Sapsucker, Northern Flicker, Downy Woodpecker, and Hairy Woodpecker, drumming functions much as song does to proclaim territorial boundaries and to attract mates.

By altering the spacing of wing or tail feathers and causing them to vibrate, birds can create a variety of whistling, rattling, buzzing, or other sounds as air passes through those feathers in flight. These sounds are evi-

Antillean Nighthawk

Supersp #21
Chordeiles gundlachii Lawrence

NG–250; G–182; PE–184; AM(II)–182

 NO NEST ?
I: ? DAYS
1 SEMIPRECOCIAL
(1–2) F: ? DAYS
? MF

BREEDING: Open and semiopen habitats. ? broods. **DISPLAYS:** Aerial courtship by male includes wing-produced "boom" as in Common Nighthawk, but much higher pitched and does not carry very far. **NEST:** Eggs laid on open bare ground. **EGGS:** White/olive, with olive mottling; more heavily marked with larger and darker spots than are eggs of Common Nighthawk. 1.2″ (29 mm). **DIET:** Insects. **CONSERVATION:** Wintering area is unknown but probably in S.A. Deforestation on FL Keys in 1960s and 1970s enabled increase. **NOTES:** Biology largely unknown. Formerly considered subspecies of Common Nighthawk. Call notes distinctively different from Common Nighthawk. Interspecifically territorial with Common Nighthawk; not clear whether mixed pairs occur. **ESSAYS:** Nonvocal Sounds, p. 313; Interspecific Territoriality, p. 385; Hybridization, p. 501; How Do We Find Out About Bird Biology?, p. 319. **REFS:** Kale, 1978; Stevenson et al., 1983.

Lesser Nighthawk

Chordeiles acutipennis Hermann

NG–250; G–182; PE–184; PW–pl 38; AW–pl 251; AM(II)–180

 NO NEST F
I: 18–19 DAYS
2 SEMIPRECOCIAL
? F: 21? DAYS
MF

BREEDING: Open desert, scrub, savanna, and arid cultivated areas. ? broods. **DISPLAYS:** Aerial courtship display by male. **NEST:** Eggs laid on bare sand or gravel substrate, occ at base of shrub or on flat roof. **EGGS:** Light-gray/light-cream/pinkish-white, marked with tan/gray/lilac. 1.1″ (27 mm). **DIET:** Oft feeds after sunset, in glow of city lights; oft flies low and mothlike over open ground. Occ feeds in morning. Young fed regurgitant. **CONSERVATION:** Winters n w Mexico s to c S.A. **NOTES:** Not territorial, minimally aggressive, and wanders widely in search of food. Largely excludes Common Nighthawk from desert habitats. Becomes torpid ("hibernates") when food unavailable or when temperatures cool. **ESSAYS:** Nonvocal Sounds, p. 313; Interspecific Territoriality, p. 385; Temperature Regulation, p. 149. **REFS:** Caccamise, 1974; Grant, 1982.

dent in the courtship displays of the American Woodcock, Common Snipe, several swifts, and in the booming sound of Common Nighthawk flight. Sound made by the two wings or their carpal bones actually striking each other occur in the display flights of Short-eared and Long-eared Owls. One of the best-known woodland sounds of spring, the drumming of male Ruffed Grouse, is performed from a low perch such as a fallen log. The sound is produced by the cupped wings of the male grouse striking the air as he flaps them forward and upward. Grouse drumming serves for both territorial defense and mate attraction and is easily detectable as much as a quarter of a mile away.

Males of the eight hummingbird species that breed widely north of the Mexican border employ wind-and-feather-derived sounds in their territorial and courtship displays. Male Broad-tailed Hummingbirds use a shrill wing whistle when defending courting territories. Birds experimentally silenced by placing a thin film of glue on the tips of the noisemaking primary feathers defended their territories less effectively. Presumably they could not communicate threat and were generally less aggressive because they did not hear their own buzzing flight.

The most spectacular courtship sound of hummers is the explosive noise made by a male Anna's Hummingbird at the bottom of its U-shaped dive as it passes near a perched female. The name "hummingbird" was acquired from the early English colonists who knew only the Ruby-throated Hummingbird of the east with its buzzing flight. The majority of hummingbird species, however, produce only relatively inconspicuous flight sounds, and instead use song to a much greater extent in their courtship display.

SEE: Visual Displays, p. 5; What Do Birds Hear?, p. 299; Vocal Functions, p. 471; Bills, p. 209; Feathers, p. 309. REFS: Lawrence, 1967, Miller and Inouye, 1983; Skutch, 1973.

Nest Sanitation

The very fragility of nests may be adaptive in forcing many birds to build a new nest every year; nests that do not deteriorate over the winter can harbor potentially lethal numbers of parasites or pathogens that may withstand the cold and await returning nesters. Indeed, despite their appearance as peaceful retreats, nests are often alive with invertebrates feeding on the birds, on the birds' waste products, or on each other. Infestations of parasites (fly maggots, fleas, ticks, and mites) or pathogens (bacteria and fungi) are discouraged by various means. One that is widely used is, of course, removal of the fecal sacs of the young.

Recent work has shown that many birds repeatedly add green leaves or cedar bark with pesticidal properties to their nests. This behavior has been

Black Swift

Cypseloides niger Gmelin

NG–252; G–184; PW– 130; AW–pl 360; AM(II)–190

```
                        MF
                        I: 24–27 DAYS
    ?           1       ALTRICIAL
            MONOG       F: 45–49 DAYS
                        MF
```

BREEDING: Montane habitats, sea cliffs and caves. 1? brood. **DISPLAYS:** Courtship and cop performed in flight. **NEST:** On ledge or in crevice, oft near or behind waterfall; of moss, ferns, algae, little or no mud. Lined with fine rootlets, conif needles. Layers added annually. **EGGS:** Dull white, may be nest-stained. 1.2″ (29 mm). **DIET:** Flying insects. **CONSERVATION:** Winters in Mexico s to Costa Rica and in Greater Antilles (except PR). **NOTES:** Nest in colonies, generally of a few pairs. Strong, fast fliers; foraging height varies with weather, usu high in air. Forages over wide area, oft far from breeding site. Young have very weak feet relative to our other swifts, and remain in the nest until fledging. Natal down absent on young, instead have downlike semiplume covering before acquiring contour feathers. **ESSAYS:** Nonvocal Sounds, p. 313; Migration, p. 183; Feathers, p. 309; Site Tenacity, p. 189. **REFS:** Knorr, 1961; Kondla, 1973.

Chimney Swift

Supersp #22
Chaetura pelagica Linnaeus

NG–252; G–184; PE–204; AE–pl 335; AW–pl 361; AM(II)–192

```
CHIMNEY                      MF
                             I: 19–21 DAYS
TREE        MF       4–5     ALTRICIAL
   HOLLOW            (3–6)   F: 28–30 DAYS
                     COOP    MF +
```

BREEDING: Woodland, open areas, esp near human habitation. 1? brood. **DISPLAYS:** Courtship in flight; pair fly in "V-ing" display: following bird then leading bird raise wings in V, both then glide with wings fixed in V. **NEST:** Half saucer, attached to chimney wall, other suitable human-built structure, avg 22′ from top; prehistorically in hollow tree; of twigs, glued together and to wall with saliva. Built in 18–30 days, but eggs oft laid before complete. **EGGS:** White, unmarked. 0.8″ (20 mm). **DIET:** Flying insects. **CONSERVATION:** Winters in w Peru, upper Amazon Basin of e Peru, n Chile, and n w Brazil. Greatly benefited by arrival of Europeans providing superabundance of nest sites. **NOTES:** Nest in colonies, usu of a few pairs. Pairs oft assisted by male or female helper (occ 2 or 3). Except for first-year nesters, reproductive success not increased with helpers. Helpers feed young, occ incubate. Polygyny and polyandry reported but frequency unknown. Clutch size of first-year nesters <older nesters. Nest materials are collected while in flight. Young oft leave nest at three weeks and use sharp, strong claws to cling and crawl on vertical walls. Postbreeding flocks, oft numbering several thousand, commonly roost together in chimneys. **ESSAYS:** Feet, p. 239; Nonvocal Sounds, p. 313; Migration, p. 183; Cooperative Breeding, p. 283; Coloniality, p. 173; Communal Roosting, p. 615. **REFS:** Dexter, 1981; Zammuto et al., 1981.

recorded in numerous birds of prey that often reuse old nests (some kites, many hawks, and most eagles) and in some passerines (especially secondary cavity nesters, such as European Starlings and Purple Martins). Interestingly, nuthatches, which are also secondary cavity nesters, ritually smear pine pitch and rub insects around the entrance of their holes instead of adding fresh greenery. Both the pitch and the defensive chemicals of the insects may discourage parasites.

Many birds avoid reusing old nests, even if the nests do not deteriorate over the winter. When heavy parasite infestations do occur, nestling mortality rises, nests may be deserted, and in extreme cases, entire colonies have been known to move to a new location.

SEE: Masterbuilders, p. 445; Nest Materials, p. 369; Nest Lining, p. 391; Feathered Nests, p. 605; Disease and Parasitism, p. 399; Incubation: Heating Eggs, p. 393. REFS: Clark and Mason, 1985; Collias and Collias, 1984; Wimberger, 1984.

Copulation

Unlike the testes of mammals, those of birds vary greatly in size with the seasons. During the breeding season they may be several hundred times larger than they are during the rest of the year and can account for as much as a tenth of the male's body weight. The massive enlargement of the testes is triggered in temperate-zone birds by day length (curiously enough not timed by the amount of light received by the eyes, but by light passing through the skull and stimulating photoreceptors on the brain). As the days lengthen in the spring, increases in hormones produced by the brain initiate the enlargement of the testes. This stimulus occurs weeks in advance of the actual breeding season, so that the male arrives on the breeding grounds with the testes fully developed. A similar sequence results in the enlargement of the female reproductive organs, development of eggs in the ovaries, formation of the brood patch, and so on.

Enlarged testes secrete greater amounts of male hormones that may brighten skin (not feather) colors and stimulate singing and courtship behavior. During copulation, the male mounts the female from behind. Both sexes hold their tails to the side and turn back the feathers around the cloaca (the common opening of the bird's alimentary canal and excretory and reproductive systems), so that the swollen lips of the male's and female's cloacae can come into contact. In some birds, such as geese, ducks, and game birds, there is a grooved, erectile penis inside the male's cloaca. The penis guides the sperm, which have been stored in a nearby sac, into the female. In passerines, there is no penis, and copulation amounts to a brief "cloacal kiss" during which the sperm are transferred.

Once transferred, the sperm remain for a while in storage at the lower end of the oviduct, and then swim to the upper end of that duct to fertilize

Vaux's Swift

Supersp #22
Chaetura vauxi Townsend

NG–252; G–184; PE–204; PW– 130; AW–701; AM(II)–192

CHIMNEY   MF(?)   4–5   MF
0.6′–2′   (3–7) I: 18–20 DAYS
(To 20′)   MONOG ALTRICIAL
                           F: 28 DAYS
                           MF

BREEDING: Forests, esp burned or cutover areas providing snags. ? broods. **DISPLAYS:** Courtship and cop performed in flight. Lacks "V-ing" flight display of Chimney Swift. **NEST:** Attached to inside wall of hollow tree, occ in chimney, usu near bottom; of twigs or conif needles glued together and to wall with saliva. **EGGS:** White, unmarked. 0.7″ (18 mm). **DIET:** Flying insects. **CONSERVATION:** Winters from c Mexico s to Venezuela. **NOTES:** Polygyny reported but frequency unknown. To gather nest materials, birds break off twigs while in flight. Has not commonly accepted chimneys as nest sites. Young fed bolus of food brought by adult, not actually regurgitated. Both parents brood. Young oft leave nest at 3 weeks and use sharp, strong claws to cling and crawl on vertical walls. Postbreeding flocks, numbering several hundred, commonly roost together in chimneys. Roosting may be influenced by ambient temperature: birds roost earlier on colder days. **ESSAYS:** Feet, p. 239; Nonvocal Sounds, p. 313; Migration, p. 183; Communal Roosting, p. 615; Temperature Regulation, p. 149. **REFS:** Baldwin and Hunter, 1963; Baldwin and Zaczkowski, 1963.

White-throated Swift

Aeronautes saxatalis Woodhouse

NG–252; G–184; PW– 130; AW–781; AM(II)–192

?   4–5   ?
                    (3–6) I: ? DAYS
                    MONOG? ALTRICIAL
                            F: ? DAYS
                             MF(?)

BREEDING: Mountainous country near cliffs and canyons, occ coastal sea cliffs. ? broods. **DISPLAYS:** Courtship and cop performed in flight; male and female come together from opposite directions, engage, and may tumble slowly downward end over end for as much as 500′. **NEST:** Deep in crack or crevice of rock wall, occ in suitable building; of feathers glued together and to rock with saliva. Construction very prolonged. **EGGS:** White or creamy white, unmarked. 0.8″ (21 mm). **DIET:** Flying insects. **CONSERVATION:** Winters s through Mexico to Honduras. **NOTES:** Nests in small colonies of up to a dozen pairs. Traditional use of nest and roost sites over long time periods. Postbreeding flocks of up to 200 roost together in rock crevices. Able to become torpid during periods of cool temperatures and low food availability. Said to be the fastest of the N.A. swifts. Feet adapted for lateral grasping enable clinging to soft material such as feathers which compose the nest. **ESSAYS:** Site Tenacity, p. 189; Copulation, p. 317; Temperature Regulation, p. 149; Communal Roosting, p. 615. **REFS:** Collins, 1983; Dobkin et al., 1986.

the egg. A single copulation is usually sufficient to fertilize the eggs laid over a period of about a week. In some birds the sperm remain viable for much longer—turkeys have been reported to lay fertile eggs more than two months after copulation. Consequently, there is considerable variation among species in the frequency of copulations. If copulation is observed in the field, the habitat, time of day, position used, duration, and any associated behavior should be recorded.

In most terrestrial species, copulation takes place either on the ground, on a tree limb, or on some other perch. Some aquatic birds (phalaropes, ducks) copulate primarily in the water. Among the most spectacular sights North American bird enthusiasts can see is a mating flight of White-throated Swifts. A group may come swooping down a canyon at high speed, shortly after dawn, with pairs tumbling together as they copulate in midair.

Goshawks may copulate as many as 500 to 600 times per clutch of eggs, while the Eurasian Skylark (which has been introduced onto Vancouver Island) copulates but once. The reason for the difference appears to be related to the chances that other males will manage to copulate with the female in a "monogamous" pair. In birds of prey and many colonial species, males must spend long periods away from females and therefore cannot guard their mates from other males. It is in those species that multiple matings seem to occur, as the male attempts to dilute any other male's semen that the female may have acquired in his absence.

SEE: Monogamy, p. 597; Breeding Season, p. 55; Brood Patches, p. 427; Courtship Feeding, p. 181. REF: Birkhead and Moller, 1986.

How Do We Find Out About Bird Biology?

Many of the essays in this book are loaded with "weasel" words—birds *appear* to do this, or *seem* to behave in a certain manner, or *may* respond in a particular way for the following reason. Surely, one would think scientists could be more definitive about the biology of such a well-known group of animals. But they cannot.

One reason for the uncertainty is the difficulty of finding out what a rapidly flying animal does. Two White-throated Swifts that touch briefly in flight may appear to be copulating, but how (short of bringing them down for a biological assay) can we be sure? How can we even be sure that the two birds tumbling in midair as they sweep past us down a canyon at forty miles an hour are a male and a female? Finding answers in such cases may require detailed, logistically difficult, and time-consuming research involving such things as netting, trapping, examining and banding birds, photographing them with high-speed cameras, and often clever experimental alterations of the birds or their environments.

Suppose, after completing such a detailed study, a scientist is con-

Buff-bellied Hummingbird

Amazilia yucatanensis Cabot

NG–254; G–190; PW–pl 39; AE–pl 481; AM(II)–198

3'–8'   F?   2
PROMISC

F?
I: ? DAYS
ALTRICIAL
F: ? DAYS
F?

INSECTS

BREEDING: Open woodland, clearings, scrub. 2? broods. **DISPLAYS:** ? **NEST:** On small drooping limb or in fork of shrub or small tree; of plant fibers, plant down, covered with lichen, shredded bark, blossoms, bound with spider's silk, lined with plant down. **EGGS:** White, unmarked. 0.5″ (13 mm). **DIET:** Incl spiders. **CONSERVATION:** Winters s through Caribbean lowlands of Mexico to Belize. **NOTES:** Virtually unstudied. **ESSAYS:** Hummingbirds, Nectar, and Water, p. 333; Hovering Flight, p. 323; Hummingbird Foraging Bouts, p. 331; Coevolution, p. 405; Optimally Foraging Hummers, p. 335; How Do We Find Out About Bird Biology?, p. 319; Promiscuity, p. 145. **REFS:** Johnsgard, 1983; Tyrell and Tyrell, 1984.

Berylline Hummingbird

Amazilia beryllina Lichtenstein

NG–254; AM(II)–196

17'–25'   F?   2?
PROMISC

F?
I: ? DAYS
ALTRICIAL
F: ? DAYS
F?

INSECTS

BREEDING: Open pine and pine-oak woodland. ? broods. **DISPLAYS:** ? **NEST:** On slender branch of decid tree, occ shrub or conif tree; of plant fibers, plant down, covered with lichen, bound with spider's silk, oft with streamer of grass blades attached to bottom by spider's web, lined probably with plant down. **EGGS:** White, unmarked. 0.6″ (14 mm). **DIET:** Incl spiders. **CONSERVATION:** Winters in n w Mexico s through Honduras. **NOTES:** Virtually unstudied. **ESSAYS:** Hummingbirds, Nectar, and Water, p. 333; Hovering Flight, p. 323; Hummingbird Foraging Bouts, p. 331; Coevolution, p. 405; Optimally Foraging Hummers, p. 335; How Do We Find Out About Bird Biology?, p. 319; Promiscuity, p. 145. **REFS:** Johnsgard, 1983; Tyrell and Tyrell, 1984.

vinced that White-throated Swifts in one part of Arizona copulate in midair. How far can the researcher generalize such findings? Does it mean that White-throated Swifts everywhere copulate in midair? Do all other species of swifts copulate in midair? Ornithologists think all swifts are aerial maters. In fact, they assume that swifts are the only birds that do so on the wing. But they cannot be *certain* of either point. Maybe one obscure population of Palm Swifts in Asia actually mates only in their nests. And just possibly an Amazonian hummingbird, on occasion, copulates aerially above the canopy. That's why the authoritative *Dictionary of Birds* says, "Swifts are *apparently* unique in copulating in the air" (our emphasis). In short, statements by scientists are always provisional; they represent the best current evaluation of the situation, but are *always* subject to revision.

A related problem is that there are more than 8,000 species of birds, and, as we know, they are a rather diverse lot. Suppose, for instance, we wished to know whether female birds prefer males that hold superior territories. Just determining whether females of one species in one habitat have that preference is not a simple task. The territories of males must be mapped and criteria to judge territorial quality must be found. For example, to compare territories within a population of insect eaters an ecologist may be required to do many careful censuses of insect abundance during the breeding season, without disturbing the breeding birds. Finally, of course, the female choices must be evaluated, most likely by counting the number of nests and the number of young fledged within each male's territory, often a difficult task in itself.

So much for finding the answer for one species in one locality—how about other localities? And, since male birds of most species are territorial, what about other species? Obviously, it would be a mistake to generalize from the behavior of one population living in one habitat to all species of birds in all habitats. It would be necessary to see if female choices were made not only in a variety of species, but also in different habitats. If this were done, a pattern should emerge slowly, and with it an opportunity to draw tentative conclusions. Further studies may tend to confirm or refute those initial conclusions, and after enough studies have been completed, a consensus will emerge. For instance, territoriality in most male birds is so well documented that it is treated as fact. That females tend to mate with the holders of the better territories is not so well established, but many ecologists think that it eventually will be.

Learning about bird communities can be even more difficult than drawing conclusions about the behavior of single species. Suppose, for example, we wished to know whether Downy and Hairy Woodpeckers were competing in three square miles of forest. One way to find out would be to remove all the Downy Woodpeckers in one square mile, all the Hairy Woodpeckers in another, and leave the third square mile undisturbed. Then comparing the fledging rates in the three localities should provide substantial information on the degree of competition. The logistics of doing such an experiment would be daunting, but more important, we and many others

Lucifer Hummingbird

Calothorax lucifer Swainson

NG–254; G–190; PW–pl 39; AW–514; AM(II)–202

AGAVE 4'–6'	F?	2 PROMISC	F? I: 15–16 (?) DAYS ALTRICIAL F: 21–24 (?) DAYS F?	NECTAR

BREEDING: Arid scrub, semidesert, brushy slopes. ? broods. **DISPLAYS:** Male performs repeated lateral flights between two perches. Also vertical spiraling flight by male followed by rapid descent toward female, ending with series of pendulum-like swings. **NEST:** Of plant fibers and down, lichen, bud scales, blossoms, bound with spider's silk. **EGGS:** White, unmarked. 0.5" (13 mm). **DIET:** Incl spiders. **CONSERVATION:** Winters from n Mexico s to s c Mexico. **NOTES:** Little studied. Oft excluded from nectar resources by territorial male Black-chinned Hummingbirds. **ESSAYS:** Hummingbirds, Nectar, and Water, p. 333; Hovering Flight, p. 323; Hummingbird Foraging Bouts, p. 331; Metabolism, p. 325; Coevolution, p. 405; Optimally Foraging Hummers, p. 335; How Do We Find Out About Bird Biology?, p. 319; Promiscuity, p. 145; Interspecific Territoriality, p. 385. **REFS:** Johnsgard, 1983; Kuban et al., 1983; Tyrell and Tyrell, 1984.

Broad-billed Hummingbird

Cynanthus latirostris Swainson

NG–256; G–190; PW–pl 39; AW–pl 394; AM(II)–194

SHRUB VINE 3'–12'	F	2 PROMISC?	F I: ? DAYS ALTRICIAL F: ? DAYS F	INSECTS

BREEDING: Arid scrub, open woodland, desert riparian, and semidesert. 2? broods. **DISPLAYS:** Male display before female: a pendulum-swing accompanied by high-pitched "zing." **NEST:** Of grass stems, plant down, covered with leaves, bark, bound with spider's silk, lined with plant down. Unusual in not having lichen attached to exterior. Thin-walled, apparently because of little need for insulation. **EGGS:** White, unmarked. 0.5" (13 mm). **DIET:** Incl spiders. **CONSERVATION:** Winters s through Mexico. **NOTES:** Male makes a dry clicking or rattling noise in agonistic encounters with other hummingbirds. Little studied. **ESSAYS:** Hummingbirds, Nectar, and Water, p. 333; Hovering Flight, p. 323; Hummingbird Foraging Bouts, p. 331; Coevolution, p. 405; Metabolism, p. 325; Optimally Foraging Hummers, p. 335; How Do We Find Out About Bird Biology?, p. 319; Promiscuity, p. 145; Masterbuilders, p. 445. **REFS:** Baltosser, 1986; Johnsgard, 1983; Tyrell and Tyrell, 1984.

would consider its impact on the birds to raise serious ethical questions. Physical scientists generally ask whether the knowledge that might be gained from an experiment would justify the effort; biologists must also consider an experiment's effects on the organisms and natural systems being investigated.

In our essays we try to indicate how well established the conclusions are and, wherever possible, to describe the evidence on which they are based. The length of the treatments generally reflects how much is known about the birds, although the length of some of the most thoroughly studied species had to be shortened because of space constraints. You should be cautioned that there often appears to be more certainty in the data from poorly studied species; for instance, if only a few nests have been found, the range of heights above ground or clutch sizes will almost always be smaller than if hundreds of nests had been examined.

You may be disappointed by how little is known about so many aspects of avian ecology and behavior, even though many birds have been thoroughly studied. But looking at the bright side, that means that there are numerous opportunities for birder and ornithologist alike to add to the understanding of these fascinating creatures.

SEE: Facts, Hypotheses, and Theories, p. 567; Territoriality, p. 387; Polygyny, p. 443. REF: Ehrlich, 1986a.

Hovering Flight

Some birds, such as kestrels, remain motionless "wind hovering" above a point on the ground by flying into the wind at a speed equal to that of the wind, and other birds hover momentarily while foraging. Hummingbirds, on the other hand, are able to remain in the same place in still air as long as they wish—they are true hoverers. A hovering hummer keeps its body at about a 45° angle to the ground and moves its wings in more or less a figure-eight pattern, with the "eight" lying on its side. Hummers have an extremely mobile shoulder joint, permitting them to twist the wing in such a way as to generate lift on both the backward and the forward strokes. The front edge of the wing leads on both strokes, and on the backstroke it is the underside of the feathers that face upward, the shoulder rotation having, in effect, turned the wing upside down. In each stroke the bird is able to make use of some of the energy transferred into the motion of air on the previous sweep of its wings. For instance, on the forward stroke the airspeed of the wing is increased because it is traveling through air pushed toward the rear of the bird by the previous backstroke. The direction of thrust changes between the forward and backward strokes, so that they cancel each other out. Since the wings beat more than 20 times per second (sometimes as rapidly as 80 beats per second), inertia holds the bird's body essentially stationary.

White-eared Hummingbird
Hylocharis leucotis Vieillot

NG–256; G–190; PW–pl 39; AW–648; AM(II)–196

| TREE 5'–20' | F | 2 PROMISC | F I: 14–16 DAYS ALTRICIAL F: 23–26 DAYS F | INSECTS | HAWKS |

BREEDING: Open woodland, clearings, brushy slopes. 2 broods. **DISPLAYS:** Males gather in singing assemblies, a form of lek. Chosen male led to nesting area by female, where male performs aerial display to perched female followed by pair's nuptial flight incl alternating looping maneuvers. **NEST:** Of moss, plant down, pine needles, covered with lichen, occ small leaves, bound with spider's silk, lined with plant down. Lichen and spider webs continue to be added to exterior and plant down to interior, during incubation. Built in 15–20 days. **EGGS:** White, unmarked. 0.5" (12 mm). **DIET:** Incl spiders. **CONSERVATION:** Winters from n Mexico through highlands to n Nicaragua. **NOTES:** Extremely pugnacious, regularly dominates larger hummingbird species at feeding areas. **ESSAYS:** Hummingbirds, Nectar, and Water, p. 333; Hovering Flight, p. 323; Hummingbird Foraging Bouts, p. 331; Coevolution, p. 405; Optimally Foraging Hummers, p. 335; Leks, p. 259; Promiscuity, p. 145. **REFS:** Johnsgard, 1983; Tyrell and Tyrell, 1984.

Violet-crowned Hummingbird
Amazilia violiceps Gould

NG–256; G–190; PW–pl 39; AW–pl 397; AM(II)–198

| 6'–40' | F? | 2 PROMISC | F? I: ? DAYS ALTRICIAL F: ? DAYS F? | INSECTS | |

BREEDING: Arid or semiarid open woodland, riparian groves. 2? broods. **DISPLAYS:** ? **NEST:** Of plant down, twigs, lichen, bound with spider's silk, lined with plant down. **EGGS:** White, unmarked. 0.6" (14 mm). **DIET:** Incl spiders. **CONSERVATION:** Winters s through Mexico. **NOTES:** Virtually unstudied. **ESSAYS:** Hummingbirds, Nectar, and Water, p. 333; Hovering Flight, p. 323; Hummingbird Foraging Bouts, p. 331; Coevolution, p. 405; Optimally Foraging Hummers, p. 335; Metabolism, p. 325; How Do We Find Out About Bird Biology?, p. 319; Promiscuity, p. 145. **REFS:** Baltosser, 1986; Johnsgard, 1983; Tyrell and Tyrell, 1984.

This system makes hummingbirds extremely maneuverable and permits them to hover while they extract nectar from flowers that might otherwise be inaccessible. But the hovering flight is quite expensive: about 30 percent of the total body weight of hummingbirds is invested in the breast muscles (which power the wings), whereas other strong-flying birds have about 20 percent, and weak fliers may have only about 15 percent. The hummers would require an even greater investment in muscle if it were not for the way that their wings are always moving through air accelerated by the previous wing stroke.

SEE: How Do Birds Fly?, p. 161; How Fast and High Do Birds Fly?, p. 81; Adaptations for Flight, p. 507; Wing Shapes and Flight, p. 227.

Metabolism

The physical and chemical processes that maintain a bird's life are called, collectively, its "metabolism." A flow of energy is required to run the metabolism of any organism, and the basic energy source for all birds is the sun. Green plants "capture" the sun's energy in the process of photosynthesis, and birds then acquire it by eating plants or by eating other animals that eat plants. The energy is used to do the work of building tissues, contracting muscles, manufacturing eggs, processing information in the brain, and powering all the other activities of a living bird.

The entire metabolic process is run by biological catalysts known as enzymes. They are long, chainlike protein molecules that are twisted into characteristic three-dimensional shapes. Enzyme molecules function rather like templates to hold reacting molecules together in the proper position to speed their interactions. If your enzymes lose their shape ("denature"), they stop functioning, your metabolism ceases, and you're dead. Birds are no different. That's why boiling kills; it denatures enzymes.

To compare rates at which different animals use energy, scientists calculate for each the rate at which a resting animal under no stress consumes oxygen. That consumption is then used to calculate the basal metabolic rate, which is expressed as the number of kilocalories of energy used per kilogram of body weight, per hour. Small birds have proportionately larger surfaces (through which heat is lost) in relation to their mass of metabolizing tissue than do large birds. A Bushtit can maintain a body temperature like a Tundra Swan's because it has such a higher basal metabolism (i.e., uses proportionately more energy). Hummingbirds, with their tiny bodies and high levels of activity, have the highest metabolic rates of any animals —roughly a dozen times that of a pigeon and a hundred times that of an elephant. To maintain those rates, hummers have to consume about their weight in nectar daily. In fact, a warm-blooded animal can't be smaller than a hummer or a shrew. Further reduction in size would make it impossible

Blue-throated Hummingbird
Lampornis clemenciae Lesson

NG–256; G–190; PW–pl 39; PW–pl 396; AM(II)–200

HERB			F?		
			I: 17–18 DAYS		
TREE	F	2	ALTRICIAL	NECTAR	HAWKS
1'–30'		(1–2)	F: 24–29 DAYS		
		PROMISC?	F?		

BREEDING: Pine-oak and decid woodland, mountain canyons. ? broods. **DIS-PLAYS:** ? **NEST:** Usu covered from above by veg, occ on wire; of moss, plant fibers, bound with spider's silk, lined with plant down. Occ builds nest on top of old nest or on flycatcher nest. Built in 15–30 days. **EGGS:** White, unmarked. 0.6" (15 mm). **DIET:** Incl spiders. **CONSERVATION:** Winters s through Mexico. **NOTES:** Nests are generally well spaced. Males oft forage outside of their territories. Usu dominates smaller hummingbird species; forages with impunity in feeding territories of other species. Males separated from nesting females during breeding season, males usu occurring at higher elevations in the mountains. **ESSAYS:** Hummingbirds, Nectar, and Water, p. 333; Hovering Flight, p. 323; Hummingbird Foraging Bouts, p. 331; Coevolution, p. 405; Optimally Foraging Hummers, p. 335; Territoriality, p. 387; Promiscuity, p. 145. **REFS:** Johnsgard, 1983; Kuban and Neill, 1980; Lyon et al., 1977; Rio and Eguiarte, 1987; Tyrell and Tyrell, 1984.

Magnificent Hummingbird
Eugenes fulgens Swainson

NG–256; G–190; PW–pl 39; AW–pl 395; AM(II)–200

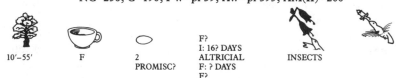

			F?		
			I: 16? DAYS		
10'–55'	F	2	ALTRICIAL	INSECTS	
		PROMISC?	F: ? DAYS		
			F?		

BREEDING: Pine-oak woodland, mountain canyons at higher elevations. ? broods. **DISPLAYS:** ? **NEST:** On horizontal limb of decid, occ conif tree; of mosses, plant fibers, coated with lichen, bound with spider's silk, lined with feathers. **EGGS:** White, unmarked. 0.6" (15 mm). **DIET:** Incl spiders. **CONSERVATION:** Winters from n c Mexico s to Panama. **NOTES:** Interspecifically aggressive around food resources, excluding other species of hummingbirds but not other avian nectar feeders such as orioles and thrashers. Depending on distribution of food resources, may be territorial or follow a "trapline," regularly visiting widely dispersed flowers on a repeated circuit. **ESSAYS:** Hummingbirds, Nectar, and Water, p. 333; Hovering Flight, p. 323; Hummingbird Foraging Bouts, p. 331; Coevolution, p. 405; Interspecific Territoriality, p. 385; Optimally Foraging Hummers, p. 335; Promiscuity, p. 145. **REFS:** Johnsgard, 1983; Rio and Eguiarte, 1987; Tyrell and Tyrell, 1984.

for the creature to eat fast enough to maintain its body temperature.

The basal metabolic rates of nonpasserine birds are very similar to those of some mammals. Passerines, however, tend to have 30–70 percent higher metabolic rates than either nonpasserines or mammals, for reasons that are not understood. Birds do not generally use more energy than mammals to get the same job done—indeed they often use less. Flying is faster and energetically cheaper than walking or running for comparably heavy animals. But, overall, birds and mammals are metabolically very similar.

When they are active, birds, of course, have metabolic rates well above their basal metabolism. When hovering, hummingbirds are using energy at as much as eight times the resting rate. At the other extreme of their activity range, hummingbirds may become torpid at night—that is, they let their body temperature drop, often until it is close to that of the surrounding air. A torpid individual may have a temperature 50° F below its normal 104° F, and a metabolic rate a third that of the basal metabolism. Generally, the temperature of torpid individuals is regulated at a level which may be correlated with the environment, being higher in tropical than in temperate zone species.

Hummingbirds do not become torpid every night. The ability to "lower their thermostats" appears to have evolved as a device for conserving energy, as when surviving periods of food shortage. At their active metabolic rate, hummers are only a few hours from starving to death; periods of bad weather threaten them severely even at their basal rate. Some other birds, such as swifts and poorwills, can also become torpid, but their lowered metabolic states have not been as thoroughly studied as those of hummingbirds.

When you are observing hummingbirds, you may see hummingbird (sphinx) moths hovering around flowers and sucking nectar through their long tongues. The parallels between the behavior of these day-flying moths and the hummers are striking. The larger of the sphinx moths are, in fact, heavier than the lightest birds. Interestingly, both birds and moths operate at similar body temperatures when hovering and feeding; the moths use metabolic heat generated by vibrating their wing muscles to raise their temperature to as high as 104° F. The "warm-blooded" (endothermic) birds drop their temperature during the night (when they are at rest) to conserve energy. The "cold-blooded" (ectothermic) sphinx moths become endotherms and use metabolic heat to raise their temperature only when they must to reach operating temperature for flight.

In cold weather, all nontorpid birds must operate at well above their basal metabolic rates in order to maintain their body temperatures. Small species, such as Black-capped and Boreal Chickadees that overwinter in temperate and subarctic areas, are at particular risk of freezing. They have proportionately large surface areas through which to lose heat and thus must eat continuously during short daylight hours to stoke their metabolic fires. If they do not, they will not reserve enough energy to see them through the long night. A wintering chickadee living at forty degrees below

Ruby-throated Hummingbird

NG–258; G–186; PE–186; PW–pl 39; AE–pl 479; AM(II)–204

10'–20' (6'–50')	F	2 PROMISC?	F I: 11–14? DAYS ALTRICIAL F: 14–28 DAYS F	INSECTS	

BREEDING: Decid or mixed woodland, open areas with scattered trees, gardens, parks. 2, occ 3 broods. **DISPLAYS:** Male swings pendulumlike before female, rising 8'–10' above and 5'–6' to each side of her. Preceding cop, male and female face each other, alternately ascend ca. 10' and descend, eventually dropping to ground and copulating. **NEST:** On small, downward-inclined decid, occ conif limb, oft near or over stream; of bud scales, lichen on exterior, bound with spider's silk, lined with plant down. Old nests occ occupied several seasons, refurbished annually. **EGGS:** White, unmarked. 0.5" (13 mm). **DIET:** Incl spiders; also takes tree sap from woodpecker drilling. **CONSERVATION:** Winters s through n c Mexico to c Costa Rica. Blue List 1978–86; widely reported to be declining. **NOTES:** Sexes apparently migrate separately; males first to arrive and to depart. Northern distribution may depend on availability of tree sap provided by sapsuckers' drilling. During hovering, wings beat 55 times/second, 61/second when moving backward, and at least 75/second when moving forward. **ESSAYS:** Blue List, p. 11; Nonvocal Sounds, p. 313; Hummingbirds, Nectar, and Water, p. 333; Hovering Flight, p. 323; Hummingbird Foraging Bouts, p. 331; Coevolution, p. 405; Optimally Foraging Hummers, p. 335; Commensal Feeding, p. 35. **REFS:** Johnsgard, 1983; Miller and Nero, 1983.

Black-chinned Hummingbird

NG–258; G–188; PW–pl 39; AW–pl 398; AM(II)–204

4'–8' (To 30')	F	2 (1–3) PROMISC?	F I: 13–16 DAYS ALTRICIAL F: 21 DAYS F	INSECTS	HAWKS

BREEDING: Open woodland, arid scrub, riparian woodland, chapparal, parks and gardens, most oft in arid regions. 2, occ 3 broods. **DISPLAYS:** Aerial courtship: male swings pendulumlike before female, rises 15' above her, pauses at apex and, flapping wings together, descends with a whizzing noise. Also described as following a narrow figure-8 pattern. **NEST:** On small limb, oft near or over stream, occ on vine or herb; of plant down bound with spider's silk, lichen absent from exterior, replaced by small leaves or flowers, lined with plant down. Nest may be perennial. Built in 3–7 days. **EGGS:** White, unmarked. 0.5" (13 mm). **DIET:** Incl spiders. **CONSERVATION:** Winters from n Mexico s to c Mexico. **NOTES:** Sexes apparently migrate separately in spring; males arrive first. Male roosts near female during courtship period. Bathes in water. **ESSAYS:** Hummingbirds, Nectar, and Water, p. 333; Hovering Flight, p. 323; Hummingbird Foraging Bouts, p. 331; Coevolution, p. 405; Optimally Foraging Hummers, p. 335; Nonvocal Sounds, p. 313; Bathing, p. 429; Promiscuity, p. 145; Migration, p. 183. **REFS:** Baltosser, 1986; Ewald, 1985; Johnsgard, 1983; Kuban et al., 1983.

freezing must spend something like twenty times as much time feeding per day as it would in the warmth of spring.

Birds have only slightly higher body temperatures than mammals; avian temperatures range from around the human level of 98.6° F (penguins, Whip-poor-wills) to 104° (most resting birds). But in general, the temperature ranges of the two groups, like their overall metabolisms, are remarkably similar, considering their different modes of life. Both have evolved to function at temperatures just below those at which the crucial protein enzymes begin to lose their stability, change their shape, and cease to function (denature). Maintaining constant body temperature is thus not just a problem for birds trying to keep from chilling in cold weather; it is an even more critical problem when the air temperature rises above that of the body. Then birds must avoid overheating and sudden death. The relatively large body surfaces of small birds take in environmental heat (and lose cooling water) quickly. That is one reason few songbirds are evident at midday during heat waves; they seek shade and become inactive. Soaring birds, in contrast, may take advantage of "thermals"—rising packets of warm air—to avoid midday heat and the denaturation of their proteins in the cool air of high altitudes.

Why do birds (and mammals) run these risks of maintaining a high, constant temperature, especially since it costs them to do so? A small bird must consume many times more food than an ectothermal lizard of the same weight that warms to operating temperature in the sun and cools again at night. One obvious reason for the constancy of their temperatures is so that birds and mammals can be active at night and during cold weather—they can penetrate areas and take on activities from which reptiles are barred. No lizard could feed alongside a Boreal Chickadee in winter. Another advantage to constancy is that the thousands of temperature-sensitive reactions that compose the metabolism can be better coordinated if they are in a relatively uniform thermal environment.

But why are temperatures of endotherms (and ectotherms when they are active) so close to the point of overheating? High temperatures, besides increasing the rate of chemical reactions, permit important physical functions that depend on diffusion to go on more rapidly. Heat speeds the diffusion of transmitter chemicals in nerve connections; the hotter a bird can be, the more rapidly vital information can be processed and commands sent to the bird's muscles. This allows birds to react more quickly. So high operating temperatures have clear advantages for both avian predators and prey; and unlike lizards and other ectotherms, birds are not dependent on the sun's warmth to attain those temperatures. It has also been suggested that maintaining a constant high brain temperature aids memory and facilitates learning.

SEE: Temperature Regulation and Behavior, p. 149; Drinking, p. 123; Hummingbird Foraging Bouts, p. 331; Spread-Wing Postures, p. 25; Black and White Plumage, p. 177. REFS: Calder, 1974, 1984; Calder and King, 1974; Paynter, 1974.

Costa's Hummingbird

Calypte costae Bourcier

NG–258; G–188; PW–pl 39; AW–pl 401; AM (II)–208

DECID   F   2   F   INSECTS
3′–5′   PROMISC?   I: 15–18 DAYS
(1′–30′)   ALTRICIAL
                               F: 20–23 DAYS
                               F

BREEDING: Desert, arid brushy foothills, and chaparral. 1 brood. **DISPLAYS**: Courtship: male flies in U-shaped pattern, rising to 100′, passing over female and shooting downward with a shrill continuous whistle or shriek, apparently of vocal origin. **NEST**: Also in yucca; loosely made of plant down, forb leaves, bud scales, flowers, bark strips, bound with spider's silk, lined with plant down. Distinctly grayish in appearance. **EGGS**: White, unmarked. 0.5″ (12 mm). **DIET**: Incl spiders. **CONSERVATION**: Winters s to n w Mexico. **NOTES**: Oft nests far from water. Males depart breeding grounds while late-nesting females are still incubating. **ESSAYS**: Hummingbirds, Nectar, and Water, p. 333; Hovering Flight, p. 323; Hummingbird Foraging Bouts, p. 331; Coevolution, p. 405; Optimally Foraging Hummers, p. 335; Migration, p. 183. **REFS**: Baltosser, 1986; Johnsgard, 1983.

Anna's Hummingbird

Calypte anna Lesson

NG–258; G–186; PW–pl 39; AW–pl 399; AM(II)–206

SHRUB   F   2   F   INSECTS   HAWKS
1.5′–30′   (1–3)   I: 14–19 DAYS
                     PROMISC   ALTRICIAL
                               F: 18–23 DAYS
                               F

BREEDING: Open woodland, chaparral, gardens. 2, possibly 3 broods. **DISPLAYS**: Male flight describes arc of vertical circle before female; rising very high, plummets downward making explosive chirp sound at lowest point, then rises straight above female, hovers and faces her at top of ascent, delivering brief squeaky song. Male chases female to nesting area, then, with body held horizontally, male flies rapidly back and forth in short, tight arcs above female. **NEST**: Varied; oft in oak, also vine, brush, and human-built structures; thick, well insulated, of plant down bound with spider's silk, lined with plant down and feathers. Building continues after eggs laid; lichen added to exterior. Usu built in 7 (range 3–14) days. **EGGS**: White, unmarked. 0.5″ (13 mm). **DIET**: Incl spiders; tree sap. **CONSERVATION**: Winters s to c Baja and to n w Mexico. Range expanding to n. Widespread planting of eucalyptus and provision of artificial and exotic floral nectar sources year-round in gardens have led to permanent residency by many birds in coastal CA and likely increased abundance. **NOTES**: Fond of bathing, usu in dew-covered foliage. Post-breeding movement of migrants from coast to montane habitats. Defends feeding territories in nonbreeding season. **ESSAYS**: Nonvocal Sounds, p. 313; Hummingbirds, Nectar, and Water, p. 333; Hovering Flight, p. 323; Hummingbird Foraging Bouts, p. 331; Coevolution, p. 405; Optimally Foraging Hummers, p. 335; Range Expansion, p. 459; Bathing and Dusting, p. 429; Feeding Birds, p. 349. **REFS**: Ewald and Orians, 1983; Powers, 1987; Stiles, 1972, 1982.

Hummingbird Foraging Bouts

Like other small animals that are "warm-blooded" (that is, like us, maintain a high body temperature by generating metabolic heat), hummingbirds need a prodigious energy intake. In spite of this, Rufous Hummingbirds don't feed constantly. In fact, they make only 14–18 foraging bouts per hour, each taking less than a minute. For the remainder of the hour the bird perches quietly. Ecologists William Karasov, Duong Phan, Jared Diamond, and Lynn Carpenter discovered the reason for this inactivity.

They found that the hummers pass nectar through their digestive tracts very rapidly—average transit time through the gut is less than an hour. In this short time, they are able to extract about 97 percent of the sugars from the nectar. But why do they sit around so much "doing nothing" when they could be sipping more nectar? The answer was discovered with a clever experiment using radioactive isotopes as tracers to follow what happens to the nectar. In fact, the "resting" hummers aren't "doing nothing"—they are emptying their crops (specially modified parts of the digestive system that store food immediately after it is taken in). They apparently wait until the crop is about half empty before foraging again, and it takes about four minutes for this to happen (which would account for the roughly 15 bouts of nectar gathering per hour). They forage only as often as required to keep up with the rate at which the crop can pass nectar into the rest of the digestive system; more frequent foraging would carry a high energy cost but provide no further benefit. While it is emptying its crop, therefore, the bird conserves energy by remaining immobile.

The hummers don't have room to take in any more nectar until the crop is partly drained. What limits the rate of crop emptying is not yet clear, but it is probably how fast the intestine can absorb the sugar, or how fast the stomach can acidify the crop contents (an important step in digestion). As Diamond and his colleagues say, ". . . despite external appearances, hummingbirds may be energy maximizers, taking in energy as rapidly as their digestive processes permit."

SEE: Metabolism, p. 325; Optimally Foraging Hummers, p. 335; Hummingbirds, Nectar, and Water, p. 333.   REF: Diamond et al., 1986.

Calliope Hummingbird

Stellula calliope Gould

NG–260; G–186; PW–pl 39; AW–pl 400; AM(II)–208

			F		
DECID	F	2	I: 15–16 DAYS	INSECTS	HAWKS
SHRUB		PROMISC	ALTRICIAL		
1.8'–70'			F: 18–23 DAYS		
			F		

BREEDING: Open montane forest, mountain meadows, willow and alder thickets. ? broods. **DISPLAYS:** Courtship: male flies in U–shaped pattern before female, swooping down from a height of 65', making a short "bzt" sound at the bottom, then ascending again. **NEST:** On limb or conif cone. Well camouflaged; of moss, shredded bark and cones, plant down, covered with lichen, bound with cocoons and spider's silk, lined with plant down. Oft built on old nests in successive years. **EGGS:** White, unmarked. 0.5" (12 mm). **DIET:** Incl spiders; tree sap. **CONSERVATION:** Winters in n w Mexico s to c Mexico. **NOTES:** Smallest bird n of Mexico. Territorial males defending richer territories (more food resources) display more frequently, although access to females rather than nectar may be most important determinant of breeding territory "quality." As with many other N.A. hummingbirds, nests invariably placed directly beneath shielding branch or leaves. Males depart breeding grounds while females still incubating. More common in migration than is oft apparent because usu stay low in veg. **ESSAYS:** Nectar and Water, p. 333; Hovering, p. 323; Hummingbird Foraging, p. 331; Coevolution, p. 405; Optimally Foraging Hummers, p. 335; Territoriality, p. 387. **REFS:** Armstrong, 1987; Calder, 1971; Johnsgard, 1983; Tamm, 1985; Tyrell and Tyrell, 1984.

Broad-tailed Hummingbird

Selasphorus platycercus Swainson

NG–260; G–186; PW–pl 39; AW–pl 393; AM(II)–210

			F		
CONIF	F	2	I: 14–17 DAYS	INSECTS	HAWKS
3'–15'		PROMISC	ALTRICIAL		
(To 30')			F: 21–26 DAYS		
			F		

BREEDING: Open woodland, brushy slopes, riparian and montane thickets. 1, possibly 2 broods. **DISPLAYS:** Male flies before female in U-shaped pattern, diving from 30'–50'. Both birds may ascend to 90', one 4'–5' below the other, before descending together. **NEST:** Usu on horizontal limb, occ in forb, oft over or near mountain stream; of plant down bound with cocoons or spider's silk, exterior of lichen, leaves, shredded bark, plant fibers, lined with plant down or spider's silk. **EGGS:** White, unmarked. 0.5" (13 mm). **DIET:** Incl spiders; tree sap. **CONSERVATION:** Winters in highlands of n Mexico s to Guatemala. **NOTES:** In forward flight, characteristic shrill, buzzing whistle made by air rushing through slots created by tapered tips of male's outer wing feathers; esp important in maintaining courtship territories. Females show strong breeding site fidelity, esp if previously successful there. Females oft long-lived. Fond of bathing, oft on flat rocks in shallow mountain streams. **ESSAYS:** Nonvocal Sounds, p. 313; Nectar and Water, p. 333; Temperature Regulation, p. 149; Hovering, p. 323; Foraging Bouts, p. 331; Optimally Foraging Hummers, p. 335; Site Tenacity, p. 189; Bathing, p. 429; How Long Can Birds Live?, p. 643. **REFS:** Calder et al., 1983; Miller and Inouye, 1983; Waser, 1976.

Bird Names—VI

Hummingbirds are, of course, named for the sound their wings make, but why is one called the Calliope hummer? It has nothing to do with the steam-powered musical instrument often heard at fairs and circuses. Instead it was named after the Muse of epic poetry, whose name in Greek means "beautiful voiced." Why the famous English ornithologist and artist John Gould gave that name to our smallest hummer, hardly "epic" in any dimension and more notable for its relative silence, is mysterious.

Chuck-will's-widow, Whip-poor-will, and Poorwill all have names suggesting their songs. The song of the European Nightjar is said to be "jarring," and the name carries to our Buff-collared representative. All are "goatsuckers," from the myth, going back at least to Aristotle's time, that they sucked on the udders of goats.

Owl is a name originating in the birds' calls—the old joke that it is a cockney version of "howl" is not far off.

REF: Choate, 1985; Owen, 1985.

Hummingbirds, Nectar, and Water

Hummingbirds feed on copious quantities of nectar. When, for example, a Broad-tailed or Rufous Hummingbird is subsisting on the nectar of scarlet gilias in subalpine areas of Colorado, it must take in more than its normal body water content every day in order to get enough sugar to fuel its metabolism. (It gets fats and protein by also feeding on small insects.) Its kidneys must work very effectively to retain needed body salts while removing the excess water that floods them after sugar is absorbed from the nectar. In spite of their small size, and thus natural susceptibility to evaporative loss of water (since they have a huge area relative to their volume), small hummingbirds in the laboratory fed on synthetic gilia nectar produced urine and cloacal fluid (the latter being water passed directly through the gut) amounting to 75–85 percent of their body weight daily. That is the rough equivalent of a human adult voiding 20 gallons of water a day!

SEE: Determining Diets, p. 535; Hummingbird Foraging Bouts, p. 331: Optimally Foraging Hummers, p. 335; Diet and Nutrition, p. 587; Salt Glands, p. 29; Bird Droppings, p. 263.   REFS: Calder and Hiebert, 1983; Diamond et al., 1986.

Rufous Hummingbird

NG–260; G–188; PE–186; PW–pl 39; AE–pl 480; AW–pl 391; AM(II)–212

DECID	F	2	F I: 12–14? DAYS ALTRICIAL	INSECTS	HAWKS
VINE		(1–3)	F: 20 DAYS		
1'–15' (To 50')		PROMISC	F		

BREEDING: Conif forest, thickets and brushy slopes, foraging in adjacent meadows. 1, occ 2 broods. **DISPLAYS:** Male flies before female in U-shaped, or occ complete oval, pattern. Male ascends with back to female and dives with gorget facing her (as in other hummingbirds). Whining note made at bottom of dive, caused by air rushing through wing feathers. **NEST:** Usu on drooping limb; of plant down, covered with lichen, moss, bud scales, leaves, shredded bark, plant fibers, bound with spider's silk, lined with plant down. Oft reused and built upon in succeeding years. **EGGS:** White, unmarked. 0.5" (13 mm). **DIET:** Incl spiders; tree sap. **CONSERVATION:** Winters s to s c Mexico. **NOTES:** Nests oft clustered, appearing semicolonial. Pugnacious defender of nest area. Males arrive well in advance of females on breeding grounds. Fall migration through mountains at high elevation, defending temporary feeding territories; preferentially exploit flowers (along territory periphery) in early morning which are most subject to being usurped by intruding birds. **ESSAYS:** Hummingbird Foraging Bouts, p. 331; Optimally Foraging Hummers, p. 335; Nonvocal Sounds, p. 313; Nectar and Water, p. 333; Coevolution, p. 405; Hovering Flight, p. 323. **REFS:** Gass, 1979; Johnsgard, 1983; Kodric-Brown and Brown, 1978; Paton and Carpenter, 1984; Tyrell and Tyrell, 1984.

Allen's Hummingbird

NG–260; G–188; PW–pl 39; AW–pl 392; AM(II)–212

SHRUB	F	2	F I: 17–22 DAYS ALTRICIAL	INSECTS	HAWKS
VINE		PROMISC?	F: 22–25 DAYS		
1'–20' (To 90')			F		

BREEDING: Chaparral, thickets, brushy slopes, open conif forest. 2 broods. **DISPLAYS:** Male flies before female in J–shaped pattern, swooping down from a height of 75', making a prolonged metallic buzz at the bottom, then curving upward ca. 25' and hovering. Oft preceded and followed by pendulumlike rocking display covering ca. 25'. **NEST:** Oft on limb of conif or decid tree; of moss, forb stems, plant down, covered with lichen, bound with spider's silk, lined with plant down. Lichens continue to be added to exterior during incubation. Built in 8–11 days. **EGGS:** White, unmarked. 0.5" (13 mm). **DIET:** Incl spiders. **CONSERVATION:** Winters in Baja and c Mexico. **NOTES:** Nests oft clustered, appearing semicolonial. Pugnacious defender of nest area. Adult males depart breeding grounds half a month before females; young males are last to leave, departing one month after adult males. **ESSAYS:** Hummingbird Foraging Bouts, p. 331; Optimally Foraging Hummers, p. 335; Hummingbirds, Nectar, and Water, p. 333; Coevolution, p. 405; Hovering Flight, p. 323; Migration, p. 183; Promiscuity, p. 145. **REFS:** Johnsgard, 1983; Phillips, 1975; Tyrell and Tyrell, 1984.

Optimally Foraging Hummers

Do animals gather food efficiently—that is, in a way that maximizes their intake per unit of effort? This question has long interested ecologists and has led to the formulation of *optimal foraging theory,* which describes what sorts of behavior should be observed if the foragers are feeding with a minimum of wasted effort. For example, an animal defending a feeding territory should make that territory large enough to maximize its energy "profit." Territory size would be optimal when there is the greatest possible difference between the amount of energy that could be obtained from the territory and the expenditure of energy required to gather food from it and patrol and defend it.

So much for what *should* happen according to the theory. But does the theory reasonably describe what actually goes on in nature? It has proven quite difficult to test optimal foraging theory in the field. Among other things, periodically catching an animal to measure its weight gain (or loss) under different conditions is almost certain to modify its behavior. But biologists F. Lynn Carpenter, David C. Paton, and Mark A. Hixon found an ingenious way to test optimal foraging theory, using Rufous Hummingbirds. These hummers establish feeding territories during stops on their 2,000-mile migration between their breeding grounds in the Pacific Northwest and their wintering habitat in southern Mexico. They zealously guard those territories, driving off hawkmoths, butterflies, other hummers, and even bees that might compete for the nectar. In addition, they deplete the nectar resources around the periphery of their territories as early in the day as they can, in order to outcompete other nectar-sippers that might try to sneak a drink at the territory edge.

When half of the flowers in a territory were covered with cloth so the birds could not drain them, Carpenter and her coworkers found that the resident hummer increased its territory size. This showed that territoriality was tied to the availability of nectar, and that the bird could in some way assess the amount of nectar it controlled. Then, by substituting a sensitive scale topped by a perch for the territory-holder's traditional perch, they were able to measure the bird's weight each time it alighted. The researchers found that the hummers optimized their territory size by trial and error, making it larger or smaller until their daily weight gain was at a maximum.

In this case of migrant-territorial hummers, theory accurately predicted how a bird behaves in nature. But when hummingbirds are not migrating, things seem to get more complicated. For example, hummingbird student William Calder of the University of Arizona observed that, near the Rocky Mountain Biological Laboratory in Colorado, territories were larger than usual in 1986. That was a year when hummers were rare and, as a result, nectar resources were superabundant. Apparently males made their territories larger in order to increase their chances of finding a mate. So theory that explains behavior in one set of circumstances may have to be modified

Belted Kingfisher

Ceryle alcyon Linnaeus

NG–262; G–192; PE–186; PW–pl 44; AE–pl 433; AW–pl 503; AM(II)–216

SNAG   CAVITY   6–7   MF
              MF   (5–8)   I: 23–24 DAYS
                    MONOG? ALTRICIAL
                            F: 23 + ? DAYS
                            MF?

BREEDING: Usu along watercourses, both freshwater and marine. 1 brood. **DISPLAYS:** Prolonged rapid succession of mewing calls. **NEST:** Horizontal (or slightly upward-sloping) burrow in vertical bank near water; prefer soil with high sand, low clay composition. Male and female alternately dig and remove detritus. Usu 3′–6′, may reach 15′ in length. Nest chamber holds grass or leaf saucer. Occ in tree cavity. **EGGS:** White. 1.4″ (34 mm). **DIET:** Occ also takes aquatic inverts, amphibians, reptiles, insects, young birds, mice; rarely berries. Also oysters and squid on coast. Young fed regurgitant. Ejects pellets. Dives from perch or hovers and dives from above. **CONSERVATION:** Winters s to n S.A. **NOTES:** Nestlings cling together and can maintain body heat in a group at 6 days, whereas lone nestling requires 16 days. Mates can recognize each other by distinctive calls given when approaching nest. After fledging, parents teach fishing to perched young by dropping dead meals into water for retrieval; at 10 days postfledging, young catch live food and are forced from parental territory. Fish fills throat while rapid digestion allows it to inch down gullet. Solitary when not breeding, defends individual feeding territories, size inversely correlated with food abundance. **ESSAYS:** Birds and the Law, p. 293; Swimming, p. 73; Vocal Functions, p. 471; Pellets, p. 297; Temperature Regulation, p. 149; Territoriality, p. 387; Parental Care, p. 555. **REFS:** Brooks and Davis, 1987; Davis, 1982, 1986.

Ringed Kingfisher

Ceryle torquata Linnaeus

NG–262; G–192; AE–pl 434; AM(II)–216

           MF   4–5   MF
                  (3–6)   I: ? DAYS
                  ?   ALTRICIAL
                        F: 34–35 DAYS
                        ?

BREEDING: Lakes, rivers, streams, lagoons. 1 brood. **DISPLAYS: ?** **NEST:** Tunnels 5′–6′ into perpendicular banks, occ far from water. Leisurely excavation limited to drier seasons. Working alternately, each member of pair emerges from excavation head-first, removing the detritus piled up by the other. **EGGS:** White. 1.7″ (44 mm). **DIET:** Also takes frogs, aquatic reptiles. Dives from high perch or hovers and dives from above. **CONSERVATION:** Winter resident. **NOTES:** Largest N.A. kingfisher. Adults switch incubation stints twice daily. Breeding biology little studied. **ESSAYS:** Pellets, p. 297; Swimming, p. 73; Masterbuilders, p. 445; Who Incubates?, p. 27; How Do We Find Out About Bird Biology?, p. 319. **REF:** McGrew, 1971.

before it accurately predicts what will happen in other circumstances, as when reproductive and foraging strategies cannot simultaneously be optimized.

SEE: Territoriality, p. 387; Migration, p. 183; Facts, Hypotheses, and Theories, p. 567; Hummingbirds, Nectar, and Water, p.333. REFS: Carpenter et al., 1983; Diamond, 1984b.

Bird Names—VII

The term kingfisher comes from Anglo-Saxon and means "king of the fishes." The Belted Kingfisher is so-named because of the belt of blue-gray feathers across its white breast. The generic name of that kingfisher, *Ceryle*, comes from the Greek for "seabird" or "kingfisher." The trivial name (second part of the species name), *alcyon*, comes from the Greek also; a lady of that name so grieved after her drowned husband that the gods turned them both into kingfishers.

Vaux's Swift was named by John K. Townsend, a contemporary of Audubon's, in honor of his friend, William S. Vaux. John K. Townsend was an early explorer of the far west, and Audubon named Townsend's Solitaire after him because he collected the first specimen near the Columbia River.

Kingbirds are probably named for their aggressive, domineering behavior, indicated also by their generic name, *Tyrannus* from the Latin for "tyrant." Pileated, as in Pileated Woodpecker, means "capped," in this case referring to the bird's red crest. Interestingly it is not clear whether woodpecker itself refers to a "pecker of wood" or a "pecker in the woods."

Becard is from French and German, meaning "big beak." Lark is based on the Anglo-Saxon word for the same bird. Martin is from the proper name "Martin" in French; robin is the French diminutive of "Robert." The generic name of the Purple Martin, *Progne*, remembers the Latin version of a figure in Greek mythology, Procne, who was transformed by the gods into a swallow. "*Turdus*," the generic name of the American Robin, is the Latin word for "thrush."

REFS: Choate, 1985; Owen, 1985.

Green Kingfisher

Chloroceryle americana Gmelin

NG–262; G–192; PW–pl 44; AE–pl 482; AW–pl 523; AM(II)–218

	5	MF	
?	(3–6)	I: 19–21 DAYS	
	?	ALTRICIAL	
		F: 22–26 DAYS	
		MF	

BREEDING: Streams, rivers, lakes, marshes, swamps. ? broods. **DISPLAYS:** ? **NEST:** Burrow in sandy bank near water. Tunnel usu 5'–8' above waterline, 2'–3' long. Eggs may be surrounded by fishbone, scale and shell pellets, but usu no nesting materials added. Unlike other kingfishers, entrance oft hidden. **EGGS:** White. 1.0" (25 mm). **DIET:** Dives for fish from low perch; usu does not hover. **CONSERVATION:** Winter resident. **NOTES:** More nests destroyed by fire ants than by all other enemies combined. Oft driven from territory by Belted Kingfisher. Female incubates at night; male takes turn, leaving female free for longest period in afternoon. Vocal exchange at incubation changeover. Young forced from parental territory one month postfledging. Requires less water depth and less perch height than do other kingfishers. **ESSAYS:** Pellets, p. 297; Swimming, p. 73; Hawk-Eyed, p. 229; Who Incubates?, p. 27. **REF:** Oberholser, 1974.

Northern Flicker

Colaptes auratus Linnaeus

NG–264; G–194; PE–190; PW–pl 40; AE–pl 348; AW–pl 370; AM (II)–244

6'–15' (To 100')	MF (?)	5–8 (3–12) MONOG	MF I: 11–14 DAYS ALTRICIAL F: 25–28 DAYS MF		HAWKS BARK GLEAN

BREEDING: Nearly ubiquitous below tree line where nest sites and open ground for feeding occur together. 1 brood, 2 in s. **DISPLAYS:** Courtship: noisy, active, with calling, drumming, wing and tail flashing, billing, and bobbing while pair face each other. Aggressive displays include bill pointing, head swinging/bobbing, tail spreading. **NEST:** Prefer snag; will use variety of cavities: poles and posts, houses, banks, haystacks, boxes. Occ usurp kingfisher and Bank Swallow burrows. Cavities oft perennial. Excavation time varies, avg 12 days; male usu selects site. **EGGS:** White. 1.1" (28 mm). **DIET:** Esp ants (more than any other N.A. bird); also occ seeds, acorns, nuts, grain. Young fed regurgitant. **CONSERVATION:** Winters within N.A. **NOTES:** Most terrestrial of N.A. woodpeckers. Starlings, squirrels, screech owls, kestrels may usurp holes. Large clutch sizes usu represent output of 2 females. Both sexes brood, but mostly female. Hybrid zone between Yellow- and Red-shafted subspecies appears stable; no evidence for preferential mating of birds with similar plumage-types within hybrid zone. Early clutches larger than later ones; clutches larger in n. Clutches of Gilded Flicker subspecies significantly smaller, avg 4. **ESSAYS:** Variation in Clutch Sizes, p. 339; Great Plains Hybrids, p. 625; Walking vs. Hopping, p. 69; Species and Speciation, p. 355; Average Clutch Size, p. 51; Hybridization, p. 501. **REFS:** Grudzien et al., 1987; Koenig, 1984; Moore and Koenig, 1986.

Variation in Clutch Sizes

The number of eggs in a set laid by a female bird tends to vary among taxonomic groups. Usually petrels, albatrosses, and shearwaters lay 1 egg, auks and vultures lay 1 or 2, terns and gulls 2–3, shorebirds and cormorants 3–4, hawks and songbirds 2–5, grouse and ptarmigan 5–12, ducks 7–12, and pheasants and partridges 8–18. Clutch sizes differ not only among major taxonomic groups and among species, but also among populations and individuals of the same species (as is apparent from the ranges of clutch sizes given for many species in this guide). For instance, both the European Robin (a thrush only distantly related to our robin) and the Snow Bunting lay larger clutches in the northern than in the southern parts of their ranges. In addition, older females of some species lay more eggs than do younger females.

Few topics have fascinated students of birds more than the causes of such variations in clutch size. Why do birds near the equator lay fewer eggs than related birds near the poles do? Why do seabirds that forage close to shore lay more eggs than those that forage far from shore? Why do tropical rain-forest birds generally have smaller clutches than those that dwell on tropical savannas? Why do birds that are colonial or nest at relatively high densities often lay fewer eggs than solitary relatives do? Why, in multiple-brooded birds, does clutch size often decline as the breeding season progresses? Why do small species tend to have larger clutches than large species do?

The quick answer to all of these questions is that birds lay the number of eggs that will permit them to produce the maximum number of offspring —but that number varies with latitude, habitat, body size, etc. That answer is provided by evolutionary theory, which says that winning the game of natural selection involves producing as many surviving young as possible. A female laying too many eggs may lose them all as a result of being unable to properly incubate them, may attract nest robbers, may be too weakened by the reproductive effort to survive the winter, or (most likely) may be unable to properly care for the young. On the other hand, by laying too few eggs, the bird will fledge fewer young than it is capable of rearing.

Consider some more detailed explanations of trends in clutch size. Ornithologist N. P. Ashmole has offered an explanation of one of these trends —the increase in the number of eggs per set from equator to pole. Such "latitudinal variation" in clutch size is related to the amount of food produced per unit area of habitat. More specifically, clutch size is positively related to resource abundance during the breeding season relative to the density of bird populations (abundance per unit area) at that time. If, when the birds are not breeding, their population sizes are limited by food shortages, then population density would be low at egg-laying time. And if resources increase only slightly during the breeding season, then natural selection would not favor large clutches, since food for the hatchlings would

Red-bellied Woodpecker

NG–264; G–196; PE–190; AE–pl 349; AM(II)–226

<40'	MF(?)	4–5	MF	NUTS	HAWKS?
(5'–120')		(3–8)	I: 12–14 DAYS	FRUIT	FOLIAGE
		MONOG	ALTRICIAL	SEEDS	GLEAN
			F: 24–27 DAYS		
			MF		

BREEDING: Decid, occ conif woodland, riparian forest, swamps, parks and towns. 1 brood in n, 2–3 in s. **DISPLAYS:** Include crest raising, wing and tail spreading, bowing, V–shaped flight. Courtship of mutual tapping and reverse mounting. **NEST:** Usu in decid snag; oft more than one hole/tree; may be perennial. Also use poles and birdhouses. Nest excavated in 7–10 days. **EGGS:** White, unmarked. 1.0″ (25 mm). **DIET:** Incl acorns. In s, favor oranges (may be pests, tap sap). Occ usurp sapsucker wells. Hoard nuts, fruit and insects. Young fed insects, berries. Oft work upward on trees. Occ feed on ground. **CONSERVATION:** Winter within U.S.; irregular wandering is food-dependent, some flocking in s U.S., oft in assoc with Yellow-bellied Sapsuckers. **NOTES:** Starlings usurp completed excavations. Male incubates and broods at night. Interspecifically territorial with Red-headed Woodpeckers in fall/winter. Hybridizes with Golden-fronted Woodpecker in area of overlap. **ESSAYS:** Feeding Birds, p. 349; Great Plains Hybrids, p. 625; Superspecies, p. 375; Hoarding Food, p. 345; Interspecific Territoriality, p. 385; Hybridization, p. 501. **REFS:** Jackson, 1976; Reller, 1972; Smith, 1987.

Gila Woodpecker

NG–264; G–196; PW–pl 40; AW–pl 375; AM(II)–224

CACTUS			MF	
DECID	?	3–4	I: 12–14 DAYS	HAWKS
15'–30'		(3–5)	ALTRICIAL	
		MONOG	F: ? DAYS	
			MF (?)	

BREEDING: Desert with large cacti, semidesert, riparian woodland and towns in arid regions. 2–3 broods if food abundant. **DISPLAYS:** Aggressive interactions: bowing (head bobbing), bill pointing, and head shaking. **NEST:** Saguaro hole usu not used in year excavated; sap surrounding excavation must first harden. Unlined. Perennial. Excavations made after brood raised. **EGGS:** White, unmarked. 1.0″ (25 mm). **DIET:** Insects, bird eggs; fruit (esp cactus), berries (esp mistletoe), some cactus pulp, acorns. Occ caches acorns. **CONSERVATION:** Winter resident. **NOTES:** Competes with other species for nest sites; defends nest sites and nest holes from Northern Flickers and European Starlings by excluding them from territory. Old holes also used by owls, kestrels, and martins. Young are fed for prolonged period beyond fledging. **ESSAYS:** Superspecies, p. 375; Hoarding Food, p. 345; Interspecific Territoriality, p. 385; Parental Care, p. 555. **REFS:** Brenowitz, 1978; Korol and Hutto, 1984; Short, 1982.

be limited. But if the increase in food were large during the breeding season, then, everything else being equal, raising a large brood should be possible. Thus the largest clutches should be found in high latitudes, where there is an enormous increase in productivity in the spring and summer (as anyone who has braved northern mosquitoes knows only too well), and the smallest clutch sizes might be expected in nonseasonal tropical rain forests, where productivity is rather uniform throughout the year.

According to Ashmole's hypothesis, there should be considerable uniformity of clutch size within a locality, since the seasonality of production should affect all the local birds. Such uniformity is precisely what has been found in tests conducted by avian ecologist Robert Ricklefs. In both the Western and Eastern Hemispheres, for instance, the most common number of eggs in the wet tropics is 2 or 3, but in temperate and arctic regions it is 4 to 6. For one series of 13 localities spread from Borneo to Alaska, 48–88 percent of the passerine species in each locality fall within a range of 1 egg. For example, in an equatorial rain forest in Borneo, 86 percent of the species laid an average of 2–3 eggs, and in another rain forest in west Java 75 percent were in that range. In a thorn forest in Oaxaca, Mexico, about one half of the bird species laid an average of 3–4 eggs, and on an Alaskan tundra all of the species averaged between 4.5 and 5.5.

Most important, average clutch size under Ashmole's hypothesis is predicted to be closely and inversely related to resource productivity during the *nonbreeding* season; the lower the off-season productivity, the larger should be the clutch. In order to test the hypothesis, woodpecker specialist Walter Koenig of the University of California tabulated the sizes of 411 complete clutches of Northern Flickers from a wide range of localities. He found that, as predicted, clutch size declined significantly as one moved from localities where resources are scarce in the winter to ones where they are abundant. Koenig found that, as predicted by Ashmole's hypothesis, flicker clutch size is not related to resource productivity during the breeding season; he found no correlation between the two.

On the other hand, average clutch size should be positively related to breeding season resource productivity *per breeding pair* of birds. Such a relationship was found in a series of localities spread from Costa Rica to Alaska. Thus it isn't the breeding season productivity per se that counts, but that productivity in relationship to the bird density at that season. When there are few winter survivors, so that breeding density is low, the breeders will not seriously compete for resources, and so will have a chance to raise large broods.

Seasonal differences in food resources seem to explain latitudinal (and, similarly, other geographic and habitat) trends in clutch size. Food is also obviously the key to the difference between onshore and offshore feeding seabirds—the former can rear more chicks because they can visit the nest with food more often. Competition for food also probably explains why clutch sizes are smaller in dense rather than sparse populations. Declining

Golden-fronted Woodpecker

Supersp #25
Melanerpes aurifrons Wagler

NG–264; G–196; PW–pl 40; AE–pl 350; AW–pl 374; AM(II)–224

6'–25'	MF	4–5 (4–7) MONOG	MF I: 12–14 DAYS ALTRICIAL F: 30 DAYS MF	NUTS FRUIT	GROUND GLEAN HAWKS

BREEDING: Dry woodland, scrub, semidesert, river bottom, towns and parks. 2? broods. **DISPLAYS:** ? (Like Red-bellied?) **NEST:** In live or dead tree, pole, post, artificial box; unlined. Occ uses old holes. Excavation takes 6–10 days. **EGGS:** White, unmarked. 1.0" (26 mm). **DIET:** Incl acorns, berries. Forages at base of tree and on ground. **CONSERVATION:** Winter resident; wander in pairs. Once considered telecommunications-pole pest (soft pine easy to excavate compared with much harder mesquite) and consequently persecuted: railroad personnel stocked with shotguns to clear lines. **NOTES:** Vocal in spring; does not drum as frequently as woodpeckers of other genera. Male spends night in cavity from before egg laying through incubation. Young separate from family before winter. Caches food in bark crevices. Area of overlap and frequency of hybridization with Red-bellied Woodpecker have greatly increased in past 50 years. **ESSAYS:** Great Plains Hybrids, p. 625; Hybridization, p. 501; Hoarding Food, p. 345; Finding Hidden Caches, p. 411; Nonvocal Sounds, p. 313. **REFS:** Short, 1982; Skutch, 1969; Smith, 1987.

Red-headed Woodpecker

Melanerpes erythrocephalus Linnaeus

NG–266; G–198; PE–188; PW–pl 40; AE–pl 351; AM(II)–222

    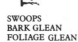

8'–80'	M – F	4–5 (3–7) MONOG	MF I: 12–13 DAYS ALTRICIAL F: 27–30 DAYS MF	SWOOPS BARK GLEAN FOLIAGE GLEAN

BREEDING: Decid woodland (esp with beech or oak), open areas with scattered trees, parks. Attracted to old burns, recent clearings. Oft 2 broods. **DISPLAYS:** Courtship: incl horizontal pose with neck stretched forward, plumage sleeked, shoulders humped. Female inspection of prospective nest cavity incl tapping on cavity. Aggression: usu bow, wing and tail spread. **NEST:** Usu in barkless dead tree or dead stub on live tree. On treeless prairie uses pole, fence, roof, etc. Lined with chips. Excavated in 6–17 days. Will use natural cavities. **EGGS:** White. 1.0" (25 mm). **DIET:** Insects, bird eggs, nestlings, occ adult birds, mice; corn, berries, fruit, various seeds, nuts. Caches insects, acorns, and beechnuts, breaking them to fit natural cavities. Young fed insects, spiders, worms, berries. **CONSERVATION:** Winters within U.S. Blue List 1972, 1976–81, Special Concern 1982–86. Widely reported as decreasing due to loss of nesting habitat. Avoids birdhouses. **NOTES:** Creosote-coated utility poles lethal to eggs and young reared there. Male incubates and broods at night. Starlings, small woodpeckers, kestrels, compete for cavities. Blue Jays and starlings steal caches. **ESSAYS:** Avian Invaders, p. 633; Hoarding Food, p. 345; Blue List, p. 11; Nonvocal Sounds, p. 313. **REFS:** Ingold, 1987; Jackson, 1976; Kilham, 1977; Reller, 1972.

food resources also explain the evolution of smaller clutch sizes in late breeders.

Although the broad evolutionary influences on clutch size seem reasonably well understood, a great deal remains to be done before the full array of factors determining the number of eggs per clutch are worked out in detail. Some biologists feel, for example, that clutch size in passerines will be negatively related to the chance that the nest will be robbed—vulnerable populations should produce smaller clutches. The reasons that have been given include: smaller nests should be more difficult for predators to find, the adults will have more energy to invest in a second brood if the first clutch is lost, and (since less time is invested in the first nest) renesting can begin earlier while spring conditions still prevail. But it has not yet been possible to sort out such factors definitely, so it seems likely that the determinants of clutch size will be the subject of ornithological research for some time to come.

SEE: Average Clutch Size, p. 51; Indeterminate Egg Layers, p. 165; Brood Patches, p. 427; Natural Selection, p. 237. REFS: Ashmole, 1963; Koenig, 1984; Lack, 1947, 1968; Ricklefs, 1980; Slagsvold, 1982; Winkler and Walters, 1983.

Bird Biologist—Joel Asaph Allen

The first curator of birds at Harvard's Museum of Comparative Zoology was Joel Asaph Allen (1838–1921). Allen was also a founder of the Nuttall Ornithological Club in Cambridge (1873) and the American Ornithologists' Union (1883); he was the first president of the AOU, and first editor of its journal, *The Auk*. Allen did important work on geographic variation in birds, and concluded that environmental influences were more responsible than selection for observed inherited differences. In short he supported not Darwin's evolutionary view, but Lamarck's—one now known to be erroneous but subscribed to by many eminent ornithologists of that day. He is remembered by ecologists for "Allen's rule" of geographic variation, which states that populations of both birds and mammals in cooler climates will have shorter extremities than those of the same species in warmer climates; in the first instance they will have less surface area to dissipate heat, in the second, more cooling area.

SEE: Temperature Regulation p. 149, Natural Selection, p. 237 REFS: Kastner, 1986; Stresemann, 1975.

Acorn Woodpecker

Melanerpes formicivorus Swainson

NG–266; G–198; PW–pl 40; AW–pl 376; AM (II)–222

20'–25'	MF+	3–7
(6'–60')		(7+)
		COOP

MF
I: 11–12 DAYS
ALTRICIAL
F: 30–32 DAYS
MF+

BARK
DRILL
HAWKS

BREEDING: Oak and mixed oak/conif woodland, oft in foothills. Requires acorns and storage trees. 1, rarely 2 broods. **DISPLAYS:** Bowing and wing spreading commonly seen; some aerial displays. **NEST:** Usu decid snag, esp oak, also poles. Lined with chips. **EGGS:** White. 1.0″ (25 mm). **DIET:** Mostly insects; also acorns, fruit, sap, corn. In fall/winter groups hoard by studding "storage" trees, utility poles, other wooden structures with up to 50,000 acorns. Also hoard almonds/walnuts/pecans. **CONSERVATION:** Winter resident. **NOTES:** Live in communal groups of up to 16, consisting of at least 2 breeding adults plus their young of previous nestings and cousins. Large clutches result of 2 females. Reproduction highly dependent on size of acorn crop. In CA maintain all-year communal territories, with communal acorn stores. In AZ, some nest as lone pairs and migrate if insufficient food is stored; some AZ populations do not hoard. Young independent at ca. 2 months. Oft evicted from nest cavity by starlings. Attack squirrels, jays, nuthatches, titmice, and esp Lewis' Woodpecker (which also store acorns) that raid caches. **ESSAYS:** Cooperative Breeding, p. 283; Hoarding Food, p. 345; Parental Care, p. 555; Monogamy, p. 597; Island Biogeography, p. 549; Interspecific Territoriality, p. 385. **REFS:** Koenig and Mumme, 1987; Stacey and Bock, 1978.

Lewis' Woodpecker

Melanerpes lewis Gray

NG–266; G–198; PW–pl 40; AW–pl 377; AM (II)–220

SNAG	M –F	6–7
5'–100'		(4–9)
(To 170')		MONOG

MF
I: 13–14 DAYS
ALTRICIAL
F: 28–34 DAYS
MF

NUTS
BERRIES

GROUND
GLEAN
BARK GLEAN

BREEDING: Open woodland and forest, oft logged or burned, incl oak, conif forest (usu ponderosa pine), riparian woodland and orchard edge, occ piñon-juniper habitat, as high as 9,000' where burned forest available. ? broods. **DISPLAYS:** Wing spreading and circular flight around nest tree used as both aggressive and courtship displays. **NEST:** Oft in dead stub of live tree, also uses pole. Perennial. Male usu selects nest site. **EGGS:** White. 1.0″ (26 mm). **DIET:** Incl acorns, commercial nuts, pine seeds, fruit. Caches acorns and nuts for use only in nonbreeding season, but does not drill holes—tailors food to fit natural crevices; does not store communally. **CONSERVATION:** Winters s to n w Mexico. Blue List 1975–81, Special Concern 1982, Local Concern 1986; populations now apparently stable. Occ orchard pest. **NOTES:** Territorially defends only immediate nest site and guards nut stores; defends stores from Acorn and other woodpeckers. Pair bond may be permanent. Male incubates and broods at night, pair alternate in day. No apparent foraging differences between sexes. Very acrobatic in pursuit of prey. Only woodpecker that perches on wires. **ESSAYS:** Hoarding, p. 345; Interspecific Territoriality, p. 385; Blue List, p. 11; Nonvocal Sounds, p. 313. **REFS:** Bock, 1970; Short, 1982.

Hoarding Food

Birds living in environments that produce food in abundance during one season of the year, and relatively little (or none) during others, may cope with the uneven supply in several different ways. One strategy is to leave the area for the periods of shortage, as many North American birds do in migrating from barren, cold, temperate, or polar regions to the relatively food-rich, warm tropics for the winter. The hazards of migration are accepted in return for continuity of food supply. Another strategy is to stay through the times of shortage and scrounge hard for the food that is available, as do ptarmigan and even chickadees, although throughout the northern winter the latter remain daily poised on the razor's edge of starvation.

A third strategy is to harvest more food than is needed during periods of seasonal abundance and to store it. This strategy, too, has its dangers; the store may be robbed or may spoil. Long-term storage—what might be called hoarding—is practiced in North America by various woodpeckers, some jays, Clark's Nutcrackers, and nuthatches. Techniques of storing differ from species to species. Groups of Acorn Woodpeckers place surplus acorns in one or two storage sites near the center of the group territory—dead trunks and limbs are studded with acorns jammed into shallow holes. Up to 50,000 acorns may be stored in a single snag (standing remains of a dead tree), which is known as a granary. The woodpeckers aggressively defend their acorns, which are so tightly hammered into the holes that it is difficult for potential robbers to retrieve them without being detected or, in many cases, to remove them from the holes at all. Other woodpeckers use cracks and cavities to store acorns and various other nuts. Interestingly, Lewis' Woodpeckers may (for unknown reasons) husk acorns before storing them, and individuals of at least one woodpecker species, the Red-bellied, apparently do not defend their stores.

Nutcrackers and jays tend to store acorns, nuts, seeds, pine cones, and other items in the soil or under loose litter, as well as in elevated niches and

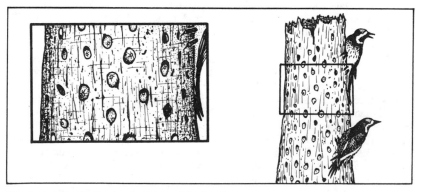

The larder of a family group of Acorn Woodpeckers.

White-headed Woodpecker

Picoides albolarvatus Cassin

NG–266; G–198; PW–pl 40; AW–pl 385; AM(II)–240

6'–15' (2'–25')	MF	4–5 (3–7) MONOG	MF I: 14 DAYS ALTRICIAL F: 26 DAYS MF	PINE SEEDS	PROBES CONES

BREEDING: Mountainous conif forest, esp pine and fir, usu from 4,000' to 9,000'. ? broods. **DISPLAYS:** Head swinging and "flutter" aerial displays. **NEST:** Esp in dying or dead pine, also oak, aspen. Lined with chips. Nest located in section no less than 2' in diameter. Stump oft used perennially. Nest height up to 50' in s. **EGGS:** White, oft pitch-stained. 1.0″ (24 mm). **DIET:** Also spiders. Esp in s part of range, diet may be >50% pine seed and other veg. **CONSERVATION:** Winter resident. **NOTES:** Males and females tend to forage separately in winter: females on ponderosa pine and incense cedar, males higher and on Coulter pines. In summer, less difference between sexes in foraging heights and tree species. Oft drinks water, esp when mostly veg diet. Performs comparatively less drilling; skull softer and less dense than most woodpeckers. Oft lands head-down on tree like Nuttall's. **ESSAYS:** Nonvocal Sounds, p. 313; Bills, p. 209; Drinking, p. 123. **REFS:** Ligon, 1973; Morrison and With, 1987; Short, 1982.

Williamson's Sapsucker

Sphyrapicus thyroideus Cassin

NG–268; G–198; PW–pl 40; AW–pl 384; AM(II)–230

CONIF TREE 3'–60'	M	5–6 (3–7) MONOG	MF I: 12–14 DAYS ALTRICIAL F: 21–28 DAYS MF	TREE SAP	GROUND GLEAN

BREEDING: Montane conif forest, esp fir, lodgepole pine, also aspen groves. 1 brood. **DISPLAYS:** Crest raising, wings up, head bobbing/wagging, fluttering and moth flight. Male and female bob. Reverse mounting common. Postnesting courtship flight and drumming, but does not produce second brood. **NEST:** Prefer aspen, pine, fir, larch, found at higher elevations, but below 7,000'. Annual nest but occ 1 tree used for life, riddling it with up to 40 cavities. Excavation 3–4 weeks. **EGGS:** White. 1.0″ (24 mm). **DIET:** Esp ants. Sap wells scar hemlock, fir, pine, and aspen; shift to ants in spring. Also berries in winter. **CONSERVATION:** Winters s to n c Mexico. **NOTES:** Males arrive on breeding grounds 2 weeks before females. Occ interspecifically territorial with Yellow-bellied Sapsucker. Male incubates at night, alternates with female in day, switching every ½ hour. Parents usu land above hole and hitch down. Family separates soon after fledging. Sexes occupy largely separate habitats in winter; females feed more than males on berries. **ESSAYS:** Interspecific Territoriality, p. 385; Nonvocal Sounds, p. 313; Hormones and Nest Building, p. 547; Who Incubates?, p. 27. **REFS:** Bock and Larson, 1986; Crockett and Hansley, 1977.

cracks. A Clark's Nutcracker may store more than 30,000 pinyon pine seeds during a single season, placing them in caches with 4-to-5 seeds each. The trees are not always passive victims in this game, however. For instance, pinyon and other pines are coevolving with Clark's Nutcrackers and Pinyon Jays, with the trees affecting the birds' evolution, and vice versa. The pines appear to have evolved cone and seed structures and fruiting times that increase the chance for their seeds to be buried (planted) by the birds. For example, whitebark pines have been shown to be dependent on Clark's Nutcrackers for their reproduction. Other animals harvest and feed on their seeds, but only the nutcrackers cache them in places favorable to the growth of the tree and at an appropriate depth for seedling establishment.

The nutcrackers and jays, in turn, have evolved to exploit this resource. Clark's Nutcracker has evolved both a long, sharp bill for use in prying the pine seeds from their cones, and a special pouch under the tongue for carrying them. One individual was found with 38 seeds, weighing a total of more than an ounce, in its pouch. A powerful flier, the nutcracker can carry its burden of seeds a long distance. It can start breeding as early as February by exploiting its hoarded seeds.

North American Jays have not proceeded quite as far down that evolutionary path as the nutcracker. Pinyon Jays store seeds in an expandable esophagus, but are unable to transport as large a load as the nutcracker. Steller's Jays have a less specialized bill, and an esophagus of smaller capacity, and Scrub Jays (which are the least dependent of all on stored food in the winter) can carry only one seed at a time.

Both birds and pines benefit from the relationship. The birds get fed and the trees get millions of their seeds buried, not just in the immediate vicinity, but in adjacent areas for miles around. Movement by the birds promotes rapid colonization by the pines of new areas made suitable for them as a result of climatic change. In contrast to these mutually beneficial relationships, Acorn Woodpeckers seem to be predators on oaks, because generally they do not place the acorns in sites suitable for germination. Thus the oaks gain little, if any, benefit from the relationship.

Some birds, especially parids (titmice, chickadees), some raptors, owls, shrikes, and (occasionally) woodpeckers, store animal prey, but this seldom extends beyond short-term storage of a few days, because such prey soon decay. Exceptions may be the victims of northern owls and parids, for fall-stored mammals and insects may be preserved by cold and used over a longer period. This is indicated by the recent discovery that Great Horned, Boreal, and Saw-whet Owls thaw frozen prey by incubating them as they would eggs! All the thoroughly studied, long-term-storing birds use conifer seeds, acorns, and other nuts that are energy rich and yet have a hard, impervious coat that retards spoilage. Some acorns apparently can be stored for up to a year or more.

Careful observations are needed of nuthatch hoarding behavior, about which little is know. Also desirable would be information on the elapsed time before hoards are recovered. Marking of the stores and repeated obser-

Red-breasted Sapsucker

NG–268; G–198; PW–pl 40; AW–pl 379; AM(II)–230

			MF (?)		
			I: 12–13 DAYS		
SNAG	MF (?)	4–5	ALTRICIAL	TREE	HAWKS?
15'–60'		(4–7)	F: 25–29 DAYS	SAP	
(To 100'?)		MONOG	MF (?)	FRUIT	

BREEDING: Aspen-pine assoc and conif forest, incl humid coastal lowlands. N populations breed at lower elevations than s populations. ? broods. **DISPLAYS:** Not well known, but probably similar to Yellow-bellied Sapsucker's. **NEST:** At low elevation prefers live decid tree (alder, cottonwood, aspen); at higher elevations fir, riparian alder or willow preferred. Decid snags also used. Lined with chips. **EGGS:** White. 1.0" (24 mm). **DIET:** Esp ants; drill and strip bark to produce perennial sap wells. Fledglings taught sapsucking while clinging to nest tree, but still fed insects, fruit. **CONSERVATION:** Winters s to n Baja. **NOTES:** Warblers, hummingbirds, other species use sap wells. Hybridization between Red-breasted and Red-naped Sapsuckers restricted to narrow zone in s c OR, n e CA, and along CA/NV border to s NV; hybrid zone stable because hybrids are less successful. **ESSAYS:** Species and Speciation, p. 355; Superspecies, p. 375; Commensal Feeding, p. 35; Hybridization, p. 501. **REFS:** Johnson and Johnson, 1985; Short, 1982.

Yellow-bellied Sapsucker

NG–268; G–198; PE–190; AE–pl 346; AM(II)–228

			MF		
			I: 12–13 DAYS		
25'	MF	5–6	ALTRICIAL	TREE	HAWKS
(8'–40')		(3–7)	F: 25–29 DAYS	SAP	
		MONOG	MF		

BREEDING: Mixed decid/conif forest. 1 brood. **DISPLAYS:** Bill raising (exposing throat patch), crest raising, bowing, wing flicking and drooping; mostly agonistic but bowing more oft in courtship. Fluttering or undulating courtship flights; ritual tapping at nest entrance very prominent; male and female perform drumming duets. **NEST:** Prefers live birch, poplar, aspen, oft near water. Same tree, but not necessarily same hole, oft used perennially. Lined with chips. For nesting, favors trees affected by heart-softening tinder fungus (nest encased in unaffected hard protective wood). Male usu selects nest site. **EGGS:** White. 1.0" (24 mm). **DIET:** Also cambium, fruit, berries. Sap taken from 246 native species. Occ caches nuts, fruit. Young offered sap, fruit, and insects; fed regurgitant (in some populations) first two weeks. **CONSERVATION:** Winters s to C.A. **NOTES:** Male incubates and broods at night. Young taught sapsucking upon fledging, then dependent on parents for only 1–2 more weeks. Guard sap wells from other birds, incl Ruby-throated Hummingbirds, also from small mammals. **ESSAYS:** Species and Speciation, p. 355; Superspecies, p. 375; Nonvocal Sounds, p. 313; Commensal Feeding, p. 35; Decline of Eastern Songbirds, p. 495. **REFS:** Kilham, 1962; Lawrence, 1967.

vations should help to solve the question of their "shelf life" and their relative importance to the birds.

SEE: Finding Hidden Caches, p. 411; Coevolution, p. 405; Bills, p. 209. REFS: George and Sulski, 1984; Hutchins and Lanner, 1982; Roberts, 1979; Vander Wall and Balda, 1981.

Feeding Birds

Feeding backyard birds began in earnest in the 1950s. Today, at an estimated expenditure of more than one-half billion dollars, one in three North American households makes available an average of 60 pounds of supplemental seed each year. New Englanders are our most dedicated providers. In the city of Amherst, Massachusetts, for example, more than 40 percent of the households provide winter feed. The effect that this artificial resource may have on the survival, population stability, and migration patterns of our birds is uncertain, but ornithologists speculate that if handouts were to stop tomorrow, there would be neither species extinctions nor major population declines, although some recently enlarged ranges would contract and there might be detectable decreases in some regions.

Recent range expansion thought to be related to supplemental feeding is evident among finches, especially the House Finch, which has spread from Long Island to the Mississippi River within the past 45 years. Several other beneficiaries of feeding (Northern Cardinal, Tufted Titmouse, Red-bellied Woodpecker, and Mourning Dove) are working their way northward. In a number of areas where supplemental food is plentiful, some species, such as the Mourning Dove, no longer migrate.

Feeding may pull many birds, especially weak individuals, through the extremes of winter. Birds increase their visits to feeders in harsh weather, particularly after snowfalls and ice storms that make natural foods inaccessible. Small species, which are more constrained energetically, benefit greatly from feeding. In one experiment, chickadees raised their daily fat deposits by about 4 percent of their body weight when offered sunflower seeds in place of their normal diet of conifer seeds, berries, etc. During extreme cold spells, juncos, finches, and other winter residents unable to find sufficient food before sunset often will not survive the night.

In some circumstances, however, taking advantage of handouts may be a mistake. Feeding stations may attract weakened or sick individuals and promote the spread of avian diseases. In addition, many birds will readily approach damp grain or bread contaminated with the mold *Aspergillus fumigatus*, which, if inhaled, can cause a potentially lethal infection, aspergillosis. Irregular feeding can be hazardous to birds which establish habitual foraging patterns; oversupply may attract undesirable species such as pigeons, starlings, and grackles, which crowd out other birds. Feeding on the

Red-naped Sapsucker

NG–268; PW–pl 40; AW–pl 378; AM(II)–228

10′–20′   MF   4–5   MF   TREE   HAWKS
(3′–35′)   (3–7)   I: 12–13 DAYS   SAP
         MONOG   ALTRICIAL
               F: 25–29 DAYS
               MF

BREEDING: Usu conif forest that incl aspen, montane riparian woodland. 1 brood. **DISPLAYS**: Bill raising (exposing throat patch), crest raising, bowing, wing flicking and drooping; mostly agonistic but bowing more oft in courtship. Fluttering or undulating courtship flights; ritual tapping at nest entrance very prominent; male and female perform drumming duets. **NEST**: Prefers live birch, cottonwood, aspen, oft near water. Same tree, but not necessarily same hole, oft used perennially. Lined with chips. **EGGS**: White. 1.0″ (24 mm). **DIET**: Also cambium, fruit, berries. Pine pitch oft used instead of sap from decid trees. **CONSERVATION**: Winters s to C.A. **NOTES**: Oft serve "keystone" function in mountainous habitats where it is the only abundant woodpecker: provide tree cavities for smaller nonwoodpecker species that require them for nesting. Male incubates and broods at night. Young taught sapsucking upon fledging, remaining dependent on parents for only short additional period. Guard sap wells from other species, incl hummingbirds, juvenile warblers, and chipmunks. **ESSAYS**: Species and Speciation, p. 355; Nonvocal Sounds, p. 313; Commensal Feeding, p. 35. **REFS**: American Ornithologists' Union, 1985; Crockett and Hadow, 1975; Dobkin and Wilcox, 1986; Johnson and Zink, 1983.

Downy Woodpecker

Picoides pubescens Linnaeus

NG–270; G–200; PE–192; PW–pl 40; AE–pl 339; AW–pl 364; AM (II)–236

3′–50′   ?   4–5   MF
          (3–6)   I: 12 DAYS
         MONOG   ALTRICIAL
              F: 20–25 DAYS
              MF

BREEDING: Decid and mixed decid-conif woodland, riparian woodland, parks, orchards. 1 brood in n, 2? in s. **DISPLAYS**: "Dancing," drumming, bill waving, crest raising used in territorial displays and with duetting in courtship. Stilted, floating flight occurs in both aggression and courtship. **NEST**: New hole yearly, entrance oft camouflaged by surrounding fungus/lichen/moss. Lined with chips. Excavated in 13–20 days (avg 16). Female usu selects site. **EGGS**: White. 0.8″ (19 mm). **DIET**: Insects (75%–85%); fruit, seeds, sap from sapsucker holes. **CONSERVATION**: Winter resident. Occ uses birdhouse for roost but not for nest. **NOTES**: Pair initially hold large territory which shrinks after nest site selected and excavated. Male reportedly performs most of brooding. Fledglings dependent for up to 3 weeks. Sexes forage separately: males prefer small branches, upper canopy and branches <60° from horizontal. Other hole-nesting species may invade roosting holes or nests. Each bird excavates winter roost. **ESSAYS**: Island Biogeography, p. 549; Bird Guilds, p. 493; How Do We Find Out About Bird Biology?, p. 319; Feeding Birds, p. 349; Nonvocal Sounds, p. 313; Mixed-Species Flocking, p. 433; Territoriality, p. 387. **REFS**: Kilham, 1983; Lawrence, 1967; Short, 1982.

ground encourages predation by cats and, much more desirable from a birder's viewpoint, as the number of visitors increases, so does the number of hawks that are able to find their food around the station.

The provisions themselves may also cause problems. Beef suet brings 80 species of birds (including woodpeckers, catbirds, mockingbirds, nuthatches, chickadees, titmice, wrens, orioles, shrikes, thrushes, warblers, grackles, and starlings) into backyards. Unfortunately, many feeders are kept stocked as spring advances. Sun-warmed suet mats feathers, which can result in reduced insulation and waterproofing, inflamed or infected follicles, and loss of facial feathers. In Iowa, more suet is taken by birds in May than during the rest of the year. Many Downy Woodpeckers that eat this warm suet become barefaced in the spring. Bird enthusiasts also encourage more than 50 species of birds (mostly hummingbirds, orioles, tanagers, and various warblers) to sip ersatz nectar from backyard feeders. But the liquid ferments within two to three days while continuing to lure birds, resulting in enlarged hummingbird livers.

In addition to seed-, suet- and nectar-eating species (and their predators) that forage at backyard feeders, many other species take advantage of food wastes generated by people and industry. The size of opportunistic Brewer's Blackbird, European Starling, and Rock Dove populations varies as people directly and indirectly alter available food supplies. Similarly, Red-winged Blackbirds have expanded beyond their marshland habitat to cultivated areas where leftover grain is abundant. Profiting from dumped refuse or offal released from fish-processing plants and from boats and ships in sea lanes, local populations of petrels and Herring, Ring-billed, Great Black-backed, and other gulls may build giant colonies.

Today, in spite of the farsighted efforts of many bird enthusiasts, the provision of supplemental food remains somewhat uneven. But this is likely to change. Bird watching has become the second most popular passive sport (after gardening) in North America; with some 30 million participants. As more information about avian nutrition is made available to the well-intentioned public, safer, more effective bird feed will be made available in backyards. This change should not take very long; more farmers have been discovering how to increase their profits (up to five times) by selling their grain as bird feed. In addition many birders are participating in "Project Feederwatch" of the Laboratory of Ornithology of Cornell University, by recording which birds visit their feeders on one of two days of each week in the winter. They will both help the birds and add to knowledge of wintering bird populations.

Along with improvements in feeds, we should see modification of public trash and waste disposal policies, which will influence which species are common in the vicinity of cities and towns. Whereas garbage fosters population growth in some colonial seabirds, oil contamination and chemical pollution remain the major threats to others. As laws controlling refuse dumping and regulating maritime industries become commonplace, the population density and distribution of "garbage birds" and of some species

Hairy Woodpecker

Picoides villosus Linnaeus

NG–270; G–200; PE–192; PW–pl 40; AE–pl 340; AW–pl 365; AM(II)–236

			MF	
			I: 11–15 DAYS	
SNAG	MF	4	ALTRICIAL	
4'–60'		(3–6)	F: (24?–) 28–30 DAYS	
		MONOG	MF	

BREEDING: Decid or conif forest, wooded swamps, orchards, woodland, well-wooded towns and parks. 1 brood. **DISPLAYS:** Pair bonds formed in winter. Duet drumming; female may tap at symbolic (unsuitable) nest site or at suitable sites, and perform quivering, fluttering flight to attract male. Many apparent courtship displays may be aggressive or appeasement. **NEST:** Excavation takes 1–3.5 weeks (avg 20 days). Usu annual. Lined with chips. Male usu selects site. **EGGS:** White. 1.0" (25 mm). **DIET:** Insects (75% to 95%), sap from sapsucker hole. Winter diet incl acorns, hazelnuts, beechnuts. May cache insects. **CONSERVATION:** Winter resident. Blue List 1975–82, Special Concern 1986; widely reported as declining. **NOTES:** Female incubates in day, male at night; female does most of brooding. Male forages away from nest, making few visits but brings large prey; female feeds at start and end of day, foraging within hearing distance of young and making frequent trips. Parental care continues several weeks beyond fledging. Nest cavities oft appropriated by House Sparrows and starlings. Males tend to forage higher than females in winter. **ESSAYS:** Island Biogeography, p. 549; How Do We Find Out About Bird Biology?, p. 319; Nonvocal Sounds, p. 313; Hoarding Food, p. 345; Who Incubates?, p. 27. **REFS:** Kilham, 1968, 1969, 1983; Morrison and With, 1987.

Three-toed Woodpecker

Picoides tridactylus Linnaeus

NG–270; G–200; PE–192; PW–pl 40; AE–pl 344; AW–pl 382; AM(II)–242

			MF	
			I: 11 (to 14?) DAYS	
3'–15'	MF	4	ALTRICIAL	TREE
(1'–45')		(2–6)	F: 22–26 DAYS	SAP
		MONOG	MF	

BREEDING: Conif forest (usu spruce), occ mixed conif-decid forest, occ riparian willows; prefer burned tracts and montane spruce (e) or aspen (w). 1 brood. **DISPLAYS:** Male attracts female by drumming, then performs head swaying and calls; similar displays also used in antagonistic context. **NEST:** Prefer balsam fir but will use decid snags, esp near burns, also use poles. Lined with chips. Excavated in ca. 12 days. Annual. **EGGS:** White. 0.9" (23 mm). **DIET:** Esp wood-boring beetles (>75%). **CONSERVATION:** Winter resident. **NOTES:** Nests in loose colonies where food abundant. Pair bond occ maintained all year and in successive years; strong breeding site tenacity. Male roosts nightly in nest throughout incubation. Both adults brood. Family cohesion continues well into summer. In CO, abundance correlates with abundance of spruce bark beetles. Pair forage separately in nesting territory. Forage lower in trees in winter but females tend to forage higher than males. Range overlaps with related Black-backed Woodpecker, but less common, esp in e. Less irruptive than Black-backed Woodpecker. Easily approached. **ESSAYS:** Feet, p. 239; Nonvocal Sounds, p. 313; Irruptions, p. 639; Site Tenacity, p. 189. **REFS:** Cramp, 1985; Short, 1982; Yunick, 1985.

considered more desirable will change. How similar the mix of bird species around centers of human population will be at that point compared to today's avifauna is, in many respects, up to us.

SEE: Irruptions, p. 639; Helping to Conserve Birds—Local Level, p. 361; Metallic Poisons, p. 137; Disease and Parasitism, p. 399; European Starlings, p. 489; Urban Birds, p. 629.   REFS: Beecher, 1955; De Graaf and Payne, 1975; Kress, 1985; Leck, 1978; U.S. Fish and Wildlife Service and U.S. Bureau of the Census, 1980.

How Woodpecker Tongues Work

Hairy Woodpecker tongue retracted (left) and extended (right). The exceptionally long tongue wraps around the skull and is anchored at the base of the bill. It is extended by a complex system which includes very long hyoid (tongue-base) bones. The tips of such wood-pecker tongues are barbed to help in extracting insects from holes, and the tongue is coated with sticky saliva, which helps to retain the prey. Sapsucker tongues are shorter and have fine, hairlike processes on their tips for capturing sap by capillary action.

Black-backed Woodpecker

Picoides arcticus Swainson

NG–270; G–200; PE–192; PW–pl 40; AE–pl 343; AW–pl 383; AM(II)–244

  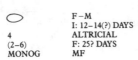

CONIF	MF	4	F–M		
2'–15'		(2–6)	I: 12–14(?) DAYS		
(2'–80')		MONOG	ALTRICIAL		
			F: 25? DAYS		
			MF		

BREEDING: Conif forest (usu spruce and fir), esp windfalls and burned areas with standing dead trees, swamps, occ mixed conif-decid forest, usu over 3,000'. 1 brood. **DISPLAYS:** Aggressive displays with Hairy Woodpeckers; oft use complex of wing spreading and scream-rattle-snarl calls. **NEST:** Oft in fir; prefer new nest annually, entrance usu below branch. Oft debark snag; abort holes. Lined with chips. **EGGS:** White. 0.9" (22 mm) **DIET:** Mostly larvae of wood-boring beetles, ants; may consume >13,500 annually. Some fruit, mast, and cambium. **CONSERVATION:** Winter resident, with some wandering within N.A. **NOTES:** Preferentially forages in trees with easily peeled bark. Irrupts irregularly but usu for several consecutive winters. Breeding biology not well known. **ESSAYS:** Feet, p. 239; Irruptions, p. 639; Nonvocal Sounds, p. 313. **REFS:** Short, 1982; Yunick, 1985.

Ladder-backed Woodpecker

Supersp #27
Picoides scalaris Wagler

NG–272; G–196; PW–pl 40; AE–pl 345; AW–pl 368; AM(II)–232

AGAVE	?	4–5	MF	FRUIT	GROUND
6'–14'		(2–6)	I: 13 DAYS		GLEAN
(3'–30')		MONOG	ALTRICIAL		
			F: ? DAYS		
			MF		

BREEDING: Deserts, arid scrub, riparian woodland, piñon-juniper woodland, pine-oak assoc, pine savanna, towns. Oft at lower elevations. ? broods. **DISPLAYS:** Head bobbing and turning, crest raising, bill directing and raising, wing spreading and aerial displays, apparently mostly territorial. **NEST:** Oft in dead or decaying branches. Will use posts and poles if other suitable sites unavailable. Lined with chips. **EGGS:** White. 0.8" (21 mm). **DIET:** Fruit incl esp cactus. **CONSERVATION:** Winter resident. **NOTES:** Little overlap between sexes in foraging: females tend to forage higher and on different substrates than males. Males forage by probing and pecking more than females, which primarily glean from bark surfaces. **ESSAYS:** Nonvocal Sounds, p. 313; Feet, p. 239; Superspecies, p. 375. **REFS:** Austin, 1976; Short, 1982.

Species and Speciation

Species are distinctly different kinds of organisms. Birds of one species are, under most circumstances, incapable of interbreeding with individuals of other species. Indeed, the "biological species concept" centers on this inability to successfully hybridize, and is what most biologists mean by "distinctly different." That concept works very well when two different kinds of birds live in the same area. For example, Townsend's and Yellow-rumped Warblers are clearly distinct kinds because their breeding ranges overlap, but they do not mate with one another. If they did, they might produce hybrid young, which in turn could "backcross" to the parental types, and (eventually) this process could cause the two kinds of warblers to lose their distinctness.

On the other hand, when relatively similar populations occur in different areas, it is much more difficult to decide whether to classify them as different species. For example, the western populations of the Yellow-rumped Warbler (which have yellow throats) were previously considered a species, Audubon's Warbler, distinct from the eastern Myrtle Warblers (which have white throats), largely because of differences in appearance. Then it was discovered that the breeding ranges of Audubon's and Myrtle Warblers overlap broadly in a band from southeastern Alaska through central British Columbia to southern Alberta, and that the two "species" hybridize freely within this area. The forms intergrade, and taxonomists now consider them to be *subspecies* of a single species, the Yellow-rumped Warbler. Subspecies are simply populations or sets of populations within a species that are sufficiently distinct that taxonomists have found it convenient to formally name them, but not distinct enough to prevent hybridization where two populations come into contact.

Judgments about whether two populations should be considered different species or just different subspecies may be very difficult to make. For instance, in some areas where populations of Red-breasted and Yellow-bellied Sapsuckers meet, they hybridize, whereas in other areas of overlap they do not. As a result, ornithologists do not agree upon whether to consider the two forms as separate species or as subspecies of the same species. In situations where differentiated, but clearly closely related forms replace one another geographically, taxonomists often consider them to be separate species within a superspecies.

These complications are a natural result of applying a hierarchical taxonomic system, developed a century before Darwin, to the results of a continuous evolutionary process. Geographic variation—birds showing different characteristics in different areas—is inevitable among the populations of all species with extensive breeding distributions. It is largely the result of populations responding to different pressures of natural selection in different habitats. If populations of a single bird species become geographically isolated, those different selection pressures may, given enough time, cause the populations to differentiate sufficiently to prevent inter-

Red-cockaded Woodpecker

Picoides borealis Vieillot

NG–272; G–196; PE–190; AE–pl 347; AM(II)–240

10'–40'	– FM +	2–5	MF +
(4'–100')		COOP	I: 10–15(?) DAYS
			ALTRICIAL
			F: 22?–29 DAYS
			MF +

BREEDING: Open, mature (80–120-year-old) pine (esp longleaf) woodland; leaves habitat if logged. 1 brood. **DISPLAYS:** Head bobbing/swinging, fluttering, wing spreading used in variety of contexts. Drumming uncommon. **NEST:** In tall, live pine. Cavities used for several years; excavation occ requires >year. Lined with chips. **EGGS:** White. 1.0″ (24 mm). **DIET:** Esp wood-boring beetles, grubs; occ fruit, berries, seeds. **CONSERVATION:** Winter resident. Endangered Species: depends on mature open pine woodland maintained by fire but habitat now rare because forestry practices exclude fire and harvest immature trees. Continued drastic decline even since Endangered status conferred in 1970. **NOTES:** Live in family groups composed of mated pair, offspring of the year, and occ unmated male helpers; groups are strongly territorial all year, defending 100–200 acres. Groups with helpers fledge more young than unassisted pairs. Dependent on pines infected with heart fungus for nest cavities; hardened sap from drill holes ("wells") characteristically surround nest and roost cavities. Male and female incubate during day; male at night. Preferentially forage in large live pines; males forage primarily in crown and at midtrunk, females primarily on lower trunk. **ESSAYS:** Cooperative Breeding, p. 283; Birds and the Law, p. 293; Nonvocal Sounds, p. 313. **REFS:** Hooper and Lennartz, 1981; Jackson, 1977, 1986; Lennartz et al., 1987; Ligon et al, 1986.

Nuttall's Woodpecker

Supersp #27
Picoides nuttallii Gambel

NG–272; G–196; PW–pl 40; AW–pl 369; AM (II)–234

DECID	M – F	4–5	MF	BERRIES	HAWKS
TREE		(3–6)	I: 14 DAYS		
2.5'–60'		MONOG	ALTRICIAL		
			F: 29 DAYS		
			MF		

BREEDING: Oak woodland, chaparral, riparian (esp willow-cottonwood) woodland; oft foothill canyons. ? broods. **DISPLAYS:** Mostly territorial: head bobbing and turning, crest raising, bill directing and raising, wing spreading and aerial displays. **NEST:** Usu in dead riparian decid tree. Unlined. Excavation ca. 13 days, not reused. **EGGS:** White. 0.9″ (22 mm). **DIET:** Insects (80%); also few acorns, sap, occ grain. Nuthatch style of gleaning from underside of limbs. **CONSERVATION:** Winter resident. **NOTES:** Pairs remain on year-round territories. Male performs most of incubation incl all nocturnal incubation and brooding. Preferentially forage on oaks; females forage on smaller branches and twigs more frequently than do males. Occ hybridizes with Ladder-backed and Downy, with which it is especially territorial. Breeding biology similar to that of Ladderback. **ESSAYS:** Island Biogeography, p. 549; Nonvocal Sounds, p. 313; Feet, p. 239; Hybridization, p. 501; Interspecific Territoriality, p. 385; Who Incubates?, p. 27. **REFS:** Jenkins, 1979; Miller and Bock, 1972.

breeding if contact is reestablished. In nature, degrees of differentiation and of abilities to hybridize fall along a continuum, so one finds what is expected in an evolving avifauna—some populations intermediate between subspecies and species, populations (members of superspecies) that have differentiated to the point where they will not hybridize but have not yet regained full contact, and populations so distinct that they can be recognized as full species whether or not they occur together. As an example of the latter, the Three-toed Woodpecker and the Red-cockaded Woodpecker have separate distributions, but clearly are separate species.

Biologists differ on the details of both the definition of species and the mechanisms of speciation, and our treatment is necessarily simplified. Changing views of the specific status of North American birds can be an annoyance, since they may result in new names for familiar birds. But changes reflect increasing knowledge of the biology of the birds involved, and by careful observations of hybrids, mating pairs, and species distributions, you should be able to add to that knowledge.

SEE: Taxonomy and Nomenclature, p. 515; Natural Selection, p. 237; Superspecies, p. 375; Sibling Species, p. 383; Great Plains Hybrids, p. 625; Hybridization, p. 501. REFS: Futuyma, 1979; Mayr, 1963; Milkman, 1982.

Bird Biologist—Thomas Nuttall

The author of the first book that could be described as a "field guide" to North American birds was Thomas Nuttall (1786–1859), an English acquaintance of Audubon. Trained as a printer, Nuttall was a self-taught naturalist who made major contributions to botany. His *A Manual of the Ornithology of the United States and Canada* (1832–34) was compact, cheap, clearly illustrated with woodcuts, and replete with useful information. It went through many editions, and was still in print in this century. Elliot Coues (p. 565) said of the *Manual*, "Nuttall, like good wine, does not deteriorate with age." REFS: Choate, 1985; Kastner, 1986.

Disappearing Ivorybill

A century and a half ago Audubon wrote: "The Ivory-billed Woodpecker confines its rambles to a comparatively very small portion of the United States." It actually was found in much of the Southeast, but it had very special habitat requirements—mature, swampy, riverine forests about which the great artist waxed poetic:

> . . . Would that I could describe the extent of those deep morasses, overshadowed by millions of gigantic dark cypresses, spreading their sturdy moss-covered branches, as if to admonish intruding man to pause and reflect on the many difficulties which he must

Strickland's Woodpecker

Picoides stricklandi Malherbe

NG–272; G–200; PW–pl 40; AW–pl 380; AM(II)–238

20'	?	3–4	MF I: 14 DAYS ALTRICIAL F: ? DAYS MF		FOLIAGE
(9'–50')		MONOG			GLEAN

BREEDING: Open woodland, esp oak or pine-oak in mountains and canyons. ? broods. **DISPLAYS:** Poorly known; wing flicking and spreading observed. Displays presumably much like those of Hairy Woodpecker. **NEST:** Usu dead or dying branches and snags of oak, sycamore, maple, walnut, or agave. Excavation oft on underside of limb. **EGGS:** White. 1.0" (25 mm). **DIET:** Also some fruit, acorns. Forages on tree from base, working upward; performs little drilling. **CONSERVATION:** Winter resident, but moves to lower elevation. **NOTES:** Like Red-cockaded, oft travels in flocks of 5 to 15. Nonbreeding mixed flocks with titmice, bushtits, and nuthatches. Previously known as Arizona Woodpecker and Brown-backed Woodpecker. **ESSAYS:** Nonvocal Sounds, p. 313; Feet, p. 239; How Do We Find Out About Bird Biology?, p. 319; Mixed-Species Flocking, p. 433. **REFS:** Davis, 1965; Short, 1982.

Ivory-billed Woodpecker

Campephilus principalis Linnaeus

NG–274; G–194; PE–188; AM(II)–248

TREE	MF?	2–3	MF I: 20 DAYS ALTRICIAL F: 35 DAYS MF		GROUND
25'		(1–5)			GLEAN
(15'–70')		MONOG			

BREEDING: Mature decid forest swamps, mature riverine bottomlands, occ in pines. 1 brood. **DISPLAYS:** Atop dead tree, pair preen and call until female climbs below male, who leans downward to clasp bill, followed by ritual feeding. **NEST:** Excavated in 8–14 days. **EGGS:** White. 1.5" (38 mm). **DIET:** Mostly wood-boring insects; also seeds, nuts, berries. **CONSERVATION:** Winter resident. Endangered Species; presumably extinct in U.S., but confirmed sighting in mountains of Cuba in 1986. U.S. loss due to logging of bottomland and virgin cypress forests. **NOTES:** Sedentary, remaining within several miles of natal cavity. Large, powerful, chisellike bill; only woodpecker able to pry off unloosened bark. Male incubates at night. Young remain with adults for up to 8 months. Known to make 4" gashes in cambium when hunting insects but more bark-scaling in feeding than seen in Pileated. **ESSAYS:** Disappearing Ivorybill, p. 357; Birds and the Law, p. 293; Fate of Bachman's Warbler, p. 505; Who Incubates?, p. 27; Courtship Feeding, p. 181. **REFS:** Halliday, 1978; Short, 1982, 1985; Short and Horne, 1986.

encounter, should he persist in venturing farther into their almost inaccessible recesses, extending for miles before him, where he should be interrupted by huge projecting branches, here and there the massy trunk of a fallen and decaying tree, and thousands of creeping and twining plants of numberless species.

He goes on to describe the "dangerous nature of the ground...the hissing of serpents...the bellowing of alligators" and "the sultry pestiferous atmosphere...in those gloomy and horrible swamps."

The bills of these woodpeckers were valued by Indians as decorations, and their hunting of them may have had some impact on Ivorybill populations. But the desire of the European invaders of North America for timber was the major reason for the bird's decline. Forbidding and impassable as the swampy forests seemed to Audubon, they represented opportunity to lumber companies, and the number of Ivorybills dropped precipitously between 1885 and 1900 as the timbering industry expanded. The species' decline was especially swift since a single breeding pair requires some three square miles of undisturbed forest for its territory. By 1939 an estimated two dozen breeding Ivorybills remained in the continental United States, and by 1968, only six were reported to exist. It seems very unlikely that any persist today—habitat destruction, perhaps combined with inbreeding as population sizes declined, has done them in.

A remnant population was suspected to be hanging on in the mountains of eastern Cuba, the last retreat of forests replaced elsewhere by sugarcane plantations. Although woodlands are now expanding on that island (fortunately, since many North American warblers winter there), as yet the Ivorybill does not seem to have benefitted. There are too few of the mature trees they require. In early 1985, woodpecker specialist Lester Short searched unsuccessfully for Cuban Ivorybills, but found only what appeared to be trees recently worked by the birds.

At Short's urging, and with the support of their government, Cuban ornithologists made three trips to the mountains subsequently and, on the last, spotted a single female Ivorybill. In April 1986 another group led by Short to the same area sighted a male Ivorybill and at least one female (six persons saw a female on seven separate occasions). All this is exciting news for conservationists everywhere, especially since the Cuban government is taking steps to try to preserve the birds. It looks as if it will be touch and go, since the population is clearly *very* small. With luck, however, as Short suggests, the Cuban population may one day recover, and this largest of North American woodpeckers could be reintroduced into the United States —if there are any of the old-growth swampy forests they require left to receive them.

SEE: Island Biogeography, p. 549; Habitat Selection, p. 463; The Fate of Bachman's Warbler, p. 505. REFS: Audubon, 1842; Halliday, 1978; Short, 1985; Short and Horne, 1986.

Pileated Woodpecker

Dryocopus pileatus Linnaeus

NG–274; G–194; PE–188; PW–139; AE–pl 352; AW–pl 381; AM(II)–246

45'	MF	4	MF	
(15'–80')		(3–5)	I: 15–18 DAYS	
		MONOG	ALTRICIAL	
			F: 26–28 DAYS	
			MF	

BREEDING: Decid-conif forest, open woodland, parks, wooded suburbs. 1 brood. **DISPLAYS**: Crest raising, wing spreading, head swinging, bobbing, etc. Flight display in pair formation with male circling. **NEST**: Holes oft face e or s (depending on cover), oft on bark-free surfaces. Lined with chips. Excavation may continue during incubation. **EGGS**: White. 1.3" (33 mm). **DIET**: Mostly insects (75%); some fruit, acorns, nuts, sap. In winter, when ground snow-covered, diet largely of dormant ants. In fall: fruit, nuts, acorns (n). Young fed regurgitant. **CONSERVATION**: Winter resident. Absent from agricultural areas, small woodlots; requires large territories. Will reappear after reforestation. Indians used crests in calumets. Returned to many sites in New England after changes in lumbering practices, farming, and protective laws in early 1900s. **NOTES**: Year-round territory and pair bond. Male roosts in nest cavity prior to egg laying; at other times, roosts in nest cavity of previous years. Male incubates at night. Male and female brood up to 10 days. **ESSAYS**: Carrying Eggs, p. 361; Nonvocal Sounds, p. 313; Territoriality, p. 387; Who Incubates?, p. 27. **REFS**: Kilham, 1979; Short, 1982.

Eastern Kingbird

Tyrannus tyrannus Linnaeus

NG–276; G–206; PE–194; PW–pl 41; AE–pl 423; AW–pl 474; AM(II)–288

SHRUB	MF	3–4	F	FRUIT	HOVER &
8'–25'		(2–5)	I: 16–18 DAYS		GLEAN
(2'–60')		MONOG	ALTRICIAL		
			F: 16–18 DAYS		
			MF		

BREEDING: Farmland, open or riparian woodland, forest edge. 1 brood. **DISPLAYS**: Courtship: erratic flights, tumbling, hovering; male may display orange crown patch and white tail band to female. **NEST**: Usu at midheight of tree, midway between trunk and canopy edge on horizontal limb of isolated tree, or occ on fence post, stump; bulky, of weed stems, grass, plant down, lined with fine grass, rootlets, hair, feathers. **EGGS**: White, creamy, pinkish, mottled with browns, olive, lavender, occ wreathed. 1.0" (24 mm). **DIET**: Insects; some fruit. Occ hovers and pounces. **CONSERVATION**: Winters from Colombia s to n Chile and n Argentina. Common cowbird host, but usu ejects or damages parasites' eggs. **NOTES**: Fearless, oft harasses larger birds. Pairs may defend nest vigorously against people. Timing of breeding appears to be related to insect abundance. Older females tend to lay earlier in season and lay larger clutches; clutch size decreases through season. Extended postfledging period of parental care oft >5 weeks. **ESSAYS**: Visual Displays, p. 5; Passerines and Songbirds, p. 395; Bills, p. 209; Cowbirds, p. 619; Breeding Season, p. 55. **REFS**: Blancher and Robertson, 1985b; Murphy, 1983, 1986.

Carrying Eggs

While parental transport of chicks has been documented in a number of species, egg carrying by birds appears to be far less common, and few instances have been recorded. Published photographs of a female Pileated Woodpecker document her retrieval of her eggs after the sudden collapse of the nest tree. Within 20 minutes of the crash, the female transferred the clutch of three to a new site. The male apparently discovered the catastrophe on his return to the site nearly two hours later. After a very active search of the surrounding area, he located the female, and they resumed their breeding efforts.

Abandoning disturbed nests and losing the opportunity to breed for the year typifies many species with insufficient time to produce a replacement clutch. But because of the scarcity of suitable nest sites, cavity nesters only rarely succeed in reestablishing their clutch elsewhere if forced to desert the original site. Careful observations of egg transportation are obviously badly needed.

SEE: Transporting Young, p. 103; Masterbuilders, p. 445; Eggs and Their Evolution, p. 301; Life in the Egg, p. 457.   REF: Truslow, 1967.

Helping to Conserve Birds—Local Level

Once people are aware of the escalating extinction crisis, "How can I help?" becomes a frequent question asked of conservation biologists. Fortunately individuals can do a great deal to fend off the silent spring that will surely come if degradation of North American habitats and the tropical wintering grounds of many of our birds continues. In fact, you can make substantial contributions to the conservation of birds not only at local and national levels but at the international level as well.

In some ways working at the local level is most personally rewarding. Results come more quickly, and are more easily recognized. For example, if you have a back yard you can make it a haven for birds by planting native ground cover, shrubs, and trees. Your local Audubon Society chapter as well as the excellent *Audubon Society Guide to Attracting Birds* by Stephen Kress can provide information on both the plants that are important for birds in your area and on the diets of these birds. In many areas, providing a source of fresh water may be as important as supplemental feeding.

You should also limit the use of garden pesticides as much as possible —something that could benefit you as well. If you must tackle a pest problem, start with conservative techniques; use powerful jets of water from a hose to decimate insect infestations on trees, or use pesticides based on the natural chemical pyrethrum. If you must resort to synthetics, restrict the area in which they are used. Paint the chemicals on plants with a brush or

Gray Kingbird

Tyrannus dominicensis Gmelin

NG–276; G–206; PE–194; AE–pl 426; AM(II)–288

| SHRUB
3'–12'
(To 50') | ? | 3–4
(3–5)
MONOG | ?
I: ? DAYS
ALTRICIAL
F: ? DAYS
? | BERRIES | FOLIAGE
GLEAN |

BREEDING: Coastal woodland, esp mangroves, along beaches, inland in towns. ? broods. **DISPLAYS:** Male and female perform rising courtship flight, oft spiral, with twittering and occ snapping of bills. Male sings to nearby female from perch, repeatedly spreads tail, occ spreads wings. **NEST:** Oft in mangrove or oak; flimsy, eggs usu visible through bottom; of sticks, vines, rootlets, lined with fine grass, rootlets. **EGGS:** Pinkish, mottled with rich browns, olive, lavender, oft wreathed or capped. 1.0″ (25 mm). **DIET:** Occ small lizards, other small verts; also fruit. Insects oft taken in air close to water surface, occ from surface. **CONSERVATION:** Winters from Antilles and c Panama s to Venezuela, Colombia, and Guianas. **NOTES:** Fearless, oft harasses larger birds. Pairs may defend nest vigorously against people. Breeding biology virtually unknown. **ESSAYS:** Passerines and Songbirds, p. 395; Bills, p. 209; Masterbuilders, p. 445; How Do We Find Out About Bird Biology?, p. 319. **REFS:** Lefebvre and Spahn, 1987; Ricklefs and Cox, 1977.

Thick-billed Kingbird

Tyrannus crassirostris Swainson

NG–276; G–206; PW–pl 41; AW–655; AM(II)–286

| 50'–60' | ? | 3–4
MONOG | ?
I: ? DAYS
ALTRICIAL
F: ? DAYS
? |

BREEDING: Riparian woodland esp with sycamores, savanna. ? broods. **DISPLAYS:** ? **NEST:** In sycamore; unfinished in appearance, flimsy, eggs usu visible through bottom; of grass, twigs. **EGGS:** White, spotted with brown. ?″ (? mm). **DIET:** Insects. **CONSERVATION:** Winters from n w Mexico s to w Guatemala. **NOTES:** Breeding biology unknown. Very loud; oft calls upon returning to perch after successfully capturing an insect. **ESSAYS:** Passerines and Songbirds, p. 395; Bills, p. 209; Masterbuilders, p. 445; How Do We Find Out About Bird Biology?, p. 319. **REF:** Phillips et al., 1964.

use large-droplet sprays that drift less readily than fine aerosols. To limit their spread, spray and dust pesticides when the air is calm.

Whether you become a lone activist or join with your neighbors, the main focus of political action at the local level should be preservation of quality bird habitats. Wherever areas of natural vegetation are destroyed, local bird populations are likely to decline, but this does not mean that you have to resist all development. The challenge is to encourage development and conservation to go hand in hand. One way is to steer development into areas that have already been seriously disturbed—to focus on redevelopment rather than the destruction of relatively undisturbed habitat. The provision of greenbelts, of course, should be encouraged wherever possible. Strips of habitat along streams can make urban areas much more hospitable to birds and other wildlife, as well as to people. Turning waterways that run through cities and towns into concrete canals should be resisted politically wherever flood control is not a serious consideration. Similarly, old railroad rights-of-way and hedgerows can provide homes for a diversity of birds. Even the edges of freeways can provide important patches of habitat; they need not be manicured grasslands or vistas of imported iceplant, offering neither perches nor cover. City parks can be designed, within the limits of security requirements, to host a maximum of species. Central Park is the only haven for birds that some New York City bird watchers can frequent. Even though it is in the middle of the busiest city in North America, the park is visited by hundreds of bird species annually.

SEE: Helping to Conserve Birds—National Level, p. 363; Helping to Conserve Birds—Global Level, p. 367 (see list of organizations appended to this essay); Feeding Birds, p. 349; The Decline of Eastern Songbirds, p. 495; Island Biogeography, p. 549; Birds and the Law, p. 293. REFS: Ehrlich and Ehrlich, 1981, 1987; Kress, 1985; Soulé, 1986; Soulé and Wilcox, 1980.

Helping to Conserve Birds—National Level

Participation in bird conservation on the national level generally involves group political activities. As a member of the Audubon Society, which disseminates information on bird conservation through its magazines, *Audubon* and *American Birds,* or other conservation-oriented groups such as the Sierra Club, Friends of the Earth, and the National Wildlife Federation, you can remain informed about issues of importance. You can support the activities of The Nature Conservancy, which raises money to purchase habitats that are important for conserving various species. You can also become an associate of the Laboratory of Ornithology at Cornell University, which (as described on p. xxx) is a major center for documenting the conservation status of North American birds. It needs your financial support, and in return will send you its interesting publication, *The Living Bird Quarterly.*

Participation in bird conservation on the national level can, however,

Western Kingbird

Tyrannus verticalis Say

NG–278; G–206; PE–194; PW–pl 41; AE–pl 467; AW–pl 421; AM(II)–286

SHRUB	?	3–4	F I: 18–19 DAYS ALTRICIAL	BERRIES	HOVER & POUNCE
15'–30' (5'–40')		(3–7) MONOG	F: 16–17 DAYS MF		

BREEDING: Savanna, dry open country, agricultural lands, riparian woodland. ? broods. **DISPLAYS:** Male performs frenetic courtship flight, darting into air, fluttering, vibrating feathers, and trilling. **NEST:** Usu on horizontal branch against or near trunk of tree or on human-built structure; of variable materials, thickly and finely lined with hair, cotton, plant down. **EGGS:** White, creamy, pinkish, mottled with browns, gray, lavender, occ concentrated at large end. 1.0″ (24 mm). **DIET:** Insects; berries. **CONSERVATION:** Winters from s Mexico s (except Yucatan) to s w Costa Rica. Rare cowbird host. Range has expanded since 1900 as suitable nest sites became available due to expanding agriculture. **NOTES:** Reproductive success varies with insect abundance; when insects abundant, clutches are larger and initiated earlier, nestlings are fed more oft and grow faster. On territory very aggressive toward crows, hawks, etc. **ESSAYS:** Passerines and Songbirds, p. 395; Bills, p. 209; Masterbuilders, p. 445; Range Expansion, p. 459. **REFS:** Blancher and Robertson, 1984, 1987; MacKenzie and Sealy, 1981.

Cassin's Kingbird

Tyrannus vociferans Swainson

NG–278; G–206; PW–pl 41; AW–546; AM(II)–284

20'–55' (8'–55')	?	3–4	F I: 18–19 DAYS ALTRICIAL	BERRIES	HOVER & POUNCE
		(2–5) MONOG	F: 16–17 DAYS MF		

BREEDING: Oak-piñon and pine-juniper-sycamore woodlands, dry savanna, scrub. 2 broods in s. **DISPLAYS:** Male performs frenetic zigzag courtship flight. **NEST:** Usu on horizontal branch near trunk; bulky, of wide variety of materials, oft thickly and finely lined with rootlets, grass, plant down. **EGGS:** White, creamy, mottled with browns, lavender, occ concentrated at large end. 0.9″ (23 mm). **DIET:** Insects; berries. Consumes more fruit than other kingbirds. **CONSERVATION:** Winters from s Baja, n Mexico s to c Guatemala. **NOTES:** On territory, aggressive toward crows, hawks, etc. Although regularly forages from perches located up to 630' from nest, captures only insects that fly to within ca. 65' of perch. **ESSAYS:** Passerines and Songbirds, p. 395; Bills, p. 209; Masterbuilders, p. 445. **REFS:** Blancher and Robertson, 1984, 1987; Ohlendorf, 1974.

also involve individual contributions such as those offered in exchange for the annual $7.50 duck stamp which is available through most U.S. post offices. Although its purchase is required by waterfowl hunters over the age of 15, popularity of the stamps is increasing as non-hunters begin to collect them. As of 1984 some 3.5 million acres of wetland had been purchased with the $285 million revenue from stamp sales. The program happily weds the harvesting of a living resource and the preservation of its habitat, helping to assure that the resource will be available to future generations.

The conservation of birds can hardly be separated from the broader problem of conserving Earth's organic diversity as a whole. The Center for Conservation Biology at Stanford University has a mission somewhat different from other conservation groups. It is concerned with providing current scientific thinking on conservation issues to those involved in the design and management of nature preserves. It holds workshops for preserve managers on strategies of conservation for organisms as diverse as Spotted Owls and grizzly bears. Center scientists also carry out research projects. For instance, they have used the array of isolated mountain range "islands" of moist habitat in Utah and Nevada as a model to identify the essential characteristics (size, shape, habitat diversity) for preserves for birds, mammals, and butterflies. Another of the center's research programs is aimed at developing projections of the rates of bird species extinctions in tropical rain forests by applying island biogeographic theory to a computer data base of bird distributions and rates of forest destruction.

Some conservation organizations help to coordinate national political action (letter writing, lobbying, reporting on the activities of congressmen and of members of Parliament, etc.) needed to encourage our leaders to take the steps necessary to preserve the biological riches of the United States and Canada. These steps include legislation such as the United States' Endangered Species Act and laws protecting migratory birds, as well as more general environmental legislation. It is important, for example, that you support legal abatement of acid precipitation, which is damaging freshwater and forest habitats. Many avian populations ranging from those of aquatic birds, such as loons, which depend on freshwater fishes, to those of woodland species are threatened.

Too many American and Canadian decision-makers seem unaware that, to a large degree, humans compete with birds (and most other animals) for both habitat and food resources. Pressing for steps to limit (and then gradually reduce) the scale of human activities on our continent is perhaps the most basic action we can take to ensure a future for its nonhuman residents.

SEE: The Decline of Eastern Songbirds, p. 495; Wintering and Conservation, p. 513; Island Biogeography, p. 549; Loon Nurseries and Populations, p. 3; Birds and the Law, p. 293; Helping to Conserve Birds—Global Level, p. 367 (see list of organizations appended to essay); Helping to Conserve Birds—Local Level, p. 361. REFS: Ehrlich and Ehrlich, 1981, 1987; Soulé, 1986; Soulé and Wilcox, 1980.

Tropical Kingbird

Tyrannus melancholicus Vieillot

NG–278; G–206; PW–pl 41; AE–pl 468; AW–pl 420; AM(II)–282

| 8'–20' | F | 3–4
(3–5)
MONOG | F
I: 15–16 DAYS
ALTRICIAL
F: 18–19 DAYS
MF | BERRIES | HOVER &
POUNCE |

BREEDING: Open woodland, parks, suburbs. 1 brood. **DISPLAYS:** ? **NEST:** Broad and shallow, of sticks, moss, rootlets, bark, plant down, finely lined with moss, rootlets. **EGGS:** Pink, buff, mottled with browns, purples, oft concentrated at large end. 1.0″ (25 mm). **DIET:** Insects; berries. **CONSERVATION:** Winters from n Mexico s through S.A. Rare host to Bronzed Cowbird. **NOTES:** Only the female broods. Of the 3 relatively common kingbirds in AZ, Tropical is latest to arrive and earliest to depart. Range overlaps widely in Mexico with closely similar Couch's Kingbird, with limited hybridization. **ESSAYS:** Passerines and Songbirds, p. 395; Bills, p. 209; Masterbuilders, p. 445; Hybridization, p. 501; Species and Speciation, p. 355. **REFS:** Fitzpatrick, 1980; Phillips et al., 1964; Skutch, 1960.

Couch's Kingbird

Tyrannus couchii Baird

NG–278; G–206; AM(II)–284

| 8'–20' | ? | 3–4
(3–5)
MONOG | ?
I: ? DAYS
ALTRICIAL
F: ? DAYS
MF (?) | BERRIES | |

BREEDING: Open and riparian woodland, parks, suburbs. ? broods. **DISPLAYS:** ? **NEST:** Of twigs, moss, rootlets, bark, plant down, finely lined with moss, rootlets. **EGGS:** Pink, buff, mottled with browns, purples, oft concentrated at large end. 1.0″ (25 mm). **DIET:** Insects; berries. **CONSERVATION:** Winters s to Belize. Ejects Bronzed Cowbird eggs from nest. **NOTES:** Range widely overlaps with similar Tropical Kingbird in Mexico, with limited hybridization. Occ forms small, loose flocks in nonbreeding season. Breeding biology virtually unknown but probably similar to Tropical Kingbird's. **ESSAYS:** Passerines and Songbirds, p. 395; Bills, p. 209; Masterbuilders, p. 445; How Do We Find Out About Bird Biology?, p. 319; Hybridization, p. 501; Species and Speciation, p. 355. **REF:** Oberholser, 1974.

Helping to Conserve Birds—Global Level

In addition to protecting birds on a local and national level, you can also help to preserve the global avifauna. Many of the conservation organizations that you can join try to help protect species and habitat outside of the United States. The World Wildlife Fund is preeminent here, and the Nature Conservancy, although primarily active on the national level, is increasing its efforts overseas. North Americans can also take political action that will help to protect birds elsewhere. For example, meat import policies of both the United States and Canada affect the Central American forests that are the winter homes of so many of our birds. Substantial areas of those forests have already been cut to provide temporary pastures for cattle destined for consumption here, something you should inform your representatives of.

Assisting other nations with population control programs is obviously an important activity from the viewpoint of conserving both birds and humans. There are recurring political battles over whether foreign aid should be provided for such purposes. Indeed, limiting the growth of the human population, and then gradually (and humanely) reducing its size, are essential if bird populations are to thrive. In the 1980s *Homo sapiens* was already diverting almost 40 percent of the food resources of the planet into ecological systems dominated by people, domestic animals, and pests. If the human population continues to expand, most kinds of birds gradually will give way to those "weedy" species that thrive in human-altered environments. But we can avoid declining into a world of hungry, unhappy people whose avian companions are largely European Starlings, House Sparrows, and grackles. Protecting birds both by supporting conservation organizations with your money and your time and by becoming politically informed and active can only help.

The odds are very much against declaring victory in the war against environmental destruction during your lifetime. Nonetheless, you are far from helpless when it comes to aiding in the battles to see to it that a wide variety of birds will survive to eat insects, pollinate plants and disperse their seeds, return phosphorous fertilizer from the sea in their guano, and carry out all of the other roles birds play in keeping our planet's ecosystems functioning—while giving future generations of people the kinds of pleasure they have given to us. To the degree you have the interest, the time, and the dollars, we hope that you will get involved in the battles to help our feathered companions and ourselves.

Some important addresses for conservationists are appended to this essay on the next page.

SEE: The Decline of Eastern Songbirds, p. 495; Wintering and Conservation, p. 513; Island Biogeography, p. 549; Birds and the Law, p. 293; Helping to Conserve Birds —Local Level, p. 361; Helping to Conserve Birds—National Level, p. 363.   REFS: Ehrlich and Ehrlich, 1981, 1987; Soulé, 1986; Soulé and Wilcox, 1980; Vitousek et al., 1986.

Scissor-tailed Flycatcher

Tyrannus forficatus Gmelin

NG–280; G–204; PE–194; PW–pl 42; AE–pl 418; AW–pl 469; AM(II)–290

			F		
			I: 14–17 DAYS		
SHRUB	F	3–5	ALTRICIAL		FOLIAGE
5'–20'		(3–6)	F: 14–16 DAYS		GLEAN
(5'–40')		MONOG	MF		GRND GLEAN

BREEDING: Open prairie, scrub, open country with scattered trees. 1 brood. **DISPLAYS:** Male performs dramatic up-down and zigzag courtship flight, with cackling-snapping call; may end with reverse somersaults. Flowing tail well displayed. **NEST:** Usu on horizontal limb, occ in fork or crotch, low in tree or shrub, also on human-built structure; roughly built of twigs, rootlets, weed stems, moss, plant down, occ feathers, hair. Built in 2–4 days. **EGGS:** White, creamy, pinkish, lightly mottled with red, browns, gray, olive. 0.9″ (23 mm). **DIET:** Almost entirely insects; few berries. **CONSERVATION:** Winters s to Panama. Rare host to both cowbird species. **NOTES:** Drops to ground to hunt more than other flycatchers. Roosts communally (up to 250 birds), except females with eggs or nestlings. Usu seen sitting quietly on wire, bare branches of treetops, etc., but can engage in impressive acrobatics. Spirited defender of territory against crows, hawks, etc. Gregarious in non-breeding season. **ESSAYS:** Feathers, p. 309; Sexual Selection, p. 251; Pellets, p. 297. **REF:** Fitch, 1950.

Sulphur-bellied Flycatcher

Myiodynastes luteiventris Sclater

NG–280; G–204; PW–pl 41; AW–655; AM(II)–282

			F		
			I: 15–16 DAYS		
20'–45'	F	3–4	ALTRICIAL		BERRIES
		MONOG	F: 16–18 DAYS		
			MF		

BREEDING: Decid (esp sycamore or walnut) or decid-conif riparian woodland in mountain canyons. ? broods. **DISPLAYS:** Male and female vigorously shake heads, snap their beaks, and duet. Pair then fly closely following each other, occ perch together, all within a small area. **NEST:** Usu in cavity of sycamore; nest usu built almost to level of opening, bulky, oft on base of twigs and sticks, cup of decid leaf petioles, pine needles, without soft lining. Perennial. **EGGS:** White, creamy, buff, heavily marked with browns, red, olive, lavender. 1.0″ (26 mm). **DIET:** Incl small fruit. **CONSERVATION:** Winters e of Andes in Peru and Bolivia. **NOTES:** Begins nesting later than most other birds in its range. Not as aggressive as kingbirds, but will persistently defend nest. Male does not feed incubating female. Young hatch asynchronously. **ESSAYS:** Territoriality, p. 387; Incubation Time, p. 481; Brood Reduction, p. 307; Passerines and Songbirds, p. 395. **REFS:** Ligon, 1971; Skutch, 1960.

Nest Materials

Like a carton for store-bought eggs, nest materials help to cushion, insulate, and keep the clutch together. These materials may be of little importance for birds such as terns and murres, which require little more than a resting spot for their eggs. In contrast, nest materials can be critical for some species—as in the case of Bald Eagles, whose young require a durable playpen that an adult pair may maintain for decades.

An important function of nest materials gathered by ground-nesting precocial birds is to prevent their eggs from becoming embedded in sand or mud after heavy rains or flooding due to exceptionally high tides. Often only enough material is collected to create a buffer that raises the eggs off the substrate. Such a buffer also helps to guard against cracking when the eggs are rotated for uniform heating during incubation. In the case of many marsh-dwelling birds, the buffering layer may be expanded to form sides and sometimes extended to create a relatively fragile canopy, helping to hide the site.

Because the form of the nest varies from habitat to habitat, and must be adapted to fit a bewildering diversity of supporting structures, it is not surprising that an almost limitless variety of materials (including stones and mud, animal and plant products, and human-made artifacts) have at one time or another been incorporated into nests. Avian products that become part of nests include saliva (the main ingredient in cave swiftlet nests used in Chinese "bird's nest" soup), ejected pellets, feathers, down, and guano. Feathers are highly valued, in part because of their capacity to trap air and provide insulation. Products of other animal species may include silk from cocoons and spider webs, cast snake skins, hair, fur, bits of cow pats, shells,

Great Kiskadee

Pitangus sulphuratus Linnaeus

NG–280; G–204; PE–300; PW–pl 41; AE–pl 390; AM(II)–280

SHRUB	?	4–5	?	FISH	HIGH
20'		(3–6)	I: ? DAYS	BERRIES	DIVES
(6'–50')		MONOG	F: ? DAYS		
			?		

BREEDING: Savanna, woodland, dense forests, esp near water. ? broods. **DISPLAYS:** ? **NEST:** Oft in crotch of thorny tree, occ in vine tangle; bulky, globular mass of grass, weed stems, moss, feathers, lined with fine materials; entrance on side. **EGGS:** Creamy white, small spots of browns, lavender. 1.1" (28 mm). **DIET:** Also takes tadpoles, frogs; seeds. Dives for fish like kingfisher. **CONSERVATION:** Winter resident. Believed capable of fending off cowbirds. **NOTES:** Aggressive and noisy; vigorously pursues larger birds that intrude in territory. Breeding biology not well known, although widespread, abundant, and conspicuous in Latin America s to Argentina. **ESSAYS:** Nest Materials, p. 369; Territoriality, p. 387; Cowbirds, p. 619; How Do We Find Out About Bird Biology?, p. 319. **REF:** Oberholser, 1974.

Great Crested Flycatcher

Supersp #30
Myiarchus crinitus Linnaeus

NG–282; G–208; PE–194; AE–pl 469; AM(II)–278

SNAG	MF	5	F	BERRIES	GROUND
20'–50'		(4–8)	I: 13–15 DAYS		GLEAN
		MONOG	ALTRICIAL		
			F: 12–21 DAYS		
			MF		

BREEDING: Decid forest edge, woodland, orchards, parks. Usu 1 brood. **DISPLAYS:** In courtship, male repeatedly dashes after female; hovers close to hole where female retreats. **NEST:** In natural or woodpecker-excavated cavity, nest built to within 1' of opening; bulky, of leaves, variety of other materials, esp fur and feathers, occ snakeskin. **EGGS:** Creamy white, buff, marked with browns, olive, lavender. 0.9" (23 mm). **DIET:** Occ small lizards; also small fruit. May occ glean from bark. **CONSERVATION:** Winters in c and s FL, c Mexico s to Colombia and n Venezuela. Rare cowbird host. Occ uses nest box. Starlings usurp cavities. **NOTES:** Defends territory against woodpeckers, squirrels, etc., but not hawks, possibly because cavity nest more secure from latter. **ESSAYS:** Decline of Eastern Songbirds, p. 495; Great Plains Hybrids, p. 625; Territoriality, p. 387; European Starlings, p. 484. **REF:** Godfrey, 1986.

etc. The variety of plant and manufactured products found in nests is enormous, including virtually anything that can be carried.

Some adhesive materials are required to bind and to provide support in adherent and hanging nests. Such materials include mud (swallows), saliva (swifts), caterpillar silk (hummingbirds, vireos), certain plant fibers, and leaf mold (Wood Thrushes). These binding materials can be remarkably durable. For example, cellulose, the major constituent of plant fibers, is waterproof and, ounce for ounce, stronger than steel. Other water-shedding substances used in nests include lichens and spider webs.

Some materials are selected specifically to help sanitize the nest. More than half of our hawk species routinely add fresh green leaves that contain natural pesticides such as hydrocyanic acid, which may inhibit infestation by insect parasites. Such preventive efforts are not limited to birds of prey. Users of old nest sites, such as starlings, can discriminate between helpful and ornamental leaves and select those that deter lice and bacteria for inclusion in their nests.

Avian ingenuity is seemingly boundless. For example, the Great Kiskadee is known to add the entire nest of the Vermilion Flycatcher to its own, presumably to increase its cushioning/insulating properties. Lists of nesting materials published by early ornithologists provide a sort of fossil record allowing us to trace changing patterns of use. Comparison of these records with contemporary observations of nest materials helps to document changes in the availability of materials. For instance, the Chipping Sparrow, at the turn of the century, was commonly referred to as the "hairbird" from its practice of lining its nest with horse hair. With the advent of mechanized travel and the decline of horses, both the trait and the name disappeared. Similarly, a number of contemporary inventions such as plastic insulation and cellophane may substitute for snake skin in nests of some flycatchers and titmice or replace other once common materials. Thus, nests used perennially could serve as storehouses of data. A White Stork nest still in use in 1930 dated to 1549. One 36-year-old nest of a Bald Eagle, which finally collapsed along with its supporting tree in a storm, contained two tons of accumulated material. Dissection of either nest could have proved a fascinating (if messy) enterprise.

SEE: Nest Lining, p. 391; Masterbuilders, p. 445; Disease and Parasitism, p. 399; Hormones and Nest Building, p. 547; Eggs and Their Evolution, p. 301; Incubation: Heating Eggs, p. 393; Preocial and Altricial Young, p. 581.   REFS: Collias and Collias, 1984; Greig-Smith, 1986; Skutch, 1976.

Bird Names—VIII

Pewees, phoebes, kiskadees, and chickadees are named after their calls, and nutcrackers after their diets. The generic name of the *Empidonax* fly-

Brown-crested Flycatcher

Supersp #30
Myiarchus tyrannulus Müller

NG–282; G–208; PW–pl 41; AE–pl 471; AW–pl 520; AM(II)–280

| CACTUS 5'–30' | MF | 4–5 (3–6) MONOG | F I: 13–15 DAYS ALTRICIAL F: 12–21? DAYS MF | BERRIES | HAWKS GROUND GLEAN |

BREEDING: Savanna, open and riparian woodlands in arid regions, desert with larger cacti. ? broods. **DISPLAYS:** ? **NEST:** In natural cavity or old hole in saguaro made by Gila Woodpecker or flicker; nest soft, of hair, fur, feathers, bark. **EGGS:** Creamy, buff, marked with browns, olive. 1.0" (24 mm). **DIET:** Incl some small fruit. Reported eating hummingbirds in s AZ. Occ gleans from bark of branches and trunks. **CONSERVATION:** Winters from n Mexico s to s Mexico. **NOTES:** Defends territory against woodpeckers, wrens, etc., but less so against hawks, possibly because cavity nest more secure from latter. Departs breeding grounds in midsummer. Formerly known as Wied's Crested Flycatcher. Breeding biology not well known. **ESSAYS:** Superspecies, p. 375; How Do We Find Out About Bird Biology?, p. 319; Masterbuilders, p. 445. **REFS:** Gamboa, 1977; Lanyon, 1960; Phillips et al., 1964.

Ash-throated Flycatcher

Supersp #30
Myiarchus cinerascens Lawrence

NG–282; G–208; PE–194; PW–pl 41; AE–pl 472; AW–pl 548; AM(II)–276

| 3'–20' | MF | 4–5 (3–7) MONOG | F I: 15 DAYS ALTRICIAL F: 14–16 DAYS MF | BERRIES | HAWKS GROUND GLEAN |

BREEDING: Scrub, chaparral, open and riparian woodlands, esp oak and piñon juniper. ? broods. **DISPLAYS:** Little geographic variation exists in the basic vocal repertoire of 4 call patterns; repertoire fully developed by time of fledging. **NEST:** In natural cavity, old Cactus Wren or woodpecker hole, or oft hole in fence post; nest soft, of hair, fur, feathers, grass, occ snakeskin. **EGGS:** Creamy, marked with browns, purples, olive. 0.9" (22 mm). **DIET:** Incl some small fruit. Occ gleans from bark of branches and trunks. **CONSERVATION:** Winters s to n e Costa Rica. **NOTES:** May usurp nest holes from small woodpeckers. Will occ defend territory like kingbird against hawks. **ESSAYS:** Great Plains Hybrids, p. 625; Vocal Development, p. 601; Natural Selection, p. 237; Territoriality, p. 387. **REF:** Lanyon, 1961.

catchers means "king of the gnats" in Greek. Swallow comes from the Anglo-Saxon *swalewe*, raven from the same language, *hraefn*, and crow, *crawe* (also in imitation of the call). The generic names of the raven and crow are the Latin *corvus* meaning "crow." The Common Raven's trivial name, *corax* is onomatopoetic; that of the American Crow, *brachyrhynchos* is Greek for "short-beaked"—and the crow's beak is shorter than the raven's.

Jay may be a reference to bright ("gay") plumage, or it may trace back to a nickname for the Roman name "Gaius." Steller's Jay was named for the German naturalist George Steller, who accompanied Vitus Bering on the trip which discovered what is now known as Bering Strait. The first part of Magpie is a nickname for "Margaret" (or the French or Latin versions of the same name), and is thought to refer to "a chattering female." The last part traces to the Latin *pica* and before that to early Indo-European languages, as a name of the bird.

Titmouse is a combination of "tit" of the Icelandic *tittr* for anything small and the Anglo-Saxon *mase*, "a small bird." "Tit" is a contraction of titmouse. The generic name of these birds and the chickadees, *Parus* is just Latin for "titmouse." The name of the Black-capped chickadee, *Parus atricapillus*, means in Latin "the titmouse with black hair on its head."

REFS: Choate, 1985; Owen, 1985.

Bird Voices

The organ that birds use to produce vocalizations (songs and calls) is very different in location and structure from our own. The mammalian larynx is located at the top of the "windpipe" (trachea), and contains hard membranes (vocal cords) whose vibration as air passes is controlled by a complex of muscles and cartilage. The vocal organ of birds, in contrast, is a unique bony structure called a syrinx, which lies at the lower end of the trachea, is surrounded by an air sac, and may be deep in the breast cavity. Thus situated, the syrinx becomes a resonating chamber (the air sac may resonate also) in conjunction with highly elastic vibrating membranes. Specialized sets of syringeal muscles control the movement of the syrinx, including the tension on the membranes (which can be adjusted like the skin of a drum). Birds can vary both the intensity (loudness) and frequency (pitch) of sounds by altering the air pressure passing from the lungs to the syrinx and by varying the tension exerted by the syringeal muscles on the membranes. The attributes of song that characterize individual species appear to result mostly from differences in the learning process rather than from differences in the structure of the vocal apparatus.

Neurobiologist Fernando Nottebohm has shown that the two sides of

Dusky-capped Flycatcher

Myiarchus tuberculifer
d'Orbigny and Lafresnaye

NG–282; G–208; PW–pl 41; AW– 631; AM(II)–276

11'–50'	?	4–5 MONOG	? I: 14 DAYS ALTRICIAL F: 14? DAYS MF(?)	BERRIES	HAWKS

BREEDING: Open and riparian woodland (esp oak), scrub. ? broods. **DISPLAYS:** ? **NEST:** In natural cavity or old Cactus Wren or woodpecker hole; nest of soft fibrous materials such as hair, fur, feathers. **EGGS:** Creamy, finely marked with browns, purples, olive. 0.8″ (20 mm). **DIET:** Oft hovers while gleaning insects from leaves. **CONSERVATION:** Winters from n Mexico s to s Mexico. **NOTES:** Adults vigorously defend nest containing young. Numbers fluctuate widely from year to year. Breeding biology little known. Widespread in Latin America s to Argentina where oft participates in mixed-species foraging flocks. Formerly known as Olivaceous Flycatcher. **ESSAYS:** Bills, p. 209; Passerines and Songbirds, p. 395; How Do We Find Out About Bird Biology?, p. 319; Mixed-Species Flocking, p. 433; Bathing and Dusting, p. 429. **REFS:** Phillips et al., 1964; Skutch, 1960.

Greater Pewee

Contopus pertinax Cabanis and Heine

NG–284; G–216; PW–pl 42; AW–739; AM(II)–252

DECID TREE 10'–40' +	F?	3–4 MONOG	? I: ? DAYS ALTRICIAL F ? DAYS ?

BREEDING: Montane decid (esp sycamore) and decid-conif (oak-pine) woodland. ? broods. **DISPLAYS:** ? **NEST:** Oft high in horizontal fork of pine; compact, firmly attached with cobwebs, of grass, weeds, decorated with lichen, lined with fine grass. **EGGS:** White, creamy, sparsely marked (oft wreathed) with browns, olive. 0.8″ (21 mm). **DIET:** Insects. **CONSERVATION:** Winters from n Mexico s to n c Nicaragua. **NOTES:** Defends territory vigorously against hawks, jays, squirrels, etc. Details of breeding biology unknown. Formerly known as Coues' Flycatcher. **ESSAYS:** How Do We Find Out About Bird Biology?, p. 319; Bills, p. 209; Passerines and Songbirds, p. 395; Territoriality, p. 387. **REF:** Phillips et al., 1964.

the syrinx are independently controlled, which explains the "two-voice" phenomenon seen in sonagrams of some species: simultaneous double tones that are nonharmonically related and therefore must be derived from two independent acoustic sources. Our understanding of how the syrinx works is based on studies of only a very few species (including the domestic chicken and Mallard, which hardly typify birds in general), and many of our ideas about how the passerine syrinx functions are based on "informed guesswork."

Recent work on the neural basis of song in passerines by Nottebohm and his colleagues not only identified the specific regions in the brain that control song production but also demonstrated differences between the sexes in the size of these regions. The substantially smaller size of these areas in female Canaries and Zebra Finches suggests an explanation for their inability to sing. The assertion that singing ability is dependent on the amount of brain space allocated to it is further supported by Nottebohm's demonstration that superior singers among male Canaries, Zebra Finches, and Marsh Wrens have larger song control regions in their brains. In fact, Pacific Coast Marsh Wrens, which have song repertoires that are three times larger than Atlantic Coast birds, have 30–40 percent larger song control areas in their brains.

SEE: Vocal Development, p. 601; Sonagrams: Seeing Bird Songs, p. 563; Adaptations for Flight, p. 507.   REFS: Brackenbury, 1982; Gaunt and Gaunt, 1977, 1985; Nottebohm, 1981.

Superspecies

What do Eastern and Western Screech-Owls, Plain and Tufted Titmice, and Eastern and Western Meadowlarks have in common? They are species that diverged from one another in isolation rather recently, and have remained largely or entirely geographically separated. Taxonomists group such closely related species that are allopatric (that is, with nonoverlapping distributions) into superspecies.

Superspecies are especially interesting because they represent a "snapshot" of the process of speciation—evolution caught in the act, as it were. There is no sharp dividing line between very well-differentiated subspecies and members of a superspecies, so designation of superspecies is usually tentative and sometimes controversial. In regions where their mapped ranges approach one another, it is important to look for evidence of members of a superspecies occurring together (being partially "sympatric"

Olive-sided Flycatcher

Contopus borealis Swainson

NG–284; G–216; PE–196; PW–pl 42; AE–pl 470; AW–pl 547; AM(II)–252

5'–75' F? 3
(3–4)
MONOG

F
I: 14 DAYS
ALTRICIAL
F: 21–23 DAYS
MF

BREEDING: Open montane and boreal conif and conif-decid forests, esp with abundant dead trees. ? broods. **DISPLAYS:** Males pursue females in courtship chase. **NEST:** Oft high in conif (decid in some areas) tree, on horizontal branch, far from trunk; compact, firmly attached with cobwebs; of twigs, rootlets, lichen, pine needles, most lined with lichen, grass, rootlets. **EGGS:** White, buff, pale salmon, lightly but clearly marked (oft wreathed) with browns, olive. 0.8" (22 mm). **DIET:** Exclusively insects that can be captured in air; many honeybees. **CONSERVATION:** Winters in montane S.A. from Colombia and Venezuela s to s e Peru. Rare cowbird host. **NOTES:** Vigorous defender of nest area against potential predators incl humans. Usu seen on exposed perch at top of or high in tree. **ESSAYS:** Territoriality, p. 387; Bathing and Dusting, p. 429; Incubation: Heating Eggs, p. 393. **REF:** Godfrey, 1986.

Eastern Wood-Pewee

Supersp #28
Contopus virens Linnaeus

NG–284; G–216; PE–196; PW–pl 42; AE–pl 465; AM(II)–254

15'–35' F 3
(8'–60') (2–4)
MONOG

F
I: 12–13 (–17?) DAYS
ALTRICIAL
F: 14–18 DAYS
MF

HOVER &
GLEAN

BREEDING: Decid and decid-conif forests, forest edge, woodland. 1 brood. **DISPLAYS:** Males pursue females vigorously in courtship chase. **NEST:** On horizontal limb far from trunk; small, well camouflaged, usu with lichen on outside, of grass, weed stems, bark, lichen, cocoons, lined with fine materials. **EGGS:** White to creamy, marked with browns, purples, oft wreathed. 0.7" (18 mm). **DIET:** Almost entirely insects; few berries. **CONSERVATION:** Winters from Colombia and Venezuela s to Peru and w Brazil in a variety of habitats, where it is solitary and active. Uncommon cowbird host. **NOTES:** Male feeds incubating female. **ESSAYS:** Decline of Eastern Songbirds, p. 495; Great Plains Hybrids, p. 625; Superspecies, p. 375; Nest Lining, p. 391. **REF:** Bent, 1942.

as opposed to allopatric). Birds often change their distributions quickly, and in many regions there are relatively few observers. If you are fortunate enough to find such a situation, you should be on the alert for the formation of mixed-species pairs or even successful hybridization. If the two forms overlap with little or no interbreeding, taxonomists would consider them separate species; if there is extensive interbreeding they would be given subspecific rank.

Following is a list of somewhat more than 100 North American species that are now considered members of 53 superspecies of North American birds. We have not listed numerous cases where North American species are members of superspecies whose other members breed *only* outside of our area. The list is based primarily on the judgments of the 1983 American Ornithologists' Union (AOU) checklist. The high frequency of question marks indicates the difficulty of taxonomically pigeonholing organisms at various stages within the continuous process of differentiation. In many cases where there is a narrow zone of overlap and a slight degree of hybridization, as in Ladder-backed and Nuttall's Woodpeckers, most (but not all) taxonomists would prefer the two forms to be considered allospecies within a superspecies. When the ranges of two very closely related forms do not overlap so that one cannot determine the degree of natural hybridization (if any), as in the case of Pygmy and Brown-headed Nuthatches, some taxonomists will claim they should be considered subspecies of the same species, and others that they should be members of superspecies. In the gulls, the situation is so complex that our classification is somewhat arbitrary. The bottom line is that it really makes little difference exactly how they are categorized—understanding their biology is the crucial point. This list serves to "flag" situations where allopatric speciation seems to be reaching its terminal stages, and where you might make a contribution to understanding the process.

SEE: Species and Speciation, p. 355; Sibling Species, p. 383; Hybridization, p. 501; Great Plains Hybrids, p. 625. REFS: Amadon, 1966; AOU, 1983.

North American Superspecies

A question mark (?) in this list indicates that there is some question about the status of the species listed. The numbers in parentheses refer to the pages in the AOU checklist where the taxonomic status of the superspecies is discussed. In many cases there are taxonomists who think the species of a superspecies should be reduced to the status of subspecies within a species, and to indicate this we've added an "s" to the AOU page number. In some cases there is taxonomic opinion that the species are sufficiently distinct or

Western Wood-Pewee

NG–284; G–216; PW–pl 42; AE–664; AW–pl 513; AM(II)–254

15′–35′	F	3	F		HOVER &
(2′–75′)		(2–4)	I: 12–13 DAYS		GLEAN
		MONOG	ALTRICIAL		
			F: 14–18? DAYS		
			MF		

BREEDING: Conif and conif-decid forests, forest edge, riparian woodland. 1 brood. **DISPLAYS:** ? **NEST:** Usu on horizontal limb far from trunk; larger, deeper than that of Eastern Wood-Pewee, well camouflaged but usu without lichen, of plant fibers, plant down, oft bound to branch with spider webs, lined with fine materials. **EGGS:** White to creamy, marked with browns, purples, oft wreathed. 0.7″ (18 mm). **DIET:** Almost entirely insects; few berries. **CONSERVATION:** Winters from Colombia and Venezuela s to Peru and Bolivia. Rare cowbird host. **NOTES:** Reportedly polygynous, but frequency unclear, perhaps only rarely. **ESSAYS:** Superspecies, p. 375; Decline of Eastern Songbirds, p. 495; Great Plains Hybrids, p. 625. **REFS:** Eckhardt, 1976; Verbeek, 1975.

Eastern Phoebe

Sayornis phoebe Latham

NG–286; G–210; PE–196; PW–pl 42; AE–pl 466; AM(II)–272

BRIDGE			F		
CLIFF	F	4–5	I: 16 DAYS		
0′–20′?		(3–8)	ALTRICIAL		
		MONOG	F: 15–16 DAYS		
			MF		

BREEDING: Open and riparian woodlands, rocky ravines, farmland with scattered trees. 2 broods. **DISPLAYS:** Courtship: brief, erratic flight-chases; pair formation is rapid. **NEST:** Originally in niches in cliff or bank, now mostly in or on variety of human-built structures, esp beneath bridges, in culverts, wells, etc.; of mud pellets, plant fibers, moss, lined with hair, feathers, grass. Built in 7–12 days. Oft renovate old nests (occ those of Barn Swallow); second clutches oft in same nest as first, esp if first was successful. **EGGS:** White, mostly unmarked, some (last laid) with small brown spots. 0.8″ (19 mm). **DIET:** Occ small fish and frogs. Berries, few seeds, mostly in winter. **CONSERVATION:** Winters s to s Mexico. Common cowbird host; may build new nest floor over cowbird eggs. Blue List 1980, Special Concern 1981–1986, apparently declining in many parts of e and midwest. **NOTES:** Energetic cost of building a new adherent nest translates into a reduced clutch size. Females known to sing. Learning not involved in development of songs. Oft feeds just above water surface. **ESSAYS:** Vocal Development, p. 601; Blue List, p. 11; Brood Parasitism, p. 287; Cowbirds, p. 619; Bills, p. 209. **REFS:** Kroodsma, 1985a; Weeks, 1978.

too widely overlapping in range to be considered parts of a superspecies, and there we've added a "d." A question mark after the superspecies and no letter after the page number shows more general uncertainty.

1. Common and Yellow-billed Loons (6)
2. Arctic and Pacific Loons (5)
3. Western and Clark's Grebes (10)
4. Double-crested and Olivaceous Cormorants? (38)
5. Glossy and White-faced Ibis? (56s)
6. Tundra and Trumpeter Swans? (63)
7. Blue-winged and Cinnamon Teal? (79d)
8. Greater and Lesser Prairie-Chickens? (140s)
9. Gambel's and California Quail (147)
10. Clapper and King Rail? (152s)
11. American and American Black Oystercatchers? (173s)
12. Ruddy and Black Turnstones? (190)
13. Purple and Rock Sandpipers? (199s)
14. Short- and Long-billed Dowitchers (203)
15. California, Herring, Western, Glaucous-winged, Glaucous, and Great Black-backed Gulls? (218–223)
16. Thayer's and Iceland Gulls? (218–223)
17. Black and Pigeon Guillemots (243)
18. Atlantic and Horned Puffins (249)
19. Eastern and Western Screech-Owls (293)
20. Spotted and Barred Owls? (302)
21. Common and Antillean Nighthawks (309)
22. Chimney and Vaux's Swifts? (319)

23. Ruby-throated and Black-chinned Hummingbirds? (356d)
24. Rufous and Allen's Hummingbirds (360)
25. Gila, Golden-fronted, and Red-bellied Woodpeckers (387)
26. Yellow-bellied, Red-breasted, and Red-naped Sapsuckers (388)
27. Ladder-backed and Nuttall's Woodpeckers (390)
28. Western and Eastern Wood-Pewees? (449s)
29. Alder and Willow Flycatchers (452)
30. Great Crested and Brown-crested or Ash-throated Flycatchers? (464)
31. Steller's and Blue Jays? (500d)
32. Black-billed and Yellow-billed Magpies (508)
33. American and Northwestern Crows (509s)
34. Black-capped and Carolina Chickadees (513)
35. Mexican and Mountain Chickadees? (513d)
36. Siberian Tit and Boreal and Chestnut-backed Chickadees? (514)
37. Plain and Tufted Titmice (516)
38. Pygmy and Brown-headed Nuthatches? (519s)
39. Brown and Long-billed Thrashers? (571s)
40. California, Crissal and LeConte's Thrashers? (573)
41. Northern and Loggerhead Shrikes? (585s)
42. Red-eyed and Black-whiskered Vireos? (597d)
43. Nashville, Virginia's, and Colima Warblers (604)

(List continues on next page.)

Black Phoebe
Sayornis nigricans Swainson

NG–286; G–210; PW–pl 42; AW–pl 610; AM(II)–270

WALL	F?	4 (3–6) MONOG	F I: 15–17 DAYS ALTRICIAL F: 14–21 DAYS MF		HOVER & GLEAN

BREEDING: Near water in woodland, canyon, suburb, farmland with scattered trees, coastal cliff. 2 (occ 3?) broods. **DISPLAYS:** In courtship, male performs song flight of fluttering and calling, then slowly descends. **NEST:** Adherent also on or under other structures; of mud pellets, plant fibers, hair, lined with hair, rootlets, grass, bark. **EGGS:** White, mostly unmarked, some (last laid) with small red spots. 0.8″ (19 mm). **DIET:** Almost exclusively insects, occ small fish. Regurgitates pellets. **CONSERVATION:** Winter resident, but wanders after breeding season. Rare cowbird host. **NOTES:** Oft feeds just above water surface. Sexes maintain separate winter feeding territories. In winter, also gleans insects from ground. **ESSAYS:** Bills, p. 209; Pellets, p. 297; Passerines and Songbirds, p. 395. **REFS:** Verbeek, 1975a, b.

Say's Phoebe
Sayornis saya Bonaparte

NG–286; G–210; PE–196; PW–pl 42; AW–pl 521; AM(II)–272

WALL	F?	4–5 (3–7) MONOG	F I: 12?–14 DAYS ALTRICIAL F: 14–16 DAYS MF	BERRIES	HOVER & GLEAN

BREEDING: Farmland, savanna, open woodland, usu near water. 2–3 broods. **DISPLAYS:** ? **NEST:** Adherent also under eaves, bridges, in wells; of grass, forbs, moss, plant fibers, lined with fine materials, esp hair. **EGGS:** White, mostly unmarked, some (last laid) with small red spots. 0.8″ (19 mm). **DIET:** Almost exclusively insects. Regurgitates pellets. **CONSERVATION:** Winters s to s Mexico. Rare cowbird host. **NOTES:** Frequently seen hovering. Oft feeds just above water surface. **ESSAYS:** Pellets, p. 297; Passerines and Songbirds, p. 395; Bills, p. 209. **REF:** Phillips et al., 1964.

Songbird Foraging

We usually see passerines more often than other kinds of birds, and very frequently it is while they are looking for food. Songbird foraging is thus one of the most frequent behaviors birders encounter—and one of the most interesting. Different birds go about it in different ways. A Black Phoebe can provide many minutes of entertainment as it sallies from a perch and snatches up mayflies as they emerge from a pond. Warblers seem always on the move as they glean insects from foliage and bark—and take on added interest when one realizes that different species tend to search in somewhat different places. Chickadees and Bushtits scramble through trees, often in flocks, frequently hanging upside down to search out an insect morsel. Crossbills also move in gangs, and resemble small parrots, as they too often hang upside down. But instead of insects, they use their unusual bills to pry the seeds out of pine cones. Berry-eating waxwings also flock but are more sedate. In the fall, groups of Lesser Goldfinches make a lively sight as they swarm over the seed heads of thistles. Swallows zoom along acting as speedy insect nets engulfing "aerial plankton"—small flying insects.

Rufous-sides Towhees and Fox Sparrows use both feet simultaneously

A Black Phoebe sallies from its perch to hawk insects over the surface of a pond.

Vermilion Flycatcher

Pyrocephalus rubinus Boddaert

NG–286; G–204; PE–196; PW–pl 42; AE–pl 415; AW–pl 451; AM(II)–274

8'–20'	F	3	F		HOVER &
(4'–60')		(2–4)	I: 14–15 DAYS		POUNCE
		MONOG	ALTRICIAL		
			F: 14–16 DAYS		
			MF		

BREEDING: Riparian woodland, roadsides, deserts. 2 broods. **DISPLAYS:** Male ascends high performing flight song, red crest erect, tail spread, then hovers with rapidly beating wings and slowly flutters down. **NEST:** Deep in horizontal fork; flat, well constructed, of twigs, grass, forbs, rootlets, plant fibers, cocoons, spider web, lined with down, hair, feathers. **EGGS:** White to creamy, boldly marked (oft wreathed) with browns, olive, lavender. 0.7" (17 mm). **DIET:** Almost exclusively insects; takes many bees. Regurgitates pellets. **CONSERVATION:** Winters s to s Mexico. Rare cowbird host. **NOTES:** Male feeds female during incubation and brooding. Female broods. Oft feeds just above water surface. Oft pumps tail up and down while perched. **ESSAYS:** Nest Materials, p. 369; Color of Birds, p. 111; Pellets, p. 297. **REFS:** Smith, 1970; Taylor and Hanson, 1970.

Gray Flycatcher

Empidonax wrightii Baird

NG–288; G–214; AW–pl 490; AM(II)–266

TREE	F?	3–4	F		GROUND
2'–9'		MONOG	I: 14 DAYS		GLEAN
			ALTRICIAL		
			F: 16 DAYS		
			MF		

BREEDING: Sagebrush, arid open woodland (usu piñon-juniper, occ oak-pine). ? broods. **DISPLAYS:** ? **NEST:** In crotch of juniper or sage, near base of thornbush; of bark, plant down, weed stems, grass, lined with feathers, hair. **EGGS:** Creamy white, unmarked. 0.7" (18 mm). **DIET:** Exclusively insects. **CONSERVATION:** Winters s to c Mexico. **NOTES:** Closely related to Dusky Flycatcher; where their ranges overlap, territories are defended interspecifically. Whether male aids in incubation in this species (as reported for Dusky Flycatcher) is unknown. **ESSAYS:** Interspecific Territoriality, p. 385; Sibling Species, p. 383; Bills, p. 209; Who Incubates?, p. 27; How Do We Find Out About Bird Biology?, p. 319. **REFS:** Johnson, 1963, 1966.

to scratch up litter and uncover edible items; thrashers sweep and dig with their bills for the same purpose. Thrushes run along the ground, pause, and pounce on insects or earthworms. Meadowlarks walk along bobbing their heads and spearing prey. Cactus Wrens often lift leaves or stones with their bills to search for food underneath. Shrikes and bluebirds may hover before dropping on prey on the ground.

A given species of bird will often change its foraging behavior from area to area, from season to season, and even from moment to moment, depending on the kinds of food items that are available. Watching and recording patterns of foraging can thus be a fascinating and useful activity. Ecologists have approached foraging theoretically, trying to create models that predict how an animal should behave when confronted by numerous food items that differ in how difficult they are to find, the time each takes to "handle" (e.g., to kill an insect, husk a seed), their relative nutritional value, how long it takes an individual to travel from one concentration of food items (say, a seed-rich weed patch) to another, and so on. Much of the work testing foraging models has been done with birds. Some of the models have proven capable of predicting with considerable accuracy such things as when a bird should leave a certain patch of habitat where it has been feeding and seek another, and how a bird should select food items from a mix of big scarce and small common ones.

So whether you are a bird lover who just enjoys watching them, or an ecologist interested in the details of how nature works, observing the foraging of songbirds has a great deal to offer.

SEE: Mixed-Species Flocking, p. 433; MacArthur's Warblers, p. 523; European Starlings, p. 489; Shorebird Feeding, p. 125; Raptor Hunting, p. 223; Facts, Hypotheses, and Theories, p. 567.   REFS: Krebs et al., 1977, 1983; Orians and Angell, 1985.

Sibling Species

Empidonax flycatchers, especially species such as the Dusky and the Gray Flycatchers, are notoriously difficult to identify. In general, birds of this group are more readily separated by their songs than by their appearance; indeed, it is suspected that even the birds depend heavily on song to sort out who is who in order to avoid hybridizing.

These flycatchers are examples of "sibling species"—species that are extremely similar in appearance but are nonetheless reproductively isolated from one another. Sibling species are often thought to be the result of fairly recent differentiation—relatively new products of the speciation process. If, however, new species remain subject to very similar selection pressures, there is no reason why they cannot remain siblings for a very long time.

SEE: Species and Speciation, p. 355; Natural Selection, p. 237; Interspecific Territoriality, p. 385.   REF: Mayr, 1963.

Dusky Flycatcher

Empidonax oberholseri Phillips

NG–288; G–214; AW–pl 546; AM(II)–264

TREE	F?	3–4	F–M I: 12–15 DAYS ALTRICIAL		HOVER &
3'–7' (2'–15')		MONOG	F: 18 DAYS MF		GLEAN?

BREEDING: Open conif forest, aspen groves, willows, montane chaparral. ? broods. **DISPLAYS**: ? **NEST**: In crotch of juniper or sage, near base of thorny shrub; of weed stems, grass, lined with feathers, grass, hair. **EGGS**: Creamy white, unmarked. 0.7″ (18 mm). **DIET**: Exclusively insects. **CONSERVATION**: Winters s to s Mexico. Rare cowbird host. **NOTES**: Closely related to Gray Flycatcher; where their ranges overlap, territories are defended interspecifically. Adult (female?) performs distraction display at nest. Reports of male helping with incubation need to be confirmed. Oft flicks tail while perched. **ESSAYS**: Interspecific Territoriality, p. 385; Sibling Species, p. 383; Bills, p. 209; Distraction Displays, p. 115; Who Incubates?, p. 27; How Do We Find Out About Bird Biology?, p. 319. **REFS**: Johnson, 1966; Morton and Pereyra, 1985.

Least Flycatcher

Empidonax minimus Baird and Baird

NG–290; G–212; PE–196; AE–pl 464; AM(II)–260

SHRUB	F	4	F I: 13–14 DAYS ALTRICIAL	BERRIES	HAWKS
10'–40' (2'–60')		(3–6) MONOG	F: 12–16 DAYS MF		

BREEDING: Open decid or decid-conif woodland, suburbs. 1 brood, 2 in s (rarely in n). **DISPLAYS**: Males pursue females in courtship chase. **NEST**: On horizontal limb of tree (occ conif); compact, of bark, weed stems, grass, lined with grass, hair, plant down, feathers. **EGGS**: Creamy white, unmarked. 0.6″ (16 mm). **DIET**: Also few seeds. **CONSERVATION**: Winters from n Mexico s to Panama. Blue List 1980, Special Concern 1981–82, Local Concern 1986; continuing decline in some portions of range. Uncommon cowbird host. **NOTES**: Rare polygyny documented. Pugnacious in vicinity of nest. Male occ feeds female on nest. Aggressively excludes ecologically similar American Redstarts from nesting territories. Territorial on wintering grounds. **ESSAYS**: Sibling Species, p. 383; Blue List, p. 11; Interspecific Territoriality, p. 385; Polygyny, p. 443; Bills, p. 209. **REFS**: Briskie and Sealy, 1987; Holmes et al., 1979; Sherry, 1979; Walkinshaw, 1966a.

Interspecific Territoriality

Most birds defend their territories only against members of the same species; some, however, defend against individuals of other species as well. Generally such interspecific territoriality occurs between species that are very similar—as might be expected if territoriality is a way of guarding resources or mates. Closely related species are most likely to have similar resource requirements, and are also most likely to attempt to copulate with the territory owner's mate. For instance, interspecific territoriality is found in two extremely similar *Empidonax* flycatchers, the Gray and Dusky Flycatchers. These birds are so much alike that they can be told apart with assurance only by their songs or by careful measurements of specimens. The Gray Flycatcher breeds in small trees and sagebrush and tends to forage in the open; the Dusky Flycatcher lives in forest and chaparral. Logging operations in eastern California in the mid-1800s brought these two flycatchers together by opening clearings in the forest, where the species retain their habitat separation but defend their territories interspecifically. The birds' appearances and challenge calls are so similar that each respects the other's domains. Even with the high degree of similarity, there is no sign that the species hybridize.

Similarly, on a Scottish island, Great Tits (relatives of chickadees) and Chaffinches (relatives of goldfinches) defend their territories against one another, even though the birds belong to entirely different taxonomic families. On the mainland the two species do not exclude each other. Great Tits and Chaffinches have similar feeding habits and areas, and presumably the simpler island environment provides less opportunity for each to use different resources. Ecologists generally expect to find interspecific territoriality when the habitat is relatively simple, restricting the variety of resources (usually kinds of food) available, and when the birds involved are specialists in their use of resources (so that it is not easy for one or both species to change its resource use in the face of competition from the other). When breeding, North American hummingbirds usually live in separate habitats, but during migration, more than one species often occur together and all use the same nectar resources—and then interspecific territories are defended.

Some groups of birds defend interspecific territories communally. Acorn Woodpecker groups attempt to exclude Acorn Woodpeckers belonging to other groups, Lewis' Woodpeckers, jays, and squirrels from the territories that they establish around their large caches of acorns. They also defend against European Starlings, which may appropriate the woodpeckers' nest holes.

Finally, birds may defend their territories against insects; some tropical hummingbirds chase bees and butterflies away from nectar sources. This behavior has not been reported in North American hummers, but you should watch for it.

Hammond's Flycatcher
Empidonax hammondii Xántus de Vesey

NG–288; G–214; AW–pl 517; AM(II)–262

DECID
10'–40'
(6'–60')

F?

3–4
MONOG

F
I: 12–15 DAYS
ALTRICIAL
F: 17–18 DAYS
MF

BREEDING: Boreal conif forest, esp dense fir, aspen forest. 1? brood. **DISPLAYS**: ? **NEST**: On horizontal limb of tall conif, occ decid tree; of leaves, bark, grass, lined with feathers, grass, hair. **EGGS**: Creamy white, unmarked. 0.7" (18 mm). **DIET**: Exclusively insects. **CONSERVATION**: Winters s to Honduras. **NOTES**: Interspecifically territorial with Western Flycatcher in Pacific n w. Usu found near tops of trees. **ESSAYS**: Sibling Species, p. 383; Interspecific Territoriality, p. 385; Bills, p. 209. **REFS**: Beaver and Baldwin, 1975; Davis, 1954.

Acadian Flycatcher
Empidonax virescens Vieillot

NG–290; G–212; PE–198; AE–pl 461; AM(II)–256

SHRUB
CONIF
8'–20' (3'–25')

F

3
(2–4)
MONOG

F
I: 14 (13–15) DAYS
ALTRICIAL
F: 13–15 DAYS
MF

BERRIES

BREEDING: Heavily wooded decid bottomland and swamp, riparian thickets, wooded ravines. 2 broods. **DISPLAYS**: Courtship mostly of erratic, swift chases; male oft hovers above perched female. **NEST**: Well out on horizontal limb of tree, placed hammocklike between spreading twigs; shallow, of bark, twigs, weed stems, grass, cobweb, sloppy with hanging streamers of grass, lined with grass, hair, plant down. Female selects site. **EGGS**: Creamy white, spotted with browns. 0.7" (18 mm). **DIET**: Also few seeds. **CONSERVATION**: Winters from e Nicaragua, Costa Rica, s to n and w Colombia, n Venezuela, and w Ecuador. Range reportedly expanding in n e. Common cowbird host. **NOTES**: Long-term pair bond; rarely polygynous. Strong fidelity to breeding territory. Male rarely feeds incubating female. Female broods. Fledglings fed only by male when female begins incubating second clutch. **ESSAYS**: Decline of Eastern Songbirds, p. 495; Masterbuilders, p. 445; Polygyny, p. 443; Site Tenacity, p. 189; Sibling Species, p. 383; Range Expansion, p. 459. **REFS**: Mumford, 1964; Walkinshaw, 1966b.

SEE: Territoriality, p. 387; Sibling Species, p. 383; Hoarding Food, p. 345; Hybridization, p. 501; Species and Speciation, p. 355. REFS: Boyden, 1978; Cody, 1974; Johnson, 1963; Orians and Willson, 1964; Reed, 1982.

Territoriality

Many birds attempt to exclude other birds from all or part of their "home range"—the area they occupy in the course of their normal daily activities. When they do, we say they are defending a "territory." Most often this behavior occurs during the breeding season and is directed toward members of the same species. Territoriality appears, in most cases, to be an attempt to monopolize resources, especially food resources, or access to mates. But territoriality may also serve, in part, as a predator defense mechanism.

Some birds defend their entire home range. Others defend only their food supply, a place to mate, or the site of their nest. Some tropical hummingbirds chase most other hummingbirds and other nectar-feeding birds (and some butterflies) away from favorite patches of nectar-bearing flowers. On their leks (patches of ground traditionally used for communal mating displays) grouse, some sandpipers, and some other birds defend small territories. Most colonial-nesting seabirds simply defend the immediate vicinity of their nests—presumably to protect their eggs and, at least in the case of some penguins, the pebbles from which the nest is constructed.

Territoriality tends to space some species of camouflaged birds and their nests rather evenly throughout their habitat; it prevents them from occurring in flocks or clusters while breeding. This, in turn, may reduce the danger from predation, since many predators will concentrate on one kind of prey after one or a few individuals of that prey type are discovered (that is, the predator forms a "search image"). Clustering can promote the formation of a search image by predators and thus reduce the security of each individual prey (birds that are not cryptic, however, may gain protection in clustering).

To minimize the need for actual physical contact in order to defend territories, animals have evolved "keep-out" signals to warn away potential intruders. In birds, of course, the most prominent are the songs of males. Far from being beautiful bits of music intended to enliven the human environment (as was long assumed), bird songs are, in large part, announcements of ownership and threats of possible violent defense of an area. If, of course, the aural warning is ineffective, the territory owner will often escalate its activities to include visual displays, chases, and even combat. This territorial behavior is typically quite stereotyped, and can usually be elicited experimentally with the use of recorded songs or with stuffed taxidermy mounts.

Willow Flycatcher

Supersp #29
Empidonax traillii Audubon

NG–290; G–212; PE–198; AE–pl 462; AW–pl 518; AM(II)–258

			F		
			I: 12–13 DAYS		
DECID	F	3–4	ALTRICIAL	BERRIES	HOVER &
2'–10'		(2–4)	F: 12–14 DAYS		GLEAN
(1'–18')		MONOG	MF		

BREEDING: Swamps and thickets, esp willow. 1 brood. **DISPLAYS**: Courtship chase. **NEST**: In upright or slanting fork; compact, of bark, weed stems, grass, lined with grass, hair, plant down, feathers. Female selects nest site, accompanied by male. **EGGS**: Buff, occ white, spotted with browns near large end. 0.7" (18 mm). **DIET**: Also few seeds. **CONSERVATION**: Winters from s Mexico to Panama. Common cowbird host; occ bury cowbird egg in bottom of nest. Blue List 1980–82, Special Concern 1986; w coast populations apparently declining. Populations increase with reduction of cattle grazing and the cessation of poisoning and removal of riparian willows. **NOTES**: In contrast to typical songbirds, song is entirely innate, rather than learned or partly learned. Females also sing territorial song. Interspecifically territorial with Alder Flycatcher in BC and in n e U.S. Rare polygyny documented. Female broods young for 7–8 days. Formerly known as Traill's Flycatcher, which included Alder Flycatcher. **ESSAYS**: Blue List, p. 11; Superspecies, p. 375; Vocal Development, p. 601; Sibling Species, p. 383; Interspecific Territoriality, p. 385; Polygyny, p. 443; Bills, p. 209. **REFS**: Ettinger and King, 1980; Frakes and Johnson, 1982; Kroodsma, 1984; Seutin, 1987; Taylor and Littlefield, 1986.

Alder Flycatcher

Supersp #29
Empidonax alnorum Brewster

NG–290; G–212; PE–198; PW–pl 42; AW–pl 519; AM(II)–258

			F	
			I: 12–13 DAYS	
1'–4'	F?	3–4	ALTRICIAL	BERRIES
(To 30')		(2–4)	F: 13–14 DAYS	
		MONOG	MF	

BREEDING: Swamps and thickets, esp alder and willow. ? broods. **DISPLAYS**: ? **NEST**: In upright or slanting fork; compact, untidy, of bark, weed stems, grass, lined sparsely with grass, pine needles. **EGGS**: White, spotted with browns near large end. 0.7" (18 mm). **DIET**: Also few seeds. **CONSERVATION**: Winters in S.A. (members of Alder-Willow superspecies reported from Colombia and n w Venezuela s to e Peru, Bolivia and n Argentina). Occ cowbird host. **NOTES**: In contrast to typical songbirds, song is entirely innate, rather than wholly or partly learned. Interspecifically territorial with Willow Flycatcher in BC and in n e U.S. Formerly known as Traill's Flycatcher, which included Willow Flycatcher. **ESSAYS**: Superspecies, p. 375; Vocal Development, p. 601; Sibling Species, p. 383; Interspecific Territoriality, p. 385; Bills, p. 209. **REFS**: Kroodsma, 1984; Stein, 1963.

Territory size varies enormously from species to species, and even within species, from individual to individual. Golden Eagles have territories of some 35 square miles; Least Flycatchers' territories are about 700 square yards; and sea gulls have territories of only a few square feet in the immediate vicinity of the nest. Territory size often varies in the same species from habitat to habitat. In relatively resource-poor Ohio shrublands, Song Sparrows have territories several thousand square yards in extent. In the resource-rich salt marshes of the San Francisco baylands they are about one-fifth to one-tenth as large. The San Francisco birds need to defend much less area to assure an adequate food supply.

SEE: Interspecific Territoriality, p. 385; Sandpipers, Social Systems, and Territoriality, p. 155; Population Dynamics, p. 575; Leks, p. 259; Spacing of Wintering Shorebirds, p. 147; Vocal Dialects, p. 595; Vocal Functions, p. 471. REF: Nice, 1964.

Bird Biologist—Ernst Mayr

When one thinks of ornithologists who have had an enormous impact on science outside of the world of birds, Ernst Mayr's name always comes to mind. Like Darwin (p. 475), Mayr's scientific career was influenced early on by his experiences with island birds; he did research on the avifauna of the Solomon Islands and New Guinea in the late 1920s. Born in Germany in 1904, Mayr emigrated to the United States and became curator of birds at the American Museum of Natural History in 1932; in 1953 he moved to Harvard as Agassiz Professor of Zoology. With his book *Systematics and the Origin of Species* (1942) Mayr brought the field of taxonomy firmly into the "Neo-Darwinian" evolutionary synthesis that was developing at that time. His monumental *Animal Species and Evolution* (1963) summarized his ideas on speciation, which were similar to those of Joseph Grinnell (p. 411), another great student of birds. Those ideas are now accepted by the vast majority of zoologists. In later years Mayr has written brilliantly on the history of biology, and in 1987 at the age of 83 he was still "retired" in name only, hard at work on papers about birds of the South Pacific.

SEE: Species and Speciation, p. 355.

Yellow-bellied Flycatcher

Empidonax flaviventris
Baird and Baird

NG–292; G–212; PE–198; AE–pl 463; AM(II)–256

| 0'–2' | F | 3–4
(3–5)
MONOG | F
I: 12–13 DAYS
ALTRICIAL
F: 13–14 DAYS
MF | BERRIES | HOVER &
GLEAN |

BREEDING: Boreal conif forests and bogs. ? broods. **DISPLAYS:** ? **NEST:** On or close to ground in sphagnum hummocks, roots of upturned stumps, etc.; primarily of moss, also rootlets, grass, lined with grass, pine needles, rootlets. **EGGS:** White, spotted with browns, esp near large end. 0.7" (17 mm). **DIET:** Also few seeds. **CONSERVATION:** Winters from s Mexico s to Panama, where, like other *Empidonax*, it tends to be solitary (although oft seen in "waves" at peak of migration); found in woodland and woodland edge. Rare cowbird host. **NOTES:** Adults quiet and unaggressive at nest; female occ calls when returning to nest with building materials and when resuming incubation. **ESSAYS:** Decline of Eastern Songbirds, p. 495; Sibling Species, p. 383; Bills, p. 209. **REFS:** Walkinshaw, 1967; Walkinshaw and Henry, 1957.

Western Flycatcher

Empidonax difficilis Baird

NG–292; G–214; PW–pl 42; AW–pl 549; AM(II)–268

| CLIFF
GROUND
0'–30' | F | 3–4
(3–5)
MONOG | F
I: 14–15 DAYS
ALTRICIAL
F: 14–18 DAYS
MF | | HOVER &
GLEAN |

BREEDING: Decid and conif forests and woodlands, esp near water. ? broods. **DISPLAYS:** ? **NEST:** Wide variety of situations from stream bank or roots of upturned tree to eaves, cliff ledge, cavity in small tree; of moss, lichen, rootlets, grass, leaves, bark, lined with shredded bark, hair, feathers. **EGGS:** White to creamy, spotted with browns, occ lavender, esp near large end. 0.7" (17 mm). **DIET:** Also few berries and seeds. **CONSERVATION:** Winters from n Mexico to s Mexico. Rare cowbird host. **NOTES:** Oft interspecifically territorial with Hammond's Flycatcher in Pacific n w. Female broods. **ESSAYS:** Interspecific Territoriality, p. 385; Sibling Species, p. 383; Birds in the Bush, p. 541. **REFS:** Beaver and Baldwin, 1975; Davis et al., 1963; Johnson, 1980.

Nest Lining

At first glance, a display of the materials birds have used to line their nests might be linked to an avian pawnshop. On closer scrutiny, however, these sometimes incongruous substances can be grouped into five more or less discrete classes: *finer materials, feathers, concealing ornaments, remnants,* and *artifacts.* To save space in some species treatments these terms may be used to label materials lining the nests; here we describe them in greater detail.

First, the lining may consist of loose, smaller bits of the same materials that have been incorporated into the latticework of the nest. These *finer materials* are utilized to shed water, deter pests, conceal the eggs from predators, insulate, and cushion them. Typically, finer materials are bits of vegetation (including leaves, needles, twigs, sticks, reeds, mosses, lichen, grass, seaweed, etc.), but birds may also take advantage of a variety of other readily available and portable animal products such as hair, fur, or shreds of dry cow pats.

The second lining material, *feathers* (including down), usually comes from the brooding birds themselves, but those of other species may be gathered, as well. They also serve to insulate and cushion the eggs.

A third type of lining, often found in the minimal scrapes made by ground nesters, consists of *concealing ornaments*—collections of nearby objects whose main value lies in providing camouflage for otherwise exposed eggs. In some situations they may help to keep the eggs in place, provide additional insulation, or prevent the eggs from becoming embedded in mud or sand after inadvertent flooding of the nest. These objects include stones, rock shards, shells, bits of wood, moss, lichen, withered leaves, or nearby grasses that sometimes may be simply plucked by the incubating adult as it sits.

A fourth type, *remnants,* is material that has not been placed deliberately in the nests by the birds. Wood chips found in the arboreal excavations of cavity-nesting species, the remains from the winter nests of squirrels and mice occasionally found in tunnels and chambers of burrow-nesting species, bits of vegetation deposited by wind, and pieces of surrounding plants broken as ground-nesting adults mat down the vegetation to form their depressionlike nest are a few of the many items coincidentally cradling eggs. In simple scrapes some remnants may function as concealing ornaments as well.

A fifth lining type, *artifacts,* includes a vast array of manufactured or natural, shiny, eye-catching objects. These materials are sometimes poorly suited for use in a nest, and their choice by adults is perplexing. In one study of Wrynecks (*Jynx torquilla* a distinctive member of the woodpecker family), the stomachs of 4 out of 14 young that had died in their nests were found to contain a potentially lethal shiny stone or piece of glass. Why the adults included such items in their nests is unknown. Certainly the ingested artifacts did not serve to supplement the diet of the young. If their presence illustrates nothing more than a misguided attraction that some birds have

Buff-breasted Flycatcher

Empidonax fulvifrons Giraud

NG–292; G–214; AW–632; AM(II)–270

DECID
TREE
9′–45′

F?

4
(3–5)
MONOG?

F?
I: 14–15 (?) DAYS
ALTRICIAL
F: 14–17 (?) DAYS
MF (?)

BREEDING: Dry montane canyons with sycamore, pine, and pine-oak forests. ? broods. **DISPLAYS:** ? **NEST:** On horizontal limb near trunk or in crotch of tree; of plant fibers, grass, leaves, rootlets, blossoms, lined with plant down, grass, hair, feathers. **EGGS:** Creamy white, unmarked. 0.6″ (15 mm). **DIET:** Insects. **CONSERVATION:** Winters from n Mexico to s Mexico. Numbers have declined and range has decreased markedly since 1920. Rare cowbird host. **NOTES:** Reportedly nests in small colonies. Oft forages from top of forb or small shrub. Breeding biology not well known. **ESSAYS:** How Do We Find Out About Bird Biology?, p. 319; Bills, p. 209; Birds in the Bush, p. 541; Passerines and Songbirds, p. 395. **REF:** Phillips et al. 1964.

Northern Beardless-Tyrannulet

Camptostoma imberbe
Sclater

NG–292; G–214; PW–pl 42; AE–617; AW–673; AM(II)–250

4′–50′

F?

3
(1–3)
MONOG?

F?
I: ? DAYS
ALTRICIAL
F: ? DAYS
MF (?)

BREEDING: Open riparian woodland (esp cottonwood), river bottom thickets. ? broods. **DISPLAYS:** ? **NEST:** On limb (usu far from trunk) or in mistletoe; globular, with side entrance near top, of plant fibers, lined with down, feathers, etc. **EGGS:** White, spotted with browns, olive, esp near large end. 0.6″ (16 mm). **DIET:** Little known: mostly insects; few berries and seeds. **CONSERVATION:** Winters from n Mexico to n Costa Rica. **NOTES:** Breeding biology unknown. In winter, reportedly forages mostly by gleaning from bark of twigs. **ESSAYS:** How Do We Find Out About Bird Biology?, p. 319; Bills, p. 209; Birds in the Bush, p. 541; Bathing and Dusting, p. 429; Determining Diets, p. 535. **REF:** Phillips et al., 1964.

for adding dangerous materials to their nests, one wonders why natural selection has not operated more strongly against such behavior.

If by default or by design, the nest or incubation site has no lining, then eggs simply rest directly on the substrate or on the supporting nest lattice. Such nests or sites are described as *unlined* and are typical of a number of colonial cliff-nesting birds.

SEE: Nest Materials, p. 369; Masterbuilders, p. 445; Eggs and Their Evolution, p. 301; Incubation: Heating Eggs, p. 393; Feathered Nests, p. 605; Brood Patches, p. 427. REFS: Greig-Smith, 1986; Terhivuo, 1977, 1983.

Incubation: Heating Eggs

For an egg to develop normally, it must be exposed for a considerable length of time to temperatures a few degrees below the normal 104° F (40° C) avian body temperature. Indeed, the ideal incubation temperature for many birds' eggs is about human body temperature, 98.6° F. Almost all birds create the required temperature by sitting on the eggs and incubating them, often transferring heat via a temporarily bare area of abdominal skin called the "brood patch." A few birds, like penguins, pelicans, and gannets, transfer heat through their webbed feet. A unique form of incubation is found in the turkeylike megapodes of Australia. They heat their eggs by depositing them in a large mound of decaying vegetation, which the birds have scratched together. By opening and closing the mound as needed, the birds carefully regulate the heat of decomposition, which takes the place of the parental body heat used in normal incubation.

On the other hand, the embryo inside the egg is also very sensitive to high temperatures, so that in some situations eggs must be protected from the sun. Ducks with open nests, for example, will pull downy feathers (originally plucked to form their brood patches) over the nest to cover the eggs when they leave it, providing shade if the weather is hot and helping to retard heat loss when it is cold. Open-nesting ducks usually have camouflage down that does not reveal the nest's location; hole-nesting ducks have white down. Other species may stand over the nest and shade the eggs when temperatures rise. Killdeer and some other shorebirds soak the feathers of their bellies and use them to wet the eggs before shading, thus helping to cool the developing embryos by evaporative heat loss.

Embryos are less sensitive to cold than to heat, particularly before incubation has started. Mallard eggs have been known to crack by freezing and still hatch successfully. Eggs cool when incubation is interrupted, but this is not usually harmful, and few birds incubate continuously. Instead egg temperature is regulated in response to changes in the temperature of the environment by varying the length of time that a parent bird sits on them or the tightness of the "sit." For instance, female House Wrens

Rose-throated Becard

Pachyramphus aglaiae Lafresnaye

NG–294; G–204; PW–pl 42; AE–pl 430; AW–pl 493; AM(II)–292

15'–50' F–M 4–6 MONOG F I: ? DAYS ALTRICIAL F: 19+ DAYS MF BERRIES SEEDS HAWKS

BREEDING: Woodland, open forest, scrub, mangroves. ? broods. **DISPLAYS:** In courtship, male spreads and displays white epaulets. **NEST:** Suspended from branch tip: large, globular, with small cavity, entrance low; of lichen, bark, vine, pine needles, spider web, feathers. Female lines nest, does most of building. Female, and to a lesser extent male, continue adding material throughout incubation. **EGGS:** White, cinnamon, buff, spotted with brown, occ concentrated at large end. 0.9″ (23 mm). **DIET:** Incl fruit. **CONSERVATION:** Winters from n Mexico s to Costa Rica. Rare Bronzed Cowbird host. **NOTES:** Usu hidden in tree foliage, rather than perched in open like flycatchers. Strong nest site tenacity. Not clear how eggs avoid being shaken from nest when wind whips slender branches supporting nest. Female broods. Occurs in mixed winter flocks. **ESSAYS:** Passerines and Songbirds, p. 395; Masterbuilders, p. 445; Site Tenacity, p. 189; Mixed–Species Flocking, p. 433. **REFS:** Runnels, 1975; Skutch, 1969.

Eurasian Skylark

Alauda arvensis Linnaeus

NG–294; G–218; PW–pl 60; AW–pl 574; AM(II)–294

F 3–4 (3–7) MONOG F I: 11–12 DAYS ALTRICIAL F: 9–10 DAYS FM? INSECTS FOLIAGE GLEAN

BREEDING: Open country. Possibly 2 broods. **DISPLAYS:** Male pursues female, performs elaborate song-flight reaching great heights; male runs around female with erect crest and drooping wings. **NEST:** In shallow depression, lined with roots, grass, occ hair. **EGGS:** Grayish-white, yellowish, heavily spotted with browns, olive. 1.0″ (24 mm). **DIET:** Incl other terrestrial inverts; grass and forb seeds. **CONSERVATION:** Winter resident. Introduced in 1902 or 1903 to Vancouver Island, BC, and has spread to San Juan Island in WA. **NOTES:** Breeding biology virtually unknown in N.A. **ESSAYS:** Avian Invaders, p. 633; Bird Voices, p. 373; How Do We Find Out About Bird Biology?, p. 319. **REF:** Weisbrod and Stevens, 1974.

(which incubate without help from the males) sat on the eggs for periods averaging 14 minutes when the temperature was 59° F (15° C), but an average of only 7.5 minutes when it rose to 86° F (30° C).

Many birds apparently sense the egg temperature with receptors in the brood patches, which helps them to regulate their attentiveness (time spent incubating) more accurately. Since the embryo itself increasingly generates heat as it develops, periods of attentiveness should generally decline as incubation progresses. Attentiveness is also influenced by the insulating properties of a particular nest.

Eggs are also turned periodically—from about every eight minutes by American Redstarts to once an hour by Mallards. The turning presumably helps to warm the eggs more evenly, and to prevent embryonic membranes from sticking to the shell.

SEE: Who Incubates?, p. 27; Incubation Time, p. 481; Life in the Egg, p. 457. REFS: Schardien and Jackson, 1979; White and Kinney, 1974.

Passerines and Songbirds

Passerines are the perching birds—technically members of the order Passeriformes. Birds in this order are characterized by having four toes, three directed forward and one backward, all joining the foot at the same level. Orders are primary taxonomic subdivisions of classes. Birds compose the class Aves (we are in the class Mammalia; bees are in the class Insecta).

Roughly 60 percent of all bird species are passerines, but only about 40 percent of the families. Thus, this order makes up an extremely large fraction of bird diversity, and the families within it have a disproportionately high average number of species. Both facts indicate the great success of the passerine way of life: not only have a great many passerine species evolved, but the existence of so many similar species within families suggests a relatively low rate of extinctions, a high rate of speciation, or both.

Because the diversity of passerine species is so extensive, and perhaps because they are the most familiar of birds, the class Aves is often conveniently divided simply into passerines and nonpasserines. Within the Passeriformes, two suborders which differ in the structure of the vocal apparatus are usually recognized: the Oscines and the Suboscines. Only one of eighteen passerine families represented in North America are Suboscines: the Tyrannidae (tyrant flycatchers—flycatchers, kingbirds, phoebes, etc.).

The Oscines, divided into about 70 families, are the "songbirds." This is the group of birds in which singing is most highly developed. The calls of some birds in other groups are quite musical, but it is in the Oscines that we perceive songs to reach their full beauty and complexity.

SEE: Feet, p. 239; Bird Voices, p. 373; Vocal Functions, p. 471; Birds, DNA, and Evolutionary Convergence, p. 419; Taxonomy and Nomenclature, p. 515.

Horned Lark
Eremophila alpestris Linnaeus

NG–294; G–218; PE–200; PW–pl 54; AE–pl 556; AW–pl 603; AM(II)–296

		F I: 11–12 DAYS	
F	3–4 (2–5) MONOG	ALTRICIAL F: 9–12 DAYS MF	INSECTS

BREEDING: Open country, tundra, grassland, agricultural areas. 1 brood in n, 2 (3?) in s. **DISPLAYS:** Male performs elaborate song-flight: rises to 800′, circles, then dives to ground with wings folded. Male struts before female with erect horns and drooped wings. **NEST:** In shallow depression, lined with roots, grass, plant down, hair, oft with rim of pebbles or dirt clods on most exposed side. Female selects nest site. **EGGS:** Variable, gray, greenish, heavily speckled with brown. 0.8″ (22 mm). **DIET:** Incl spiders, snails; grass and forb seeds. **CONSERVATION:** Winters s to S.A. Uncommon cowbird host. Adoption of farm fields for breeding has greatly increased numbers and expanded range eastward since 1800, although farming operations destroy many nests. **NOTES:** Female may fly low and far from nest when intruder detected, or perform fluttering distraction display if intruder is close. Female renests ca. 7 days after brood fledges. Juveniles form postbreeding flocks. Winter flocks, oft immense, occ with Snow Buntings, Lapland Longspurs. **ESSAYS:** Dusting, p. 429; Walking vs. Hopping, p. 69; Distraction Displays, p. 115; Range Expansion, p. 459; Mixed-Species Flocking, p. 433. **REFS:** Beason and Franks, 1974; Hurley and Franks, 1976; Wiens et al., 1986.

Tree Swallow
Tachycineta bicolor Vieillot

NG–296; G–220; PE–204; PW–pl 43; AE–pl 331; AW–pl 356; AM(II)–300

			F I: (13–) 16 DAYS		
5′+	F–M	4–6 MONOG (POLYGYN)	ALTRICIAL F: 20 (16–24) DAYS MF	BERRIES	FOLIAGE GLEAN

BREEDING: Open country, woodland edge, usu near water. 1 brood, rarely 2. **DISPLAYS:** Complex courtship flight. **NEST:** In tree hole or other cavity; of grass, oft lined with feathers. **EGGS:** White, unmarked. 0.8″ (19 mm). **DIET:** Berries taken when insects unavailable. Occ glean ground. **CONSERVATION:** Winters s to Honduras, Nicaragua, and c Costa Rica. Rare cowbird host. Forestry practice of removing standing dead trees has greatly reduced availability of natural nest sites; will use nest boxes. **NOTES:** Oft nest in loose colonies. Occ polygynous, possibly when food supplies are superabundant. Juveniles oft seen as attendants at nonkin nests but do not serve as helpers—in fact, they attempt to steal food from nestlings and parents! Clutch size larger and nestling survival greater when food very abundant. Hatch asynchronously. Nestlings brooded by female for 5 days. Starlings, House Sparrows, House Wrens, bluebirds compete for nest cavities. Only N.A. passerine in which females do not attain full breeding plumage at one year. Form large premigratory communal roosts; huge flocks perform preroosting aerial displays. **ESSAYS:** Cooperative Breeding, p. 283; Polygyny, p. 443; Brood Reduction, p. 307; Variation in Clutch Sizes, p. 339; Communal Roosting, p. 615. **REFS:** Hussell and Quinney, 1987; Leffelaar and Robertson, 1986; Lombardo, 1987; Quinney, 1986.

Origin of Flight

There is an ongoing argument about the evolution and behavior of the famous fossil *Archaeopteryx*, which combined characteristics of both birds and reptiles. Some paleontologists, notably John Ostrom of Yale University, believe that it was a ground dweller, racing after insects and clapping its feathered forelimbs together like nets to trap its prey. Its feathers, like mammalian hair, may have originally evolved from reptilian scales as a general insulating body covering. Those individuals able to speed their pursuit (or escape predators) by employing their feather nets to glide down slopes or extend leaps over obstacles would have left more offspring than slower individuals, and natural selection would have opened the road to more skillful flight. There are birds today, including the Greater Coucal, a close relative of cuckoos that lives in southeast Asia, that fly reluctantly and clumsily (much as did *Archaeopteryx* in this view), indicating that "partial flight" is a viable mode of locomotion.

A more classic view is that the immediate ancestors of *Archaeopteryx* were arboreal, and gradually enlarged scales into feathers to help cushion falls. Eventually they evolved primitive wings in order to glide between trees. In this scenario, gliding gradually evolved into flapping flight, and off the first birds went. A problem with this arboreal scenario is that the ancestors of *Archaeopteryx* were certainly bipedal, and today all reptiles and mammals that live in trees are quadrupedal, and able to hang on with all four feet.

Most recently a team of physical and biological scientists, Gerald Caple, Russel Balda, and William Willis, have developed a mathematical/physical model of the evolution of flight. It postulates a bipedal insectivore that jumps after its prey evolving into an animal able not only to fly but eventually to land with precision on a tree branch. They agree with Ostrom that a runner, rather than a glider, was ancestral to the birds; gliding quadrupeds would have to make too many unlikely transitions to be plausible bird ancestors. On the other hand, they could not envision how "insect nets" could develop into functional wings.

On the basis of their model, the team concluded that movements of forelimbs in a jumping animal would have been a great advantage in controlling its orientation, which, in turn, would have added to its rate of success at capturing aerial prey such as insects. Furthermore, those movements would be similar to those required for both control and propulsion during powered flight, so that no novel nerve-muscle pathways would have to evolve, as would be the case with the transition from glider to flier. The model predicts rapid evolution of powered flight, and that feathers near the end of the wing would have developed before those near the base, since small lift-developing surfaces far from the body's center of gravity would have been most efficient at providing control. The latter prediction might eventually be supported if a transitional fossil with well-developed primaries and poorly developed secondaries should be discovered.

Violet-green Swallow

Tachycineta thalassina Swainson

NG–296; G–220; PW–pl 43; AW–pl 357; AM(II)–300

5' +

F–M (?)

4–6
MONOG

F
I: 13–14 DAYS
ALTRICIAL
F: 16–24 DAYS
F–M

BREEDING: Conif or decid open forest or woodland, oft at higher altitudes. 1 brood. **DISPLAYS:** Predawn song-flights may be part of courtship. **NEST:** In tree hole or other cavity; of grass and weed stems, lined with feathers. **EGGS:** White, unmarked. 0.8" (19 mm). **DIET:** Insects only rarely taken on ground. **CONSERVATION:** Winters s to Honduras. Forestry practice of removing standing dead trees has greatly reduced availability of natural nest sites; will use nest boxes. **NOTES:** Occ nest in loose colonies of up to 20 pairs. Defends area around nest hole from other cavity-nesting species of swallows. Several pairs have been documented helping Western Bluebirds to rear nestlings and subsequently breeding in the nest box after the bluebirds fledge. Like other swallows, oft perches in long rows on wire. House Sparrows compete for nest cavities. Flocks occ with Tree Swallows. **ESSAYS:** Communal Roosting, p. 615; Wing Shapes and Flight, p. 227; Bathing and Dusting, p. 429; Coloniality, p. 173. **REFS:** Brown, 1983; Eltzroth and Robinson, 1984; Erskine, 1984.

Purple Martin

Progne subis Linnaeus

NG–296; G–220; PE–202; PW–pl 43; AE–pl 332; AW–pl 359; AM(II)–298

5' +

MF

4–5(3–8)
MONOG
(POLYGYN)

F
I: 15–18 DAYS
ALTRICIAL
F: 26–31 DAYS
MF

BREEDING: Open country, savanna, rural areas, esp near water. 1–3 broods. **DISPLAYS: ?** **NEST:** In tree hole, cliff niche, or other cavity, oft in birdhouse (esp in e); of grass, leaves, mud, feathers, occ with dirt rim to keep eggs from rolling out. **EGGS:** White, unmarked. 1.0" (24 mm). **DIET:** Occ feeds on ground taking ants and other insects. **CONSERVATION:** Winters in S.A. e of Andes from Venezuela s to n Bolivia and s e Brazil. Blue List 1975–81, Special Concern 1982–86. Forestry practice of removing standing dead trees has greatly reduced availability of natural nest sites; readily accepts colonial nest boxes. Currently the focus of a concerted effort to locate and monitor all active breeding colonies. **NOTES:** Usu nest in colonies. Occ polygynous. Oft drinks and bathes on the wing. Generally, very few birds return to their natal colony to breed. House Sparrows and starlings compete for nest cavities. Gather in enormous premigratory communal roosts (up to 100,000 birds) at end of summer. **ESSAYS:** Blue List, p. 11; Coloniality, p. 173; Polygyny, p. 443; Communal Roosts, p. 615; Bathing and Dusting, p. 429. **REFS:** Brown, 1979; Finlay, 1976; Morton and Patterson, 1983.

Needless to say, we may never have answers to all the puzzles of the origins of flight, but evolutionists are agreed that *Archaeopteryx* was either an ancestor of modern birds or a rather close relative of such an ancestor. The nearly identical nature of the feathers of *Archaeopteryx* and modern birds, both in their structural details and in their division into primaries and secondaries, shows this. It is extremely unlikely that such similar organs evolved twice independently.

SEE: Feathered Dinosaurs?, p. 31; How Do Birds Fly?, p. 161; Adaptations for Flight, p. 507; Natural Selection, p. 237. REFS: Caple et al., 1983; Martin, 1983; Ostrom, 1979.

Disease and Parasitism

Many organisms obtain energy and nutrients by feeding on birds. If they are animals big enough to kill and devour a bird all at once, the consumers are called predators. If the consumers are small animals that live on or in birds indefinitely, they are called parasites. Parasites may or may not have a sufficient impact on a bird to make it sick. When a bird's tenants are microorganisms—protozoans, bacteria, fungi, viruses, or rickettsiae (tiny bacteri-alike organisms)—that cause diseases, we call them pathogens.

There is a great variety of avian diseases. Birds get malaria (caused by close relatives of the protozoans that cause human malaria), aspergillosis (a fungal infection), tuberculosis (not the same pathogen that causes human tuberculosis), Newcastle disease (viral), fowl plague (viral), avian pox (viral), avian influenza (viral), and hundreds of other infections. People cannot catch most avian diseases, but birds can serve as hosts of pathogens that cause serious human illnesses. The rickettsia that causes psittacosis is sometimes contracted by people from pets in the parrot family (Psittacidae), but the disease name is misleading, as the pathogen has been found in at least 140 species of 17 orders of birds. Psittacosis may be fatal in people. So may the equine encephalitis virus, for which some 80 species of North American birds can serve as reservoirs. The virus can be carried from bird to person by mosquitoes. Migrating birds have been implicated in the transport of virulent encephalitis strains between continents.

Birds usually do not suffer heavily from mosquito-transmitted viruses, but there are exceptions. The mosquito species, *Culex pipiens*, accidentally introduced into the Hawaiian Islands in 1826, was an agent (vector) for transmitting the avian pox virus, malarial protozoans, and other pathogens. Many lowland species of the wonderful Hawaiian honeyeaters proved extremely susceptible to the pathogens and were wiped out; highland forms were spared because the mosquito could not survive at altitudes above 2,000 feet.

Birds also are dined upon by a great variety of parasites. Chewing bird-lice (Mallophaga) invade plumage and live on accumulated "dandruff,"

Bank Swallow

Riparia riparia Linnaeus

NG–298; G–220; PE–204; PW–pl 43; AE–pl 334; AW–pl 355; AM(II)–302

4' + MF 4–5 (3–7) MONOG

MF
I: 14–16 DAYS
ALTRICIAL
F: 18–24 DAYS
MF

BREEDING: Open country, savanna, esp near running water. 1 brood. **DISPLAYS:** Courtship flight, incl passing of white feather in flight; oft followed by cop usu in burrow. **NEST:** At end of burrow 2'–3' (1'–4') deep, mostly in disturbed sites; of grass, rootlets, weed stems, usu abundant feathers. Usu pair excavate own burrow, but may use deserted kingfisher burrow. **EGGS:** White, unmarked. 0.7" (18 mm). **DIET:** Almost entirely insects; rarely feed on ground. **CONSERVATION:** Winters in S.A. e of Andes from Venezuela s to Peru, n Argentina, and Paraguay. Rare cowbird host. **NOTES:** Colonial. Pairs within colonies tend to breed synchronously. The main advantages of coloniality in this species are reduced predation on eggs and nestlings resulting from group mobbing and "selfish herd" effects, and as information center for food finding—birds follow each other to patchy food resources. Nest site tenacity not as strong as in cavity-nesting swallows, presumably due to the more transient nature of colony nest sites (stream banks, road cuts, etc.). Gather in enormous premigratory communal roosts. Known as Sand Martin in Europe. **ESSAYS:** Parent-Chick Recognition, p. 193; Geometry of the Selfish Colony, p. 19; Site Tenacity, p. 189; Coloniality, p. 173; Mobbing, p. 425; Flock Defense, p. 235; Communal Roosting, p. 615. **REFS:** Beecher et al., 1981; Birchard and Kilgore, 1980; Freer, 1979; Hoogland and Sherman, 1976; Sieber, 1980.

Northern Rough-winged Swallow

Stelgidopteryx serripennis Audubon

NG–298; G–220; PE–204; PW–pl 43; AE–pl 333; AW–pl 354; AM(II)–302

CLIFF
CULVERT
4' +

CREVICE
MF

5–6
(4–8)
MONOG

F
I: 12 DAYS
ALTRICIAL
F: 19–21 DAYS
MF

BREEDING: Open country, savanna, esp near running water. 1 brood. **DISPLAYS:** In courtship flight, males pursue females, displaying white feathers at lower base of tail. **NEST:** At end of burrow 4'–5' (1'–6') deep, or in other cavity or niche; of grass, leaves, weed stems, occ moist horse dung, no feather lining. In addition to occ excavating burrows, nest in deserted kingfisher burrows, rodent holes, and a wide variety of niches under bridges and wharves, in culverts, sewer pipes, etc. **EGGS:** White, unmarked. 0.7" (18 mm). **DIET:** Entirely insects; occ taken from ground. **CONSERVATION:** Winters s to Panama. **NOTES:** Usu solitary, occ loosely colonial. Oft nest in Bank Swallow colony, where they perch on roots protruding from bank, something Bank Swallows never do. Function of serrations on outer primary feathers (from which name is derived) is unknown; possibly function to produce sounds in courtship flight. **ESSAYS:** Masterbuilders, p. 445; Nest Materials, p. 369; Birds, DNA, and Evolutionary Convergence, p. 419; Nonvocal Sounds, p. 313. **REFS:** Lunk, 1962; Ricklefs, 1972.

on blood, or on other fluids. Fleas, louse flies (Hippoboscidae), small bugs (Hemiptera, relatives of bedbugs), ticks, and mites suck blood. Internally, birds host roundworms, tapeworms, flukes and so on, which live either in the digestive tract or in the blood vessels. Little is known about the impact of parasites on natural populations of birds, but there are indications that it can be considerable, especially in populations of colonially nesting species.

For instance, biologists Charles and Mary Brown of Princeton University found that the number of "swallow bugs" (bedbuglike parasites) per nest went up as the size of Cliff Swallow colonies increased. In addition, the weight of ten-day-old chicks declined as the number of bugs per nestling rose. By fumigating some nests and leaving others infested, they showed that the bugs also increased fledgling mortality in large colonies but not in small ones. In response to the threat of the parasites, the swallows apparently construct new nests (rather than reuse old ones) in large colonies more frequently than in the less heavily infested small colonies. The swallow may also switch sites in alternate years (or return to the same sites even less frequently), leaving its parasites to starve in empty nests in the meantime.

SEE: Coevolution, p. 405; Coloniality, p. 173; Nest Materials, p. 369; Nest Sanitation, p. 315; European Starlings, p. 489; Bird Droppings, p. 263; Hawaiian Bird Biology, p. 651. REFS: Brown and Brown, 1986; Moss and Camin, 1970.

Parasitic Swallows

Cowbirds laying eggs in the nests of other species exemplify avian brood parasitism. Some solitary breeding birds (especially waterfowl) occasionally parasitize their own species, producing abnormally large clutches, and cooperative breeders often have strategies for getting other members of the group to incubate their eggs. Such parasitization of conspecifics had been thought to occur widely in colonial birds as well, although it was only recently demonstrated. Cliff Swallows have now been shown to have an unusually high degree of intraspecific brood parasitism, a phenomenon enhanced by the synchronized breeding within their colonies.

In southwestern Nebraska, Cliff Swallow colonies contain up to 3,000 nests, making them among the densest known aggregations of vertebrates. They cluster their gourd-shaped mud nests under bridges, in culverts, beneath the eaves of buildings, and on the faces of cliffs.

Attention was drawn to brood parasitism in this species in the course of a study that recorded egg-laying intervals in over 700 swallow nests. More than two eggs often appeared in a nest within a 24-hour period. As no bird is known to lay more than one egg daily, this indicated that more than one female was laying in the same nest. Following that discovery, a colony of 190 nests was observed for the entire period of egg laying, and 30 nests were selected for intensive scrutiny. About three-quarters of the swallows using

Cliff Swallow

Hirundo pyrrhonota Vieillot

NG–298; G–218; PE–202; PW–pl 43; AE–pl 330; AW–pl 353; AM(II)–304

BRIDGE	GOURD	🥚	MF
			I: 14–16 DAYS
CLIFF	MF	4–5	ALTRICIAL
BUILDING		(3–6)	F: 21–24 DAYS
3' +		MONOG	MF

BREEDING: Open country, savanna, esp near running water. Usu 1, occ 2–3 broods. **DISPLAYS:** Courtship flight followed by cop on ground. **NEST:** Plastered on underside of bridge or culvert, on cliff, wall under eaves, or other vertical surface; of mud pellets, tubular entrance to a spherical cavity sparsely lined with grass, feathers. Built in 5–14 days. Oft repaired and reused. **EGGS:** White, creamy, or pinkish white, spotted with brown. 0.8" (20 mm). **DIET:** Almost entirely insects, but occ gorge on berries. **CONSERVATION:** Winters in S.A. from Paraguay and c and s e Brazil, s to c Argentina. Blue List 1976–77, 1981, Special Concern 1982, Local Concern, 1986; status unclear in n e. Rare cowbird host. House Sparrows usurp nests. **NOTES:** Nest in colonies, occ to >1,000 pairs. Colonies serve as information centers for good foraging spots: unsuccessful foragers observe successful foragers feeding nestlings and follow them from colony. Colony site occ alternated between years to avoid heavy infestations of nest parasites. Mutual vocal recognition between parents and offspring occurs shortly before fledging. Occ forage with Barn Swallows. **ESSAYS:** Parasitic Swallows, p. 401; Parent-Chick Recognition, p. 193; Coloniality, p. 173; Blue List, p. 11; Disease, p. 399; Masterbuilders, p. 445. **REFS:** Beecher et al., 1985; Brown, 1986; Brown and Brown, 1986; Withers, 1977.

Barn Swallow

Hirundo rustica Linnaeus

NG–298; G–218; PE–202; PW–pl 43; AE–pl 329; AW–pl 352; AM(II)–306

BUILDING	☕	🥚	F–M
			I: 13–17 DAYS
6'–40' +	MF	4–5 (4–7)	ALTRICIAL
		MONOG	F: 18–23 DAYS
		(POLYGYN)	MF

BREEDING: Open country, savanna, esp near water, agricultural areas. 2 broods. **DISPLAYS:** Males pursue females in long, graceful courtship flights; on landing, pair rub heads and necks, interlock bills or mutually preen. **NEST:** Usu plastered on ledges and walls of building, occ in cave, culvert, under bridge, or in cliff crevice; of mud pellets, straw, heavily lined with feathers. Built in 7–14 days. **EGGS:** White, spotted with brown. 0.8" (19 mm). **DIET:** Also occ berries, seeds. **CONSERVATION:** Winters from Lesser Antilles, Puerto Rico, and Panama s to s tip of S.A. Rare cowbird host. **NOTES:** Oft nest in small colonies. Helpers oft seen at nests, occ feed nestlings; helpers usu yearlings or immatures from first clutch aiding their parents. Breeders tend to return to same colony, same cluster of nests within colony, occ same nest and same mate. In spite of not having brood patch, male incubates effectively although not routinely. House Sparrows and phoebes occ usurp nests. Drink and bathe on wing. After fledging, young return to roost in nest for few days. **ESSAYS:** Clutch Sizes, p. 339; Parasitic Swallows, p. 401; Cooperative Breeding, p. 283; Coloniality, p. 173; Site Tenacity, p. 189; Incubation, p. 393. **REFS:** Grzybowski, 1979; Medvin et al., 1987; Shields, 1984; Snapp, 1976.

those 30 nests were color banded for individual recognition. On five occasions, banded birds were seen to enter the nests of others and lay a single egg when the owners of the nest were absent; one bird was responsible for two of the parasitic incidents. All of the parasitic birds also had clutches in their own nests. It was estimated that nearly a quarter of the swallow nests in large colonies were parasitized.

Typical brood parasites such as cowbirds are notoriously quick egg layers. The parasitic swallows were also fast, each spending less than a minute in the host nest during laying. Indeed, one parasitic bird managed to lay an egg in a mere 15-second visit, while the host swallow was distracted by a battle with another intruder.

Eggs of parasites sometimes appeared in nests several days after the hosts had started to incubate their own eggs. In spite of this, the parasite eggs hatched synchronously with the host eggs. This means that they required less incubation time than the host eggs, an adaptation frequently found in brood parasites that attack members of other species. Swallows were also frequently observed entering neighbors' nests and tossing out eggs. Presumably many of the vandals were parasites that later replaced a tossed egg with one of their own. If this is the case, then the frequency of parasitism in the study colony may be even higher than estimated from the number of appearances of "extra" eggs within a day—since many parasitic eggs would go undetected by the daily egg census. It is therefore possible that well over a quarter of the nests in some colonies harbored parasites.

Parasitized swallows fledged fewer of their own young, on average, than did swallows not burdened with "adopted" offspring. Parasitic swallows, on the other hand, increased their fitness. Not only were they successful in fledging all of their young, but all of their eggs identified as having been laid in host nests were fledged by the foster parents, as well. Instead of averaging about three young, they managed to produce four or five.

So far, it has not been possible to determine what distinguishes parasitic from host swallows. Are they genetically different, or is their parasitic behavior related to their environment? It is not clear whether the presence of a certain percentage of parasites is a stable situation, or whether high levels of parasitism might, in some manner, lead to the decline of entire colonies. Theoretically, if all birds in a colony were to take up parasitism, the fitness of all should be reduced simply from the mutual destruction of eggs.

Just as the *Handbook* was about to be printed Charles and Mary Brown reported (*Nature* 331:66–68, 7 January 1988) that Cliff Swallows actually *carry* their eggs in their beaks to the nests of other individuals. This is a previously unknown mode of brood parasitism, and the first systematic study of egg transport in North American birds.

SEE: Brood Parasitism, p. 287; Cowbirds, p. 619; Cooperative Breeding, p. 283; Coloniality, p. 173; Variation in Clutch Sizes, p. 339.   REF: Brown, 1984.

Cave Swallow

Hirundo fulva Vieillot

NG–298; G–218; PE–300; PW–pl 43; AE–604; AW–780; AM(II)–306

CAVE			MF (?)
			I: 15 (–18) DAYS
CULVERT	MF (?)	3–4	ALTRICIAL
3′ +		(3–5)	F: 21–23 DAYS
		MONOG	MF (?)

BREEDING: Open country, savanna, esp near running water. 2 broods. **DISPLAYS:** ? **NEST:** Plastered on walls of caves or culverts; of mud pellets, guano, sparsely lined with grass, feathers. Oft repaired and reused. **EGGS:** White, spotted with brown. 0.8″ (20 mm). **DIET:** Almost entirely insects. **CONSERVATION:** Wintering unknown; populations from s Mexico to S.A. are resident. Recent adoption of culvert nesting has enabled range expansion. **NOTES:** Nest in colonies. Birds may enter cave in high-speed plunge, then circle around inside to lose momentum before landing. Oft nest with Barn, occ with Cliff Swallows; occ hybridize with Barn Swallows. **ESSAYS:** Parasitic Swallows, p. 401; Parent-Chick Recognition, p. 193; Coloniality, p. 173; Wing Shapes and Flight, p. 227; Range Expansion, p. 459; Hybridization, p. 501. **REFS:** Martin, 1980; Martin and Martin, 1978; Martin et al., 1977.

Scrub Jay

Aphelocoma coerulescens Bosc

NG–300; G–222; PE–208; PW–pl 44; AE–pl 436; AW–pl 505; AM(II)–312

SHRUB	MF	3–6 (2–7)	F
3′–30′		MONOG	I: 15–17 DAYS
		(COOP)	ALTRICIAL
			F: 18–19 DAYS
			MF(+)

BREEDING: Scrub (esp oak, piñon and juniper), brush, chaparral, pine-oak woodland. 1 brood, rarely 2. **DISPLAYS:** Courting male hops around female with his head erect, tail spread and dragging. **NEST:** Occ in small conif; supported by platform of twigs, occ moss, cup of grass lined with fine rootlets, hair. **EGGS:** Pale green marked with reddish browns or greens. 1.1″ (28 mm). **DIET:** Mostly insects; also other inverts and small verts, incl bird eggs, nestlings, fledglings. In nonbreeding season, largely acorns, piñon nuts, fruit, seeds. **CONSERVATION:** Winter resident. Florida subspecies on Blue List 1973–86. Through at least 1930s organized "shoots" held by farmers and fruit growers in CA to reduce jay numbers because of ostensible damage to crops; nearly 1,500 birds occ killed in one day. **NOTES:** Long-term pair bond, pair or flock remain year-round on permanent territory; cooperative breeder in FL. In FL clutch size usu 3–4; predation primary cause of nest failure, reduced in pairs with helpers. Male feeds female before and during incubation. Female does most of brooding. Cache food and steal from Acorn Woodpecker caches; likely serve as major disperser for oaks and piñon pines by burying acorns and seeds and failing to recover them. Perch on deer and remove ticks. **ESSAYS:** Cooperative Breeding, p. 283; Blue List, p. 11; Hoarding Food, p. 345; Finding Hidden Caches, p. 411; Population Dynamics, p. 575; Natural Selection, p. 237. **REFS:** Atwood, 1980; Ehrlich and McLaughlin, 1988; Goodwin, 1976; Woolfenden and Fitzpatrick, 1984.

Bird Names—IX

The generic name of the Chimney Swift, *Chaetura*, means "bristle-tail" in Greek. We suspect this bird's inappropriate trivial name *"pelagica"* traces to an ancient myth (current before migration was understood) that fishermen sometimes drew up in their nets masses of torpid swallows. Plovers owe their generic name, *Charadrius*, to the Greek *charadra*, gully, suggesting their nesting sites. *Lagopus,* the genus of ptarmigans, means "hare-footed" in Greek, a reference to the birds' feathered feet, which help them navigate on snow.

Ptarmigan itself seems to come from the Gaelic for "mountaineer" or "white game." Grouse may come from an old French word meaning speckled, and be a cognate of "grizzled." Quail imitates the call of the European Quail. It is a cognate of "quack." Partridge is derived from the Latin "perdix," Latin for partridge and the generic name of the bird.

SEE: Avian Snowshoes, p. 255. REFS: Choate, 1985; Mead, 1983.

Coevolution

When organisms that are ecologically intimate—for example, predators and prey, or hosts and parasites—influence each other's evolution, we say that "coevolution" is occurring. Birds are often important actors in coevolutionary systems. For example, predation by birds largely drives the coevolution of model and mimetic butterflies. Some butterflies have evolved the ability to store poisonous chemicals from the food plants they eat as caterpillars, thus becoming distasteful. This reduces their chances of being eaten, since birds, once they have tried to devour such butterflies, will avoid attacking them in the future. Other butterflies have gradually evolved color patterns that mimic those of the distasteful butterflies (called "models"). It is disadvantageous for the models to be mimicked, because if the mimics become common then most of the butterflies with the model's color pattern taste good, the birds may resume attacking the models. Being tasted and spit out by a bird is a most dangerous experience for a butterfly. Therefore, mimicry presumably leads to a "coevolutionary race"—the mimics evolving toward the color patterns of the models, and the models evolving away from the converging mimics. The birds actually may be directly involved in the entire coevolutionary complex, since they may be under selection for better powers of discrimination. Individuals that can tell the mimetic butterflies from the models will gain more nourishment at less cost in time and effort.

Birds, of course, are presumed to be directly involved in many coevolutionary relationships with their competitors, predators, prey, and parasites. The relationship of seed-hoarding Clark's Nutcrackers and Pinyon Jays with pinyon pines is a relatively well-studied example; and the evolu-

Gray-breasted Jay

Aphelocoma ultramarina Bonaparte

NG–300; G–222; PW–pl 44; AW–pl 506; AM(II)–314

10'–25'	MF+	4–5 (4–7)	F		
(6'–30')		MONOG	I: 16–18 DAYS		
		(COOP)	ALTRICIAL		
			F: 24–25 DAYS		
			MF+		

BREEDING: Oak, pine-oak, and juniper woodland, scrub, rarely riparian woodland. 1 brood. **DISPLAYS:** Courting male circles female with his wings and tail tilted toward her; aligns himself sideways to female, oft reversing direction through 180° jump. **NEST:** Usu on horizontal limb or in crotch of oak tree, occ conif; conspicuous and bulky with platform of twigs supporting cup of rootlets lined with fine grass and hair. No mud. **EGGS:** Pale green marked with green; AZ race unmarked. 1.2" (30 mm). **DIET:** Very dependent on acorns. **CONSERVATION:** Winter resident. **NOTES:** Live in communal flocks of 5–22 within which 2 pairs generally breed each year, the remainder serving as helpers in nest building and care of the young. Permanently resident on breeding territories. Likely serve as major disperser for oak trees by burying acorns and then failing to recover them. N limit of range set by availability of adequate mast crops. Formerly known as Mexican Jay. **ESSAYS:** Cooperative Breeding, p. 283; Hoarding Food, p. 345; Finding Hidden Caches, p. 411; Walking vs. Hopping, p. 69. **REFS:** Brown and Brown, 1985; Edwards, 1986; Goodwin, 1976.

Pinyon Jay

Gymnorhinus cyanocephalus Wied

NG–300; G–222; PW–pl 44; AW–pl 507; AM(II)–314

3'–26'	MF	4–5	F		FOLIAGE
(To 85')		(3–5)	I: 16–17 DAYS		GLEAN
		MONOG	ALTRICIAL		HAWKS
			F: 21 DAYS		
			MF		

BREEDING: Piñon-juniper woodland, pine woodland. 1, occ 2 broods. **DISPLAYS:** Courtship pursuit flight of female by males; male feeds female. **NEST:** In juniper or pine, occ oak; bulky outer platform of twigs and bark supporting cup of shredded bark, plant fibers, rootlets, paper, hair. Male selects site. Built in 5–9 days. **EGGS:** Bluish, greenish, or grayish white, marked with browns. 1.2" (29 mm). **DIET:** Pine nuts, conif and other seeds, fruits, insects, bird eggs and nestlings. Young fed mostly insects, few pine seeds. **CONSERVATION:** Nonmigratory, but wander in winter flocks of 100s to 1,000. **NOTES:** Highly gregarious, breeding in colonies of up to 150. Breeding triggered largely by consumption of piñon seeds. Availability of caches of piñon seeds permits breeding in late winter (oft while snow still present); breeding in late summer triggered by bumper crop of piñon seeds. Long-term pair bond; pairing is assortative for age i.e., birds select mates close to their own age. Female fed by male during incubation and early brooding. Flying and foraging flocks move in a wheeling mass with rear birds constantly replacing birds in front. Roost communally in conif trees in nonbreeding season. Many unrecovered pine seed caches germinate. **ESSAYS:** Hoarding, p. 345; Coevolution, p. 405; Caches, p. 411; Coloniality, p. 173; Courtship Feeding, p. 181; Breeding Season, p. 55. **REFS:** Balda and Bateman, 1972; Balda et al., 1977; Ligon, 1978; Marzluff and Balda, 1988.

tion of long bills and sickle-shaped bills in some Latin American humming-birds which match the long or sharply curved flowers from which they sip nectar (and which they pollinate) is another obvious case of coevolution.

Hermit hummingbirds and the curved flowers of the genus *Heliconia* (seen increasingly as horticultural cut flowers) provide widespread and con-spicuous examples of the latter phenomenon throughout the lowland moist forests of Central and South America.

Many fruit-eating birds, especially in tropical rain forests are coevolv-ing with the plants whose fruits they eat. The birds get nourishment, and in the process the plants get their digestion-resistant seeds dispersed by regur-gitation or along with the birds' droppings. Many characteristics of the plants have evolved to facilitate dispersal, and the behavior and diets of the birds have responded to those changes. In particular, the plants have evolved conspicuously colored, relatively odorless fleshy fruits to attract the avian dispersers of their seeds. They are coevolving in response to the finely honed visual systems of the birds; plant species coevolving with color-blind mammalian seed-dispersers have, in contrast, dull-colored but smelly fruits. The bird-dispersed plants often have evolved fruits with giant seeds covered by a thin, highly nutritious layer of flesh. This forces the bird to swallow the fruit whole, since it is difficult or impossible just to nip off the flesh. In response, birds that are specialized frugivores (that is, that do not take other kinds of food) have evolved both bills with wide gapes (so they can swallow the fruit whole) and digestive tracts that can rapidly dissolve the flesh from the large impervious seed, which then can be regurgitated.

The most dramatic examples of avian coevolution are probably those involving brood parasites, such as cuckoos and cowbirds, and their hosts. The parasites have often evolved eggs that closely mimic those of the host, and young with characteristics that encourage the hosts to feed them. In response, some hosts have developed the ability to discriminate between their own and parasitic eggs, and various methods of destroying the latter. As one might expect, Brown-headed Cowbirds have their most serious im-pact on hosts, such as Kirtland's Warblers, that are thought to have only recently been subjected to cowbird attack and have not yet had time to evolve defensive reactions.

Many examples of coevolution in response to competition between bird species can be inferred from studies of dietary habits and bill structures in various guilds of birds. Here, as in the other cases mentioned, direct evi-dence of coevolution is lacking. It is lacking for the same reason that there are very few cases of plain old single-population evolution actually being observed in nature. The process occurs over hundreds or thousands of gen-erations, and extraordinary circumstances are required for it to be "caught in the act."

SEE: Natural Selection, p. 237; Hoarding Food, p. 345; Bird Guilds, p. 493; Bird Communities and Competition, p. 605; Brood Parasitism, p. 287; Cowbirds, p. 619. REFS: Diamond, 1984a; Dobkin, 1984; Ehrlich, 1970; Futuyma and Slat-kin, 1983; Thompson, 1982; Willson, 1986.

Blue Jay

NG–302; G–222; PE–208; PW–pl 44; AE–pl 435; AM(II)–310

5′–20′	MF	4–5	F–M		HAWKS
(To 50′)		(3–7)	I: 16–18 DAYS		
		MONOG?	ALTRICIAL		
			F: 17–21 DAYS		
			MF		

BREEDING: Decid and mixed conif-decid forest, open woodland, parks, residential areas. 1 brood in n, 2 or 3 in s. **DISPLAYS:** Male courtship flight, up-and-down bobbing, and courtship feeding of female. **NEST:** On horizontal branch or in crotch, occ in decid tree, shrub, or vine tangle; bulky but compact, of twigs, bark strips, moss, lichen, paper, rags, string, and grass, occ cemented together with mud, lined with fine rootlets. **EGGS:** Variable: greenish, buff, or bluish, spotted with browns. 1.1″ (28 mm). **DIET:** Insects, other inverts and small verts, carrion, bird eggs, nestlings, but mostly acorns, fruit, nuts, seeds. **CONSERVATION:** Winter resident except northernmost populations partially migratory. Rare cowbird victim. Has become markedly tolerant of humans in past 100 years. Range expanding westward in urban and suburban areas. **NOTES:** Occ forcefully appropriate nests from other passerines. Cache food. Scream strongly resembles Red-shouldered Hawk's. Oft mob owls. Male feeds incubating female; male rarely broods. Travel in small flocks and family groups in late summer and fall. Hybridizes with Steller's Jay where ranges contact in Colorado. **ESSAYS:** Nest-Robbing, p. 409; Decline of Songbirds, p. 495; Kirtland's Warbler, p. 527; Plains Hybrids, p. 625; Range Expansion, p. 459; Vocal Copying, p. 469; Mobbing, p. 425. **REFS:** Goodwin, 1976; Laine, 1981.

Steller's Jay

NG–302; G–222; PW–pl 44; AW–pl 502; AM(II)–310

8′–25′	MF	4	F		FOLIAGE
(To 100′)		(2–6)	I: 16 DAYS		GLEAN
		MONOG?	ALTRICIAL		
			F: ? DAYS		
			MF		

BREEDING: Conif and mixed conif-decid forest, arid pine-oak woodland. 1 brood. **DISPLAYS:** Courtship feeding of female by male; male circles female, aligns sideways to her, oft reversing direction through 180° jump. **NEST:** On horizontal branch or in crotch, occ in decid tree, shrub; bulky foundation of twigs, dry leaves, cemented with mud, lined with rootlets, pine needles, grass. **EGGS:** Pale greenish-blue or bluish-green, marked with dark browns. 1.2″ (30 mm). **DIET:** 30% insects, other inverts and small verts, bird eggs, nestlings; 70% acorns or pine seeds, fruit, seeds. December–January diet 90%–99% acorns or pine seeds. **CONSERVATION:** Winter resident; some movement to lower elevations in winter. **NOTES:** Pair defend territory of immediate vicinity around nest. Oft congregate at feeding sites, even when breeding. Cache food and steal from Acorn Woodpecker caches. Postbreeding family groups remain together until fall. Scream strongly resembles Red-tailed Hawk's. Hybridizes with Blue Jay where their ranges contact along the Front Range of Colorado. **ESSAYS:** Hoarding Food, p. 345; Great Plains Hybrids, p. 625; Vocal Copying, p. 469; Finding Hidden Caches, p. 411; Courtship Feeding, p. 181; DDT and Birds, p. 21. **REFS:** Brown, 1964; Goodwin, 1976.

Nest-Robbing Blue Jays

One of the most common birds in the eastern half of our continent, the Blue Jay, eats mostly insects, seeds, and nuts. But in the spring it adds to its diet the eggs and young of other species. This habit has long been known—it attracted the attention of Audubon, who wrote of the Blue Jay:

"Everywhere it manifests the same mischievous disposition. It imitates the cry of the Sparrow Hawk so perfectly that the little birds in the neighborhood hurry into thick coverts, to avoid what they believe to be the attack of that marauder. It robs every nest it can find, sucks the eggs like the Crow, or tears to pieces and devours the young birds." Audubon's painting of Blue Jays eating purloined eggs, upon which our illustration is based, is a classic example of the ways in which Audubon worked the biology of birds into his art.

Reduction and fragmentation of eastern forests have given Blue Jays and other nest robbers more access to the nests of woodland birds, and the abundance of this beautiful albeit aggressive species is paid for in part by a decline in other beautiful but relatively defenseless birds such as warblers and vireos.

SEE: The Decline of Eastern Songbirds, p. 495; Bird Biology and the Arts, p. 47. REFS: Angell, 1978; Audubon, 1842.

Gray Jay
Perisoreus canadensis Linnaeus

NG–302; G–224; PE–208; PW–pl 44; AE–pl 425; AW–pl 471; AM(II)–308

4'–30' (To 85')	MF	3–4 (2–5) MONOG	F I: 16–18 DAYS ALTRICIAL F: 15 DAYS MF		FOLIAGE GLEAN

BREEDING: Conif and mixed conif-decid forest, open woodland, bogs. 1 brood. **DISPLAYS:** Courtship feeding of female. **NEST:** Usu on horizontal branch near trunk or in crotch, occ in decid tree; bulky and well woven, of sticks, bark strips, moss, grass, fastened together with spider silk, insect cocoon, lined with feathers, bark strips, grass, fur. Very well insulated. **EGGS:** Grayish-white, finely spotted with olive buff. 1.2" (29 mm). **DIET:** Primarily insects, fruit, carrion. Nestlings fed partially digested food. **CONSERVATION:** Winters throughout breeding range with altitudinal migration to lower elevations in late fall through winter. **NOTES:** Oft nest very early when snow is still deep. Cache boli of saliva-permeated food in variety of locations on conifers; caches oft robbed by Steller's and Blue Jays. Very tame, bold, and curious, showing no fear of humans and brazenly raiding camps, picnic tables, etc. Occ seen s of breeding range in winter, likely related to insufficient food resources in n. **ESSAYS:** Irruptions, p. 639; Hoarding Food, p. 345; Finding Hidden Caches, p. 411; Courtship Feeding, p.181; Breeding Season, p. 55. **REFS:** Goodwin, 1976; Rutter, 1969.

Clark's Nutcracker
Nucifraga columbiana Wilson

NG–302; G–224; PW–pl 44; AW–pl 470; AM(II)–316

8'–50'	MF	2–4 (2–6) MONOG?	MF I: 16–18 DAYS ALTRICIAL F: 18–21 DAYS MF		GROUND GLEAN HAWKS

BREEDING: Conif forest, primarily in mountains. 1 brood. **DISPLAYS:** Long courtship flights of male following female, oft ending at or near starting point. **NEST:** On horizontal limb; platform of twigs secured with bark strips supports inner cup of fine bark strips, grass, conif needles, hair, feathers. Incubating bird well hidden by nest. **EGGS:** Pale green, marked with browns, olive, or gray. 1.3" (32 mm). **DIET:** Pine nuts, conif and other seeds, fruit, insects, small verts, bird eggs and nestlings. **CONSERVATION:** In winter, wanders in small flocks depending on status of cone crop; oft seen in lowlands. **NOTES:** Oft breed early at high elevations while snow still deep on ground. Caches 22,000–33,000 conif seeds in late summer and fall in ground on s-facing slopes; major food from winter to midsummer. Caches found by memory; a bird must recover >1,000 seed caches each year. Sublingual pouch enables transport of up to 95 pine seeds per trip. Female is a close sitter on nest. Both parents brood. Young fed regurgitated hulled piñon nuts from caches; reportedly fed by regurgitation as fledglings, as well. Individuals are either "left-" or "right-footed" when handling pine seeds but not known whether foot preference is learned or innate. **ESSAYS:** Migration, p. 183; Hoarding, p. 345; Coevolution, p. 405; Finding Hidden Caches, p. 411; Breeding Season, p. 55 **REFS:** Goodwin, 1976; Johnson et al., 1987; Tomback, 1980; Vander Wall and Balda, 1977.

Finding Hidden Caches

How does a long-term hoarder like Clark's Nutcracker recover stored seeds when it needs them to feed its young? Ornithologists at first thought that the food was stored only in certain kinds of areas, and that the birds redis-covered it by later foraging in the same areas. But recent experiments with nutcrackers in aviaries, done by Stephen Vander Wall of Utah State Univer-sity, have shown clearly that individuals are able to recall where they have cached seeds. The birds remember where the seeds are in relation to certain landmarks, such as rocks. If the landmarks are moved, the areas the birds search are displaced an equivalent amount.

The results of these experiments confirmed observations by behaviorist Diana Tomback, who examined the distribution of beak marks in earth and snow where nutcrackers had searched for caches. The marks were not ran-dom, but rather unsuccessful probes were clustered in the vicinity of suc-cessful ones (indicated by the presence of pinyon-seed coats, which the birds removed before eating the seeds, next to the hole). In addition, early in the year before rodents started to find the caches, the birds found caches on about two out of three attempts, far more frequently than one would expect if they were searching at random. This capacity to remember the sites of stored food seems to be an evolutionary enhancement of a spatial memory that is more widespread in birds. For example, titmice often store food in diverse places when it is abundant. They show excellent short-term (hours-days) memory for the storage locations, as elegant experiments by British avian behaviorist John Krebs and his colleagues have shown.

SEE: Hoarding Food, p. 345. REFS: Sherry et al., 1981; Shettleworth, 1983; Tom-back, 1980; Vander Wall, 1982.

Bird Biologist—Joseph Grinnell

Joseph Grinnell (1877–1939) was born at an Indian agency forty miles from Fort Sill, in what is now Oklahoma. He published over 500 scientific papers, mostly on birds, and was instrumental in establishing the Museum of Vertebrate Zoology at the University of California. That institution has long been a center of the study of bird biology. Grinnell, a superb scientist, was elected the youngest Fellow of the American Ornithologists' Union in 1901. In 1904 he made the first explicit statement of the principle of specia-tion in isolation: "It is *isolation*, either by barriers or by sufficient distance to more than counterbalance inheritance from the opposite type, that seems to me to be the absolutely essential condition for the differentiation of two species, at least in birds." He was one of many students of birds who has made important contributions to biology as a whole.

SEE: Species and Speciation, p. 355.

Brown Jay

Cyanocorax morio Wagler

NG–304; G–224; AM(II)–312

SHRUB
23'–70'

MF+

3–5 (1–8)
MONOG
(COOP)

F+
I: 18–20 DAYS
ALTRICIAL
F: 22–31 DAYS
MF+

FOLIAGE
GLEAN

BREEDING: Open woodland, forest edge, clearings. 1, occ 2 broods. **DISPLAYS:** Courtship feeding of female by male: perched in tree, female spreads wings, lifts tail, rapidly and intensely whines. Variety of complex, poorly understood displays within and between groups. **NEST:** Oft far out from trunk; cup of twigs, lined with veg. Up to 6 birds may build the nest. Rarely reused. **EGGS:** Blue-gray, marked with browns. ?" (? mm). **DIET:** Terrestrial inverts, small verts, occ nestlings; nectar, fruit. **CONSERVATION:** Winter resident. **NOTES:** Variable breeding system: from cooperative breeding with one monogamous pair breeding per flock and helpers-at-the-nest, to communal breeding producing single brood of mixed parentage. Communal females may toss each other's eggs from shared nest. Flocks number 6–15 birds; new flocks formed by 5–10 birds splitting away from original group. Each flock attends only 1 nest. Female on nest gives loud whining call to attract other flock members to feed her. Young fed by all flock members. Fledglings become helpers in their natal flocks. Breeding success increases with number of older, experienced birds in the flock. Breeding behavior and flock structure more variable than other N.A. jays. **ESSAYS:** Cooperative Breeding, p. 283; Courtship Feeding, p. 181. **REFS:** Goodwin, 1976; Lawton and Lawton, 1985.

Green Jay

Cyanocorax yncas Boddaert

NG–304; G–224; PW–pl 44; AE–pl 483; AM(II)–312

SHRUB
5'–30'

MF+

4 (3–5)
MONOG
(COOP)

F
I: 17–18 DAYS
ALTRICIAL
F: 19–22 DAYS
F–M

GROUND
GLEAN
HAWKS

BREEDING: Brush, pine-oak woodland, riparian thickets. 1 brood. **DISPLAYS:** Mated pair perch close together, female bobs several times, male responds with sleeked posture, followed by bill caressing. **NEST:** In small tree or shrub in dense thicket; bulky platform of thorny twigs supports cup lined with fine rootlets, vine, moss, grass, and leaves. **EGGS:** Grayish-white marked with brown, gray, and lavender. 1.1" (27 mm). **DIET:** Insects, small inverts and verts, bird eggs, nestlings; seeds, fruit. **CONSERVATION:** Winter resident. Rare victim of Bronzed Cowbird. **NOTES:** Family flocks of 4–9 remain on permanent territories. Only one pair breed in each flock. Young incorporated into flock and remain with parents for 1 year; do not help at the nest (except in C.A. populations), only in territorial defense. After young fledge, the yearlings from previous season are evicted from territory by the breeding male. Female does not flush easily from nest; fed by male during incubation. Both parents brood. Hoard food and steal from Acorn Woodpecker caches; likely serve as major disperser for oak trees by burying acorns, then failing to recover them. **ESSAYS:** Cooperative Breeding, p. 283; Tool Using, p. 435; Hoarding Food, p. 345; Finding Caches, p. 411. **REFS:** Alvarez, 1975; Gayou, 1986.

Bird Biologist—John James Audubon

John James Audubon (1785–1851) was born in Santo Domingo (now Haiti), the son of a sea captain, and raised in France where he received formal training as an artist. Audubon migrated to the United States in 1803 and went into business in Pennsylvania. There he became fascinated with birds, and for four decades, whenever time was available, traveled through America east of the Rockies observing, shooting, and making life-sized watercolor paintings of North American birds. After 1819 he devoted full time to this enterprise, carrying his trademark, a huge folder holding his paintings, as he roamed on boats, horseback, and foot.

About 170 copies were made of the 435 "Elephant Folio" prints (roughly 30×40 inches), produced from the paintings by engraving and hand coloring. These magnificent folios were published without text, apparently to avoid supplying free copies to English libraries, which was required by British copyright law if the work were to be sold in England. Audubon also published a five-volume *Ornithological Biography, or An Account of the Habits of the Birds of the United States* which contained his observations on the birds he had painted. A later octavo edition of the prints was produced by hand-colored lithography (first edition estimated to be 1,200 copies), this time accompanied by a text similar to that of the *Ornithological Biography*. These three works guarantee Audubon's position as a great pioneering student of bird biology.

Audubon had met the other leading North American ornithologist of his era, Alexander Wilson (p. 277); they had taken bird walks together, seeing Passenger Pigeons and Sandhill Cranes. The two were competitors, and Audubon "borrowed" information and even occasionally images from Wilson's work. In retrospect, however, the two really could not compete. Wilson's work was scientifically superior and started before Audubon's. He was the *scientific* father of American Ornithology. Audubon's paintings were incomparably superior—he was the first to attempt to portray birds as they actually lived their lives. He was the *artistic* father of American Ornithology.

SEE: Bird Biology and the Arts, p. 47; Nest-Robbing Blue Jays, p. 409. REFS: Bannon and Clark, 1985; Choate, 1985; Kastner, 1986.

Black-billed Magpie

NG–304; G–224; PE–208; PW–pl 44; AE–pl 584; AW–pl 617; AM(II)–316

SHRUB	MF	5–8	F
20'–30'		(1–13)	I: 16–21 DAYS
(5'–50')		MONOG	ALTRICIAL
			F: 25–29(23-32) DAYS
			MF

BREEDING: Open country esp with scattered trees, brushy habitats, riparian and open woodland, farmland. 1 brood. **DISPLAYS:** Courtship: males strut, flash wings, chase females. **NEST:** Occ in conif; large and conspicuous with bulky dome covering entire structure; base and outer walls of heavy, oft thorny sticks enclose bowl of mud or cow dung, lined with rootlets, fine plant stems, and hair. Built in 40–50 days. Old nests occ repaired and reused or new nest built on top. **EGGS:** Greenish-gray, marked with browns. 1.3″ (33 mm). **DIET:** 85% insects, carrion, inverts, small verts; 15% fruit, seeds. Nestlings fed 95% animal food. Most insectivorous N.A. corvid. **CONSERVATION:** Winter resident; some upslope movement in fall. Through at least 1930s organized contests periodically held to "exterminate" magpies; also thousands died from poisoned baits intended for predators. **NOTES:** Gregarious, breed in small colonies with scattered nests. Long-term pair bond. First-year birds usu do not breed. Male feeds female throughout laying and incubation. Female broods. Cache food. Travel and roost in winter flocks of 8–10, occ to 40. Pairs may remain together throughout year. **ESSAYS:** Piracy, p. 159; Hoarding, p. 345; Roosting, p. 615. **REFS:** Buitron, 1988; Hayworth and Weathers, 1984; Mugaas and King, 1981; Reese and Kadlec, 1985.

Yellow-billed Magpie

NG–304; G–224; PW–pl 44; AW–pl 616; AM(II)–318

40'–60'	MF	7	F	FOLIAGE
		(5–8)	I: 16–18 DAYS	GLEAN
		MONOG?	ALTRICIAL	HAWKS
			F: ? DAYS	
			MF	

BREEDING: Oak or riparian woodland, savanna. 1 brood. **DISPLAYS:** Wing raising with bowing oft performed by mated pair; courtship feeding. **NEST:** Large and conspicuous with bulky dome covering entire structure; base and outer walls of heavy sticks enclose bowl of mud, lined with rootlets, fine plant stems, and hair. Old nests occ repaired and reused or new nest built on top. **EGGS:** Olive, marked with brown or olive. 1.2″ (31 mm). **DIET:** 70% insects, carrion, inverts, small verts; 30% fruit, seeds. In some years, acorns provide much of diet for several months starting in September. **CONSERVATION:** Winter resident. In 1800s, persistent attempts made to exterminate by shooting, direct and indirect poisoning; perceived as threat to livestock and crops. **NOTES:** Gregarious, breed in small colonies, more compact than Black-billed Magpie's. Roost in dense groves of trees. Pairs may remain together throughout year. Male feeds incubating female. Female broods. Fledglings fed, at least partly, up to 7 weeks. Cache acorns and carrion in ground or in trees. In winter, travel and roost in flocks. **ESSAYS:** Piracy, p. 159; Hoarding, p. 345; DDT, p. 21; Finding Hidden Caches, p. 411; Courtship Feeding, p. 181. **REFS:** Goodwin, 1976; Hayworth and Weathers, 1984; Verbeek, 1973.

Bird-Brained

To say the very least, birds do not have a reputation for great intelligence. Much of their behavior is strictly stereotyped—a male meadowlark will determinedly assault a stuffed male that is placed in its territory, seemingly unable to recognize that its "rival" poses no threat. Growing evidence indicates, however, that birds have been getting a bum rap. It appears that birds are more capable of learning and reasoning than had been assumed, and that they are, in fact, in the same intellectual league as most mammals.

One of the first bits of evidence from "nature" on the ability of birds to learn was uncovered in the 1920s with the spread of the habit of dipping into milk bottles left on doorsteps in Great Britain. Titmice led the way, puncturing foil tops and removing cardboard lids (or dissecting lids layer by layer). Flocks of tits were reported to follow milk carts and pilfer milk when carts were left unguarded. Other species of birds, even those not as adept as tits at tearing things open (in nature, tits often tear bark while searching for insects), soon learned to follow this example, and by the end of World War II at least eleven species, including the Chaffinch, English Robin, European Starling, and Great Spotted Woodpecker, were performing the trick.

This behavior had to spread by learning; there was not enough time for natural selection to produce the milk-robbing behavior in tits and other birds. Similarly, by the middle of this century kestrels were following slow trains in Mexico, catching small birds disturbed by the trains' passage. Trains had not been around long enough for the behavior to evolve; it had to be learned. There is a great deal of evidence that many birds learn by experience. For example, older birds are often more successful at both foraging and breeding than younger, less experienced individuals. Male bowerbirds, fascinating passerines that are confined to New Guinea and Australia, often erect complex, decorated structures to woo their mates. Young males spend about two years improving their building skills, gradually moving from constructing simple rudimentary bowers to producing the complex structures of the breeding adult. The character of the bowers produced by a single species may show dramatic geographic variation. Ecologist Jared Diamond, who has studied these birds extensively in New Guinea, has suggested that the variation in bower styles may be culturally transmitted, just like styles in human art.

Learning ability in birds has also been repeatedly demonstrated in laboratory experiments. Classic work by Jane Van Zandt Brower demonstrated that naive Blue Jays, once they had tried to eat a distasteful monarch butterfly, learned immediately to avoid its black and orange color pattern. They subsequently refused even to sample palatable viceroy butterflies, which closely resemble the monarchs. Indeed, the entire story of the evolution of mimicry in butterflies and other insects depends on the ability of birds to learn that certain color or behavior patterns are associated with unpleasant experiences—bad tastes or vomiting following ingestion (the emetic substance in monarchs is a heart poison). Furthermore, Blue Jays in cages

American Crow

Supersp #33
Corvus brachyrhynchos Brehm

NG–306; G–226; PE–206; PW–165; AE–pl 579; AW–pl 625; AM(II)–318

			FM?
			I: 18 DAYS
SHRUB	MF+	4–6 (3–9)	ALTRICIAL
0'–70'		MONOG?	F: 28–35 DAYS
		(COOP)	MF+

BREEDING: Woodland, farmland, orchards, and tidal flats; riparian woodland in arid regions. 1 brood, 2 in s. **DISPLAYS:** Courtship: males wheel and dive in flight pursuit of female; in tree or on ground, male spreads wings and tail, fluffs body feathers and bows several times to female while singing "rattling" song. Pair perch together, preen and bill. Male occ performs song-flight. **NEST:** In conif or decid tree, shrub, rarely on ground; of branches, twigs, and bark, lined with shredded bark, moss, grass, feathers, hair, leaves. Built in 5–13 days. **EGGS:** Bluish-green to olive green, marked with browns, grays. 1.6" (41 mm). **DIET:** Insects, other inverts, carrion, small verts, bird eggs, nestlings; seeds, esp corn, fruit, nuts. Ejects pellets. **CONSERVATION:** In winter partially migratory within N.A. Rare cowbird host. Damage to poultry, game, songbirds, and variety of crops has led to extensive control efforts, oft using dynamite, directed at fall and winter roosts killing tens of thousands per roost. **NOTES:** Occ breed cooperatively with yearling helpers; usu breed in small colonies in w. Female fed during incubation. Break mollusk shells by dropping onto rocks from above. Immense winter roosts of up to hundreds of thousands. **ESSAYS:** Decline of Eastern Songbirds, p. 495; Eye Color, p. 233; Cooperative Breeding, p. 283; Pellets, p. 297; Communal Roosting, p. 615. **REFS:** Goodwin, 1976; Kilham, 1984; Knight et al., 1987.

Northwestern Crow

Supersp #33
Corvus caurinus Baird

NG–306; G–226; AW– 624; AM(II)–318

			F?
			I: ? DAYS
SHRUB	?	4–5	ALTRICIAL
GROUND		MONOG	F: ? DAYS
0'–70'		(COOP)	MF+

BREEDING: Coastal tidelands near conif forest, forest edge, farmland and around dwellings. 2? broods. **DISPLAYS:** ? **NEST:** In crotch of conif or decid tree, ground nests beneath boulder, shrub, or windfall; of fine sticks and mud, lined with bark, grass, hair. Nests oft perennial. **EGGS:** Bluish- or grayish-green, marked with browns and grays. 1.6" (40 mm). **DIET:** Marine inverts, insects, carrion, bird eggs and nestlings (esp in seabird colonies); fruit, few seeds. **CONSERVATION:** Winter resident. **NOTES:** Breed in small colonies, occ as scattered pairs. Yearlings occ serve as helpers in territory defense, feeding of young, caching of mollusks. Adults with helper (only one per territory) produce more young than adults without helper. Break mollusk shells by dropping onto rocks from above; compared with adults, yearlings take smaller clams and are less efficient at opening them. Form roosts of up to 1,000 in fall and winter. **ESSAYS:** Cooperative Breeding, p. 283; Bird-Brained, p. 415; Wing Shapes and Flight, p. 227; Hoarding Food, p. 345; Communal Roosting, p. 615. **REFS:** Goodwin, 1976; Richardson and Verbeek, 1987; Verbeek and Butler, 1981.

adjacent to those in which other jays were fed edible butterflies were able to learn from the other birds. When the observer jays were offered the choice of the same butterfly species as the other jays had been eating, or an edible butterfly of a distinctly different species, they chose the species that they had already observed the other jays to consume.

There is a large literature on pigeons, canaries, and other birds in cages learning to do such things as peck at keys in certain patterns, discriminate between symmetrical and asymmetrical figures, or recognize unique objects in a series (a screw in a group of aspirin tablets or an aspirin in a collection of screws) in order to gain food rewards.

There is also evidence that some birds have much higher intelligence than the sort involved in learning to open milk bottles, peck keys, and recognize unique objects. Anyone who has tried to hunt crows by parading first before their roosts carrying a broom handle until the crows do not flee, and then substituting a shotgun in an attempt to deceive the birds, has had a quick lesson in bird intelligence.

Parrots have a remarkable capacity to acquire language, and apparently considerable powers of association to go with it. One African Grey Parrot has been trained to name over 40 items, and demonstrates the ability to grasp abstract ideas such as color and shape. If it is shown a green square and asked "what color?" it usually says "green." If asked "what shape?" it usually says "square." But parrots have long been recognized to be intelligent. More surprising is the recently discovered ability of pigeons to deal with problems whose solutions were once considered indications of insightful thinking in chimpanzees. Pigeons were taught to peck at a banana while standing on a box placed right under it and, in a separate experiment, to push a box along the ground. Then they were presented with a banana hung too high for them to peck at, combined with a box at some distance from the banana. The pigeons solved the problem by combining their learned skills—they pushed the box under the banana, jumped up on it, and pecked away.

An even more stunning report of avian problem solving, this time by crows, has come from Moscow University. A crow is presented with a row of caps, with some food hidden under the first cap. The crow is allowed to find the food by trial and error. Then the experiment is rerun, with the food under the second cap. After the crow finds it again, the next run has the food under the third cap, and so on. The experimenters claim that the bird soon learns the progression and uses it to find the food. If confirmed, this experiment would mean that the bird has grasped a concept as complex as "increase in number" or distance.

There is other impressive evidence of learned purposive behavior in birds. A Rook (a close relative of crows) appears to have figured out that by putting a plug in the drain hole of its aviary and tapping it firmly in place, it could help form a pool of water in which to bathe. The behavior occurred most often on hot days when bathing was most desirable, so it was not simply a version of the Rook's standard food-caching behavior.

Fish Crow

Corvus ossifragus Wilson

NG–306; G–226; PE–206; AE–pl 580; AM(II)–320

SHRUB
5.5'–90'

?

4–5
MONOG?

FM?
I: 16–18 DAYS
ALTRICIAL
F: 21+ DAYS
MF (?)

BREEDING: Beaches, bays, swamps, etc., and inland along major watercourses; occ in woodland. 1 brood. **DISPLAYS**: In gliding courtship flight, male and female touch wings and heads. **NEST**: Usu in topmost crotch of conif, occ decid, tree, shrub; of sticks, twigs, lined with bark, feathers, pine needles, hair, grass, leaves, dung. **EGGS**: Bluish- or grayish-green, marked with browns and grays. 1.5" (37 mm). **DIET**: Marine and other inverts, carrion, bird eggs, (esp of water birds); berries, fruit, seeds. **CONSERVATION**: Winter resident. Said to cause immense damage in southern heronries by preying on eggs in unattended nests. **NOTES**: Breed in loose colonies consisting of a few pairs. If first clutch is lost, will produce replacement, oft in same nest. More sociable and gregarious than other N.A. crows. Break mollusk shells by dropping onto rocks from above. When foraging, occ hover to scan ground or water surface below. Gather in winter roosts of thousands. **ESSAYS**: Bird-Brained, p. 415; Wing Shapes and Flight, p. 227; Communal Roosting, p. 615; Walking vs. Hopping, p. 69; Geometry of the Selfish Colony, p. 19. **REF**: Goodwin, 1976.

Chihuahuan Raven

Corvus cryptoleucus Couch

NG–306; G–226; PE–206; AE–pl 582; AW–pl 627; AM(II)–320

SHRUB
9'–40'

F

5–7
(3–8)
MONOG?

FM?
I: 21 DAYS
ALTRICIAL
F: 30? DAYS
MF (?)

BREEDING: Arid and semiarid grassland, scrub, and desert. 1 brood. **DISPLAYS**: Male performs acrobatic aerial display of soaring, wheeling, and tumbling. When displaying to female, male fluffs neck feathers. **NEST**: Usu in solitary tree or shrub, occ on human-built structure; loosely constructed exterior of twigs (oft thorny, occ barbed wire), lined with strips of bark, hair, grass, trash. Old nests oft repaired and used perennially. Building takes several weeks. **EGGS**: Pale or grayish-green, marked with brown, lilac. 1.8" (44 mm). **DIET**: Insects, carrion, other inverts, small verts, bird eggs, nestlings; seeds, fruit. Nestlings fed 100% animal food. **CONSERVATION**: Winter resident except n e populations, which migrate s, possibly into Mexico. Expanded into CO, KS, and NE feeding on slaughtered buffalo, subsequently range receded southward. Control measures (largely unsuccessful) incl persistent trapping, in some cases removing 10,000 birds from one locality in less than a year. **NOTES**: Breeds late in season, possibly timed to onset of summer rains and subsequent food supply. Cache food temporarily. Flocks form soon after fledging. Foraging flocks move as rolling mass, with rear birds constantly replacing birds in front. Highly gregarious, forming immense winter feeding and roosting flocks, oft in thousands. **ESSAYS**: Monogamy, p. 597; Feet, p. 239; Hoarding Food, p. 345; Breeding Season, p. 55; Communal Roosting, p. 615. **REF**: Goodwin, 1976.

When we watch the behavior of birds in nature we should be alert to evidence of them learning and acting intelligently to solve problems. They are clearly not automata, but we have yet to determine how often intelligence replaces instinct, and what differences in the capacity to do so there may be between the various groups of birds.

SEE: Metabolism, p. 325; Tool Using, p. 435. REFS: Brower, 1958; Crocker, 1985; Diamond, 1982, 1986; Kenyon, 1942.

Birds, DNA, and Evolutionary Convergence

Tracing genealogies fascinates many people, and reconstructing the genealogies (which they call "phylogenies") of groups of organisms is a favorite sport of biologists. A persisting mystery has been the evolutionary relationships of various groups of birds. Which birds are similar because they are descended from relatively recent common ancestors (true evolutionary relationship), and which are similar because, although coming from different recent ancestors, they have evolved similar structures in response to similar ways of life (evolutionary convergence). This mystery is exemplified by a long debate over who are the relatives of the Wrentit. Confusion is indicated by its name: does it share recent common ancestors with wrens, or titmice, or members of some entirely different group? At one time or another, the Wrentit has been declared a near relative of wrens, bushtits, titmice, mockingbirds, Old World warblers (which include Dusky and Arctic Warblers which stray into North America), and babblers (Eastern Hemisphere insect eaters).

Normally evolutionary family trees are constructed by carefully comparing details of structural features, because taxonomists known that overall similarity in form can be misleading. In spite of their fishlike shapes, whales have long been recognized as phylogenetically much more closely related to people than to fishes, because the presence of mammary glands and hair (scanty as it is) and the structure of their brains, hearts, and many other features show them to be mammals. The superficial similarity of fishes and whales is an example of convergence. The whale-fish convergence indicates that streamlining is the evolutionary solution to minimizing drag on large creatures moving rapidly through water.

Since most birds have also had to solve the problem of moving rapidly through a fluid, air, they tend to be very convergent in shape. There also is great potential for convergence in bill structure (if two unrelated birds have the same diets) and leg structure (if, say, they both perch, wade, or paddle). All birds are also much more recently and closely related to one another than are whales and fishes, making structural differences among them relatively slight. Not surprisingly, taxonomists have had considerable problems reconstructing the phylogeny of the birds. A classic example of avian con-

Common Raven
Corvus corax Linnaeus

NG–306; G–226; PE–206; PW– 165; AE–pl 581; AW–pl 626; AM(II)–322

CONIF   MF   4–6
TREE   (3–7)
                       MONOG

F
I: 18–21 DAYS
ALTRICIAL
F: 38–44 DAYS
MF

BREEDING: Wide variety of habitats, oft mountainous or hilly areas. 1 brood. **DISPLAYS:** Male performs acrobatic aerial display of soaring, wheeling, and tumbling; pair oft soar together, wingtips touching, male above female; perch together, preen, and bill. **NEST:** Occ in decid tree (to 100′), on human-built structure; of branches, twigs (occ wire), lined with shreds of bark, hair. Oft repaired and used perennially. Built over several weeks. Old nests oft used by hawks and owls. **EGGS:** Greenish, marked with browns, olive. 2.0″ (50 mm). **DIET:** Primarily carrion, also small verts, bird eggs and nestlings (esp in seabird colonies), insects, other inverts; garbage, seeds, fruit. Eject pellets. **CONSERVATION:** Winter resident. Alleged damage to domestic animals and wild game led to intensive trapping in past. **NOTES:** Never retrieve building materials that fall from nest; large accumulations of sticks, etc., may occur below nest site. Long-term pair bond. If initial clutch is lost, a second smaller clutch occ produced in same nest. Male feeds incubating female. Female broods. Cache food temporarily, oft burying it. Break mollusk shells by dropping onto rocks from above. Occ hunt cooperatively in groups. Aerial acrobatics and spectacular dives said to be play. Winter communal roosts in trees, occ in marsh, in flocks of up to several hundred, oft perennial. Largest passerine. **ESSAYS:** Monogamy, p. 597; Hoarding Food, p. 345; Communal Roosting, p. 615. **REFS:** Goodwin, 1976; Harlow et al., 1975; Stiehl, 1985.

Wrentit
Chamaea fasciata Gambel

NG–308; G–232; PW–pl 45; AW–pl 484; AM(III)–60

1′–15′   MF   4
                   (3–5)
                   MONOG

MF
I: 15–16 DAYS
ALTRICIAL
F: 15–16 DAYS
MF

BARK
GLEAN

BREEDING: Chaparral, scrub, well planted suburban areas. 2? broods. **DISPLAYS:** ? **NEST:** Base of cobwebs supporting coarse bark, with deep cup of fine bark, lined with fine fibers, hair. Outside oft decorated with lichen. **EGGS:** Pale greenish-blue, unmarked. 0.7″ (18 mm). **DIET:** Incl spiders; adults feed heavily on fruit, esp when insects scarce in fall and winter. Young fed 100% insects. **CONSERVATION:** Winter resident. Uncommon cowbird host. **NOTES:** "Bouncing ping pong ball" song is heard much more often than bird is seen; secretive in thick undergrowth. Extremely sedentary: mate for life and remain in 1–2.5–acre area. Young still beg from adults at 30–35 days. Tends to avoid singing when Bewick's Wrens sing (so as to avoid acoustic interference); usu follows wren by few minutes. Recent taxonomic work indicates neither a wren nor a tit (as chickadees are called in England), but a babbler (Timaliidae), an otherwise Old World family of insectivores. **ESSAYS:** Birds and DNA, p. 419; DNA and Classification, p. 662; Bathing and Dusting, p. 429. **REFS:** Fleischer et al., 1985; Sibley and Ahlquist, 1984b.

vergence is that between swallows and swifts. Both are specialized for scooping up flying insects, and early ornithologists grouped them together. But detailed analysis of their anatomy revealed swifts to be distant relatives of hummingbirds and swallows to be songbirds.

New techniques, however, are coming to the rescue of bird taxonomy. It is now possible to compare directly the DNAs in different organisms, and evolutionists Charles Sibley and Jon Ahlquist have been diligently assaying the similarities of these molecules (which encode the genetic information) of diverse groups of birds. A brief summary of their techniques and an outline of their recent classification of North American passerines is given in an appendix (p. 662).

Before the reality of continental drift had been established in the 1960s, it had been argued by some bird taxonomists that each of the flightless ratites—the African Ostrich, South American rheas, Australian Emu, New Guinea cassowaries, and New Zealand Kiwis—was more closely related to various flying birds than to one another. After all, how could a group of flightless birds spread across ocean barriers? But when it became clear that the southern homelands of these birds were once united, the idea that they were all more closely related to one another than to flying birds gained popularity. Sibley and Ahlquist made comparisons of the DNAs of ratites which show them to be, indeed, each other's closest relatives, with South American tinamous (ground-dwelling, short-winged, partridgelike birds) their nearest flying relatives.

Continental drift has, in turn, permitted Sibley and Ahlquist to estimate an absolute time scale of divergence for all groups of birds. The scale calibrates relative rates of DNA divergence against the time of known geological events. For example, the genetic distance between the Ostrich of Africa and the rheas of South America represent about 80 million years of DNA evolution, since it was roughly 80 million years ago that Africa and South America had drifted far enough apart to make the Atlantic Ocean a barrier for flightless animals. Using this DNA "clock," it seems that the last common ancestor of finches and mockers-thrashers lived about 50 million years ago, and the split between the mockers and thrashers took place about 10 million years ago.

Sibley and Ahlquist have also shown that a large number of Australian passerines, often thought to be relatives of robins, wrens, nuthatches, and so on, are rather like the marsupials, the product of an independent "radiation" (evolution of great diversity) on the island continent. Thus, the beautiful Australian fairy wrens are not related to our wrens at all, the nuthatchlike sittellas and tree-creepers are not related to nuthatches and creepers, and the red- and yellow-breasted Australian robins are not even thrushes. In fact, all share more recent common ancestors with crows and shrikes than with their American and Eurasian namesakes.

Interestingly the Australian birds converge in more than appearance. The fairy wrens characteristically cock their tails, and many of their calls are often very wrenlike trills. The sittellas often forage head-downward, and the

Tufted Titmouse

NG–308; G–230; PE–210; AE–pl 432; AM(II)–330

SNAG	F	5–7	F	SEEDS	BARK
3'–90'		(4–8)	I: 13–14 DAYS	FRUIT	GLEAN
		MONOG	ALTRICIAL		
			F: 15–18 DAYS		
			MF		

BREEDING: Forest, woodland, scrub, parks; from decid and mixed decid-conif woodland in n e to oak-juniper scrub, mesquite and riparian woodland in s w. 1 brood, 2 in s. **DISPLAYS:** Courtship: simple pursuit of female by male. **NEST:** In natural or woodpecker-excavated cavity; lined with moss, fur, bark, leaves, grass, and snake skin. Built in 6–11 days. Occ perennial. **EGGS:** White to creamy white, spotted with browns, occ wreathed. 0.7" (18 mm). **DIET:** Incl spiders and their eggs, a few snails. Acorns may form most of diet from November to February. **CONSERVATION:** Winter resident. Uncommon cowbird host. Will use nest boxes. **NOTES:** Long-term pair bond. Young of previous brood occ help at nest. Male feeds female from courtship through early hatching. Close sitter on nest. Move about in family groups in fall. Form mixed-species flocks with a variety of other species (esp chickadees, nuthatches, small woodpeckers) in nonbreeding season. Formerly regarded as separate species from Black-crested Titmouse until studies showed that they interbreed freely in a narrow zone through e c TX. **ESSAYS:** Visual Displays, p. 5; Feeding Birds, p. 349; Nest Materials, p. 369; Mixed-Species Flocking, p. 433; Great Plains Hybrids, p. 625; Hybridization, p. 501; Monogamy, p. 597; Cooperative Breeding, p. 283. **REFS:** Brackbill, 1970; Elder, 1985; Waite, 1987b; Waite and Grubb, 1987.

Plain Titmouse

NG–308; G–230; PW–pl 45; AW–pl 486; AM(II)–330

SNAG	?	6–8	F	FRUIT	BARK
3'–10'		(3–9)	I: 14–16 DAYS	SEEDS	GLEAN
(To 32')		MONOG	ALTRICIAL		
			F: 16–21 DAYS		
			MF		

BREEDING: Piñon-juniper and oak woodland. ? broods. **DISPLAYS:** ? **NEST:** In natural or woodpecker-excavated cavity, oft partially excavated by pair; of moss, grass, forbs, lined with fur, feathers. Female selects nest site. **EGGS:** White, unmarked or faintly marked with reddish-browns. 0.7" (17 mm). **DIET:** Incl few spiders; acorns. **CONSERVATION:** Winter resident. Readily use nest boxes. **NOTES:** Pairs usu remain together from year to year; with rare exception, mates are replaced only if they disappear. Female is a tight sitter on nest. Young fed by regurgitation through fourth day; driven from territory as soon as they are able to care for themselves. Roost in cavities. Occ join mixed-species flocks in nonbreeding season. **ESSAYS:** Bird Guilds, p. 493; Mixed-Species Flocking, p. 433; Bathing and Dusting, p. 429; Monogamy, p. 597. **REFS:** Hertz et al., 1976; Wagner, 1981.

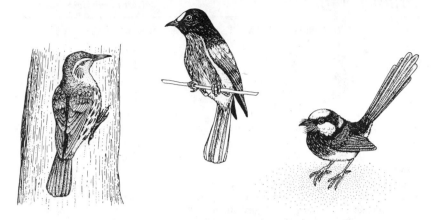

Australian birds that are much more closely related to crows than to the groups indicated by their common names. Top: Scarlet Robin (Petroica multicolor). *Left: Brown Tree-creeper* (Climacteris picumnus). *Right: Superb Blue Wren* (Malurus cyaneus).

tree-creepers climb up tree trunks seeking prey under the bark. The robins, however, have a mode of hunting not found in the North American bird fauna. They are "pounce predators," often clinging to the sides of tree trunks 3–6 feet high and pouncing on insects on the ground. All in all, the Australian bird convergence is even more spectacular than the convergence of various marsupials with the placental mammals that dominate on all other continents—after all the mammalian convergence was recognized early on, while the birds fooled biologists until very recently.

Closer to home, another problem that long bedeviled ornithologists was the identity of the birds that had colonized the Hawaiian Islands and evolved into the group known as Hawaiian honeycreepers. Although obviously closely related to one another, the honeycreepers have radiated to fill a wide variety of habitats. Many have evolved remarkably different bills—some finchlike, some long and downcurved, some parrotlike, etc. Comparisons of honeycreeper DNA with that of other groups has confirmed the suspicion of ornithologists that honeycreepers are most closely related to the cardueline finches: goldfinches, crossbills, grosbeaks, siskins, etc. Sibley and Ahlquist estimate that an ancestral finch reached the Hawaiian area some 15–20 million years ago—long before the current islands emerged from the sea. That finch colonized one of the pre-Hawaiian islands that has long since been worn away by the sea. That island was produced by the same volcanic "hot spot" that has been producing the present group. The remains of that first home of the honeycreepers, now represented by one of the submerged volcanic remnants called the Emperor Seamounts, are being carried northward away from the hot spot from which it emerged by the drifting Pacific tectonic plate. Such drifting is the same kind of motion that causes continents to move with their tectonic plates.

Now what about the Wrentit? DNA comparisons show it to be geneti-

Bridled Titmouse

Parus wollweberi Bonaparte

NG–308; G–230; PW–pl 45; AW–pl 489; AM(II)–328

		⬭	?		
			I: ? DAYS		
SNAG	?	5–7	ALTRICIAL		BARK
3.5'–28'		?	F: ? DAYS		GLEAN
			?		

BREEDING: Oak and pine-oak woodland, occ in cottonwood-willow-mesquite. ? broods. **DISPLAYS:** ? **NEST:** In natural cavity; foundation of forbs, grass, lined with plant down, fur. **EGGS:** White, unmarked. 0.6″ (16 mm). **DIET:** Poorly known; mostly insects. **CONSERVATION:** Winter resident. **NOTES:** Details of breeding biology virtually unknown. During nonbreeding season forms flocks of 25 or more; occ serve as core species of insectivorous mixed-species flocks. **ESSAYS:** Mixed-Species Flocking, p. 433; Bird Badges, p. 591; Bathing and Dusting, p. 429; Determining Diets, p. 535; How Do We Find Out About Bird Biology?, p. 319. **REFS:** Austin and Smith, 1972; Phillips et al., 1964.

Black-capped Chickadee

Supersp #34
Parus atricapillus Linnaeus

NG–310; G–228; PE–210; PW–pl 45; AE–pl 428; AW–pl 487; AM(II)–324

			MF		
			I: 11–13 DAYS		
SNAG	MF	6–8	ALTRICIAL	CONIF	BARK
4'–8'		(5–10)	F: 14–18 DAYS	SEEDS	GLEAN
(To 40')		MONOG?	MF	FRUIT	

BREEDING: Decid or mixed decid-conif woodland, riparian woodland, thickets, parks. 1? brood. **DISPLAYS:** Courtship: simple pursuit of female by male. **NEST:** Excavate or enlarge cavity; rarely in conif; lined with plant down, moss, feathers, hair, insect cocoons. Require 10–14 days to excavate and line cavity. **EGGS:** White, finely marked with reddish-browns. 0.6″ (16 mm). **DIET:** Incl spiders and their eggs. **CONSERVATION:** Winter resident. Rare cowbird host. Will use nest boxes. **NOTES:** Excavated material from nest carried from vicinity and scattered. Male feeds female during incubation. If disturbed on nest, female makes explosive snakelike hiss. After cavity is lined and throughout incubation, female roosts in nest. Fledglings stay with parents ca. 3 weeks then disperse to future breeding areas; extent of spring dispersal may vary regionally. In winter, forage and roost in stable flocks of up to 12; flocks incl a few young low-ranked birds that lack pair bonds and oft switch flocks. Dense conifers and empty nests used as winter roosts; occ join in mixed flocks. Hybridizes with Carolina Chickadee in parts of contact zone between NJ and KS. **ESSAYS:** Great Plains Hybrids, p. 625; Metabolism, p. 325; Irruptions, p. 639; Mobbing, p. 425; Dominance Hierarchies, p. 533. **REFS:** Elder and Zimmerman, 1983; Smith, 1984; Weise and Meyer, 1979.

cally similar to the babblers and the Old World warblers—two groups that are closely related. Ecologically and behaviorally it most resembles babblers. Wrentits and babblers build similar nests, and many babblers, like Wrentits, inhabit semiarid regions, sing a great deal, and dine on insects and small fruits. Interestingly, however, Australian "babblers" turn out to be unrelated to Asian and African babblers but, like Australian robins, are instead relatives of crows.

SEE: DNA and Passerine Classification, p. 662; Species and Speciation, p. 355; Hawaiian Bird Biology, p. 651. REFS: Sibley and Ahlquist, 1984a, b, 1985, 1986.

Mobbing

It is not uncommon to see a group of blackbirds or swallows chasing a hawk or eagle, or a group of songbirds fluttering and calling around a perched owl. Such "mobbing" behavior is probably the most frequently observed overt antipredator strategy. Nevertheless, the exact purpose of such noisy group demonstrations remains a matter of some debate.

Mobbing tends to occur most intensely on the breeding grounds. For instance, in April a tape recording of the cries of an Eastern Screech-Owl brought Prothonotary Warblers, Blue-gray Gnatcatchers, and other small songbirds swarming in from their newly established territories in the swamps of South Carolina. A week later the same tape had no discernible effect on warblers moving northward along a ridge in Nashville. Presumably the migrating warblers had less reason to mob, perhaps because they would be leaving the vicinity of the predator anyway. Mobbing may thus function to divert the predator from areas where there are fledglings, or simply to confuse and annoy the predator, in the hope of getting it to move away.

This "move-along" hypothesis, first put forth by E. Curio, a specialist in the biology of predation from Ruhr University in Germany, is supported by the research of ornithologist Douglas Shedd of Randolph-Macon Women's College. Shedd has shown that Black-capped Chickadees will respond to predators in fall and winter, even in January with the temperature 25 below zero. The chickadees, which remain in residence all year long, still find it profitable to mob in winter. Migratory robins, in contrast, sometimes approached a stuffed screech-owl and tape combination outside the breeding season, but never mobbed.

Careful experiments have shown that birds can learn from each other which predators to mob (indeed, one bird in an experiment was taught by another to "mob" a many-colored plastic bottle, although the mobbing was halfhearted). Therefore one function of mobbing may be educational—to teach young birds the identity of the enemy. Another may be to alert other

Carolina Chickadee

NG–310; G–228; PE–210; AE–pl 427; AM(II)–324

			MF		
			I: 11–12 DAYS		
SNAG	MF	6	ALTRICIAL	CONIF	BARK
5'–15'		(5–8)	F: 13–17 DAYS	SEEDS	GLEAN
(1'–23')		MONOG	MF	FRUIT	

BREEDING: Decid woodland (esp riparian), swamps, thickets, parks. ? broods. **DISPLAYS:** ? **NEST:** Excavate or enlarge cavity, occ in pine, artificial structure; lined with moss, grass, plant down, feathers, hair. **EGGS:** White, marked with reddish-browns. 0.6" (15 mm). **DIET:** Incl spiders and their eggs; seeds. **CONSERVATION:** Winter resident. Rare cowbird host. Will use nest boxes. **NOTES:** When disturbed, female on nest produces an explosive snakelike hiss. Pair remain together throughout year. In winter, forage in small mixed-species flocks with titmice, warblers, nuthatches, woodpeckers, and kinglets. Hybridizes with Black-capped Chickadee in parts of contact zone between NJ and KS; in s w MO, hybrids are intermediate in morphology and/or vocalizations and respond aggressively to territorial songs of both Black-capped and Carolina Chickadees. **ESSAYS:** Great Plains Hybrids, p. 623; Mixed-Species Flocking, p. 433; Feeding Birds, p. 349; Mobbing, p. 425; Monogamy, p. 597; Hybridization, p. 501. **REFS:** Dixon, 1963; Robbins et al., 1986.

Mexican Chickadee

NG–310; G–228; PW–pl 45; AW–733; AM(II)–325

			?		
			I: ? DAYS		
TREE	?	6	ALTRICIAL	SEEDS?	BARK
5'–45'		MONOG	F ? DAYS		GLEAN
			MF		

BREEDING: Mesic montane pine, spruce-fir, and pine-oak woodland. ? broods. **DISPLAYS:** ? **NEST:** In cavity usu in snag; lined with plant down, fur. **EGGS:** White, finely marked with reddish-browns. 0.6" (14 mm). **DIET:** Presumably mostly insects. **CONSERVATION:** Winter resident. **NOTES:** Unlike other closely related chickadee species, uses songs with complex syllables rather than simple whistles for territorial proclamation. Female likely does all of brooding. Reported to sweep nest cavity entrance with crushed insects held in bill; noxious chemicals released from insects possibly deter nest predators from entering. Breeding biology virtually unknown. **ESSAYS:** How Do We Find Out About Bird Biology?, p. 319; Mobbing, p. 425; Bathing and Dusting, p. 429; Determining Diets, p. 535; How Long Can Birds Live?, p. 643. **REFS:** Dixon and Martin, 1979; Ficken and Ficken, 1987.

birds to the presence of the predator, either getting them to join in the mobbing or protecting them, since a predator is unlikely to be able to sneak up on an alert victim. The original mobber may benefit directly by the predator being moved along, or indirectly if the protected birds are its kin.

Much is lacking in our understanding of mobbing. It is not clear why predators don't simply turn on their tormentors and snatch up one or two of the mobbing birds. If they did, presumably mobbing would quickly disappear; that it persists suggests that surprise is an essential element in raptor hunting.

SEE: Altruism, p. 453; Flock Defense, p. 235; Hawk-Eyed, p. 229.   REFS: Curio et al., 1978; Shedd, 1985.

Brood Patches

Once a bird's egg is laid, it must be heated if it is to develop. With rare exceptions, birds use their body (metabolic) heat to incubate their eggs. This presents them with a problem, however. Since birds are "warm-blooded," they must be very careful about losing heat yet be able to transfer heat to their eggs.

Heat is lost from a bird's surface, and the more surface it has relative to its volume, the more readily it will lose heat. The smaller of two objects with the same shape will always have the greater surface/volume ratio. (A 1-inch cube has a surface area of 6 square inches, and a volume of 1 cubic inch—a surface/volume ratio of 6/1. A 2-inch cube has a surface area of 24 square inches [6 sides, each with 4 square inches] and a volume of 8 cubic inches. Its ratio then is 3/1—only half the surface/volume ratio of the smaller cube.) Most birds are relatively small, and thus have a large surface-to-volume ratio.

One of the main functions of the feathers is to insulate the bird—to prevent its body heat from being dissipated through the skin surface. Most birds have "solved" the dilemma posed by the need to both transfer and preserve heat by evolving "brood patches." These are areas of skin on the belly that lose their feathers toward the end of the egg-laying period. In most birds the feathers are shed automatically, but geese and ducks pluck their brood patch and use the plucked feathers to make an insulating lining for their nests. The brood patch also develops a supplemental set of vessels that bring hot blood close to the surface of the skin. When birds return to the nest to resume incubating, they go through characteristic settling movements in order to bring the brood patch into contact with the eggs. In precocial birds, after the chicks have hatched the insulating feathers grow back. In passerines, and presumably other altricial birds, the regrowth of the feathers is delayed, and the patches remain functional through early brooding. Then they gradually disappear, restoring the adult's thermoregulatory integrity about the time the young are fledged.

Mountain Chickadee

Supersp #35
Parus gambeli Ridgway

NG–310; G–228; PW–pl 45; AW–pl 488; AM(II)–326

			?		
SNAG	?	5–9	I: 14 DAYS	CONIF	BARK
4′–8′		(5–12)	ALTRICIAL	SEEDS	GLEAN
(0.5′–80′)		MONOG	F: 21 DAYS		
			MF		

BREEDING: Montane conif. forest. 2? broods. **DISPLAYS**: Male and female give series of high-pitched calls in precopulatory display. **NEST**: In natural or wood-pecker-excavated cavity, occ excavate their own; lined with moss, fur, feathers, shredded bark. **EGGS**: White, unmarked, occ spotted with reddish-browns. 0.6″ (16 mm). **DIET**: Incl spiders and their eggs. **CONSERVATION**: Winter resident, may move downslope in winter. Will use nest boxes. **NOTES**: Female is a close sitter on the nest; if disturbed, will lunge and emit explosive snakelike hiss. Young fed by regurgitation until 4 days old. Male collects more food for young than does female; female spends more time tending young at the nest. In winter, form mixed-species flocks with warblers, sparrows, Brown Creepers, vireos, and bushtits. **ESSAYS**: Mixed-Species Flocking, p. 433; Bird Badges, p. 591; Vocal Copying, p. 469; Parental Care, p. 555. **REFS**: Gaddis, 1985; Grundel, 1987; Man-olis, 1977; Minock, 1971.

Chestnut-backed Chickadee

Supersp #36
Parus rufescens Townsend

NG–312; G–228; PW–pl 45; AW–pl 545; AM(II)–328

			?		
TREE	?	6–7	I: ? DAYS	SEEDS	BARK
1.5′–12′		(5–9)	ALTRICIAL	FRUIT	GLEAN
(To 80′)		MONOG?	F: ? DAYS		
			?		

BREEDING: Conif and mixed conif-decid forest, primarily in humid regions. ? broods. **DISPLAYS**: ? **NEST**: In natural or excavated cavity; lined with moss, fur, plant down, feathers. **EGGS**: White, sparsely marked with reddish-browns. 0.6″ (16 mm). **DIET**: Incl spiders and their eggs; seeds incl mostly conif. **CONSERVA-TION**: Winter resident. **NOTES**: Bird on nest hisses and flutters wings in response to disturbance. May compete for food resources with ecologically similar Hutton's Vireo where both are resident. In winter, form mixed-species flocks with other chickadees, kinglets, nuthatches, warblers, bushtits, Brown Creepers, and juncos. **ESSAYS**: Bird Guilds, p. 493; Bathing and Dusting, p. 429; Mixed-Species Flocking, p. 433. **REFS**: Hertz et al., 1976; Wagner, 1981.

The placement of brood patches differs among groups of birds. There may be a single brood patch in the middle of the belly, as in hawks, pigeons, and most songbirds. Shorebirds, auks, and skuas have one on each side, and gulls and game birds combine these two patterns by having three brood patches. Pelicans, boobies, and gannets have none at all. They cradle the eggs in their webbed feet, cover them with the abdomen, and apparently warm them from both above and below.

When just one parent incubates, it alone develops a brood patch. If both parents incubate, both may grow brood patches, or one may cover the eggs without a patch, warming it less efficiently, but at least retarding heat and water loss from the egg.

SEE: Incubation: Heating Eggs, p. 393; Temperature Regulation and Behavior, p. 149; Feathers, p. 309.   REF: Bailey, 1952.

Bathing and Dusting

When birds bathe in water or saturate themselves with dust they are actively maintaining their plumage. In well-watered areas bathing is most common, in arid ones dusting is more often observed. Experiments with quail show that frequent dusting helps to maintain an optimum amount of oil on the feathers. Excess plumage lipids, including preen oil, are absorbed by the dust and expelled along with dry skin and other debris. If quail are prevented from dusting, their feathers quickly become oily and matted. Dusting may also help to discourage bird lice, but no experimental evidence exists as yet showing that to be the case.

Wrens and House Sparrows frequently follow a water bath with a dust bath (one reason to suspect an antiparasite function for dusting). Overall, the amount of time and effort birds put into bathing and dusting indicates how critical feather maintenance may be. Feathers are marvelous and intricate devices, but keeping them functional requires constant care.

A bird is considered to be bathing whenever it uses any of several stereotyped movements to wet its feathers. One pattern, wading, is commonly observed in birds with strong feet and broad, short, flexible wings. In a typical sequence a bird stands in the water, fluffs the feathers to expose the bare skin between their bases, and rapidly flicks the wings in and out of the water. The breast is submerged and rolled vigorously back and forth, and then, as the front end emerges, the head is thrown back, forming a cup with the partially elevated wings and tail, and dousing the feathers of the back. Those feathers are elevated so that the water reaches the skin, and then lowered, forcing the water between them. The sequence may be repeated, with the bird submerging farther in each cycle, until it is a mass of soaked, disarranged feathers. Variations on this theme can be seen in different species, such as robins, thrushes, mockingbirds, jays, and titmice.

Siberian Tit

Supersp #36
Parus cinctus Boddaert

NG–312; G–228; PW–pl 45; AW–664; AM(II)–326

TREE	F?	6–9	F?	CONIF	BARK
5'–7'		?	I: 14? DAYS	SEEDS	GLEAN
			ALTRICIAL	FRUIT	
			F: ? DAYS		
			MF (?)		

BREEDING: Boreal conif forest, riparian willow and aspen thickets. 1? brood. **DISPLAYS:** ? **NEST:** In natural or woodpecker-excavated cavity; lined with moss, fur. **EGGS:** White, finely marked with reddish-browns. 0.6" (16 mm). **DIET:** Incl spiders and their eggs; berries. **CONSERVATION:** Winter resident. **NOTES:** Also found in boreal Eurasia; virtually unstudied in N.A. Formerly known as Grayheaded Chickadee. **ESSAYS:** How Do We Find Out About Bird Biology?, p. 319; Superspecies, p. 375; Mobbing, p. 425; How Long Can Birds Live?, p. 643. **REF:** Gabrielson and Lincoln, 1959.

Boreal Chickadee

Supersp #36
Parus hudsonicus Forster

NG–312; G–228; PE–210; PW–pl 45; AE–pl 511; AW–pl 544; AM(II)–328

SNAG	F – M	5–8	F	SEEDS	BARK
1'–10'		(4–9)	I: 15 (11–16) DAYS		GLEAN
		MONOG?	ALTRICIAL		
			F: 18 DAYS		
			MF		

BREEDING: Boreal conif and mixed conif-decid woodland. 1 brood. **DISPLAYS:** From top of tree, male chases female in downward spiral around tree, until female gives solicitation calls. After pairing, female begs food from male. **NEST:** In natural or woodpecker-excavated cavity, occ excavate their own; lined with moss, fur, plant down, inner bark, lichen. Female and male excavate, but only female builds nest. **EGGS:** White, finely marked with reddish-browns. 0.6" (16 mm). **DIET:** Incl spiders and their eggs. **CONSERVATION:** Winter resident. **NOTES:** As for other members of the genus, possibly mate for life. Male feeds female on nest or near cavity during incubation. Young fed mostly by male in days following hatching. Fledglings leave territory by 3 weeks posthatching. Formerly known as Brown-capped Chickadee. In winter, form mixed-species flocks with other chickadees, kinglets, nuthatches, and small woodpeckers. **ESSAYS:** Metabolism, p. 325; Irruptions, p. 639; Mixed-Species Flocking, p. 433; Courtship Feeding, p. 181; Monogamy, p. 597; Parental Care, p. 555. **REFS:** McLaren, 1975, 1976.

Birds with weak feet, such as swifts and swallows, which spend most of their time flying, dip into the water in flight, thus getting their baths "on the wing." As the body is dipped, the tail is raised to direct a spray of water over the back, and the feathers are vibrated. Flycatchers dive repeatedly from their perches into water, and vireos, which may combine both wading and diving, stand briefly and dip in the water between dives.

Chickadees, yellowthroats, wrens, buntings, and waterthrushes dart in and out of water, immersing and rolling briefly, before returning to shore to flick their wings and vibrate their feathers before jumping in again. The Wrentit, which often lives in habitats where pools of water are scarce, wets its plumage with dew from vegetation.

For birds with stubby, weak legs not adapted to wading, bathing is passive. Most woodpeckers and nuthatches, for example, simply expose their feathers when it is drizzling. They have characteristic bathing postures, extending their wings and spreading their tails.

The frequency of bathing by land birds typically is related to the weather. On a hot summer day titmice or chickadees may take five baths; in midwinter they still may bathe several times a week, often in snowmelt found in protected areas.

Waterbirds and seabirds also bathe with stereotyped routines. Terns that spend most of their time flying bathe in the same way as swifts. Grebes, ducks, geese, and swans bathe either on the surface or while diving, opening their feathers and wings. Gulls and some rails bathe while wading.

After bathing, birds dry themselves using ritualized movements. Even swimming birds must force the surplus water from between their feathers to protect their insulating properties. Anhingas and cormorants, which often sit in a characteristic sunbathing posture with drying wings spread, are perhaps also thermoregulating. (Vultures take on similar sunbathing postures in the morning. Sunbathing, which occurs in many birds, may stimulate skin parasites into activity so they can be more readily picked off.) Songbirds shake themselves to throw off water by vibrating wings and tail and ruffling feathers. All birds normally follow bathing with preening.

For some species that live in areas where standing water is not readily available, dusting appears to substitute for water bathing. Birds create dust wallows by scraping the ground. They throw dust over their bodies and rub their heads in the wallow. The dust is first worked through the feathers and then shaken out. Wrens, House Sparrows, Wrentits, larks, game birds, and some raptors are among the North American birds known to dust. As with water bathing, different species tend to have somewhat different dusting routines.

SEE: Preening, p. 53; Head Scratching, p. 543; Anting, p. 487; Disease and Parasitism, p. 399.   REFS: Simmons, 1986; Slessers, 1970.

Verdin

Auriparus flaviceps Sundevall

NG–312; G–232; PW–pl 45; AE–pl 381; AW–pl 422; AM(II)–332

| CACTUS 2'–20' | M | 4–5 (3–6) MONOG? | F I: 10 DAYS ALTRICIAL F: 21 DAYS MF | FRUIT SEEDS | BARK GLEAN |

BREEDING: Desert and arid brush, esp mesquite and creosote bush. 2 broods. **DISPLAYS**: ? **NEST**: Conspicuous oval ball of interlaced thorny twigs, placed well out toward end of branch; of leaves and grass bound with spider web and cocoons, lined with feathers, plant down. Well protected and insulated, may last several seasons, giving appearance of greater nesting density than is actually the case. Early season nests oriented so entrances protected from prevailing winds (to avoid cooling), late season nests oriented to face winds (to facilitate cooling). **EGGS**: Bluish-green to greenish-white, marked with reddish-browns. 0.6″ (15 mm). **DIET**: Incl spiders; berries. **CONSERVATION**: Winter resident. **NOTES**: Male builds several nests from which female selects the one in which to lay. Young initially fed by female by regurgitation; after fledging, return nightly to roost in nest. Reduce activity and seek shade each day when temperatures are high. Build roosting or winter nests, as well as breeding nests. In nonbreeding season, forage in small, loosely associated family groups and occ join mixed flocks that cross winter territory. **ESSAYS**: Masterbuilders, p. 445; Mixed-Species Flocking, p. 433; Temperature Regulation, p. 149. **REFS**: Austin, 1976, 1978; Buttemer et al., 1987.

Bushtit

Psaltriparus minimus Townsend

NG–312; G–232; PW–pl 45; AW–pl 485; AM(II)–334

| SHRUB 4'–25' (To 50') | MF | 5–7 MONOG? | MF I: 12 DAYS ALTRICIAL F: 14–15 DAYS MF | SEEDS FRUIT | BARK GLEAN |

BREEDING: Woodland, scrub, chaparral. 2 broods. **DISPLAYS**: Courtship of calls, trills, and posturing. **NEST**: Gourd-shaped hanging pocket, woven around and supported by twigs; of moss, lichen, leaves, cocoons, grass, flowers, secured by spider web, lined with plant down, hair, feathers. Built in 13–51 days. **EGGS**: White, unmarked. 0.6″ (14 mm). **DIET**: Incl spiders. Young fed undigested, solid food. **CONSERVATION**: Winter resident. Rare cowbird host. **NOTES**: Pairs disturbed during nest building, egg laying, or incubation oft desert, change mates, and build new nest. When clutch complete, male and female roost in nest. Both sexes brood. Pair show high tolerance for other Bushtits in territory, allowing them to forage and even take part in nesting activities. Highly gregarious except when breeding, moving about in family groups after nesting, then in loose flocks of 6–30 (up to 70), oft assoc with kinglets, wrens, titmice, warblers, and chickadees. Groups roost huddled in tight mass, saving energy from reduced heat loss. Iris of eye is pale cream in adult females, dark brown in juveniles and adult males. Populations in s w with black-eared males previously regarded as separate species, Black-eared Bushtit. **ESSAYS**: Metabolism, p. 325; Guilds, p. 493; Birds, DNA, p. 419; Eye Color, p. 233; Flocking, p. 433; Temperature, p. 149. **REFS**: Chaplin, 1982; Ervin, 1977.

Mixed-Species Flocking

It is not uncommon to find birds of several species flocking together. One reason may be that such flocking increases the number of eyes and ears available to detect predators and may confuse them as many individuals flee at once. Also a mixture of species can take advantage of different abilities. Just as nearsighted zebras with keen hearing associate on African plains with species such as wildebeest and giraffes with keen eyesight, so nearsighted gleaning birds such as Red-eyed Vireos move in groups (on their tropical wintering grounds) with farsighted salliers like Yellow-margined Flycatchers. The former lose some prey to the latter, but apparently are more than compensated by the latter's early detection of approaching danger. Similarly, it has been shown experimentally that chickadees and titmice are used as sentinels by Downy Woodpeckers foraging in mixed-species flocks.

Next to predator defense, however, the most popular hypothesis to explain the formation of mixed-species flocks is an increase in feeding efficiency. Flocks may function to overwhelm territorial defenses, because moving groups are able to feed in areas from which single individuals would be ejected by the "owner" of the territory. Having more individuals searching for food also increases the likelihood that a rich feeding patch will be located. By moving together in a mixed-species flock, birds with the same sorts of diets can avoid areas that have already been searched for food. Individuals in mixed flocks can also learn about new food sources from other species; tits have been observed to visit the site where a woodpecker was pecking at bark and to begin pecking in the same place. Finally, by associating with birds of different species that have somewhat different food preferences and foraging techniques, each individual faces less competition than it would in a similar flock of conspecifics.

If the feeding efficiency hypothesis is correct, then the amount of flocking should be related to the availability of food; when food is superabundant, little can be gained by flocking. A test of this hypothesis was carried out in two Ohio woodlots. One woodlot was left undisturbed; the other was provisioned in early November with an ample supply of sunflower seed and beef suet. Downy Woodpeckers, Tufted Titmice, Carolina Chickadees, Brown Creepers, and White-breasted Nuthatches all participated much less frequently in mixed-species flocks in the provisioned woodlot than they did in the control woodlot. This result supports the hypothesis that increased feeding efficiency is a major cause of mixed-species flocking.

Similarly, flocks may occur because one species, in the course of its feeding, flushes prey that can be caught by the others. Such foraging associations are called commensal feeding. In Australian rain forests, Yellow Robins follow Brush Turkeys, pouncing on insects the turkeys stir up as they scratch through the dead leaves of the forest floor. Cattle Egrets "flock" with cattle and tractors for similar reasons.

Brown Creeper

Certhia americana Bonaparte

NG–314; G–234; PE–212; PW–pl 45; AE–pl 355; AW–pl 388; AM(II)–340

DECID
TREE
3'–50'

UNDER
BARK

F – M

5–6
(4–8)
MONOG

F
I: 14–17 DAYS
ALTRICIAL
F: 13–16 DAYS
MF

NUTS
SEEDS

HAWKS

BREEDING: Pine forests (esp ponderosa, yellow, Jeffrey). ? broods. **DISPLAYS:** Courtship: male display flights, chases, wing fluttering, and courtship feeding; male spirals rapidly around tree trunk in pursuit of female. **NEST:** Hammocklike cup, usu beneath loose bark, rarely in cavity; of bark, moss, conif needles, silk, on base of twigs which nearly close opening between bark and trunk, lined with shredded bark, feathers. Pair select site. Built in 6–30 days. **EGGS:** White, sparsely flecked with reddish-browns, oft wreathed, occ almost unmarked. 0.6" (15 mm). **DIET:** Incl spiders, other inverts; some acorns, beechnuts. Young may be fed 100% animal food. **CONSERVATION:** n populations winter s to Nicaragua, remainder within breeding range. Rare cowbird host. **NOTES:** Use camouflage pattern when pursued: land on tree trunk, flatten, spread wings and remain motionless. Normally feed by ascending trunk in spiral or straight course, then dropping to repeat on another trunk. Male feeds incubating female. Female broods. Young can creep upward as soon as mobile. Fledglings roost in tight circle, heads to center. **ESSAYS:** Bird Guilds, p. 493; Mixed-Species Flocking, p. 433; Communal Roosting, p. 615; Temperature Regulation, p. 149; The Color of Birds, p. 111; Courtship Feeding, p. 181. **REFS:** Davis, 1978; Franzreb, 1985.

White-breasted Nuthatch

Sitta carolinensis Latham

NG–314; G–234; PE–212; PW–pl 45; AE–pl 354; AW–pl 387; AM(II)–338

10'–60'
(3'–60')

F – M

5–8
(3–10)
MONOG

F
I: 12 DAYS
ALTRICIAL
F: 14 DAYS
MF

BREEDING: Decid (esp), mixed decid-conif forest, woodland, forest edge, occ conif forest; prefers mature stands with decaying large trees. 1? brood. **DISPLAYS:** Courting male carries food to female, performs bowing and singing ritual with head feathers raised, tail spread. **NEST:** In natural cavity or deserted woodpecker hole; bed of soft bark shreds, hair, feathers. **EGGS:** White to pinkish-white, usu heavily marked with reddish-brown, esp at large end. 0.8" (19 mm). **DIET:** Incl spiders; in winter takes many acorns, nuts. Young may be fed 100% animal food. **CONSERVATION:** Winter resident. Rare cowbird host. **NOTES:** Pairs maintain feeding territories throughout year. Within pairs, males always dominant over females, e.g., in gaining access to food. In winter, roost singly in cavity; occ join mixed foraging flocks with Brown Creepers, chickadees, Downy Woodpeckers. **ESSAYS:** Bird Guilds, p. 493; Mixed-Species Flocking, p. 433; Territoriality, p. 387; Courtship Feeding, p. 181. **REFS:** Kilham, 1972; Waite, 1987a.

There are other interesting aspects of mixed-species flocks. For instance, some species appear to take the lead in forming the flock—to serve as "nuclear" or "core" species. Such species often have conspicuous plumage or behavior. Titmice in North America (and tits in Europe and Africa) play this role, as do antbirds (which often "flock" with army ants and snap up insects their raiding columns disturb) in tropical America, babblers in tropical Asia, fairy wrens and thornbills (titlike birds) in Australia, and Gerygone warblers in New Guinea.

Mixed-species flocks in North America are seen primarily in the non-breeding season. They tend to have a rapid turnover of species when they are just beginning to form in the late summer as migratory species depart or pass through from more northern locations. It is not in the temperate zones, however, that such flocking reaches its highest development. Mixed-species flocks are a dominant feature in tropical moist forests—so much so that their arrival can quickly transform an almost birdless patch of forest into an area alive with activity and calling. The composition of these tropical flocks and the complex relationships among their members are just beginning to be elucidated. Some of "our" birds join these flocks on the wintering grounds in Central and South America, and provide one reason for everyone interested in birds to make at least one trip to a tropical forest.

SEE: Flock Defense, p. 235; Bird Guilds, p. 493; Commensal Feeding, p. 35; Geometry of the Selfish Colony, p. 19. REFS: Berner and Grubb, 1985; Diamond, 1981; Morse, 1970; Munn, 1984; Wagner, 1984.

Tool Using

At one time it was assumed that humans were unique among creatures in their ability to use tools. Now it is clear that tool using is widespread in the animal kingdom. For instance, chimps use twigs to fish termites out of termite mounds, and small wasps use pebbles to tamp down earth over their nests. Birds are no exception—tool use has been demonstrated in several species.

Perhaps the best-known avian tool user is the Woodpecker Finch, one of "Darwin's finches," on the Galapagos Islands. It uses a cactus spine or wooden splinter to dig grubs or other insects out of holes. Although in general the Woodpecker Finch forages much like a true woodpecker, the two birds are unrelated. The woodpecker pries up bark with its bill, uncovering insects underneath and in holes and immediately devours those it can reach. But the finch has not evolved the long tongue that permits real woodpeckers to extract wood-boring insects from their deep holes. When such insects are found, the finch flies to a cactus, breaks off a spine, and returns to spear its prey. If a cactus spine is not available, the Woodpecker Finch may break a twig off a bush or tree, and if necessary even trim it of twiglets. In these cases the bird not only uses a tool, it "manufactures" it.

Red-breasted Nuthatch

Sitta canadensis Linnaeus

NG–314; G–234; PE–212; PW–pl 45; AE–pl 353; AW–pl 386; AM(II)–336

5'–40'	F–M	5–6	F		HAWKS
(To 120')		(4–7)	I: 12 DAYS		
		MONOG	ALTRICIAL		
			F: 14–21 DAYS		
			MF		

BREEDING: Conif (esp) and mixed decid-conif forest, aspen woodland, prefers mature stands with decaying large trees. ? broods. **DISPLAYS:** Courtship: male with head and tail raised, wings drooped, back feathers fluffed, sways from side to side with back turned to female and oft sings. Courtship feeding. **NEST:** In cavity excavated in rotten branch or stump, occ in deserted woodpecker hole; bed of soft bark shreds, grass, roots. **EGGS:** White to pinkish-white, marked with reddish-brown. 0.6" (15 mm). **DIET:** In winter, takes many conif seeds. Young may be fed 100% animal food. **CONSERVATION:** Winters in breeding range except in n and at higher elevations; some move s to n Baja. Breeding range in e expanding s. **NOTES:** Pairs may remain together on feeding territory through winter if food resources are adequate. **ESSAYS:** Birds, DNA, and Evolutionary Convergence, p. 419; Irruptions, p. 639; Territoriality, p. 387; Courtship Feeding, p. 181. **REF:** Kilham, 1973.

Pygmy Nuthatch

Supersp #38
Sitta pygmaea Vigors

NG–314; G–234; PW–pl 45; AW–pl 389; AM(II)–338

SNAG	MF+	6–8 (4–9)	F	CONIF	HOVER &
6'–60'		MONOG	I: 15–16 DAYS	SEEDS	GLEAN
		(COOP)	ALTRICIAL		HAWKS
			F: 20–22 DAYS		
			MF+		

BREEDING: Pine forests (esp ponderosa, yellow, Jeffrey), piñon-juniper woodland. 1 brood. **DISPLAYS:** ? **NEST:** Oft excavated in pine, also in post, occ uses deserted woodpecker hole; bed of plant down, bark shreds, hair, feathers. **EGGS:** White, sparsely flecked with reddish-browns. 0.6" (15 mm). **DIET:** Incl spiders. Young fed insects and spiders. **CONSERVATION:** Winter resident. **NOTES:** Long-term pair bond. Breeding units consist of 2-5 birds: helpers are unmated males, mostly yearling offspring or siblings of the pair; assist in nest building, maintenance, feeding female on nest, and feeding nestlings and fledglings. Territories maintained all year, defense limited to vicinity of nest cavity. Female broods. Pairs with helpers fledge more young than do unaided pairs. Cache conif seeds. Western equivalent, ecologically, of Brown-headed Nuthatch. In winter, groups of 4–15 forge as a flock and roost communally in nest cavities; occ form loose mixed-species flocks with warblers, titmice, chickadees. **ESSAYS:** Birds, DNA and Evolutionary Convergence, p. 419; Tool Using, p. 435; Superspecies, p. 375; Communal Roosting, p. 615; Hoarding Food, p. 345; Cooperative Breeding, p. 283; Mixed-Species Flocking, p. 433. **REFS:** Norris, 1958; Sydeman et al., 1988.

Egyptian Vultures use stones as tools to assault the eggs of ostriches, often throwing rock after rock until an egg is breached and its contents can be consumed. White-winged Choughs, ravenlike Australian birds, are reported to employ pieces of mussel shell as hammers in their attempts to open other mussels. Another Australian bird, the Brush Turkey, builds gigantic mounds of soil and decaying vegetation (as much as 36 feet across and 16 feet high) in which to incubate its eggs; the turkey kicks these materials into a pile with its powerful legs. It seems a natural transition for the bird to use debris as a tool (a weapon), by kicking it toward competitors —large monitor lizards that share their rain-forest habitats and compete for the insects and seeds that compose the turkey's diet.

One of the most astonishing examples of the employment of tools by a bird is the use of bait by fishing Green-backed Herons (*Butorides striatus*) in southern Japan. The herons obtain bait as diverse as live insects, berries, twigs, and discarded crackers, and cast them on the waters. They then crouch and wait for the curious or hungry fish that comes to inspect the lure. The birds have even been observed carefully trimming oversized twigs to the proper dimensions—so that like the Woodpecker Finch, the herons actually engage in tool manufacturing. Young herons are less successful bait-fishers than their elders, in part because they tend to use twigs that are too large. While the herons can fish successfully without bait, their use of bait seems to enlarge the catch. You should be on a sharp lookout for similar behavior in North American herons.

Green Jays in Texas have been observed using twigs to extract food from crevices, and an American Robin is recorded as having used a twig to sweep aside leaves, but the only North American bird to habitually use tools is the Brown-headed Nuthatch. At least in one longleaf pine forest in Louisiana, it employs bits of bark to pry off other bits of bark when it searches for insects. Sometimes several pieces of bark are removed and the exposed area searched before a single bark tool is dropped, and the birds have been observed flying from place to place carrying the tools.

This behavior is most common in years when pine seeds, normally a major item in the nuthatches' diet during the fall and winter, are scarce. Tool use may have evolved from the nuthatches' habit of wedging pine seeds into cracks in the flaky bark of the longleaf pines while they hammer them open. That wedging behavior may have led to the accidental prying off of pieces of bark and the exposure of previously hidden insects. Using flakes of bark roughly the size of the pine seeds to remove other bark flakes may have followed. Interestingly Australian sittellas, which look and behave like nuthatches in many ways, but are not even remotely related to them, also use tools. They dip strips of wood into cavities to evict hiding insects.

Finally, it is not unusual to find birds using ants as tools for cleaning or disinfecting their plumage.

Additional careful observation of North American birds will probably reveal other examples of tool use and answer several questions about this interesting behavior. Is the use of tools by Brown-headed Nuthatches wide-

Brown-headed Nuthatch

Supersp #38
Sitta pusilla Latham

NG–314; G–234; PE–212; AE–pl 356; AM(II)–338

2'–10' (0.5'–90')	MF+	4–5 (3–7) MONOG (COOP)	F I: 14 DAYS ALTRICIAL F: 18–19 DAYS MF+	CONIF SEEDS	HAWKS ?

BREEDING: Open stands of pines, mixed pine-hardwood woodland. 1 brood. **DIS-PLAYS:** ? **NEST:** Excavated usu in pine, occ in post, rarely use deserted woodpecker hole; bed of soft bark shreds, grass, forbs, wood chips, hair, feathers. Male selects nest site. **EGGS:** White or off-white, heavily marked with reddish-brown, esp large end. 0.6″ (15 mm). **DIET:** Incl spiders; esp pine seeds. Young fed insects and spiders. **CONSERVATION:** Winter resident. Will use nest boxes. **NOTES:** Occ use bark chip as tool to pry off bark on tree and expose insects. Occ nests attended by 3 birds: helper is unmated male, assists in nest building, maintenance, feeding female on nest, and feeding nestlings and fledglings. Territories maintained all year, defense limited to vicinity of nest cavity. Most frequent clutch size in FL is 4, elsewhere 5. Female broods. Cache pine seeds. Eastern equivalent, ecologically, of Pygmy Nuthatch. When not nesting, form mixed-species flocks with woodpeckers, kinglets, titmice, warblers. **ESSAYS:** Birds, DNA, and Evolutionary Convergence, p. 419; Tool Using, p. 435; Superspecies, p. 375; Hoarding Food, p. 345; Cooperative Breeding, p. 283; Territoriality, p. 387; Mixed-Species Flocking, p. 433. **REFS:** McNair, 1983, 1984; Norris, 1958.

House Wren

Troglodytes aedon Vieillot

NG–316; G–236; PE–214; PW–pl 46; AE–pl 486; AW–pl 529; AM(II)–350

SNAG 0'–20'+?	MF	6–8 (5–12) MONOG (POLYGYN)	FM? I: 13 DAYS ALTRICIAL F: 12–18 DAYS ?	INVERTS	FOLIAGE GLEAN

BREEDING: Open woodland (esp in w), shrubland, farmland, suburbs. 2, rarely 3 broods. **DISPLAYS:** Courtship: male sings while quivering wings, tail raised; female quivers wings. Oft male has already started nests, and dual nest inspection follows. **NEST:** Usu in natural hole, occ in nests of other birds, variety of other cavities. Of twigs, grass, lined with fine materials. **EGGS:** White, marked with browns, occ wreathed. 0.6″ (16 mm). **DIET:** Incl millipedes, spiders, snails. **CONSERVATION:** Winters s throughout Mexico. Rare cowbird host. Readily uses nest boxes. **NOTES:** Male oft builds crude "dummy" nests. Males exhibit strong fidelity to breeding territory. Both male and female oft destroy eggs of other House Wrens and of other species nesting nearby; this behavior is inhibited while birds are tending their own eggs. Carolina Wrens, House Sparrows, and European Starlings compete for nest holes. **ESSAYS:** Incubation: Heating Eggs, p. 393; Polygyny, p. 443; Eggs and Their Evolution, p. 301; DDT and Birds, p. 21; Site Tenacity, p. 189. **REF:** Belles-Isles and Picman, 1986.

A Brown-headed Nuthatch uses a sliver of bark as a tool to pry up another piece of bark.

spread in longleaf pine forests, or highly localized? Is this the only nuthatch species to use tools, or does the western Pygmy Nuthatch do the same? How about the other nuthatches? Was that "sweeping" robin a one-time fluke, or do other robins (or other birds that forage on the ground) occasionally take up tools? Once you've identified a feeding bird, take the time to observe it and note its behavior.

SEE: Anting, p. 487; Bird-Brained, p. 415; Songbird Foraging, p. 381.   REFS: Higuchi, 1986; Morse, 1968.

Bird Biologist—Charles Bendire

Among the army men who helped Spencer Fullerton Baird (p. 569) by collecting specimens and making natural history observations in the West was Charles Emil Bendire (1836–97). A German immigrant, Bendire started in the medical corps as a surgical assistant and eventually became a major. He received medals for bravery in both the Civil and Indian wars. Bendire's principal fascination was with birds' eggs. He became Curator of Oology at the United States National Museum (a division of the Smithsonian Institution), and was author of an outstanding book, *Life Histories of North American Birds, with Special Reference to Their Breeding Habits and Eggs.* He is memorialized by Bendire's Thrasher.

REFS: Choate, 1985; Kastner, 1986.

Winter Wren
Troglodytes troglodytes Linnaeus

NG–316; G–236; PE–214; PW–pl 46; AE–pl 487; AW–pl 527; AM(II)–352

0'–6'	MF	5–6	F I: 11?–16 DAYS ALTRICIAL		FOLIAGE
(To 7'+)		(4–7) POLYGYN	F: 19 DAYS F		GLEAN

BREEDING: Near water in dense conif (rarely decid) forest, oft with heavy understory. 2? broods. **DISPLAYS:** Male squats, quivers wings, moves tail from side to side, gives modified alarm call, then erects back feathers and fans wings. **NEST:** Usu in natural cavity in or under stump, amid roots of upturned tree, and in tree, occ in old woodpecker hole or rock crevice (in arctic); bulky, of moss on base of twigs, lined with feathers, hair. **EGGS:** White, flecked with browns, oft mostly at large end. 0.6" (17 mm). **DIET:** Incl spiders; in winter, rarely takes juniper or cedar berries. **CONSERVATION:** Winter resident along w coast; remainder migratory within U.S. **NOTES:** Male oft builds crude "dummy" nests. Highly polygynous in Europe, apparently so in N.A., as well. Secretive, usu seen in low tangles of veg, around logs, etc. Habitually teeters and bobs. May immerse entire head to obtain aquatic insects. Widespread in Eurasia; only member of wren family found in Old World where known as "the Wren." **ESSAYS:** Vocal Functions, p. 471; Polygyny, p. 443; Island Biogeography, p. 549. **REF:** Kroodsma, 1980.

Carolina Wren
Thryothorus ludovicianus Latham

NG–316; G–236; PE–214; PW–pl 46; AE–pl 489; AM(II)–348

SNAG	MF	5	F I: 12–14 DAYS ALTRICIAL	INVERTS	FOLIAGE
0'–10'		(4–8) MONOG	F: 12–14 DAYS MF	SMALL VERTS	GLEAN BARK GLEAN

BREEDING: Open decid woodland, esp with good cover, farmland, suburbs (less commonly than House Wren). 2 broods in n, oft 3 in s. **DISPLAYS:** ? **NEST:** In natural hole, also amid roots of upturned tree, in variety of other cavities, center of brushpile; of twigs, bark strips, leaves, grass, lined with fine materials. **EGGS:** White, oft pinkish or creamy, usu heavily flecked with browns, purple, oft wreathed. 0.8" (19 mm). **DIET:** Also few seeds. **CONSERVATION:** Winter resident. Uncommon cowbird host. Blue List 1980–81, Special Concern 1982–86; declining in n e, parts of midwest. **NOTES:** Pairs remain together throughout year on permanent territories. Each male sings 27–41 different song types, singing one song repeatedly before switching to a different song type; neighboring males frequently match song types. Male and female duet. Some song elements appropriated from other species. Male prepares nest and takes charge of feeding young while female begins next clutch. **ESSAYS:** Environmental Acoustics, p. 441; Vocal Functions, p. 471; Vocal Copying, p. 469; Blue List, p. 11; Monogamy, p. 597; Territoriality, p. 387. **REFS:** Morton, 1982; Richards, 1981a; Simpson, 1985.

Environmental Acoustics

Two people standing on opposite sides of a rushing stream and attempting to talk to one another are faced with a communication problem. If they shout loudly, their voices may carry above the noise of the water, depending on the distance between them, but their words may not be discernible. In transmitting their songs and calls, birds face similar challenges posed by such obvious problems as running water, wind, rain, physical barriers (rocks and vegetation), and more subtle influences on sound transmission such as humidity and temperature. Only recently have ornithologists begun to consider the role of the environment through which a vocalization must travel as a selective force in the evolution of songs and calls.

A sound traveling through air is attenuated and degraded by an array of environmental features. "Attenuation," the progressive reduction of intensity (loudness), is frequency-dependent and determines the distance that a sound will carry. "Degradation," a change in the pattern of frequency and intensity, is a problem where communication clearly requires more than simple detection of the signal by the receiver. Especially in bird song, receivers must discriminate among signals with different acoustic structures.

The pioneering studies of ornithologist Eugene Morton demonstrated that different habitats pose different problems for successful sound transmission. For instance, in general, the higher the frequency, the greater the attenuation due to absorption and scattering. Thus higher-frequency sounds are less satisfactory for communication in forests (where there is much vegetation to absorb and scatter) than lower-frequency sounds. Lower-frequency sounds are also less influenced by absorption and scattering by the ground, and so would tend to be the frequencies used by birds that generate their sound signals from close to the ground in both densely vegetated and open habitats.

Although Morton found that birds of dense tropical forest habitats have songs with lower average frequencies than birds of adjacent open habitat, no differences were found in song frequencies between birds in similarly contrasting North American habitats. That our forest birds (in contrast to many tropical forest species) rarely sing while standing on the ground or from very low perches may explain this apparent lack of difference. On the other hand, the booming calls of many grouse species and the wing drumming by Ruffed Grouse are very-low-frequency signals that are invariably produced from on or near the ground, both in open and in forested habitats.

Recent studies have shown that the acoustic features of songs used by a species may be closely adapted to habitat characteristics in order to avoid loss of information during singing. Morton and his associates working in Maryland and Florida found that the physical characteristics of songs of Carolina Wrens native to one habitat were retained over a greater distance than were those of Carolina Wrens recorded in another habitat and experi-

Bewick's Wren

Thryomanes bewickii Audubon

NG–316; G–236; PE–214; PW–pl 46; AE–pl 490; AW–pl 526; AM(II)–350

SNAG
0'–20'+?

MF

5–7
(4–11)
MONOG

F
I: 12?–14 DAYS
ALTRICIAL
F: 14 DAYS
MF

FOLIAGE
GLEAN

BREEDING: Open woodland, shrubland, farms, suburbs. >1? brood. **DISPLAYS:** ? **NEST:** In natural cavity, also amid roots of upturned tree, in variety of other cavities, in center of brushpile; of twigs, grass, lined with feathers, grass. **EGGS:** White, flecked with browns, purple, occ wreathed; occ almost unmarked. 0.7" (17 mm). **DIET:** Incl spiders. **CONSERVATION:** In winter, largely resident but some move s to c Mexico. Uncommon cowbird host. Blue List 1972–86; declining everywhere e of Mississippi River. **NOTES:** Male songs show marked geographic variation: males in AZ sing short simple songs but have song repertoires of 15 + songs each; males in CO sing long complex songs but have song repertoires of only ca. 10 songs each; population density, habitat structure, and possibly the vocal milieu associated with avian community composition may influence the nature of geographic variation of songs. Male may build crude "dummy" nests. Occ attack nests of other Bewick's Wrens and of other species nesting nearby. **ESSAYS:** Bird Guilds, p. 493; Blue List, p. 11; Vocal Development, p. 601; Vocal Functions, p. 471. **REF:** Kroodsma, 1985.

Marsh Wren

Cistothorus palustris Wilson

NG–318; G–238; PE–214; PW–pl 46; AE–pl 488; AW–pl 528; AM(II)–354

REEDS

1'–9'
(To 15')

M–F

4–6
(3–10)
POLYGYN

F
I: 12–16 DAYS
ALTRICIAL
F: 13–16 DAYS
F–M

SNAILS

FOLIAGE
GLEAN
HAWKS

BREEDING: Fresh and brackish water marshes with abundant reeds. 2 broods. **DISPLAYS:** Courtship: male takes position 1'–2' above female, fluffs breast feathers, cocks tail over back; looking like ball of feathers, flaps partly folded wings, wags head rapidly from side to side. Male accompanies female as she inspects nest. **NEST:** Attached to reeds, built in layers with entrance usu near top (usu facing s or w); of reeds, grass, lined with fine plant materials, feathers. Male builds, female lines. **EGGS:** Dull brown, usu marked with darker brown, occ wreathed, occ unmarked. 0.7" (17 mm). **DIET:** Incl aquatic insects, occ contents of other birds' eggs. **CONSERVATION:** Winter resident in coastal areas, elsewhere s to c Mexico. **NOTES:** Polygyny more common in w. May actually be 2 species, range divided in e c NE; singing quality strikingly different in the two groups: e birds sing 30–70 songs each, w birds sing 110–210 songs each. Oft destroy eggs and nestlings of other Marsh Wrens and of marsh-nesting blackbirds; blackbirds recognize Marsh Wren as enemy and destroy wren's eggs. Male builds 14–22 nests, only 1–3 used for nesting. Male sings at night. Female broods. Roost in dummy nests in nonbreeding season. Formerly known as Long-billed Marsh Wren. **ESSAYS:** Voices, p. 373; Sexual Selection, p. 251; Polygyny, p. 443; Sibling Species, p. 383. **REFS:** Kroodsma and Canady, 1985; Leonard and Picman, 1987; Picman, 1984; Verner, 1965.

mentally played back in the first. Whether other species show such close local adaptation in song characteristics remains to be explored.

SEE: Sonagrams: Seeing Bird Songs, p. 563; Vocal Dialects, p. 595; Bird Voices, p. 373.   REFS: Gish and Morton, 1981; Morton, 1975; Wiley and Richards, 1982.

Polygyny

Polygyny, where one male mates with more than one female while each female mates with only one male, is thought to be the fundamental mating system of animals. The reason is straightforward. By definition, the sex that produces the larger reproductive cells (eggs) is the female, and the one that produces the smaller (sperm) is the male. Males therefore make a smaller investment in the embryos that result from the fusion of egg and sperm cells. The difference is especially pronounced in birds, since the sperm is microscopic and the egg (relatively) gigantic. The male thus puts proportionately little effort into any single embryo, while the female has a great stake in each one, since she can produce relatively few eggs in her lifetime. Females must therefore exercise care in choosing the fathers of their limited number of young. It would seem, in contrast, that male birds should be much less choosy and attempt to have as many mates as possible, since evolution favors behavior that leads to leaving a maximum number of offspring. A male that mates with a weak or otherwise unfit female loses a small part of his reproductive potential; a female making a similar mistake may sacrifice all or almost all of hers.

Most birds, however, are monogamous. Apparently both parents must help to rear the young if the adults are to have much chance of leaving any genes to posterity. Under what circumstances, then, can polygyny occur? One idea is that polygyny is likely when males hold territories that vary greatly in the quality of resources. Females will tend to choose superior males—by inference those that have high-quality territories. When those males already have mates, females have a choice. They can either select a male that holds an inferior territory, or they can become the second mate of one of the superior males. If the difference between high- and low-quality territories is great enough, the latter strategy will be better—little or no aid from a male holding a resource-rich territory will yield a better chance of producing surviving offspring than the full cooperation of a male with an inferior territory. The male with a superior territory will benefit by increased reproduction, as will the second female.

Often that is precisely what is found. For example, female Marsh Wrens near Seattle, Washington, sometimes mate with already-mated males, even when bachelor males are available. The number of females mated to each male is related to the amount of emergent vegetation in the males' territories, which, in turn, is presumably an indicator of the availability of insect food. Studies of Red-winged and Yellow-headed Blackbirds,

Sedge Wren

Cistothorus platensis Latham

NG–318; G–238; PE–214; PW–pl 46; AE–pl 485; AM(II)–352

GRASS

0'–2'   MF   7   F
                       (4–8)   I: 12–16 DAYS
                       POLYGYN   ALTRICIAL   FOLIAGE
                                  F: 12–14 DAYS   GLEAN
                                  F – M   HAWKS?

BREEDING: Wet meadows, drier marshes with mostly sedges rather than cattails. 2? broods. **DISPLAYS:** ? **NEST:** Ball of dry and green grass interwoven with growing grass, partially hiding it; entrance well concealed on side; lined with fine grass, feathers, hair. **EGGS:** White, unmarked. 0.6″ (16 mm). **DIET:** Incl spiders. **CONSERVATION:** Winters s to c Mexico. Blue List 1979, 1981, Special Concern 1982–86; declining in n e, parts of midwest. **NOTES:** Opportunistic breeder, readily shifting nesting area between years; little apparent site fidelity from year to year. Oft destroy eggs of other Sedge Wrens and of other small species nesting nearby. Males build dummy nests. Unlike Marsh Wrens, neighboring males do not share song-type repertoires and thus do not countersing by matching song types. Roost in nests in nonbreeding season. Formerly known as Short-billed Marsh Wren. **ESSAYS:** Polygyny, p. 443; Blue List, p. 11; Habitat Selection, p. 463; Bird Voices, p. 373; Vocal Functions, p. 471; Site Tenacity, p. 189. **REFS:** Crawford, 1977; Kroodsma and Verner, 1978; Picman and Picman, 1980.

Canyon Wren

Catherpes mexicanus Swainson

NG–318; G–238; PW–pl 46; AE–pl 491; AW–pl 530; AM(II)–346

MF   5–6   ?
            (4–7)   I: ? DAYS
            MONOG   ALTRICIAL   FOLIAGE
                       F: ? DAYS   GLEAN
                       FM?

BREEDING: Arid and semiarid rocky canyons and rock outcrops, occ suburban areas with old stone buildings or other structures providing suitable nesting sites. 2? broods. **DISPLAYS:** ? **NEST:** Also in cave, deserted building; cup of moss, spider web, leaves, catkins, on base of twigs, lined with fine materials. Nests maintained and reused. **EGGS:** White, lightly flecked with reddish-brown, rarely wreathed. 0.7″ (18 mm). **DIET:** Little known; likely insects, perhaps small verts. **CONSERVATION:** Winter resident. **NOTES:** Virtually unstudied. **ESSAYS:** Birds, DNA, and Evolutionary Convergence, p. 419; Bathing and Dusting, p. 429; How Long Can Birds Live?, p. 643; How Do We Find Out About Bird Biology?, p. 319; Determining Diets, p. 535. **REF:** Kroodsma, 1977.

Dickcissels, Indigo Buntings, and Lark Buntings also show clear relationships between various aspects of territory quality and the likelihood that a male holding a given territory will have more than one mate.

Polygyny is not always associated with territoriality. Certain seed-eating savanna species of African weavers (relatives of House Sparrows) have superabundant resources and the males are not territorial, presumably because defending an area does not increase their access to food. The females apparently do not need help from males to raise the young, and the weavers nest in colonies, minimizing the need for a partner in nest defense. The female is thus free to choose any male to father her offspring, regardless of his other attachments. Here, as in situations where males are territorial, polygyny is related to the availability of resources—in this case their super-abundance rather than their uneven distribution.

SEE: Monogamy, p. 597; Polyandry, p. 133; Promiscuity, p. 145; Natural Selection, p. 237; Territoriality, p. 387; Cooperative Breeding, p. 283; Leks, p. 259. REFS: Emlen and Oring, 1977; Orians, 1967; Oring, 1982; Verner, 1964; Verner and Willson, 1966

Masterbuilders

Ornithologists can only speculate on the origins of nest building in birds, but it is thought to have arisen from a shortage of natural cavities for use in sheltering eggs and young. Birds unable to find satisfactory nest holes modified and moved into crevices that were originally unsuitable. With continued shortage, natural selection favored tendencies to excavate compartments in soil and decayed soft wood, to chisel new holes in firm wood, or to search for and assemble materials to augment otherwise marginal sites. The entire panoply of avian construction, from typical open cups and anchored platforms to mud or saliva structures plastered onto firm supports, is thought to have evolved from that simple beginning. The diversity of nests among bird species gives testimony to the numerous kinds of structure that can provide satisfactory shelter, whereas the similarity of nests within a species indicates how highly ritualized nest-building behavior has become.

Many nonpasserines, however, do not use shelters to protect their eggs. Ground-nesting birds with precocial young often simply lay their clutch on the substrate. Others make minimal scrapes or pile available materials into a buffering pad beneath the eggs. Digging shallow scrapes or using ground-level natural cavities is thought to have led to scratching short burrows like those of the Rough-winged Swallow, and eventually to excavating the longer tunnels of kingfishers and puffins. In general, North American birds that do not place their nests under shelter keep their eggs just as warm as those that do. To compensate for the reduced insulation, these birds spend more time on the nest, but the price of being a "sitting duck" includes additional

Rock Wren

Salpinctes obsoletus Say

NG–318; G–238; PE–214; PW–pl 46; AE–pl 492; AW–pl 531; AM(II)–346

| MF | 5–6 (4–8) MONOG | F? I: ? DAYS ALTRICIAL F: ? DAYS MF | | FOLIAGE GLEAN |

BREEDING: Arid and semiarid canyons, valleys with rock outcrops, cliffs, to 10,000' in mountains. 2? broods. **DISPLAYS:** ? **NEST:** In hole or crevice oft under or around rocks, entrance paved with small stone chips; of grass, forbs, rootlets, many other materials, lined with fine materials. **EGGS:** White, lightly flecked with reddish-brown. 0.7" (18 mm). **DIET:** Little known; likely insects, spiders, earthworms, perhaps small vertebrates. **CONSERVATION:** Winters in s and w portions of breeding range. Occ cowbird host. **NOTES:** Neighboring territorial males tend to countersing with similar song types. Individual males have song repertoires of >100 songs each. Little studied in the field. **ESSAYS:** Vocal Functions, p. 471; Island Biogeography, p. 549; How Do We Find Out About Bird Biology?, p. 319; Determining Diets, p. 535. **REFS:** Kroodsma, 1975; Wolf et al., 1985.

Cactus Wren

Campylorhynchus brunneicapillus Lafresnaye

NG–318; G–238; PW–pl 46; AE–pl 493; AW–pl 532; AM(II)–344

CACTUS

| 2'–6' (To 30') | MF | 3–4 (2–5) MONOG | F I: 16 DAYS ALTRICIAL F: 19–23 DAYS MF | SM VERTS FRUIT SEEDS | FOLIAGE GLEAN |

BREEDING: Desert with large cacti, other thorny plants capable of supporting bulky nests at least 2'–3' above ground, desert suburbs. 2 broods, occ 3. **DISPLAYS:** Pair perform display-growl greeting: male extends wings and tail and "growls"; female does same in response, then crouches and refolds wings. **NEST:** Esp in cholla cactus, tree yucca, also in desert shrub or tree. Pouch-shaped mass ca. 1' across with internal chamber reached by narrow passage; of forbs, grass, lined usu with feathers, occ grass. Nests maintained and used for roosting. Completed in 7–10 days; lining added throughout incubation. Female selects site. **EGGS:** Pinkish, usu marked with reddish-brown, occ wreathed. 0.9" (24 mm). **DIET:** 15%–20% fruit, berries, seeds (more than other wrens), nectar. **CONSERVATION:** Winter resident. **NOTES:** Pairs resident on year-round territories. Female roosts in breeding nest, oft starting before laying. Male constructs new nest while female incubates; used for second clutch or for roosting by adult or fledgling. Hatching asynchronous; female broods. Females disperse farther than males. Roost singly in old nests within territory in winter, occ building new nest. **ESSAYS:** Habitat Selection, p. 463; Masterbuilders, p. 445; Territoriality, p. 387. **REFS:** Anderson and Anderson, 1973; Ricklefs, 1975.

exposure to predators. There is speculation that a shift from nesting on the ground to building elevated nests or moving breeding colonies to offshore islands paralleled the evolutionary diversification of mammalian predators.

Cavity nesting protects eggs and young not only from predators but also from harsh weather. Thus, the orientation of the entrance may be intentionally selected to modify the temperature of the nest. The entrances of woodpeckers' holes, for example, often face in a direction that increases solar exposure. Similarly, the first broods of Cactus Wrens and Verdins are raised in nests with entrances facing away from cold winds, whereas the nest entrances containing second broods are oriented toward cool afternoon breezes.

Of the approximately 470 passerine species (perching birds) in North

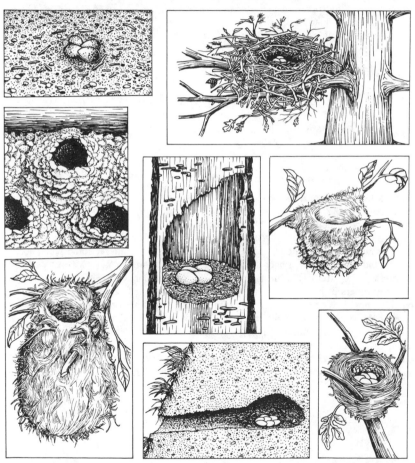

Examples of nests. Center: woodpecker. Outer, clockwise from upper left: Killdeer, Red-shouldered Hawk, vireo, finch, kingfisher, oriole, Cliff Swallow.

Arctic Warbler
Phylloscopus borealis Blasius

NG–320; G–254; PW–pl 51; AW–667; AM(III)–34

 OVEN F
I: ? DAYS
ALTRICIAL
F: 11–12 (?) DAYS
MF (?)
  HOVER &
GLEAN

F   6–7
(5–7)
MONOG ?

BREEDING: Northern conif and conif-decid woodland, shrubland, riparian thickets. 1 brood. **DISPLAYS:** ? **NEST:** Domed, with entrance hole on one side, loosely constructed of fine grass, leaves, moss, lined with fine grass, hair. **EGGS:** White, spotted with pink or reddish-brown, occ wreathed. 0.6″ (16 mm). **DIET:** Incl esp mosquitoes. **CONSERVATION:** Winters from s e Asia to Phillippines, Moluccas, and East Indies. **NOTES:** Oft assoc with willows; remains mostly in canopies of larger trees. Widespread in n Eurasia. Unstudied in N.A. **ESSAYS:** Birds, DNA, and Evolutionary Convergence, p. 419; How Do We Find Out About Bird Biology?, p. 319; Masterbuilders, p. 445. **REF:** Gabrielson and Lincoln, 1959.

Golden-crowned Kinglet
Regulus satrapa Lichtenstein

NG–322; G–252; PE–216; PW–pl 49; AE–pl 458; AW–pl 509; AM(III)–36

   F
I: 14–15 DAYS
ALTRICIAL
F: 14–19 DAYS
MF
TREE
SAP
FRUIT
HOVER &
GLEAN
HAWKS

4′–60′   F   8–9
(5–11)
MONOG

BREEDING: Open conif forest. 2 broods. **DISPLAYS:** Courtship feeding. Cop on or near nest. **NEST:** Near trunk, usu hung from branches; open at top with oblong cavity, of moss, lichen, spider web, plant down, dead leaves, lined with fine materials. Built in ca. 5 days. **EGGS:** Creamy white to muddy cream, variably spotted with browns, usu wreathed. 0.5″ (14 mm). **DIET:** Incl spiders; some fruit, seeds. Young fed only insects, reject spiders. Also gleans from bark. **CONSERVATION:** Winters s to Guatemala. Blue List 1980–81, Special Concern 1982, Local Concern 1986; numbers in most regions appear to have recovered from earlier decline. Rare cowbird host. **NOTES:** Adults very tame at nest. Eggs are crowded into two layers in nest. Male occ feeds incubating female. Second clutch oft as large as first. Flicks wings when moving amongst foliage. Winters in mixed-species flocks with chickadees, Brown Creepers, small woodpeckers. **ESSAYS:** Blue List, p. 11; Mixed-Species Flocking, p. 433; Variation in Clutch Sizes, p. 339; Courtship Feeding, p. 181; Incubation: Heating Eggs, p. 393. **REF:** Galati and Galati, 1985.

America, only 23 percent use holes or build domed structures while 77 percent have open nests. Assuming that enclosed sites offer more protection, why do so many passerines build open nests? One answer may be that both the birds and their nests are usually small. Small birds may have shifted to open-nest construction because a larger species could readily usurp a tree hole from them. To take over a hole, a bigger bird simply needed to enlarge the entrance. The absence of doming reduces overall size, presumably making open nests less obvious to predators. Detection of open nests by predators can be minimized by using, as does the Purple Finch, only nest materials that blend into the nest site. Pendulous nests (suspended nests typified by those of orioles) may be more obvious, but are often attached to the far end of slender branches where they are relatively safe from climbing predators and larger avian nest robbers. Some species nest in plants that have sharp thorns or other physical defenses. Cactus and House Wrens, Curve-billed and Bendire's Thrashers, and Mourning, White-winged and Inca Doves, among others, may place their nests within the protection provided by cacti. Vireos, among others, incorporate spiderwebs and lichens, which not only help conceal and bind the structure, but also help it to shed water.

A few birds seek the assistance of other animal species. Such protective associations usually involve nesting near organisms that may discourage predators or parasites from approaching. Mississippi Kites, Aplomado Falcons, and other raptors have been known to associate with bees and wasps, which may ward off botflies that feed on their chicks. Numerous raptors seek out ants, which may clean parasites from the nests. Raptors may also permit small birds such as House Sparrows and kingbirds to build their tiny nests in the raptors' ample platforms or to be close neighbors. These small birds sound the alarm when an intruder approaches, but are not threatened by their predatory "hosts," which ordinarily do not hunt near their own nests.

Numerous bird species now find themselves associating with people. It is evident that avian nest placement is undergoing a transition as human and bird populations increasingly interact. Ground-nesting Herring Gulls, Common Nighthawks, and Killdeers are opportunistic and adapt particularly well to urban sites, especially rooftops. Precocial roof-reared Killdeer young have been known to withstand roof surface temperatures of 138° F and to survive falls from 50-foot heights. These young, however, have been unable to cope with parapets—traps from which they cannot escape before starving. The abundance and distribution of many bird species in the future will be determined in no small part by their ability to nest in human-created habitats.

SEE: Nest Materials, p. 369; Nest Lining, p. 391; Nest Sanitation, p. 315; Feathered Nests. p. 605; Hormones and Nest Building, p. 547; Disease and Parasitism, p. 399; Incubation: Heating Eggs, p. 393; Cooperative Breeding, p. 283. REFS: Collias and Collias, 1984; Fisk, 1978; Inouye, 1976; Inouye et al., 1981; Louther, 1977; Parker, 1981; Skutch, 1976

Ruby-crowned Kinglet

Regulus calendula Linnaeus

NG–322; G–252; PE–216; PW–pl 49; AE–pl 459; AW–pl 510; AM(III)–36

15'–30'	F?		7–9	F I: 12? DAYS ALTRICIAL	TREE	HOVER &
(2'–100')			(5–11)	F: 12? DAYS	SAP	GLEAN
			MONOG	MF	BERRIES	HAWKS

BREEDING: Conif and conif-decid forests. ? broods. **DISPLAYS:** Male displays with red crest erect, singing a "wheezy, subdued song." **NEST:** Hung from limb, open at top with cavity deep enough to conceal incubating bird; of moss, lichen, down, twigs, dead leaves, lined with fine materials. **EGGS:** Creamy white to muddy cream, variably spotted with brown, usu wreathed. 0.5″ (14 mm). **DIET:** Incl spiders; few seeds. **CONSERVATION:** Winters s to w Guatemala. Rare cowbird host. **NOTES:** Winter studies suggest that size of N.A. breeding populations may be limited by conditions experienced during the winter. Forms loose, mixed-species winter flocks with titmice, nuthatches, Brown Creepers, Golden-crowned Kinglets, and warblers. **ESSAYS:** Bird Guilds, p. 493; Mixed-Species Flocking, p. 433; Population Dynamics, p. 575. **REF:** Laurenzi et al., 1982.

Blue-gray Gnatcatcher

Polioptila caerulea Linnaeus

NG–322; G–252; PE–216; PW–pl 46; AE–pl 443; AW–pl 495; AM(III)–38

2'–25'	MF		4–5	MF I: 13 DAYS ALTRICIAL	HOVER &
(To 80')			MONOG	F: 10–12 DAYS	GLEAN
				MF	HAWKS

BREEDING: A habitat generalist: decid forest, woodland, swamp, scrub, chaparral, desert. 1 brood, 2 in far s. **DISPLAYS:** No well-marked courtship ritual. **NEST:** Saddled on horizontal limb or in fork; compact, of plant down and similar materials held together with insect and spider silk, covered on outside with bits of lichen, lined with fine materials. **EGGS:** Pale blue to bluish-white, flecked with browns, occ wreathed, rarely unmarked. 0.6″ (14 mm). **DIET:** Incl spiders. **CONSERVATION:** Winters s to Bahamas, w Greater Antilles, Guatemala and Honduras. Common cowbird host. **NOTES:** Territorial boundaries shift as food resources change through nesting cycle. Extremely active, tail always flicking up and down or side to side. At some nests only female broods, at others task shared. **ESSAYS:** Decline of Eastern Songbirds, p. 495; Bird Guilds, p. 493; Mobbing, p. 425; Territoriality, p. 387; Cowbirds, p. 619; Parental Care, p. 555. **REF:** Root, 1967.

Bird Names—X

The generic name of the gnatcatchers, *Polioptila*, means "gray-feathered" in Greek, noting the gray edging on the primaries. That of the kinglets, *Regulus*, is Latin for "little king." *Ortalis*, the genus of the chachalacas is Greek for "young bird"; chachalaca itself is a good imitation of the noisy birds' calls. Pigeon goes back to the Old French *pijon*, also a "young bird." Passenger Pigeon was a "bird of passage." Dove probably derives from the Anglo-Saxon word for "dive," referring to a dove's erratic flight. The Mourning Dove has a mournful call.

The Wild Turkey got its name from an erroneous notion of its country of origin. Its scientific name, *Meleagris gallopavo* means in Latin "a Guinea fowl, a peacock," thus having been named by Linnaeus for African and Asian species. Trogons are more accurately named, from the Latin for "gnawer," referring to their tooth-edged bills. One of the seemingly least appropriate generic names of birds, *Protonotaria*, belongs to the Prothonotary Warbler. Baird (p. 569) gave it the name, which means in Latin "authorized scribe." Coues (p. 565), quite logically asked, "why?" Perhaps Baird was honoring his secretary.

Auk comes from the Old Norse "alka" given to several seabirds. Murre is probably a name in a Celtic dialect for "auk" or "guillemot." Kittlitz's Murrelet and Xantus' Murrelets are named after their collectors. Guillemot is a diminutive of the French for "William." Puffin means "little puff," and may refer either to the appearance of the adults or the downy young.

REF: Choate, 1985; Owen, 1985.

Black-tailed Gnatcatcher
Polioptila melanura Linnaeus

NG–322; G–252; PW–pl 46; AW–pl 494; AM(III)–38

1'–4' MF 4 MF
              (3–5) I: 14 DAYS
              MONOG ALTRICIAL
                      F: 9–15 DAYS
                      MF

HOVER &
GLEAN

BREEDING: Mesquite and creosote bush, other desert scrub. ? broods. **DISPLAYS:** ? **NEST:** Usu in fork of small shrub; compact, of plant down and similar materials bound with insect and spider silk, lined with fine materials. **EGGS:** Pale blue to bluish-white, lightly spotted with browns, occ wreathed, rarely almost unmarked. 0.6" (14 mm). **DIET:** Incl few spiders; occ seeds. **CONSERVATION:** Winter resident. Special Concern 1982, Local Concern 1986; status unclear. Uncommon cowbird host. **NOTES:** Very active, with tail flicking up and down or side to side. Plumage and vocalizations of coastal CA populations ("Plumbeous Gnatcatcher") differ from inland populations; may be separate species, but field studies are needed. **ESSAYS:** Blue List, p. 11; Species and Speciation, p. 355; Sibling Species, p. 383; How Do We Find Out About Bird Biology?, p. 319. **REF:** Phillips et al., 1964.

Eastern Bluebird
Sialia sialis Linnaeus

NG–324; G–250; PE–220; PW–pl 48; AE–pl 440; AM(III)–46

2'–50'? F 4–5 F
              (2–7) I: 12–14 DAYS
              MONOG ALTRICIAL
                      F: 15–20 DAYS
                      MF

FRUIT

FOLIAGE
GLEAN

BREEDING: Forest edge, burned or cutover woodland, open country with scattered trees. 2, occ 3 broods. **DISPLAYS:** Courting male sings and flutters in front of female, wings half open, tail spread, then perches beside and preens female, and may offer food. **NEST:** Oft in woodpecker-excavated cavity; loose cup of grass, weed stems, pine needles, twigs, occ with hair or feathers. Built in avg 10–11 days. Female occ builds >1 nest. **EGGS:** Pale blue, occ white, unmarked. 0.8" (21 mm). **DIET:** Incl earthworms, snails, other inverts; esp berries. Young fed primarily insects. Hawking oft from low perch, catching insects near ground. Very dependent on berries in winter. **CONSERVATION:** Winters mostly within U.S. Blue List 1972, 1978–82, Special Concern 1986. Felling dead trees and removing dead branches reduces nest holes and increases competition with other cavity-nesting species (esp House Sparrows and European Starlings). Nest boxes now maintain populations that have declined by up to 90% this century. Rare cowbird host. **NOTES:** Young from previous brood occ help at parent's nest. Broods oft derived from >1 female and/or >1 male, indicating less than total fidelity by both sexes, and egg dumping by some females. Oft successfully defend nest hole against swallows or House Sparrows (but not starlings), although sparrows occ kill bluebird adults and nestlings. Female broods. Winter flocks to 100+; oft roost singly or in small groups in nest boxes. **ESSAYS:** Avian Invaders, p. 633; Great Plains Hybrids, p. 625; Monogamy, p. 597; Blue List, p. 11; Helping to Conserve Birds—Local Level, p. 361; Starlings, p. 489. **REFS:** Gowaty, 1985; Pinkowski, 1979; Zeleny, 1976.

Altruism

Some kinds of bird behavior can be interpreted as altruistic—that is, one bird seems to put itself at risk to help another. A classic example is the bird in a flock that spots a predator and gives an alarm call, alerting the rest of the group. Another is the bird that joins in mobbing a hawk, perhaps teaching juveniles that the hawk is an enemy. Why doesn't the first bird keep quiet and keep to the far side of the flock, rather than risk attracting the attention of the predator by calling? What evolutionary explanation could there be for a bird spending its time and energy (and perhaps getting injured or killed) to teach others about the danger of hawks? After all, the rule in natural selection is to leave as many offspring as possible, and self-sacrifice rarely seems a route to reproductive success. Intuitively, one would think that there would be strong selection *against* altruistic behavior, making its evolution unlikely.

How, then, does behavior that appears altruistic evolve? There are two ways. One is when the so-called altruistic behavior actually turns out to be selfish. For instance, the "altruistic" alarm call could be ventriloquial, preventing the predator from locating the caller. By scaring the rest of the flock into flight, the caller may be manipulating the other birds into rising from the grass, thereby calling themselves to the attention of the predator. The caller, presumably having seen the predator first, may be improving its chances to get away in the ensuing confusion—at the expense of its unprepared colleagues.

Similarly, a small bird mobbing a hawk may not be truly altruistic; it may be protecting itself. Perhaps it is safer to keep the enemy close and in view and try to drive it away, than to wonder where the hawk is and what it is doing.

The second way such behavior could evolve works even if the actions are truly altruistic from the viewpoint of immediate individual survival (and there is evidence in mammals that some alarm calls are altruistic in this sense). Altruism of that sort *can* be favored by natural selection if the individual or individuals helped are relatives of the altruist. The most obvious case is when a parent sacrifices its life to help its offspring, in the process assuring the parent's genes are well represented in the breeders of the next generation. The act is directly altruistic but evolutionarily selfish. Altruism toward more distant relatives can also be favored through a form of natural selection called "kin selection." In this case, the altruist is helping to pass on, not its own genes (as it does when aiding its offspring), but genes that are identical with its own but are carried by its kin.

For instance, half of a hatchling's genes are duplicates of genes of the father, passed on through the sperm; the other half come from the mother, passed on through the egg. Parents each share 50 percent of their genes with their offspring. Brothers and sisters also share half of each other's genes on average, as can be seen from the following example: A mother bird can be thought of as having two versions of each of her thousands of kinds of

Western Bluebird

Sialia mexicana Swainson

NG–324; G–250; PW–pl 48; AW–pl 500; AM(III)–46

| 2'–50'? | MF | 4–6 (3–8) MONOG? | F I: ? DAYS ALTRICIAL F: ? DAYS MF | FRUIT | FOLIAGE GLEAN |

BREEDING: Open, riparian, burned, or cutover woodlands, other open country with scattered trees. 2? broods. **DISPLAYS:** Courting male sings and flutters in front of female, wings half open, tail spread, then perches beside and preens female, and may offer food. **NEST:** Oft in woodpecker-excavated cavity; loose cup of grass, weed stems, pine needles, twigs, occ with hair or feathers. **EGGS:** Pale blue to bluish-white, occ white, unmarked. 0.8″ (21 mm). **DIET:** Incl earthworms, snails, other inverts; esp berries. Young presumably fed primarily insects. Hawking oft from low perch catching insects near ground. **CONSERVATION:** Winters mostly within U.S. Blue List 1972, 1978–81, Special Concern 1982, Local Concern 1986; decline continues in some areas. Felling dead trees and removing dead branches reduces nest holes and increases competition with other cavity-nesting species (esp House Sparrows and European Starlings). Will use nest boxes. Rare cowbird host. **NOTES:** Oft successfully defend nest hole against swallows, House Wrens, and House Sparrows. **ESSAYS:** European Starlings, p. 489; Blue List, p. 11; Helping to Conserve Birds—Local Level, p. 361; Great Plains Hybrids, p. 625; Avian Invaders, p. 633. **REF:** Bent, 1949.

Mountain Bluebird

Sialia currucoides Bechstein

NG–324; G–250; PE–220; PW–pl 48; AE–pl 441; AW–pl 496; AM(III)–48

| 2'–50'? | | 5–6 (4–8) MONOG | F I: 13–14 DAYS ALTRICIAL F: 22–23 DAYS MF | | HOVER & POUNCE HOVER & GLEAN |

BREEDING: Open conif and decid forests, subalpine meadows, other open country, usu above 7000'. Usu 2 broods. **DISPLAYS:** ? **NEST:** Oft in woodpecker-excavated cavity; loose cup of grass, weed stems, pine needles, twigs, occ with hair or feathers. Female selects site. **EGGS:** Pale blue to bluish-white, rarely white, unmarked. 0.8″ (22 mm). **DIET:** Also takes fruit, esp in winter. Young fed insects. Oft hovers while foraging from ground or hawking from low perch. **CONSERVATION:** Winters s to c Mexico. Populations have declined markedly this century. Flickers, swallows, House Sparrows, and starlings compete for nesting sites. Rare cowbird host. **NOTES:** Oft successfully defends nest hole against swallows, House Wrens, and House Sparrows. Female broods through day 6. Young independent at 22–28 days postfledging. Birds reared in nest box imprint to it and preferentially select that type of box for breeding. **ESSAYS:** Great Plains Hybrids, p. 625; Color of Birds, p. 111; Helping to Conserve Birds—Local Level, p. 361; European Starlings, p. 489. **REFS:** Herlugson, 1981; Power, 1980.

genes, but only one of the two goes into each egg. Suppose the two kinds of her "A" gene are A^1 and A^2. Each nestling has a 50 percent chance of getting A^1, and a 50 percent chance of getting A^2. What, then, are the chances of two nestlings from the same clutch both getting A^1 or both getting A^2 from mom? This problem is analogous to the probability that two people, each flipping a coin, will both get the same result. That will occur half of the time, since the possible outcomes are HT (Joe gets a head and Sam a tail), HH (both get heads), TH (Joe a tail and Sam a head), and TT (both tails). The chances of one offspring getting A^1 and the other A^1 or of one offspring getting A^2 and the other A^2 is the same as getting either HH or TT—that is, 50 percent.

The same reasoning applies not just to "A" genes but to all the kinds of genes in both the mother and the father, so that half of the genes of one sibling are identical with those found in the other sibling. Thus a brother and sister have the same "genetic relatedness" as a parent and child. By similar reasoning it can be shown that grandparents and grandchildren share a quarter of their genes with each other, first cousins an eighth of their genes, and so on. From an evolutionary perspective, then, natural selection could favor a bird sacrificing its life to save four of its siblings—unless in the process that bird was giving up the chance to fledge more than four offspring of its own (four siblings or four offspring represent identical genetic "contributions" for an individual). On the other hand, a bird should not sacrifice itself to save one first cousin unless it "knew" it would have no additional offspring and its death would not jeopardize either its own young or siblings.

Of course, neither birds nor people keep precise track of relatives and make conscious decisions about the probabilities of a given act promoting a certain proportion of genes identical with their own. Nevertheless, there is considerable evidence that kin selection can cause directly altruistic behaviors to evolve. All that is required is for the altruist to help close relatives more than nonrelatives and for the risk to the altruist to be relatively small. This is commonly seen among cooperatively breeding birds, where some individuals forgo the opportunity of breeding in a given year when the probability of breeding success is low, and instead help to rear their brothers and sisters. The probability of the altruists breeding successfully in the following year presumably will be greater or, at least, no worse.

SEE: Natural Selection, p. 237; Cooperative Breeding, p. 283; Flock Defense, p. 235; Mobbing, p. 425. REF: Krebs and Davies, 1984.

Townsend's Solitaire

Myadestes townsendi Audubon

NG–324; G–246; PE–218; PW–pl 48; AW–pl 476; AM(III)–50

SNAG	CAVITY	4	? I: ? DAYS	FRUIT	FOLIAGE
0'–10'	?	(3–5) MONOG	ALTRICIAL F: ? DAYS MF		GLEAN GRND GLEAN

BREEDING: Open montane conif forest on steep rocky slopes in about a 3,000' band below timberline. 1 brood, 2? in s. **DISPLAYS:** ? **NEST:** Oft amid tree roots or other shelter on ground; on base of trash, twigs, sticks, faded grass, with neat shallow cup of fine dry grass stems. **EGGS:** Dull white to light blue, marked with browns, occ wreathed. 0.9″ (24 mm). **DIET:** Incl spiders, worms; esp berries. Young fed mostly insects. Winter diet occ exclusively berries. **CONSERVATION:** Winters s to c Mexico. **NOTES:** Breeding biology little known. Defends exclusive winter territories to protect supply of berries; each territory supplies total food for duration of winter. When berry supply is poor, winter territories also defended interspecifically to ensure adequate berry supply. **ESSAYS:** Territoriality, p. 387; Interspecific Territoriality, p. 385; How Do We Find Out About Bird Biology?, p. 319. **REF:** Salomonson and Balda, 1977.

Wood Thrush

Hylocichla mustelina Gmelin

NG–326; G–248; PE–222; PW–pl 48; AE–pl 500; AM(III)–54

CONIF	F	3–4	F I: 13–14 DAYS	FRUIT	FOLIAGE
TREE 6'–50'		(2–4) MONOG	ALTRICIAL F: 12 DAYS MF		GLEAN

BREEDING: Decid or decid-conif forest, esp near water, occ near human habitation. Oft 2 broods. **DISPLAYS:** Female fluffs feathers and raises wings, then swift circling flights, with male following female; pair then feed together. **NEST:** Bulky, compact cup of weed stalks, grass, on base of leaves, middle layer of mud, lined with fine dark rootlets. Frequent use of white paper or rag in base of nest may serve to break up its outline. **EGGS:** Greenish-blue, unmarked. 1.0″ (25 mm). **DIET:** Incl spiders, etc.; fruit oft over ⅓ diet. Reportedly at least some fruit fed to young. **CONSERVATION:** Winters s through e Mexico to Panama and n w Colombia. Frequent cowbird host. **NOTES:** Prefers nest habitat with moist substrate; expands range of breeding habitats in the absence of Veery. Young begin to forage at 20–23 days, may still beg up to 32 days. Experimental displacements of breeding birds from their territories demonstrated an ability to navigate successfully and return from distances of 4 to >10 miles. Exhibits relatively little geographic variation in song patterns. **ESSAYS:** Decline of Eastern Songbirds, p. 495; Navigation and Orientation, p. 559; Cowbirds, p. 619; Habitat Selection, p. 463; Vocal Dialects, p. 595. **REFS:** Able et al., 1984; Bertin, 1977; Noon, 1981; Whitney and Miller, 1987.

Life in the Egg

Life is a continuum, but in people, birds, and most other organisms it is a continuum of alternating stages defined by the chromosomal complement of cells. Chromosomes are tiny structures of the cell that contain most of the DNA, the giant molecules (in the form of a double helix) that contain the coded genetic information. In the "haploid" stage, the cells contain a single set of chromosomes—each represented only once. In the "diploid" stage, which alternates with the haploid, each chromosome is represented twice in the cells. Eggs and sperm are the haploid stage; embryos and adults are the diploid stage.

In birds, the fusion of egg and sperm cells occurs while the egg cell is still high in the female's oviduct, before the shell is put on, and development is initiated. (In chickens and turkeys, development has been observed to occur without fertilization, leading to an individual carrying copies of only the mother's chromosomes. This parthenogenetic type of development is presumed to be abortive in wild populations.) The "genes," the genetic information in the chromosomes, control the development of the alternating stages. In the cell that results from the fusion of sperm and egg (the "zygote"), genes oversee the transformation of that single cell into an adult bird containing many billions of cells. The process consists of a sequence of cell divisions; the zygote gives rise to 2 daughter cells, each of which divides to produce 2 granddaughters of the zygote. Division after division follows, through 8, 16, 32, 64 cells, and so on. At each division, the chromosomes are copied, and a complete set is deposited in each daughter cell.

Each cell, then, gets the same genetic information. A skin cell that helps form a feather, a muscle cell, and a brain cell, are all quite different from the original zygote, and from each other, but they all have the same instructions. How they get to be so different is the central mystery of the science of embryology (or, as it is more commonly called today, "developmental biology").

The cell nucleus, the tiny structure containing the chromosomes, has been experimentally removed from a frog zygote and replaced by the nucleus of a cell from an adult frog's intestine. That modified zygote, containing the nucleus with the genetic instructions from a gut cell, proceeded to develop into a complete adult frog. Why, then, isn't every gut cell in a frog producing adults? It is because the environment of the gut is very different from that of a zygote, and in the intestinal environment genes different from those that function in a zygote are active.

Thus a general solution to the mystery of development is known. It is believed that it is the environment of a cell—the chemical substances to which it is exposed and the other cells with which it is in contact—that turns genes on and off. Genes appropriate to cellular functioning in that environment give "instructions" to the cell; inappropriate genes remain quiescent. In that way, the environment determines how the cells, and thus the tissues and organs of which the cells are the basic structural and functional

Veery

Catharus fuscescens Stephens

NG–326; G–248; PE–222; PW–pl 48; AE–pl 499; AW–pl 540; AM(III)–52

			F		
			I: 10–12 DAYS		
SHRUB	F	4	ALTRICIAL	FRUIT	SWOOPS
0'–6'		(3–5)	F: 10 DAYS		FOLIAGE
(To 25')		MONOG	MF		GLEAN

BREEDING: Shaded moist woodland (esp poplar, aspen) with understory. 1 brood, 2? in s. **DISPLAYS:** Agonistic: birds draw heads back, bills up at 45° and slightly to side, may also flick wings, raise crests. **NEST:** Substantial, of grass, bark strips, weed stems, twigs, moss, lining of soft bark, dry leaves. **EGGS:** Pale blue, usu unmarked, rarely marked with browns. 0.9" (23 mm). **DIET:** Incl spiders; some fruit, esp in fall and winter. Young fed insects. Oft feed by flying from low perch to ground and then returning to perch; also hawks insects. **CONSERVATION:** Winters in S.A. from n Colombia e to Guyana and s to Amazonia and c Brazil. Common cowbird host. **NOTES:** Prefers nest habitat with moist substrate; expands range of breeding habitats where Hermit and Swainson's Thrushes are absent. **ESSAYS:** Decline of Eastern Songbirds, p. 495; Habitat Selection, p. 463; Bathing and Dusting, p. 429; Cowbirds, p. 619. **REFS:** Bertin, 1977; Dilger, 1956a, b; Noon, 1981.

Swainson's Thrush

Catharus ustulatus Nuttall

NG–326; G–248; PE–222; PW–pl 48; AE–pl 502; AW–pl 538; AM(III)–52

			F		
			I: 12–14 DAYS		
CONIF	F	3–4	ALTRICIAL	FRUIT	HAWKS
4'–20'		(3–5)	F: 10–13 DAYS		HOVER &
(0'–40')		MONOG	MF		GLEAN

BREEDING: Woodland, conif forest edge (esp where damp), orchards, riparian thickets. ? broods. **DISPLAYS:** Agonistic: wing flicking, crest raising, also sleeked erect posture with bill pointed upward. **NEST:** In shrubs (usu in w) or low in conif tree (e); bulky, of weeds, rotten wood, bark, twigs, grass, moss, occ middle layer of mud, lining of skeletonized leaves, plant fibers, fine rootlets, lichen. **EGGS:** Pale blue, spotted with browns, occ nearly unmarked. 0.8" (22 mm). **DIET:** Incl spiders; berries, esp in winter. Young fed insects, perhaps some fruit. Also gleans from ground. **CONSERVATION:** Winters from c Mexico s to Guyana, w Brazil, Peru, Bolivia, n w Argentina, and Paraguay. Rare cowbird host. **NOTES:** The least terrestrial of the eastern "ground-dwelling" thrushes. Unlike most N.A. passerines, postbreeding molt is oft begun after departure from breeding grounds. **ESSAYS:** Decline of Eastern Songbirds, p. 495; Island Biogeography, p. 549; Molting, p. 529; Bathing and Dusting, p. 429. **REFS:** Cherry, 1985; Dilger, 1956a, b; Noon, 1981.

units, develop in the proper manner. It sees to it that beaks do not get placed on wingtips, and feathers do not grow inside kidneys.

Some of the details of bird embryology are well known, thanks to intensive research on the domestic chicken. Indeed, generations of biology students have studied the embryology of the chick. The zygote begins development on the surface of the yolk, which is the main energy source for the chick embryo. The "white" (albumen) of the egg provides a sterile, protective, cushioned surrounding for the yolk and the developing embryo. A series of membranes carries out functions for the developing embryo; one (the amnion) cushions it so that no matter how an egg is turned, the embryo always remains "up."

Division of the zygote produces a flat disk of cells, which exist in different microenvironments. For instance, cells at the edge of the disk have less contact with other cells and more contact with the environment outside of the embryo than do those at the center. These differences lead in a complex process to the formation of three layers of cells, creating further environmental differences among cells in different positions, and providing them with different destinies. For example, the skin and nervous system will be derived from the upper layer, the gut and lungs from the lower, and muscles and bones from the middle. Gradually, within two to three days after fertilization, the beginnings of a head, tail, nervous system, and limbs can be seen under a microscope. At this stage a chick embryo looks much like a pig or human embryo. Gradually the chick embryo takes on its avian character. Within eight to ten days the forelimbs can be seen developing into wings, and the start of feather development can be detected. How far that development will go before hatching will depend on whether the bird is altricial or precocial—the former are hatched at an earlier developmental stage than the latter.

SEE: Eggs and Their Evolution, p. 301; Hatching, p. 233; Precocial and Altricial Young, p. 581; Incubation: Heating Eggs, p. 393; Facts, Hypotheses, and Theories, p. 567.

Range Expansion

The geographic areas occupied by bird species change through time. For example, various woodland and forest edge species moved into the Great Plains as farmyards, suburbs, and city parks provided nesting trees. The Inca Dove, having adapted to life in Mexican pueblos, first arrived at Laredo, Texas, in 1866 and then gradually spread north of the border as human settlements created suitable habitat. Inca Doves have been seen as far north as Kansas and Arkansas, and as far west as southern California. Gardens

Gray-cheeked Thrush

Catharus minimus Lafresnaye

NG–326; G–248; PE–222; PW–pl 48; AE–pl 498; AW–pl 539; AM(III)–52

			F		
0'–10'	F	3–5	I: 13–14 DAYS	FRUIT	
(To 20')		(3–6?)	ALTRICIAL		
		MONOG	F: 11–13 DAYS		
			MF		

BREEDING: Moist woodland to arctic tundra, conif forest edge, riparian thickets. 1 brood, 2? in s. **DISPLAYS:** Courting male pursues female in swift flight with crest erect and bill gaping. **NEST:** Substantial, of grass, sedge, bark, weed stems, twigs, moss, lining of grass, fine rootlets, occ few dry leaves. **EGGS:** Pale blue, usu faintly spotted with browns, some nearly unmarked. 0.9″ (23 mm). **DIET:** Incl berries, esp in fall and winter. Young fed insects. **CONSERVATION:** Winters in S.A. from Colombia, Venezuela, Trinidad, and Guyana s to n Peru and n w Brazil. **NOTES:** Habitat generalist in migration, found in virtually any habitat. **ESSAYS:** Decline of Eastern Songbirds, p. 495; Island Biogeography, p. 549; Bathing and Dusting, p. 429; Migration, p. 183. **REFS:** Dilger, 1956a, b; Noon, 1981.

Hermit Thrush

Catharus guttatus Pallas

NG–326; G–248; PE–222; PW–pl 48; AE–pl 501; AW–pl 541; AM(III)–54

			F		
TREE	F	4	I: 12–13 DAYS	FRUIT	FOLIAGE
0'–8'		(3–6)	ALTRICIAL		GLEAN
		MONOG	F: 12 DAYS		HOVER & GLEAN
			MF		

BREEDING: Conif, mixed, or decid forest and forest edge. 2 broods, 3? in s. **DISPLAYS:** Agonistic: wing flicking, crest raising, also sleeked erect posture with bill pointed upward. **NEST:** On ground (usu in e) or low in decid or conif tree (w); of weeds, rotted wood, twigs, grass, moss, occ middle layer of mud, lining of fine materials. **EGGS:** Greenish-blue, usu unmarked, rarely flecked with black. 0.8″ (22 mm). **DIET:** Incl spiders, earthworms, also small salamanders; much fruit, esp in winter. Young fed insects, perhaps some fruit. **CONSERVATION:** Winters s to Bahamas, Guatemala, and El Salvador. Rare cowbird host. **NOTES:** Tends to select nest sites where conditions are relatively moist. Habitually flips (or "twinkles") wings. Has been observed anting. **ESSAYS:** Anting, p. 487; Bathing and Dusting, p. 429; Nest Lining, p. 391. **REFS:** Dilger, 1956a, b; Martin and Roper, 1988; Noon, 1981.

and hummingbird feeders may have been responsible for the eastward advance of Anna's Hummers, which appear to have colonized the Davis Mountains of west Texas, and for the northward expansion of ranges of Violet-crowned and Berylline Hummingbirds in Arizona. For instance, Beryllines attempted to nest near a feeder in the Chiricahua Mountains of southern Arizona in 1976, and a pair nested near feeders in the Huachuca Mountains in 1978 and fledged two young.

Similarly, Great-tailed Grackles have followed irrigated farmland and lawns northward out of Mexico. In the middle of the last century they were rare visitors to the Rio Grande Valley; now they nest in central California, central Nevada, southeastern Colorado, and southwestern Nebraska. It was reported that when this species first came into contact with the very similar Boat-tailed Grackles in southeastern Texas and southwestern Louisiana, hybrids were formed. The species now occur together without interbreeding, suggesting that the hybrids were less successful than "pure" offspring and that the process of speciation is complete.

The consequences of range expansion of one species for closely related species in the communities that are invaded can be considerable. The interesting example of the Wood Thrush, which expanded its range northward in this century, has been described by ecologist Douglass Morse of Brown University. Sometime after 1950, this species started to breed in Maine localities previously occupied by two other woodland thrushes, the Hermit Thrush and the Veery. The latter two, presumably displaced by the Wood Thrushes, moved into different habitats, the Hermit Thrush into relatively dry situations, especially pine-oak woodland, and the Veeries into damp deciduous forests.

The habitat preference of the invading Wood Thrushes lies in between the other two, and its ecological distribution overlaps both. The Wood Thrushes are socially dominant over the Hermits and Veeries, and defend their territorial boundaries against them. Interestingly, these interspecific territories are set up over a period of about a week in the spring, after which there are few if any obvious encounters between the species. To avoid missing the action, birders must be in the woods at precisely the right time. While the amount of habitat available to Hermits and Veeries is reduced by the presence of Wood Thrushes, all three species should coexist in areas that have habitats ranging from dry to wet woodlands.

Thus range expansions are of interest because they often signal important changes in habitats, because they may bring together populations that have partially (or just) completed the process of speciation, and because they may have interesting consequences for the communities that are invaded. They are also one of the many areas where observations by the numerous amateur birders in North America have contributed to scientific knowledge of birds—for without the help of the birding community, professional biologists would be hard pressed to maintain even a skeletal knowledge of avian distributions. Fortunately, ornithologists David De-

Varied Thrush

Ixoreus naevius Gmelin

NG–328; G–246; PE–220; PW–pl 48; AW–pl 444; AM(III)–60

9'–25'	F	3–4 (2–5) MONOG	F I: 14? DAYS ALTRICIAL F: ? DAYS MF	FRUIT	FOLIAGE GLEAN

BREEDING: Moist conif forest and decid forest with dense understory. 2? broods. **DISPLAYS:** Agonistic: head extended forward with body held in horizontal crouch, plumage sleeked; at highest intensity, tail lifted and spread, wings spread and rotated forward. **NEST:** Usu against trunk in small conif; bulky, of mud, dried leaves, inner bark strips, soft moss, reinforced with twigs, lining of grass or rootlets. **EGGS:** Pale blue, flecked with brown. 1.2″ (30 mm). **DIET:** Incl sowbugs, myriapods, snails, worms; much fruit, weed seeds, and acorns in winter. Young probably fed exclusively animal diet. **CONSERVATION:** Winters s to n Baja. **NOTES:** Song is an eerie, bell-like, prolonged whistle that slowly fades away from the listener. Breeding biology not well known. Aggressive toward other species at winter feeding sites. **ESSAYS:** Feeding Birds, p. 349; Bathing and Dusting, p. 429; How Do We Find Out About Bird Biology?, p. 319. **REF:** Martin, 1970.

American Robin

Turdus migratorius Linnaeus

NG–330; G–244; PE–220; PW–pl 48; AE–pl 400; AW–pl 445; AM(III)–58

CONIF 10'–20' (0'–75')	F–M	4 (3–7) MONOG	F I: 12–14 DAYS ALTRICIAL F: 14–16 DAYS F–M	FRUIT	FOLIAGE GLEAN

BREEDING: Habitat generalist: forest, woodland, gardens, parks. 2 broods, occ 3. **DISPLAYS:** Courting groups of males chase female, or male struts around female with tail spread, wings shaking, throat inflated. **NEST:** Now also buildings, other structures offering sufficient support, also shrubs, occ on ground; unkempt foundation of protruding twigs and grass, cup of mud lined with fine grass. **EGGS:** Pale blue, occ white, usu unmarked, occ flecked with brown. 1.1″ (28 mm). **DIET:** Incl earthworms, snails, etc.; much fruit. Young fed insects. **CONSERVATION:** Winters s to Bermuda and Guatemala. Rare cowbird host. Once widely hunted for food. Has expanded range into Great Plains and drier lowlands of w as trees have been planted, structures erected, and irrigation extended, creating suitable nesting sites and moist grassland for foraging. **NOTES:** Experiments demonstrate that earthworms are located by sight, not by sound. Adults oft belligerently defend nest. Male cares for fledged first brood while female incubates second clutch. Oft roost communally when fledged young are strong enough. Poisoning by spraying of DDT for Dutch elm disease in 1950s was instrumental in generating concern over potential "Silent Spring"; DDT-coated elm leaves eventually processed by earthworms, which were then devoured by robins, leading to death or reproductive failure. **ESSAYS:** Birds and the Law, p. 293; Tool Using, p. 435; DDT and Birds, p. 21; Mobbing, p. 425; Bathing and Dusting, p. 429; Range Expansion, p. 459. **REFS:** Eiserer, 1976; Knupp et al., 1977, Paszkowski, 1982; Wheelwright, 1986.

Sante and Peter Pyle have produced an excellent *Distributional Checklist of North American Birds* that will make it much easier to detect range changes.

SEE: Great Plains Hybrids, p. 625; Avian Invaders, p. 633; Species and Speciation, p. 355; Superspecies, p. 375; Feeding Birds, p. 349; Habitat Selection, p. 463; Bird Communities and Competition, p. 605; Interspecific Territoriality, p. 385. REFS: DeSante and Pyle, 1986; Gehlbach, 1981; Holmes et al., 1985; Morse, 1971.

Bird Biologist—Charles Bonaparte

One of the important early figures in North American ornithology was the younger brother of Napoleon. Charles Lucian Jules Laurent Bonaparte, Prince of Canino and Musignano (1803–57), spent 1823 to 1828 in the United States after Waterloo cast a pall over the family's prospects in Europe. His major contribution in America was a series of supplemental volumes to Alexander Wilson's *American Ornithology*. His contributions were more systematic and zoogeographic in nature than Wilson's, since Bonaparte was not primarily a talented field observer like Wilson. For his work in America and his later *Conspectus Generum Avium,* he has been called the father of systematic ornithology.

SEE: Taxonomy and Nomenclature, p. 515. REF: Stresemann, 1975.

Habitat Selection

Charles Darwin visited the Falkland Islands in the South Atlantic during his 1831–1836 globe-girdling expedition in H.M.S. *Beagle*. He reported: "Two kinds of geese frequent the Falklands. The upland species (*Anas magellanica*) is common, in pairs and in small flocks, throughout the island. . . . The rock goose, so called from living exclusively on the sea-beach (*Anas antarctica*), is common both here and on the west coast of America, as far north as Chile." The names of the geese have since changed (to *Chloeophaga picta* and *C. hybrida,* respectively), but these two closely related species each live, as Darwin described, in a different range of habitats.

Ornithologists are interested in answering two major questions about habitat selection—what determines the range of habitats in which a species occurs, and how does each individual determine when it's in an appropriate habitat? The first question is evolutionary: how has natural selection shaped habitat choices? The second is behavioral: what cues does a bird use in "choosing" its home? We put choosing in quotes to emphasize the presumed

Northern Wheatear

Oenanthe oenanthe Linnaeus

NG–332; G–246; PE–220; PW– 250; AE–pl 510; AW–pl 482; AM(III)–44

BURROW MF	5–6 (3–8) MONOG		F –M I: 14 DAYS ALTRICIAL F: 15–16 DAYS MF	SEEDS FRUIT	HAWKS

BREEDING: Arctic tundra and mountains, esp on rocky slopes. 1? brood. **DISPLAYS:** Courtship: male hops and bows around female with tail fanned, occ springs back and forth very rapidly and then prostrates himself before female with wings and tail spread for a few seconds; in song flight, male rises high, glides down with tail spread while singing. **NEST:** In cavity under rock or in deserted rodent burrow; loosely built of grass, roots, moss, lined with fine materials. **EGGS:** Pale blue, usu unmarked, occ flecked with red-brown. 0.8″ (21 mm). **DIET:** Incl snails. Young probably fed exclusively insects. **CONSERVATION:** Transoceanic migrant: winters in n Africa, Arabia, India, Mongolia and n China s to c Africa. **NOTES:** Parents divide brood 3 or 4 days after fledging and continue to feed their respective groups for another 10–11 days. Appears restless or nervous when foraging, oft making short flights. Widely distributed across Eurasian arctic. **ESSAYS:** Breeding Season, p. 55; Hatching, p. 233; Parental Care, p. 555. **REF:** Moreno, 1984.

Bluethroat

Luscinia svecica Linnaeus

NG–332; G–246; PW– 250; AW–pl 499; AM(III)–42

MF	6 (4–7) MONOG	F I: 14 DAYS ALTRICIAL F: 14 DAYS MF	

BREEDING: Arctic tundra and mountains, esp on rocky slopes. ? broods. **DISPLAYS:** Courting male displays with head thrown back, tail cocked, and wings drooped, while moving around female and singing. **NEST:** Oft at base of shrub; loosely built of grass, inner bark, roots, moss, lined with fine materials. **EGGS:** Green, faintly flecked with browns, occ capped, some almost unmarked. 0.8" (19 mm). **DIET:** Incl some aquatic insects, snails; few seeds and berries, esp in autumn. **CONSERVATION:** Winters in n Africa, Near East, s and s e Asia. **NOTES:** A secretive bird that remains near the ground and under cover. Highly variable singer. Widely distributed across Eurasian arctic. Virtually unstudied in N.A. **ESSAYS:** Bathing and Dusting, p. 429; Breeding Season, p. 55; How Do We Find Out About Bird Biology?, p. 319. **REF:** Gabrielson and Lincoln, 1959.

absence of conscious choice. Indeed, some ecologists employ the term "habitat *use*" rather than "habitat selection" to avoid the connotation of birds making deliberate decisions among habitat alternatives.

Birds are nearly ideal subjects for studies of habitat selection, because they are highly mobile, often migrating thousands of miles (and in the process passing over an enormous range of environments), and yet ordinarily forage, breed, and winter in very specific habitats. Indeed, the lives of small migrant songbirds are replete with habitat choices—where to feed, where to seek a mate, where to build a nest, where to stop to replenish depleted stores of fat when migrating, and so on. Choices can be so finely tuned that often the two sexes of a species use habitats differently. In grassland, male Henslow's Sparrows forage farther from the nest than females; in woodlands, female Red-eyed Vireos seek their food closer to the height of their nest (10–30 feet), and males forage closer to the height of their song perches (20–60 feet).

Many studies have demonstrated the special habitat requirements of different species. Belted Kingfishers choose nesting sites at those points along streams where particular kinds of riffles shelter fish. Broad-tailed Hummingbirds in the Colorado Rockies select nest sites under a canopy of conifer branches; the nighttime microclimate is warmer there, and the chance of daytime overheating is less. Red-cockaded Woodpeckers settle in woodlands offering the tall, old pines infected with heartwood fungus that their clans require for nests. Spotted Owls may require a habitat that includes cool spots in deep canyons in which to roost, and Ferruginous Hawks select open country with low cover and suitable perch sites.

Some groups of birds are much more habitat-specific than others. Our wood warblers (tribe Parulini) are generally much more tied to certain habitats, and tend to restrict the height at which they forage much more closely than do many Old World warblers (family Sylviidae). In most cases the latter do not show the sort of specialization that restricts the Pine Warbler largely to pine and cedar groves, and separates and Ovenbird and Black-and-white Warbler (which occur in a wide variety of vegetation types) by foraging preference. The former searches the ground and the latter gleans tree trunks and limbs. The behavioral differences between the superficially similar New World and Old World warblers indicate that evolution has, to a degree, genetically programmed habitat choice.

But the habitat preferences that evolution has programmed into a species are not cast in concrete. Local populations may respond either genetically or behaviorally to special conditions by changing the habitats they occupy. For instance, in a classic study ornithologist Kenneth Crowell compared the ecology of Northern Cardinals, Gray Catbirds, and White-eyed Vireos in eastern North America and on the island of Bermuda. On the mainland all three species prefer forest edge sites, and the catbird and vireo tend to select habitats near water. On Bermuda, which is largely dry and devoid of forest, dense populations of all three species are found in areas of scrub.

Northern Shrike

NG–334; G–260; PE–224; PW–pl 47; AE–pl 421; AW–pl 473; AM(III)–88

DECID	?	4–6	F?	SMALL	AERIAL
6′–12′		(4–9)	I: 15–16 (?) DAYS	MAMMALS	PURSUIT
(To 20′)		MONOG	ALTRICIAL	INSECTS	
			F: 20 DAYS		
			MF(?)		

BREEDING: Open decid and conif woodland, taiga, scrub, thickets. ? broods. **DISPLAYS:** ? **NEST:** Usu in spruce, occ in shrub; bulky, symmetrical, of twigs, matted grass, inner bark, moss, feathers, hair. **EGGS:** Grayish- or greenish-white, heavily blotched with olive, brown, lavender. 1.1″ (27 mm). **DIET:** Incl esp mice, large insects. **CONSERVATION:** Winters within N.A., occ irruptive. A man in Boston shot 50 one winter protecting House Sparrows in the days when that pest was being imported! **NOTES:** Winter range and abundance may be strongly influenced by cycles in small mammal populations. Lacking the talons of raptors, it stuns or kills flying birds with a blow from its powerful beak, and oft caches prey by impaling on plant spine or barbed wire—leading to the common name of "butcher bird." Details of breeding biology not well known. **ESSAYS:** Irruptions, p. 639; Hoarding Food, p. 345; Feet, p. 239; Raptor Hunting, p. 223. **REFS:** Cade, 1967; Godfrey, 1986.

Loggerhead Shrike

NG–334; G–260; PE–224; PW–pl 47; AE–pl 422; AW–pl 472; AM(III)–90

SHRUB	MF	5–6	F	SMALL	AERIAL
3′–30′		(4–7)	I: 16–17 DAYS	VERTS	PURSUIT
(To 50′)		MONOG	ALTRICIAL	CARRION	
			F: 17–21 DAYS		
			MF		

BREEDING: Open fields with scattered trees, open woodland, scrub. 2, occ 3 broods in s. **DISPLAYS:** Courtship: male feeds female and performs flight display back and forth about 20′ from female. Mock pursuits occur also. **NEST:** Usu hidden below crown in crotch or on large branch, occ in vine tangle; bulky, well made of twigs, forbs, bark strips woven together, lined with fine materials. **EGGS:** Grayish-buff, marked with gray, browns, black, oft near large end. 1.0″ (24 mm). **DIET:** Mostly large insects, esp in w; incl esp birds, mice, lizards. **CONSERVATION:** Winters s to c Mexico. Blue List 1972–86; declining everywhere, esp in c U.S.; San Clemente (CA) subspecies Endangered. Habitat loss and pesticides (esp in c portion of range) implicated in decline. **NOTES:** Oft sits immobile for long periods watching for prey (vision is excellent). Lacking the talons of raptors, it stuns or kills flying birds with a blow from its powerful beak; oft caches prey by impaling on plant spine or barbed wire—leading to the common name "butcher bird." Strong male fidelity to breeding territory. Nests earlier than most passerines. Male feeds incubating female, occ from his food cache; occ most of food fed by female to nestlings comes from male caches. Young fed 3–4 weeks postfledging. Sexes hold separate territories in nonbreeding season. **ESSAYS:** Blue List, p. 11; Hoarding Food, p. 345; Site Tenacity, p. 189; DDT and Birds, p. 21. **REFS:** Applegate, 1977; Bohall-Wood, 1987; Fraser and Luukkonen, 1986; Morrison, 1980; Smith, 1973.

Similarly, ecologist Martin Cody found that when drought greatly reduced the availability of insects in an Arizona pine-oak woodland, the density of birds was also greatly reduced and the composition of the bird community altered. Those species typical of more moist, higher elevation habitats as well as pine-oak woodland (such as Painted Redstarts, Western Wood-Pewees, and Pygmy Nuthatches), departed. In contrast, species normally found in drier, lower elevation habitats such as mesquite scrub (including Ash-throated Flycatchers, Lucy's Warblers, and House Finches), chose to move into the now more arid woodland.

Avian habitat selection is a vast topic in part because both amateur and professional students of birds have accumulated an enormous body of information on which birds live where, and how they operate in their environments. But detailed observations can still add to our understanding of habitat selection—especially observations of bird behavior made when habitats are being altered either by "natural experiments" such as droughts and insect outbreaks or by human activities.

SEE: Birds in the Bush, p. 541; Bird Guilds, p. 493; Bird Communities and Competition, p. 605; Dabblers vs. Divers, p. 75; Seabird Nesting Sites, p. 197.   REFS: Cody, 1981, 1985; Crowell, 1962; Robins, 1971; Williamson, 1971.

Loggerhead Shrike which has skewered a grasshopper on a barbed-wire fence. Shrikes have the interesting habit of impaling prey on thorns or other pointed objects, either to eat them immediately or to establish a larder for future use. Shrikes show an amazing memory for the placement of their victims: in Texas, shrikes were reported returning to mummified frogs they had stored eight months before.

Gray Catbird

Dumetella carolinensis Linnaeus

NG–334; G–240; PE–218; PW–pl 47; AE–pl 420; AW–pl 477; AM(III)–62

			F		
			I: 12–13 DAYS		
2′–10′	F –M	4	ALTRICIAL	FRUIT	FOLIAGE
(1′–50′)		(2–6)	F: 10–11 DAYS		GLEAN
		MONOG	MF		

BREEDING: Dense brush (oft bordering woodland swamp or stream), shrubland, wooded suburbs, forest edge, absent from deep forest. 2 broods. **DISPLAYS:** Courtship: male pursues female, pauses to sing, struts with wings lowered, tail erect, turns to display chestnut undertail coverts. **NEST:** Oft in dense thicket; bulky, of grass, forbs, twigs, leaves, lined with fine materials. **EGGS:** Blue-green, unmarked, rarely spotted with red. 0.9″ (24 mm). **DIET:** Incl spiders, berries; occ >50% fruit. Young fed almost 100% insects. **CONSERVATION:** Winters s to c Panama, Bermuda, Greater Antilles. Uncommon cowbird host; ejects cowbird eggs from nest. **NOTES:** Appropriates sounds of other birds. Hatching asynchronous. Female broods; male makes far more feeding trips for nestlings. **ESSAYS:** Visual Displays, p. 5; DDT, p. 21; Brood Parasitism, p. 287; DNA and Passerine Classification, p. 662; Vocal Copying, p. 469; Brood Reduction, p. 307; Parental Care, p. 555. **REFS:** Fletcher and Smith, 1978; Johnson and Best, 1982; Nickell, 1965.

Northern Mockingbird

Mimus polyglottos Linnaeus

NG–336; G–240; PE–218; PW–pl 47; AE–pl 419; AW–pl 475; AM(III)–62

			F		
			I: 12–13 DAYS		
TREE	MF	3–5	ALTRICIAL	FRUIT	FOLIAGE
3′–10′		(2–6)	F: 11–13 DAYS		GLEAN
(0.5′–20′)		MONOG	MF		

BREEDING: Habitat generalist: wide range of open and partly open habitats, abundant in suburbs. 2 broods, occ 3 or 4. **DISPLAYS:** Male and female perform mating "dance" facing each other with heads and tails high, darting at each other and retreating; may also serve as territorial display, oft occurring between males. **NEST:** Usu in conif or decid shrub, also occ in vines; of twigs, lined with grass, rootlets. Male usu builds foundation, female lines it. Built in 4–8 days. **EGGS:** Blue-green, usu heavily marked with browns. 1.0″ (24 mm). **DIET:** Incl crayfish, sowbugs, snails, few small verts; berries. Nestlings fed mostly insects, some fruit. **CONSERVATION:** In winter largely resident; few migrate s to s Mexico, Bahamas, Greater Antilles. Rare Brown-headed Cowbird host, occ Bronzed Cowbird host. **NOTES:** Uses songs and calls of other birds; unmated males sing more than mated males, only unmated males sing at night in spring. Vigorously defends territory against many other species. Long-term pair bond; polygyny and polyandry rare. Young brooded up to 4 days, almost entirely by female. Male assumes feeding of fledglings while female renests. Conspicuous "wing-flashing" ostensibly functions to stir up insects and to distract predators, esp snakes. Sexes oft defend separate winter feeding territories. **ESSAYS:** Vocal Copying, p. 469; Vocal Development, p. 601; Natural Selection, p. 237; Bathing and Dusting, p. 429; Birds, DNA, and Evolutionary Convergence, p. 419; Visual Displays, p. 5. **REFS:** Breitwisch and Whitesides, 1987; Breitwisch et al., 1986; Laskey, 1962; Logan, 1983.

Vocal Copying

Many species of songbirds learn the specific song elements of their repertoires from one or more adult tutors, most often from the male parent. Such learning, for at least some species, is not confined to the period prior to sexual maturity. For example, territorial male Swamp Sparrows listen to songs from adjacent territorial males and incorporate those songs into their own repertoire. Generally, this type of vocal copying, where the individual copied (the model) is a member of the same species, is referred to as "vocal imitation" and serves as the basic mechanism underlying the evolution of dialect systems—variation in songs among local populations.

There are, however, many examples of vocalizations characteristic of ône species being copied by a second species. Such "vocal mimicry" is well known in the Northern Mockingbird and European Starling. The function(s) of acquired alien sounds is still debated. Even the term "vocal mimicry" is a source of dispute among ornithologists. In biology, mimicry generally connotes deception by the mimic directed toward some signal-receiver, generally a predator or competitor. With most mimicked bird vocalizations, the true identity of the singer is quite clear because the mimic imparts some characteristic tonal quality, temporal pattern, or context of use that serves to differentiate it from the model's vocalizations. The human ear can detect these differences, and the model's more sensitive avian ear would certainly be expected to detect the rendition of a mimic. In short, in the vast majority of examples it is unlikely that anyone is fooled by vocal mimicry.

Why, then, are sounds of other species (as well as nonavian sounds such as the barking of dogs, screeching of machinery, or human whistling) sometimes incorporated into a bird's repertoire? The answer seems to be that selection has favored a large and diverse repertoire in some species and that one way of increasing repertoire size and diversity is to incorporate sounds from the surrounding acoustic environment, even sounds that do not belong to the bird's own species. Evidence from several studies indicates that an expanded repertoire may improve ability to attract a mate, intimidate rivals, and stimulate females. Thus the effects of sexual selection tend to favor an increasingly large and diverse song repertoire within the limits imposed by the need for species recognition and by the capacity of the singer to memorize sounds. The common, nondeceptive use of such vocalizations has been termed "vocal appropriation" to eliminate the connotation of deceit implicit in the biological use of the term "mimicry."

SEE: Vocal Dialects, p. 595; Vocal Functions, p. 471; Territoriality, p. 387; Sexual Selection, p. 251. REF: Dobkin, 1979.

Sage Thrasher

Oreoscoptes montanus Henry

NG–336; G–240; PW–pl 47; AE–pl 497; AW–533; AM(III)–64

			MF		
GROUND	MF?	3–5	I: 15 (13–17) DAYS	FRUIT	
0′–3′		(1–7)	ALTRICIAL		
(To 5′)		MONOG	F: 11–14 DAYS		
			MF		

BREEDING: Sagebrush communities. 2? broods. **DISPLAYS:** Male does flight display with peculiar tremor of wings; lands and holds wings up and briefly flutters them. **NEST:** Concealed in or occ beneath sagebrush; bulky, of coarse twigs, forbs, grass, lined with fine materials. **EGGS:** Deep or greenish blue, heavily spotted with browns. 1.0″ (25 mm). **DIET:** Incl berries. **CONSERVATION:** Winters s to n Mexico. Rejects cowbird eggs. **NOTES:** Highly terrestrial, but male sings from prominent elevated perch. Unlike most N.A. mimids, hatching is synchronous. **ESSAYS:** Brood Parasitism, p. 287; Cowbirds, p. 619; DNA and Passerine Classification, p. 662; Brood Reduction, p. 307. **REFS:** Reynolds, 1981; Reynolds and Rich, 1978.

Brown Thrasher

Supersp #39
Toxostoma rufum Linnaeus

NG–336; G–240; PE–218; PW–pl 47; AE–pl 494; AM(III)–66

			MF		
2′–5′	MF	4–5	I: 11–14 DAYS		
GROUND		(2–6)	ALTRICIAL		FOLIAGE
(0′–10′)		MONOG	F: 9–13 DAYS		GLEAN
			MF		

BREEDING: Brush and shrubland, decid forest edge and clearings, suburbs (esp in w part of range). 2 broods, rarely 3? **DISPLAYS:** Courtship: male song elicits female response of picking up twig and hopping to male, fluttering wings vigorously and chirping; male may pick up dead leaves and hop to female. **NEST:** On ground mostly in e, also in vines or small tree; of twigs, dead leaves, grass, usu lined with grass, rootlets. **EGGS:** Pale bluish-white, occ greenish, spotted with reddish-brown, occ wreathed, occ almost unmarked. 1.0″ (26 mm). **DIET:** Insects, inverts, small verts; berries, fruit, nuts. **CONSERVATION:** Winters within U.S. Occ cowbird host; largest passerine to rear them. **NOTES:** Male has largest documented song repertoire of all N.A. birds (>1,100 song types); occ appropriates sounds of other species. Hatching asynchronous, except in early nests. Uses long, strong bill to dig and sweep aside debris in search of food. Boldly defends nest and young. Maintains winter territories interspecifically with Long-billed Thrasher where both occur. **ESSAYS:** Vocal Functions, p. 471; Vocal Copying, p. 469; Interspecific Territoriality, p. 385; Brood Parasitism, p. 287; Cowbirds, p. 619; Bills, p. 209. **REFS:** Boughey and Thompson, 1981; Fischer, 1981a, b; Murphy and Fleischer, 1986.

Vocal Functions

The advent of the breeding season in spring is heralded each dawn by a chorus of bird song that continues intermittently throughout the day. With practice, we can identify a species by its songs and calls even without seeing the vocalizer, and we infer that birds can similarly distinguish between members of their own and other species by voice alone. This assumption has been verified experimentally for numerous passerine species by playing tapes of vocalizations in the field carefully observing responses of individual listeners. By altering the tempo, frequency characteristics, length, or other features of tape-recorded songs, and then observing birds' responses to them, the actual components of songs used for species recognition have been identified in several instances. For example, the duration of intervals between elements within songs is important for species recognition in Common Yellowthroat, Rufous-sided Towhee, and Field, Song, and White-throated Sparrows. Other species, such as Winter Wren and Brown Thrasher, encode identification mainly in the syntax (sequence of elements) of their songs.

Ornithologists differentiate, somewhat arbitrarily, between a call and a song by the length and complexity of the vocalization. Calls tend to serve specific functions and are generally innate rather than learned. For example, alarm calls serve to alert all within earshot that danger is present; they tend to be rather similar among groups of birds and often communicate their message across species. Contact calls are used among members of a flock or between mates to indicate the location of the caller. Many species in groups that lack song (such as gulls and parrots) have complex repertoires of calls that serve varied functions.

Song is a well-developed feature primarily of oscine passerines (hence, they are referred to as "songbirds"), and generally must be partly or entirely learned. Songs identify the species of the singer. In addition, the territorial or advertising song of males serves the dual function of territorial proclamation directed at other males and of mate attraction directed toward females. Thus the song warns the former to keep out of the defended territory and invites the latter to join the singer. There are other, more subtle functions and messages, as well. The motivation of the singer can be conveyed by the amount that he sings; in order to attract a mate, unpaired males devote more time to singing than do paired males. When excited, such as during and immediately following a territorial encounter with a rival male, the rapidity of singing often increases. Song length also may increase or decrease when the bird is agitated.

Males of approximately three-quarters of all songbirds sing two or more different songs and are said to possess "song repertoires." Each song having a particular configuration of syllables and phrases repeated in a stereotyped fashion is referred to as a "song-type." At the extreme end of the range in repertoire size is the male Brown Thrasher, estimated to sing in excess of 3,000 song-types. The evolution of elaborate song repertoires is

Long-billed Thrasher

Supersp #39
Toxostoma longirostre Lafresnaye

NG–336; G–240; PW–pl 47; AE–pl 495; AM(III)–66

			MF		
			I: 13–14 DAYS		
TREE	?	3–4	ALTRICIAL		FOLIAGE
4'–10'		(2–5)	F: 12–14 DAYS		GLEAN
		MONOG	MF		

BREEDING: Brush and shrubland, esp in bottomland willow and dense forests along resacas (stagnant watercourses). 2? broods. **DISPLAYS:** ? **NEST:** In thorny shrub, small tree; of twigs, dead leaves, grass, usu lined with grass, rootlets. **EGGS:** Greenish-white, densely spotted with reddish-brown, occ wreathed, occ almost unmarked. 1.1" (28 mm). **DIET:** Insects, inverts, small verts; berries, other fruit. **CONSERVATION:** Winter resident. Common victim of Bronzed Cowbird. **NOTES:** Unlike most N.A. mimids, hatching is synchronous. Nests usu well shaded in very hot environment, so nestlings brooded only 2 days because high ambient temperatures preclude need for warmth normally supplied by brooding adult, and shade usu sufficient to prevent overheating. Maintain winter territories interspecifically with Brown Thrashers where both occur. **ESSAYS:** Interspecific Territoriality, p. 385; Bills, p. 209; DNA and Passerine Classification, p. 662; Cowbirds, p. 619; Temperature Regulation, p. 149; Brood Reduction, p. 307. **REFS:** Fischer, 1980, 1983.

Curve-billed Thrasher

Toxostoma curvirostre Swainson

NG–338; G–242; PW–pl 47; AE–pl 496; AW–pl 535; AM(III)–68

			F –M		
			I: 12–15 DAYS		
TREE	MF	3–4	ALTRICIAL	FRUIT	FOLIAGE
2'–8'		(1–5)	F: 11–18 DAYS	INVERTS	GLEAN
(1'–15')		MONOG	MF		

BREEDING: Shrubland, semidesert (esp with cholla cactus and mesquite), desert suburbia. 2 broods, occ a third produced after summer rains. **DISPLAYS:** Courting male follows female singing softly. **NEST:** Mostly in spiny shrub or cactus, rarely in cavity; bulky, of twigs, grass, usu lined with fine materials. Occ reused. **EGGS:** Pale blue green, spotted with pale brown, rarely wreathed. 1.2" (29 mm). **DIET:** Incl spiders, snails, isopods; berries, fruit (esp cactus), nectar. **CONSERVATION:** Winter resident. Rare cowbird host. **NOTES:** Remain paired throughout year in same area used for nesting. Only female incubates at night. Young hatch asynchronously. Female broods for 13+ days where nests very exposed, necessitating shading of nestlings by female. Cactus Wren roosting nests routinely destroyed if found within thrasher's territory. Attracted to water. In winter, individuals occ build roosting platform which may become nest site in following spring. **ESSAYS:** Brood Reduction, p. 307; Territoriality, p. 387; DNA and Passerine Classification, p. 662; Who Incubates?, p. 27. **REFS:** Anderson and Anderson, 1973; Fischer, 1980, 1983; Ricklefs, 1965.

presumed to be the result of sexual selection arising from competition between males for females. In selecting a male with which to pair, females may use size and complexity of the song repertoire to assess a male's overall potential "fitness" as a partner. In some species, these characteristics are known to increase with age, and may serve as an indirect gauge of breeding experience and health. Increased complexity and size of repertoire also have been shown to correlate with measures of territory quality in some species, thus providing further information to a female about to invest her immediate reproductive future on the basis of what she hears.

There is some experimental evidence that song is important in coordinating the reproductive cycle between mates in addition to its presumed role in maintaining the pair bond. Male song is known to stimulate ovarian development and egg laying in Budgerigars and to accelerate nest-building activity in female Canaries. In fact, ornithologist Don Kroodsma has shown that female Canaries exposed to large repertoires are more stimulated to build nests than are females exposed to impoverished repertoires. Laboratory experiments with female Song Sparrows demonstrate that larger song repertoires elicit more copulation-soliciting displays; females prefer repertoires of 4 song-types compared to 1, 8 compared to 4, and 16 compared to 8. Observations of pairing in the field, however, revealed no relationship between repertoire size and either date of initial pair formation or the speed with which a second mate was acquired following removal of the first female. Thus, although larger song repertoires appear to serve as stronger stimuli in sexual and nesting behavior, there is little field evidence that they influence female choice of mates in species where song repertoire size is not correlated with male age (as in the Song Sparrow).

Individual males often can be identified by characteristic features of their songs, and birds of many species have been tested in the field for their ability to discriminate between the songs of neighbors (males that are already established on territories and pose no real threat) and strangers (males that are searching for a territory on which to establish themselves). The ability to distinguish between neighbors and strangers without being able to see them should afford considerable energy savings to a territory holder. The song of an established neighbor can be answered with a song or can be ignored; the song of a stranger, however, necessitates a vigorous physical as well as vocal rebuff. Territorial males identify each other using both song features and location from which the song originates. Interestingly, species with large repertoires show a somewhat reduced ability to discriminate between neighbors and strangers than do species with limited repertoires. For example, Song Sparrows, with repertoires of 8–10 songs, show weaker discrimination than closely related Swamp Sparrows, with repertoires of 4–5 songs.

The ability to recognize neighbors by vocalizations alone has not been found in species that nest in dense colonies. This is true even for species (such as the Northern Gannet, Laughing Gull, and Black-legged Kittiwake) that can recognize their young or their mates by vocalizations. Presumably

Bendire's Thrasher

Toxostoma bendirei Coues

NG–338; G–242; PW–pl 47; AW–pl 534; AM(III)–68

2'–4'	?	3–4	?	FRUIT	FOLIAGE
(To 8')		(3–5)	I: ? DAYS		GLEAN
		MONOG	ALTRICIAL		
			F: ? DAYS		
			?		

BREEDING: Desert, esp with tall cholla cactus, yucca, creosote bush. 2 broods, occ 3. **DISPLAYS:** Male sings from high perch (8'–15'), typical rambling thrasher-type song. **NEST:** In thorny shrub, small tree; finer and more compact than most thrashers'; of fine twigs, leaves, grass, usu lined with fine materials. **EGGS:** Pale gray-green to greenish-white, spotted with reddish-brown, mostly at large end, variable. 1.0" (25 mm). **DIET:** Esp caterpillars, beetles. **CONSERVATION:** Winters s to n w Mexico. Rare cowbird host. **NOTES:** Tends to prefer more open habitat than Curve-billed Thrasher. Oft cocks tail somewhat when running. Little studied. **ESSAYS:** Birds, DNA and Evolutionary Convergence, p. 419; Bills, p. 209; How Do We Find Out About Bird Biology?, p. 319. **REF:** Phillips et al., 1964.

Crissal Thrasher

Supersp #40
Toxostoma crissale Henry

NG–338; G–242; PW–pl 47; AM(III)–70

3'–8'	MF	2–3	MF	FRUIT	DIGGING
		(1–4)	I: 14 DAYS		
		MONOG	ALTRICIAL		
			F: 11–13 DAYS		
			MF		

BREEDING: Desert scrub (esp stands of mesquite or saltbush), riparian brush. 2 broods. **DISPLAYS:** Male sings from high perch, typical thrasherlike rambling song. **NEST:** In dense willows, mesquite, sagebrush; of forbs, grass, shreds of inner bark, lined with fine grass, occ feathers. Usu not as deep a cup as in other similar thrashers. **EGGS:** Blue-green, unmarked. 1.0" (26 mm). **DIET:** Mostly insects, inverts, small verts; <10% fruit, berries. Forage mostly by digging with bill. **CONSERVATION:** Winter resident. Strongly discriminate between own eggs and cowbirds'; eject cowbird eggs from nest. **NOTES:** Highly terrestrial, but male sings from elevated perch. Young cannot fly until 3–5 days after leaving nest. Mated pairs remain in home range all year. **ESSAYS:** Bills, p. 209; Cowbirds, p. 619; Brood Parasitism, p. 287; Territoriality, p. 387; Precocial and Altricial Young, p. 581. **REF:** Finch, 1982.

under conditions of unobstructed visual contact, natural selection has not favored vocal recognition of neighbors.

SEE: Vocal Development, p. 601; Vocal Copying, p. 469; Sonagrams: Seeing Bird Songs, p. 563; Visual Displays, p. 5; Sexual Selection, p. 251. REFS: Becker, 1982; Krebs and Kroodsma, 1980; Searcy, 1984.

Bird Biologist—Charles Darwin

Charles Darwin (1809–82) was the most important scientist in the history of biology. His theory of evolution by natural selection provides a coherent framework for all biological observations—which is why we run into his ideas whenever we investigate questions of North American ornithology, even though Darwin never visited our continent. Darwin originally studied medicine and then seemed destined for the clergy, but that changed when he became naturalist on H.M.S. *Beagle,* a naval ship on an exploratory trip circumnavigating the globe (1831–36). His observations on birds, especially those of the finches of the Galapagos Islands, were important to the development of his evolutionary ideas. At the urging of colleagues he began a book on evolution in 1856, and his theory was finally publicly presented to the Linnaean Society in 1858. Darwin had received a paper from Alfred Russel Wallace that year giving essentially identical views to his own. Always the Victorian gentleman, he had intended to step aside, but friends persuaded him to present both Wallace's and his own ideas at the same time.

The notion that life had evolved had been around for a long time, but Darwin and Wallace came up with the mechanism of natural selection. Darwin alone then made a second major contribution, without which the idea of evolution by natural selection might have never gained currency—he produced a heavily documented, brilliant book supporting it: *On the Origin of Species by Means of Natural Selection, or the Preservation of Favored Races in the Struggle for Life* (1859). He later wrote a series of books on other biological subjects, any one of which would have won him recognition as a distinguished scientist, but *Origin of Species,* which is still a fascinating read, makes clear that he was one of the intellectual giants of all time.

SEE: Natural Selection, p. 237; Sexual Selection, p. 251; Facts, Hypotheses, and Theories, p. 567; Habitat Selection, p. 463.

Le Conte's Thrasher

NG–338; G–242; PW–pl 47; AW–pl 537; AM(III)–72

2'–4'	MF	3–4	MF		DIGGING
(1'–6')		(2–4)	I: 15 DAYS		
		MONOG	ALTRICIAL		FOLIAGE
			F: 15 (13–17) DAYS		GLEAN
			MF		

BREEDING: Desert scrub, esp with scattered creosote bush. 2, perhaps 3 broods. **DISPLAYS:** Male sings from elevated (4'–8') perch; presents twig or insect to female; cop on ground (rarely in shrub), female begs before male mounts. **NEST:** Mostly in dense, thickly branching cholla cactus, palo verde, creosote bush; bulky, deep, of thorny twigs, sticks, lined with flower clusters, feathers (rarely), fibers, rootlets. Uniquely double-lined with inner lining of plant down (derived from seeds, leaves, etc.). **EGGS:** Blue-green, spotted with pale brown, mostly at large end, some nearly unmarked. 1.1" (28 mm). **DIET:** Incl other terrestrial arthropods, occ small verts; <3% seeds, fruit. Forage mostly by digging with bill. **CONSERVATION:** Winter resident. Intolerant of habitat disruption by humans. Rare host to Bronzed Cowbird. **NOTES:** Pairs mate for life and remain year-round in home range. Very rarely polygynous. Hatching asynchronous. Runs very rapidly, reminiscent of miniature roadrunner. Uncommon. **ESSAYS:** Bills, p. 209; Monogamy, p. 597; Polygyny, p. 443; Brood Reduction, p. 307. **REFS:** Phillips et al., 1964; Sheppard, 1970.

California Thrasher

NG–338; G–242; PW–pl 47; AW–pl 536; AM(III)–70

2'–4'	MF	3–4	MF	FRUIT	DIGGING
(To 9')		(2–4)	I: 14 DAYS	NUTS	
		MONOG	ALTRICIAL		FOLIAGE
			F: 12–14 DAYS		GLEAN
			MF		

BREEDING: Chaparral, moist woodland with dense ground cover, brush along stream, suburbs with abundant plantings. 2 broods (occ 3?). **DISPLAYS:** Male sings from elevated perch. Female performs begging display; male presents food to or feeds female; cop on or near ground. **NEST:** Mostly hidden in shrub or low tree; bulky, of stiff twigs, lined with grass, rootlets. **EGGS:** Pale blue, spotted with pale brown, oft faint. 1.1" (29 mm). **DIET:** Mostly insects, spiders; some fruit, acorns, forb seeds. Forages primarily by digging and raking with bill. **CONSERVATION:** Winter resident. **NOTES:** Incorporates sounds of other species in its vocal repertoire. Male takes charge of fledglings while female renests. Young cannot fly until several days after leaving nest. Although highly terrestrial, male will ascend small bush to sing. Seldom forages >few feet from protective cover. Runs rapidly. **ESSAYS:** Natural Selection, p. 237; Vocal Copying, p. 469; Bills, p. 209; Courtship Feeding, p. 181; Parental Care, p. 555; Precocial and Altricial Young, p. 581. **REF:** Grinnell and Miller, 1986.

Selection in Nature

Natural selection, the differential reproduction of different genetic types in a population, is the creative force in evolution, and in our essays we often attempt to show how selection has shaped the physical and behavioral characteristics of birds. The effects of selection are well known from both genetic theory and laboratory experiments. It has less frequently been investigated in natural populations, and there several classic studies have involved birds.

In the winter of 1898, following an unusually severe ice and snow storm, a biologist named H. C. Bumpus brought 136 stunned House Sparrows into his laboratory at Brown University. Seventy-two of the sparrows recovered, and 64 died. Bumpus measured both groups, and modern analyses of his measurements indicate that large males were more likely to survive than small ones, and that intermediate-sized females were more likely to survive than either large or small ones. Thus it appeared that the storm acted as a selective agent on the sparrow population.

Since Bumpus' work, population geneticists have shown that very small differentials in survival or reproduction are sufficient to account for the evolution of extremely simple ancestral organisms, living in the seas shortly after life originated, into House Sparrows, people, and oak trees. The reason that such small changes could lead to such big differences is that billions of years were available for the transformation. This means that selection may often occur at undetectably slow rates. For example, if birds with a wing length of 150 mm have a 1 percent better chance of surviving and reproducing than members of the same population with 155-mm wings, then selection pressure could, over hundreds of years, lead to shorter wing length in a population. But that differential in reproduction is small enough and that period long enough to make it virtually impossible for observers to record the measurements and reproductive success of a sufficient number of individuals to demonstrate selection at work.

This problem accounts for the relative paucity of examples in which selection has actually been documented (rather than inferred) in nature. While the Bumpus case is one of the very few in which selection operating on birds has been shown, several important examples involve birds as selective agents. In the industrial midlands of 19th-century England, pollution had blackened tree trunks and killed the lichens that grew on them. Simultaneously, populations of the peppered moths in those areas had changed from mostly variegated, black-and-white (peppered) individuals to mostly all-black (melanic) individuals. It has been shown that this phenomenon of "industrial melanism" in British moths was largely the result of selective predation by birds. In the 1950s motion pictures were made of both kinds of moths sitting on both pollution-blacked tree trunks near factories and lichen-covered tree trunks in unpolluted countryside. The films showed clearly that flycatchers, nuthatches, thrushes, and other birds found and ate

Water Pipit

Anthus spinoletta Linnaeus

NG–340; G–256; PE–200; PW–pl 54; AE–pl 546; AW–pl 571; AM(III)–78

F	4–5 (4–7) MONOG	F I: 13–15 DAYS ALTRICIAL F: 13–15 DAYS MF	AQUATIC INVERTS SEEDS	HAWKS FROM GROUND	

BREEDING: Alpine and arctic tundra. 1 brood. **DISPLAYS:** Male performs repeated courtship flight ascending 50′–200′, floats downward singing, with legs extended and tail held upward at sharp angle. **NEST:** Sunk in ground and partially overhung by rock or veg; of grass or grass and twigs, lined with fine grass, occ hair. Rarely a shallow scrape or built on old nest. Built in 4–5 days. **EGGS:** Dull or gray white, marked with grays, browns, occ so blotched as to be solid brown. 0.8″ (20 mm). **DIET:** Incl mollusks, crustaceans; also some berries. Occ forages in shallow water. **CONSERVATION:** Winters s to Guatemala and El Salvador. **NOTES:** Habitually bobs or swings tail when walking. Occ migrates to lower elevation during breeding to escape adverse weather. Male feeds female during incubation, but away from nest. Young birds gather in late summer flocks. Forms large winter flocks, oft in cultivated fields and along beaches. Widespread across Eurasia. **ESSAYS:** Walking vs. Hopping, p. 69; DNA and Passerine Classification, p. 662; Breeding Season, p. 55. **REFS:** Catzeflis, 1978; Miller and Green, 1987; Verbeek, 1970.

Sprague's Pipit

Anthus spragueii Audubon

NG–340; G–256; PE–200; PW–pl 54; AW–562; AM(III)–80

F?	4–5 (4–6) MONOG?	F? I: ? DAYS ALTRICIAL F: 10–11+ DAYS F?	SEEDS	

BREEDING: Shortgrass prairie. 2? broods. **DISPLAYS:** Male performs extended aerial courtship, ascending up to 500′ and spiraling down while singing. **NEST:** In ground hollow usu overarched by grass; of grass, unlined. **EGGS:** Pale buff or grayish-white, flecked with browns, or gray, oft with fine dark brown lines at large end. 0.8″ (21 mm). **DIET:** Mostly insects; grass and forb seeds. Young fed mostly or exclusively insects. **CONSERVATION:** Winters s to c Mexico. Rare cowbird host. **NOTES:** Female difficult to flush from nest. Breeding biology little known. Flocks in winter. **ESSAYS:** Walking vs. Hopping, p. 69; DNA and Passerine Classification, p. 662; How Do We Find Out About Bird Biology?, p. 319. **REF:** Bent, 1950.

mostly peppered moths on blackened trunks and discovered and devoured melanic moths on the lichen-covered trunks.

Also in England, biologists measured selection under natural conditions in the field by taking advantage of thrushes' propensity to crack the shells of many-patterned *Cepaea* land snails against favorite rocks (thrush anvils) within their territories. By comparing samples of snail shells from around the anvils with samples of live snails, they were able to show that the thrushes were selective in their choice of prey. They found that the birds differentially ate individuals with banded shells in an area where the background was rather uniform; snails with unbanded shells were apparently better camouflaged and thus somewhat protected from detection by the birds. When the snail population lived in rough herbage, the reverse was true, and the birds found and ate more unbanded individuals.

Another demonstration that birds act as selective predators was provided by a study by ecologists Deane Bowers, Irene Brown, and Darryl Wheye. They found the remains of over 300 chalcedon checkerspot butterflies on Stanford University's Jasper Ridge Biological Preserve. Most of the wings were found with characteristic triangular beak marks where they were pulled from the body before it was eaten. California Thrashers were apparently the main culprit.

Bowers and her colleagues compared the characteristics of the black-red-cream checkerspot butterflies eaten by birds with those of the butterfly population at large, and found that the birds preferentially attacked individuals with less red on their wings. The reason is not certain, but red is a "warning color" in many distasteful insects and the birds may simply avoid the redder individuals. Such field observations suggest that the butterfly-eating birds have at least some role in determining the evolution of wing color in their prey.

There is every reason to believe that feeding birds are important evolutionary agents, helping to shape the characteristics not only of insects and other animals they prey upon, but also of such things as seed-size, fruit-color, and flower shape in certain plants.

SEE: Natural Selection, p. 237; Coevolution, p. 405; Sexual Selection, p. 251. REFS: Bowers et al., 1985; Cain and Sheppard, 1954; Ehrlich, 1986a; Ehrlich and Roughgarden, 1987; Futuyma, 1979; Johnston et al., 1972; Kettlewell, 1973.

Red-throated Pipit

Anthus cervinus Pallas

NG–340; G–256; AW–768; AM(III)–78

F?

5–6
(4–7)
MONOG?

F
I: 12–14(?) DAYS
ALTRICIAL
F: 11–13(?) DAYS
MF

BREEDING: High, rocky tundra in coastal mountains. 1? brood. **DISPLAYS:** Male performs repeated courtship flight ascending 50'–200' and floats downward while singing. **NEST:** Under the edge of a mossy hummock, oft sheltered by willow or shrub; of grass, lined with fine grass, occ hair. **EGGS:** Blue or olive gray, marked with browns, black. 0.8" (19 mm). **DIET:** Insects; in winter small freshwater mollusks and seeds. **CONSERVATION:** Winters from n Africa, Asia Minor, to s e China, s to c Africa, s e Asia, East Indies and Philippines. **NOTES:** Performs "broken-wing" display to distract predators from nest. Details of breeding biology largely unknown; little studied in N.A. Found mostly in Eurasia. **ESSAYS:** Walking vs. Hopping, p. 69; DNA and Passerine Classification, p. 662; Distraction Displays, p. 115; How Do We Find Out About Bird Biology?, p. 319. **REF:** Gabrielson and Lincoln, 1959.

White Wagtail

Motacilla alba Linnaeus

NG–342; G–254; PW– 250; AW–767; AM(III)–76

0'–10'

F

5–6
(4–8)
MONOG

F –M
I: 12–14 DAYS
ALTRICIAL
F: 14–15 DAYS
MF

SNAILS

HAWKS

BREEDING: Tundra near water. ? broods. **DISPLAYS:** Variable courtship: male approaches female with tail spread and depressed, wings drooped, or with tail spread and erected vertically, bill pointed upward, and wings drooped, slightly spread, or fluttered. **NEST:** Among or under rocks, also in cavity in stream bank; of grass, forbs, leaves, roots, twigs, lichen, moss, occ held together with mud, lined with grass, hair, feathers. **EGGS:** Grayish- or bluish-white, flecked with brown. 0.8" (20 mm). **DIET:** Incl spiders. Occ forages in shallow water. **CONSERVATION:** Winters from s Eurasia to s Africa, Indian Ocean coasts, East Indies, Philippines. **NOTES:** Named for continuous up and down motion of tail; when walking or running, head characteristically moves backwards and forwards. Widespread in Eurasia. Uncommon and unstudied in AK. **ESSAYS:** Brood Parasitism, p. 287; DNA and Passerine Classification, p 662; How Do We Find Out About Bird Biology?, p. 319. **REF:** Gabrielson and Lincoln, 1959.

Incubation Time

How much time different species actually spend sitting on the eggs during the incubation period is even more variable than who does the sitting. Individual bouts of incubation by many small passerines such as wrens may last less than ten minutes; an albatross, in contrast, may sit on its eggs continuously for weeks at a stretch. Where only one parent incubates, it usually spends about two-thirds to three-quarters of the daytime hours on the eggs, and the remainder feeding. Flycatchers and others that hunt flying insects spend only slightly over half their time on the nests. Small birds have high metabolic rates, and stoking their fast-burning fires exhausts fat reserves rapidly. They could not survive even a small part of a normal albatross incubating session.

The constancy of incubation often is genetically controlled and adapted to the habitat of the species. It may have a profound effect on the ability of different species to colonize new areas. For example, two starling species, the European Starling and the Asian Crested Myna, were both introduced into North America in the late 1800s. The species have very similar breeding habits, but the former has spread over virtually the entire continent; the latter has remained restricted to the vicinity of Vancouver where it was introduced. One hypothesis to explain the different successes of these two close relatives is that the myna's incubation constancy is genetically attuned to its subtropical homeland. It sits on its eggs for only about half of the day; the starling incubates for almost three-quarters of the hours of daylight. Although both lay clutches of 5 eggs, the starling successfully rears an average of 3.5 young per clutch; the myna manages to fledge an average of 2. This relatively low reproductive rate may account for the myna's limited success in Vancouver, compared with the explosive spread of the European Starling.

Since, in general, birds do not begin incubating until the clutch is complete, "incubation time" is defined as the period from the laying of the *last* egg of the clutch until that egg hatches (or, if individual eggs can't be identified, from the last egg laid to the first egg hatched). It is one more aspect of incubation that varies a great deal. Incubation time is roughly correlated with the weight of the egg. The eggs of small songbirds generally hatch in about 11 days; those of the Royal Albatross in about 80 days.

More information on incubation, based on careful, long-term observations of nests, is needed for most species of North American birds. Data to be gathered include who incubates (and if both parents do, how the load is shared), the proportion of time the eggs are covered in different kinds of weather, egg turning frequency, and elapsed time from laying to hatching.

SEE: Incubation: Heating Eggs, p. 393; Hatching Asynchrony and Brood Reduction, p. 307; Who Incubates?, p. 27. REF: White and Kinney, 1974.

Yellow Wagtail
Motacilla flava Linnaeus

NG–342; G–254; PW–250; AW–pl 425; AM(III)–74

		F –M?		
		I: 10–13 DAYS		
F?	5–6	ALTRICIAL	SNAILS	HAWKS?
	(4–7)	F: 15–16 DAYS	BERRIES	
	MONOG	MF(?)		

BREEDING: Low tundra. Occ 2? broods. **DISPLAYS:** In courtship, male flies up 60'–90' and floats downward on stiff, decurved wings, singing and slowly spreading and elevating tail; nearing ground, male glides to bush or rise, repeats display. **NEST:** Under edge of tussock or overhanging bank; variable, of grass, forbs, leaves, club moss, lined with hair, feathers. **EGGS:** Buff to off-white, marked with browns. 0.8″ (19 mm). **DIET:** Incl aquatic insects, worms. **CONSERVATION:** Winters from n Africa, s Asia, and e China to s Africa and East Indies. **NOTES:** Named for continuous up and down motion of tail. Widespread in Eurasia, locally common but unstudied in N.A. **ESSAYS:** DNA and Passerine Classification, p. 662; Visual Displays, p. 5; How Do We Find Out About Bird Biology?, p. 319. **REF:** Gabrielson and Lincoln, 1959.

American Dipper
Cinclus mexicanus Swainson

NG–342; G–232; PW– 173; AW–pl 492; AM(II)–356

 OVEN   ON ROCKS IN WATER

			F		
			I: 13–17 DAYS		
BRIDGE	F	4–5 (3–6)	ALTRICIAL	FISH	
0' +		MONOG	F: 18–25 DAYS		
		(POLYGYN)	F –M		

BREEDING: Swift mountain streams. 2 broods in most of range. **DISPLAYS:** Courtship: male stretches neck upward, bill vertical, wings down and partly spread, struts and sings before female; occ male and female perform together, ending in upward jump with breasts touching. **NEST:** On cliff face among moss and ferns, behind waterfall, or on midstream rock; like hut or oven with arched opening near bottom; of interwoven moss, unlined or lined with moss. **EGGS:** White, unmarked. 1.0″ (26 mm). **DIET:** Fish are small (2″–3″); possibly aquatic plants? **CONSERVATION:** Winter resident. Favored habitat threatened by pollution in some areas. **NOTES:** Oft forages underwater: "flies" to depths of 20' +. Adaptations for semiaquatic life incl much larger oil glands than other passerines' and scales that close nostrils when underwater. "Dips" up and down with entire body on alighting, possibly to signal mate. Pair bonds may last as little as 3 weeks, then pair with new mates. Polygynous females aggressive toward each other. Young somewhat more precocial than most passerines: can climb, dive, and swim on departing nest. Winter territories range from solitary to harmonious group occupation. Also known as Water Ouzel. **ESSAYS:** Dipping, p. 483; Swimming, p. 73; Polygyny, p. 443; Preening, p. 53; Precocial and Altricial Young, p. 581; Helping to Conserve Birds—Local Level, p. 361,—National Level, p. 363. **REFS:** Morse, 1979; Price and Bock, 1983.

Dipping

The most unusual foraging strategy of any North American songbird is that of the American Dipper. This bird is often seen flying rapidly along mountain streams, perching on emergent rocks, wading in the water, and frequently disappearing beneath its surface. Although dippers occasionally glean insects from streamside rocks or even flycatch, they extract most of their prey from the water. Often they wade along with their heads beneath the surface snapping up prey. They also stride along the bottom completely submerged and "fly" underwater using powerful beats of their wings as they search for food. Dipper plumage is very soft, dense, and difficult to satu-

rate, and a white nictitating membrane (third eyelid) can be drawn across the eye to help keep it clear of dirt suspended in the water. Amazingly, these birds are able to forage on the bottom of streams in which the current is too fast and the water too deep for people to stand.

Dippers are completely dependent on stream and river productivity, since even those prey captured out of water mostly have aquatic larvae. The food preferences of dippers overlap those of trout, but the degree of competition between them has not been determined. However much competition may exist between the birds and the fishes, the need to preserve their common habitat gives ornithologists common cause with anglers.

SEE: Swimming, p. 73; Songbird Foraging, p. 381.   REF: Price and Bock, 1983.

Bohemian Waxwing

Bombycilla garrulus Linnaeus

NG–344; G–258; PE–224; PW–190; AE–pl 507; AW–pl 565; AM(III)–82

| 4'–50' | ? | 4–6 (2–6) MONOG | F? I: 14? DAYS ALTRICIAL F: 13–16(?) DAYS MF (?) | BERRIES FRUIT | HAWKS |

BREEDING: Conif and conif-decid woodland. 1? brood. **DISPLAYS:** One recorded observation of courtship: male (?) struts before female with partially spread tail, drooped wings, raised crest, body held stiffly upright. **NEST:** Variable in position and height; of twigs, grass, moss, lined with fine materials. **EGGS:** Pale bluish-gray, marked with black, esp at large end. 1.0" (25 mm). **DIET:** Also flowers. In winter, berries, fruit, tree sap. Young fed berries as well as insects. Like Cedar Waxwing, has reputation for gluttony. **CONSERVATION:** Winters within N.A. **NOTES:** Named for bright red waxy substance exuded from feather shafts of adults' secondaries (function unknown but may serve as in Cedar Waxwing). Nomadic, moving about in flocks, and not territorial. Winter flocks oft with Cedar Waxwings and American Robins; in some winters, irrupts to s. Very tame. Breeding biology not well known. **ESSAYS:** Irruptions, p. 639; Determining Diets, p. 535; Mixed-Species Flocking, p. 433; How Do We Find About Bird Biology?, p. 319. **REF:** Bent, 1950.

Cedar Waxwing

Bombycilla cedrorum Vieillot

NG–344; G–258; PE–224; PW– 190; AE–pl 506; AW–pl 566; AM(III)–84

| CONIF TREE 6'–50' | MF | 3–5 (2–6) MONOG | FM? I: 12 (10–16) DAYS ALTRICIAL F: 16 (14–18) DAYS MF | INSECTS | HAWKS |

BREEDING: Woodland, forest edge, well-planted suburbs. 1, occ 2 broods. **DISPLAYS:** Food sharing, beak rubbing, male-female "dances," all interpreted as courtship. **NEST:** Variable in position in tree; bulky or compact, of twigs, grass, moss, lined with fine grass, moss, rootlets, pine needles, hair. **EGGS:** Pale bluish-gray, dotted with black, brown. 0.8" (22 mm). **DIET:** Incl berries, flowers, tree sap; ca. 70% fruit avg over the year. Young fed insects first, but berries added within a few days. Like Bohemian Waxwing, has reputation for gluttony. **CONSERVATION:** Winters s to c Panama. Uncommon cowbird host; rejects cowbird eggs, usu by deserting nest (esp early in nesting cycle), ejecting egg from nest, or occ by damaging cowbird egg. **NOTES:** Occ nests in small colonies. Named for bright red waxy substance exuded from feather shafts of adults' secondaries; function unknown but may serve as a signal of age and social status used in pair formation: second-year birds lack entirely or have very few waxy tips. Older birds pair preferentially with each other and have greater nesting success than pairs of younger birds. Conflicting reports on whether both male and female incubate. Moves about in feeding flocks, esp in winter. Berries oft passed from bird to bird. Very tame. **ESSAYS:** Irruptions, p. 639; Brood Parasitism, p. 287; Cowbirds, p. 619; Who Incubates?, p. 27. **REFS:** Leck and Cantor, 1979; McPherson, 1987; Mountjoy and Robertson, 1988; Rothstein, 1976.

Bird Names—XI

Waxwings are so called because the red, drop-shaped, waxlike tips of the secondaries (prolongations of their shafts) reminded people of sealing wax. The Cedar Waxwing is fond of cedar berries, but debate surrounds the naming of the Bohemian Waxwing. It does occur in that region of western Czechoslovakia (as well as in much of the rest of the northern parts of Eurasia), but the name is thought to refer to the way the bird moves around without appearing to have a permanent home.

Phainopepla is both the scientific and common name of our representative of the family of silky flycatchers. It comes from the Greek meaning "shining robe," in reference to its plumage. Its specific name is *Phainopepla nitens*, which makes it redundant, since the trivial name, *nitens*, also means "shining"—this time in Latin.

The origins of the name starling are lost in Anglo-Saxon antiquity. The name may actually derive from "little star," referring to its silhouette in flight. *Sturnus vulgaris* just means "common starling" in Latin. Pipit comes from the Latin "to chirp." The Water Pipit is said to have that name because in Europe it is found near water. Sprague's Pipit was named by Audubon after Isaac Sprague, who collected the first specimen while accompanying him on a trip on the Missouri River.

Thrashers are, curiously enough, so named because they were once called "thrushers" (same Anglo-Saxon root as thrush)—not because they "thrash around." The Crissal Thrasher has a rusty colored "crissum" (undertail coverts). Thrush may also be related to the Greek verb "to twitter."

The Gray Catbird is named for its color and call. The mockingbird, of course, imitates the songs of other species. Its scientific name, *Mimus polyglottos*, is Latin for "mimic with many tongues."

The name shrike has the same Anglo-Saxon roots as "shriek." Shrikes have heads that are larger in proportion to their bodies than most birds, and this is noted in Loggerhead, which has the same origins as "blockhead." The generic name of the shrikes, *Lanius*, is Latin for "butcher" (and shrikes are often termed "butcherbirds"). The Northern Shrike, *Lanius excubitor* was given its trivial name, the Latin word for "sentinel" by Linnaeus, who thought the bird looked out for hawks and warned little birds. Actually, of course, an erect stationary shrike *is* looking for little birds or insects, but not to warn them. The trivial name of the Loggerhead, *ludovicianus* means "of Louisiana" in Latin.

Wheatear, interestingly, appears to have nothing to do with ears. The name seems to be a euphemistic version of "white arse," for its distinctive white rump.

The Hermit Thrush spends its winters alone; solitaire comes from the French "alone," and recognizes that it is not a bird commonly found in flocks. Veery is thought simply to imitate the bird's song.

REF: Choate, 1985; Owen, 1985.

Phainopepla

Phainopepla nitens Swainson

NG–344; G–258; PW– 190; AW–pl 613; AM(III)–86

| | | | MF
I: 14 DAYS | | |
| SHRUB
4'–50' | M–F | 2–3
(2–4)
MONOG | ALTRICIAL
F: 19–20 DAYS
MF | INSECTS | HAWKS
HOVER &
GLEAN |

BREEDING: Desert scrub, semiarid and riparian woodland. 2 broods, possibly 3. **DISPLAYS:** Courtship: male rises to 300', circles or zigzags above territory; usu performed simultaneously by several birds over respective territories. Small feeding groups, chases, and courtship feeding also occur. **NEST:** Oft in upright crotch of mistletoe; compact, shallow, of twigs, flowers, plant down, leaves, bound with spider silk, lined with hair, down. Male occ builds 2 or 3 nests. **EGGS:** Grayish, dotted with violet, black. 0.8" (22 mm). **DIET:** Esp mistletoe berries in deserts. Young fed insects for 2–3 days, then also fruit. **CONSERVATION:** Winters s to c Mexico. Rare cowbird host. **NOTES:** Nests early in desert, then moves to more moist habitat and renests. Where berries are clumped, large nesting/feeding territories occur; where berries are scattered, territories consist of only the nesting tree, breeding is in loose colonies, and foraging is social. Hawking has "fluttery" quality. Rarely lands on ground. Defends mistletoe clumps from other species. Winter territories held separately by both sexes. **ESSAYS:** Territoriality, p. 387; Interspecific Territoriality, p. 385; Courtship Feeding, p. 181. **REF:** Walsberg, 1977.

Crested Myna

Acridotheres cristatellus Linnaeus

NG–346; G–260; PW– 193; AW–591; AM(III)–94

| | | | MF
I: 14–15 DAYS | | |
| BUILDING
10'–25'
(2'–60') | MF | 4–5
(4–7)
MONOG | ALTRICIAL
F: 27 DAYS
MF | | FOLIAGE
GLEAN |

BREEDING: Open fields, open woodland, suburbia, cities. 1 brood. **DISPLAYS:** ? **NEST:** In any almost fully enclosed cavity; slovenly accumulation of grass, forbs, rootlets, paper, snakeskin. **EGGS:** Greenish-blue. 1.2" (30 mm). **DIET:** Insects and other inverts (predominant food of nestlings); fruit, berries, seeds (esp in winter). Much food obtained at garbage dumps and manure piles (housefly larvae at the latter). Reported to eat eggs of other birds. **CONSERVATION:** Winter resident. Introduced around 1897 in Vancouver, BC, from where it has not spread; apparently declining, at least partly due to competition with an expanding (and climatically better adapted) European Starling population. **NOTES:** Roost in flocks like starlings on buildings and in trees. **ESSAYS:** Avian Invaders, p. 633; Incubation Time, p. 481; Helping to Conserve Birds—Local Level, p. 361; Communal Roosting, p. 615; European Starlings, p. 489. **REFS:** Godfrey, 1986; Johnson and Cowan, 1974.

Anting

Many different songbird species have been observed picking up single ants or small groups and rubbing them on their feathers. Less commonly, other songbirds "ant" by spreading their wings and lying on an anthill, and squirming or otherwise stimulating the ants to swarm up among their feathers.

The purpose of anting is not well understood, but the most reasonable assumption seems to be that it is a way of acquiring the defensive secretions of ants, primarily for their insecticidal, miticidal, fungicidal, or bactericidal properties and, perhaps secondarily, as a supplement to the bird's own preen oil. The former explanation is reinforced by a growing body of evidence on the biocidal properties of ant secretions and by an observation of a Jungle Myna (*Acridotheres fuscus*) actively "anting" with a millipede, whose potent defensive secretions (evolved to fend off the millipede's enemies) could be smelled from 15 feet away. Likewise, the observed correlation of anting activity with high humidity might be explained by the documented fungicidal properties of ant secretions. Because the seasonal timing of anting and molting (spring and summer) often correspond, some have suggested that anting may soothe the skin during feather replacement. It seems more likely that the seasonal relationship simply reflects the greater activity of ants during those periods.

Recording anting and related behavior is an activity where birders can easily gather information of interest to biologists. Those who live in or visit the Vancouver area, for example, should be alert to the possibility that the Crested Myna might show behavior similar to its close jungle relative. If you see anting, be sure to make detailed notes of the circumstances in which it is taking place.

SEE: Preening, p. 53; Disease and Parasitism, p. 399; Bathing and Dusting, p. 429; Head Scratching, p. 543; Tool Using, p. 435.   REFS: Beattie, 1985; Ehrlich et al., 1986; Potter 1970; Simmons, 1966.

European Starling
Sturnus vulgaris Linnaeus

NG–346; G–260; PE–256; PW–pl 52; AE–pl 565; AW–pl 611; AM(III)–92

			F–M		
			I: 12–14 DAYS		
BUILDING	MF	4–6	ALTRICIAL	FRUIT	FOLIAGE
10'–25'		(4–8)	F: 18–21 DAYS	SEEDS	GLEAN
(2'–60')		MONOG	MF		

BREEDING: Habitat generalist: open fields, woodland, suburbia, cities (usu absent from deep forest). 2, occ 3 broods. **DISPLAYS:** Courting male adopts variety of postures while vocalizing; highest intensity incl flailing wings in hunched stance. **NEST:** In any handy cavity; slovenly cup of grass, twigs, forbs, rootlets, straw. Male initiates nest, female completes it, adds lining. **EGGS:** Pale bluish or greenish white, marked with browns. 1.2″ (30 mm). **DIET:** Incl other inverts, berries. **CONSERVATION:** Although resident in winter, many individuals tend to wander s. Successfully introduced into N.A. in New York City in 1890–91, now a pest. **NOTES:** Occ nest in loose colony, laying initiated synchronously. Males outnumber females in many populations. Occ polygynous. Females occ lay eggs in nests of other females. Male incubates for only small part of day. Territory does not extend much beyond nest hole. Fly and roost in huge flocks oft with blackbirds, cowbirds, grackles, and American Robins. Thought to be important competitors of bluebirds and other hole nesters. Incorporate sounds of other species and of inanimate objects (mechanical squeaks, grinding) into own vocalizations. **ESSAYS:** Avian Invaders, p. 633; European Starlings, p. 489; Vocal Copying, p. 469; Helping to Conserve Birds—National Level, p. 363; Communal Roosting, p. 615; Coloniality, p. 173; Polygyny, p. 443. **REFS:** Feare, 1984; Kessel, 1957.

White-eyed Vireo
Vireo griseus Boddaert

NG–348; G–264; PE–228; AE–pl 383; AM(III)–96

			MF		
			I: 12–16 DAYS		
1'–8'	MF	4	ALTRICIAL		
(1'–8'+)		(3–5)	F: ? DAYS		
		MONOG	MF		

BREEDING: Brushy, moist areas near streams, old fields with thickets, scrub in open forest. 1 brood in n, 2 in s. **DISPLAYS:** Courtship: male postures before female, fluffs feathers, fans tail, gives "whining" or "snarling" call. **NEST:** Rim suspended by forked twig in scrub oak, shrub, sapling; of twigs, rootlets, bark strips, coarse grass, leaves, bound with silk, veg fiber, lined with fine grass, fibers. **EGGS:** White, spotted with brown, black. 0.8″ (19 mm). **DIET:** Almost entirely insects during breeding season; 20%–30% berries in autumn and winter. **CONSERVATION:** Winters from Bahamas and Bermuda s along e slope of Mexico to Honduras. Common cowbird host. **NOTES:** Fearless around nest. Song repertoires of most males consist of 10–14 song types (range 5–17). Reportedly a vocal appropriator. **ESSAYS:** Vocal Copying, p. 469; Vocal Functions, p. 471; Cowbirds, p. 619. **REFS:** Adkisson and Conner, 1978; Barlow, 1980; Borror, 1987; Bradley, 1980.

European Starlings

The first two attempts to introduce the European Starling into North America failed. The third did not, and what has followed since those 60 starlings were released in 1890 in New York City's Central Park has kept ornithologists alternately astounded, puzzled, and infuriated. Much as European human settlers did in the preceding years, the invading birds pushed their way across the continent, taking advantage of its riches and, where necessary, usurping the habitat of residents. What enabled the starling to advance all the way to the Pacific within a mere 60 years?

Starlings were not always pests, although, according to historical records, they have associated with people since the advent of agriculture. They were described in detail by Aristotle and Pliny, and the Romans taught them to mimic human speech. The meager mention of starlings by European chroniclers before 1830 is thought to indicate rather limited numbers. After 1830, however, milder European winters eliminated starlings' need to migrate or shortened the migration route, and the conversion of forest into farms created more favorable open habitats and provided cereal grains for food. These concurrent changes are thought to have favored double-brooding, breeding at an earlier age, and formation of ever larger starling colonies (which probably have higher breeding success than small ones) and led to a rapid increase in those populations. Before the turn of the century, the species was brought to our shores.

Few people like starlings. But disdain of the species may be tempered by knowledge of its biology. Take, for example, its bill. Unlike most of the 130-member starling family, Sturnidae, the European Starling has jaw muscles that work "backward." Instead of using most of their power to clamp the bill shut, these muscles use it to spring the bill open. Thus the bill functions not just to grip prey but also to pry apart obscuring plants. The closed bill is inserted between blades of grass in thick turf or other cover, and then sprung open to expose hidden prey. As the bill opens, the eyes move forward toward each other, permitting binocular vision. This readily observed foraging technique enables the starling to detect not only active prey but also dormant or stationary prey, as well. William Beecher, who made this discovery during a seven-year study of songbird head musculature and skull adaptations, suggests that this unique hunting maneuver was also key to the high rate of survival of starlings during winter.

Consider, as well, starlings' housekeeping. Even more than most cavity nesters, starlings use a wide array of sites and an endless variety of human-built structures. Typically cavity nesters lay their eggs on nothing more than a bed of chips or feathers, but starlings build nests inside their chambers. In addition to gathering dead grasses for those nests, starlings carefully select fresh green vegetation rich in chemicals that act as fumigants against parasites and pathogens. Green sprigs are added to the nest until the eggs hatch. To maintain its insulating properties the nest is kept dry by removing the fecal sacs of the nestlings. Once the chicks are feathered, nest

Black-capped Vireo

Vireo atricapillus Woodhouse

NG–348; G–262; PE–228; PW–pl 49; AE–583; AM(III)–100

MF
I: 14–17 DAYS

1'–6'   MF   4   ALTRICIAL   SEEDS
(1'–15')   (3–5)   F: 10–12 DAYS   FRUIT
                          MONOG   MF

BREEDING: Oak-juniper woodland and scrub. 2 broods. **DISPLAYS:** Male follows female singing courtship song; male also performs courtship song-flight with fluttering wings. **NEST:** Rim suspended by forked twig usu in scrub oak or other short tree; of bark strips, coarse grass, leaves, bound with silk, veg fiber, lined with fine grass. Female selects nest site. Built in 4–16 days. **EGGS:** White, unmarked. 0.7" (18 mm). **DIET:** Incl spiders. **CONSERVATION:** Winters from n w Mexico (w slope) s to s w Mexico. Breeding range has decreased this century. Endangered Species threatened by habitat losses and cowbird parasitism; cowbird control measures being taken on Edwards Plateau of TX where >90% of nests are usu parasitized. **NOTES:** Males show strong site tenacity to breeding territory. Female incubates at night, male and female alternate in day. Female broods. Male brings 75% of nestlings' food. Fledglings tended 4–7 days, female then renests, occ with different male. Moves restlessly in dense cover as it forages. **ESSAYS:** Decline of Eastern Songbirds, p. 495; Site Tenacity, p. 189; Brood Parasitism, p. 287; Cowbirds, p. 619; Birds and the Law, p. 293; Who Incubates?, p. 27. **REFS:** Barlow, 1978, 1980; Grzybowski et al., 1986.

Yellow-throated Vireo

Vireo flavifrons Vieillot

NG–348; G–264; PE–228; AE–pl 362; AM(III)–102

MF
I: 14 DAYS

20'–60'   MF   4   ALTRICIAL
(3'–60')   (3–5)   F: 14 DAYS
                          MONOG   MF

BREEDING: Open decid woodland and forest edge, decid-conif woodland. ? broods. **DISPLAYS:** In pairing, male gives nest-building display slightly crouched with body horizontal, usu without nest material in bill. **NEST:** Very well made, deep cup, suspended by rim from prongs of forked twig, generally rounded; of grass, forbs, shredded bark, plant fibers, spider web, cocoons, decorated with lichen, lined with fine grass, pine needles. Male selects site. **EGGS:** White to pinkish-white, spotted with browns, esp near large end (most heavily marked of vireo eggs). 0.7" (18 mm). **DIET:** Almost entirely insects; berries compose 2%–10% of diet, mostly in fall. **CONSERVATION:** Winters s through n e Mexico to Colombia, n Venezuela. Common cowbird host, occ builds second floor of nest over cowbird eggs, killing them. Pesticide spraying of shade trees has reduced numbers in suburban areas, esp in New England. **NOTES:** Males occ start building one or more nests before pairing. Fearless around nest. Parents divide fledged brood and leave nest area. Territorial on wintering grounds. **ESSAYS:** Decline of Eastern Songbirds, p. 495; Fate of Bachman's Warbler, p. 505; DDT and Birds, p. 21; Cowbirds, p. 619. **REFS:** James, 1978, 1984; Smith et al., 1978.

insulation becomes superfluous, the fecal sacs are no longer removed, and fresh anti-parasite greenery is no longer added. Thus, even before fledging, starling nests resemble a pest-ridden compost. But starlings are hardier than many other cavity nesters. They can, for example, withstand the infestation of tens of thousands of mites per nest hole without an increase in mortality. Therefore nest construction includes early (but not late) incorporation of leaves containing fumigants, and minimal, but precisely timed, efforts in nest sanitation, the starling has reduced the energy costs of housekeeping while decreasing the value of its hole for reuse by its competitors.

Starlings are colonial breeders. There are reports of bachelor males feeding the young and, along with the male parent, guarding the nest tree after the fledglings and female parent depart to forage. There may thus be a tendency toward cooperative breeding (which has been found in some tropical members of the starling family) in European Starlings. Observers should be alert for signs of such behavior.

Breeding males may attempt to father a second and even third brood. Their fidelity to mates depends, in part, on the success of the previous brood, but apparently it is not uncommon for males to select a new female for a second brood, perhaps on the basis of her previous success. A family unit usually forages within 200–500 yards of its nest. During nest building and egg laying, unit members make, on average, 30 visits a day to the nest; during incubation this decreases to 18, but when young are being fed, visits jump to 260. Also, visits to the nest may not be restricted to members of a unit. Evidence points to intraspecific nest parasitism—visiting female starlings are known to dump their eggs in the active nests of other females.

In the winter, starlings become somewhat nomadic but are able to find dormant insects under snow wherever it is not too deep. They show a marked preference for foraging for insects in short grass but are extremely opportunistic and will even rely on fungus to get by in the absence of preferred foods.

Exotic "weeds" often escape the natural controls that limit their numbers at home and may, quite quickly, become pests. Is it possible to control our weedlike starlings? Some think starlings could serve humanity well by ridding pastures of insect infestations, although benefits have been demonstrated under only very special conditions. Nonetheless, a reputation for controlling pests has apparently paved the way for starlings in New Zealand, where nest boxes for them can be found atop many pastureland fence posts. The use of starlings to suppress North American insect outbreaks, however, is unlikely. Instead, programs to control starlings probably will become more common.

Starlings form aggregations with other species which may reach 10 million birds and can be astonishingly difficult to control. Congregations on trees have been discouraged by thinning the canopy. Loudspeakers have been wired throughout vineyards and orchards to broadcast distress calls, which may be effective under some conditions in keeping the birds from roosting. During the past 15 years, where massive winter roosts have oc-

Bell's Vireo

Vireo bellii Audubon

NG–350; G–264; PE–228; PW–pl 49; AE–pl 449; AW–pl 508; AM(III)–98

1'–5'   MF   4   MF
(To 25')   (3–5)   I: 14 DAYS
                MONOG ALTRICIAL
                           F: 11–12 DAYS
                           MF

BREEDING: Dense riparian thickets, mesquite, scrub oak (usu near water in semiarid areas), hedgerows between fields. 2 broods. **DISPLAYS:** In pair formation, male rapidly chases female, occ leaps and flutters before female; also follows female while singing and spreading tail. **NEST:** Suspended by rim between two twigs; usu rounded, deep, of dried leaves, shredded bark, plant fibers, spider cocoons, lined with fine grass, down, hair. Female selects site. Built in ca. 5 days. **EGGS:** White, with scattered brown spots, esp near large end, occ unmarked. 0.7″ (18 mm). **DIET:** Some fruit taken after July. **CONSERVATION:** Winters from n w Mexico s to Honduras. Blue List 1972–82, Special Concern 1986; declining in s w. CA subspecies found in valley riparian habitats now Endangered due to habitat loss. Common cowbird host, occ destroys cowbird eggs by building second floor of nest over them. **NOTES:** A restless forager. Fearless around nest. **ESSAYS:** Blue List, p. 11; Birds and the Law, p. 293; Cowbirds, p. 619. **REFS:** Barlow, 1962; Nolan, 1960.

Hutton's Vireo

Vireo huttoni Cassin

NG–350; G–264; PW–pl 49; AW–737; AM(III)–102

CONIF   MF   4   MF   BERRIES
TREE   (3–5)   I: 14 DAYS
6'–25'   MONOG ALTRICIAL
                             F: 14? DAYS
                             MF

BREEDING: Woodland, esp oak and pine-oak. ? broods. **DISPLAYS:** Courting male postures before female, fluffs feathers, fans tail, and gives "whining" or "snarling" call. **NEST:** Suspended by rim in fork of twig usu of evergreen oak; deep and round, of "Spanish moss" (lichen) bound with spider web, lined with fine dry grass. **EGGS:** White, spotted with browns, mostly near large end, occ unmarked. 0.7″ (18 mm). **DIET:** Incl spiders. **CONSERVATION:** Winter resident. Uncommon cowbird host. **NOTES:** Fearless around nest. May compete for food resources with ecologically similar Chestnut-backed Chickadee where both are resident. **ESSAYS:** Bird Guilds, p. 493; Masterbuilders, p. 445; Nest Materials, p. 369. **REFS:** Wagner, 1981; Weathers, 1983.

curred, a million or more individuals have been killed at one time by spraying with detergent (which destroys the insulating properties of the plumage). But even these local losses have not put a significant dent in starling populations.

Human modification of North American habitats permitted rapid colonization of the entire continent. Starlings are now ubiquitous, outcompeting other such cavity nesters as Eastern Bluebirds, Red-headed Woodpeckers, Northern Flickers, and Great Crested Flycatchers. Within one century, 60 starlings introduced to North America have increased to over 200,000,000 (one-third of the world's European Starling population). How fast and for how long their numbers will continue to grow is uncertain, but it is likely that managing the consequences of their introduction will continue to be difficult, expensive, and (considering the nature of the foe) often unsuccessful.

SEE: Avian Invaders, p. 633; Range Expansion, p. 459; Communal Roosting, p. 615; Bird Droppings, p. 263; Mixed-Species Flocking, p. 433; Vocal Copying, p. 469; Cooperative Breeding, p. 283; Brood Parasitism, p. 287. REFS: Beecher, 1985; Clark and Mason, 1985; Feare, 1984; Suthers, 1978; Yom-Tov et al., 1974.

Bird Guilds

Guilds are groups of species in a community that exploit the same set of resources in a similar manner, but are not necessarily closely related taxonomically. Birds that hunt for insects on the floor of a deciduous forest constitute a guild; tropical American hummingbirds and butterflies jointly form a guild of daytime nectar feeders; desert sparrows, ants, and rodents constitute a seed-eating guild. Members of guilds often differ in their precise food requirements, thus reducing the potential for competition among them when resources are limited. In a given locality, the membership of a guild can change through the year as migrants are added or subtracted.

For example, in the oak woodland on Stanford University's Jasper Ridge Biological Preserve, Chestnut-backed Chickadees, Hutton's Vireos, and Plain Titmice are resident species that form the core of a foliage- and bark-gleaning guild of insectivores. These are joined as core species by Ruby-crowned Kinglets and Yellow-rumped Warblers fall and winter, and by Blue-gray Gnatcatchers in the spring. Other guild members include Downy Woodpeckers, Bushtits, White-breasted Nuthatches, Brown Creepers, Wrentits, Bewick's Wrens, Warbling Vireos, and Townsend's Warblers. The arrival and departure of the migrants do not seem to influence the foraging of the resident guild members. In general, guild members with similar foraging sites differ in bill size, suggesting they eat prey of different sizes.

Although the bill sizes of the closely related kinglet and gnatcatcher are

Gray Vireo

Vireo vicinior Coues

NG–350; G–262; PW–pl 49; AW–616; AM(III)–100

			MF I: 13–14 DAYS		
2'–6'	MF	4 (3–5) MONOG	ALTRICIAL F: 13–14 DAYS MF		GROUND GLEAN

BREEDING: Arid thorn scrub, chaparral, piñon-juniper and oak-juniper woodland. 2 broods. **DISPLAYS:** ? **NEST:** Rim suspended from forked twig; usu rounded, deep, of grass, forbs, shredded bark, leaves, plant fibers, spider web, cocoons, lined with fine grass, long, hairlike fibers. **EGGS:** Rosy, with scattered brown spots, esp near large end. 0.7" (18 mm). **DIET:** Little known but presumably almost entirely insects. **CONSERVATION:** Winters s to n w Mexico. Frequent cowbird host, occ builds second floor of nest over cowbird eggs, killing them. **NOTES:** A restless forager, flicks tail like gnatcatcher; takes ca. 5% of prey from ground. Fearless around nest. **ESSAYS:** Nest Materials, p. 369; Masterbuilders, p. 445; Cowbirds, p. 619; Determining Diets, p. 535. **REFS:** Barlow et al., 1970; Barlow and Waver, 1971.

Solitary Vireo

Vireo solitarius Wilson

NG–350; G–262; PE–228; PW–pl 49; AE–pl 450; AW–pl 516; AM(III)–100

			MF I: 14? DAYS		
DECID TREE 4'–30'	MF	4 (3–5) MONOG	ALTRICIAL F: 14? DAYS MF		HAWKS BARK GLEAN

BREEDING: Conif-decid woodland. Occ 2 broods. **DISPLAYS:** Courting male fluffs conspicuous yellow flank feathers while bobbing, bowing, and singing to female. Male performs nest-building display while slightly crouched with body horizontal, usu without nest material in bill. **NEST:** Usu in conif tree (in e) or in oak (in w); well made, basketlike deep cup, suspended by rim from prongs of forked twig, usu rounded, of grass, forbs, shredded bark, plant fibers, spider web, cocoons, decorated with lichen, lined with fine grass, hair. Male selects site. **EGGS:** White, spotted with browns, black, esp near large end. 0.8" (20 mm). **DIET:** Almost entirely insects; fleshy fruits compose 25% of diet in January, but only 4% year-round. **CONSERVATION:** Winters s to Costa Rica, Cuba. Common cowbird host; if cowbird egg laid first, oft builds second floor of nest to cover it. **NOTES:** Males occ start building one or more nests before pairing. Fearless around nest; female is a close sitter. Parents divide fledged brood and leave nest area. Recent studies indicate w and e populations are actually two separate species. **ESSAYS:** Decline of Eastern Songbirds, p. 495; Fate of Bachman's Warbler, p. 505; Cowbirds, p. 619; Species and Speciation, p. 355; Parental Care, p. 555. **REFS:** James, 1978; Martindale, 1980.

similar, the species forage in different sites and are present in different seasons. Only the chickadee and Hutton's Vireo are potentially close competitors. If they actually are in competition, experimental removal of either species should lead to an increase in the other, although capturing enough of either to sufficiently decrease its population would be very difficult. One major problem in understanding guilds, and the communities to which they belong, is the great practical difficulty in doing such critical experiments. Scientists must also always consider the ethical question of how much disturbance is justified to gain knowledge about the birds.

SEE: Bird Communities and Competition, p. 605; Bills, p. 209; Songbird Foraging, p. 381; How Do We Find Out About Bird Biology?, p. 319. REFS: Root, 1967; Wagner, 1981.

The Decline of Eastern Songbirds

Since the end of World War II there has been a decline in forest songbird populations over much of the eastern United States. For example, in Rock Creek Park in the middle of Washington, D.C., populations of Red-eyed Vireos have dropped by 79 percent and Ovenbirds by 94 percent. Acadian Flycatchers, Yellow-throated Vireos, Black-and-white Warblers, and Hooded Warblers have disappeared entirely. The decline has not been uniform for all species; the Acadian Flycatcher and others that migrate long distances to tropical America have suffered more than residents or those like robins and towhees that can overwinter in the southern United States. Nor has the decline been equal in all types of forest; the loss of species from woodlots and small forest tracts exceeds the loss from large stretches of forest such as those of the Great Smoky Mountains National Park.

One suspected cause is, quite naturally, the rapid destruction of tropical forests where many migrants overwinter. Perhaps deforestation in Mexico, Costa Rica, and Jamaica, for instance, is responsible for the decline of some species, such as the Worm-eating Warbler. But in the last century about half of the forest breeding habitat of that species in eastern North America was destroyed, while there was relatively much less loss of tropical forests in that period. The result may well have been a *surplus* of wintering habitat. More recent deforestation has wiped out on the order of half of the tropical forests, and perhaps has just about restored the balance between available breeding and wintering habitat.

Other possible explanations of declines in eastern migratory songbirds have to do with changes within North America. They include increased cowbird parasitism, loss and fragmentation of habitat, and increased nest predation in habitat patches. When Christopher Columbus landed, cowbirds are thought to have been largely confined to open country west of the

Red-eyed Vireo

NG–352; G–266; PE–226; PW–pl 49; AE–pl 453; AW–pl 515; AM(III)–106

| DECID 5'–35' (2'–60') | F | 4 (3–5) MONOG | F I: 11–14 DAYS ALTRICIAL F: 10–12 DAYS MF | FRUIT | FOLIAGE GLEAN |

BREEDING: Decid forest and woodland, well-planted suburbs, occ conif forest. ? broods. **DISPLAYS:** Courtship: male draws feathers close, female fluffs up, male rocks body and head from side-to-side while facing female; male and female quiver wings simultaneously. **NEST:** Dainty, well made, basketlike deep cup, suspended by rim from prongs of forked twig, usu rounded; of grapevine bark, fine grass, forbs, rootlets, spider web, cocoons. Female selects site. **EGGS:** White, spotted with browns, black, esp toward large end, occ almost unmarked. 0.8" (20 mm). **DIET:** Almost entirely insects; snails, spiders also fed to young. On wintering grounds, entirely fruit. **CONSERVATION:** Winters in w Amazonia. One of the most frequent cowbird hosts, only occ buries parasites' eggs under nest floor. Once considered one of the three most common species in e decid forest, now declining. **NOTES:** Interspecifically territorial with Philadelphia Vireo in structurally simple forests; in more complex forests, territories overlap and aggression varies with food abundance and stage of nesting. Male song repertoires average 40 song types; rarely sings same song type in succession. Recently split into separate species: birds breeding in s TX s through C.A. are Yellow-green Vireo (*Vireo flavoviridis*) and apparently do not interbreed with Red-eyed Vireos. **ESSAYS:** Decline of Eastern Songbirds, p. 495; Interspecific Territoriality, p. 385; Birds in the Bush, p. 541; Mixed-Species Flocking, p. 433; Cowbirds, p. 619; Species and Speciation, p. 355; Vocal Functions, p. 471. **REFS:** Barlow and Rice, 1977; Lawrence, 1953; Robinson, 1981.

Black-whiskered Vireo

NG–352; G–266; PE–226; AE–pl 452; AM(III)–106

| 3'–20' | F | 3 (2–3) MONOG | F I: ? DAYS ALTRICIAL F: ? DAYS MF(?) | BERRIES | |

BREEDING: Mangrove swamps. ? broods. **DISPLAYS:** ? **NEST:** In mangrove; well made, basketlike deep cup, suspended by rim from prongs of forked twig; usu rounded, of grass, forbs, plant fibers, spider web, cocoons, lichen, lined with fine grass, pine needles, hair. **EGGS:** White, spotted with browns, purple, black. 0.8" (21 mm). **DIET:** Incl spiders, some fruit. Up to 50% fruit on wintering grounds. **CONSERVATION:** Winters from e Colombia, Venezuela, and Guianas s (e of Andes) to Amazonia. **NOTES:** Males sing for much of day on breeding territory. A restless forager high in trees. Fearless around nest. **ESSAYS:** Masterbuilders, p. 445; Nest Materials, p. 369; Vocal Functions, p. 471. **REFS:** Barlow and Bortolotti, 1987; Cruz, 1980; Kale, 1978.

Mississippi, because the continuous forests of the eastern United States did not provide suitable habitat for their ground feeding or social displays. As the forests were cleared, cowbirds extended their range, occupying most of the East but remaining rare until this century. Then increased winter food supply, especially the rising abundance of waste grain in southern rice fields, created a cowbird population explosion. The forest-dwelling tropical migrants—especially vireos, warblers, tanagers, thrushes, and flycatchers—have proven very vulnerable to cowbird parasitism. And that vulnerability is highest for those birds nesting near the edge of wooded habitat and thus closest to the open country preferred by the cowbirds.

This provides one explanation for the much sharper decline of songbirds in forest fragments than in large areas of continuous forest: nest sites in a forest fragment are on average closer to open land than those in continuous forest because there is more "edge" per unit area. In addition, there is evidence that fragmentation *per se*, with both reduction of total habitat area and increased isolation of habitat remnants, has strong negative effects on forest-dwelling long-range migrants that need forest habitat, while often favoring short-range migrants and residents that do not have such strict habitat requirements.

Ecologist David Wilcove of the Wilderness Society has tested the nest predation hypothesis experimentally by putting quail eggs in straw-colored wicker baskets either on or above the ground, and placing large numbers of such pseudonests in forest patches of various sizes. He also constructed some artificial cavity nests to compare with the artificial cup nests. Wilcove found that predation was heavier in suburban woodlots (70 percent) than in rural woodlots (48 percent), and much lower in large continuous forests than in smaller fragments. In the Great Smoky Mountains, eggs in only 2 percent of the experimental nests were destroyed. Several of the species that are most sensitive to forest fragmentation, such as the Ovenbird and Black-and-white Warbler, nest on or near the ground, and most of the migrants make cup nests rather than nesting in cavities. Predation on cup nests was much higher than on the cavity nests, and more ground nests were destroyed than those placed above ground level.

The pseudonests were more conspicuous than normal nests, so Wilcove's experiments cannot be used to determine actual predation rates, but they do strongly indicate that higher levels of nest predation are at least a partial explanation for the decline of migrant songbirds in forest fragments. Again, the increased proportion of forest edge in fragments is implicated; many important nest predators, especially the Blue Jay, American Crow, and Common Grackle, are most common along woodland borders. In addition jays and crows have benefited greatly from other human-induced changes in the landscape, such as increased suburbanization. High losses of songbird eggs in suburban areas are doubtless due to the abundance there not just of nest-robbing birds, but of dogs, cats, rats, raccoons, and gray squirrels as well.

So it looks as if many factors may be contributing to the decline of

Warbling Vireo

Vireo gilvus Vieillot

NG–352; G–266; PE–226; PW–pl 49; AE–pl 454; AW–pl 514; AM(III)–104

SHRUB	MF	4	MF
30'–90'		(3–5)	I: 12 DAYS
(4'–90')		MONOG	ALTRICIAL
			F: 16 DAYS
		BERRIES	HOVER &
			MF GLEAN

BREEDING: Open decid and decid-conif woodland, riparian forest and thickets. ? broods. **DISPLAYS:** Female quivers wings, oft in response to courtship song of male. Most courtship occurs within 30' of nest. Audubon reported that male struts around female with wings and tail spread. **NEST:** Usu high in tree, oft lower (<30') in w in tree or shrub; very well made, compact, basketlike deep cup, suspended by rim from prongs of forked twig; of bark strips, leaves, veg fibers, grass. **EGGS:** White, spotted with browns, black. 0.8" (19 mm). **DIET:** Almost entirely insects, some spiders; few berries. **CONSERVATION:** Winters from n w Mexico s to El Salvador. Common cowbird host, does not attempt to destroy their eggs. Has declined in urban areas from pesticide spraying of shade trees. **NOTES:** Forages and sings mostly in treetops. Fearless around nest. Both sexes brood. **ESSAYS:** Bird Guilds, p. 493; Brood Parasitism, p. 287; DDT and Birds, p. 21; Cowbirds, p. 619. **REF:** Howes-Jones, 1985.

Philadelphia Vireo

Vireo philadelphicus Cassin

NG–352; G–266; PE–226; PW–pl 49; AE–pl 451; AM(III)–104

30'–80'	F	4	MF
(10'–90')		(3–5)	I: 14 DAYS
		MONOG	ALTRICIAL
			F: 12–14 DAYS
		BERRIES	MF
			FOLIAGE GLEAN HAWKS

BREEDING: Decid and decid-conif forest. ? broods. **DISPLAYS:** In courtship and pair-bond maintenance: male and female wing quiver; male sways with feathers erect, tail fanned. **NEST:** Well made, basketlike deep cup, suspended by rim from prongs of forked twig; of birch bark, lichen, fine grass, forbs, spider web, cocoons, lined with pine needles, fine grass, feathers. Female selects site. **EGGS:** White, spotted with browns, black, esp toward large end, occ almost unmarked. 0.8" (19 mm). **DIET:** Almost entirely insects; fruit ca. 20% of diet in September but only 7% year-round. **CONSERVATION:** Winters from Guatemala s to c Panama. Rare cowbird host. **NOTES:** Interspecifically territorial with Red-eyed Vireo in structurally simple forests; in more complex forests, territories overlap and aggression varies with food abundance and stage of nesting. Forages more actively than Red-eyed Vireo; oft hangs chickadee-like from clusters of leaves when feeding. Fearless around nest. **ESSAYS:** Decline of Eastern Songbirds, p. 495; Interspecific Territoriality, p. 385. **REFS:** Barlow and Rice, 1977; Robinson, 1981.

songbirds. Thus, sadly, the prognosis is grim. Ornithologists think that cowbirds are likely to continue to increase, and the now-thriving nest predators are unlikely to decline. The loss of songbirds might be halted if conservation depended entirely on temperate zone events, because habitat fragmentation in the United States and Canada could be stopped or its effects controlled. But the inexorable destruction of tropical rain forests shows no sign of abating. If it continues at current rates for another few decades, it seems likely that many of our passerine species will become much rarer or even disappear.

North American migrants that overwinter in mature tropical forest are listed here (this tabulation is based on the work of Princeton ecologist John Terborgh with additions by David Wilcove). These species are ones that tend to shun disturbance, but may do well in second-growth tropical forest, edges, or woodlots. Unfortunately, however, deforestation in the tropics rarely leads to such habitats, but rather to vast expanses of overgrazed pastures, canefields, and the like. Thus the following should be the North American birds most at risk as the destruction of tropical forests continues. If possible, you might want to do long-term censuses of breeding populations of one or more of these species should they occur in your area. And should your birding take you to the tropics at the right season, watch for "our" migrants. We have much to learn about their wintering ecology.

Mississippi Kite	Black-throated Gray Warbler
Swallow-tailed Kite	Golden-cheeked Warbler
Broad-winged Hawk	Bachman's Warbler (extinct?)
Chuck-will's Widow	Tennessee Warbler
Whip-poor-will	Northern Parula
Yellow-billed Cuckoo	Magnolia Warbler
Black-billed Cuckoo	Cape May Warbler
Yellow-bellied Sapsucker	Townsend's Warbler
Great Crested Flycatcher	Black-throated Green Warbler
Yellow-bellied Flycatcher	Cerulean Warbler
Acadian Flycatcher	Yellow-throated Warbler
Eastern Wood-Pewee	Grace's Warbler
Western Wood-Pewee	Blackburnian Warbler
Wood Thrush	Chestnut-sided Warbler
Swainson's Thrush	Bay-breasted Warbler
Gray-cheeked Thrush	Blackpoll Warbler
Veery	Ovenbird
Blue-gray Gnatcatcher	Northern Waterthrush
Black-capped Vireo	Louisiana Waterthrush
Solitary Vireo	Kentucky Warbler
Yellow-throated Vireo	Hooded Warbler
Red-eyed Vireo	Canada Warbler
Philadelphia Vireo	American Redstart
Black-and-white Warbler	Northern Oriole (western form)
Prothonotary Warbler	Western Tanager
Swainson's Warbler	Scarlet Tanager
Worm-eating Warbler	Hepatic Tanager
Golden-winged Warbler	Black-headed Grosbeak
Blue-winged Warbler	

Prothonotary Warbler

Protonotaria citrea Boddaert

NG–354; G–270; PE–230; AE–pl 360; AM(III)–162

5'–10'	F	4–6	F I: 12–14 DAYS ALTRICIAL	SNAILS	FOLIAGE
(2'–32')		(3–8) MONOG	F: 11 DAYS MF		GLEAN

BREEDING: Swampy lowland forest and river bottom woodlands subject to flooding. 2 broods in s. **DISPLAYS:** Courting male fluffs plumage, displays intensively around female. **NEST:** Variety of natural cavities, oft over water; some excavation in very rotten stumps; mostly of moss, dry leaves, twigs, bark, lined with fine materials. Cavity usu filled to near entrance hole. **EGGS:** Creamy, blotched with browns, variable, markings sparse to very dense. 0.8" (19 mm). **DIET:** Insects, snails. **CONSERVATION:** Winters from Yucatan and Dutch Antilles s to n S.A. Frequent cowbird host; record of one nest with 7 cowbird eggs and no warbler eggs. May be declining due to loss of habitat. Will use nest boxes. **NOTES:** Interspecifically aggressive toward bluebirds, woodpeckers, wrens, and robins. Territorial males build dummy nests; females alone make real one. Little geographic variation in song. Young supposedly can swim. House Wrens compete for nesting sites. Roost communally in nonbreeding season. Relatively tame. **ESSAYS:** Decline of Eastern Songbirds, p. 495; Mobbing, p. 425; Vocal Dialects, p. 595; Interspecific Territoriality, p. 385; Cowbirds, p. 619; Communal Roosting, p. 615. **REFS:** Bryan et al., 1987; Petit et al, 1987; Petit and Petit, 1987.

Blue-winged Warbler

Vermivora pinus Linnaeus

NG–354; G–272; PE–238; AE–pl 361; AM(III)–110

VINE	F?	5	F I: 10–11 DAYS ALTRICIAL	
TANGLE 0'–1'		(4–7) MONOG	F: 8–10 DAYS MF	

BREEDING: Second growth, brushy hillsides, bogs, old fields, stream edges. ? broods. **DISPLAYS:** ? **NEST:** Hidden in grass or vines; bulky, deep and narrow, of dead leaves, grass strips, grapevine bark, smoothly lined with grapevine fibers. **EGGS:** White, finely spotted with brown, mostly at large end. 0.6" (16 mm). **DIET:** Incl spiders. Commonly feeds by probing into live and dead curled leaves. **CONSERVATION:** Winters mostly from c Mexico s to Honduras, also to c Panama. Frequent cowbird host. Range expanding to n e and w. **NOTES:** Each male sings two song types, using one in territorial interactions and one in other contexts; territorial song shows little variation among neighboring males but varies geographically ("dialects"). Hybridizes with Golden-winged Warbler to produce birds known as Brewster's and Lawrence's Warblers. Hybrids, although fertile, rarely breed with each other, instead mostly backcross to parental species. More of a habitat generalist than the Golden-winged Warbler. **ESSAYS:** Hybridization, p. 501; Decline of Eastern Songbirds, p. 495; Vocal Dialects, p. 595; Range Expansion, p. 459; Cowbirds, p. 619. **REFS:** Confer and Knapp, 1981; Gill, 1980; Kroodsma et al., 1984.

SEE: Helping to Conserve Birds—National Level, p. 363; Island Biogeography, p. 549; Brood Parasitism, p. 287; The Fate of Bachman's Warbler, p. 505; Conservation of Kirtland's Warbler, p. 527. REFS: Ambuel and Temple, 1982; Briggs and Criswell, 1979; Brittingham and Temple, 1983; Gates and Geysel, 1978; Lynch and Whigham, 1984; Robbins, 1980; Terborgh, 1980; Wilcove, 1985; Wilcove and Terborgh, 1984.

Hybridization

When two populations of distinct but closely related birds come into contact, members of those populations may mate with each other and successfully reproduce. That process of "hybridization" creates problems for taxonomists, but is one sign of the continuous nature of the process of speciation—the evolutionary formation of new kinds of organisms. If hybrids are formed between two populations that are barely differentiated, they may remain undetected, since their features may fall within the range of variability of one or both of the populations. One would expect, if those populations were to remain in contact, that they would blend together and lose their distinctness. On the other hand, two populations may each have diverged so far from their common ancestor that their individuals no longer recognize each other as potential mates. In that case, biologists are agreed that the two populations should be considered separate species. They will not fuse back into a single species.

It is between those two extremes of complete blending and total distinctness that hybridization can provide glimpses of the complex process of differentiation—of evolution in action. Speciation normally occurs in geographic isolation, but the distributions of birds are complicated and ever changing. Populations once isolated often come into contact, and when they do, the amount, duration, and results of hybridization will vary from instance to instance.

Something on the order of 10 percent of North American birds that are considered specifically distinct hybridize with other species. One of the most thoroughly investigated examples involves two warblers. In the middle of the last century, the Blue-winged Warbler was restricted to the central Midwest (Missouri, southern Iowa, southern Illinois, southern Indiana, Kentucky, Tennessee, etc.), but it expanded its range into New England as tracts of farmland began to revert to brush and woodland. There it came into contact with the very closely related Golden-winged Warbler, which, like the Blue-winged, breeds in successional habitats—woodland edges, brushy fields, etc.

When the ranges of the two warblers began to overlap, they began to hybridize. At first the offspring of their matings were considered to be separate species. Before their hybrid origin was uncovered, the most common hybrid type was called Brewster's Warbler, and a rarer one was known

Golden-winged Warbler
Vermivora chrysoptera Linnaeus

NG–354; G–272; PE–242; AE–pl 378; AM(III)–114

F?   4–5   F?
          (4–7)   I: 10 DAYS
          MONOG   ALTRICIAL
                      F: 9–10 DAYS
                      MF

BREEDING: Habitat specialist: early successional habitats of old fields. ? broods. **DISPLAYS:** ? **NEST:** Hidden in grass clump or against tree; of long grass strips, grapevine bark, smoothly lined with fine grapevine fibers. Outer layers unkempt with protruding grass blades. **EGGS:** White, marked with brown, variable, oft wreathed. 0.7″ (17 mm). **DIET:** Incl spiders. Commonly forage by probing in dead leaves. **CONSERVATION:** Winters from Yucatan and Guatemala s (mostly on e slope) to n S.A., but mostly in highlands of Costa Rica and Panama. Blue List 1981–82, Special Concern 1986. Uncommon cowbird host. Range expanded n and e during past 175 years bringing it into contact with Blue-winged Warbler; has now disappeared from most of s part of range. Decrease in recently abandoned farmland, and resultant increase of land in later successional stages (woodland unsuitable for this species), coupled with competition from increasingly abundant Blue-winged Warbler, have led to large declines in abundance of Golden-winged Warblers. **NOTES:** Hybridizes with Blue-winged Warblers to produce birds known as Brewster's and Lawrence's Warblers. Hybrids, although fertile, rarely breed with each other, instead mostly backcross to parental species. **ESSAYS:** Hybridization, p. 501; Decline of Eastern Songbirds, p. 495; Head Scratching, p. 543; Blue List, p. 11; Range Expansion, p. 459. **REFS:** Confer and Knapp, 1981; Gill, 1980.

Tennessee Warbler
Vermivora peregrina Wilson

NG–356; G–274; PE–240; PW–pl 51; AE–pl 457; AW–pl 512; AM(III)–114

F   5–6   F
          (4–7)   I: 11–12(?) DAYS   FRUIT
          MONOG   ALTRICIAL
                      F: ? DAYS
                      MF(?)

BREEDING: Bogs, swamps, conif and conif-decid forest edge. ? broods. **DISPLAYS:** Male performs high (60′) song-flight that may be part of courtship. **NEST:** Oft hidden at base of bush or on sphagnum hummock (occ in dry area); of coarse grass, lined with fine materials. **EGGS:** White, variably marked with brown, occ wreathed. 0.6″ (16 mm). **DIET:** Incl some berries. In winter, also nectar and protein-rich structures that cecropia trees produce at base of leaf petioles as attractants for ants which protect the trees from other insects. **CONSERVATION:** Winters from c Mexico to n S.A. Rare cowbird host. **NOTES:** Occ nest in loose colonies with many nests in small areas of ideal habitat. Male sings and moves constantly in treetops; female secretive, remains near ground, not easily flushed from nest. Clutch size larger than most northern warblers; increases in response to outbreaks of forest insects, esp spruce budworm. Gregarious on wintering grounds, oft form flocks of 10–200. **ESSAYS:** Decline of Eastern Songbirds, p. 495; Head Scratching, p. 543; Variation in Clutch Sizes, p. 339. **REF:** Harrison, 1984.

as Lawrence's Warbler. Hybridization has continued wherever the species live together. The hybrids are fertile, being able both to mate with each other and with the parental types. There is, however, no sign that the two species are fusing back into one. Instead, the Blue-winged appears to be replacing the Golden-winged. The mechanism of replacement is not clear, but the Blue-wings may simply be outcompeting the Golden-wings, and simultaneously acquiring (through backcrossing) further ability to penetrate into the historical range of the Golden-wings.

Some studies suggest that the decline of the Golden-wings is not entirely due to the expansion of the Blue-wings, but that changes in habitats may also be involved. The Golden-wings, more than the Blue-wings, need to breed in those early stages of the succession that gradually changes abandoned farm fields into woodland. Thus increased reestablishment of forests and the destruction of bogs and fields by advancing suburbia may both be important factors in the Golden-wing's troubles. Whatever the exact mechanism, the overlap of these two hybridizing species may lead to the replacement of one by the other within about 50 years. If the trends of the middle half of this century continue, the Golden-winged Warbler could be threatened with extinction before 2025.

The relationship between these warblers is simple compared with those found between gulls of the Herring Gull group, where varying degrees of hybridization between species occur (and lead to endless debates on which should be considered "good species"!). The Herring Gull itself, for example, is involved in a "ring of races" with the Lesser Black-backed Gull. The Herring and Black-backed overlap widely with little hybridization in Europe, but they are connected by a circle of hybridizing populations that extends across Siberia, North America, and then the North Atlantic.

The situation is made more complex by the propensity of the Herring Gull to also hybridize with the Glaucous Gull (in Iceland), the Glaucous-winged Gull (in Alaska), and the Slaty-backed Gull (in Siberia). In turn, the Glaucous and Glaucous-winged gulls hybridize around the Bering Sea. Furthermore, the Iceland Gull hybridizes with Thayer's Gull (on Baffin Island). All of these gulls, together with the California and Western Gulls, and the Mexican Yellow-footed Gull, compose one of the most interesting groups of birds—illustrating many degrees of genetic differentiation. So when you are in the field trying to sort out which of these gulls you have in your binoculars, take heart. The gulls themselves also have problems telling who is who.

SEE: Species and Speciation, p. 355; Natural Selection, p. 237; Range Expansion, p. 459; Great Plains Hybrids, p. 625. REFS: Confer and Knapp, 1979; Gill, 1980; Pierotti, 1987.

Orange-crowned Warbler

Vermivora celata Say

NG–356; G–274; PE–240; PW–pl 51; AE–pl 456; AW–pl 511; AM(III)–116

0'–3'   F?   4–5   F?
                  (3–6)   I: 12–14 DAYS
                  MONOG   ALTRICIAL   FRUIT
                               F: 8–10 DAYS   NECTAR
                               MF(?)   TREE SAP

BREEDING: Decid and decid-conif woodland, chaparral, riparian woodland. ? broods. **DISPLAYS:** ? **NEST:** Usu hidden on ground, but in s CA (occ elsewhere) low in shrub or vine; of coarse grass, bark strips, lined with fine materials. **EGGS:** White, marked with reds or browns; oft mostly at large end. 0.6" (16 mm). **DIET:** Incl berries, plant galls. **CONSERVATION:** Winters s to Guatemala. Rare cowbird host. Occ visits hummingbird feeders. **NOTES:** Widespread and fairly common (esp in w) but many details of breeding biology largely unknown. Regularly feeds at Red-naped Sapsucker wells. Oft feeds on floral nectar in tropical wintering areas. Reproduction by blood-feeding lice found only on Orange-crowns is triggered by the birds' own reproductive hormones; synchronized breeding by parasites and their hosts maximizes dispersal opportunities for lice onto uninfected hosts (i.e., nestlings). **ESSAYS:** Birds in the Bush, p. 541; Disease and Parasitism, p. 399; Bills, p. 209; Mobbing, p. 425; How Do We Find Out About Bird Biology?, p. 319. **REFS:** Foster, 1969; Harrison, 1984.

Bachman's Warbler

Vermivora bachmanii Audubon

NG–356; G–272; PE–242; AE–651; AM(III)–108

2'–3'   F?   4   F
                  (3–5)   I: ? DAYS
                  MONOG   ALTRICIAL
                               F: ? DAYS
                               MF(?)

BREEDING: Palmetto and cypress swamps. ? broods. **DISPLAYS:** ? **NEST:** Also in brambles, cane, or other undergrowth; of dried leaves, weed and grass stalks, lined with rootlets and Spanish moss. **EGGS:** Unlike all other wood warblers except Swainson's: white, unmarked, with a pink blush early in incubation from yolks showing through translucent shell. 0.6" (16 mm). **DIET:** Insects, as far as known. Does not flycatch; slowly and deliberately gleans from foliage. **CONSERVATION:** Winters in Cuba and Isle of Pines. Endangered Species. Always very rare, now possibly extinct; last confirmed sightings in Cuba in mid-1980s. Destruction of extensive canebrakes in s e U.S. for agriculture and flood control, coupled with destruction of wintering habitat are the likely causes of decline. **NOTES:** Thought to have been a bamboo thicket ("canebrake") specialist for nesting. Irruptive nature of this species possibly linked to episodic nature of bamboo reproductive cycles (slow growth followed by synchronous flowering and death). **ESSAYS:** Fate of Bachman's Warbler, p. 505; Decline of Eastern Songbirds, p. 495; Birds and the Law, p. 293; Wintering and Conservation, p. 513; Conservation of Kirtland's Warbler, p. 527. **REFS:** Hamel, 1986; Remsen, 1986; Stevenson, 1972.

The Fate of Bachman's Warbler

In the late 1800s Bachman's Warbler was the seventh most common migrant along the lower Suwannee River of Florida, being more abundant than, for example, Red-eyed, Yellow-throated, and Solitary Vireos. In those days it bred in swampy forests throughout much of the southeastern United States. By the 1920s, however, Bachman's Warbler was considered a very rare bird. Today, it is our rarest native songbird. No individuals have been seen on territory since 1962 or 1963, and the last sighting was a wintering female in Cuba in 1981. It is a species on the verge of extinction if not already gone.

The reasons for the decline of this pretty warbler are somewhat mysterious. Certainly, widespread clearing of river-bottom forest may have been a factor, but wooded swamps large enough to contain numerous warbler territories remain in roughly the same condition they were in a hundred years ago. Unlike the Ivory-billed Woodpeckers, Bachman's Warblers did not require huge territories and thus would not have suffered so much from the logging of great expanses of swamp. The degree to which Bachman's wintering habitat in Cuba and on the Isle of Pines has been destroyed is not clear, however, since that habitat has never been identified.

It seems likely that a combination of factors has been responsible for this warbler's decline. Fragmentation of forests unquestionably would have reduced its population sizes and led to more breeding near forest edges where nests are more vulnerable to cowbirds and nest robbers. It also has been suggested that Bachman's Warbler had a very narrow migration corridor. That not only would account for the relative abundance of transients in some locations, but would also make a large portion of the species' population vulnerable to relatively localized severe storms and other disasters during peak migration time.

Another possibility is that this warbler was a bamboo specialist, nesting in the vast "canebrakes" (bamboo thickets) that once occupied seasonally flooded swamps in the southeastern United States. Canebrakes were severely reduced by clearing for agriculture and by flood and fire control measures (the bamboo thrived on periodic flooding, and stands required occasional burning to maintain their productivity). Overall, the area of canebrake seems to have dwindled even more than the swamp forests in which bamboo used to form a major part of the understory.

We may never know the precise reason for the decline of Bachman's Warbler, but the simplest hypothesis would seem to be that it may never have been an abundant bird and was simply very susceptible to the environmental changes that are now depressing the numbers of many other small forest birds in the East. Unlike Kirtland's Warbler it did not tend to breed semicolonially, so that once numbers were reduced mate finding would have been very difficult. Many of the last sitings were of unmated males.

SEE: The Decline of Eastern Songbirds, p. 495; Island Biogeography, p. 549; Disappearing Ivorybill, p. 357; Conservation of Kirtland's Warbler, p. 527. REFS: Hamel, 1986; Remsen, 1986; Stevenson, 1972.

Nashville Warbler

NG–358; G–274; PE–244; PW–pl 51; AE–pl 373; AW–pl 412; AM(III)–118

| F | 4–5 MONOG | F –M I: 11–12 DAYS ALTRICIAL F: 11 DAYS F –M | | GRND GLEAN HOVER & GLEAN |

BREEDING: Decid, conif, and riparian woodlands, bogs, thickets. ? broods. **DIS-PLAYS:** ? **NEST:** Well hidden; of coarse grass, bark strips, occ rimmed with moss, lined with fine materials. **EGGS:** White, marked with reddish-brown, brown, usu wreathed. 0.6″ (16 mm). **DIET:** Entirely insectivorous. **CONSERVATION:** Winters s to El Salvador and c Honduras. Uncommon cowbird host. **NOTES:** Little studied. Breeding range does not overlap with the closely related Virginia's Warbler. **ESSAYS:** Superspecies, p. 375; Species and Speciation, p. 355; Wintering and Conservation, p. 513; How Do We Find Out About Bird Biology?, p. 319. **REF:** Johnson, 1976.

Virginia's Warbler

NG–358; G–276; PW–pl 51; AW–pl 478; AM(III)–120

| F? | 4 (3–5) MONOG | F –M? I: ? DAYS ALTRICIAL F: ? DAYS MF | HAWKS FOLIAGE GLEAN |

BREEDING: Dry montane woodland, rocky canyons with scrub oak, chaparral, piñon-juniper brushland. 2? broods. **DISPLAYS:** ? **NEST:** Hidden by veg; of coarse grass, bark strips, lined with fine materials. **EGGS:** White to creamy, marked with reddish-brown or brown. 0.6″ (16 mm). **DIET:** Entirely insectivorous. **CONSERVATION:** Winters in c and s Mexico. Rare cowbird host. **NOTES:** Many details of breeding biology unknown. Breeding range does not overlap with that of closely related Nashville Warbler. **ESSAYS:** Superspecies, p. 375; Species and Speciation, p. 355; Wintering and Conservation, p. 513; How Do We Find Out About Bird Biology?, p. 319. **REF:** Johnson, 1976.

The evolution of flight has endowed birds with many physical features in addition to wings and feathers. One of the requirements of heavier-than-air flying machines, birds included, is a structure that combines strength and light weight. One way this is accomplished in birds is by the fusion and elimination of some bones and the "pneumatization" (hollowing) of the remaining ones. Some of the vertebrae and some bones of the pelvic girdle of birds are fused into a single structure, as are some finger and leg bones—all of which are separate in most vertebrates. And many tail, finger, and leg bones are missing altogether. Not only are some bones of birds, unlike ours, hollow, but many of the hollows are connected to the respiratory system. To keep the cylindrical walls of a bird's major wing bones from buckling, the bones have internal strutlike reinforcements.

The pneumatization of bird bones led to the belief that birds had skeletons that weighed proportionately less than those of mammals. Careful studies by H. D. Prange and his colleagues have shown this not to be the case. More demands are placed on a bird's skeleton than on that of a terrestrial mammal. The bird must be able to support itself either entirely by its forelimbs or entirely by its hindlimbs. It also requires a deep, solid breastbone (sternum) to which the wing muscles can be anchored. Thus, while some bones are much lighter than their mammalian counterparts, others, especially the leg bones, are heavier. Evolution has created in the avian skeleton a model of parsimony, lightening where possible, adding weight and strength where required. The results can be quite spectacular: the skeleton of a frigatebird with a seven-foot wingspan weighs less than the feathers covering it!

Not all birds have the same degree of skeletal pneumatization. To decrease their buoyancy and make diving easier, some diving birds, such as loons and auklets, have relatively solid bones. Those birds are generally less skillful fliers than ones with lighter skeletons.

Birds have found other ways to lighten the load in addition to hollowing out their bones. For instance, they keep their reproductive organs (testes, ovaries and oviducts) tiny for most of the year, greatly enlarging them only during the breeding season.

The respiratory system of birds is also adapted to the demands of flight. A bird's respiratory system is proportionately larger and much more efficient than ours—as might be expected, since flight is a more demanding activity than walking or running. An average bird devotes about one-fifth of its body volume to its respiratory system, an average mammal only about one-twentieth. Mammalian respiratory systems consist of lungs that are blind sacs and of tubes that connect them to the nose and mouth. During each breath, only some of the air contained in the lungs is exchanged, since the lungs do not collapse completely with each exhalation, and some "dead air" then remains in them.

In contrast, the lungs of birds are less flexible, and relatively small, but

Colima Warbler

Supersp #43

Vermivora crissalis Salvin and Godman

NG–358; G–276; PW–pl 51; AW–652; AM(III)–122

    ?

MF   4   MF   GROUND
     MONOG   I: ? DAYS   GLEAN?
       ALTRICIAL   HAWKS?
       F: ? DAYS
       MF

BREEDING: Above 6,000′ in montane oak forests. ? broods. **DISPLAYS:** ? **NEST:** Well hidden by veg in leaf litter or beneath clumps of grass; of coarse grass, bark strips, lined with fine materials. **EGGS:** Creamy white, marked with browns forming wreath at large end. 0.7″ (18 mm). **DIET:** Presumably largely insectivorous. **CONSERVATION:** Winters in c and s w Mexico. **NOTES:** Young independent within a few days following fledging. Virtually unstudied in the field. **ESSAYS:** Superspecies, p. 375; Sibling Species, p. 383; How Do We Find Out About Bird Biology?, p. 319; Species and Speciation, p. 355; Parental Care, p. 555. **REFS:** Harrison, 1984; Waver, 1973.

Lucy's Warbler

Vermivora luciae Cooper

NG–358; G–276; PW–pl 51; AW–515; AM(III)–122

3′–11′   MF   4–5(?)   F –M?   HAWKS
(0′–11′)   (3–7)(?)   I: ? DAYS
       MONOG   ALTRICIAL
         F: ? DAYS
         MF(?)

BREEDING: Riparian brush and woodland in desert areas. 2? broods. **DISPLAYS:** ? **NEST:** In old woodpecker hole, under loose bark, in deserted Verdin nest, and rarely in hole in eroded stream bank; of coarse weeds, bark strips, mesquite leaf stems, etc., lined with fine materials. **EGGS:** White to creamy, marked, usu near large end, with brown or reddish-brown. 0.6″ (15 mm). **DIET:** Largely or entirely insectivorous. **CONSERVATION:** Winters in w Mexico from Jalisco to Guerrero. Occ cowbird host. **NOTES:** Details of breeding biology unknown. With the Prothonotary, one of the two hole-nesting N.A. warblers. **ESSAYS:** Birds in the Bush, p. 541; Bills, p. 209; How Do We Find Out About Bird Biology?, p. 319; Cowbirds, p. 619. **REF:** Harrison, 1984.

they are interconnected with a system of large, thin-walled air sacs in the front (anterior) and back (posterior) portions of the body. These, in turn, are connected with the air spaces in the bones. Evolution has created an ingenious system that passes the air in a one-way, two-stage flow through the bird's lungs. A breath of inhaled air passes first into the posterior air sacs and then, on exhalation, into the lungs. When a second breath is inhaled into the posterior sacs, the air from the first breath moves from shrinking lungs into the anterior air sacs. When the second exhalation occurs, the air from the first breath moves from the anterior air sacs and out of the bird, while the second breath moves into the lungs. The air thus moves in one direction through the lungs. All birds have this one-way flow system; most have a second two-way flow system which may make up as much as 20 percent of the lung volume.

In both systems, the air is funneled down fine tubules which interdigitate with capillaries carrying oxygen-poor venous blood. At the beginning of the tubules the oxygen-rich air is in close contact with that oxygen-hungry blood; farther down the tubules the oxygen content of air and blood are in equilibrium. Birds' lungs are anatomically very complex (their structure and function are only barely outlined here), but they create a "crosscurrent circulation" of air and blood that provides a greater capacity for the exchange of oxygen and carbon dioxide across the thin intervening membranes than is found in mammalian lungs.

Contrary to what was once believed, the rhythm of a bird's respiratory "two-cycle pump" is not related to the beats of its wings. Flight movements and respiratory movements are independent. The heart does the pumping required to get oxygenated blood to the tissues and to carry deoxygenated blood (loaded with carbon dioxide) away from them. Because of the efficiency of the bird's breathing apparatus, the ratio of breaths to heartbeats can be quite low. A mammal takes about one breath for every four and one-half heartbeats (independent of the size of the mammal), a bird about one every six to ten heartbeats (depending on the size of the bird).

A bird's heart is large, powerful, and of the same basic design as that of a mammal. It is a four-chambered structure of two pumps operating side by side. One two-chambered pump receives oxygen-rich blood from the lungs and pumps it out to the waiting tissues. The other pump receives oxygen-poor blood from the tissues and pumps it into the lungs. This segregation of the two kinds of blood (which does not occur completely in reptiles, amphibians, and fishes) makes a bird's circulatory system, like its respiratory system, well equipped to handle the rigors of flight.

The flight muscles of most birds are red in color ("dark meat") because of the presence of many fibers containing red oxygen-carrying compounds, myoglobin and cytochrome. They are also richly supplied with blood and are designed for sustained flight. Lighter-colored muscles ("white meat"), with many fewer such fibers, are found in pheasants, grouse, quail, and other gallinaceous birds. These are also well supplied with blood, are apparently capable of carrying a heavy work load for a short time, but fatigue

Northern Parula

NG–358; G–276; PE–230; AE–pl 447; AM(III)–124

5'–55'	F	4–5	F –M I: 12–14 DAYS ALTRICIAL		HOVER &
(0'–55')		(3–7) MONOG	F: ? DAYS F –M		GLEAN HAWKS

BREEDING: Open conif and decid woods, esp with abundant tree lichens. ? broods. **DISPLAYS:** ? **NEST:** Pocket hollowed in hanging lichens; lined with fine materials. Where lichen not available, nest may be made of hanging clusters of conif twigs, or in flood-deposited rubbish in branches overhanging stream. **EGGS:** White to creamy, marked with brown or reddish-brown, variable, may be almost immaculate. 0.7″ (17 mm). **DIET:** Largely or entirely insectivorous. Very agile and active forager, oft hovering at branch tips and clinging to leaf cluster upside down like chickadee; also occ forages on ground. **CONSERVATION:** Winters most commonly in Greater Antilles; also c Mexico s to Guatemala and Belize in Atlantic drainage. Uncommon cowbird host. **NOTES:** Same nesting site oft used in successive years. **ESSAYS:** Decline of Eastern Songbirds, p. 495; Birds in the Bush, p. 541; Site Tenacity, p. 189. **REF:** Harrison, 1984.

Tropical Parula

NG–358; G–276; PW–pl 51; AE–614; AM(III)–126

8'–40'	?	3–4 MONOG	? I: ? DAYS ALTRICIAL F: ? DAYS ?		HAWKS?

BREEDING: Subtropical forest with abundant Spanish moss. ? broods. **DISPLAYS:** ? **NEST:** Pocket hollowed in Spanish moss, occ in orchid or dangling cactus, lined with fine materials. **EGGS:** White to creamy, variably marked with brown, usu loosely wreathed. 0.7″ (17 mm). **DIET:** Largely or entirely insectivorous. **CONSERVATION:** Winter resident. Common cowbird host. Pesticide pollution in Rio Grande valley threatens populations. **NOTES:** Details of breeding biology virtually unknown. Formerly known as Olive-backed Warbler. **ESSAYS:** Superspecies, p. 375; DDT and Birds, p. 21; Cowbirds, p. 619; How Do We Find Out About Bird Biology?, p. 319. **REF:** Harrison, 1984.

more rapidly. If a quail is flushed a few times in a row, it will become so exhausted it will be incapable of further flight.

Finally, of course, it does little good to be able to sustain flight or fly rapidly if you are always crashing into things. Although birds have found many ways to streamline, lighten, or totally eliminate unnecessary parts (like urinary bladders), they have not stinted on nervous systems. Birds have brains that are proportionately much larger than those of lizards and comparable, in fact, with those of rodents. The brain is connected to sharp eyes, and has ample processing centers for coordinating the information received from them. A bird's nerves can rapidly transmit commands of the brain to the muscles operating the wings. It is the combination of visual acuity, quick decision making, and high-speed nerve transmission along short nerves that permits a Golden-crowned Sparrow to weave rapidly among the branches of a thicket, escaping the clutches of a pursuing Sharp-shinned Hawk.

SEE: Temperature Regulation and Behavior, p. 149; Metabolism, p. 325; Feathered Dinosaurs?, p. 31; Hawk-Eyed, p. 229. REFS: Calder, 1984; Dunker, 1974; Prange et al., 1979; Scheid, 1982.

Bird Biologist—Rachel Carson

Why should Rachel L. Carson (1907–64) be listed as a bird biologist? Her research career was in marine biology, and she never did any research on birds. But if it were not for Rachel Carson there would be many fewer birds for us to appreciate and study. Carson was a broadly knowledgeable biologist and a superb writer. She assembled the entire picture of the threat that misuse of pesticides represented to all animals in North America, including birds, and presented it to the public in a very readable book, *Silent Spring* (1962). The silence to which the book's title referred was an absence of bird song. Popular concern for the environment can very largely be traced to the publication of that landmark volume, and the many honors she received for it were richly deserved.

SEE: DDT and Birds, p. 21; Conservation of Raptors, p. 247.

Black-and-white Warbler
Mniotilta varia Linnaeus

NG–360; G–270; PE–232; PW–pl 50; AE–pl 564; AM(III)–160

0'–2'	F	5 (4–5) MONOG	F I: 10 DAYS ALTRICIAL F: 8–12 DAYS MF		HAWKS

BREEDING: Decid and decid-conif forests, esp on hillsides and in ravines. ? broods. **DISPLAYS:** Courting male pursues female intermittently over a long period, with much song and display of plumage. **NEST:** Also rarely on platform near ground, concealed under dead leaves or branches; of leaves, coarse grass, etc., lined with fine materials. **EGGS:** White to creamy, flecked over entire surface with brown or markings mostly at large end, occ wreathed. 0.7" (17 mm). **DIET:** In early spring, insects incl dormant forms, gleaned nuthatch-like from trunks and limbs. **CONSERVATION:** Winters s through Bahamas, C.A. and Caribbean (less frequent in Lesser Antilles) to n S.A. Frequent cowbird host. Very sensitive to fragmentation of forested breeding habitat. **NOTES:** One of the earliest warblers to arrive on breeding grounds; by foraging from bark, need not wait for trees to leaf out. Female performs distraction display if flushed from nest. **ESSAYS:** Decline of Eastern Songbirds, p. 495; Breeding Season, p. 55; Island Biogeography, p. 549; Cowbirds, p. 619; Distraction Displays, p. 115. **REF:** Harrison, 1984.

Black-throated Blue Warbler
Dendroica caerulescens Gmelin

NG–360; G–282; PE–232; AE–pl 446; AM(III)–132

     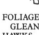

CONIF TREE 0.5'–3'	F –M?	4 (3–5) MONOG	F I: 12–13 DAYS ALTRICIAL F: 11–12 DAYS MF		FOLIAGE GLEAN HAWKS

BREEDING: Decid and decid-conif forests with heavy undergrowth, rhododendron bogs, partially cleared forest. ? broods. **DISPLAYS:** ? **NEST:** In shrub, small tree, vine tangle; bulky, rough exterior of inner bark strips, birch bark, pieces of pithy wood, dried grass, dried leaves, pine needles, moss, lined with hair, rootlets. **EGGS:** White to creamy, marked with browns, mostly at large end, occ wreathed or capped. 0.7" (17 mm). **DIET:** Also forages by bark gleaning. In winter, up to 25% seeds and other veg matter. **CONSERVATION:** Winters s through C.A., Bahamas, and Caribbean (except Lesser Antilles) to n S.A. Uncommon cowbird host. **NOTES:** Sexes differ more in appearance than any other wood warbler. Female may slip away quietly or perform distraction display if flushed from nest. Female broods. Males tend to forage higher than females. Largely restricted to shrubby understory when foraging in forest. **ESSAYS:** Habitat Selection, p. 463; Sexual Selection, p. 251; Distraction Displays, p. 115. **REFS:** Holmes et al., 1979; Robinson and Holmes, 1984.

Wintering and Conservation

In the species treatments we have placed information on the wintering range of North American birds under the **CONSERVATION** heading. The connection between wintering range and conservation is emphasized because *the greatest threat to the preservation of many North American birds occurs south of the U.S.–Mexican border.* At current growth rates, human populations in tropical America will double in the next 30 years, and remaining areas of undisturbed natural environment will be greatly reduced. Especially critical for North American migrants is the likely decimation of tropical rain forests, which host many of our songbirds. If current trends continue, those forests will be largely gone before the middle of the next century, in part because of a desire by North Americans for cheap fast-food hamburgers, TV dinners, and meaty dog food. Many rain forests in Central and South America are being cleared so that they can be used to raise beef cattle. Grazing is poor to begin with, and usually in less than a decade new range becomes wasteland. Even so, large landowners make a handsome profit in the process, selling beef raised relatively cheaply to rich nations.

In addition, numerous shorebirds depend upon tropical estuarine and other wetland environments either for wintering or for resting habitat during migration. These areas also are likely to be destroyed as the numbers of people expand. And, finally, the use of those pesticides dangerous to birds is not well regulated in most Latin American nations. Some of our birds doubtless never make it back, or suffer breeding failures when they do, because they were poisoned.

In short, much of the winter habitat required by some members of North America's avifauna is likely to disappear or be contaminated in the next few decades. Outlining the south-of-the border winter distribution of each species both gives a clue to its vulnerability and provides a reminder that conservation of many of our bird species requires steps to save tropical habitats. Preservation of birds gives us one more reason to do all we can to help our southern neighbors solve their environmental problems. Of course, we must remember that our avifauna, both migratory and nonmigratory, is also threatened in diverse ways by environmental changes within the United States and Canada.

SEE: The Decline of Eastern Songbirds, p. 495; DDT and Birds, p. 21; Metallic Poisons, p. 137; Shorebird Migration and Conservation, p. 119; Helping to Conserve Birds—Global Level, p. 367; Loon Nurseries and Populations, p. 3. REFS: Ehrlich and Ehrlich, 1981; Keast and Morton, 1980.

Cerulean Warbler

Dendroica cerulea Wilson

NG–360; G–282; PE–232; AE–pl 444; AM (III)–158

30'–60' +   F?   4   F?   HAWKS
(15'–60' +)   (3–5)   I: 12–13 (?) DAYS
                  MONOG   ALTRICIAL
                             F: ? DAYS
                             MF (?)

BREEDING: Mature decid forest. ? broods. **DISPLAYS:** ? **NEST:** On high horizontal limb far from trunk (usu oak); small, compact, shallow, of bark, weed stalks, lichen, moss, smoothly lined with moss, occ hair. **EGGS:** Grayish, creamy or greenish-white, marked with browns, variable, most finely spotted, some strongly blotched, usu loosely wreathed. 0.7". (17 mm). **DIET:** Little known, largely or entirely insectivorous. **CONSERVATION:** Winters from Venezuela and Colombia s to e Peru and n Bolivia. Uncommon cowbird host. Range reportedly expanding in s and n e. Very sensitive to fragmentation of forested breeding habitat. **NOTES:** Forages with great agility, moving rapidly between branches; remains high in trees. Breeding biology not well known. **ESSAYS:** Decline of Eastern Songbirds, p. 495; Island Biogeography, p. 549; Determining Diets, p. 535; How Do We Find Out About Bird Biology?, p. 319; Range Expansion, p. 459. **REF:** Harrison, 1984.

Cape May Warbler

Dendroica tigrina Gmelin

NG–362; G–278; PE–236; PW–pl 50; AE–pl 368; AM(III)–132

35'–60'   F?   6–7   F?   HAWKS
(11'–60')   (4–9)   I: ? DAYS
                  MONOG   ALTRICIAL
                             F: ? DAYS
                             MF(?)

BREEDING: Open conif (spruce-fir) forest, conif forest edge. ? broods. **DISPLAYS:** Courting male flies with rigid wings above female. **NEST:** In crown of spruce or fir tree; of moss, vine stems, weed stalks, lined thickly with fine materials, smoothly felted. **EGGS:** Creamy white, heavily marked with reddish-browns, mostly at large end. 0.7" (17 mm). **DIET:** During fall migration occ punctures cultivated grapes and drinks juice, occ damaging crop. Feeds heavily on nectar in winter, oft defending flowering plants. **CONSERVATION:** Winters s through West Indies. Rare cowbird host. **NOTES:** Nest difficult to locate since female does not fly directly to it but works her way up trunk; on leaving nest dives toward ground. Compared with other warblers, male very aggressively defends territory, oft perching atop conifer and flying out to chase away all other warblers, regardless of species or size. Clutch size (largest of any wood warbler), reproductive success, and population density apparently correlated positively with outbreaks of spruce budworm. **ESSAYS:** Decline of Eastern Songbirds, p. 495; MacArthur's Warblers, p. 523; Variation in Clutch Sizes, p. 339; Nest Lining, p. 391; Population Dynamics, p. 575; Territoriality, p. 387. **REF:** Morse, 1978.

Bird Biologist—John Cassin

Until John Cassin (1813–69) became curator of Ornithology at the Academy of Natural Sciences of Philadelphia, all of the top-notch students of native American birds had been non-natives themselves. Cassin volunteered for the Union army, was captured, and survived the hell of the Confederate's Libby Prison. After the war he published the first comprehensive work on western birds, *Illustrations of the Birds of California, Texas, Oregon, British and Russian America . . . 1853 to 1855.* Working with the superb global collection that he was instrumental in building at the Academy, he described and named 193 species of birds and was the only American of his era to gain an international reputation as an ornithologist.

SEE: Taxonomy and Nomenclature, p. 515. REFS: Choate, 1985; Kastner, 1986.

Taxonomy and Nomenclature

Taxonomy (sometimes called "systematics") is the science of classifying organisms. The Linnean system of classification, used for both plants and animals, was developed more than two centuries ago by the great Swedish botanist Carolus Linnaeus (born Carl von Linné). It is a hierarchical system—that is, each organism belongs to a series of ranked taxonomic categories, such as a subspecies, species, genus, family, etc. At any rank (level) in the hierarchy any organism can belong to only one taxon, or taxonomic group. For instance, the Yellow-rumped Warbler can be a member of only one genus and one class. Each taxon is given a formal, latinized name that is recognized by scientists around the world. Nomenclature is a formal system of names used to label taxonomic groups.

Birds compose the class Aves, which is in the phylum Chordata (Chordata also includes mammals, reptiles, fishes, and tunicates—everything with an internal skeletal rod called a "notochord," which in vertebrates is enclosed in cartilage or within a backbone). The living (nonfossil) members of the class Aves are placed into more than two dozen orders, such as the Passeriformes (perching birds), Piciformes (woodpeckers, etc.), Columbiformes (pigeons and doves), Procellariiformes (albatrosses, petrels, etc.), Apodiformes (swifts and hummingbirds), and so on. The orders are divided into about 160 families—an average 6–7 families per order. Family names can be recognized because they all end in "idae." For example, in the order Passeriformes are such families as the Tyrannidae (the tyrant flycatchers), the Laniidae (the shrikes), and the Emberizidae, a large family that includes, among others, the wood warblers, sparrows, blackbirds, and orioles.

Families, in turn, are divided into subfamilies, with names ending in "inae." The wood warblers make up the subfamily Parulinae and the black-

Chestnut-sided Warbler
Dendroica pensylvanica Linnaeus

NG–362; G–284; PE–236; PW–pl 50; AE–pl 377; AM (III)–128

1'–3'	F	4 (3–5) MONOG	F I: 12–13 DAYS ALTRICIAL F: 10–12 DAYS MF	BERRIES	HAWKS HOVER & GLEAN

BREEDING: Brushy thickets, open decid woodland and borders, second growth. ? broods. **DISPLAYS**: ? **NEST**: Usu loosely constructed, occ compact, of fine plant material, lined with fine materials. **EGGS**: White to off-white, marked with browns. 0.7" (17 mm). **DIET**: Takes berries when insects scarce. **CONSERVATION**: Winters mostly in C.A. (esp on Caribbean slope of Costa Rica, where it is one of the commonest birds). Frequent cowbird host; may destroy cowbird eggs by burying in bottom of nest. Very rare in Audubon's time, then became abundant as modification of landscape produced successional habitats suitable for breeding; now declining slightly as shrubby fields change back into woodland. **NOTES**: Males use different song types to convey different messages in territorial advertisement; song used for territorial proclamation varies little among neighboring males but varies geographically (dialects). Adults may closely approach observer in defense of young. When foraging, hops rapidly between branches, usu with tail cocked exposing bright white undertail coverts. Persistent member of tropical mixed-species flocks on wintering grounds. **ESSAYS**: Decline of Eastern Songbirds, p. 495; Head Scratching, p. 543; Vocal Functions, p. 471; Vocal Dialects, p. 595; Mixed-Species Flocking, p. 433; Cowbirds, p. 619. **REFS**: Greenberg, 1984; Lein, 1978.

Blackburnian Warbler
Dendroica fusca Müller

NG–360; G–284; PE–236; PW–pl 50; AE–pl 404; AM (III)–144

20'–50' (5'–85')	F	4 (4–5) MONOG	F I: 11–12(?) DAYS ALTRICIAL F: ? DAYS MF		HOV GLEAN HAWKS BARK GLEAN

BREEDING: Mature conif (mostly balsam fir) and conif-decid forests. ? broods. **DISPLAYS**: ? **NEST**: High in dense branches of conif; of conif twigs, weed stalks, plant down, lichen, spider silk, lined with fine grass, black rootlets, hair. **EGGS**: White to greenish-white, marked with browns, usu wreathed. 0.7" (17 mm). **DIET**: Feeds on berries when insects scarce. **CONSERVATION**: Winters from Costa Rica s to c Peru and Bolivia. Uncommon cowbird host. **NOTES**: Forages predominantly in treetops; males tend to forage higher than females. Details of breeding biology not well known. **ESSAYS**: Decline of Eastern Songbirds, p. 495; MacArthur's Warblers, p. 523; Wintering and Conservation, p. 513; How Do We Find Out About Bird Biology?, p. 319. **REFS**: Holmes, 1986; Morse, 1980.

birds and orioles are the Icterinae. Within subfamilies, tribes (name ending "ini") are often recognized: blackbirds are the Agelaiini and orioles the Icterini within the Icterinae. The next commonly used category is the genus: the Yellow-rumped Warbler is in the genus *Dendroica*, along with more than two dozen very similar species. Its latinized specific name is *Dendroica coronata*, made up of the name of the genus combined with a "trivial name" to distinguish it from congeners (other members of the same genus).

Because the Linnean system features a two-part specific name, it is often referred to as a system of "binomial nomenclature." Often, as in this book, the name of the author who first described and named the species in the scientific literature is added to the specific name—thus, *Dendroica coronata* Linnaeus. Traditionally, generic and specific names are set in italic type, and in some works the name of the author is put in parentheses if he or she originally placed the species in a different genus. Thus if you find the Yellow-rumped Warbler listed as *Dendroica coronata* (Linnaeus), it is because Linnaeus originally placed it in the genus *Motacilla*, not *Dendroica*. We have not followed this procedure, since most bird species have long since been moved from their original genera as the taxonomic system has been refined.

Finally, subspecies may be recognized with trinomial nomenclature—by adding a third name to the specific name. Thus the eastern Yellow-rumped Warbler (formerly the Myrtle Warbler) is *Dendroica coronata coronata* Linnaeus, and the western Yellow-rumped Warbler (formerly Audubon's Warbler) is *Dendroica coronata auduboni* Townsend.

The taxonomic-nomenclatural system is a device for communicating about the complexly interrelated products of evolution. Generally it works well, even though many aspects of it are arbitrary. For example, whether *Dendroica* is distinct enough to be recognized as a full genus, or should be merged with *Vermivora* and *Parula* is not self-evident, and ornithological taxonomists disagee on it. Some taxonomists are "lumpers" and would like to combine the three; others are "splitters" and wish to keep them separate. Furthermore, as new studies of the relationships of various higher categories are published, scientists must modify the taxonomic system, and as a result names of taxonomic groups may change, as may the organisms included in them. For example, recent DNA-DNA hybridization studies have led some scientists to conclude that the Emberizidae should be considered a subfamily (Emberizinae) of the family Fringillidae, the wood warblers a tribe (Parulini) of that subfamily, and both the orioles and blackbirds combined in yet another emberizine tribe, Icterini, with the tribal name Agelaiini disappearing.

Changes in latinized specific names are inevitable as knowledge about birds increases, and most should simply be accepted as the price of progress. Common names, at least within North America, show more stability and facilitate regional communication. But for worldwide communication, the level on which professional ornithologists often operate, the latinized

Magnolia Warbler

Dendroica magnolia Wilson

NG–362; G–278; PE–234; PW–pl 50; AE–pl 366; AW–713; AM(III)–130

SHRUB	MF	4	F		BARK
1'–10'		(3–5)	I: 11–13 DAYS		GLEAN
(1'–35')		MONOG	ALTRICIAL		HAWKS?
			F: (8–)10 DAYS		
			MF		

BREEDING: Open conif (spruce-fir-hemlock) forest. ? broods. **DISPLAYS:** Courtship: male pursues female, oft pausing and posturing. **NEST:** Well hidden, usu loosely built and not well attached to support; of weed stalks, fine twigs, fine grass; lined with fine materials, always incl some black rootlets. **EGGS:** White to creamy, marked with browns, olive, usu wreathed or capped. 0.7″ (17 mm). **DIET:** Takes less fruit than any other *Dendroica* in winter. **CONSERVATION:** Winters from c Mexico s to c Panama and e to Puerto Rico. Uncommon cowbird host. **NOTES:** Female gives unusual "squeaky" alarm note when disturbed on nest. Usu forages by hopping between branches with tail fanned; commonly picks insects from bottom surface of leaves. Males tend to forage higher than females. **ESSAYS:** Decline of Eastern Songbirds, p. 495; Head Scratching, p. 543; Wintering and Conservation, p. 513; Nest Lining, p. 391. **REFS:** Harrison, 1984; Morse, 1980.

Yellow-rumped Warbler

Dendroica coronata Linnaeus

NG–362; G–278; PE–234; PW–pl 50; AE–pl 379; AW–pl 414; AM(III)–134

4'–50'	F	4–5	F	BERRIES	HAWKS
		(3–5)	I: 12–13 DAYS		HOVER &
		MONOG	ALTRICIAL		GLEAN
			F: 10–12 DAYS		
			MF (?)		

BREEDING: Conif and conif-decid forests. Oft 2 broods. **DISPLAYS:** Courting male follows female, fluffs side feathers, raises wings, erects crown feathers, calls, and flutters. **NEST:** Usu on horizontal branch; of shredded bark, weed stalks, twigs, rootlets, some lined with feathers interwoven so tips curve over and screen eggs, other linings incl hair. **EGGS:** White to creamy, marked with browns, grays, occ wreathed. 0.7″ (18 mm). **DIET:** Tends to be more insectivorous in w than in e; berries of shrubs, esp in winter. **CONSERVATION:** Some sedentary in winter, some s to C.A. Common (e) or rare (w) cowbird host; female may destroy cowbird eggs by burying in base of nest. **NOTES:** One of the most generalized and opportunistic of all our insectivorous birds. Gregarious, oft assoc in flocks. Males tend to forage higher than females. May skim swallow-like over water eating insects from surface. One of last warblers to migrate. Most abundant wood warbler in Canada. Occ roost communally in winter. Until recently, e and w populations were considered separate species, Myrtle (e) and Audubon's (w) Warblers. **ESSAYS:** Taxonomy and Nomenclature, p. 515; MacArthur's Warblers, p. 523; Migration, p. 183; Bird Guilds, p. 493; Species and Speciation, p. 355; Cowbirds, p. 619. **REFS:** Harrison, 1984; Morse, 1980.

names are essential. One need only note that the "robin" in North America is *Turdus migratorius,* while in England it is *Erithacus rubicula* (which, in turn, is "roodborst" in Holland, "rotkehlchen" in Germany, "rödhake" in Switzerland, and "rougegorge" in France). An American birdwatcher told by a traveling friend returning from Europe that she had added the "Ring Ousel" and "Blackbird" to her life list might be left pretty much in the dark. But if the American knew that those birds were *Turdus torquatus* and *Turdus merula,* he or she would at least know that both were sizable thrushes.

SEE: Species and Speciation, p. 355; Birds, DNA, and Evolutionary Convergence, p. 419; Passerines and Songbirds, p. 395; Superspecies, p. 375; Sibling Species, p. 383. REFS: American Ornithologists' Union, 1983, 1985; Mayr, 1969.

Eating Wax

Many berries, such as those of wax myrtle and bayberry bushes, have a waxy coating. Waxes are a chemical grab-bag of waterproof organic materials that are solid at room temperature. Few animals can digest them, but some birds can turn the trick.

Honeyguides, Old World relatives of woodpeckers, eat insects, but also consume wax. They attack bee nests and devour the bee larvae and wax honey combs and they eat waxy scale insects. In experiments, some species of honeyguides have survived for a month on a diet of wax alone, but whether these birds produce the enzymes necessary to break it down or depend upon the action of bacteria that live in their digestive tracts is not known. Recent investigations have shown that Yellow-rumped Warblers have evolved the appropriate enzymes to digest wax. This ability is probably why Yellow-rumped Warblers can overwinter farther north than most wood warblers; Yellow-rumps can gain energy from the coatings of berries that arc indigestible to the others.

The young of some pelagic birds are also able to extract energy from waxes. Waxes are abundant in marine environments, constituting, for example, up to 70 percent of the dry weight of some shrimps. Many young tubenoses collect masses of wax in their stomachs during the relatively infrequent feeding visits of their parents. The chicks then are able to draw energy from that reserve. Many fledgling seabirds continue to live on waxes stored in their guts during their first few weeks at sea, while they are learning to fish. They survive by digesting the "whole ball of wax."

SEE: Diet and Nutrition, p. 587; Determining Diets, p. 535. REF: Roby et al., 1986.

Black-throated Gray Warbler
Dendroica nigrescens Townsend

NG–364; G–282; PE–232; PW–pl 50; AW–pl 608; AM(III)–136

			F?		
DECID	F?	4	I: ? DAYS		HOVER &
5'–50'		(3–5)	ALTRICIAL		GLEAN
(1'–50')		MONOG	F: ? DAYS		HAWKS
			MF		

BREEDING: Open, dry conif and conif-decid forests, chaparral, scrub, oak and piñon montane woodlands. 1 brood. **DISPLAYS:** ? **NEST:** Usu far out on horizontal branch; neat, of weed stalks, grass, plant fibers, lining always contains feathers, oft hair, moss. **EGGS:** White to creamy, marked with browns, usu wreathed. 0.6" (16 mm). **DIET:** Largely or entirely insects during nesting. **CONSERVATION:** Winters s to s Mexico. Rare cowbird host. **NOTES:** Very active and agile forager. Details of breeding biology little known. **ESSAYS:** Bird Communities and Competition, p. 605; Mobbing, p. 425; Bills, p. 209; Feathered Nests, p. 605; How Do We Find Out About Bird Biology?, p. 319. **REF:** Morrison, 1982.

Townsend's Warbler
Supersp #45
Dendroica townsendi Townsend

NG–364; G–280; PW–pl 50; AW–pl 415; AM(III)–138

			FM?		
8'–15'	MF(?)	4–5	I: 12? DAYS		HAWKS
(7'–60')		(3–5)	ALTRICIAL		
		MONOG	F: 8–10 (?) DAYS		
			F –M?		

BREEDING: Conif and conif-decid forests. ? broods. **DISPLAYS:** ? **NEST:** Usu far out on horizontal branch of fir; relatively shallow, of grass, moss, cedar bark, fir twigs, plant fibers, lined with moss, feathers, hair. **EGGS:** White, marked with browns, usu mostly at large end but not wreathed. 0.7" (18 mm). **DIET:** Largely or entirely insects; also few seeds, plant galls. **CONSERVATION:** Winters s through highlands of Mexico to Costa Rica. Rare cowbird host. **NOTES:** Female allows close approach when incubating, then drops to ground and disappears. During summer, activities confined to highest parts of trees. In winter in N.A., joins mixed-species flocks of chickadees, nuthatches, etc.; in Mexico and C.A., oft gregarious, forming single-species flocks and feeding on fruit and nectar. Birds breeding on islands off BC winter in U.S. and have longer wings and smaller bills than birds breeding elsewhere and wintering s of U.S. **ESSAYS:** Species and Speciation, p. 355; Superspecies, p. 375; Bird Guilds, p. 493; Decline of Eastern Songbirds, p. 495; Mixed-Species Flocking, p. 433; Wintering and Conservation, p. 513. **REFS:** Harrison, 1984; Morrison, 1983.

News About Bird Biology

There are quite a few popular (as opposed to technical) magazines that provide lively reports of recent developments in North American ornithology. A number of these magazines are offered with membership in conservation organizations and museums. The Audubon Society's *Audubon* and *American Birds*, and the Cornell University Ornithological Laboratory's *Living Bird Quarterly*, feature well-illustrated and well-written accounts; the latter two journals are entirely devoted to birds. The American Museum of Natural History's *Natural History*, the Chicago Field Museum's *Bulletin*, the California Academy of Sciences' *Pacific Discovery*, and *Smithsonian Magazine* also frequently carry articles on avian biology.

The number and variety of journals appears to be increasing: the *Bird Watcher's Digest* achieved a circulation of 60,000 eight years after its first issue in 1978, and *Birder's World*, *Wildbird*, and *Wingtips* recently began publication. To keep apprised of current works available you can also refer to a newsletter, *Books About Birds*, which lists and reviews books, publications, reports, and artwork of possible interest to bird enthusiasts. *Birding*, the journal of the American Birding Association, is a goldmine of information on how to find and identify birds—the first step in learning about their biology.

For *subscription* information, write to:

American Museum of Natural History
Natural History
Box 5000
Harlan, IA 51537

Chicago Field Museum
Bulletin
Roosevelt Road at Lake Shore Drive
Chicago, IL 60605-2499

California Academy of Sciences
Pacific Discovery
Golden Gate Park
San Francisco, CA 94118-9961

Bird Watcher's Digest
P.O. Box 110
Marietta, OH 45750

Birder's World
720 E 8th Street
Holland, MI 49423

Wildbird
P.O. Box 6040
Mission Viejo, CA 92690-9983

Wingtips
Box 226
Lansing, NY 14882

Books about Birds
P.O. Box 106
Jamaica, NY 11415

Joe Taylor
American Birding Association
P.O. Box 31
Honeoye Falls, NY 14472

For addresses of *Audubon, American Birds,* and *Living Bird Quarterly,* see p. 369.

SEE: Helping to Conserve Birds—National Level, p. 363; Sources of Information Used in this Guide, p. 670.

Hermit Warbler

NG–364; G–280; PW–pl 50; AW–pl 416; AM(III)–140

15'–100' +	F	4–5 (3–5) MONOG	FM? I: 12? DAYS ALTRICIAL F: 8–10(?) DAYS F –M ?		HOVER & GLEAN HAWKS

BREEDING: Mature conif forest. ? broods. **DISPLAYS:** ? **NEST:** On horizontal branch; compact, deep, of weed stems, pine needles, fine twigs, lichen, lined with soft, fine materials. **EGGS:** Creamy white, finely flecked with browns, usu wreathed. 0.6" (17 mm). **DIET:** Largely or entirely insects during nesting. **CONSERVATION:** Winters s to n c Nicaragua. Rare cowbird host. **NOTES:** Spends most of the time actively foraging high in trees; males tend to forage higher than females. Incubating female is a "tight sitter" on nest. Occ hybridizes with Townsend's Warbler. **ESSAYS:** Superspecies, p. 375; Hybridization, p. 501; Wintering and Conservation, p. 513. **REF:** Morrison, 1982.

Black-throated Green Warbler

NG–364; G–280; PE–230; PW–pl 50; AE–pl 375; AM(III)–142

    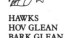

20'–35' (3'–40')	MF	4–5 MONOG	F I: 12 DAYS ALTRICIAL F: 8–10 DAYS F –M		HAWKS HOV GLEAN BARK GLEAN

BREEDING: Open conif and conif-decid (occ decid) forests, cypress swamps in coastal Carolinas. ? broods. **DISPLAYS:** ? **NEST:** Oft on horizontal limb; compact, deep, of grass, moss, inner bark, plant fibers, lined with fine materials. **EGGS:** Off-white, marked with browns, usu wreathed. 0.6" (17 mm). **DIET:** Largely or entirely insects during nesting. **CONSERVATION:** Winters s through Bahamas, Cuba, Jamaica, and s to Panama; found mostly on the mainland—reported in 1938 as one of the most common winter birds in El Salvador. Uncommon cowbird host. **NOTES:** Male sings one song type at territorial boundaries, another in vicinity of female or nest. Male tends to forage higher in trees than female. **ESSAYS:** Superspecies, p. 375; MacArthur's Warblers, p. 523; Decline of Eastern Songbirds, p. 495; Head Scratching, p. 543; Vocal Functions, p. 471; Wintering and Conservation, p. 513. **REFS:** Holmes, 1986; Morse, 1980; Rabenold, 1980.

MacArthur's Warblers

Five species of insectivorous wood warblers—Cape May, Yellow-rumped, Black-throated Green, Blackburnian, and Bay-breasted—were the subject of a classic study of community ecology (the science of interpreting species interactions). These species often share the same breeding grounds in mature coniferous forests. They had been thought by some ornithologists to occupy the same "niche"—in other words, they appeared to assume identical roles in the same bird community. These five warblers would thus be an exception to the ecological rule of competitive exclusion. The rule states that two species with essentially the same niche cannot coexist because one will always outcompete and displace the other.

For his doctoral dissertation, the late Robert MacArthur, who became one of the nation's leading ecologists, set out to determine whether the five species of warblers actually did occupy the same niche. By measuring distances down from the top and outward from the trunk of individual spruce, fir, and pine trees, MacArthur divided the trees into zones and recorded feeding positions of the different warblers within each. A record in zone "T3" indicated a bird feeding among the abundant new needles and buds of the *tip* of a branch, between 20 and 30 feet from the top of the tree. A record of "M3" signified feeding mostly among dead needles at the same height but in the *middle* zone of a branch. A record of "B2" represented a warbler feeding on the bare, lichen-covered *base* of a branch. In all, 16 different positions were distinguished,

MacArthur found that each warbler species divided its time differently among various parts of the tree. The Cape May, for instance, stayed mostly toward the outside on the top, the Bay-breasted fed mostly around the middle interior, while the Yellow-rumped moved from part to part more than either of the other two. This is shown in the accompanying diagrams,

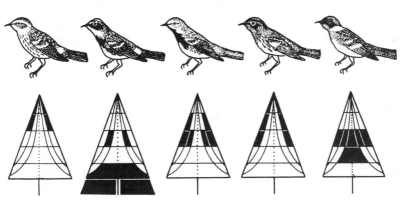

Left to right: Cape May, Yellow-rumped, Black-throated Green, Blackburnian, and Bay-breasted Warblers. Black areas in stylized conifers show where feeding is concentrated.

Golden-cheeked Warbler
Dendroica chrysoparia Sclater and Salvin

NG–364; G–280; PW–pl 50; AE–609; AM(III)–144

			F		
15′–21′	F	3–4	I: 12 DAYS		HAWKS
(6′–32′)		(3–5)	ALTRICIAL		
		MONOG	F: 9 DAYS		
			MF		

BREEDING: Stands of mature Ashe juniper ("cedar brakes"). 1 brood. **DISPLAYS:** Courtship inconspicuous; male fluffs feathers, gives "chip" notes, occ faces female and spreads wings. **NEST:** In tree fork (usu juniper); compact, deep, outside *always* of camouflaging bark strips from mature Ashe juniper secured by spider web, some grass, lined with rootlets, feathers, hair. Female chooses site. Built in 4 days. **EGGS:** White to creamy, usu finely flecked with browns, oft wreathed. 0.7″ (17 mm). **DIET:** Entirely insectivorous. **CONSERVATION:** Winters in highlands of Guatemala, Honduras, and Nicaragua in pine-oak forest. Frequent cowbird host. Rare, threatened by destruction of habitat on Edwards Plateau in c TX; remaining cedar brakes should be preserved to protect this endemic. Total population estimated at only 15,000 in 1974. Cowbird parasitism has severe impact on reproductive success. **NOTES:** Like Kirtland's Warbler, an extreme habitat specialist. Both sexes show strong site tenacity to breeding territory. Female (occ male) performs distraction display with spread tail and rapid fluttering among tree branches. Female broods continuously for first 3 days. Parents divide fledged brood; provide care for 4–7 weeks. **ESSAYS:** Birds and the Law, p. 293; Cowbirds, p. 619; Site Tenacity, p. 189; Decline of Eastern Songbirds, p. 495; Helping to Conserve Birds—National Level, p. 363; Parental Care, p. 555. **REF:** Pulich, 1976.

Yellow-throated Warbler
Dendroica dominica Linnaeus

NG–366; G–282; PE–230; AE–pl 376; AM(III)–146

			?		
20′–50′	F –M	4	I: 12–13 (?) DAYS		FOLIAGE
(3′–100′)		(4–5)	ALTRICIAL		GLEAN
		MONOG	F: ? DAYS		HAWKS
			?		

BREEDING: Pine-oak woodland, sycamore-bald cypress swamps with Spanish moss, pine forest. 2 broods in s. **DISPLAYS:** ? **NEST:** In s e, buried in Spanish moss; when inland, on high horizontal branch of pine; of fine grass, bark strips, weed stems, caterpillar silk, plant down, lined with down, occ feathers. **EGGS:** Dull greenish gray-white, marked with purples, reds, browns, occ wreathed. 0.6″ (17 mm). **DIET:** Not well known; incl spiders. **CONSERVATION:** Winters s through Greater Antilles, Caribbean slope to Costa Rica. Rare cowbird host. **NOTES:** Oft forages like Brown Creeper, searching under bark on vertical surfaces; has longest bill of wood warblers. Bathes more than most warblers. Occ mortality in swamps from entanglement in spider webs. Details of breeding biology little known. **ESSAYS:** Decline of Eastern Songbirds, p. 495; Bills, p. 209; Determining Diets, p. 535; Bathing and Dusting, p. 429; How Do We Find Out About Bird Biology?, p. 319. **REF:** Harrison, 1984.

in which the zones that contained 50 percent of the birds' feeding activity are blackened.

MacArthur also recorded details of the warblers' foraging habits and discovered that they differed too. For example, the Cape May warbler hawks flying insects much more often than does the Blackburnian and tends to move vertically rather than horizontally (matching its tendency to remain on the outside of the tree). The Black-throated Green hovers much more than the Bay-breasted, and the more variable Yellow-rumped has the most varied feeding habits. In addition, MacArthur found evidence that food shortage limited the size of the warbler populations.

Overall, MacArthur concluded that "the birds behave in such a way as to be exposed to different kinds of food." They also have somewhat different nesting times, and thus the times of their peak food requirements are not the same. They are partitioning a limiting resource—their supply of insects, and, in the process, occupying different niches.

SEE: Bird Communities and Competition, p. 605; Bird Guilds, p. 493; Songbird Foraging, p. 381. REF: MacArthur, 1958.

Bird Biologist—Robert MacArthur

History will view Robert MacArthur (1930–72) as a leader in bringing mathematical theory into ecology. Those who knew him personally are more likely to think of him as a birder with a great talent for seeing the essence of biological problems. Along with his great teacher G. Evelyn Hutchinson of Yale University, MacArthur was a major force in changing how ecologists think about the world—and much of his work was focused on the biology of birds, from how they divided up resources to the number of bird species found in a given community. He died tragically young, but in his short life accomplished more than most scientists ever hope to.

SEE: MacArthur's Warblers, p. 523; Birds in the Bush, p. 541; Island Biogeography, p. 549; Facts, Hypotheses, and Theories, p. 567.

Grace's Warbler

NG–366; G–282; PW–pl 50; AW–717; AM(III)–148

20'–60'	F	4 (3–4) MONOG	? I: ? DAYS ALTRICIAL F: ? DAYS ?		HAWKS HOVER & GLEAN

BREEDING: Montane pine forest and oak-pine forest. 2 broods. **DISPLAYS:** ? **NEST:** On horizontal branch or in crown of pine; compact, flat, of oak catkins, plant fibers, lined with fine materials. **EGGS:** White to creamy, marked with browns, usu wreathed. 0.6″ (17 mm). **DIET:** Not well known, presumably largely or entirely insects. **CONSERVATION:** Winters from n Mexico s to Honduras and Nicaragua. Rare cowbird host. **NOTES:** Mostly remains high in pine trees, where it hunts primarily for active, mobile insects. Details of breeding biology unknown. **ESSAYS:** Decline of Eastern Songbirds, p. 495; How Do We Find Out About Bird Biology?, p. 319; Wintering and Conservation, p. 513. **REF:** Harrison, 1984.

Kirtland's Warbler

Dendroica kirtlandii Baird

NG–366; G–286; PE–234; AE–pl 374; AM(III)–150

	MF	4–5 (3–5) MONOG (POLYGYN)	F I: 14–15 DAYS ALTRICIAL F: 12–13 DAYS MF	TREE SAP BERRIES	GRND GLEAN HAWKS HOV GLEAN?

BREEDING: Large stands of 6'–20' jack pines on sandy soil with low cover. Extreme habitat specialist. ? broods. **DISPLAYS:** Courting male may perform display flight, descending from 6' to 8' directly over female. **NEST:** Concealed close to pine, of grass or other fibrous plant material, lined with fine grass, moss, hair. **EGGS:** White, creamy-pinkish, marked with brown, mostly at large end. 0.7″ (18 mm). **DIET:** Incl esp pine sap, blueberries. **CONSERVATION:** Winters in Bahamas only. Endangered Species, largely because of exacting requirements for breeding habitat. About 170 breeding males remained in 1987. Frequent cowbird host; cowbirds reached breeding range only within past 100 years. Cowbird removal, habitat maintenance, and other protective measures now being taken. **NOTES:** Longest incubation of any N.A. warbler. Male song is unusually loud. Male feeds incubating female. Bathes in dew. Habitually wags tail. Very tame. **ESSAYS:** Conservation of Kirtland's Warbler, p. 527; Cowbirds, p. 619; Birds and the Law, p. 293; Fate of Bachman's Warbler, p. 505. **REFS:** Hayes et al., 1986; Mayfield, 1978; Probst and Hayes, 1987; Walkinshaw, 1983.

Conservation of Kirtland's Warbler

Ever since its discovery in the middle of the last century, Kirtland's Warbler has been considered a rarity. The first individual known to science was a migrant shot near Cleveland, Ohio, in May 1851. The breeding range in Michigan and the wintering range in the Bahamas were discovered in the 1870s, but relatively few birds were seen in either place. A total of 71 specimens were taken in the Bahamas in the two decades after Kirtland's Warbler was discovered there, and only 6 in Michigan in roughly the same period. In 1903 the bird's nesting grounds in central Michigan were located, and in the 1980s its wintering grounds were found to extend farther south (to the Dominican Republic) and into drier habitat than previously thought.

A survey of Kirtland's Warblers in 1951 turned up 432 singing males. In 1961 the number had increased to 502, but by 1971 it had declined sharply to 201. The species is now restricted to just six Michigan counties. It is an extreme habitat specialist, nesting only in areas of 5- to 6-year-old jack pines (1–5 feet tall)—*if* the stand is extensive enough and contains grassy clearings. Such areas are produced when a fire of appropriate intensity sweeps through a mature stand of pines permitting the germination of their seeds. The birds will start to nest in an area when the pines are young. Wildfires once provided abundant habitat, but now improved forest firefighting capability has greatly reduced burned areas. To compensate, jack pine stands specifically designed to meet the needs of Kirtland's Warblers rather than the needs of forestry have been planted.

In addition to habitat shrinkage in this century, population increases of Brown-headed Cowbirds threaten the warblers. Cowbirds have been abundant in Kirtland's habitat only recently as forests in the area were cleared for agriculture. The warblers are not adapted to defend against them. The percentage of parasitized nests increased from about 55 percent in the 1940s and 1950s to over 70 percent in the 1960s. The cowbird is an especially dangerous enemy because it parasitizes numerous species and is thus not dependent on Kirtland's Warbler. As it reduces the warbler population, its own population size will not necessarily decline—its assault can be unrelenting. Thus when the decline in warbler populations was observed, the U.S. Fish and Wildlife Service (with the aid of several state agencies and the Detroit and Pontiac Audubon Societies) began a program of trapping and removing cowbirds. By about 1980 over 40,000 cowbirds had been removed, and as a result the level of parasitism of warbler nests became negligible. Kirtland's fledging rates have tripled, so that their nesting success is now higher than that known for any other warbler. By 1977 the decrease in warbler numbers had clearly been halted, and 219 singing males were counted, a slight increase over 1971. There were 210 pairs censused in 1986, but a sharp decline to 167 in 1987.

That rate of recovery seems quite low, however, considering the great increase in reproductive success. Survival through the first year of life seems to be less than 20 percent. This could be due to high fledgling mortal-

Prairie Warbler

Dendroica discolor Vieillot

NG–366; G–286; PE–238; AE–pl 363; AM(III)–152

TREE	F	4 (3–5)	F		HAWKS
1'–10'		MONOG	I: 12 (11–14) DAYS		HOV GLEAN
(To 45')		(POLYGYN)	ALTRICIAL		SWOOPS
			F: 9–10 (8–11) DAYS		
			MF		

BREEDING: Dry brushy clearings, forest margin, pine barrens. Occ 2 broods. **DISPLAYS:** Courtship: male performs short, low display flights ("mothlike") interspersed with chases. **NEST:** In upright fork, on limb, or against trunk, rarely in vines; compact, of closely felted plant materials. Female selects site. Usu built in 3–5 days. **EGGS:** White to off-white, marked with brown, usu wreathed. 0.6" (16 mm). **DIET:** Nestlings fed mostly caterpillars. **CONSERVATION:** Winters s to Caribbean. Frequent cowbird host; oft deserts parasitized nest. **NOTES:** Strong site tenacity by breeding males, but only by few females, which occ pair with former mate. Ca. 15% of males polygynous; polygynous bonds formed mostly midseason. Female broods. Adults perform wing-quivering distraction display with vocalizations. Adults divide and care separately for fledglings. Young independent usu at 40–50 days. Name a misnomer; Wilson found it in area of barrens in KY locally called "prairie." Twitches tail when foraging. Joins loose mixed-species flocks of warblers in winter. **ESSAYS:** Polygyny, p. 443; Monogamy, p. 597; Site Tenacity, p. 189; Cowbirds, p. 619; Distraction Displays, p. 115. **REF:** Nolan, 1978.

Bay-breasted Warbler

Dendroica castanea Wilson

NG–368; G–284; PE–236; PW–pl 51; AE–pl 403; AM(III)–154

4'–40'	?	4–5	F	BERRIES	HAWKS
		(3–7)	I: 12–13 DAYS		
		MONOG	ALTRICIAL		
			F: 11–12 DAYS		
			MF		

BREEDING: Conif forest, occ adjoining decid second growth. ? broods. **DISPLAYS:** ? **NEST:** Usu on horizontal branch; loose or compact, of grass, conif twigs, lined with fine rootlets, occ hair. **EGGS:** White to off-white, marked with browns, occ black, mostly at large end. 0.7" (17 mm). **DIET:** Largely insects; few berries. **CONSERVATION:** Winters from c Panama s to n S.A. Rare cowbird host. **NOTES:** Number of eggs oft correlated with abundance of spruce budworms. Foraging movements are short and along branches, imparting a sluggish appearance; wags tail slightly as it forages. Commonly joins mixed-species canopy-foraging flocks in tropical wintering areas. **ESSAYS:** MacArthur's Warblers, p. 523; Decline of Eastern Songbirds, p. 495; Island Biogeography, p. 549; Mixed-Species Flocking, p. 433; Variation in Clutch Sizes, p. 339. **REFS:** Greenberg, 1984; Morse, 1978.

ity before migration or perhaps unusual mortality during migration in recent years. Other possibilities are that the now limited breeding habitat makes too small a "target" for inexperienced birds returning from the Bahamas, that there is simply not enough of that habitat to support a larger population (although it seems uncrowded), or that some change unrecognized by ornithologists has made the northern West Indies a less satisfactory wintering ground. Ecologists John Terborgh and David Wilcove have speculated, however, that the main reason that Kirtland's has not gone extinct already is its semicolonial breeding behavior which keeps individuals returning to the small target area. Were it not for that, failure to find mates might have pushed it down the path taken by Bachman's Warbler, where returning migrants scattered over the entire southeastern United States, and many of the last sightings were of apparently unmated males.

The future of Kirtland's Warbler remains in doubt. Some Blue Jays, important nest predators, are removed in the course of the cowbird control program, but more intensive predator control may be required, along with increased production of suitable pine stands, if the species is to be saved. The only long-range solution will be to maintain enough habitat in Michigan for Kirtland's Warblers to persist without constant human interference to control the warblers' parasites and predators, and good luck (or constant vigilance) to keep the West Indian wintering grounds in suitable condition.

SEE: Nest-Robbing Blue Jays, p. 409; Brood Parasitism, p. 287; The Fate of Bachman's Warbler, p. 505; Cowbirds, p. 619. REFS: Mayfield, 1978; Walkinshaw, 1983.

Molting

Birds must spend a great deal of time caring for their feathers, since their lives depend on them. Preening, bathing, dusting, and other feather care operations, however, cannot prevent the feathers from wearing out. Because formed feathers (like our fingernails) are lifeless, horny structures, incapable of being repaired, worn feathers must be replaced. This process of replacement is termed molting. The old, worn feathers are loosened in their follicles (sockets) by the growth of new intruding feathers, which eventually push them out. Molting occurs in regular patterns over a bird's body. The adaptiveness of such patterns can be illustrated by the arboreal woodpeckers, which retain the key inner pair of long tail feathers used in bracing and climbing until the outer feathers have been replaced. This is the reverse of the pattern found in most birds, which molt tail feathers from the center of the tail first, and then progressively toward each side. The majority of adult birds molt once or twice a year, and the temporal pattern, not unexpectedly, is related to the wear rate on the feathers. Feathers of species that migrate enormous distances or live in thick brush, dodging among twigs and spines, wear more rapidly than those of birds resident in one place or

Blackpoll Warbler

Dendroica striata Forster

NG–368; G–284; PE–232; PW–pl 50; AE–pl 563; AW–pl 609; AM(III)–156

2'–7'	F	4–5 (3–5)	F I: 12? DAYS ALTRICIAL	BERRIES	BARK
(To 33')		MONOG (POLYGYN)	F: 11–12 DAYS MF		GLEAN HAWKS

BREEDING: Low n conif forest (primarily spruce). 1, occ 2 broods. **DISPLAYS:** Courtship unusually prolonged for a wood warbler. **NEST:** Against trunk, supported by horizontal branches; bulky, of conif twigs, bark, dried grass, lined with feathers. **EGGS:** White to off-white, marked with browns, lavender, occ wreathed. 0.7" (18 mm). **DIET:** Incl spiders; few seeds. **CONSERVATION:** Winters in S.A., mostly e of Andes, as far s as s Brazil and n Argentina. Range does not overlap with cowbirds. **NOTES:** Champion long-distance migrant among warblers with a round trip of at least 2,500 miles, incl overwater flight from e U.S. to n S.A. in autumn; departs rather late on migration s. Strong nest site tenacity by females is primary factor resulting in polygynous matings for 10%–30% of males; female mates with male holding territory closest to her previous nest site, whether or not he is already paired. Forages in very deliberate fashion, creeping along branches. **ESSAYS:** Migration, p. 183; Decline of Eastern Songbirds, p. 495; Island Biogeography, p. 549; Navigation and Orientation, p. 559; Polygyny, p. 444; Site Tenacity, p. 189. **REFS:** Eliason, 1986; Morse, 1979.

Pine Warbler

Dendroica pinus Wilson

NG–368; G–286; PE–238; AE–pl 364; AM(III)–148

25'–40'	F	4	F I: 10? DAYS ALTRICIAL	SEEDS	FOLIAGE
(10'–135')		(3–5) MONOG	F: 10? DAYS MF	FRUIT	GLEAN HAWKS

BREEDING: Pine forests. ? broods. **DISPLAYS:** ? **NEST:** Oft far out on limb, concealed from below by leaves; compact, lined with feathers. **EGGS:** White to off-white, marked with browns, mostly toward large end. 0.7" (18 mm). **DIET:** Largely insects, spiders; when insects scarce, takes pine, grass, and forb seeds, fruit, berries. **CONSERVATION:** Winters s to n e Mexico, Caribbean. Uncommon cowbird host; may destroy cowbird eggs by burying in bottom of nest. **NOTES:** Nests only in pines, where it forages by creeping along branches. In winter, oft assoc with other warblers and bluebirds, and occurs in a wider range of habitats. **ESSAYS:** Head Scratching, p. 543; Habitat Selection, p. 463; Mixed-Species Flocking, p. 433. **REF:** Harrison, 1984.

live in open country. The former tend to molt twice a year, and the latter only once.

Molting is timed to meet various needs. For example, resident temperate-zone birds require more insulating feathers in the winter than in the summer. The number is changed in the process of molting; winter plumage may contain more than half again as many feathers as summer plumage. Since the feathers, which carry the colors of birds, are "dead," a bird cannot totally change its colors without changing its feathers (although its appearance can change substantially just from wear). Therefore a male bird usually molts into his most colorful plumage prior to the breeding season. Molting in most passerines takes from 5 to 12 weeks, but some raptors may require two years or more to completely replace their feathers.

Some birds, such as ducks, swans, grebes, pelicans, and auks, are "synchronous molters"—they change their feathers all at once in a period as short as two weeks, but sometimes stretching over a month. During this period, they cannot fly, and males, in particular, often complete the process on secluded lakes in order to minimize their vulnerability to predators.

Why should synchronous molters have evolved this seemingly risky process instead of undergoing a gradual molt like most birds? These birds tend to be heavy relative to their wing surfaces—they have high "wing loadings." The loss of only a few flight feathers would seriously compromise their flying ability, and so evolution has favored being grounded for a "quick overhaul" rather than a longer period of difficult flying.

SEE: Feathers, p. 309; Avian Snowshoes, p. 255; The Color of Birds, p. 111; Preening, p. 53; Eclipse Plumage, p. 61.

Bird Names—XII

The name warbler refers to "singing with trills, runs, or quavers." The name was originally applied to European warblers, which are not related to North American warblers and are properly called wood warblers. Two wood warblers were named in honor of relatives of certain ornithologists: Grace's Warbler after Grace Coues, sister of Elliot Coues (p. 565); and Lucy's Warbler after Lucy Baird, daughter of Spencer Fullerton Baird (p. 569). MacGillivray's Warbler was named by Audubon for his Scottish friend, ornithologist William MacGillivray. The same species, however, had previously been scientifically described and named, so that the scientific name is now *Oporornis tolmiei*. *Oporornis* means "end of summer bird" in Greek; *tolmiei* honors Dr. William F. Tolmie, a friend of John K. Townsend, the describer of the bird. Since the latinized name given by Townsend was published first, it takes priority over Audubon's name honoring MacGillivray.

The Prairie Warbler does not live on the prairies, but it does spend its winters in grassy woodland clearings known locally in the south as "prairies."

Palm Warbler

Dendroica palmarum Gmelin

NG–368; G–286; PE–238; PW–pl 50; AE–pl 365; AM(III)–154

| CONIF
TREE
(To 4') | F | 4–5
MONOG
(POLYGYN) | FM?
I: 12 DAYS
ALTRICIAL
F: 12 DAYS
MF | BERRIES | FOLIAGE
GLEAN
HAWKS |

BREEDING: Sphagnum bogs with scattered spruce, dry pine stands in boreal forests. 2? broods. **DISPLAYS:** ? **NEST:** On ground or low in spruce close to trunk; of dry grass and other plant fibers, lined with fine plant material, feathers. **EGGS:** White to creamy, marked with browns, oft wreathed. 0.7″ (17 mm). **DIET:** Almost entirely insects. Also forages by hover gleaning. **CONSERVATION:** Winters primarily in West Indies, but occurs s to lowland pine savannas of n e Nicaragua and e Honduras. Uncommon cowbird host; may destroy cowbird eggs by burying in bottom of nest. **NOTES:** Wintering birds oft seen in FL and Caribbean assoc with palm trees, which doubtless explains seemingly inappropriate common name. Wags tail as it forages on ground. **ESSAYS:** Cowbirds, p. 619; Brood Parasitism, p. 287; Wintering and Conservation, p. 513. **REF:** Harrison, 1984.

Yellow Warbler

Dendroica petechia Linnaeus

NG–370; G–278; PE–238; PW–pl 50; AE–pl 357; AW–pl 410; AM(III)–126

| TREE
1′–14′
(To 60') | F | 4–5
(3–6)
MONOG | F
I: 11–12 DAYS
ALTRICIAL
F: 9–12 DAYS
MF | BARK GLEAN
HAWKS
HOV GLEAN |

BREEDING: Habitat generalist in e: well-watered second-growth woodland, gardens, scrub; in w, riparian thickets. ? broods. **DISPLAYS:** Courtship: male persistently pursues female for 1–4 days. **NEST:** Usu compact, neat, strong, of weed stalks, shredded bark, grass, lined with fine materials. **EGGS:** Off-white, occ pale green, marked with browns, olive, gray, from barely spotted to strongly blotched, usu wreathed. 0.7″ (16 mm). **DIET:** Also few berries. **CONSERVATION:** Winters s to Bahamas, n Mexico, s to Peru, Bolivia, and Brazilian Amazon. Blue List 1973–82; Special Concern 1986. Populations in w increase where reduction of grazing and cessation of herbiciding willows has led to regrowth of riparian veg. One of the 3 most frequent cowbird hosts; oft destroys cowbird egg by burying in bottom of nest where egg cools and dies. **NOTES:** Occ polygynous. Males forage higher in trees than females, and in trees with less dense foliage than those used by females; presumably this enables male to more efficiently advertise his territorial ownership while foraging, and minimizes conspicuousness of female. Females occ steal nesting material from each other. Quite tame garden bird in e. **ESSAYS:** Head Scratching, p. 543; Determining Diets, p. 535; Cowbirds, p. 619; Blue List, p. 11; Polygyny, p. 443 **REFS:** Biermann and Sealy, 1982; Busby and Sealy, 1979; DellaSala, 1986; Taylor and Littlefield, 1986.

Dominance Hierarchies

It all started with hens. Norwegian scientist Thorleif Schjelderup-Ebbe wondered how peace was kept in their flocks, and conducted a series of experiments to find out. He discovered that things were tranquil only in *established* flocks—ones in which each hen knew its place. And the hens learned their places in fights over chicken feed. Once a hen had been bested in a squabble, it henceforth would defer to the victor. Each hen knew whom it could dominate, and by whom it would be dominated. A "peck order" was thus established in the flock and functioned to maintain social stability. Hens can recognize many other hens and can remember their dominance status relative to each. One hen demonstrated the ability to recognize 27 other individuals belonging to four different flocks. As you would expect, the birds at the top of the peck order benefited both by increased access to food and by avoidance of injuries (even bullies can get hurt in fights). The birds at the bottom, while having to wait until those higher up had eaten their fill, at least were not subjected to continuous fights that they were likely to lose.

In all but polyandrous species of birds (those where one female mates with more than one male), males are normally dominant over females. That is especially true in the early stages of pair formation, although in some buntings and other finches and in some gulls, a reversal of dominance, with the male becoming subordinate, reportedly occurs after the pair bond is established. In experiments, females have been able to assume higher ranks in dominance hierarchies after receiving injections of male hormones and by dyeing their feathers to resemble male plumage. Results of such experiments varied from species to species; doses of male hormone increased the social status of female European Chaffinches and Japanese Quail, but not of starlings.

It is usually assumed that a high position in a dominance hierarchy increases the chances of survival and also increases reproductive output. In species where males display on leks, the dominant male generally holds the best territory on the lek and successfully copulates with the most females. But there is relatively little evidence in monogamous species that dominant individuals have a better chance of survival than subordinates.

A study of juvenile Song Sparrows on an island near Victoria, British Columbia, showed that dominance relationships at millet-provisioned feeders during summer were reflected in chances for surviving the subsequent winter and establishing a territory the following spring. In two consecutive years, dominant males showed 35 and 22 percent better survival than subordinate males. For dominant females the equivalent figures were 32 and 33 percent. The effects on successful settlement of territories were similar for both sexes—dominant individuals were more likely to settle into territories than subordinates.

The same study showed that sex and age were the major determinants of dominance. Males more frequently dominated females than vice versa;

Mourning Warbler

NG–370; G–290; PE–244; PW–pl 51; AE–pl 372; AM(III)–172

			F		
			I: 12 DAYS		
SHRUB	MF(?)	3–4	ALTRICIAL		GROUND
0'–2.5'		(3–5)	F: 7–9 DAYS		GLEAN
		MONOG?	MF		

BREEDING: Dense shrubbery in open decid woods, bog and marsh edges. ? broods. **DISPLAYS:** Territorial: bobs, flicks wings and tail. **NEST:** At base of shrub, on or close to ground; of leaves with core of weed stems, grass, lined with fine plant materials. **EGGS:** White to creamy, marked with browns, from finely spotted to strongly blotched. 0.7" (18 mm). **DIET:** Little known, reportedly insects, spiders. **CONSERVATION:** Winters from s Nicaragua to n S.A. Uncommon cowbird host. **NOTES:** Male feeds incubating female. Female broods, esp initial 3–4 days. Adults perform distraction displays. Fledglings stay with adults 2–3 weeks. Hybridizes with MacGillivray's Warbler, its western counterpart, where ranges overlap. Hops, unlike similar-looking Connecticut Warbler, which walks. Forages low in thickets. Male oft sings from high perch. Solitary and oft territorial on wintering grounds. **ESSAYS:** Head Scratching, p. 543; Hybridization, p. 501; Determining Diets, p. 535; Walking vs. Hopping, p. 69; Wintering and Conservation, p. 513. **REF:** Cox, 1960.

MacGillivray's Warbler

NG–370; G–290; PW–pl 51; AW–pl 411; AM(III)–174

     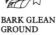

			F?		
			I: 11 DAYS		
2'–3'	MF?	4	ALTRICIAL		BARK GLEAN
(1'–5')		(3–5)	F: 8–9 DAYS		GROUND
GROUND		MONOG	MF		GLEAN

BREEDING: Dense thickets (esp riparian willow and alder), edge of conif or mixed woods. ? broods. **DISPLAYS:** ? **NEST:** Usu close to ground in thick shrubbery; of weed stems, grass, lined with fine materials. **EGGS:** White to creamy, marked with browns. 0.7" (18 mm). **DIET:** Little known, mostly insects. Juveniles in CO oft take sap from Red-naped Sapsucker wells excavated in willows; visits are frequent but short, as sapsuckers chase warblers away. **CONSERVATION:** Winters from c Mexico s to Panama. Uncommon cowbird host. **NOTES:** Hybridizes with its eastern equivalent, the Mourning Warbler, where ranges overlap. Hops, unlike similar-looking Connecticut Warbler, which walks. Solitary and oft territorial on wintering grounds. **ESSAYS:** Hybridization, p. 501; Superspecies, p. 375; Wintering and Conservation, p. 513; Determining Diets, p. 535; Walking vs. Hopping, p. 69. **REF:** Hutto, 1981.

males tended to win about 60 percent of their encounters with females at the feeders, females about 40 percent. Time since hatching had a strong effect on the success of encounters, even when only 24 days separated the oldest juvenile from the youngest. In contrast, no effect of body size on dominance was detected; a small bird was as likely to dominate a larger one as the reverse. Overall, it appeared that next after sex and age, previous experience in encounters was the most important factor in achieving dominance. Thus, early nesting would appear to be the best reproductive strategy for Song Sparrows. Young produced early in the season will gain the most experience and are the most likely to survive to reproduce. But if nesting is started too early, offspring may be killed by food shortage or late winter storms. Undoubtedly, there is a fine ecological line between reaping the advantages of early nesting and suffering the consequences of premature breeding.

In another study of Yellow Warblers, however, Michael Studd and Raleigh Robertson of Queens University in Ontario discovered that the nestlings of subordinate birds grew just as fast as those of dominant birds. At least by that measure (to be sure, not an exhaustive one), natural selection was not operating in favor of dominant birds. It has been suggested that in many circumstances being dominant is no more advantageous than being subordinate. For example, a dominant male may obtain a territory which is more resource-rich than that of a subordinate, but it may have to spend much more energy to protect it. Therefore, costs and benefits may more or less balance one another at each level in a dominance hierarchy, and evolution may favor the maintenance of the hierarchy itself, rather than just those near the top (which could lead to the disappearance of differences in dominance). Such a situation in which selection leads to the coexistence of several different modes of behavior has been called by British evolutionist John Maynard Smith a "mixed evolutionarily stable strategy."

SEE: Bird Badges, p. 591; Natural Selection, p. 237; Visual Displays, p. 5; Leks, p. 259.   REFS: Arcese and Smith, 1985; Roper, 1986; Studd and Robertson, 1985a.

Determining Diets

Considering how many people are interested in birds, a surprising amount remains to be learned about exactly what they eat. Determining by observation what birds consume is both tedious and difficult. It may be evident that a warbler working over bark or leaves high in a tree is catching insects, but which insects, and how many, cannot be assessed readily. A Willet or Marbled Godwit probing in shallow water along a mud bar occasionally may be seen swallowing a worm, but how can we record what kind it was, or what else the bird may be feeding on that is simply too small to see?

Because of such problems, ornithologists long relied on careful exami-

Connecticut Warbler

Oporornis agilis Wilson

NG-370; G-290; PE-244; PW-pl 51; AE-pl 460; AM(III)-170

| SHRUB | ? | 4–5 MONOG | ? I: ? DAYS ALTRICIAL F: ? DAYS MF(?) | | FOLIAGE GLEAN |

BREEDING: Muskeg bogs with black spruce or tamarack, open poplar stands. ? broods. **DISPLAYS:** ? **NEST:** Usu concealed in sphagnum hummock, dried grass or weeds; cup made of leaves or simple depression in moss lined with fine materials. **EGGS:** Creamy white, marked with browns. 0.8″ (19 mm). **DIET:** Not well known but reports of insects, spiders, snails; occ seeds, berries. **CONSERVATION:** Winters in n and c S.A. Uncommon cowbird host. **NOTES:** Lands 30′–40′ from nest and walks to it to conceal location. Walks rather than hops when on ground. Male sings from top of tree, oft remaining motionless for long periods. Details of breeding biology unknown. Very shy and oft overlooked in migration; location of wintering grounds essentially unknown, based on only a few records. **ESSAYS:** Walking vs. Hopping, p. 69; Wintering and Conservation, p. 513; How Do We Find Out About Bird Biology?, p. 319; Determining Diets, p. 535. **REF:** Harrison, 1984.

Kentucky Warbler

Oporornis formosus Wilson

NG–372; G–290; PE–244; AE–pl 370; AM(III)–168

| SHRUB 0′–0.5′ | MF | 4–5 (3–6) MONOG | F I: 12–13 DAYS ALTRICIAL F: 8–10 DAYS F –M | | FOLIAGE GLEAN |

BREEDING: Woodlands with dense, damp undergrowth. ? broods. **DISPLAYS:** Each male has only one song type in his repertoire but can alter frequency characteristics of song to "match" song of nearby males when countersinging. **NEST:** At base of bush, on or close to ground; of leaves with core of weed stems, grass, lined with rootlets, occ hair. **EGGS:** White to creamy, marked with browns, most finely spotted, some strongly blotched, mostly at large end. 0.8″ (19 mm). **DIET:** Also few berries. **CONSERVATION:** Winters from s Mexico and Caribbean s to n S.A. Frequent cowbird host. Very sensitive to fragmentation of forested breeding habitat. **NOTES:** Female may perform distraction display when flushed from nest. Forages by hopping on ground and leaping up to pick insects off leaf undersurface of forest herbs. One of the most forest-dependent warblers on wintering grounds where they defend small territories and occ follow army ant swarms as commensal foragers. **ESSAYS:** Decline of Eastern Songbirds, p. 495; Island Biogeography, p. 549; Vocal Functions, p. 471; Commensal Feeding, p. 35; Helping to Conserve Birds—National Level, p. 363; Wintering and Conservation, p. 513; Distraction Displays, p. 115. **REFS:** Harrison, 1984; Morton and Young, 1986.

nation of stomach contents to assess feeding habits. This procedure is reasonably accurate, although, for example, marine worms are often omitted from diet descriptions because they are digested too rapidly to be identified. The main exception to the need to dissect stomachs are the birds, especially owls, that regurgitate the remains of their meals as pellets that can subsequently be collected and analyzed. Very large samples of diets can be obtained this way. It has been estimated that some 30,000 prey items of Long-eared Owls have been identified from North America, and more than 300,000 from Europe. This makes the food habits of these owls the best-known aspect of their ecology.

Stomach-content analysis is less commonly used today because large numbers of birds would have to be killed to develop a detailed knowledge of the diet of even a single population. We know that individual birds, like individual people, differ in their food intake at any given time, and that the average diet of a population will often change dramatically throughout the year. Many species that are primarily insectivorous specialize in devouring one common kind of insect at one time, switch to another insect species when the first kind of bug completes its flight season (or is decimated by predators), and then move on to others until insect activity becomes less common in the fall. The birds then may begin to supplement their diets with vegetable matter such as berries, or else depart for southern climes where insects are still active (and where many species that eat insects in the north eat primarily, if not exclusively, fruit).

Birds frequently form "search images"—i.e., they learn to find certain abundant (although often camouflaged) prey and then specialize in eating that prey as long as it remains abundant. Thus the diet of a population shifts dramatically as increasing numbers of individuals form new search images. Diets may change from week to week or from year to year as the abundance of food items changes. For example, when there is a mass emergence of 13- or 17-year cicadas, many birds will gorge on those superabundant insects. A naive observer sampling at that time might conclude that, say, the Red-winged Blackbird was a specialist on cicadas.

To make assessment even more difficult, diets differ from place to place. Yellow Warblers in Nebraska eat many more grasshoppers than do Yellow Warblers in Massachusetts, where gypsy moth caterpillars and plant lice are more favored. We suspect that winter diets of Yellow Warblers in Central America are quite different from spring and summer diets on the breeding grounds. Obviously, Peregrines living near the sea dine much more often on seabirds than those living inland, and inland Peregrines eat more doves than their coastal cousins. It is no surprise that Herring Gulls near big cities eat a lot more garbage than those on pristine coasts.

Nevertheless, there are limits to the variation in the diet of a species. Herring Gulls do not feed on plant lice, and Yellow Warblers eat neither fish nor doves. Birds, being adaptable creatures, usually dine on a spectrum of different kinds of foods, but even closely related species tend to have different spectra. Observations of foraging behavior and studies of stomach con-

Canada Warbler

Wilsonia canadensis Linnaeus

NG–372; G–292; PE–234; PW–pl 50; AE–pl 367; AM(III)–180

0'–0.5'	F	4 (3–5) MONOG	F –M? I: ? DAYS ALTRICIAL F: ? DAYS MF		FOLIAGE GLEAN GRND GLEAN

BREEDING: Decid woodland, riparian thickets. ? broods. **DISPLAYS:** ? **NEST:** On sphagnum hummocks, among roots of upturned stumps, etc.; bulky, of dead leaves, grass, ferns, dried plant fibers, lined with fine materials. **EGGS:** White to creamy, marked with browns; variable, oft wreathed. 0.7" (17 mm). **DIET:** Largely or exclusively insects. **CONSERVATION:** Winters in S.A. from n Colombia and Venezuela to e Peru and n Brazil in wide range of habitats from forest to scrub. Common cowbird host. **NOTES:** Male oft shows "anticipatory feeding" by offering food to eggs. Female may perform distraction display when flushed from nest. Details of breeding biology largely unknown. Very active forager, commonly flushing and chasing insects from leaves. Occurs in male-female pairs during migration in C.A. **ESSAYS:** Decline of Eastern Songbirds, p. 495; Cowbirds, p. 619; Distraction Displays, p. 115; How Do We Find Out About Bird Biology?, p. 319; Wintering and Conservation, p. 513. **REF:** Greenberg and Gradwohl, 1980.

Wilson's Warbler

Wilsonia pusilla Wilson

NG–372; G–292; PE–242; PW–pl 51; AE–pl 358; AW–pl 409; AM(III)–180

VINE TANGLE 0'–3'	F	4–6 (2–7) MONOG (POLYGYN)	F I: 10–13 DAYS ALTRICIAL F: 8–11 DAYS MF		HOV GLEAN HAWKS BARK GLEAN

BREEDING: Thickets and brush in well-watered locations (esp willow and alder bogs), riparian woodland. 1 brood. **DISPLAYS:** ? **NEST:** Variably placed: high-elevation nests are smaller and built on ground; coastal nests larger and above ground. Bulky, esp for such a small bird; of dead leaves, grass, moss, lined with fine grass, occ hair. Built in 5 days. **EGGS:** White to creamy, marked with browns, variable, oft wreathed. 0.6" (16 mm). **DIET:** Also occ berries. **CONSERVATION:** Winters s to w Panama. Uncommon cowbird host. **NOTES:** Breeds over a wide range of elevations: coastal populations have smaller clutches, lower nesting success, and are monogamous; high-elevation populations have larger clutches, higher nesting success, and polygyny occurs regularly. Females brood. Much more common in w than in e. **ESSAYS:** Polygyny, p. 443; Monogamy, p. 597; Average Clutch Size, p. 51; Variation in Clutch Sizes, p. 339. **REF:** Stewart et al., 1977.

tents have outlined major features of the diets of North American birds, but detailed knowledge is lacking for many species. Information reported in the literature is often based on small samples of birds recorded in too few places and limited portions of the year. To get a thorough picture of the diet of a single population would require examination of the stomach contents of dozens of birds at numerous different times throughout the year, and repeating the process over a series of years. To document the diet of a species thoroughly, such studies would have to be carried out on many populations over the species' entire range. It is the prospect of such a slaughter that makes ornithologists forgo the use of stomach-content analysis as a method for fine tuning knowledge of feeding habits (although when specimens are collected for other scientific purposes, the contents are always recorded).

Yet it is important to understand the similarities and differences of avian diets in much greater detail. If students of birds continue to record and publish careful observations of feeding habits, much of the needed information will accumulate gradually. During the breeding season, the nature of the diet tends to be of basic scientific interest, because, for example, one often wants to know whether two species breeding in the same place are competing for food. Scientists studying a population sometimes are able to assay diets by gently placing pipe cleaners around the throats of nestlings, so that they cannot swallow but can still breathe. The food delivered by the parents can then be retrieved and analyzed. This technique must be left to experts so that the nestlings are not injured or deprived of too much food. It is, however, often possible to identify what is being fed to nestlings by observation alone. So if you spend time monitoring nests, note what the parents bring to the young. If you are not familiar with the major groups of insects, bird watching can introduce you to another fascinating group of organisms. A good book to start with is *A Field Guide to the Insects*, by D. J. Borror and R. E. White (Houghton Mifflin, Boston, 1970).

SEE: Pellets, p. 297; Diet and Nutrition, p. 587; Swallowing Stones, p. 269. REF: Marks, 1984.

Bird Biologist—Waldo Lee McAtee

Waldo McAtee (1883–1962) was stimulated to become a professional ornithologist through lectures he heard as a teenager given by Frank M. Chapman (p. 43). Later he worked for the U.S. Biological Survey and became the leading economic ornithologist in the nation and an expert on the food habits of birds and other vertebrates. Almost alone, he pioneered the use of the analysis of stomach contents in determining diets. He published over 1,200 books, articles, reviews, and letters.

Hooded Warbler

Wilsonia citrina Boddaert

NG–372; G–292; PE–242; AE–pl 369; AM(III)–178

			MF		
2'–3'	F	3–4	I: 12 DAYS		HAWKS
(1'–6')		(3–5)	ALTRICIAL		GROUND
		MONOG	F: 8–9 DAYS		GLEAN
			MF		

BREEDING: Undergrowth in well-watered mature decid forest, esp in ravines. Usu 1 brood. **DISPLAYS:** ? **NEST:** Compact, on base of dead leaves; of bark, dried plant fibers, lined with fine materials. **EGGS:** Creamy white, marked with browns; variable, occ wreathed. 0.7" (18 mm). **DIET:** Entirely insectivorous. **CONSERVATION:** Winters from s e Mexico s mostly to s Costa Rica. Frequent cowbird host. **NOTES:** Females oft feed by gleaning near or on ground; males frequently hawk insects or sally to ground from elevated perch, thus decreasing competition for food between mated male and female. Persistently renests when nest destroyed by predator. Males and females defend separate feeding territories in winter, and occupy different habitats; no apparent differences in foraging behavior between sexes in winter. Both sexes show strong site tenacity to winter territories. **ESSAYS:** Decline of Eastern Songbirds, p. 495; Cowbirds, p. 619; Territoriality, p. 387; Site Tenacity, p. 189; Wintering and Conservation, p. 513; Songbird Foraging, p. 381. **REFS:** Lynch et al., 1985; Morton et al., 1987; Powell and Rappole, 1986.

Worm-eating Warbler

Helmitheros vermivorus Gmelin

NG–374; G–270; PE–240; AE–pl 509; AM(III)–164

			F		
	F	4–5	I: 13 DAYS		BARK GLEAN
		(3–6)	ALTRICIAL		GROUND
		MONOG	F: 10 DAYS		GLEAN
			MF		

BREEDING: Ravines and hillsides in thick decid woods. ? broods. **DISPLAYS:** Male performs a varied and musical flight song in courtship. **NEST:** Usu on hillside, tucked beneath low shrub, occ concealed by drifts of dead leaves; of partly skeletonized leaves lined with fine materials, always incl mycelia of hair fungi. **EGGS:** White, marked with brown, from barely spotted to strongly blotched, usu wreathed. 0.7" (18 mm). **DIET:** Entirely insects. **CONSERVATION:** Winters in Bahamas, Greater Antilles, s Mexico, s to Panama. Rare cowbird host. Very sensitive to fragmentation of forested breeding habitat. **NOTES:** Name is a misnomer, since there are no records of it taking earthworms. Hops rather than walks when foraging and is primarily arboreal. Large bill and short legs enable acrobatic maneuvers (incl grabbing leaves) when foraging on insects in curled dead leaves. Female reportedly performs distraction display. **ESSAYS:** Decline of Eastern Songbirds, p. 495; Birds in the Bush, p. 541; Island Biogeography, p. 549; Nest Lining, p. 39; Walking vs. Hopping, p. 69; Wintering and Conservation, p. 513; Distraction Displays, p. 115. **REF:** Greenberg, 1987.

Birds in the Bush

The late Robert MacArthur, one of the most distinguished ecologists of this century, had a lifelong interest in birds. One of his earliest scientific works was based on his observation that keen ornithologists seemed to have an "intuition" about which species of birds would be found in a given habitat. He reasoned that if a birder could predict that Northern Parulas, Ovenbirds, or Red-eyed Vireos would be found in a given woodlot, then he or she must have based the prediction on a visible feature or combination of features of the woodlot. MacArthur endeavored to discover what those features were and to see, for a start, if they could be used to forecast, not exactly *which* species of birds would be found in a woodlot, but how many different species would live there.

Using his own experience as a bird watcher, he started with the hypothesis that bird species diversity had something to do with the vertical structure of the vegetation—whether most of the foliage was concentrated near the ground, up high, evenly distributed, or whatever. It was a reasonable starting point because, after all, some birds are associated with open fields and others with mature forests. One does not seek Worm-eating Warblers in prairies or meadowlarks on heavily wooded slopes. To test his hypothesis, MacArthur developed a quantitative index for the distribution of vegetation density from the ground to the tops of the trees (if any). He called that index "foliage height diversity."

To calculate the index, a white board is mounted at different heights on a pole, and the proportion of it obscured by leaves at each height is recorded. The proportions are combined into a single number that is high if roughly the same amount of vegetation is found at each height (grass, shrubs, and trees intermixed), and low if the foliage is concentrated at a single height—as in a grassland or in a forest with no undergrowth.

MacArthur counted the bird species and calculated his index in a series of habitats. He found that the diversity of bird species was proportional to the index of foliage height diversity. He had made an important discovery. From an avian point of view, the physical structure ("physiognomy") of a plant community (how the foliage is distributed vertically) is often more important than the actual species of plants making up the vegetation.

Subsequent work by ecologists John Wiens and John Rotenberry has shown that, on a more local scale, floristic composition *can* hold the key to bird diversity. Association with particular floras appears to be largely a result of the differential ability of plant species to provide food for birds. The basis of the association is obvious for fruit, seed, and nectar feeding birds, but less so for insectivores. However, different kinds of plants can support quite dissimilar faunas of insect herbivores, and thus be more or less attractive to warblers, flycatchers, and the like.

MacArthur's discovery was the kind of principle that science seeks: a

Swainson's Warbler
Limnothlypis swainsonii Audubon

NG–374; G–270; PE–240; AE–670; AM(III)–164

VINES	F	3	F	FOLIAGE
2'–6'		(2–5)	I: 13–15 DAYS	GLEAN
(0.8'–10')		MONOG	ALTRICIAL	BARK GLEAN
			F: 10–12 DAYS	
			MF	

BREEDING: Canebrakes, swamps, thickets in moist lowland forests and woodland, ravines filled with laurel and rhododendron (up to 3000') in montane forests. Occ 2 broods. **DISPLAYS:** Courtship: male chases female; male may flutter wings in crouched posture. One report of male "moth-flight" aerial display. Cop follows male pouncing on female. **NEST:** Also in canes, etc.; bulky, of leaves, lined with fine materials. Built in 2–3 days. **EGGS:** Unlike all other wood warblers except Bachman's: white, unmarked, occ some faint speckling. 0.8" (20 mm). **DIET:** Forages for insects on or near ground by flipping leaves and probing long heavy bill into soil. **CONSERVATION:** Winters in n Bahamas, Cuba, Jamaica, s e Mexico and Belize. Uncommon and secretive, may be threatened by loss of prime canebrake habitat and by expanding cowbird populations; locally common cowbird host. **NOTES:** Oft appears semicolonial in small areas of prime habitat. Males occ return to same territory in successive years. Female is close sitter on nest. **ESSAYS:** Decline of Eastern Songbirds, p. 495; Cowbirds, p. 619; Site Tenacity, p. 189; Wintering and Conservation, p. 513; Nest Lining, p. 391. **REFS:** Eddleman et al., 1980; Meanley, 1971.

Ovenbird
Seiurus aurocapillus Linnaeus

NG–374; G–288; PE–246; PW–pl 50; AE–pl 503; AM(III)–164

	OVEN		F	
0'–3'	F	4–5 (3–6)	I: 11–13 DAYS	
		MONOG	ALTRICIAL	
		(POLYGYN)	F: 8–10 DAYS	
			MF	

BREEDING: Decid, rarely pine forests. Occ 2 broods. **DISPLAYS:** Male displays above and near female; oft pursues female in wild courting flight, singing throughout. **NEST:** In open, on leaf-covered floor of decid woods; of dried grass, leaves, moss, other veg matter, oft lined with hair. Always roofed with leaves, branches, etc. (like a Dutch oven, hence the name "ovenbird"); entrance merely small slit. **EGGS:** White, marked with browns, gray, usu wreathed. 0.8" (20 mm). **DIET:** Incl worms, spiders, snails; seeds and other veg reportedly compose part of winter diet. **CONSERVATION:** Winters s through C.A. and Caribbean to n Venezuela in a variety of forest and scrub habitats. Frequent cowbird host. Very sensitive to fragmentation of forested breeding habitat. **NOTES:** Appears to respond to spruce budworm outbreaks by increasing clutch size and producing up to 3 broods. Occ forages in conifs during budworm outbreaks. Birds usu walk (rather than hop or fly), oft wagging tail. Incubating female flushes only when approached closely and performs distraction display. Territory size decreases as prey density increases; prey density is related to veg structure of habitat. **ESSAYS:** Decline of Eastern Songbirds, p. 495; Birds in the Bush, p. 541; Head Scratching, p. 543; Island Biogeography, p. 549; Polygyny, p. 443; Territoriality, p. 387; Habitat Selection, p. 463; Variation in Clutch Sizes, p. 339. **REFS:** Smith and Shugart, 1987; Zach and Falls, 1975.

simple pattern underlying seemingly great complexity, and one that stimulates research that leads to further understanding of how nature works.

SEE: Facts, Hypotheses, and Theories, p. 567; Habitat Selection, p. 463; MacArthur's Warblers, p. 523; Bird Communities and Competition, p. 605. REFS: MacArthur and MacArthur, 1961; Rotenberry, 1985; Wiens, 1985; Wiens and Rotenberry, 1981.

Head Scratching

Head scratching is so essential to birds that even one-legged individuals will attempt it. As far as we can tell, it has several functions related to plumage maintenance. Since a preening bird cannot reach its head with its beak, scratching helps to spread preen oil there. Indeed, some species gather preen oil on the bill, scrape the bill with the foot, and then scratch the head. Head scratching may also remove molted feathers. The area of the head most frequently scratched is near the ear, and it has been suggested that the behavior is associated with pressure changes in the eustachian tubes. This, however, seems counterintuitive since claws are not inserted inside. But chronic ear scratching suggests that there may be another function in addition to spreading preen oil and cleaning. It could be removing ectoparasites (those that live on the outside of the host) and their eggs, something that is done with the bill on other parts of the body.

The motions used for head scratching are quite ritualized, and vary from species to species. For instance, among North American wood warblers, seven species, including the Tennessee Warbler, Mourning Warbler, and Ovenbird, scratch their heads by directly raising a leg toward the front. In contrast, 31 wood warbler species, including all of the genus *Dendroica* (e.g., Golden-winged, Chestnut-sided, Yellow, Pine, Black-throated Green,

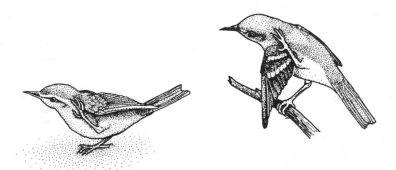

Left: A Swainson's Warbler scratches under the wing. Right: A Northern Parula scratches over the wing.

Louisiana Waterthrush

Seiurus motacilla Vieillot

NG–374; G–288; PE–246; AE–pl 504; AM(III)–168

BANK	F?	5	F I: 13 DAYS	INSECTS	FOLIAGE
0'–2'		(4–6)	ALTRICIAL		GLEAN
		MONOG?	F: 10 DAYS MF		HAWKS

BREEDING: Humid forests with running water (esp in mountains), swamps. ? broods. **DISPLAYS:** ? **NEST:** Usu hidden amid roots of tree or under overhang of bank, oft only few feet from water; of leaves, moss, twigs, inner bark, lined with fine materials. A platform or walkway of leaves is oft constructed from nest to water. **EGGS:** White to creamy, marked with browns, purplish-gray, variable, from nearly immaculate to boldly blotched. 0.8" (19 mm). **DIET:** Aquatic and terrestrial insects, mollusks, crustaceans, occ small fish. Mostly insects in winter. Tends to take larger prey than does Northern Waterthrush. **CONSERVATION:** Winters s through C.A. and Caribbean to n S.A., e Ecuador and n e Peru. Common cowbird host. **NOTES:** Spends much time walking on ground, along water's edge, and wading; bobs head, tilts tail upward suddenly and repeatedly. Oft flips dead leaves or pulls them from water when foraging. Feeding behavior reminiscent of small sandpiper. Breeding territories may overlap with Northern Waterthrush, but the two exclude each other from winter territories. **ESSAYS:** Decline of Eastern Songbirds, p. 495; Bathing and Dusting, p. 429; Interspecific Territoriality, p. 385; Cowbirds, p. 619. **REF:** Craig, 1987.

Northern Waterthrush

Seiurus noveboracensis Gmelin

NG–374; G–288; PE–246; PW–pl 50; AE–pl 505; AW–pl 542; AM(III)–166

BANK	F?	4–5	F? I: 13? DAYS	INSECTS	FOLIAGE
0'–2'		(3–6)	ALTRICIAL		GLEAN
		MONOG	F: 10? DAYS MF(?)		HAWKS

BREEDING: Wooded swamps, forests (oft conif) with standing or slow-moving water. ? broods. **DISPLAYS:** ? **NEST:** Usu hidden amid roots of uprooted tree or under overhanging bank, close to water; of leaves, moss, twigs, inner bark, lined with fine materials. **EGGS:** Off-white, marked with browns, purplish-gray, variable, from finely spotted to boldly blotched. 0.8" (20 mm). **DIET:** Aquatic and terrestrial insects, mollusks, crustaceans, occ small fish. Insects in winter. Tends to take smaller prey than does Louisiana Waterthrush. **CONSERVATION:** Winters s through C.A. and Caribbean to n S.A., e Ecuador and n e Peru; esp favors mangrove swamps. Uncommon (?) cowbird host. **NOTES:** Spends much time walking on ground, along water's edge, and wading; bobs head, tilts tail upward suddenly and repeatedly. Feeding behavior generally reminiscent of small sandpiper; oft flips dead leaves or pulls them from water when foraging. Breeding territories may overlap with Louisiana Waterthrush, but the two are interspecifically territorial in winter. Details of breeding biology not well known. **ESSAYS:** Decline of Eastern Songbirds, p. 495; Interspecific Territoriality, p. 385; How Do We Find Out About Bird Biology?, p. 319; Bird Guilds, p. 493. **REF:** Craig, 1987.

and other warblers), are "overwing scratchers." They scratch their heads by extending the leg over a drooping wing that is held close to the body.

Within a species, the pattern of scratching is constant, but it is not related to the taxonomy of the warblers. Of two closely related species, one may scratch under, and the other over, the wing. There is, however, an intriguing and as yet unexplained correlation between the ecology of the warblers and their scratching method. Species that dwell mostly on the ground tend to scratch under the wing; those that are primarily arboreal, over the wing. Perhaps underwing scratching helps to keep the wings of ground-dwelling birds clean.

SEE: Preening, p. 53; Bathing and Dusting, p. 429; Anting, p. 487; Disease and Parasitism, p. 399. REF: Burtt and Hailman, 1978.

Bird Names—XIII

Waterthrushes, of course, are not thrushes but wood warblers, but they do live near water. The Northern Waterthrush does breed north of the Louisiana Waterthrush, but the latter breeds in most of the eastern United States, although only south to central Louisiana. The latinized name of the Louisiana, *Seirus motacilla,* shows further confusion about the affinities of the bird, since it is derived from Greek and Latin meaning "wagtail wagtail." It was named, however, in 1808 before there was even a semblance of a sensible bird taxonomy. The Ovenbird is a close relative of the waterthrushes and is named for its domed, ovenlike nest.

Chat may be derived from "chatterer"; redstarts were so-called because of their resemblance to the European bird of the same name (a thrush). The name derives from the Anglo-Saxon for "red tail." The root of cardinal is Latin for "important." Cardinals are important officials of the Catholic Church, and their red robes gave both common and scientific names to *Cardinalis cardinalis.* The trivial part of the species name *Cardinalis sinuatus* means "curved" in Latin (referring to its bill). The common name of that bird, however, is Pyrrhuloxia—held over from the genus where it had once been placed. Pyrrhuloxia means "bullfinch" in Greek.

REF: Choate, 1985; Owen, 1985.

Common Yellowthroat

Geothlypis trichas Linnaeus

NG–376; G–288; PE–246; PW–pl 51; AE–pl 371; AW–pl 419; AM(III)–176

0'–3'	F	3–5 (3–6)	F	HOV GLEAN
		MONOG	I: 12 DAYS	BARK GLEAN
		(POLYGYN)	ALTRICIAL	HAWKS
			F: 10 DAYS	
			MF	

BREEDING: Overgrown fields, hedgerow, woodland margin, freshwater and salt marshes. 2 broods. **DISPLAYS**: Courtship: male follows female closely; occ performs flight display: ascends from low perch to 25'–100', swoops to another low perch giving call notes and garbled song. **NEST**: Bulky, loosely made of weed stems, grass, bark, ferns, lined with fine materials. **EGGS**: White to creamy, marked with browns, black, occ wreathed. 0.7" (18 mm). **DIET**: Incl spiders; few seeds. Occ gleans from ground. **CONSERVATION**: Winters s to Bahamas, West Indies, and s to Panama. One of the three most frequent cowbird hosts. **NOTES**: Perhaps the most abundant warbler. Female leaves nest unobtrusively; does not perform distraction display. Young remain dependent on parents for longer than most warblers; second brood may be fed up to migration time. May begin migration as family group. **ESSAYS**: Vocal Functions, p. 471; Bathing and Dusting, p. 429; Cowbirds, p. 619; Distraction Display, p. 115; Parental Care, p. 555. **REF**: Wunderle, 1978.

Rufous-capped Warbler

Basileuterus rufifrons Swainson

NG–376; AM(III)–184

	OVEN			
		?	?	?
	F	4	I: ? DAYS	HAWKS?
		MONOG?	ALTRICIAL	
			F: ? DAYS	
			?	

BREEDING: Brushy hillsides, open woodland. ? broods. **DISPLAYS**: ? **NEST**: Oven-shaped (roofed or arched) nest on ground. **EGGS**: ? **DIET**: Essentially unknown but insects likely. **CONSERVATION**: Winter resident. **NOTES**: Breeding biology virtually unknown. One nesting record in Cave Creek Canyon, Chiricahua Mts., AZ, but may be more common. Recent sightings in TX and AZ suggest possible range expansion from Mexico. Holds long tail cocked like a wren. **ESSAYS**: How Do We Find Out About Bird Biology?, p. 319; Masterbuilders, p. 445; Range Expansion, p. 459; Determining Diets, p. 535. **REF**: Harrison, 1984.

Hormones and Nest Building

Passerines may make more than one thousand trips to carry construction materials to their nests. Just what prompts such dedication has been the focus of numerous studies. Physiological ecologists have been piecing together how the complex practice of nest building is driven by hormones (chemical messengers) and triggered by environmental factors.

The springtime production of hormones involved in nest building is initially activated by increased day length. This solar trigger is, of course, especially apparent in birds that live some distance from the equator, where seasonal change in day length is substantial. Lengthening days stimulate the pituitary gland to produce hormones that promote the enlargement of the gonads (ovaries and testes). Once enlarged, these organs release a flood of hormones that, in concert with environmental cues (such as the presence or absence of females or other males, bird song, or the time of day when food is available), lead to courtship and mating.

The combination of gonadal hormones, including estradiol and progesterone, and external factors helps to stimulate nest-building behavior and the onset of ovulation. The gonadal hormones also prompt the release of yet another chemical messenger, prolactin, which may induce brooding behavior. This sequence is typically reinforced in females by the sight of the egg and in males by the sight of the incubating female. Coming full circle, when prolactin reaches a critical level it suppresses further release of hormones from the pituitary gland. No longer stimulated by pituitary hormones, the gonads (in birds that produce only one brood a year) begin to regress and residual sexual interest is rechanneled into parental behavior. For species that produce more than one brood annually, however, the gonads do not regress between broods.

The transitions from courtship, to nest building, to brooding, and to parenting are not always clear-cut. Since nest building requires a lower level of hormonal stimulation than does sexual behavior, building may begin early in the courtship cycle or continue during incubation, and may account for some of the so-called dummy nests that are constructed and never used. Apparently, by responding to early hormonal signals some birds incorporate portions of the nesting ritual into their pair-bonding displays. And by responding to late secretion of chemical messengers that occasionally reassert their influence in the fall, some birds appear to reinitiate nest-building behavior. Called "autumnal recrudescence," this partial postseason reactivation of breeding behavior is likely responsible for some incongruous interactions you may witness.

Nest building may involve more than this. Experimental evidence indicates that building simple nests is indeed instinctive, but constructing complex ones improves over time as skills in choosing and preparing nesting sites and materials are sharpened. For such complex nests the hormone-en-

Yellow-breasted Chat

Icteria virens Linnaeus

NG–376; G–288; PE–246; PW–pl 51; AE–pl 359; AW–pl 413; AM(III)–184

			F		
			I: 11 DAYS		
1'–5'	F	3–4	ALTRICIAL	BERRIES	
(To 8')		(3–6)	F: 8 DAYS		
		MONOG	MF		

BREEDING: Dense brush or scrub, esp along streams and at swamp margins. 2 broods. **DISPLAYS:** Courtship: male rises from high perch with head raised and legs dangling, sings a complex song, hovers, then drops back to perch. **NEST:** Large but well concealed; base of dead leaves, straw, and weed stems supporting tightly woven inner nest of vine bark with thin lining of fine weed stems, grass. **EGGS:** White to creamy, marked with browns, usu sharply defined and mostly at large end. 0.8″ (22 mm), largest of any warbler. **DIET:** Insects and berries about equally. Young apparently fed only insects. **CONSERVATION:** Winters s to Panama. Frequent host of Brown-headed, rare host of Bronzed Cowbirds. **NOTES:** Occ nests in loose colonies, although males defend individual territories. Has many unwarbler-like characteristics (thick bill, unscaled tarsi, oft holds food with its foot), yet DNA studies show its affinity with other wood warblers; behaves and sings more like a mockingbird or thrasher than a warbler. Oft sings at night. **ESSAYS:** DNA and Passerine Classification, p. 662; Visual Displays, p. 5; Cowbirds, p. 619; Vocal Functions, p. 471; Wintering and Conservation, p. 513. **REFS:** Thompson, 1977; Thompson and Nolan, 1973.

American Redstart

Setophaga ruticilla Linnaeus

NG–378; G–292; PE–236; PW–pl 51; AE–pl 402; AW–pl 441; AM(III)–160

			F		
			I: 12 DAYS		
SHRUB	F	4	ALTRICIAL		FOLIAGE
10'–20'		(2–5)	F: 9 DAYS		GLEAN
(4'–70')		MONOG	MF		

BREEDING: Open decid and decid-conif woodland, forest edge, second growth. ? broods. **DISPLAYS:** Territorial and courtship displays: short, horizontal, semicircular flights by male with wings held stiff. **NEST:** Oft in fork of low tree, rarely on ground; compact, of plant fibers, grass, rootlets, ornamented with bits of lichen, birch bark, feathers, lined with fine materials. Occ use old or newly deserted nests of other birds such as vireos. **EGGS:** White to off-white, marked with browns, usu wreathed. 0.6″ (16 mm). **DIET:** Also rarely seeds, berries. **CONSERVATION:** Winters in Baja, c FL, c Mexico s through C.A. and West Indies to Ecuador and n w Brazil. Frequent cowbird host; occ destroys cowbird eggs by burying in bottom of nest. **NOTES:** One case reported of two pairs sharing common nest with 7 eggs which females took turns incubating. Competes for food with ecologically similar Least Flycatcher and oft subjected to aggressive attacks by it. When foraging, actively flashes tail and wing patches and chases insects and spiders from foliage. Has flycatcher-like rictal bristles around mouth. **ESSAYS:** Island Biogeography, p. 549; Decline of Eastern Songbirds, p. 495; Irruptions, p. 639; Bird Communities and Competition, p. 605; Cowbirds, p. 619; Feathers, p. 309. **REF:** Sherry, 1979.

vironment interaction can guide the building process, but only practice makes perfect.

SEE: Breeding Season, p. 55; Masterbuilders, p. 445; Migration, p. 183; Nest Materials, p. 369; Copulation, p. 317; Vocal Functions, p. 471; Courtship Feeding, p. 181. REF: Collias and Collias, 1984.

Island Biogeography

Why do many more species of birds occur on the island of New Guinea than on the island of Bali? One answer is that New Guinea has more than fifty times the area of Bali, and numbers of species ordinarily increase with available space. This does not, however, explain why the Society Islands (Tahiti, Moorea, Bora Bora, etc.), which collectively have about the same area as the islands of the Louisiade Archipelago off New Guinea, play host to many fewer species, or why the Hawaiian Islands, ten times the area of the Louisiades, also have fewer native birds.

Two eminent ecologists, the late Robert MacArthur of Princeton University and E. O. Wilson of Harvard, developed a theory of "island biogeography" to explain such uneven distributions. They proposed that the number of species on any island reflects a balance between the rate at which new species colonize it and the rate at which populations of established species become extinct. If a new volcanic island were to rise out of the ocean off the coast of a mainland inhabited by 100 species of birds, some birds would begin to immigrate across the gap and establish populations on the empty, but habitable, island. The *rate* at which these immigrant species could become established, however, would inevitably decline, for each species that successfully invaded the island would diminish by one the pool of possible future invaders (the same 100 species continue to live on the mainland, but those which have already become residents of the island can no longer be classed as potential invaders).

Equally, the rate at which species might become extinct on the island would be related to the number that have become residents. When an island is nearly empty, the extinction rate is necessarily low because few species are available to become extinct. And since the resources of an island are limited, as the number of resident species increases, the smaller and more prone to extinction their individual populations are likely to become. The rate at which additional species will establish populations will be high when the island is relatively empty, and the rate at which resident populations go extinct will be high when the island is relatively full. Thus, there must be a point between 0 and 100 species (the number on the mainland) where the two rates are equal—where input from immigration balances output from extinction. That equilibrium number of species would be expected to remain constant as long as the factors determining the two rates did not

Painted Redstart

Myioborus pictus Swainson

NG–378; G–292; PW–pl 51; AW–pl 456; AM(III)–182

| BANK (To 10') | F | 3–4 MONOG (POLYGYN) | F
I: 13–14 DAYS
ALTRICIAL
F: 9–13 DAYS
MF | BARK GLEAN
HOVER &
GLEAN |

BREEDING: Oak and pine forests and riparian woodland of steep canyons above 7,000'. Oft 2 broods. **DISPLAYS:** Male pursues female in erratic courtship flight. Female occ duets with male. **NEST:** Occ beneath overhanging bank; flat, shallow, of grass, pine needles, leaves, bark, thinly lined with fine grass, hair. Male and female select site together. Built in 4–14 days. **EGGS:** Creamy white, finely flecked with browns, mostly at large end, not wreathed. 0.7″ (17 mm). **DIET:** Exclusively insects. **CONSERVATION:** Winters from n Mexico to Nicaragua. Rare cowbird host. **NOTES:** Polygyny occurs regularly. Males arrive on breeding grounds 2–10 days ahead of females. Female broods. Young of first brood leave territory at 27–30 days. Behavior similar to American Redstart, to which (in spite of its name) it is only distantly related. Both sexes frequently fan their tails while foraging and in display, oft accompanied by wing spreading; likely functions to help individuals locate each other. **ESSAYS:** Polygyny, p. 443; Visual Displays, p. 5; Taxonomy and Nomenclature, p. 515. **REF:** Marshall and Balda, 1974.

Red-faced Warbler

Cardellina rubrifrons Giraud

NG–378; G–292; PW–pl 51; AW–pl 458; AM(III)–182

| ? | 3–4 MONOG? | ?
I: ? DAYS
ALTRICIAL
F: ? DAYS
MF (?) | HAWKS |

BREEDING: Conif, oak, and aspen high mountain forests, mostly between 6,400' and 8,000'. ? broods. **DISPLAYS:** ? **NEST:** Concealed in low veg or under log on ground; base of dry leaves, conif needles, cup of plant stems, bark, lined with fine materials. **EGGS:** White, finely flecked with browns, usu mostly at large end. 0.7″ (17 mm). **DIET:** Little known but likely insects. **CONSERVATION:** Winters from highlands of Mexico and Guatemala s to El Salvador and Honduras. **NOTES:** Details of breeding biology unknown. Oft feeds chickadee-like in conif trees. Migrates only a short distance compared with most warblers. **ESSAYS:** How Do We Find Out About Bird Biology?, p. 319; Wintering and Conservation, p. 513. **REFS:** Harrison, 1984; Phillips et al., 1964.

change. But the exact species present *should* change continuously as some species go extinct and others invade (including some that have previously gone extinct), so that there is a steady *turnover* in the composition of the fauna.

That is the essence of the MacArthur-Wilson equilibrium theory of island biogeography. How well does it explain what we actually observe in nature? One famous "test" of the theory was provided in 1883 by a catastrophic volcanic explosion that devastated the island of Krakatoa, located between the islands of Sumatra and Java. The flora and fauna of its remnant and of two adjacent islands were completely exterminated, yet within 25 years (1908) thirteen species of birds had recolonized what was left of the island. By 1919–21 twenty-eight bird species were present, and by 1932–34, twenty-nine. Between the explosion and 1934, thirty-four species actually became established, but five of them went extinct. By 1951–52 thirty-three species were present, and by 1984–85, thirty-five species. During this half century (1934–1985), a further fourteen species had become established, and eight had become extinct. As the theory predicted, the rate of increase declined as more and more species colonized the island. In addition, as equilibrium was approached there was some turnover. The number in the cast remained roughly the same while the actors gradually changed.

The theory predicts other things, too. For instance, everything else being equal, distant islands will have lower immigration rates than those close to a mainland, and equilibrium will occur with fewer species on distant islands. Close islands will have high immigration rates and support more species. By similar reasoning, large islands, with their lower extinction rates, will have more species than small ones—again everything else being equal (which it frequently is not, for larger islands often have a greater variety of habitats and more species for that reason).

Island biogeographic theory has been applied to many kinds of problems, including forecasting faunal changes caused by fragmenting previously continuous habitat. For instance, in most of the eastern United States only patches of the once-great deciduous forest remain, and many species of songbirds are disappearing from those patches. One reason for the decline in birds, according to the theory, is that fragmentation leads to both lower immigration rates (gaps between fragments are not crossed easily) and higher extinction rates (less area supports fewer species).

Indications of such changes in species composition during habitat fragmentation were found in studies conducted between 1953 and 1976 in a 16-acre nature preserve in Connecticut in which a forest was reestablishing itself. During that period development was increasing the distance between the preserve and other woodlands. As the forest grew back, species such as American Redstarts that live in young forest colonized the area, and birds such as the Field Sparrow, which prefer open shrublands, became scarce or disappeared. In spite of the successional trend toward large trees, however, two bird species normally found in mature forest suffered population declines, and five such species went extinct on the reserve. The extinctions are

Olive Warbler
Peucedramus taeniatus Du Bus de Gisignies

NG–378; G–274; PW–pl 51; AW–712; AM(III)–186

30'–65'	F	3–4 MONOG	F? I: ? DAYS ALTRICIAL F: ? DAYS MF(?)		BARK GLEAN

BREEDING: Open, montane pine forests around 9,000'. ? broods. **DISPLAYS:** ? **NEST:** Usu in pine tree; of moss, lichen, pine bud hulls, pine needles, plant down, lined with plant down supported by rootlets. **EGGS:** Off-white, pale blue, marked with olive, browns, mostly at large end, but entire egg more darkly smudged than other warblers'. 0.7″ (17 mm). **DIET:** Little known, but largely insects. **CONSERVATION:** In winter, most individuals move s into Mexico. **NOTES:** Morphologically an unusual wood warbler; may be more closely related to Old World warblers, New World kinglets and gnatcatchers. Nests oft soiled with excrement by young, which does not occur in any other wood warbler because adults remove fecal sacs of the nestlings. **ESSAYS:** Birds, DNA, and Evolutionary Convergence, p. 419; Nest Sanitation, p. 315; Taxonomy and Nomenclature, p. 515; DNA and Passerine Classification, p. 662. **REFS:** Harrison, 1984; Phillips et al., 1964.

Rose-breasted Grosbeak
Supersp #48
Pheucticus ludovicianus Linnaeus

NG–380; G–310; PE–276; PW–pl 56; AE–pl 408; AM(III)–204

SHRUB 5'–15' (To 50')	F –M	4 (3–5) MONOG	MF I: 13–14 DAYS ALTRICIAL F: 9–12 DAYS MF	SEEDS FRUIT BUDS	HOV GLEAN BARK GLEAN HAWKS

BREEDING: Decid forest, woodland, second growth. 1 or 2 broods. **DISPLAYS:** Courtship: male sings in flight pursuit of female; male crouches, spreads and droops wings with tail spread and slightly elevated, retracts head with nape against back; male sings and waves head and body in erratic dance. **NEST:** Loosely built of twigs, coarse plant material, lined with fine twigs, rootlets, hair. Male may select site. **EGGS:** Pale green, blue, or bluish-green, marked with browns, purples; usu wreathed or capped. 1.0″ (25 mm). **DIET:** Incl some flowers. Occ gleans from ground. **CONSERVATION:** Winters from c Mexico to n S.A., but most abundant in n portion of range, most commonly in highlands. Common cowbird host. Popular cage bird in wintering range. **NOTES:** Male sings from nest while incubating or brooding; occ sings at night. Female occ sings softer, shorter song than male. When double brooded, male cares for fledged young while female builds new nest. Females forage by hover gleaning more than males and tend to forage higher than males. Forms winter flocks of up to 20 in plantations, clearings. **ESSAYS:** Great Plains Hybrids, p. 625; Decline of Eastern Songbirds, p. 495; Birds, DNA, and Evolutionary Convergence, p. 419; Cowbirds, p. 619; Parental Care, p. 555. **REFS:** Holmes, 1986; Kroodsma, 1974.

thought to have resulted from lowering immigration rates caused by the preserve's increasing isolation and by competition from six invading species characteristic of suburban habitats.

Long-term studies of a bird community in an oak wood in Surrey, England, also support the view that isolation can influence the avifauna of habitat islands. A rough equilibrium number of 32 breeding species was found in that community, with a turnover of three additions and three extinctions annually. It was projected that if the wood were as thoroughly isolated as an oceanic island, it would maintain only five species over an extended period—two species of tits (same genus as titmice), a wren, and two thrushes (the English Robin and Blackbird).

Island biogeographic theory can be a great help in understanding the effects of habitat fragmentation. It does not, however, address other factors that can greatly influence which birds reside in a fragment. Some of these include whether nest-robbing species are present in such abundance that they could prevent certain invaders from establishing themselves, whether the fragment is large enough to contain a territory of the size required by some members of the pool of potential residents, or whether other habitat requirements of species in that pool can be satisfied. To take an extreme example of the latter, a grass-covered, treeless habitat in California would not be colonized by Acorn, Nuttall's, Downy, or Hairy Woodpeckers, even if it were large and all four woodpeckers are found in adjacent woodlands. Ecological theory is designed to help us think about the real world, but it is not a substitute for an intimate knowledge of nature's ways.

SEE: The Decline of Eastern Songbirds, p. 495; The Fate of Bachman's Warbler, p. 505; Facts, Hypotheses, and Theories, p. 567; Habitat Selection, p. 463.   REFS: Butcher et al., 1981; MacArthur and Wilson, 1967; Rusterholz and Howe, 1979; Williamson, 1981.

Black-headed Grosbeak

NG-380; G-310; PE-276; PW-pl 56; AE-pl 399; AW-pl 443; AM(III)-206

			MF I: 12–13 DAYS		
SHRUB	F	3–4	ALTRICIAL	SEEDS
4'–12'		(2–5)	F: 11–12 DAYS	FRUIT
		MONOG	MF	

BREEDING: Riparian woodland and thickets, edges of ponds, open woodland. 1? brood. **DISPLAYS:** Courting male performs song-flights above female with his wings and tail spread while singing nearly continuously, then returns to original perch. Song-flights also occur during incubation. **NEST:** Bulky, loosely built of twigs, plant stems, rootlets, lined with finer stems and rootlets. Built in 3–4 days. **EGGS:** Pale green, blue, or bluish-green, marked with browns or purples, esp at larger end. 1.0" (25 mm). **DIET:** Incl spiders, occ buds. **CONSERVATION:** Winters s through Mexico to Oaxaca and Veracruz. Uncommon cowbird host. **NOTES:** Both sexes occ sing on nest and are difficult to flush from nest; female songs less complex, more variable than male songs. Female very aggressive in defending territory against other Black-headed Grosbeaks. Both sexes brood. Young able to fly at ca. 15 days; may recognize parents' songs. **ESSAYS:** Great Plains Hybrids, p. 625; Decline of Eastern Songbirds, p. 495; Bills, p. 209; Territoriality, p. 387. **REFS:** Kroodsma, 1974; Ritchison, 1983, 1985.

Northern Cardinal

Cardinalis cardinalis Linnaeus

NG-382; G-308; PE-268; PW-pl 55; AE-pl 407; AW-pl 448; AM(III)-200

			F –M I: 12–13 DAYS		
SAPLING	?	3–4	ALTRICIAL	SEEDS
1'–15'		(2–5)	F: 9–10 DAYS	FRUIT
		MONOG	MF	

BREEDING: Thickets, dense shrubs, undergrowth, residential areas; riparian thickets in w. 2, 3, occ 4 broods. **DISPLAYS:** Male and female with outstretched necks and erect crests sway bodies from side to side while singing softly. **NEST:** Compact and well lined to flimsy and scarcely lined; of weed stems, pliable twigs, bark strips, grass, rootlets, with leaves and paper interwoven, lined with fine grass, hair. **EGGS:** Grayish-, bluish-, greenish-white, marked with browns, grays, purples. 1.0" (25 mm). **DIET:** Insects; fruit, seeds. **CONSERVATION:** Winter resident although some e birds tend to move n e and n in late summer and early fall. Common cowbird host, esp in c portion of range. Range extending steadily n. Introduced to Hawaii. **NOTES:** Female sings usu after male establishes territory but before nesting starts; likely functions in pair bonding and reproductive synchronization of pair. Male cares for first brood while female incubates second clutch. May form winter flocks of up to 60–70 birds. **ESSAYS:** Color of Birds, p. 111; How Long Can Birds Live?, p. 643; Feeding Birds, p. 349; Parental Care, p. 555; Cowbirds, p. 619; Range Expansion, p. 459; Vocal Functions, p. 471. **REFS:** Anderson and Conner, 1985; Ritchison, 1986.

Parental Care

The young of most egg-laying reptiles hatch long after the parents have abandoned the eggs; a few lizards and snakes guard them, and pythons incubate their eggs for a while. The young of those female snakes that carry their eggs inside the body until they hatch also receive no parental care. Among reptiles only crocodiles and their relatives tend both eggs and hatchlings. In contrast, nearly all birds provide extended care for their offspring. The exceptions are brood parasites, which foist their responsibility onto other species, and some megapodes, turkeylike birds of the southwest Pacific.

Most megapodes scratch together mounds (sometimes astonishingly large) of vegetation or sand and lay their eggs inside. The heat for incubation is provided by decay of the vegetation, the sun, or (occasionally) volcanic activity. Some megapodes tend the mound, opening and closing it to regulate the incubation temperature; others desert the mound. A few megapodes do not build mounds, but simply lay their eggs in warm spots on sand or between rocks and cover them with leaves.

Patterns of care in precocial birds (those with young ready to leave the nest almost immediately after hatching) vary a great deal. The major parental duties for most are to keep the young safe from predators and to watch over them as they feed. In many, however, the adults also help instruct the chicks in what's good to eat, how to find it, and how to handle it. Oystercatchers first present food to their young and then train them to find food for themselves. The latter is a long process; oystercatchers specialize in opening mussels and other bivalve mollusks, a difficult task that can be accomplished in less than a minute by an experienced individual, but one that requires many months to learn.

The young of passerines, and thus of most birds, are altricial (born naked, blind, and helpless) and require much more care and feeding than precocial young. One or both parents must bring food to altricial young until they are ready to leave the nest, and in most species the offspring are fed by the parents for a while after fledging. Most passerines are monogamous, and usually both parents help in rearing the young. Often the male does more of the food gathering and the female more of the brooding—covering the young to keep them warm (or to shield them from sun or rain) and protecting them from predators. Frequently, the male also feeds the female, and she in turn may pass food on to her helpless chicks. In some cases, however, those caretaking roles are reversed. Female Red-eyed Vireos, for example, gather about three-quarters of the food their young receive. In cooperative breeders, such as Acorn Woodpeckers, nonbreeding adults or juveniles may help care for the young.

In polygynous species (where one male mates with more than one female), the male's parental role is reduced in both precocial and altricial birds. Polyandrous species (one female with more than one male) are all

Pyrrhuloxia

Cardinalis sinuatus Bonaparte

NG–382; G–308; PW–pl 55; AE–pl 405; AW–pl 468; AM(III)–202

THICKET	F	2–3	F I: 14 DAYS ALTRICIAL	INSECTS	
5'–15'		(2–5) MONOG?	F: 10? DAYS MF	FRUIT	

BREEDING: Arid brush, thorn scrub, and thickets, esp mesquite. 1 brood. **DISPLAYS:** Male feeds female during courtship and incubation. **NEST:** Compact, of twigs, inner bark, coarse grass, lined with rootlets, fine grass, plant fiber. **EGGS:** Grayish- or greenish-white, marked with browns over pale grays. 1.0" (24 mm). **DIET:** Insects; fruit, seeds. **CONSERVATION:** Winter resident but not sedentary. Uncommon cowbird host. **NOTES:** Male and female actively defend territory during its establishment but subsequent maintenance by male only. Forms small flocks during nonbreeding season. **ESSAYS:** Territoriality, p. 387; Monogamy, p. 597; Courtship Feeding, p. 181. **REFS:** Bent, 1968; Phillips et al., 1964.

Blue Grosbeak

Guiraca caerulea Linnaeus

NG–382; G–310; PE–274; PW–pl 56; AE–pl 439; AW–pl 498; AM(III)–206

TREE	?	4	F I: 11–12 DAYS ALTRICIAL	SEEDS	FOLIAGE
3'–12'		(2–5) MONOG	F: 9–10 DAYS MF		GLEAN
(0.5'–15')					

BREEDING: Riparian thickets, overgrown fields, open woodland, hedgerows, orchards. 2 broods. **DISPLAYS:** ? **NEST:** Also occ in vine tangle. Composed of twigs, rootlets, inner bark strippings, lined with fine rootlets, tendrils, grass, hair. Snakeskin, dried leaves, or paper characteristically woven into exterior. **EGGS:** Pale bluish-white, unmarked. 0.9" (22 mm). **DIET:** Incl snails, grain, occ fruit. **CONSERVATION:** Winters from n Mexico s to Panama, Bahamas, and Cuba. Frequent cowbird host. **NOTES:** After breeding season, forms flocks and feeds in grainfields, grasslands, and ricefields prior to migration. **ESSAYS:** Bills, p. 209; Color of Birds, p. 111; Birds, DNA, and Evolutionary Convergence, p. 419; Cowbirds, p. 619; Wintering and Conservation, p. 513. **REF:** Bent, 1968.

precocial, and the burden of caring for the offspring either falls exclusively on the males or is shared.

Generally parent birds feed their offspring a diet similar to their own, but during the breeding season the diet of the adults (and thus of the young) shifts toward higher-protein foods. Many passerine birds that during the winter subsist mainly on vegetable foods eat insects and feed them to their young during the breeding season. There is a tendency for the birds to consume the smaller insects themselves and, for the sake of efficiency, to carry larger ones back to the nest.

Other parents swallow the food as they forage and then regurgitate it for the young when they return to the nest. As the young mature, the proportion of solid food in the regurgitant increases—perhaps an avian analogue to weaning. Some birds, such as pigeons, produce a special "crop milk," which is also regurgitated for the young. Petrels regurgitate for their young an oil along with half-digested food from which the oil is derived. Raptors usually carry their prey back to the nest and tear it into bite-sized chunks for their chicks.

The feeding instinct in parental birds is very strong, and feeding behavior is usually elicited by feeding calls and gaping on the part of the chicks. When a bird's own brood is destroyed, it may transfer its attention to the young of others; observations of birds feeding the young of other parents of the same species, and even of other species, are quite common. One Northern Cardinal was even observed to have adopted a school of gaping goldfish at a pond where the fish were accustomed to begging from people!

Presumably, the length of time that adults will care for their young is determined by several factors. In most cases, the longer the care, the better the chances that the young will survive to maturity. Counterbalancing prolonged dependence in the "calculations" of evolution, however, are the possibility of the parents rearing a second brood and the physical cost of extended care. These factors affect the probability of the adults being able to survive migration or wintering to breed again the next season. As far as possible, evolution will favor the strategy that maximizes the reproductive output of an individual *over its entire lifetime;* this may limit the amount of care given to any one set of offspring. There is, in fact, often a conflict between the evolutionary interests of parents and young, it being best for the parents to cease care before it is best for the young to be on their own. This conflict is not restricted to birds (as some of us well know) and is one of the more interesting topics in sociobiology.

SEE: Precocial and Altricial Young, p. 581; Incubation: Heating Eggs, p. 393; Oystercatchers and Oysters, p. 109; Monogamy, p. 597; Polygyny, p. 443; Polyandry, p. 133; Cooperative Breeding, p. 283; Creches, p. 191; Bird Milk, p. 271.

Indigo Bunting

NG–384; G–312; PE–274; PW–pl 56; AE–pl 438; AM(III)–210

TREE	F	3–4 (2–4)	F I: 12–13 DAYS ALTRICIAL	SEEDS	GROUND
TANGLE		MONOG	F: 9–10 DAYS	FRUIT	GLEAN
1'–15'		(POLYGYN)	F –M		

BREEDING: Decid forest edge and clearings, open woodland, weedy fields, shrublands, orchards. 2 broods. **DISPLAYS:** Courtship: song-flight by male; on ground, male spreads wings and dances around female. **NEST:** Well woven of dried grass, dead leaves, bark strips, Spanish moss, snakeskin, and weed stems, lined with rootlets, fine grass, cotton, feathers, hair. Female selects site. **EGGS:** Pale bluish-white to pure white, usu unmarked. 0.8" (19 mm). **DIET:** Incl grain, berries. **CONSERVATION:** Winters from s FL and c Mexico s to Panama, Greater Antilles, Bahamas. Frequent cowbird host; occ buries cowbird eggs by building new floor in nest. Increased abundance since 1900 with creation of favored habitat following logging and abandonment of pastures. **NOTES:** Amount of male parental care highly variable: most do little if any feeding of nestlings or fledglings. Forms interspecific territories with Lazuli Buntings in w; male song repertoires oft contain elements typical of both species. Occ mixed pairs result in hybrids. Oft forms mixed winter flocks with other finches. **ESSAYS:** Navigation and Orientation, p. 559; Polygyny, p. 443; Vocal Development, p. 601; Great Plains Hybrids, p. 625; Interspecific Territoriality, p. 385; Cowbirds, p. 619. **REFS:** Carey and Nolan, 1979; Emlen et al., 1975; Westneat, 1988.

Lazuli Bunting

NG–384; G–312; PE–274; PW–pl 56; AE–pl 437; AW–pl 501; AM(III)–208

TANGLE	F	4 (3–5)	F I: 12 DAYS ALTRICIAL	SEEDS	FOLIAGE
1.5'–4'		MONOG	F: 10–12 DAYS		GLEAN
(To 10')		(POLYGYN)	F –M		

BREEDING: Arid brushy canyons, riparian thickets, chaparral, open woodland. 2, occ 3 broods. **DISPLAYS:** Courtship: male flutters on ground with extended trembling wings. **NEST:** Coarsely woven of dried grass, forbs, lined with fine grass, hair. **EGGS:** Pale bluish-white, unmarked. 0.8" (19 mm). **DIET:** Insects; seeds. **CONSERVATION:** Winters s to s Mexico, absent from e Mexico. Uncommon cowbird host. Increased abundance this century with creation of early successional stages following logging, and growth of riparian thickets formed by agricultural irrigation systems in arid regions. However, seems to have disappeared from former areas of range in face of encroaching suburbanization. **NOTES:** Forms interspecific territories with Indigo Buntings; male song repertoires oft contain elements typical of both species. Occ mixed pairs result in hybrids. Female aggressively defends territory against other females. Commonly flocks and moves to higher elevations after breeding. Assoc with Chipping Sparrows and other finches during migration. **ESSAYS:** Great Plains Hybrids, p. 625; Interspecific Territoriality, p. 385; Vocal Development, p. 601. **REFS:** Emlen et al., 1975; Thompson 1976.

The question of how birds find their way between breeding and wintering grounds has puzzled people for as long as they have been aware of the phenomenon of migration. Today we know many more parts of the puzzle's solution than we did even twenty-five years ago. Some would argue that there are really two puzzles: (1) how birds navigate over thousands of miles to find their way between breeding and wintering sites, and (2) how birds find their way back to precise nesting or roosting sites (homing behavior). To do either, birds must be able to orient (that is, determine compass direction) and to navigate (judge their position while traveling).

The short explanation of these complex phenomena is that birds find their way by using a variety of cues in a hierarchical fashion. Different species may use these cues in different orders of priority, and some cues may always be used in preference to others. Birds acquire directional information from five primary sources: (1) topographic features, including wind direction which can be influenced by major land forms, (2) stars, (3) sun, (4) Earth's magnetic field, and (5) odors.

Some of the most convincing experiments demonstrating the navigational abilities of birds were performed by behavioral ecologist Stephen Emlen. He took advantage of the "migratory restlessness" of caged migrant birds—fluttering and hopping that tend to be oriented in the direction of migration. Using Indigo Buntings in a planetarium, Emlen found that the birds oriented in the proper migratory direction using the stellar cues projected onto the planetarium ceiling. When Emlen shifted the position of the planetarium's stars, the birds shifted their orientation as well. The buntings were shown to learn a "sky map" as they watch the rotation of the stars while they grow up. The young birds learn to recognize the area of least apparent movement around the pole; if maturing buntings were exposed to a false sky rotating around the star Betelgeuse (in the constellation Orion), they acted as if Betelgeuse were the North Star.

But how do birds find their way on overcast nights? Apparently, they are able to set course by the setting sun, unless this too is obscured by cloud cover. Lacking either stars or sun for information, birds will orient by wind direction, although not always correctly. Ornithologist Kenneth Able used radar and portable ceilometers (electronic devices for measuring the altitude of overcasts) to track nocturnal migrants and reported that birds frequently flew in the wrong direction by using wind as a cue when stars were unavailable. Interestingly, while most ornithologists believe that birds employ topographic features like mountains, rivers, tall buildings, etc., to navigate in the vicinity of the home site, there is little evidence of the use of such cues.

Recent experiments have revealed that pigeons are capable of detecting the Earth's magnetic field and can use it to orient and possibly to navigate. We still do not understand just how pigeons manage to sense such weak electromagnetic fields, but birds are far more sensitive to them than are

Painted Bunting

Passerina ciris Linnaeus

NG–384; G–312; PE–274; PW–pl 56; AE–pl 476; AW–pl 525; AM(III)–212

TREE	?	3–4	F	INSECTS	FOLIAGE
3'–6'		(3–5)	I: 11–12 DAYS		GLEAN
(To 25')		POLYGYN	ALTRICIAL		
			F: 12–14 DAYS		
			F–M		

BREEDING: Areas of scattered brush and trees, riparian thickets, weedy and shrubby areas. 2, 3, occ 4 broods. 1 or 2 broods near n limit of range. **DISPLAYS:** Courtship: male flattens out with wings and tail spread, and fluffs plumage; actions are jerky and stiff, with alternating periods of activity and quiet. **NEST:** Also occ in vine tangle. Well made deep cup of grass, forbs, leaves, lined with fine grass, hair. **EGGS:** Pale bluish-white or grayish-white, spotted with reddish-brown concentrated toward large end. 0.8″ (19 mm). **DIET:** Primarily seeds. **CONSERVATION:** Winters in n FL, Bahamas, Cuba, Jamaica, c Mexico s to Panama. Frequent cowbird host. Popular as cage bird in mainland wintering grounds s of U.S. **NOTES:** Male extremely pugnacious on territory; territorial disputes between males described as frequently bloody and sometimes fatal. **ESSAYS:** Polygyny, p. 443; Territoriality, p. 387; Cowbirds, p. 619; Wintering and Conservation, p. 513. **REFS:** Lanyon and Thompson, 1984; Parmelee, 1959.

Varied Bunting

Passerina versicolor Bonaparte

NG–384; G–312; PW–pl 56; AE–613; AW–525; AM(III)–212

TREE	?	3–4	?	SEEDS?	FOLIAGE
TANGLE		(3–5)	I: 12? DAYS	?	GLEAN?
1.5'–10'		?	ALTRICIAL		?
			F: ? DAYS		
			MF		

BREEDING: Arid thorny brush and thickets, dry washes, arid scrub. ? broods. **DISPLAYS:** ? **NEST:** Compactly built of dried grass, stems, cotton, snake-skin, paper, lined with fine grass, rootlets, hair. **EGGS:** Pale bluish-white, unmarked. 0.7″ (18 mm). **DIET:** Not well known; presumably similar to other *Passerina*. **CONSERVATION:** Winters from n Mexico and southernmost TX s to Guatemala. Rare cowbird host. May have decreased in abundance in U.S. due to habitat loss as arid brushlands have been converted to agriculture. **NOTES:** Little is known of the natural history and ecology of this species. **ESSAYS:** How Do We Find Out About Bird Biology?, p. 319; Bathing and Dusting, p. 429; Determining Diets, p. 535; Wintering and Conservation, p. 513. **REF:** Bent, 1968.

human beings. We have yet to learn how widespread this ability may be among other species of birds.

Homing pigeons, in addition to sensing magnetic fields, recently have been shown to use smell for at least short-distance orientation in returning to their loft. Earlier studies indicated that Leach's Storm-Petrels (and probably other "tubenoses") might possibly use their sense of smell to locate their nest burrows, although they rely on other cues to find the colony. Shearwaters, like pigeons, are capable of spectacular homing feats. Many Shearwaters were taken from their nest burrows off the coast of England, transported across the Atlantic Ocean, and released near Boston. Twelve and a half days later some of these individuals were back in their nest burrows. How they accomplished the feat is unknown, but they certainly didn't sniff their way home.

One clear message emerges from studies of avian orientation and navigation: birds do not rely on a single source of information to guide them on their travels. Instead, they possess the ability, shaped over evolutionary time, to use redundant cues from a variety of sources. Such a system enables birds to find their way under most conditions that they routinely encounter.

SEE: Migration, p. 183; The Avian Sense of Smell, p. 15; How Do We Find Out About Bird Biology?, p. 319; Shorebird Migration and Conservation, p. 119.   REFS: Able, 1983; Emlen, 1975; James, 1986; Mead, 1983; Walcott and Lednor, 1983.

Bird Names—XIV

No one knows where the name bunting came from—some think it was from the German "bunt" meaning "mottled," others from a French diminutive. The name of the Lazuli Bunting is from the same source as the name of the semiprecious stone lapis lazuli, the Latin "azulis" meaning "azure." The root of the "Indigo" in Indigo Bunting is the same as "Indian." It refers to the subcontinent that is the source of the blueish plant dye bearing the same name.

Sparrow is based on the Anglo-Saxon word meaning "flutterer." Henslow's Sparrow was named by Audubon (p. 413) after the famous English botanist John S. Henslow to whom Audubon was indebted for getting Cambridge University to subscribe to his *Birds of America*. Henslow was also the person who had recommended that Darwin become expedition naturalist on H.M.S. *Beagle*. Le Conte's Sparrow is named after Dr. John LeConte, a physician, physicist, and chemist from Georgia who became president of the University of California at Berkeley. Its generic name, *Ammodramus*, means "sand runner" in Greek, and is not terribly apt. The Vesper Sparrow is supposed to "sing at dusk," but when breeding it sings all day. REFS: Choate, 1985; Owen, 1985.

Olive Sparrow
Arremonops rufivirgatus Lawrence

NG–386; G–324; PW–pl 56; AE–pl 478; AM(III)–216

CACTUS	?	3–5	?	SEEDS ?	
2'–5'		?	I: ? DAYS		
			ALTRICIAL		
			F: ? DAYS		
			?		

BREEDING: Thickets, thorn scrub, mesquite, riparian brush. 2 broods. **DISPLAYS:** ? **NEST:** Very well concealed. Nearly round, domed and oversized; of dried forbs, grass, bark, twigs, leaves, lined with hair, fine herbaceous stems. Entrance on side. **EGGS:** White, unmarked. 0.9″ (22 mm). **DIET:** Not well known; presumably insects and seeds. **CONSERVATION:** Winter resident. Uncommon host of Brown-headed and Bronzed Cowbirds. **NOTES:** Resembles a small version of Green-tailed Towhee in foraging, as it scratches in leaf litter within dense undergrowth. Virtually nothing known of the biology of this primarily Mexican species. **ESSAYS:** How Do We Find Out About Bird Biology?, p. 319; Masterbuilders, p. 445; Determining Diets, p. 535. **REF:** Oberholser, 1974.

Rufous-sided Towhee
Pipilo erythrophthalmus Linnaeus

NG–386; G–324; PE–276; PW–pl 56; AE–pl 401; AW–pl 442; AM(III)–218

SHRUB	F	3–4	F –M?	SEEDS	FOLIAGE
0'–5'		(2–6)	I: 12–13 DAYS	FRUIT	GLEAN
(To 18')		MONOG	ALTRICIAL		
			F: 10–12 DAYS		
			MF		

BREEDING: Forest edge, chaparral, riparian thickets, woodland. 2 broods, occ 3 in s. **DISPLAYS:** From elevated perch male spreads tail showing white spots, raises wings and fluffs body feathers; may rapidly spread and fold tail and wings to flash white spots. **NEST:** Oft in scratched depression, rim of cup flush with ground surface; of leaves, grass, bark, twigs, rootlets, lined with fine grass, hair. Female selects site. **EGGS:** Grayish to creamy white, spotted with browns, oft wreathed or capped. 1.0″ (24 mm). **DIET:** Incl terrestrial inverts, grass and forb seeds, acorns (esp in winter), berries. Nestlings fed insects, some fruit. **CONSERVATION:** Winter resident, except in n portion of range; found s to Guatemala. Frequent cowbird host; apparently does not cover or eject parasite eggs. **NOTES:** Double-scratch foraging and mouselike run of female as in Green-tailed Towhee. Female broods nestlings; male then does most of feeding. Female occ feigns injury to distract predator from nest. Female may sing in early spring. Second broods normally produced by same mates within original territory; first egg produced 8–21 days after first brood fledges. Family groups remain together through summer. Oft bathes in dew or fog drip on veg. Forms loose winter flocks. **ESSAYS:** Vocal Functions, p. 471; Vocal Dialects, p. 595; Great Plains Hybrids, p. 625; Cowbirds, p. 619; Bathing and Dusting, p. 429. **REFS:** Ewert, 1980; Greenlaw, 1978; Richards, 1981b.

Bird Biologist—Roger Tory Peterson

In this century no one has done more to promote an interest in living creatures than Roger Tory Peterson, the inventor of the modern field guide. Born in 1907, 122 years after Audubon, Peterson was also an artist who developed a lifelong passion for birds. He was appalled at the clumsiness of existing guides, and set out to produce the first true *field* guide to birds—a pocket-sized volume that emphasized in illustrations and text the characteristics of birds that distinguished them when seen in nature. Peterson's *A Field Guide to the Birds* is a monument to his ability to paint and describe the very essence of a bird. It was an immediate success, and eventually sold over three million copies. The name Peterson will be forever associated with the series of guides to birds and other organisms that he authored or edited. Roger Tory Peterson has been a lifelong active conservationist, but his greatest contribution to the preservation of biological diversity has been in getting tens of millions of people outdoors with Peterson field guides in their pockets.

SEE: Helping to Conserve Birds—Local Level, p. 361. REF: Kastner, 1986.

Sonagrams: Seeing Bird Songs

Two people attempting to describe a Green-tailed Towhee song verbally may conjure two entirely different sound images. Both would agree that it includes some whistlelike phrases, some trills and some buzzes. But such a description is most unsatisfying to anyone who has never heard the song. It is equally unsatisfactory for the ornithologist wishing to examine questions of individual repertoire size and variation, the amount of song and syllable sharing among individuals, the existence of dialects, or the degree of geographic variation in songs among populations. With the development of the sound spectograph or sonagraph, it became possible to objectively and quantitatively approach these questions, and the sonagraph has been used in an impressive number of studies over the past 25 years. This work has been facilitated by the development of high-quality portable tape recorders used in conjunction with microphones mounted in parabolic reflectors or with very sensitive directional microphones.

The sonagraph produces on paper a graphic picture (a sonagram) of sound showing frequency (measured in kilohertz—thousands of cycles per second) on the vertical axis and time (in seconds) on the horizontal axis. Thus displayed, complex songs can be objectively separated into their constituent components, as shown in the sonagram (below) of a Green-tailed Towhee song. The song consists of an introductory note-complex followed

Green-tailed Towhee

Pipilo chlorurus Audubon

NG–386; G–324; PE–276; PW–pl 56; AW–pl 524; AM(III)–218

GROUND	?	3–4	? I: ? DAYS ALTRICIAL	SEEDS	
0'–2.5'		(2–5) MONOG	F: ? DAYS MF(?)	BERRIES	

BREEDING: Thickets, chaparral, shrublands with interspersed conifs, riparian scrub, all primarily in mountains. 2 broods. **DISPLAYS: ?** **NEST:** Large, thick-walled, of grass, bark, twigs, stems, lined with hair, fine stems, rootlets. **EGGS:** White, heavily spotted with browns, grays, oft forming solid cap at large end. 0.9″ (22 mm). **DIET:** Incl only grass and forb seeds. **CONSERVATION:** Winters s to c Mexico. Uncommon cowbird host. **NOTES:** Song resembles Fox Sparrow's and commonly incorporates notes from other species breeding nearby. Characteristically forages with double-scratch movement in leaf litter. If nest is approached, female drops straight down and runs away in mouselike fashion, presumably to distract predator. Usu moves upslope prior to migration. Breeding biology of this species has not been systematically studied. **ESSAYS:** Sonagrams: Bird Songs, p. 563; Vocal Copying, p. 469; Bird Voices, p. 373; Distraction Displays, p. 115. **REF:** Bent, 1968.

Brown Towhee

Pipilo fuscus Swainson

NG–386; G–324; PW–pl 56; AW–pl 563; AM(III)–220

TREE	?	3–4	F I: 11 DAYS ALTRICIAL	INSECTS	
4'–12'		(2–6)	F: 8 DAYS	FRUIT	
(0.5'–35')		MONOG	MF		

BREEDING: Chaparral, riparian thickets, brushland, arid scrub, and around human habitations. 2 or 3 broods. **DISPLAYS:** Courting male approaches female with wings drooped and quivering. Male and female "squeal duet" and posture when meeting after being apart within their territory. **NEST:** Bulky, of forb stems, twigs, grass, inner bark, lined with fine materials. **EGGS:** Bluish-white, marked with brown, purple. 1.0″ (25 mm). **DIET:** Young fed 100% insects. Drinks morning dew from grass. **CONSERVATION:** Winter resident. Uncommon cowbird host (both species). Has spread and increased in abundance as favored edge-type habitat increased through grazing, logging, farming, and suburbanization. **NOTES:** Far w populations highly territorial and males aggressively defend against intruders, incl reflections in windows and hubcaps! E populations evidence little territorial interaction and appear more peaceable. Female does not flush easily from nest. "Mouse-runs" like other towhees. Young remain with parents 4–6 weeks; driven from territory when next clutch hatches. Differences in behavior, vocalizations, and genetics indicate that populations in CA and OR are distinct from populations e of CA, and should be considered separate species. **ESSAYS:** Walking vs. Hopping, p. 69; Territoriality, p. 387; Species and Speciation, p.355; Drinking, p. 123; Range Expansion, p. 459. **REF:** Zink, 1988.

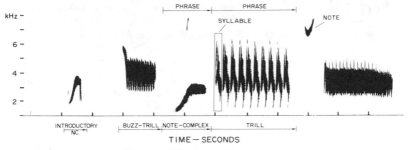

Sonagram of Green-tailed Towhee Song, Nc = note complex. See essay for details.

by a buzzy trill, another note-complex, a trill composed of separable, repeated syllables, a single note, and ends with a buzzy trill of essentially continuous syllables.

Although the sonagraph was a major advance in the study of bird vocalizations, its effectiveness is somewhat limited. The production of sonagrams is slow and laborious, and each is limited to only two and a half seconds of recording. These limitations have been overcome by a new generation of modern frequency spectrum analyzers that display sonagrams instantaneously on a visual display unit, and can selectively print "hard copy" of 10 seconds of continuous sound. Thus, thousands of songs can be scanned and analyzed in a relatively short time.

SEE: What Do Birds Hear?, p. 299; Bird Voices, p. 373; Vocal Copying, p. 469; Vocal Dialects, p. 595.

Bird Biologist—Elliot Coues

One of the most productive students of birds in the last century was army surgeon Elliot Coues (1842–99). Like many other army officers in the West, Coues braved the perils of the Indian wars to collect specimens and make observations on birds. Coues had more sensibility than many of his era—he was a notorious complainer, and one of the things he complained about was having to take part in "the massacre" of an Indian tribe. He was also an early champion of women's rights. Coues, however, had an acid tongue and was at the center of controversy, often taking positions less attractive than defending Native Americans or promoting equality of the sexes. He was an inconstant friend, and a vicious opponent in scientific disputes. But his talents were undeniable. In 1872 he published a major contribution to North American birding, *Key to North American Birds*. The work was a landmark, taking information on birds out of the technical literature and making it available to everyone; it provided a great stimulus to the expansion of knowledge of bird biology.

REF: Kastner, 1986.

Abert's Towhee

Pipilo aberti Baird

NG–386; G–324; PW–pl 56; AW–pl 564; AM(III)–222

			F		
TREE	?	3–4	I: ? DAYS	INSECTS	
(To 30')		(2–5)	ALTRICIAL		
		MONOG	F: 12–13 DAYS		
			MF		

BREEDING: Desert scrub, esp near water, riparian thickets and woodland. ? broods. **DISPLAYS:** ? **NEST:** Bulky, loose; of forb stems, vines, bark strips, green leaves, lined with bark strips, dried grass, hair. **EGGS:** Pale bluish or creamy white with scattered marks of dark brown, black, mostly toward large end. 0.9" (24 mm). **DIET:** Insects; seeds. **CONSERVATION:** Winter resident. Common cowbird host. Future status of this endemic, sedentary species is threatened by increasing adverse cowbird impact and rapid disappearance of desert riparian habitat. **NOTES:** Forms long-term pair bonds on permanent territories. Shy and wary. During the extremely hot summers, activity restricted to cooler parts of day: early morning and late afternoon. Male and female sing duets. Young hatch asynchronously, leading to brood reduction if food supply is poor, as adults selectively feed only larger nestlings. Female broods. **ESSAYS:** Cowbirds, p. 619; Monogamy, p. 597; Brood Reduction, p. 307; Temperature Regulation, p. 149; Vocal Functions, p. 471. **REFS:** Finch, 1983, 1984.

Grasshopper Sparrow

Ammodramus savannarum Gmelin

NG–388; G–328; PE–282; PW–pl 57; AE–pl 536; AW–pl 568; AM(III)–252

			F		
	F?	4–5	I: 11–12 DAYS	SEEDS	
		(3–6)	ALTRICIAL		
		MONOG	F: 9 DAYS		
			MF		

BREEDING: Grassland, cultivated fields, prairie, old fields, open savanna. 2 broods, 3? in FL. **DISPLAYS:** Courtship: low fluttering flight by male, silent or with song, the latter answered by female trill. Male may chase female while singing. **NEST:** Sunk in slight depression, rim flush with ground level, well concealed by overhanging grass and forbs, arched or domed at back; of dried grass, lined with fine materials. **EGGS:** Creamy white, marked with reddish-brown, occ wreathed. 0.8" (19 mm). **DIET:** Incl inverts, grass and forb seeds. **CONSERVATION:** Winters s to n S.A., Greater Antilles. Blue List 1974–86; declining in many areas, esp FL and Appalachians. FL subspecies Endangered. Nests oft destroyed by mowing in cultivated grassland; despite loss of cover, birds stay and then suffer increased losses from predators. Uncommon cowbird host. **NOTES:** Semicolonial breeding groups of 3–12 pairs. Local abundance fluctuates greatly between years. Male territorial display directed at other males alternates song with crouched display of lowered head and fluttering wings; territorial defense declines after young hatch. Female performs distraction display of short fluttering flight followed by feigned injury with spread wings and tail. Does not form winter flocks. **ESSAYS:** Blue List, p. 11; Birds and the Law, p. 293; Territoriality, p. 387; Distraction Displays, p. 115. **REFS:** Kale, 1978; Wiens, 1973.

Facts, Hypotheses, and Theories

In the technical language of science, a "fact" is something on which any group of ordinary observers would agree—the time given by a clock, the number of eggs in a gull's nest, the shape of a hawk's bill. Facts are as close to "certainty" as science gets; there is, after all, no guarantee against something distorting the perceptions of all the observers. Quite different from a fact, indeed at the opposite end of the spectrum of certainty–uncertainty, lies the "hypothesis." An hypothesis is an explanatory *idea*, a notion worthy of testing. That older birds have different reasons for joining breeding colonies or communal roosts than do younger birds is a hypothesis. It is a bright idea that may explain a large number of observations.

If, over time, careful studies of aggregating birds repeatedly demonstrate that older and younger birds consistently behave differently, and their behavior conforms to that expected under the hypothesis, then the hypothesis gradually becomes a "theory." A theory is an explanatory *framework* supported by a large number of observations and/or experiments. It is not necessarily "correct"; rather it is the best (most useful) framework available. Newton's theories about how the universe worked were supplanted by Einstein's, but the former were an enormous advance for their time, and many aspects of them remain quite useful.

In biology the best-known and most useful theory is the theory of evolution—the theory that living organisms today are the modified descendants of organisms from the distant past. It unifies what otherwise would be a huge conglomeration of fascinating, but often unrelated, facts. For instance, evolution, as Darwin pointed out more than a century ago, explains why birds on islands resemble birds from nearby mainlands more than they resemble birds on environmentally similar islands in other parts of the world. Without the theory, the observations of similarities would make no sense at all. Evolution, indeed, ties virtually everything about birds and other organisms into a single explanatory web.

Laypersons are often confused by the status of evolution as "just" a theory. But in the less precise language of everyday life, the theory of descent with modification is a "fact," just as the scientific theory that Earth circles the sun and not vice versa is also a layperson's "fact."

There is another way in which the word "theory" is used in biology. It sometimes means "mathematical theory"—a quantitative model that attempts a simplified description of the real world and can help us to understand it. A simple example is the notion that the chance of an adult bird dying remains constant—that, say, under certain environmental conditions a sparrow having a 70 percent chance of dying in 1990 will, if it is lucky enough to survive that year, again have a 70 percent chance of dying in 1991. If the model holds, simple mathematical manipulations will permit prediction of the average life expectancy of an adult sparrow under those conditions. (It would be about 11 months.) Of course, we know that it is impossible for a bird's chances of dying to remain exactly the same for years

Baird's Sparrow
Ammodramus bairdii Audubon

NG–388; G–328; PE–286; PW–pl 57; AW–555; AM(III)–250

| F? | 4–5
(3–6)
MONOG? | | F
I: 11–12 DAYS
ALTRICIAL
F: 8–10 DAYS
MF | SEEDS |

BREEDING: Shortgrass prairie. 1 brood. **DISPLAYS:** Courtship: male walks slowly and silently with head withdrawn, tail spread, and wings vibrated alternately over his back, occ bobs head low to ground; flies with rapid fluttering wing beats. **NEST:** In natural or scratched depression, oft concealed by overhead veg; bulky, well woven of dried grass, forbs, lined with fine materials. Female selects site. **EGGS:** Grayish-white, marked with reddish-brown, occ wreathed. 0.8" (19 mm). **DIET:** Incl spiders, grass and forb seeds. Young fed 100% insects. **CONSERVATION:** Winters s to n Mexico. Uncommon cowbird host. In 1878, Coues noted this species as more abundant than all other species combined in parts of the Dakotas; agriculture and grazing have since decreased habitat; now declining and confined to disappearing native prairie. **NOTES:** Semicolonial breeding groups of a few pairs. Males fight vigorously over initial territory establishment. Female extremely close sitter. Initially female alone feeds and broods young. Reluctance to fly is characteristic at all seasons, as is mouselike running along ground. Does not form winter flocks. **ESSAYS:** Territoriality, p. 387; Walking vs. Hopping, p. 69; Helping to Conserve Birds—National Level, p. 363. **REF:** Bent, 1968.

Henslow's Sparrow
Ammodramus henslowii Audubon

NG–388; G–328; PE–286; AE–pl 537; AM(III)–254

| 0'–0.3'
(To 1.6') | F –M | 3–5
MONOG ? | F
I: 11 DAYS
ALTRICIAL
F: 9–10 DAYS
MF | SEEDS |

BREEDING: Fields and meadows, preferably moist, with combination of grass, forbs, and scattered shrubs. 2 broods. **DISPLAYS:** Courtship: male holds nesting material in beak while hopping or singing on ground; leads female on ground and flutters wings at potential nest sites. **NEST:** On or very near ground, occ in depression, well concealed by overhead grass oft forming partial roof; some nests elevated, attached to vertical stems, lack roof; of coarse grass, forbs, lined with fine materials. **EGGS:** Creamy or pale greenish-white, marked with reddish-brown, oft wreathed. 0.7" (18 mm). **DIET:** Incl some spiders, snails; takes seeds of grass, forbs, sedges. Young fed 100% insects. **CONSERVATION:** Winters within U.S. Uncommon cowbird host. Blue List 1974–81, Special Concern 1982–86. Widespread forest clearing enabled range expansion and increased abundance, but drainage of lowlands and intense cultivation have reduced breeding habitat this century. Uses unmowed hayfields, but abandons when cut. **NOTES:** Tends to form loose breeding colonies, with males holding territories lacking rigid boundaries. If nest destroyed, new site selected and nest built in 5–6 days. Both sexes brood. Male oft sings at night. Characteristically skulks and runs mouselike on ground. **ESSAYS:** Blue List, p. 11; Bills, p. 209; Habitat Selection, p. 463. **REF:** Bent, 1968.

(winters change in severity, predator populations change in size, the abundance of food varies, the bird both becomes more experienced and also ages, and so on), but it turns out that in spite of that variability, this model is *close enough* (on the average) to be very informative about changes in real bird populations.

Another example of a useful mathematical theory is that of island biogeography. That theory suggests that the number of species on an island should be at an equilibrium established by opposing rates of immigration and extinction of species. Although the theory ignores many of the complexities of "real" biology, such as differences in the variety of habitats available on large and small islands and the possibility of competition between different species, the island biogeographic theory has proven a very useful tool for ecologists, especially those interested in conservation.

Theory must interact with the other great tools of science, observation and experiment. Observations and experiments stimulate theoreticians to build mathematical models, and those models are in turn tested by observations and experiments. Through such cycles, science is continually working to improve its explanations, and scientists are perpetually testing each other's ideas. Whether science is, in the process, approaching some final set of "truths" is a matter of debate among scientists and philosophers, but most are agreed that the entire enterprise is at least moving away from error.

SEE: How Do We Find Out About Bird Biology?, p. 319; Coloniality, p. 173; How Long Can Birds Live?, p. 643; Population Dynamics, p. 575; Island Biogeography, p. 549. REFS: Ehrlich, 1986a; Ehrlich and Roughgarden, 1987.

Bird Biologist—Spencer Fullerton Baird

Baird's Sandpiper, a denizen of arctic tundras, and Baird's Sparrow, which breeds in short-grass prairies of the northern plains, are named after Spencer Fullerton Baird (1823–87). He began his career at the age of 16 by reading Wilson's (p. 277) *Ornithology* and corresponding with Audubon (p. 413) in the artist's later years, and he went on to begin the modern era of North American ornithology.

Baird established the Smithsonian Institution (where he served first as scientific head and then as Secretary) as a major scientific center. By encouraging military men who accompanied government expeditions of railroad exploration to collect specimens during their travels, he greatly expanded the museum's bird collection. He co-authored the monumental *A History of North American Birds* (1874) with Thomas Brewer (p. 647) and Robert Ridgway (p. 119), a work which started an American tradition of careful description of life histories and detailed documentation of conclusions. Baird was also one of the first American supporters of Darwin (p. 475). REFS: Kastner, 1986; Stresemann, 1975.

Le Conte's Sparrow

Ammodramus leconteii Audubon

NG–390; G–330; PE–288; PW–pl 57; AE–pl 538; AM(III)–254

0'–0.6'	F?	4 (3–5) ?	F I: 12–13 (?) DAYS ALTRICIAL F: ? DAYS ?	SEEDS	

BREEDING: Moist meadows, marsh and bog edges. ? broods. **DISPLAYS:** ? **NEST:** On or slightly above ground, beneath tangles of rushes, grass, or sedges, very well concealed; of dried grass, rushes, interwoven with standing stems, lined with fine materials. **EGGS:** Grayish-white, marked with browns. 0.7" (18 mm). **DIET:** Incl spiders; takes grass and forb seeds. Young fed almost entirely on insects. **CONSERVATION:** Winters within U.S. Uncommon victim of cowbird. **NOTES:** Reluctant to fly, oft runs along ground in mouselike fashion. Secretive and poorly known. **ESSAYS:** How Do We Find Out About Bird Biology?, p. 319; Diet and Nutrition, p. 587; Bills, p. 209. **REF:** Bent, 1968.

Seaside Sparrow

Ammodramus maritimus Wilson

NG–390; G–330; PE–288; AE–pl 534; AM(III)–258

GRASS			F	SEEDS	FOLIAGE GLEAN
0.3'–5' (To 14')	F?	3–5 (2–6) MONOG	I: 12–13 DAYS ALTRICIAL F: 8–10 DAYS MF		

BREEDING: Salt marsh. 2 broods; 1 in n, 3 in FL. **DISPLAYS:** Courtship: male slowly flutters straight up 20'–30', pauses, slowly descends, singing throughout (rare or absent in habitats with elevated perches). Conspicuous wing raising by male in aggressive territorial encounters. **NEST:** Usu in grass, rush, sedge (occ in shrub), oft canopied by interweaving with surrounding grass; of dried grass, sedge, lined with fine grass. **EGGS:** White to greenish-white, marked with reddish-brown. 0.8" (21 mm). **DIET:** Incl spiders, amphipods, seeds of various marsh plants. **CONSERVATION:** In winter, partly or wholly resident in coastal marshes. Rare cowbird host. Destruction of salt marshes severely decreased breeding habitat. DDT, draining, development, and flooding for mosquito control have led to extinction of one subspecies (Dusky Seaside Sparrow) and virtual extinction of another (Cape Sable Sparrow); both listed as Endangered. **NOTES:** Nests in loose, oft isolated, colonies. Both sexes perform distraction display by running and fluttering wings. Female broods. Runs raillike through grass with body held erect. Common clutch size in n, 4–5; 3–4 in s. Rice rats destroy many clutches in s. Although usu separated from Sharp-tailed Sparrow by nesting in wetter portions of marsh, hybrids are known. **ESSAYS:** Saving a Subspecies, p. 571; Birds and the Law, p. 293; Walking vs. Hopping, p. 69; Average Clutch Size, p. 51; DDT and Birds, p. 21; Hybridization, p. 501. **REF:** Quay et al., 1983.

Saving a Subspecies

The Dusky Seaside Sparrow (*Ammodramus maritimus nigrescens*) was a subspecies of the Seaside Sparrow (see p. 570), which bred in salt marshes from New England south to Florida and west across the Gulf Coast. The subspecies (a group of populations within a species that is different enough genetically to require a formal, latinized name) was once common on Florida's east coast, but rapid development of the Sunshine State drastically reduced its habitat and its numbers. Major efforts to save the birds ensued, including the expenditure of five million dollars by the U.S. Fish and Wildlife Service (USFWS) to buy a chunk of its remaining habitat. But even the Habitat Protection Program failed. It was unsuccessful because the habitat (now the St. John's National Wildlife Refuge) was subjected to degradation from drainage and underwent continued deterioration from fires originating outside of its borders.

By 1980, the Dusky Seaside Sparrow was represented by a mere six individuals. Its preservation presented a considerable challenge to conservation biologists, because all six survivors were males. For their protection, five of those males were brought into captivity (the sixth eluded capture). Project coordinators concluded that there was just one way to save the subspecies—by mating those males with females of the closely related subspecies, Scott's Seaside Sparrow (*Ammodramus maritimus peninsulae*), which breeds in Florida's Gulf Coast marshes. The surviving Dusky males could then be mated with any hybrid daughters (50 percent Dusky, 50 percent Scott's) that were obtained, yielding "backcross" individuals that were mathematically 75 percent Dusky and 25 percent Scott's. If the backcrossing process (mating the original males with females of each generation) could be continued for three more generations, individuals that were 96.9 percent Dusky could be produced. Then, if further breeding could produce a flock of those "mostly Duskies," an attempt could be made to reestablish them in nature.

In 1980 a male Dusky was mated to a female Scott's, and three hybrids were produced. But for the following two years the USFWS refused to permit further experiments, so it was not until 1983 that a single 75 percent Dusky female was available. That year one of the original males died. In 1984 another 75 percent chick, a male, hatched, along with an 87.5 percent chick, which accidentally died by flying into the side of its cage. The 1985 breeding season found the surviving three original Dusky males almost a decade old—quite ancient for a small songbird. Two 87.5 percent chicks, a male and a female, were born in 1985, but two of the remaining adult males died. The next-to-last male died in 1986, and the last in 1987. The "pure" Dusky Seaside Sparrow is gone forever.

It is problematical whether this attempt to save the subspecies will succeed. It started late, and the number of available birds was very small. Only old male birds (which tend to be poor breeders) were used; one was unable to convince females to mate with him, and another's mates produced

Sharp-tailed Sparrow

Ammodramus caudacutus Gmelin

NG–390; G–330; PE–288; PW–pl 57; AE–pl 533; AM(III)–256

GRASS
0'–0.3'

F

3–5
(3–7)
PROMISC

F
I: 11 DAYS
ALTRICIAL
F: 10 DAYS
F

SEEDS

BREEDING: Marshes, wet meadows; w race exclusively freshwater marshes, e races primarily saltwater marshes. 2 broods, possibly 1 in n. **DISPLAYS:** Agonistic interactions among a group of males oft precedes cop. **NEST:** Occ in depression, oft suspended a few inches by sedges or grass, usu well concealed; of coarse grass, sedges, lined with fine grass. **EGGS:** Greenish-white, marked with reddish-brown. 0.8″ (19 mm). **DIET:** Mostly insects, spiders, amphipods, snails; takes seeds of grass, sedges, and, in w, forbs. **CONSERVATION:** Winters in coastal marshes within U.S. Rare cowbird host. Destruction of e salt marshes has markedly decreased breeding habitat. **NOTES:** Colonial breeding of a few to <20 "pairs." Males do not defend territories. Characteristic mouselike run through grass with head held low. Undergoes two complete molts per year. Several hybridization records with Seaside Sparrow. **ESSAYS:** Promiscuity, p. 145; Hybridization, p. 501; Molting, p. 529; Bird Guilds, p. 493. **REF:** Woolfenden, 1956.

Vesper Sparrow

Pooecetes gramineus Gmelin

NG–392; G–332; PE–284; PW–pl 57; AE–pl 550; AW–pl 575; AM(III)–240

?

3–4
(2–6)
MONOG?

F –M
I: 11–13 DAYS
ALTRICIAL
F: 9 (7–14) DAYS
MF

SEEDS

BREEDING: Grassland, prairie, savanna, old fields, arid scrub, woodland clearings. 1–3 broods, usu 2. **DISPLAYS:** Male walks or runs with wings raised, wings and tail spread widely, and periodically rises into air to give short flight song. **NEST:** In excavated depression, usu well concealed by mat of dead veg or concealed by fresh growth as incubation progresses; bulky, loosely built of grass, forbs, rootlets, lined with fine materials. **EGGS:** Creamy white or pale greenish-white, marked with browns. 0.8″ (21 mm). **DIET:** 50% insects; 50% grass and forb seeds. **CONSERVATION:** Winters s to c Mexico. Common cowbird host. Nests oft placed in cropland and destroyed by agricultural operations. **NOTES:** Female (occ male) broods. Young fed mostly by male when female begins second nest. Female distraction display: spreads tail and drags wing or leg. Male requires elevated song perches. Strong propensity for dust bathing; neither drinks nor bathes in water. **ESSAYS:** Walking vs. Hopping, p. 69; Distraction Displays, p. 115; Drinking, p. 123; Bathing and Dusting, p. 429; Cowbirds, p. 619. **REFS:** Best and Rodenhouse, 1984; Wray and Whitmore, 1979.

only infertile eggs. Although in 1984 a 50 percent Dusky female laid eight clutches totaling twenty eggs, only five hatched, and only one chick survived. Small numbers of experimental birds mean that the enterprise is extremely vulnerable to a single accident. According to the last report we had from Herbert W. Kale of the Florida Audubon Society (which with Disney World's Discovery Island Zoological Park is cooperatively running the breeding project) was that none of the eggs of the mate of the last male were fertile in 1986. Kale and Charles Cook, curator of Discovery Island, plan to crossbreed the remaining part-Duskies with Scott's Seasides, and then do backcrossing, with the goal of producing a population whose individuals approach being 75 percent Duskies.

Even if it fails, the Dusky Seaside Sparrow breeding program shows the potential for preserving genetic diversity in species by reestablishing subspecies through backcrossing. The hybrids are fertile, and the 75 and 87.5 percent Dusky birds do resemble the original Duskies. But they are not, and cannot be, the "original" subspecies. The USFWS even claimed that it could no longer spend money on protecting habitat for reintroductions of the hybrid birds because *legally* they would not be Duskies.

But there is a much larger question. How much money should be spent on captive breeding programs for subspecies, or even species? Sadly, we well know that funds available for conservation efforts are very limited. Dollars spent on captive breeding and habitat preservation must come from the same pocket, and it is degradation and destructive of habitat that is the major threat to Earth's avifauna. The question of allocation of funds is a matter of great debate among conservation biologists, and is likely to remain so as the necessity of protecting individual species and smaller and smaller plots of land inevitably increases.

What is certain is that a great deal of attention must be paid to preserving diverse populations of each species. That helps ensure against the entire species being wiped out by a calamity that destroys one or two populations. Saving populations will also conserve genetic diversity which can be critical to a species' ability to evolve in response to environmental change (and thus to survive). Furthermore, populations provide humanity with both important services (as when your local chickadees and warblers help suppress insect pests on shade trees) and with esthetic enjoyment. Conservation should start with populations—if they are preserved, then so will be species.

SEE: How Long Can Birds Live?, p. 643; Conservation of the California Condor, p. 219; Natural Selection, p. 237; Species and Speciation, p. 355; Helping to Conserve Birds—National Level, p. 363. REFS: Diamond, 1985a; Soulé, 1986; Soulé and Wilcox, 1980.

Savannah Sparrow

Passerculus sandwichensis Gmelin

NG–392; G–328; PE–286; PW–pl 57; AE–pl 548; AW–pl 569; AM(III)–248

| 0′–0.5′ | F | 3–5 (2–6) MONOG (POLYGYN) | F –M I: (10–)12–13 DAYS ALTRICIAL F: 7–10 (–14?) DAYS MF | SEEDS SNAILS |

BREEDING: Grassland, meadow, tundra, marsh, bog, cultivated grassy areas. 2 broods; 1 in far n. **DISPLAYS:** Courtship: on ground, male rapidly vibrates wings above back; low, slow flight on rapidly vibrating wings with head and tail raised; flight song. **NEST:** Usu in natural or excavated depression, rim flush with ground, well concealed by overhanging veg; of coarse grass, lined with fine materials. **EGGS:** Pale greenish-blue, off-white, marked with brown, occ wreathed. 0.8″ (20 mm). **DIET:** Incl spiders; seeds mostly of grass. **CONSERVATION:** Winters s through Mexico to Honduras; also Bahamas, Cuba, assoc islands; resident in s CA salt marshes. Uncommon cowbird host. One of several distinct races, the Ipswich Sparrow breeds only on Sable Island off Nova Scotia and numbers <1000. **NOTES:** Occ appears semicolonial, esp marsh populations. Polygyny common in some populations. First clutches oft larger than second. 85% of brooding by female. Female occ performs distraction display: low flight with shallow wingbeats, feigns injury with spread wings and tail. Runs mouselike on ground. Roosts in small compact groups on ground in short grass. Forms small, loose winter aggregations. **ESSAYS:** Polygyny, p. 443; Distraction Displays, p. 115; Variation in Clutch Sizes, p. 339. **REFS:** Bédard and LaPointe, 1985; Bédard and Meunier, 1983; Weatherhead, 1979; Williams, 1987.

Lark Sparrow

Chondestes grammacus Say

NG–394; G–332; PE–282; PW–pl 58; AE–pl 527; AW–pl 577; AM(III)–242

| SHRUB 0′–7′ (To 25′) | F | 4–5 (3–6) MONOG (POLYGYN) | F I: 11–12 DAYS ALTRICIAL F: 9–10 DAYS MF | INSECTS |

BREEDING: Grassland, prairie, savanna, cultivated areas, fields with scattered trees and shrubs. 1 brood. **DISPLAYS:** Courtship: male struts before female with bill pointed up, tail spread, wings fluttering; flight song on rapidly beating wings with spread tail. Twig oft held by female or passed to her during cop. **NEST:** Oft hollow depression in ground lined with fine grass; nest in shrub or rock crevice bulky, of grass, forbs, foundation of twigs, lined with fine materials. Oft reuse their own nests and those of other species (esp mockingbird and thrashers). Male and female select site together. **EGGS:** Creamy to grayish-white, marked with dark browns, blacks, oft wreathed. 0.8″ (20 mm). **DIET:** Incl grass and forb seeds. **CONSERVATION:** Winters s to c Mexico. Occ cowbird host. **NOTES:** Gregarious, feeding in flocks even in breeding season. Weak territoriality disappears entirely when incubation begins. Male oft presents food to female on nest and she feeds nestlings. Distraction display by ground-nesting female: spreads tail and flutters one or both wings. Male oft sings at night. **ESSAYS:** Distraction Displays, p. 115; Vocal Functions, p. 471. **REF:** McNair, 1984.

Population Dynamics

The "dynamics" of bird populations, the ways in which their numbers grow and shrink as time goes by, are controlled by the same general factors that control the size of human populations. An avian or human population has two kinds of input—birth (natality) and immigration. And each population has the same two outputs—death (mortality) and emigration. If the inputs are greater than the outputs, the population will grow. If the outputs are higher than the inputs, it will shrink. If the two are in balance, the population size will not change, or as ecologists would say, the population "density" is constant. Population density is, technically, the number of individuals per unit area. But since a population normally occupies a limited area of suitable habitat, its size increases, decreases, or remains stable along with its density.

In an average lifetime, the average female in each bird population lays many more eggs than are required to replace her and her mate, if the chicks from all of her eggs were to mature into reproducing adults. Mortality, however, intervenes. Eggs are destroyed by nest robbers, chicks starve, freeze, are killed by disease or parasites, or are carried off by predators, juveniles are devoured by hawks, crash into obstacles on migration, or die of cold or starvation in their first winter. As a result, in spite of their large reproductive potential, populations are often more or less stable. Over the long run each female in one generation of a bird population is replaced in the next generation by, on the average, just one female. If she were replaced by two females, and there were one generation per year, and if each bird weighed a pound, then in less than a century the bird population would outweigh Earth. Such is the power of exponential increase. If each female were replaced by much less than one female each generation, then the population would soon be extinct. In the following example, the constraints of mortality have been relaxed, and one can see a bird population begin expansion in the direction of Earth weight.

In 1937, two male and six female Ring-necked Pheasants were introduced onto a 450-acre island off the coast of Washington State. The island had not previously had a pheasant population, but with superabundant food and few predators, the population exploded. Even though many birds died each winter, the original flock of eight became a horde of nearly two thousand within six breeding seasons. During that period, however, the rate of growth of the population was gradually slowed. This decrease in growth rate was probably due, at least in part, to diminishing space for male territories and possibly to decreased food supply, leading to higher juvenile mortality.

Limited space for territories may often put a cap on the size of bird populations. In his well-known study of Florida Scrub Jays, Glen Woolfenden found that the density of breeding pairs remained quite constant. In a stretch of about 550 acres of prime habitat, there was very close to one pair per 25 acres for each of the nine years from 1971 to 1979. In contrast, at the

Song Sparrow

Melospiza melodia Wilson

NG–392; G–342; PE–284; PW–pl 57; AE–pl 542; AW–pl 573; AM(III)–262

SHRUB   F   3–4 (2–6)   F   SEEDS   FOLIAGE
0′–3′   MONOG   I: 12–14 DAYS   GLEAN
(To 12′)   (POLYGYN)   ALTRICIAL
                          F: 9–12 (–16) DAYS
                          MF

BREEDING: Dense veg along watercourses and coasts, marshes, and, mostly in n and e, forest edge, clearings, bogs, gardens. 2 or 3 broods, occ 4. **DISPLAYS:** Courting male chases female, flutters wings, oft sailing and singing; flies among perches with neck outstretched, head and tail held high, wings vibrating. **NEST:** Beneath grass tuft, shrub, brushpile, rarely in cavity; of grass, forbs, leaves, bark strips, lined with fine materials. Built in 4–10 days. Occ reused for second clutch. Later nests oft higher. **EGGS:** Pale blue to greenish-white, marked with reddish-browns. 0.8″ (20 mm). **DIET:** Incl grass and forb seeds, some berries. Crustaceans and mollusks along coast. **CONSERVATION:** Winter resident in many areas, remainder mostly within N.A. Most frequent cowbird host (dubious honor shared with Yellow Warbler); occ recognize and attack cowbird. **NOTES:** Most variable N.A. bird with 31 subspecies. Polygyny occurs 1) when male dies and mate joins another mated male, and 2) when females outnumber males. Some pairs stay together in successive years. Residents stay on or near territory all year. Female broods. Adult distraction display: runs about, wings held stiffly erect, tail depressed. Fledglings oft divided, each tended by only one adult; male takes charge when young fly well and female begins next clutch. By 21–30 days, young leave nesting territory. **ESSAYS:** Vocal Development, p. 601; Vocal Functions, p. 471; Population Dynamics, p. 575; Brood Parasitism, p. 287; Cowbirds, p. 619; Polygyny, p. 443; Dominance Hierarchies, p. 533. **REFS:** Arcese, 1987; Smith and Merkt, 1980; Smith et al., 1982.

Black-throated Sparrow

Amphispiza bilineata Cassin

NG–394; G–332; PW–pl 58; AE–pl 528; AW–pl 593; AM(III)–242

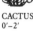

CACTUS   ?   3–4   ?   SEEDS   FOLIAGE
0′–2′   (2–4)   I: ? DAYS   GLEAN
                 MONOG?   ALTRICIAL   HAWKS
                          F: ? DAYS
                          ?

BREEDING: Desert scrub, esp rocky uplands. 2 broods. **DISPLAYS:** ? **NEST:** sturdy, of grass, plant fibers, lined with fine materials. **EGGS:** Bluish-white, unmarked. 0.7″ (17 mm). **DIET:** Incl new shoots of grass and forbs. Young fed insects. Requires water to drink in summer and autumn until rains begin; water needs then satisfied by water in green veg, subsequently by body fluids of insects. **CONSERVATION:** Winters s to c Mexico. Uncommon cowbird victim. **NOTES:** Timing of breeding varies from year to year, likely related to rainfall and food abundance. Highly variable singers. Details of breeding biology largely unknown. Forms small winter flocks with other species, esp Sage, Brewer's, and White-crowned Sparrows. **ESSAYS:** Mixed-Species Flocking, p. 433; Drinking, p. 123; Diet and Nutrition, p. 587; How Do We Find Out About Bird Biology?, p. 319. **REF:** Heckenlively, 1970.

start of the breeding season in those same years, the overall density of jays in the area was three to four times as great. Interestingly, there was no relationship between the density of jays just before the breeding season and the breeding density. Apparently the habitat is saturated with breeding pairs; surplus mature birds must wait until space opens for them, often in the interim helping at the nests of their parents.

Florida Scrub Jay territories tend to be relatively constant in size, but those of other birds may vary. When territorial males are abundant, territories may be small. If, in contrast, few males seek territories, territories may expand—and if a severe winter or some other factor significantly reduces the number of potentially breeding males, parts of the habitat that previously were used for territories will remain unoccupied in the spring.

These phenomena were well described in a classic study of Song Sparrows by pioneer American ornithologist Margaret Morse Nice. She carefully mapped territories in one locality in Ohio from 1930 to 1935, inclusive, as shown in the accompanying figure (in each map the Olentangy River is the left-hand border of the map, a street the right, the other straight lines are dikes; the scale line represents 200 yards). The number of males fluctuated between 17 (much habitat unoccupied, territories large) and 44 (most habitat occupied, territories small). The difference can be seen easily in the right-hand pair of maps. Note the five small territories along the southern dike at the bottom of the upper map and the four larger ones at the bottom of the lower map.

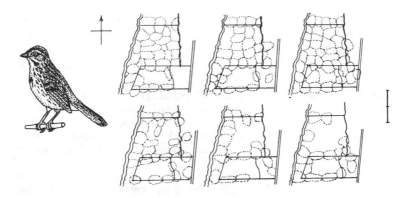

The two-and-a-half-fold range of population sizes of the sparrow may seem far from constancy, but compared with fluctuations of, say, the sort found in insect populations, the Song Sparrow population was quite stable. For example, in 25 years of study, a single population of checkerspot butterflies in California has gone through more than 20-fold changes in size, and enormously greater changes are commonly observed in organisms ranging from phytoplankton (minute water plants) to lemmings.

Homo sapiens is, of course, subject to the same basic population dy-

Five-striped Sparrow
Amphispiza quinquestriata Sclater and Salvin

NG–394; G–336; AM(III)–246

| GRASS 0.5'–4.5' | F | 3–4 MONOG | F I: 12–13 DAYS ALTRICIAL F: 9–10 DAYS MF | SEEDS | FOLIAGE GLEAN |

BREEDING: Mixture of dense shrubs and grass usu on steep arid slopes. 1–3 broods, usu 2. **DISPLAYS:** Upon meeting in territory after separation, male and female give distinctive warbling pair-bond call. **NEST:** In low shrub, grass clump; deep cup of grass, lined with grass, hair. Built in 3–5 days. **EGGS:** Dull white, unmarked. 0.8" (20 mm). **DIET:** Young fed insects. **CONSERVATION:** Winters usu s to c Mexico, occ resident. Frequent cowbird host. **NOTES:** Reportedly defends territories against Rufous-crowned and Black-throated Sparrows. Later clutches larger. Female broods. Male alone cares for fledglings when female begins incubating second clutch. Male song repertoires are large (>150 song types per bird); male sings each song type many times before switching to a different one. First recorded nesting in U.S. in 1969. In winter may join loose mixed flocks with other ground-foraging finches. **ESSAYS:** Interspecific Territoriality, p. 385; Vocal Functions, p. 471; Cowbirds, p. 619; Mixed-Species Flocking, p. 433; Variation in Clutch Sizes, p. 339. **REFS:** Groschupf and Mills, 1982; Mills et al., 1980.

Sage Sparrow
Amphispiza belli Cassin

NG–394; G–332; PW–pl 58; AW–pl 602; AM(III)–244

| GROUND 0'–3.3' | ? | 2–4 (2–5) MONOG | ? I: 13–16 DAYS ALTRICIAL F: 9–11 DAYS ? | SEEDS | FOLIAGE GLEAN |

BREEDING: Sagebrush, arid brushland, chaparral. 2? broods. **DISPLAYS:** Males occ walk-in-line parallel to each other along mutual territorial boundary in territorial/dominance display. **NEST:** Usu in sagebrush; of twigs, grass, forbs, bark, lined with fine materials. **EGGS:** Bluish-white, marked with dark browns, black, occ wreathed. 0.8" (19 mm). **DIET:** Incl spiders. Young fed insects. **CONSERVATION:** Winters s to n Mexico; resident in coastal CA. Distinctive subspecies endemic to San Clemente Island, CA, is Endangered (sub)Species. Uncommon cowbird host. **NOTES:** Males show strong site tenacity to breeding territory, even if habitat changes markedly. Incubating bird very tight sitter; leaves nest by dropping to ground and running. Tail raised perpendicularly when running, suggesting wren or thrasher. Male twitches tail while singing from elevated perch; each male sings a single song with only minor variations. Late summer loose flocks of mixed ages oft found at water sources. Some upslope movement by flocks of young birds after breeding season. **ESSAYS:** Birds and the Law, p. 293; Vocal Functions, p. 471; Site Tenacity, p. 189; Drinking, p. 123. **REFS:** Reynolds, 1981; Rich, 1981, 1983; Petersen et al., 1986; Wiens et al., 1986.

namic factors as birds. The human population has increased about 40-fold in the eighty generations since the time of Christ, as mortality rates have dropped without compensating declines in natality. One result of human population growth has been a decline in many bird populations, as *Homo sapiens* has hunted them, appropriated their food, and destroyed their habitats. In contrast, other bird populations, such as those of some gulls, European Starlings, and House Sparrows have increased through exploitation of resources supplied by humanity and occupation of human-modified habitats.

Migration can greatly influence the size of a bird population in a given area. Crossbills, for example, may move in large numbers into a habitat providing a rich, seasonal supply of conifer seeds. The crossbills breed and then move on. Immigration creates a large local population, and emigration removes it. Crossbills are an extreme case, and their sort of nomadic behavior is normally not considered in studies of the dynamics of individual populations (since birds are not moving into and out of a population, but into and out of a location). The major influence of immigration on the size of bird populations is through the short-range movement of nonterritorial males into unoccupied space that is suitable for territories.

Note also that migration between wintering and breeding grounds is not ordinarily important in the dynamics of populations except as it affects the mortality of migrants. Birds of a given breeding population usually return to nest in the same area each year (a phenomenon known as "site tenacity" or "philopatry," meaning "site faithfulness")—the entire population moves south and then returns north.

SEE: Territoriality, p. 387; Irruptions, p. 639; Site Tenacity, p. 189; Avian Invaders, p. 633; Cooperative Breeding, p. 283.   REFS: Carrick, 1963; Einarsen, 1945; Krebs, 1970; Nice, 1964; Watson, 1967; Woolfenden and Fitzpatrick, 1984.

Bird Biologist—Margaret Morse Nice

The most important woman in the history of North American ornithology, a great leader in the field, and one of the most impressive scholars ever to work on our continent was Margaret Morse Nice (1883–1974). Nice had done graduate work in ornithology, but when her husband took a faculty job in the Ohio State medical school they did not (as many young couples would today) press for a teaching position for her also. Instead she kept the house and began an intensive study of birds. The title of her autobiography says it all: *Research Is a Passion with Me*. Nice authored some 60 articles on various aspects of avian ecology and behavior, on topics as diverse as nesting habits, the role of territoriality in bird life, and the development of precocial birds. Her fame, however, rests on a detailed eight-year field study of a population

Bachman's Sparrow

Aimophila aestivalis Lichtenstein

NG–396; G–336; PE–282; AE–594; AM(III)–224

F 3–5
MONOG?
F
I: 14 DAYS
ALTRICIAL
F: 10–11 DAYS
MF
INSECTS

BREEDING: Open pine woods with understory, brushy slopes, old fields. 2, possibly 3 broods. **DISPLAYS:** Rare evening flight song: erratic ascent to ca. 150' with fluttering wings. **NEST:** Open or domed, well concealed; of coarse grass, forbs, lined with fine grass, hair. **EGGS:** White, unmarked. 0.8" (19 mm). **DIET:** Incl some spiders, snails, millipedes; seeds of grass, sedge, forbs. **CONSERVATION:** Winters within U.S. Blue List 1972–86. Uncommon cowbird host. Logging of unbroken s e pinewoods, creating second growth and abundant edge habitat, enabled spread to n and n w and increased abundance. Now absent or very local breeder in n e portion of expanded range, and apparently declining everywhere. **NOTES:** Female is close sitter on nest; female performs distraction display by fluttering and dragging wing along ground. **ESSAYS:** Blue List, p. 11; Distraction Displays, p. 115; Range Expansion, p. 459; Bills, p. 209. **REF:** Allaire and Fisher, 1975.

Botteri's Sparrow

Aimophila botterii Sclater

NG–396; G–336; PW–pl 57; AE–625; AW–553; AM(III)–226

? 4?
(2–5)
?
?
I: ? DAYS
ALTRICIAL
F: ? DAYS
?
SEEDS

BREEDING: Grassland, savanna, esp with scattered bushes. ? broods. **DISPLAYS:** ? **NEST:** Constructed of grass. **EGGS:** Bluish-white, unmarked. 0.8" (20 mm). **DIET:** Incl esp grasshoppers; grass and forb seeds. **CONSERVATION:** Winters from n Mexico s to Costa Rica. Range in U.S. apparently has decreased since overgrazing of the late 1800s. **NOTES:** Details of the biology of this secretive and difficult to identify species are unknown. **ESSAYS:** How Do We Find Out About Bird Biology?, p. 319; Bird Guilds, p. 493; Bills, p. 209; Walking vs. Hopping, p. 69. **REFS:** Bent, 1968; Phillips et al., 1964.

of Song Sparrows living on a section of flood plain created by the Olentangy River in Columbus, Ohio—a site Nice called "Interpont." That pioneering work, based on careful following of scores of color-banded individuals, remains a keystone in our understanding of the dynamics of populations of territorial vertebrates.

Nice was a friend of Konrad Lorenz (p. 57), with whom she studied briefly. She also published on the development of children's vocabularies, and could search the ornithological literature in seven languages. The great behaviorist Nikolaas Tinbergen (p. 71) once said of her that "an American housewife was the greatest scholar of them all."

SEE: Population Dynamics, p. 575.   REF: Kastner, 1986.

Precocial and Altricial Young

"Precocial" and "altricial," two words describing the degree of development in young birds at hatching, are good examples of *useful* scientific jargon. They save ornithologists from repeatedly using phrases when single words will do. A precocial bird is "capable of moving around on its own soon after hatching." The word comes from the same Latin root as "precocious." Altricial means "incapable of moving around on its own soon after hatching." It comes from a Latin root meaning "to nourish"—a reference to the need for extensive parental care required before fledging in altricial species. If you consult some of the literature we have cited, you may sometimes see the term "nidifugous" used to describe precocial young that leave the nest immediately, and "nidicolous" to describe young that remain in the nest. All nidifugous birds are precocial, but some nidicolous birds are precocial, too—they remain in the nest even though capable of locomotion. These terms are less widely used than precocial and altricial, and we will not employ them outside of this essay.

Instead of a sharp dividing line between hatchlings that are precocial and those that are altricial, there is a gradient of precociality. In this guide, we recognize the following categories of young:

Precocial: Hatched with eyes open, covered with down, and leave the nest within two days. There are four levels of precociality, although only three are found in North American birds. Level 1 of development (precocial 1) is the pattern found in the chicks of megapodes (Australian Malee fowl, Brush Turkeys, etc.), which are totally independent of their parents. The megapode young are incubated in huge piles of decaying vegetation, and upon hatching dig their way out, already well feathered and able to fly. No

Cassin's Sparrow

Aimophila cassinii Woodhouse

NG–396; G–336; PW–pl 57; AE–526; AW–553; AM(III)–226

SHRUB   ?   4   ?   I: ? DAYS
0'–1'   (3–5)   ALTRICIAL
                     MONOG ?   F: ? DAYS
                                  MF

BREEDING: Grassland, shortgrass prairie with scattered bushes, mesquite, cactus, or yucca. ? broods. **DISPLAYS**: Male flight song initiated from elevated perch, rather than from ground. Male descends in floating fashion, with head up, tail spread, and legs stretched downward; usu flies 15'–30', rarely returns to same perch from which he started. Male displays toward female with elevated, spread tail, head held down and wings held outward while fluttering wings and tail. **NEST**: Built of forbs, grass, occ flowers, lined with fine grass, rootlets, hair. **EGGS**: White, unmarked. 0.8" (19 mm). **DIET**: Insects during breeding season; grass and forb seeds during rest of year. **CONSERVATION**: Winters s to n w and e c Mexico. Uncommon cowbird host. **NOTES**: Male territorial song delivered from perch, and in flight if another male enters his territory. Reported to sing at night. Apparently does not require drinking water. Details of breeding biology largely unknown. **ESSAYS**: Drinking, p. 123; Vocal Functions, p. 471; Bills, p. 209; Diet and Nutrition, p. 587; Territoriality, p. 387. **REF**: Bent, 1968.

Rufous-winged Sparrow

Aimophila carpalis Coues

NG–398; G–336; PW–pl 57; AW–554; AM(III)–228

CACTUS   F   4   F   SEEDS   HAWKS
0.5'–7'   (2–5)   I: ? DAYS
                   MONOG ?   ALTRICIAL
                             F: 8–9 DAYS
                             MF

BREEDING: Flat, open areas with scattered thorny brush and mixed bunchgrass. 2 broods. **DISPLAYS**: Courting pair perform billing, but unclear if courtship feeding involved. **NEST**: Materials vary with habitat; of forbs, grass, twigs, bark, lined with fine materials. **EGGS**: Pale bluish-white, unmarked. 0.8" (19 mm). **DIET**: Mostly insects; some grass and forb seeds. **CONSERVATION**: Winter resident. Uncommon cowbird host. Overgrazing has caused loss of preferred habitat and shift into previously marginal habitats. **NOTES**: Breeding triggered by an ill-defined combination of unpredictable rainfall and high temperatures. Numbers fluctuate greatly from year to year. Female not easily flushed from nest. Fledglings dependent on parents for 3–4 weeks; last brood stays with parents through autumn and possibly winter. Does not form flocks. In winter, small groups assoc with flocks of Black-throated, Chipping, and Brewer's Sparrows. Natural history not well known. **ESSAYS**: Breeding Season, p. 55; Mixed-Species Flocking, p. 433; Population Dynamics, p. 575; Habitat Selection, p. 463; Parental Care, p. 555; How Do We Find Out About Bird Biology?, p. 319. **REFS**: Austin and Ricklefs, 1977; Phillips et al., 1964.

North American birds show this extreme precociality. Precocial 2 development is found in ducklings and the chicks of shorebirds, which follow their parents but find their own food. The young of game birds, however, trail after their parents and are shown food; they are classified as precocial 3. Precocial 4 development is represented by the young of birds such as rails and grebes, which follow their parents and are not just shown food but are actually fed by them.

Semiprecocial: Hatched with eyes open, covered with down, and capable of leaving the nest soon after hatching (they can walk and often swim), but stay at the nest and are fed by parents. Basically precocial but nidicolous, this developmental pattern is found in the young of gulls and terns.

Semialtricial: Covered with down, incapable of departing from the nest, and fed by the parents. In species classified as semialtricial 1, such as hawks and herons, chicks hatch with their eyes open. Owls, in the category semialtricial 2, hatch with the eyes closed. If all young were divided into only two categories, altricial and precocial, these all would be considered altricial.

Altricial: Hatched with eyes closed, with little or no down, incapable of departing from the nest, and fed by the parents. All passerines are altricial.

Note that in the species treatments in this book we use the term "fledging" (F:) for the number of days it takes for the young of an altricial or semi-altricial bird to acquire its full set of feathers, after which it leaves the nest. Thus for altricial and semialtricial birds, the time needed to get fully feathered and time spent in the nest are essentially the same. In precocial and semiprecocial birds, F: indicates *not* the number of days that pass before the young leave the nest, but the time from hatching until they can fly.

Why have these different modes of development evolved? They are

Left: House Sparrow hatchling (altricial—naked, blind and helpless on hatching). Right: Ruffed Grouse hatchling (precocial 3—downy, open-eyed, mobile on hatching, follows parents and is shown food).

Rufous-crowned Sparrow

Aimophila ruficeps Cassin

NG–398; G–336; PE–280; PW–pl 58; AW–pl 591; AM(III)–228

SHRUB	?	3–4	? I: ? DAYS ALTRICIAL	SEEDS	FOLIAGE
0'–2.5'		(2–5)	F: ? DAYS		GLEAN
(To 25')		MONOG ?	MF		

BREEDING: Dry, rocky slopes with scattered scrub and patches of grass and forbs. 1, possibly 2 broods. **DISPLAYS:** Squealing "pair-reunion duet" given when male and female meet within their territory (similar to Brown Towhee display). **NEST:** In shallow depression, rim flush with ground surface, occ in shrub (esp in e portion of range); of grass, twigs, forbs, bark, lined with fine grass, hair. **EGGS:** Pale bluish-white, unmarked. 0.8" (20 mm). **DIET:** Also young grass and forb shoots. **CONSERVATION:** Winter resident except n e populations. **NOTES:** Territories tend to be clumped. Female is close sitter on nest. Female distraction display: flutters wings feigning injury. Song said to resemble Lazuli Bunting's. Postbreeding family groups of up to 6 are seen. Details of breeding biology not well known. Does not flock in winter. **ESSAYS:** Distraction Displays, p. 115; Bird Guilds, p. 493; Diet and Nutrition, p. 587; How Do We Find Out About Bird Biology?, p. 319. **REF:** Bent, 1968.

American Tree Sparrow

Spizella arborea Wilson

NG–398; G–338; PE–280; PW–pl 58; AE–pl 531; AW–pl 589; AM(III)–230

SHRUB	F	3–5	F I: 12–13 DAYS ALTRICIAL	SEEDS	FOLIAGE
0'–5'		(3–7)	F: 8–10 DAYS	BUDS	GLEAN
		MONOG?	MF		

BREEDING: Open areas with scattered trees, brush, along tundra edge. 1 brood. **DISPLAYS:** Courting male puffs out plumage, spreads wings, flutters rapidly. **NEST:** Usu on ground in grass tussock or shallow depression, rarely in shrub, low tree; compact, of grass, rootlets, moss, forbs, inner bark, lined with feathers or fur. **EGGS:** Pale bluish- or greenish-white, marked with browns, blacks. 0.8" (19 mm). **DIET:** Incl few spiders; seeds of grass, sedge, forbs, buds and catkins of willows and birches, few berries. Young fed nearly 100% insects; initially, parents masticate food for nestlings. **CONSERVATION:** Winters within N.A. **NOTES:** Female broods and is a close sitter. Drinks and bathes in water, eats snow. Roosts individually in shelters on ground or in conif trees (winter). Winter flocks loosely defined, with apparent flock territory and social hierarchy. Males tend to winter farther n than females. **ESSAYS:** Dominance Hierarchies, p. 533; Drinking, p. 123; Bathing and Dusting, p. 429; Migration, p. 183. **REF:** Bent, 1968.

CHARACTERISTICS OF NESTLINGS
(modified from O'Connor, 1984)

TYPE OF DEVELOPMENT	DOWN PRESENT?	EYES OPEN?	MOBILE?	FEED SELVES?	PARENTS ABSENT?	EXAMPLES
Precocial 1	Yes	Yes	Yes	Yes	Yes	Megapodes
Precocial 2	Yes	Yes	Yes	Yes*	No	Ducks, Plovers
Precocial 3	Yes	Yes	Yes	Yes†	No	Quail, Turkey
Precocial 4	Yes	Yes	Yes	Yes/No	No	Grebes, Rails
Semiprecocial	Yes	Yes	Yes/No	No	No	Gulls, Terns
Semialtricial 1	Yes	Yes	No	No	No	Herons, Hawks
Semialtricial 2	Yes	No	No	No	No	Owls
Altricial	No	No	No	No	No	Passerines

* = Precocial 2 follow parents but find own food.
† = Precocial 3 are shown food.

obviously tied into two important aspects of the bird's environment: food availability and predation pressure. Precociality puts a premium on the ability of females to obtain abundant resources before laying. They must produce energy-rich eggs to support the greater in-egg development of the chicks (eggs of precocial birds may contain almost twice the calories per unit weight as those of altricial birds). Females of altricial species do not have such large nutritional demands before egg laying, but must be able (with their mates) to find sufficient food to rush their helpless young through to fledging. While the young are in the nest, the entire brood is extremely vulnerable to predation and is dependent on concealment of the nest and parental defense for survival. In contrast, precocial young, having left the nest, have some ability to avoid predation, and there is a much smaller chance of the entire brood (as opposed to single chicks) being devoured.

Interestingly, there seems to be an evolutionary trade-off in bird brain sizes related to the degree of precocity. Precocial species have relatively large brains at hatching—as one might expect since the young, to one degree or another, must be able to fend for themselves. But precocial species trade for this advantage an adult brain that is small in relation to their body size. Altricial young, in contrast, are born small-brained, but on the protein-rich diet provided by the adults (and with their highly efficient digestive tracts) postnatal brain growth is great, and the adults have proportionally larger brains than precocial species.

Parrots have evolved their way into the best of both worlds. They are altricial, but the female invests in a nutrient-rich egg just like females of precocial species. Parrots are among the most intelligent of birds; they have adopted the same evolutionary strategy as we have. People (like other primates, elephants, and antelopes, but unlike rodents and marsupials) are

Field Sparrow

Spizella pusilla Wilson

NG–398; G–338; PE–280; PW–pl 58; AE–pl 532; AM(III)–236

			F		
			I: 12 (10–17) DAYS		
SAPLING	F	3–5 (2–6)	ALTRICIAL	SEEDS	FOLIAGE
SHRUB		MONOG	F: 7–8 DAYS		GLEAN
0'–2.5'		(POLYGYN?)	MF		

BREEDING: Old fields, brush, decid forest edge, thorn scrub. 2, occ 3 broods. **DISPLAYS**: ? **NEST**: Also occ in vine tangle. Built of grass, forbs, lined with fine materials. Female selects site; usu built in 4–5 days, later nests 2–3 days, located higher. **EGGS**: Creamy, pale greenish-bluish white, marked with browns, occ wreathed. 0.7" (18 mm). **DIET**: Incl few spiders; seeds of forbs and grass. Nestlings fed 100% insects, spiders. **CONSERVATION**: Winters mostly within U.S. Frequent cowbird host; when cowbird seen, ceases work on nest until cowbird leaves. **NOTES**: In n, older males arrive first, followed by younger males, later by females. Older males return to previous territories. Male song decreases markedly upon pairing. Male occ feeds incubating female; female does most of brooding. Later clutches smaller. Male does most of feeding of young while female begins second nest. Occ forages in low foliage within 3' of ground. Young from initial nests move in flocks of 10–12, tolerated by territorial males. Postbreeding flocks of >100 roost in small trees, shrubs, prior to migration. Small flocks in winter occ with Chipping, other related sparrows. **ESSAYS**: Island Biogeography, p. 549; Vocal Functions, p. 471; Site Tenacity, p. 189; Cowbirds, p. 619; Variation in Clutch Sizes, p. 339; Mixed-Species Flocking, p. 433. **REFS**: Best, 1977, 1978; Evans, 1978.

Chipping Sparrow

Spizella passerina Bechstein

NG–400; G–338; PE–280; PW–pl 58; AE–pl 530; AW–pl 590; AM(III)–232

			F		
			I: 11–14 DAYS		
DECID	F	4 (2–5)	ALTRICIAL	SEEDS	FOLIAGE
0'–11'		MONOG	F: 10 (8–12) DAYS		GLEAN
(To 60')		(POLYGYN)	MF		HAWKS

BREEDING: Open conif forest, forest edge, oak and pine-oak woodland, thickets, parks. 2 broods. **DISPLAYS**: ? **NEST**: Also in vine tangle and rarely on ground; compact, of grass, forb stalks, rootlets, lined with hair or fur. **EGGS**: Bluish-green, marked with dark browns, blacks, oft wreathed. 0.7" (18 mm). **DIET**: Incl few spiders; seeds of grass and forbs. Can subsist on dry seeds without drinking for up to 3 weeks. **CONSERVATION**: Winters s throughout Mexico. Frequent cowbird host. **NOTES**: Polygyny occurs in ca. 5% of population; males advertise for additional female during first 5 days of incubation when male is free of other obligations, but very few females are available then. Female does most of brooding; close sitter. Male occ feeds incubating female. Male known to sing at night. Later clutches smaller. Oft feeds in low foliage and in trees. Wanders in family groups after breeding, prior to migration; in w, oft drifts upslope. In winter, may forage in small flocks of 25–50 birds, occ with Field Sparrows and juncos. **ESSAYS**: Nest Materials, p. 369; Polygyny, p. 433; Variation in Clutch Sizes, p. 339; Cowbirds, p. 619; Drinking, p. 123; Mixed-Species Flocking, p. 433. **REFS**: Allaire and Fisher, 1975; Buech, 1982; Dawson et al., 1979; Hebrard, 1978.

precocial—born with hair, open eyes, and large brains. But our brains and those of parrots, both large at birth, also grow a great deal after birth as a result of large parental investments of food energy.

Thus a complex evolutionary problem of balancing the need to provide nourishment to the young and to protect them from predation has been "solved" by each group of birds—and the solutions are the different avian developmental patterns we now observe. Similar problems have been solved, also in diverse ways, in the course of mammalian evolution. But many more groups of mammals than birds have managed to become big-brained as both young and adults.

SEE: Parental Care, p. 555; Hatching, p. 233; Life in the Egg, p. 457; Bird-Brained, p. 415. REFS: Ar and Yom-Tov, 1979; Bennett and Harvey, 1985; O'Connor, 1984; Ricklefs, 1984.

Diet and Nutrition

Birds eat many things that seem none-too-appealing to us: beetles, flies, spiders, earthworms, rotting fish, offal, poison oak berries, weed seeds, and so on. Not only that, most birds have diets that are quite monotonous—some passerines may go for weeks on a diet composed largely of grasshoppers, Brants dine almost exclusively on eelgrass, and Snail Kites rarely if ever taste anything but snails. In spite of this, the nutritional requirements of birds are not very different from ours; they need proteins, fats, carbohydrates, vitamins, and minerals.

Carbohydrates and fats are used primarily as energy sources, but proteins—more specifically the nitrogen-containing amino acids that are the building blocks of proteins—are needed for construction of tissues, enzymes, and so on. Reproduction, growth, and molting all require more nitrogen than simple maintenance of the body, and proteins are the source of that nitrogen. Birds, such as Red-winged Blackbirds, that are omnivorous (eating both plant and animal food) increase the proportion of protein-rich animal food they eat in the breeding season. Many that are herbivorous (primarily eating plant foods), such as sparrows, may subsist for much of the year on a relatively low-protein vegetable diet, but in the breeding season they take as many insects as possible, and often provide their young with a diet comprised entirely of insects.

Similarly, wood warblers, which are considered carnivorous (dining mostly on animal food), will feed themselves and their young virtually exclusively on insects in the breeding season. Like many thrushes and other more omnivorous species, they may have berries and other plant foods as a substantial portion of their fall-winter intake. And nectarivores, such as hummingbirds, must also catch insects to provide protein to balance their energy-rich but nitrogen-poor intake of nectar, especially when breeding. It

Clay-colored Sparrow

Spizella pallida Swainson

NG–400; G–338; PE–282; PW–pl 58; AE–pl 535; AW–pl 578; AM(III)–234

GROUND	F	3–4	F –M I: 10–12 DAYS ALTRICIAL	SEEDS	
0'–2'		(3–5)	F: 8–9 DAYS		
(To 4.5')		MONOG	MF		

BREEDING: Thickets, esp near water, forest openings, fields with scattered shrubs. Oft 2 broods. **DISPLAYS:** Billing in courtship. **NEST:** In grass tuft, at base of herb or shrub, on low branch of shrub or small tree; compact, of grass, forb stalks, twigs, rootlets, lined with fine materials. Built in 2–4 days. Later nests oft higher. Tendency to select one type of nest site within a local population. **EGGS:** Bluish-green, marked with dark browns, blacks, oft wreathed. 0.7" (17 mm). **DIET:** Incl forb and grass seeds, also catkins, decid tree buds in spring. **CONSERVATION:** Winters s in highlands to c Mexico. Common cowbird host; parasitized nests occ deserted. Breeding range extended e and n since 1900 as suitable habitat was created by lumbering. **NOTES:** Males arrive on breeding grounds shortly before females; territories rather small (<acre), vigorously defended by male; reportedly excludes Chipping and Song Sparrows. Female does most of brooding; close sitter. Male occ feeds incubating female. Adult (female?) distraction display: drags wings, moves slowly, and calls. Small postbreeding flocks prior to migration. Winter flocks occ with Brewer's and White-crowned Sparrows in open weedy or brushy habitats. **ESSAYS:** Territoriality, p. 387; Cowbirds, p. 619; Distraction Displays, p. 115; Range Expansion, p. 459. **REFS:** Buech, 1982; Knapton, 1978.

Brewer's Sparrow

Spizella breweri Cassin

NG–400; G–338; PW–pl 58; AW–pl 600; AM(III)–236

0'–4'	?	3–4	? I: 11–13 DAYS ALTRICIAL	SEEDS	
		(3–5)	F: 8–9 DAYS		
		MONOG?	?		

BREEDING: Arid brushland; low thickets at high elevations and latitudes. ? broods. **DISPLAYS:** ? **NEST:** In shrub or low tree; of grass, rootlets, forbs, lined with fine materials. **EGGS:** Bluish-green, marked with dark browns. 0.7" (17 mm). **DIET:** Incl few spiders; seeds of forbs and grass. Can tolerate diet of dry seeds without water for up to 3 weeks. **CONSERVATION:** Winters s through highlands to c Mexico. Uncommon cowbird host. **NOTES:** Close sitter on nest. Oft drops from nest and runs rather than flies. Fond of bathing in water. Oft drifts upslope after nesting. Winter flocks with White-crowned, Black-throated, and other sparrows in brushland and desert scrub. **ESSAYS:** Mixed-Species Flocking, p. 433; Bird Guilds, p. 493; Bathing and Dusting, p. 429; Drinking, p. 123. **REFS:** Dawson et al., 1979; Petersen et al., 1986; Reynolds, 1981; Wiens et al., 1986.

is, of course, no miracle that protein-rich food sources just happen to be more abundant during the breeding season. Just the reverse—evolution has timed the breeding season so that it occurs when the needed nitrogen can be obtained.

Birds' mineral requirements seem much like ours. Calcium, which is needed in large quantities for egg production, is a critical mineral nutrient for reproductively active female birds. It is thought that shortage of calcium may restrict the reproductive output of vultures, which devour only the soft, calcium-poor parts of carcasses. This may be the reason that some African vultures, as well as our Black and Turkey Vultures, supplement their diets with small vertebrate prey that can be swallowed whole. Calcium, is of course, also critical for reproductively active female human beings, who must produce large amounts of calcium-rich milk. Avian needs for vitamins are also similar to the human requirements. Unlike us, however, many birds manufacture vitamin C in their kidneys or liver, or in both.

As with human beings, what birds eat is determined by more than their brute nutritional requirements. Various kinds of learning play an important role. For instance, once a bird has discovered a certain kind of palatable prey, it may form a "search image" for that prey and specialize for a time in eating it. Experiments also indicate that a bird's feeding preferences can be influenced by its diet as a nestling. The best-documented learning pattern in birds is the speed with which Blue Jays learn to avoid foods that make them sick. Many monarch butterflies contain heart poisons, cardiac glycosides, which they obtain as caterpillars from the milkweed plants they feed on. A jay that has never seen such a monarch before will eat it and then suffer a bout of vomiting brought on by the glycosides. Subsequently the bird will not touch a monarch butterfly or even a viceroy butterfly, which closely mimics the monarch. Here again bird behavior is much like human behavior. A person who gets violently ill soon after eating a particular food may be unable to stomach that food again, even if he or she knows that the sickness was caused, not by food, but by a virus. Nausea is a powerful teacher for both mammals and birds.

Changing availability of different kinds of food can also be a crucial factor in what is eaten. Many birds will opportunistically switch to a new food source that suddenly becomes abundant. The immortalized sea gulls that saved the Mormons' crops from a locust plague did that; when seventeen-year cicada ("locust") broods emerge, many birds switch from whatever they have been eating to gorge on cicadas. Hobbies (Eurasian falcons that look like small Peregrines) are reported to catch and eat more swifts in cool cloudy weather than in warm sunny weather. Apparently the lack of insects in the gloom weakens the swifts, making them easier prey for the Hobbies.

SEE: Breeding Season, p. 55; Feeding Young Petrels, p. 15; Hummingbirds, Nectar, and Water, p. 333; Hoarding Food, p. 345; Drinking, p. 123; Swallowing Stones, p. 269.

Black-chinned Sparrow

Spizella atrogularis Cabanis

NG–402; G–338; PW–pl 58; AW–pl 601; AM(III)–238

1.5′–3′	?	2–4 (2–5) MONOG?	? I: 13? DAYS ALTRICIAL F: ? DAYS MF	SEEDS	FOLIAGE GLEAN

BREEDING: Chaparral, sagebrush, arid scrub, and brushy slopes. ? broods. **DISPLAYS:** ? **NEST:** Oft in sagebrush; of grass, lined with fine materials. **EGGS:** Pale blue, marked with dark browns or unmarked. 0.7″ (18 mm). **DIET:** Insects; seeds. **CONSERVATION:** Winters s to s Mexico. Uncommon cowbird host. **NOTES:** Female is close sitter on nest. Little known of ecology and behavior. **ESSAYS:** Bills, p. 209; Diet and Nutrition, p. 587; How Do We Find Out About Bird Biology?, p. 319. **REF:** Bent, 1968.

Dark-eyed Junco

Junco hyemalis Linnaeus

NG–402; G–334; PE–266; PW–pl 56; AE–pl 429; AW–pl 483; AM(III)–272

BANK (To 20′)	CAVITY F–M	3–5 (3–6) MONOG ?	F I: 12–13 DAYS ALTRICIAL F: 9–13 DAYS MF	INSECTS	HAWKS

BREEDING: Conif and decid forest and edge, open woodland, bogs. 2 broods, occ 3 in s, 1 at higher elevation and latitude. **DISPLAYS:** Courting pair hop with wings drooped, tail fanned displaying white outer feathers; from low perch male droops wings, spreads and droops tail, sings softly. **NEST:** Usu in shallow depression with overhead protection, oft against vertical surface; rarely in shrub, tree, or building; of coarse grass, moss, rootlets, forbs, bark, twigs, lined with fine materials. **EGGS:** White to pale bluish-white, marked with reddish-browns, oft wreathed. 0.8″ (19 mm). **DIET:** Incl few spiders; wide variety of seeds. Nestlings fed 100% insects, initially partly regurgitated. **CONSERVATION:** Winters s to n Mexico. Uncommon cowbird host. **NOTES:** Territorial conflict uncommon. Female broods nestlings. Later clutches smaller. Rapid tarsal development enables nestlings to run from nest if threatened before they can fly. Foraging flocks occ with chickadees, bushtits, nuthatches, kinglets, sparrows, in spring and fall. Roosts in conif trees, old nests, rock crevices, on ground. Winter flocks of 10–30 with definite social ranking and mutually exclusive foraging territories. Males tend to winter farther n than females. Several races, formerly regarded as species, now combined in Dark-eyed Junco: Slate-colored, Oregon, White-winged, Gray-headed, and Guadalupe Junco. **ESSAYS:** Eye Color, p. 233; Walking vs. Hopping, p. 69; Birds and the Law, p. 293; Dominance Hierarchies, p. 533; Taxonomy and Nomenclature, p. 515. **REFS:** Balph, 1979; Ketterson and Nolan, 1982; Smith and Andersen, 1982.

Bird Badges

Bulging muscles and jeweled adornments are nonarbitrary symbols in human society, denoting strength and wealth, respectively. On the other hand, many arbitrary symbols—the bishop's mitre, the admiral's gold braid, the karate master's black belt, the judge's gown, the knight's title of "Sir"—are also recognized. Such symbols are arbitrary because they signal status without having any inherent connection with the status signaled.

Nonarbitrary status symbols are readily found in nonhuman animals, the classic example being the size of horns in mountain sheep. In those creatures a small-horned male will avoid a large-horned stranger seen at a distance, even though the two have never determined their relative positions in a dominance hierarchy by actual combat. The existence of arbitrary symbols outside of human society has been more problematic. British evolutionists Richard Dawkins and John Krebs adopted the term "badge" for arbitrary animal symbols, and avian biologists, especially Sievert Rohwer, have carried out investigations to see if badges play a role in dominance relationships in bird flocks.

Harris' Sparrows assemble in flocks of mixed ages in the winter. Individuals within the flocks show a great deal of variation in their plumage characteristics, especially in the amount of darkness on their heads and "bibs." In a series of experiments Rohwer darkened relatively light first-year birds with dye to make them look like adults. He found, for example, that dyed first-year birds are initially avoided by undyed "control" first-year birds. Then the dyed birds began actively to dominate the controls. Rohwer thus concluded that the dominance status of a Harris' Sparrow can be communicated by a badge, a dark head and bib. The alternate explanation (that the dye in some way actually enhanced the combat ability of dyed birds) is too unlikely to merit serious consideration.

Differences in darkness do not, however, always correlate with status, as behaviorist Doris Watt has shown. In experiments Watt showed that within age classes, at least in small groups, darker birds are not always dominant over lighter individuals. She believes the darkness to be basically a badge of age, which signals to first-year birds the potential dominance of adults. Apparently among both young and adults, variation in breast spot patterns (as opposed to overall breast darkness) aids individuals in recognizing one another, but does not indicate status.

Status signals may allow associations to form between dominant and subordinate individuals so that both may benefit, as Rohwer and his colleague, Paul Ewald, have suggested. Subordinates, for instance, may learn what foods are most nutritious, while dominants may be able to place subordinates between themselves and potential predators.

Badges also exist in White-crowned Sparrows, as Gary Fugle and his coworkers at the University of California have demonstrated. Adult males, which have bright black and white striping on the head, have the highest dominance status, juvenile females with dull striping the lowest, and adult

Yellow-eyed Junco

Junco phaeonotus Wagler

NG–402; G–334; PE–266; PW–pl 56; AW–pl 479; AM(III)–274

| SHRUB TREE (To 15') | CAVITY F –M | 3–4 (3–5) MONOG? | F I: 15 DAYS ALTRICIAL F: 10 DAYS MF | SEEDS | FOLIAGE GLEAN |

BREEDING: Open conif forest, pine-oak forest, brush, fields. 2–3 broods. **DISPLAYS:** On ground or from perch, courting male struts with spread tail, alternately dragged and held upright, and sings softly. **NEST:** Usu in shallow depression with overhead protection; of coarse grass, moss, lined with fine materials. **EGGS:** Pale bluish-grayish white, marked with reddish-browns, usu wreathed. 0.8" (20 mm). **DIET:** Also occ flowers and fruits of forbs. **CONSERVATION:** Winter resident, moves to lower elevations during severe weather. **NOTES:** Unlike Dark-eyed Junco, territorial conflicts common; males frequently engage in tenacious fights with locked bills and flailing feet. Fledglings do not fly well until ca. 6 days postfledging. Parents evict offspring from breeding territory at 22–28 days postfledging, whereupon young form juvenile flocks of up to 40 birds; at end of breeding season adults combine with juveniles to form fall flocks before moving to lower elevations. Walks with characteristic shuffle. **ESSAYS:** Walking vs. Hopping, p. 69; Territoriality, p. 387; How Do We Find Out About Bird Biology?, p. 319. **REF:** Sullivan, 1988.

Harris' Sparrow

Zonotrichia querula Nuttall

NG–404; G–340; PE–278; PW–pl 58; AE–pl 529; AW–pl 594; AM(III)–270

| | | ? 4–5 (3–5) MONOG? | ? I: 13–14 DAYS ALTRICIAL F: ? DAYS ? | SEEDS BERRIES | FOLIAGE GLEAN |

BREEDING: Stunted trees and shrubs in conif forest–tundra ecotone. 1 brood. **DISPLAYS:** Social dominance in winter flocks signaled visually by extent of black feathering on throat and crown, which is under hormonal control. **NEST:** Sunken into ground beneath low woody veg or in mossy hummock among stunted trees; of grass, coarse rootlets, lined with finer grass. **EGGS:** White, greenish-white, marked with browns. 0.9" (22 mm). **DIET:** Incl spiders, few snails; forb, grass, sedge, and rush seeds. **CONSERVATION:** Winters within N.A. **NOTES:** When alarmed, flies up, rather than seeking cover in low-growing veg. Details of breeding biology largely unknown. Forms winter flocks. Strong site attachment to wintering territory. **ESSAYS:** Bird Badges, p. 591; Dominance Hierarchies, p. 533; Site Tenacity, p. 189; How Do We Find Out About Bird Biology?, p. 319. **REF:** Rohwer and Rohwer, 1978.

females with intermediate striping intermediate status. Experiments in which the heads of juvenile and adult females were painted to resemble adult males revealed that brighter striping added to the status of the painted birds relative to unpainted controls. Similarly, experiments with stuffed birds (mounts) indicate that a male Yellow Warbler signals his status, in particular his level of aggressive motivation, by the amount of brown streaking on his breast. Brighter (more streaked) mounts, elicited more aggressive responses from males than duller mounts, while brighter males responded more aggressively to mounts than did duller males.

Perhaps the most ingenious experiment on avian badges involved the European Great Tit, a close relative of North American chickadees and titmice (all are members of the same genus, *Parus*). This species has a dark cap, white cheeks, and a dark breast stripe/bib. Torbjorn Järvi and Marten Bakken of Norway's University of Trondheim used radio-controlled motorized stuffed birds at a feeder to test the efficacy of the breast stripe as a badge. When a Great Tit approached the feeder, the stuffed bird could be rotated to face the incoming individual and to perform a "head-up" aggressive display. When, and only when, the stuffed bird had a breast stripe wider than that of the incoming bird was the latter frightened away.

Evidently badges can signal status in avian societies—but this presents evolutionists with a considerable mystery. Since they are arbitrary symbols, why isn't cheating widespread? Why don't first-year Harris' Sparrows grow dark plumage just like adults? Why don't weakling Great Tits develop broad breast stripes and monopolize the food at feeders? Badge systems seem to have built into them the seeds of their own evolutionary destruction, since frequent cheating should soon make all the signals ambiguous.

One way out of this seeming dilemma has been suggested. Perhaps dominance in monogamous birds (as opposed to polygynous ones, where dominant males may get many more matings) does not in itself confer a selective advantage. Subordinate birds may not get access to the best resources, but they also may not have to expend much energy defending what they've got. Being subordinate may be just as good an evolutionary strategy as being dominant—both kinds of individual may be equally successful reproductively. If that is the case, there would be no advantage to cheating, and one would not expect such behavior to evolve.

SEE: Redwing Coverable Badges, p. 611; Visual Displays, p. 5; Sexual Selection, p. 251; Dominance Hierarchies, p. 533; Geometry of the Selfish Colony, p. 19. REFS: Fugle et al., 1984; Järvi and Bakken, 1984; Rohwer, 1985; Rohwer and Ewald, 1981; Roper, 1986; Studd and Robertson, 1985a; Watt, 1986.

Golden-crowned Sparrow
Zonotrichia atricapilla Gmelin

NG–404; G–340; PE–278; PW–pl 58; AW–pl 588; AM(III)–268

TREE	?	3–5	F?	SEEDS	
0'–2.5'		MONOG ?	I: ? DAYS	BERRIES	
			ALTRICIAL		
			F: ? DAYS		
			MF		

BREEDING: Montane thickets and shrubs, dwarf conifs, brushy canyons. 1? brood. **DISPLAYS**: ? **NEST**: Usu sunk in ground at base of small tree or on horizontal branch of low tree; bulky, of grass, leaves, twigs, bark, moss, lined with fine grass, feathers, fur. **EGGS**: Creamy or pale bluish-white, marked with reddish-browns. 0.9″ (23 mm). **DIET**: Nestlings probably fed 100% insects. In winter, buds, flowers, fresh seedlings (esp of annuals), seeds. **CONSERVATION**: Winters s to n Baja. **NOTES**: Male feeds incubating female. Details of breeding biology largely unknown. Stable winter flocks, oft with White-crowned Sparrows, show site attachment to wintering territory. **ESSAYS**: Adaptations for Flight, p. 507; Site Tenacity, p. 189; Mixed-Species Flocking, p. 433; How Do We Find Out About Bird Biology?, p. 319. **REF**: Pearson, 1979.

White-crowned Sparrow
Zonotrichia leucophrys Forster

NG–404; G–340; PE–278; PW–pl 58; AE–pl 540; AW–pl 586; AM(III)–268

GROUND	F	3–5 (2–6)	F	SEEDS	FOLIAGE
1'–5'		MONOG	I: 12 (11–14) DAYS	BERRIES	GLEAN
(0'–35')		(POLYGYN)	ALTRICIAL		HAWKS
			F: 7–12 DAYS		
			MF		

BREEDING: Stunted woody veg, coastal scrub, wet meadows, thickets, chaparral, gardens, parks. 2–3, occ 4 broods, 1 in far n. **DISPLAYS**: Courtship: female flutters wings and trills. **NEST**: Built of grass, twigs, rootlets, forbs, leaves, shredded bark, lined with fine materials. Built in 2–9 days. Female chooses site. **EGGS**: Pale greenish-blue, creamy white, marked with reddish-browns. 0.8″ (21 mm). **DIET**: Incl spiders; forb and grass seeds, fruit, moss capsules, blossoms, fresh leaves. **CONSERVATION**: Winters s to c Mexico. Uncommon cowbird host. **NOTES**: In nonmigratory populations, pair may stay on territory all year and pair for life. Polygynous females may show antagonism (even singing) toward each other and divide up their male's territory. In far n, males arrive 2–3 weeks before females. Female broods; mouse-runs off ground nest if disturbed. Young usu fed only by female for first 3–4 days; fledge at earlier age in far n. Male assumes most of feeding while female begins second nest. Interval between fledging first brood and laying first egg of second clutch varies from 9–20 days. Male oft sings at night. Stable winter flocks of 10–50 show strong site attachment to wintering territory. Females tend to winter farther s than males. **ESSAYS**: Bird Badges, p. 591; Vocal Development, p. 601; Vocal Dialects, p. 595; Polygyny, p. 443; Birds and the Law, p. 293; Site Tenacity, p. 189; Distraction Displays, p. 115. **REFS**: King and Hubbard, 1981; Morton et al., 1972; Petrinovich and Patterson, 1983.

Vocal Dialects

Just as our speech patterns vary regionally, the songs of many avian species also show geographic variation. For example, in states and provinces east of the Mississippi, the songs of Rufous-sided Towhees consist of two introductory notes followed by a buzzy trill. Songs in the Rocky Mountain states begin with a single introductory note followed by the trill, and West Coast populations have dropped the introductory notes entirely—their songs are composed of just the buzzy trill. Although such geographic variation is quite evident to the human ear, we still recognize the singer as a Rufous-sided Towhee.

The songs of populations often differ markedly on a much smaller geographic scale. Local variants are called dialects. They are commonly found in songbirds with populations restricted to particular habitats and separated from other populations by unsuitable terrain. The separation can be on the order of a mile or so, but in some species it can be much less. Among the White-crowned Sparrow populations of coastal California, distint dialects may be separated by as little as a few yards in what appears to be essentially continuous habitat!

Vocal dialects appear to be learned. Young birds hear the songs sung around their natal territories by their fathers and neighboring males, and acquire the peculiarities of these renditions. Factors that determine the geographic pattern of dialects include the accuracy with which the pitch and temporal characteristics of individual song components are learned, the distance young males disperse from where they hatch to where they breed, and the timing of dispersal relative to the sensitive period for learning.

The "why" of dialects, their functional significance, has proven more elusive than the question of how they arise. Many ornithologists have assumed that dialects serve as indicators of genetic adaptation to local conditions. The dialects thus enable females to choose males from their own birth area, who presumably are carrying genes closely adapted to the specific environment in which breeding occurs. In other words, dialects function to promote "positive assortative mating"—the breeding together of similar individuals. Experimental work with several species has shown that females are more responsive to their own song dialects than to more distant song dialects. Genetic studies of White-crowned Sparrows along the coast of northern California have shown genetic differences between birds of different dialects.

But nature is rarely that straightforward. Additional work has shown that females of some species are more responsive to songs of males with dialects other than their own, so that the assumption that a female breeds within the dialect region in which she was hatched is not always warranted. In a series of experiments, paired female White-crowned Sparrows were captured on their territories and injected with the male hormone testosterone (to induce singing). Surprisingly, they sang the song of nearby dialects, rather than their own local dialect. Presumably this indicates that they had

White-throated Sparrow

Zonotrichia albicollis Gmelin

NG–404; G–340; PE–278; PW–pl 58; AE–pl 539; AW–pl 587; AM(III)–266

SHRUB	F	4–6	F I: 11–14 DAYS ALTRICIAL	SEEDS	FOLIAGE
(To 3')		(3–6) MONOG ?	F: 8–9 (7–12) DAYS MF	FRUIT	GLEAN HAWKS

BREEDING: Conif and mixed conif-decid forest, edge and clearings, thickets, open woodland. 1, occ 2 broods. **DISPLAYS:** Courtship: female flutters wings and trills. **NEST:** Usu at edge of clearing, well concealed; of coarse grass, wood chips, twigs, pine needles, rootlets, lined with fine materials. Female probably selects site. **EGGS:** Greenish-, bluish-, or creamy-white, marked with reddish-browns. 0.8" (21 mm). **DIET:** Incl few spiders, millipedes, snails; forb, grass and tree seeds. **CONSERVATION:** Winters s to n e Mexico. Uncommon cowbird host. **NOTES:** White-striped (WS) and tan-striped (TS) adults tend to mate with opposite-colored morphs; experiments show that male WS are more aggressive than male TS toward singing birds and that female WS sing, thus WS males likely drive off WS females and mate with TS females, which do not sing. Males tend to return to same breeding territory each year. Oft sing at night. Foraging behavior largely determined by proximity to cover. Immature and first-year females tend to winter farther s than adults; adult males tend to winter in n. Oft assoc with other sparrows in winter. Birds in winter flocks form stable dominance hierarchies. **ESSAYS:** Vocal Functions, p. 471; Dominance Hierarchies, p. 533; Migration, p. 183; Site Tenacity, p. 189. **REFS:** Atkinson and Ralph, 1980; Knapton et al., 1984; Schneider, 1984.

Fox Sparrow

Passerella iliaca Merrem

NG–406; G–342; PE–284; PW–pl 57; AE–pl 543; AW–pl 572; AM(III)–260

SHRUB	F?	2–5	F I: 12–14 DAYS ALTRICIAL	SEEDS
0'–3' (To 20')		MONOG ?	F: 9–11 DAYS MF	BERRIES

BREEDING: Conif or decid forest undergrowth, edge, woodland thickets, scrub, chaparral, riparian woodland, montane brushland. 2 broods. **DISPLAYS:** ? **NEST:** Rarely in tree. Built of grass, moss, lichen, rootlets, shredded bark, leaves, and, if above ground, twigs; lined with fine grass, rootlets, fur, feathers, and finely shredded bark. Earlier nests higher, perhaps due to presence of snow and snowmelt. **EGGS:** Pale green to greenish-white, marked with reddish-browns. 0.9" (23 mm). **DIET:** Incl few spiders, millipedes, buds. Nestlings likely fed 100% insects. **CONSERVATION:** Winters s to n Baja. Uncommon cowbird host. **NOTES:** Males on breeding territory occ pugnacious toward other species. Female broods. Adult known to give broken-wing display in defense of young fledglings. Average clutch in n is 4–5, in s 2–3. Male sings each song once until entire repertoire is sung, then starts over. **ESSAYS:** Vocal Functions, p. 471; Interspecific Territoriality, p. 385; Bills, p. 209; Variation in Clutch Sizes, p. 339; Distraction Displays, p. 115. **REFS:** Martin, 1979; Threlfall and Blacquiere, 1982; Zink, 1986.

chosen to mate with males from "foreign" dialects and had dispersed out of their native dialect region. In addition, reanalysis of the genetic data from the White-crowned Sparrow studies has demonstrated that the results may be attributable to other factors. The data could be interpreted as indicating that environments are as heterogeneous within a dialect region as they are between dialect areas. If so, one might expect to find as much genetic differentiation between groups living in dramatically different habitats within a dialect region as between different dialects.

Thus, the adaptive significance of dialects remains to be demonstrated. It may be that no selective force has acted to promote dialects. Instead, dialects may simply be "epiphenomena"—that have arisen simply as a consequence of vocal learning—and have no evolutionary significance.

SEE: Vocal Development, p. 601; Vocal Functions, p. 471; Vocal Copying, p. 469; Hybridization, p. 501. REFS: Kroodsma et al., 1985; Mundinger, 1982.

Monogamy

An estimated 90 percent of all bird species are monogamous. Monogamy is defined as one male mating with one female and forming a "pair bond." That bond may last for a single nesting (House Wrens), an entire breeding season (most bird species, including most passerines), several successive breeding seasons (observed in some pairs of American Robins, Tree Swallows, Mourning Doves, etc.), or life (albatrosses, petrels, swans, geese, eagles, and some owls and parrots).

Presumably monogamy evolved in situations where young have a much better chance of surviving if both parents cooperate in rearing them. Nonetheless, the amount of time and energy invested by monogamous male parents varies greatly. The Willow Ptarmigan male serves only as a sentinel watching for danger. The Eastern Bluebird male provides a site for the rearing of young (by defending a territory containing a nest cavity), but experimental removal of males has shown that they are not essential for successful brood-rearing. In some monogamous species, the male defends a territory in which his mate collects the food required by the offspring, but does not himself feed the nestlings. Levels of male parental investment are even higher in most passerines, where males feed brooding females and/or help to feed the young. In herons, egrets, some woodpeckers, and others, males not only provide food for the young but share in incubation as well. The ante is raised even further in such ground-nesting birds as geese, swans, gulls, terns, and shorebirds in which males also commonly place themselves in danger by vigorously defending the nest and young from predators.

The traditional view of why more or less permanent monogamous bonds are formed is changing, as interest has become focused on the parent-

Lincoln's Sparrow

Melospiza lincolnii Audubon

NG–406; G–342; PE–284; PW–pl 57; AE–pl 544; AW–pl 599; AM(III)–264

			F I: 12–14 DAYS ALTRICIAL F: 9–12 DAYS MF		
F	4–5 (3–6) MONOG?			SEEDS	

BREEDING: Bogs, wet meadows, riparian thickets mostly in n and montane areas. 1 brood, possibly 2. **DISPLAYS:** ? **NEST:** In grass tussock or sunk in shallow depression on sphagnum or moss; of grass or sedge, lined with fine grass, hair. **EGGS:** Pale green to greenish-white, marked with reddish-browns. 0.8" (19 mm). **DIET:** Incl few spiders, millipedes; grass and forb seeds. Nestlings likely fed 100% insects. **CONSERVATION:** Winters s to Honduras and El Salvador. Rare cowbird host. **NOTES:** Dominated by and may compete with Song Sparrows where breeding territories overlap. Male sings very little during incubation. Female leaves nest by mouse-running along ground when disturbed. Female performs broken-wing distraction display when flushed from nest containing young. Very unobtrusive in migration. **ESSAYS:** Bird Guilds, p. 493; Distraction Displays, p. 115; Territoriality, p. 387; Vocal Functions, p. 471. **REF:** Bent, 1968.

Swamp Sparrow

Melospiza georgiana Latham

NG–406; G–342; PE–280; PW–pl 58; AE–pl 541; AM(III)–264

GROUND 0'–5'	F	4–5 (3–6) MONOG ?	F I: 12–15 DAYS ALTRICIAL F: 11–13 DAYS MF (?)	SEEDS

BREEDING: Emergent veg around water, marsh, bog, wet meadow. 2 broods. **DISPLAYS:** ? **NEST:** In low bush, grass tussock, sedge, oft over water; bulky foundation of coarse grass, lined with fine grass. **EGGS:** Pale green to greenish-white, marked with reddish-browns. 0.8" (19 mm). **DIET:** Incl grass, forb, and sedge seeds. **CONSERVATION:** Winters s to c Mexico. Common cowbird host. **NOTES:** Male feeds female on nest. Female broods. Song learning occurs in first few months following hatching. Occ wades to feed. **ESSAYS:** Vocal Development, p. 601; Vocal Functions, p. 471; Cowbirds, p. 619. **REFS:** Kroodsma, 1982; Marler, 1984.

age of offspring reared by "monogamous" pairs. Increasingly, ornithologists and behavioral ecologists have come to view monogamy as part of a "mixed" reproductive strategy in which matings may occur outside the primary pair bond, but both members of the pair still contribute substantially only to the care and feeding of the young from their own nest. Some species are viewed as facultatively monogamous; that is, if released from certain environmental constraints, they would typically exhibit some other form of mating system such as polygyny (one male mating with more than one female) or promiscuity (mating without forming pair bonds). According to this view, for example, North American dabbling ducks are monogamous only because males are unable to monopolize more than one female. These ducks breed synchronously and their populations typically contain more males than females.

Two lines of evidence have contributed to the shift in viewpoint about the nature of monogamy. First, ecologist Yoram Yom-Tov showed intraspecific nest parasitism ("egg dumping" by females in nests other than their own) to be much more frequent than previously assumed. Consequently, females of birds as different as Common Goldeneyes, Cliff Swallows, and Savannah Sparrows may often incubate clutches containing one or more eggs laid by another female that may or may not have been sired by her mate. The parasitic female may be monogamous, but she is "stealing" parental investment from another pair. Therefore the situation is not one in which mated pairs rear only their own offspring, as traditional use of the term monogamy has implied.

Second, a few recent studies employing new techniques of genetic analysis have allowed investigators to determine whether one or both members of a pair are the parents of all of the nestlings or fledglings they are rearing. Investigations of cooperatively breeding Acorn Woodpeckers and "monogamous" Eastern Bluebirds demonstrate conclusively that clutches with mixed parentage (containing offspring of more than one female, more than one male, or both) are not infrequent, indicating some infidelity by either or both sexes and/or egg dumping by females. Because so few species have been investigated using this technique, the results of future analyses may lead to a further reevaluation of the evolutionary significance of monogamy. At the moment it is perhaps best simply to consider monogamy as a social pattern in which one male and one female associate during the breeding season, and not to make too many assumptions about fidelity or parentage.

SEE: Polygyny, p. 443; Polyandry, p. 133; Cooperative Breeding, p. 283; Promiscuity, 145; Leks, p. 259; Parasitized Ducks, p. 89. REFS: Gowaty and Mock, 1985; Weatherhead and Robertson, 1978; Yom-Tov, 1980.

Chestnut-collared Longspur

Calcarius ornatus Townsend

NG–408; G–344; PE–264; PW–pl 54; AE–pl 552; AW–pl 597; AM(III)–280

| F | 3–5
(3–6)
MONOG ? | F
I: 10–13 DAYS
ALTRICIAL
F: 9–14 DAYS
MF | SEEDS | |

BREEDING: Shortgrass prairie. 2 broods. **DISPLAYS:** Conspicuous flight song: male rises from ground on rapidly beating wings, circles and undulates at peak of ascent, glides down on rapidly beating wings. **NEST:** In shallow depression, rim flush with ground surface, usu well concealed under tuft or clump of grass; of dried grass, lined with fine grass, occ feathers, hair, rootlets. **EGGS:** Creamy white, marked with dark browns, black, occ wreathed. 0.8″ (19 mm). **DIET:** Incl spiders; grass, forb, and sedge seeds. Young fed 100% insects. **CONSERVATION:** Winters s to n c Mexico. Uncommon cowbird host. **NOTES:** As hatching approaches, female increasingly reluctant to flush from nest. Female performs distraction display by fluttering 2′–3′ into air in series of jumps with head held low and tail spread. Female broods. Hatching takes 1–2 days, resulting in smallest young dying before, or being left behind when, siblings fledge. Will regularly visit water, if available, to drink and bathe. Prefers denser, more vegetated prairie than McCown's Longspur. **ESSAYS:** Bathing and Dusting, p. 429; Distraction Displays, p. 115; Brood Reduction, p. 307. **REF:** Bent, 1968.

McCown's Longspur

Calcarius mccownii Lawrence

NG–408; G–344; PE–264; PW–pl 54; AE–pl 553; AW–pl 595; AM(III)–276

| F | 3–4
(3–6)
MONOG ? | F
I: 12 DAYS
ALTRICIAL
F: 10–12 DAYS
MF | INSECTS | |

BREEDING: Shortgrass prairie, stubble fields. 2? broods. **DISPLAYS:** Courting male circles female while singing, his near wing stretched upward showing bright white lining. Conspicuous flight song: male rises from ground to 20′–30′, glides down with wings outstretched and tail expanded. **NEST:** In shallow natural or scraped depression, occ in open, oft at base of grass, cactus; of coarse grass, occ with shredded bark, lichen, lined with fine grass, occ feathers. **EGGS:** White, grayish-white to olive, marked with browns, purple, gray. 0.8″ (20 mm). **DIET:** Incl grass and forb seeds. Young fed all or mostly insects. **CONSERVATION:** Winters s to n Mexico. Uncommon cowbird host. Breeding and, to a lesser extent, wintering range have strongly contracted this century; reasons unclear. **NOTES:** Female is close sitter, oft not flushing until practically stepped on. Female and male both brood. Commonly drinks at artificial sources of water. Prefers drier, more sparsely vegetated prairie than Chestnut-collared Longspur. Forms large winter flocks. **ESSAYS:** Drinking, p. 123; Diet and Nutrition, p. 587; Walking vs. Hopping, p. 69; Flock Defense, p. 235; Wintering and Conservation, p. 513. **REF:** Bent, 1968.

Vocal Development

With practice, most birders learn to identify many species by their characteristic calls and songs. What are the underlying mechanisms that lead to "standardized" repertoires for each species? Are these characteristic sounds learned or are they genetically determined and fixed without learning (innate)? Where learning is involved, when does it take place? And how does each species "know" which sounds are appropriate and should be learned? The answers to these questions are as varied as birds themselves and have long served as a focus of research by ornithologists, ethologists, and neurobiologists.

Most of this research has been concerned with song development in species of songbirds, but relatively few species have been examined in detail. Most songbirds must learn at least part of their song repertoire. What little we know of vocal development in nonpasserines indicates that calls of those species (Mallard, American Coot, Ring-billed and Franklin's Gulls, domestic chicken, and Ringed Turtledove) are innate rather than learned, and that precocial young tend to have larger, better-developed repertoires of calls than do altricial young. Two exceptions among non-passerines are hummingbirds and parrots, for which there is some evidence of vocal learning (there also is suggestive evidence for Greater Prairie-Chicken and Sharp-tailed Grouse). Studies of many groups have yet to be done.

The learning of songs is a gradual process that takes place over a period of weeks or months. Typically, a vague, jumbled "subsong" appears first which then gradually is transformed into a more structured, but still quite variable, "plastic song." The end point of this process is the production of a stable repertoire of "crystallized" songs. Much more material may be developed than is actually needed for the eventual crystallized repertoire, leading to a process of attrition as the mature song takes shape. Swamp Sparrows, for example, generate four to five times more song material during development than they eventually retain in the adult repertoire.

The most thorough studies of song development, pioneered by ethologists W. H. Thorpe and Peter Marler, involve detailed experimental procedures using birds that have been isolated in soundproof chambers as hatchlings or nestlings. The development of songs and calls can then be followed in these birds, which have been deprived of any chance to hear the normal song of their species. In most species that have been examined, the resulting songs bear only a slight resemblance to normal songs, and are not recognized by others of the same species. Isolated birds allowed to hear the singing attempts of other isolates form better, but still imperfect, songs, whereas isolates allowed to hear normal song during their "sensitive period" (the limited period of time during which song learning can take place) develop normal songs.

The social bonds to the song tutor (usually the male parent) have been shown to be important in determining which vocalizations are copied by young birds. In addition, territorial males appear to also copy song charac-

Smith's Longspur

Calcarius pictus Swainson

NG–410; G–344; PE–264; PW–pl 54; AE–pl 554; AW–pl 596; AM(III)–280

?   4–5 (4–6) MONOG?   F I: 11–12 DAYS ALTRICIAL F: ? DAYS MF (?)   SEEDS

BREEDING: Arctic tundra in dry, grassy, hummocky areas. ? broods. **DISPLAYS:** ? **NEST:** In shallow depression in hummock or grass tussock; of grass, lined with fine grass, feathers, hair. **EGGS:** Grayish, marked with dark browns, lavender. 0.8″ (21 mm). **DIET:** Incl grass, sedge, and forb seeds. **CONSERVATION:** Winters within U.S. **NOTES:** Female distraction display similar to Lapland Longspur's. Largely solitary in winter, occ in small loose flocks. One of the least known N.A. birds. **ESSAYS:** Distraction Displays, p. 115; How Do We Find Out About Bird Biology?, p. 319. **REF:** Bent, 1968.

Lapland Longspur

Calcarius lapponicus Linnaeus

NG–410; G–344; PE–264; PW–pl 54; AE–pl 551; AW–pl 576; AM(III)–278

F   4–6 (3–7) MONOG (POLYGYN)   F I: 12–13 (10–14) DAYS ALTRICIAL F: 8–10 DAYS MF   SEEDS

BREEDING: Arctic tundra in wet meadows and scrub. 1 brood. **DISPLAYS:** Courtship: male fluffs breast feathers, holds head high with bill pointed slightly up, wings half spread, drooped and quivering, and runs after female while singing. Conspicuous flight song: male rises from ground, glides down on outstretched wings, tail spread; in presence of female, sings close to ground. **NEST:** In shallow depression of moss, sedge, or grass; of grass, occ with moss, lined with fine grass, occ feathers, hair, plant down. Built in 3 days. **EGGS:** Pale greenish-white or -gray, marked with browns, black. 0.8″ (21 mm). **DIET:** Incl spiders; grass, sedge, and forb seeds. Young fed 100% insects. **CONSERVATION:** Winters in N.A. **NOTES:** Unequaled in extent of circumpolar breeding range and consistently high density. Migrants retain much fat as buffer against unpredictable weather of Arctic spring. Striking synchronicity across entire range in onset of courtship, nest building, etc. Flocks of males arrive few days to 2 weeks before females. Male feeds incubating female only in years of very low food abundance. Female distraction display: wings slightly spread and drooped, tail spread against ground, runs from nest with fluttering wings. Hatching takes 1–3 days; smallest young oft left behind at fledging. Parents divide fledglings equally and care separately. Large winter flocks, oft with Horned Larks, pipits, Snow Buntings. **ESSAYS:** Breeding Season, p. 55; Polygyny, p. 443; Parental Care, p. 555; Brood Reduction, p. 307. **REFS:** Custer et al., 1986; Lyon and Montgomerie, 1987; McLaughlin and Montgomerie, 1985; Seastedt and MacLean, 1979.

teristics of surrounding territorial males, indicating that males of some species may have the ability to expand their repertoires and replace song components each breeding season.

Studies of song learning have led to the "auditory template hypothesis" —the idea that each species is born with a neurological model of what its song should sound like and it develops that song by matching sounds that it hears with the template in its brain. This process enables a young bird to filter out inappropriate sounds and to produce sounds matching the template, which are then stored for future use when breeding the following spring. Swamp Sparrows are able to store and precisely reproduce song syllables without rehearsal after as long as nine months.

The template model is exemplified by studies of young White-crowned Sparrows, which manifest a sensitive period for song acquisition roughly from day 10 through day 50 after hatching. Around day 150 they begin to practice what they have learned, and by day 200 they have developed a stable "crystallized" song that matches parts of the song heard during their sensitive period. Song learning is selective, so that if offered a choice, birds will learn their own species' song. If offered only songs of other species or if reared in isolation, learning does not occur and only a simplified approximation to the normal song develops. The importance of auditory feedback is shown by birds that have been experimentally deafened after exposure to normal song during the sensitive period but prior to day 150. Such birds fail to develop anything melodic. In contrast, birds deafened after their own song had crystallized will continue to sing normally. In essence, vocal learning appears to consist of two phases: (1) exposure to and memorization of species-specific sounds by matching them to the template during a sensitive period, and (2) production of those sounds.

The duration and timing of the sensitive period varies among species. Bewick's Wrens, Song and Swamp Sparrows, and meadowlarks acquire their songs during the first few months following hatching. In contrast, Northern Mockingbirds, Indigo Buntings, and Red-winged Blackbirds continue to incorporate new songs and song elements into their repertoires beyond their first breeding season. As additional field studies are conducted on individually identifiable birds over several seasons, many more species may be added to the latter category.

SEE: Vocal Dialects, p. 595; Vocal Functions, p. 471. REFS: Kroodsma, 1982; Marler, 1984.

Bird Names—XV

Longspur is a sensible common name, referring to "the elongated claw on the hind toe." Junco is a less sensible name than Longspur, since it comes from the Latin for "rush" (reed) and juncos are not swamp dwellers. Dickcissel and Bobolink were apparently named for the sound of their songs. Grackle comes from the Latin meaning "jackdaw" or "chough" (both Eur-

Snow Bunting

NG–412; G–344; PE–266; PW–pl 250; AE–pl 547; AW–pl 605; AM(III)–284

CLIFF	CAVITY	4–7	F	SEEDS
	F	(3–9)	I: 10–16 DAYS	
		MONOG ?	ALTRICIAL	
			F: 10–17 DAYS	
			MF	

BREEDING: Arctic rocky shores, cliffs, scree, and tundra. 1 brood, occ 2 in s. **DISPLAYS**: Courtship: male stands erect, tail spread widely, wings spread backward and downward; directs back and tail toward female, runs from her, returns, repeats sequence. Conspicuous flight song: male rises 15′–30′, flutters down with wings set high or held level, sings mostly during descent and after landing. **NEST**: Beneath or in rocks, in artificial cavity, occ under moss or in ground depression; bulky, loosely built of grass, moss, lichen, roots, leaves, lined with grass, rootlets, plant down, feathers, fur. Built in 4 days. Female oft adds lining for 2–3 days after laying first egg. Old nests occ reused. **EGGS**: Greenish, pale bluish, grayish, creamy white, marked with browns, black, occ wreathed or capped. 0.9″ (23 mm). **DIET**: Incl spiders; grass and forb seeds, buds (leaves in spring migration); also crustaceans and mollusks along coast. Young fed 100% insects. **CONSERVATION**: Winters in N.A. **NOTES**: Males arrive on breeding grounds 3–4 weeks ahead of females; older males arrive first. Male feeds female during egg laying and incubation. Asynchronous hatching leads to staggered fledging. Young form large flocks at independence. Gregarious in winter, occ assoc with Horned Larks, Lapland Longspurs; flocks oft roost in rock cavities or crevices or in sheltered areas on ground. Snow-bathe in winter. **ESSAYS**: Variation in Clutch Sizes, p. 339; Feathered Nests, p. 605; Brood Reduction, p. 307. **REFS**: Bazely, 1987; Lyon and Montgomerie, 1987; Nethersole-Thompson, 1966.

McKay's Bunting

NG–412; G–344; PW– 250; AW–pl 604; AM(III)–286

CLIFF	CAVITY	5?	F?	SEEDS
	F?	MONOG ?	I: 10–16(?) DAYS	
			ALTRICIAL	
			F: 10–17(?) DAYS	
			FM?	

BREEDING: Open, rocky ground, beaches, shores of tundra pools. 2 broods. **DISPLAYS**: Males perform wide, circular nuptial flight song. **NEST**: Beneath or among rocks, driftwood; of grass, lined with fine grass. **EGGS**: Pale greenish, dotted with pale browns. 0.9″ (23 mm). **DIET**: Presumably insects, spiders; grass and forb seeds. **CONSERVATION**: Winters on coast of w Alaska. **NOTES**: Closely related to Snow Bunting and considered to be the same species by some; limited hybridization occurs on St. Lawrence Island. Highly restricted distribution and virtually unstudied in the field; breeding biology likely very similar to Snow Bunting's. **ESSAYS**: Hybridization, p. 501; Superspecies, p. 375; How Do We Find Out About Bird Biology?, p. 319; Bills, p. 209; Species and Speciation, p. 355. **REF**: Gabrielson and Lincoln, 1959.

asian corvids) or "cormorant." Oriole comes from the Latin "aureolus," golden. Tanager doesn't have classical roots—the name comes from *tangara*, the Native American name for a South American species of tanager.

Siskin seems to mean "a chirper" in several European languages. Grosbeaks have big beaks. Finch is from the Anglo-Saxon "finc" for the same bird, possibly an imitation of the song. REFS: Choate, 1985; Owen, 1985.

Feathered Nests

Much as we keep warm under down comforters in winter, many birds improve nest insulation during incubation by adding feathers and down to their nests. The advantage of insulation must be weighed, however, against possible added conspicuousness of the nest to predators and brood parasites and the danger of overheating the nestlings. Zoologist Anders Moller surveyed European passerine nests to determine which birds feathered their nests and how much feather lining they added. Moller found that feathers are more likely to be incorporated into nests of birds that breed early in the year, particularly if they are small and have a more northerly distribution and especially if they are cavity nesters. The latter, of course, need not worry about feathers increasing the conspicuousness of their nests.

The source of feathers for nests is often the brood patch (a ventral area plucked bare to facilitate heat flow from the adult to the eggs). Grebes, waterfowl, shorebirds, gallinaceous birds, passerines, and birds of prey are among those that pluck brood patches. Interestingly, some birds incorporate feathers from other species into their nests. Molted feathers of ptarmigan are routinely used by redpolls, Snow Buntings, and some longspurs. You might try making available a handful of down from an old pillow to northern backyard breeders in early spring and see whether it is taken.

SEE: Masterbuilders, p. 445; Nest Lining, p. 391; Nest Materials, p. 369; Eggs and Their Evolution, p. 301; Incubation: Heating Eggs, p. 393; Brood Patches, p. 427. REF: Moller, 1984.

Bird Communities and Competition

A biological community consists of all of the organisms—microbes, plants, and animals—that live in an area. A community, together with the physical environment to which it is tied by a series of processes (such as the production of oxygen by plants and its use by animals, and the reciprocal production of carbon dioxide by animals and its use by plants), is called an ecosystem. How the species composition of communities is determined, and how those species interact with each other and with their inanimate surroundings, are major foci of ecological research.

In order to simplify the investigation of communities, ecologists usually study some subset of the organisms present, either a functional complex such as a group of herbivores and the plant species they feed on, or a

Dickcissel

Spiza americana Gmelin

HERBS

0'–2'　　　F　　　4　　　F
(To 6')　　　　　　(2–6)　I: 12–13 DAYS
　　　　　　　　　POLYGYN　ALTRICIAL　　SEEDS
　　　　　　　　　　　　　F: 9(7–10) DAYS
　　　　　　　　　　　　　F

BREEDING: Grasslands, meadows, savanna, cultivated and abandoned fields. 1 brood; second may be raised after move to new area. **DISPLAYS**: ? **NEST**: Bulky, of coarse forbs, grass, or cornstalk interwoven with a few leaves and grass, lined with fine grass, rootlets, hair. **EGGS**: Pale blue, unmarked. 0.8″ (21 mm). **DIET**: Younger birds predominantly (70%) grain, grass and forb seeds, remainder insects. Adults the reverse, 70% insects, 30% seeds. **CONSERVATION**: Winters from s w Mexico s, primarily on Pacific slope, to n S.A., esp in rice-growing areas. Blue List 1978–82, Special Concern 1986. Frequent cowbird host. Mowing machines destroy nests and nestlings in clover and alfalfa fields. **NOTES**: Erratic breeding distribution; in 1800s, commonly nested from Carolinas to New England but disappeared by 1905; began to reappear in 1920s and small numbers continue to nest there sporadically. Female broods. Young unable to fly until 2–3 days after leaving nest; some remain partially dependent on adults for food until after forming large premigratory flocks. Form roosts of up to several hundred after nesting. Males may sing in winter. Forms small to large winter flocks. **ESSAYS**: Blue List, p. 11; Polygyny, p. 443; Cowbirds, p. 619; Communal Roosting, p. 615. **REFS**: Fretwell, 1986; Harmeson, 1974; Zimmerman, 1982.

Lark Bunting

Calamospiza melanocorys Stejneger

?　　　4–5 (3–7)　FM?
　　　　MONOG　I: 11–12 DAYS
　　　　(POLYGYN)　ALTRICIAL　　SEEDS　　HAWKS
　　　　　　　F: 8–9 DAYS
　　　　　　　MF

BREEDING: Grassland, prairie, meadows, sagebrush. 2? broods. **DISPLAYS**: Conspicuous male flight song and display begin by rapid ascent to 20'–30'; male pauses at top of ascent, then with jerky movements of extended wings, floats butterfly-like to ground opposite starting point. Occ flight is circular, male landing near starting point. **NEST**: Usu rim of cup flush with ground level, occ slightly elevated, oft sheltered by overhead veg; woven of grass, forbs, fine roots, lined with finer grass, stems, hair, plant down. **EGGS**: Pale blue, greenish-blue, occ spotted with reddish-brown. 0.9″ (22 mm). **DIET**: Esp grasshoppers; grass and forb seeds. During breeding season, 80% animal. **CONSERVATION**: Winters s to c Mexico. Uncommon cowbird host. Destruction of native prairie in midwest has caused disappearance from e and n e portions of historic breeding range. **NOTES**: Later arriving females in spring oft mate polygynously; these secondary females lose more weight from lack of male help rearing brood, but manage to fledge as many young as primary females. Gregarious, lives in flocks throughout year except when breeding. Large winter flocks of hundreds. **ESSAYS**: Polygyny, p. 443; Parental Care, p. 555; Flock Defense, p. 235. **REFS**: Pleszczynska, 1978; Pleszczynska and Hansell, 1980.

taxonomic group, such as the resident insects or birds. Thus one may read about "mammal communities" or "bird communities." Unlike mammals (which are often nocturnal and secretive), birds are relatively easy to observe; hence, a great deal of research has been done on avian communities.

Much of that research has been focused on a seemingly simple question: Are the birds that compose a community merely a chance association of species that share similar tolerances to a physical environment, or do biological interactions among the birds determine which species are included in a community and which are excluded from it? In particular, interest has centered on whether competition—two or more species using the same limited resource—is responsible both for excluding some species from communities and for causing certain kinds of differences to evolve between the species that do live together. So far, no simple answers to these questions about species composition have emerged.

Many avian ecologists do believe that competition can be an important factor influencing both the composition of bird communities and the behavioral and morphological characteristics (structure, color, etc.) of the birds themselves. That belief is based on diverse lines of evidence, such as many observations of closely related birds apparently dividing up resources such as food or suitable space for territories, or one species excluding another from apparently desirable habitat. For example, in the northwestern United States males of both Red-winged and Yellow-headed Blackbirds set up territories in open marshes. The Redwings arrive earlier in the spring and occupy the entire marsh. When the Yellowheads fly in, they take over the best territories (areas of cattails and other plants in deep water that harbor the richest insect life) and force the Redwings into the shallower, drier, more marginal habitats. The Redwings are able to breed successfully in these areas, however, while the Yellowheads are unable to exploit the less productive sites successfully.

The Yellowheads are bigger, perhaps a result of natural selection favoring the ability to oust Redwings from high-quality areas, perhaps to eat larger seeds in the winter, or perhaps both—or perhaps neither! Many such details remain uncertain, but it is clear that the Redwings have a broader niche (loosely, "way of life") than do the Yellowheads. Nevertheless, Yellowheads are better competitors within their own narrow niche, and thus are able to exclude the Redwings from it. Territorial habitat is a scarce resource; the Yellowheads take the richest and the Redwings get the rest.

Dividing up resources (resource partitioning) often takes the form of similar bird species either feeding in different parts of the same habitat (as do some closely related warblers that live together) or else taking food of different sizes. The former is evident from differences in foraging behavior; the latter is often inferred from differences in bill size of the species.

One approach to detecting the existence of competitive interactions in bird communities is to determine whether closely related species are distributed independently over a large sample of similar habitats, or whether the presence of one or more species has an influence on the others. For four

Bobolink

Dolichonyx oryzivorus Linnaeus

| F | 5–6 (4–7) POLYGYN | F
I: 10–13 DAYS
ALTRICIAL
F: 10–14 DAYS
MF | SEEDS | FOLIAGE GLEAN |

BREEDING: Tall grass, flooded meadows, prairie, dense grain fields. 1 brood. **DISPLAYS:** Courtship: male spreads and drags tail, nape feathers erect, bill pointed down, wings partly open, while softly singing; song-flight on rapidly vibrating wings, hovers slightly above veg. **NEST:** In dense cover of forbs in natural or scraped depression; of coarse grass, forbs, lined with finer grass. Well concealed. **EGGS:** Gray to pale reddish-brown, marked with browns, purples. 0.8″ (21 mm). **DIET:** Incl few spiders; grass and forb seeds. Also fruit and nectar in winter. Young fed insects almost exclusively. **CONSERVATION:** Winters in s S.A., mostly e of Andes, from Brazil s to n Argentina. Largely disappeared from breeding range in e and n e N.A. likely due to earlier cutting of hayfields and to past extensive shooting for food and for rice crop protection in s e. Wintering habitat conversion to rice agriculture leading to situation similar to earlier one in s e U.S. Uncommon cowbird host. **NOTES:** Little territorial defense by males. Female runs from nest before taking flight. Forms large postbreeding flocks, oft congregating in marshes, and remains in large open flocks except when breeding. **ESSAYS:** Polygyny, p. 443; Sexual Selection, p. 251; Parental Care, p. 555; Wintering and Conservation, p. 513. **REFS:** Martin, 1974; Orians, 1985; Wittenberger, 1980.

Western Meadowlark

Supersp #51
Sturnella neglecta Audubon

| F | 5 (3–7) MONOG (POLYGYN) | F
I: 13–15 DAYS
ALTRICIAL
F: 12 DAYS
F –M | SEEDS | |

BREEDING: Grassland, savanna, pasture, cultivated fields. 2 broods. **DISPLAYS:** Similar to Eastern Meadowlark. **NEST:** In natural or scraped depression; of coarse grass, lined with finer grass, hair. Domed canopy of grass, bark, forbs interwoven with surrounding veg; opening on one side. **EGGS:** White, marked with browns, purples. 1.1″ (28 mm). **DIET:** Incl few spiders, sowbugs, snails; grass and forb seeds. **CONSERVATION:** Winters s to c Mexico. Range expanding in n e. Uncommon cowbird host. **NOTES:** Interspecifically territorial where both meadowlarks overlap; some males sing songs of both species. Males have repertoires of 5–12 song types. Roosts on ground in small groups. Winter flocks of 40–100. **ESSAYS:** Vocal Development, p. 601; Polygyny, p. 443; Great Plains Hybrids, p. 625; Interspecific Territoriality, p. 385; Sibling Species, p. 383. **REFS:** Falls and Krebs, 1975; Lanyon, 1957; Orians, 1985; Rohwer, 1973.

years, ecologists Catherine Toft, David Trauger, and Horatio Murdy analyzed statistically the distribution of five duck species breeding in 236 ponds in the Northwest Territories of Canada. Three of the ducks were dabblers: Mallard, American Wigeon, and Green-winged Teal. Two were divers: Lesser Scaup and Ring-necked Duck. The species showed significant differences in both time of hatching and pond-size use. For instance, the dabblers nested early, running the risks of springtime inclement weather. The divers nested later, risking the loss of their broods with the arrival of the fall freeze. Mallards showed little preference for pond size, teal strongly preferred small ponds, and wigeon and divers preferred large ponds (and were almost never found in small ones). Detailed analysis of the results led to the conclusion that competition, past and present, was responsible for patterns of pond use, and partially responsible for the temporal differences in dabbler and diver breeding. The most dramatic current competition was between the two divers; the scaup and Ring-necks would often occupy the same pond in different years, but not occur there together.

Some of the most interesting studies of avian communities that consider the distributions of related species have been done not on North American birds, but on assemblages of birds found in different parts of New Guinea and on other islands of the southwest Pacific. The species compositions of these communities have been documented by ecologist Jared Diamond, who found many cases of "checkerboard" distributions, sort of an expanded version of the scaup and Ring-neck situation, with certain combinations of closely related species never found. For instance, Diamond searched for two species of *Macropygia* cuckoo doves on 33 islands of the Bismarck Archipelago. He found one of the species on 14 islands, the second on 6 other islands, and neither on 13 islands. The two kinds of cuckoo doves never lived together on the same island. Similarly, two small nectarivores, the Black Sunbird (*Nectarinia sericea*) and the Bismarck Black Honeyeater (*Myzomela pammelaena*) occupy 41 islands in the archipelago. The sunbird is found on 18, the honeyeater on 23, but no island plays host to both. The two birds, although they belong to different families, are quite similar in color, size, foraging techniques, and habitat preference. Diamond concluded from finding such patterns in several groups of ecologically similar species that certain combinations of species were "forbidden" by competition. That conclusion has been challenged, but Diamond's interpretation seems correct to us. His work provides some of the most persuasive evidence that competition can play a key role in determining which species are found in a given bird community.

So competition occurs, but how common it is, and the degree to which it is responsible for the composition of bird communities worldwide, remain unresolved. The arguments are complex and technical. They involve a wide range of questions, some of which reflect the difficulties of studying birds. How are the resources fed upon by birds best measured? How can accurate censuses of bird populations be obtained? Do spot observations of birds feeding provide unbiased information about foraging behavior? Might birds

Eastern Meadowlark

NG–418; G–296; PE–256; AE–pl 392; AW–pl 424; AM(III)–292

F	3–5 (3–7) MONOG (POLYGYN)		F I: 13–15 DAYS ALTRICIAL F: 11–12 DAYS F – M	SEEDS

BREEDING: Grassland, savanna, fields. 2 broods. **DISPLAYS:** Courting male stands erect on ground, points bill skyward with tail fanned and jerked up and down; wings waved alternately or together, breast feathers fluffed. Male then may jump straight up into air; female occ responds with similar display but remains on ground. **NEST:** In dense cover in natural or scraped depression; of coarse grass, lined with finer grass, hair. Domed canopy of grass interwoven with surrounding veg; opening on one side. Several nests may be started, only one completed; built in 3–18 days. **EGGS:** White, marked with browns, purples. 1.1″ (28 mm). **DIET:** Incl few spiders; grass and forb seeds, some fruit. **CONSERVATION:** Winters s through C.A. to Brazil. Blue List 1980–82, Special Concern 1986; declining in n e. Common cowbird host. Many nests destroyed by mowing of cultivated fields. **NOTES:** Clutch size in n commonly 5, second clutch 4; 3–4 most common in s. Female broods. Female continues feeding young while building second nest and laying; male assumes major role when female begins incubating. Interspecifically territorial where both meadowlarks overlap; some males sing songs of both species. Forms small cohesive winter flocks. **ESSAYS:** Vocal Development, p. 601; Polygyny, p. 443; Great Plains Hybrids, p. 625; Interspecific Territoriality, p. 385; Blue List, p. 11; Variation in Clutch Sizes, p. 339. **REFS:** Knapton, 1987; Lanyon, 1957; Orians, 1985; Rohwer, 1973; Roseberry and Klimstra, 1970.

Tricolored Blackbird

Agelaius tricolor Audubon

NG–420; G–298; AW–pl 615; AM(III)–292

REEDS					
SHRUB 0.5′–5′ (To 12′)	F	3–4 (2–6) POLYGYN		F I: 11–13 DAYS ALTRICIAL F: 11–14 DAYS F –M	SEEDS SNAILS	FOLIAGE GLEAN

BREEDING: Freshwater marshes, croplands. 2 broods. **DISPLAYS:** Similar to Red-winged Blackbird, but lacks flight display. **NEST:** Near or over water, also in agricultural crops. Woven of sedges, grass, forbs, lined with fine grass. Built in 4 days. **EGGS:** Pale green, marked with browns, black. 1.1″ (28 mm). **DIET:** Incl clams; grass and forb seeds, grain. Proportion of seeds and grain much higher in nonbreeding season. Young fed 90% insects, snails, clams. **CONSERVATION:** Winters in CA breeding range and adjacent agricultural areas, s to n w Mexico. Lives in enormous flocks that occ damage grain crops, esp in fields near large breeding colonies. Control measures usu entail baiting fields with poisoned grain. **NOTES:** Highly gregarious in all seasons. Colonies formerly numbered up to 200,000 + nests, now to 20,000, still the highest nest density of any marsh-nesting blackbird. Feeds in flocks even when breeding. **ESSAYS:** Variation in Clutch Sizes, p. 339; Polygyny, p. 443; Badges, p. 611; Coloniality, p. 173; Sibling Species, p. 383. **REFS:** Orians, 1985; Orians and Christman, 1968; Payne, 1969; Skorupa et al., 1980.

behave differently in relatively open situations where they are readily observed from the way they behave when out of sight in thick foliage? How does one interpret observed differences in bill size or shape among closely related species? Are these differences a result of natural selection produced by competition, by the need for members of the same species to recognize one another, or by other factors?

Other questions involve difficult statistical issues—such as how one determines if an assembly of bird species is a "random" assortment, that is, a chance subset of the species that theoretically might be members of a community. How strongly do factors (such as predation and random disturbances) other than competition affect community composition? Careful observations and experiments on many more bird communities will be required before these questions can be answered with assurance.

SEE: Bird Guilds, p. 493; Bills, p. 209; Dabblers vs. Divers, p. 75; MacArthur's Warblers, p. 523; Metabolism, p. 325. REFS: Diamond, 1975; Diamond and Case, 1986; Gilpin and Diamond, 1982; Simberloff, 1983; Toft et al., 1982; Wiens, 1983.

A male Eastern Meadowlark (right) courts a female by jumping up and displaying the bright yellow and black markings of its breast.

Redwing Coverable Badges

A corporal can tell that another soldier is a sergeant by the number of stripes on the sergeant's sleeve; we are informed of the status of a plainclothes detective when he flashes his shield at us. Badges play significant roles in human societies. Do they also serve important functions in avian societies?

In nonhuman animals, "badges" may simply be defined as arbitrary visual cues, often taking the form of especially prominent patches of color, that signal social status. One of the most familiar badges in the bird world is

Red-winged Blackbird

Agelaius phoeniceus Linnaeus

NG–420; G–298; PE–252; PW–pl 52; AE–pl 568; AW–pl 614; AM(III)–290

REEDS			F I: 10–12 DAYS		
1′–8′ (0.5′–20′)	F	3–4 (2–6) POLYGYN	ALTRICIAL F: 11–14 DAYS MF	SEEDS	FOLIAGE GLEAN HAWKS

BREEDING: Freshwater and brackish marshes, riparian habitats, fields. 2, occ 3 broods. **DISPLAYS:** Elevated on emergent veg, male spreads tail, droops wings, raises colored patches, fluffs feathers, leans forward with head pointing downward and "sings." Slow, stalling song-flight with tail spread, head down. **NEST:** Near or over water, usu in emergent veg or shrub, rarely in low tree; woven of sedges, grass, lined with fine grass, rushes. Built in 3–6 days. **EGGS:** Pale bluish-green, marked with dark colors. 1.0″ (25 mm). **DIET:** Incl few spiders; grass and forb seeds, rarely fruit. Young fed 100% insects. **CONSERVATION:** Winters s to Costa Rica. Frequent cowbird host. Late summer and fall flocks occ damage grain crops, esp in midwest. **NOTES:** Strongly territorial on clumped territories. Marsh Wrens oft puncture and occ steal eggs. Young can swim at 5–6 days. In addition to large fall and winter roosts, males may roost together in early summer. Males oft form fall flocks separate from females and young; flocks oft feed in uplands, roost in marshes. Enormous mixed winter flocks with grackles, Rusty Blackbirds, starlings, and cowbirds. Possibly most numerous N.A. land bird. **ESSAYS:** Polygyny, p. 443; Badges, p. 611; Visual Displays, p. 5; Roosting, p. 615; Sexual Selection, p. 251; Cowbirds, p. 619. **REFS:** Orians, 1980, 1985; Ewald and Rohwer, 1982; Yasukawa, 1979.

Yellow-headed Blackbird

Xanthocephalus xanthocephalus
Bonaparte

NG–420; G–298; PE–252; PW–pl 52; AE–pl 583; AW–pl 428; AM(III)–296

REEDS			F I: 11–13 DAYS		
0.5′–3′	F	4 (3–5) POLYGYN	ALTRICIAL F: 9–12 DAYS F –M	SEEDS	HAWKS FOLIAGE GLEAN

BREEDING: Freshwater marshes. 2? broods. **DISPLAYS:** Elevated on emergent veg, male spreads tail, half-opens wings, leans forward with head pointing downward or upward and "sings." **NEST:** Over water in emergent veg; bulky, firmly woven of wet veg, lined with dried grass. Nest shrinks as it dries, drawing nest supports tight. Built in 2–4 days **EGGS:** Grayish-white to pale greenish-white, marked with browns, gray. 1.0″ (26 mm). **DIET:** Incl few spiders; grass and forb seeds. **CONSERVATION:** Winters s to s Mexico. Rare cowbird host. **NOTES:** Strongly territorial on clumped territories, usu in portion of marsh with deeper water (2′–4′), thus separating them from Red-winged Blackbird nests. Nests occ destroyed by Marsh Wrens; recognizes wrens and excludes them from nesting territories. Young fed by regurgitation during first two days, and partially by regurgitation for two more. Males oft form fall flocks separate from females and young. Enormous mixed winter flocks with grackles, Red-winged Blackbirds, and cowbirds. **ESSAYS:** Visual Displays, p. 5; Bird Communities and Competition, p. 605; Polygyny, p. 443; Interspecific Territoriality, p. 385; Mixed-Species Flocking, p. 433. **REFS:** Bump, 1986; Leonard and Picman, 1986; Orians, 1980, 1985.

the bright red epaulette of the Red-winged Blackbird. Rare indeed is the birder who has not enjoyed the spectacle of a male Redwing, perched on a reed, singing while flashing forward the brilliant patches that give him his name.

What is the function of the Redwing's badge; does it serve to distinguish Redwings from other blackbirds, or does it signal status within Redwing society? That the epaulettes are important within the Redwing social system was suggested by experiments in which the patches of adult males were dyed black. Such males had much more difficulty holding their territories than "control" males with unmodified red epaulettes. In two separate experiments, over 60 percent of the blackened males lost their territories; less than 10 percent of the control males were evicted. These results, however, do not definitively answer the question of whether the badges function as intraspecific or interspecific signals. It could be that the epaulettes are species-recognition signals, and that other male Redwings did not realize that the dyed males were members of their own species. Since no other Redwings appeared to be present, male Redwings may have continued intruding into the dyed males' territories until the latter became exhausted and gave up the defense.

Experiments with mounted dead birds (mounts) by Andrew Hansen and Sievert Rohwer allowed the "social status" and "species recognition" hypotheses to be distinguished. Territorial male Redwings responded to mounts by approaching or attacking them or by displaying to them. The researchers found that the males responded more strongly to Redwing mounts with their epaulettes darkened than to mounts of male Brewer's Blackbirds, a species that shares the Redwing habitat and whose males resemble the dyed Redwings. In fact, the Brewer's mounts were largely ignored. The Redwings' ability to discriminate between the two species in the absence of the badge indicates that the epaulette is not necessary for species recognition and supports the social status hypothesis.

Hansen and Rohwer further tested and expanded that hypothesis. They recorded the responses of territorial males to Redwing mounts that had epaulettes totally blackened, half-blackened, normal, and twice as large as normal (the supplemental epaulettes were cut from Redwing study skins and glued behind normal ones on the mounts). The males invariably showed aggression that was proportional to epaulette size; some of the mounts with double epaulettes were violently attacked and suffered substantial damage.

This explains another of Hansen and Rohwer's observations—that males intruding into occupied territories greatly limit the exposure of their epaulettes. While searching for territories of their own or seeking food within another male's territory, keeping one's epaulettes covered reduced the chances of being assaulted. When the experimenters removed territorial males, however, intruders into the newly empty territories at first kept their epaulettes covered, but within a few minutes began to expose them. Within about half an hour the intruders were displaying like owners. The time that

Rusty Blackbird

Euphagus carolinus Müller

NG–422; G–298; PE–254; PW–pl 52; AE–pl 569; AW–pl 623; AM(III)–296

| SHRUB 2'–8' (To 20') | F | 4–5 MONOG | F I: 14 DAYS ALTRICIAL F: 11–13? DAYS MF | SEEDS | |

BREEDING: Moist conif woodland, bogs, riparian habitats. ? broods. **DISPLAYS:** ? **NEST:** Usu near or over water; bulky, of moss, twigs, lichens, grass, duff, lined with fine grass. **EGGS:** Pale bluish-green, marked with brown, gray. 1.0" (26 mm). **DIET:** Incl few spiders, crustaceans, snails, salamanders, fish; little fruit. **CONSERVATION:** Winters in N.A. Rare cowbird host. **NOTES:** Nests in loose colonies. Male feeds female on nest. In winter forms large flocks, oft joined by other blackbirds. **ESSAYS:** Communal Roosting, p. 615; Coloniality, p. 173; Mixed-Species Flocking, p. 433. **REFS:** Godfrey, 1986; Orians, 1985.

Brewer's Blackbird

Euphagus cyanocephalus Wagler

NG–422; G–298; PE–254; PW–pl 52; AE–pl 570; AW–pl 622; AM(III)–298

| GROUND SHRUB 0'–150' | F | 4–6 (3–7) MONOG (POLYGYN) | F I: 12–14 DAYS ALTRICIAL F: 13–14 DAYS MF | SEEDS FRUIT | FOLIAGE GLEAN HAWKS |

BREEDING: Shrubby, brushy areas (esp near water), riparian woodland, aspen parks, cultivated lands, marshes, around human habitations. 1, occ 2 broods. **DISPLAYS:** Courtship (or threat between birds of same sex): male, occ female, holds bill horizontally or pointed upward, fluffs body feathers, spreads wings, tail, and vocalizes. **NEST:** Variably placed; also occ in decid tree, emergent marsh veg; sturdy, of twigs, grass, matrix of mud or cow dung, lined with fine materials. **EGGS:** Grayish, marked with brown. 1.0" (25 mm). **DIET:** Incl few spiders, also crustaceans, snails; grass and some forb seeds. Young fed 90% insects, spiders. Occ wades to feed. **CONSERVATION:** Winters s to s Mexico. Common cowbird host. Increased range and abundance with spread of agriculture; expanding eastward. Oft assoc with humans, using urban, suburban, agricultural habitats. **NOTES:** Nests in colonies of 3–100 pairs. Pairs oft rejoin for up to 5 yr. Monogamous females tend to remain monogamous; secondary females of polygynous males tend to remain polygynous but change males yearly. Male occ feeds incubating female. Incubation occ starts before clutch completed, causing hatching to take up to 3 days. Large winter flocks with other blackbirds, esp Red-winged and Tricolored, but greatly outnumbered by them. **ESSAYS:** Feeding Birds, p. 349; Eye Color and Development, p. 233; Redwing Coverable Badges, p. 611; Polygyny, p. 443; Coloniality, p. 173; Range Expansion, p. 459. **REFS:** Balph, 1975; Furrer, 1975; Horn, 1968; Orians, 1985.

elapsed before ownerlike behavior appeared was roughly the same as the length of absences of owners from their territories in the ordinary course of events, time enough for the intruder to be reasonably certain the owner would not return.

All of this work supports what Hansen and Rohwer call the "coverable badge hypothesis." It assumes that Redwings (and other birds with badges that can be either displayed or covered, such as kinglets) benefit from being able to signal their intentions either to fight as owner of a territory or to depart submissively. They predict that coverable badges will evolve in territorial systems where (1) owners have a high probability of evicting intruders; (2) males frequently "trespass" in search of food or vacant territories; (3) fighting involves a high risk of injury to both combatants; and (4) adult males cannot predict whether they are going to be owners or "floaters" (males unable to establish territories). These conditions seem to be met in the Redwing system—intruders presumably searching for territories conceal their badges and leave without a battle when owners display theirs.

So, when you watch Redwings, see if you can spot trespassers into territories, and record whether they normally cover their badges and depart when the owner displays at them or chases them. Hansen and Rohwer studied Redwings in Grant County, Washington. It would be interesting to ascertain whether their observations apply to other populations of these widely distributed birds. If you have the opportunity of studying Tricolored Blackbirds, try to determine whether they make the same use of their prominent epaulettes. And, of course, it would be fascinating to discover if kinglets employ their red and gold crowns in a similar manner.

SEE: Bird Badges, p. 591; Visual Displays, p. 5; Territoriality, p. 387.   REF: Hansen and Rohwer, 1986.

Communal Roosting

When flocks of a million or more starlings and blackbirds make pests of themselves by spending the night close to human habitation, the phenomenon of communal roosting comes to public attention. These gigantic swarms, however, hardly approach the record for communally roosting birds. The Red-billed Quelea (a weaver, related to the House Sparrow) is so abundant that it may be considered the avian equivalent of a locust plague when invading African grain fields en masse. Quelea roosts may number tens of millions of individuals; poisons, explosives, and even flamethrowers have been used in attempts to control local outbreaks. The record-holding communal rooster, however, was North American; the now-extinct Passenger Pigeon roosted (and nested) in gigantic colonies containing billions of individuals and covering square miles.

All birds roost—that is, have a period of inactivity analogous to sleep

Brown-headed Cowbird

Molothrus ater Boddaert

NG–422; G–300; PE–252; PW–pl 52; AE–pl 571; AW–pl 620; AM(III)–306

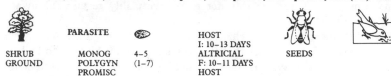

	PARASITE		HOST I: 10–13 DAYS	
SHRUB	MONOG	4–5	ALTRICIAL	SEEDS
GROUND	POLYGYN	(1–7)	F: 10–11 DAYS	
	PROMISC		HOST	

BREEDING: Woodland, forest (esp decid), forest edge, grassland. **DISPLAYS:** Courting male ruffles feathers of upper body, bows toward female, and calls. In air, male ruffles feathers as on ground, bends head, arches wings and sings. On elevated perch, male points bill straight up, fluffs feathers on nape, breast, and flanks, sings, then arches neck, spreads tail, raises wings, and bows. **NEST:** Does not build nest; deposits eggs in nests of other species, esp flycatchers, warblers, finches, and vireos. **EGGS:** White to grayish-white, marked with browns. 0.8″ (21 mm). **DIET:** Incl spiders, few snails; grain, grass and forb seeds. **CONSERVATION:** Winters s to s Mexico. Range has expanded e and w from Great Plains with clearing of forests and introduction of cattle, with which it is now assoc (originally assoc with American bison). **NOTES:** See Cowbirds, p. 619. Highly gregarious at all seasons; postbreeding fall flocks generally 50–200. Feeds and roosts in enormous flocks with other blackbirds and starlings, esp in winter. **ESSAYS:** Brood Parasitism, p. 287; Conservation of Kirtland's Warbler, p. 527; Communal Roosting, p. 615; European Starlings, p. 489; Range Expansion, p. 459. **REFS:** Darley, 1982; Friedmann and Kiff, 1985; Teather and Robertson, 1986.

Bronzed Cowbird

Molothrus aeneus Wagler

NG–422; G–300; PW–pl 52; AE–pl 574; AW–pl 621; AM(III)–304

	PARASITE	HOST I: 10–12 DAYS	
SHRUB		ALTRICIAL	SEEDS
	?	F: 11 DAYS	
	?	HOST	

BREEDING: Partially open habitats with scattered trees or scrub, cultivated fields, pastures, around human habitation. **DISPLAYS:** Courtship: on ground near female, male throws head back, ruffles feathers, quivers wings, and walks stiffly; male may also ruffle feathers, spread and bend tail, arch wings, bend head down, and bounce up and down while calling. **NEST:** Does not build nest; deposits eggs in nests of other species, esp orioles. **EGGS:** Pale bluish-green, unmarked. 0.9″ (23 mm). **DIET:** Incl grain, grass and forb seeds. **CONSERVATION:** Winter resident; populations in n are partially migratory. **NOTES:** A generalist parasite known to parasitize at least 77 species. Females pierce host eggs and previously laid cowbird eggs. Population sex ratios are skewed; some studies report an excess of males, others an excess of females. Gregarious, flocking at all seasons except when breeding. Flocks generally 25–30, exceptionally to 500. **ESSAYS:** Brood Parasitism, p. 287; Cowbirds, p. 619. **REFS:** Carter, 1986; Friedmann and Kiff, 1985.

in human beings. Some birds do it alone; others with mobs of compatriots. Some change their roosting habits with the season: male Red-winged Blackbirds usually roost alone on their territories when breeding, but crowd together at night during the rest of the year. Birds that roost communally do so in a wide variety of situations. Small groups of nuthatches or creepers spend the night together in tree cavities. Some vultures roost on cliffs, and others on the tops of cacti; many seabirds roost on islands, and swallows may roost on telephone lines. Starlings choose an enormous diversity of roost sites—many kinds of woodlands, cattails and other reeds, and numerous kinds of buildings, to name a few.

The question of why some birds roost communally and others roost solitarily is related to the question of why there are both communal and solitary nesters. One possibility is that older, more experienced birds are better able to find food; hence younger birds roost with them in order to follow their elders to better foraging grounds. The older birds accept this social parasitism because they tend to be dominant, and are able to appropriate more central and therefore safer positions in the roosting crowd. As long as the costs of increased competition are outweighed by the benefits of increased safety from predators for the older birds, and the benefits of locating rich food supplies for the young outweigh reduced nighttime safety for them, roosting should be communal. In fact, some studies have reported that older Red-winged Blackbirds and Brown-headed Cowbirds are concentrated in the centers of their roosts.

In a Mexican mixed-species roost of egrets, herons, and other species, Snowy Egrets and Great Egrets displaced other species from the higher (and presumably safer) positions in the trees; other species have been found to get more food if they forage near Snowy Egrets, and other birds tend to be attracted more to dummies of Snowy Egrets placed in foraging sites than to dummies of other species. No studies have yet been done to determine whether the egrets are actually followed to foraging sites from the mixed-species roosts, however. These observations, and those of the blackbirds and cowbirds, are consistent with the notion that older and younger birds (or species with divergent capacities to locate food) join communal roosts for different reasons.

Further support for this notion comes from observations of swallows in Denmark. Older birds were more successful in finding food than younger ones, and also displaced the youngsters from the safest roosting positions. Evidence was also found that the young swallows were somehow able to evaluate the feeding success of adults and preferentially follow the well-fed ones when they left the roost the next day.

One further advantage can accrue to birds that roost together at night —they may be able to huddle together to keep warm. For nuthatches that jam together in cavities this might be the main advantage, as they significantly reduce their heat loss. Even in large roosts in which huddling does not occur, more central positions may often be thermally advantageous as a result of denser vegetation (relative to the periphery of the roost) and a

Common Grackle

Quiscalus quiscula Linnaeus

NG–424; G–300; PE–254; PW–pl 52; AE–pl 573; AW–pl 618; AM(III)–302

			F		
			I: 13–14 DAYS		
CONIF	CAVITY	4–5 (2–6)	ALTRICIAL		FOLIAGE
2'–12'	F	MONOG	F: 16–20 DAYS		GLEAN
(To 100')		(POLYGYN)	MF		

BREEDING: Partly open areas with scattered trees, open woodland, around human habitation. 1, occ 2 broods. **DISPLAYS:** Male fluffs body feathers, spreads wings, tail, and vocalizes. Male then strikes pose with bill pointed skyward. **NEST:** Oft near water; also in shrub, emergent marsh veg, tree cavity, artificial structure; bulky, of grass, forbs, twigs, rushes, sedges, mud, lined with fine materials, trash. **EGGS:** Greenish-white to light brown, marked with dark brown, purple. 1.2" (29 mm). **DIET:** Insects, crustaceans, other terrestrial and aquatic inverts, fish, small verts, bird eggs, nestlings; fruit, grain, grass and forb seeds, acorns, nuts. Young fed 75% insects, spiders. Steals food from ground-foraging birds, esp robins. Occ wades to forage. **CONSERVATION:** Winters within U.S. Rare cowbird host. Large post-breeding flocks, occ to hundreds of thousands, can damage grain crops; control measures incl baiting with poisoned grain. Large urban roosts create nuisance leading to control efforts. **NOTES:** Usu nests in colonies of few pairs to >100. Large late summer to fall and immense winter roosts (up to several million birds) with starlings and other blackbirds. **ESSAYS:** Decline of Eastern Songbirds, p. 495; Eye Color and Development, p. 233; Communal Roosting, p. 615; European Starlings, p. 489; Bird Droppings, p. 263. **REFS:** Caccamise et al., 1983; Howe, 1978, 1979; Maxwell and Putnam, 1972; Orians, 1985.

Boat-tailed Grackle

Supersp #52
Quiscalus major Vieillot

NG–424; G–300; PE–254; PW–pl 52; AE–pl 575; AM(III)–300

			F		
			I: 13–15 DAYS		
SHRUB	F	2–4	ALTRICIAL		HAWKS
3'–12'		(1–5)	F: 12–15 DAYS		
(To 50')		PROMISC	F		

BREEDING: Coastal marshes and adjacent open habitats, pastures, cultivated fields. 2, occ 3 broods. **DISPLAYS:** As in Great-tailed Grackle, but vocalizations differ markedly. Males oft display in groups. **NEST:** Also in emergent veg. Built as in Great-tailed Grackle. Female chooses site. **EGGS:** Pale greenish-blue, marked with dark brown, black, gray. 1.3" (32 mm). **DIET:** As in Great-tailed Grackle; young fed 100% animal diet, from insects to small verts. Oft wades in shallow water and fishes like a heron. Steals food from Glossy Ibis and probably herons. **CONSERVATION:** Winter resident. Expanding range northward. **NOTES:** Nests in colonies. Nestling and adult sex ratio usu 2 females to 1 male. Females breed as yearlings, but males do not breed until second year. Early nests contain smaller eggs. Forms relatively small winter flocks. Long considered as one species with Great-tailed Grackle, but hybridization does not occur in area of overlap from s w LA to s e TX. **ESSAYS:** Superspecies, p. 375; Hybridization, p. 501; Coloniality, p. 173; Range Expansion, p. 459; European Starlings, p. 489; Piracy, p. 159. **REFS:** Bancroft, 1986; Orians, 1985.

greater mass of bird bodies per unit area. Both of these factors may act to reduce the loss of heat from individual birds, primarily by reducing the cooling effects of wind. That reduction, however, would rarely be enough to compensate for the energy lost flying the extra distance to the roosting site. In addition, there is some evidence that birds in the lower positions in colonial roosts lose heat because the rain of droppings from higher birds reduces the insulating properties of their plumage. It thus seems unlikely that thermoregulation is a prime reason for communal roosting in most species.

SEE: Coloniality, p. 173; Mixed-Species Flocking, p. 433; Temperature Regulation and Behavior, p. 149; Commensal Feeding, p. 35; Flock Defense, p. 235; Geometry of the Selfish Colony, p. 19.   REF: Yom-Tov, 1979.

Cowbirds

Only two species of cowbirds, Brown-headed and Bronzed, are found in North America. Both cowbird species are generalist parasites, laying their eggs in the nests of a wide range of other species. The Bronzed Cowbird occurs only in the arid southwest and extends south into Mexico and through Central America; it has been little studied because it occupies a relatively restricted range in North America and a somewhat inhospitable habitat. The Brown-headed Cowbird, in contrast, occupies most of our continent south of the Arctic. This reflects the remarkable population explosion and range expansion it has undergone during this century. It has spread from its original home in the Great Plains as humanity has converted forest lands into farms and pastures. In fact, it is now sufficiently numerous to pose a major threat to the continued survival of several species and subspecies that it regularly parasitizes. As a result, much research effort has recently been directed at understanding the breeding biology of Brown-headed Cowbirds, and a surprisingly complex and fascinating picture is emerging.

Although the nests of many species are acceptable places for cowbirds to deposit eggs, all of those species are not necessarily appropriate hosts. Many parasitized species routinely recognize and reject cowbird eggs (by either destroying the egg, rebuilding the nest to cover the egg, or abandoning the nest), while many others are simply inadequate as foster parents and never successfully rear cowbird chicks. Blue-winged Teal, Ferruginous Hawk, Virginia Rail, Killdeer, Spotted Sandpiper, Upland Sandpiper, Wilson's Phalarope, California Gull, Common Tern, Ruby-throated Hummingbird, and Red-headed Woodpecker are among the species that fail as foster parents. The Brown-headed Cowbird now has been recorded as successfully parasitizing 144 of 220 species in whose nests its eggs have been observed.

Great-tailed Grackle

Supersp #52
Quiscalus mexicanus Gmelin

NG–424; G–300; PE–254; PW–pl 52; AE–pl 576; AW–pl 619; AM(III)–300

SHRUB	F	3–4	F
REEDS		(3–5)	I: 13–14 DAYS
2'–30'		PROMISC	ALTRICIAL
			F: 20–23(?) DAYS
			F

BREEDING: Open areas with scattered trees, cultivated areas, pastures, riparian thickets, swamps, around human habitation. 1, occ 2 broods. **DISPLAYS:** Male fluffs body feathers, spreads wings, tail, vibrates wings making crashing or brushing sound, and vocalizes. Male then strikes pose with bill pointed skyward.   **NEST:** Oft near water, oft in heronry; large, bulky, rim woven to supports, built of twigs, forbs, rushes, sedges, mud or cow dung, lined with fine grass, rootlets, trash. Built in 5–10 days. **EGGS:** Greenish-blue, marked with dark colors. 1.3″ (33 mm). **DIET:** Insects, lizards, aquatic inverts and verts, ectoparasites from domestic stock, bird eggs, nestlings; fruit, grain, grass seeds. **CONSERVATION:** Winter resident except at n fringe of range. Ejects eggs of Bronzed Cowbird. Agricultural irrigation in arid regions enabled continuing range expansion this century. **NOTES:** Nests placed close together in colonies of few to thousands. Male disputes are low key, but females squabble over choice of nest site and steal nest materials from each other. Incubation occ starts before clutch complete, hatching then takes up to 3 days. Male nestlings require more food than females of equal age. **ESSAYS:** Superspecies, p. 375; Parasitized Ducks, p. 89; Hybridization, p. 501; Range Expansion, p. 459; Promiscuity, p. 145; Coloniality, p. 173. **REFS:** Holmes et al., 1985; Orians, 1985; Smith, 1977; Teather, 1987.

Scott's Oriole

Icterus parisorum Bonaparte

NG–426; G–302; PW–pl 53; AW–pl 427; AM(III)–320

YUCCA	F	3	F	FRUIT
4'–18'		(2–4)	I: 12–14 DAYS	NECTAR
		MONOG?	ALTRICIAL	
			F: 14 DAYS	
			MF	

BREEDING: Yucca, piñon-juniper, arid oak scrub, riparian woodland, palm oases. 2 broods. **DISPLAYS:** ? **NEST:** Also in palm; woven through overhanging leaves or suspended from twigs; of yucca fibers, fine grass, lined with fine grass, cotton waste, hair. **EGGS:** Pale blue, marked with browns, black, purples, grays. 1.0″ (24 mm). **DIET:** Young fed insects, fruit, berries, by regurgitation for 4–5 days. **CONSERVATION:** Winters from n and n w Mexico s to s and s w Mexico. Rare Bronzed Cowbird host. **NOTES:** Natural history little known. **ESSAYS:** Masterbuilders, p. 445; Bird Badges, p. 591; Taxonomy and Nomenclature, p. 515; How Do We Find Out About Bird Biology?, p. 319. **REF:** Orians, 1985.

The Bronzed Cowbird has been successful with 28 of 77 species, and of those 28, only 18 occur north of Mexico.

Recent studies estimate that only 3 percent of Brown-headed Cowbird eggs result in adults. In spite of these tremendous losses, the Brown-headed and Bronzed Cowbirds in North America and the Shiny Cowbird in parts of South America and the Caribbean continue to expand their breeding range and numbers. This apparent paradox is explained by the unusual breeding behavior and physiology of Brown-headed Cowbirds (behavior presumably shared by the less-studied Bronzed Cowbirds).

A female Brown-headed Cowbird has a long reproductive period with an extraordinarily short interval between clutches. In fact, this cowbird is the only wild passerine ever reported not to show regression of ovaries and oviducts following clutch completion. Indeed, the physiological demarcation between clutches sometimes is not at all clear, leading ornithologists to characterize female cowbirds as "passerine chickens!" Each female's laying cycle appears adapted to take advantage of a continuous supply of host nests for about a two-month period. An average female lays about 80 eggs, 40 per year for two years. About 3 percent of those 80 eggs end up as adults—an average of 2.4 adults per female. Clearly, such numbers more than compensate for the excessive loss of eggs and young in the nests of inappropriate hosts. Each pair of cowbirds replaces itself with an average of 1.2 pairs— which will double a cowbird population in eight years.

The mating system of Brown-headed Cowbirds shows similar flexibility, ranging from monogamy, to a mixture of monogamy and polygyny, to total promiscuity. The type of mating system seen in a given area is influenced by the spatial distribution of host nests and by the sex ratio (proportions of males and females) of the local cowbird population. Although both sexes occupy distinct breeding home ranges, these areas are not defended and are not exclusive. Where host nests are dense, female home ranges are small, enabling males to guard their mates and resulting in monogamous or polygynous relationships. Where host nests are widely dis-

A Kirtland's Warbler feeding a young Brown-headed Cowbird. The cowbirds represent a major threat to this rare warbler.

Orchard Oriole

Icterus spurius Linnaeus

NG–426; G–302; PE–258; PW–pl 53; AE–pl 396; AM(III)–308

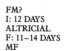

SHRUB
4'–50'

FM?

3–5
(3–7)
MONOG

FM?
I: 12 DAYS
ALTRICIAL
F: 11–14 DAYS
MF

FRUIT

BREEDING: Scrub, open woodland, mesquite, orchards. 1 brood. **DISPLAYS:** ? **NEST:** Rarely in conif tree. Suspended from forked terminal twig, hidden by leaves; woven of long green grass blades, lined with fine grass, plant down. Built in 3–6 days. **EGGS:** Pale bluish-white, marked with browns, purples, grays. 0.8″ (20 mm). **DIET:** Occ takes tree blossoms. Also nectar in winter. **CONSERVATION:** Winters from c Mexico s to n S.A. Common cowbird host. Special Concern 1982–86, reportedly declining in many areas esp in w portion of range. **NOTES:** Has nested colonially with 114 nests on 7-acre tract in LA. Male and female brood. Parents oft divide fledglings and care for them separately. Family units remain together until departing in fall. Solitary in some areas in winter, flocks in others; roosts in flocks. **ESSAYS:** Blue List, p. 11; Masterbuilders, p. 445; Bird Badges, p. 591; Taxonomy and Nomenclature, p. 515; Cowbirds, p. 619; Parental Care, p. 555; Wintering and Conservation, p. 513. **REF:** Sealy, 1980.

Audubon's Oriole

Icterus graduacauda Lesson

NG–426; G–302; PW–pl 53; AE–pl 387; AM(III)–314

6'–14'

?

3–5
MONOG?

?
I: ? DAYS
ALTRICIAL
F: ? DAYS
?

FRUIT

BREEDING: Scrub, mesquite, riparian thickets, open oak woodland, pine-oak assoc. 2? broods. **DISPLAYS:** ? **NEST:** Oft in mesquite, attached by top and sides to upright terminal twigs; woven of fine green grass blades, lined with fine grass. **EGGS:** Pale bluish- or grayish-white, marked with browns, purples. 1.0″ (25 mm). **DIET:** Insects, fruit. **CONSERVATION:** Winter resident. Frequent Bronzed Cowbird host. Habitat alteration and increased cowbird populations have led to declining numbers since 1920s. **NOTES:** Inconspicuous in its behavior and not abundant. Oft seen in pairs(?) throughout year. Little known and virtually unstudied. Formerly known as Black-headed Oriole. **ESSAYS:** Masterbuilders, p. 445; Bird Badges, p. 591; Taxonomy and Nomenclature, p. 515; Cowbirds, p. 619; How Do We Find Out About Bird Biology?, p. 319. **REF:** Oberholser, 1974.

persed, female home ranges are rather large, resulting in promiscuous matings as females move over large areas.

Female home ranges are thought to overlap, since eggs of more than one female frequently are found in a single host's nest; a cowbird generally will lay only one egg per nest. Approximately one-third of all parasitized nests hold more than one cowbird egg. A female Brown-headed Cowbird often locates a potential host nest during its construction. She then regularly visits the nest prior to laying while the owners are absent. One day prior to, or on the day she lays her egg, the female cowbird usually removes (and occasionally eats) one host egg from the nest. If only one host egg is present, she does not remove it (otherwise the hosts might abandon their now eggless nest).

Circumstantial evidence indicates that in some areas, at least some female cowbirds specialize in particularly vulnerable host species, to the apparent exclusion of other species nesting nearby that serve as common hosts in other parts of the cowbird's range. A partial explanation could be that host species that have been in contact with cowbirds for a long time have evolved the ability to recognize the parasite or its eggs. As a result, many of these otherwise suitable host species make poor hosts because they aggressively attack female cowbirds, eject or destroy cowbird eggs found in their nests, or abandon their nests altogether upon detection of a parasite's egg. In contrast, many of the most accepting and most heavily affected host species may have been subjected to cowbird parasitism for only a short time because their ranges did not overlap prior to the cowbird's recent range expansion. Examples of species that may have been recently contacted and are now imperiled are Kirtland's Warbler and the California subspecies of Bell's Vireo, the Least Bell's Vireo. There is, however, little evidence as yet to support these "time of contact" explanations.

The only adaptation for parasitism seen in nestling and fledgling cowbirds is their rapid development. Cowbird eggs usually hatch one day ahead of the host's eggs. In addition cowbird nestlings usually are larger and grow faster than the host's young, which enable them to garner more than their fair share of the food brought to the nest. Cowbird fledglings do not recognize their foster parents as individuals, but respond positively to all adults of their foster parents' species. Fledglings receive more food than would the equivalent weight of host young, probably because their loud and persistent calling causes them to be fed more.

Even though some 97 percent of cowbird eggs and nestlings fail to reach adulthood, cowbird parasitism reduces production of young by the parasitized species. Abandonment of a nest by a parasitized host may preclude renesting and result in zero reproduction for that pair that breeding season. The reproductive effort of birds that suffer the presence of a cowbird chick in their nest will be significantly lower than that of unparasitized conspecifics in the same population. Because the cowbirds represent a major threat to many species of passerines, we have paid particular attention to the relative frequency of cowbird parasitism for all documented hosts in the

Northern Oriole

Icterus galbula Linnaeus

NG–426; G–304; PE–258; PW–pl 53; AE–pl 393; AW–pl 446; AM(III)–316

15'–30' (6'–60')	F –M	4–5 (3–6) MONOG?	F I: 12–14 DAYS ALTRICIAL F: 12–14 DAYS MF	FRUIT NECTAR	HAWKS

BREEDING: Open and riparian woodland, decid forest edge, open areas with scattered trees, around human habitation. 1 brood. **DISPLAYS:** Courting male rises to full height, bows low to female with tail spread and wings slightly raised; alternates between these two postures. **NEST:** Rarely in conif tree, attached at rim or secured at sides to drooping branch; woven of plant fiber strips, lined with fine grass, plant down, hair. Built in 4.5–15 days. **EGGS:** Pale grayish- to bluish-white, marked with dark colors. 0.9" (23 mm). **DIET:** Incl few spiders, snails; some buds in spring. **CONSERVATION:** Winters from c Mexico s to n e S.A., Greater Antilles; increasingly remains in e U.S. and CA due to feeders. Uncommon cowbird host; may eject cowbird eggs. **NOTES:** Formerly considered as two species, Baltimore and Bullock's Orioles. Loosely colonial in riparian woodland as a consequence of nest site scarcity. Female (Bullock's) sings early in nesting season. Males sexually mature at 1 year but acquire adult plumage in year 2. Postbreeding flocks of juveniles and females; adult males solitary. Solitary to slightly gregarious in winter in groups of up to 4. **ESSAYS:** Great Plains Hybrids, p. 625; Decline of Eastern Songbirds, p. 495; Feeding Birds, p. 349; Taxonomy and Nomenclature, p. 515. **REFS:** Flood, 1984; Pleasants, 1979; Sealy, 1980.

Hooded Oriole

Icterus cucullatus Swainson

NG–428; G–304; PW–pl 53; AE–pl 398; AW–pl 447; AM(III)–308

PALM YUCCA 12'–45'	MF?	3–4 (3–5) MONOG?	F I: 12–14 DAYS ALTRICIAL F: 14 DAYS MF	NECTAR FRUIT	

BREEDING: Riparian woodland, palm groves, mesquite, arid scrub, decid woodland, around human habitation. 2, occ 3 broods. **DISPLAYS:** Courtship: on elevated perch, male performs series of exaggerated bows toward female as he approaches, then hops around her singing softly and posturing with head pointed skyward, bill open; female may respond with similar posture. **NEST:** Suspended from twigs, or woven through overhanging leaves of palm or palmetto; woven of wiry green grass blades or shredded palm or yucca fibers, unlined or lined with plant down. Built in 3–4 days. If suspended from palm, nest opening on side. **EGGS:** Dull white, marked with browns, purples, grays. 0.9" (22 mm). **DIET:** Insects; nectar; fruit. **CONSERVATION:** Winters from n Mexico s to Oaxaca. Frequent Bronzed Cowbird host. Range expanding northward in CA, likely due to extensive plantings of palms and flower-bearing ornamentals. **NOTES:** Generally an "illegitimate" visitor to flowers—obtains nectar by piercing base of flower without pollinating. Young fed by regurgitation for 4–5 days. **ESSAYS:** Masterbuilders, p. 445; Bird Badges, p. 591; Taxonomy and Nomenclature, p. 515; Cowbirds, p. 619; Range Expansion, p. 459. **REF:** Orians, 1985.

species treatments, and we have designated the frequency with which they are parasitized as "rare," "uncommon," "common," and "frequent."

SEE: Brood Parasitism, p. 287; Conservation of Kirtland's Warbler, p. 527; Decline of Eastern Songbirds, p. 495. REFS: Darley, 1982; Friedmann and Kiff, 1985; Scott and Ankney, 1983; Teather and Robertson, 1986; Woodward, 1983.

Great Plains Hybrids

The grasslands and prairies of the Great Plains once presented an impenetrable barrier to avian dwellers of forests, woodland edges, and thickets in the East and West. All that changed with the advent of European-style agriculture and the planting of trees. Fingers and islands of deciduous forest along rivers and streams, on farms, and in towns began to reach out across the plains. They created suitable habitats for range expansion that affected 14 pairs of closely related, ecologically similar but geographically separated species. These closely related pairs of species had evolved in isolation from each other, and bringing them into contact resulted in hybridization (interbreeding) between members of most pairs of congeners (members of the same genus), as shown in the following table:

Eastern Form	Western Form	Hybrids	Studied?
E. Screech-Owl	W. Screech-Owl	Rare	No
Yellow-shafted Flicker	Red-shafted Flicker	Common	Yes
Red-bellied Woodpecker	Golden-fronted Woodpecker	Rare	No
Great Crested Flycatcher	Ash-throated Flycatcher	Unknown	No
E. Wood-Pewee	W. Wood-Pewee	Unknown	No
Blue Jay	Steller's Jay	Rare	No?
Carolina Chickadee	Black-capped Chickadee	Rare	No
Tufted Titmouse	Black-crested Titmouse	Common	Yes
E. Bluebird	Mountain Bluebird	Very rare*	No
Rose-breasted Grosbeak	Black-headed Grosbeak	Various	—†
Indigo Bunting	Lazuli Bunting	Common	Yes
Rufous-sided Towhee	Spotted Towhee	Common	Yes
E. Meadowlark	W. Meadowlark	Rare	Yes
Baltimore Oriole	Bullock's Oriole	Common	Yes

*Only a single hybrid known
†Common only along Platte River in central Nebraska; hybrids rare or unknown elsewhere; well studied in only a few locales

Although this "spread of agriculture and planting of trees" scenario appears likely for at least some of these species (e.g., the jays), extensive

Altamira Oriole

Icterus gularis Wagler

NG–428; G–304; PW–pl 53; AE–pl 397; AM(III)–314

12'–35' (To 80')	F	3–4 MONOG ?	F? I: ? DAYS ALTRICIAL F: ? DAYS MF	FRUIT	

BREEDING: Decid forest, arid scrub, open woodland, semidesert. 2 broods. **DISPLAYS:** ? **NEST:** Very exposed, suspended from twigs near end of branch; long, woven of plant fibers, epiphyte rootlets, lined with plant fiber, hair. Built in 18–26 days. **EGGS:** Bluish-white, marked with browns, purples, grays. 1.2" (29 mm). **DIET:** Occ forages on ground. **CONSERVATION:** Winter resident. Frequent Bronzed Cowbird host. Oft kept as cage bird in C.A. **NOTES:** Male and female both sing and are very vocal; songs and calls carry far. Young of first brood fed by male while female builds second nest. Details of breeding biology largely unknown. Previously known as Lichtenstein's Oriole. **ESSAYS:** Masterbuilders, p. 445; Bird Badges, p. 591; Taxonomy and Nomenclature, p. 515; Cowbirds, p. 619; Vocal Functions, p. 471; How Do We Find Out About Bird Biology?, p. 319. **REFS:** Oberholser, 1974; Skutch, 1960.

Spot-breasted Oriole

Icterus pectoralis Wagler

NG–428; G–304; PE–258; AE–pl 395; AM(III)–312

?	F	2–5? MONOG?	F? I: ? DAYS ALTRICIAL F: ? DAYS MF	NECTAR INSECTS	

BREEDING: Open woodland, arid scrub, decid forest, brushy areas. 2? broods. **DISPLAYS:** ? **NEST:** Long, well woven pouch attached near end of slim branch. Exterior woven in 5–6 days. **EGGS:** Pale blue or white, marked with dark colors. ?" (? mm). **DIET:** Primarily fruit and nectar. **CONSERVATION:** Introduced in Miami Beach, FL area around 1949. (Resident in Pacific lowlands from c Mexico s to Costa Rica, in arid interior valleys and on Caribbean slope of Guatemala and Honduras.) **NOTES:** Male exceptionally fine singer; female also sings. FL population stable but not expanding. Travels and roosts in small flocks, possibly family groups, in winter. **ESSAYS:** Avian Invaders, p. 633; Masterbuilders, p. 445; Bird Badges, p. 591; Taxonomy and Nomenclature, p. 515; Feral Birds, p. 654. **REFS:** Owre, 1973; Skutch, 1960.

field studies and better understanding of the dynamics of hybridization over the past 20 years have led to challenges of this view. The stability of hybrid zones for several species pairs has led some ornithologists to conclude that contact between them predates the arrival of European agriculture. In fact, Audubon recorded a mixed pair of flickers and their brood near the present Montana–North Dakota border, an area where hybrid flickers still predominate.

Across the range of locales where they overlap, only seven of the 14 species pairs have been adequately studied. Based on these studies, members of four of the hybridizing pairs previously treated as separate species have been combined into single species (Northern Flicker, Tufted Titmouse, Rufous-sided Towhee, Northern Oriole).

The orioles and buntings are particularly well studied and provide some interesting examples of hybrid zone dynamics. It appears that the Baltimore Oriole form is extending its range westward and replacing the Bullock's Oriole form both in the Canadian prairies and along the Platte River in Nebraska and Colorado. Along the Platte River, the geographic center of the hybrid zone between the two orioles has shifted 200 km westward over the past two decades. In contrast, the Bullock's appears to be extending eastward across southern Kansas and replacing the Baltimore at a similar pace, with the hybrid zone center shifting by 100 km eastward over the past decade. In spite of these shifts, the width of the hybrid zone has not increased. For the most part, there is little indication of assortative mating (the preferential mating of each oriole with individuals of the same form) or of selection against the hybrids.

Although an estimated one-third of Indigo and Lazuli Buntings hybridize in areas of contact where they are equally abundant, hybrids appear to have reduced viability, putting them at a selective disadvantage relative to pure Indigos or Lazulis. For this reason, the two buntings are, unlike the orioles, considered sufficiently distinct to be classified as separate species. The range of the Indigo has expanded westward by 200 km over a 15-year period in northern Nebraska and in western Kansas. In areas of regular contact, song switching between the species and interspecific territoriality both occur.

The extent of hybridization between members of the other seven pairs is poorly known for most areas of contact. The amateur as well as professional ornithologist can help clarify the relationships between these closely related species by carefully noting the composition of breeding pairs in these areas and their reproductive success.

SEE: Hybridization, p. 501; Species and Speciation, p. 355; Natural Selection, p. 237; Superspecies, p. 375; Sibling Species, p. 383; Taxonomy and Nomenclature, p. 515. REF: Rising, 1983.

Scarlet Tanager

Piranga olivacea Gmelin

NG–430; G–306; PE–260; PW–pl 53; AE–pl 416; AM(III)–194

CONIF	F	4	F I: 13–14 DAYS ALTRICIAL	FRUIT	FOLIAGE
20'–30'		(2–5)	F: 9–11 DAYS		GLEAN
(6'–60')		MONOG	MF		HAWKS

BREEDING: Decid forest and woodland, mixed decid-conif forest. 1 brood. **DIS-PLAYS:** Courtship: male hops about on low perches, spreads wings and displays his back to female perched above. **NEST:** On horizontal branch, well out from trunk; loosely built of grass, rootlets, forbs, twigs, lined with fine grass, forbs, rootlets. Female selects site. Built in 2–7 days. **EGGS:** Bluish, greenish, marked with browns, oft wreathed. 0.9″ (23 mm). **DIET:** Incl few other terrestrial inverts. Young fed insects, few berries. Also gleans from bark. **CONSERVATION:** Winters from Panama and Colombia s, e of Andes, to n w Bolivia, in variety of forest, woodland, and scrub. Common cowbird host; adults recognize female cowbird as enemy. **NOTES:** Where range overlaps with Summer Tanager, the two species respond aggressively to each other's songs and countersing; coexist by partial habitat shift maintained by interspecific aggression. Male occ feeds incubating female. Female broods for ca. 3 days, and in cold and rain. Females tend to forage higher than males; females forage by hawking far more than do males. No apparent dialects in advertising song. **ESSAYS:** Decline of Eastern Songbirds, p. 495; Vocal Dialects, p. 595; Interspecific Territoriality, p. 385; Vocal Functions, p. 471; Cowbirds, p. 619. **REFS:** Holmes, 1986; Shy 1984a, b.

Western Tanager

Piranga ludoviciana Wilson

NG–430; G–306; PE–260; PW–pl 53; AE–pl 389; AW–pl 454; AM(III)–196

6'–65'	?	3–5	F I: 13 DAYS ALTRICIAL	FRUIT	HAWKS
		MONOG?	F: 13–15(?) DAYS		
			MF		

BREEDING: Conif and mixed conif-decid woodland, mostly in mountains. ? broods. **DISPLAYS:** ? **NEST:** Rarely in decid tree; in fork on horizontal branch, well out from trunk; of twigs, rootlets, moss, lined with hair, rootlets. **EGGS:** Bluish, marked with browns, oft wreathed. 0.9″ (23 mm). **DIET:** Incl few buds. **CONSERVATION:** Winters mostly in highlands from c Mexico to Costa Rica, in variety of forest, woodland, and scrub, esp pine, pine-oak, forest edge and clearings. Rare cowbird host. **NOTES:** Female does not flush easily when incubating. **ESSAYS:** Decline of Eastern Songbirds, p. 495; Colors of Birds, p. 111; Wintering and Conservation, p. 513. **REF:** Bent, 1958.

Bird Biologist—Carolus Linnaeus

The father of biological taxonomy, the Swedish botanist Carolus Linnaeus (1707–78), was, of course, much more than a bird biologist. He was made professor of medicine and botany at Uppsala University in 1741, and died still holding that position. Linnaeus was, according to his biographer, a "complete naturalist," a man who thought God had given him the mission of bringing order out of chaos by naming and classifying living organisms. He not only studied specimens sent to him but also traveled to collect his own (although he never visited the Western Hemisphere).

The Linnaean system of binomial nomenclature is used today for all organisms, and the tenth edition of his great work *Systema Naturae* (1758), is now the official starting point of zoological (and bird) nomenclature. Animal names given prior to its publication have no standing; those Linnaeus coined in that edition, and those given subsequently, do.

Linnaeus formally described and gave scientific names to a large number of a birds that live in North America. These include Arctic Loon, Pied-billed Grebe, Brown Pelican, Anhinga, Great Blue Heron, Little Egret, White Ibis, Wood Stork, Snow Goose, Canada Goose, Wood Duck, Northern Pintail, Red-breasted Merganser, Sora, Northern Jacana, Parasitic Jaeger, Bald Eagle, American Kestrel, Snowy Owl, Belted Kingfisher, Eastern Kingbird, Winter Wren, Golden-winged Warbler, Summer Tanager, Northern Oriole, and House Sparrow, to name just a few.

SEE: Taxonomy and Nomenclature, p. 515.   REF: Owen, 1985.

Urban Birds

Referring to an inner-city bird perched on a neglected dumpster as an avian cockroach or feathered rat may well raise appreciative nods. In fact, the ability of vast numbers of birds to make their homes in cities regularly calls upon the ingenuity of people to establish bird-free zones. This situation is not restricted to North America. In Moscow, for example, to keep Hooded Crows from sliding down renowned and easily scratched gold-leaf on onion domes, recordings of falcons and Northern Goshawks (the crow's major predators) were played and trained falcons released. Animal rights activists periodically disapprove of such niche-emptying efforts, but when birds are in conflict with people, it is the avian populations that are reduced and the human populations appeased.

But not all city dwellers consider urban birds as candidates for extermination. More and more people, in addition to those who enjoy feeding pigeons and sparrows in parks, are viewing their avian neighbors with interest. For birders who cannot often venture into a natural setting there is

Summer Tanager

Piranga rubra Linnaeus

NG–430; G–306; PE–260; PW–pl 53; AE–pl 417; AW–pl 449; AM(III)–194

CONIF	?	4	? I: 12 DAYS ALTRICIAL	FRUIT	HAWKS
TREE		(3–5)	F: ? DAYS		HOVER &
10'–35'		MONOG?	MF		GLEAN

BREEDING: Decid forest, open and riparian woodland, pine-oak association, parks. ? broods. **DISPLAYS:** ? **NEST:** On horizontal branch; loosely built of grass, forbs, Spanish moss, lined with fine grass. **EGGS:** Pale blue, pale green, marked with browns, occ wreathed or capped. 0.9" (23 mm). **DIET:** Incl esp bees and wasps, few spiders. **CONSERVATION:** Winters from c Mexico s to w Ecuador s e to Amazonian Brazil, but most abundant in lowlands in wide variety of forest, woodland, and scrub. Range reportedly contracting in e U.S. Uncommon cowbird host. **NOTES:** Frequently raids beehives and paper wasp nests to obtain larvae and adults. Where range overlaps with Scarlet Tanager, the two species respond aggressively to each other's songs and countersing; coexist by partial habitat shift maintained by interspecific aggression. Solitary in winter, apparently holding exclusive feeding territories. **ESSAYS:** Interspecific Territoriality, p. 385; Vocal Functions, p. 471; Territoriality, p. 387. **REF:** Shy, 1984b.

Hepatic Tanager

Piranga flava Vieillot

NG–430; G–306; PW–pl 53; AW–pl 450; AM(III)–192

DECID	?	4	? I: ? DAYS ALTRICIAL	FRUIT	HAWKS
TREE		(3–5)	F: ? DAYS		
18'–50'		MONOG?	?		

BREEDING: Open conif forest (esp pine and piñon-juniper), montane pine-oak assoc, riparian woodland, lowland pine savanna. ? broods. **DISPLAYS:** ? **NEST:** In fork of horizontal branch, well out from trunk; of grass and forb stems, lined with finer grass. **EGGS:** Bluish, greenish, marked with browns, oft wreathed. 1.0" (24 mm). **DIET:** Insects; fruit. **CONSERVATION:** Winters from n Mexico s to n Nicaragua, in a variety of forest and woodland. Rare Bronzed Cowbird host. **NOTES:** Breeding biology not well known. Male sings from high perch. **ESSAYS:** Decline of Eastern Songbirds, p. 495; How Do We Find Out About Bird Biology?, p. 319; Wintering and Conservation, p. 513. **REF:** Phillips et al., 1964.

a wealth of avian activity to watch right in the city. Some urban birds become uncharacteristically tame and relatively simple to observe. It is easier, for example, to witness the maintenance of dominance hierarchies in slow-gaited city pigeons (Rock Doves) than in their fast-flying country cousins. Similarly, city crows, park ducks, outdoor restaurant House Sparrows, and parking lot Brewer's Blackbirds are more approachable than their rural brethren.

The artificial concrete and steel ecosystems of cities, including occasional small, manicured parks, can support a surprisingly large number of birds. The birds are often most visible where people have congregated to buy, sell, eat, and discard food. The commensal relationship (whereby birds vacuum up bits of food that people do not value for themselves—items dropped, discarded, or purposely provided) is evident near benches in city parks, in playgrounds, sports stadiums, and the parking lots of fast-food restaurants, at deserted farmers' markets and fairgrounds, around refuse disposal areas, and at window ledge feeders.

Urban birds differ from wild populations in several ways, besides just being easier to observe. A number of ornithologists have looked at the ways birds have adapted to urban foraging. For example, in cities that lie in the snowbelt, birds may seek underground heating ducts over which plants can grow, and have also learned to feed in areas illuminated by artificial light where they can prolong their foraging schedule. In another case, although feral (country) pigeons usually eat twice a day, filling their crops at each session and digesting the food between the feeding bouts, city pigeons face a less predictable food supply, and are much more opportunistic, having a relatively irregular feeding schedule.

Beyond foraging strategies, however, we know little about other aspects of urban bird behavior. Do different neighborhoods, for example, support different dialects in House Sparrows? Do fluctuating population sizes and uncertain resources cause changes in avian behavior? Will, for example, group territoriality eventually evolve so that gangs of grackles, European Starlings, and blackbirds stake claims when the available "turf" is limited? And how do fluctuations in the number of city birds affect their avian predators? Domestic pigeons, for example, are the favored prey of Peregrine Falcons. If the number of pigeons is reduced, will Peregrines living around urban areas resort to a different prey or suffer substantial losses? In the 1940s a scarcity in feed led to such a reduction in the German pigeon population and resulted in a decline of Peregrines. As yet, however, no parallel trends have been described or predicted in North America.

Urban habitats favor species that are less affected by toxic substances flowing through cities, that are better able to adapt to artificial light, to communicate over the noise of traffic and automation, to breed successfully on human built structures, and to rebound after city council decisions to decimate their populations. As more of the natural habitat of Earth is destroyed, urban birds will become more "typical" of our avifauna. As tongue-in-cheek evolutionists claim, birds may, indeed, be feathered dino-

Eurasian Tree Sparrow

Passer montanus Linnaeus

NG–432; G–296; PE–262; PW–pl 58; AE–pl 524; AM(III)–350

? MF(?) 4–6
(4–8)
MONOG?

MF
I: 13–14 DAYS
ALTRICIAL
F: 12–14 DAYS
MF(?)

INSECTS

BREEDING: Woodland, cultivated and old fields, around human habitation. 2, occ 3 broods. **DISPLAYS:** ? **NEST:** In natural or previously excavated tree hole, or artificial cavity; of grass, forbs, lined with feathers. **EGGS:** White to pale gray, marked with browns; darker than House Sparrow's. 0.8″ (20 mm). **DIET:** Incl grass and forb seeds. **CONSERVATION:** Winter resident. 20 birds introduced in 1870 in St. Louis, MO from Germany; has spread only into e c MO and w IL. **NOTES:** Generally in flocks of 50–100, occ with House Sparrows. Neither aggressive nor pugnacious like House Sparrow; competition with House Sparrow may be primary factor limiting spread and holding total numbers to ca. 150,000. **ESSAYS:** Avian Invaders, p. 633; Bathing and Dusting, p. 429; Communal Roosting, p. 615. **REFS:** Anderson, 1977; Barlow, 1973; Lang and Barlow, 1987.

House Sparrow

Passer domesticus Linnaeus

NG–432; G–296; PE–262; PW–pl 60; AE–pl 525; AW–pl 592; AM(III)–348

BUILDING

TREE
To 40′

SPHERICAL
MF

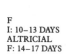

4–6
(3–7)
?

F
I: 10–13 DAYS
ALTRICIAL
F: 14–17 DAYS
MF

INSECTS
FRUIT

FOLIAGE
GLEAN

BREEDING: Cultivated lands, woodland and edge, around human habitation. 2, oft 3 broods. **DISPLAYS:** Courting male hops around female, back flattened, head up, tail down, wings extended, and tips of primaries nearly touching the ground. **NEST:** In artificial or natural cavity; also rarely ball-shaped with entrance on side, placed in fork or tree branch; of grass, forbs, lined with feathers, hair. Male or female may select site. **EGGS:** White, greenish, or bluish, marked with gray or brown. 0.9″ (23 mm). **DIET:** Incl spiders; grass and forb seeds, blossoms. Young fed mostly insects. **CONSERVATION:** Winter resident. Introduced and established between 1850 and 1867. Aggressively appropriates nests, esp of bluebirds and swallows, oft destroying eggs and nestlings. **NOTES:** Most abundant species in U.S. in early 1900s except in densely forested, alpine and desert regions. Decreased with advent of automobile and decline of horse, esp in e urban areas; presumably because of disappearance of grain fed to horses and spread in their manure. Still abundant in agricultural areas. Competition for nest sites begins in autumn for the following spring. Mostly female broods young. Large winter roosts in or near human dwellings or in dense evergreen trees. Has differentiated geographically since introduction to N.A.; races now vary in color and body size in different parts of N.A. range. **ESSAYS:** Avian Invaders, p. 633; Natural Selection, p. 237; Wing Shapes and Flight, p. 227; Bathing and Dusting, p. 429; Species and Speciation, p. 355; Communal Roosting, p. 615. **REFS:** Hegner and Wingfield, 1986, 1987; Johnston and Selander, 1964; Murphy, 1978; Robbins, 1973.

saurs. Many species of birds may soon follow the dinosaurs into extinction, but it seems likely that urban birds will be around as long as there are people to build cities.

SEE: Helping to Conserve Birds—Local Level, p. 361; Feeding Birds, p. 349; Dominance Hierarchies, p. 533; Population Dynamics, p. 575; Habitat Selection, p. 463; Commensal Feeding, p. 35. REFS: Lefebvre and Giraldeau, 1984; Ratcliffe, 1980; Tudge, 1986.

Avian Invaders

Some of the most abundant birds in North America were deliberately introduced to our continent. We owe the presence of the extremely successful (and often pestiferous) European Starling to William Shakespeare. Toward the end of the last century, "The American Acclimatization Society" had the goal of establishing in the United States every species of bird mentioned in the works of the immortal Bard of Avon. Unfortunately, in *Henry IV*, Hotspur proclaimed, "Nay, I'll have a starling shall be taught to speak nothing but 'Mortimer'. . . ." North American birds and people have been suffering ever since.

The starlings' impact on native birds, in some cases, appears to have been severe. Starlings also devour grain put out for cattle in feedlots, damage crops, foul buildings and walkways with their droppings, and may be involved in transmitting histoplasmosis, a serious fungal disease of human beings.

A great deal of money has been spent trying to control starling populations, and many of the birds have been killed. In the 1960s, one program in California designed to alleviate starling depredations on cattle feed resulted in the slaughter of some 9 million birds, but left 5,000 starlings in the area alive to reproduce. In spite of such massive efforts to reduce the numbers of descendants of those birds introduced by the Acclimatization Society, starlings are today ubiquitous on the North American continent except for the Far North.

It is interesting to speculate on why some introduced birds thrive, while others do not. The Crested Myna, a close relative of the starling, has never spread beyond the Vancouver, British Columbia, area, where it became established during the last century. Apparently it has remained localized because it retains incubating habits more suitable to its tropical homeland than to the temperate zone, thus limiting its reproductive success.

More mysterious is the case of the House (or English) Sparrow and its close relative, the Eurasian Tree Sparrow. The House Sparrow formed a relationship with *Homo sapiens* shortly after people in the Middle East first settled down and started farming. The sparrows are thought to have originally been migratory, but they appear to have lost that ability over many

Pine Siskin

Carduelis pinus Wilson

NG–434; G–320; PE–272; PW–pl 55; AE–pl 557; AW–pl 598; AM(III)–338

DECID	F	3–4	F I: 13 DAYS	INSECTS	GROUND
8'–50'		(1–5)	ALTRICIAL		GLEAN
(3'–50')		MONOG	F: 14–15 DAYS MF		

BREEDING: Conif and mixed conif-decid forest, woodland, parks, suburbs. 2? broods. **DISPLAYS**: Courtship (begins prior to breakup of winter flocks): male spreads tail, flaps wings rapidly while circling over female during flight song. Courtship feeding. **NEST**: On horizontal limb well out from trunk; of twigs, rootlets, grass, lined with fine rootlets, moss, fur, feathers. Female chooses site. **EGGS**: Pale greenish-blue, spotted with browns, black, usu wreathed. 0.7″ (17 mm). **DIET**: Incl seeds of decid and conif trees, forbs, and grass, floral buds and nectar (of trees), sap. **CONSERVATION**: Winters s to n Mexico; migrates altitudinally in some areas. Uncommon cowbird host. Fondness for road salts leads to many deaths from automobiles. **NOTES**: Oft semicolonial, only few feet between nests. Social all year, oft feeds in small groups in breeding season. Male feeds female on nest from incubation to few days after hatching; during latter period, male supplies food to female for nestlings. When foraging in flocks, birds tend to move down from top of tree in compact group, then move in circular flight to another tree and repeat. Winter flocks usu 50–200, occ to 1,000. Nomadic in fall and winter; feeds in mixed flocks, esp with goldfinches, juncos, crossbills. **ESSAYS**: Irruptions, p. 639; Birds, DNA, and Evolutionary Convergence, p. 419; Mixed-Species Flocking, p. 433; Courtship Feeding, p. 181. **REF**: Bent, 1968.

Lawrence's Goldfinch

Carduelis lawrencei Cassin

NG–434; G–320; PW–pl 55; AW–pl 418; AM(III)–342

SHRUB	F	4–5	F I: ? DAYS	INSECTS	GROUND
3'–40'		(3–6)	ALTRICIAL		GLEAN
		MONOG ?	F: 11–13 DAYS MF		

BREEDING: Oak and riparian woodland, chaparral, piñon/juniper woodland, arid weedy areas near water. ? broods. **DISPLAYS**: Courting male perches near female, extends head and neck, and sings. **NEST**: Dainty cup of grass, lichen, forb stems, flower heads, hair, feathers. **EGGS**: Pale bluish-white or white, unmarked. 0.6″ (15 mm). **DIET**: Variety of native plant seeds, not as varied as Lesser Goldfinch; few insects. Fondness for salt, esp when nesting. Availability of water is important, strongly affects distribution, esp during nesting. **CONSERVATION**: Winters s to n w Mexico. Rare cowbird host. **NOTES**: Occ semicolonial. Erratic distribution during breeding season from year to year. Female incubates for long periods (up to 97% of time) with little time spent away from nest. Male feeds female from incubation to few days after hatching as male continues to supply food to female for young. Fond of bathing. Forages in flocks; flocks throughout year occ with other seed eaters, e.g., Lesser Goldfinch, House Finch, junco, Lark Sparrow. **ESSAYS**: Bird Biology and the Arts, p. 47; Mixed-Species Flocking, p. 433; Incubation Time, p. 481; Bathing and Dusting, p. 429; Drinking, p. 123. **REF**: Bent, 1968.

generations as they evolved the habit of overwintering close to settlements and feeding on grain stores, garbage, and other materials made available by human activities. Sparrow populations grew especially large in cities when horses and their seed-rich droppings were common.

Several attempts were made to introduce the House Sparrow to North America, both because people considered it attractive and because it was hoped that the bird would help control insect pests. The first successful introduction was made in Brooklyn shortly after 1850, and like the starling the House Sparrow spread rapidly, taking only 50 years to occupy suitable habitats over the entire United States. In contrast, the Tree Sparrow was established in St. Louis in 1870, but for almost 100 years remained largely confined to that area. Around 1960 it began to spread, and has since occupied adjacent parts of Missouri and Illinois, but it has shown none of the colonizing vigor of the House Sparrow. On other continents where both species have been introduced, the House Sparrow invariably has been the most successful.

Ecologists still do not understand why the two species have had such different colonization histories. The House Sparrow is somewhat larger, and a bigger bird may compete better with native finchlike species, but the size difference is not great. Pure luck might be invoked to explain the difference in the United States. For instance, the original stock of the House Sparrow might have contained a sample of the genetic traits of that species better suited for survival here than did the initial Tree Sparrow immigrants. Or the Tree Sparrow may have had the misfortune to bring more of its diseases with it. However, since the House Sparrow seems a more vigorous colonizer wherever it has been introduced, as the sole explanation chance alone seems unlikely. It is possible that the House Sparrow simply outcompetes the Tree Sparrow in areas of human disturbance. Outside of their native communities in Eurasia those may be the only areas invasible by either.

Not all introductions of birds have been intentional. Escapes and releases of caged pet birds have caused a rash of introductions of parrots, parakeets, doves, and others into the United States—mostly in Florida and southern California. The demise of the Carolina Parakeet ended the natural occurrence of parrots north of Mexico, but it remains to be seen whether any of the related introduced species will build large, sustainable populations in North America.

Finally, there are birds that have invaded North America in historic times under their own steam. Of these, the Old World Cattle Egret is the best known and most successful. Around 1880 the egret reached Suriname on the northern coast of South America, and it arrived in Florida about 1940. It is now firmly established over the eastern and southwestern United States, thriving in the pastures and among the cattle herds established by *Homo sapiens*.

The spread of the egret is, of course, just a recently observed example of a natural process that has gone on for as long as there have been birds (indeed, as long as there have been organisms)—i.e., species crossing bar-

Lesser Goldfinch

Carduelis psaltria Say

NG–434; G–320; PW–pl 55; AW–pl 417; AM(III)–340

  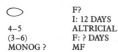

			F?		
			I: 12 DAYS		
SHRUB	F	4–5	ALTRICIAL	INSECTS	
FORB		(3–6)	F: ? DAYS		
2'–30'		MONOG ?	MF		

BREEDING: Open habitats with scattered trees or brush, forest edge, fields, suburban areas. 2? broods. **DISPLAYS:** Male song-flight display: spreads wings and tail widely and flaps wings rapidly. Courtship feeding. **NEST:** Compactly woven of plant fibers, grass stems, bark, moss, lined with plant down. Male may help build in early stages. **EGGS:** Pale blue or bluish-white, unmarked. 0.6" (15 mm). **DIET:** Incl seeds of decid trees, forbs, and grass, also floral buds, berries. Young fed regurgitant of milky seed pulp. Fond of salt. Availability of water is important and strongly affects distribution, esp in dry seasons. **CONSERVATION:** Winter resident, although e form (black-backed) reported partially migratory. Rare cowbird host. **NOTES:** Late nester. Male feeds incubating female by regurgitation. Pair may stay together in winter. Highly gregarious during winter forming flocks of up to 400, occ assoc with other goldfinches and siskins. **ESSAYS:** Bird Biology and the Arts, p. 47; Mixed-Species Flocking, p. 433; Breeding Season, p. 55; Courtship Feeding, p. 181; Drinking, p. 123. **REF:** Bent, 1968.

American Goldfinch

Carduelis tristis Linnaeus

NG–434; G–320; PE–272; PW–pl 55; AE–pl 385; AW–pl 408; AM(III)–344

			F		
			I: 10–12 DAYS		
TREE	F	4–6	ALTRICIAL	INSECTS	GROUND
1'–30'		(3–7)	F: 11–17 DAYS		GLEAN
(To 60')		MONOG	MF		

BREEDING: Weedy and cultivated fields, open decid and riparian woodland. Occ 2 broods. **DISPLAYS:** Male song-flight on level (rather than typical undulating) flight, rapidly flapping wings. **NEST:** In branch fork, oft woven so tightly that nest holds water; of forbs, other pliable veg, lined with plant down. Caterpillar webbing and spider silk oft used to bind outer rim. Male may collect some nest material and give to female. **EGGS:** Pale blue or bluish-white, unmarked. 0.6" (16 mm). **DIET:** Incl seeds of decid trees, forbs (esp composites), grass, floral buds, berries. Young fed regurgitant of milky seed pulp; few insects. **CONSERVATION:** Winters s to n Mexico (and along coast to Veracruz). Common cowbird host. Declined in n e as House Sparrows increased. **NOTES:** Commonly change mates between years; females show nest-site tenacity. Nests usu near water. Male feeds female on nest; female may call to male to be fed, begs when he appears with food. Females may sit on eggs 95% of the time! Hatching asynchronous, increasingly so as season progresses. Late nester except in CA and s w; older birds nest earlier than younger birds. Winter flocks up to 300 common, oft with siskins, redpolls. **ESSAYS:** Bird Biology and the Arts, p. 47; Site Tenacity, p. 189; Mixed-Species Flocking, p. 433; Incubation Time, p. 481; Incubation: Heating Eggs, p. 393; Brood Reduction, p. 307; Cowbirds, p. 619. **REFS:** Middleton, 1978, 1979; Skagen, 1987.

riers and extending their ranges into new areas of suitable habitat. It is a mistake to regard distribution maps as final. We should always be on the alert for expansion and shrinkage of the area occupied by a bird species—it is a normal process.

SEE: Incubation Time, p. 481; Hawaiian Bird Biology, p. 651; Feral Birds, p. 654; Urban Birds, p. 629; Population Dynamics, p. 575. REFS: Ehrlich, 1986b, 1987; Johnson and Cowan, 1974; Long, 1981.

Bird Biologist—Arthur Bent

The basic foundation on which this, and all other compilations of the biology of North American birds rests, is the 26-volume series *Life Histories of North American Birds* (1919–68). It was edited, and mostly written, by Arthur Cleveland Bent (1866–1954), a successful businessman who from boyhood had been a dedicated amateur ornithologist. He began sending papers to *The Auk* in 1901, and soon was making important contributions on distributions and nesting habits of a wide variety of species. In 1910 the Smithsonian Institution asked Bent to continue a series on the life histories of birds that had been started by Charles Bendire (p. 439) more than a decade earlier. Bent was already, in essence, doing that, and had (from the Smithsonian's viewpoint) the enormous advantage of not requiring a salary. Bent accepted, but instead of continuing began afresh, and for the remaining 44 years of his life devoted himself to the project. When he died, the penultimate volume, *Blackbirds, Orioles, Tanagers, and Allies,* was ready to go to the printer; it remained only for the three parts on finches to be completed, which they were in 1968.

SEE: Bibliography for complete listing of Bent's *Life Histories*.

Red Crossbill
Loxia curvirostra Linnaeus

NG–436; G–322; PE–268; PW–pl 55; AE–pl 412; AW–pl 452; AM(III)–332

			F		
			I: 12–18 DAYS		
6'–40'	F	3–4	ALTRICIAL	BUDS	
		(2–5)	F: 15–20 DAYS		
		MONOG	MF		

BREEDING: Conif and mixed conif-decid forest. 1 brood; 2 in Rockies. **DISPLAYS:** In flight song, male vibrates wings and circles above female. Courtship feeding. **NEST:** Bulky, loosely built far from trunk on horizontal branch; of twigs, grass, moss, rootlets, bark strips, lined with feathers, hair, moss, lichen. Female selects site. **EGGS:** Pale bluish- or greenish-white, spotted with browns, purples, mostly at large end. 0.8″ (21 mm). **DIET:** Esp conif tree seeds (also decid buds and seeds), spruce buds, forb seeds, few insects, berries. Occ feeds on ground on fallen seeds. Young fed regurgitant of milky seed pulp. **CONSERVATION:** Wanders s to n w Mexico in winter. Breeding range in e expanding s. **NOTES:** Usu breeds from late winter to early spring. Male feeds incubating and brooding female by regurgitation; accompanied by mutual calling. Tips of mandibles cross gradually over few weeks after fledging. Individuals right- or left-handed in opening cones, according to which way mandibles cross. Mandibles inserted into cone to force and hold apart the scales, seed then lifted out by tongue. Reminiscent of small parrots when climbing slowly among branches using both bills and feet. In Rockies, may breed in year hatched. **ESSAYS:** Winter Feeding, p. 641; Irruptions, p. 639; Population Dynamics, p. 575; Courtship Feeding, p. 181; Bills, p. 209. **REFS:** Benkman, 1987a, b.

White-winged Crossbill
Loxia leucoptera Gmelin

NG–436; G–322; PE–268; PW–pl 55; AE–pl 413; AW–pl 453; AM(III)–334

			F		
			I: 12–14(?) DAYS		
3'–70'	F?	4	ALTRICIAL	GROUND	
		(2–5)	F: ? DAYS	GLEAN	
		MONOG ?	F – M?		

BREEDING: Conif and mixed conif-decid forest. ? broods. **DISPLAYS:** Continuous flight song as male slowly beats wings while circling above female. **NEST:** Usu far from trunk on horizontal branch; of twigs, moss, lichen, grass and forb stems, insect cocoons, bark, lined with fine materials. **EGGS:** Pale bluish- or greenish-white, marked with browns, purples. 0.8″ (21 mm). **DIET:** Mostly conif seeds; also seeds of decid trees, grass, and forbs; few berries, insects. Young fed regurgitant of milky seed pulp. Commonly feed on ground on fallen cones. Fond of salt. **CONSERVATION:** Wanders erratically and sporadically within N.A. in winter. Range expanding to s in w. Fondness for road salt produces occ heavy mortality as listless birds are run over. **NOTES:** Usu breeds from late winter to early spring. Male feeds incubating female by regurgitation; lands near nest and calls before flying to her; after feeding, male occ gives flight song display. Tameness and feeding behavior as in Red Crossbill. Winter flocks of 12–50, occ to 300; occ mixed with Red Crossbills, redpolls, Pine Siskins, Pine and Evening Grosbeaks, waxwings. **ESSAYS:** Winter Feeding by Redpolls and Crossbills, p. 641; Irruptions, p. 639; Population Dynamics, p. 575; Range Expansion, p. 459; Bills, p. 209. **REFS:** Benkman, 1987a, b.

Irruptions

Southward autumn invasions (irruptions) by normally northern seed-eating birds are dramatic but apparently irregular events. Irruptive North American species include Bohemian and Cedar Waxwings, Pine and Evening Grosbeaks, Black-capped and Boreal Chickadees, Red-breasted Nuthatch, Pine Siskin, Common and Hoary Redpolls, Purple Finch, and Clark's Nutcracker. The species perhaps best associated with these occurrences, however, are the Red and White-winged Crossbills. Three major questions are raised by these irruptive migrations: What causes them? Are they really irregular events? Are they synchronized among populations within a species and between species?

Ornithologists generally concur that irruptions are triggered by food shortages, such as failure of the coniferous cone crops over a large geographic area. Analysis by ornithologists Carl Bock and Larry Lepthien of many years of Audubon Christmas Counts indicate that a synchronization of seed crop failures in some high-latitude tree species leads to southward irruptions of species normally dependent on those seeds.

Years of good crops, which presumably result in higher population densities of seed-eating birds, are often followed by years with poor crops. Thus, in a year of crop failure that followed one of abundant seeds, bird populations may be larger than normal. This adds to pressure on scarce food resources and serves as additional impetus to migrate. It appears, then, that seed crop size is the primary cause of irruptions and that large population sizes may sometimes be a contributing factor. However, because many other factors (such as insect abundance during the breeding season) can affect population density in any given year, not all species will be affected synchronously by a seed crop failure that leads to irruptions of some species.

Diurnal and nocturnal raptors that feed on small mammals with cyclic population fluctuations constitute another group of irruptive species which also eat foods that fluctuate from year to year in boreal regions. Among North American species, Rough-legged Hawk, Northern Goshawk, Snowy, Great Horned, and Short-eared Owls are known to irrupt periodically. Two main cycles are recognized in boreal small mammals: a four-year cycle among tundra and grassland rodents, and a ten-year cycle that characterizes snowshoe hares. Why populations of these species explode and crash with these approximate periodicities is not clear, but when they crash the predictable result is a southward irruption of many of their avian predators. As in northern seed-eating birds, problems of food scarcity caused by the crash are often exacerbated by dense raptor populations that resulted from preceding years of relatively high prey abundance. Invasions by Rough-legged Hawks and Snowy Owls often occur in the same year, with about a four-year periodicity, because both of these species feed largely on rodents. In contrast, invasions by Northern Goshawks, which feed to a great extent on hares and rabbits, occur roughly in ten-year cycles.

Pine Grosbeak

Pinicola enucleator Linnaeus

NG–436; G–316; PE–270; PW–pl 55; AE–pl 414; AW–pl 466; AM(III)–326

SHRUB
2'–25'

?

4
(2–5)
MONOG ?

F
I: 13–15 DAYS
ALTRICIAL
F: 13–20 DAYS
MF

BUDS
FRUIT
INSECTS

GROUND
GLEAN

BREEDING: Open conif forest and forest edge. 1? brood. **DISPLAYS**: Male feeds female as part of courtship. **NEST**: Bulky, loose; of moss, twigs, grass, lichens, lined with fine grass, rootlets, moss, lichens, occ fur. Nests at lower latitudes usu higher because trees are usu taller. **EGGS**: Bluish-green, marked with purple, brown, black, scattered over entire egg or concentrated at large end. 1.0" (26 mm). **DIET**: Incl buds, fruit, and seeds of conif and decid trees, forb seeds. Esp favor crab apples, mountain ash fruit, pine seeds, maple buds. **CONSERVATION**: Winters within N.A., wandering sporadically, occ far to s, perhaps due to reduced supplies of fruit, cones, and seeds in n. **NOTES**: In breeding season, male and female develop a pair of pouches in floor of mouth for transporting food to young. Male feeds female during incubation, but female reportedly leaves nest to receive food. Ridiculously tame and approachable in winter; feeds in flocks of 5–30, occ with Bohemian Waxwings. Bathes in soft snow. **ESSAYS**: Irruptions, p. 639; Winter Feeding by Redpolls and Crossbills, p. 641; Courtship Feeding, p. 181; Bathing and Dusting, p. 429. **REFS**: Adkisson, 1981; Pullianinen, 1979.

Common Redpoll

Supersp #53
Carduelis flammea Linnaeus

NG–438; G–318; PE–270; PW–pl 55; AE–pl 411; AW–pl 463; AM(III)–336

ROCKS
3'–6'

CREVICE
F?

4–5
(4–7)
MONOG ?

F
I: 10–11 DAYS
ALTRICIAL
F: 12 DAYS
F –M

INSECTS

GROUND
GLEAN

BREEDING: Subarctic forest, shrubby areas, open tundra with scattered shrubs. 1, occ 2 broods. **DISPLAYS**: Courtship: female crouches with drooped wings and twitters while male stands stiffly before her and bows. **NEST**: Foundation of twigs with woven cup of fine twigs, rootlets, grass, lichen, moss, lined with ptarmigan feathers, plant down, fur. **EGGS**: Pale green or bluish, spotted with purples esp at large end. 0.7" (17 mm). **DIET**: Primarily seeds of decid and conif shrubs, forbs, and grass; insects taken when abundant. **CONSERVATION**: Winters within N.A.; biennial invasion into s portion of range likely related to reduced availability of food farther n. **NOTES**: Apparently not territorial, nests occ close together. Little fidelity to breeding or wintering areas. Song most common prior to breakup of winter flocks. Study of captive flock revealed rigid social hierarchy: males dominant over females during nonbreeding season, reversed with approach of breeding season. Male feeds incubating female. Winter flocks of a few individuals to >100 of mixed forms and species of redpolls; tame and easily approached. Bathes in winter in snow or water. **ESSAYS**: Irruptions, p. 639; Winter Feeding by Redpolls and Crossbills, p. 641; Feathered Nests, p. 605; Dominance Hierarchies, p. 533; Bathing and Dusting, p. 429. **REFS**: Evans, 1969; Hilden, 1969; Troy, 1983.

SEE: Population Dynamics, p. 575; Range Expansion, p. 459; Bird Guilds, p. 493; Raptor Hunting, p. 223; How Owls Hunt in the Dark, p. 291. REFS: Bock and Lepthien, 1976; Newton, 1979.

Winter Feeding by Redpolls and Crossbills

One of the most important adaptations enabling redpolls and crossbills to cope with the energy demands imposed by severe arctic and subarctic winters is a structure that is somewhat analogous to the substantial crop of gallinaceous birds. The structure is a partially bilobed pocket situated about midway down the neck, technically an "esophageal diverticulum." The pocket is used to store seeds, especially toward nightfall and during particularly severe weather. The "extra" food helps carry the bird through low nighttime temperatures and permits energy to be saved during bad weather by reducing foraging time and allowing the bird to "feed" while resting in a sheltered spot.

Redpolls in winter feed primarily on birch seeds, and the presence of an esophageal diverticulum permits feeding behavior consisting of three distinct phases. In phase I, the birds acrobatically knock seeds from the birch catkins to the ground below. In phase II the birds gather the seeds from the often snow-covered ground and store them in their diverticula. The birds can then fly to a sheltered spot (phase III) where they are better protected from predators and where they can shell and consume the seeds at their leisure. Redpolls and crossbills seek the wind-protected shelter provided by dense coniferous foliage, remain stationary, and adopt a "fluffed-ball" posture that further reduces heat loss.

Redpolls appear to be able to survive colder temperatures than any other songbirds that have been studied in detail. Large birds, of course, have a great advantage in saving heat because they have a relatively small surface area for their volume. Birds as large as ptarmigans and as small as Snow Buntings may burrow into loose snow to sleep. Two feet down in the snow the temperature can be 25°F when the air above the snow is colder than − 50°F. But neither a large bird nor a small one can survive long in an arctic or subarctic winter without an ample supply of food.

The diversity of species you will encounter, should you have the opportunity to watch birds in the northern winter, will be low, but observing the ways they manage to cope with an extremely severe environment can be fascinating.

SEE: Feeding Birds, p. 349; Swallowing Stones, p. 269; Irruptions, p. 639; Feathered Nests, p. 605; Temperature Regulation and Behavior, p. 149; Metabolism, p. 325. REF: Brooks, 1978.

Hoary Redpoll
Supersp #53
Carduelis hornemanni Holböll

NG–438; G–318; PE–270; PW–pl 55; AE–579; AW–pl 464; AM(III)–338

| ROCKS 1'–7' | CREVICE F | 4–5 (3–7) MONOG ? | F I: 11 DAYS ALTRICIAL F: 9–14 DAYS ? | BUDS INSECTS | GROUND GLEAN |

BREEDING: Shrubby areas of tundra. 1 brood (occ 2?). **DISPLAYS:** Courtship feeding. **NEST:** Of grass, rootlets, forbs, twigs, lined with feathers (ptarmigan), willow down, fur. Nests usu near water. **EGGS:** Pale green, bluish, spotted with reddish-browns, mostly toward large end. 0.7″ (17 mm). **DIET:** Primarily seeds of decid shrubs, forbs, and grass. Young fed mash of seed kernels with small amount of insect material mixed in. **CONSERVATION:** Winters within N.A.; biennial pattern of invasion and fluctuation in numbers from year to year, esp in s portion of wintering range. **NOTES:** Reportedly not territorial, nests oft close together. Gregarious during breeding season, as well as winter. Shows little fidelity to breeding or wintering areas. Female begs food from male during incubation; male feeds her on nest. Jaegers and Peregrine Falcons are main predators. Winter flocks of few to >100 of mixed forms and species of redpolls. **ESSAYS:** Irruptions, p. 639; Winter Feeding by Redpolls and Crossbills, p. 641; Feathered Nests, p. 605; Courtship Feeding, p. 181. **REF:** Troy, 1983.

Rosy Finch
Leucosticte arctoa Pallas

NG–438; G–318; PW–pl 55; AW–pl 465; AM(III)–324

| CLIFF 0'–25' | CREVICE F | 4–5 (3–6) MONOG | F I: 12–14 DAYS ALTRICIAL F: 18 (16–22) DAYS MF | INSECTS | |

BREEDING: Barren rocky or grassy areas on alpine tundra in high mountains; maritime island tundra; rocky cliffs. 1 brood in mountains, 2 elsewhere. **DISPLAYS:** Courtship: facing female, male droops wings, slowly raises and lowers them, or holds still. **NEST:** Occ on human-built structures; bulky, of moss, grass, forbs, lichen, rootlets, lined with fine grass, feathers (esp ptarmigan), hair. Female selects site. Same nest oft used for second brood and in successive years. **EGGS:** White, unmarked. 0.9″ (23 mm). **DIET:** Esp seeds of grass and forbs. Nestlings fed entirely insects. **CONSERVATION:** Winters within N.A. **NOTES:** Semicolonial, males weakly territorial; gregarious all year. Males outnumber females by up to 6:1 all year. In breeding season, males spend much time fighting. Incubating female fed by male. Male and female develop buccal pouches (openings from floor of mouth) used for carrying food to nestlings. Alpine nests, eggs, and young oft destroyed by Clark's Nutcrackers. Winter roosts of >1,000 in cave entrances, mine shafts, abandoned Cliff Swallow nests, artificial structures; oft assoc with juncos, House Sparrows, Pine Siskins. Three major color forms occur in w N.A., regarded by some as distinct species comprising a superspecies. Mixed flocks (to several hundred) of various forms common in winter; unwary and easily approached. **ESSAYS:** Communal Roosting, p. 615; Taxonomy and Nomenclature, p. 515; Mixed-Species Flocking, p. 433; Feathered Nests, p. 605. **REFS:** Johnson, 1983; Shreeve, 1980.

How Long Can Birds Live?

Precise information on the longevity of birds is not easy to come by. It is usually impossible to follow large groups of individuals from hatching to death, so in addition to collecting data directly by banding and recapturing individuals, many indirect methods of estimating age are used. Generally, it appears that the heaviest postfledging mortality occurs among inexperienced young birds, and that for adults, after they have successfully reared young, the probability of death each year remains roughly constant. In other words, few birds die of "old age"—they just run the same gamut of risks year in and year out until they are killed. The annual risk of being killed varies from about 70 percent in small temperate-zone songbirds (adult life expectancy about 10 months; in the tropics adult songbirds are thought to be much longer-lived) to 3 percent in Royal Albatrosses (life expectancy slightly over 30 years). If a bird lasts long enough, however, the probability of it dying in a given year may once again rise. Common Terns reach old age after about 19 years, and their annual risk of dying then goes up.

Life expectancy in birds is closely correlated with size—the larger the species, the longer it is likely to live. But the relationship is far from exact. Some groups of birds tend to have long lives for their sizes, especially the Procellariiformes (tubenoses—albatrosses, shearwaters, and petrels) and Charadriiformes (shorebirds, gulls and terns, and auks). Other groups, for instance titmice and chickadees, wrens, and game birds, are shorter-lived than their sizes would predict.

Birds can be very long-lived in captivity. One Sulphur-crested Cockatoo (a common Australian parrot made famous by the TV show "Baretta") lived most of his 80-plus years in a zoo. Captive Canada Geese have lived for 33 years, House Sparrows 23 years, and Northern Cardinals 22 years. In nature, the life-spans of these species are much shorter. As luck would have it, however, the record for a European Starling in the wild, 20 years, is 3 years *longer* than for any starling captives.

The table on the next page gives longevity *records* (years-months) of wild birds. Small differences among these figures should not be taken too seriously. For one thing, they represent the upper end of a range—and the range of any measurement is a statistic that almost always increases with the number of measurements. If, for instance, you record the heights of a random sample of 10 American women, and then of another sample of a million American women, both the tallest and the shortest woman are virtually certain to be in the larger sample. So the minimum life-spans of bird species that are frequently banded are more likely to be greater than those of species rarely banded, everything else being equal. It seems likely, for example, that the short record for the Northern Shrike is simply a result of a low frequency of banding. At any rate, remember that with the exception of errors that may later be corrected, *the numbers on the list can only increase.* Remember also that these figures are maximum recorded ages. While at one

Purple Finch

Carpodacus purpureus Gmelin

NG–440; G–316; PE–270; PW–pl 55; AE–pl 409; AW–pl 461; AM(III)–328

| DECID TREE 6'–40' | MF | 4–5 (3–6) MONOG ? | F I: 13 DAYS ALTRICIAL F: 14 DAYS MF | INSECTS FRUIT | FOLIAGE GLEAN |

BREEDING: Open conif and mixed conif-decid forest, forest edge, open woodland. 1 brood in e, 2 in w. **DISPLAYS:** Courting male hops about dangling wings and puffing out chest. With wings vibrating rapidly and tail cocked, male softly vocalizes and may rise 6"–12" off the ground, occ while holding nest material in beak and singing. **NEST:** Usu in conif tree in e, on horizontal branch, far from trunk. Neat shallow cup of twigs, fine roots, grass, lined with rootlets, hair, moss. **EGGS:** Pale greenish-blue, marked with browns, blacks. 0.8" (20 mm). **DIET:** Primarily seeds; some tree buds and blossoms from winter to early spring. Adds insects in spring, feeds heavily on fruit in summer. Young fed mostly seeds. **CONSERVATION:** Winters within N.A.; erratic in distribution. Uncommon cowbird host. Competition with House Sparrow suggested cause of decrease in New England breeding range, esp in urban and suburban areas; competition with House Finch important in disappearance from e areas where ranges now overlap. **NOTES:** Occ forms postbreeding unisexual flocks of 20–30. Remains somewhat gregarious during winter and may flock with siskins and goldfinches; w populations migrate altitudinally. **ESSAYS:** How Long Do Birds Live?, p. 643; Irruptions, p. 639; Masterbuilders, p. 445; Bird Communities and Competition, p. 605; Avian Invaders, p. 633. **REFS:** Popp, 1987; Wootton, 1987.

Cassin's Finch

Carpodacus cassinii Baird

NG–440; G–316; PW–pl 55; AW–pl 462; AM(III)–330

| 10'–80' | ? | 4–5 (3–6) MONOG | F I: 12–14 DAYS ALTRICIAL F: 14? DAYS MF | INSECTS BUDS BERRIES | FOLIAGE GLEAN |

BREEDING: Semiarid open conif forest at higher elevations. 2? broods. **DISPLAYS:** ? **NEST:** Usu placed near end of large limb, rarely in shrub; of twigs, weed stems, rootlets, lichen, lined with rootlets, hair, shredded bark. **EGGS:** Bluish-green, spotted with browns, blacks, oft loosely wreathed. 0.8" (20 mm). **DIET:** Primarily buds, berries, and seeds of conifers. **CONSERVATION:** Winters s through highlands of c Mexico. **NOTES:** Semicolonial breeder, usu nomadic, nesting at different locale each year. Flocks throughout year except during 3 month nesting season, when flocks of nonbreeding(?) males still occur. From nest site selection through egg laying, male defends only small zone around female. Pair bonds may last >1 year. Male feeds female on nest during incubation and brooding. Young and adults depart nesting area as soon as fledged. Postbreeding flocks move to higher elevations, then in autumn to lower elevations. **ESSAYS:** Monogamy, p. 597; Swallowing Stones, p. 269; Bills, p. 209. **REFS:** Mewaldt and King, 1985; Samson, 1976.

point the maximum record for the Purple Finch was 10 years (it has since been extended to almost 12), of 1,746 recoveries from 21,715 banded individuals, only 1 lived 10 years, 6 lived 8 years, and 18 lived 7 years. All the remainder lived less than 7 years. In short, the maximum life-span is far longer than the median life-span (the length of the life of the individual that lives longer than half the population and shorter than the other half), which in songbirds is usually only a year or two.

MAXIMUM RECORDED LIFESPAN

SPECIES	YR.-MO.	SPECIES	YR.-MO.
Laysan Albatross	37-05	White-crowned Sparrow	13-04
Arctic Tern	34-00	House Sparrow	13-04
Great Frigatebird	30-00	Warbling Vireo	13-01
Western Gull	27-10	Brown Thrasher	12-10
Common Murre	26-05	Black-bellied Plover	12-08
Trumpeter Swan	23-10	Wrentit	12-07
Great Blue Heron	23-03	Wild Turkey	12-06
Canada Goose	23-06	Black-capped Chickadee	12-05
Mallard	23-05	Peregrine Falcon	12-03
American Coot	22-04	Sanderling	12-01
Osprey	21-11	American Kestrel	11-07
Bald Eagle	21-11	Song Sparrow	11-04
Red-tailed Hawk	21-06	Black-and-white Warbler	11-03
Brown Pelican	19-08	Tree Swallow	11-00
Mourning Dove	19-03	Broad-tailed Hummingbird	11-00
Sandhill Crane	18-06	Acadian Flycatcher	10-11
Great Horned Owl	17-04	Killdeer	10-11
Northern Harrier	16-05	Dark-eyed Junco	10-09
Blue Jay	16-04	Scarlet Tanager	10-01
Hairy Woodpecker	15-10	Cassin's Auklet	9-01
Brown-headed Cowbird	15-10	Ruby-throated Hummingbird	9-00
Northern Cardinal	15-09	House Wren	7-01
Red-winged Blackbird	15-09	Golden-crowned Kinglet	5-04
American Crow	14-07	Allen's Hummingbird	3-11
Great Crested Flycatcher	13-11	Northern Shrike	3-03
American Robin	13-11	Blackpoll Warbler	3-05
Lesser Prairie-Chicken	13-06		

Recent work on seabirds by ornithologist Ralph Schreiber of the Los Angeles County Museum indicates that dramatic increases in longevity records of seabirds can be expected as more data are gathered. For example, there are now thousands of banded Laysan Albatrosses that are in their 30s. It is likely that these and some others will eventually be shown to have life-spans of 50–70 years, longer than those of the rings used to band them!

The records presented in our list are from Dr. M. Kathleen Klimkiewicz of the Bird Banding Laboratory of the U.S. Fish and Wildlife Service (with the exception of the Broad-tailed Hummingbird, which is courtesy of

House Finch
Carpodacus mexicanus Müller

NG–440; G–316; PE–270; PW–pl 55; AE–pl 410; AW–pl 460; AM(III)–332

			F		
			I: 12–14 DAYS		
SHRUB	CAVITY	4–5 (2–6)	ALTRICIAL	FRUIT	FOLIAGE
BUILDING	F	MONOG	F: 11–19 DAYS	BUDS	GLEAN
5'–35'		(POLYGYN)	MF	TREE SAP	

BREEDING: Arid scrub, open woodland, urban areas, cultivated land. 1–3 broods, possibly dependent on age of adults. **DISPLAYS:** Courtship: singing male follows female, fluttering wings; hops about female with raised tail, drooped wings, raised head and crest feathers, continues singing. Female may sing short song. **NEST:** Variable placement incl appropriation of other species' nests; of twigs, grass, debris, leaves, rootlets, hair. Oft reused for later broods. **EGGS:** Bluish-white or pale bluish-green, sparsely marked with brown, black, oft wreathed. 0.8" (19 mm). **DIET:** Consumes virtually no insects; feeds nestlings almost entirely on seeds. **CONSERVATION:** Winters within N.A. Uncommon cowbird host in w, common host in e. Historic range confined to w; established in early 1940s on Long Island and now spread throughout e. Range in w also expanding. **NOTES:** Competition with House Sparrow in n e appears to be important factor in the sparrow's decline there. Incubating female occ fed by male. Avg clutch size in w is 4, in e 5. Young highly variable in rate of posthatching development. Songs more complex in CA than in e. Flocks in nonbreeding season. **ESSAYS:** Feeding Birds, p. 349; Vocal Functions, p. 471; Average Clutch Size, p. 339. **REFS:** Aldrich and Weske, 1978; Bitterbaum and Baptista, 1979; Kricher, 1983; Leck, 1987; Wootton, 1987.

Evening Grosbeak
Coccothraustes vespertinus Cooper

NG–442; G–310; PE–272; PW–pl 55; AE–pl 384; AW–pl 426; AM(III)–346

			F		
			I: 11–14 DAYS		
DECID	F	3–4	ALTRICIAL	FRUIT	FOLIAGE
TREE		(2–5)	F: 13–14 DAYS	INSECTS	GLEAN
20'–100'		MONOG ?	MF		

BREEDING: Conif and mixed conif-decid forest, second growth, parks. Primarily at higher altitudes in conif forest in w. 2? broods. **DISPLAYS:** Courting male crouches low, puffs out plumage, extends and rapidly quivers wings; male and female may alternately bow. Male does not sing during display but female may occ call; male may occ feed female. **NEST:** Frail structure usu well out on horizontal limb; of twigs, sticks, roots, lined with fine materials. **EGGS:** Blue or blue-green, marked with brown, gray, purple, occ black. 1.0" (24 mm). **DIET:** Insects only in breeding season, for up to 20% of diet; seeds of trees and shrubs, occ of forbs; juniper berries and piñon nuts in w mountains. Fond of maple sap and buds of decid trees and shrubs. Nestlings fed well-masticated insect larvae and crushed seeds of fleshy fruits. Oft feeds on dirt and gravel for minerals and salts. **CONSERVATION:** Winters s sporadically to Oaxaca. Frequent highway casualty when seeking road salts. Rare cowbird host. Breeding range expanded e since 1900. **NOTES:** Male feeds incubating female. Very tame. Highly irruptive. Wings longest relative to body size of all N.A. finches. **ESSAYS:** Irruptions, p. 639; Feeding Birds, p. 349; Range Expansion, p. 459; Wing Shapes and Flight, p. 227. **REF:** Bekoff et al., 1987.

Dr. William Calder). They are updated to September 1, 1986. Records for all North American species may be found in three papers by Dr. Klimkiewicz and her colleagues published (and one soon to be published) in the *Journal of Field Ornithology*. Updates of the records in the earlier papers will appear in the same journal.

SEE: Population Dynamics, p. 575; Bird Banding and Marking, p. 95. REFS: Clapp et al., 1982, 1983; Diamond, 1985b; Fry, 1980; Klimkiewicz et al., 1983; Lindstedt and Calder, 1976.

Bird Biologist—Thomas Brewer

Thomas Mayo Brewer (1814–80), a physician who gave up medicine to write for a Boston newspaper, was a dedicated birder, and a correspondent who supplied John James Audubon (p. 413) with much information on bird biology. Brewer, like Spencer Fullerton Baird (p. 569), connected the early and modern eras of North American ornithology. He is best known not for his book on bird eggs, *North American Oology*, but as being a staunch defender of the House Sparrow when it was introduced into the United States. For taking that position, he earned the eternal emnity of Elliot Coues (p. 565), another physician-birder who considered the sparrow "public enemy number one." Brewer is remembered in the names of Brewer's Blackbird and Brewer's Sparrow.

SEE: Avian Invaders, p. 633. REFS: Choate, 1985; Kastner, 1986.

APPENDICES

Hawaiian Bird Biology

While the fiftieth state of the United States is outside of the area covered by this guide, it is frequently visited by mainland birders from both the continental 49 and Canada. Should you take a Hawaiian vacation, there is every reason to take your binoculars with you. Some lessons in avian biology are more conveniently learned in the islands than anywhere else, and the Hawaii Audubon Society has produced a fine, inexpensive identification guide, *Hawaii's Birds,* which is widely available in the state.

Hawaii is the site of one of the most remarkable avian "adaptive radiations" (diversification of a single ancestral type into a variety of species playing different ecological roles). The family of the Hawaiian Honeycreepers (Drepanididae) is found nowhere else. The 16 genera, 28 species, and 18 subspecies of honeycreepers are all thought to be descendants of a single invader species, probably a cardueline finch, that arrived several million years ago. Presumably the ancestral stock diversified by a process of geographic speciation on isolated islands followed by multiple colonizations by newly formed species. No other family of birds shows such a spectacular radiation, particularly in the form of the beak.

Although most of the honeycreepers are now extinct or extremely rare, it is still possible to observe an interesting sample of species on the island of Kauai. On the trail that leads northeast along the rim of the beautiful Kalalau Valley from the Pu'u o Kila Lookout, on the right-hand side you can look down on the canopy of a relatively undisturbed native forest consisting primarily of 'ohi'a trees (*Metrosideros collina polymorpha,* family Myrtaceae). The forest stretches over a rugged plateau which holds the Alakai swamp— the wettest place in the world and the last refuge of some of the rarest drepanidids. The Alakai sometimes receives as much as 600 inches of rain annually (you're likely to get misted or rained on along the ridge, but fortunately the birds remain active in the wet). There, at an altitude of some 4,000 feet, you should find abundant 'Apapane (*Himatione sanguinea*), with medium-length, slightly downcurved bills used primarily to extract nectar from flowers but also to snap up insects. Second in abundance among the drepanidids will probably be the 'Anianiau (*Hemignathus parvus*), a smaller, extremely active species, which has a rather short, slightly downcurved bill and feeds like a warbler, primarily on insects. The closely related, slightly larger Common 'Amakihi (*Hemignathus virens*) should also be present. It has a medium-sized downcurved bill with which it takes proportionately less nectar, especially from blossoms of mamane trees (*Sophora chrysophylla,* family Leguminosae) and more caterpillars, spiders, bugs, flies, and so on than the 'Apapane. It also drinks juice from fruits, and is very common elsewhere in mamane forests.

If you listen for its raucous call, you should also get a look at a larger, bright red, nectarivorous drepanidid with a very long, very downcurved bill, the 'I'iwi (*Vestiaria coccinea*). These birds can be observed feeding on 'ohi'a blooms and, like the 'Apapane, fly relatively high above the forest canopy. Scarcer than the 'I'iwi, but present in the canopy, is the 'Akepa (*Loxops coccineus*), which has a short, cone-shaped bill with the tips of the upper and lower mandible twisted somewhat in opposite directions (the beginnings of the "crossbill" are not visible in the field). The precise function of this unusual bill is not certain, but 'Akepas seem to use it for twisting buds off the 'ohi'a trees and also, reputedly, to take insects and occasionally nectar. The 'Akepas often forage in the open on the top of the canopy.

Finally, with some patience and luck you may catch a glimpse of a sixth drepanidid in this area, the Hawaiian Creeper (*Oreomystis bairdi*). This secretive species gleans insects from trunks and branches, and occasionally from canopy foliage. Its bill is short, sharply pointed, and slightly downcurved.

With some effort, other drepanidids can be seen on other islands. For example, high on the slopes of Haleakala volcano one can see the Crested Honeycreeper or 'Akohekohe (*Palmeria dolei*), which feeds on 'ohi'a blooms, those of other plants, and insects. There is also a small population of the endangered Maui Parrotbill (*Pseudonestor xanthophrys*), whose heavy lower mandible splits open wood as it forages for grubs, and whose sharp, hooked upper mandible pries them out. Above 3,500 feet on the island of Hawaii lives another endangered species, the 'Akiapola'au (*Hemignathus munroi*). This unusual bird has a short, straight lower mandible with which it pecks like a woodpecker. Its upper mandible is twice as long and sharply downcurved, and is used to probe for insects exposed by the pecking.

But no amount of effort is likely to bring into view the bright yellow Kauai 'Akiola (*Hemignathus procerus*), a 7.5-inch bird with a downcurved sickle bill extending 2.5 inches. It may still be hanging on in the nearly impassible depths of the Alakai, but most believe it has become extinct, a fate that has already overtaken more than a third of the species and subspecies of honeycreepers that were present when Europeans first landed on the "Sandwich Islands."

Recently discovered fossils make it clear that many drepanidids and other Hawaiian birds (including some flightless forms) were wiped out by the Polynesians—presumably partly by hunting for food and feathers (magnificent feather cloaks were made for Hawaiian kings, some of which can be seen in Honolulu's Bishop Museum), partly by lowland deforestation, and partly by the inadvertent importation of the Polynesian rat. Subsequent extinctions seem to have been caused by massive habitat destruction as virtually all of the lowland native forests have been cleared for sugarcane, pineapple, condominiums, and so on, probably combined with the introduction of predators such as the roof rat and mongoose and of a mosquito capable of carrying avian diseases.

A large number of exotic species of birds have been introduced into Hawaii, more than into any other area of comparable size. Some of them will make North American birders feel right at home. The Northern Cardinal was brought in in 1929, and is now common on all the islands, and the

House Finch, introduced before 1870, can now be seen both in tourist-saturated lowlands and sharing the high forests with drepanidids. Northern Mockingbirds can also be seen on all the islands, although they seem to have declined in the Hololulu area. There they may be suffering from competition with Red-whiskered and Red-vented Bulbuls (*Pycnonotus jocosus* and *P. cafer*), aggressive birds which are increasing rapidly around Hawaii's only big city. The House Sparrow, introduced from New Zealand, is pervasive in urban and surburban areas, and on Kauai Western Meadowlarks are frequent in open fields.

There are dozens more exotics. Common Mynas (*Acridotheres tristis*), close relatives of the Crested Mynas that have invaded Vancouver, British Columbia, are ubiquitous and brazen enough to snatch the toast from your balcony breakfast if you don't watch it. Asian Shama Thrushes (*Copsychus malabaricus*) sing one of the prettiest songs on the islands, and do so in the high forests alongside the tooting of 'I'iwis. Red-crested Cardinals (*Paroaria coronata*) from South America are common in several areas, and sing a more melodius version of the Northern Cardinal's song. And Japanese White-eyes (*Zosterops japonicus*) are now probably the most abundant Hawaiian birds, penetrating the high native forests and perhaps competing with drepanidids for nectar and with the little endemic monarch flycatcher, the 'Elepaio (*Chasiempis sandwichensis*), for insects. The 'Elepaio, which can be seen with the drepanidids, not only hawks but gleans foliage and pounces on insects on the ground like a miniature robin.

Most of the several dozen introduced land birds in Hawaii are largely restricted to disturbed areas at low altitudes—for reasons that are not entirely clear. Similarly, native Hawaiian passerines are confined almost exclusively to the high-altitude remnants of native forest, but why at least some of them do not mix with the rich community of introduced birds has not been determined with assurance. Both questions are under active investigation at the present time.

In addition to both native and introduced communities of land birds available to observe, there are also the famous endemic and endangered Hawaiian Goose (Nene), an endemic species of duck, Hawaiian races of the American Coot, Common Gallinule, and Black-necked Stilt (the latter especially distinctive), migratory ducks, and migratory shorebirds. Overwintering Lesser Golden Plovers are among the most common nonpasserine birds during the winter months.

Pelagic birds can be seen both offshore and nesting. For instance, at Kilauea Lighthouse on Kauai there is a large colony of Red-footed Boobies (*Sula sula*) nesting in shrubs and trees on land, and one of Brown Boobies (*Sula leucogaster*) breeding on an island just offshore. Piracy is easily observed there as Great Frigatebirds often "double-team" to force the boobies returning to their nests to disgorge the fish intended for the boobies' young. In the same area Wedge-tailed Shearwaters (*Puffinus pacificus*) dig their burrows and swarm around the lighthouse like graceful moths when they return at dusk to feed their young. If you visit Oahu you might call the public information office of the Marine Corps Air Station at Kaneohe Bay on the windward shore. The marines, under the leadership of their Environmental Protection Specialist, Dr. Diane C. Drigot, have been doing a superb job of protecting a Red-footed Booby colony, and visits into the heart of the colony can easily be arranged. The base is less than an hour's drive from downtown Honolulu, and is a fine place to see other pelagic birds and shorebirds as well.

We have the space here to only scratch the surface of the fascinating biology of the Hawaiian avifauna. The islands are a place where the process of extinction that threatens our planet's birds is already well advanced, with only the remnants of an intriguing endemic fauna hanging on, and where a constantly changing fauna of introduced species, dominated by Common Mynas, can be observed. It is the sort of monument to human disturbance of natural systems that may soon be found in North America if great care is not taken to prevent it.

SEE: Species and Speciation, p. 355; Birds, DNA, and Evolutionary Convergence, p. 419; Avian Invaders, p. 633; Piracy, p. 159. REFS: Berger, 1981; Hawaiian Audubon Society, 1984; Moulton and Pimm, 1986; Olson and James, 1982.

Feral Birds

Feral birds are ones that have escaped from domestication and have managed to establish breeding populations in the wild. Feral populations are the results of accidents—not of releases by people who intended to add new birds to the local fauna. A substantial proportion of exotic species that "get away" are doves, parrots and their relatives, and waterfowl, because of the popularity of these groups in the pet trade. In most cases, pet escapees (and those "given their freedom") have not gone feral. In the past two decades, however, several species of tropical and subtropical doves and parrots have managed to establish breeding populations in the United States.

Most of these localized populations are found in southern California and southeastern Florida, both because of their hospitable climates and because Miami and Los Angeles are major importation centers for the pet trade derived from Latin America and from tropical Asia and Australia, respectively. The Mediterranean climate of coastal California and the subtropical climate of south Florida have also been conducive to the widespread introduction of exotic plants which create familiar habitats for exotic bird species.

Chief among our feral doves are the Ringed Turtledove and the Spotted Dove, both of which are well established in southern California. The turtledove is also feral in central and southern Florida, Houston, and Mobile. The Spotted Dove's range extends from Santa Barbara south to San Diego, and seems to be strongly associated with eucalyptus trees. In contrast to the

Spotted Dove, which apparently was released intentionally at first, the Ringed Turtledove appears to have established itself through multiple escapes in and around the several cities it inhabits.

Parrots and parakeets have long been favorites with exotic-bird fanciers. There are probably a few escapees somewhere of every species of parrot imported into the United States. Rose-ringed, Canary-winged, and Monk Parakeets, Budgerigars, and several of the large *Amazona* parrots (especially the Yellow-headed Parrot) each now exist in small, stable, feral populations.

The Monk Parakeet illustrates the potential harm (real or imagined) that could be engendered by the establishment and expansion of a feral psittacine. The species is native to temperate regions of southern South America, so that unlike most parrots, it is not dependent on tropical climatic conditions. The Monk Parakeet was first reported in the "wild" in 1967; in the following three years, nearly 35,000 birds were imported legally into the United States. Numbers in the wild continued to increase, and by 1972 nesting Monk Parakeets were scattered across much of the East Coast and were found in locations as diverse as California, Nebraska, Oklahoma, Michigan, and Ohio.

The Monk Parakeet is considered a major agricultural pest in its native Argentina. That reputation, coupled with reports in the popular press putting the U.S. feral population at 4,000 to 5,000 birds, led to a coordinated eradication program, especially in New York, New Jersey, California, and Virginia. The program was highly successful, and small feral populations now persist only in a few Florida locations and in Chicago. In retrospect, the fears may have been groundless. The actual number of feral birds probably was overestimated considerably, and population expansion was mostly confined to the metropolitan New York area, with lesser numbers in Florida, Pennsylvania, and Illinois. Nonetheless, it has been estimated that the Monk Parakeet could cause millions of dollars in agricultural losses should it become abundant.

The fate of feral psittacines in the United States is more likely to be typified by the Canary-winged Parakeet, a tropical species from South America. From 1968 to 1974, more than 260,000 individuals were brought into the United States by the pet trade, making it the most common psittacine import during that period. Small feral populations have been reported in California, Florida, Connecticut, and New York. Ethologist Patricia Arrowood had studied the San Francisco population of Canary-wings for several years and reports that although breeding is successful each year, juveniles suffer inordinately high mortality rates. Nesting and roosting occur in (introduced) palm trees, and the birds feed primarily on buds, flowers, nectar, seeds, and fruit of mostly exotic species of trees. Winter survival is largely dependent on food supplied at backyard feeders. Although the birds are very conspicuous as they fly noisily over the rooftops between their nesting trees in Dolores Park, their primary foraging site on

Telegraph Hill, and their nonbreeding-season roost in Fort Mason, their numbers remain stable at fewer than 20 birds.

The Canary-winged Parakeet appears to be more successful in south Florida, where nearly 700 birds were reported in a single winter roost in 1973. Black-hooded Parakeets (Nanday Conures), another tropical American species, have, however, replaced the Canary-winged Parakeet as the most popular psittacine import. It seems likely that they will become widely feral in the coming years, with the most successful populations in warmer areas.

Members of the parrot family are not the only cage birds to have gone feral in the mainland United States. Red-whiskered Bulbuls (passerines related to kinglets), from southeast Asia, escaped from a bird farm near Miami around 1960. The species, at last report, occupied about three square miles and was slowly spreading. Escaped bulbuls also established feral populations in the Los Angeles area, where attempts have been made to eliminate them by shooting. The Java Finch and Indian Hill Myna, both popular as pets, are also feral in the Miami area. The Spot-breasted Oriole from Central America is also well established in southeastern Florida following escapes from captivity. The most spectacular feral bird in the United States, however, is the Greater Flamingo. This Caribbean species has repeatedly escaped from captive flocks in Florida, and a free-flying colony lives around Hialeah Race Track in Miami.

The establishment of feral birds is, by definition, unintentional. Some birds, of course, have been deliberately introduced into North America. They fall into two categories: game and nongame species. Several game birds, such as the Ring-necked Pheasant, Chukar, Black Francolin, and Himalayan Snowcock, have been released by fish and game departments for the express purpose of providing recreational hunting, and are now well established as breeding populations. Introductions of nongame species for a variety of ill-considered reasons include the European Starling, House Sparrow, Eurasian Tree Sparrow, Crested Myna, and Eurasian Skylark, of which the first two species have become widespread, major pests.

Feral birds, like the European Starling, always have the potential of harming native species. Monk Parakeets have been reported killing Blue Jays and a robin, but there is no documented case of serious interference with natives. So far we have been lucky, but unless the pet trade is carefully controlled, that luck may run out.

SEE: Avian Invaders, p. 633; Our Only Native Parrot, p. 279; Birds and the Law, p. 293; Hawaiian Bird Biology, p. 651.   REFS: Arrowood, 1981; Bull, 1973; Hardy, 1973; Long, 1981; Neidermyer and Hickey, 1977; Owre, 1973.

Pelagic Birds

Some birds have largely cut their ties with the land. They are *pelagic*, spending most of their lives in the open ocean, returning to land only to breed. Why, like whales, seals, and other marine mammals, their progenitors deserted the land is not clearly understood, but some informed guesses can be made. The ancestors of today's pelagic birds and mammals may have reentered the seas (the ancestral home of all life) in order to exploit its rich food resources, to take advantage of reduced pressures of competition or predation, or, perhaps, because of a combination of these factors. North American birders are fortunate, since they have the opportunity to acquaint themselves with pelagic species more readily than do their European counterparts. From both coasts, small charter boats regularly make day or overnight trips specifically designed for observing species rarely, if ever, seen from shore; the price is usually reasonable, and the rewards can be great.

Perhaps the most spectacular birds easily observed off our coasts are the albatrosses—members of one family of tubenoses that do not breed in North America (and thus are not included in the treatments of this guide). These huge petrels are usually seen soaring gracefully with their long, slender wings held characteristically bowed, or floating with the wings held in a characteristic half-open threat posture when they alight among other seabirds to feed. On the water they lose their graceful appearance and float like giant gawky gulls. Normally they are surface feeders, but they will very occasionally submerge entirely in pursuit of a sinking scrap. Albatrosses cannot take off in calm air but must run across the surface of the sea (or, during the breeding season, the ground) into the wind to become airborne.

The most common albatross in the Pacific off of North America is the Black-footed, a species often attracted to offal jettisoned from shrimp or fishing boats. Its breeding grounds include remote atolls in the Hawaiian archipelago and other isolated islands in the central and western Pacific. The Black-footed albatross has an elaborate courtship ritual, which includes much bill snapping and bowing. Like other tubenoses, it is monogamous, the same pairs breeding together year after year. It breeds colonially, but does not build impressive mud nests like those of Southern Hemisphere species such as the Black-browed Albatross, but rather lays its single egg in a depression rimmed with packed-down sand. The young are fed by regurgitation, first on stomach oil and then primarily on squid, for the nearly five months they require to fledge. Although the Laysan Albatross outnumbers the Black-footed, it is less frequently encountered off the California and Alaskan coasts. The Laysan breeds primarily on the leeward (northwestern) Hawaiian Islands, and its biology is similar to the Black-footed. The Short-tailed Albatross, driven to the brink of extinction, was once a regular visitor off the North American West Coast. It's numbers have increased slightly and in recent years there have been a few new sightings after an absence of many years. It used to breed on several island groups south of Japan and near Taiwan, but now appears to be confined to one or two sites.

All three of these West Coast visitors were persecuted by feather hunters around the turn of the century (the Japanese killed many Short-tails). The breeding success of the surviving Black-footed and Laysan Albatrosses also appears to have been reduced by the introduction of rabbits to Laysan and possibly other islands. The rabbits mowed down the vegetation, probably increasing mortality from storm-blown sand. The Laysan Albatross is the famous "Gooney Bird" of Midway Island, where it often was struck by aircraft. More than 50,000 were killed there in "control programs" between 1955 and 1964, but recently as the activities of the U.S. Navy at Midway have declined, the bird populations have recovered. Both the Black-footed and Laysan Albatrosses previously bred more widely in the Pacific, and may be recolonizing parts of their former range. Neither species is endangered at the moment.

East Coast birders must be very lucky to see an occasional Yellow-nosed or Black-browed Albatross (species that breed on islands in the southern oceans). But, like westerners, they can enjoy those graceful cousins of albatrosses, the shearwaters, arcing near the ocean surface in search of food.

Some aspects of the biology of shearwaters that occur in our offshore waters are summarized in the following table.

SHEARWATER BREEDING BIOLOGY

SPECIES (U.S. Coast)	BREEDING SITES	NESTING LOCATION
Flesh-footed (Pacific, rare)	Isles off New Zealand, Australia, of Indian O.	Burrows
Sooty (Both)	Isles off s South America and in Australasia	Burrows
Short-tailed (Pacific)	Isles off s Australia	Burrows
Cory's (Atlantic)	Isles of e Atlantic and Mediterranean	Burrows and rock crevices
Greater (Atlantic)	Isles of s Atlantic	Burrows
Manx (Atlantic)	e Atlantic, isles off Newfoundland and Massachusetts	Burrows; cliffs of rocky isles
Audubon's (s Atlantic)	Caribbean, e Atlantic, Indian O., Pacific	Rock crevices; under thick vegetation
Pink-footed (Pacific)	Isles off Chile	Burrows
Buller's (Pacific)	Isles off North Island of New Zealand	Burrows
Black-vented (s Pacific)	Isles off w coast of Baja California	Burrows and in small caves

Relatively thin-billed, shearwaters feed primarily on fish (but also on squid and crustaceans), snapping them up at the surface or diving to pursue them, reportedly "flying" underwater with partially spread wings. Like the albatrosses, they do not breed in North America. The species most likely to be seen off our West Coast, the Sooty Shearwater, breeds in large colonies on islands off southern South America and in the Australasian region, and, like most shearwaters nests in burrows. The world population of Sooty Shearwaters is estimated to number above a billion individuals. The beautiful Buller's Shearwater is lighter in both color and weight, and has a more graceful, albatrosslike flight than the Sooty, with which it occurs off the West Coast. It nests on islets off the North Island of New Zealand, sometimes sharing those burrows with tuataras, primitive lizardlike reptiles. From this center the birds range to the west coasts of South as well as North America.

The only representative of the gadfly (*Pterodroma*) petrels—which, in spite of their name, are members of the shearwater family—seen regularly off North America, the Black-capped Petrel, rarely alights but snatches food from the surface in its bill. It was long thought to be extinct, having been heavily exploited on Dominica, Guadeloupe, and Martinique for food and fuel (the fat young are a source of oil), and attacked by the imported Small Indian Mongoose, which has helped decimate Caribbean bird populations. In 1961, however, the Black-capped was discovered in the inland mountains of southeast Haiti breeding on high, inaccessible cliff faces, a location which the mongoose apparently cannot penetrate. Subsequently, small breeding colonies were discovered on Cuba and in the Dominican Republic, and it is still reported on Dominica, which is free of the mongooses. Additional colonies may exist in remote Caribbean areas, since pelagic surveys have shown the birds to be not uncommon over the inner edge of the Gulf Stream off the southeast coast of the United States. Unfortunately the Haitian petrel population appears still to be exploited for food by the human population of that desperately poor nation, so concern over the security of this species is still warranted.

There are other gadfly petrels out there. For the truly dedicated birder, there are now overnight boat trips from the San Francisco area out to the Cordell Bank, about 20 miles seaward of Point Reyes. In that area of shallow water surrounded by deep, some of the rarest vagrants to North America–Solander's, Murphy's, and Cook's Petrels—have recently been sighted. All three nest in burrows on islands in the South Pacific. Mottled and Stejneger's petrels also occur off the Pacific coast, the former mostly in the north and the latter in the south. The Mottled breeds on inland mountain bluffs and in burrows on offshore islands of New Zealand. Stejneger's also breeds on small islands of New Zealand, as well as on one island of the Juan Fernandez group off the Chilean coast. Little is known about the biology of this entire group of sturdy birds with stubby, rounded tails and a strong, arcing flight. They apparently feed largely on octopus and squid taken at night, and have a highly specialized, twisted gut designed to absorb oil from their prey. To avoid being taken by Peregrines and predaceous gulls, they fly to their burrows at night.

In contrast to the shearwaters and gadfly petrels, most of the storm-petrels seen on pelagic birding trips—Ashy, Black, Leach's, and Fork-tailed—breed in the United States or Canada. Exceptions are Wilson's, Least, and White-faced Storm-Petrels. Wilson's is common off the Atlantic and Gulf coasts but breeds on subantarctic islands off southern South America and in the southern Indian Ocean, nesting in burrows or rock crevices. The Least Storm-Petrel, which can often be seen off southern California, travels a much smaller distance to visit us, breeding in crevices or among loose stones on islands off the Pacific coast of Baja California and in the northern part of the Gulf of California. The White-faced Storm-Petrel, which breeds mostly in the Southern Hemisphere, is a rare treat for Atlantic coast pelagic birders. Like their larger relatives, storm-petrels often locate their food by odor. Known to seaman as "Mother Carey's chickens," they all feed at the surface primarily on small fishes and crustaceans or on oil slicks leaking from wounded marine mammals. Their sudden appearance

Marine birds show a wide variety of foraging strategies. From left to right above the waterline: a skimmer skims fish from near the surface; a gull picks up floating offal; a tern, gannet, and pelican plunge after fishes near the surface; and a storm-petrel "walks on water" as it forages on the surface. Below the waterline: a cormorant uses its legs to propel itself after a fish; a shearwater (above the cormorant) and a razorbill use their wings to "fly" in pursuit of prey; and a scaup "flies" down to forage for crabs on the bottom.

was thought to signal the approach of severe storms. These birds, which range from sparrow- to robin-size, often have a fluttery, erratic flight, and frequently hover, pattering their feet along the surface while they feed. This habit of "walking on water" gave them the name "petrel" that has subsequently been applied to many tubenoses. It is a diminutive of Peter, and refers to the story of St. Peter walking on water with the help of Jesus.

Of course, on a pelagic trip you will probably see many other birds that breed in North America. Bull-necked Northern Fulmars (birds of the shearwater family) may be seen in large flocks, often mixed in with swarms of gulls following fishing boats. Some gulls whose breeding grounds are not easily reached are readily seen on pelagic trips: arctic-breeding Sabine's Gulls and Black-legged Kittiwakes are frequently seen off the West Coast, with the former found closer to shore. In the same swarms you may see all three species of jaegers when they are migrating. These predatory gulls may even be observed chasing migratory songbirds that have strayed out to sea. (Chunky relatives of the jaegers, the South Polar and Great Skuas, may also be seen off North America. The former breeds in the Antarctic, and the latter in northern Europe and Iceland.) Alcids, in contrast, are seldom attracted to vessels, but are frequently encountered. Whereas observing them on their breeding grounds may be difficult or require expensive trips, birds like Common Murres, Cassin's and Rhinoceros Auklets, Marbled, Xantus', and Ancient Murrelets, Dovekies, Atlantic, Tufted and (rarely) Horned Puffins, and Razorbills may be seen on pelagic trips. Similarly ducks (including wintering King and Common Eiders), Northern Gannets, loons, phalaropes, and cormorants are often observed on such expeditions.

We wish we could say that pelagic birds at sea are beyond the reach of the destructive activities of humanity, but that sadly is not the case. Seabirds suffer from oil spills, and thousands upon thousands of alcids drown annually in fishing nets. Ninety percent of Laysan Albatross chicks examined had plastics in their guts. This is not surprising since ships throw overboard some five million plastic containers daily, and commercial fishermen add some 175,000 tons of plastics to the ocean annually. Huge additional amounts are carried into the oceans by rivers and garbage scows. The exact impact of these huge quantities of plastic on marine birds is unknown, but, as on land, the adding of nonbiodegradable plastics to the environment should be a cause for concern.

Proven serious hazards to marine birds in the north Pacific are huge, fine-mesh, nylon drift nets used by some 1,600 fishing boats from South Korea, Taiwan, and Japan. The nets, which may be miles long, entangle birds (and many marine mammals) during fishing operations, and the trapped individuals drown. Nets continue to kill when, too damaged for use, they are cast loose. The abandoned nets deteriorate very slowly, and float for long times as gigantic random deathtraps. Drift nets are thought to kill more than a million birds annually; some nine percent of the Tufted Puffins breeding in the Aleutians are thought to be entrapped and die each year, and hundreds of thousands of Short-tailed Shearwaters are slaughtered, far from their Australian breeding grounds, in each northern summer. Steps are being taken to get the U.S. State and Commerce departments to apply pressure to halt fishing with drift nets; these efforts should be applauded and supported.

Every land-bound bird enthusiast should take an antiseasickness pill and get an introduction to the birdlife that lives largely hidden a few miles beyond our shores. On the same trips one often gets to see whales or porpoises, a wonderful bonus.

SEE: Swimming, p. 73; The Avian Sense of Smell, p. 15; Soaring, p. 215; Seabird Nesting Sites, p. 197; Salt Glands, p. 29; Birds and Oil, p. 207.   REFS: Croxall et al., 1984; Harrison, 1983; Norris, 1986.

DNA and Passerine Classification

A new laboratory technique is beginning to solve persistent mysteries of the evolutionary relationships of various groups of birds. Evolutionists Charles Sibley and Jon Ahlquist have been comparing the DNA (the molecules that encode the genetic information) of different birds. In outline the technique is simple. DNA from one species is boiled briefly, which causes it to "melt" —that is, to separate into its two complementary component strands. Then the single strands of one species are labeled with a radioactive isotope, mixed with unlabeled strands from a different species, and incubated at 140° F for 120 hours. At that temperature complementary DNA strands bond together chemically. Sibley and Ahlquist then determine how much they must heat the DNA to melt the hybrid molecules that have formed. The more similar the genetic information coded into the DNA from the two species, the more tightly the two halves of their hybrid DNA molecules stick together (nonhybrid DNA, both halves from the same species, has the highest melting temperature). The lower the melting temperature, the more dissimilar the two DNA strands and more distantly related the two birds supplying the strands.

Fascinating results have emerged from these DNA-DNA hybridization studies. Sibley and Ahlquist's tens of thousands of DNA-DNA hybrid comparisons have revealed that each of two close relatives, say, a mockingbird and a thrasher, show the same genetic distance from a third less-related bird. For example, a mockingbird and a thrasher each form hybrid DNA with a finch that melts at roughly the same temperature. This means that the genetic distance between evolving bird species with the same generation time (e.g., passerines, which all mature at one year) always increases at roughly the same rate. As you can see from the following diagram, both the mocker and thrasher must have been separated for the same amount of time from the last common ancestor the two shared with the finch.

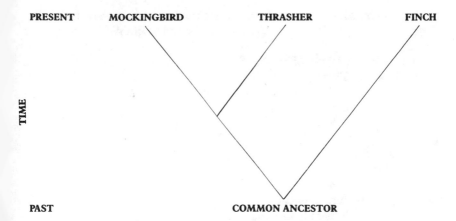

PRESENT   MOCKINGBIRD   THRASHER   FINCH

TIME

PAST   COMMON ANCESTOR

On the next two pages we give Sibley and Ahlquist's proposed classification of the passerine birds of North America, based on their DNA-DNA
hybridization studies. It has features that will strike those familiar with
older classifications as quite unusual. For instance, vireos and wood warblers have usually been thought to be closely related, but here they are not.
Mockingbirds, thrashers, and catbirds are placed in the starling family, and
wagtails and pipits are shown as relatives of African weaver finches and the
House Sparrow group. On the other hand, the Yellow-breasted Chat is confirmed as a close relative of the wood warblers.

We believe that the Sibley-Ahlquist classification is much closer to biological reality than that recognized in the 1983 AOU Checklist. Since the
Sibley-Alquist proposal is somewhat controversial and unfamiliar to most
bird enthusiasts, however, the higher classification (arrangement of groups
above the generic level—subfamilies, families, etc.) used elsewhere in this
book follows the AOU treatment.

SEE: Species and Speciation, p. 355; Hawaiian Bird Biology, p. 651; Birds, DNA,
and Evolutionary Convergence, p. 419. REFS: Houde, 1987; Sibley and Ahlquist,
1984a, 1984b, 1985, 1986.

A CLASSIFICATION OF THE PASSERINE BIRDS OF NORTH AMERICA
(See pages 662–63 for explanation)

Order Passeriformes, Perching Birds
  Suborder Tyranni, Suboscines
    Infraorder Tyrannides, New World Suboscines
      Parvorder Tyrannida
        Family Tyrannidae
          Subfamily Tyranninae, Tyrant Flycatchers
  Suborder Passeri, Oscines (Songbirds)
    Parvorder Corvida
      Superfamily Corvoidea
        Family Corvidae
          Subfamily Corvinae
            Tribe Corvini, Crows, Jays, Magpies, Nutcrackers
        Family Vireonidae, Vireos
        Family Laniidae, Shrikes
    Parvorder Passerida
      Superfamily Muscicapoidea
        Family Bombycillidae
          Tribe Ptilogonatini, Phainopepla
          Tribe Bombycillini, Waxwings
        Family Cinclidae, Dippers
        Family Muscicapidae
          Subfamily Turdinae, typical Thrushes
        Family Sturnidae
          Tribe Sturnini, Starlings (introduced)
          Tribe Mimini, Mockingbirds, Thrashers, Catbirds
      Superfamily Sylvioidea
        Family Sittidae
          Subfamily Sittinae, Nuthatches
        Family Certhiidae
          Subfamily Certhiinae, Northern Creepers
          Subfamily Troglodytinae, Wrens
          Subfamily Polioptilinae, Verdin, Gnatcatchers
        Family Paridae
          Subfamily Parinae, Titmice, Chickadees
        Family Aegithalidae, Bushtits
        Family Hirundinidae, Swallows
        Family Regulidae, Kinglets
        Family Sylviidae
          Subfamily Phylloscopinae, Leaf Warblers
          Subfamily Sylviinae
             Tribe Sylviini, Old World Warblers
             Tribe Timaliini, Babblers
             Tribe Chamaeini, Wrentit

Superfamily Passeroidea
  Family Alaudidae, Larks
  Family Passeridae
    Subfamily Passerinae, House Sparrow (introduced)
    Subfamily Motacillinae, Pipits
  Family Fringillidae
    Subfamily Peucedraminae, Olive Warbler
    Subfamily Fringillinae
      Tribe Carduelini, Goldfinches, Crossbills, etc.
      Tribe Drepanidini, Hawaiian Honeycreepers
    Subfamily Emberizinae
      Tribe Emberizini, Northern "Sparrows," Buntings,
        Longspurs, Towhees, etc.
      Tribe Parulini, Wood Warblers
      Tribe Cardinalini, Cardinals
      Tribe Icterini, Troupials (= New World Orioles),
        Meadowlarks, Blackbirds, etc.
      Tribe Thraupini, Tanagers

North American Birds
Omitted from Species Treatments

Here we list species dealt with in the National Geographic *Field Guide to the Birds of North America* (1987) that have not been included in our species treatments because they do not reliably breed in North America or because they are recent introductions whose status is in doubt.

Accentor: Siberian
Albatross: Black-browed; Black-footed; Laysan; Short-tailed; Yellow-nosed
Bananaquit
Booby: Blue-footed; Brown; Masked; Red-footed
Brambling
Budgerigar
Bulbul: Red-whiskered
Bullfinch: Eurasian
Bunting: Blue; Gray; Little; Rustic
Coot: Caribbean; Eurasian
Crake: Corn
Crane: Common
Crow: Mexican
Cuckoo: Common; Oriental
Curlew: Eurasian; Far Eastern
Dotterel: Eurasian
Dove: Ringed Turtle-; Ruddy Ground-; Key West Quail-; Ruddy Quail-; Spotted; Zenaida
Duck: Garganey; Mandarin; Muscovy; Spot-billed; Tufted
Eagle: Steller's Sea-; White-tailed
Emerald: Cuban
Fieldfare
Flamingo: Chilean; Lesser
Flycatcher: Fork-tailed; Gray-spotted; Red-breasted; Variegated
Francolin: Black
Garganey
Gnatcatcher: Black-capped
Godwit: Black-tailed
Goose: Bar-headed; Barnacle; Bean; Chinese; Domestic; Graylag; Pink-footed; Red-breasted
Grassquit: Black-faced
Greenfinch: Oriental
Greenshank: Common
Grosbeak: Yellow
Gull: Lesser Black-backed; Slaty-backed; Yellow-footed

Hawfinch
Hummingbird: Bahama Woodstar; Cuban Emerald; Green Violet-ear
Jabiru
Jackdaw: Eurasian
Kestrel: Eurasian
Kingbird: Loggerhead
Knot: Great
Lapwing: Northern
Mockingbird: Bahama
Murrelet: Craveri's
Myna: Hill
Needletail: White-throated
Noddy: Black
Oriole: Streak-backed
Parakeet: Canary-winged; Green; Monk; Rose-ringed
Parrot: Red-crowned; Thick-billed; Yellow-headed
Partridge: Red-legged
Petrel: Black-capped; Cook's; Mottled; Solander's; Stejneger's
Pintail: White-cheeked
Pipit: Olive Tree-; Pechora
Plover: Common Ringed; Greater Golden-; Mongolian
Pochard: Common
Quail: Japanese
Quail-Dove: Key West; Ruddy
Redshank: Spotted
Redstart: Slate-throated
Reed-Bunting: Common; Pallas'
Robin: Clay-colored; Rufous-backed
Rosefinch: Common
Rubythroat: Siberian
Ruff
Sandpiper: Broad-billed; Common; Curlew; Green; Sharp-tailed, Spoonbill; Terek
Seedeater: White-collared
Shearwater: Audubon's; Black-vented; Buller's; Cory's; Flesh-footed;

Greater; Little; Pink-footed; Short-
tailed; Sooty; Streaked; Townsend's
Shelduck: Northern; Ruddy
Skua: Great; South Polar
Smew
Snowcock: Himalayan
Sparrow: Java
Starthroat: Plain-capped
Stint: Little; Long-toed; Rufous-
necked; Temminck's
Storm-Petrel: Band-rumped; Least;
Wedge-rumped; White-faced;
Wilson's
Swallow: Bahama
Swan: Black; Whooper
Swift: Fork-tailed; White-collared

Tanager: Stripe-headed
Tattler: Gray-tailed
Teal: Baikal; Falcated
Tern: Bridled; White-winged
Thrush: Aztec; Dusky, Eye-browed
Trogon: Eared
Tropicbird: Red-billed; Red-tailed;
White-tailed
Turtle-Dove: Ringed Violet-ear; Green
Vireo: Thick-billed
Wagtail: Black-backed; Gray
Warbler: Dusky; Golden-crowned;
Lanceolated; Middendorff's Green
Wigeon: Eurasian
Woodstar: Bahama

Acknowledgments

We are most grateful to the many people who assisted us in the preparation of this book. Mercedes Foster of the National Museum of Natural History reviewed all of the essays and called our attention to more oversights and ambiguities than we care to remember. Jared Diamond of the University of California at Los Angeles made countless suggestions that improved the manuscript and also read many of the essays. Similarly, William Calder of the University of Arizona at Tucson, Pete Myers of the National Audubon Society, and Judith Wagner of Los Altos, CA, gave extensive and very helpful criticism of essays and helped to review treatments as well. David Wilcove of the Wilderness Society must also be singled out for having reviewed materials above and beyond the call of duty. Others who kindly reviewed or provided information for treatments or essays include Tony Angell, Seattle, WA; George A. Archibald, International Crane Foundation; Patricia C. Arrowood, University of California, Irvine; Russell P. Balda, Northern Arizona University; Jon C. Barlow, Royal Ontario Museum, Toronto; Frank C. Bellrose, Illinois Natural History Survey; Clait E. Braun, Wildlife Research Center, Fort Collins, CO; Joanna Burger, Rutgers University; Gregory Butcher, Tom J. Cade, Scott Sutcliffe, David W. Winkler, Cornell University; Arthur R. Clark, Richard Laub, Buffalo Museum of Science; Charles T. Collins, California State University, Long Beach; Francesca J. Cuthbert, Unversity of Minnesota; Benjamin Dane, Tufts University; David DeSante, Point Reyes Bird Observatory; Susan R. Drennan, National Audubon Society; Anne H. Ehrlich, Marcus W. Feldman, Richard W. Holm, Dennis D. Murphy, Jonathan Roughgarden, Bruce A. Wilcox, Stanford University; Gregory Florant, Swarthmore College; Valerie M. Freer, Ellenville, NY; Anthony J. Gaston, Canadian Wildlife Service; Russell Greenberg, National Zoological Park; Ralph J. Gutiérrez, Humboldt State University; John Harte, John P. Holdren, University of California, Berkeley; David Inouye, University of Maryland; Herbert Kale, Florida Audubon Society; Karl Kenyon, Seattle, WA; Walter D. Koenig, University of California, Hastings Reservation, Carmel Valley, CA; Donald E. Kroodsma, University of Massachusetts; Wesley Lanyon, American Museum of Natural History; Judith McIntyre, Utica College; Carl D. Marti, Weber State College; Helmut C. Mueller, University of North Carolina; Gary L. Nuechterlein, North Dakota State University; Gordon H. Orians, University of Washington; Colin J. Pennycuick, University of Miami; Stuart L. Pimm, University of Tennessee; Harry F. Recher, Australian Museum; Ralph Schrieber, Los Angeles County Museum; Spencer Sealy, University of Manitoba; Jay M. Sheppard, U.S. Fish and Wildlife Service; Charles Sibley, Tiburon Center; P. William Smith, Homestead, FL; Richard Stallcup, Inverness, CA; Scott B. Terrill, State University of New York, Albany; Ian Thornton, Latrobe University, Australia; Terry Wahl, Bellingham, WA.

In the midst of completing his doctorate at the University of California at Berkeley, Shahid Naeem exhibited extraordinary patience in helping us develop and then produce the essay illustrations and symbols for the treatment summary lines. We hope that this is only the first of a long list of biological books that he illustrates.

At Stanford, Gretchen C. Daily, Carol Holland, and Pam Nakaso found the time to assist us in many aspects of the *Handbook*'s production, Steven Masley and Pat Browne photocopied reams of material with care and without delay, and Christine Mullen helped with the voluminous correspondence that a project of this scope entails.

Special appreciation goes to Beth Weil and the staff of the Stanford University Falconer Biology Library. Claire Shoens, Judy Levitt, Adam Schiff, Joan Dietrich, Lisa Branard, Jill Sen, and Jennifer Nagorka patiently tracked down countless references.

Perhaps our firmest aim in producing this handbook was to provide birders with a portable mini-library to use in the field. Without the help of Bob Bender, our editor at Simon and Schuster, it would never have been possible. Bob was with us every step of the way, and we remain in his debt. Our copy editor, Philip James, did a superb job of "keeping all our ducks in a row," on a project of extraordinary complexity. His help and the continual aid of Simon and Schuster's production and design staff, especially Jay Schweitzer, Eve Metz, and Karolina Harris are deeply appreciated.

Continuing support provided by the Koret Foundation enabled us to proceed with work on this project. Also, many members of the Rocky Mountain Biological Laboratory, where a portion of the *Handbook* was produced, were very helpful—especially the director, Susan Allen.

But, more than anyone else, we thank LuEsther. This is one more book that would be little more than an idea without her support.

Sources of Information Used in this Guide

The scientific literature on North American birds is vast. In preparing this guide we have surveyed it in the following manner. First, we extracted the key information from all 26 volumes of Arthur Cleveland Bent's *Life Histories of North American Birds*. That compendium provided material which was current to roughly 1920–1965 (depending on group) and provided a foundation on which to build. Our species treatments, originally based on information provided in the Bent series and the AOU's 1983 *Checklist of North American Birds* (and entered into word-processing files), were then completely revised and updated on the basis of additional information from the last 20 to 30 years of four major North American ornithological journals, *The Auk, The Condor, Journal of Field Ornithology (Bird-Banding)*, and *The Wilson Bulletin*, and two monograph series, *Ornithological Monographs* and *Studies in Avian Biology*. And to cover the past decade or so in broader terms, we reviewed other bird journals and more general biological journals such as *Ibis, Ecology, Evolution, American Naturalist, Animal Behaviour, Behavioral Ecology and Sociobiology, Canadian Journal of Zoology*, and *Journal of Wildlife Management*, as well as numerous monographs, symposium volumes, and (especially with regard to the essays) more popular journals such as *New Scientist, Audubon, American Birds*, and *Natural History*.

Next we cross-checked the information in our species treatments against dozens of books dealing with specific groups of birds, such as Harrison's work on wood warblers, Bellrose on waterfowl, Johnsgard on hummingbirds, Brown and Amadon on raptors, Cade on falcons, Nettleship and Birkhead on alcids, Short on picids, Orians on blackbirds, etc. They were also checked against J. K. Terres' *The Audubon Society Encyclopedia of North American Birds* (Knopf, New York, 1980). Terres was especially useful in suggesting pre-1975 literature that we had overlooked. Similarly, the excellent first four volumes of *The Birds of the Western Palearctic* edited by S. Cramp and K. E. L. Simmons were checked for species that breed in both North America and Europe. Where information differed (e.g., in clutch size) between European and North American populations, we usually give only the latter on the assumption that the discrepancies may represent real geographic variation. Finally, to uncover mistakes and add information that had not yet been published or that we had missed, and to settle points on which various published sources differed, we divided the treatments of the book draft into sections and sent them for review to ornithologists specializing in each taxonomic group. We, of course, also had the essays reviewed by specialists.

Sources of information are cited at the end of most species treatments and essays and complete references are given in the bibliography, p. 672. These are selected primarily from the scientific literature, with emphasis on recent articles with bibliographies that will provide access to further publications. Three widely used sources are *not cited:* B. Campbell and E. Lack (eds.), *A Dictionary of Birds* (Buteo Books, Vermillion, South Dakota, 1985); J. C. Welty, *The Life of Birds*, 3rd edition (W. B. Saunders, Philadelphia, 1982; new edition, coauthored by Luis Baptista, published in 1988); and Terres' *Encyclopedia*. Every serious birder should be familiar with these books, especially the superb *Dictionary*.

Our procedures do not guarantee that this book is free of omissions and errors—doubtless, both are present. We will discover some, and reviewers and colleagues will point out others. We will try to correct the mistakes and oversights, and add new information, in the next edition.

Bibliography

Able, K.P. 1983. A migratory bird's Baedeker. Natural History, September, pp. 22–27.

Able, K.P., W.F. Gergits, J.D. Cherry, and S.B. Terrill. 1984. Homing behavior of Wood Thrushes (*Hylocichla mustelina*). Behav. Ecol. Sociobiol. 15:39–43.

Adamcik, R.S., and L.B. Keith. 1978. Regional movements and mortality of Great Horned Owls in relation to snowshoe hare fluctuations. Can. Field-Nat. 92:228–234.

Adkisson, C.S. 1981. Geographic variation in vocalizations and evolution of North American Pine Grosbeaks. Condor 83:277–288.

Adkisson, C.S., and R.N. Conner. 1978. Interspecific vocal imitation in White-eyed Vireos. Auk 95:602–606.

Afton, A.D. 1979a. Incubation temperatures of the Northern Shoveler. Can. J. Zool. 57:1052–1056.

Afton, A.D. 1979b. Time budget of breeding Northern Shovelers. Wilson Bull. 91:42–49.

Afton, A.D. 1984. Influence of age and time on reproductive performance of female Lesser Scaup. Auk 101:255–265.

Ainley, D.G., D.W. Anderson, and P.R. Kelly. 1981. Feeding ecology of marine cormorants in southwestern North America. Condor 83:120–131.

Aldrich, J.W., and J.S. Weske. 1978. Origin and evolution of the eastern House Finch population. Auk 95:528–536.

Alison, R.M. 1975. Breeding Biology and Behavior of the Oldsquaw (*Clangula hyemalis* L.). Ornithol. Monogr. No. 18.

Alison, R.M. 1976. Oldsquaw brood behavior. Bird-Banding 47:210–213.

Allaire, P.N., and C.D. Fisher. 1975. Feeding ecology of three resident sympatric sparrows in eastern Texas. Auk 92:260–269.

Allen, G.T., R.K. Murphy, K. Steenhof, and S.W. Platt. 1986. Late fledging dates, renesting, and large clutches of Prairie Falcons. Wilson Bull. 98:463–465.

Allen, J.N. 1980. The Ecology and Behavior of the Long-billed Curlew in Southeastern Washington. Wildl. Monogr. No. 73.

Alvarez, H. 1975. The social system of the Green Jay in Colombia. Living Bird 14:5–44.

Alvo, R. 1986. Lost loons of the northern lakes. Natural History, September, pp. 60–64.

Amadon, D. 1966. The superspecies concept. Syst. Zool. 15:245–249.

Amat, J.A., and R.C. Soriguer. 1984. Kleptoparasitism of coots by Gadwalls. Ornis Scand. 15:188–194.

Ambuel, B., and S.A. Temple. 1982. Songbird populations in southern Wisconsin forests: 1954 and 1979. J. Field Ornithol. 53:149–158.

American Ornithologists' Union. 1983. Check-list of North American Birds, 6th Edition. Allen Press, Lawrence, KS.

American Ornithologists' Union. 1985. Thirty-fifth Supplement to the American Ornithologists' Union Check-list of North American Birds. Auk 102:680–686.

American Ornithologists' Union. 1987. Thirty-sixth Supplement to the American Ornithologists' Union Check-list of North American Birds. Auk 104: 591–596.

Anderson, A.H., and A. Anderson. 1973. The Cactus Wren. Univ. Arizona Press, Tucson, AZ.

Anderson, G.L., and E.J. Braun. 1985. Postrenal modifications of urine in birds. Am. J. Physiol. 248 17:R93–R98.

Anderson, M.E., and R.N. Conner. 1985. Northern Cardinal song in three forest habitats in eastern Texas. Wilson Bull. 97:436–449.

Anderson, M.G. 1974. American Coots feeding in association with Canvasbacks. Wilson Bull. 86:462–463.

Anderson, M.G. 1985. Variations on monogamy in Canvasbacks (Aythya valisineria). Ornithol. Monogr. 37:57–67.

Anderson, T.R. 1977. Population Studies of European Sparrows in North America. Occ. Pap. Mus. Nat. Hist. Univ. Kans. No. 70.

Anderson, W.L. 1978. Vocalizations of Scaled Quail. Condor 80:49–63.

Andersson, M. 1982. Female choice selects for extreme tail length in a widowbird. Nature 299:818–820.

Andersson, M., and M.O.G. Eriksson. 1982. Nest parasitism in goldeneyes Bucephala clangula: some evolutionary aspects. Amer. Nat. 120:1–16.

Andersson, S., and C.G. Wiklund. 1987. Sex role partitioning during offspring protection in the Rough-legged Buzzard Buteo lagopus. Ibis 129:103–107.

Andrew, R.J. 1961. The displays given by passerines in courtship and reproductive fighting: a review. Ibis 103A: 315–348; 549–579.

Angell, T. 1969. A study of the Ferruginous Hawk: adult and brood behavior. Living Bird 8:225–241.

Angell, T. 1974. Owls. Univ. Washington Press, Seattle.

Angell, T. 1978. Ravens, Crows, Magpies and Jays. Univ. Washington Press, Seattle.

Ankney, C.D., D.G. Dennis, L.N. Wishard, and J.E. Seeb. 1986. Low genic variation between Black Ducks and Mallards. Auk 103:701–709.

Applegate, R.D. 1977. Possible ecological role of food caches of Loggerhead Shrike. Auk 94:391–392.

Ar, A., and Y. Yom-Tov. 1979. The evolution of parental care in birds. Evolution 32:655–668.

Arbib, R. 1971. Announcing—The Blue List: an "early warning system" for birds. Amer. Birds 25:948–949.

Arcese, P. 1987. Age, intrusion pressure and defense against floaters by territorial male Song Sparrows. Anim. Behav. 35:773–784.

Arcese, P., and J.N.M. Smith. 1985. Phenotypic correlates and ecological consequences of dominance in Song Sparrows. J. Anim. Ecol. 54:817–830.

Archibald, H.L. 1976. Spring drumming patterns of Ruffed Grouse. Auk 93:808–829.

Armbruster, J.S. 1982. Wood Duck displays and pairing chronology. Auk 99:116–122.

Armstrong, D.P. 1987. Economics of breeding territory in male Calliope Hummingbirds. Auk 104:242–253.

Armstrong, E.A. 1949. Diversionary display: the nature and origin of distraction display. Ibis 91:88–97; 179–188.

Arnold, K.A., and D.J. Jirovec. 1978. Arrivals and departures of wintering Common Snipe in Central Brazos Valley of Texas. North American Bird Bander 3:45–47.

Arrowood, P.C. 1981. Importation and status of Canary-winged Parakeets (Brotogeris versicolurus P.L.S. Müller) in California. In R.F. Pasquier (ed.), Conservation of New World Parrots, Proc. I.C.B.P. Parrot Working Group Meeting, St. Lucia, 1980, Smithsonian Institution Press, Washington, DC, pp. 425–429.

Ashkenazie, S., and U.N. Safriel. 1979. Breeding cycle and behavior of the Semipalmated Sandpiper at Barrow, Alaska. Auk 96:56–67.

Ashmole, N.P. 1963. The regulation of numbers of tropical oceanic birds. Ibis 103B:458–473.

Atkinson, C.T., and C.J. Ralph. 1980. Acquisition of plumage polymorphism in White-throated Sparrows. Auk 97:245–252.

Atwood J.L. 1980. Social interactions in the Santa Cruz Island Scrub Jay. Condor 82:440–448.

Atwood, J.L. 1986. Delayed nocturnal occupation of breeding colonies by Least Terns (*Sterna antillarum*). Auk 103:242–244.

Audubon, J.J. 1840–1844. Birds of America, Vols. 1–9. (Published by the author).

Austin, G.T. 1976. Behavioral adaptations of the Verdin to the desert. Auk 93:245–262.

Austin, G.T. 1978. Daily time budget of the postnesting Verdin. Auk 95:247–251.

Austin, G.T., and R.E. Ricklefs. 1977. Growth and development of the Rufous-winged Sparrow (*Aimophila carpalis*). Condor 79:37–50.

Austin, G.T., and E.L. Smith. 1972. Winter foraging ecology of mixed insectivorous bird flocks in oak woodland in southern Arizona. Condor 74:17–24.

Autenrieth, R.E. 1986. Sage Grouse. *In* R.L. Di Silvestro (ed.), Audubon Wildlife Report 1986, National Audubon Soc., NY, pp. 763–779.

Babcock, R.E. 1975. Another instance of incubation by a male Whip-poor-will. Wilson Bull. 87:284.

Baerends, G.P. 1975. An evaluation of the conflict hypothesis as an explanatory principle for the evolution of displays. *In* G. Baerends, C. Beer, and A. Manning (eds.), Function and Evolution in Behavior, Clarendon Press, Oxford, pp. 187–227.

Bailey, R.E. 1952. The incubation patch of passerine birds. Condor 54:121–136.

Baird, P. 1978. Comparative ecology of Arctic and Aleutian Terns. Proc. Seabird Group Bull. 5:45–46.

Baker, M.C. 1974. Foraging behavior of Black-bellied Plovers (*Pluvialis squatarola*). Ecology 55:162–167.

Balda, R.P., and G.C. Bateman. 1972. The breeding biology of the Piñon Jay. Living Bird 11:5–42.

Balda, R.P., B.C. McKnight, and C.D. Johnson. 1975. Flammulated Owl migration in the southwestern United States. Wilson Bull. 87:520–533.

Balda, R.P., M.L. Morrison, and T.R. Bement. 1977. Roosting behavior of the Piñon Jay in autumn and winter. Auk 94:494–504.

Baldwin, P.H., and W.H. Hunter. 1963. Nesting and nest visitors of the Vaux's Swift in Montana. Auk 80:81–85.

Baldwin, P.H., and N.K. Zaczkowski. 1963. Breeding biology of the Vaux Swift. Condor 65:400–406.

Balph, M.H. 1975. Development of young Brewer's Blackbirds. Wilson Bull. 87:207–230.

Balph, M.H. 1979. Flock stability in relation to social dominance and agonistic behavior in wintering Dark-eyed Juncos. Auk 96:714–722.

Baltosser, W.H. 1986. Nesting success and productivity of hummingbirds in southwestern New Mexico and southeastern Arizona. Wilson Bull. 98:353–367.

Bancroft, G.T. 1986. Nesting success and mortality of the Boat-tailed Grackle. Auk 103:86–99.

Bang, B.G., and B.M. Wenzel. 1985. The nasal cavity and olfactory system. *In* A.S. King and J. McLelland (eds.), Form and Function in Birds, vol. 3. Academic Press, New York, pp. 195–225.

Banko, W.E. 1960. The Trumpeter Swan. North American Fauna, No. 155, U.S. Dept. Interior, Fish and Wildlife Service, Washington, DC.

Bannon, L.E., and T. Clark. 1985. Handbook of Audubon Prints. Pelican Pub., Gretna, LA.

Barash, D.P. 1975. Evolutionary aspects of parental behavior: distraction behavior of the Alpine Accentor. Wilson Bull. 85:367–373.

Barbour, D.B. 1982. Communal roosting in wintering Hooded Mergansers. J. Field Ornithol. 53:279–280.

Barklow, W.E. 1979. Graded frequency variations of the tremolo call of the Common Loon (Gavia immer). Condor 81:53–64.

Barlow, J.C. 1962. Natural history of the Bell Vireo, Vireo bellii Audubon. Univ. Kans. Mus. Nat. Hist. Publ. 12:241–296.

Barlow, J.C. 1973. Status of the North American population of the European Tree Sparrow. Ornithol. Monogr. 14:10–23.

Barlow, J.C. 1978. Effects of habitat attrition on vireo distribution and population density in the northern Chihuahuan Desert. In R.H. Wauer and D.H. Riskind (eds.), Transactions of the Symposium on the Biological Resources of the Chihuahuan Desert Region—United States and Mexico. U.S. Natl. Park Service Transactions and Proc. Ser. No. 3, pp. 591–596.

Barlow, J.C. 1980. Patterns of ecological interactions among migrant and resident vireos on the wintering ground. In A. Keast and E.S. Morton (eds.), Migrant Birds in the Neotropics—Ecology, Behavior, Distribution and Conservation. Smithsonian Institution Press, Washington, DC, pp. 79–107.

Barlow, J.C., and G.R. Bortolotti. 1988. Adaptive divergence in morphology and behavior in some New World island birds, with special reference to Vireo altiloquus. Proc. 19th Int. Ornithol. Congr. In press.

Barlow, J.C., R.D. James, and N. Williams. 1970. Habitat cooccupancy among some vireos of the subgenus Vireo (Aves: Vireonidae). Can. J. Zool. 48:395–398.

Barlow, J.C., and J.C. Rice. 1977. Aspects of the comparative behavior of Red-eyed and Philadelphia Vireos. Can. J. Zool. 55:528–542.

Barlow, J.C., and R.H. Waver. 1971. The Gray Vireo (Vireo vicinior Coues, Aves: Vireonidae) wintering in the Big Bend region, west Texas. Can J. Zool. 49:953–955.

Barrentin, C.D. 1980. Ingestion of grit by nesting Barn Swallows. J. Field Ornithol. 51:368–371.

Barrows, C.W. 1981. Roost selection by Spotted Owls: an adaptation to heat stress. Condor 83:302–309.

Bartholomew, G.A., and W.R. Dawson. 1979. Thermoregulatory behavior during incubation in Heermann's Gulls. Physiol. Zool. 52:422–437.

Bateson, P.P.G., and R.C. Plowright. 1959. Some aspects of the reproductive behavior of the Ivory Gull. Ardea 47:157–176.

Bazely, D.R. 1987. Snow Buntings feeding on leaves of salt-marsh grass during spring migration. Condor 89:190–192.

Beason, R.C., and E.C. Franks. 1974. Breeding behavior of the Horned Lark. Auk 91:65–74.

Beattie, A.J. 1985. The Evolutionary Ecology of Ant-Plant Mutualisms. Cambridge Univ. Press, Cambridge.

Beaver, D.L. 1980. Recovery of an American Robin population after early DDT use. J. Field Ornithol. 51:220–228.

Beaver, D.L., and P.H. Baldwin. 1975. Ecological overlap and the problem of competition and sympatry in the Western and Hammond's Flycatchers. Condor 77:1–13.

Bechard, M.J. 1982. Effect of vegetative cover on foraging site selection by Swainson's Hawk. Condor 84:153–159.

Becker, D.M. 1985. Food habits of Richardson's Merlins in southeastern Montana. Wilson Bull. 97:226–230.

Becker, P.H. 1982. The coding of species-specific characteristics in bird sounds. *In* D.E. Kroodsma and E.H. Miller (eds.), Acoustic Communication in Birds, vol. 1. Academic Press, New York, pp. 213–252.

Bédard, J. 1969. The nesting of the Crested, Least, and Parakeet Auklets on St. Lawrence Island, Alaska. Condor 71:386–398.

Bédard, J., and G. LaPointe. 1985. Influence of parental age and season on Savannah Sparrow reproductive success. Condor 87:106–110.

Bédard, J., and M. Meunier. 1983. Parental care in the Savannah Sparrow. Can. J. Zool. 61:2836–2843.

Bednarz, J.C. 1987a. Successive nesting and autumnal breeding in Harris' Hawks. Auk 104:85–96.

Bednarz, J.C. 1987b. Pair and group reproductive success, polyandry, and cooperative breeding in Harris' Hawks. Auk 104:393–404.

Beecham. J.J., and M.N. Kochert. 1975. Breeding biology of the Golden Eagle in southwestern Idaho. Wilson Bull. 87:506–513.

Beecher, M.D., I.M. Beecher, and S. Hahn. 1981. Parent-offspring recognition in Bank Swallows *(Riparia riparia)*: II. Development and acoustic basis. Anim. Behav. 29:95–101.

Beecher, M.D., P.K. Stoddard, and P. Loesche. 1985. Recognition of parents' voices by young Cliff Swallows. Auk 102:600–605.

Beecher, W.J. 1955. Attracting Birds to Your Backyard. All-Pets Books, Inc. Fond du Lac, WI.

Beecher, W.J. 1985. In quest of starlings. Bull. Field Mus. Nat. Hist. (Chicago). 56 (September):16–21.

Beer, C.G. 1979. Vocal communication between Laughing Gull parents and chicks. Behaviour 70:118–146.

Beissinger, S.R. 1986. Demography, environmental uncertainty, and the evolution of mate desertion in the Snail Kite. Ecology 67:1445–1459.

Beissinger, S.R. 1987. Anisogamy overcome: female strategies in Snail Kites. Amer. Nat. 129:486–500.

Beissinger, S.R., and N.F.R. Snyder. 1987. Mate desertion in the Snail Kite. Anim. Behav. 35:477–487.

Bekoff, M., A.C. Scott, and D.A. Conner. 1987. Nonrandom nest-site selection in Evening Grosbeaks. Condor 89:819–829.

Belles-Isles, J.-C., and J. Picman. 1986a. House Wren nest-destroying behavior. Condor 88:190–193.

Belles-Isles, J.-C., and J. Picman. 1986b. Nesting losses and nest site preferences in House Wrens. Condor 88:483–486.

Bellrose, F.C. 1976. Ducks, Geese and Swans of North America, second edition. Stackpole Books, Harrisburg, PA.

Bengtson, S.A. 1984. Breeding ecology and extinction of the Great Auk *(Pinguinus impennis):* anecdotal evidence and conjectures. Auk 101:1–12.

Benkman, C.W. 1987a. Food profitability and the foraging ecology of crossbills. Ecol. Monogr. 57:251–267.

Benkman, C.W. 1987b. Crossbill foraging behavior, bill structure, and patterns of food profitability. Wilson Bull. 99:351–368.

Bennett, A.F., and W.R. Dawson. 1979. Physiological responses of embryonic Heermann's Gulls to temperature. Physiol. Zool. 52:413–421.

Bennett, P., and P. Harvey, 1985. Why mammals are not bird-brained. New Scientist, 4 April, pp. 16–17.

Bent, A.C. 1919–1968. Life Histories of North American Birds. United States National Museum: Washington, DC. 26 Vols. Reprinted by Dover, New York, 1962–1968. The volumes and their original publication dates are: Diving Birds (1919); Gulls and Terns (1921); Petrels, Pelicans, and Their Allies (1922); Wild Fowl, vol. 1 (1923), vol. 2 (1923); Marsh Birds (1926); Shorebirds, vol. 1 (1927), vol. 2 (1929); Gallinaceous Birds (1932); Birds of Prey, vol. 1 (1937), vol. 2 (1937); Woodpeckers (1939); Cuckoos, Goatsuckers, Hummingbirds, and Their Allies, vol. 1 (1940), vol. 2 (1940); Flycatchers, Larks, Swallows, and Their Allies (1942); Jays, Crows, and Titmice, vol. 1 (1946), vol. 2 (1946); Nuthatches, Wrens, Thrashers, and Their Allies (1948); Thrushes, Kinglets, and Their Allies (1949); Wagtails, Shrikes, Vireos, and Their Allies (1950); Wood Warblers, vol. 1 (1953), vol. 2 (1953); Blackbirds, Orioles, Tanagers, and Their Allies (1958); Cardinals, Grosbeaks, Buntings, Towhees, Finches, Sparrows, and Their Allies, vol. 1 (1968), vol. 2 (1968), Vol.3 (1968).

Berger, A.J. 1981. Hawaiian Birdlife. Univ. Hawaii Press, Honolulu.

Bergman, C.A. 1983. Flaming owl of the Ponderosa. Audubon, November, pp. 66–70.

Bergman, R.D., P. Swain, and M.W. Weller. 1970. A comparative study of nesting Forster's and Black Terns. Wilson Bull. 82:435–444.

Bergstrom, P.W. 1986. Daylight incubation sex roles in Wilson's Plover. Condor 88:113–115.

Berner, T.O., and T.C. Grubb, Jr. 1985. An experimental analysis of mixed-species flocking in birds in deciduous woodland. Ecology 66:1229–1236.

Bertin, R.I. 1977. Breeding habitats of the Wood Thrush and Veery. Auk 79:303–311.

Best, L.B. 1977. Territory quality and mating success in the Field Sparrow. Condor 79:192–204.

Best, L.B. 1978. Field Sparrow reproductive success and nesting ecology. Auk 95:9–22.

Best, L.B., and N.L. Rodenhouse. 1984. Territory preference of Vesper Sparrows in cropland. Wilson Bull. 96:72–82.

Biermann, G.C., and S.G. Sealy. 1979. Parental feeding of nestling Yellow Warblers in relation to brood size and prey availability. Auk 99:332–341.

Bildstein, K.L. 1987. Energetic consequences of sexual size dimorphism in White Ibises (*Eudocimus albus*). Auk 104:771–775.

Binkley, C.S., and R.S. Miller. 1983. Population characteristics of the Whooping Crane, *Grus americana*. Can. J. Zool. 61:2768–2776.

Birchard, G.F., and D.L. Kilgore. 1980. Conductance of water vapor in eggs of burrowing and nonburrowing birds: implications for gas exchange. Physiol. Zool. 53:284–292.

Birkhead, T., and A. Moller, 1986. Avian mating games. New Scientist, 18 December, pp. 34–36.

Birt, V.L., and D.K. Cairns. 1987. Kleptoparasitic interactions of Arctic Skuas *Stercorarius parasiticus* and Black Guillemots, *Cepphus grylle* in northeastern Hudson Bay, Canada. Ibis 129:190–196.

Bitterbaum, E., and L.F. Baptista. 1979. Geographical variation in songs of California House Finches (*Carpodacus mexicanus*). Auk 96:462–474.

Blake, R.W. 1985. A model of foraging efficiency and daily energy budget in the Black Skimmers (*Rynchops niger*). Can. J. Zool. 63:42–48.

Blancher, P.J., and R.J. Robertson. 1984. Resource use by sympatric kingbirds. Condor 86:305–313.

Blancher, P.J., and R.J. Robertson. 1985a. Site consistency in kingbird breeding performance: implications for site fidelity. J. Anim. Ecol. 54:1017–1027.

Blancher, P.J., and R.J. Robertson, 1985b. A comparison of Eastern Kingbird breeding biology in lakeshore and upland habitats. Can. J. Zool. 63:2305–2312.

Blancher, P.J., and R.J. Robertson. 1987. Effect of food supply on the breeding biology of Western Kingbirds. Ecology 68:723–732.

Blockstein, D.E., and H.B. Tordoff. 1985. Gone forever: a contemporary look at the extinction of the Passenger Pigeon. Amer. Birds 39:845–851.

Boag, D.A., and M. Alexander. 1986. The Atlantic Puffin. Blandford Press, New York.

Boag, D.A., K.H. McCourt, P.W. Herzog, and J.H. Alway. 1979. Population regulation in Spruce Grouse: a working hypothesis. Can. J. Zool. 57:2275–2284.

Bock, C.E., and L.W. Lepthien. 1976. Synchronous eruptions of boreal seed-eating birds. Amer. Nat. 110:559–571.

Boersma, P.D. 1986. Ingestion of petroleum by seabirds can serve as a monitor of water quality. Science 231:373–376.

Boersma, P.D., and J.P. Ryder. 1983. Reproductive performance and body condition of earlier and later nesting Ring-billed Gulls. J. Field Ornithol. 54:374–380.

Boersma, P.D., N.T. Wheelwright, M.K. Nerini, and E.S. Wheelwright. 1980. The breeding biology of the Fork-tailed Storm-Petrel (*Oceanodroma furcata*). Auk 97:268–282.

Bohall-Wood, P. 1987. Abundance, habitat use, and perch use of Loggerhead Shrikes in north-central Florida. Wilson Bull. 99:82–86.

Bolen, E.G., and R.E. McCamant. 1977. Mortality rates for Black-bellied Whistling Ducks. Bird-Banding 48:350–353.

Bollinger, R.C., and E. Bowes. 1973. Another chapter in the "ornithological mystery story." Amer. Birds 27:741–742.

Bondrup-Nielsen, S. 1977. Thawing of frozen prey by Boreal and Saw-whet Owls. Can. J. Zool. 55:595–601.

Bonney, R.E. 1986. Dicofol stays on the market. Audubon, January, pp. 124–125.

Bookhout, T.A., and J.R. Stenzel. 1987. Habitat and movements of breeding Yellow Rails. Wilson Bull. 99:441–447.

Borror, D.J. 1987. Song in the White-eyed Vireo. Wilson Bull. 99:377–397.

Bossema, I., and E. Roemers. 1985. Mating strategy, including mate choice, in Mallards. Ardea 73:147–157.

Boughey, M.J., and N.S. Thompson. 1981. Song variety in the Brown Thrasher (*Toxostoma rufum*). Zeit. Tierpsychol. 56:47–58.

Bowers, M.D., I.L. Brown, and D. Wheye. 1985. Bird predation as a selective agent in a butterfly population. Evolution 39:93–103.

Boxall, P.C., and M.R. Lein. 1982. Territoriality and habitat selection of female Snowy Owls (*Nyctea scandiaca*) in winter. Can. J. Zool. 60:2344–2350.

Boyce, M.S., and R.S. Miller. 1985. Ten-year periodicity in Whooping Crane census. Auk 102:658–660.

Boyd, H., G.J. Smith, and F.G. Cooch. 1982. The Lesser Snow Goose (*Anser c. caerulescens*) of the Eastern Canadian Arctic: Their Status in 1964–1979 and Their Management in 1981–1990. Can Wildl. Serv. Occas. Pap. No. 46.

Boyden, T.C. 1978. Territorial defense against hummingbirds and insects by tropical hummingbirds. Condor 80:216–221.

Brackbill, H. 1970. Tufted Titmouse breeding behavior. Auk 87:522–536.

Brackenbury, J.H. 1982. The structural basis of voice production and its relationship to sound characteristics. *In* D.E. Kroodsma and E.H. Miller (eds.), Acoustic Communication in Birds, vol. 1. Academic Press, New York, pp. 53–73.

Bradbury, J.W., and R. Gibson. 1983. Leks and mate choice. *In* P. Bateson, (ed.), Mate Choice. Cambridge Univ. Press, Cambridge, pp. 109–138.

Bradley, R.A. 1980. Vocal and territorial behavior in the White-eyed Vireo. Wilson Bull. 92:302–311.

Braune, B.M. 1987a. Body morphometrics and molt of Bonaparte's Gulls in the Quoddy region, New Brunswick, Canada. Condor 89:150–157.

Braune, B.M. 1987b. Seasonal aspects of the diet of Bonaparte's Gulls (*Larus philadelphia*) in the Quoddy region, New Brunswick, Canada. Auk 104:167–172.

Braune, B.M. and D.E. Gaskin. 1982. Feeding methods and diving rates of migrating larids off Deer Island, New Brunswick. Can J. Zool. 60:2190–2197.

Braune, B.M., and G.L. Hunt, Jr. 1983. Brood reduction in Black-legged Kittiwakes. Auk 100:469–476.

Braune, C.E., T. Britt, and R.O. Wallestad. 1977. Guidelines for maintenance of Sage Grouse habitats. Wildl. Soc. Bull. 5:99–106.

Brearey, D., and O. Hilden. 1985. Nesting and egg-predation by Turnstones *Arenaria interpres* in larid colonies. Ornis Scand. 16:283–292.

Breitwisch, R., P.G. Merritt, and G.H. Whitesides. 1986. Parental investment by the Northern Mockingbird: male and female roles in feeding nestlings. Auk 103:152–159.

Breitwisch, R. and G.H. Whitesides. 1987. Directionality of singing and nonsinging behavior of mated and unmated Northern Mockingbirds, *Mimus polyglottos*. Anim. Behav. 35:331–339.

Brennan, L.A., W.M. Block, and R.J. Gutiérrez. 1987. Habitat use by Mountain Quail in northern California. Condor 89:66–74.

Brent, R., P.F. Pedersen, C. Bech, and K. Johansen. 1985. Thermal balance in the European Coot *Fulica atra* exposed to temperatures from −28°C to 40°C. Ornis Scand. 16:145–150.

Briggs, K.T., W.B. Tyler, D.B. Lewis, P.R. Kelly, and D.A. Croll. 1983. Brown Pelicans in central and northern California. J. Field Ornithol. 54:353–373.

Briggs, S.A., and J.H. Criswell. 1979. Gradual silencing of spring in Washington. Atlantic Naturalist 32:19–26.

Brisbin, I.L. 1968. The Passenger Pigeon, a study in the ecology of extinction. Modern Game Breeding 4:13–20.

Briskie, J.V., and S.G. Sealy. 1987. Polygyny and double-brooding in the Least Flycatcher. Wilson Bull. 99:492–494.

Brittingham, M.C., and S.A. Temple. 1983. Have cowbirds caused forest songbirds to decline? BioScience 33:31–35.

Brooks, R.P., and W.J. Davis. 1987. Habitat selection by breeding Belted Kingfishers (*Ceryle alcyon*). Amer. Midl. Nat. 117:63–70.

Brooks, W.S. 1978. Triphasic feeding behavior and the esophageal diverticulum in redpolls. Auk 95:182–183.

Brower, J.V.Z. 1958. Experimental studies of mimicry in some North American butterflies. 1. *Danaus plexippus* and *Limenitis archippus archippus*. Evolution 12:32–47.

Brown, C.R. 1979. Territoriality in the Purple Martin. Wilson Bull. 91:583–591.

Brown, C.R. 1983. Vocalizations and behavior of Violet-green Swallows in the Chiricahua Mountains, Arizona. Wilson Bull. 95:142–145.

Brown, C.R. 1984. Laying eggs in a neighbor's nest: benefit and cost of colonial nesting in swallows. Science 224:518–519.

Brown, C.R. 1986. Cliff Swallow colonies as information centers. Science 234:83–85.

Brown, C.R., and M.B. Brown. 1986. Ectoparasitism as a cost of coloniality in Cliff Swallows (*Hirundo pyrrhonota*). Ecology 67:1206–1218.

Brown, J.L. 1964. The integration of agonistic behavior in the Steller's Jay *Cyanocitta stelleri* (Gmelin). Univ. Calif. Publ. Zool. 60:223–328.

Brown, J.L. 1978. Avian communal breeding systems. Ann. Rev. Ecol. Syst. 9:123–155.

Brown, J.L. 1987. Helping and Communal Breeding in Birds. Princeton Univ. Press, Princeton, NJ.

Brown, J.L., and E.R. Brown. 1985. Ecological correlates of group size in a communally breeding jay. Condor 87:309–315.

Brown, L., and D. Amadon. 1968. Eagles, Hawks, and Falcons of the World. 2 vols. McGraw-Hill Book Company, New York.

Brown, P.W., and M.A. Brown. 1981. Nesting biology of the White-winged Scoter. J. Wildl. Manage. 45:38–45.

Brown, P.W., and L.H. Frederickson. 1987. Time budget and incubation behavior of breeding White-winged Scoters. Wilson Bull. 99:50–55.

Brown, W.Y. 1977. Temporal patterns in laying, hatching and incubation of Sooty Terns and Brown Noddies. Condor 79:133–136.

Bruce, J.A. 1973. Tail-flashing display in the Whip-poor-will. Auk 90:682.

Bryan, K., R. Moldenhauer, and D.E. Kroodsma. 1987. Geographic uniformity in songs of the Prothonotary Warbler. Wilson Bull. 99:369–376.

Buchheister, C.W., and F. Graham, Jr. 1973. From the swamp back: a concise and candid history of the Audubon movement. Audubon, January, pp. 4–43.

Buckley, F.G., and P.A. Buckley. 1972. The breeding ecology of Royal Terns *Sterna (Thalasseus) maxima maxima*. Ibis 114:344–359.

Buckley, F.G., and P.A. Buckley. 1979. Do Aleutian Terns exhibit extraordinary anti-predator adaptations? Proc. Conf. Colonial Waterbird Group 3:99–107.

Buckley, P.A., and F.G. Buckley. 1977. Hexagonal packing of Royal Tern nests. Auk 94:36–43.

Buech, R.R. 1982. Nesting ecology and cowbird parasitism of Clay-colored, Chipping, and Field Sparrows in a Christmas tree plantation. J. Field Ornithol. 53:363–369.

Bull, J. 1973. Exotic birds in the New York City area. Wilson Bull. 85:501–505

Bump, S.R. 1986. Yellow-headed Blackbird nest defense: aggressive responses to Marsh Wrens. Condor 88:328–335.

Bundy, G. 1976. Breeding biology of the Red-throated Diver. Bird Study 23:249–256.

Bunn, D.S., A.B. Warburton, and R.D.S. Wilson. 1982. The Barn Owl. Buteo Books, Vermillion, SD.

Burger, A.E., and M. Simpson. 1986. Diving depths of Atlantic Puffins and Common Murres. Auk 103:828–830.

Burger, J. 1972. Dispersal and post-fledging survival of Franklin's Gulls. Bird-Banding 43:267–275.

Burger, J. 1974. Breeding adaptations of Franklin's Gull (*Larus pipixcan*) to a marsh habitat. Anim. Behav. 22:521–567.

Burger, J. 1976. Daily and seasonal activity patterns in breeding Laughing Gulls. Auk 93:308–323.

Burger, J. 1978. Competition between Cattle Egrets and native North American herons, egrets, and ibises. Condor 80:15–23.

Burger, J. 1981. Sexual differences in parental activities of breeding Black Skimmers. Amer. Nat. 117:975–984.

Burger, J. 1982. The role of reproductive success in colony-site selection and abandonment in Black Skimmers *(Rynchops niger)*. Auk 99:109–115.

Burger, J. 1983. Competition between two species of nesting gulls: on the importance of timing. Behav. Neurosci. 97:492–501.

Burger, J. 1984. Pattern, Mechanism, and Adaptive Significance of Territoriality in Herring Gulls *(Larus argentatus)*. Ornithol. Monogr. No. 34.

Burger, J. 1985. Factors affecting bird strikes on aircraft at a coastal airport. Biol. Cons. 33:1–28.

Burger, J. 1988. Foraging behavior in gulls: differences in method, prey and habitat. Colonial Waterbirds, vol. II, *In Press.*

Burger, J., and M. Gochfeld. 1985. Nest site selection by Laughing Gulls: comparison of tropical colonies (Culebra, Puerto Rico) with temperate colonies (New Jersey). Condor 87:364–373.

Burger, J., and M. Gochfeld. 1988. Nest site selection in Mew Gulls *(Larus canus)*: a comparison of marsh and dry land colonies. Wilson Bull. *In Press.*

Burger, J., and F. Lesser. 1979. Breeding behavior and success in salt marsh Common Tern colonies. Bird-Banding 50:322–337.

Burger, J., and L.M. Miller. 1977. Colony and nest-site selection in White-faced and Glossy Ibises. Auk 94:664–676.

Burger, J., L.M. Miller, and D.C. Hahn. 1978. Behavior and sex roles of nesting Anhingas at San Blas, Mexico. Wilson Bull. 90:359–375.

Burger, J., and B.L. Olla (eds.). 1984. Shorebirds: Migration and Foraging Behavior, Behavior of Marine Animals, vol. 6. Plenum, New York.

Burton, J.A. (ed.). 1984. Owls of the World: Their Evolution, Structure and Ecology, 2nd edition. Tanager Books, Dover, NH.

Burtt, E.H., and J.P. Hailman. 1978. Head-scratching among North American wood-warblers (Parulidae). Ibis 120:153–170.

Burtt, W.G., III. 1987. Deceiving a feathered mouse. Audubon, September, pp. 78, 80–83.

Busby, D.G., and S.G. Sealy. 1979. Feeding ecology of a population of nesting Yellow Warblers. Can. J. Zool. 57:1670–1681.

Butcher, G.S., W.A. Niering, W.J. Barry, and R.H. Goodwin. 1981. Equilibrium biogeography and the size of nature reserves: an avian case study. Oecologia 49:29–37.

Butler, R.G., and S. Janes-Butler. 1983. Sexual differences in the behavior of adult Great Black-backed Gulls *(Larus marinus)* during the pre- and post-hatch periods. Auk 100:63–75.

Butler, R.G., and W. Trivelpiece. 1981. Nest spacing, reproductive success, and behavior of the Great Black-backed Gull *(Larus marinus)*. Auk 98:99–107.

Butler, R.W., G.W. Kaiser, and G.E.J. Smith. 1987. Migration chronology, length of stay, sex ratio, and weight of Western Sandpipers *(Calidris mauri)* on the south coast of British Columbia. J. Field Ornithol. 58:103–111.

Buttemer, W.A., L.B. Astheimer, W.W. Weathers, and A.M. Hayworth. 1987. Energy savings attending winter-nest use by Verdins *(Auriparus flaviceps)*. Auk 104:531–535.

Byrd, G.V. 1978. Red-legged Kittiwake colonies in the Aleutian Islands, Alaska. Condor 80:250.

Caccamise, D.F. 1974. Competitive relationships of the Common and Lesser Nighthawks. Condor 76:1–20.

Caccamise, D.F., L.A. Lyon, and J. Fischl. 1983. Seasonal patterns in roosting flocks of starlings and Common Grackles. Condor 85:474–481.

Cade, T.J. 1967. Ecological and behavioral aspects of predation by a Northern Shrike. Living Bird 6:43–86.

Cade, T.J. 1982. The Falcons of the World. Cornell Univ. Press, Ithaca, NY.

Cade, T.J., J.L. Lincer, C.M. White, D.G. Roseneau, and L.G. Swartz. 1971. DDE residues and eggshell changes in Alaskan falcons and hawks. Science 172:955–957.

Cain, A.J., and P.M. Sheppard. 1954. Natural selection in *Cepaea*. Genetics 39:89–116.

Cairns, D.K. 1987. The ecology and energetics of chick provisioning by Black Guillemots. Condor 89:627–635.

Cairns, D.K., K.A. Bredin, and W.A. Montevecchi. 1987. Activity budgets and foraging ranges of breeding Common Murres. Auk 104:218–224.

Cairns, W.E., and I.A. McLaren. 1980. Status of the Piping Plover on the east coast of North America. Amer. Birds 34:206–208.

Calder, W.A. 1971. Temperature relationships and nesting of the Calliope Hummingbird. Condor 73:314–321.

Calder, W.A. 1974. Consequences of body size for avian energetics. *In* R.A. Paynter, Jr. (ed.), Avian Energetics, Nuttall Ornith. Club, Publ. 15. Cambridge, MA, pp. 86–151.

Calder, W.A. 1984. Size, Function, and Life History. Harvard Univ. Press, Cambridge.

Calder, W.A., and S.M. Hiebert. 1983. Nectar feeding, diuresis, and electrolyte replacement of hummingbirds. Physiol. Zool. 56:325–334.

Calder, W.A., and J.R. King. 1974. Thermal and caloric relations in birds. *In* D.S. Farner, J.R. King, and K.C. Parkes (eds.), Avian Biology. Academic Press, New York, vol. 4, pp. 259–413.

Calder, W.A., N.M. Waser, S.M. Hiebert, D.W. Inouye, and S. Miller. 1983. Site-fidelity, longevity, and population dynamics of Broad-tailed Hummingbirds: a ten-year study. Oecologia 56:359–364.

Campbell, B., and E. Lack. 1985. A Dictionary of Birds. Buteo Books, Vermillion, SD.

Campbell, H., D.K. Martin, P.E. Ferkovich, and B.K. Harris. 1973. Effects of Hunting and Some Other Environmental Factors on Scaled Quail in New Mexico. Wildl. Monogr. No. 34.

Caple, G., R.P. Balda, and W.R. Willis. 1983. The physics of leaping animals and the evolution of preflight. Amer. Nat. 121:455–476.

Carey, C. 1983. Structure and function of avian eggs. Current Ornithology 1:69–103.

Carey, M., and V. Nolan, Jr. 1979. Population dynamics of Indigo Buntings and the evolution of avian polygyny. Evolution 33:1180–1192.

Carpenter, F.L., D.C. Paton, and M.A. Hixon. 1983. Weight gain and adjustment of feeding territory size in migrant hummingbirds. Proc. Nat. Acad. Sci. U.S.A. 80:7259–7263.

Carrick, R. 1963. Ecological significance of territory in the Australian magpie, *Gymnorhina tibicen*. Proc. XIII Inter. Ornith. Congress, pp. 740–753.

Carson, R. 1962. Silent Spring. Houghton Mifflin, Boston, MA.

Cartar, R.V., and R.D. Montgomerie. 1987. Day-to-day variation in nest attentiveness of White-rumped Sandpipers. Condor 89:252–260.

Carter, H.R., and S.G. Sealy. 1986. Year-round use of coastal lakes by Marbled Murrelets. Condor 88:473–477.

Carter, M.D. 1986. The parasitic behavior of the Bronzed Cowbird in south Texas. Condor 88:11–25.

Catzeflis, F. 1978. Reproductive biology of the Water Pipit. Nos Oiseaux 34:287–302.

Chaplin, S.B. 1982. The energetic significance of huddling behavior in Common Bushtits (*Psaltriparus minimus*). Auk 99:424–430.

Chaplin, S.B., D.A. Diesel, and J.A. Kasparie. 1984. Body temperature regulation in Red-tailed Hawks and Great Horned Owls: responses to air temperature and food deprivation. Condor 86:175–181.

Chappell, M.A., D.L. Goldstein, and D.W. Winkler. 1984. Oxygen consumption, evaporative water loss, and temperature regulation of California Gull chicks (*Larus californicus*) in a desert rookery. Physiol. Zool. 57:204–214.

Charig, A. 1979. A New Look at the Dinosaurs. Mayflower Books, New York.

Chartier B., and F. Cooke. 1980. Ross' Gulls *Rhodostethia rosea* nesting at Churchill, Manitoba, Canada. Amer. Birds 34:839–841.

Cherry, J.D. 1985. Early autumn movements and prebasic molt of Swainson's Thrushes. Wilson Bull. 97:368–370.

Choate, E.A. 1985. The Dictionary of American Bird Names, Rev. Ed. Harvard Common Press, Cambridge, MA.

Clapp, R.B., M.K. Klimkiewicz, and A.G. Futcher. 1983. Longevity records of North American birds: Columbidae through Paridae. J. Field Ornithol. 54:123–137.

Clapp, R.B., M.K. Klimkiewicz, and J.H. Kennard. 1982. Longevity records of North American birds: Gaviidae through Alcidae. J. Field Ornithol. 53:81–124.

Clark, A.B., and D.S. Wilson. 1981. Avian breeding adaptations: hatching asynchrony, brood reduction, and nest failure. Quart. Rev. Biol. 56:253–277.

Clark, G.A., Jr. 1969. Spread-wing postures in Pelecaniformes, Ciconiiformes, and Falconiformes. Auk 86:136–139.

Clark, L., and J.R. Mason. 1985. Use of nest material as insecticidal and anti-pathogenic agents by the European Starling. Oecologia 67:169–176.

Clark, R.G., and R.D. Ohmart. 1985. Spread-wing posture of Turkey Vultures: single or multiple function? Condor 87:350–355.

Clark, R.J. 1975. A Field Study of the Short-eared Owl, *Asio flammeus* (Pontoppidan), in North America. Wildl. Monogr. No. 47.

Cody, M.L. 1974. Competition and the Structure of Bird Communities. Princeton Univ. Press, Princeton.

Cody, M.L. 1981. Habitat selection in birds: the roles of habitat structure, competitors, and productivity. BioScience 31:107–113.

Cody, M.L. (ed.). 1985. Habitat Selection in Birds. Academic Press, New York.

Collias, N.E., and E.C. Collias. 1984. Nest Building and Bird Behavior. Princeton Univ. Press, Princeton.

Collins, C.T. 1983. A reinterpretation of pamprodactyly in swifts: a convergent grasping mechanism in vertebrates. Auk 100:735–737.

Collopy, M.W. 1977. Food caching by female American Kestrels in winter. Condor 79:63–68.

Collopy, M.W. 1984. Parental care and feeding ecology of Golden Eagle nestlings. Auk 101:753–760.

Colvin, B.A. 1985. Common Barn-Owl population decline in Ohio and the relationship to agricultural trends. J. Field Ornithol. 56:224–235.

Confer, J.L., and K. Knapp. 1979. The changing proportion of Blue-winged and Golden-winged Warblers in Tompkins County and their habitat selection. Kingbird 29:8–14.

Confer, J.L., and K. Knapp. 1981. Golden-winged Warblers and Blue-winged Warblers: the relative success of a habitat specialist and a generalist. Auk 98:108–114.

Connors, P.G. 1983. Taxonomy, distribution, and evolution of Golden Plovers (Pluvialis dominica and Pluvialis fulva). Auk 100:607–620.

Conover, M.R. 1984. Frequency, spatial distribution and nest attendants of supernormal clutches in Ring-billed and California Gulls. Condor 86:467–471.

Cooch, F.G. 1965. The breeding biology and management of the Northern Eider (Somateria mollissima borealis) in the Cape Dorset area, Northwest Territories. Can. Wildl. Serv. Rep., Ser. 6.

Cooper, J.A. 1979. Trumpeter Swan nesting behaviour. Wildfowl 30:55–71.

Cottam, C., and J.B. Trefethen (eds.). 1968. White-wings: The Life History, Status, and Management of the White-winged Dove. D. Van Nostrand, Princeton, NJ.

Coulson, J.C. 1966. The influence of the pair bond and age on the breeding biology of the Kittiwake Gull, Rissa tridactyla. J. Anim. Ecol. 35:269–279.

Council on Environmental Quality. 1977. The Evolution of National Wildlife Law. U.S. Government Printing Office, Washington, DC.

Courser, W.E., and J.J. Dinsmore. 1975. Foraging associates of White Ibis. Auk 92:599–610.

Cox, G.W. 1960. A life history of the Mourning Warbler. Wilson Bull. 72:5–28.

Craig, G. 1986. Peregrine Falcon. In R.L. Di Silvestro (ed.), Audubon Wildlife Report 1986, National Audubon Soc., N.Y., pp. 807–824.

Craig, R.J. 1987. Divergent prey selection in two species of waterthrushes (Seiurus). Auk 104:180–187.

Cramp, S. (ed.). 1985. Handbook of the Birds of Europe, the Middle East, and North Africa: The Birds of the Western Palearctic, vol. 4. Terns to Woodpeckers. Oxford Univ. Press, Oxford.

Cramp, S., and K.E.L. Simmons (eds.). 1977. Handbook of the Birds of Europe, the Middle East, and North Africa: The Birds of the Western Palearctic, vol. 1. Ostrich to Ducks. Oxford Univ. Press, Oxford.

Cramp, S., and K.E.L. Simmons (eds.). 1980. Handbook of the Birds of Europe, the Middle East, and North Africa: The Birds of the Western Palearctic, vol. 2. Hawks to Bustards. Oxford Univ. Press, Oxford.

Cramp, S., and K.E.L. Simmons (eds.). 1983. Handbook of the Birds of Europe, the Middle East, and North Africa: The Birds of the Western Palearctic, vol. 3. Waders to Gulls. Oxford Univ. Press, Oxford.

Craven, S.R. 1984. Fall food habits of Canada Geese in Wisconsin. J. Wildl. Manage. 48:169–173.

Crawford, J.A., and E.G. Bolen. 1975. Spring lek activity of the Lesser Prairie Chicken in west Texas. Auk 92:808–810.

Crawford, J.A., and E.G. Bolen. 1976. Fall diet of Lesser Prairie Chickens in west Texas. Condor 78:142–144.

Crawford, J.A., and F.A. Stormer. 1980. A Bibliography of the Lesser Prairie Chicken, 1873–1980. U.S. Dept. Agric., For. Serv. General Tech. Report RM-80. Rocky Mountain Forest and Range Experiment Station, Ft. Collins, CO.

Crawford, R.D. 1977. Polygynous breeding of Short-billed Marsh Wrens. Auk 94:359–362.

Crocker, J. 1985. Respect your feathered friends. New Scientist, 10 October, pp. 47–50.

Crockett, A.B., Jr., and P.L. Hansley. 1977. Coition, nesting, and post-fledging behavior in Williamson's Sapsucker in Colorado. Living Bird 16:7–19.

Crowell, K. 1962. Reduced interspecific competition in the birds of Bermuda. Ecology 43:75–88.

684 BIBLIOGRAPHY

Croxall, J.P., P.G.H. Evans, and R.W. Schreiber. 1984. Status and Conservation of the World's Seabirds. International Council for Bird Preservation, Technical Publication No. 2.

Cruz, A. 1980. Feeding ecology of the Black-whiskered Vireo and associated gleaning birds in Jamaica. Wilson Bull. 92:40–52.

Curio, E., U. Ernst, and W. Veith. 1978. The adaptive significance of avian mobbing. II. Zeit. Tierpsychol. 21:223–234.

Custer, T.W., G.L. Hensler, and T.E. Kaiser. 1983. Clutch size, reproductive success, and organochlorine contaminants in Atlantic Coast Black-crowned Night-Herons. Auk 100:699–710.

Custer, T.W., R.G. Osborn, F.A. Pitelka, and J.A. Gessaman. 1986. Energy budget and prey requirements of breeding Lapland Longspurs near Barrow, Alaska, U.S.A. Arctic and Alpine Research 18:415–427.

Cuthbert, F.J. 1985a. Mate retention in Caspian Terns. Condor 87:74–78.

Cuthbert, F.J. 1985b. Intraseasonal movement between colony sites by Caspian Terns. Wilson Bull. 97:502–510.

Dagy, A.I. 1977. The walk of the Silver Gull (*Larus novaehollandiae*) and of other birds. J. Zool. (London) 182:529–540.

Dane, B., and W. Van Der Kloot. 1964. An analysis of the display of the Goldeneye Duck (*Bucephala clangula*). Behaviour 22:282–328.

Dane, B., C. Walcott, and W. Drury. 1959. The form and duration of the display actions of the Goldeneye (*Bucephala clangula*). Behaviour 14:265–281.

Darley, J.A. 1982. Territoriality and mating behavior of the male Brown-headed Cowbird. Condor 84:15–21.

Davis, C.M. 1978. A nesting study of the Brown Creeper. Living Bird 17:237–263.

Davis, D.E. 1954. The breeding biology of Hammond's Flycatcher. Auk 71:164–171.

Davis, J., G.F. Fisler, and B.S. Davis. 1963. The breeding biology of the Western Flycatcher. Condor 65:337–382.

Davis, T.A. and R.A. Ackerman. 1985. Adaptations of Black Tern (*Chlidonias niger*) eggs for water loss in a moist nest. Auk 102:640–643.

Davis, T.A., M.F. Platter-Reiger, and R.A. Ackerman. 1984. Incubation water loss by Pied-billed Grebe eggs: adaptation to a hot, wet nest. Physiol. Zool. 57:384–391.

Davis, W.J. 1982. Territory size in *Megaceryle alcyon* along a stream habitat. Auk 99:353–362.

Davis, W.J. 1986. Acoustic recognition in the Belted Kingfisher: cardiac response to playback vocalizations. Condor 88:505–512.

Dawson, W.R., C. Carey, C.S. Adkisson, and R.D. Ohmart. 1979. Responses of Brewer's and Chipping Sparrows to water restriction. Physiol. Zool. 52:529–541.

Dawson, W.R., J.D. Ligon, J.R. Murphy, J.R. Myers, D. Simberloff, and J. Verner. 1987. Report of the scientific advisory panel on the Spotted Owl. Condor 89:205–229.

Day, R.H., K.L. Oakley, and D.R. Barnard. 1983. Nest sites and eggs of Kittlitz's and Marbled Murrelets. Condor 85:265–273.

Degen, A.A., B. Pinshow, and P.J. Shaw. 1984. Must desert Chukars (*Alectoris chukar sinaica*) drink water? Water influx and body mass changes in response to dietary water content. Auk 101:47–52.

De Graaf, R., and B. Payne. 1975. Economic values of non-game birds and some urban wildlife research needs. Trans. N.A. Wildlife and Natural Resources Conf. 40:281–287.

Delacour, J., and D. Amadon. 1973. Curassows and Related Birds. American Museum of Natural History, New York.

DellaSala, D.A. 1986. Polygyny in the Yellow Warbler. Wilson Bull. 98:152–154.

Delnicki, D., and E.G. Bolen. 1976. Renesting by the Black-bellied Whistling Duck. Auk 93:535–542.

DeSante, D., and P. Pyle, 1986. Distributional Checklist of North American Birds. Vol. 1: United States and Canada. Artemisia Press, Lee Vining, CA.

De Smet, K.D. 1987. Organochlorines, predators, and reproductive success of the Red-necked Grebe in southern Manitoba. Condor 89:460–467.

Desmond, A.J. 1975. The Hot-Blooded Dinosaurs. Warner Books, New York.

Dexter, R.W. 1981. Nesting success of Chimney Swifts related to age and the number of adults at the nest, and the subsequent fate of the visitors. J. Field Ornithol. 52:228–232.

Diamond, J. 1975. Assembly of species communities. In M.L. Cody and J.M. Diamond (eds.), Ecology and Evolution of Communities. Harvard Univ. Press, Cambridge, MA, pp. 342–444.

Diamond, J. 1981. Mixed-species foraging groups. Nature 292:408–409.

Diamond, J. 1982a. How eggs breathe while avoiding desiccation and drowning. Nature 295:10–11.

Diamond, J. 1982b. Evolution of bowerbird's bowers: animal origins of the aesthetic sense. Nature 297:99–102.

Diamond, J. 1984a. Evolution of stable exploiter-victim systems. Nature 310:632.

Diamond, J. 1984b. Optimal foraging theory tested. Nature 311:603–604.

Diamond, J. 1985a. Salvaging single-sex populations. Nature 316:104.

Diamond, J. 1985b. Mass mortality in Pacific seabirds. Nature 315:712.

Diamond, J. 1986. Animal art: variation in bower decorating style among male bowerbirds Amblyornis inornatus. Proc. Nat. Acad. Sci. USA 83:3042–3046.

Diamond, J., and T.J. Case (eds.). 1986. Community Ecology. Harper and Row, New York.

Diamond, J., M. Fraga, J. Wiakibu, T. Maru, and S. Feni. 1977. Fruit consumption and seed dispersal by New Guinea birds. Wildlife in Papua New Guinea Publication 77:9.

Diamond, J., W.H. Karasov, D. Phan, and F.L. Carpenter. 1986. Digestive physiology is a determinant of foraging bout frequency in hummingbirds. Nature 320:62–63.

Dilger, W.C. 1956a. Adaptive modifications and ecological isolating mechanisms in the thrush genera Catharus and Hylocichla. Wilson Bull. 68:171–199.

Dilger, W.C. 1956b. Hostile behavior and reproductive isolating mechanisms in the avian genera Catharus and Hylocichla. Auk 73:313–353.

Dinsmore, J.J. 1972. Sooty Tern behavior. Bull. Florida State Museum Biol. Sci. 16:129–179.

Divoky, G.J. 1976. The pelagic feeding habits of Ivory and Ross' Gulls. Condor 78:85–90.

Dixon, K.L. 1963. Some aspects of social organization in the Carolina Chickadee. Proc. 13th Intern. Ornithol. Congr. 1:240–258.

Dixon, K.L., and D.J. Martin. 1979. Notes on the vocalizations of the Mexican Chickadee. Condor 81:421–423.

Dobkin, D.S. 1979. Functional and evolutionary relationships of vocal copying phenomena in birds. Zeit. Tierpsychol. 50:348–363.

Dobkin, D.S., J.A. Holmes, and B.A. Wilcox. 1986. Traditional nest-site use by White-throated Swifts. Condor 88:252–253.

Dobkin, D.S., and B.A. Wilcox. 1986. Analysis of natural forest fragments: riparian birds in the Toiyabe Mountains, Nevada. *In* J. Verner, M.L. Morrison, and C.J. Ralph (eds.), Wildlife 2000: Modeling Habitat Relationships of Terrestrial Vertebrates. Univ. Wisconsin Press, Madison, pp. 293–299.

Dooling, R.J. 1982. Auditory perception in birds. *In* D.E. Kroodsma and E.H. Miller (eds.), Acoustic Communication in Birds, vol. 1. Academic Press, New York, pp. 95–130.

Doughty, R.W. 1975. Feather Fashions and Bird Preservation. Univ. California Press, Berkeley.

Drent, R.H. 1965. Breeding biology of the Pigeon Guillemot, *Cepphus columba*. Ardea 53:99–160.

Drobney, R.D., and L.H. Fredrickson. 1979. Food selection by Wood Ducks in relation to breeding status. J. Wildl. Manage. 43:109–120.

Drury, W.H., and J.J. Hatch. 1985. Great Cormorants nesting on New England coast. Amer. Birds 39:259.

Dunker, H.-R. 1974. Structure of the avian respiratory tract. Respir. Physiol. 22:1–19.

Dunn, E.H. 1976. Development of endothermy and existence energy expenditure of nestling Double-crested Cormorants. Condor 78:350–356.

Dunn. E.H. 1979. Nesting biology and development of young in Ontario Black Terns. Can. Field-Nat. 93:276–281.

Dunn, E.K. 1972. Effect of age on the fishing ability of Sandwich Terns *Sterna sandvicensis*. Ibis 114:360–366.

Dunn, E.K. 1973. Robbing behavior of Roseate Terns. Auk 90:641–651.

Eadie, J. McA., and G. Gauthier. 1985. Prospecting for nest sites by cavity-nesting ducks of the genus *Bucephala*. Condor 87:528–534.

Earhart C.M., and N.K. Johnson. 1970. Size dimorphism and food habits of North American owls. Condor 72:251–264.

Eckhardt, R.C. 1976. Polygyny in the Western Wood Pewee. Condor 78:561–562.

Eddleman, W.R., K.E. Evans, and W.H. Elder. 1980. Habitat characteristics and management of Swainson's Warbler in southern Illinois. Wildl. Soc. Bull. 8:228–233.

Edwards, T.C., Jr. 1986. Ecological distribution of the Gray-breasted Jay: the role of habitats. Condor 88:456–460.

Ehrlich, A.H. and P.R. Ehrlich. 1987. Earth. Methuen, London; Franklin Watts, New York.

Ehrlich, P.R. 1970. Coevolution and the biology of communities. *In* K.L. Chambers (ed.), Biochemical Coevolution. Oregon State Univ. Press, Corvallis, pp. 1–11.

Ehrlich, P.R. 1986a. The Machinery of Nature. Simon and Schuster, New York.

Ehrlich, P.R. 1986b. Which animal will invade? *In* H.A. Mooney and J.A. Drake (eds.), Ecology of Biological Invasions of North America and Hawaii. Springer-Verlag, New York, pp. 79–95.

Ehrlich, P.R. 1988. Attributes of invaders and invading processes: vertebrates. *In* H.A. Mooney and J.A. Drake (eds.), Summary Volume of SCOPE Biological Invasions Program. *In press*.

Ehrlich, P.R., D.S. Dobkin, and D. Wheye. 1986. The adaptive significance of anting. Auk 103:835.

Ehrlich, P.R. and A.H. Ehrlich. 1981. Extinction: The Causes and Consequences of the Disappearance of Species. Random House, New York.

Ehrlich, P.R., A.H. Ehrlich, and J.P. Holdren. 1975. Ecoscience: Population, Resources, Environment. Freeman, San Francisco.

Ehrlich, P.R., and J.F. McLaughlin. 1988. Scrub Jay predation on starlings: attack and interspecific defense. Condor *In Press*.

Ehrlich, P.R., and J. Roughgarden. 1987. The Science of Ecology. Macmillan, New York.

Einarsen, A.S. 1945. Some factors affecting Ring-necked Pheasant population density. Murrelet 26:3–9, 39–44.

Eisenmann, E. 1971. Range expansion and population increase in North and Middle America of the White-tailed Kite (*Elanus leucurus*). Amer. Birds 25:529–536.

Eiserer, L.A. 1976. The American Robin: A Backyard Institution. Nelson Hall Co., Chicago.

Elder, W.H. 1985. Survivorship in the Tufted Titmouse. Wilson Bull. 97:517–524.

Elder, W.H., and D. Zimmerman. 1983. A comparison of recapture versus resighting data in a 15-year study of the survivorship of the Black-capped Chickadee. J. Field Ornithol. 54:138–145.

Elgar, M. and P. Harvey. 1987. Colonial information centers. Trends in Ecol. and Evol. 2:34.

Eliason, B.C. 1986. Female site fidelity and polygyny in the Blackpoll Warbler (*Dendroica striata*). Auk 103:782–790.

Elliot, R.D., and R.I.G. Morrison. 1979. The incubation period of the Yellow Rail. Auk 96:422–423.

Ellis, H.I. 1980. Metabolism and solar radiation in dark and white herons in hot climates. Physiol. Zool. 53:358–372.

Ellison, L.N. 1973. Seasonal social organization and movements of Spruce Grouse. Condor 75:375–385.

Elowson, A.M. 1984. Spread-wing postures and the water repellency of feathers: a test of Rijke's hypothesis. Auk 101:371–383.

Eltzroth, E.K., and S.R. Robinson. 1984. Violet-green Swallows help Western Bluebirds at the nest. J. Field Ornithol. 55:259–261.

Ely, C.R., and D.B. Raveling. 1984. Breeding biology of Pacific White-fronted Geese. J. Wildl. Manage. 48:823–837.

Emlen, S.T. 1975. The stellar-orientation system of a migratory bird. Sci. Amer. 233:102–111.

Emlen, S.T., and L.W. Oring. 1977. Ecology, sexual selection, and the evolution of mating systems. Science 197:215–223.

Emlen, S.T., J.D. Rising, and W.L. Thompson. 1975. A behavioral and morphological study of sympatry in the Indigo and Lazuli Buntings of the Great Plains. Wilson Bull. 87:145–177.

Emlen, S.T. and S.L. Vehrencamp. 1983. Cooperative breeding strategies among birds. *In* A.H. Brush and G.A. Clark, Jr. (eds.), Perspectives in Ornithology. Cambridge Univ. Press, Cambridge, pp. 93–120.

Emslie, S.D. 1987. Age and diet of fossil California Condors in Grand Canyon, Arizona. Science 237:768–770.

Enderson, J.H. 1964. A study of the Prairie Falcon in the central Rocky Mountain region. Auk 81:332–352.

Erckmann, W.J. 1983. The evolution of polyandry in shorebirds: an evaluation of hypotheses. *In* S.K. Wasser (ed.), Social Behavior of Female Vertebrates. Academic Press, New York, pp. 113–168.

Erskine, A.J. 1972a. Buffleheads. Can. Wildl. Serv. Monogr. Ser. No. 4.

Erskine, A.J. 1972b. The Great Cormorant of Eastern Canada. Can. Wildl. Serv. Occ. Pap. No. 14.

Erskine, A.J. 1984. Swallows foraging on the ground. Wilson Bull. 96:136–137.

Ervin, S. 1977. Flock size, composition, and behavior in a population of Bushtits. Bird-Banding 48:97–109.

Erwin, R.M. 1983. Feeding habitats of nesting wading birds: spatial use and social influences. Auk 100:960–970.

Ettinger, A.O., and J.R. King. 1980. Time and energy budgets of the Willow Flycatcher (*Empidonax traillii*) during the breeding season. Auk 97:533–546.

Evans, E.W. 1978. Nesting responses of Field Sparrows (*Spizella pusilla*) to plant succession on a Michigan old field. Condor 80:34–40.

Evans, K.E., and A.N. Moen. 1975. Thermal exchange between Sharp-tailed Grouse (*Pedioecetes phasianellus*) and their winter environment. Condor 77:160–168.

Evans, P.R. 1969. Ecological aspects of migration and premigratory fat deposition in the Lesser Redpoll, *Carduelis flammea cabaret*. Condor 71:316–330.

Evans, P.R., J.D. Goss-Custard, and W.G. Hale. 1984. Coastal Waders and Wildfowl in Winter. Cambridge Univ. Press, Cambridge.

Evans, P.R., and P.C. Smith. 1975. Studies of shorebirds at Lindisfarne, Northumberland. 2. Fat and pectoral muscle as indicators of body condition in the Bar-tailed Godwit. Wildfowl 26:64–76.

Evans, R.M., and K.J. Cash. 1985. Early spring flights of American White Pelicans: timing and functional role in attracting others to the breeding colony. Condor 87:252–255.

Evans, R.M., and B.F. McMahon. 1987. Within-brood variation in growth and condition in relation to brood reduction in the American White Pelican. Wilson Bull. 99:190–201.

Evenleigh, E.S., and W. Trelfall. 1976. Population dynamics of lice (Mallophaga) on auks (Alcidae) from Newfoundland. Can. J. Zool. 54:1694–1711.

Ewald, P.W. 1985. Influence of asymmetries in resource quality and age on aggression and dominance in Black-chinned Hummingbirds. Anim. Behav. 33:705–719.

Ewald, P.W., and G.H. Orians. 1983. Effects of resource depression on use of inexpensive and escalated aggressive behavior: experimental tests using Anna Hummingbirds. Behav. Ecol. Sociobiol. 12:95–101.

Ewald, P.W., and S. Rohwer. 1982. Effects of supplemental feeding on timing of breeding, clutch size, and polygamy in Red-winged Blackbirds. J. Anim. Ecol. 51:429–450.

Ewert, D.N. 1980. Recognition of conspecific song by the Rufous-sided Towhee. Anim. Behav. 28:379–386.

Falls, J.B. 1982. Individual recognition by sounds in birds. *In* D.E. Kroodsma and E.H. Miller (eds.), Acoustic Communication in Birds, vol. 2. Academic Press, New York, pp. 237–278.

Falls, J.B., and J.R. Krebs. 1975. Sequence of songs in repertoires of Western Meadowlarks (*Sturnella neglecta*). Can. J. Zool. 53:1165–1178.

Falls, J.B., and M.K. McNicholl. 1979. Neighbor-stranger discrimination by song in male Blue Grouse. Can. J. Zool. 57:457–462.

Feare, C. 1984. The Starling. Oxford Univ. Press, Oxford.

Fears, O.T. 1975. Observations on the aerial drinking performance of a Poorwill. Wilson Bull. 87:284.

Ferguson, R.S., and S.G. Sealy. 1983. Breeding ecology of the Horned Grebe, *Podiceps auritus*, in s w Manitoba. Can. Field-Nat. 97:401–408.

Ficken, M.S., and R.W. Ficken. 1987. Bill-sweeping behavior of a Mexican Chicadee. Condor 89:901–902.

Finch, D.M. 1982. Rejection of cowbird eggs by Crissal Thrashers. Auk 99:719–724.

Finch, D.M. 1983. Brood parasitism of the Abert's Towhee: timing, frequency, and effects. Condor 85:355–359.

Finch, D.M. 1984. Parental expenditure of time and energy in the Abert's Towhee (*Pipilo aberti*). Auk 101:473–486.

Findlay C.S., and F. Cooke. 1982. Synchrony in the Lesser Snow Goose (*Anser caerulescens*). II. The adaptive value of reproductive synchrony. Evolution 36:786–799.

Finlay, J.C. 1976. Some effects of weather on Purple Martin activity. Auk 93:231–244.

Fischer, D.H. 1980. Breeding biology of Curve-billed Thrashers and Long-billed Thrashers in southern Texas. Condor 82:392–397.

Fischer, D.H. 1981a. Wintering ecology of thrashers in southern Texas. Condor 83:340–346.

Fischer, D.H. 1981b. Winter time budgets of Brown Thrashers. J. Field Ornithol. 52:304–308.

Fischer, D.H. 1983. Growth, development, and food habits of nestling mimids in south Texas. Wilson Bull. 95:97–105.

Fischer, D.L. 1985. Piracy behavior of wintering Bald Eagles. Condor 87:246–251.

Fisk, E.J. 1975. Least Tern: beleaguered, opportunistic, and roof-nesting. Amer. Birds 29:15–16.

Fisk, E.J. 1978. The growing use of roofs by nesting birds. Bird-Banding 49:134–141.

Fitch, F.W., Jr. 1950. Life history and ecology of the Scissor-tailed Flycatcher, *Muscivora forficata*. Auk 67:145–168.

Fitch, H.S. 1974. Observations of the food and nesting of the Broad-winged Hawk (*Buteo platypterus*) in northeastern Kansas. Condor 76:331–360.

Fitzner, R.E., D. Berry, L.L. Boyd, and C.A. Rieck. 1977. Nesting of Ferruginous Hawks (*Buteo regalis*) in Washington 1974–75. Condor 79:245–249.

Fitzpatrick, J.W. 1980. Foraging behavior of Neotropical tyrant flycatchers. Condor 82:43–57.

Fitzpatrick, J.W., and G.E. Woolfenden. 1984. The helpful shall inherit the scrub. Natural History, May, pp. 55–63.

Fleischer, R.C., W.I. Boarman, and M.L. Cody. 1985. Asynchrony of song series in the Bewick's Wren and Wrentit. Anim. Behav. 33:674–676.

Fletcher, L.E., and D.G. Smith. 1978. Some parameters of song important in conspecific recognition by Gray Catbirds. Auk 95:338–347.

Flickinger, E.L. 1975. Incubation by a male Fulvous Tree Duck. Wilson Bull. 87:106–107.

Flood, N.J. 1984. Adaptive significance of delayed plumage maturation in male Northern Orioles. Evolution 38:267–279.

Forsman, E., and E.C. Meslow. 1986. The Spotted Owl. *In* R. L. Di Silvestro (ed.), Audubon Wildlife Report 1986, National Audubon Soc., NY, pp. 743–761.

Forsman, E.D., E.C. Meslow, and H.M. Wight. 1984. Distribution and Biology of the Spotted Owl in Oregon. Wildl. Monogr. 87:1–64.

Frakes, R.A., and R.E. Johnson. 1982. Niche convergence in *Empidonax* flycatchers. Condor 84:286–291.

Franzreb, K.E. 1985. Foraging ecology of Brown Creepers in a mixed-coniferous forest. J. Field Ornithol. 56:9–16.

Fraser, J.D., and D.R. Luukkonen. 1986. The Loggerhead Shrike. *In* R.L. Di Silvestro (ed.), Audubon Wildlife Report 1986, National Audubon Soc., NY, pp. 933–941.

Frederick, P. 1986. Conspecific nest takeovers and egg destruction by White Ibises. Wilson Bull. 98:156–157.

Frederick, P. 1987. Chronic tidally-induced nest failure in a colony of White Ibises. Condor 89:413–419.

Freer, V.M. 1979. Factors affecting site tenacity in New York Bank Swallows. Bird-Banding 50:349–357.

Fretwell, S. 1986. Distribution and abundance of the Dickcissel. Current Ornithol. 4:211–242.

Friedmann, H., and L.F. Kiff. 1985. The parasitic cowbirds and their hosts. Proc. Western Foundation Vert. Zool. 2:226–304.

Fry. C.H. 1980. Survival and longevity among tropical land birds. Proc. IV Pan-Afr. Ornith. Congr., pp. 333–343.

Fugle, G.N., S.I. Rothstein, C.W. Osenberg, and M.A. McGinley. 1984. Signals of status in wintering White-crowned Sparrows, *Zonotrichia leucophrys gambelii.* Anim. Behav. 32:86–93.

Furrer, R.K. 1975. Breeding success and nest site stereotypy in a population of Brewer's Blackbirds *(Euphagus cyanocephalus).* Oecologia 20:339–350.

Futuyma, D.J. 1987. Evolutionary Biology, 2nd edition. Sinauer Associates, Sunderland, MA.

Futuyma, D.J., and M. Slatkin. 1983. Coevolution. Sinauer Associates, Sunderland MA.

Gabrielson, I.N., and F.C. Lincoln. 1959. The Birds of Alaska. The Stackpole Co., Harrisburg, PA and The Wildlife Management Inst., Washington, DC.

Gaddis, P.K. 1985. Structure and variability in the vocal repertoire of the Mountain Chickadee. Wilson Bull. 97:30–46.

Galati, B., and C.B. Galati. 1985. Breeding of the Golden-crowned Kinglet in northern Minnesota. J. Field Ornithol. 56:28–40.

Galbraith, H. 1983. Diet and feeding ecology of breeding Kittiwakes *Rissa tridactyla.* Bird Study 30:109–120.

Gallup, F.M., and B.H. Bailey. 1960. Elegant and Royal Terns nesting in California. Condor 62:65–66.

Gamboa, G.J. 1977. Predation on Rufous Hummingbird by Wied's Flycatcher. Auk 94:157–158.

Gashwiler, J.G. 1960. The hunting behavior of a Pygmy Owl. Murrelet 41:12–13.

Gass, C.L. 1979. Territory regulation, tenure and migration in Rufous Hummingbirds. Can J. Zool. 57:914–923.

Gaston, A.J. 1985a. The diet of Thick-billed Murre chicks in the eastern Canadian Arctic. Auk 102:727–734.

Gaston, A.J. 1985b. Energy invested in reproduction by Thick-billed Murres *(Uria lomvia).* Auk 102:447–458.

Gaston, A.J. 1987. Seabird citadels in the Arctic. Natural History, April, pp. 54–59.

Gaston, A.J., and D.N. Nettleship. 1981. The Thick-billed Murres of Prince Leopold Island. Can. Wildl. Serv. Monogr. No. 6.

Gates, J.E., and L.W. Geysel. 1978. Avian nest dispersion and fledging success in field-forest ecotones. Ecology 59:871–883.

Gaunt, A.S., and S.L.L. Gaunt. 1977. Mechanics of the syrinx in *Gallus gallus.* J. Morph. 152:1–20.

Gaunt, A.S., and S.L.L. Gaunt. 1985. Syringeal structure and avian phonation, *In* R.F. Johnston (ed.), Current Ornithology 2:213–245.

Gauthier, G. 1987. Further evidence of long-term pair bonds in ducks of the genus *Bucephala.* Auk 104:521–522.

Gauthreaux, S.A., Jr. 1982. The ecology and evolution of avian migration systems. Avian Biology, vol. 6. Academic Press, New York, pp. 93–168.

Gayou, D.C. 1986. The social system of the Texas Green Jay. Auk 103:540–547.

Gehlbach, F.R. 1981. Mountain Islands and Desert Seas: a Natural History of the U.S.–Mexican Borderlands. Texas A&M Press, College Station, TX.

Gehlbach, F.R. 1986. Odd couples of suburbia. Natural History, June, pp. 56–66.

Gehlbach, F.R., and R.S. Baldridge. 1987. Live blind snakes (*Leptotyphlops dulcis*) in Eastern Screech Owl (*Otus asio*) nests: a novel commensalism. Oecologia 71:560–563.

George, W.G., and R. Sulski. 1984. Thawing of frozen prey by a Great Horned Owl. Can. J. Zool. 62:314–315.

Gibbs, J.P., S. Woodward, M.L. Hunter, and A.E. Hutchinson. 1987. Determinants of Great Blue Heron colony distribution in coastal Maine. Auk 104:38–47.

Gibson, F. 1971. The breeding biology of the American Avocet (*Recurvirostra americana*) in central Oregon. Condor 73:444–454.

Gibson, F. 1978. Ecological aspects of the time budget of the American Avocet. Amer. Midl. Nat. 99:65–82.

Gibson, R.M., and J.W. Bradbury. 1986. Male and female mating strategies on Sage Grouse leks. *In* D.I. Rubenstein and R.W. Wrangham (eds.), Ecological Aspects of Social Evolution. Princeton Univ. Press, Princeton, pp. 379–398.

Gibson, R.M., and J.W. Bradbury. 1987. Lek organization in Sage Grouse: variations on a territorial theme. Auk 104:77–84.

Giesen, K.M., and C.E. Braun. 1979. Nesting behavior of female White-tailed Ptarmigan in Colorado. Condor 81:215–217.

Giesen, K.M., C.E. Braun, and T.A. May. 1980. Reproduction and nest-site selection of White-tailed Ptarmigan in Colorado. Wilson Bull. 92:188–199.

Gill, F.B. 1980. Historical aspects of hybridization between Blue-winged and Golden-winged Warblers. Auk 97:1–18.

Gill, R.E., Jr., and L.R. Mewaldt. 1983. Pacific coast Caspian Terns: dynamics of an expanding population. Auk 100:369–381.

Gilmer, D.S., and R.E. Stewart. 1983. Ferruginous Hawk populations and habitat use in North Dakota. J. Wildl. Manage. 47:146–157.

Gilmer, D.S., and R.E. Stewart. 1984. Swainson's Hawk nesting ecology in North Dakota. Condor 86:12–18.

Gilpin, M.E., and J.M. Diamond. 1982. Factors contributing to non-randomness in species co-occurrences on islands. Oecologia 52:75–84.

Giraldeau, L.-A., and L. Lefebvre. 1985. Individual feeding preferences in feral groups of Rock Doves. Can. J. Zool. 63:189–191.

Giroux, J. 1981. Interspecific nest parasitism by Redheads on islands in southeastern Alberta. Can. J. Zool. 59:2053–2057.

Gish, S.L., and E.S. Morton. 1981. Structural adaptations to local habitat acoustics in Carolina Wren songs. Zeit. Tierpsychol. 56:74–84.

Glinski, R.L., and R.D. Ohmart. 1983. Breeding ecology of the Mississippi Kite in Arizona. Condor 85:200–207.

Goad, M.S., and R.W. Mannan. 1987. Nest site selection by Elf Owls in Saguaro National Monument, Arizona. Condor 89:659–662.

Gochfeld, M., and J. Burger. 1981. Age-related differences in piracy of Frigatebirds from Laughing Gulls. Condor 83:79–82.

Godfrey, W.E. 1986. The Birds of Canada. Revised Edition. Natl. Museum, Canada, Ottawa.

Goldsmith, T.H. 1980. Hummingbirds see near ultraviolet light. Science 207:786–788.

Goldstein, D.L. 1984. The thermal environment and its constraint on activity of desert quail in summer. Auk 101:542–550.

Goldstein, D.L., and K.A. Nagy. 1985. Resource utilization by desert quail: time and energy, food and water. Ecology 66:378–387.

Gollop, J.B., T.W. Barry, and E.H. Iverson. 1986. Eskimo Curlew a Vanishing Species? Special Publ. No. 17, Saskatchewan Nat. Hist. Soc., Regina, Saskatchewan.

Gooders, J., and T. Boyer. 1986. Ducks of North America and the Northern Hemisphere. Facts on File, New York.

Goodwin, D. 1976. Crows of the World. Cornell Univ. Press, Ithaca, NY.

Goodwin, D. 1983. Pigeons and Doves of the World, 3rd edition. Cornell Univ. Press, Ithaca, NY.

Gorenzel, W.P., R.A. Ryder, and C.E. Braun. 1982. Reproduction and nest site characteristics of American Coots at different altitudes in Colorado. Condor 84:59–65.

Goslow, C.E., Jr. 1971. The attack and strike of some North American raptors. Auk 88:815–827.

Gould, L.L., and F. Heppner. 1974. The vee formation of Canadian Geese. Auk 91:494–506.

Gould, S.J. 1985. The Flamingo's Smile. Natural History, March, pp. 6–19.

Gowaty, P.A. 1985. Multiple parentage and apparent monogamy in birds. Ornithol. Monogr. 37:11–21.

Gowaty, P.A., and D.W. Mock (eds.). 1985. Avian Monogamy. Ornithol. Monogr. No. 37.

Grant, G.S. 1982. Avian Incubation: Egg Temperature, Nest Humidity, and Behavioral Thermoregulation in a Hot Environment. Ornithol. Monogr. No. 30.

Grant, P.J. 1986. Gulls: A Guide to Identification. Buteo Books, Vermillion, SD.

Gratto, C.L., F. Cooke, and R.I.G. Morrison. 1983. Nesting success of yearling and older breeders in the Semipalmated Sandpiper, *Calidris pusilla*. Can. J. Zool. 61:1113–1137.

Gratto, C.L., R.I.G. Morrison, and F. Cooke. 1985. Philopatry, site tenacity, and mate fidelity in the Semipalmated Sandpiper. Auk 102:16–24.

Graul, W.D. 1975. Breeding biology of the Mountain Plover. Wilson Bull. 87:6–31.

Graul, W.D., and L.E. Webster. 1976. Breeding status of the Mountain Plover. Condor 78:265–267.

Green, N. 1985. The Bald Eagle. *In* R.L. Di Silvestro (ed.), Audubon Wildlife Report 1985. National Audubon Soc., NY, pp. 509–531.

Greenberg, R. 1981. Dissimilar bill shapes in New World tropical versus temperate forest foliage-gleaning birds. Oecologia 49:143–147.

Greenberg, R. 1984. The winter exploitation systems of Bay-breasted and Chestnut-sided Warblers in Panama. Univ. Calif. Publ. Zool. 116:1–107.

Greenberg, R. 1987. Seasonal foraging specialization in the Worm-eating Warbler. Condor 89:158–168.

Greenberg, R., and J. Gradwohl. 1980. Observations of paired Canada Warblers *Wilsonia canadensis* during migration in Panama. Ibis 122:509–512.

Greenlaw, J.S. 1978. The relation of breeding schedule and clutch size to food supply in the Rufous-sided Towhee. Condor 80:24–33.

Greenway, J.C., Jr. 1967. Extinct and Vanishing Birds of the World. Dover, New York.

Gregg, L.E., and J.B. Hale. 1977. Woodcock nesting habitat in northern Wisconsin. Auk 94:489–493.

Greig-Smith, P. 1986. Avian ideal homes. New Scientist, 2 January, pp. 29–31.

Grinnell, J., and A.H. Miller. 1986. The Distribution of the Birds of California. Pacific Coast Avifauna No. 27, publ. 1944, reprinted by Artemisia Press, Lee Vining, CA.

Groschupf, K., and G.S. Mills. 1982. Singing behavior of the Five-striped Sparrow. Condor 84:226–236.

Grover, J.J., and B.L. Olla. 1983. The role of Rhinoceros Auklet (*Cerorhinca monocerata*) in mixed-species feeding assemblages of seabirds in the Strait of Juan de Fuca, Washington. Auk 100:979–982.

Groves, S. 1984. Chick growth, sibling rivalry, and chick production in American Black Oystercatchers. Auk 101:525–531.

Grubb, T.C., Jr. 1974. Olfactory navigation to the nesting burrow in Leach's Petrel (*Oceanodroma leucorhoa*). Anim. Behav. 22:192–202.

Grudzien, T.A., W.S. Moore, J.R. Cook, and D. Tagle. 1987. Genic population structure and gene flow in the Northern Flicker (*Colaptes auratus*) hybrid zone. Auk 104:654–664.

Grundel, R. 1987. Determinants of nestling feeding rates and parental investment in the Mountain Chickadee. Condor 89:319–328.

Grzybowski, J.A. 1979. Responses of Barn Swallows to eggs, young, nests, and nest sites. Condor 81:236–246.

Grzybowski, J.A., R.B. Clapp, and J.T. Marshall, Jr. 1986. History and current population status of the Black-capped Vireo in Oklahoma. Amer. Birds 40:1151–1161.

Gullion, G.W. 1952. The displays and calls of the American Coot. Wilson Bull. 61:83–97.

Gullion, G.W. 1953. Territorial behavior of the American Coot. Condor 55:169–185.

Gullion, G.W. 1954. Reproductive cycle of American Coots in California. Auk 71:366–412.

Gullion, G.W. 1960. The ecology of Gambel's Quail in Nevada and the arid Southwest. Ecology 41:518–536.

Gullion, G.W. 1984. Grouse of the North Shore. Willow-Creek Press, Oshkosh, WI.

Gutiérrez, R.J. 1979–80. Comparative ecology of the Mountain and California Quail in the Carmel Valley, CA. Living Bird 18:71–93.

Gutiérrez, R.J., C.E. Braun, and T.P. Zapatka. 1975. Reproductive biology of the Band-tailed Pigeon in Colorado and New Mexico. Auk 92:665–677.

Gutiérrez, R.J., R.M. Zink, and S.Y. Yang. 1983. Genic variation, systematic, and biogeographic relationships of some galliform birds. Auk 100:33–47.

Hagar, J.A. 1966. Nesting of the Hudsonian Godwit at Churchill, Manitoba. Living Bird 5:5–43.

Haig, S.M., and L.W. Oring. 1987. The Piping Plover. *In* R.L. Di Silvestro (ed.), Audubon Wildlife Report 1987. Academic Press, New York, pp 509–519.

Hailman, J.P. 1973. Double-scratching and terrestrial locomotion in Emberizines: some complications. Wilson Bull. 85:348–350.

Halliday, T. 1978. Vanishing Birds: Their Natural History and Conservation. Holt, Rinehart and Winston, New York.

Hamel, P.B. 1986. Bachman's Warbler: A Species in Peril. Smithsonian Institution Press, Washington, DC.

Hamerstrom, F. 1963. Sharptail brood habitat in Wisconsin's northern pine barrens. J. Wildl. Manage. 27:793–802.

Hamerstrom, F. 1980. Strictly for the Chickens. Iowa State Univ. Press, Ames, IA.

Hamerstrom, F. and F. Hamerstrom. 1973. The Prairie Chicken in Wisconsin. Dept. Nat. Resources, Tech. Bull. No. 64, Madison, WI.

Hamerstrom, F., F.N. Hamerstrom, and C.J. Burke. 1985. Effect of voles on mating systems in a central Wisconsin population of Harriers. Wilson Bull. 97:332–346.

Hamilton, R.B. 1975. Comparative Behavior of the American Avocet and Black-necked Stilt (Recurvirostridae). Ornithol. Monogr. No. 17.

Hamilton, W.D. 1971. Geometry for the selfish herd. J. Theor. Biol. 31:295–311.

Hamilton, W.J., III, and M.E. Hamilton. 1965. Breeding characteristics of Yellow-billed Cuckoos in Arizona. Proc. Calif. Acad. Sci. (4th ser.) 32:405–432.

Hancock, J., and J. Kushlan. 1984. The Herons Handbook. Harper and Row, New York.

Hand, J.L., G.L. Hunt, Jr., and M. Warner. 1981. Thermal stress and predation: influences on the structure of a gull colony and possibly on breeding distributions. Condor 83:193–203.

Hannon, S.J., and J.N.M. Smith. 1984. Factors influencing age-related reproductive success in the Willow Ptarmigan. Auk 101:848–854.

Hansen, A.J., and S. Rohwer. 1986. Coverable badges and resource defense in birds. Anim. Behav. 34:69–76.

Hardy, J.W. 1973. Feral exotic birds in southern California. Wilson Bull. 85:506–512.

Hardy, J.W. 1978. Damage to loblolly pine by winter roosting blackbirds and starlings. Proc. Ann. Conf. Southeast Assoc. Fish and Wildl. Agencies 30:466–470.

Harlow, R.F., R.G. Hooper, D.R. Chamberlain, and H.S. Crawford. 1975. Some winter and nesting season foods of the Common Raven in Virginia. Auk 92:298–306.

Harmeson, J.P. 1974. Breeding ecology of the Dickcissel. Auk 91:348–359.

Harrington, B.A. 1986. Red Knot. In R.L. Di Silvestro (ed.), Audubon Wildlife Report 1986, National Audubon Soc., NY, pp. 871–886.

Harrington, B.A., Schreiber, R.W., and G.E. Woolfenden. 1972. The distribution of male and female Magnificent Frigatebirds, *Fregata magnificens*, along the Gulf Coast of Florida. Amer. Birds 26:927–931.

Harris, M.P. 1984. The Puffin. T. and A.D. Poyser, Ltd., Calton, England.

Harrison, P. 1983. Seabirds: An Identification Guide. Houghton Mifflin, New York.

Hartwick, E.B., and W. Blaylock. 1979. Winter ecology of a Black Oystercatcher population. Studies in Avian Biol. 2:207–215.

Hatch, S.A. 1983. Mechanism and ecological significance of sperm storage in the Northern Fulmar with reference to its occurrence in other birds. Auk 100:593–600.

Hatch, S.A. 1987. Copulation and mate guarding in the Northern Fulmar. Auk 104:450–461.

Hawaiian Audubon Society. 1984. Hawaii's Birds, 3rd ed. Hawaiian Audubon Society, Honolulu.

Hayes, J.P., J.R. Probst, and D. Rakstad. 1986. Effect of mating status and time of day on Kirtland's Warbler song rates. Condor 88:386–388.

Hayward, G.D., P.H. Hayward, E.O. Garton, and R. Escano. 1987. Revised breeding distribution of the Boreal Owl in the northern Rocky Mountains. Condor 89:431–432.

Hayworth, A.M., and W.W. Weathers. 1984. Temperature regulation and climatic adaptation in Black-billed and Yellow-billed Magpies. Condor 86:19–26.

Hebrard, J.J. 1978. Habitat selection in two species of *Spizella:* a concurrent laboratory and field study. Auk 95:404–410.

Heckenlively, D.B. 1970. Song in a population of Black-throated Sparrows. Condor 72:24–36.

Hector, D.P. 1985. The diet of the Aplomado Falcon (*Falco femoralis*) in eastern Mexico. Condor 87:336–342.

Hector, D.P. 1986. Cooperative hunting and its relationship to foraging success and prey size in an avian predator. Ethology 73:247–257.

Hegde, S. 1973. Composition of pigeon milk and its effect on growth in chicks. Ind. J. Exp. Biol. 11:238–239.

Hegner, R.E., and J.C. Wingfield. 1986. Gonadal development during autumn and winter in House Sparrows. Condor 88:269–278.

Hegner, R.E., and J.C. Wingfield. 1987. Effects of brood-size manipulations on parental investment, breeding success, and reproductive endocrinology of House Sparrows. Auk 104:470–480.

Heinrich, B. 1986. Why is a robin's egg blue? Audubon, July, pp. 65–71.

Hennemann, W.W., III. 1982. Energetics and spread-winged behavior of Anhingas in Florida. Condor 84:91–96.

Hennemann, W.W., III. 1983. Environmental influences on the energetics and behavior of Anhingas and Double-crested Cormorants. Physiol. Zool. 56:201–216.

Hennemann, W.W., III. 1985. Energetics, behavior and the zoogeography of Anhingas and Double-crested Cormorants. Ornis Scand. 16:319–323.

Henny, C.J., L.J. Blus, A.J. Krynitsky, and C.M. Bunck. 1984. Current impact of DDE on Black-crowned Night-Herons in the intermountain west. J. Wildl. Manage. 48:1–13.

Henny, C.J., F.C. Schmid, E.M. Martin, and L.L. Hood. 1973. Territorial behavior, pesticides, and the population ecology of Red-shouldered Hawks in central Maryland 1943–1971. Ecology 54:545–554.

Hepp, G.R. 1985. Effects of environmental parameters on the foraging behavior of three species of wintering dabbling ducks (Anatini). Can. J. Zool. 63:289–294.

Heppleston, P.B. 1971. Feeding techniques of the Oystercatcher. Bird Study 18:15–20.

Herlugson, C.J. 1981. Nest site selection of Mountain Bluebirds. Condor 83:252–255.

Hertz, P.E., J.V. Remsen, and S.I. Zones. 1976. Ecological complementarity of three sympatric parids in a California oak woodland. Condor 78:307–316.

Hewitt, O.H. 1967. The Wild Turkey and Its Management. Wildlife Society, Washington, DC.

Higgins, K.F., and L. Kirsch. 1975. Some aspects of the breeding biology of the Upland Sandpiper in North Dakota. Wilson Bull. 87:96–102.

Higuchi, H. 1986. Bait-fishing by the Green-backed Heron, *Ardeola striata* in Japan. Ibis 128:285–290.

Hilden, O. 1969. The occurrence and breeding of the Redpoll in northern Lapland 1968. Ornis Fenn. 46:109–110.

Hilden, O., and P. Helo. 1981. The Great Gray Owl *Strix nebulosa*—a bird of the northern taiga. Ornis Fenn. 58:159–166.

Hill, W.L. 1986. Clutch overlap in American Coots. Condor 88:96–97.

Hinde, R.A. 1954a. Factors governing the changes in strength of a partially inborn response, as shown by the mobbing behaviour of the Chaffinch (*Fringilla coelebs*). I. The nature of the response and examination of its course. Proc. Roy. Soc. Lond. B Biol. Sci. 142:306–330.

Hinde, R.A. 1954b. Factors governing the changes in strength of a partially inborn response, as shown by the mobbing behaviour of the Chaffinch (*Fringilla coelebs*). II. The waning of the response. Proc. Roy. Soc. Lond. B Biol. Sci. 142:331–358.

Hinde, R.A. 1955. A comparative study of the courtship of certain finches (Fringillidae). Ibis 97:706–744; 98:1–222.

Hines, J.E., and G.J. Mitchell. 1983. Breeding ecology of the Gadwall at Waterhen Marsh, Saskatchewan. Can. J. Zool. 61:1532–1539.

Hines, J.E., and G.J. Mitchell. 1984. Parasitic laying in nests of Gadwalls. Can. J. Zool. 62:627–630.

Hoffman, W., J.A. Wiens, and J.M. Scott. 1978. Hybridization between gulls (*Larus glaucescens* and *L. occidentalis*) in the Pacific Northwest. Auk 95:441–458.

Hohman, W.L. 1985. Feeding ecology of Ring-necked Ducks in northwestern Minnesota. J. Wildl. Manage. 49:546–557.

Hohman, W.L. 1986. Incubation rhythms of Ring-necked Ducks. Condor 88:290–296.

Hohn, E.O. 1977. The "snowshoe effect" of the feathering on ptarmigan feet. Condor 79:380–382.

Holmes, J.A., D.S. Dobkin, and B.A. Wilcox. 1985. Second nesting record and northward advance of the Great-tailed Grackle (*Quiscalus mexicanus*) in Nevada. Great Basin Naturalist 45:483–484.

Holmes, R.T. 1973. Social behaviour of breeding Western Sandpipers *Calidris mauri*. Ibis 115:107–123.

Holmes, R.T. 1986. Foraging patterns of forest birds: male-female differences. Wilson Bull. 98:196–213.

Holmes, R.T., C.P. Black, and T.W. Sherry. 1979. Comparative population bioenergetics of three insectivorous passerines in a deciduous forest. Condor 81:9–20.

Holt, D.W., J.P. Lortie, B.J. Nikula, and R.C. Humphrey. 1986. First record of Common Black-headed Gulls breeding in the United States. Amer. Birds 40:204–206.

Hoogland, J.L., and P.W. Sherman. 1976. Advantages and disadvantages of Bank Swallow (*Riparia riparia*) coloniality. Ecol. Monogr. 46:33–58.

Horak, G.J. 1970. A comparative study of the foods of the Sora and Virginia Rail. Wilson Bull. 82:206–213.

Horn, H.S. 1968. The adaptive significance of colonial nesting in the Brewer's Blackbird (*Euphagus cyanocephalus*). Ecology 49:682–694.

Houde, P. 1987. Critical evaluation of DNA hybridization studies in avian systematics. Auk 104:17–32.

Howe, H.F. 1978. Initial investment, clutch size, and brood reduction in the Common Grackle (*Quiscalus quiscula* L.). Ecology 59:1109–1122.

Howe, H.F. 1979. Evolutionary aspects of parental care in the Common Grackle, *Quiscalus quiscula* L. Evolution 33:41–51.

Howe, M.A. 1975. Social interactions in flocks of courting Wilson's Phalaropes (*Phalaropus tricolor*). Condor 77:24–33.

Howe, M.A. 1982. Social organization in a nesting population of eastern Willets (*Catoptrophorus semipalmatus*). Auk 99:88–102.

Howes-Jones, D. 1985. Relationships among song activity, context, and social behavior in the Warbling Vireo. Wilson Bull. 97:4–20.

Hoyt, S.F. 1953. Incubation and nesting behavior of the Chuck-will's-widow. Wilson Bull. 65:204–205.

Hunt, G.L., Jr., Z.A. Eppley, and D.C. Schneider. 1986. Reproductive performance of seabirds: the importance of population and colony size. Auk 103:306–317.

Hunt, G.L., Jr., and M.W. Hunt. 1975. Reproductive ecology of the Western Gull: the importance of nest spacing. Auk 92:270–279.

Hunter, L. 1987. Acquisition of territories by floaters in cooperatively breeding Purple Gallinules. Anim. Behav. 35:402–410.

Hunter, L.A. 1985. Kin cannibalism in the Purple Gallinule. Wilson Bull. 97:560–561.

Hurley, R.J., and E.C. Franks. 1976. Changes in the breeding ranges of two grassland birds. Auk 92:108–115.

Hurxthal, L.M. 1986. Our gang, ostrich style. Natural History, December, pp. 34–41.

Hussell, D.B., and P. Page. 1976. Observations on the breeding biology of Black-bellied Plovers on Devon Island, N.W.T., Canada. Wilson Bull. 88:632–653.

Hussell, D.J.T., and T.E. Quinney. 1987. Food abundance and clutch size of Tree Swallows *Tachycineta bicolor*. Ibis 129:243–258.

Hutchins, H.E., and R.M. Lanner. 1982. The central role of Clark's Nutcracker in the dispersal and establishment of whitebark pine. Oecologia 55:192–201.

Hutchinson, G.E. 1978. Zoological iconography in the West after A.D. 1200. Amer. Sci. 66:675–684.

Hutto, R.L. 1981. Seasonal variation in the foraging behavior of some migratory western wood warblers. Auk 98:765–777.

Ingold, D.J. 1987. Documented double-broodedness in Red-headed Woodpeckers. J. Field Ornithol. 58:234–235.

Inouye, D.W. 1976. Nonrandom orientation of entrance holes to woodpecker nests in aspen trees. Condor 78:101–102.

Inouye, R.S., N.J. Huntley, and D.W. Inouye. 1981. Non-random orientation of Gila Woodpecker nest entrances in Saguaro cacti. Condor 83:88–89.

Irons, D.B., R.G. Anthony, and J.A. Estes. 1986. Foraging strategies of Glaucous-winged Gulls in a rocky intertidal community. Ecology 67:1460–1474.

Jackson, J.A. 1977. Red-cockaded Woodpeckers and pine red heart disease. Auk 94:160–163.

Jackson, J.A. 1986. Biopolitics, management of federal lands, and the conservation of the Red-cockaded Woodpecker. Amer. Birds 40:1162–1168.

James, P.C. 1986. How do Manx Shearwaters *Puffinus puffinus* find their burrows? Ethology 71:287–294.

James, P.C., and L.W. Oliphant. 1986. Extra birds and helpers at the nests of Richardson's Merlin. Condor 88:533–534.

James, R.D. 1978. Pairing and nest site selection in Solitary and Yellow-throated Vireos with a description of a ritualized nest building display. Can. J. Zool. 56:1163–1169.

James, R.D. 1984. Structure, frequency of usage, and apparent learning in the primary song of the Yellow-throated Vireo, with comparative notes on Solitary Vireos (Aves: Vireonidae). Can. J. Zool. 62:468–472.

Janes, S.W. 1984a. Influences of territory composition and interspecific competition on Red-tailed Hawk reproductive success. Ecology 65:862–870.

Janes, S.W. 1984b. Fidelity to breeding territory in a population of Red-tailed Hawks. Condor 86:200–203.

Järvi, T., and M. Bakken. 1984. The function of variation in the breast stripe of the Great Tit *(Parus major)*. Anim. Behav. 32:590–596.

Jehl, J.R., Jr. 1979. The autumnal migration of Baird's Sandpiper. Studies in Avian Biol. 2:55–68.

Jenkin, P.M. 1957. The filter feeding and food of flamingoes (Phoenicopteri). Phil. Trans. Roy. Soc. London, Ser. B 240:401–493.

Jenkins, M.A. 1978. Gyrfalcon nesting behavior from hatching to fledging. Auk 95:122–127.

Jenkinson, M.A., and R.M. Mengel. 1970. Ingestion of stones by goatsuckers (Caprimulgidae). Condor 72:236–237.

Jenni, D.A., and B.J. Betts. 1978. Sex differences in nest construction, incubation, and parental behaviour in the polyandrous American Jacana (*Jacana spinosa*). Anim. Behav. 26:207–218.

Johnsgard, P.A. 1965. Handbook of Waterfowl Behavior. Cornell Univ. Press, Ithaca, NY.

Johnsgard, P.A. 1973. Grouse and Quails of North America. Univ. Nebraska Press, Lincoln.

Johnsgard, P.A. 1981. The Plovers, Sandpipers, and Snipes of the World. Univ. Nebraska Press, Lincoln.

Johnsgard, P.A. 1983a. Cranes of the World. Indiana Univ. Press, Bloomington, IN.

Johnsgard, P.A. 1983b. The Hummingbirds of North America. Smithsonian Institution Press, Washington, DC.

Johnsgard, P.A., and J. Kear. 1968. A review of parental carrying of young by waterfowl. Living Bird 7:89–102.

Johnson, E.J., and L.B. Best. 1982. Factors affecting feeding and brooding of Gray Catbird nestlings. Auk 99:148–156.

Johnson, L.S., J.M. Marzluff, and R.P. Balda. 1987. Handling of pinyon pine seed by the Clark's Nutcracker. Condor 89:117–125.

Johnson, N.K. 1963. Biosystematics of sibling species of flycatchers in the *Empidonax hammondii-oberholseri-wrightii* complex. Univ. Calif. Publ. Zool. 66:79–238.

Johnson, N.K. 1966. Bill size and the question of competition in allopatric and sympatric populations of Dusky and Gray Flycatchers. Syst. Zool. 15:70–87.

Johnson, N.K. 1976. Breeding distribution of Nashville and Virginia's Warblers. Auk 93:219–230.

Johnson, N.K. 1980. Character variation and evolution of sibling species in the *Empidonax difficilis-flavescens* complex (Aves: Tyrannidae). Univ. Calif. Publ. Zool. 112:1–151.

Johnson, R.E. 1983. Nesting biology of the Rosy Finch on the Aleutian Islands, Alaska. Condor 85:447–452.

Johnson, R.R., and J.J. Dinsmore. 1985. Brood-rearing and postbreeding habitat use by Virginia Rails and Soras. Wilson Bull. 97:551–554.

Johnson, S.R., and I.M. Cowan. 1974. Thermal adaptation as a factor affecting colonizing success of introduced Sturnidae (Aves) in North America. Can. J. Zool. 52:1559–1576.

Johnston, D.W. 1979. The uropygial gland of the Sooty Tern. Condor 81:430–432.

Johnston, R.F. 1960. Behavior of the Inca Dove. Condor 62:7–24.

Johnston, R.F., D.M. Miles, and S.A. Rohwer. 1972. Hermon Bumpus and natural selection in the House Sparrow *Passer domesticus*. Evolution 26:20–31.

Johnston, R.F., and R.K. Selander. 1964. House Sparrows: rapid evolution of races in North America. Science 141:548–550.

Jones, I.L., J.B. Falls, and A.J. Gaston. 1987. Colony departure of family groups of Ancient Murrelets. Condor 89:940–943.

Joyner, D.E. 1977. Behavior of Ruddy Duck broods in Utah. Auk 94:343–349.

Joyner, D.E. 1983. Parasitic egg laying in Redheads and Ruddy Ducks in Utah: incidence and success. Auk 100:717–725.

Kagarise, C.M. 1979. Breeding biology of the Wilson's Phalarope in North Dakota. Bird-Banding 50:12–22.

Kale, H.W., II (ed.). 1978. Rare and Endangered Biota of Florida, vol. 2, Birds. Univ. Presses of Florida, Gainesville.

Kastner, J. 1986. A World of Watchers. Knopf, New York.

Kaufmann, G.W. 1987. Growth and development of Sora and Virginia Rail chicks. Wilson Bull. 99:432–440.

Keast, A., and E.S. Morton (eds.). 1980. Migrant Birds in the Neotropics: Ecology, Behavior, Distribution, and Conservation. Smithsonian Institution Press, Washington, DC.

Kennedy, P.L., and D.R. Johnson. 1986. Prey-size selection in nesting male and female Cooper's Hawks. Wilson Bull. 98:110–115.

Kenyon, K.W. 1942. Hunting strategy of Pigeon Hawks. Auk 59:443–444.

Kerbes, R.H., M.R. McLandress, G.E.J. Smith, G.W. Beyersbergen, and B. Godwin. 1983. Ross' Goose and Lesser Snow Goose colonies in the central Canadian Arctic. Can. J. Zool. 61:168–173.

Kerlinger, P., and P.H. Lehrer. 1982. Owl recognition and antipredator behaviour of Sharp-shinned Hawks. Zeit. Tierpsychol. 58:163–173.

Kessel, B. 1957. A study of the breeding biology of the European Starling (*Sturnus vulgaris*) in North America. Amer. Midl. Nat. 58:257–331.

Ketterson, E.D., and V. Nolan, Jr. 1982. The role of migration and winter mortality in the life history of a temperate-zone migrant, the Dark-eyed Junco, as determined from demographic analyses of winter populations. Auk 99:243–259.

Ketterson, E.D., and V. Nolan, Jr. 1983. The evolution of differential bird migration. Current Ornithology 1:357–402.

Kettlewell, H.B.D. 1973. The Evolution of Melanism. Clarendon Press, Oxford.

Kilham, L. 1972. Reproductive behavior of White-breasted Nuthatches. II. Courtship. Auk 89:115–129.

Kilham, L. 1973. Reproductive behavior of the Red-breasted Nuthatch. I. Courtship. Auk 90:597–609.

Kilham, L. 1980a. Association of Great Egret and White Ibis. J. Field Ornithol. 51:73–74.

Kilham, L. 1984. Cooperative breeding of American Crows. J. Field Ornithol. 55:349–356.

King, J.R., and J.D. Hubbard. 1981. Comparative patterns of nestling growth in White-crowned Sparrows. Condor 83:362–369.

Kirkham, I.R., P.L. McLaren, and W.A. Montevecchi. 1985. The food habits and distribution of Northern Gannets, *Sula bassanus*, off eastern Newfoundland and Labrador. Can. J. Zool. 63:181–188.

Kistchinski, A.A. 1975. Breeding biology and behaviour of the Grey Phalarope *Phalaropus fulicarius* in East Siberia. Ibis 117:285–301.

Klein, T. 1985. Loon Magic. Paper Birch Press, Ashland, WI.

Klimkiewicz, M.K., R.B. Clapp, and A.G. Futcher. 1983. Longevity records of North American birds: Remizidae through Parulinae. J. Field Ornithol. 54:287–294.

Knapton, R.W. 1978. Breeding ecology of the Clay-colored Sparrow. Living Bird 17:137–158.

Knapton, R.W. 1987. Intraspecific avoidance and interspecific overlap of song series in the Eastern Meadowlark. Auk 104:775–779.

Knapton, R.W., R.V. Cartar, and J.B. Falls. 1984. A comparison of breeding ecology and reproductive success between morphs of the White-throated Sparrow. Wilson Bull. 96:60–71.

Knight, R.L., D.J. Grout, and S.A. Temple. 1987. Nest-defense behavior of the American Crow in urban and rural areas. Condor 89:175–177.

Knopf, F.L. 1979. Spatial and temporal aspects of colonial nesting of White Pelicans. Condor 81:353–363.

Knorr, O.A. 1961. The geographical and ecological distribution of the black Swift in Colorado. Wilson Bull. 73:155–170.

Knowles, C.J., C.J. Stoner, and S.P. Gieb. 1982. Selective use of black-tailed prairie dog towns by Mountain Plovers. Condor 84:71–74.

Knudsen, E.I. 1980. Sound localization in birds. *In* A.N. Popper and R.R. Fay (eds.), Comparative Studies of Hearing in Vertebrates. Springer-Verlag, New York, pp. 289–322.

Knudtson, E.P., and G.V. Byrd. 1982. Breeding biology of Crested, Least and Whiskered Auklets on Buldir Island, Alaska. Condor 84:197–202.

Knupp, D.M., R.B. Owen, Jr., and J.B. Dimond. 1977. Reproductive biology of American Robins in northern Maine. Auk 94:80–85.

Kodric-Brown, A., and J.H. Brown. 1978. Influence of economics, interspecific competition, and sexual dimorphism on territoriality of migrant Rufous Hummingbirds. Ecology 59:285–296.

Koenig, W.D. 1984. Geographic variation in clutch size in the Northern Flicker *(Colaptes auratus)*: support for Ashmole's hypothesis. Auk 101:698–706.

Koenig, W.D., and R.L. Mumme. 1987. Population Ecology of the Cooperatively Breeding Acorn Woodpecker. Princeton Univ. Press, Princeton.

Koenig, W.D., R.L. Mumme, and F.A. Pitelka. 1984. The breeding system of the Acorn Woodpecker in central coastal California. Zeit. Tierpsychol. 65:289–308.

Koford, C.B. 1953. The California Condor. Natl. Audubon Soc. Research Report No. 4, New York.

Kondla, N.G. 1973. Nesting of the Black Swift at Johnston's Canyon, Alberta. Can. Field-Nat. 87:64–65.

Konishi, M. 1983. Night owls are good listeners. Natural History, September, pp. 56–59.

Korol, J.J., and R.L. Hutto. 1984. Factors affecting nest site location in Gila Woodpeckers. Condor 86:73–78.

Kotliar, N.B., and J. Burger. 1986. Colony site selection and abandonment by Least Terns *Sterna antillarum* in New Jersey, USA. Biol. Cons. 37:1–21.

Krebs, J.R. 1970. Territory and breeding density in the Great Tit, *Parus major.* Ecology 52:2–22.

Krebs, J.R. 1974. Colonial nesting and social feeding as strategies for exploiting food resources in the Great Blue Heron *(Ardea herodias)*. Behaviour 51:99–131.

Krebs, J.R. 1977. The significance of song repertoires: the Beau Geste hypothesis. Anim. Behav. 25:475–478.

Krebs, J.R., and N.B. Davies (eds.). 1984. Behavioural Ecology: An Evolutionary Approach, 2nd edition. Sinauer Associates, Sunderland, MA.

Krebs, J.R., J.T. Erickson, M.I. Webber, and E.L. Charnov. 1977. Optimal prey selection in the Great Tit *(Parus major)*. Anim. Behav. 25:30–38.

Krebs, J.R., and D.E. Kroodsma. 1980. Repertoires and geographical variation in bird song. Advances in the Study of Behaviour 11:143–177.

Krebs, J.R., D.W. Stephens, and W.J. Sutherland. 1983. Perspectives in optimal foraging. *In* G.A. Clark and A.H. Brush (eds.), Perspectives in Ornithology. Cambridge Univ. Press, New York.

Krekorian, C.O. 1978. Alloparental care in the Purple Gallinule. Condor 80:382–390.

Kress, S.W. 1985. Audubon Society Guide to Attracting Birds. Charles Scribner's Sons, New York.

Kricher, J.C. 1983. Correlation between House Finch increase and House Sparrow decline. Amer. Birds 37:358–360.

Kroodsma, D.E. 1975. Song patterning in the Rock Wren. Condor 77:294–303.

Kroodsma, D.E. 1977. Correlates of song organization among North American wrens. Amer. Nat. 111:995–1008.

Kroodsma, D.E. 1980. Winter Wren singing behavior: a pinnacle of song complexity. Condor 82:357–365.

Kroodsma, D.E. 1982. Learning and the ontogeny of sound signals in birds. *In* D.E. Kroodsma and E.H. Miller (eds.), Acoustic Communication in Birds, vol. 2. Academic Press, New York, pp. 1–23.

Kroodsma, D.E. 1984. Songs of the Alder Flycatcher (*Empidonax alnorum*) and Willow Flycatcher (*Empidonax traillii*) are innate. Auk 101:13–24.

Kroodsma, D.E. 1985a. Development and use of two song forms by the Eastern Phoebe. Wilson Bull. 97:21–29.

Kroodsma, D.E. 1985b. Geographic variation in songs of the Bewick's Wren: a search for correlations with avifaunal complexity. Behav. Ecol. Sociobiol. 16:143–150.

Kroodsma, D.E., M.C. Baker, L.F. Baptista, and L. Petrinovich. 1985. Vocal "dialects" in Nuttall's White-crowned Sparrow. Current Ornithology 2:103–133.

Kroodsma, D.E., and R.A. Canady. 1985. Differences in repertoire size, singing behavior, and associated neuroanatomy among Marsh Wren populations have a genetic basis. Auk 102:439–446.

Kroodsma, D.E., W.R. Meservey, A.L. Whitlock, and W.M. VanderHaegen. 1984. Blue-winged Warblers (*Vermivora pinus*) "recognize" dialects in type II but not type I songs. Behav. Ecol. Sociobiol. 15:127–131.

Kroodsma, D.E., and J. Verner. 1978. Complex singing behaviors among *Cistothorus* wrens. Auk 95:703–716.

Kruuk, H. 1976. The biological function of gulls' attraction towards predators. Anim. Behav. 24:146–153.

Kuban, J.F., J. Lawley, and R.L. Neill. 1983. The partitioning of flowering century plants by Black-chinned and Lucifer Hummingbirds. Southwest. Nat. 28:143–148.

Kuban, J.F., and R.L. Neill. 1980. Feeding ecology of hummingbirds in the highlands of the Chisos Mountains, Texas. Condor 82:180–185.

Kus, B.E., P. Ashman, G.W. Page, and L.E. Stenzel. 1984. Age-related mortalilty in a wintering population of Dunlin. Auk 101:69–73.

Kushlan, J.A. 1977. Population energetics of the American White Ibis. Auk 94:114–122.

Kushlan, J.A. 1978a. Nonrigorous foraging by robbing egrets. Ecology 59:649–653.

Kushlan, J.A. 1978b. Commensalism in the Little Blue Heron. Auk 95:677–681.

Kushlan, J.A. 1979. Feeding ecology and prey selection in the White Ibis. Condor 81:376–389.

Kushlan, J.A., and P.C. Frohring. 1986. The history of the southern Florida Wood Stork population. Wilson Bull. 98:368–386.

Kyllingstad, H.C. 1987. In search of an Alaskan curlew. Birder's World, May/June, pp. 22–26.

Lack, D. 1947. The significance of clutch-size. I, II. Ibis 89:302–352.

Lack, D. 1958. The significance of colour in turdine eggs. Ibis 100:145–166.

Lack, D. 1968. Ecological Adaptations for Breeding in Birds. Methuen, London.

Laine, H. 1981. Male participation in incubation and brooding in the Blue Jay. Auk 98:622–623.

Lang, A.L., and J.C. Barlow. 1987. Syllable sharing among North American populations of the Eurasian Tree Sparrow. Condor 89:746–751.

Lang, E.M. 1963. Flamingos raise their young on a liquid containing blood. Experientia 19:532–533.

Langham, N.P.E. 1974. Comparative breeding biology of the Sandwich Tern. Auk 91:255–277.

Lanier, G.A. 1982. A test for conspecific egg discrimination in three species of colonial passerine birds. Auk 99:519–525.

Lank, D.B., L.W. Oring, and S.J. Maxson. 1985. Mate and nutrient limitation of egg-laying in a polyandrous shorebird. Ecology 66:1513–1524.

Lanyon, S.M., and C.F. Thompson. 1984. Visual displays and their context in the Painted Bunting. Wilson Bull. 96:396–407.

Lanyon, W.E. 1957. The Comparative Biology of the Meadowlarks (*Sturnella*) in Wisconsin. Publ. Nuttall Ornithol. Club No. 1.

Lanyon, W.E. 1960. The Middle American populations of the Crested Flycatcher *Myiarchus tyrannulus*. Condor 62:341–350.

Lanyon, W.E. 1961. Specific limits and distribution of the Ash-throated and Nutting Flycatchers. Condor 63:421–449.

Larochelle, J., J. Delson, and K. Schmidt-Nielsen. 1982. Temperature regulation in the Black Vulture. Can. J. Zool. 60:491–494.

Laskey, A.R. 1962. Breeding biology of Mockingbirds. Auk 79:596–606.

Laurenzi, A.W., B.W. Anderson, and R.D. Ohmart. 1982. Wintering biology of Ruby-crowned Kinglets in the lower Colorado River Valley. Condor 84:385–398.

Lawes, G., and M. Kenwood. 1970. Poultry droppings feed cows and reclaim tips. New Scientist, 12 March, p. 508.

Lawrence, L. de K. 1953. Nesting life and behaviour of the Red-eyed Vireo. Can. Field-Nat. 67:47–87.

Lawrence, L. de K. 1967. A Comparative Life-history Study of Four Species of Woodpeckers. Ornithol. Monogr. No. 5.

Lawton, M.F., and R.O. Lawton. 1985. The breeding biology of the Brown Jay in Monteverde, Costa Rica. Condor 87:192–204.

Laycock, G. 1987. Keeping a key pigeon in the Keys. Natural History, March, pp. 76–80.

Layne, J.N. 1983. Productivity of Sandhill Cranes in south central Florida. J. Wildl. Manage. 47:178–185.

Leck, C.F. 1978. Temperature and snowfall effects on feeding station activity. Bird-Banding 49:283–284.

Leck, C.F. 1987. Update on House Finch range. Records of NJ Birds 13:18–19.

Leck, C.F., and F.L. Cantor. 1979. Seasonality, clutch size, and hatching success in the Cedar Waxwing. Auk 96:196–198.

LeCroy, M., and C.T. Collins. 1972. Growth and survival of Roseate and Common Tern chicks. Auk 89:595–611.

Lefebvre, L., 1985. Stability of flock composition in urban pigeons. Auk 102:886–888.

Lefebvre, L., and L.-A. Giraldeau. 1984. Daily feeding site use of urban pigeons. Can. J. Zool. 62:1425–1428.

Lefebvre, L., and D. Spahn. 1987. Gray Kingbird predation on small fish (*Poecilia* sp.) crossing a sandbar. Wilson Bull. 99:291–292.

Leffelaar, D., and R.J. Robertson. 1986. Equality of feeding roles and the maintenance of monogamy in Tree Swallows. Behav. Ecol. Sociobiol. 18:199–206.

Lein, M.R. 1978. Song variation in a population of Chestnut-sided Warblers (*Dendroica pensylvanica*): its nature and suggested significance. Can. J. Zool. 56:1266–1283.

Lendrem, D.A. 1983. Safer life for the peeking duck. New Scientist, 24 February, pp. 514–515.

Lenington, S., and T. Mace. 1975. Mate fidelity and nesting site tenacity in the Killdeer. Auk 92:149–151.

Lennartz, M.R., R.G. Hooper, and R.F. Harlow. 1987. Sociality and cooperative breeding of Red-cockaded Woodpeckers, *Picoides borealis*. Behav. Ecol. Sociobiol. 20:77–88.

Leonard, M.L., and J. Picman. 1986. Why are nesting Marsh Wrens and Yellow-headed Blackbirds spatially segregated? Auk 103:135–140.

Leonard, M.L., and J. Picman. 1987. Nesting mortality and habitat selection by Marsh Wrens. Auk 104:491–495.

Leopold, A.S. 1977. The California Quail. Univ. California Press, Berkeley.

Leopold, A.S., and M.F. Dedon. 1983. Resident Mourning Doves in Berkeley, California. J. Wildl. Manage. 47:780–789.

Leopold, A.S., M. Erwin, J. Oh, and B. Browning. 1976. Phytoestrogens: adverse effects on reproduction in California Quail. Science 191:98–100.

Leopold, A.S., R.J. Gutiérrez, and M.T. Bronson. 1981. North American Game Birds and Mammals. Charles Scribner's Sons, New York.

Leopold, A.S., and R.A. McCabe. 1957. Natural history of the Montezuma Quail in Mexico. Condor 59:3–26.

Lessells, C.M. 1984. The mating system of Kentish Plovers (*Charadrius alexandrinus*). Ibis 126:474–483.

Levenson, H. 1979. Time and activity budget of Ospreys nesting in northern California. Condor 81:364–369.

Lewin, R. 1985. Why are male hawks so small? Science 228:1299–1300.

Lewin, R. 1986. Egg laying is for the birds. Science 234:285.

Lewis, J.C. 1973. The World of the Wild Turkey. J.B. Lippincott Co., Philadelphia.

Lewis, R.A. 1985. Do Blue Grouse form leks? Auk 102:180–184.

Lewis, R.A., and I.G. Jamieson. 1987. Delayed breeding in yearling and male grouse: an evaluation of two hypotheses. Condor 89:182–185.

Ligon, J.D. 1968. The Biology of the Elf Owl, *Micrathene whitneyi*. Univ. Michigan Mus. Zool. Misc. Publ. No. 136.

Ligon, J.D. 1971. Notes on the breeding of the Sulphur-bellied Flycatcher in Arizona. Condor 73:250–252.

Ligon, J.D. 1978. Reproductive interdependence of Piñon Jay and Piñon Pines. Ecol. Monogr. 48:111–126.

Lincer, J.L., W.S. Clark, and M.N. LeFranc, Jr. 1979. Working Bibliography of the Bald Eagle. National Wildlife Federation, Scientific and Technical Series No. 2.

Lind, H. 1984. The rotation display of the Mute Swan *Cygnus olor:* synchronised neighbour responses as instrument in the territorial defence strategy. Ornis Scand. 15:98–104.

Lindstedt, S.L., and W.A. Calder. 1976. Body size and longevity in birds. Condor 78:91–145.

Linkhart, B.D., and R.T. Reynolds. 1987. Brood division and postnesting behavior of Flammulated Owls. Wilson Bull. 99:240–243.

Lissaman, P.B.S., and C.A. Schollenberger. 1970. Formation flight of birds. Science 168:1003–1005.

Loftin, R.W., and S. Sutton. 1979. Ruddy Turnstones destroy Royal Tern colony. Wilson Bull. 91:133–135.

Logan, C.A. 1983. Reproductively dependent song cyclicity in mated male Mockingbirds (*Mimus polyglottos*). Auk 100:404–413.

Lombardo, M.P. 1987. Attendants at Tree Swallow nests. II. The exploratory-dispersal hypothesis. Condor 89:138–149.

Long, J.L. 1981. Introduced Birds of the World. Universe Books, New York.

Louther, J.K. 1977. Nesting biology of the Sora at Vermilion, Alberta. Can. Field-Nat. 91:63–67.

Lowe, V.P.W. 1972. Distraction display by a Woodcock with chicks. Ibis 114:106–107.

Lundberg, C.-A., and R.A. Vaisanen. 1981. Selective correlation of egg size with chick mortality in the Black-headed Gull *(Larus ridibundus)*. Condor 81:146–156.

Lunk, W.A. 1962. The Rough-winged Swallow, *Stelgidopteryx serripennis:* A Study Based on Its Breeding Biology in Michigan. Nuttall Ornith. Club Publ. No. 4, Cambridge, MA.

Luoma, J.R. 1987. Black Duck decline: an acid rain link. Audubon, May, pp. 19–24.

Lustick, S., B. Battersby, and M. Kelty. 1978. Behavioral thermoregulation: orientation toward the sun in Herring Gulls. Science 200:81–83.

Lynch, J.F., E.S. Morton, and M.E. Vander Voort. 1985. Habitat segregation between the sexes of wintering Hooded Warblers *(Wilsonia citrina)*. Auk 102:714–721.

Lynch, J.F., and D.F. Whigham. 1984. Effects of forest fragmentation on breeding bird communities in Maryland, USA. Biol. Cons. 28:287–324.

Lyon, B.E., and R.D. Montgomerie. 1987. Ecological correlates of incubation feeding: a comparative study of high arctic finches. Ecology 68:713–722.

Lyon, D.L., J. Crandall, and M. McKone. 1977. A test of the adaptiveness of interspecific territoriality in the Blue-throated Hummingbird. Auk 94:448–454.

MacArthur, R.H. 1958. Population ecology of some warblers of northeastern coniferous forests. Ecology 39:599–619.

MacArthur, R.H., and J. MacArthur. 1961. On bird species diversity. Ecology 42:594–598.

MacArthur, R.H., and E.O. Wilson. 1967. The Theory of Island Biogeography. Princeton Univ. Press, Princeton.

MacDonald, S.D. 1970. The breeding behavior of the Rock Ptarmigan. Living Bird 9:195–238.

MacKenzie, D.I., and S.G. Sealy. 1981. Nest site selection in Eastern and Western Kingbirds: a multivariate approach. Condor 83:310–321.

MacLean, A.A.E. 1986. Age-specific foraging ability and the evolution of deferred breeding in three species of gulls. Wilson Bull. 98:267–279.

McGill, P.A., and M.E. Richmond. 1979. Hatching success of Great Black-backed Gull eggs treated with oil. Bird-Banding 50:108–113.

McGilvrey, F.B. 1966. Nesting of Hooded Mergansers on the Patuxent Wildlife Research Center, Laurel, Maryland. Auk 83:477–479.

McGrew, A. 1971. Nesting of Ringed Kingfisher in the United States. Auk 88:665–666.

McHargue, L.A. 1981. Black Vulture nesting, behavior, and growth. Auk 98:182–185.

McIntyre, J.W. 1978. Wintering behavior of Common Loons. Auk 95:396–403.

McIntyre, J.W. 1983. Nurseries: a consideration of habitat requirements during the early chick-rearing period in Common Loons. J. Field Ornithol. 54:247–253.

McIntyre, J.W. 1986a. A louder voice in the wilderness. National Wildlife 24:46–50.

McIntyre, J.W. 1986b. Common Loon. *In* R.L. Di Silvestro (ed.), Audubon Wildlife Report 1986, National Audubon Soc., NY, pp. 679–695.

McKee, R. 1987. Rock knockers and egg trails. Audubon, September, pp. 79, 84–87.

McKinney, F. 1975. The evolution of duck displays. *In* G. Baerends, C. Beer, and A. Manning (eds.), Function and Evolution in Behaviour. Clarendon Press, Oxford, pp. 331–357.

McKinney, F. 1986. Ecological factors influencing the social systems of migratory dabbling ducks. *In* D.I. Rubenstein and R.W. Wrangham (eds.), Ecological Aspects of Social Evolution. Princeton Univ. Press, Princeton, pp. 153–171.

McLandress, M.R. 1983. Temporal changes in habitat selection and nest spacing in a colony of Ross' and Lesser Snow Geese. Auk 100:335–343.

McLaren, M.A. 1975. Breeding biology of the Boreal Chickadee. Wilson Bull. 87:344–354.

McLaren, M.A. 1976. Vocalizations of the Boreal Chickadee. Auk 93:451–463.

McLaughlin, R.L., and R.D. Montgomerie. 1985. Brood division by Lapland Longspurs. Auk 102:687–695.

McNair, D.B. 1983. Brown-headed Nuthatches store pine seeds. Chat 47:47–48.

McNair, D.B. 1984a. Reuse of other species nests by Lark Sparrows. Southwest. Nat. 29:506–509.

McNair, D.B. 1984b. Clutch-size and nest placement in the Brown-headed Nuthatch. Wilson Bull. 96:296–301.

McNeil, R., and C. Léger. 1987. Nest-site quality and reproductive success of early- and late-nesting Double-crested Cormorants. Wilson Bull. 99:262–267.

McNicholl, M.K. 1975. Larid site tenacity and group adherence in relation to habitat. Auk 92:98–104.

McNicholl, M.K. 1982. Factors affecting reproductive success of Forster's Terns at Delta Marsh, Manitoba. Colonial Waterbirds 5:32–38.

McPherson, J.M. 1987. A field study of winter fruit preferences of Cedar Waxwings. Condor 89:293–306.

Mader, W.J. 1978. A comparative nesting study of Red-tailed Hawks and Harris' Hawks in southern Arizona. Auk 95:327–337.

Mader, W.J. 1979. Breeding behavior of a polyandrous trio of Harris' Hawks in southern Arizona. Auk 96:776–788.

Maher, W.J. 1974. Ecology of Pomarine, Parasitic and Long-tailed Jaegers in Northern Alaska. Pacific Coast Avifauna No. 37, Los Angeles.

Mahoney, S.A. 1984. Plumage wettability of aquatic birds. Auk 101:181–185.

Mahoney, S.A., and J.R. Jehl, Jr. 1985. Adaptations of migratory shorebirds to highly saline and alkaline lakes: Wilson's Phalarope and American Avocet. Condor 87:520–527.

Mallory, F.F. 1987. Foraging behavior and diet of Lesser Sandhill Cranes in low arctic tundra near Eskimo Point, Northwest Territories, Canada. Wilson Bull. 99:495–496.

Manolis, T. 1977. Foraging relationships of Mountain Chickadees and Pygmy Nuthatches. Western Birds 8:13–20.

Manuwal, D.A. 1979. Reproductive commitment and success of Cassin's Auklet. Condor 81:111–121.

Marion, W.R. 1976. Plain Chachalaca food habits in south Texas. Auk 93:376–379.

Marion, W.R., and J.D. Shamis. 1977. An annotated bibliography of bird marking techniques. Bird-Banding 48:42–61.

Marks, J.S. 1984. Feeding ecology of breeding Long-eared Owls in southern Idaho. Can. J. Zool. 62:1528–1533.

Marks, J.S. 1986. Nest site characteristics and reproductive success of Large-eared Owls in southwestern Idaho. Wilson Bull. 98:547–560.

Marks, J.S., and V.A. Marks. 1981. Comparative food habits of the Screech Owls and Long-eared Owl in southwestern Idaho. Murrelet 62:80–82.

Marler, P. 1984. Song learning: innate species differences in the learning process. *In* P. Marler and H.S. Terrace (eds.), The Biology of Learning. Springer-Verlag, Berlin, pp. 289–309 (Dahlem Konferenzen).

Marriott, R.W. 1973. The manurial effect of Cape Barren Goose droppings. Wildfowl 24:131–133.

Marshall, A.J., and D.L. Serventy. 1959. The experimental demonstration of an internal rhythm of reproduction in a transequatorial migrant, the Short-tailed Shearwater, *Puffinus tenuirostris*. Nature 184:1704–1705.

Marshall, J., and R.P. Balda. 1974. The breeding ecology of the Painted Redstart. Condor 76:89–101.

Marti, C.D. 1974. Feeding ecology of four sympatric owls. Condor 76:45–61.

Marti, C.D. 1976. A review of prey selection by the Long-eared Owl. Condor 78:331–336.

Marti, C.D., and C.E. Braun. 1975. Use of tundra habitats by Prairie Falcons in Colorado. Condor 77:213–214.

Marti, C.D., and J.G. Hogue. 1979. Selection of prey by size in Screech Owls. Auk 96:319–327.

Marti, C.D., and P.W. Wagner. 1985. Winter mortality in Common Barn-Owls and its effect on population density and reproduction. Condor 87:111–115.

Martin, D.J. 1973. Selected aspects of Burrowing Owl ecology and behavior. Condor 75:446–456.

Martin, D.J. 1974. Copulatory and vocal behavior of a pair of Whiskered Owls. Auk 91:619–624.

Martin, D.J. 1979. Songs of the Fox Sparrow II. Intra- and interpopulation variation. Condor 81:173–184.

Martin, G. 1986. The owl's key to a successful nightlife. New Scientist, 18 September, pp. 42–44.

Martin, K. 1984. Reproductive defence priorities of male Willow Ptarmigan (*Lagopus lagopus*): enhancing mate survival or extending paternity options? Behav. Ecol. Sociobiol. 16:57–63.

Martin, K. 1987. Grouse and spouse. Natural History, February, pp. 62–68.

Martin, K., and F. Cooke. 1987. Bi-parental care in Willow Ptarmigan: a luxury? Anim. Behav. 35:369–379.

Martin, L.D. 1983. The origin and early radiation of birds. *In* A.H. Brush and G.A. Clark, Jr. (eds.), Perspectives in Ornithology. Cambridge Univ. Press, Cambridge, pp. 291–338. See also commentaries by D.W. Steadman (pp. 338–345) and P.V. Rich (pp. 345–353), following this article.

Martin, M., and T.W. Barry. 1978. Nesting behavior and food habits of Parasitic Jaegers at Anderson River Delta, Northwest Territories. Can. Field-Nat. 92:45–50.

Martin, R.F. 1980. Analysis of hybridization between the hirundinid genera *Hirundo* and *Petrochelidon* in Texas. Auk 97:148–159.

Martin, R.F., and S.R. Martin. 1978. Niche and range expansion of Cave Swallows in Texas. Amer. Birds 32:941–946.

Martin, R.F., G.O. Miller, M.R. Lewis, S.R. Martin, and W.R. Davis, II. 1977. Reproduction of the Cave Swallow: a Texas cave population. Southwest. Nat. 22:177–186.

Martin, S.G. 1970. The agonistic behavior of Varied Thrushes (*Ixoreus naevius*) in winter assemblages. Condor 72:452–459.

Martin, S.G. 1974. Adaptations for polygynous breeding in the Bobolink, *Dolichonyx oryzivorus*. Amer. Zool. 14:109–119.

Martin, S.G., P.H. Baldwin, and E.B. Reed. 1974. Recent records of birds from the Yampa Valley, northwestern Colorado. Condor 76:113–116.

Martindale, S. 1980. A numerical approach to the analysis of Solitary Vireo songs. Condor 82:199–211.

Massey, B.W., R. Zembal, and P.D. Jorgensen. 1984. Nesting habitat of the Light-footed Clapper Rail in southern California. J. Field Ornithol. 55:67–80.

Maunder, J.E., and W. Threlfall. 1972. The breeding biology of the Black-legged Kittiwake in Newfoundland. Auk 89:798–816.

Maxson, S.J., and L.W. Oring. 1978. Mice as a source of egg loss among ground-nesting birds. Auk 95:582–584.

Maxwell, G.R., II, and L.S. Putnam. 1972. Incubation, care of young, and nest success of the Common Grackle (Quiscalus quiscula) in northern Ohio. Auk 89:349–359.

May, R.M. 1979. Flight formations in geese and other birds. Nature 282:778–780.

Mayfield, H.F. 1978a. Brood parasitism: reducing interactions between Kirtland's Warblers and Brown-headed Cowbirds. In S.A. Temple (ed.), Symposium on Endangered Birds: Management Techniques for Endangered Species. Univ. Wisconsin Press, Madison, pp. 85–92.

Mayfield, H.F. 1978b. Red Phalaropes breeding on Bathurst Island. Living Bird 17:7–39.

Mayr, E. 1963. Animal Species and Evolution. Harvard Univ. Press, Cambridge, MA.

Mayr, E. 1969. Principles of Systematic Zoology. McGraw-Hill, New York.

Mead, C. 1983. Bird Migration. Facts on File, New York.

Meanley, B. 1969. Natural history of the King Rail. North Amer. Fauna, No. 67, U.S. Dept. Interior, Fish and Wildlife Service, Washington, DC.

Meanley, B. 1971. Natural history of the Swainson's Warbler. North American Fauna, No. 69, U.S. Dept. Interior, Fish and Wildlife Service, Washington, DC.

Meanley, B. 1985. The Marsh Hen—a Natural History of the Clapper Rail of the Atlantic Coast Salt Marsh. Tidewater Publishers, Centreville, MD.

Medvin, M.M., M.D. Beecher, and S.J. Andelman. 1987. Extra adults at the nest in Barn Swallows. Condor 89:179–182.

Mewaldt, L.R., and J.R. King. 1985. Breeding site faithfulness, reproductive biology, and adult survivorship in an isolated population of Cassin's Finches. Condor 87:494–510.

Middleton, A.L.A. 1978. The annual cycle of the American Goldfinch. Condor 80:401–406.

Middleton, A.L.A. 1979. Influence of age and habitat on reproduction by the American Goldfinch. Ecology 60:418–432.

Milkman, R. (ed.). 1982. Perspectives on Evolution. Sinauer, Sunderland, MA.

Miller, E.H. 1983a. Structure of display flights in the Least Sandpiper. Condor 85:220–242.

Miller, E.H. 1983b. The structure of aerial displays in three species of Calidridinae (Scolopacidae). Auk 100:440–451.

Miller, E.H. 1984. Communication in breeding shorebirds. In J. Burger and B.L. Olla (eds.), Shorebirds: Breeding Behavior and Populations. Plenum, New York, pp. 169–241.

Miller, E.H., W.W.H. Gunn, and R.E. Harris. 1983. Geographic variation in the aerial song of the Short-billed Dowitcher (Aves: Scolopacidae). Can. J. Zool. 61:2191–2198.

Miller, E.H., W.W.H. Gunn, and S.F. MacLean, Jr. 1987. Breeding vocalizations of the Surfbird. Condor 89:406–412.

Miller, E.H., W.W.H. Gunn, J.P. Myers, and B.N. Veprintsev. 1984. Species-distinctiveness of Long-billed Dowitcher song (Aves: Scolopacidae). Proc. Biol. Soc. Wash. 97:804–811.

Miller, J.H., and M.T. Green. 1987. Distribution, status, and origin of Water Pipits breeding in California. Condor 89:788–797.

Miller, L.M., and J. Burger. 1978. Factors affecting nesting success of the Glossy Ibis. Auk 95:353–361.

Miller, R.S., and R.W. Nero. 1983. Hummingbird-sapsucker associations in northern climates. Can. J. Zool. 61:1540–1546.

Miller, S.J., and D.W. Inouye. 1983. Roles of the wing whistle in the territorial behaviour of male Broad-tailed Hummingbirds (*Selasphorus platycercus*). Anim. Behav. 31:689–700.

Mills, A.M. 1986. The influence of moonlight on the behavior of goatsuckers (Caprimulgidae). Auk 103:370–378.

Mills, G.S. 1976. American Kestrel sex ratios and habitat separation. Auk 93:740–748.

Mills, G.S., J.R. Silliman, K.D. Groschupf, and S.M. Speich. 1980. Life history of the Five-striped Sparrow. Living Bird 18:95–110.

Milton, G.R., and P. Austin-Smith. 1983. Changes in the abundance and distribution of Double-crested Cormorants (*Phalacrocorax auritus*) and Great Cormorants (*P. carbo*) in Nova Scotia. Colonial Waterbirds 6:130–138.

Minock, M.E. 1971. Social relationships among Mountain Chickadees. Condor 73:118–120.

Mock, D.W. 1978. Pair-formation displays of the Great Egret. Condor 80:159–172.

Mock, D.W. 1984. Infanticide, siblicide, and avian nestling mortality. *In* G. Hausfater and S.B Hrdy (eds.), Infanticide—Comparative and Evolutionary Perspectives. Aldine, New York, pp. 3–30.

Møller, A.P. 1981. Breeding cycle of the Gull-billed Tern, *Gelochelidon nilotica*, especially in relation to colony size. Ardea 60:193–198.

Møller, A.P. 1982. Coloniality and colony structure in Gull-billed Tern *Gelochelidon nilotica*. J. f. Ornithologie 123:41–53.

Møller, A.P. 1984. On the use of feathers in birds' nests: predictions and tests. Ornis Scand. 15:38–42.

Montevecchi, W.A. 1978. Nest site selection and its survival value among Laughing Gulls. Behav. Ecol. Sociobiol. 4:143–161.

Montevecchi, W.A., R.E. Ricklefs, I.R. Kirkham, and D. Gabaldon. 1984. Growth energetics of nestling Northern Gannets (*Sula bassanus*). Auk 101:334–341.

Moreno, J. 1984. Parental care of fledged young, division of labor, and the development of foraging techniques in the Northern Wheatear (*Oenanthe oenanthe* L.). Auk 101:741–752.

Morrell, S.H., H.R. Huber, T.J. Lewis, and D.G. Ainley. 1979. Feeding ecology of Black Oystercatchers on South Farallon Island, California. Studies in Avian Biol. 2:185–186.

Morris, R.D., and G.T. Haynes. 1977. The breeding biology of two Lake Erie Herring Gull colonies. Can. J. Zool. 55:796–805.

Morris, R.D., and D.A. Wiggins. 1986. Ruddy Turnstones, Great Horned Owls, and egg loss from Common Tern clutches. Wilson Bull. 98:101–109.

Morrison, M.L. 1980. Seasonal aspects of the predatory behavior of Loggerhead Shrikes. Condor 82:296–300.

Morrison, M.L. 1982. The structure of western warbler assemblages: ecomorphological analysis of the Black-throated Gray and Hermit Warblers. Auk 99:503–513.

Morrison, M.L. 1983. Analysis of geographic variation in the Townsend's Warbler. Condor 85:385–391.

Morrison, M.L., R.D. Slack, and E. Shanley, Jr. 1978. Age and foraging ability relationships of Olivaceous Cormorants. Wilson Bull. 90:414–422.

Morrison, M.L., and K.A. With. 1987. Interseasonal and intersexual resource partitioning in Hairy and White-headed Woodpeckers. Auk 104:225–233.

Morse, D.H. 1968. The use of tools by Brown-headed Nuthatches. Wilson Bull. 80:220–224.

Morse, D.H. 1970. Ecological aspects of some mixed-species foraging flocks of birds. Ecology 40:119–168.

Morse, D.H. 1971. Effects of the arrival of a new species upon habitat utilization by two forest thrushes in Maine. Wilson Bull. 83:57–65.

Morse, D.H. 1978. Populations of Bay-breasted and Cape May Warblers during an outbreak of the spruce budworm. Wilson Bull. 90:404–413.

Morse, D.H. 1979. Habitat use by the Blackpoll Warbler. Wilson Bull. 91:234–243.

Morse, D.H. 1980. Foraging and coexistence of spruce-woods warblers. Living Bird 18:7–25.

Morse, D.H., and S.W. Kress. 1984. The effect of burrow loss on mate choice in the Leach's Storm-Petrel. Auk 101:158–160.

Morse, P.J. 1979. Pairing and courtship in the North American Dipper. Bird-Banding 50:62–65.

Morton, E.S. 1971. Nest predation affecting the breeding season of the Clay-colored Robin, a tropical songbird. Science 171:920–921.

Morton, E.S. 1975. Ecological sources of selection in avian sounds. Amer. Nat. 109:17–34.

Morton, E.S. 1982. Grading, discreteness, redundancy, and motivation-structural rules. In D. Kroodsma and E.H. Miller (eds.), Acoustic Communication in Birds, vol. 1. Academic Press, New York, pp. 183–212.

Morton, E.S., J.F. Lynch, K. Young, and P. Mehlhop. 1987. Do male Hooded Warblers exclude females from nonbreeding territories in tropical forest? Auk 104:133–135.

Morton, E.S., and R.M. Patterson. 1983. Kin association, spacing, and composition of a post-breeding roost of Purple Martins. J. Field Ornithol. 54:36–41.

Morton, E.S., and K. Young. 1986. A previously undescribed method of song matching in a species with a single song "type," the Kentucky Warbler (Oporornis formosus). Ethology 73:334–342.

Morton, M.L., J.L. Horstmann, and J.M. Osborn. 1972. Reproductive cycle and nesting success of the Mountain White-crowned Sparrow (Zonotrichia leucophrys oriantha) in the central Sierra Nevada. Condor 74:152–163.

Morton, M.L., and M.E. Pereyra. 1985. The regulation of egg temperatures and attentiveness patterns in the Dusky Flycatcher (Empidonax oberholseri). Auk 102:25–37.

Moseley, L.J. 1979. Individual auditory recognition in the Least Tern (Sterna albifrons). Auk 96:31–39.

Moss, W. W., and J.H. Camin. 1970. Nest parasitism, productivity, and clutch size in Purple Martins. Science 168:1000–1003.

Moulton, M.P., and S.L. Pimm. 1986. The extent of competition in shaping an introduced avifauna. In J. Diamond and T.J. Case (eds.), Community Ecology. Harper and Row, New York, pp. 80–97.

Moyles, D.L.J. 1981. Seasonal and daily use of plant communities by Sharp-tailed Grouse (Pedioecetes phasianellus) in the parklands of Alberta. Can. Field-Nat. 95:287–291.

Mueller, H.C. 1977. Prey selection in the American Kestrel: experiments with two species of prey. Amer. Nat. 111:25–29.

Mueller, H.C., D.D. Berger, and G. Allez. 1977. The periodic invasions of Goshawks. Auk 94:652–663.

Mueller, H.C., and K. Meyer. 1985. The evolution of reversed sexual dimorphism in size: a comparative analysis of the Falconiformes of the western Palearctic. Current Ornithology 2:65–101.

Mugaas, J.N., and J.R. King. 1981. Annual Variation of Daily Energy Expenditure by the Black-billed Magpie: A Study of Thermal and Behavioral Energetics. Studies in Avian Biol. 5:1–78.

Mumford, R.E. 1964. The breeding biology of the Acadian Flycatcher. Misc. Publ. Mus. Zool. Univ. Mich., Ann Arbor.

Mundinger, P.C. 1982. Microgeographic and macrogeographic variation in acquired vocalizations of birds. In D.E. Kroodsma and E.H. Miller (eds.), Acoustic Communication in Birds, vol. 2. Academic Press, New York, pp. 147–208.

Munn, C.A. 1984. Birds of different feather also flock together. Natural History, November, pp. 34–42.

Munro, J., and J. Bédard. 1977. Creche formation in the Common Eider. Auk 94:759–771.

Murphy, E.C. 1978. Breeding ecology of House Sparrows: spatial variation. Condor 80:180–193.

Murphy, E.C., R.H. Day, K.L. Oakley, and A.A. Hoover. 1984. Dietary changes and poor reproductive performance in Glaucous-winged Gulls. Auk 101:532–541.

Murphy, E.C., A.M. Springer, and D.G. Roseneau. 1986. Population status of Common Guillemots Uria aalge at a colony in western Alaska: results and simulations. Ibis 128:348–363.

Murphy, K. 1986. Train to be a bird brain. Aero, August, pp. 6–10.

Murphy, M.T. 1983. Nest success and nesting habits of Eastern Kingbirds and other flycatchers. Condor 85:208–219.

Murphy, M.T. 1986. Temporal components of reproductive variability in Eastern Kingbirds (Tyrannus tyrannus). Ecology 67:1483–1492.

Murphy, M.T., and R.C. Fleischer. 1986. Body size, nest predation, and reproductive patterns in Brown Thrashers and other mimids. Condor 88:446–455.

Murray, K.G., K. Winnett-Murray, Z.A. Eppley, G.L. Hunt, Jr., and D.B. Schwartz. 1983. Breeding biology of the Xantus' Murrelet. Condor 85:12–21.

Myers, J.P. 1979. Leks, sex, and Buff-breasted Sandpipers. Amer. Birds 33:823–825.

Myers, J.P. 1981. A test of three hypotheses for latitudinal segregation of the sexes in wintering birds. Can. J. Zool. 59:1527–1534.

Myers, J.P. 1982. The promiscuous Pectoral Sandpiper. Amer. Birds 36:119–122.

Myers, J.P. 1983. Space, time and the pattern of individual associations in a group-living species: Sanderlings have no friends. Behav. Ecol. Sociobiol. 12:129–134.

Myers, J.P. 1984. Spacing behavior of nonbreeding shorebirds. In J. Burger and B.L. Olla (eds.), Shorebirds: Migration and Foraging Behavior, Behavior of Marine Animals, vol. 6. Plenum Press, New York, pp. 271–321.

Myers, J. P. 1986. Sex and gluttony on Delaware Bay. Natural History, May, pp. 69–76.

Myers, J.P., P.G. Connors, and F.A. Pitelka. 1979. Territoriality in non-breeding shorebirds. Studies in Avian Biology No. 2, Cooper Ornithol. Soc., pp. 231–246.

Myers, J.P., O. Hilden, and P. Tomkovich. 1982. Exotic Calidris species of the Siberian tundra. Ornis Fenn. 59:175–182.

Myers, J.P., R.I.G. Morrison, P.Z. Antas, B.A. Harrington, T.E. Lovejoy, M. Sallaberry, S.E. Senner, and A. Tarak. 1987. Conservation strategy for migratory species. Amer. Sci. 75:19–26.

Myers, J.P., and L.P. Myers. 1979. Shorebirds of coastal Buenos Aires Province, Argentina. Ibis 121:186–200.

Myers, J.P., S.L. Williams, and F.A. Pitelka. 1980. An experimental analysis of prey availability for Sanderlings (Aves: Scolopacidae) feeding on sandy beach crustaceans. Can. J. Zool. 58:1564–1574.

Necker, R. 1985. Observations on the function of a slowly adapting mechanoreceptor associated with filoplumes in the feathered skin of pigeons. J. Comp. Physiol. A 156:391–394.

Neidermyer, W.J., and J.J. Hickey. 1977. The Monk Parakeet in the United States, 1970–75. Amer. Birds 31:273–278.

Nelson, D.A. 1987. Factors influencing colony attendance by Pigeon Guillemots on Southeast Farallon Island, California. Condor 89:340–348.

Nelson, J.B. 1975. The breeding biology of Frigatebirds—a comparative review. Living Bird 14:113–155.

Nelson, J.B. 1978. The Gannet. Buteo Books, Vermillion, SD.

Nelson, R.W. 1968. Nest robbing by Cooper's Hawks. Auk 85:696–697.

Nero, R.W. 1980. The Great Gray Owl—Phantom of the Northern Forest. Smithsonian Institution Press, Washington, DC.

Nethersole-Thompson, D. 1966. The Snow Bunting. Oliver and Boyd, Edinburgh.

Nettleship, D.N., and T.R. Birkhead (eds.). 1985. The Atlantic Alcidae: The Evolution, Distribution and Biology of the Auks Inhabiting the Atlantic Ocean and Adjacent Water Areas. Academic Press, London.

Newton, I. 1979. Population Ecology of Raptors. Buteo Books, Vermillion, SD.

Newton, I., E.R. Meek, and B. Little. 1984. Breeding season foods of Merlins *Falco columbarius* in Northumbria. Bird Study 31:49–56.

Nice, M. 1964. Studies in the Life History of the Song Sparrow, vols. 1, 2. Dover, New York (originally published 1937, 1943).

Nickell, W.P. 1965. Habitats, territory and nesting of the Catbird. Amer. Midl. Nat. 73:433–478.

Nisbet, I.C.T. 1977. Courtship-feeding and clutch size in Common Tern *Sterna hirundo*. *In* B. Stonehouse and C.M. Perrins (eds.), Evolutionary Ecology. Macmillan, London.

Nisbet, I.C.T. 1983. Defecation behavior of territorial and nonterritorial Common Terns *(Sterna hirundo)*. Auk 100:1001–1002.

Nol, E., A.J. Baker, and M.D. Cadman. 1984. Clutch initiation dates, clutch size, and egg size of the American Oystercatcher in Virginia. Auk 101:855–867.

Nolan, V., Jr. 1960. Breeding behavior of the Bell Vireo in southern Indiana. Condor 61:223–244.

Nolan, V., Jr. 1978. The Ecology and Behavior of the Prairie Warbler *Dendroica discolor*. Ornithol. Monogr. No. 26.

Nolan, V., Jr., and C.F. Thompson. 1975. The occurrence and significance of anomalous reproductive activities in two North American non-parasitic cuckoos *Coccyzus* spp. Ibis 117:496–503.

Noon, B.R. 1981. The distribution of an avian guild along a temperate elevational gradient: the importance and expression of competition. Ecol. Monogr. 51:105–124.

Norris, R. 1986. A tide of plastic. Audubon, September, pp. 19–23.

Norris, R.A. 1958. Comparative biosystematics and life history of the nuthatches *Sitta pygmaea* and *Sitta pusilla*. Univ. Calif. Publ. Zool. 56:119–300.

Norton-Griffiths, M. 1967. Some ecological aspects of the feeding behaviour of the Oystercatcher *(Haematopus ostralegus)* on the edible mussel *(Mytilus edulis)*. Ibis 109:412–424.

Nottebohm, F. 1981. Brain pathways for vocal learning in birds: A review of the first 10 years. *In* J.M.S. Sprague and A.N.E. Epstein (eds.), Progress in Psychobiology and Physiological Psychology, vol. 9. Academic Press, New York, pp. 85–124.

Noyes, J.H., and R.L. Jarvis. 1985. Diet and nutrition of breeding female Redhead and Canvasback ducks in Nevada. J. Wildl. Manage. 49:203–211.

Nuechterlein, G.L. 1981a. Variations and multiple functions of the advertising display of Western Grebes. Behaviour 76:289–317.

Nuechterlein, G.L. 1981b. Courtship behavior and reproductive isolation between Western Grebe color morphs. Auk 98:335–349.

Nuechterlein, G.L. 1985. Experiments on the functions of the bare crown patch of downy Western Grebe chicks. Can. J. Zool. 63:464–467.

Nuechterlein, G.L., and R.W. Storer. 1982. The pair-formation displays of the Western Grebe. Condor 84:351–369.

Nugent, D.P., and D.A. Boag. 1982. Communication among territorial female Spruce Grouse. Can. J. Zool. 60:2624–2632.

Nuttall, P.A., C.M. Perrins, and K.A. Harrap. 1982. Further studies on puffinosis, a disease of the Manx Shearwater *(Puffinus puffinus)*. Can. J. Zool. 60:3462–3465.

Oberholser, H.C. 1974. The Bird Life of Texas. Univ. Texas Press, Austin.

O'Connor, R.J. 1978. Brood reduction in birds: selection for fratricide, infanticide, and suicide? Anim. Behav. 26:79–96.

O'Connor, R.J. 1984. The Growth and Development of Birds. Wiley, New York.

O'Donald, P. 1983. The Arctic Skua: A Study of the Ecology and Evolution of a Seabird. Cambridge Univ. Press, Cambridge.

Ogden, J.C. 1985a. The Wood Stork. *In* R.L. Di Silvestro (ed.), Audubon Wildlife Report 1985, National Audubon Soc., NY, pp. 459–470.

Ogden, J.C. 1985b. The California Condor. *In* R.L. Di Silvestro (ed.), Audubon Wildlife Report 1985, National Audubon Soc., NY, pp. 389–399.

Ogden, J.C., J.A Kushlan, and J.T. Tilmant. 1976. Prey selectivity by the Wood Stork. Condor 78:324–330.

Ohlendorf, H.M. 1974. Competitive relationships among kingbirds *(Tyrannus)* in Trans-Pecos Texas. Wilson Bull. 86:357–373.

Ohmart, R.D. 1973. Observations on the breeding adaptations of the Roadrunner. Condor 75:140–149.

Olendorff, R.R. 1974. A courtship flight of the Swainson's Hawk. Condor 76:215.

Ollason, J.C., and G.M. Dunnet. 1986. Relative effects of parental performance and egg quality on breeding success of Fulmars, *Fulmarus glacialis*. Ibis 128:290–296.

Olson, S.L., and A. Feduccia. 1980. Relationships and Evolution of Flamingos (Aves: Phoenicopteridae). Smithsonian Contrib. Zool. No. 316.

Olson, S.L., and H.F. James. 1982. Fossil birds from the Hawaiian Islands: evidence for wholesale extinction by man before western contact. Science 217:633–635.

Orians, G.H. 1967. On the evolution of mating systems in birds and mammals. Amer. Nat. 103:589–603.

Orians, G.H. 1980. Some Adaptations of Marsh-nesting Blackbirds. Monogr. Pop. Biol. No. 14, Princeton Univ. Press, Princeton.

Orians, G.H. 1985. Blackbirds of the Americas. Univ. Washington Press, Seattle.

Orians, G.H., and G.M. Christman. 1968. A comparative study of the behavior of Red-winged, Tricolored, and Yellow-headed Blackbirds. Univ. Calif. Publ. Zool. 84:1–81.

Orians, G.H., and M.F. Willson. 1964. Interspecific territories of birds. Ecology 45:736–745.

Oring, L.W. 1964. Displays of the Buff-breasted Sandpiper at Norman, OK. Auk 81:83–86.

Oring, L.W. 1973. Solitary Sandpiper early reproductive behavior. Auk 90:652–663.

Oring, L.W. 1982. Avian mating systems. *In* D.S. Farner, J.R. King, and K.C. Parkes (eds.), Avian Biology, vol. 6. Academic Press, New York, pp. 1–92.

Oring, L.W. 1986. Avian polyandry. Current Ornithology 3:309–351.

Oring, L.W., and D.B. Lank. 1986. Polyandry in Spotted Sandpipers: the impact of environment and experience. *In* D.I. Rubenstein and R.W. Wrangham (eds.), Ecological Aspects of Social Evolution, Princeton Univ. Press, Princeton, NJ, pp. 21–42.

Oring, L.W., D.B. Lank, and S.J. Maxson. 1983. Population studies of the polyandrous Spotted Sandpiper. Auk 100:272–285.

Ostrom, J.H. 1979. Bird flight: how did it begin? Amer. Sci. 67:46–55.

Owen, D. 1985. What's in a Name. British Broadcasting Corporation, London.

Owre, O.T. 1967. Adaptations for Locomotion and Feeding in the Anhinga and Double-crested Cormorant. Ornithol. Monogr. No. 6.

Owre, O.T. 1973. A consideration of the exotic avifauna of southeastern Florida. Wilson Bull. 85:491–500.

Palmer, R.S. (ed.). 1962. Handbook of North American Birds, vol. 1. Yale University Press, New Haven, CT.

Parker, J.W. 1981. Nest associates of the Mississippi Kite. J. Field Ornithol. 52:144–145.

Parmelee, D.F. 1959. The breeding behavior of the Painted Bunting in southern Oklahoma. Bird-Banding 30:1–18.

Parmelee, D.F., and R.B. Payne. 1973. On multiple broods and the breeding strategy of arctic Sanderlings. Ibis 115:218–226.

Paszkowski, C.A. 1982. Vegetation, ground, and frugivorous foraging of the American Robin. Auk 99:701–709.

Paton, D.C., and F.L. Carpenter. 1984. Peripheral foraging by territorial Rufous Hummingbirds: defense by exploitation. Ecology 65:1808–1819.

Paulson, D.R. 1983. Flocking in the Hook-billed Kite. Auk 100:749–750.

Payne, R.B. 1969. Breeding seasons and reproductive physiology of Tricolored and Redwinged Blackbirds. Univ. Calif. Publ. Zool. 90:1–115.

Payne, R.B. 1977. The ecology of brood parasitism in birds. Ann. Rev. Ecol. Syst. 8:1–28.

Payne, R.B. 1984. Sexual Selection, Lek and Arena Behavior, and Sexual Size Dimorphism in Birds. Ornithol. Monogr. No. 33.

Paynter, R.A., Jr. (ed.). 1974. Avian Energetics. Nuttall Ornith. Club. Publ. No. 15, Cambridge, MA.

Pearson, O.P. 1979. Spacing and orientation among feeding Golden-crowned Sparrows. Condor 81:278–285.

Pennycuick, C.J. 1975. Mechanics of flight. *In* D.S. Farner and J.R. King (eds.), Avian Biology, vol. 5. Academic Press, New York, pp. 1–76.

Pennycuick, C.J. 1982. The flight of petrels and albatrosses (Procellariiformes), observed in South Georgia and its vicinity. Phil. Trans. R. Soc. Lond. B 300:75–106.

Petersen, K.L., L.B. Best, and B.M. Winter. 1986. Growth of nestling Sage Sparrows and Brewer's Sparrows. Wilson Bull. 98:535–546.

Petersen, M.R. 1979. Nesting ecology of Arctic Loons. Wilson Bull. 91:608–617.

Petersen, M.R. 1981. Populations, feeding ecology and molt of Steller's Eiders. Condor 83:256–262.

Petersen, M.R. 1985. The Emperor Goose. *In* R.L. Di Silvestro (ed.), Audubon Wildlife Report 1985, National Audubon Soc., NY, pp. 453–457.

Peterson, R.T. 1969. Population trends of Ospreys in the northeastern United States. *In* J.J. Hickey (ed.), Peregrine Populations: Their Biology and Decline. Univ. Wisconsin Press, Madison.

Petit, D.R., and L.J. Petit. 1987. Fecal sac dispersal by Prothonotary Warblers: Weatherhead's hypothesis re-evaluated. Condor 89:610–613.

Petit, L.J., W.J. Fleming, K.E. Petit, and D.R. Petit. 1987. Nest-box use by Prothonotary Warblers *(Protonotaria citrea)* in riverine habitat. Wilson Bull. 99:485–488.

Petrie, M. 1986. Reproductive strategies of male and female Moorhens *(Gallinula chloropus)*. *In* D.I. Rubenstein and R.W. Wrangham (eds.), Ecological Aspects of Social Evolution. Princeton Univ. Press, Princeton, pp. 43–63.

Petrinovich, L., and T.L. Patterson. 1983. The White-crowned Sparrow: reproductive success (1975–1980). Auk 100:811–825.

Phillips, A., J. Marshall, and G. Monson. 1964. The Birds of Arizona. Univ. Arizona Press, Tucson.

Phillips, A.R. 1975. The migrations of Allen's and other hummingbirds. Condor 77:196–205.

Phillips, R.E. 1972. Sexual and agonistic behaviour in the Killdeer *(Charadrius vociferus)*. Anim. Behav. 20:1–9.

Piatt, J.F., and D.N. Nettleship. 1985. Diving depths of four alcids. Auk 102:293–297.

Picman, J. 1984. Experimental study on the role of intra- and inter-specific competition in the evolution of nest-destroying behavior in Marsh Wrens. Can. J. Zool. 62:2353–2356.

Picman, J., and A.K. Picman. 1980. Destruction of nests by the Short-billed Marsh Wren. Condor 82:176–179.

Pierotti, R. 1987. Isolating mechanisms in seabirds. Evolution 41:559–570.

Pinkowski, B.C. 1979. Annual productivity and its measurement in a multi-brooded passerine, the Eastern Bluebird. Auk 96:562–572.

Pitelka, F.A. 1959. Numbers, breeding schedule, and territoriality in Pectoral Sandpipers of northern Alaska. Condor 61:233–263.

Pitelka, F.A., R.T. Holmes, and S.F. MacLean. 1974. Ecology and evolution of social organization in arctic sandpipers. Amer. Zool. 14:185–204.

Platt, J.B. 1976. Sharp-shinned Hawk nesting and nest site selection in Utah. Condor 78:102–103.

Pleasants, B.Y. 1979. Adaptive significance of the variable dispersion pattern of breeding Northern Orioles. Condor 81:28–34.

Pleszczynska, W.K. 1978. Microgeographic prediction of polygyny in Lark Bunting. Science 201:935–937.

Pleszczynska, W.K., and R. Hansell. 1980. Polygyny and decision theory: testing of a model in Lark Buntings *(Calamospiza melanocorys)*. Amer. Nat. 116:821–830.

Poole, A. 1985. Courtship feeding and Osprey reproduction. Auk 102:479–492.

Popp, J.W. 1987. Agonistic communication among wintering Purple Finches. Wilson Bull. 99:97–100.

Potter, E.F. 1970. Anting in wild birds, its frequency and probable purpose. Auk 87:692–713.

Potter, E.F. 1980. Notes on nesting Yellow-billed Cuckoos. J. Field Ornithol. 51:16–29.

Powell, G.V.N., and J.H. Rappole. 1986. The Hooded Warbler. *In* R.L. Di Silvestro (ed.), Audubon Wildlife Report 1986, National Audubon Soc., NY, pp. 827–853.

Power, H.W. 1980. The Foraging Behavior of Mountain Bluebirds with Emphasis on Sexual Foraging Differences. Ornithol. Monogr. No. 28.

Powers, D.R. 1987. Effects of variation in food quality on the breeding territoriality of the male Anna's Hummingbird. Condor 89:103–111.

Prange, H.D., J.F. Anderson, and H. Rahn. 1979. Scaling of skeletal mass to body mass in birds and mammals. Amer. Nat. 113:103–122.

Pratt, H.M., and D.W. Winkler. 1985. Clutch size, timing of laying, and reproductive success in a colony of Great Blue Herons and Great Egrets. Auk 102:49–63.

Prevett, J.P., and J.F. Barr. 1976. Lek behavior of the Buff-breasted Sandpiper. Wilson Bull. 88:500–503.

Prevett, J.P., I.F. Marshall, and V.G. Thomas. 1985. Spring foods of Snow and Canada Geese at James Bay. J. Wildl. Manage. 49:558–563.

Price, F.E., and C.E. Bock. 1983. Population Ecology of the Dipper (Cinclus mexicanus) in the Front Range of Colorado. Studies in Avian Biol. No. 7, Cooper Ornithol. Soc., Los Angeles.

Probst, J.R., and J.P. Hayes. 1987. Pairing success of Kirtland's Warblers in marginal vs. suitable habitat. Auk 104:234–241.

Pugekse, B.H. 1983. The relationship between parental age and reproductive effort in the California Gull (Larus californicus). Behav. Ecol. Sociobiol. 13:161–171.

Pulich, W.M. 1976. The Golden-cheeked Warbler. Texas Parks and Wildlife Dept., Austin, TX.

Pullianinen, E. 1979. On the breeding of the Pine Grosbeak Pinicola enucleator in NE Finland. Ornis Fenn. 56:156–162.

Purdue, J.R. 1976. Thermal environment of the nest and related parental behavior in Snowy Plovers, Charadrius alexandrinus. Condor 78:180–185.

Quay, T.L., J.B. Funderburg, Jr., D.S. Lee, E.F. Potter, and C.S. Robbins (eds.). 1983. The Seaside Sparrow: Its Biology and Management. North Carolina State Mus. Occ. Papers, Raleigh, NC.

Quay, W.B. 1982. Seasonal calling, foraging, and flocking of Inca Doves at Galveston, Texas. Condor 84:321–326.

Quinlan, S.E. 1983. Avian and river otter predation in a storm-petrel colony. J. Wildl. Manage. 47:1036–1043.

Quinney, T.E. 1986. Male and female parental care in Tree Swallows. Wilson Bull. 98:147–150.

Rabe, D.L., H.H. Prince, and D.L. Beaver. 1983. Feeding-site selection and foraging strategies of American Woodcock. Auk 100:711–716.

Rabenold, K.N. 1980. The Black-throated Green Warbler in Panama: geographic and seasonal comparison of foraging. In A. Keast and E.S. Morton (eds.), Migrant Birds in the Neotropics: Ecology, Behavior, Distribution, and Conservation. Smithsonian Institution Press, Washington, DC, pp. 297–307.

Rabenold, P.P. 1986. Family associations in communally roosting Black Vultures. Auk 103:32–41.

Rabenold, P.P. 1987. Roost attendance and aggression in Black Vultures. Auk 104:647–653.

Raspet, A. 1950. Performance measurements of a soaring bird. Aeronautical Engineering Review 9:1–4.

Ratcliffe, D. 1980. The Peregrine Falcon. Buteo Books, Vermillion, SD.

Raye, S.S.C., and J. Burger. 1979. Behavioral determinants of nestling success of Snowy Egrets (Leucophoyx thula). Amer. Midl. Nat. 102:76–85.

Ream, C.H. 1976. Loon productivity, human disturbance, and pesticide residues in northern Minnesota. Wilson Bull. 88:427–432.

Recher, H., and J. Recher. 1980. Why are there different kinds of herons? Trans. Linn. Soc. NY 9:135–158.

Redmond, R.L., and D.A. Jenni. 1982. Natal philopatry and breeding area fidelity of Long-billed Curlews *(Numenius americanus)*: patterns and evolutionary consequences. Behav. Ecol. Sociobiol. 10:277–279.

Redmond, R.L., and D.A. Jenni. 1986. Population ecology of the Long-billed Curlew *(Numenius americanus)* in western Idaho. Auk 103:755–767.

Reed, T.M. 1982. Interspecific territoriality in the Chaffinch and Great Tit on islands and the mainland of Scotland: playback and removal experiments. Anim. Behav. 30:171–181.

Reese, J.G. 1977. Reproductive success of Ospreys in central Chesapeake Bay. Auk 94:202–221.

Reese, J.G. 1980. Demography of European Mute Swans in Chesapeake Bay. Auk 97:449–464.

Reese, K.P., and J.A. Kadlec. 1985. Influence of high density and parental age on the habitat selection and reproduction of Black-billed Magpies. Condor 87:96–105.

Reid, W.V. 1987. Constraints on clutch size in the Glaucous-winged Gull. Studies in Avian Biol. 10:8–25.

Reimchen, T.E., and S. Douglas. 1984. Feeding schedule and daily food consumption in Red-throated Loons *(Gavia stellata)* over the prefledging period. Auk 101:593–599.

Reinecke, K.J., and G.L. Krapu. 1986. Feeding ecology of Sandhill Cranes during spring migration in Nebraska. J. Wildl. Manage. 50:71–79.

Remsen, J.V., Jr. 1986. Was Bachman's Warbler a bamboo specialist? Auk 103:216–219.

Remsen, J.V., Jr., and L.C. Binford. 1975. Status of the Yellow-billed Loon *(Gavia adamsii)* in the western United States and Mexico. Western Birds 6:7–20.

Repking, C.F., and R.D. Ohmart. 1977. Distribution and density of Black Rail populations along the lower Colorado River. Condor 79:486–489.

Reynard, G.B. 1974. Some vocalizations of the Black, Yellow, and Virginia Rails. Auk 91:747–756.

Reynard, G.B., and S.T. Harty. 1968. Ornithological "mystery" song given by male Virginia Rail. Casinia 50:3–8 (1966–67 issue; issued Nov. 1968).

Reynolds, J.D. 1987. Mating system and nesting biology of the Red-necked Phalarope, *Phalaropus lobatus*: what constrains polyandry? Ibis 129:225–242.

Reynolds, J.D., M.A. Colwell, and F. Cooke. 1986. Sexual selection and spring arrival times of Red-necked and Wilson's Phalaropes. Behav. Ecol. Sociobiol. 18:303–310.

Reynolds, R.T., and E.C. Meslow. 1984. Partitioning of food and niche characteristics of coexisting *Accipiter* during breeding. Auk 101:761–779.

Reynolds, T.D. 1981. Nesting of the Sage Thrasher, Sage Sparrow, and Brewer's Sparrow in southeastern Idaho. Condor 83:61–64.

Reynolds, T.D., and T.D. Rich. 1978. Reproductive ecology of the Sage Thrasher *(Oreoscoptes montanus)* on the Snake River Plain in southeastern Idaho. Auk 95:580–582.

Rice, W.R. 1982. Acoustical location of prey by the Marsh Hawk: adaptation to concealed prey. Auk 99:403–413.

Rich, T. 1981. Microgeographic variation in the song of the Sage Sparrow. Condor 83:113–119.

Rich, T. 1983. "Walking-in-line" behavior in Sage Sparrow territorial encounters. Condor 85:496–497.

Rich, T. 1986. Habitat and nest site selection by Burrowing Owls in the sagebrush steppe of Idaho. J. Wildl. Manage. 50:548–555.

Richards, D.G. 1981a. Estimation of distance of singing conspecifics by the Carolina Wren. Auk 98:127–133.

Richards, D.G. 1981b. Alerting and message components in songs of Rufous-sided Towhees. Behaviour 76:223–249.

Richardson, H., and N.A.M. Verbeek. 1987. Diet selection by yearling Northwestern Crows (*Corvus caurinus*) feeding on littleneck clams (*Venerupis japonica*). Auk 104:263–269.

Ricklefs, R.E. 1965. Brood reduction in the Curve-billed Thrasher. Condor 67:505–510.

Ricklefs, R.E. 1975. Patterns of growth in birds. III. Growth and development of the Cactus Wren. Condor 77:34–45.

Ricklefs, R.E. 1979. Ecology, 2nd edition. Chiron Press, Concord, MA.

Ricklefs, R.E. 1980. Geographical variation in clutch size among passerine birds: Ashmole's hypothesis. Auk 97:38–49.

Ricklefs, R.E. 1984. Avian postnatal development. *In* D.S. Farner and J.R. King (eds.), Avian Biology, vol. 7. Academic Press, New York, pp. 2–84.

Ricklefs, R.E. 1987. Response of adult Leach's Storm-Petrels to increased food demand at the nest. Auk 104:750–756.

Ricklefs, R.E., and G.W. Cox. 1977. Morphological similarity and ecological overlap among passerine birds on St. Kitts, British West Indies. Oikos 29:60–66.

Ricklefs, R.E., C.H. Day, C.E. Huntington, and J.B. Williams. 1985. Variability in feeding rate and meal size of Leach's Storm-Petrel at Kent Island, New Brunswick. J. Anim. Ecol. 54:883–898.

Ringelman, J.K., J.R. Longcore, and R.B. Owen, Jr. 1982. Nest and brood attentiveness in female Black Ducks. Condor 84:110–116.

Rio, C.M. del, and L.E. Eguiarte. 1987. Bird visitation to *Agave salmiana*: comparisons among hummingbirds and perching birds. Condor 89:357–363.

Ripley, S.D. 1977. Rails of the World. David R. Godine, Boston, MA.

Rising, J.D. 1983. The Great Plains hybrid zones. Current Ornithology 1:131–157.

Riska, D.E. 1984. Experiments on nestling recognition by Brown Noddies (*Anous stolidus*). Auk 101:605–609.

Riska, D.E. 1986. An analysis of vocal communication in the adult Brown Noddy (*Anous stolidus*). Auk 103:359–369.

Ritchison, G. 1983. The function of singing in female Black-headed Grosbeaks (*Pheucticus melanocephalus*): family-group maintenance. Auk 100:105–116.

Ritchison, G. 1985. Variation in the songs of female Black-headed Grosbeaks. Wilson Bull. 97:47–56.

Ritchison, G. 1986. The singing behavior of female Northern Cardinals. Condor 88:156–159.

Robbins, C.S. 1973. Introduction, spread, and present abundance of the House Sparrow in North America. Ornithol. Monogr. 14:3–9.

Robbins, C.S. 1980. Effect of forest fragmentation on breeding bird populations in the piedmont of the mid-Atlantic region. Atlantic Naturalist 33:31–35.

Robbins, J. 1985. Anatomy of a sting. Natural History, July, pp. 4–10.

Robbins, M.B., M.J. Braun, and E.A. Tobey. 1986. Morphological and vocal variation across a contact zone between the chickadees *Parus atricapillus* and *P. carolinensis*. Auk 103:655–666.

Roberts, R.C. 1979. The evolution of avian food-storing behavior. Amer. Nat. 114:418–438.

Robertson, P.B., and A.F. Schnapf. 1987. Pyramiding behavior in the Inca Dove: adaptive aspects of day-night differences. Condor 89:185–187.

Robertson, W.B., Jr., L.L. Breen, and B.W. Patty. 1983. Movement of marked Roseate Spoonbills in Florida with a review of present distribution. J. Field Ornithol. 54:225–236.

Robins, J.D. 1971. Differential niche utilization in a grassland sparrow. Ecology 52:1065–1070.

Robinson, S.K. 1981. Ecological relations and social interactions of Philadelphia and Red-eyed Vireos. Condor 83:16–26.

Robinson, S.K., and R.T. Holmes. 1984. Effects of plant species and foliage structure on the foraging behavior of forest birds. Auk 101:672–684.

Robinson, W.L. 1980. Fool Hen: the Spruce Grouse on the Yellow Dog Plains. Univ. Wisconsin Press, Madison.

Roby, D.D., and K.L. Brink. 1986. Breeding biology of Least Auklets on the Pribilof Islands, Alaska. Condor 88:336–346.

Roby, D.D., K.L. Brink, and D.N. Nettleship. 1981. Measurements, chick meals and breeding distribution of Dovekies (Alle alle) in northwest Greenland. Arctic 34:241–248.

Roby, D.D., A.R. Place, and R.E. Ricklefs, 1986. Assimilation and deposition of wax esters in planktivorous seabirds. J. Exper. Zool. 238:29–41.

Rodgers, J.A., Jr. 1980. Little Blue Heron breeding behavior. Auk 97:371–384.

Rohwer, S.A. 1971. Molt and annual cycle of the Chuck-will's-widow, Caprimulgus carolinensis. Auk 88:485–519.

Rohwer, S.A. 1973. Significance of sympatry to behavior and evolution of Great Plains meadowlarks. Evolution 27:44–57.

Rohwer, S.A. 1977. Status signalling in Harris Sparrows: some experiments in deception. Behaviour 61:107–129.

Rohwer, S.A. 1985. Dyed birds achieve higher social status than controls in Harris' Sparrows. Anim. Behav. 33:1325–1331.

Rohwer, S.A., and P.W. Ewald. 1981. The cost of dominance and advantage of subordination in a badge signalling system. Evolution 35:441–454.

Rohwer, S.A., and F.C. Rohwer. 1978. Status signalling in Harris' Sparrows: experimental deceptions achieved. Anim. Behav. 26:1012–1022.

Root, R.B. 1967. The niche exploitation pattern of the Blue-gray Gnatcatcher. Ecol. Monogr. 37:317–350.

Roper, T. 1986. Badges of status in avian societies. New Scientist, 6 February, pp. 38–40.

Roseberry, J.L., and W.D. Klimstra. 1970. The nesting ecology and reproductive performance of the Eastern Meadowlark. Wilson Bull. 82:243–267.

Roseberry, J.L., and W.D. Klimstra. 1984. Population Ecology of the Bobwhite. Southern Illinois Univ. Press, Carbondale, IL.

Rosene, W. 1969. The Bobwhite Quail: It's Life and Management. Rutgers Univ. Press, New Brunswick, NJ.

Rotenberry, J.T. 1985. Physiognomy or floristics? Oecologia 67:213–217.

Rothstein, S.I. 1971. Observation and experiment in the analysis of interactions between brood parasites and their hosts. Amer. Nat. 105:71–74.

Rothstein, S.I. 1975a. Evolutionary rates and host defenses against avian brood parasitism. Amer. Nat. 109:161–176.

Rothstein, S.I. 1975b. An experimental and teleonomic investigation of avian brood parasitism. Condor 77:250–271.

Rothstein, S.I. 1976a. Cowbird parasitism of the Cedar Waxwing and its evolutionary implications. Auk 93:498–509.

Rothstein, S.I. 1976b. Experiments on defenses Cedar Waxwings use against cowbird parasitism. Auk 93:675–691.

Rudolph, S.G. 1982. Foraging strategies of American Kestrels during breeding. Ecology 63:1268–1276.

Rueppell, G. 1977. Bird Flight. Van Nostrand and Reinhold, New York.

Rummel, L., and C. Goetzinger. 1978. Aggressive display in the Common Loon. Auk 95:183–186.

Rundle, W. D. 1982. A case for esophageal analysis in shorebird food studies. J. Field Ornithol. 53:249–257.

Rundle, W.D., and M.W. Sayre. 1983. Feeding ecology of migrant Soras in southeastern Missouri. J. Wildl. Manage. 47:1153–1159.

Runnels, S.R. 1975. Rose-throated Becard in Jeff Davis County, Texas. Condor 77:221.

Rusch D.H., and P.D. Doerr. 1972. Broad-winged Hawk nesting and food habits. Auk 89:139–145.

Rusterholz, K.A., and R.W. Howe. 1979. Species-area relations of birds on small islands in a Minnesota lake. Evolution 33:468–477.

Rutter, R.J. 1969. A contribution to the biology of the Gray Jay (*Perisoreus canadensis*). Can. Field-Nat. 83:300–316.

Ryan, M.R. 1981. Evasive behavior of American Coots to kleptoparasitism by waterfowl. Wilson Bull. 93:274–275.

Ryan, M.R., and J.J. Dinsmore. 1979. A quantitative study of the behavior of breeding American Coots. Auk 96:704–713.

Ryan, M.R., and J.J. Dinsmore. 1980. The behavioral ecology of breeding American Coots in relation to age. Condor 82:320–327.

Ryan, M.R., and R.B. Renken. 1987. Habitat use by breeding Willets in the northern Great Plains. Wilson Bull. 99:175–189.

Ryan, M.R., R.B. Renken, and J.J. Dinsmore. 1984. Marbled Godwit habitat selection in the northern prairie region. J. Wildl. Manage. 48:1206–1218.

Ryder, R.A. 1967. Distribution, migration, and mortality of the White-faced Ibis (*Plegadis chihi*) in North America. Bird-Banding 38:257–277.

Salomonson, M.G., and R.P. Balda. 1977. Winter territoriality of Townsend's Solitaires (*Myadestes townsendi*) in a Pinon-Juniper-Ponderosa Pine ecotone. Condor 79:148–161.

Salt, G.W., and D.E. Willard. 1971. The hunting behavior and success of Forster's Tern. Ecology 52:989–998.

Salwasser, H. 1986. Conserving a regional Spotted Owl population. *In* National Research Council (eds.), Ecological Knowledge and Environmental Problem-Solving, Concepts and Case Studies. National Academy Press, Washington, DC, pp. 227–247.

Samson, F.B. 1976. Territory, breeding density, and fall departure in Cassin's Finch. Auk 93:477–497.

Sanderson, G.C., and F.C. Bellrose. 1986. A review of the problem of lead poisoning in waterfowl. Illinois Natural History Survey, Special Publication No. 4.

Sanger, G.A. 1987. Winter diets of Common Murres and Marbled Murrelets in Kachemak Bay, Alaska. Condor 89:426–430.

Savard, J-P.L. 1982. Intra- and inter-specific competition between Barrow's Goldeneye (*Bucephala islandica*) and Bufflehead (*Bucephala albeola*). Can. J. Zool. 60:3439–3446.

Savard, J-P.L. 1985. Evidence of long-term pair bonds in Barrow's Goldeneye (*Bucephala islandica*). Auk 102:389–391.

Savard, J-P.L. 1986. Polygyny in Barrow's Goldeneye. Condor 88:250–252.

Schaeffer, F.S. 1973. Tactile bristles of Saw-whet Owls are sensitive to touch. Bird-Banding 44:125.

Schaffner, F.C. 1986. Trends in Elegant Tern and northern anchovy populations in California. Condor 88:347–354.

Schamel, D. 1977. Breeding of the Common Eider (*Somateria mollissima*) on the Beaufort Sea Coast of Alaska. Condor 79:478–485.

Schamel, D., and D. Tracy. 1977. Polyandry, replacement clutches, and site tenacity in the Red Phalarope (*Phalaropus fulicaria*) at Barrow, Alaska. Bird-Banding 48:314–324.

Schardien, B.J., and J.A. Jackson. 1979. Belly-soaking as a thermoregulatory mechanism in nesting Killdeers. Auk 96:604–606.

Scheid, P. 1982. Respiration and control of breathing. *In* D.S. Farner and J.R. King (eds.), Avian Biology, vol. 6. Academic Press, New York, pp. 406–454.

Schmutz, J.K., and R.W. Fyfe. 1987. Migration and mortality of Alberta Ferruginous Hawks. Condor 89:169–174.

Schneider, K.J. 1984. Dominance, predation, and optimal foraging in White-throated Sparrow flocks. Ecology 65:1820–1827.

Schnell, G.D., and J.J. Hellack. 1978. Flight speeds of Brown Pelicans, Chimney Swifts, and other birds. Bird-Banding 49:109–112.

Schnell, G.D., and J.J. Hellack. 1979. Bird flight speeds in nature: optimized or a compromise? Amer. Nat. 113:53–66.

Schorger, A.W. 1955. The Passenger Pigeon: Its Natural History and Extinction. Univ. Oklahoma Press, Norman.

Schreiber, E.A., and R.W. Schreiber. 1980. Breeding biology of Laughing Gulls in Florida. Part II: Nestling parameters. J. Field Ornithol. 51:340–355.

Schreiber, R.W. 1977. Maintenance Behavior and Communication in the Brown Pelican. Ornithol. Monogr. No. 22.

Schreiber, R.W. 1980. The Brown Pelican: an endangered species? BioScience 30:742–747.

Scott, D. 1977. Breeding behaviour of the wild Whistling Swans. Wildfowl 28:101–106.

Scott, D.M., and C.D. Ankney. 1983. The laying cycle of Brown-headed Cowbirds: passerine chickens? Auk 100:583–592.

Scott, T.G. 1985. Bobwhite Thesaurus. International Quail Foundation, Edgefield, SC.

Sealy, S.G. 1975a. Feeding ecology of the Ancient and Marbled Murrelets near Langara Island, British Columbia. Can. J. Zool. 53:418–433.

Sealy, S.G. 1975b. Aspects of the breeding biology of the Marbled Murrelet in British Columbia. Bird-Banding 46:141–154.

Sealy, S.G. 1976. Biology of nesting Ancient Murrelets. Condor 78:294–306.

Sealy, S.G. 1978. Possible influence of food on egg-laying and clutch size in the Black-billed Cuckoo. Condor 80:103–104.

Sealy, S.G. 1980a. Breeding biology of Orchard Orioles in a new population in Manitoba. Can. Field-Nat. 94:154–158.

Sealy, S.G. 1980b. Reproductive responses of Northern Orioles to a changing food supply. Can. J. Zool. 58:221–227.

Sealy, S.G. 1984. Interruptions extend incubation by Ancient Murrelets, Crested Auklets, and Least Auklets. Murrelet 65:53–56.

Sealy, S.G. 1985. Erect posture of the young Black-billed Cuckoo: an adaptation for early mobility in a nomadic species. Auk 102:889–892.

Sealy, S.G., and J. Bédard. 1973. Breeding biology of the Parakeet Auklet (*Cyclorhynchus psittacula*) on St. Lawrence Island, Alaska. Astarte 6:59–68.

Searcy, W.A. 1984. Song repertoire size and female preferences in Song Sparrows. Behav. Ecol. Sociobiol. 14:281–286.

Sears, H.F. 1978. Nesting behavior of the Gull-billed Tern. Bird-Banding 49:1–16.

Sears, H.F. 1981. The display behavior of the Gull-billed Tern. J. Field Ornithol. 52:191–209.

Seastedt, T.R., and S.F. MacLean, Jr. 1979. Territory size and composition in relation to resource abundance in Lapland Longspurs breeding in arctic Alaska. Auk 96:131–142.

Semel, B., and P.W. Sherman. 1986. Dynamics of nest parasitism in Wood Ducks. Auk 103:813–816.

Seutin, G. 1987. Female song in Willow Flycatchers (Empidonax traillii). Auk 104:329–330.

Seymour, N.R., and R.D. Titman. 1978. Changes in activity patterns, agonistic behavior, and territoriality of Black Ducks (Anas rubripes) during the breeding season in a Nova Scotia tidal marsh. Can. J. Zool. 56:1773–1785.

Shaffer, M.L. 1981. Minimum population sizes for species conservation. BioScience 31:131–134.

Shedd, D.H. 1985. A propensity to mob. Living Bird 4:8–11.

Sheldon, W.G. 1967. The Book of the American Woodcock. Univ. Massachusetts Press, Amherst, MA.

Sheppard, J.M. 1970. A study of the Le Conte's Thrasher. California Birds 1:85–95.

Sherry, D.F., J.R. Krebs, and R.J. Cowie. 1981. Memory for the location of stored food in Marsh Tits. Anim. Behav. 29:1260–1266.

Sherry, T.W. 1979. Competitive interactions and adaptive strategies of American Redstarts and Least Flycatchers in a northern hardwoods forest. Auk 96:265–283.

Shettleworth, S.J. 1983. Memory in food-hoarding birds. Sci. Amer. 248:102–110.

Shields, W.M. 1984. Factors affecting nest and site fidelity in Adirondack Barn Swallows (Hirundo rustica). Auk 101:780–789.

Short, L.L. 1982. Woodpeckers of the World. Delaware Museum Natural History, Greenville.

Short, L.L. 1985. Last chance for the Ivorybill. Natural History, August, pp. 66–68.

Short, L.L., and J.F.M. Horne. 1986. The Ivorybill still lives. Natural History, July, pp. 26–28.

Shreeve, D.F. 1980. Behaviour of the Aleutian Grey-crowned and Brown-capped Rosy Finches Leucosticte tephrocotis. Ibis 122:145–165.

Shy, E. 1984a. The structure of song and its geographical variation in the Scarlet Tanager (Piranga olivacea). Amer. Midl. Nat. 112:119–130.

Shy, E. 1984b. Habitat shift and geographical variation in North American tanagers (Thraupinae: Piranga). Oecologia 63:281–285.

Sibley, C.G., and J.E. Ahlquist. 1984a. The classification of the passerine birds of North and Central America. Connecticut Warbler 4:50–56.

Sibley, C.G., and J.E. Ahlquist. 1984b. The relationships of the Wrentit as indicated by DNA-DNA hybridization. Condor 84:40–44.

Sibley, C.G., and J.E. Ahlquist. 1985. The phylogeny and classification of the Australo-Papuan passerine birds. Emu 85:1–14.

Sibley, C.G., and J.E. Ahlquist. 1986. Reconstructing bird phylogeny by comparing DNA's. Sci. Amer., February, pp. 82–92.

Sibley, S.C. 1985. Peregrine Falcon. Living Bird 4:25

Sidle, J.G. 1986. Wanted: Dakota ducks. Living Bird 5:6–11.

Sidle, J.G., W.H. Koonz, and K. Roney. 1985. Status of the American White Pelican: an update. Amer. Birds 39:859–864.

Sieber, O. 1980. Causal and functional aspects of brood distribution in Sand Martins (Riparia riparia L.). Zeit. Tierpsychol. 52:19–56.

Siegel-Causey, D., and G.L. Hunt, Jr. 1981. Colonial defense behavior in Double-crested and Pelagic Cormorants. Auk 98:522–531.

Siegfried, W.R. 1976. Social organization in Ruddy and Maccoa Ducks. Auk 93:560–570.

Siegfried, W.R., and B.D.J. Batt. 1972. Wilson's Phalaropes forming associations with Shovelers. Auk 89:667–668.

Siegfried, W.R., and L.G. Underhill. 1975. Flocking as an antipredator strategy in doves. Anim. Behav. 23:504–508.

Simberloff, D. 1983. Biogeography: the unification and maturation of a science. *In* A.H. Brush and G.A. Clark, Jr. (eds.), Perspectives in Ornithology. Cambridge Univ. Press, Cambridge, pp. 411–455.

Simmons, K.E.L. 1966. Anting and the problem of self-stimulation. J. Zool. London 149:145–162.

Simmons, K.E.L. 1986. The Sunning Behaviour of Birds. Bristol Ornithological Club, Bristol.

Simons, T.R. 1981. Behavior and attendance patterns of the Fork-tailed Storm-Petrel. Auk 98:145–158.

Simpson, B.S. 1985. Effects of location in territory and distance from neighbors on the use of repertoires by Carolina Wrens. Anim. Behav. 33:793–804.

Sjolander, S., and G. Agren. 1976. Reproductive behavior of the Yellow-billed Loon, *Gavia adamsii*. Condor 78:454–463.

Skagen, S.K. 1987. Hatching asynchrony in American Goldfinches: an experimental study. Ecology 68:1747–1759.

Skeel, M.A. 1983. Nesting success, density, philopatry, and nest-site selection of the Whimbrel *(Numenius phaeopus)* in different habitats. Can. J. Zool. 61:218–225.

Skipnes, K. 1983. Incubation behaviour of the Arctic Tern *Sterna paradisaea*, in relation to time of day and stage of incubation. Ardea 41:211–215.

Skorupa, J.P., R.L. Hothem, and R.W. DeHaven. 1980. Foods of breeding Tricolored Blackbirds in agricultural areas of Merced County, California. Condor 82:465–467.

Skutch, A.F. 1954. Life Histories of Central American Birds. Pacific Coast Avifauna No. 31, Cooper Ornithological Society, Berkeley, CA.

Skutch, A.F. 1960. Life Histories of Central American Birds. II. Pacific Coast Avifauna No. 34, Cooper Ornithological Society, Berkeley, CA.

Skutch, A.F. 1969. Life Histories of Central American Birds. III. Pacific Coast Avifauna No. 35, Cooper Ornithological Society, Berkeley, CA.

Skutch, A.F. 1973. The Life of the Hummingbird. Crown, New York.

Skutch, A.F. 1976. Parent Birds and Their Young. Univ. Texas Press, Austin, TX.

Skutch, A.F. 1987. Helpers at Birds' Nests: A Worldwide Survey of Cooperative Breeding and Related Behavior. Univ. Iowa Press, Iowa City.

Slagsvold, T. 1982. Clutch size variation in passerine birds: the nest predation hypothesis. Oecologia 54:159–169.

Slater, P.J.B. 1986. The cultural transmission of bird song. Trends in Ecology and Evolution 1:94–97.

Slessers, M. 1970. Bathing behavior of land birds. Auk 87:91–99.

Smith, D.G., A. Devine, and D. Gendron. 1982. An observation of copulation and allopreening of a pair of Whiskered Owls. J. Field Ornithol. 53:51–52.

Smith, D.G., and R. Gilbert. 1984. Eastern Screech-Owl home range and use of suburban habitats in southern Connecticut. J. Field Ornithol. 55:322–329.

Smith, D.G., J.R. Murphy, and N.D. Woffindin. 1981. Relationships between jackrabbit abundance and Ferruginous Hawk reproduction. Condor 83:52–56.

Smith, J.I. 1987. Evidence of hybridization between Red-bellied and Golden-fronted Woodpeckers. Condor 89:377–386.

Smith, J.N.M. 1977. Feeding rates, search paths, and surveillance for predators in Great-tailed Grackle flocks. Can. J. Zool. 55:891–898.

Smith, J.N.M., and J.R. Merkt. 1980. Development and stability of single-parent family units in the Song Sparrow. Can. J. Zool. 58:1869–1875.

Smith, J.N.M., Y. Yom-Tov, and R. Moses. 1982. Polygyny, male parental care, and sex ratio in Song Sparrows: an experimental study. Auk 99:555–564.

Smith, K.G., and D.C. Andersen. 1982. Food, predation, and reproductive ecology of the Dark-eyed Junco in northern Utah. Auk 99:650–661.

Smith, L.M., Vangilder, L.D., and R.A. Kennamer. 1985. Foods of wintering Brant in eastern North America. J. Field Ornithol. 56:286–288.

Smith, M. 1986. From a strike to a kill. New Scientist, 29 May, pp. 44–47.

Smith, N.G. 1966. Evolution of Some Arctic Gulls (*Larus*): An Experimental Study of Isolating Mechanisms. Ornithol. Monogr. No. 40.

Smith, P.C., and P.R. Evans. 1973. Studies of shorebirds at Lindisfarne, Northumberland. I. Feeding ecology and behaviour of the Bar-tailed Godwit. Wildfowl 24:135–139.

Smith, S.A., and R.A. Paselk. 1986. Olfactory sensitivity of the Turkey Vulture (*Cathartes aura*) to three carrion-associated odorants. Auk 103:586–592.

Smith, S.M. 1973. An aggressive display and related behavior in the Loggerhead Shrike. Auk 90:287–298.

Smith, S.M. 1984. Flock switching in chickadees: why be a winter floater? Amer. Nat. 123:81–98.

Smith, T.B., and S.A. Temple. 1982a. Feeding habits and bill polymorphism in Hook-billed Kites. Auk 99:197–207.

Smith, T.B., and S.A. Temple. 1982b. Grenada Hook-billed Kites: recent status and life history notes. Condor 84:131.

Smith, T.M. and H.H. Shugart. 1987. Territory size variation in the Ovenbird: the role of habitat structure. Ecology 68:695–704.

Smith, W.J. 1970. Courtship and territorial display in the Vermilion Flycatcher, *Pyrocephalus rubinus*. Condor 72:488–491.

Smith, W.J., J. Pawlukiewicz, and S.T. Smith. 1978. Kinds of activities correlated with singing patterns of the Yellow-throated Vireo. Anim. Behav. 26:862–884.

Snapp, B.D. 1976. Colonial breeding in the Barn Swallow (*Hirundo rustica*) and its adaptive significance. Condor 78:471–480.

Snow, D.W. 1981. Coevolution of birds and plants. *In* P.L. Forey (ed.), The Evolving Biosphere. British Museum (Natural History), London, pp. 169–178.

Snyder, A.W., and W.H. Miller. 1978. Telephoto lens system of falconiform eyes. Nature 275:127–129.

Snyder, N.F.R. 1974. Breeding biology of Swallow-tailed Kites in Florida. Living Bird 13:73–97.

Snyder, N.F.R., and J.A. Hamber. 1985. Replacement-clutching and annual nesting of California Condors. Condor 87:374–378.

Snyder, N.F.R., R.R. Ramey, and F.C. Sibley. 1986. Nest-site biology of the California Condor. Condor 88:228–241.

Snyder, N.F.R., and H.A. Snyder. 1969. A comparative study of mollusc predation by Limpkins, Everglade Kites and Boat-tailed Grackles. Living Bird 8:177–223.

Snyder, W.D. 1984. Ring-necked Pheasant nesting ecology and wheat farming on the high plains. J. Wildl. Manage. 48:878–888.

Soikkeli, M. 1970. Mortality and reproductive rates in a Finnish population of Dunlin *Calidris alpina*. Ornis Fenn. 47:149–158.

Solheim, R. 1983. Bigyny and biandry in the Tengmalm's Owl, *Aegolius funereus*. Ornis Scand. 14:51–57.

Sordahl, T.A. 1979. Vocalizations and behavior of the Willet. Wilson Bull. 91:551—574.

Soulé, M.E. (ed.). 1986. Conservation Biology: The Science of Scarcity and Diversity. Sinauer Associates, Sunderland, MA.

Soulé, M.E., and B.A. Wilcox (eds.). 1980. Conservation Biology: An Evolutionary-Ecological Approach. Sinauer Associates, Sunderland, MA.

Southern, W.E., S.R. Patton, L.K. Southern, and L.A. Hanners. 1985. Effects of nine years of fox predation on two species of breeding gulls. Auk 102:827–833.

Spear, L.B., D.G. Ainley, and R.P. Henderson. 1986. Post-fledging parental care in the Western Gull. Condor 88:194–199.

Spear, L.B., T.M. Penniman, J.F. Penniman, H.R. Carter, and D.G. Ainley. 1987. Survivorship and mortality factors in a population of Western Gulls. Studies in Avian Biol. 10:44–56.

Speiser, R. and T. Bosakowski. 1987. Nest site selection by Northern Goshawks in northern New Jersey and southeastern New York. Condor 89:387–394.

Spencer, H.E., Jr. 1986. Black Duck. *In* R.L. Di Silvestro (ed.), Audubon Wildlife Report 1986, National Audubon Soc., NY, pp. 855–869.

Spitzer, P.R., R.W. Risebrough, W. Walker, R. Hernandez, A. Poole, D. Puleston, and I.C.T. Nisbet. 1978. Productivity of Ospreys in Connecticut–Long Island increases as DDE residues decline. Science 202:333–335.

Squibb, R.C., and G.L. Hunt, Jr. 1983. A comparison of nesting-edges used by seabirds on St. George Island. Ecology 64:727–734.

Stacey, P.B., and C.E. Bock. 1978. Social plasticity in the Acorn Woodpecker. Science 202:1298–1300.

Stacey, P.B., and W.D. Koenig. 1984. Cooperative breeding in the Acorn Woodpecker. Sci. Amer., August, pp. 114–121.

Stager, K.E. 1964. The role of olfaction in food location by the Turkey Vulture *(Cathartes aura)*. Los Angeles County Mus. Contrib. Sci. 81:1–63.

Steenhof, K., M.N. Kochert, and J.H. Doremus. 1983. Nesting of subadult Golden Eagles in southwestern Idaho. Auk 100:743–747.

Stein, R.C. 1963. Isolating mechanisms between populations of Traill's Flycatchers. Proc. Amer. Phil. Soc. 107:21–50.

Stempniewicz, L. 1983. Hunting methods of the Glaucous Gull and escape maneuvers of its prey, the Dovekie. J. Field Ornithol. 54:329–331.

Stephens, D.W., and J.R. Krebs. 1986. Foraging Theory. Princeton Univ. Press, Princeton, NJ.

Stephens, M.L. 1984. Interspecific aggressive behavior of the polyandrous Northern Jacana *(Jacana spinosa)*. Auk 101:508–518.

Stevenson, H.M. 1972. The recent history of Bachman's Warbler. Wilson Bull. 84:344–347.

Stevenson, H.M., E. Eisenmann, C. Winegarner, and A. Karlin. 1983. Notes on Common and Antillean Nighthawks of the Florida Keys. Auk 100:983–988.

Stewart, G.R., and R.D. Titman. 1980. Territorial behaviour by prairie pothole Blue-winged Teal. Can. J. Zool. 58:639–649.

Stewart, R.E., and J.H. Manning. 1958. Distribution and ecology of Whistling Swans in the Chesapeake Bay region. Auk 75:203–212.

Stewart, R.M., R.P. Henderson, and K. Darling. 1977. Breeding ecology of the Wilson's Warbler in the high Sierra Nevada, California. Living Bird 16:83–102.

Stiehl, R.B. 1985. Brood chronology of the Common Raven. Wilson Bull. 97:78–87.

Stiles, F.G. 1972. Food supply and the annual cycle of the Anna Hummingbird. Univ. Calif. Publ. Zool. 97:1–109.

Stiles, F.G. 1982. Aggressive and courtship displays of the male Anna's Hummingbird. Condor 84:208–225.

Stinson, C.H. 1979. On the selective advantage of fratricide in raptors. Evolution 33:1219–1225.

Stonehouse, B. (ed.). 1975. The Biology of Penguins. Macmillan, London.

Storer, R.W. 1969. The behavior of the Horned Grebe in spring. Condor 71:180–205.

Storer, R.W. 1976. The behavior and relationships of the Least Grebe. Trans. San Diego Soc. Nat. Hist. 18:113–126.

Storer, R.W. 1987. The possible significance of large eyes in the Red-legged Kittiwake. Condor 89:192–194.

Storer, R.W., and G.L. Nuechterlein. 1985. An analysis of plumage and morphological characters of the two color forms of the Western Grebe (Aechmophorus). Auk 102:102–119.

Storey, A.E., and J. Lien. 1985. Development of the first North American colony of Manx Shearwaters. Auk 102:395–401.

Stresemann, E. 1975. Ornithology: From Aristotle to the Present. Harvard Univ. Press, Cambridge, MA.

Strom, D. 1986. Birdwatching with American Women. Norton, New York.

Studd, M.V., and R.J. Robertson. 1985a. Evidence for reliable badges of status in territorial Yellow Warblers (Dendroica petechia). Anim. Behav. 33:1102–1113.

Studd, M.V., and R.J. Robertson. 1985b. Sexual selection and variation in reproductive strategy in male Yellow Warblers (Dendroica petechia). Behav. Ecol. Sociobiol. 17:101–109.

Sugden, L.G. 1977. Horned Grebe breeding habitat in Saskatchewan Parklands. Can. Field-Nat. 91:372–376.

Sullivan, K.A. 1986. Influence of prey distribution on aggression in Ruddy Turnstones. Condor 88:376–378.

Suthers, H.B. 1978. Analysis of a resident flock of starlings. Bird-Banding 49:35–46.

Sutton, G.M., and D.F. Parmelee. 1955. The breeding of the Semipalmated Plover on Baffin Island. Bird-Banding 26:137–196.

Swanson, G.A., M.I. Meyer, and V.A. Adomaitis. 1985. Foods consumed by breeding Mallards on wetlands of south-central North Dakota. J. Wildl. Manage. 49:197–203.

Swennen, C. 1974. Observations on the effect of ejection of stomach oil by the fulmar Fulmarus glacialis on other birds. Ardea 62:111–117.

Sykes, P.W., Jr. 1983. Recent population trend of the Snail Kite in Florida and its relationship to water levels. J. Field Ornithol. 54:237–246.

Sykes, P.W., and H.W. Kale. 1974. Everglade Kite feeds on nonsnail prey. Auk 91:818–820.

Tamm, S. 1985. Breeding territory quality and agonistic behavior: effects of energy availability and intruder pressure in hummingbirds. Behav. Ecol. Sociobiol. 16:203–207.

Tasker, C.R., and J.A. Mills. 1981. A functional analysis of courtship feeding in the Red-billed Gull, Larus novaehollandiae scopulinus. Behaviour 77:221–241.

Tate, J., Jr. 1981. The Blue List for 1981: the first decade. Amer. Birds 35:3–10.

Tate, J., Jr., 1986. The Blue List for 1986. Amer. Birds 40:227–236.

Taylor, D.M., and C.D. Littlefield. 1986. Willow Flycatcher and Yellow Warbler response to cattle grazing. Amer. Birds 40:1169–1173.

Taylor, P.S. 1973. Breeding behavior of the Snowy Owl. Living Bird 12:137–154.

Taylor, W.K., and H. Hanson. 1970. Observations on the breeding biology of the Vermilion Flycatcher in Arizona. Wilson Bull. 82:315–319.

Teather, K.L. 1987. Intersexual differences in food consumption by hand-reared Great-tailed Grackle (*Quiscalus mexicanus*) nestlings. Auk 104:635–639.

Teather, K.L., and R.J. Robertson. 1986. Pair bonds and factors influencing the diversity of mating systems in Brown-headed Cowbirds. Condor 88:63–69.

Temeles, E.J. 1985. Sexual size dimorphism of bird-eating hawks: the effect of prey vulnerability. Amer. Nat. 125:485–499.

Temeles, E.J. 1986. Reversed sexual size dimorphism: effect on resource defense and foraging behaviors of nonbreeding Northern Harriers. Auk 103:70–78.

Temple, S.A. (ed.). 1978. Endangered Birds: Management Techniques for Preserving Threatened Species. Univ. Wisconsin Press, Madison.

Terborgh, J.W. 1980. The conservation status of neotropical migrants: present and future. *In* A. Keast and E.S. Morton (eds.), Migrant Birds in the Neotropics: Ecology, Behavior, Distribution, and Conservation. Smithsonian Institution Press, Washington, DC, pp. 21–30.

Terhivuo, J. 1977. Occurrence of strange objects in nests of the Wryneck, *Jynx torquilla*. Ornis Fenn. 54:66–72.

Terhivuo, J. 1983. Why does the Wryneck *Jynx torquilla* bring strange items to the nest? Ornis Fenn. 60:51–57.

Terres, J.K. 1980. The Audubon Society Encyclopedia of North American Birds. Knopf, New York.

Terrill, S.B., and R.D. Ohmart. 1984. Facultative extension of fall migration by Yellow-rumped Warblers (*Dendroica coronata*). Auk 101:427–438.

Theberge, J.B., and J.F. Bendell. 1980. Differences in survival and behaviour of Rock Ptarmigan (*Lagopus mutus*) chicks among years in Alaska. Can. J. Zool. 58:1638–1642.

Thompson, C.F. 1977. Experimental removal and replacement of territorial male Yellow-breasted Chats. Auk 94:107–113.

Thompson, C.F., and V. Nolan, Jr. 1973. Population biology of the Yellow-breasted Chat (*Icteria virens* L.) in southern Indiana. Ecol. Monogr. 43:145–171.

Thompson, J.N. 1982. Interaction and Coevolution. Wiley, New York.

Thompson, S.C., and D.G. Raveling. 1987. Incubation behavior of Emperor Geese compared with other geese: interactions of predation, body size, and energetics. Auk 104:707–716.

Thompson, W.L. 1976. Vocalizations of the Lazuli Bunting. Condor 78:195–207.

Thomsen, L. 1971. Behavior and ecology of Burrowing Owls on the Oakland Municipal Airport. Condor 73:177–192.

Thoresen, A.C. 1983. Diurnal activity and social displays of Rhinoceros Auklets on Teuri Island, Japan. Condor 85:373–375.

Threlfall, W. 1985. Stacked on a cliff. Int. Wildlife 15:40–43.

Threlfall, W., and J.R. Blacquiere. 1982. Breeding biology of the Fox Sparrow in Newfoundland. J. Field Ornithol. 53:235–239.

Tinbergen, N. 1953. The Herring Gull's World. Collins, London.

Tinbergen, N. 1963. The shell menace. Natural History 72:28–35.

Tinbergen, N., M. Impekoven, and D. Franck. 1967. An experiment in spacing-out as a defense against predation. Behaviour 28:307–321.

Tinbergen, N., and M. Norton-Griffiths. 1964. Oystercatchers and mussels. Brit. Birds 57:64–70.

Toft, C.A., D.L. Trauger, and H.W. Murdy. 1982. Tests for species interactions: breeding phenology and habitat use in subarctic ducks. Amer. Nat. 120:586–613.

Toland, B.R. 1985. Double brooding by American Kestrels in central Missouri. Condor 87:434–436.

Tomback, D.F. 1980. How nutcrackers find their seed stores. Condor 82:10–19.

Trauger, D.L. 1974. Eye color of female Lesser Scaup in relation to age. Auk 91:243–254.

Tremblay, J., and L.N. Ellison. 1980. Breeding success of the Black-crowned Night Heron in the St. Lawrence Estuary. Can. J. Zool. 58:1259–1263.

Trivelpiece, W.Z., and J.D. Ferraris. 1987. Notes on the behavioural ecology of the Magnificent Frigatebird *Fregata magnificens*. Ibis 129:168–174.

Troy, D.M. 1983. Recaptures of redpolls: movements of an irruptive species. J. Field Ornithol. 54:146–151.

Truslow, F.K. 1967. Egg-carrying by the Pileated Woodpecker. Living Bird 6:227–235.

Tuck, L.M. 1972. The Snipes: A Study of the Genus *Capella*. Can. Wildl. Serv. Monogr. Ser. No. 5, Ottawa.

Tudge, C. 1986. Natural niches in artificial worlds. New Scientist, 9 October, p. 57.

Turner, J.C., Jr., and L. McClanahan, Jr. 1981. Physiogenesis of endothermy and its relation to growth in the Great Horned Owl *(Bubo virginianus)*. Comp. Biochem. Physiol. 68A:167–173.

Turner, J.L. 1985. The deadly wild-bird trade. Defenders 60:20–29.

Tyrrell, E.Q., and R.A. Tyrrell. 1984. Hummingbirds: Their Life and Behavior. Crown, New York.

Ulfstrand, S. 1979. Age and plumage associated differences of behavior among Black-headed Gulls *Larus ridibundus:* foraging success, conflict, victoriousness and reaction to disturbance. Oikos 33:160–166.

U.S. Fish and Wildlife Service and U.S. Bureau of the Census. 1980. National Survey of Fishing, Hunting, and Wildlife-Associated Recreation. Washington, DC.

Van Camp, L.F., and C.J. Henny. 1975. The Screech Owl: Its Life History and Population Ecology in Northern Ohio. North Amer. Fauna No. 71, U.S. Dept. Int., Fish and Wildl. Serv., Washington, DC.

Vance, D.R., and R.L. Westemeier. 1979. Interactions of pheasants and Prairie Chickens in Illinois. Wildl. Soc. Bull. 7:221–225.

Van Daele, L.J., and H.A. Van Daele. 1982. Factors affecting the productivity of Ospreys nesting in west-central Idaho. Condor 84:292–299.

Vander Wall, S.B. 1982. An experimental analysis of cache recovery in Clark's Nutcracker. Anim. Behav. 30:84–94.

Vander Wall, S.B., and R.P. Balda. 1977. Coadaptations of the Clark's Nutcracker and the piñon pine for efficient seed harvest and dispersal. Ecol. Monogr. 47:89–111.

Vander Wall, S.B., and R.P. Balda. 1981. Ecology and evolution of food-storage behavior in conifer-seed-caching corvids. Zeit. Tierpsychol. 56:217–242.

Van Wormer, J. 1972. The World of the Swan. J.B. Lippincott, New York.

Veen, J. 1980. Breeding behaviour and breeding success of a colony of Little Gulls *Larus minutus* in the Netherlands. Limosa 53:73–83.

Vehrencamp, S.L. 1977. Relative fecundity and parental effort in communally nesting anis, *Crotophaga sulcirostris*. Science 197:403–405.

Vehrencamp, S.L. 1978. The adaptive significance of communal nesting in Groove-billed Anis *(Crotophaga sulcirostris)*. Behav. Ecol. Sociobiol. 4:1–33.

Vehrencamp, S.L. 1982. Body temperatures of incubating versus non-incubating Roadrunners. Condor 84:203–207.

Verbeek, N.A.M. 1970. Breeding ecology of the Water Pipit. Auk 87:425–451.

Verbeek, N.A.M. 1973. The exploitation system of the Yellow-billed Magpie. Univ. California Publ. Zool. No. 99.

Verbeek, N.A.M. 1975a. Northern wintering of flycatchers and residency of Black Phoebes in California. Auk 92:737–749.

Verbeek, N.A.M. 1975b. Comparative feeding behavior of three coexisting tyrannid flycatchers. Wilson Bull. 87:231–240.

Verbeek, N.A.M. 1979. Some aspects of the breeding biology and behavior of the Great Black-backed Gull. Wilson Bull. 91:575–582.

Verbeek, N.A.M. 1986. Aspects of the breeding biology of an expanded population of Glaucous-winged Gulls in British Columbia. J. Field Ornithol. 57:22–33.

Verbeek, N.A.M., and R.W. Butler. 1981. Cooperative breeding of the Northwestern Crow *Corvus caurinus* in British Columbia. Ibis 123:183–189.

Vermeer, K. 1979. Nesting requirements, food and breeding distribution of Rhinoceros Auklets *(Cerorhinca monocerata)* and Tufted Puffins *(Lunda cirrhata)*. Ardea 67:101–110.

Vermeer, K. 1984. The diet and food consumption of nestling Cassin's Auklets during summer, and a comparison with other plankton-feeding alcids. Murrelet 65:65–77.

Vermeer, K., and L. Cullen. 1979. Growth of Rhinoceros Auklets and Tufted Puffins, Triangle Islands, British Columbia. Ardea 67:22–27.

Vermeer, K., and K. DeVito. 1986. The nesting biology of Mew Gulls *(Larus canus)* on Kennedy Lake, British Columbia, Canada: comparison with Mew Gulls in northern Europe. Colonial Waterbirds 9:95–103.

Vermeer, K., and K. Devito. 1987. Habitat and nest-site selection of Mew and Glaucous-winged Gulls in coastal British Columbia. Studies in Avian Biol. 10:105–118.

Vermeer, K., and L. Rankin. 1984. Population trends in nesting Double-crested and Pelagic Cormorants in Canada. Murrelet 65:1–9.

Vermeer, K., R.A. Vermeer, K.S. Summers, and R.R. Billings. 1979. Numbers and habitat selection of Cassin's Auklet breeding on Temple Island, British Columbia. Auk 96:143–151.

Verner, J. 1964. Evolution of polygamy in the Long-billed Marsh Wren. Evolution 18:252–261.

Verner, J. 1965. Breeding biology of the Long-billed Marsh Wren. Condor 67:6–30.

Verner, J., and M.F. Willson. 1966. The influence of habitats on mating systems of North American passerine birds. Ecology 47:143–147.

Vitousek, P.M., P.R. Ehrlich, A.H. Ehrlich, and P.A. Matson. 1986. Human appropriation of the products of photosynthesis. BioScience 36:368–373.

Vleck, C.M., and G.J. Kenagy. 1980. Embryonic metabolism of the Fork-tailed Storm Petrel: physiological patterns during prolonged and interrupted incubation. Physiol. Zool. 53:32–42.

Wagner, J.L. 1981. Seasonal change in guild structure: oak woodland insectivorous birds. Ecology 62:973–981.

Wagner, J.L. 1984. Post-breeding avifauna and mixed insectivorous flocks in a Colorado spruce-fir forest. Western Birds 15:81–84.

Waite, T.A. 1987a. Vigilance in the White-breasted Nuthatch: effects of dominance and sociality. Auk 104:429–434.

Waite, T.A. 1987b. Dominance-specific vigilance in the Tufted Titmouse: effects of social context. Condor 89:932–935.

Waite, T.A., and T.C. Grubb, Jr. 1987. Dominance, foraging and predation risk in the Tufted Titmouse. Condor 89:936–940.

Walcott, C., and A.J. Lednor. 1983. Bird navigation. *In* A.H. Brush and G.A. Clark, Jr. (eds.), Perspectives in Ornithology. Cambridge Univ. Press, Cambridge, pp. 513–542.

Walkinshaw, L.H. 1966a. Summer observations of the Least Flycatcher in Michigan. Jack-Pine Warbler 44:151–168.

Walkinshaw, L.H. 1966b. Studies of the Acadian Flycatcher in Michigan. Bird-Banding 37:227–257.

Walkinshaw, L.H. 1967. The Yellow-bellied Flycatcher in Michigan. Jack-Pine Warbler 45:2–9.

Walkinshaw, L.H. 1983. Kirtland's Warbler: The Natural History of an Endangered Species. Cranbrook Institute of Science, Bloomfield Hills, MI.

Walkinshaw, L.H., and C.J. Henry. 1957. Yellow-bellied Flycatcher nesting in Michigan. Auk 74:293–304.

Walsberg, G.E. 1977. Ecology and energetics of contrasting social systems in *Phainopepla nitens* (Aves: Ptilogonatidae). Univ. Calif. Publ. Zool. 108:1–63.

Walsberg, G.E. 1982. Coat color, solar heat gain, and conspicuousness in the *Phainopepla*. Auk 99:495–502.

Walsberg, G.E. 1983. Avian ecological energetics. *In* D.S. Farner and J. R. King (eds.), Avian Biology, Vol. 7. Academic Press, New York, pp. 161–220.

Walsberg, G.E., G.S. Campbell, and J.R. King. 1978. Animal coat color and radiative heat gain: a re-evaluation. J. Comp. Physiol. 126:211–222.

Wander, W. 1985. Sharing the shore. Living Bird 4:12–19.

Ward, P., and A. Zahavi. 1973. The importance of certain assemblages of birds as "information-centres" for food-finding. Ibis 115:517–534.

Warham, J. 1983. The composition of petrel eggs. Condor 85:194–199.

Warner, J.S., and R.L. Rudd. 1975. Hunting by the White-tailed Kite (*Elanus leucurus*). Condor 77:226–230.

Warriner, J.S., J.C. Warriner, G.W. Page, and L.E. Stenzel. 1986. Mating system and reproductive success of a small population of polygamous Snowy Plovers. Wilson Bull. 98:15–37.

Waser, N.M. 1976. Food supply and nest timing of Broad-tailed Hummingbirds in the Rocky Mountains. Condor 78:133–135.

Watanuki, Y. 1986. Moonlight avoidance behavior in Leach's Storm-Petrels as a defense against Slaty-backed Gulls. Auk 103:14–22.

Watson, A. 1967. Population control by territorial behavior in Red Grouse. Nature 215:1274–1275.

Watt, D.J. 1986. Relationship of plumage variability, size, and sex to social dominance in Harris' Sparrows. Anim. Behav. 34:16–27.

Watt, D.J., and D.W. Mock. 1987. A selfish herd of martins. Auk 104:342–343.

Waver, R.H. 1973. Birds of Big Bend National Park and Vicinity. Univ. Texas Press, Austin.

Weatherhead, P.J. 1979. Ecological correlates of monogamy in tundra-breeding Savannah Sparrows. Auk 96:391–401.

Weatherhead, P.J. 1985. The birds' communal connection. Natural History, February, pp. 34–40.

Weatherhead, P.J., and R.J. Robertson. 1978. Intraspecific nest parasitism in the Savannah Sparrow. Auk 95:744–745.

Weathers, W.W. 1983. Birds of Southern California's Deep Canyon. Univ. California Press, Berkeley.

Weber, W.J. 1975. Notes on Cattle Egret breeding. Auk 92:111–117.

Weeden, R.B. 1965. Further notes on Wandering Tattlers in central Alaska. Condor 67:87–89.

Weeden, R.B., and J.B. Theberge. 1972. The dynamics of a fluctuating population of Rock Ptarmigan in Alaska. Int. Ornithol. Congr. 15:90–106.

Weeks, H.P., Jr. 1978. Clutch size variation in the Eastern Phoebe in southern Indiana. Auk 95:656–666.

Wehle, D.H.S. 1983. The food, feeding, and development of young Tufted and Horned Puffins in Alaska. Condor 85:427–442.

Weigand, J.P. 1980. Ecology of the Hungarian Partridge in North-central Montana. Wildl. Monogr. No. 74.

Weisbrod, A.R., and W.F. Stevens. 1974. The Skylark in Washington. Auk 91:832–835.

Weise, C.M., and J.R. Meyer. 1979. Juvenile dispersal and development of site-fidelity in the Black-capped Chickadee. Auk 96:40–55.

Weller, M.W. 1971. Experimental parasitism of American Coot nests. Auk 88:108–115.

Welty, J.C., and L.F. Baptista. 1988. The Life of Birds, 4th edition. Saunders, Philadelphia, PA.

Wenzel, B.M. 1973. Chemoreception. In D.S. Farner and J.R. King (eds.), Avian Biology, Vol. 3. Academic Press, New York, pp. 389–416.

Werschkul, D.F. 1982. Nesting ecology of the Little Blue Heron: promiscuous behavior. Condor 84:381–384.

Westmoreland, D., L.B. Best, and D.E. Blockstein. 1986. Multiple brooding as a reproductive strategy: time-conserving adaptations in Mourning Doves. Auk 103:196–203.

Whaley, W.H. 1986. Population ecology of the Harris' Hawk in Arizona. Raptor Res. 20:1–15.

Wheelwright, N.T. 1986. The diet of American Robins: an analysis of U.S. Biological Survey records. Auk 103:710–725.

White, D.H., A.K. King, C.A. Mitchell, and A.J. Krynitsky. 1981. Body lipids and pesticide burdens of migrant Blue-winged Teal. J. Field Ornithol. 52:23–28.

White, D.H., C.A. Mitchell, and E. Cromartie. 1982. Nesting ecology of Roseate Spoonbills at Nueces Bay, Texas. Auk 99:275–284.

White, D.H., C.A. Mitchell, L.D. Wynn, E.L. Flickinger, and E.J. Kolbe. 1982. Organophosphate insecticide poisoning of Canada Geese in the Texas panhandle. J. Field Ornithol. 53:22–27.

White, F.N., and J.L. Kinney. 1974. Avian incubation. Science 186:107–115.

Whiteside, R.W., and F.S. Guthery. 1983. Ring-necked Pheasant movements, home ranges, and habitat use in west Texas. J. Wildl. Manage. 47:1097–1104.

Whitfield, D.P. 1987. Plumage variability, status signalling and individual recognition in avian flocks. Trends in Ecol. and Evol. 2:13–18.

Whitney, C.L., and J. Miller. 1987. Distribution and variability of song types in the Wood Thrush. Behaviour 103:49–67.

Whitson, M. 1975. Courtship behavior of the Greater Roadrunner. Living Bird 14:215–255.

Wickler, W. 1968. Mimicry in Plants and Animals. McGraw-Hill, New York.

Wiens, J.A. 1973. Interterritorial habitat variation in Grasshopper and Savannah Sparrows. Ecology 54:877–884.

Wiens, J.A. 1983. Avian community ecology: an iconoclastic view. In A.H. Brush and G.A. Clark, Jr. (eds.), Perspectives in Ornithology. Cambridge Univ. Press, Cambridge, pp. 355–403.

Wiens, J.A. 1985. Habitat selection in variable environments: shrub-steppe birds. In M.L. Cody (ed.), Habitat Selection in Birds. Academic Press, New York, pp. 227–251.

Wiens, J.A., and J.T. Rotenberry. 1981. Habitat associations and community structure of birds in shrubsteppe environments. Ecol. Monogr. 51:21–41.

Wiens, J.A., J.T. Rotenberry, and B. Van Horne. 1986. A lesson in the limitations of field experiments: shrubsteppe birds and habitat alteration. Ecology 67:365–376.

Wiggins, D.A., R.D. Morris, I.C.T. Nisbet, and T.W. Custer. 1984. Occurrence and timing of second clutches in Common Terns. Auk 101:281–287.

Wijnandts, H. 1984. Ecological energetics of the Long-eared Owl (Asio otus). Ardea 72:1–92.

Wilbur, S.R., and J.A. Jackson. 1983. Vulture Biology and Management. Univ. California Press, Berkeley.

Wilcove, D.S. 1985. Nest predation in forest tracts and the decline of migratory songbirds. Ecology 66:1211–1214.

Wilcove, D.S., and R.M. May. 1986. The fate of the California Condor. Nature 319:16

Wilcove, D.S., and J.W. Terborgh. 1984. Patterns of population decline in birds. Amer. Birds 38:10–13.

Wilcox, L. 1980. Observations of the life history of Willets on Long Island, New York. Wilson Bull. 92:253–258.

Wiley, J.W. 1975. The nesting and reproductive success of Red-tailed Hawks and Red-shouldered Hawks in Orange County, California, 1973. Condor 77:133–139.

Wiley, R.H. 1973. Territoriality and non-random mating in Sage Grouse, Centrocercus urophasianus. Anim. Behav. Monogr. 6:87–169.

Wiley, R.H. 1978. The lek mating system of the Sage Grouse. Sci. Amer. 238:114–125.

Wiley, R.H., and D.G. Richards. 1982. Adaptations for acoustic communication in birds: sound transmission and signal detection. In D.E. Kroodsma and E.H. Miller (eds.), Acoustic Communication in Birds, vol. 1. Academic Press, New York, pp. 131–181.

Williams, G.G. 1953. Wilson Phalaropes as commensals. Condor 55:158.

Williams, J.B. 1987. Field metabolism and food consumption of Savannah Sparrows during the breeding season. Auk 104:277–289.

Williamson, M. 1981. Island Populations. Oxford Univ. Press, Oxford.

Williamson, P. 1971. Feeding ecology of the Red-eyed Vireo (Vireo olivaceus) and associated foliage-gleaning birds. Ecol. Monogr. 41:129–152.

Willis, E.O. 1963. Is the Zone-tailed Hawk a mimic of the Turkey Vulture? Condor 65:313–317.

Willis, E.O., and Y. Oniki. 1978. Birds and army ants. Ann. Rev. Ecol. Syst. 9:243–263.

Willson, M.F. 1986. Avian frugivory and seed dispersal in eastern North America. Current Ornithology 3:223–279.

Wilson, A. 1808–1824. American Ornithology, vols. 1–9. Bradford and Inskeep, Philadelphia, PA.

Wilson, E.O. 1975. Sociobiology: The New Synthesis. Harvard Univ. Press, Cambridge, MA.

Wilson, U.W., and D.A. Manuwal. 1986. Breeding biology of the Rhinoceros Auklet in Washington. Condor 88:143–155.

Wimberger, P. H. 1984. The use of green plant material in bird nests to avoid ectoparasites. Auk 101:615–618.

Winkler, D.W. 1985. Factors determining a clutch size reduction in California Gulls (Larus californicus): a multi-hypothesis approach. Evolution 39:667–677.

Winkler, D.W., and S.D. Cooper. 1986. Ecology of migrant Black-necked Grebes Podiceps nigricollis at Mono Lake, California. Ibis 128:483–491.

Winkler, D.W., and J.R. Walters. 1983. The determination of clutch size in precocial birds. Current Ornithology 1:33–68.

Wishart, R.A. 1983. Pairing chronology and mate selection in the American Wigeon *(Anas americana)*. Can. J. Zool. 61:1733–1743.

Wishart, R.A., and S.G. Sealy. 1980. Late summer time budget and feeding behavior of Marbled Godwits *(Limosa fedoa)* in southern Manitoba. Can. J. Zool. 58:1277–1282.

Withers, P.C. 1977. Energetic aspects of reproduction by the Cliff Swallow. Auk 94:718–725.

Wittenberger, J.F. 1978. The evolution of mating systems in grouse. Condor 80:126–137.

Wittenberger, J.F. 1980. Feeding of secondary nestlings by polygynous male Bobolinks in Oregon. Wilson Bull. 92:330–340.

Wittenberger, J.F., and G.L. Hunt, Jr. 1985. The adaptive significance of colonality in birds. *In* D.S. Farner, J.R. King, and K.C. Parkes (eds.), Avian Biology, vol. 8. Academic Press, New York, pp. 1–78.

Wolf, L., R.M. Lejnieks, and C.R. Brown. 1985. Temperature fluctuations and nesting behavior of Rock Wrens in a high-altitude environment. Wilson Bull. 97:385–387.

Woodward, P.W. 1983. Behavioral ecology of fledgling Brown-headed Cowbirds and their hosts. Condor 85:151–163.

Woolfenden, G.E. 1956. Comparative breeding behavior of *Ammospiza caudacuta* and *A. maritima*. Univ. Kansas Publ. Mus. Nat. Hist. 10:45–75.

Woolfenden, G.E., and J.W. Fitzpatrick. 1978. The inheritance of territory in group-breeding birds. BioScience 28:104–108.

Woolfenden, G.E., and J.W. Fitzpatrick. 1984. The Florida Scrub Jay. Monogr. Pop. Biol. No. 20. Princeton Univ. Press, Princeton, NJ.

Woolfenden, G.E., and J.W. Fitzpatrick. 1986. Sexual asymmetries in the life history of the Florida Scrub Jay. *In* D.I. Rubenstein and R.W. Wrangham (eds.), Ecological Aspects of Social Evolution. Princeton Univ. Press, Princeton, NJ, pp. 87–107.

Wooten, J.T. 1987. Interspecific competition between introduced House Finch populations and two associated passerine species. Oecologia 71:325–331.

Wray, T., II, and R.C. Whitmore. 1979. Effects of vegetation on nesting success of Vesper Sparrows. Auk 96:802–805.

Wunder, B.A. 1979. Evaporative water loss from birds: effects of artificial radiation. Comp. Biochem. Physiol. 63A:493–494.

Wunderle, J.M., Jr. 1978. Differential response of territorial Yellowthroats to the songs of neighbors and non-neighbors. Auk 95:389–395.

Yasukawa, K. 1979. Territory establishment in Red-winged Blackbirds: importance of aggressive behavior and experience. Condor 81:258–264.

Yom-Tov, Y. 1979. The disadvantage of low positions in colonial roosts: an experiment to test the effect of droppings on plumage quality. Ibis 121:331–332.

Yom-Tov, Y. 1980. Intraspecific nest parasitism in birds. Biological Review 55:93–108.

Yom-Tov, Y., G.M. Dunnet, and A. Anderson. 1974. Intraspecific nest parasitism in the starling *Sturnus vulgaris*. Ibis 116:87–90.

Yunick, R.P. 1985. A review of recent irruptions of the Black-backed Woodpecker and Three-toed Woodpeckers in eastern North America. J. Field Ornithol. 56:138–152.

Zach, R., and J.B. Falls. 1975. Response of the Ovenbird (Aves: Parulidae) to an outbreak of the spruce budworm. Can. J. Zool. 53:1669–1672.

Zammuto, R.M., E.C. Franks, and C.R. Preston. 1981. Factors associated with the interval between feeding visits in brood-rearing Chimney Swifts. J. Field Ornithol. 52:134–139.

Zeleny, L. 1976. The Bluebird—How You Can Help Its Fight for Survival. Indiana Univ. Press, Bloomington.

Zimmerman, D.A. 1976. Comments on feeding habits and vulture-mimicry in the Zone-tailed Hawk. Condor 78:420–421.

Zimmerman, J.L. 1982. Nesting success of Dickcissels (*Spiza americana*) in preferred and less preferred habitats. Auk 99:292–298.

Zink, R.M. 1986. Patterns and Evolutionary Significance of Geographic Variation in the *schistacea* Group of the Fox Sparrow (*Passerella iliaca*). Ornithol. Monogr. No. 40.

Zink, R.M., D.F. Lott, and D.W. Anderson. 1987. Genetic variation, population structure, and evolution of California Quail. Condor 89:395–405.

Zusi, R.L., and G.D. Bentz. 1978. The appendicular morphology of the Labrador Duck (*Camptorhynchus labradorius*). Condor 80:407–418.

Supplemental Bibliography

Anderson, D.J., N.C. Stoyan, and R.E. Ricklefs. 1987. Why are there no viviparous birds? A comment. Am. Nat. 130:941–947.

Bednarz, J.C., and J.J. Dinsmore. 1981. Status, habitat use, and management of Red-shouldered Hawks in Iowa. J. Wildl. Manage. 45:236–241.

Blackburn, D.G., and H.E. Evans. 1986. Why are there no viviparous birds? Am. Nat. 128:165–190.

Buitron, D. 1988. Female and male specialization in parental care and its consequences in Black-billed Magpies. Condor 90:29–39.

Clark, W.S. 1987. A Field Guide to Hawks of North America. Houghton Mifflin Co., Boston.

Devereux. J.G., and J.A. Mosher. 1984. Breeding ecology of Barred Owls in the central Appalachians. Raptor Res. 18:49–58.

Dobkin, D.S. 1984. Flowering patterns of long-lived *Heliconia* inflorescences: implications for visiting and resident nectarivores. Oecologia 64:245–254.

Dunkle, S.W. 1977. Swainson's Hawks on the Laramie plains, Wyoming. Auk 94:65–71.

Foster, M.S. 1969. Synchronized life cycles in the Orange-crowned Warbler and its mallophagan parasites. Ecology 50:315–323.

Henny, C.J., R.A. Olson, and T.L. Fleming. 1985. Breeding chronology, molt, and measurements of Accipiter hawks in northeastern Oregon. J. Field Ornithol. 56:97–112.

Hubbard, J.P. 1974. Flight displays in two American species of *Buteo*. Condor 76:214–215.

Kilham, L. 1980b. Pre-nesting behavior of the Swallow-tailed Kite (*Elanoides forficatus*), including interference by an unmated male with a breeding pair. Raptor Res. 14:29–31.

Kroodsma, R.L. 1974. Species-recognition behavior of territorial male Rose-breasted and Black-headed Grosbeaks (*Pheucticus*). Auk 91:54–64.

Marion, W.R., and R.J. Fleetwood. 1978. Nesting ecology of the Plain Chachalaca. Wilson Bull. 90:386–395.

Martin, T.E., and J.J. Roper. 1988. Nest predation and nest-site selection of a western population of the Hermit Thrush. Condor 90:51–57.

Marzluff, J.M., and R.P. Balda. 1988. Pairing patterns and fitness in a free-ranging population of Pinyon Jays: what do they reveal about mate choice? Condor 90:201–213.

Matray, P.F. 1974. Broad-winged Hawk nesting and ecology. Auk 91:307–324.

Morrison, M.L. 1978. Breeding characteristics, eggshell thinning, and population trends of White-tailed Hawks in Texas. Bull. Texas Ornithol. Soc. 11:35–40.

Mountjoy, D.J., and R.J. Robertson. 1988. Why are waxwings "waxy"? Delayed plumage maturation in the Cedar Waxwing. Auk 105:61–69.

Ricklefs, R.E. 1972. Latitudinal variation in breeding productivity of the Rough-winged Swallow. Auk 89:826–836.

Rosenfield, R.N. 1984. Nesting biology of Broad-winged Hawks in Wisconsin. Raptor Res. 18:6–9.

Sullivan, K.A. 1988. Ontogeny of time budgets in Yellow-eyed Juncos: adaptation to ecological constraints. Ecology 69:118–124.

Sydeman, W.J., M. Güntert, and R.P. Balda. 1988. Annual reproductive yield in the cooperative Pygmy Nuthatch (*Sitta pygmaea*). Auk 105:70–77.

Westneat, D.F. 1988. Male parental care and extrapair copulations in the Indigo Bunting. Auk 105:149–160.

Zink, R.M. 1988. Evolution of Brown Towhees: allozymes, morphometrics and species limits. Condor 90:72–82.

Guide to Essay Topics

As described in *How to Use this Book*, each species treatment paragraph expands upon the information listed in each summary line. The essays, in turn, expand upon the information covered in the treatments. This *Guide to Essay Topics* is organized as far as possible in the same sequence as the information presented in the species treatments. Thus, we first list essays offering background on bird nomenclature, which will be helpful in interpreting the treatment heading, follow with essays that expand on information found in the summary line (categories in italics), and finally list the essays that expand the material covered in the treatment paragraph under boldfaced headings that match those in the paragraph. Many topics are clustered under various categories of **NOTES**, which is unavoidable because of the great diversity of subjects that do not fall logically under the other headings. In some instances an essay could logically be placed in more than one category, and we have made an arbitrary decision on its position. In a few cases we have listed essays more than once. An asterisk (*) indicates essays that will be especially helpful in understanding the abbreviated information listed in the species treatment.

TREATMENT HEADING

SUMMARY LINE

Parental Care, p. 555
see also EGGS AND DEVELOPMENT
  (below)

Diet
Determining Diets, p. 535

Diet and Nutrition, p. 587
see also DIET (below)

Foraging Techniques
see DIET (below)

TREATMENT PARAGRAPH

BREEDING:
Habitat
  Habitat Selection, p. 463
  Bird Communities and
    Competition, p. 605
  Dabblers vs. Divers, p. 75
  Seabird Nesting Sites, p. 197

DISPLAYS:
Territoriality
  Territoriality, p. 387
  Interspecific Territoriality, p. 385
  Sandpipers, Social Systems, and
    Territoriality, p. 155
  Spacing of Wintering Shorebirds,
    p. 147

Visual Displays
  Visual Displays, p. 5
  Duck Displays, p. 63
  Shorebird Communication,
    p. 139
  Dominance Hierarchies, p. 533
  Bird Badges, p. 591
  Redwing Coverable Badges,
    p. 611
  Courtship Feeding, p. 181

Song and Singing
  Bird Voices, p. 373
  Vocal Development, p. 601
  Vocal Functions, p. 471
  Vocal Dialects, p. 595
  Vocal Copying, p. 469
  Nonvocal Sounds, p. 313

Environmental Acoustics, p. 441
Sonagrams: Seeing Bird Songs,
    p. 563

NEST:
Onset of Nesting
  Breeding Season, p. 55
  Hormones and Nest Building,
    p. 547

Nest Structure and Location
  Masterbuilders, p. 445
  *Nest Lining, p. 391
  Nest Materials, p. 369
  Feathered Nests, p. 605
  Nest Sanitation, p. 315

Nesting in Colonies
  Coloniality, p. 173
  Site Tenacity, p. 189

EGGS AND DEVELOPMENT:
Clutches and Broods
  *Average Clutch Size, p. 51
  *Variation in Clutch Sizes, p. 339
  Indeterminate Egg Layers,
    p. 165
  *Hatching Asynchrony and
    Brood Reduction, p. 307

Prenatal Development
  Eggs and Their Evolution,
    p. 301
  *Color of Eggs, p. 305

SUBJECT INDEX

*(Page numbers in **boldface** refer to entire essays devoted to a subject. For mentions of North American birds in the essays, see* Index of North American Birds, *pp. 765–785; for* Guide to Essay Topics, *see pp. 736–742.)*

Able, Kenneth, 559
Aborigines, Australian, and crane
   courtship, 49
Academy of Natural Sciences of
   Philadelphia, 515
acceptor species of Cowbird eggs,
   623
acid precipitation, damage to bird
   habitats, 3–5, 365
acorns, 345, 385
acoustics, environmental, and
   vocalizations, **441**
Acridotheres tristis, 653
adaptive radiation of birds in Hawaii,
   651
aerodynamics, 291, 397
   and bird flights, **161–63**
   of skimming, **194**
   of soaring, **215–17**
   of vee formations, **59**
   and wing shape, **227–29**
age, maximum attained, *see* longevity
aggregations, *see* flocks; coloniality
Ahlquist, Jon, 421, 423, 662–65
Ainu, and cranes in dance, 49
aircraft, birds struck by, **83–85**, 658
   see also flight, speed of
'Akepa, 652
'Akiapola'au, 652
'Akiola, Kauai, 652
'Akohekohe, 652
Albatrosses, 15, 29, 209, 211, 217, 227,
   235, 313, 339, 481, 643, 657–58
   Black-browed, 657, 658
   Black-footed, 657, 658
   Laysan, 645–47, 661
   Royal, 643
   Short-tailed, 657–58
   Yellow-nosed, 658
Alison, Robert, 65
Allen, Joel Asaph, biography of, **343**
allopatric, defined, 375
allospecies, 377
altricial, precocial vs., **581–87**
altruism, **453–55**
   and creche formation, 191–93

evolution of, 453–55
and flock defense, 237
kin selection and, 285, 453
mobbing and, 425, 453
Alvo, Robert, 3
'Amakihi, Common, 651
American Acclimatization Society and
   introduced species, 633
American Birds, 11, 363, 521
American Museum of Natural History,
   37, 43, 215, 389, 521
American Ornithologists' Union (AOU),
   41, 119, 219, 343, 377, 411
American Ornithology (Wilson), 129,
   277, 463
amphibians, eggs of, 123
Amphispiza belli clementeae (threatened
   subspecies), 297
'Anianiau, 651
Animal Species and Evolution (Mayr),
   389
antbirds:
   as commensal feeders, 35
   in mixed-species flocks, 435
anting, to control parasites, **487**
'Apapane, 651
Archaeopteryx, 397, 399
   and evolution of birds, 31–33
Aristotle, and starlings, 489
Arrowood, Patricia, 655
artifacts in nests, 371, 391
arts, history of birds in the, **47–51**, 409
Ashmole, N. P., 339, 341
aspergillosis, infection of birds by, 349,
   399
assortative mating, 595, 627
asynchronous hatching, **307–9**
attendants, in commensal feeding, 35
Audubon (magazine), 43, 363, 521
Audubon, John James, 49, 85, 99, 129,
   133, 201, 247, 273, 277, 279, 293,
   333, 357–59, 409, 485, 531, 561,
   569, 627, 647
   biography of, **413**
Audubon Society, 11, 41, 121, 219,
   363, 365, 369, 521, 527, 573, 651

Audubon Society Encyclopedia of North American Birds (Terres), 670
Audubon Society Guide to Attracting Birds (Kress), 361
Auk, The, 343, 637
Auk, Great, **199–203**
 diving depth of, 205
Austin, Oliver, 189
Australia:
 bird trade in, 654
 evolutionary convergence of birds in, 421–23
 Peregrine Falcons in, 223
 Short-tailed Shearwaters in, 57, 662
autumnal recrudescence, 547

babblers, 419, 425, 435
Bachman's Warbler, as threatened species, **505**
back-crossing as conservation technique, 571–73
badges, as arbitrary status symbols in dominance hierarchy, **591–93**
 redwing coverable, **611–15**
 see also displays
Baird, Lucy, 531
Baird, Spencer Fullerton, 95, 119, 439, 451, 531
 biography of, **569**
Baja California, condors in, 219
Bakken, Marten, 593
Balda, Russel, 397
Bald Eagle Protection Act, 295
banding of birds, **95–99**
Baptista, Luis, 670
barbs, barbules, *see* feathers
Bartram, William, biography of, **129**
bathing and dusting, **429–31**
 see also preening
beaks, *see* bills
bears, polar, and the Great Auk, 201
beaters in commensal feeding, 35
Beecher, William, 489
Beer, Colin, 193
bees:
 competition with hummingbirds, 335, 385
 and wasps defend bird nests, 449
begging displays, 7
behavior, *see* displays; vocalizations; feeding; preening; anting; head scratching; bathing; courtship

Bendire, Charles, 637
 biography of, **439**
Bent, Arthur, 95
 biography of, **637**
Bering, Vitus, 373
Bernoulli, Daniel, 161
bills, **209–13**
 Clark's Nutcracker, 347
 and coevolution, 405–7
 crossbill, 381
 European Starling, 489
 evolution of, 419
 flamingo, 45
 guilds and, 493
 of Hawaiian birds, 651–52
 of Ivorybill Woodpecker, 359
 of oystercatchers, 109
 of Pinyon Jays, 347
 resource partitioning and, 493–95
 of shorebirds, 125–27
 sounds made with, 313
 woodpecker tongue and, 353
biocentration of pesticides, 23
biogeography, island, **549–53**
 see also communities; conservation efforts; theory
biological calendars, clocks, and breeding cycle, 57
 see also hormones
Biological Survey, U.S., 539
biology of birds, how it is studied, **319–23**
bird banding, **95–97**
Bird Banding Laboratory (BBL), 95, 99, 647
Bird Watcher's Digest, 521
Birder's World, 521
birding, popularity of, and feeding efforts, 351
Bird-Lore, 43
 see also Audubon (magazine)
Birds of America (Audubon), 49, 99, 273, 293, 561
Birds of North and Middle America (Ridgway), 119
birds of paradise, leks of, 261
bird trade (illegal), 654
Birds of Western Palearctic (Cramp and Simmons), 670
bird preservation, *see* conservation
Blackburn, Daniel, 303
Blue List, **11**, 29

California Academy of Sciences, 521
California Fish and Game Commission, 221
calls, *see* vocalizations
camouflage, 63
countershading as, 113
   and disruptive coloration, 113
   and eclipse plumage, 61–63
   of eggs, 167, **305–7**
   in King Eiders, 113
   of nests, 391, 393
   in rails, 99–101
   see also color
Canada, laws protecting birds, *see* laws
canaries and song, 375, 473
Caple, Gerald, 397
Caracaras, fruit feeding, 225
Cardinal, Red-crested, 653
Carpenter, F. Lynn, 331, 335
Carson, Rachel:
   biography of, **511**
   DDT and, 21
carrying, *see* transporting
Cassin, John, biography of, **515**
cassowaries, 421
cats, as predators of birds, 257, 351, 497
cattle:
   as beaters for Cattle Egrets, 35, 433, 625
   clearing of wintering grounds for, 367, 513
Center for Conservation Biology (Stanford), 365, 369
Chaffinches, 385, 415
   European, 533
Chapman, Frank M., 37, 39, 215, 539
   biography of, **43**
Charig, Alan, 33
Chasiempis sandwichensis, 653
Chatterjee, Sankar, 33
Check-list of North American Birds (AOU), 119
checkerboard distributions, *see* communities
chicken, domestic, 257, 265, 375, 457, 459, 533
   as indiscriminant layer, 165
chicks:
   care of by parents, **555–57**
   creches and, **191–93**
   cuckoo, 287

distanced from eggshells, 165–67
   and distraction displays, **115–17**
   feeding and, 113, 171, 271–73, 555
   gull, 151–53, 171
   and hatching asynchrony, **307–9**
   loon, 3–5
   oystercatcher, extended care of, 109–11
   parent recognition by, 191, **193–95**
   of petrels, how fed, **15**
   precocial vs. altricial, **581–87**
   transporting of, **103–5**
   see also hatching
China, taxidermy in, 247
Chloeophaga:
   hybrida, 463
   picta, 463
chlorinated hydrocarbons, and eggshell thinning, 21–23
Choate, Ernest, 247
Chough, White-winged, 437
Chukar, 656
cinematographic studies:
   of duck displays, 67
   of flock defense, 235–37
   of raptor hunting, 233
   of vee formation, 59
circulatory system, 509
cities, birds in, **629–33**
Clark, Anne, 309
claws, *see* feet
cloacal kiss, *see* copulation
Clostridium botulinum, 69
clothing, feathers decorating, **37–41**, 652
clover, quail eggs and, **265–67**
clutch size:
   average, **51–53**
   and courtship feeding, 181
   hormonal control of, 165
   indeterminate, **165**
   and lifetime reproduction, 51
   in parasitized ducks, 89–91
   in parasitized swallows, 401–3
   in petrels, 15
   and resources in breeding season, 339–41
   variation in, **339–43**
Cockatoo, Sulphur-crested, 643
Cody, Martin, 467
coevolution, 345–47, **405–7**
   see also evolution

creches, for care of chicks, **191–93**
and onset of parent-chick recognition, 193
Creepers, Hawaiian, 652
crocodiles, and bird evolution, 33
crop:
  and bird milk, 271, 557
  and nectar in hummingbirds, 331
Crowell, Kenneth, 465
Crows:
  Carrion, 167
  Hooded, 629
cuckoldry, prevention in ducks, 61
cuckoo doves, 609
Cuckoos, European, as brood parasite, **287–91**
Curio, E., 425

dabblers vs. divers, **75–79**
  and piracy, 159–61
Dane, Benjamin, 67
Darwin, Charles, 237–39, 343, 389, 463, 561, 567
  biography of, **475**
Dawkins, Richard, 591
DDT, **21–25**
  and California Condor, 219–21
  and raptor conservation, 249
  and wintering birds, 513
Delaware, shorebirds in, 121
Dendroica warblers and head scratching, 543–45
DeSante, David, 461–63
development:
  eye color and, **233**
  of gulls, **171**
  vocalizations and, **601–3**
dialects, vocal, **595–97**
Diamond, Jared, 331, 415, 609
Diatryma (extinct predatory bird), 93
dicofol (pesticide), 23–25, 249
Dictionary of American Bird Names (Choate), 247
Dictionary of Birds (Campbell and Lack), 321, 670
diets, how determined, **535–39**
  and nutrition, **587–89**
  see also feeding
differentiation, *see* species
differential migration, 185
digestion, 35, 407

feathers in, **13**, 269
in hummingbirds, 331
pellets and, 297
stones (grinding aids) in, **269–71**
of wax, **519**
dimorphism, sexual:
  in raptors, **243–45**
  reverse, 133
  and sexual selection, **251–55**
  in vocal apparatus, 375
dinosaurs, bird evolution and, **31–33**
  see also flight; *Hesperornis*
Dipper, American, foraging of, **483**
  swimming of, 75
dipping as foraging strategy, **483**
diseases, **399–401**
  avian pox, 399
  botulism, **69**
  encephalitis, 399
  and Hawaiian birds, 652
  and Heath Hen decline, 257
  histoplasmosis, 265, 633
  Newcastle disease, 399
  from pollution, 207
  psittacosis, 399
  spread at feeding stations, 349
  spread from birds to humans, 633
  tuberculosis, 399
displacement activities, 9
displays, **5–9**, 139–43
  aerial, in shorebirds, 139–41
  of badges in hierarchy, 611–15
  by coots, 105–7
  in courtship, 5–9, 141–43, 253, 259–61, 315
  distraction, 105, 107, **115–17**
  by ducks, **63–67**
  non-vocal sounds in, **315–17**
  by rails, 101
  rodent run, as, 115
  by shorebirds, 139–43
  in shorebird territories, 147
  see also vocalizations
disruptive coloration and camouflage, 113
Distributional Checklist of North American Birds (DeSante and Pyle), 463
distributions, checkerboard, 609
  see also competition
divers vs. dabblers, **75–79**
diversity of bird communities,

determination of, 541–43
see also communities
diving, 75–79
  by American Dippers, 483
  buoyancy and, 25, 507
  depths attained, 205
  flightlessness and, 203–5
  and swimming underwater, 73–75
DNA, 517
  and evolutionary convergence,
    419–25
  and hybridization studies, 517
  and passerine classification, 662–63
Dobkin, David, 191
domain of danger, *see* flock defense
dominance, *see* badges; hierarchies;
    Leks
Dominican Republic, 527, 659
double-scratching (foraging technique),
    71
Doves:
  Emerald, as commensal feeder, 35
  Laughing, and flock defense, 235
Drigot, Diane C., 654
drinking, 123–25
  in hummingbirds and, 333
  salt glands and, 29
drongos, African, and commensal
    feeding, 35
droppings, 263–65
  commercial value of, 263
  disposal by starlings, 489–91
  and drinking, 123
  and egg coloration, 305
  as fertilizer, 367
drumming (non-vocal communication),
    313, 315
Ducks:
  brood parasitism of, 89–93
  displays of, 63–67
  Labrador, extinction of the, 85–87
  Pied, *see* Ducks, Labrador
  Sand-shoal, *see* Ducks, Labrador
  dummy nests, construction of, 547
  see also American Coot
dusting and bathing, 429–31

Eagles:
  Black, 307
  Fish, 225
ears, *see* hearing

eclipse plumage in waterfowl, 61–63
ecosystem, defined, 605
ectoparasites, *see* diseases
egg mimic, *see* brood parasitism
eggs, 301–5
  calcium for, 269
  carrying of, 361, 403
  collecting of, 219, 295, 439
  color of, 165–67, 287, 305–7
  coot, 107
  cowbird, 289
  cuckoo, mimicking host, 287
  development in, 457–59
  evolution of, 301–5
  insurance, 51–53, 309
  pollution and, 23, 207
  of precocial birds, 585
  predators on, 129, 155, 157, 165–67,
    409, 497
  quail, 265–67
  rejection of, 305
  sandpiper, 131, 155
  size of, 181
  turning of, *see* incubation; nestlining
  transportation of, 361, 403
  wastes in, 123–25
  see also brood parasitism; clutch
    size; hatching; incubation
eggshells:
  empty, removal of, 165–67
  weakened by pollution, 23, 303
egg tooth, and hatching, 233–35
egg tossing, *see* brood parasitism;
    cooperative breeding
'Elepaio, 653
embryos:
  development of, 457–59
  and incubation, 393–95
  see also eggs
Emlen, Stephen, 559
Emu, 421
encephalitis, birds as reservoirs of, 399
endangered species, 11, 97, 247–51,
    295–97, 365
  'Akiapola'au, 652
  Blue List as early warning, 11
  Condor, California, 175, 217,
    219–23, 247, 297
  Crane, Whooping, 51–53, 297
  Curlew, Eskimo, 293, 297
  Eagle, Bald, 23, 47, 49, 137, 225,
    233, 249, 295, 297, 369, 371, 645

endangered species (*cont.*)
  Falcon, Peregrine, 21, 23, 81, 159,
    223, 225, 245, 249, 297, 537, 631,
    645, 659
  Goose, Hawaiian, 267, 653
  and legal protection, **293–97**
  Parrotbill, Maui, 652
  Pelican, Brown, 23, 25, 297, 645
  Plover, Piping, 297
  raptors, **247–51**
  Stork, Wood, 297
  Tern, Least, 189, 297, 449
  Warbler, Bachman's, 297
  Warbler, Kirtland's, 297, 407, 505,
    527–29, 623
  Woodpecker, Ivory-billed, 297,
    357–59, 505
  Woodpecker, Red-cockaded, 297,
    357, 465
Endangered Species Act, U.S., 249,
  295–97, 365
endangered subspecies, 297
environmental acoustics, **441**
enzymes in metabolism, 325, 329
  and wax digestion, 519
escaped birds, *see* feral birds
Eskimo Year (Sutton), 87
esophagus, carrying seeds in, 347
ethics, research and, 323
etymology, *see* names of birds
European robins as commensal feeders, 35
Evans, Howard, 303
evolution, 93, 261, 339, 347, 475, 567
  of altruism, **453–55**
  coevolutionary, **405–7**
  convergence in, **419–25**
  of duck displys, **63–67**
  of eggs, **301–5**
  of flight, **397–99**
  of flocking, 235–37
  in habitat choices, 463, 465
  history of birds, **31–33**
  of hawk eyes, 231
  natural selection in, **237–39**, **477–79**
  sexual selection and, 251–55
  species formation in, 355
Ewald, Paul, 591
excrement, *see* droppings
extinct species:
  Archaeopteryx, **31–32**, 43, 397, 399
  Auk, Great, **199–203**, 205, 303
  Diatryma, 93

  Duck, Labrador, **85–87**
  Hesperornis, *93*
  Ichthyornis, *93*
  on islands, 549–53
  Parakeet, Carolina, **279–81**, 635
  Pigeon, Passenger, 175, 265, **273–77**,
    293, 295, 451, 615
  see also threatened species
extinct subspecies:
  Hen, Heath, **257–59**
  Sparrow, Dusky Seaside, 297
  see also endangered subspecies; Blue
    List
eyes, 15
  color and develpment, **233**
  of raptors, **229–31**
  of starlings, 489

facial bristles, *see* feathers
fact, defined, **567–69**
Falco cherrug, 247
falconry, 245, 247
families, as a taxonomic unit, 515–17
feathers, **309–13**
  black and white, **177–79**
  and brood patch, 427
  on clothing, **37–41**, 652
  color of, 63, **111–15**, **177–79**
  in courtship, 5, 7
  in diving, 25, 75
  eating of, **13**, 269
  eclipse plumage of waterfowl and,
    61–63
  in flight, 163
  in hearing, 291
  matting of, 207, 351
  molting of, **529–31**
  in nest building, 369, 391, **605**
  origin of, 397
  preening of, 53
  and sense of touch, 211
  sounds made with, 313–15
  specialized in owls, 291
  in thermoregulation, 151, 177
  trade in, **37–41**
  and walking on snow, **255–57**
  wingtip wear of, 113–14
feeders, bird, *see* feeding stations
feeding:
  begging in, 7
  by Blue Jays, **409**
  breeding and, 55, 57, 131, 265–67,

339–43, 491
caching food and, 411
chicks and, 15, 113, 171, 271–73, 555
in cities, 631
color on bill used to induce, 113
commensal, 35–37
communities and, 617
by coots, 107
in courtship, 181
by crossbills in winter, 641
determining diets in, 535–39
by dippers, 483
droppings and, 263
by ducks, 77–79
by European Starlings, 489, 491
in evolution, 407
on feathers, 13, 269
by flamingos, 43–45, 269–71
flight and, 325
flocks and, 433
gizzard and, 269–71
in Hawaiian birds, 651–54
hopping in, 71
by hummingbirds
    efficiency of, 335–37
    frequency of, 331
in incubation, 27–29
during irruptions, 639–41
and leg length, 71
in loons, 3
by marine birds, 660
in migration, 121, 183, 185, 639
milk to young, 271–73, 557
by Northern Phalaropes, 133
nutrition and, 587–89
by oystercatchers, 109–11
pellets and, 297–99
of petrel young, 15
piracy in, 107, 159–61
pollution and, 137
by redpolls in winter, 641
resource partitioning in, 75–79, 125–27, 245, 607
and sexual dimorphism in raptors, 245
by Shearwaters, 658–59
by Shining Starlings, 35
by shorebirds, 121, 125–27
smell in, 17
by songbirds, 381–83
storing as strategy in, 345–49, 411

territoriality of shorebirds and, 147–49, 173–77
tools in, 435–37
by warblers, 523–25
wax in, 519
see also digestion
feeding stations, 349–53
    Canary-winged Parakeets and, 655
    range expansion and, 349, 459–61
feet, 239–43
    in bathing and dusting, 431
    of dabblers vs. divers, 77
    in diving, 73
    in hunting, 223
    in incubation, 393, 429
    of passerines, 395
    in thermoregulation, 149–51
    and walking on snow, 255–57
feigning injury, see displays, distraction
feral birds, 654–56
    parrots as, 281, 635
Field Guide to Birds, A (Peterson), 563
Field Guide to Insects, A (Borror and White), 539
fighting:
    by Black-tailed Godwits, 141
    by coots, 105–7
    by Spotted Sandpipers, 131
filter feeding, see feeding, Flamingos
Finches:
    Java, 656
    Woodpecker, 435
    Zebra, 375
Fish and Wildlife Service (FWS), U.S., 11, 95, 99, 137, 221, 249, 297, 527, 571, 573, 647
fishes:
    in courtship feeding, 181
    and creches, 191–93
    as diet item, 13, 211, 225, 243, 263, 365, 437, 465, 483
    and DDT in birds' diet, 21–23
    eggs of, 123
    as predators, 3, 101
fishing nets, birds entangled in, 203, 661–62
Fitzpatrick, John, 283
Flamingo feeding, 43–45
    Lesser vs. Greater, diet of, 43, 271
flamingo tongue, 45
flight, 291, 303, 397
    adaptations for, 203–5, 507–9

flight *(cont.)*
   altitude of, 81–83
   in *Archaeopteryx*, 31, 33
   copulation in, 319
   displays in shorebirds, 139–41
   diving and, 73, **203–5**
   in duck displays, 63
   hovering in, **323–25**
   mechanics of, **161–63**
   muscles in, **509–11**
   origin of, **397–99**
   of owls, 291
   skimming in, **195**
   swimming and, **73**
   soaring in, **215–17**
   speed of, **81–83**
   takeoff and landing in, 79
   in vee formation, **59**
   wing shape and, 161–63, **227–29**
flightlessness and diving depths, **203–5**
   and eclipse plumage, 61–63
flocks, 19–21, 453
   defense of, 19, **235–37**, 425, 433
   evolution of, **19–21**
   flight of, 59
   hierarchies in, **533–35**
   mixed-species, 125–27, **433–35**
   parent-chick recognition in, 193–95
   roosting in, **615–17**
   of sleeping ducks, **61**
   spacing in shorebird, **147–49**
   vs. territoriality, 387
   see also coloniality
Florida:
   Bachman's Warblers in, 505
   Condor fossils in, 219
   Dusky Seaside Sparrows in, 571
   feral birds in, 281, 635, 654, 655, 656
   loons poisoned in, 3
   Scrub Jays in, 283, 575–77
Flycatcher, Yellow-margined, 433
flyways, in migration, 185
foliage, diversity and bird diversity,
   541–43
   see also communities
food:
   birds as, 45, 97, 257
   chains, 21–23
   history of birds as, 293–95
   passenger pigeons as, 273–75
   see also feeding
foraging, *see* feeding

Forest and Stream, 275
forest fragmentation, *see* habitat
   destruction; island biogeography
Forster, Johann Reinhold, 187
fossils, 31, 93, 219
foxes as predators of birds, 129, 155,
   169–71
Francolin, Block, 656
Franklin, Sir John, 187
Friends of the Earth, 363, 369
Frigatebird, Great, 645, 653
Fugle, Gary, 591–93
furcula (wishbone), 31, 33
   see bones

game birds, 227, 243, 431, 583, 643
Garefowl, *see* Auk, Great
Garganey, 65
Geese:
   Falklands, 463
   Hawaiian, 267, 653
genetic drift, 257–59
genetics:
   and development, 457
   DNA and, **419–25**, 517, **662–63**
   and evolution of altruism, 453–55
   and extinction, 257, 259
   and natural selection, 239
   random changes in, 257–59
   see also DNA; evolution
geographical variation, 355
   in clutch size, 339–41
geography, biology and, **549–53**
gizzard:
   and feather consumption, **13**
   and grinding materials, **269–71**
   see also pellets
glands:
   pituitary and nesting behavior, 547
   preen, **53**
   salt, **29–31**
goatsuckers, 333
Godwit, Black-tailed, 141
gonads, *see* reproductive system
Gould, John, 331
Gould, Stephen Jay, 45
Grand Canyon, as possible condor
   habitat, 221–23
Great Plains:
   hybridization in, **625–27**
Grebe, Great Crested, 9

Edward Grey Institute of Field
Ornithology, 187
Grinnell, Joseph, 267, 389
biography of, **411**
ground-nesting birds, **129**
Grouse, Red, 259–61, 269
Grzimek, Bernhard, 83
Grzimek, Michael, 83
guano, *see* droppings
guilds, bird, **493–95**
foraging, 433
habitat selection, 463–67
see also communities; flocks (mixed
species)
Gulls:
attracted to predators, **169–71**
development of, **171**
ring of races in, 503

habitat destruction, 249, 251, 361, 363,
367, 503, 652, 658
in Bachman's Warbler decline, 505
in California Condor decline, 221–23
in Common Loons, 3–5
in Dusky Seaside Sparrow decline,
571
in eastern songbird decline, **495–501**
in Heath Hen's decline, 257
in Ivory-billed Woodpecker decline,
359
in Kirtland's Warbler decline, 527
in Passenger Pigeon's decline, 275
in rails, 103
in tropical wintering grounds, 513
see also extinct species; extinct
subspecies; migrants; threatened
species; threatened subspecies
habitat selection by birds, **463–67**
Hamilton, W. D., 19
Hansen, Andrew, 613–15
hare population cycles and bird
irruptions, 639
Harris, Edward, 247
hatching, **233–35**
asynchrony in, **307–9**
and eggshell removal, **165–71**
see also chicks; eggs; incubation
hats, and plume trade, **37–41**
Hawaii, 549, **651–54**
albatrosses in, 657
coots in, 109

honeycreepers in, 423
honeyeaters and mosquitoes in, 399
Hawaiian Creeper, 652
Hawaii's Birds, 651
head scratching, **543–45**
see also preening; parasites
hearing, **299**
in owls, 291–93
vs. seeing, 15
in song development, 603
heart adapted to flight, 509
Heermann, Adolphus, 187
Heinrich, Bernd, 305
Hellack, Jenna, 81
helpers at the nest, *see* cooperative
breeding
Hemignathus:
munroi, 652
parvus, 651
procerus, 652
virens, 651
Hen, Heath, factors leading to
extinction of, **257–59**
Henry IV (Shakespeare) and introduced
species, 633
Henslow, John S., 561
Herons:
European Gray, 7
Green-backed, 437
Herring Gull's World, The (Tinbergen),
71
Hesperornis, **93**
see also evolution
hierarchies, dominance, 7, **533–35**
badges in, **591–93**, 613
in leks, 259
sexual selection and, 251–53
Himatione sanguinea, 651
histoplasmosis, *see* diseases
History of North American Birds, A
(Baird, Brewer and Ridgway), 119,
569
Hixon, Mark A., 335
hoarding of food, **345–49**, 385, 411
see also storage of food
hoatzins and evolution of birds, 31
Hobbies (falcons), 589
European, 225
home range defined, 387
see also territoriality
Honeycreepers, 651, 652
Crested ('Akohekohe), 652

Honeyeaters, 299, 399
  Bismarck Black, and checkerboard
    distributions, 609
honeyguides and wax eating, 519
hopping vs. walking, **69–71**
hormones, 267, 317
  nest building and, **547–49**
hornbills and incubation, 27–29
horses as a source of nest materials, 371
hovering, **323–25**
Hummingbirds:
  foraging of, **331–33, 335**
  hermit and leks in tropics, 261
  Sicklebill and bill shape, 211
Hunt, G. L., Jr., 199
hunting:
  by birds as natural selection, 477–79
  in California Condor's decline, 219
  of coots, 109
  of ducks, 85, 87
  of Golden Plovers, 295
  lead poisoning from, 137, 219, 221,
    271
  limits determined by banding, 95
  by owls, **291–93**
  in Passenger Pigeon's decline,
    273–77
  by piracy, **159**
  by raptors, **223–25,** 229–31, 243–45,
    589
  of raptors, 247
  see also raptors
Hutchinson, G. Evelyn, 525
Huxley, Julian, 9
hybridization, **501–3**
  in conservation efforts, 571–73
  display differences minimize, 67
  in Great Plains, **625–27**
  and range expansion, 461–63
  and sibling species, 383
  and speciation, 355–57
  and superspecies, 377
hypothermia, regulated, 153
hypothesis, defined, **567**

Ichthyornis, 93
'I'iwi, 651
*Illustrations of the Birds of California,
  Texas, Oregon, British and Russian
  America* (Cassin), 515
incubation, **393–95**
  brood patches in, 317, 393, 395,

  427–29, 605
  and feathered nests, **605**
  and hatching asynchrony, 307
  and indeterminate laying, 165
  length of, **481**
  by males, 135, 271–73
  by sandpipers, 155, 157
  by which sex, **27–29**
  see also brood patches; eggs; nests
Indians, American, 49, 359
infanticide, polygamy and, 135
influenza, avian, 399
  see diseases
information-center hypothesis, 173, 175
  see also flocks
insurance eggs, 51–53, 309
intelligence, **415–19**
  and development at hatching,
    585–87
  and tool using, 435–39
Internatonal Association of Fish and
    Wildlife Agencies, 121
invasions (and introductions), **633–35,**
    651–55
  see also irruptions; range expansion;
    Starlings
irruptions, **639–41**
  see also population dynamics
island biogeography, **549–53**
Ivory-billed Woodpecker as threatened
    species, **357–59**

Järvi, Torbiorn, 593
Jays, nest-robbing Blue, **409**
Job, Herbert, 39
Journal of Field Ornithology, 647
Journal of Wildlife Management, 539
Jynx torquilla, 391

Kale, Herbert W., 573
Karasov, William, 331
Kendeigh, S. C., biography of, **153**
Kestrels and information center
    hypothesis:
  Common, 175
  Eurasian Lesser, 175
Key to North American Birds (Coues),
    565
kidneys and excretion, 123, 333
  manufacture of vitamin C in, 589
  salt glands vs., 29
Kinney, James, 385

Kirtland's Warbler as threatened species, **527–29**
Kites, pesticidal leaves in nests of, 317
Kittlitz, 451
Kiwis, sense of smell, 17
  relationship to other flightless birds, 421
kleptoparasitism, 159
  see also piracy
Klimkiewicz, M. Kathleen, 647
Knudsen, Eric, 291
Koenig, Walter, 285, 341
Koford, Carl, 221
Komodo dragons and bird evolution, 33
Konishi, Marc, 291
Krakatoa and island biogeography, 551
Krebs, John, 411, 591
Kress, Stephen, 361
Kroodsma, Don, 473
Kushlan, James, 35

Laboratory of Ornithology (Cornell), 351, 363, 521
Lacey Act, 295
Lack, David, 307, 309
  biography of, **187**
Lamarck, Chevalier de, 343
Lammergeir, in derivation of name "osprey," 247
language, acquired by parrots, 417
  see intelligence
Lascaux Cave, bird art in, 47
Laub, Richard, 219
laws, U.S. and Canadian, **293–97**, 365
  on banding and trapping, 97
  on parrot selling, 281
  on pesticide usage, 249
  on plume trade, 41
  to protect Passenger Pigeon, 275
  to protect raptors, 247
  on refuse dumping, 351
lead poisoning from shotgun pellet:
  and California condors, 219–21
  as metallic poison, 137
  taken as grinding material, 271
LeConte, John, 561
learning, 415–19
  of songs, **601–3**
legs:
  of dabblers vs. divers, 77
  evolution of, 419
  in locomotion, 69, 71

in thermoregulation, 149–51
  see also feet; thermoregulation
leks, 5, **259–61**
  dominance hierarchies on, 533
  promiscuous breeders and, 145
  of sandpipers, 155–57
  sexual selection and, 251
  territoriality and, 387
  visual displays and, 5
  see also displays; hierarchies
Lendrem, Dennis, 61
Lepthien, Larry, 639
lice, 399–401, 429
  see also parasites
Life Histories of North American Birds (Bendire), 439
Life Histories of North American Birds (Bent, ed.), 637, 670
Life of Birds, The (Welty and Baptista), 670
life span, **643–47**
lining of nests, **391–93**
Linnaean Society, 475
Linnaeus, Carolus, 485, 515
  biography of, **629**
Linnean system of classification, **515–519**
  see also taxonomy
Linsdale, Jean, 191
liver, manufacture of vitamin C in, 589
Living Bird Quarterly, 363, 521
Logbook for Grace (Murphy), 215
longevity, **643–47**
  methods for estimating, 643
Loons:
  breeding declines, **3–5**
  nurseries, **3**
Lorenz, Konrad, 71, 581
  biography of, **57–59**
Loxops coccineus, 652
lumber industry:
  bird damage to, 265
  and decline of Ivory-billed Woodpecker, 359
  see also forest fragmentation
lungs and demands of flight, 83, 507–9

MacArthur, Robert, 125
  biography of, **525**
  and foliage height diversity, 541–43
  and island biogeography, 549
  and study of warbler foraging, 523

McAtee, Waldo Lee, biography of, **539**
MacGillivray, William, 531
McIntyre, Judith, 3
MacRoberts, B. R., 285
MacRoberts, M. H., 285
Macropygia cuckoo doves and
    checkerboard distributions, 609
magazines for bird enthusiasts, 521, 670
Malthus, Thomas, 237
mammal–bird comparisons:
    birth vs. hatching, 303
    bones, 507
    excrement, 123, 263
    intelligence, 415
    lungs, 83, 509
    metabolism, 327, 329
    milk, 271
    polygamy and infanticide, 135
    testes, 317
    vocal organs, 373
mammals:
    birds as commensal feeders with, 35
    as predators, 19, 129, 155, 169–71,
      201, 257, 351, 445, 497
    as prey, 225, 245, 347, 639
management programs, *see* conservation
manakins and leks, 261
*Manual of the Ornithology of United
    States and Canada, A* (Nuttall),
    357
marking birds for study, **95–99**
Marler, Peter, 601
Marsh Hen, hunting of, 101
Martin, Gray-breasted roosting in, 19
mathematical theory, role in science,
    567–69
    of island biogeography, **551–53**
    see also theory
mating systems, **597–99**
    of Brown-headed Cowbirds, 621–23
    chick care and, 555–57
    cooperative breeding, 283–87, 491
    hierarchies and, 553
    incubation and, 27
    leks and, 259–61
    monogamy, 155, 283, 319, **597–99**
    polyandry, 27, **131–33**, 155–57, 185,
      251–53, 533, 555–57
    polygyny, 155, **443–45**, 555
    promiscuity, **145**
    of sandpipers, **155–57**
    see also breeding; courtship; displays

Maxson, Stephen, 129
Mayr, Ernst, biography of, **389**
megapodes, life history of, 301, 393,
    555, 581–85
Mendel, Gregor, 237–39
mercury poisoning, 3, 137
metabolism, **325–29**, 331, 333
    and spread-wing thermoregulation,
    25
mice:
    burrows used as nest, 391
    as predators on eggs, **129**
    as prey, 225
Middle East, falconry in, 247
migrants threatened by tropical forest
    destruction, 499, 513
    see also forest fragmentation; habitat
    destruction
migration, **183–87**
    altitude in, 81–83
    feeding in, 121, 183, 185, 639
    flyways in, 185
    irruptive, **639–41**
    navigation, orientation and, **559–61**
    patterns revealed by banding, 95
    population and, 579
    research on, 95
    of shorebirds, **119–21**
    stopped by bird feeding, 349
    vs. hoarding food, 345
    and wintering, 513
    see also navigation; orientation
Migratory Bird Treaty, 295
milk, crop, **271–73**, 557
Miller, Alden H., biography of, **267**
Miller, Edward H., 139
Mimicry:
    in butterflies, 405
    of host eggs by cuckoo eggs, 287
mixed-species flocking, 235–37, **433**
    and commensal feeding, 35
mobbing, **425–27**
    and altruism, 453
    and gulls, 169–71
Moller, Anders, 605
molting, **529–31**
    see also brood patch; eclipse plumage;
    feathers
Mongoose, Small Indian, 659
monogamy, **597–99**
    among cooperative breeders, 283
    and frequency of copulation, 319

territoriality and, 155
see also mating systems
Morse, Douglass, 461
Morton, Eugene, 441
mosquitoes and bird disease in Hawaii, 399
see also diseases
moths:
  evolving under bird predation, 477–479
  Hawk, as hummingbird competitor, 335
Mumme, Ron, 285
Murdy, Horatio, 609
Murphy, Robert Cushman, biography of, **215**
mussels, as prey items, 127, 437, 555
  of Labrador Duck, 85–87
Myers, Pete, 119
Mynas:
  Common, 653, 654
  Jungle, 487
Myzomela pammelaena, 609

names of birds, origins of, **13, 117, 143–45, 187, 245–47, 331–33, 337, 371–73, 405, 451, 485, 531, 545, 561, 603–4**
Napoleon I, Emperor of France, 463
National and International Wildlife Federations, 369
National Audubon Society, *see* Audubon Society
National Museum, U.S., 119, 439
National Wildlife Federation, 363
natural experiments, 465–67, **477–79**
Natural History, 521, 670
Natural Regulation of Animal Numbers, The (Lack), 187
natural selection, *see* evolution
Nature Conservancy, 363, 367, 369
navigation and orientation, **559–61**
  and sense of smell, 17
nectar as food for birds, 299
  and backyard feeders, 351
  bills adapted for, 211, 327
  hovering to obtain, 325
  hummingbird capacity for, 331, **333**
  territorial defense of, 335, 385
Nectarinia sericea, 609
Nene, *see* Geese, Hawaiian
nervous system, adapted to flight, 511

nest robbing:
  and clutch size, 343
  and Jays, **409**
nests:
  and disease, 399–401
  of European Starlings, 489–91
  evolution and types of, **445–49**
  feathers in, **605**
  on ground, **129**
  hormones and building, **547–49**
  materials for building, 369–71, 605
  materials for lining, 341–43
  predators on, 129, 155, 157, 409, 497
  sanitation of, **315–17**, 371
nest sites, **189–91**
  faithfulness to (tenacity), **189–91**
  and protective associations, 449
  of seabirds, **197–99**
  shortage of, 91
  see also coloniality
nets:
  to capture birds, 97
  fishing, birds entangled in, 203, 661–62
Newcastle disease, *see* diseases
news about bird biology, **521**
Nice, Margaret Morse, 577
  biography of, **579–81**
nidicolous vs. nidifugous, 581
Nightjars, European, 333
Nobel Prize, won by Lorenz, Tinbergen and von Frisch, 59, 71
nomenclature, **515–19**
  see also taxonomy
North American Loon Fund, 5
North American Oology (Brewer), 647
nostrils and bills, 209
  see also salt glands; smell, sense of
Nottebohm, Fernando, 373–75
nurseries, loon, **3–5**
nutrition, diet and, **587–89**
Nuttall, Thomas, biography of, **357**
Nuttall Ornithological Club, 343

Oceanic Birds of South America (Murphy), 215
O'Donald, Peter, 255
Ohmart, Robert, 185
oil, as pollution, **207–9**, 661
oil, preen, 53
  bathing and dusting and, 429
  headscratching and, 543

Oilbirds, 299
olfaction, *see* smell, sense of
oology, 219, 295
opportunistic social systems in
    sandpipers, 157
Oreomystis bairdi, 652
orientation and navigation, **559–61**
Origin of Species (Darwin), 239, 475
Oring, Lewis, 129, 131
Ornithological Biography (Audubon),
    413
oscines (songbirds) and suboscines, 395
Ostriches, 89, 191, 269, 301, 437
    African, 241
Ostrom, John, 33, 397
Owls:
    hunting by, **291–93**
    Tawny, 293
Oystercatchers:
    Eurasian, 109
    and oysters, **109–11**

Pachyptila, flamingo-like feeding in, 45
Pacific Discovery, 521
pair bond:
    and courtship, 181
    and monogamy, 397
paleontology and the evolution of birds,
    33, 397
Palmeria dolei, 652
Panama, Clay-colored Robin breeding
    in, 55
Parakeet, Carolina, extinction of, **279–
    281**
parasites of birds, **399–401**
    nest materials selected to control, 371
    nest sanitation and, **315–16**
    removal of, 543
parasitism, brood, *see* brood parasitism
parathion and waterfowl kill, 23
parents, *see* chicks
Parrotbill, Maui, 652
Parrot, Grey, 417
passerines (songbirds), **395**
    classification of, **662–65**
    see also feet; names of groups
pathogens, 399
    see also diseases
Paton, David C., 335
PCBs and eggshell thinning, 21
Peacocks, 49, 113, 251
peck order, *see* hierarchies

pelagic birds, **657–62**
    diving depths attained by, 203–5
    nesting sites of, 197–99
    oil pollution and, **207–9**
    wax consumption by, 519
    see also seabirds
pellets ejected by birds, **297–99**
    and gizzard, 269
    used in determining diets, 537
Penguins, 173
    Adelie, 7
    body temperature and, 329
    creches and, 101
    Emperor, diving depths, 203, 205
    feeding techniques, 45
    feet heating eggs, 393
    King, diving depth, 203
    Little Blue, 203
    swimming and, 73
Pennycuick, Colin, 203, 217
pesticides:
    California Condor and, 219–21
    DDT, **21–25**
    dicofol, 23
    natural, in nest materials, **315–17,**
        371
    lead and mercury, 137
    parathion, 23
    Rachel Carson and, 511
    raptors and, 247–49
    reducing use of, 361–63
    TEPP, 23
    and wintering birds, 513
pests, birds as, 107–9, 489–93, 615
Peterson, Roger Tory, biography of,
    563
Phan, Duong, 331
philopatry (site tenacity), 189, 579
phytoestrogens and quail reproduction,
    267
Pigeon, Passenger, extinction of, **273–
    277**
pioneering species, sandpipers as, 131
piracy as foraging strategy, 107, **159–61**
Pitelka, Frank, 285
pituitary gland and nesting behavior,
    547
platypus and egg evolution, 301
Pliny the Elder and starlings, 489
plumage, *see* feathers; color; eclipse
        plumage in waterfowl
plume trade, *see* feathers, trade in

shorebirds, 29, 35, 83, 145, 159, 165, 229, 261, 269, 301, 339, 393, 429, 513, 597, 605, 643, 653
  communication in, **139–43**
  conservation of, **119–21**
  cryptic color of, 113–15
  feeding in, **125–27**
  feet of, 241–43
  migration of, **119–21**, 513
  polyandry in, **131–33**
  precocial young of, **583–85**
  spacing of in winter, **147–48**
  thermoregulation in, 151–53
Short, Lester, 359
Shreiber, Ralph, 645
Siberia, gulls in, 503
Sibley, Charles, 421, 423, 662–65
siblicide and hatching asynchrony, 307–8
sibling species, 383
sidestepping, 69
  see also walking
Sierra Club, 363, 369
sight, **229–31**
  vs. smell, 15
  see also vision
Silent Spring (Carson), 21, 511
site tenacity (fidelity), 185, **189–91**
sittellas, convergent on nuthatches, 421–23, 437
skimming as a foraging technique, **194**
sleep, **61, 615–17**
slots, *see* wings, shape of
smell, avian sense of, **15–17**, 207, 229
  in navigation, 559, 561
Smith, John Maynard, 535
Smithsonian Institution, and the history of bird biology, 95, 119, 439, 569, 637
Smithsonian Magazine, 521
smuggling of parrots, 281
snails as prey items, 225, 269, 479
Snowcocks, Himalayan, 656
snowshoes of ptarmigans, **255–57**
soaring, **215–17**
social systems, of sandpipers, **155–57**
  see also mating systems
sonagrams, 299, 375, **563–65**
  see also vocalizations
songbirds:
  and cowbirds, 619–25
  decline in east, **495–99**

defined, **395**
foraging by, **381–83**
wintering and conservation of, 513
see also names of groups
songs, *see* vocalizations
sounds, nonvocal, **313–15**
  see also acoustics, enviromental
spacing of wintering shorebirds, **147–149**
Sparrowhawk, European, 159
speciation, 355–57, 383, 419–25
  in Hawaii, 651
  and hybridization, 501–3
  and taxonomy, 515–19
species as taxonomic category, **355–57**
  latinized ("scientific") names of, 517–19
  sibling, **383**, 385
  see also hybridization; subspecies; superspecies; speciation
speed of flight, 81
Spencer, Herbert, 239
sperm precedence and storage, *see* copulation
spinning as foraging technique in phalaropes, 133
Sprague, Isaac, 485
Squibb, R. C., 199
squirrels:
  as bird competitor, 385
  as bird enemy, 129, 497
  as prey, 245
  as source of nest materials, 391
stamps, duck, 365
Starlings, European, success as invader, **489–93**
  Shining, 35
Stedman, David, 219
Steller, George, 373
Stonehouse, Bernard, 203
stones (grit), swallowing of, **269–71**
  see also gizzard
storage of food, **345–49**
  remembering sites, 411
  see also caches; hoarding
Storks, White, 137, 371
Studd, Michael, 535
suboscines, 395
subspecies, conservation of, **571–73**
  defined, 355, 377
Sunbird, Black and checkerboard distributions, 609

superspecies, 375–81
  list of North American, 379
Sutton, George Miksch, biography of, 87
Swainson, William, 247
Swallows, brood parasitism in, **401–3**
Swiftlet, Cave, 299
Swift:
  Chestnut-collared, 191
  Short-tailed, 191
swimming, **73–75**
  while transporting chick, 103
  in duck courtship, 63
  territoriality and, 105
  webbed feet for, 243
  see also diving; feet
switch-sidling and walking, 69
Swordbill, 211
symbols:
  bird badges as, **591–93**, 611–15
  birds in art as, 47–51
sympatric, defined, 375
syrinx as part of vocal apparatus, 373–375
Systema Naturae (Linnaeus), 629
systematics, *see* taxonomy
Systematics and the Origin of Species (Mayr), 389

tame birds and distraction displays, 117
taxidermy, 247
taxonomy:
  evolutionary convergence and, **419–421**
  nomenclature and, **515–19**
  of passerines based on DNA, **662–65**
  subspecies, species, and, 355–57
  superspecies and, **375–81**
teeth, egg, 233–35
temperature regulation, *see* thermoregulation
Teratornis merriami, 219
Terborgh, John, 499, 529
Terrill, Scott, 185
territoriality, 321, **387–89**
  badges in, 613–15
  in breeding, 147, 251, 253, 259, 443
  communities and, 607
  in coots, 105
  in ducks, 65
  feeding and, 147–49, 173, 175, 177

intra- and interspecific, 383, **385–87**, 627
  in leks, 259–61
  in loons, 7
  optimal foraging theory and, 335
  population and, 575–77
  "portable," 147
  in sandpipers, 133, **155–57**
  in sibling species, 383
  vocalizations and, 471, 473
  in winter, **147–49**
  see also displays; hierarchies
testes, enlargement in breeding season, 317
thecodonts and bird evolution, 33
theory, defined, **567–69**
  see also mathematical theory
thermoregulation:
  behavior and, **149–53**
  coloration and, 177
  in communities, 617–19
  feet and, 107, 151, 243, 255–57
  improved by preening, 53
  metabolism and, 327–29
  wing posture in, 25–27
thornbills and mixed species flocking, 435
Thorpe, W. H., 601
Threatened and Endangered Species List, *see* Blue List
threatened species:
  Bachman's Warbler, **505**
  California Condor, **219–23**
  Ivory-billed Woodpecker, **357–59**
  Kirtland's Warbler, **527–29**
  see also Blue List
threats to bird populations:
  from disease and parasitism, 349, 399
  and fate of Heath Hen, 257
  from harvesting sea, 659
  ingested artifacts, 391
  natural calamities, 101
  plume trade, 37–41
  see also diseases; habitat destruction; hunting; pollution
Thrush, Shama, 653
timber industry, *see* lumber industry
Tinbergen, Nikolaas, 9, 57, 165–69, 581
  biography of, **71**
Tits, 373, 435
  Great, 385, 593

weavers, largely African House Sparrow
relatives, 173, 253, 261, 289, 395,
443
webbed feet, 241, 243
swimming and, 73
Weller, Milton, 107
Wetmore, Alexander, biography of, 95
Wheye, Darryl, 479
White, Fred, 395
White, R. E., 539
White-eyes, Japanese, 653
Widowbird, Long-tailed, and sexual
selection, 253–55
Wiens, John, 541
Wilcove, David, 497, 499, 529
Wildbird, 521
Wilderness Society, 497
Wildlife Review, 539
Willis, William, 397
Wilson, Alexander, 85, 87, 117, 129,
273, 279, 413, 463
biography of, 277
Wilson, David, 209
Wilson, E. O., 549–51
wings:
while diving, 73
duck, 63, 79
in flight, 161–63, 215–17
hummingbird, 323
origin of, 397

shape of, 227–29
silent, of owls, 291
spread postures of, 25–27
Wingtips, 521
wintering, conservation and, 513
and shorebird territoriality, 147–49
see also migrants threatened
wishbone (furcula), 31, 33
see also bones
Woodcock, Eurasian, feigns carrying
young, 105
Woodpeckers, how tongues work, 353
disappearance of Ivory-bill, 357–59
Great Spotted and milk theft, 415
Woolfenden, Glen, 283, 575–77
World Wildlife Fund, 121, 367, 369
worms:
as prey, 109
robins poisoned by DDT in, 21
Wrens:
Fairy, and mixed-species flocking,
435
superb Blue, 423

Yom-Tov, Yoram, 599

zoo-breeding of California Condors,
219–21
Zosterops japonicus, 653

INDEX OF
NORTH AMERICAN BIRDS

*(Page numbers in **boldface** refer to species treatment paragraphs; page numbers in roman type refer to essays.)*

Chickadees, 181, 327–29, 345, 347,
    349, 371, 373, 381, 385, **424–30**,
    431, 433, 643
  Black-capped, 327, 373, **424**, 425,
    645
  Boreal, 327, **430**
  Carolina, **426**, 433
  Chestnut-backed, **428**, 493, 495
  Gray-headed, *see* Tits, Siberian
  Mexican, **426**
  Mountain, **428**
  see also Tits
Chlidonias niger, **188**
Chloroceryle americana, **338**
Chondestes grammacus, **576**
Chondrohierax uncinatus, **224**
Chordeiles, **312–14**
  acutipennis, **314**
  gundlachii, **314**
  minor, **312**
Chuck-will's-widow, **308**, 333
Chukar, **266**
Cinclus mexicanus, **482**
Circus cyaneus, **226**
Cistothorus, **442–44**
  palustris, **442**
  platensis, **444**
Clangula hyemalis, **88**
Coccothraustes vespertinus, **646**
Coccyzus, **286–88**
  americanus, **286**
  erythropthalmus, **286**
  minor, **288**
Colaptes auratus, **338**
Colinus virginianus, **260**
Columba, **270–74**
  fasciata, **270**
  flavirostris, **272**
  leucocephala, **272**
  livia, **274**
Columbina, **276**
  inca, **276**
  passerina, **276**
Condor, California, 175, 217, **218**,
    219–23, 247, 297
Contopus, **374–78**
  borealis, **376**
  pertinax, **374**
  sordidulus, **378**
  virens, **376**
Conuropsis carolinensis, **280**
Coots, **104**, 223

American, 35, 103, **104**, 105–9,
    159–61, 243, 601, 645, 653
  Caribbean, 666
  Eurasian, 666
Coragyps atratus, **216**
Cormorants, **24–30**, 25, 27, 29, 35, 73,
    75, 305, 339, 431, 660, 661
  Brandt's, **28**
  Double-crested, **26**, 27
  Great, 9, **24**
  Neotropic, *see* Olivaceous
  Olivaceous, **26**
  Pelagic, **28**
  Red-faced, **30**, 199
Corvus, 373, **416–20**
  brachyrhynchos, 373, **416**
  caurinus, **416**
  corax, 373, **420**
  cryptoleucus, **418**
  ossifragus, **418**
Coturnicops noveboracensis, **100**
Cowbirds, 289, 297, 307. 401, 403,
    495–97, 505, **616**, 619–25
  Bronzed, 289, **616**, 619, 621
  Brown-headed, 289, 407, 527, **616**,
    617, 619–21, 645
  Red-eyed, *see* Bronzed
Crake, Corn, 666
Cranes, 13, 17, **48–50**, 49, 261, 309
  Common, 666
  Sandhill, **48**, 645
  Whooping, **50**, 51–53, 297
Creepers, 211, 421, **434**, 617
  Brown, 433, **434**, 493
Crossbills, 181, 381, 579, **638**, 641
  Red, 213, **638**, 639
  White-winged, **638**, 639
Crotophaga, **282–84**
  ani, **282**
  sulcirostris, **284**
Crows, 159, 167, 211, 227, 313, 373,
    416–18, 417, 421
  American, 213, 233, 373, **416**, 497,
    645
  Fish, **418**
  Mexican, 666
  Northwestern, **416**
Cuckoos, 103, **284–88**, 395, 407
  Black-billed, **286**, 289
  Common, 666
  Mangrove, **288**
  Oriental, 666

Rufous-sided, 381–83, 469, **562**, 595, 627
Spotted, *see* Towhees, Rufous-sided
Toxostoma, **470–76**
  bendirei, **474**
  crissale, **474**
  curvirostre, **472**
  lecontei, **476**
  longirostre, **472**
  redivivum, **476**
  rufum, **470**
Tree Ducks, *see* Whistling Ducks
Tree Sparrow, Eurasian, *see* Sparrows, Eurasian Tree
Tringa, **126–28**, 132
  flavipes, **128**
  glareola, **132**
  melanoleuca, **126**
  solitaria, **128**
Troglodytes, **438–40**
  aedon, **438**
  troglodytes, **440**
Trogon elegans, **282**
Trogons, **282**, 451
  Eared, 667
  Elegant, **282**
Tropicbirds:
  Red-billed, 667
  Red-tailed, 667
  White-tailed, 667
Tryngites subruficollis, **156**
tubenoses, 15, 17, 207–9, 561, 643, 657
Turdus migratorius, 337, **462**
Turkeys, Wild, **268**, 269, 319, 451, 457, 585, 645
Turnstones, **140–42**
  Black, **140**, 147
  Ruddy, 113, 119, 125, 127, **142**
Turtledoves:
  Ringed, 601, 654–55
Tympanuchus, **256–58**
  cupido, 256, 257–59
  pallidicinctus, **256**
  phasianellus, **258**
Tyrannulet, Northern Beardless-, **392**
Tyrannus, 337, **360–68**
  couchii, **366**
  crassirostris, **362**
  dominicensis, **362**
  forficatus, **368**
  melancholicus, **366**
  tyrannus, **360**

verticalis, **364**
vociferans, **364**
Tyto alba, **288**

Uria, **196–98**
  aalge, **196**
  lomvia, **198**

Veery, **458**, 461, 485
Verdin, **432**, 447
Vermivora, **500–8**
  bachmanii, **504**
  celata, **504**
  chrysoptera, **502**
  crissalis, **508**
  luciae, **508**
  peregrina, **502**
  pinus, **500**
  ruficapilla, **506**
  virginiae, **506**
Violet-ear, green, 666
Vireo, **488–98**
  altiloquus, **496**
  atricapillus, **490**
  bellii, **492**
  flavifrons, **490**
  gilvus, **498**
  griseus, **488**
  huttoni, **492**
  olivaceus, **496**
  philadelphicus, **498**
  solitarius, **494**
  vicinior, **494**
Vireos, 371, 409, 431, 447, 449, **488–498**, 497
  Bell's, **492**, 623
  Black-capped, **490**
  Black-whiskered, **496**
  Gray, **494**
  Hutton's, **492**, 493, 495
  Philadelphia, **498**
  Red-eyed, 289, 433, 465, 495, **496**, 555
  Solitary, **494**
  Thick-billed, 667
  Warbling, 493, **498**, 645
  White-eyed, 465, **488**
  Yellow-green, *see* Red-eyed
  Yellow-throated, **490**, 495
Vultures, 17, 25, 83, 175, 177, 215–17, **216–18**, 225, 229, 243, 339, 617
  Black, 149, **216**, 217, 589